Psychology

SEVENTH EDITION

Dedicated to the students at Purdue, who taught me so much over the last 30 years.

—JSN

Dedicated to Ruth Grzesnikowski, 1927–2018.

—DMM

Sara Miller McCune founded SAGE Publishing in 1965 to support the dissemination of usable knowledge and educate a global community. SAGE publishes more than 1000 journals and over 600 new books each year, spanning a wide range of subject areas. Our growing selection of library products includes archives, data, case studies and video. SAGE remains majority owned by our founder and after her lifetime will become owned by a charitable trust that secures the company's continued independence.

Los Angeles | London | New Delhi | Singapore | Washington DC | Melbourne

Psychology

SEVENTH EDITION

JAMES S. NAIRNE
Purdue University

DAWN M. MCBRIDE
Illinois State University

Los Angeles | London | New Delhi
Singapore | Washington DC | Melbourne

FOR INFORMATION:

SAGE Publications, Inc.
2455 Teller Road
Thousand Oaks, California 91320
E-mail: order@sagepub.com

SAGE Publications Ltd.
1 Oliver's Yard
55 City Road
London, EC1Y 1SP
United Kingdom

SAGE Publications India Pvt. Ltd.
B 1/I 1 Mohan Cooperative Industrial Area
Mathura Road, New Delhi 110 044
India

SAGE Publications Asia-Pacific Pte. Ltd.
18 Cross Street #10-10/11/12
China Square Central
Singapore 048423

Acquisitions Editor: Lara Parra

Production Editor: Tracy Buyan

Copy Editor: Melinda Masson

Typesetter: diacriTech

Proofreader: Barbara Coster

Cover Designer: Janet Kiesel

Marketing Managers: Victoria Velasquez, Katherine Hepburn

Printed in Canada

Library of Congress Cataloging-in-Publication Data
Names: Nairne, James S., 1954- | McBride, Dawn M., author.
Title: Psychology / James S. Nairne, Purdue University, Dawn M. McBride, Illinois State University.
Description: 7th Edition. | Thousand Oaks, California : SAGE Publications, Inc, 2022. | Revised edition. | Includes bibliographical references and index.
Identifiers: LCCN 2021021744 | ISBN 9781544362953 (paperback ; alk. paper) | ISBN 9781544362960 (looseleaf) | ISBN 9781544362977 (epub)
Subjects: LCSH: Psychology.
Classification: LCC BF121 .N27 2022 | DDC 150--dc23
LC record available at https://lccn.loc.gov/2021021744

This book is printed on acid-free paper.

22 23 24 25 26 10 9 8 7 6 5 4 3 2 1

BRIEF CONTENTS

DETAILED CONTENTS

PREFACE

CRITICAL THINKING. FROM PSYCHOLOGY TO LIFE.

Psychology, Seventh Edition takes a fresh approach to basic psychological science by stressing the adaptability of human behavior and cognition as its central theme. It uses a unique problem-solving approach in which behavior, as well as the tools of the discipline, is introduced as a solution to pressing adaptive and conceptual problems, particularly those encountered in everyday living. This central theme presents an effective organizing framework for within-chapter development and naturally affords critical thinking, recognition of diversity, and the use of pedagogical devices. Written in an accessible and conversational style, the text draws on the decades of teaching experience of the two authors, both regular instructors of introductory psychology. The text also taps their extensive backgrounds in research scholarship to stress methodology and the research process, as well as highlighting cutting-edge developments such as the use of active learning and retrieval practice to aid in comprehension and retention.

PREFACE TO THE STUDENT

Psychology is the scientific study of behavior and mind. It can be a tough subject, but we're confident that you'll find it fun and even surprising at the same time. There are scores of research studies and hundreds of isolated facts scattered throughout this book, but our main goal is to help you understand the function of psychology in your life—to tell you what psychology is for! Toward that end, we'll show you how your behaviors, thoughts, and emotions help you solve important problems every day.

Everything we do is influenced, in part, by our need to adapt to rapidly changing situations. We're constantly dipping into our psychological "tool kit" to solve specific social, personal, or environmental problems. For example, before you can react, your brain needs to communicate with the environment and with the rest of your body. To communicate internally, your body uses the nervous system, the endocrine system, and, to some extent, even the genetic code. We also must translate the messages from the environment, which come in a variety of forms, into the internal language of the nervous system (which is electrochemical). We solve this problem through our various sensory systems, such as vision and audition. Our survival also depends on our ability to communicate through language and other, nonverbal forms of communication.

You'll soon see that many of our behaviors and thoughts can be viewed as solutions to such problems or demands. We don't think you should be expected to understand a topic unless you first know what it's for! Therefore, each chapter begins with a brief preview section, *The Problems to Be Solved*. In this section, we discuss the function and purpose of the psychological processes that we'll be examining and the particular problems that they help us solve. Throughout the chapter, we'll then show you how these psychological processes help people meet the challenges that they face. At the end of the chapter, a review section, *The Problems Solved*, summarizes the function and purpose of the psychological processes discussed in the chapter.

We invite you to browse through the rest of the preface for a preview of how this book is organized. And we hope you will soon begin applying what you learn to situations in your daily life. The study of psychology may be challenging, but above all else it is relevant to everything we do. Have fun!

PREFACE TO THE INSTRUCTOR

One of the first hurdles we face as instructors of introductory psychology is convincing students that psychology is more than just the study of abnormal behavior. Introduce yourself as a psychologist, and you're likely to get a response like "Don't analyze me!" or "I'd better watch what I say around you!" It takes time for students to realize that psychology is a vast interdisciplinary field that includes all aspects of both normal and abnormal behavior. Even after exposure to its breadth, the topics of psychology can remain mysterious and forbidding. Take a look at a typical chapter on learning, for example, and its contents seem to bear little resemblance to our everyday understanding of what it means to "learn." There are extended discussions of drooling dogs and key-pecking pigeons, but little about the connection between conditioning procedures and the learning problems we face on a daily basis.

In *Psychology, Seventh Edition*, we once again focus extensively on the function and purpose of psychological processes. Instead of leading with the facts and methods specific to a topic, we introduce each topic as a kind of "solution" to a pressing environmental or conceptual challenge. For example, if you want to understand how we learn about the signaling properties of events (problem), you can look to classical conditioning (solution). Notice the shift in emphasis: Instead of topic followed by function, it's function followed by topic. We believe this kind of "functional approach" offers a number of advantages:

1. The student has a reason to follow the discussion.

2. Because the discussion is about an adaptive or conceptual problem, it naturally promotes critical thinking. The student sees the connection between the problem and the solution.

3. The functional problem-solving theme extends across chapters.

4. The organization provides an effective learning framework.

Each chapter is organized around a set of topics that (a) focus the discussion on the functional relevance of the material and (b) demonstrate that we think and act for adaptive reasons. When we view behavior as the product of adaptive systems, psychology begins to make more sense. Students learn that behaviors (including the methods of psychologists!) are reactions to particular problems. When we emphasize adaptiveness, we relax our egocentric view of the world and increase our sensitivity to why behavior is so diverse, both within and across species. Our appreciation of individuality and diversity is enhanced by understanding that differences are natural consequences of adaptations to the environment.

Organization

Psychology, Seventh Edition uses the problem-solving framework to organize its 16 chapters. Traditional textbooks organize chapters around standard topic areas (vision, short-term memory, attribution theory, etc.), but students often have little idea why these particular topics are important. In *Psychology, Seventh Edition*, "topics" are presented as solutions to problems—for example, classical conditioning is discussed as a "solution" to the problem of how people and animals learn about the signaling properties of events. Each of the 16 chapters introduces a set of adaptive or conceptual problems that are then "solved" through topical discussions in the chapters.

As outlined here, the text follows a conventional chapter-by-chapter organization. We begin with a conceptual introduction to the field in Chapter 1, followed by a separate chapter on the "tools" of psychological research. Given the strong emphasis that we place on the research enterprise throughout the text, we felt that it was important to present basic methods in detail. The methods chapter is followed by a chapter on biological processes, which treats neural transmission and general brain activity in detail. We chose to place the developmental chapter next because it serves as a kind of précis for the remaining topics in the book. It too is organized around adaptive problems, namely developing physically, intellectually, and socially. Chapters 5 through 9 cover the basics of cognitive psychology (sensation and perception, consciousness, learning, memory, and cognitive processes). Chapters 10 and

11 focus on intelligence and personality; both use similar organizational structures to help students understand the commonalities in the study of individual differences. Chapter 12 combines the topics of motivation and emotion and argues forcefully that the two topic areas are interrelated. Chapter 13 is a lengthy chapter covering social psychology, focusing on social cognition followed by social influence. Chapter 14 introduces the study of psychological disorders and includes discussions of how disorders should be conceptualized and understood. Chapter 15 focuses on therapy, using the framework developed in Chapter 14 to organize therapies around the factors that explain the development of disorders (biological, cognitive, and environmental). Finally, Chapter 16 concludes the text with a treatment of stress and health and includes discussions of how psychological science can play a role in the treatment and prevention of global pandemics (including COVID-19).

Chapter 1: An Introduction to Psychology

Chapter 1 introduces psychological science by focusing on the basics: how to define and describe the field, trace its historical roots, and identify its modern focus.

- Expanded and updated discussion of retrieval practice and the benefits of testing to learning

- New emphasis on "Big Data" and the replication crisis in psychology

- Extended coverage of underrepresented groups

- Focused research examining women's interactions with gay and straight men

Chapter 2: The Tools of Psychological Research

Chapter 2 introduces students to the methods that psychologists use as tools for observing and describing behavior, predicting and explaining behavior, and treating participants ethically. Experimental and correlational approaches are covered in detail, with an emphasis on the difference between correlation and causation.

- Targeted coverage of the use of Big Data in psychological research

- Additional focus on diversity issues in sampling

- Expanded discussion of the "replicability crisis" in psychological research

Chapter 3: Biological Processes

Chapter 3 introduces and outlines solutions for four major problems in neuroscience: How do we communicate internally, how do we initiate behavior, how is growth regulated, and how is the genetic code adapted and transmitted?

- New coverage of optogenetics as an investigative tool

- Extended and reworked discussion of sex differences in brain function

- Additional section on genome-wide complex trait analysis (GCTA)

- Targeted research on the role of the hippocampus in learning activities

Chapter 4: Human Development

Chapter 4 presents developmental processes as they operate within different areas of behavior: perception, cognition, biology, social psychology, and personality. The major sections explore how humans solve the problems of developing physically, intellectually, and socially.

- New section on the stages of the birth process

- Updated discussion of cultural issues in development

- Targeted research on social media use and effects of the pandemic
- Contemporized discussion of gender and gender roles

Chapter 5: Sensation and Perception

Chapter 5 describes the processes of sensation and perception organized by sense system—vision, hearing, tactile, and chemical senses—along with basic concepts from psychophysics. An emphasis is placed on how the sense systems solve the adaptive problems of translating environmental stimuli into neural activity, identifying the message components, and producing stable interpretations.

- Addition of neuroscientific studies in sensation and perception
- Inclusion of cultural influences on perception
- New section on perception–action

Chapter 6: Consciousness

Chapter 6 describes influences on our conscious awareness. The major sections discuss how we set priorities for mental functioning (attention), sleep and dream, alter awareness through psychoactive drugs, and induce states such as hypnosis and meditation.

- Revised section on ADHD and its effects on attention
- Updated research studies on effects of psychoactive drugs
- New content and research studies on the benefits of mindfulness

Chapter 7: Learning From Experience

Chapter 7 explains the key concepts of learning as a means of adapting behavior in the changing world. We discuss how people and animals learn about events (habituation), learn about what events signal (classical conditioning), learn about the consequences of behavior (operant conditioning), and learn from others (observational learning).

- New and updated examples of learning in everyday life
- Additional section on effects of violent video games on behavior

Chapter 8: Memory

Chapter 8 helps students understand the purpose of remembering and how it operates as a key cognitive process. The major sections cover how we remember over the short term, store information for the long term, recover information from cues, and update memory.

- Current examples to help students connect concepts with their own behaviors
- New section on the seven "sins" of memory
- Updated studies on the neuroscience of memory

Chapter 9: Language and Thought

Chapter 9 connects language and thought as related cognitive processes that aid in everyday life. The major sections treat communicating with others, classifying and categorizing, solving problems, and making decisions.

- Expanded and updated language development section
- Extended discussion of the role of culture in language use and development and other cognitive processes

Chapter 10: Intelligence

Chapter 10 introduces and outlines solutions for basic conceptual problems in the study of intelligence: How do we conceptualize intelligence, how do we measure individual differences, and how do we discover the sources of those differences?

- Added coverage of labeling effects

- Increased discussion of emotional intelligence and test bias

- New application of GCTA to the study of intelligence

- Targeted research assessing the effectiveness of working memory training on intelligence

Chapter 11: Personality

Chapter 11 introduces and outlines solutions for basic conceptual problems in the study of personality: How do we conceptualize and measure personality, how do we determine how personality develops, and how do we conceptualize and resolve the person–situation debate?

- Expanded discussion of sex differences in personality

- Up-to-date coverage on the genetics of personality

- New research investigating the use of psychological targeting as an effective approach to mass persuasion

Chapter 12: Motivation and Emotion

Chapter 12 explores the basic processes underlying motivation and emotion. Separate sections discuss how people activate behavior; meet the biological needs of hunger, eating, and sex; and express and experience emotion.

- Extended coverage of gender effects in motivation

- Updated discussion of the factors involved in sexual orientation

- New critique of the facial-feedback hypothesis

- Focused research on the effect of graphic warnings on sugary-drink purchasing

Chapter 13: Social Psychology

Chapter 13 describes how our behavior is influenced by other people and groups and how our attitudes about others are created and maintained. Our focus is on the adaptive problems of interpreting the behavior of others, behaving in the presence of others, and establishing relations with others.

- New research on racial and other biases

- Updated discussion of attitudes on gender roles

- Current examples included throughout the chapter

- Revised coverage of the role of culture in social interactions and attitudes

- Contemporized discussion of romantic love with new research studies

Chapter 14: Psychological Disorders

Chapter 14 introduces the study of psychological disorders by focusing on three main conceptual problems: How should we conceptualize abnormality, how should psychological disorders be classified, and how should disorders be understood? In the last section, we consider biological, cognitive, and environmental accounts.

- New critical assessment of the Rosenhan study
- Expanded discussion of DSM-5 categories
- Increased coverage of genetics
- Targeted research on positive thinking and depression

Chapter 15: Therapy

Chapter 15 discusses the treatment of psychological disorders and assesses the overall effectiveness of psychotherapy. The chapter is organized around how psychologists treat the body (biomedical therapies), the mind (insight therapies), and the environment (behavioral therapies).

- Extended discussion of neurotransmitters and disorders
- Updated section on culture and disorders
- Expanded coverage of clinical evaluation studies
- New research on PTSD and catastrophic thinking in combat

Chapter 16: Stress and Health

Chapter 16 deals with the topics of stress and health. The chapter addresses four major problems: experiencing stress, reacting to prolonged stress, reducing and coping with stress, and how to live a healthy lifestyle.

- Revised opening section featuring pandemic stress
- Increased discussion of the positive effects of stress
- Integrated coverage focusing on the effects of COVID-19
- New research on social resilience after a terrorist attack

Chapter Pedagogy

Additionally, the text contains special features designed to highlight each chapter's functional organization, provide in-depth treatment of a particular topic, focus on recent original research studies, and summarize and test for current knowledge.

- **Problems to Be Solved** sections introduce and frame each chapter. These sections describe how psychological processes are tools designed to help people solve important adaptive and practical problems in their lives.
- **Problems Solved** sections summarize and review the main content of the chapters and focus specifically on how the major adaptive and conceptual problems of the chapter are solved by the major processes and tools covered in the chapter.
- **Practical Solutions** sections give students an inside look at a particular study or topic in psychological science with applications to everyday living.

- **Video Enrichment:** Bite-sized videos support learning by digging deeper into foundational experiments in the world of psychology and further exploring tough concepts.
  - Psychology Experiment Exercises: Learn more about some of psychology's most classic experiments, such as Gibson's Visual Cliff and Bandura's social learning theory. These add another perspective to the text about the real-world significance and application of these well-known experiments.
  - Concepts in Action: Dig deeper into tough concepts, such as differentiating between classical and operant conditioning, difficult biological functions, and types of stress.

- **Concept Reviews** are included in each chapter to help students understand and review the main points in the section.

- **Knowledge Checks** focus on the important role that retrieval practice can play in promoting active learning and the retention of knowledge.

- **Thinking About Research:** At the end of each chapter, we present a summary of the main sections of a research article that relates the chapter's concepts. Critical thinking questions about the study are included to help students tie the research study to what they are learning in the chapter.

A NOTE ON CULTURE AND LANGUAGE

Writing a book that discusses topics related to culture and identity, as well as our understanding of human behavior, is fraught with issues related to history and the very identities we will discuss. Cultures are not static. Cultures are fluid, in flux, transforming, and evolving—some slowly, some quickly. As you read through this book, please know that a conscious attempt has been made to be inclusive and nonjudgmental when describing cultural groups and cultural traditions. Language, too, is fluid and evolving. The language spoken today is not the language of our ancestors. And so the language we use to describe cultures can sometimes unintentionally mischaracterize the culture. That's the nature of writing about humans and their interactions.

A thoughtful attempt has been made to use language throughout this book that is sensitive to these issues and, in so doing, to recognize the evolving historical, social, and political dimensions across the globe and the resulting cultural transformations, particularly as they relate to race, ethnicity, and sex and gender issues. The following terms are used in the seventh edition, although regional designations and nationalities are used when they are more accurate and specific.

- *African American* or *Black* is used, whichever is truer to the study being cited. If the person or group is not American, then *African* or *Black* (whichever is most accurate) is used.

- *Native North American* is used to refer to groups or individuals who are members or descendants of indigenous peoples of North America. When referring to groups including Hawaiians and Samoans, the broader term *Native North American* is used.

- *Asian American is used for U.S. citizens of Asian descent. Asian is used to describe things or people of or from Asia.*

- *Hispanic/Latino* is used at first reference; for subsequent references, *Hispanic* or *Latino* may be used as a collective noun depending on the study being cited.

- *White* is used to refer to citizens of the United States who are of European ancestry.

We are grateful to all the scholars from different walks of life who have reviewed the seventh edition of *Psychology* and to our colleagues with whom we've had extensive conversations about how to use the "right" terminology. To be sure, there is no consensus among them. The "correct" terminology depends on who you ask.

ABOUT THE AUTHORS

James S. Nairne, Purdue University

James S. Nairne, PhD, is Distinguished Professor Emeritus at Purdue University in West Lafayette, Indiana. He received his undergraduate training at the University of California, Berkeley, and his PhD in psychology from Yale University. His original training was in Pavlovian conditioning, but his current research specialty is human memory and cognition. He is a fellow of the Society of Experimental Psychologists, the Psychonomic Society, the Association for Psychological Science, and the Midwestern Psychological Association. His editorial positions have included editor-in-chief of *Memory & Cognition* and associate editor for the *Psychonomic Bulletin & Review* and the *Journal of Memory and Language*, and he has served on numerous editorial boards. For over three decades, he has taught introductory psychology at Purdue and served as the founding director for the Research-Focused Honors Program in psychological science. He was the recipient of the 2000 Excellence in Education Award from Purdue University and the 2001 Charles B. Murphy Award. In 2003, Dr. Nairne was inducted into the Book of Great Teachers.

Dawn M. McBride, Illinois State University

Dawn M. McBride is a professor of psychology at Illinois State University. Her research interests include various forms of memory, including false memory, prospective memory, and forgetting. In addition to research methods, she teaches courses in introductory psychology, cognition and learning, and human memory, as well as a graduate course in experimental design. She is a recipient of the Illinois State University Teaching Initiative Award and the Illinois State University SPA/Psi Chi Jim Johnson Award for commitment to undergraduate mentorship, involvement, and achievement. Her nonacademic interests include spending time with her family, traveling, watching Philadelphia sports teams (go, Eagles!), and reading British murder mysteries. She earned her PhD in cognitive psychology from the University of California, Irvine, and her BA from the University of California, Los Angeles.

ACKNOWLEDGMENTS

From Dr. Nairne: Special thanks are due to Abbie Rickard, who convinced me to move to SAGE and provided unwavering support throughout the early stages of the revision. Abbie also suggested my friend Dawn McBride as a potential co-author. Dawn has provided keen insight and a fresh perspective to *Psychology*, clearly making the 7th edition the best yet. Lara Parra, Reid Hester, Sam Rosenberg, and Liz Cruz provided terrific support as well; I'm so pleased to be working with the folks at SAGE.

From Dr. McBride: Many important people in my life have provided needed balance during my text writing endeavors. First is Jeff Wagman, who supports me in so many ways and talks me out of all my bad ideas. Next is Connor Wagman, who keeps me young. In addition, my family, friends, and colleagues provide support and helpful feedback during the writing process. The folks at SAGE provided much appreciated support to us during the production of this text: Abbie Rickard, Lara Parra, Reid Hester, Sam Rosenberg, and Liz Cruz. My thanks also go to the students at Illinois State University who have taken my courses and influenced my perspectives on the teaching of psychology.

I am so honored to have been able to work with Jim on the revision of his text. He's a wonderful author to work with and a valued friend.

STUDENT SUCCESS GUIDE

Suppose you are taking a college course for the first time. You purchase your course material and begin to peruse its contents. Within moments you realize that there is a lot of information to learn. You wonder how you are going to understand all this material by the end of the course. You might feel a mix of emotions, from intimidated to overwhelmed to excited. These emotions are all quite common among college students. Learning is a process of growth, and growth is not always comfortable. One reason is that learning is similar to exercising. You exercise to become stronger, faster, and more agile. Your goal is to be healthier, and this does not come without times of being tired or exhausted. But you work through it so that you can reach your goal of being healthier. Similarly, as a student, you learn to become more knowledgeable and capable, and to be smarter, and this also does not come without times of being tired or exhausted. But you work through it so that you can reach your goal of being educated. This parallel brings to light a key to your success in college: to set goals. Setting goals helps you to stay focused and motivated to "work through" the challenging times. Of course, it is also helpful to have a plan or guide that can help you achieve your goals. For this reason, we have prepared the following guide to help you achieve your academic goals and to support your success.

TIPS AND TRICKS FOR STUDENT SUCCESS: THE BASICS

Textbooks typically do not provide a "How-to-Rock-This-Class Manual," yet every student would love to have one. How do you study efficiently? How do you know what to say to your professors? Who can you reach out to for help? What strategies can you use to be a successful student? If these types of questions are what students seek answers for, then this guide is a great place to start. So, let's start at the very beginning—the basics:

- It is important to want to be a great student. Being a great student does not mean getting straight A's, but it does mean that you are truly committed to learning. As a student, you should embrace the opportunity to learn, be genuinely curious about the information being taught, and take the time to study it, question it, and think critically about it. This perspective captures the spirit of what it means to be a great student.

- Take the time on the first day of class to introduce yourself to your professor and teaching assistants (if applicable). Whether your class is online, in person, or a hybrid course, go out of your way to introduce yourself. Your professors are more than just teachers. They are experts in their fields of study, and this makes them excellent people to connect with. Additionally, getting to know your professors can benefit your learning in class and even into your career as possible people you can reach out to for a professional recommendation.

- Attend each class session if it is in a synchronous or face-to-face format. What is taught in class is very often the bulk of the material that is tested and/or assessed. Not only are you putting your best foot forward by attending each class session, but you are also doing your due diligence to be a great student and setting yourself up for success. If your class is asynchronous (fully online), then make sure you watch each lecture. Professors who teach asynchronous classes offer good information in the recorded lectures, and it is important to watch the full lecture—from beginning to end—so that you are not missing important information.

- Be prepared—have your materials ready, put your distracting technology away, and read before attending class. If you are in a fully online class, the same rules apply. When you are ready to watch your lecture, put the technology away. Research has demonstrated that being distracted because of multitasking—specifically by looking at your phone at the same time you are listening to a lecture—lowers your performance and retention. Students often think they are good at multitasking, but the science says that's not accurate.

GETTING THE MOST OUT OF YOUR COURSE

On the first day, the professor is going to give you the owner's manual to the class: the **syllabus**. This document will give you all the information you need for the class. In general, the first bit of information you see on the syllabus is your professor's contact information. This information generally includes the professor's email address, office hours, office location (if applicable), and availability. When it comes to professors, there are a few things to remember:

- Be respectful when you email. This is a professional communication. Start the email with "Dear Professor _____."

- When you do email, make sure it does not sound like a text. You are conducting a formal business-like exchange.

- Use correct grammar and punctuation.

- Always let professors know what class you are in by typing it in the subject header, so that they can appropriately answer your questions—most professors teach multiple classes.

- Allow for at least 24–48 hours for a response from your professor. Allow a bit more time if you email on a Friday or the weekend.

- Ask questions. If you have questions, other students likely do too!

- If you have a few questions, consider making an appointment with your professor to meet during office hours. Having a conversation with your professor might answer many questions in one sitting; and, as most of us know, sometimes answers can be lost in translation in an email.

- Just a reminder—teachers love to teach—and they appreciate enthusiastic students. So, make an appointment with your professors and say hello.

FIGURE 1 ■ Professional Communication

Next, you need to sit down and *read all of the syllabus*. The syllabus is like your road map. You will be able to find *exactly* which textbook to obtain (never assume an older edition is going to be "good enough") and any other course requirements. Additionally, the syllabus will include course policies, course materials, a course calendar, and grading and assessment policies.

Helpful tip: Note in your calendar when you should start each assignment and when it is due. That will make it easier to keep on track (in other words, put it in your calendar RIGHT NOW). Multiple research studies have found that 80–95% of college students put off doing their work and studying on "a regular basis." Procrastination is not your friend, so start projects and assignments as early as possible. Life happens, and you do not want to turn in work late. Plan to start working on written work at least two weeks in advance if assignments are available to you that far in advance.

Also add to your calendar the dates for all quizzes and exams. A general rule of thumb is to start studying for quizzes and exams one week in advance. Never, ever cram. And get good sleep.

Many students color-code their schedules to keep all of their classes organized. This might sound like a lot of work, but you will be glad you did it!!

COURSE MATERIALS

It's important to have a plan—and to use science to help you out. Researchers have found that certain strategies work well for learning—particularly when it comes to reading the textbook. So, use them! For starters, many students do not read before class, and they often try to start reading without any real plan for reading a textbook efficiently. *Helpful tip*: Read BEFORE CLASS. It will save you time and improve your grades! Research has shown that if you have no idea what the professor is going to teach about, and then you sit down and try to take notes and listen, your brain will literally put you in a "time out." It is too much! *You will have cognitive overload*. So, be fair to your brain and give yourself the information you need to be able to absorb the material.

As part of your plan, figure out how to tackle your weekly reading, which is often approximately 40 pages of generally dense material. Use tools that will help you want to keep going rather than stop before you have even begun. So, make a plan of action:

- First, skim over the chapter that you are preparing to read. Whether your book is in a hardcopy format or a digital ebook, it's important to get a sense of the formatting of the book such as the illustrations, applied sections, questions, summaries, and text size. If this is your first time using an ebook, spend some extra time familiarizing yourself with the basics such as how to "turn" pages and enlarge the font if needed, as well as the general format of the book. Many students prefer digital ebooks, but if this is your first one, it can be a very different experience for you. It may take a bit of adjusting on your part. Also, no matter the format, get familiar with the interactive elements that are often included with the book.

- When you are ready to start working on a specific chapter, consider starting at the back of the chapter. The end of the chapter will give you a clear and concise **summary** of the chapter. You can also review **key words**, which will acquaint you with what the professor is going to discuss in class.

- Read over the **thought questions** at the end of each chapter. Obviously, you will not know the answers, but it'll give you an idea of what is important.

- When you begin a chapter, peruse the first page. Read the **chapter outline**, or scan the **section headings**, and, if present, review the **learning objectives**. The learning objectives state what you should be able to accomplish when you truly learn the material. They'll also give insight into the chapter.

- Divide your reading into reasonable portions. Researchers recommend setting a timer for 20–30 minutes (approximately 7–10 pages) to serve as a reminder to take a break. When the timer goes off, take a moment or two to stretch and move around a little. It is also recommended that you not have your phone close by or that you put it on silent mode, so that random alerts and messages won't interrupt you and break your flow.

- **Learning is not about being fast. Learning is about appropriately retaining important information.** When you read those 7–10 pages, try to understand the *main points*, not every point. Do not take notes initially. You don't want to break your cognitive flow. As you go back and review the pages you've read, notetaking can be beneficial. Research has shown that taking notes (pen-to-paper notetaking) can help students understand and retain the material better. *Helpful tip*: Paraphrase what the authors are saying and write it in your notes. This will help you articulate, and therefore understand, the material better. We call this approach *deep processing*, compared to memorizing, which is *surface processing*.

- It is highly recommended that you create a learning community (aka a study group) and then discuss the chapters with that group. This will help you with deep processing, and you are more likely to remember the material. *Helpful tip*: If you are unsure how to go about creating a learning community, consider discussing this with your professor. Professors can make announcements in class, start an online forum for the class, or offer you and your classmates other ways to connect. Many study groups create their own Google Docs so that they can exchange notes with others or post questions. Other study groups may use social media as a way to connect. No matter how you do it, be sure to do it *early* in the term. The sooner you have a study support team, the better.

STUDYING: NOW THAT YOU KNOW HOW TO READ THE MATERIAL, HOW DO YOU STUDY IT?

General Studying

We have talked about ways to tackle the book, but studying involves more than that. Reading, paraphrased notetaking, time with a learning community—all of those are great strategies, but sometimes (to use a saying from my grandfather) "you don't know what you don't know." Well, how are you ever going to *know* what you are supposed to *know*, then? Again, let's turn back to science for help. The cognitive psychologist Regan Gurung posits that, based on his extensive research, the ways people try to learn are not necessarily helpful. Yes, highlighting helps and rereading is good, but if you want GREAT results, start paying attention to what science is saying!!!

Gurung suggests three things you need to keep in mind if you want the best learning outcomes:

1. What do you **NEED** to know? This requires reviewing the syllabus.

2. What **DO** you know? This requires testing yourself and reviewing those tests.

3. What do you **NOT** know? Again, review the tests. Many books offer sets of knowledge checks and flashcards to help you in this process.

It is important for you to fully understand the professor's learning objectives. In other words, what exactly does the professor want you to know? Between the syllabus and the learning objectives in the textbook, you should have a pretty good idea what you need to know. If it's still not clear to you, ask your study group. At that point you should have it figured out, but if not, that is okay. *Helpful tip:* Do not spend more time trying to figure it out. It's time to write to the teaching assistant, or TA, if there is one. TAs are good "first contacts." If you're still unclear or there isn't a TA, then ask the professor. Do not be shy to ask questions. If you can't figure it out, many other students probably can't either. Too, there are great webinars and free materials available online from some of the best researchers out there. Search for reputable online resources on studying, notetaking, and test preparation.

Prepping for a Test

Never, ever, ever cram for a test! Cramming is bad in a multitude of ways:

- Cramming is associated with anxiety and stress, which results in lower scores.

- You will have cognitive overload, which means your brain is overworked.

- Learning takes *time*, and one night of cramming will not help you learn.

- Lack of sleep results in lower test scores.

You get the idea. Do not cram for a test. Here are a few scientifically supported practices for prepping for a test. Recent research by John Dunlosky and colleagues found that a key component for doing well on exams is **space practicing**:

- The idea of space practicing is to study the same content on different occasions. Think of it like this: If you were a softball player, you might practice catching and throwing three of the five days of the week (the same drill on different days). You would schedule these specific days and times to practice your throwing and catching. *Practicing the same thing over and over embeds it into your memory and recall.* It works for softball, and it works for psychology exams!

Next, work on **retrieval practicing**:

- Retrieval practicing involves bringing key information to mind to increase learning and retention.

- Test yourself frequently to make sure you know what you need to know.

- This can be done by using the flashcards and practice tests that go with your textbook. Many researchers believe that practice tests are the most underutilized resource that students have.

- Often, textbook authors work hard to provide the student resources to use in retrieval practicing. If you have them available, be sure to use them.

WHAT ABOUT YOU? SCHOOL-WORK-FAMILY BALANCE

Research has demonstrated that there is no simple, easy answer to balancing multiple roles such as being a student, an employee, a parent, a friend, a partner, and a family member, to name just a few roles. In fact, many psychologists have suggested that "balancing" these roles isn't the correct way to think about them. Is your life ever really balanced? And with one more major life role added to the list—student—it is important to keep expectations in check. This is going to be difficult, but that's okay. It can be done if you use the resources you have around you . . . and science:

- Time management is key to reducing stress and anxiety. Plan out your day and week, and stick to a schedule. *Helpful tip*: It's easy to lose track of time, so setting reminders on your phone or watch will help you to keep track of what you need to be doing and when you should be doing it. Set a timer when you are studying so that you remember to get up and move and take a break, but also set a timer to remind yourself to get back to studying.

- Pick your method of tracking (e.g., when assignments are due, when you should start studying for a test) and stick to it. Many people like to use paper calendars so that they can check off what they've done and color-code what needs to be done. If you choose this method, pick a calendar that fits in your bag and take it everywhere.

- You may choose to use an online calendar. That's a great method, too. You certainly can color-code assignments, due dates, and deadlines, as well as prioritize activities and set alerts. The key to using a calendar (electronic or paper) is to *remember to look at it . . . every day*. Without exception. Do not rely on your memory.

- Prioritize sleeping and exercising. These two activities go together; research has demonstrated that the relationship between sleep and exercise is bidirectional. More specifically, exercise helps you sleep better. And when you sleep better, you are more likely to exercise. Also, research has shown that increasing both activities increases recall. That is a win-win-win! You might think that it's more important to study than to sleep for a full 7 or 8 hours, or take a brisk walk, but that is a myth. The less sleep you get, the less efficient your brain will be. The same goes for exercise. Your brain needs oxygen to function at its best, and there is no better way to get oxygen to your brain than through exercise.

- Ask your academic adviser about your school's counseling center. The transition to college can be difficult. It's always a great idea to build a support system as early as possible, and counselors are trained to provide exactly that. They can also direct you to support groups on and off campus.

- You might be a first-generation college student or a student who is a caretaker of others. There will be times when you might feel pulled in different directions, or times when your family will not understand why you need to spend so many hours on your studies. *Helpful tip*: Keep the lines of communication open with your family, which will help them get a better grasp of what you need to succeed. If you must be in a quiet room for 3 hours a day to study, let them know. If you need to be on campus late that week to prepare for a big project, tell them! Many students who try to balance school and family have found that discussing needs and responsibilities can create a supportive environment.

- Practice mindfulness throughout the day. Many smartphone apps are available that provide guided meditation. Also, many smartwatches have a 2-minute mindfulness activity. For some, it might be praying. For others, it could just be sitting still and being fully present in the moment. There are many ways to practice mindfulness. Pick a technique that works for you and practice consistently. *Helpful tip*: Schedule "mindfulness moments" into your day.

EFFECTIVE DISTANCE LEARNING

More and more people are deciding to become distance learners, and they need a game plan, too. Not attending college in a more traditional manner can make students feel isolated and not connected to their peers or professors. There are ways to address those issues, many of which have already been mentioned. But here's a refresher:

- Ideally, try to designate a specific area for studying. Keep it organized and clean so that when you are ready to study, your study space is prepared. If you cannot do this, make sure you are studying in a nondistracting environment that has all the "tools" (e.g., computer, paper, pen) that you need for studying.

- Create a study community. If you are unsure how to go about it, talking to your professor is a great place to start.

- Study groups give you the opportunity to articulate what you are learning (paraphrasing the content), which helps with deep processing.

- Study groups allow you to test each other on the content.

- Because many people are deciding to take classes from home, try to keep distractions to a minimum when studying and testing. It's easy to get distracted when laundry and other chores need to be done. Also, other family members can be a distraction, so try to communicate what you need and how long you need it to the others in your home. Communication is key when it comes to keeping the distractions at bay.

SECRET WEAPONS

Sometimes it may feel that being a student is a solitary endeavor, but it should not be. A wealth of resources are available to you. Here are a few:

- **Teaching Assistants**. They know so much about the inner workings of the department, faculty, university, and your specific class. They are an amazing resource! If your class is not face-to-face, TAs will often have virtual office hours. Be sure to schedule a short appointment to introduce yourself, and if you have questions, come prepared. *Helpful tip*: Write down all your questions ahead of time so that you can use your time efficiently.

- **Librarians.** Each department has a dedicated librarian. Get to know those wonderful people! They can help you in so many ways. If you're not able to meet with them on campus, you can email them and ask for a quick phone call to introduce yourself. Or you can ask for an online video session to say hello and ask for any resources that you may need. Again, be prepared for the meeting.

- **Writing Center.** The people who work at your school's writing center are focused on helping students. Many writing centers are set up to help students by subject area, and then there are more "generalists" (people who can help in any discipline). Commonly, it is recommended that students go to subject-specific tutors, if possible. Be sure to bring your assignment with you. Writing center tutors do not know every assignment for every class, but they are great with helping you understand the writing component. Keep in mind that if you do not live on campus, most writing centers have evening hours, and most universities offer online sessions.

- **Other Students.** So many students are struggling with school-work-family balance, so creating a support and study group can be extremely beneficial. If you can't find one, ask your TA or professor. Research suggests that the more connections you have, the better you will do in school.

ATTEND OFFICE HOURS

One of the first things students should do at the beginning of the term is to attend their professors' office hours (whether in person or virtually). For many students, the idea of attending office hours can be a scary prospect, but that one-on-one time with the professor is priceless. Specifically, you can ask questions you might not want to ask in class. Additionally, it is a chance for you to find out how nice and caring your professors really are! To make the most of the time with your professors, do the following:

- Read the syllabus before you go and think about any questions you have.

- Write down your questions before you go. This will help you use the time effectively.

- Do not be late.

- Discuss "best practices" with your professor. This means, ask what your professor believes are the best study methods for the class and how long it might take to properly prepare for exams.

- Inquire about any additional resources. It never hurts to ask.

- If you have questions about a grade, now is the time to ask for clarity.

- Take notes during your meeting because you might be covering a lot of ground and you do not want to rely on your memory.

- If you are unsure about what the professor suggested or said, do not hesitate to ask for clarification. Professors appreciate it when you are honest about not understanding an explanation. They would rather clarify during this one-on-one time rather than you leave confused.

- Lastly, thank your professors for their time. That's the best way to leave your appointment.

FIGURE 2 ■ Advice From an Undergraduate Adviser

- It is not recommended that students take classes back-to-back. It's better to have some time to absorb what you just learned, and then maybe write down a few more thoughts.
- If possible, do not take classes at times when you know you cannot do your best. For example, if you are not an 8 AM person, do not take a class first thing in the morning.
- Make sure you are a good fit for the instructor. Ask other students about the instructor and visit the instructor during office hours.
- Do not overload your schedule. You are in college to learn, not to stress yourself out. Be realistic with what you can do.
- We want you to be successful!

LIMIT MEDIA EXPOSURE

Being a student is stressful. If you add in personal or global events, it can be downright unmanageable. It is important that you take care of yourself so that you can prosper as a student, friend, family member, and community member. To help manage stress today, the American Psychological Association offers some great tips. One of the best tips is to limit media exposure. Media are there to keep you interested, so they often focus on the negative so that viewers will have a more visceral reaction. Keep that in mind . . . and limit the amount of time you spend on social media and news outlets.

SUMMARY OF HELPFUL TIPS

- **Planning.** Note in your calendar when you should be starting assignments and when they are due.

- **Reading.** Read *before class*. It will save you time and improve your grades.

- **Studying.** Paraphrase what the authors are saying and write it in your notes.

- **Study group.** If you are unsure how to go about creating a learning community, discuss it with your professor or teaching assistant.

- **Course goals.** If you do not fully understand what the course learning goals are, write to the teaching assistant (if there is one) or the professor (if there is no teaching assistant).

- **Reminders.** Setting reminders on your phone or watch will help remind you what you need to be doing and when you should be doing it.

- **Communication.** Keep the lines of communication open with your family and/or roommates to help them get a better grasp of what you need to succeed.

- **Take a moment:** Schedule mindfulness moments into your day.

- **Questions.** Write down all of your questions for instructors, teaching assistants, or study groups ahead of time so that you can use your time efficiently.

College is an exciting time in a person's life, but it can be stressful at times. By practicing good study habits and connecting to your college community—online or in person—you will be well suited to handle any bumps in the road!

MOMENTS IN PSYCHOLOGY AROUND THE WORLD

Date	Milestone
BCE	
387	Plato argues that the brain is the center of mental process.
335	Aristotle argues that the heart is the center of mental process.
CE	
1637	René Descartes (France) publishes *A Discourse on Method*. Descartes asserts that ideas are innate to humans from birth.
1690	John Locke (England) publishes *An Essay Concerning Human Understanding*. Locke asserts that ideas come from experience and the human ability to reason.
1774	Franz Mesmer (Austria) presents a treatment for mental illnesses, originally called mesmerism and now known as hypnosis.
1794	Philippe Pinel (France) publishes *Memoir on Madness*. It argues for humane treatment of mentally ill patients. Pinel made significant contributions to the classification of mental disorders.
1808	Franz Joseph Gall (Germany) proposes the idea of phrenology, the belief that the shape of a person's skull reveals personality traits.
1848	Phineas Gage (United States) suffers massive brain damage when his brain is pierced by a large iron rod. This leaves his intellect intact, but his personality is changed. From this, researchers study how areas in the brain play a role in personality.
1856	Hermann von Helmholtz (Germany) publishes *Handbook of Physiological Optics*. His many works make important contributions, including reports on the physiology of vision and hearing, and measurement of nerve impulse speed.
1859	Charles Darwin (England) publishes *On the Origin of Species*. Darwin asserts that species evolve, and that living beings all share a common ancestor.
1861	Paul Broca (France) presents his findings regarding the area in the left frontal lobe of the brain that is critical for the production of spoken language. This is now called Broca's area.
1869	Francis Galton (England) publishes *Hereditary Genius*. He asserts that intelligence is inherited. Galton is credited with the expression "nature and nurture" to correspond with "heredity and environment."
1874	Carl Wernicke (Germany) presents his findings that damage to a specific area in the left temporal lobe damages the ability to comprehend or produce language. This is now called Wernicke's area.
1879	Wilhelm Wundt (Germany) founds the first formal laboratory for psychological study at the University of Leipzig. Wundt, the first person to refer to himself as a psychologist, helped to establish psychology as an independent field of study.
1883	The first formal U.S. psychology laboratory is established at Johns Hopkins University.
1885	Hermann Ebbinghaus (Germany) publishes *On Memory*. Ebbinghaus made numerous contributions to the areas of learning and memory.

(Continued)

(*Continued*)

Date	Milestone
1887	G. Stanley Hall (United States) founds the *American Journal of Psychology*. Hall was the first North American to receive a Ph.D. in psychology.
1890	William James (United States) publishes *Principles of Psychology*. His research contributes to the study of functionalism. He is also the first person to teach a psychology course in the United States.
1892	The American Psychological Association (APA) is organized by G. Stanley Hall. The APA's stated mission is to promote the advancement, communication, and application of psychological science and knowledge to benefit society and improve lives.
1894	Margaret Floy Washburn (United States) is the first woman to receive a Ph.D. in psychology. She made contributions in the fields of animal behavior and motor theory development.
1896	John Dewey (United States) publishes *The Reflex Arc Concept in Psychology*. He focused on the areas of education and helped develop the psychological philosophy of functionalism.
1898	Edward Thorndike (United States) publishes *Animal Intelligence*. His work proposes that animals and humans learn similarly and leads to the development of operant conditioning.
1900	Sigmund Freud (Austria, England) publishes *The Interpretation of Dreams*. Freud is considered the founder of psychoanalysis.
1901	Mary Whiton Calkins (United States) publishes *An Introduction to Psychology*. In 1905, she is the first female elected as president of the American Psychological Association.
1903	Alfred Binet (France) publishes *Experimental Studies of Intelligence*. Binet made contributions to the study of intelligence, including the creation, along with colleague Theodore Simon, of the Binet-Simon intelligence scale.
1906	Ivan Pavlov (Russia) publishes his first studies on classical conditioning.
1912	Carl Jung (Switzerland) publishes *Psychology of the Unconscious*. Jung is considered the founder of analytical psychology.
1912	Tsuruko Haraguchi (Japan) receives a Ph.D. in psychology. She is the first Japanese woman to receive a Ph.D. in any subject.
1913	John Watson (United States) publishes *The Behaviorist Manifesto*. This puts forth a new area called behaviorism. In 1920, he and his colleague and wife, Rosalie Raynor, conducted the controversial "Little Albert" experiment.
1920	Francis Cecil Sumner (United States) receives a Ph.D. in psychology. He is the first African American to earn a Ph.D. in psychology. His work focuses on race psychology and education reform.
1921	Hermann Rorschach (Switzerland) publishes *Psychodiagnostik*. This work introduces the Rorschach Inkblot Test.
1923	Jean Piaget (Switzerland) publishes *The Language and Thought of the Child*. Piaget contributed in the area of child development, and championed child education.
1926	Leta Stetter Hollingworth (United States) publishes *Gifted Children*. Her work in the psychology of women helped to dispel myths that had been used to argue against women's rights.
1927	Anna Freud (Austria, England), the sixth and youngest child of Sigmund Freud, publishes *Introduction to the Technique of Child Analysis*. Freud developed the field of child psychoanalysis.
1929	Christine Ladd-Franklin (United States) publishes *Color and Color Theories*. Ladd-Franklin makes contributions in the field of color vision, in addition to other fields.
1929	Wolfgang Köhler (Germany) publishes *Gestalt Psychology*. This work criticizes behaviorism.
1932	Walter B. Cannon (United States) publishes *The Wisdom of the Body*. This work introduces the term *homeostasis* and discusses the fight-or-flight response.
1933	Inez Beverly Prosser (United States) becomes the first African American woman to receive a doctoral degree in psychology from a U.S. institution.

(*Continued*)

Date	Milestone
1936	Anna Freud (Austria, England) publishes her influential book, *The Ego and the Mechanisms of Defense*.
1936	Egas Moniz (Portugal) publishes work on the first human frontal lobotomies.
1936	Herman George Canady (United States) publishes *The Effect of "Rapport" on the I.Q.: A New Approach to the Problem of Race Psychology*. He was the first psychologist to examine the role of the examiner's race as a bias factor in IQ testing. His work provided suggestions for establishing a more equal testing environment.
1938	Ugo Cerletti (Italy) and Lucio Bini (Italy) use electroshock treatment on a human patient.
1939	David Wechsler (Romania, United States) publishes the Wechsler-Bellevue intelligence test, which will later evolve into the Wechsler Intelligence Scale for Children (WISC) and the Wechsler Adult Intelligence Scale (WAIS).
1940	George I. Sanchez (United States) publishes *Forgotten People: A Study of New Mexicans*. Also in 1940, he received a tenured, full professorship at the University of Texas, where he became the first professor of Latin American Studies.
1943	Starke Hathaway (United States) and J. Charnley McKinley (United States) publishes the Minnesota Multiphasic Personality Inventory (MMPI).
1945	Karen Horney (Germany, United States) publishes *Our Inner Conflicts*. Her work criticizes Freud's theory of female sexual development.
1946	Mamie Phipps Clark (United States) founds the Northside Center for Child Development. The first program of its kind in Harlem, it offered necessary therapy and assistance to children and families.
1948	Alfred Kinsey (United States) publishes *Sexual Behavior in the Human Male*, and then *Sexual Behavior in the Human Female* in 1953 with colleagues.
1948	B. F. Skinner (United States) publishes *Walden Two*. It describes a utopian community based on positive reinforcement and an experimental attitude. The book encourages the application of psychological principles to everyday life.
1949	Donald O. Hebb (Canada) publishes *The Organization of Behavior: A Neuropsychological Theory*. It offers a new and influential conceptualization about how the nervous system functions.
1950	Erik Erikson (Germany, United States) publishes *Childhood and Society*. He made contributions that advanced the study of human development across the lifespan.
1951	Carl Rogers (United States) publishes *Client-Centered Therapy*. His work advanced the humanist movement.
1952	The American Psychiatric Association publishes the first *Diagnostic and Statistical Manual of Mental Disorders (DSM)*, an influential text that is updated periodically.
1953	Janet Taylor Spence (United States) publishes her Taylor Manifest Anxiety Scale in the *Journal of Abnormal Psychology*. Her contributions advance the fields of anxiety and gender studies.
1954	Abraham Maslow (United States) publishes *Motivation and Personality*. It proposes a hierarchy of needs, ranging from physiological needs to self-actualization.
1954	Gordon Allport (United States) publishes *The Nature of Prejudice*. He was one of the first psychologists to study personality.
1955	Kenneth Clark (United States) publishes *Prejudice and Your Child*. His earlier research and experiments with his colleague and wife, Mamie Phipps Clark, explored issues of race for African American children. The findings of that research were included as evidence in the Supreme Court decision *Brown v. Board of Education* (1954) by proving that segregation psychologically harms children.
1957	B. F. Skinner (United States) publishes *Schedules of Reinforcement*. He contributed in the areas of behavior analysis and the experimental analysis of behavior.

(Continued)

(Continued)

Date	Milestone
1957	Leon Festinger (United States) proposes his theory of cognitive dissonance; in 1959, he and his colleague James Carlsmith conducts a landmark experiment to test this theory at Stanford University.
1958	Lawrence Kohlberg (United States) proposes his theory of moral development.
1960	Beatrice Ann Wright (United States) publishes *Physical Disability: A Psychological Approach*. Her contributions include developing appropriate and culturally relevant ways of working with differently abled people.
1961	Aaron Beck (United States) creates the Beck Depression Inventory, which is still used widely. Beck's contributions include the development of cognitive therapy and cognitive-behavioral therapy, along with making advances in the study of clinical depression and anxiety disorders.
1967	Zing-Yang Kuo (China) publishes *The Dynamics of Behavior in Development*. He contributed in the areas of animal and comparative psychology.
1967	Raymond Cattell (England, United States) publishes *Objective Personality and Motivation Tests*. He made contributions in the field of personality, putting forth a taxonomy of 16 different personality traits that could explain differences in peoples' personalities.
1969	Eleanor Gibson (United States) publishes *Principles of Perceptual Learning and Development*. With colleague Richard Walk (United States), Gibson conducts research on infant depth perception, known as "The Visual Cliff."
1971	Phillip Zimbardo (United States) conducts the Stanford Prison Experiment in the basement of an academic hall to examine the effects of authority in a prison environment.
1971	Albert Bandura (Canada, United States) publishes *Social Learning Theory*. His contributions advance the field of social cognitive psychology, and he is well known for his experiments regarding aggression.
1972	Elliot Aronson (United States) publishes *The Social Animal*. His contributions lead to advances in the theory of cognitive dissonance and explore the importance of situational factors on behavior.
1974	Eleanor Maccoby (United States) and Carol Jacklin (United States) publish *The Psychology of Sex Differences*. Their contributions lead to advances in the fields of gender studies and developmental psychology.
1974	Stanley Milgram (United States) publishes *Obedience to Authority: An Experimental View*. Milgram may be best known for his controversial experiments on obedience, which researched to what extent people would obey orders, even if the orders were dangerous or immoral.
1976	Robert V. Guthrie (United States) publishes *Even the Rat Was White*, the first history of African American psychologists in the United States.
1979	James J. Gibson (United States) publishes *The Ecological Approach to Visual Perception*. His contributions lead to advances in the field of visual perception.
1979	Elizabeth Loftus (United States) publishes *Eyewitness Testimony*. Her contributions lead to advances in the field of memory, misinformation, and eyewitness memory.
1983	Howard Gardner (United States) publishes *Frames of Mind*. This work outlines his theory of multiple intelligences.
1984	Hiroshi Azuma (Japan) publishes "Psychology in a Non-Western Country" in the *International Journal of Psychology*. He made contributions in the areas of cross-cultural psychology.
1986	Durganand Sinha (India) publishes *Psychology in a Third World Country: The Indian Experience*. He studied indigenous psychology; self, family, and social values; and human and socioeconomic development. He was central to the modern development of psychology from an Indian perspective.
1987	Marius Romme (Amsterdam) founds the Hearing Voices Network with Sandra Escher, a science journalist, and Patsy Hage, a person who hears voices. The network serves as a peer-mentor organization for persons who have auditory hallucinations and their supporters. The network soon spreads across the world.

Date	Milestone
1988	Muzafer Sherif (Turkey, United States) publishes *The Robbers Cave Experiment* with colleagues. One of the founders of modern social psychology, he advanced the fields of social judgment theory and realistic conflict theory.
1988	The Association for Psychological Science (APS), previously the American Psychological Society, is founded. Its stated mission is to promote, protect, and advance the interests of scientifically oriented psychology in research, application, teaching, and the improvement of human welfare.
1989	Kimberlé Williams Crenshaw (United States) publishes the paper "Demarginalizing the Intersection of Race and Sex." She is one of the founders of critical race theory, developing the theory of intersectionality.
1990	Reiko True (Japan, United States) publishes "Psychotherapeutic Issues with Asian American Women" in the journal *Sex Roles*. Her work has advanced mental health services for Asian Americans and other minorities.
1991	Martin Seligman (United States) publishes *Learned Optimism*. This work introduces the field of positive psychology.
1991	Qicheng Jing (China) publishes *Landmarks of Psychology: Contemporary Great Masters in Psychology*. He made contributions in highlighting the international aspect of psychology, advancing the exchange of international psychology, and lifting Chinese psychology onto the world stage.
1997	Beverly Daniel Tatum (United States) publishes *Why Are All the Black Kids Sitting Together in the Cafeteria?* This work examines the development of racial identity.
1997	U.S. president Bill Clinton apologizes for the Tuskegee Syphilis Study, an infamous study that violated human participant rights and led to the publishing of the Belmont Report in 1979, a U.S. code of ethics for human participants in research.
2003	Kuo-Shu Yang (China, Taiwan) publishes *Progress in Asian Social Psychology* with colleagues. A pioneer in indigenous Chinese and Taiwanese psychology, he also devoted his life to social reform in Taiwan.
2007	Alice Eagly (United States) publishes *Through the Labyrinth: The Truth about How Women Become Leaders* with colleague Linda Carli (United States). Her contributions have advanced the understanding of prejudice, sex differences, leadership styles, feminism, and stereotypes.
2008	U.S. president George W. Bush signs Mental Health Parity Act, requiring insurance to equally cover both mental and physical health.
2008	Lisa Diamond publishes *Sexual Fluidity: Understanding Women's Love and Desire*. Her research has advanced the understanding of sexual identity, sexual orientation development, and human bonding.
2010	Derald Wing Sue (United States) publishes *Microaggressions in Everyday Life: Race, Gender, and Sexual Orientation*. His contributions have advanced the fields of multicultural counseling and research.
2010	Claude Steele (United States) publishes *Whistling Vivaldi and Other Clues to How Stereotypes Affect Us*. He has advanced the areas of stereotype threat and its impact on the academic performance of minority students.
2010	The replication controversy impacts how a variety of disciplines, including psychology, validate existing studies.
2011	Michael Gazzaniga (United States) publishes *Who's in Charge? Free Will and the Science of the Brain*. His studies advance understanding of the functions of each brain hemisphere, and how they work independently and in collaboration.
2011	Daniel Kahneman (Israel) publishes *Thinking, Fast and Slow*. His contributions have advanced the fields of judgment and decision making. With colleague Amos Tversky (Israel), Kahneman has established a cognitive basis for common human errors that arise from heuristics and biases.
2013	*DSM*-5 is published by the American Psychiatric Association.

(Continued)

(*Continued*)

Date	Milestone
2014	A radio soap opera, "Musekeweya," is created by clinical psychologist Ervin Staub (Hungary, United States) and disseminated to Rwandan listeners to counteract hate speech and intolerance.
2015	The American Psychological Association bans psychologist participation in national security interrogations.
2015	Mona Amer (Egypt) and Germine Awad (United States) publish *The Handbook of Arab American Psychology*. It is the first major publication to comprehensively discuss the Arab American experience from a primarily psychological lens.
2015	David Trafimow (United States) bans null hypothesis significance testing for the journal *Basic and Applied Social Psychology*. This begins the debate about how to better determine if a hypothesis is supported or rejected.
2016	U.S. president Barack Obama signs the 21st Century Cures Act, which provides essential prevention services and treatments for populations in need and support.
2016	Mahzarin Banaji (India, United States) publishes *Blindspot: Hidden Biases of Good People* with colleague Anthony Greenwald (United States). Her work has advanced awareness of implicit or unconscious bias.
2017	Arkansas (United States) opens the first intimate partner violence shelter for men in the United States. The shelter also runs a domestic violence hotline for men.
2018	Mental Health at Work (United Kingdom) is launched by The Royal Foundation. The nonprofit provides support to employers and employees to help them improve well-being in their workplace and encourage conversations about mental health.
2019	Jennifer Eberhardt (United States) publishes *Biased: Uncovering the Hidden Prejudice That Shapes What We See, Think, and Do*. Her research advances the fields of race, bias, and inequality.
2020	In Mexico, a mental health bill that would have removed a person's right to consent to treatment was stopped by human rights activists.
2020	Telemental health availability broadens treatment options during the coronavirus pandemic.

1 AN INTRODUCTION TO PSYCHOLOGY

Welcome to the study of psychology—the scientific study of behavior and mind. If this is your first psychology course, expect to be surprised by what you find covered in this book. Most people think psychology deals mainly with the study of mental disorders—that is, depression, anxiety, or schizophrenia. Although it's true that psychologists often treat psychological problems, the image of psychology that you see in the movies or on afternoon talk shows is often misleading. Did you know that psychologists tend to focus just as much on the study of normal behavior as they do on abnormal behavior?

In fact, most of the material in this book comes from the study of normal people. Psychologists study normal behavior for two main reasons: First, to understand the abnormal, it is necessary to understand normal functioning first, in the same way that medical doctors need to understand healthy bodies before they can understand sickness and disease. Second, by understanding normal functioning, we can gain control over our environment and live more productive lives. As you'll soon see, modern psychology has something to say about everything from the treatment of irrational fears (such as the fear of spiders) to the development of effective study skills—even to the design of the kitchen stove. You can live a better life if you understand a little psychology.

At the same time, some of the things you'll learn may be difficult to match up with everyday experience. For example, you'll discover that your personal memories are not always accurate. Instead, what you remember can be an elaborate reconstruction of the past, one that bears little resemblance to what actually occurred. You will learn that your beliefs—how you think you would act and treat others—can be easily changed in the face of a demanding situation. We will even consider the possibility that free will is an illusion—instead, your thoughts may be influenced by unconscious forces and natural drives that are not under your direct control. As the behavioral neuroscientist David Eagleman put it, "The brain runs its show incognito," meaning that much of what we see and think is produced by a brain working in secret, below conscious awareness (Eagleman, 2011, p. 12). So be prepared: What you'll learn may well change the way you view yourself, the world, and others around you.

THE PROBLEMS TO BE SOLVED: WHAT IS PSYCHOLOGY?

Throughout this book, we present the topics of psychology from a "functional" perspective, which means we explain what a psychological process is *for* before explaining how it works. Our brains are filled with psychological tools, controlling everything from emotion to reason to memory. Each of these tools helps us adapt and solve problems. We'll describe these tools in detail and show you how each is used. We'll also focus on the specific situations in which they are applied. Each chapter begins with a preview section just like this, called "The Problems to Be Solved." Here we explain how and why a given psychological process is important, stressing its function and the particular problems that it helps us solve. To understand any psychological process completely, you first must have some idea of what the process is *for*.

The brain runs its show incognito.

MIGUEL MEDINA / Stringer via Getty Images

Here are a few examples: Suppose you're walking along a mountain trail and you hear a sudden rattle. You stop quickly because that sound could signal the presence of a rattlesnake. One important thing you learn about your environment is that certain events, such as rattling sounds, predict or signal other events, such as dangerous snakes. Our brains are designed to learn associations between significant events so we can better adapt to our environment. In Chapter 7, we'll discuss a procedure called *classical conditioning* that shows us how this important learning process works. As you read about this procedure, you should think about the adaptive problem that needs to be solved—how do we learn about signals in our environment? Likewise, in Chapter 13, you'll learn how we use psychological processes to interpret the behavior of others. If a shadowy figure emerges suddenly from an alleyway, it's important that you size up the situation quickly and decide on an appropriate response. Is this person a threat or just having a little fun? For a broad overview of the types of situations that we'll be considering in this book, take a look at Table 1.1.

At other times, we'll consider the methods psychologists use to understand behavior and mind. Here, too, we'll begin the discussion by examining what each technique is *for*. The methods of

TABLE 1.1 ■ Examples of Functional Problems Considered in the Book			
Chapter	**Functional Problem**	**Example**	**Solution Tools**
2	Determining the causes of behavior	Jayla watches a TV program and becomes aggressive.	Experimental research
3	Communicating internally	A bicyclist weaves suddenly into the path of your car.	Electrochemical transmission in the nervous system
7	Learning what events signal	You hear a rattling tail on a mountain path.	Associations acquired through classical conditioning
8	Remembering over the short term	You try to remember a person's name as you cross the room.	Rehearsal in short-term memory
10	Conceptualizing intelligence	Roland is excellent at fixing mechanical devices but is terrible at reading and math.	Psychometric tests designed to measure the mind
13	Interpreting the behavior of others	A shadowy figure emerges suddenly from an alleyway.	Knowledge-based social schemas used to predict outcomes
14	Defining abnormality	Lucinda hears voices and thinks she's immortal.	*Diagnostic and Statistical Manual of Mental Disorders*
15	Treating the mind	Amir is mired in the depths of depression.	Psychoactive drug therapy or "insight" therapy

psychology were not developed in a vacuum—they were developed to help psychologists understand specific aspects of behavior and mind. For example, what are the best strategies for understanding the changes we go through from infancy to adulthood (Chapter 4)? We know a great deal about the mind of a newborn, but how is this possible? Newborns can't tell us what they're feeling or thinking or seeing. What are the best ways to measure intelligence (Chapter 10)? How can abnormal behavior be treated (Chapter 15)? These are practical problems that psychologists face; and, again, the key to understanding the methods psychologists employ is to understand the specific problems that these methods are designed to solve.

Another reason we'll be discussing the methods of psychology—its techniques and strategies—is to help you develop scientific literacy. The scientific method is the "supreme court of appeal" for psychological insight. Most of the conclusions that you'll be reading about are based on controlled research, often in the laboratory but in real-world settings as well. To understand psychology, and what psychology is for, it's essential that you understand the nuts and bolts of scientific research. You'll find that our discussions will often include references to specific research studies, ones that have been published in peer-reviewed scientific journals (*peer-reviewed* means that other experts have critiqued the study prior to publication). We will also end every chapter with a feature called "Thinking About Research" that discusses a specific research study in detail and invites you to think critically about the study and its results.

This first chapter is designed to provide you with a broad introduction to the field of psychology. Our discussion will revolve around three basic questions:

Defining and Describing Psychology

Why is psychology defined as the scientific study of behavior and mind? We'll talk about the distinction between behavior and mind and about how and what psychologists do. Most scientific fields include subspecialties, and psychology is no exception.

Tracing the Development of Psychology: A Brief History

How did current psychological perspectives evolve? Psychology has a short history as a science, but scholars have been interested in psychological questions for centuries. We'll discuss some of the famous "schools" of psychological thought and how they developed. Modern psychology continues to bear the "footprints" of these schools of thought, so it's important to understand them well.

Identifying the Focus of Modern Psychology

What trends and directions are shaping modern psychology? We'll characterize how modern psychologists think and some important recent influences. Increasingly, modern psychologists are concerned with cognitive, biological, evolutionary, and cultural factors in understanding behavior and mind. Moreover, in keeping with our emphasis on research, psychologists are increasingly concerned with new data techniques, and with fine-tuning research methods to prevent false conclusions.

DEFINING AND DESCRIBING PSYCHOLOGY

Psychology is the scientific study of behavior and mind. The word comes from the Greek *psyche*, which translates as "soul" or "breath," and *logos*, which means the study or investigation of something (as in biology or physiology). The word *psychology* was not in common use before the 19th century, and the field of psychology didn't become an independent science until the middle of the 19th century (Boring, 1950). Prior to that point, "the study of the mind," as psychology was widely known, was conducted mainly by philosophers and physiologists. Neither Sigmund Freud nor Ivan Pavlov was trained in psychology, despite their reputations as famous psychologists. The field as we now know it simply didn't exist.

Notice that today's definition of psychology is quite precise—it is not simply the study of the mind; rather, it is the scientific study of behavior and mind. The emphasis on science, and particularly the scientific method, distinguishes psychology from the closely related field of philosophy. The essential characteristic of the scientific method, as you'll see in Chapter 2, is observation: Scientific knowledge is always based on some kind of direct or indirect observation. Psychologists collect observations, look for regularities, and then generate predictions based on what they've observed.

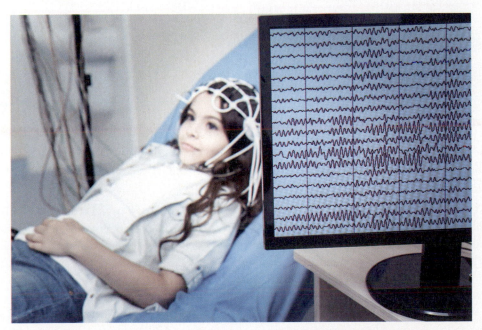

The term *behavior* can mean many things to a psychologist—even electrical activity in the brain.

iStockPhoto/yacobchuk

By **mind**, psychologists mean the contents and processes of subjective experience: sensations, thoughts, and emotions. Behavior and mind are kept separate in the definition because only behavior can be directly measured. Psychologists use the term **behavior**, though, in a quite general way. The activity of cells within the brain and even internal thoughts and feelings can be considered types of "behavior"—as long as they can be observed and measured in a systematic way.

What Psychologists Do

The work of all psychologists revolves around the scientific study of behavior and mind, but specialties abound. As summarized in Concept Review 1.1, we can divide the general job description into three main categories: *clinical psychologists, applied psychologists*, and *research psychologists*. These categories are somewhat artificial—for example, clinical psychologists often work in applied settings, and many conduct research—but the categories provide a useful way of defining the profession.

Clinical Psychologists

A **clinical psychologist** diagnoses and treats psychological problems—such as depression, anxiety, phobias, and schizophrenia. Clinical psychologists typically work in clinics or in private practice, delivering human services such as psychotherapy or counseling. To become a clinical psychologist, it is necessary to obtain a postgraduate degree such as a PhD (doctor of philosophy) or a PsyD (doctor of psychology).

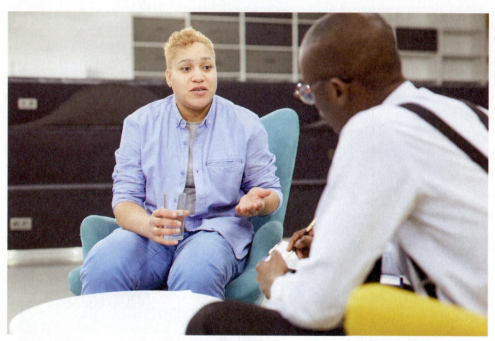

A clinical psychologist diagnoses and treats psychological problems. Clinical psychologists typically work in clinics or in private practice, delivering human services such as psychotherapy or counseling.

iStockPhoto/SeventyFour

Counseling psychologists also deliver human services, but they usually work on different kinds of problems. Counseling psychologists are more likely to deal with adjustment problems (marriage and family problems), whereas clinical psychologists tend to work with psychological disorders. Counseling psychology also requires a postgraduate degree, perhaps a PhD from a graduate program specializing in counseling psychology or an EdD (doctor of education). Together, clinical and counseling psychologists make up the majority of the profession (American Psychological Association, 2017).

What is the difference between a *psychologist* and a *psychiatrist*? Many people confuse the terms. **Psychiatrists** also specialize in the diagnosis and treatment of psychological problems, but psychiatrists are medical doctors. To become a psychiatrist, you must graduate from medical school and complete further specialized training in psychiatry. Like clinical psychologists, psychiatrists treat mental disorders, but unlike most psychologists, they are licensed to prescribe medication.

As you'll see in Chapter 15, medications are often useful in treating problems of the mind. There is an ongoing debate among mental health professionals about whether psychologists should be allowed to prescribe medication (Linda & McGrath, 2017; Nasrallah, 2017). Some states are considering legislation that will extend prescription privileges to licensed clinical psychologists; psychologists currently may prescribe in five states—Iowa, Idaho, Illinois, New Mexico, and Louisiana—as well as in the Public Health Service, the Indian Health Service, the U.S. military, and Guam. Usually, though, psychologists and medical doctors must work together. Clinical psychologists are likely to refer a client to a psychiatrist or general practitioner if they suspect that a physical problem might be involved.

Medications are often useful in treating problems of the mind.

Jb Reed/Bloomberg via Getty Images

Some clinically oriented psychologists choose to work with communities rather than individual clients. In fact, there is an entire field of psychology, known as *community psychology*, that examines and seeks to understand complex individual–environment interactions in order to bring about social change, particularly for those who have limited resources and opportunities (Jason et al., 2019). The field of community psychology typically focuses on the prevention of psychological problems rather than simply on their treatment. We'll discuss some of these prevention techniques in Chapter 16 when we focus on health psychology in general.

Applied Psychologists

Applied psychologists extend the principles of scientific psychology to practical, everyday problems in the real world. Applied psychologists work in many settings. For example, *industrial/organizational* psychologists are employed in industry to help improve morale, train new recruits, or help managers establish effective lines of communication with their employees. Industrial/organizational psychologists have developed sophisticated methodologies for assessing, evaluating, and recruiting employees, and they seek to understand what motivates performance and how workers react to stress (e.g., see Riggio, 2017).

Educational psychologists are concerned with the scientific study of how humans learn. Once again, sophisticated methodologies now exist that measure the effectiveness of classroom interventions, and educational psychologists are heavily involved in classroom management and instructional design. For example, as discussed in detail in the accompanying Practical Solutions feature, psychologists have recently been exploring the role of testing as a strategy for learning in the classroom. It turns out that actively taking a test, one that requires you to retrieve the information that you've just read about, leads to superior long-term retention, much better than retention of information that has simply been repeatedly read (see P. C. Brown, Roediger, & McDaniel, 2014).

Forensic psychologists apply psychological principles to legal issues, such as the reliability of eyewitness testimony or the evaluation of a defendant's mental competence. Forensic psychologists can also work directly with law enforcement to help with crisis management or to help officers understand the motives and emotions of both people who commit crimes and the victims of crimes. Academic researchers have been actively investigating the science of criminal confessions—both true and false—and the conditions that lead to false and true memories of a crime (e.g., E. F. Loftus, 2018; Wixted & Wells, 2017). We'll consider some of this research in detail in Chapter 8.

Human factors psychologists play a key role in the design and engineering of new products: For example, why do you think telephone numbers are seven digits long, grouped in three, then four (e.g., 555-9378)? How about traffic lights—why red and green? You'll find answers to these questions later in the book. Human factors psychologists even work on the design of the kitchen stove. Does your stove look like the one shown in the left panel of Figure 1.1? There are four burners, arranged in a rectangle, and four control knobs that line up horizontally along the front (or sometimes the back). To use the stove properly, you need to learn the relationship, or what psychologists call the *mapping*, between the control knobs and the burners. In this case, you need to learn that the far-left knob controls the back burner on the left. Or is it the front burner on the left? If you have a stove like this one, which is poorly designed from a psychological perspective, you likely have trouble remembering which knob controls which burner. We bet you've placed a pot of water on one of the burners, turned a control knob, and found moments later that you've turned on the wrong burner . . . right? The reason is simple: The stove has been designed with an unnatural mapping between its controls and the burners.

FIGURE 1.1 ■ The Human Factors of Stove Design

The stove on the left does not provide a natural mapping between the control knobs and the burners and is therefore difficult to use. The stoves in the middle and on the right provide psychologically correct designs that reduce user errors.

Illustrated by Sarah Yeh

Mapping is easier to understand when you look at a psychologically correct design, as shown in the middle panel of Figure 1.1. Notice that the arrangement of the burners naturally aligns with the controls. The left-to-right display of the control knobs matches the left-to-right arrangement of the burners. There is no need to learn the mapping in this case. It's obvious which knob you would use to turn on the appropriate burner. Alternatively, if you want to keep the rectangular arrangement of the stove top, then simply arrange the control knobs in a rectangular manner that matches the burners, as shown in the far-right panel. As these examples illustrate, there are natural and unnatural ways to express the relationship between product control and product function.

We'll be considering the work of applied psychologists throughout this book. Applied psychologists usually have a postgraduate degree, often a PhD, although a master's in psychology can be sufficient for a successful career in an industrial setting.

Research Psychologists

Some psychologists conduct basic research to discover the principles of behavior and mind. They are called **research psychologists**, and like applied psychologists, they usually specialize. *Behavioral neuroscientists* seek to understand how biological or genetic factors influence and determine behavior. *Personality psychologists* are concerned with the internal factors that lead people to act consistently across situations and also with how people differ. *Cognitive psychologists* focus on higher mental processes such as memory, learning, and reasoning. *Developmental psychologists* study how behavior and internal mental processes change over the course of the life span. *Social psychologists* are interested in how people think about, influence, and relate to each other. We're giving these psychologists only a brief mention here because you'll be reading about their work in every chapter of this book.

CONCEPT REVIEW 1.1
TYPES OF PSYCHOLOGISTS

Type of Psychologist	Guiding Focus	Primary Workplace	Examples of What They Do
Clinical psychologists	The diagnosis and treatment of psychological problems	Clinics Private practice Academic settings	Counsel clients suffering from adjustment problems or more severe psychological problems; evaluate diagnostic techniques and therapy effectiveness
Applied psychologists	Extending psychological principles to practical problems in the world	Private industry Schools Academic settings	Help performance of students in school; improve employee morale and performance at work; design computers so that humans can use them efficiently
Research psychologists	Conduct research to discover the basic principles of behavior and mind	Academic settings Private industry	Conduct experiments on the best study method for improving memory; assess the impact of day care on children's attachment to their parents; observe the effects of others on a person's helping behavior

PRACTICAL SOLUTIONS: WANT TO DO WELL ON THE TEST? TEST YOURSELF!

We've seen that psychologists focus on many different kinds of problems, but you're probably more interested in what they have to say about doing well in school. Have psychologists discovered the secret to understanding and remembering classroom material, or the subjects covered in your textbook? In fact, psychologists have a lot to say about successful learning and retention, and what they've discovered flies in the face of conventional wisdom.

The Myth: Repeated Reading

Suppose we conduct a simple experiment. Two groups of students are asked to read and remember a section of material from a college textbook. One group is given four separate opportunities during which they're allowed to read over the material and try to remember it. The other group is shown the material only once, but is required to recall what they studied on three consecutive tests. Two weeks later, everyone is asked to remember the material on a final test. Who does better—the group receiving four opportunities to read and reread the material or the group taking three tests? If you are like most people, you picked the read and reread group—after all, they're given four chances to go over the material. But if you did, you would be wrong, very wrong. In fact, the group given the three tests does substantially better. Not only does repeated testing lead to better memory for the original material; it leads to better comprehension as well (Karpicke, 2017; Karpicke & Roediger, 2008).

The Fact: Repeated Testing

The key to effective studying is effective testing. You need to practice retrieving the information, not simply read the material over and over again. In fact, repeated reading does very little to enhance either comprehension or later memory. Unfortunately, students rarely engage in repeated self-testing; their preferred technique is repeated studying, in the form of rereading or rewriting material from the book or their notes. You will learn about why repeated retrieval is so effective later in

Chapter 8, but consider the following example: Suppose you were trying to learn to play a piece of music on the piano. Which would be better—reading the sheet music over and over again or playing the piece on the piano? If the goal is to play the piano, you need to practice playing the piano. Likewise, if you want to remember something later on, you need to practice remembering it, not staring at it for hours.

Be Accurate

One final warning: Practicing retrieval through self-testing is a terrific way to study and learn material in a course. But it's very important that you practice retrieving the right information. If you test yourself and recall the wrong information, you could be in a lot of trouble. That means it's important to check your work. What you retrieve needs to be accurate, or you will "remember" the wrong thing. To make matters worse, many students tend to be overconfident about what they know—they are very poor at monitoring their learning effectively—and this leads to very poor retention and comprehension in the long term (Dunlosky & Rawson, 2011).

KNOWLEDGE CHECK 1.1

You can test your knowledge about how best to define and describe psychology by deciding whether each of the following statements is true or false. (You will find the answers in the Appendix.)

1. Psychologists use the term *behavior* to refer only to observable responses, such as moving about, talking, and gesturing. Internal events, such as thoughts and feelings, fall outside the domain of scientific psychology. *True or False?*

2. Psychology did not exist as a separate field of science 150 years ago. To explore questions about behavior and mind, it was necessary to study philosophy and physiology. *True or False?*

3. Clinical psychologists are generally interested in diagnosing and treating psychological problems such as depression or schizophrenia. *True or False?*

4. Psychiatrists differ from psychologists primarily in their focus of interest. Psychiatrists tend to work on severe and chronic problems, such as schizophrenia, whereas psychologists treat milder problems, such as phobias and anxiety disorders. *True or False?*

TRACING THE DEVELOPMENT OF PSYCHOLOGY: A BRIEF HISTORY

The field of psychology has a relatively short past, but it has a long and distinguished intellectual history. Thousands of years ago, the Greek philosopher Aristotle (384–322 BCE) wrote extensively on topics that are central to modern psychology—topics such as memory, sleep, and sensation. It was Aristotle who first argued that the mind is a kind of *tabula rasa*—a blank tablet—on which experiences are written. The idea that knowledge arises directly from experience, a philosophical position known as **empiricism**, continues to be an important theme in modern psychological thought.

Modern psychology developed out of the disciplines of philosophy and physiology. In a sense, psychology has always occupied a kind of middle ground between the two. Aristotle, Plato, and other philosophers helped frame many of the basic questions that occupy the attention of psychologists today: Where does knowledge come from? What are the laws, if any, that govern how we see and hear? What are the necessary conditions for learning and remembering? Physiologists, on the other hand, focused their attention on the workings of the human body. Before psychology was formally established, physiologists collected volumes of data on the mechanics of physical movement and the anatomy of sensory systems, which proved essential in the development of a scientific understanding of behavior and mind.

Mind and Body: Are They the Same?

What exactly is the relationship between the physical body, as studied by physiologists, and the mind, as studied by philosophers? Are the mind and body separate and distinct, or are they one and the same? In the 17th century, the French philosopher René Descartes (1596–1650) argued that the mind and body are separate: The physical body, he claimed, cannot think, nor is it possible to explain thinking by appealing to physical matter. He did allow for the possibility that one could have an important influence on the other. He believed the mind controlled the actions of a mechanical body through the *pineal gland*, a small structure at the base of the brain (see Figure 1.2). He was never clear about the details.

FIGURE 1.2 ■ Descartes and the Reflex

René Descartes introduced the concept of the reflex, which he described as an automatic, involuntary reaction of a physical body to an event in the outside world. He thought the mediating structure was the pineal gland, shown here as a tear-shaped area in the back of the head.

Oxford Science Archive/Print Collector/Getty Images

Descartes offered some ingenious descriptions of the human body, and he influenced generations of physiologists. Most of his ideas about the body turned out to be largely incorrect—the pineal gland, for example, plays a role in producing hormones, not muscle movements—but some remain influential today. It was Descartes who first introduced the concept of a *reflex*. Reflexes are automatic, involuntary reactions of the body to events in the environment (such as pulling your hand away from the hot burner on a stove). As you'll see in Chapter 3, reflexes play a very important role in our survival. But Descartes did little to advance the scientific study of the mind. To separate the mind from the physical world places psychology outside the boundaries of science. The scientific method is based on observation, and it's impossible to study something scientifically that cannot be observed in some way.

Today, most psychologists approach the mind–body problem quite differently from Descartes. They reject the separation of mind and body and assume they're one and the same. What we call the "mind" today is nothing more than brain activity; put simply, the mind is what the brain does (see Pinker, 1997). There is an extremely close link between the operation of the brain and behavior. Many psychological disorders come directly from problems in the brain, and many of the symptoms can be treated effectively through biological means (usually medication). Exactly how we infer mental "states" and processes from the study of brain action remains a tricky problem, but it's a problem that most psychologists believe will ultimately be solved.

Nature and Nurture: Where Does Knowledge Come From?

Philosophers and psychologists have always been interested in determining where knowledge comes from. Aristotle adopted an empiricist position: He believed that knowledge comes directly from our day-to-day experiences. Empiricism can be contrasted with a philosophical position called **nativism**, which holds that certain kinds of knowledge and ideas are inborn, or innate.

The Nativist Argument

Nativists believe we arrive in the world knowing certain things. The German philosopher Immanuel Kant (1724–1804) proposed that humans are born with a certain mental "structure" that determines how they perceive the world. People, he argued, are born with a natural tendency to see things in terms of cause and effect and to interpret the world in terms of space and time. Of course, it would be silly to claim that all knowledge is present at birth—we certainly learn lots of things—but some kinds of knowledge, the nativists argue, do not depend on experience.

The question of whether humans are born knowing fundamental things about their world is difficult to answer. For one thing, no one is sure at what point experience begins. We could draw a line at birth and say that any knowledge or abilities that exist at that very moment are innate, but as you'll see in Chapter 4, the environment exerts tremendous influence on embryos as they develop in the womb. We can never eliminate the influence of experience completely, so we're always faced with the problem of disentangling which portions of the knowledge we observe are inborn and which are produced by experience.

Darwin's Theory of Evolution

By the end of the 19th century, the ideas of Charles Darwin (1809–1882) began to dominate the debate about the origins of knowledge. Darwin proposed that all living things are the end products of an extended period of evolution, guided by the principles of natural selection. Cats have fur, seals have thick skin, and babies cry because these traits have been passed along—selected for—during the evolutionary history of the species. By *natural selection*, Darwin meant that some individual traits are better than others at promoting survival and enabling an individual to reproduce.

Because animals compete for survival and for opportunities to reproduce, those inherited characteristics that further survival and reproduction will be the traits most likely to persist from generation to generation. If an inborn tendency to cry helps us communicate feelings about hunger effectively, then it's more likely that we'll live long enough to pass this tendency on to our offspring. Such tendencies are selected for naturally because they are adaptive—they improve the chances of meeting the needs demanded by the environment (Darwin, 1859, 1871).

Notice that the emphasis is on inherited tendencies. Darwin believed that the principles of natural selection apply to characteristics that pass from parents to their offspring—not only physical traits, but behavioral and psychological ones as well. We now know that the principal vehicle for the transmission of inherited traits is genetic material inside the cells of the body. During development, the activity of the genes, together with other environmental influences, gives rise to the physical structure of the brain and the rest of the body.

By emphasizing the adaptive value of inherited characteristics, including psychological characteristics, Darwin had an enormous influence on psychologists (D. M.

Babies may have an inherited predisposition to learn language.

iStockPhoto/miodrag ignjatovic

Buss, 2019; Dennett, 1995). If natural selection plays a role in the evolution of mental abilities, then it's easier to accept the idea that people may inherit certain ways of thinking or of viewing the world (the nativist position). Researchers now commonly argue, for example, that humans may have an inherited predisposition to learn language, much as birds have an inherited predisposition to fly (Pinker, 1994).

Nature via Nurture

Today, virtually all psychologists accept that psychological characteristics, such as intelligence, emotion, and personality, can be influenced by genetic factors. We're born not with a blank slate but rather with a brain that is predisposed to act and think in particular ways. At the same time, genes never act alone; they always act in concert with experience. Experience (nurture) determines how genetic material is expressed, which, in turn, means that physical and psychological traits (nature) will always depend on both. Nature works via nurture and vice versa—one can't happen without the other (Ridley, 2003).

From an adaptive perspective, it makes sense that both factors are involved. Newborns arrive in the world with a set of basic reflexes that helps them survive. Yet, it would make no sense to "hardwire" the brain with fixed responses to all environmental events. We live in a constantly changing world, and it is to our advantage that we can shape our responses to best meet the needs of individual situations. One of the unique features of humans is that they do a lot of developing outside the womb, thereby allowing the environment to exert a powerful effect on our neural and psychological development.

The First Schools: Psychology as Science

The first psychology laboratory was established in 1879 at the University of Leipzig by a German professor named Wilhelm Wundt (1832–1920). Wundt was a medical doctor by training, and early in his career, he worked with some of the great physiologists of the 19th century. Fittingly, his laboratory was established during the time he spent as a professor of philosophy. (Remember, the intellectual roots of psychology lie at the union of philosophy and physiology.) Wundt is traditionally recognized as the founder, or father, of modern psychology, and 1879 is seen as the year that psychology finally started as a unique field. Prior to Wundt, it was not possible to major in psychology because there were no official psychologists or psychology departments (Bolles, 1993).

It is noteworthy that the birth of psychology began with the establishment of an experimental laboratory. Wundt's background in physiological research convinced him that the proper approach to the study of mental events was to conduct experiments. He believed that controlled observations should be collected about the mind in the same way that one might observe twitching frog legs to understand the principles of nerve conduction. Wundt didn't believe that all mental processes could be studied in this way, but he committed himself wholeheartedly to the use of scientific techniques.

Wilhelm Wundt, shown here in about 1910, established the first psychological laboratory in 1879, at the University of Leipzig.

Archiv Gerstenberg/ullstein bild via Getty Images

Structuralism

Wundt (1896) was convinced that the focus of psychology should be on the study of immediate conscious experience, by which he meant the things that people sense and perceive when they reflect inward on their own minds. This view was strongly shared by one of Wundt's students, Edward Titchener (1867–1927), who proposed that conscious experience could be broken down into elements—primarily sensations and feelings. Titchener believed it was the job of the psychologist to (1) identify these elements and then (2) discover how they combine to produce meaningful wholes. He later named this approach **structuralism**. Psychologists should seek the *structure* of the mind by breaking it down into elementary parts, much as a chemist might try to understand a chemical compound (Titchener, 1899).

Unlike a chemical compound, however, it's not easy to observe the internal workings of the human mind. Mental events are subjective, personal, and difficult to record. To solve this problem, the structuralists relied on a technique called **systematic introspection**, which required people to provide rigorous self-reports of their own internal experiences. Introspectionists were trained to describe the

Early psychology laboratories were often designed to measure basic reactions, such as sensitivity to temperature.

Bettmann / Contributor via Getty Images

elements that they perceived in simple visual stimuli, sounds, and tastes. As a result, mountains of data about elementary sensory experiences were collected. Titchener's laboratory, for example, was one of the first to document that complex tastes could be broken down into combinations of four elementary tastes: salty, bitter, sour, and sweet (W. B. Webb, 1981).

Once psychology was established as a laboratory science by Wundt and his contemporaries, psychology departments began to spring up rapidly throughout the world. This was particularly true in North America, where dozens of laboratories were established in the last two decades of the 19th century (E. R. Hilgard, 1987). Titchener immigrated to the United States and established his own psychological laboratory at Cornell University. By 1890, a number of professional journals had been established, and highly influential textbooks of psychology started to appear (e.g., W. James, 1890). In 1892, the American Psychological Association (APA) was founded. G. Stanley Hall (1846–1924), an American who had trained under Wundt in Germany, was installed as the APA's first president.

Functionalism

North American psychologists quickly moved away from the strict structuralist approach advocated by European psychologists. Rather than focusing exclusively on the content of immediate conscious experience, dissecting the mind into parts, North American psychologists worried more about the function of immediate experience. What is the purpose of immediate conscious experience? How do thoughts and feelings help us solve adaptive problems related to survival? Because of the emphasis on function rather than content, this school of thought became generally known as **functionalism** (Angell, 1903; Dewey, 1896; W. James, 1890).

Functionalists such as William James (1842–1910) and James Rowland Angell (1869–1949) believed the mind couldn't be understood by looking simply at its parts—that's like trying to understand a house by analyzing the underlying bricks and mortar (W. James, 1884). You need to determine the goal of the mental operation first, and then, perhaps, you can discover how the individual parts work together. To understand how memory works, a functionalist would argue, you first need to consider its purpose—what specific kinds of problems do our memory systems help us solve (Nairne, 2005)?

Darwin's ideas about evolution through natural selection were extremely influential in the development of functionalism. To analyze the color markings on a

William James, shown here in 1900, was convinced that to understand a mental process, its function must be considered: How does it help the individual solve problems in the environment?

CORBIS/Corbis via Getty Images

butterfly's wings, a Darwinian would argue, you must ask how those markings help the butterfly survive or reproduce. Similarly, when analyzing the operations and processes of mind, a functionalist would argue, you need to understand the adaptive value of those operations. How do they help people solve the problems they face?

Functionalism had a liberalizing effect on the development of psychology in North America. It greatly expanded the acceptable range of topics. It became fashionable to study how an organism interacts with its environment, which led to an early emphasis on how experience affects behavior (Thorndike, 1898) and to the study of individual differences among people. Later, some functionalists turned their attention to applied issues, such as how people solve practical problems in industry and in educational settings (F. W. Taylor, 1911). To a functionalist, almost any aspect of behavior was considered fair game for study, and psychology boomed in North America.

Behaviorism

Despite the differences between structuralism and functionalism, both still considered the fundamental problem in psychology to be understanding immediate conscious experience. The great functionalist William James is well known for his superb analysis of consciousness, which he compared to a flowing and ever-changing stream (see Chapter 6). Around 1900, the technique of introspection—systematic self-reflection—remained the dominant method of analysis in psychology.

Yet, not all psychologists were convinced that introspection could produce valid scientific results. In fact, throughout the early days of psychology, controversies raged over its proper role. By definition, self-observations are personal, so there is no obvious way to tell whether self-reports are accurate or representative of all people. Introspection also limited the range of populations and topics that could be covered. It's difficult to ask individuals with a severe mental disorder, for example, to introspect on their condition.

By 1910, psychologists started questioning the usefulness of studying immediate conscious experience. Increasingly, the focus shifted toward the study of observable *behavior*. The intellectual leader of this new movement was a young professor at Johns Hopkins University named John B. Watson (1878–1958). Watson was convinced that psychology should discard all references to consciousness. Mental events cannot be publicly observed, he argued, so they fall outside the proper domain of science. The task for the scientific researcher should be simply to discover how changes in the environment lead to changes in behavior. Because its entire emphasis was on behavior, Watson called this new approach **behaviorism** (Watson, 1913, 1919).

Behaviorism had an enormous impact on psychology, particularly in North America. Remember: The psychology of Wundt and James was the psychology of mind and immediate experience. Yet by the second and third decades of the 20th century, references to consciousness had largely vanished from the psychological vocabulary, as had the technique of systematic introspection. Researchers now concerned themselves with measuring behavior, especially in animals, and noting how carefully controlled laboratory experiences could change behavior (C. L. Hull, 1943; Skinner, 1938). Influential psychologists such as B. F. Skinner (1904–1990) demonstrated the practical value of the behaviorist approach. Skinner discovered the principles of behavior modification—how actions are changed by reinforcement and nonreinforcement—that are now widely used in mental hospitals, schools, and the workplace (Skinner, 1969). We'll discuss these principles in Chapter 7.

The behaviorist approach dominated psychology for decades. However, as you'll see later in this chapter, psychologists have returned to the study of mental events (but with a healthy insistence on defining those events in observational terms). Behaviorism continues to be influential in modern psychology, but it no longer commands the dominant position it once held.

B. F. Skinner, shown here with one of his famous "Skinner boxes," championed the behaviorist approach and was one of the most influential psychologists of the 20th century.

Nina Leen/The LIFE Picture Collection via Getty Images

Freud and the Humanists: The Influence of the Clinic

As American psychology was slowly drifting toward behaviorism, a medical doctor in Vienna was mounting his own psychological revolution. Sigmund Freud (1856–1939) was trained as a neurologist (someone who studies the nervous system). He regularly treated patients with physical problems that he felt were psychological in origin. His experiences led him to develop an all-encompassing theory of mind that was to have a huge impact on future psychologists and psychiatrists (Freud, 1900/1913, 1910, 1940).

Psychoanalysis

Freud called his theory and system of therapy **psychoanalysis**, because he believed that the mind and its contents—the psyche—must be analyzed extensively before effective treatments can begin. Freud believed that psychological problems are best solved through *insight*: The patient, or client, must understand exactly how memories and other mental processes lead to problem behaviors. For this reason, psychoanalysis is often referred to as a form of "insight" therapy.

Sigmund Freud
Imagno/Getty Images

One of Freud's unique contributions was his emphasis on *unconscious* determinants of behavior. Freud believed each person houses a hidden reservoir in the mind, filled with memories, urges, and conflicts that guide and control actions. By "unconscious" he meant that these conflicts and memories cannot be accessed directly through conscious introspection—you might try, but your mind prevents you from consciously experiencing certain feelings and memories on your own. Not surprisingly, Freud largely dismissed the study of immediate conscious experience. He relied instead on the analysis of dreams, which he believed were symbolic, and on the occasional slip of the tongue. He spent hours listening to his patients relate their latest dreams or fantasies in the hope of discovering a key that would unlock their unconscious minds. Freud's complex analyses of the mind and its symbols led to a theory of how the unconscious mind defends itself from those seeking to discover its secrets. We'll consider this theory, as well as its applications for the treatment of psychological disorders, in Chapters 12 and 15.

The Humanistic Response

Freud's influence was substantial, especially among clinicians seeking to treat psychological disorders. The familiar image of individual clients lying on a couch talking about their childhood, while the therapist silently jots down notes, is a fairly accurate depiction of early psychoanalysis. However, not all psychologists were comfortable with this approach. Freudian psychology painted a rather dark view of human nature, a view in which human actions are the product of unconscious urges related to sex and aggression. Moreover, it dismissed people's own thoughts and feelings about their actions; instead, behavior is primarily motivated by deeply hidden conflicts of which we are unaware.

In the 1950s, negative reactions to Freud's view of therapy and mind led to the development of a new movement, **humanistic psychology**. Humanistic psychologists such as Carl Rogers (1902–1987) and Abraham Maslow (1908–1970) rejected Freud's pessimism and focused instead on people's unique capacity for self-awareness, choice, responsibility, and growth. Humanists argued that people are not helpless unknowing animals controlled by unconscious forces—they are ultimately in control of their own destinies and can rise above whatever innate sexual or animalistic urges they possess. Humans are built for personal growth, to seek their fullest potential, to become all they are capable of being (Maslow, 1954; Rogers, 1951).

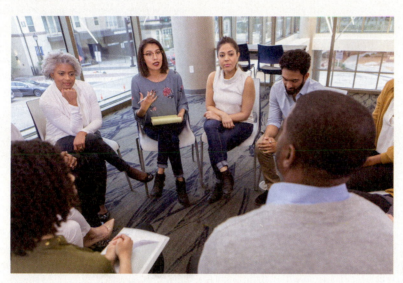

Humanistic psychologists believe people are in control of their personal destinies.

iStockPhoto/SDI Productions

The optimistic message of the humanists played a significant role in theories of personality development, as well as in the treatment of psychological disorders. Carl Rogers, for example, promoted the idea of client-centered therapy, in which the therapist is seen not as an analyst or judge but rather as a supporter and friend. Humanistic psychologists believe that all individuals have a considerable amount of untapped potential that should be nurtured by an empathetic therapist. This idea remains influential among modern psychological approaches to therapy (see Chapters 12 and 15). For a summary of how the humanistic approach compares to the other historical approaches to understanding behavior and mind, see Concept Review 1.2.

CONCEPT REVIEW 1.2
APPROACHES TO THE STUDY OF PSYCHOLOGY

General Focus	Specific Approach	Important Figure(s)	Focuses of Approach
Research	Structuralism	Wundt, Titchener	Determining the structure of immediate conscious experience through the use of systematic introspection, in which one attempts to describe the fundamental elements associated with simple thoughts and sensations.

(Continued)

(Continued)

General Focus	Specific Approach	Important Figure(s)	Focuses of Approach
	Functionalism	James, Angell	Determining the functions of conscious experience through the use of introspection, naturalistic observation, and the measurement of individual differences. Influenced by Darwin, it greatly expanded the range of topics studied in psychology.
	Behaviorism	Watson, Skinner	Establishing laws of observable behavior. The approach rejects the study of immediate conscious experience and mental events, unless they are defined in terms of observable behavior. It was the dominant approach to scientific psychology until the "cognitive revolution" of the 1950s.
Clinical	Psychoanalysis	Freud	Analyzing personality and treating psychological disorders by focusing on unconscious determinants of behavior. Also contends that childhood experiences play an important role in shaping adult behavior.
	Humanistic psychology	Rogers, Maslow	A reaction against Freud, emphasizing that humans are basically good and have a unique capacity for self-awareness, choice, responsibility, and growth.

Pioneering Women in Psychology

Mary Whiton Calkins (1863–1930) was elected president of the American Psychological Association in 1905. It's worth pausing and drawing special attention to this accomplishment because women have often been overlooked in historical treatments of psychology. Women were subject to significant discrimination in the early days of psychology. Women were denied admittance to Harvard University, and Mary Calkins was allowed to take classes with William James only as a special "guest" graduate student. She passed the final examinations for the PhD but was never officially awarded the degree. Calkins went on to make a number of contributions to the science of psychology, including the development of the paired-associate learning technique (a method for studying memory that is still in use today), and she was a major contributor to philosophy as well.

The first woman to receive a PhD in psychology (in 1894) was Margaret Floy Washburn (1871–1939), who in 1921 became the second female president of the American Psychological Association. Washburn's early contributions were in the structuralist tradition—she published her dissertation in one of Wundt's journals—and she became quite well known for her book *The Animal Mind* (1908) and for her behavioral views on consciousness. Helen Thompson Woolley (1874–1947) helped pioneer the study of sex differences, abolishing a number of myths about women that were widely accepted at the time. Never one to mince words, Woolley had this to say about the treatment of women in psychology circa 1910: "There is perhaps no field aspiring to be scientific where flagrant personal bias, logic martyred in the cause of supporting a prejudice, unfounded assertions, and even sentimental rot and drivel have run riot to such an extent as here" (H. T. Woolley, 1910, p. 340).

Calkins, Washburn, and Woolley are notable examples of female pioneers in psychology, but they were hardly alone. Many others overcame significant hardships to become active contributors to the developing science. For example, Christine Ladd-Franklin (1847–1930) was famous for her early work on color vision, and Lillien Martin (1851–1943), who made significant contributions in perception as well, rose to head the psychology department at Stanford University in 1915. Ruth Howard (1900–1997) was the first African American

Mary Whiton Calkins was the first female president of the American Psychological Association.

Psychology's Feminist Voices via Wikimedia Commons

woman to receive a PhD in psychology, and she is known for her significant contributions in clinical and developmental psychology. Martha Bernal (1931–2001), the first Latina to receive a doctorate in psychology, contributed significantly to the study of ethnic issues. Today, women work in all aspects of psychological research, and they continue to be important contributors to psychological thought. As you'll see in upcoming chapters, there is also a healthy interest in the psychology of women and in the study of gender differences (Hyde, 2014; D. I. Miller & Halpern, 2014).

Recognizing the important contributions of women to the development of psychological science is one of the success stories of the field. More recently, psychologists have begun focusing their attention on other historically underrepresented groups, such as sexual and gender minorities. The psychological community is increasingly engaged with LGBTQ+ movements in the United States and beyond, both in terms of inclusion, as well as recognition of homophobia and societal prejudice, and in terms of studying the biological factors that may contribute to personal and sexual preferences (see Hegarty, 2017). We'll discuss aspects of this work throughout the text. For a more in-depth look at how sexual orientation affects opposite-sex interactions, turn to the Thinking About Research section at the end of this chapter.

KNOWLEDGE CHECK 1.2

You can test your knowledge about the development of psychology by answering the following questions. (You will find the answers in the Appendix.)

1. Most modern psychologists believe that the mind and the body are
   a. controlled by different sections of the pineal gland.
   b. best considered as one and the same.
   c. separate, but both can be studied with the scientific method.
   d. best studied by philosophers and physiologists, respectively.

2. Fill in the blanks in the following paragraph. Choose your answers from the following set of terms: *behavior, behaviorism, emotions, empiricists, functionalists, introspection, structuralists, thoughts*.

   Functionalists and structuralists used the technique of _____ to understand immediate conscious experience. The _____ believed that it was best to break the mind down into basic parts, much as a chemist would seek to understand a chemical compound. The _____ were influenced by Darwin's views on natural selection and focused primarily on the purpose and adaptive value of mental events. _____, founded by John Watson, steered psychology away from the study of immediate conscious experience to an emphasis on _____.

3. Freud's psychoanalysis differs from Rogers's humanistic approach in which of the following ways?
   a. Psychoanalysis is "client centered" rather than "therapist centered."
   b. Psychoanalysis is designed to promote self-awareness and personal growth.
   c. Psychoanalysis minimizes the influence of early childhood experiences.
   d. Psychoanalysis is designed to reveal hidden urges and memories related to sex and aggression.

IDENTIFYING THE FOCUS OF MODERN PSYCHOLOGY

Psychology has changed a lot since Wundt established the first psychological laboratory in 1879. Psychologists continue to argue about the proper focus for psychology (mind or behavior?) and about how to conceive of human nature (e.g., is there free will?). Debates still rage about the proper form that theories should take and about the right kinds of methods to employ (L. D. Nelson et al., 2018). The presence of controversy shouldn't trouble you too much, however. Remember, the discipline is only about a century and a half old; psychology is still getting its theoretical feet wet.

In the 21st century, most psychologists refuse to accept just one school of thought, such as behaviorism or psychoanalysis, and instead adopt a more **eclectic approach**. The word *eclectic* means that one selects or adopts information from many different sources rather than relying on one perspective. Eclecticism is common among clinicians working in the field and among research psychologists working in the laboratory.

In the case of the clinical psychologist, the best technique often depends on the preferences of the client and on the particular problem. Some kinds of phobias—for example, irrational fears of heights or spiders—can be treated effectively by focusing on the fearful behavior itself and ignoring its ultimate origin. (We don't need to know why you're afraid of snakes; we can just try to deal with the fear itself.) Other kinds of problems may require the therapist to determine how factors in childhood contribute to troublesome adult behavior. Modern clinical psychologists tend to pick and choose among perspectives in an effort to find the approach that works best for their clients.

Research psychologists also take an eclectic approach. Depending on the circumstance, a researcher might try to determine the biological origins of a behavior or seek simply to describe the conditions under which it occurs. Once the conditions are cataloged, the behavior can be modified in a number of positive ways. Researchers recognize that it's possible to understand behavior and mind from many different perspectives, at many different levels of detail.

At the same time, several trends or perspectives have become influential in recent years. Modern psychologists remain eclectic, but they increasingly find themselves appealing to cognitive, biological, and cultural factors to explain behavior. In addition, there has been a recent renaissance in methodology—both in the kinds of data that are collected and in the way data are analyzed and reported. Because of the special emphasis these factors currently receive, we highlight them briefly in the following sections.

Cognitive Factors

By the 1950s, researchers began to show renewed interest in the fundamental problems of consciousness and mental processes (G. A. Miller, Galanter, & Pribram, 1960; Neisser, 1967). This return to the study of internal psychological processes has been called the **cognitive revolution**. The word *cognitive* refers to the process of knowing or perceiving; as you may remember from our earlier discussion, cognitive psychologists are research psychologists who study processes such as memory, learning, and reasoning.

Psychologists returned to the study of internal mental phenomena for several reasons. One factor was the development of research techniques that allowed them to infer the characteristics of mental processes directly from observable behavior. Changes in behavior, as measured by reaction times or forgetting rates, can provide detailed information about internal mental processes—as long as the experiments are conducted properly. You'll learn about some of these specific techniques later in the book.

Another important factor was the development of the computer, which became a model of sorts for the human mind. Computers function through hardware, the fixed features of the machine such as the processor and storage drive, and software, the programs that tell the hardware what to do. Although the human mind cannot be compared directly to a computer, behavior is often influenced by "hardwired" biological (or genetic) factors and by the strategies (the "software") that we learn from the environment. Cognitive psychologists often explain behavior by appealing to information processing systems—internal structures in the brain that process information from the environment in ways that help us solve problems (see Chapters 8 and 9).

Everything from perceptions and memories, to decisions about what foods to eat, to our choice of friends is influenced by our prior knowledge and beliefs. How we think determines how we behave. Many psychologists are convinced that to understand psychological disorders, such as depression, we need to understand a person's thought patterns. Depressed individuals tend to think in rigid and inflexible ways, and therapy is often directed specifically

The human mind cannot be compared directly to a computer. Yet, as in artificial intelligence devices, human behavior is often influenced by "hardware" (biological or genetic factors) and "software" (the strategies that we learn from the environment).

at challenging existing thoughts and beliefs. You'll see many references to "cognitive" analyses as we investigate psychological phenomena.

The Promise of Neuroscience

Modern psychologists have also benefited significantly from recent discoveries in biology. Over the years, researchers have uncovered fascinating links between structures in the brain and the phenomena of behavior and mind (see Figure 1.3). It is now possible to record the activity of brain cells directly, and we know that individual brain cells respond to particular kinds of events in the environment. For example, there are cells in the "visual" part of the brain that respond actively only when particular colors, or patterns of light and dark, are viewed.

Technology is also enabling psychologists to take "snapshots" of mental life in action. We can now create images of how mental activities change as the mind processes its environment. These pictures of the brain in action can help researchers understand normal as well as abnormal brain activity. For example, it's possible to record brain activity during depression, extreme anxiety, or even auditory and visual hallucinations. This information helps pinpoint where problems in the brain occur and acts as a road map for treatment.

Great strides have also been made in the understanding of brain chemistry—that is, how natural drugs inside the brain control a range of behaviors. It turns out that many psychological problems, such as depression and schizophrenia, can be linked to imbalances among the chemical messengers in the brain. These developments, which we'll discuss in detail in Chapters 3, 14, and 15, are shaping the way psychological problems are treated.

FIGURE 1.3 ■ Specificity in the Brain

Scientists have discovered that certain functions in the body appear to be controlled by specific areas of the brain. Biological research has an enormous impact on the thinking of psychologists.

Carolina Hrejsa/Body Scientific Intl.

Psychologists have also been influenced by Darwin's theory of natural selection. Although it was widely accepted in the 19th century that the principles of natural selection apply to psychological characteristics, few psychologists advanced these ideas after the rise of behaviorism. Instead, psychologists focused their attention on the environment (nurture) and on learning in particular. They essentially ignored evolutionary and inborn contributions (nature) to behavior. John Watson is known for claiming that any human infant might, under the right environmental conditions, be turned into a "doctor, lawyer, artist, merchant-chief and yes, even beggar-man and thief, regardless of his talents, penchants, tendencies, abilities, vocations and race of ancestors" (Watson, 1930, p. 104).

The rise of behaviorism was helped along by persistent attacks on Darwin's theory. Critics wondered why people and animals often act in ways that don't seem very adaptive. Across the animal kingdom, it's easy to find examples of social behavior that seems to occur largely for the benefit of another—often putting the actor in great personal danger. Parents might deny themselves food and water to help their children survive. In the face of a predator, some animals call attention to themselves by emitting warning cries that help save others in their group. How do these behaviors help promote an individual's "fitness" for survival and reproduction?

It wasn't until the second half of the 20th century that evolutionary theorists began to address these problems successfully. Some have argued that "altruistic" helping behavior can be handled by the mechanism of natural selection as long as one considers the unit of selection to be the gene rather than the individual (Dawkins, 1976; Hamilton, 1964). Sometimes actions that appear harmful to the individual can increase the chances that an adaptive gene, one that is shared within a family, will pass from one generation to the next. Moreover, it is now widely recognized that at least some of our actions are designed specifically to secure a mating partner and not necessarily to promote long-term survival (D. M. Buss, 2019).

Evolutionary psychology is a recent movement that seeks to identify exactly how our behaviors and thought processes have been molded by evolutionary pressures. Evolutionary psychologists believe we're born with mental software that guides our thinking and behavior. These natural tendencies, acquired through natural selection in our ancestral past, help us solve adaptive problems such as learning language, finding a mate, and acting socially in groups. For instance, it's been suggested that we're born with an ability to detect cheaters in social groups—those who violate social contracts or agreements (Cosmides & Tooby, 1992). We may also have been born with the natural distaste for incest, or sexual intercourse with relatives, because of its negative genetic consequences (Crawford, 2007). Not surprisingly, many of the claims of the evolutionary psychologists are controversial. Critics often argue that satisfactory environmental explanations can be given for behaviors that seem hardwired and universal (Buller, 2005; S. J. Gould & Lewontin, 1979).

Cultural Factors

Modern psychology is also increasingly recognizing culture and the role it plays in our thoughts and actions. By **culture**, psychologists generally mean the shared values, customs, and beliefs of a group or community (Lehman, Chiu, & Schaller, 2004). Cultural groups can be based on obvious characteristics such as ethnicity, race, or socioeconomic class but also on political, religious, or other factors (e.g., those who share the same sexual orientation might be considered a cultural group). Culture is a broad construct, and its influences can be found in virtually all aspects of behavior and mind.

Cultural influences were largely ignored in mainstream psychology for years. In the introductory textbook that one of us (JN) used as a college student, group influences were not discussed except for a mere three paragraphs covering why individuals might differ in intelligence. Moreover, virtually all research in psychology has been conducted using people from Western, educated, industrialized, rich, and democratic (often referred to as WEIRD) societies, even though such people reflect just 12% of the world's population (Henrich et al., 2010). Psychologists have always recognized that behavior is influenced by the environment, but it was the behavior of individuals in isolation rather than in groups that received the most attention. Researchers spent their time looking for universal principles of behavior that cut across all people in all groups, rather than exploring how the shared values of a community might affect how people think and act. The search for universal principles is still actively pursued today, as noted in our discussion of evolutionary psychology, but cultural influences are now considered to be a vital part of the story of psychology.

Cultural groups can reflect such obvious characteristics as shared ethnicity, race, or socioeconomic class but may also be based on political, religious, professional, or other factors.

Early on, a few notable psychologists stressed the influence of culture on cognitive and social development. Nearly a century ago, the Russian psychologist Lev Vygotsky proposed that children's thoughts and actions come from their social interactions, particularly with parents. Vygotsky didn't think it was possible to understand the mind of a child without carefully considering the child's social and cultural world. In an important sense, the properties of a child's mind are created by the child's social and cultural interactions. At first these ideas were not very influential in psychology, partly because Vygotsky died young in the 1930s, but they have recently been rediscovered by psychologists and are now being actively pursued. (You'll read a bit more about Vygotsky in Chapter 4.)

Why have cultural factors finally become so important to psychologists? There are a number of reasons, but perhaps the most important is that culture matters, even when studying basic psychological processes (see Keith, 2019). For example, it is recognized that members of Eastern societies (e.g., China and Japan), on average, think more in terms of the "group" than do Westerners (e.g., Americans), who tend to focus more on the individual. Members of these two cultures categorize and remember different things about encounters and simple visual scenes. Japanese responders, for example, are more likely to remember and report about the background elements of a visual scene ("there was a pond or lake"); Americans tend to focus on the active elements ("there was a trout swimming to the right") and ignore the background (Nisbett et al., 2001). We may even have culture-based brains, in the sense that cultural practices can powerfully shape and modify brain pathways (see Kitayama & Salvador, 2017).

The important lesson learned by psychologists, perhaps reluctantly at first, is that a full understanding of behavior cannot be achieved without considering individuals in their social and cultural context. Cultural factors play a role in how we think and interact with each other and even in how we see the world.

Big Data and Replication

Finally, psychology is undergoing a renaissance in the collection and interpretation of data. As empirical scientists, psychologists have always been concerned with data—observations of how people interact with each other and with objects in the world. But, for most of psychology's history, the techniques of data collection have been limited to relatively small sets of observations, often collected in a laboratory. The research psychologist formulates a hypothesis about the mind, brings a set of people into the lab, and then tests the hypothesis with tasks that produce observable outcomes. We discuss the methodologies behind these kinds of investigations in detail in Chapter 2.

Increasingly, however, psychologists are tapping into the power of Big Data, meaning extremely large behavioral databases that are generated by people interacting with their computers and smartphones. Every time you click a mouse, perform a Google search on your smartphone, or "like" something on Facebook, you are generating data that provide insight into your behavior and mind. As you know, advertisers already recognize this fact and have developed sophisticated algorithms designed to tailor the advertisements that you see to your particular interests. Psychologists, too, are beginning to tap into these sources of data to develop and test hypotheses about psychological issues (see Griffiths, 2015; Kosinski et al., 2016). It's an exciting development for the field, albeit one fraught with potential ethical issues, and you'll be reading about some of the insights developed with Big Data throughout this book.

The second part of the data-based renaissance centers on the replication of research findings. Psychology, as well as many other scientific fields, is undergoing a *replication crisis*, questioning whether the findings reported in peer-reviewed journals can be easily replicated, or confirmed in subsequent experiments. The crisis was fueled initially, in part, by a large study in which investigators from around the world attempted to replicate the results of 100 studies that had been reported in three high-ranking psychology journals (Open Science Collaboration, 2015). The investigators were able to replicate the original findings—that is, obtain statistically significant results that mirrored the original findings—in only 36% of the studies. The reasons for the failures to replicate are complex, and controversial, but they have led psychologists to reconsider their methods, particularly the manner in which data are analyzed (e.g., Shrout & Rodgers, 2018). We consider some of these recent trends in Chapter 2.

At the same time, it's important to understand that the methodological problems that led to the replication crisis are not unique to psychology. In fact, replication problems are commonplace in other scientific fields as well (Ioannidis, 2005), and psychologists have been among the leaders in developing new investigative techniques to handle replication concerns (L. D. Nelson et al., 2018). Moreover, the major findings that you'll be reading about in this book have been repeatedly replicated and usually generalize widely to different domains. For example, basic psychological and biological processes—learning, memory, perception, neural transmission, and so on—are well established and are associated with highly replicable experimental procedures (e.g., Zwann et al., 2018). Still, replication is one of the cornerstones of scientific knowledge, and we will be concerned with the issue throughout this book.

KNOWLEDGE CHECK 1.3

You can test your knowledge about the focus of modern psychology by answering the following questions. (You will find the answers in the Appendix.)

1. According to the eclectic approach, in choosing the best technique to use in therapy, you should consider
    a. the specific unconscious urges that are driving behavior.
    b. the training and biases of the therapist/researcher.
    c. the preferences of the client and the particular problem under investigation.
    d. the availability of relevant monitoring equipment.

2. Fill in the blanks in the following paragraph. Choose your answers from the following set of terms: *biology, cognitive, computer, cultural, philosophy.*
    Over the past several decades, psychologists have returned to the study of internal mental phenomena such as consciousness. This shift away from strict behaviorism has been labeled the _____ revolution. An important factor that helped fuel this revolution was the development of the _____, which became a model of sorts for the human mind. Developments in _____ are also playing an important role in shaping modern psychology and in creating effective treatments for psychological problems.

3. Evolutionary psychologists believe that we're born with certain mental mechanisms, acquired through natural selection in our ancestral past, that help us solve specific adaptive problems such as learning language, finding a mate, and acting socially in groups. *True or False?*

4. Increasingly, psychologists are appealing to cultural factors to help explain human behavior. Which of the following statements about culture and psychology is false?
    a. Cultural influences were largely ignored by psychologists for many years.
    b. Culture influences social processes but not basic psychological processes such as memory or reasoning.
    c. A few notable psychologists, such as Lev Vygotsky, studied cultural influences many decades ago.
    d. By "culture," psychologists mean the shared values, customs, and beliefs of a group or community.

THE PROBLEMS SOLVED: WHAT IS PSYCHOLOGY?

At the end of every chapter, you'll find a section like this, which summarizes the main points of the chapter. This is a good point to stop and think about what you've read and what it all means. Remember, the psychological processes that we'll be discussing exist for a reason—they help us solve problems every minute of every day. In this chapter, our goal was simply to introduce you to the science of psychology. We framed our discussion around three main issues.

Defining and Describing Psychology

Psychology is the scientific study of behavior and mind. Notice this definition makes no specific reference to psychological problems or to any kind of abnormal behavior. Although many psychologists (especially clinical psychologists) do indeed work to promote mental health, applied psychologists and research psychologists work primarily to understand "normal" people. The goal of the scientific study of behavior and mind is to discover general principles that can be applied widely to help people adapt more successfully—in the workplace, in school, or at home—and to unravel the great scientific mystery of how and why people do the things they do.

Tracing the Development of Psychology: A Brief History

Psychology has existed as a separate scientific subject for little more than a century, but people have pondered the mysteries of behavior and mind for thousands of years. Psychology has its primary roots in the areas of philosophy and physiology. Scholars in these fields addressed several fundamental psychological issues, including the relationship between mind and body and the origins of knowledge. Most modern psychologists solve the mind–body problem by assuming that the two are essentially one and the same—thoughts, ideas, and emotions arise out of the biological processes of the brain. It is a common belief among psychologists that many basic behaviors originate from innate tendencies (nature) as well as from lifetime experiences (nurture).

Once the discipline of psychology was established by Wundt in 1879, psychologists struggled with the proper way to characterize and study the mind. Structuralists, such as Wundt and Titchener, believed the world of immediate experience could be broken down into elements, much as a chemist seeks to understand a chemical compound. The functionalists argued that the proper focus should be on the function and purpose of behavior. The behaviorists rejected the world of immediate experience in favor of the exclusive study of behavior. Added to the mix were the insights of Sigmund Freud, with his emphasis on the unconscious mind, and the arguments of the humanists, who strongly advocated free will and the power of personal choice.

Identifying the Focus of Modern Psychology

Each of the early psychological perspectives remains influential to a certain extent today, but most modern psychologists adopt an eclectic approach—they pick and choose from the perspectives. The study of behavior remains of primary importance, but the world of inner experience is also considered fair game for study, as evidenced by the cognitive revolution and by recent developments in the biological sciences. The possibility that some of our thoughts and actions are controlled by innate mental mechanisms, acquired through natural selection, is also being actively pursued by evolutionary psychologists. Psychologists also now actively investigate the role that cultural factors play in their attempts to explain behavior and mind. Finally, in recent years, concerns have been raised about the replicability of psychological findings, and new techniques are being developed to eliminate these concerns.

THINKING ABOUT RESEARCH

A summary of a research study in psychology is given in this section. As you read the summary, think about the following questions:

1. Are women more willing to engage in intimate conversations with gay men than straight men? If so, why?
2. Do you think the results of this study would be different if the interactions were between two men—that is, a straight man talking to either a straight or gay male partner?
3. This study involved some deception—participants were not told about the true purpose of the experiment, and their interactions were secretly recorded. Are you comfortable with this kind of procedure?

4. Do you think the potential for sexual attraction is the only factor influencing these results? What other factors might be involved?

Article Reference: Russell, E. M., Ickes, W., & Ta, V. P. (2018). Women interact more comfortably with gay men—but not straight men—after learning their sexual orientation. *Psychological Science, 29,* 288–303.

Purpose of the Study: Psychologists are keenly interested in how people interact. In this study, the topic was opposite-sex interactions and how they are affected by men's often one-sided sexual attraction to women. If the element of sexual attraction is removed from an interaction, the researchers wondered, would women more readily engage in comfortable and intimate discussions with a man? To test this hypothesis, women were asked to interact with either a straight or gay man, and the nature of their interactions was assessed before and after they learned about their male partner's sexual orientation. The researchers were also interested in whether the physical attractiveness of the female participant would matter.

Method of the Study: Sixty-six heterosexual women and 66 men (34 heterosexual, 32 homosexual) participated. The women were randomly paired with either a straight or gay man, and each was told that they were participating in a study investigating how strangers convey different types of information about a discussion topic. All interactions were recorded with a hidden camera for later analysis. In the first phase of the experiment, the man's sexual orientation was kept secret; the two were simply recorded interacting for 5 minutes while they waited for the discussion topic. Next, the topic was presented: Both were asked to describe their ideal romantic partner (hence revealing the man's sexual orientation). Finally, the two were recorded for another 5 minutes. Of main interest was the nature of the interactions before and after the man's sexual orientation was revealed. The researchers also asked an independent group of participants to rate the attractiveness of each of the women.

Results of the Study: The results of the study showed a significant behavioral shift after the sexual orientation was revealed, but only when the man was discovered to be gay. Women who were paired with a gay man oriented their bodies more toward their partner, spent more time looking at their partner, and spent more time talking (see image below). The women were also found to show more positive emotions during the discussion. Again, this behavioral shift only

A straight woman with a straight man

A straight woman with a gay man

Source: Russell, E. M., Ickes, W., & Ta, V. P. (2018).

occurred after the women discovered that their partner was gay. The researchers also discovered that attractive women were more likely to show the shift than women rated somewhat lower in attractiveness.

Conclusions of the Study: From these results, the authors concluded that knowledge of a man's sexual preference increases women's comfort with a gay man (relative to a straight man), but also the extent to which women are willing to engage with a gay man at a more intimate level. The trends were more pronounced for attractive women, suggesting that worrying about a man's sexual intentions interferes with the effectiveness of opposite-sex interactions.

KNOWLEDGE CHECK: CHAPTER SUMMARY

(You will find the answers in the Appendix.)

DEFINING AND DESCRIBING PSYCHOLOGY

- Psychology is the scientific study of (1) _behavior_ and (2) _mind_. Scientific knowledge is based on (3) _sci method_. Psychologists infer how the mind works from directly measuring (4) _observation_

- (5) _Clinical_ psychologists diagnose and treat psychological problems. (6) _Applied_ psychologists extend the principles of scientific psychology to practical, everyday problems in the real world. (7) _Research_ psychologists conduct experiments and collect data to discover the basic principles of behavior and mind.

- Modern psychology developed out of the disciplines of (8) _Big Data_ and (9) _Replication_.

WEIRD
Western
Educated
Industrial
Rich
Democratic

TRACING THE DEVELOPMENT OF PSYCHOLOGY: A BRIEF HISTORY

- (10) _Descartes_ believed that the mind is separate from the body, which the mind controls through the pineal gland. Modern psychologists believe that the mind and body are the same, because the (11) _Body/mind_ is what the brain does.

- (12) _Empiricism_ holds that we learn everything through experience. (13) _Nativism_ holds that certain kinds of knowledge and ideas are innate (inborn). (14) _Darwin_ proposed that natural selection guides evolution and that certain tendencies are inherited. Today, virtually all psychologists accept that psychological characteristics are influenced by both (15) _Genes_ and (16) _Experience_.

- (17) _structuralism_ was founded by Wundt, who established an experimental lab to study the elementary components of immediate experience and how they add up to a meaningful whole. (18) _Functionalism_ was developed by North American psychologists who studied the adaptive purpose (function) of immediate experience. (19) _Behaviorism_ led by Watson, was based on the premise that because immediate conscious experience cannot be observed, measurable behavior is the proper subject of psychology.

- Freud was a neurologist and clinician who developed (20) _Psychoanalysis_, which used dreams and free association to analyze both the mind and (21) _unconscious_ determinants of behavior. Rogers and Maslow rejected Freud's pessimism and focused instead on positive traits. (22) _Humanistic_ psychology holds that we control our destinies and can attain our full potential as human beings.

- (23) _____, who developed a paired-associate technique, was the first woman president of the American Psychological Association. (24) _____ was the first woman to receive a doctorate in psychology and is well known for her behavioral views on consciousness. (25) _____ helped pioneer the study of sex differences. (26) _____ and (27) _____ did significant work on color vision and perception. (28) _____ made important contributions to the study of clinical and developmental psychology. (29) _____ contributed significantly to the study of ethnic issues.

IDENTIFYING THE FOCUS OF MODERN PSYCHOLOGY

- (30) _____ means that information is selected from many different sources rather than just one. Cognition is the process of knowing that involves learning, (31) _____, and reasoning and that importantly influences behavior. Biology influences thought and behavior. Certain psychological problems may be caused by imbalances among the (32) _____ messengers in the brain. (33) _____ factors may be the basis for the thoughts and actions that are controlled by innate mental mechanisms. Culture is influenced by the thoughts and actions of group members along with their shared (34) _____, customs, and beliefs. Finally, psychologists are increasingly recognizing the power of Big (35) ____ and the need to determine whether the results of any particular study can be repeated or (36) _____.

CRITICAL THINKING QUESTIONS

1. Psychology is the scientific study of behavior and mind. Is it surprising, then, that its intellectual roots lie in physiology and philosophy?

2. Although Freud was not technically a psychologist—he was a medical doctor—would you classify him as a clinical, applied, or research psychologist?

KEY TERMS

applied psychologists (p. 7)

behavior (p. 6)

behaviorism (p. 15)

clinical psychologists (p. 6)

cognitive revolution (p. 20)

culture (p. 22)

eclectic approach (p. 19)

empiricism (p. 10)

evolutionary psychology (p. 21)

functionalism (p. 14)

humanistic psychology (p. 17)

mind (p. 6)

nativism (p. 12)

psychiatrists (p. 6)

psychoanalysis (p. 16)

psychology (p. 5)

research psychologists (p. 8)

structuralism (p. 13)

systematic introspection (p. 13)

iStockPhoto/South_agency

2 THE TOOLS OF PSYCHOLOGICAL RESEARCH

Todd leaned back on his bed, headphones firmly in place, and cranked up the volume on his phone. He couldn't hear the hidden message, the one promoting the "Acme Weight Loss Program"; he just heard the steady "thump-thump-thump" of the bass. He noticed nothing at all in particular, but thoughts about losing weight kept entering his mind. . . .

Are there secret messages lurking about in advertisements or playing in the background of our favorite music? Maybe these messages are everywhere, hidden from the naked eye and ear by greedy advertisers and dark-natured rock stars. Some have assumed that subliminal ("below the threshold") stimuli are responsible for much of society's ills, such as sudden buying urges or especially abnormal thoughts (Key, 1973). Do you have an opinion?

Research psychologists have studied subliminal influence. Fortunately, they've found little need for concern (Greenwald et al., 1991; Merikle & Skanes, 1992). Subliminal messages may have an influence in some circumstances (Smarandescu & Shimp, 2015), but there's very little evidence that they're used by advertisers, and even if they are, their power to influence is weak at best. So, if Todd decided to buy Acme, it would almost certainly not be due to a subliminal message playing in the background of his music. It's an interesting topic for us, however, because this chapter deals with the techniques of psychological research. How do psychologists determine whether an event in the environment, such as a subliminal message, can affect our behavior?

Because psychology is a science, psychologists use the **scientific method** as their main tool for investigating behavior and mind. To understand the effect of subliminal messages, then, we must first employ the scientific method. Reduced to its barest essentials, the scientific method contains four important steps (see Figure 2.1).

FIGURE 2.1 ■ The Scientific Method: Four Major Steps

1. *Observe.* The rat jumps toward the checkerboard panel on the left. 2. *Detect regularities in behavior.* The researcher notes that the rat, over repeated trials, consistently jumps to the checkerboard on the left. 3. *Generate a hypothesis:* If I move the checkerboard to the right, the rat will jump to the right. 4. *Observe to test the hypothesis.* Here the hypothesis turns out to be wrong. The rat jumps left again instead of following the checkerboard.

Observe	Detect Regularities	Generate Hypothesis	Observe
The rat receives food for jumping through the checkerboard panel on the left.	Over trials, the rat consistently chooses to jump toward the checkerboard panel on the left.	The rat has learned to associate the checkerboard with food, so if the checkerboard is moved to the right, the rat will jump to the right.	The rat jumps to the left, suggesting it has learned that jumping left produces food.

Illustrated by Sarah Yeh

1. *Observe.* The scientific method always begins, appropriately, with observation. In psychology, we choose the behavior of interest and begin recording its characteristics as well as the conditions under which the behavior occurs.

2. *Detect regularities.* Next the researcher looks for regularities in the observations—are there certain consistent features or conditions under which the behavior commonly appears?

3. *Generate a hypothesis.* The researcher then forms a hypothesis, which is a prediction about the characteristics of the behavior under study. Hypotheses are normally expressed in the form of testable if-then statements: If some set of conditions is present and observed, then a certain kind of behavior will occur.

4. *Observe.* Finally, the predictions of the hypothesis are checked for accuracy—once again through observation. If new data are consistent with the prediction of the hypothesis, the hypothesis is supported.

Notice that the scientific method is anchored on both ends by observation: Observation always begins and ends the scientific process. This means that psychological terms must be defined in a way that allows for observation. To make certain that terms and concepts meet this criterion, psychologists use **operational definitions**, which define concepts specifically in terms of how those concepts can be measured (Levine & Parkinson, 1994; S. S. Stevens, 1939). *Intelligence* might be defined operationally as performance on a psychological test; *memory* might be defined as the number of words correctly recalled on a retention test. If your goal is to investigate the topic of *subliminal influence*, you'll need an operational definition for subliminal influence. Can you think of one? We'll return to the topic of subliminal messages later in the chapter.

THE PROBLEMS TO BE SOLVED: HOW DO WE STUDY BEHAVIOR AND MIND?

Research techniques are designed to solve specific kinds of problems for the psychologist, such as determining cause and effect or predicting and selecting. To understand a method, you must first understand its goals—what kind of information about behavior and mind is the psychologist attempting to collect?

Observing and Describing Behavior: Descriptive Research

Because the scientific process depends on observation, one of the most important steps in any psychological research project is to choose a behavior and begin recording its characteristics. However, observation in research is more than casual looking or listening—the methods of observation must be systematic. To solve problems associated with observation and description, psychologists have developed a set of procedures known collectively as descriptive research.

Predicting Behavior: Correlational Research

Once behavioral data have been collected and described, the researcher typically begins to think about the possibility of prediction. Descriptive research yields facts about behavior, but we need a different set of techniques to decide when and how the behavior will reoccur. Prediction is valuable because it allows for more effective control of future environments. To solve the problem of prediction, psychologists often employ correlational research.

Explaining Behavior: Experimental Research

To understand the cause of a behavior, it's necessary to conduct experimental research. The researcher systematically manipulates the environment to determine its effect on a particular behavior. If conducted properly, an experiment allows the researcher to understand why the behavior occurs or changes over time.

The Ethics of Research: Human and Animal Guidelines

Psychologists are interested in the behavior of others. But is it proper for the psychologist to hide in the shadows, recording someone's every move in an attempt to advance scientific knowledge? Is it acceptable to experiment on animals—depriving them of food or water or destroying portions of their brain—simply to learn about the mechanisms controlling behavior? These are not easy questions to answer, but researchers have developed a set of ethical principles to help ensure that all research participants are treated with dignity and respect.

OBSERVING BEHAVIOR: DESCRIPTIVE RESEARCH

Descriptive research consists of the methods that are used to observe and describe behavior. At face value, the act of observation seems simple enough—after all, most people can watch and record the behavior of themselves or others. However, it's easy to be misled, even when the goal is simply to record behavior passively (Rosenthal & Rosnow, 1969; Rosnow & Rosenthal, 1996).

Let's suppose you want to observe the behavior of preschoolers in the local day care center. You arrive with cameras and recording devices to observe the children at play. But you soon notice that the children distract easily—many seem uneasy and hesitant to participate in the activities suggested by the teacher. Several children show outward signs of fear and eventually withdraw, crying, to a corner of the room. You conclude that children in day care centers adjust badly, and some even show early signs of poor psychological health.

Is this a valid conclusion? Probably not. Whenever you observe the actions of another, the very act of observing can affect the behavior you're recording. In the case of the day care center, it's likely that your unexpected presence (with cameras and the like) made the children feel uncomfortable and led them to act in ways that were not representative of their normal

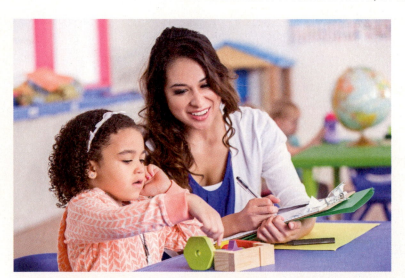

Psychologists must keep in mind the problem of reactivity: Are the behaviors they're observing simply a reaction to being observed? If this child behaves differently because of the observer's presence, the observations may not generalize well to other situations.

iStockPhoto/SDI Productions

behavior. Psychologists call this a problem of reactivity. **Reactivity** occurs when behavior is changed by the process of being observed. It's called reactivity because the behavior is essentially a reaction to the observation process (Orne, 1969; E. J. Webb et al., 1981). The children are probably not naturally hesitant and distracted—they were simply startled by your presence.

One consequence of reactivity is the loss of external validity. **External validity** tells us how well the results of an observation generalize to other situations or are representative of real life (D. T. Campbell & Stanley, 1966; Cook & Campbell, 1979). If a child's behavior is largely a reaction to your presence, it is clearly not representative of real life. More generally, even if these children are naturally fearful, your one set of observations cannot guarantee that your conclusions are representative of how children at other day care centers will act. To improve external validity, you must record the behavior of children at another day care center, or preferably many day care centers, to see whether similar behaviors emerge.

Naturalistic Observation: Focusing on Real Life

One way to reduce the problem of reactivity and improve external validity is to observe behavior in natural settings. In **naturalistic observation**, the researcher records only naturally occurring behavior, as opposed to behavior produced in the laboratory. Because the recorded behavior is natural, and the researcher has tried hard not to interfere in any way, the observations are considered to be representative of real life. (Of course, it is necessary to repeat the observations in different settings to be certain the results generalize.) Also, if the participants are unaware of being observed, their behavior cannot simply be a reaction to the observation process. Naturalistic observation has been used with great success by psychologists as well as by ethologists, biologists who study the behavior of animals in the wild (Goodall, 1990; Lorenz, 1958).

Researchers sometimes use a naturalistic technique called *participant observation*. Here, the observer attempts to become a part of the activities being studied, to blend into the group. In the 1950s, a group of psychologists joined a doomsday cult group by passing themselves off as believers. The cult members were convinced that the world was going to end, on a particular date, from a natural disaster. Once they were on the inside, the psychologists recorded and studied the reactions of the cultists when the prophesized "day of doom" failed to materialize (Festinger et al., 1956). In another classic but controversial project that you'll read more about in Chapter 14, a group of researchers committed themselves to local mental hospitals—they complained of hearing voices—in an effort to obtain an honest record of patient life inside an institution (Rosenhan, 1973). Participant observation could also have been used in our day care center example: You could introduce yourself as a new teacher, rather than as a researcher, and hide your cameras or other recording equipment.

In naturalistic observation, the researcher only records behavior that occurs naturally (in contrast to behavior produced in the laboratory), and makes an effort not to interfere in any way.

iStockPhoto/DieterMeyrl

Another way to reduce reactivity is to measure behavior indirectly, by looking at the results of the behavior rather than the behavior itself. You could learn something about the shopping habits of teenagers at the local mall by analyzing the litter they leave behind. Administrators at museums have determined the popularity of various exhibits by noting how quickly floor tiles in front of each display wear out and need to be replaced (E. J. Webb et al., 1981). Neither of these examples requires direct observation; it is the aftereffects of the behavior that provide the insightful clues.

Naturalistic observation can also be used to verify the results of laboratory experiments. To understand why a behavior occurs, researchers usually manipulate the behavior directly through an experiment. Because it is difficult to conduct an experiment in natural settings, laboratory studies generate concerns about external validity. Most studies of human memory, for example, have been conducted by having people learn lists of words in the laboratory (Bruce, 1985; Neisser, 1978). Do the principles established from such studies apply to learning and remembering in natural settings? To answer this question, psychologists also record natural instances of remembering and forgetting. There is a device, called the SenseCam, that takes digital snapshots of everything in the immediate view of an observer. SenseCam can easily be worn around the neck, and it automatically takes a new picture every 30 seconds or so. This means that the SenseCam can provide a digital record of everything the person has seen and done over the course of a day. Such a record can then be used by a researcher to verify a person's memories of the day's events. SenseCams also have a practical application, helping people with memory difficulties recover important events from the day (S. Hodges et al., 2011).

Case Studies: Focusing on the Individual

In a **case study**, the researcher focuses on a single case, usually one individual. Because lots of information can be collected about the background and behavior of a single person, case studies give researchers an important historical perspective; this, in turn, helps the researcher form hypotheses about the possible causes of a behavior or psychological problem.

Researchers can record events from participants' daily lives if they wear a camera while they perform everyday tasks.

iStockPhoto/piola666

It's easy to find examples of case studies. Just browse around at your local bookstore, and you'll find lots of books written about interesting cases; often the main characters in these books suffer from psychological problems or bizarre neurological disorders. *Sybil* is a well-known case study of multiple personality disorder (now known as dissociative identity disorder) (Schreiber, 1973). The neurologist Oliver Sacks has written a number of delightful books about clinical cases, such as *The Man Who*

Mistook His Wife for a Hat (Sacks, 1985) and *The Mind's Eye* (Sacks, 2010). One of the most influential psychological theories of the 20th century, the psychoanalytic theory of Sigmund Freud, was based primarily on descriptive data gathered from case studies.

Like naturalistic observation, case studies have limitations. By focusing on a single case, one obvious concern is external validity: Are the experiences of the research participant truly representative of others? Sybil's particular case may not be representative of how psychological disorders normally develop. Another problem is verification: It can be difficult to verify the claims of the studied person. If the observations of the participant are somehow tainted—the person is lying, for example—the entire study must be viewed with suspicion. In fact, recent evidence suggests that many of the original claims about Sybil and her disorder may have been fabrications (Nathan, 2011). Case studies can be excellent vehicles for generating hypotheses but are generally ineffective for determining cause-and-effect relationships.

Surveys: Focusing on the Group

Whereas a case study focuses on a single individual, a **survey** is used to sample behavior broadly, usually by gathering responses from many people. Most surveys use questionnaires. Individuals or groups are asked to answer questions about some personal behavior or psychological characteristic. You're familiar with the opinion surveys conducted by political campaigns. Surveys can also be used purely for research purposes to gain valuable descriptive information about behavior and mind. For example, researchers have used surveys to determine whether there are gender differences in online (internet) buying behavior (Dittmar et al., 2004), and to see whether television viewing habits in the days immediately following the September 11 terrorist attacks affected the likelihood of developing posttraumatic stress disorder (Ahern et al., 2004). Numerous surveys are currently underway to assess the immediate and long-term effects of the coronavirus pandemic (Every-Palmer et al., 2020).

Figure 2.2 shows the results of a survey conducted by Michael Yapko (1994) in which 869 psychotherapists with differing degrees of academic training responded to questions about the use of

---

FIGURE 2.2 ■ Opinions About Hypnosis

A survey of psychotherapists shows the percentage of respondents who agreed, disagreed, or gave no response to the following statements: "Hypnosis is a worthwhile psychotherapy tool," "Hypnosis can be used to recover memories of actual events as far back as birth," and "Hypnosis can be used to recover accurate memories of past lives" (Yapko, 1994).

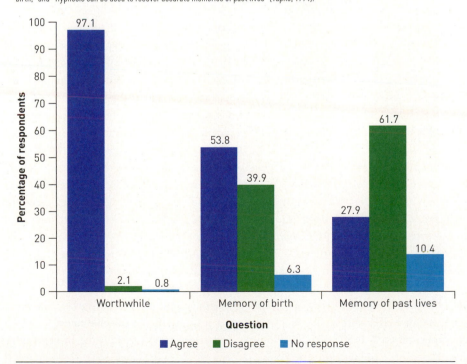

Source: Adapted from Yapko, 1994.

hypnosis for recovering forgotten or repressed memories. As you may know, hypnosis is sometimes used by therapists as a memory aid to help people recover forgotten instances of trauma. Ninety-seven percent of Yapko's survey respondents agreed that hypnosis is a worthwhile tool in psychotherapy. Nearly 54% were convinced that hypnosis could be used to recover memories of actual events as far back as birth. More than one in four of the respondents believed that hypnosis could be used to recover accurate memories of past lives. If conducted properly, surveys are useful because they provide researchers with valuable insight into what people believe. In this case, Yapko's results are alarming because they reveal how widespread misinformed views can be, even among professional psychotherapists (don't worry, the Yapko data do not represent the majority opinion among psychologists—for reasons that will be described later). As you'll discover in Chapter 6, memories recovered through hypnosis may not be especially accurate. Plus, there is certainly no scientific evidence to support the existence of past lives (remembered or otherwise)! But before survey results can be accepted as truly representative of a group, such as practicing psychotherapists, the researchers must make certain that the participants in the survey have been sampled randomly (see Lindsay & Poole, 1998).

Sampling From a Population

The purpose of a survey is to gather lots of observations to help determine the characteristics of a large group or population. If the population is extremely large, such as everyone between ages 18 and 25 in the United States, researchers must decide how to select a representative subset of individuals to measure. A subset of individuals from a target population is referred to as a *sample*.

When sampling from a population, it's easy to end up with an unrepresentative, or biased, sample unless the proper precautions are taken. Let's imagine that a researcher named Rosa wants to know how often college-aged adults practice safe sex. She puts an ad containing a telephone number in selected college newspapers. Her hope is that students will call the number and answer questions about their sexual practices. However, not every college-aged student in the country will choose to participate. This means that Rosa will end up with only a subset, or sample, of the population of interest. Do you think the data collected from her subset will be truly representative of college students? In this case, the answer is clearly "No," because the method of sampling depends on people choosing to participate. Volunteers tend to produce biased samples, because people who volunteer usually have strong feelings or opinions about the study (Rosenthal & Rosnow, 1975). Think about it—would you tell a researcher that you regularly fail to practice safe sex?

Representative samples are produced through **random sampling**, which means that everyone in the target population has an equal likelihood of being selected for the survey. Because everyone has an equal chance of participating, random sampling helps to ensure that all possible biases, viewpoints, and backgrounds will be represented. In principle, for Rosa to achieve a truly unbiased sample, she would need to sample randomly from the entire population of college students—everyone in the group must have an equal chance of being selected. Because this is difficult to achieve in practice, Rosa will probably limit herself to sampling randomly from the population of students going to her particular college.

Now let's return to Yapko's (1994) survey, in which 869 practicing psychotherapists gave their views on the use of hypnosis as an effective memory aid. The results showed that some psychotherapists wrongly believe that hypnosis can be used to recover memories from past lives. Importantly, however, Yapko did not use a random sample of psychotherapists in his study—he simply asked therapists who attended certain conventions and workshops for their opinions. His survey may therefore suffer from a volunteer problem that limits its generalizability. Only psychotherapists with strong opinions about hypnosis may have chosen to participate. To claim his results are truly representative of psychotherapists as a whole, he would need to use random sampling (for a similar study that does use random sampling, see Gore-Felton et al., 2000).

Even if a proper sample of the population has been selected, surveys can suffer from additional problems. Because large numbers of people are tested, it is usually not possible to get detailed information about the topic of interest. For example, researchers cannot obtain the in-depth historical information that can be collected in a case study. Surveys also consist mainly of self-reports, and people cannot always be counted on to provide accurate observations. Some people lie or engage in wishful thinking; others answer questions in ways they think might please the researcher.

Fortunately, psychologists have developed methods of checking for these types of strategies, but there is no perfect way to ensure honest and accurate responses from a participant. The results of a survey can also depend on the particular wording of the questions or even on the order in which the questions are asked. Surveys can be written in ways that minimize the risk of inconsistent responses—for example, particular questions can be asked several times with slightly different wording—but inaccurate responding remains a concern and is difficult to eliminate.

Another issue in sampling is the lack of diversity that has long existed in samples used in psychological research. In Chapter 1, the concept of WEIRD (Western, educated, industrialized, rich, and democratic) culture samples was described. Many researchers are now attempting to address this sampling bias by including a larger diversity of individuals in research studies and developing techniques to measure the differences across cultures (e.g., Muthukrishna et al., 2020). But even within samples that come from populations in the United States, many studies draw their samples from undergraduate student populations at colleges and universities. These populations typically contain a majority of fairly affluent, white, young adults, leaving out large sections of the U.S. population. And because many psychological research studies are published by researchers in the United States, many data sets are biased toward this population.

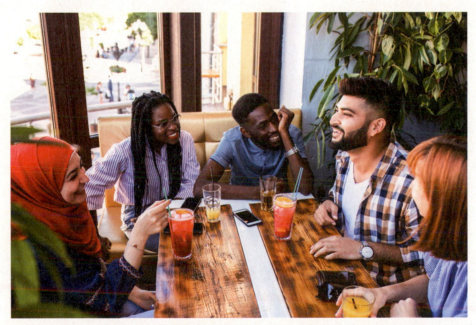

Most psychological research has focused on samples from WEIRD populations, but researchers are now correcting this bias by including more diverse samples in current research.

iStockPhoto/Evgeniia Siiankovskaia

Psychological Tests: Assessing Individual Differences

One of the most widely used descriptive research techniques is the psychological test. Psychological tests come in a variety of forms. They're designed primarily to measure differences among people. For example, *achievement tests* measure a person's current level of knowledge or competence in a particular subject (such as mathematics or psychology); *aptitude tests* measure the potential for success in a given profession or area of study. Researchers also use intelligence and personality tests to classify ability, or to characterize a person's tendencies to act in consistent ways.

Psychologists use tests to predict and select the fundamental components of the mind, as well as to help decipher them.

Lewis J. Merrim / Science Source

Psychological tests have enormous practical value, and they help to advance basic research (Kaplan & Saccuzzo, 2005). Intelligence tests can be used to identify children who might need extra help in school or who are gifted and can benefit from an enriched curriculum; for adults, intelligence test scores are sometimes used to predict future performance on the job (O'Boyle et al., 2010; Ree & Earles, 1992). Of course, tests also help diagnose psychological problems and verify the effectiveness of treatment.

Psychological tests are also used to answer fundamental questions about behavior and mind. For example, do people have a fixed amount of intelligence, present at birth, or do they have multiple kinds of intelligence that rise and fall with experience? Do people have consistent personality traits, such as honesty or pleasantness, or do their behaviors change haphazardly across situations? You'll hear more about these specific topics when we treat psychological tests in detail in Chapters 10 and 12. Table 2.1 provides an overview of the observational research methods described in this section, along with the advantages and disadvantages of each method to help you review what you've just read.

Statistics: Summarizing and Interpreting the Data

At the end of any research project, the observations are organized and summarized. Researchers look for patterns in the data so that hypotheses can be formulated and tested. If the observations can be expressed as numbers, you can calculate *statistics*, or values derived from mathematical manipulations of the data.

TABLE 2.1 ■ Observational Research Methods		
Specific Method	**Description**	**Advantages (A) and Disadvantages (D)**
Naturalistic observation	Record naturally occurring behavior	A: Behavior is natural; results are generalizable D: Research lacks control; can't determine cause
Case studies	Gather a great deal of information on a single case	A: Gives historical perspective D: Difficulties in generalization based on one case
Surveys	Gather responses from many participants	A: Can easily gather large amounts of information D: Sample bias; people misrepresenting themselves
Psychological tests	Measure individual differences among people	A: Potential practical uses; assess basics of mind D: Difficulties in test construction and validation

Central Tendencies

It's often useful to begin with a measure of central tendency, or the value around which scores tend to cluster. The **mean** is the arithmetic average of a set of scores. To calculate a mean, you simply add up the numbers for each of the observations and divide the total by the number of observations. Suppose you're a server at a local restaurant. You work a five-day week, and your tips for the week are $30, $20, $20, $60, and $70. The mean of these scores would be 40 (30 + 20 + 20 + 60 + 70 = 200; 200 / 5 = 40). The mean summarizes the data into a single representative number: On average, you made $40 in tips each day. Notice, though, you never actually made $40 on any given day. The mean provides only an estimate of central tendency; it does not indicate anything about particular scores.

Other measures of central tendency include the **mode**, which is the most frequently occurring score (in the tip example the mode is $20), and the **median**, which is the middle point in the set of scores. The mode has the advantage of representing a real score—you did actually receive $20 on some days—and it's easy to calculate. Calculating the median takes a bit more work. First order the scores from smallest to largest (20, 20, 30, 60, 70), then look for the middle score. For tips, half the scores fall below 30, and half fall above, so 30 is the median. If the number of scores is even, with no single middle score (e.g., 20, 20, 30, 40, 60, 70), the median is typically calculated by taking the midpoint of the two middle scores (the midpoint between 30 and 40 is 35).

Researchers usually like to compute several measures of central tendency. The mean is an excellent summary of the average score, but it can be misleading. Suppose instead of $70 on your last workday you actually pull in $150! If we replace the old number with the new one, we now have the following set of scores: 20, 20, 30, 60, 150. The mean will shift rather dramatically because of the extreme score, from 40 to 56, but neither the mode nor the median will change at all (see Figure 2.3). Because of the way they are calculated, means are very sensitive to extreme scores—the value shifts in the direction of the extreme score. On the other hand, the mode and the median are unaffected. In our example, the median or the mode is probably a better summary of your daily income than the mean.

FIGURE 2.3 ■ Comparing the Mean, the Median, and the Mode

The top row shows the differences between the mean (arithmetic average), the median (middle point in a set of scores), and the mode (most frequently occurring score) for tips earned per day in a restaurant. The bottom row shows how the mean can be affected by an extreme score, in this case for the day you received $150 in tips. Notice that the extreme score has no effect on the median or mode.

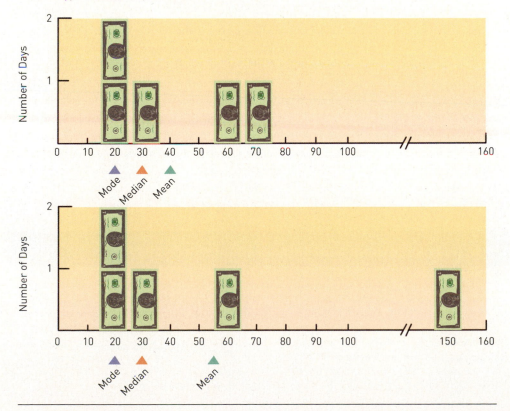

Illustrated by Sarah Yeh

Variability

In addition to calculating measures of central tendency, researchers are interested in **variability**, or how much the scores in a set differ from one another. The mean indicates the average, but it provides no information about how far apart the individual scores are from each other. Why is this important? Well, think about your last exam score. Let's assume you received a 79 and the average score was 75. How did you do? Your best guess is probably that you did about average because your score was relatively close to the mean—but perhaps not. If the scores were all bunched toward the middle, your performance might have been spectacular—in fact, a 79 could have been the highest grade in the class. As a result, researchers need to know more than the average of a set of scores; they also need to know something about variability (see Figure 2.4).

FIGURE 2.4 ■ **Variability**

Researchers are often interested in variability, the extent to which scores in a set differ from one another. Each of these two distributions has the same average, or mean, but the distribution on the left has more variability. Notice that the difference between the mean and a particular score, such as 83, is the same in the two cases. But scoring 8 points above the mean is highly unusual in the distribution on the right, and more common in the distribution on the left. If you received a score of 83, which class would you rather be in?

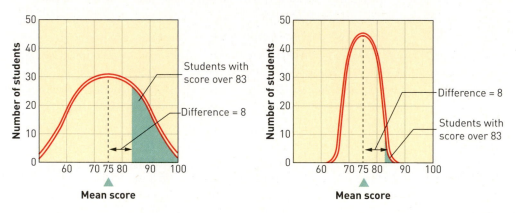

Several measures of variability are available to researchers. A simple one is the **range**, which measures the difference between the largest and smallest scores. If the highest score in the class was 90 and the lowest score was 50, the range would be 90 – 50 = 40. A more widely used statistical tool is the **standard deviation**, which provides an indication of how much individual scores vary from the mean. It's calculated by (1) finding the difference (or deviation) of each score from the mean; (2) squaring those deviations; (3) finding the average, or mean, of the squared deviations; and (4) calculating the square root of that average. Knowing the standard deviation helps you interpret individual scores. If the difference between your test score and the mean is much greater than the "standard" deviation, then we know that your score is relatively rare. We'll return to the concept of standard deviation later in the text, particularly in Chapter 10. Psychologists often define psychological characteristics, such as intelligence, by determining how far a score "sits" from the mean in a distribution of scores. (To apply what you have learned about variability, see the Practical Solutions feature.)

PRACTICAL SOLUTIONS: HOW SHOULD A TEACHER GRADE?

Now let's apply what you just learned about statistical "variability" to an important topic: *grading*! Every teacher needs a method for discriminating among people on their performance in a course. If you work really hard and perform well on tests, you should be rewarded with a higher grade than someone who skips class and never bothers to learn the material, right? Students are often skeptical about grading techniques, whatever method is employed, but most teachers adopt one of two strategies, absolute grading or relative grading (sometimes called grading "by the curve"). One depends on variability, and the other does not. Let's consider each in turn.

Absolute grading is simple and easy to understand. Your grade is determined by the number, or percentage, of items that you answer correctly on a test. So, if there are 100 questions on your final exam, you might need to answer 90 or more correctly to receive an A; if you correctly answer between 80 and 90 questions, you get a B; and so on. With this method, you immediately know where you stand once you get your test score. Your grade does not depend on how the rest of the students in the class performed. Variability, or how much the scores in the class differ from one another, is not involved in the calculation.

Relative grading, or grading by the curve, means your grade is determined by your relative performance in the class. If there are 100 students in the class, an A might be given to the top 10 students (or 10%), a B to the next 10, and so on. In this case, your absolute score means nothing by itself—you need to know something about how the test scores vary among the students in your class. Variability is critical in determining your grade, as in the example shown in Figure 2.4 .

Which is the best technique? Both are easy to justify, but they each have problems. Suppose your teacher doesn't have a very good "sense" of what the class understands, and writes an extremely difficult test—in fact, the best student in the class answers only 50% of the questions correctly. Does this mean that everyone in the class should get an F? That's what would probably happen if the grades were determined by an absolute scale. Relative grading takes the teacher's test out of the equation. It doesn't matter whether the test is easy or hard. What matters is where your test score "sits" in the distribution of class scores—how well you performed relative to everyone else in the class. So even if you only get half of the test questions correct, you might still get an A. But here's the trouble with relative grading: Suppose you happen to be in a class of brilliant students. You might learn the material quite well, perhaps you answer 90% of the test questions correctly, but you could still be at the bottom of the class distribution. Do you deserve to flunk just because you are in a "smart" class?

Lots of factors are involved in picking the best way to grade, such as the size of the class, the experience of the teacher, whether the material is introductory or advanced, and many more. Talk to your teachers about their chosen method. Try to determine the role that "variability" is playing in their method—it should help you understand why variability is important to the psychologist as well!

Inferential Statistics

Statistics, such as the mean and the standard deviation, form a part of what is called **descriptive statistics**—they help researchers describe their data. But it's also possible to use statistics to draw inferences from data—to help interpret the results. Researchers use **inferential statistics** to decide (1) whether the behaviors recorded in a sample are representative of some larger population, or (2) whether the differences among observations can be attributed to chance or to some other factor.

Inferential statistics are based on the laws of probability. Researchers always assume that the results of an observation, or group of observations, might be due to chance. For example, suppose you find that the male servers in your restaurant average $38 a day in tips for the week whereas the female servers average $42 (a difference of $4). Is there really a gender difference in tip income? Perhaps the difference is accidental and unrepresentative. Maybe if you had recorded tip income in a different week, you would have found that men produced more income. It is in your interest, then, to determine how representative your data are of true tipping behavior.

Through inferential statistics, researchers try to determine the likelihood, or probability, that results could have occurred by chance. The details of the procedures are beyond the scope of this text, but if the probability is extremely low, you can treat your findings as statistically significant. In most psychological studies, the probability that an outcome is due to chance must be lower than 0.05 (5%) for the outcome to be accepted as statistically significant. This means you can treat a female tipping advantage of $4 as significant only if that difference occurs fewer than 5 times out of 100 by chance alone. There are problems with drawing a line at a certain probability level and calling things "significant," and many researchers opt for alternative techniques, but it still represents common practice among most psychological researchers (for a discussion of the concerns, see Cumming, 2014).

Now test your knowledge of descriptive research methods by filling in these blanks with one of the following words or terms: *reactivity, external validity, case study, random sampling, survey, mean, median, mode, standard deviation*. (You will find the answers in the Appendix.)

1. The middle point in an ordered set of scores is the _____.

2. The _____ technique, which focuses on the study of a single instance of a behavior or condition, is open to criticism because its results may lack _____; that is, the results may not generalize or be representative of the population as a whole.

3. When behavior changes as a result of the observation process, the recorded data are said to suffer from a problem of _____.

4. The descriptive research technique used to gather limited amounts of information from many people is called a _____.

PREDICTING BEHAVIOR: CORRELATIONAL RESEARCH

Psychologists are rarely satisfied with just describing behavior. They're also interested in making predictions about future behavior. Prediction allows you to determine how individuals are likely to perform in the future—this is a good thing. The manager of a company can select the best potential employee based on present performance; the school administrator can manage a student's curriculum to maximize future performance.

Correlational Research

One way to predict future performance is to determine whether a relationship exists between two measures of behavior, the one recorded and the one expected. Psychologists use a statistical measure called a **correlation** to help make this determination. A correlation tells you whether two variables, or measures that can take on more than one value (such as a test score), vary together systematically. Correlations are computed by gathering observations on both measures of interest from a single set of individuals and then computing a mathematical index called a *correlation coefficient*. A correlation coefficient gives the researcher a feel for how well the value of one variable, such as job success, can be predicted if the value of a second variable, such as an achievement test score, is known.

The building skills of the young boy in the first photo may or may not predict a professional career in architecture.

When there is a correlation between two measures of behavior, those behaviors will tend to vary together in some way. For example, there is probably a strong correlation between the number of hours worked and the number of tips a server receives. The two measures vary together—the more hours you spend working, the more tips you get. In this particular case, we have a *positive* correlation, which means the two measures move in the same direction—the more of one, the more of the other. A *negative* correlation is when the two measures move in opposite directions. For example, there is a negative, or inverse, relationship between the number of hours that Beverly practices on the piano and the number of errors she makes during her recital performance. The more she practices, the fewer errors she is likely to make. A relationship still exists—we can predict one when we know the other—but the correlation is negative.

Calculating a correlation coefficient requires that you collect observations from a relatively large number of individuals. Moreover—and this is important—data must be recorded initially on both measures. The details of the calculation are beyond the scope of this text, but if calculated properly, correlation coefficients always range between +1.00 and –1.00. The absolute value of the coefficient (the range between 0 and 1 without the sign) indicates the strength of the correlation. The closer the value is to 1.00 (either positive or negative), the stronger the relationship and the more likely you'll make an accurate prediction. The sign of the coefficient tells you whether the correlation is positive or negative. Positive correlations fall within the range from 0 to +1.00; negative correlations fall within the range from 0 to –1.00.

Scatterplots

Figure 2.5 shows two examples of how positive and negative correlations can be represented graphically, in the form of a scatterplot. Each point on a scatterplot represents someone's scores on the two measures. Figure 2.5a shows a strong positive correlation between the two measures in our study of tips received by servers: hours worked and the amount of tips. Figure 2.5b shows a strong negative correlation between the two measures in our study of piano playing: hours spent practicing and errors made during the recital. Once a correlation has been computed, it can then be applied to new individuals who have a score on only one of the measures. So, based on the results of our piano study, you can predict how many errors Beverly will make during her recital by simply knowing how many hours she practiced. The closer the correlation is to 1.00 (positive or negative), the more accurate your prediction is likely to be. This is the logic used by most college admissions committees. They know there is a correlation between SAT and college performance, so they try to predict how well people will do in college by looking at their SAT scores.

FIGURE 2.5 ■   Positive and Negative Correlations

Each point in the scatterplot shows an individual's scores on each of the two variables. (a) In a strong positive correlation, the values for both variables move in the same direction; that is, as more hours are worked, more tips are received. (b) In a negative correlation, the values for the two variables move in opposite directions; that is, as more time is spent practicing, fewer errors are made during the recital.

Zero Correlations

When a correlation coefficient is not statistically different from zero, the two measures are said to be *uncorrelated*. Technically, this means knowing the value of one measure does not allow you to predict the value of the second measure with an accuracy greater than chance. Imagine, for example, trying to predict college grade point average by measuring how many times people wash their hands during the day. In this case, the correlation is almost certainly zero—you can't use hand-washing behavior to predict GPA. Note: It's important not to confuse the concept of a zero correlation with negative correlation. If the correlation between two variables is zero, no statistical relationship is present—a value on one measure reveals nothing about the other measure. In a negative correlation, a clear relationship exists; it's just that the values move in opposite directions.

Interestingly, the fact that two measures are uncorrelated (they have a zero correlation) doesn't mean that similar values can't occur on each. Look at the scatterplot in Figure 2.6 . It shows a zero correlation between hand washing and GPA. The points show how many times particular people washed their hands in a day (x-axis) along with their GPA (y-axis). If there's no correlation between the two, as the figure depicts, then we can't predict GPA simply by knowing hand-washing behavior. Yet notice that some points in the figure (marked in green) show that a high value on the hand-washing variable can be associated with a high value on the GPA variable. Suppose you only looked at these instances— "Wow, people who wash their hands a lot sure have high GPAs"—you might mistakenly conclude that the key to getting a high GPA is making sure your hands are clean.

Once again, the point to remember is that when two variables are unrelated, we can't predict what will happen. Sometimes a high value on one measure will be associated with a high value on the other measure; sometimes it will be associated with a low value. A mistake people often make is to look only at the cases where the two variables appear to be related. Consider the ability of "psychics" to predict the future. Many people believe in precognition, the ability to predict the future, based on a few anecdotal examples (e.g., "I dreamed my dog was hit by a car, and the next day it happened"). In all likelihood, however, the correlation between predictions and outcomes is zero. We ignore those instances in which our feelings ("I have a feeling something bad is going to happen to the dog tomorrow") don't come true ("My dog turned out to be fine"); instead, we focus only on those few instances where, by chance, predictions and events occur together.

Behavioral measures rarely correlate perfectly—most correlations are only moderate. When researchers make predictions about behavior based on correlations, the accuracy of their predictions is usually limited. The correlation between scores on the SAT and the GPA of college freshmen is only

FIGURE 2.6   ■   Zero Correlation

The scatterplot shows a zero correlation between number of times hands are washed and grade point average. Overall, it is not possible to predict the value on one of the variables by knowing a value on the other, although high values on each variable (orange) sometimes occur together.

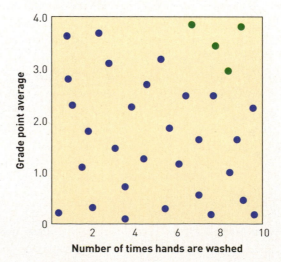

around +0.50, not 1.0 (Kunkel & Hezlett, 2010). Researchers can use SAT scores to predict college performance, but the test's predictive abilities are far from perfect. Likewise, the correlation between height and weight is only about +0.60; on average, taller people do tend to weigh more, but there are obvious exceptions to this general rule. Correlation coefficients give researchers some important predictive ability, but they do not completely capture the variability present in the world. For a summary of the different correlation patterns, see Concept Review 2.1.

CONCEPT REVIEW 2.1
CORRELATION PATTERNS

Question to Be Addressed	Pattern of Correlation	Interpretation
How does the number of hours worked relate to the tips received?	Positive	The more hours worked, the more tips received; the fewer hours worked, the fewer tips received.
How does performance on the SAT relate to college GPA?	Positive	The greater the score on the SAT, the higher the GPA; the lower the score on the SAT, the lower the GPA.
How does the amount of piano practice relate to the number of errors during a recital?	Negative	The more practice, the fewer errors are made; the less practice, the more errors are made.
How does the amount of time spent partying relate to college GPA?	Negative	The more time spent partying, the lower the GPA; the less time spent partying, the higher the GPA.
How does a person's shoe size relate to the person's score on an intelligence test?	No correlation	Knowing one's shoe size tells you nothing about the person's IQ test score, and vice versa.

Correlations and Causality

Determining that a relationship exists between two measures of behavior is important. It helps people make educated guesses about their environment. It is useful to know that if a person acts in a certain way at time 1, the person is likely to act in a predictable way at time 2. Suppose that we could demonstrate a meaningful correlation between the amount of violence that a child watches on television and how aggressively that child will act later in life. Knowing about such a relationship would probably influence the behavior of parents and might even lead to a social outcry to monitor televised violence (Bushman & Anderson, 2001).

Correlations are useful for helping psychologists describe how behaviors co-occur in our world, but they are of only limited value when it comes to understanding why. The presence of a correlation between two behaviors may help psychologists predict, but correlations do not allow them to determine causality. A correlation between watching violence on television and later aggression does not mean that television violence causes aggression, even if the correlation is perfect.

Third Variables

The main reason it's not possible to determine causality from a correlation is the presence of other potentially uncontrolled factors. Two variables can appear to be connected—that is, they might rise or fall together in a regular way—but the connection could be due to a common link with some third variable. Let's consider an example close to home. It's commonly argued, correctly, that annual income will be higher if a person graduates from college. Put in terms of a correlation, annual income is positively correlated with years of schooling. Does that mean that a good education causes better jobs and higher income? Perhaps, but not necessarily. A third factor could explain the relationship.

Think about the kinds of people who go to college. Do they represent a random sample of the population as a whole? Of course not. College students tend to be brighter, they tend to come from better schools, and they tend to be people who have worked hard and succeeded in high school. None of these other factors is controlled for in the calculation of a correlation. You can predict with a correlation, but you can't determine what is responsible for the relationship. College students might end up with higher incomes because they're smarter, because they work harder, or because they're better educated. Any or all of these factors could be contributing to the relationship that the correlation describes.

Now let's return to the example we considered earlier—the relationship between TV violence and aggression. Can you think of a third variable that might explain the correlation? One possibility is that aggressive kids like to watch violent TV programs. It is not the violence on TV that is causing the aggression; it is the child's personality that is influencing both program choice and aggression. Still other factors could be involved—perhaps children who are allowed to watch violence on television tend to be raised in households where aggression is the norm. Once again, correlations describe relationships, but they typically provide no insight into cause and effect. To determine causality, as you'll see shortly, researchers cannot simply describe and predict behavior; they must manipulate it.

Using Big Data to Predict Behavior

As we discussed in Chapter 1, a new trend in psychological research is based on the use of large data sets obtained from digital behaviors, such as social network posts, online shopping behaviors, fitness trackers, and messaging applications. The use of large digital data sets provides researchers with a convenient sample of these behaviors that is descriptive of individuals' everyday digital lives. Large data sets also allow researchers the opportunity to sample from a diverse population that is not always possible in other convenience samples (Kosinski et al., 2016). These data sets have been used by researchers to study a wide range of behaviors, including personality, language use, social networks, and decision making. Online game data can help researchers better understand the relationship between skill level and continued game play (Steyvers & Benjamin, 2019). Movie and TV reviews can be used to better

Researchers are beginning to use large data sets from social media and other sources in research studies but must be careful not to violate the privacy of participants.

iStockPhoto/hocus-focus

understand decision making and biases in those processes (Vinson et al., 2019). Researchers are also developing methods of obtaining and analyzing these data to predict a wide range of behaviors and test hypotheses about these behaviors. In the past few years, special issues of journals have been dedicated to such research as a new methodology in psychological science. However, one issue researchers have to address in such research is how use of these data may violate privacy of individuals' behavior, an issue that relates to ethical guidelines for research with human participants. For example, protecting the confidentiality of the data is an important aspect of ethical research practice. Ethical guidelines in research will be discussed more thoroughly in the last section of this chapter.

KNOWLEDGE CHECK 2.2

Now test your understanding of correlations by identifying whether the following statements represent positive, negative, or zero correlations. (You will find the answers in the Appendix.)

1. The more Larry studies for his psychology course, the fewer errors he makes on the chapter test: _____.

2. As Sadaf reduces her rate of exercising, her heart rate begins to slow: _____.

3. The longer that Yolanda waits for her date to arrive, the higher her blood pressure rises: _____.

4. Eddie finds no relationship between his dreams about plane crashes and the number of planes that actually crash: _____.

EXPLAINING BEHAVIOR: EXPERIMENTAL RESEARCH

Now let's consider techniques that help us understand why behavior occurs. Suppose you wanted to determine whether watching violent programs really does cause later aggression. If Blake becomes aggressive after watching a violent television program, is it really the program that's responsible for the change? Alternative possibilities need to be eliminated before you can confidently conclude that things are causally related. As you've just seen, the mere description of a relationship is not enough—correlation does not imply causation. Establishing causality requires *control*, one of the most important functions of an experiment.

In **experimental research**, the investigator actively manipulates the environment to observe its effect on behavior. A psychologist might manipulate the external setting (room temperature, lighting, time of day), a person's internal state (hunger, mood, motivation to perform), or social factors (presence or absence of an authority figure or popular peer group). The particular manipulation is determined by the researcher's hypothesis. As mentioned earlier, hypotheses in psychology are usually expressed as if-then statements: If some set of conditions is present, then a certain kind of behavior will occur. The purpose of the experiment is to set up the proposed conditions and see what happens.

To examine the role of television violence on aggressive behavior, an experimenter would directly manipulate the amount of violence the person watches. Perhaps one group of children would be picked to watch a violent superhero cartoon while a second group watches the playful antics of a lovable purple dinosaur. The experimenter would then carefully measure the effect of the manipulation on the behavior of interest: aggression. This strategy of directly manipulating the viewing habits, rather than simply observing them, is the essential feature of the experimental approach. Notice the difference from correlational research, where the investigator simply records the viewing habits of children and then measures later aggressive acts. It is only through a direct manipulation by the experimenter, as you'll see shortly, that control over the environment can be exercised and causality determined. Figure 2.7 compares experimental research to the other two approaches previously discussed: descriptive and correlational research.

FIGURE 2.7 ■ Major Research Methods			
	Descriptive Method	**Correlational Method**	**Experimental Method**
Purpose	Observing and describing behavior	Predicting and selecting behavior	Determining why behavior occurs: Establishing cause and effect
Research Tactics	Naturalistic observation Case studies Survey research Psychological tests	Statistical correlations based on two or more variables	Experiments manipulating the independent variable to note effects on the dependent variable

Independent and Dependent Variables

The aspect of the environment that is manipulated in an experiment is called the **independent variable**. Because it is a variable—that is, something that can take on more than one value—any experimental manipulation must consist of at least two different conditions. In our example, the independent variable is the amount of television violence, and the two conditions are (1) watching a violent program and (2) watching a nonviolent program. The aspect that is manipulated is called an independent variable because the experimenter produces the change—independently of the participant's wishes, desires, or behavior.

The behavior that is measured in an experiment is called the **dependent variable**. In our example, the dependent variable is the amount of aggressive behavior that occurs after watching the programs. The experimenter manipulates the independent variable, the level of TV violence, and observes whether the behavior measured by the dependent variable, aggression, changes. Notice that the experimenter is interested in whether the dependent variable depends on the experimental manipulation (hence the name *dependent variable*).

Now let's return to the topic that opened this chapter: subliminal perception. Can evil advertisers improve product sales by hiding messages such as "Buy Acme" in their advertising material? Remember, a subliminal message is presented below a person's normal threshold for perception. You won't be able to see or hear the message consciously, but it influences you nonetheless. Let's begin by forming a hypothesis: If people are exposed to advertising material containing a hidden message, then product sales will increase. To test this prediction, let's give two groups of people an advertisement to study. One group receives an ad containing a hidden message, and the other group receives the same

Can subliminal messages really influence our behavior? Properly controlled experiments suggest the answer is No.

Mafalda / Alamy Stock Photo

advertisement without the message. Later, we can check to see how likely the people in each group are to purchase the product.

What is the independent variable in this experiment? To answer this question, look for the aspect of the environment that is being manipulated: The independent variable is the presence or absence of the hidden message (half of the participants receive the message in the ad, and half do not). What is the dependent variable? In this case, the researcher wants to know whether sales of the advertised product will change due to the presence of the subliminal message. The dependent variable is the number of times the people in each group buy the advertised product. For other examples of experiments, see Concept Review 2.2.

CONCEPT REVIEW 2.2
THE EXPERIMENTAL METHOD

Research Question (variables in bold)	Independent Variable (experimenter *manipulates*)	Dependent Variable (experimenter *measures*)
Does **watching television violence** affect **aggression**?	Experimenter *manipulates* the amount of exposure to TV violence.	Experimenter *measures* the amount of aggression displayed.
Does **exposure to subliminal messages** have an effect on **product sales**?	Experimenter *manipulates* whether or not people receive a hidden message.	Experimenter *measures* product sales.
Does **forming images of words** to be remembered enhance **memory for those words**?	Experimenter *manipulates* whether or not people form images of words as the words are presented.	Experimenter *measures* memory for the words.

Experimental Control

To conclude that changes in the dependent variable are really caused by the independent variable, you must be certain that the independent variable is the only thing changing systematically in the experiment. This is the main reason at least two conditions are needed in an experiment. In many experiments, researchers compare people who get the change, often called the *experimental group*, with those who do not, called the *control group*. In the subliminal perception experiment, the experimental group consisted of the people who received the hidden message, and the control group consisted of those who did not. If product sales subsequently differ between these two groups, and we know that the only difference between them was the presence of the hidden message in the ad, then it's possible to conclude that hidden messages can indeed cause a change in sales.

Although our example experiment contains an experimental group and a control group, not all experiments contain a control group. In some cases, two or more conditions are manipulated as part of an independent variable that involves adding something to the participants' environment. For example, a researcher interested in whether the way something is described in an ad affects buying behavior might create two types of ads for a product: one that focuses on the consumer's improved health after using the product and another that focuses on the consumer's improved appearance after using the product. In other words, there are two experimental groups here, one that reads each type of ad, and no control group. Type of ad is the independent variable in this study. It might be more difficult to determine exactly what is responsible for a group difference in this case, but the design still qualifies as an experiment.

Confounding Variables

Determining cause and effect requires that the experimental and control groups be identical in all respects, except for the critical independent variable manipulation. But how can we ever be certain that this is the case? If some factor other than the independent variable differs across the groups, it will be difficult, if not impossible, to interpret the results. Uncontrolled variables that change with the independent variable are called **confounding variables** (the word *confound* means to throw into confusion or dismay). Suppose in our subliminal perception experiment we use one advertisement in the experimental group and a different advertisement in the control group. This would be a bad idea because any differences in sales could then be attributed to the ad itself rather than to the presence or absence of the subliminal message. For example, maybe one ad contains men and the other contains women, or one is simply more colorful than another. Changes in the dependent variable could not be attributed uniquely to the hidden message because there is a confounding variable.

To solve the problem of confounding variables, all of the factors that might vary along with the independent variable need to be controlled. You should give everyone exactly the same advertisement, and you should probably conduct the experimental session at the same time of day for both groups. You should also make certain that people in both groups are given the same amount of time to study the ad and the same length of time to buy the advertised product. Any factor that might affect the likelihood of purchase, other than the independent variable manipulation, should be controlled—that is, held constant—across the different groups. When potential confounding variables are effectively controlled, you can conclude that changes in the independent variable cause changes in the dependent variable. Under these conditions, the experiment is said to have **internal validity**.

Knowing what factors to worry about comes, in part, from experience. The more you know about the phenomenon you're studying, the more likely you are to identify and control confounding variables. Consumer researchers recognize, for example, that it's essential to give everyone the same advertisement and product in the experimental and control conditions; obviously, some ads will be liked more than others regardless of whether they contain hidden messages. But other variables, such as the length of the participants' hair or their eye color, probably have no effect on buying behavior and require no control.

Random Assignment

People differ in many ways: intelligence, personal preferences, their motivation to perform, and so on. Researchers can't possibly hold all of these factors constant. Just think about the task of finding two groups of people with exactly the same level of intelligence, likes and dislikes, and motivation. It would be impossible. So researchers typically use random assignment, which is similar to the random sampling used for survey research. In **random assignment**, the experimenter makes certain that each participant has an equal chance of being assigned to any of the groups or conditions in the experiment. At the outset, each person is assigned randomly to a group. For example, the experimenter might choose a number randomly and assign the person to one group if the number is even and a different group if the number is odd.

Random assignment does not eliminate differences among people—some participants will still be more intelligent than others, and some will be more naturally inclined to buy the advertised product. Random assignment simply increases the chances that these differences will be equally represented in each of the groups (see Figure 2.8). As a result, the researcher knows that the results of the experiment cannot easily be caused by some special characteristic of the individual participants.

FIGURE 2.8   ■   Random Assignment

Volunteers are randomly assigned to two levels of the independent variable. Each participant has an equal likelihood of being assigned to any of the groups or conditions in the experiment. Random assignment increases the chances that unique subject characteristics will be represented equally in each condition.

Hypothesis   If people are exposed to advertising that contains a hidden message, product sales will increase.

Random assignment

Subjects are asked to study an ad with a hidden message.

Subjects are asked to study an ad without the hidden message.

Measurement of dependent variable

Product sales

100

50

0

Hidden message   No hidden message

Independent variable

Carolina Hrejsa/Body Scientific Intl.

Expectancies and Biases in Experimental Research

People are rarely passive participants in research—they have expectations that can influence the results of an experiment. Let's suppose on the first day of class your teacher randomly selects half of the students, including you, to participate in a special enrichment program. You receive instruction in a special room, with carefully controlled lighting and temperature, to see whether your learning will improve. The rest of the students, forming the control group, are left in the original classroom. The end of the semester arrives, and sure enough, the enrichment group consistently outperforms the control group. What can you conclude from these results?

At first glance, this seems to be a well-designed experiment. It includes both an experimental and a control group, the students were randomly assigned to groups, and let's assume that all other known potentially confounding variables were carefully controlled. However, there is still a problem. The participants in the enrichment group were expected to perform better, based on their knowledge about the experiment. After all, they were selected to be in an enrichment group. Consequently, these students may have simply tried harder, or studied more, in an effort to live up to the expectations of the researcher. At the same time, students in the control group knew they were failing to get special instruction; this knowledge might have lowered their motivation to perform, leading to poorer performance. The fact that the groups differed in what they learned is not necessarily due to the enrichment program itself.

Researchers can control for these kinds of expectancy effects in two ways. One way is to disguise the purpose of the experiment when initially describing the study to the participants. This approach raises obvious ethical questions, although it is possible, under some conditions, to omit telling people some critical feature of the study without violating ethical standards.

Second, the investigator can match expectations for both the experimental and control groups. For example, the researchers can lead the people in the control group to believe that they, too, are receiving an experimental treatment. This technique is often used in drug studies. Participants in both groups receive a pill or an injection, but the drug is actually present only in the medication given to the experimental group. The control participants are given a **placebo**—an inactive, or inert, substance (a "sugar pill") that looks just like the true drug.

Blind Controls

The kind of experimental procedure just described for drug studies is called a **single-blind study**. That is, the participants are kept "blind" about the particular group in which they've been placed (experimental or control). Single-blind studies control for expectancies because people have no idea which group they are in. This helps keep overall expectations the same in both groups. It is even possible to inform the participants that some of them will be given a placebo—the inactive pill or injection—as long as no one knows who is in which group. Notice that the single-blind technique does not eliminate expectancies; it simply reduces the chances that expectancies will contribute more to the experimental group than to the control group (or vice versa).

The people participating in the experiment aren't the only ones who expect certain things to happen—the experimenter does too (Rosenthal, 1966). Remember, it's the experimenter who formulated the hypothesis. Experimenters are often convinced that behavior will change in a certain way, and these expectations can also influence the results. Imagine that a researcher has developed a drug designed to cure all forms of influenza. To test the drug, one group of flu patients is given the drug; another group receives a placebo. In a case like this, it's possible for the experimenter to influence the results in subtle ways. For example, the researcher might give slightly more attention to the people who receive the drug because the researcher expects these people to get well. This is not a deliberate bias on the part of the researcher. Nevertheless, these unintentional effects can make it difficult to interpret the results.

The solution to experimenter expectancy effects is to keep the researcher blind about the assignment of people to groups. If those administering the study do not know which individuals are receiving the experimental treatment, they are unlikely to treat members of each group differently. Obviously, someone needs to know the group assignments, but the information can be coded in such a way that the person doing the actual observations remains blind about the condition. After the data have been collected, based on the code, the experimenter can determine the particular manipulation that each person received. When neither the participant nor the observer is aware of who is in the experimental and control conditions, the experiment is known as a **double-blind study**. Double-blind studies, often used in drug research, are effective in reducing bias effects.

Generalizing Experimental Conclusions

Properly designed experiments help an investigator determine the causes of behavior. The determination of causality is possible whenever the experimenter has sufficient control over the situation to eliminate confounding factors. But experimental control is occasionally gained at a cost. Sometimes, in the search for appropriate controls, the researcher creates an environment that is sterile or artificial and not representative of situations in which a person normally behaves. The results of the experimental research then cannot easily be generalized to real-world situations; as you learned previously, such results are said to have little *external validity*.

Consider again the issue of television violence and aggression: Does one really cause the other? A number of experimental studies have explored this question (C. A. Anderson et al., 2003; Bushman & Anderson, 2001). Most have been conducted in the laboratory under controlled conditions. People are randomly assigned to groups who watch violent programs or neutral programs, and their behavior is then observed for aggressive tendencies, again under controlled conditions. In one study, preschool children were exposed to neutral or aggressive cartoons and then were given the opportunity to play with aggressive toys (such as toy guns); more aggressive acts were recorded for the children who watched the violent cartoon (Sanson & Di Muccio, 1993). These results clearly demonstrate that watching violence can increase the likelihood of aggressiveness. But this does not necessarily mean that these children would act similarly in their homes, or that the effects of the brief exposure to violence will be long lasting. In short, the experiment may lack external validity. Concerns about generalizability should not, however, be taken as a devastating critique of the experimental method—results demonstrated in the laboratory often do generalize to real-world environments. Moreover, the true purpose of an experiment is to gain control, not external validity. As you might expect, we'll return to the issue of external validity in later chapters.

Replicability

Another factor relevant to generalizing is replicability—whether the results of a study can be repeated with a separate sample or under slightly different conditions. Due to chance factors in the way participant samples are collected and data are analyzed with inferential statistics, not all accurate findings will replicate every time a researcher tries. As we discussed in Chapter 1, replication of research results has become an important topic in recent years due to problems replicating some well-publicized results in psychological research. Some refer to this issue as a *replication crisis*.

Consider an example: A number of studies have examined the cost of denying yourself something that you want (e.g., Baumeister et al., 1998; Hagger et al., 2010; Sripada et al., 2014). This has been called *ego depletion*—the idea is that when you engage in self-control over your behavior, you are depleting cognitive resources that could be used for other tasks. However, in an article that described results from 23 different labs across the world and over 2,000 participants (Hagger et al., 2016), the ego depletion effect described by others did not replicate. Some researchers had reported failures in replicating the effect before this study was conducted, but nonsignificant results are rarely published in journals, so many of these studies were not available to researchers in the field. (For an example of a study investigating this phenomenon, see the Thinking About Research section at the end of the chapter.)

A number of different factors can affect the replicability of results. Some issues relate to how the studies are reported, some to how the data are analyzed, some to how the study is designed and conducted, and others to how the publication process works. To counter these issues, a number of steps have been taken in the publication process to help prevent the publication of data that do not replicate. For example, researchers can now preregister a study before it is conducted to make clear the steps that will be taken to test their hypotheses ahead of time. Preregistration ensures that the data collection and analysis processes are public for a study and can be evaluated by other researchers. The Open Science

Framework, for example, allows researchers to preregister details of their study, including hypotheses, and to share their data with other researchers once they have been collected (Shrout & Rodgers, 2018).

Some journals are now reviewing the registered studies before the data have been collected to ensure that both significant and nonsignificant results are published. This prevents the problem of only significant results being published. Many journals require the uploading of data into a repository for other researchers to access when a study is published. This allows other researchers to analyze the data themselves to explore other possible ways that conclusions can be drawn from the data. Researchers have also begun to replicate their results in multiple samples before submitting results for publication to show that they replicate and to test effects in a variety of samples to ensure that the results generalize to people in different areas of the world. All of these steps help psychological researchers make positive progress in solving the "replication crisis."

KNOWLEDGE CHECK 2.3

Now test your knowledge by answering the following questions about experimental research. (You will find the answers in the Appendix.)

1. [Fill in the blanks with the term *independent* or *dependent*.] In experimental research, the researcher actively manipulates the environment to observe its effect on behavior. The aspect of the environment that is manipulated is called the IV_____ variable; the behavior of interest is measured by the DV_____ variable. To draw conclusions about cause and effect, the experimenter must make certain that the IV_____ variable is the only thing changing systematically in the environment.

2. Javier wants to determine whether the presence of Tom Cruise in a movie increases the box office take. He randomly forms two groups of people. One group sees *Mission Impossible X*, starring Cruise, and the other group sees *Barney's Great Adventure*, without Cruise. Sure enough, the Tom Cruise movie is later rated as more enjoyable than the movie starring the purple dinosaur. Javier concludes that Tom Cruise movies are sure winners. What's wrong with this experiment?
   a. The dependent variable—Tom Cruise versus Barney—is confounded with the content of the movie.
   b. The independent variable—Tom Cruise versus Barney—is not the only factor changing across the groups.
   c. Nothing has been manipulated—it's really a correlational study.
   d. Experiments of this type require independent variables with at least three conditions.

3. Random assignment is an important research tool because it helps the researcher control for potential confounding variables. Which of the following statements about random assignment is true? Random assignment
   a. eliminates individual differences among people.
   b. ensures that some participants will get the experimental treatment and others will not.
   c. increases the likelihood that participant differences will be equally represented in each group.
   d. controls for bias by ensuring that biased participants will be placed in the control group.

THE ETHICS OF RESEARCH: HUMAN AND ANIMAL GUIDELINES

Do you remember the problem of reactivity? Being observed can importantly change the way people behave. Although psychologists have developed techniques for reducing reactivity—designing noninterfering measures, keeping participants blind to their true role in the study, fooling individuals into thinking the observer is really part of the environment—each method raises significant ethical questions. Is it appropriate to deceive people under any circumstances? Is it appropriate to withhold treatment, through the use of placebos, in the interest of achieving proper experimental control? To deal with such issues, formal organizations such as the American Psychological Association (APA) develop and publish ethical guidelines and codes of conduct for their members (American Psychological Association, 2016 ; Knapp, 2012).

Psychologists have a responsibility to respect the rights and dignity of all people. The code of conduct applies to everything that psychologists do, from administering therapy, to working in the field, to giving testimony in the courtroom. Respecting the rights of others means showing concern for their health, safety, and welfare; no diabolical mind-altering treatments are allowed, even "in the name and pursuit of science." Psychologists are expected to act responsibly in advertising their services, representing themselves in the media, pricing their services, and collecting their fees.

Informed Consent

The cornerstone of the ethics code is the principle of **informed consent**. People must be informed, in easy-to-understand language, of any significant factors that could affect their willingness to participate. Physical and emotional risks should be explained, as should the general nature of the project and any therapeutic procedures to be used. Participants must then willingly give their written consent to participate in the research. They should understand as well that if for any reason they choose not to participate, they will suffer no negative consequences.

People cannot give truly informed consent unless they understand the details of the project. At the same time, full disclosure can affect the outcome of the study. Suppose you're interested in how readily bystanders at an accident will come to the aid of a victim. To gain experimental control, you stage a mock accident in the laboratory, in front of waiting research participants, to see how they react. Conducting the study in the laboratory enables you to investigate the likelihood of intervention under a variety of conditions (such as whether the person is alone or with others in the room when the accident occurs). But people in this situation would need to be misled—you certainly couldn't fully inform them about the procedure by telling them the accident isn't real.

The psychological research community recognizes that it's sometimes necessary to use deception as part of a research procedure (Kimmel, 2011). According to the APA code of ethics, deception is justified only if the scientific, educational, or applied value of the study is clear and if there is no way to answer the research questions adequately without deceiving the participants (American Psychological Association, 2016). It is also agreed that the deception should not cause physical or emotional harm or affect someone's willingness to participate in the study. Experimenters have a responsibility to respect the rights and dignity of research participants at all times. Most universities and colleges make certain that participants' rights are protected by requiring investigators to first submit detailed descriptions of their studies to oversight review committees, called institutional review boards. If the committee decides that a study will fail to protect the participant adequately, permission to conduct the study is denied.

Debriefing and Confidentiality

Two other key ingredients of the psychologist's code of ethics are debriefing and confidentiality. Psychologists are expected to debrief people fully at the end of the experimental session, meaning that everyone involved must be informed about the general purpose of the study. **Debriefing** is intended to clear up any misunderstandings about the research and to explain why certain procedures were used. Certainly, if deception was a part of the study, the full nature of the deception should be disclosed. Debriefing gives the researcher an opportunity to reduce any anxieties that individuals might have about their participation. If a participant failed to help the victim of a staged accident, for example, the experimenter could explain that bystander passivity is a characteristic of most people (Darley & Latané, 1968).

Finally, once the participation is completed, a person's right to privacy continues. All psychologists, including researchers and psychotherapists, are obligated to respect the privacy of the individual by maintaining **confidentiality**—personal information obtained in research or in therapy is not to be discussed or reported without the permission of the individual (American Psychological Association, 2016). Confidentiality makes sense for more than just ethical reasons. Research participants, as well as people seeking help for psychological problems, are likely to feel more comfortable with the process, and to act more naturally, if they are convinced that their right to privacy will be respected.

The Ethics of Animal Research

In laboratories all over the world, animals are participating in basic research. They're pressing metal bars for food, receiving small doses of electrical stimulation in the brain, and being raised in enriched environments designed to improve their ability to learn. Although animals are probably used in less than 10% of all current psychological research studies, the famous "laboratory rat" has been an important source of basic data for decades (J. L. Perry & Dess, 2012). As you'll see in later chapters, many significant psychological principles were originally discovered through the study of animal behavior.

Why use animals? The reason most often cited is experimental control. It is possible to raise and house animals in relatively ideal environments. Researchers can control diet, experience, and genetic background, thereby eliminating many of the confounding variables that plague human research studies. Researchers can also study life span development in ways that cannot be accomplished with humans. Studies that would take 70 or 80 years with people take only a few years with rats. Others use animals because they're thought to contain simple, rather than complex, internal systems. The basic biological machinery that underlies learning, for example, has been studied extensively with sea slugs; the number of neural connections in a sea slug is tiny compared with the billions of connections residing in a human brain. Research with animals often serves as a vehicle for developing hypotheses that can later be tested, when feasible, with humans (Saucier & Cain, 2006).

But is research with animals ethical? There can be no informed consent in animal research, as animal rights activists point out. Can we justify the invasive procedures sometimes used in animal research? Is it okay to destroy a part of a cat's brain to learn how localized brain structures control behavior? Obviously, the use of animals in research is a highly controversial subject. Millions of dollars are spent every year by animal rights groups; many of these groups oppose any sort of animal research (see Hubbel, 1990). Other critics question the basic value of animal studies, arguing that animals reveal little about human beings and may even mislead researchers into drawing inappropriate conclusions (see Ulrich, 1991). In one survey of animal rights activists, 85% advocated the complete elimination of all animal research (Plous, 1991).

Most psychologists are convinced that the use of animals in psychological and medical research has value. Animal studies have repeatedly led to significant breakthroughs. To cite one instance, animal research has led to significant advances in our understanding of depression, as well as to the development of drugs that lessen the symptoms of this disorder (see Chapters 14 and 15). Similarly, through the study of monkeys' natural fear of snakes in the wild, psychologists have discovered that phobias (such as the fear of heights or of being locked in small places) can be learned by imitating the behavior of others rather than through a traumatic life experience (see Chapter 7).

Many important psychological insights have come from studying animals, but using animals as laboratory subjects also raises serious ethical questions.

The American Psychological Association enforces strict guidelines with regard to the ethical treatment of nonhuman participants (American Psychological Association, 2016). Psychologists who conduct research with animals are expected to treat their participants humanely. The animals must be given proper care, and any treatments that cause discomfort, pain, or illness must be avoided unless absolutely necessary. When surgical procedures are performed, the animals must be given the appropriate anesthesia, and proper medical procedures must be followed to eliminate infection and minimize pain. Failure to stick to these standards can result in censure or termination of membership by the governing body of the association.

The issue of animal research is controversial, in part, because of misinformation. Experiments that inflict pain and suffering on animals are extremely rare and do not fairly characterize the majority of animal studies in psychological or medical research. At the same time, all researchers need to recognize that the nature of the research participant can importantly determine the results (Gluck & Bell, 2003). Findings established from research with animals may, in fact, not always apply to humans—because animals have evolved to solve different problems than humans. Despite these legitimate concerns, animal research continues to be a valuable tool in the search for an understanding of behavior and mind (J. L. Perry & Dess, 2012).

KNOWLEDGE CHECK 2.4

Now test what you've learned about ethics and research by answering the following questions. (You will find the answers in the Appendix.)

1. Fill in the blanks. Psychologists have a responsibility to respect the rights and dignity of all people. To ensure that research participants are treated ethically, psychologists use (a) informed _consent_ , which means that everyone is fully informed about the potential risks of the project; (b) _confidentiality_, which ensures that the participant's right to privacy will be maintained; and (c) _debrief_ , which is designed to provide more information about the purpose and procedures of the research.

2. Sometimes it is necessary to deceive research participants in some way, such as keeping them blind about group assignments, so that expectations won't determine the outcome. Most psychologists believe that deception
    a. is always justified as long as it furthers scientific knowledge.
    b. is never justified unless the research involves clinical treatment.
    c. is justified, but only under some circumstances.
    d. is not necessary if you design the project correctly.

3. The majority of psychologists believe that the use of animals in psychological and biomedical research has enormous value. But some question the ethics of using animals primarily because
    a. no real scientific advancements have come from animal research.
    b. animals are often treated cruelly.
    c. animals can give no informed consent.

THE PROBLEMS SOLVED: HOW WE LEARN ABOUT BEHAVIOR

Psychologists rely on a set of established research methods. Understanding research methodology is important because conclusions are importantly influenced by the methods used. Whether the behavior of children in a day care center will accurately represent real life depends on the methods of observation that have been employed. In addition, whether an experiment can determine if television violence truly causes aggression depends on the use of proper controls and the appropriate selection of participants. In this chapter, we considered various tools and guidelines that psychologists use to uncover the basic principles of behavior and mind.

Observing Behavior: Descriptive Research

To observe and describe behavior properly, psychologists use the techniques of descriptive research. In naturalistic observation, the researcher observes behavior in natural settings rather than in a laboratory environment. Naturalistic observation is a useful technique for generating ideas and for verifying whether conclusions reached in the lab generalize to more realistic settings. In case studies, the focus is on a single instance of a behavior. This technique allows the researcher to get lots of background information, but the results may not always generalize to wider populations. In survey research, behavior is sampled broadly, usually by gathering responses from many people in the form of a questionnaire. Surveys typically provide information that is representative of the group being examined, but the amount of information that can be gathered is limited. Finally, through psychological tests, differences among individuals can be measured.

Once the observational data have been collected, they are summarized through the application of statistics. Statistical applications include measures of central tendency—the mean, median, and mode—and measures of variability, or how far apart individual scores are from each other in a set of scores. Researchers use inferential statistics, based on the laws of probability, to test hypotheses. Inferential statistics can help the researcher decide whether a difference between an experimental and a control group, for example, is likely to have occurred by chance. Problems associated with the replicability of results remain a concern, and psychologists are actively developing ways to handle this concern.

Predicting Behavior: Correlational Research

In correlational research, the researcher determines whether a relationship exists between two measures of behavior. For instance, does high school GPA predict college performance? Correlation coefficients, which provide an index of how well one measure predicts another, are statistics that vary between –1.00 and +1.00. Correlations are useful because they enable the researcher to predict and select. If employers know there is a correlation between achievement test scores and job performance, they can use someone's score on an achievement test to predict that person's success on the job. Correlations are useful tools for predicting and selecting, but they do not allow us to draw conclusions about causality.

Explaining Behavior: Experimental Research

If you want to know whether an activity, such as watching violence on television, causes a change in behavior, you must conduct an experiment. In doing so, the researcher manipulates the environment in a systematic way and then observes the effect of that manipulation on behavior. The aspect of the environment that is manipulated is called the independent variable; the measured behavior is called the dependent variable. To determine that the independent variable is really responsible for the changes in behavior, the researcher must have experimental control—the only thing that can change systematically is the manipulation of the independent variable. Researchers conducting experiments encounter a variety of potential pitfalls that need to be controlled, including participant and experimenter expectancies. Control strategies include the use of random assignment and blind research designs.

The Ethics of Research: Human and Animal Guidelines

It is important to maintain a strict code of ethical conduct throughout the research process. An important safeguard is informed consent, which is designed to guarantee that participants will be informed of any significant factors that could influence their willingness to participate. Other ethical standards govern debriefing and maintaining confidentiality. All researchers, regardless of the nature of the research, have a professional responsibility to respect the rights and dignity of their participants. This applies not only to human participants but also to animals.

THINKING ABOUT RESEARCH

A summary of a research study in psychology is given in this section. As you read the summary, think about the following questions:

1. Was this study an experiment? Explain your answer.
2. Describe all variables (independent and dependent) that are present in the study.
3. Why did the researchers have one group of participants gargle with lemonade sweetened with Splenda? What does this control for?
4. What are some of the ethical issues in this study that the researchers would need to address to have the study approved by their institutional review board (IRB)?
5. A number of studies exploring the relationship between glucose and self-control have failed to replicate. Imagine that you attempted to replicate this study to verify the results and you found that reaction times for the glucose group were higher than the reaction times for the no glucose group. What would you conclude from your results? Would your results indicate that the effect is not real? Why or why not? (For more on this issue, see Vadillo et al., 2016.)

Article Reference: Sanders, M. A., Shirk, S. D., Burgin, C. J., & Martin, L. L. (2012). The gargle effect: Rinsing the mouth with glucose enhances self-control. *Psychological Science, 23*, 1470–1472.

Purpose of the Study: The researchers examined possible causes of the impairment of self-control. Previous studies have shown that there is a limited amount of self-control that one can engage in, such that if one task requires self-control, performance on a second task that requires self-control will be impaired. This study tested the idea that self-control energy is influenced by the presence of glucose, a major source of energy for the body. Two groups of subjects were compared on a task that required self-control: One group was given glucose, and one was not. The researchers predicted that the group given glucose would show better performance on the self-control task than the group not given glucose.

Method of the Study: Students completed the study to fulfill a course requirement. They first completed a task that required self-control: crossing out e's in a page of text based on a complex rule (i.e., cross out some e's, but not others). Then all subjects completed a second task requiring self-control while swishing lemonade around in their mouths. They did not swallow the drink. Participants were randomly assigned to one of two groups: For half of the subjects, the lemonade was sweetened with glucose, and for the other half, the lemonade was sweetened with Splenda (no glucose). The task they completed was a Stroop task where words were presented in colored font. Subjects were asked to name the font color as quickly as possible. On some trials, the word was a color word that was different from the font color (e.g., the word *BLUE* printed in red font). These trials require self-control because it is hard not to read the word that interferes with the font color. Reaction time to name the font color was recorded on the Stroop trials. Subjects then rated the sweetness and pleasantness of the lemonade.

Results of the Study: Figure 2.9 presents the mean reaction time results on the Stroop task for each group of subjects. Lower reaction times indicate more self-control. The statistical test run on these data showed that the glucose group has a significantly lower mean reaction time than the no glucose group.

FIGURE 2.9 ■

> **Conclusions of the Study:** The results of the study seem to support the idea that the presence of glucose can provide more "energy" for self-control in tasks that require it. However, because the participants did not swallow the glucose, it could not have affected "energy" directly in the body. Instead, the researchers proposed that rinsing with glucose may have activated portions of the brain associated with reward and/or areas associated with how we select and inhibit action. These conclusions remain controversial, though, because other studies suggest that the effects of glucose on self-control do not replicate (e.g., Lange & Eggert, 2014).

KNOWLEDGE CHECK: CHAPTER SUMMARY

(You will find the answers in the Appendix.)

Observing Behavior: Descriptive Research

- The goal of psychologists is to study behavior by using the four steps of the scientific method: observe, detect regularities, generate a hypothesis, and observe again to test the (1) __hypothesis__

- (2) __Descriptive__ research is used primarily to (3) __observe__ and describe behavior.

- (4) __Naturalistic__ is observed in natural settings with (5) __non interfering__ measures.

- (6) __Case Study__ studies focus on a single case, usually a single individual. A case study can yield historical information that is useful for generating (7) __background hypothesis__, but the results may not always generalize to the population as a whole.

- Surveys gather limited (8) __responses__ from many people. The data are likely to be (9) __representative__ of the population as a whole but often lack historical perspective.

- Psychological tests are primarily designed to measure (10) __individual__ differences.

- Data analyses reveal (11) __regularities__ in psychological observations that are used to test (12) __hypotheses__. (13) __Descriptive__ statistics summarize and describe data. (14) _____ statistics help researchers determine whether behaviors are representative of the larger population, or whether differences among observations can be attributed to chance.

Predicting Behavior: Correlational Research

- A (15) _____ helps determine whether there is a relationship between two (16) _____, or measures of behavior. When there is a correlation between two measures of behavior, it is possible to (17) _____ the value of one variable on the basis of knowledge about the other.

- A correlation between two measures of behavior allows for prediction but does not determine (18) _____. Causality requires (19) _____.

Explaining Behavior: Experimental Research

- In (20) _____ research, the investigator actively manipulates the (21) _____ to observe its effect on behavior. The particular manipulation is determined by the researcher's (22) _____.

- A(n) (23) _____ variable is the aspect of the environment that is (24) _____ in an experiment. A(n) (25) _____ variable is the behavior that is (26) _____ in an experiment.

- Experimental (27) _____ is achieved by making certain that the only thing changing systematically in an experiment is the (28) _____ variable. The independent variable must include at least (29) _____ conditions. Often there is a (30) _____, which doesn't get the experimental treatment, and a(n) (31) _____ group that does get the treatment.

- Expectations and biases, held by both participants and researchers, can influence the results of experiments. Expectancy effects on the part of the participant are controlled for with the use of

(32) _____ experiments, and (33) _____ experiments control for expectancies on the part of both the participant and the (34) _____.

- Necessary experimental (35) _____ can limit the relevance of one set of research results to other people and situations.

The Ethics of Research: Human and Animal Guidelines

- Research participants must be informed of any factors that could affect their willingness to (36) _____.

- (37) _____ is the process of explaining to research participants why the study is being conducted. (38) _____ protects the participant's privacy.

- A primary reason for using animals in psychological research is that it allows for greater experimental (39) _____. The APA enforces strict guidelines for the (40) _____ treatment of laboratory animals. However, some controversy remains over their use in psychological research.

CRITICAL THINKING QUESTIONS

1. Do you see any ethical problems with the technique of participant observation? After all, isn't the researcher misleading people by assuming a false identity?

2. Grade point average is typically calculated using the mean. Suppose the mean was replaced with a grade point mode or a grade point median. What would be the advantages and disadvantages of calculating grade point average in these ways?

3. Imagine a scenario in which every time you dreamed about your dog getting hurt, your dog was certain to be okay. Wouldn't you be truly predicting the future? What kind of correlation would this scenario represent?

4. How and why might random sampling be important to scientists seeking to find a truly representative estimate of disease (such as COVID-19) during a pandemic?

5. Can you think of any circumstances in which it might be ethical to conduct research with animals even though the results won't generalize to humans?

KEY TERMS

case study (p. 34)

confidentiality (p. 55)

confounding variable (p. 50)

correlation (p. 42)

debriefing (p. 55)

dependent variable (p. 48)

descriptive research (p. 32)

descriptive statistics (p. 41)

double-blind study (p. 53)

experimental research (p. 47)

external validity (p. 33)

independent variable (p. 48)

inferential statistics (p. 41)

informed consent (p. 55)

internal validity (p. 50)

mean (p. 39)

median (p. 39)

mode (p. 39)

naturalistic observation (p. 33)

operational definitions (p. 31)

placebo (p. 52)

random assignment (p. 50)

random sampling (p. 36)

range (p. 40)

reactivity (p. 33)

scientific method (p. 30)

single-blind study (p. 52)

standard deviation (p. 40)

survey (p. 35)

variability (p. 40)

3 BIOLOGICAL PROCESSES

LEARNING OBJECTIVES

3.1 Identify and describe the three major types of neurons—their structure and function—and explain how the steps of neural transmission solve the problem of connecting world and brain.

3.2 Identify the two major parts of the nervous system and discuss how specialized structures in the brain initiate and control the components of behavior and mind.

3.3 Explain the major functions of the endocrine system, especially the need for long-term and extended communication, and contrast this communication system with neural transmission.

3.4 Assess how psychologists determine which features of our body and mind are adaptations—that is, products of natural selection—and the role that genetics plays in the process.

3.5 For each of the major sections of the chapter, summarize how biological processes solve critical problems of behavior and mind.

CHAPTER OUTLINE

Communicating Internally: Connecting World and Brain

Initiating Behavior: A Division of Labor

  Practical Solutions: Mirror Neurons and Solving the "Other Mind Problem"

Regulating Growth and Internal Functions: Extended Communication

Adapting and Transmitting the Genetic Code

The Problems Solved: What Biological Systems Are For

Located within the confines of a protective layer of bone floats a 3- to 4-pound mass of tissue called the brain. Fueled by simple blood sugar and amino acids, the brain's billions of cells are engaged in a continuous dance of activity. The rhythms and movements of this dance are not well understood, but a "whole" is created that is collectively greater than the sum of the individual parts. From chaotic patterns of cellular activity arise the complexities of human behavior, thought, emotion, and creativity.

Psychologists assume that virtually all our actions arise from the activity of this brain—not just mundane things like breathing, maintaining a beating heart, and walking, but our intimate thoughts and feelings as well. Every time you think, act, or feel, biological activity in your brain plays a critical, if not primary, role. Disorders of the mind, such as schizophrenia and clinical depression, are products of the brain as well. This chapter introduces you to the field of **neuroscience**, which studies the connection between the brain and behavior.

THE PROBLEMS TO BE SOLVED: WHAT ARE BIOLOGICAL SYSTEMS FOR?

Our discussion of biological processes revolves around four central questions:

1. How do we communicate internally?

2. How do we initiate and control behavior?

3. How do we regulate growth and other internal functions?

4. How do we adapt and transmit the genetic code?

Each question represents a critical problem that must be solved by the systems in our bodies. Not surprisingly, each plays a critical role in explaining psychological phenomena as well. As you'll soon see, we've evolved a set of sophisticated tools to meet these needs.

Communicating Internally: Connecting World and Brain

Our actions are often adaptive because we're able to monitor the environment continuously and produce quick and appropriate responses. If a dog suddenly runs in front of your car, you quickly hit the brake, saving the animal. These nearly instantaneous world-to-behavior links are possible because of a sophisticated communication network linking the outside world to the brain. Information from the environment is translated into the language of the nervous system and relayed to appropriate processing sites throughout the body.

Initiating Behavior: A Division of Labor

The nervous system may handle the complicated task of receiving and communicating information, but information by itself does not translate into hand movements, quick reactions, or artistic creativity. Somehow the body must assign meaning to the information it receives and coordinate the appropriate responses. As you'll see, there are specific structures in the brain that initiate and coordinate our thoughts, actions, and emotions.

Regulating Growth and Internal Functions: Extended Communication

The systems in the body also have widespread and long-term internal communication needs. To resolve these needs, structures in the body control the release of chemicals into the bloodstream that serve important regulatory functions, influencing growth and development, sexual behavior, the desire to eat or drink, and even emotional expression.

Adapting and Transmitting the Genetic Code

The genetic code you inherited from your parents has been shaped by the forces of natural selection. It determines much of who you are and what you have the potential to become. Molecules carrying the genetic code influence more than eye color, height, and hair color. Intelligence, personality, and even susceptibility to mental disorders can be influenced significantly by genetic information. We'll review the basic principles of genetics and discuss how nature and nurture interact to guide and constrain behavior.

COMMUNICATING INTERNALLY: CONNECTING WORLD AND BRAIN

Strike a match and hold it an inch or so away from the tip of your index finger. Now move it a bit closer. Closer. Closer still. Let the flame approach and momentarily touch the flesh of your finger. On second thought, skip this experiment. You already know the outcome. Flame approaches flesh, and you withdraw your finger quickly, automatically, and efficiently. Let's consider the nervous system mechanisms that produce this kind of reaction, because it represents one of the simplest kinds of world-to-brain communications. The main components of the nervous system are individual cells, called **neurons**, that receive, transmit, and integrate information. The language used by the neurons to communicate is *electrochemical*—that is, it's part electrical and part chemical. There are three major types of neurons:

1. **Sensory neurons** make the initial contact with the environment and are responsible for carrying the message inward toward the spinal cord and brain. The heat of the flame excites receptor regions in the sensory neurons in your fingertip, which then pass the message along to the spinal cord.

2. **Interneurons**, the most plentiful type of neuron, make no direct contact with the world, but they convey information from one internal processing site to another. Interneurons in the spinal cord receive the message from the sensory neurons, then pass it on to the motor neurons.

3. **Motor neurons** carry the messages and commands away from the central nervous system to the muscles and glands that produce responses. In the match example in Figure 3.1, the motor neurons contact the muscles of the finger, which leads to a quick and efficient finger withdrawal.

FIGURE 3.1 ■ A Simple Reflex Pathway

The information that a hot pan has touched flesh travels through a sensory neuron to the spinal cord, which directs it to an interneuron, which sends it on to a motor neuron. The motor neuron then alerts the finger muscles, which quickly withdraw from the heat. The original information is also passed upward to the brain, which registers pain.

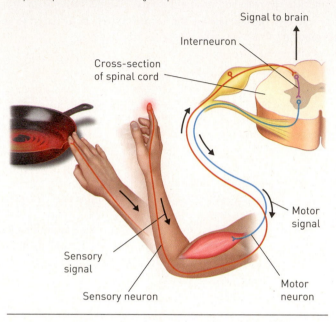

Carolina Hrejsa/Body Scientific Intl.

The nervous system also contains **glial cells**, which perform support functions such as removing waste, filling in empty space, and helping neurons to communicate efficiently. Neuroscientists used to believe that glial cells vastly outnumbered neurons in the nervous system (perhaps by as much as 10:1), but the true ratio of glial cells to neurons is probably closer to 1:1 (von Bartheld et al., 2016). Glial cells help speed up neural transmission by acting as insulation for the neuron. They form a coating called the **myelin sheath** that protects the cell, much like the rubber or plastic coating around an electrical wire protects it from environmental threats and leakage. Glial cells are thought to play a role in a wide variety of brain processes, including learning and memory (De Pitta et al., 2016) and even the control of body weight (García-Cáceres et al., 2019). The reason is that glial cells seem to be capable of modulating neuron activity in selective areas of the brain. Glial cells are also of interest because they play an important role in brain dysfunction, including brain cancer, Parkinson's disease, multiple sclerosis, and possibly even psychological disorders such as schizophrenia and bipolar disorder.

So far, the brain hasn't figured into our discussion of fingers and flames. The message is passed upward to the brain, through the activity of more interneurons, and you consciously experience the heat of the flame in the brain. But in situations requiring a quick response, as in the case of a flame touching your finger, the nervous system can produce a collection of largely automatic reactions. These reactions, called **reflexes**, are controlled primarily by spinal cord pathways. A reflex requires no input from the brain. Cut the spinal cord, blocking communication between most of the body and the brain, and you won't feel the pain or react with a facial grimace, but your finger will still twitch. Reflex pathways allow the body to respond quickly to environmental events in a simple and direct way. People don't think or feel with their spinal cords, but reflex pathways are an important part of our ability to adapt successfully to the world.

The Anatomy of Neurons

As shown in Figure 3.2, neurons have four major structural parts: *dendrites*, a *soma*, an *axon*, and *terminal buttons*. For a communication system to work properly, it must have a way to receive information, a way to process received messages, and a means for generating an appropriate response. The four components of the neuron play these roles in the communication chain.

FIGURE 3.2 ■ **The Components of a Neuron**

The dendrites are the primary information receivers, the soma is the cell body, and the axon transmits the cell's messages. The myelin sheath that surrounds the axon helps speed up neuron transmission. Terminal buttons at the end of the axon contain the chemicals that carry messages to the next neuron.

The **dendrites**, which look like tree branches extending outward from the main body of the cell, are the primary information receivers. A sensory neuron passes information about a burning flame along to an interneuron by interacting with the interneuron's dendrites. A particular neuron may have thousands of these dendritic branches, enabling the cell to receive input from many different sources. Once received, the message is processed in the **soma**, the main body of the cell. The soma is also the cell's metabolic center, and it is where genetic material is stored. The **axon** is the cell's transmitter. When a neuron transmits a message, it sends an electrical pulse called the *action potential* down its axon toward other neurons. Near its end the axon branches out to contact other cells. At the tip of each branch are tiny swellings called **terminal buttons**. Chemicals released by these buttons pass the message on to the next neuron.

Neurons don't touch. The **synapse** is a small gap between cells, typically between the terminal buttons of one neuron and the dendrite or cell body of another. The chemicals released by the terminal buttons flow into this gap. The synapse and the chemicals released into it are critical factors in the body's communication network, as you'll see next.

Solving the Transmission Problem: The Electrochemical Message

Neurons may differ in size and shape, but the direction of information flow is predictable and consistent:

Dendrites → Soma → Axon → Terminal buttons

Information arrives at the dendrites from multiple sources—many thousands of contacts might be made—and is passed along to the soma. Here all the received messages sum together; if the combined message strength exceeds a threshold, an action potential will be generated. The action potential travels down the axon toward the terminal buttons, where it causes the release of chemicals into the synapse. These chemicals move the message from the end of the axon to the dendrites of the next neuron, starting the process all over again. That's the general sequence of information flow: Messages travel electrically from one point to another within a neuron, but the message is transmitted chemically between neurons. Now let's consider each of these processes in more detail.

The Resting Potential

Neurons possess electrical properties even when they aren't receiving or transmitting messages. Specifically, a tiny electrical charge, called the **resting potential**, exists between the inside and the outside of the cell. This resting potential is created by the presence of electrically charged atoms and molecules, called *ions*, that are distributed unevenly between the inside and the outside of the cell. The main ions in neural transmission are positively charged *sodium* and *potassium* ions and negatively charged *chloride* ions. Normally, ions will distribute themselves evenly in an environment through a process called diffusion. However, the neuron's cell wall, or membrane, only allows certain ions to pass in and out through special ion channels.

As shown in Figure 3.3, when the neuron is resting, the sodium and chloride ions are concentrated outside of the cell, and the potassium ions are largely contained inside. These unequal concentrations are maintained, in part, by a sodium–potassium pump that actively moves the ions into and out of the cell. If you measured the electrical potential of the neuron, you would find that the fluid inside the cell is slightly negative with respect to the outside (between –60 and –70 millivolts). Most of the negative charge comes from large protein molecules inside the cell, which are too big to pass through the ion channels.

FIGURE 3.3 ■ The Resting Potential

Neurons possess electrical properties even when they are neither receiving nor transmitting messages. The resting potential, a tiny negative electrical charge across the inside and outside of a resting cell, is created by an uneven distribution of ions across the cell membrane.

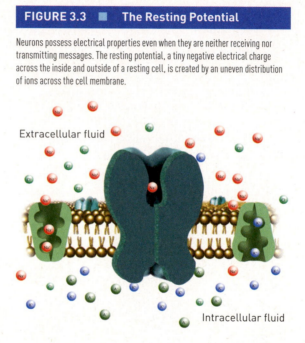

Extracellular fluid

Intracellular fluid

Generating an Action Potential

For a neuron to generate an **action potential**—that is, fire its own message—the electrical potential inside the cell needs to change. This change happens because of contact from other neurons. Two types of messages can be passed from one neuron to the next, excitatory messages and inhibitory messages. If the message is excitatory, the ion channels in the cell membrane open, and sodium ions flow into the cell. This process is called *depolarization*, and it moves the electrical potential of the cell from negative toward zero. When the message is inhibitory, the opposite happens: The cell membrane either pushes more positive ions out of the cell or allows negative ions to move in. The result is *hyperpolarization*: The electrical potential of the cell becomes more negative.

Remember, each neuron in the nervous system is in contact with many other neurons. As a result, small changes in potential occur in many input regions of the neuron as messages are received (see Figure 3.4). Near the point where the axon leaves the cell body, in a special trigger zone called the *axon hillock*, all of the excitatory and inhibitory potentials combine. If enough excitatory messages have been received—that is, if the net electrical potential inside the cell has become sufficiently less negative—the cell will "fire," and an action potential will be generated.

FIGURE 3.4   ■   Summing Excitatory and Inhibitory Messages

Each neuron is in contact with many other neurons. Some contacts initiate excitatory messages, or depolarization, and others initiate inhibitory messages, or hyperpolarization. A neuron generates its own action potential only if the summed messages produce sufficient depolarization (the negative potential moves closer to zero).

Carolina Hrejsa/Body Scientific Intl.

The firing of an action potential is an *all-or-none* process. It fires either completely or not at all. Once the firing threshold is reached, meaning there has been a sufficient change in the electrical potential around the axon hillock, the action potential begins and travels completely down the axon toward the terminal buttons. The process is somewhat like flushing a toilet. Once sufficient pressure is delivered to the handle, the toilet flushes, and it doesn't matter how hard you yank on the handle. The same is true for an action potential—increasing the intensity of the original message does not increase the intensity of the nerve impulse. There simply has to be enough of a potential change to get the message started.

The speed of the message, however, can depend on the axon's size and shape. In general, the thicker the axon, the faster the message will travel. The speed of an action potential varies among neurons in a range from about 2 to 200 miles per hour (which is still significantly slower than the speed of electricity through a wire or printed circuit). Another factor that increases the speed of transmission is the myelin sheath. Myelin provides insulation for the axon, similar to the plastic around copper wiring. At regular points there are gaps in the insulation, called *nodes of Ranvier*, that permit the action potential to jump down the axon rather than traveling from point to point. This method of transmission from node to node is called *saltatory conduction*; it comes from the Latin *saltare*, which means "to jump." The myelin sheath speeds transmission, and it also protects the message from interference by other neural signals.

Neurotransmitters: The Chemical Messengers

When the action potential reaches the end of the axon, it triggers the release of chemical messengers from small sacs, or vesicles, in the terminal buttons (see Figure 3.5). These chemical molecules, called **neurotransmitters**, spill out into the synapse and interact chemically with the cell membrane of the next neuron (called the postsynaptic membrane). Depending on the characteristics of this membrane, the neurotransmitter will transfer either an excitatory or an inhibitory message.

The released neurotransmitter acts as a kind of key in search of the appropriate lock. It flows quickly across the synapse and activates receptor molecules contained in the postsynaptic membrane. When the message is excitatory, the neurotransmitter causes channels in the cell wall to open, allowing positive sodium ions to flow into the receiving cell. When the message is inhibitory, negative chloride ions can enter the cell, and positive potassium ions are allowed to leave. It is important to note, though, that

FIGURE 3.5 ■ Releasing the Chemical Messengers

When the action potential reaches the end of the axon, chemical messengers, or neurotransmitters, are released into the synapse, where they interact with the postsynaptic membrane of the next neuron, opening or closing its ion channels.

Presynaptic neuron

Presynaptic terminal

Neurotransmitter in vesicles

Terminal releases neurotransmitter

Neurotransmitter interacts with receptors, opening ion channels

Postsynaptic neuron

neurotransmitters, by themselves, are neither excitatory nor inhibitory. It is really the nature of the receptor molecule that determines whether a particular neurotransmitter will produce an excitatory or inhibitory effect; the same neurotransmitter can produce quite different effects at different sites in the nervous system.

We don't know how many different neurotransmitters exist in our brain, but some important ones have been identified and are well studied. The most common neurotransmitter in the brain is **glutamate**. Glutamate is an excitatory neurotransmitter, and it's involved in many aspects of brain functioning, including memory. The neurotransmitter **acetylcholine** acts as the primary transmitter between motor neurons and muscles in the body. When released into the synapse between motor neurons and muscle cells, acetylcholine creates excitatory messages that lead to muscle contraction. Any voluntary motor movement, like lifting your arm or walking, involves acetylcholine. The neurotransmitter **dopamine**, which can produce either excitatory or inhibitory effects, is also involved in motor movements. Dopamine helps to dampen and stabilize communications in the brain and elsewhere. Inhibitory effects of this type keep the brain on an even keel and allow us to produce smooth voluntary muscle movements, sleep without physically acting out our dreams, and maintain posture. If neurotransmitters had only excitatory effects, there would be an endless chain of communication, producing a blooming, buzzing ball of confusion in the brain.

Dopamine is of special interest to psychologists because it's thought to play a role in reward and pleasure but also schizophrenia, a serious psychological disorder that disrupts thought processes and produces delusions and hallucinations. When patients with schizophrenia take drugs that inhibit the action of dopamine, their hallucinations and delusions are often reduced or even eliminated. It's been suggested that an inability to regulate dopamine successfully in the brain is partly responsible for this debilitating disorder (e.g., Maia & Frank, 2017). Further support linking dopamine and schizophrenia comes from the study of Parkinson's disease, a movement disorder that results from the underproduction of dopamine. Parkinson's patients are sometimes given the drug L-dopa, which increases the levels of dopamine in the brain, to reduce the tremors and other movement problems caused by the disease. For some patients, however, one of the side effects of L-dopa is a mimicking of the thought disorders characteristic of schizophrenia (Schmack et al., 2018).

Neurotransmitters in the brain control our thoughts and actions—that much is clear—but the mechanisms are not well understood. We know, for example, that people with Alzheimer's disease have suffered destruction of cells that play a role in producing acetylcholine (Kandimalla & Reddy, 2017). Because memory loss is a common problem for Alzheimer's patients, a close connection is believed to exist between acetylcholine and certain kinds of memory functioning. **Serotonin** affects sleep, dreaming, and general arousal and may be involved in a host of psychological disorders including depression, obsessive–compulsive disorder, and autism spectrum disorder (C. L. Muller et al., 2016). Many medications used to treat depression, such as Prozac (fluoxetine), act by modulating the effectiveness of serotonin. Similarly, researchers have suspected for some time that a neurotransmitter called **gamma-aminobutyric acid (GABA)** plays an important role in the regulation of anxiety. Many medications for anxiety (e.g., tranquilizers such as Valium) regulate GABA in the brain.

Researchers are trying to understand the neural pathways involved in these effects and disorders. However, much of our knowledge remains correlational at this point—we know that as the levels of particular neurotransmitters vary in the body, so too do the symptoms of disorders. This is useful information for treatment, but it doesn't establish a true cause-and-effect link between neurotransmitters and psychological characteristics. For example, current medications for schizophrenia target dopamine receptors in the brain, and can be quite effective in reducing symptoms of the disorder, but these medications affect other neurotransmitter receptor systems as well. Hence, it can be difficult to determine exactly what is responsible for any improvement (Howes et al., 2015). For a summary of neurotransmitters and their effects, see Concept Review 3.1.

CONCEPT REVIEW 3.1
NEUROTRANSMITTERS AND THEIR EFFECTS

Neurotransmitter	Nature of Effect*	What It Is Involved In
Glutamate	Excitatory	Most common neurotransmitter in the brain. Probably involved in a host of mental processes, including learning and memory.
Dopamine	Mixed	Involved in reward/pleasure systems; helps ensure smooth motor function. Plays a role in both schizophrenia and Parkinson's disease.
Acetylcholine	Excitatory	Communication between motor neurons and muscles in the body, leading to muscle contraction. May also play a role in Alzheimer's disease.
Serotonin	Inhibitory	Involved in sleep, mood, appetite, and general arousal. Thought to play a role in some psychological disorders, including depression.
GABA	Inhibitory	The regulation of anxiety; tranquilizing drugs act on GABA to decrease anxiety.

* *Note:* A neurotransmitter, on its own, can be either excitatory or inhibitory; the nature of its action depends on specific characteristics of the receiving cell's membrane.

Drugs and the Brain

Because the transmission of messages between neurons is chemical, if you consume a drug—by swallowing, smoking, snorting, or another method of ingestion—it can significantly affect the communication networks in your brain. Drugs called *agonists* enhance or mimic the action of neurotransmitters. For example, the nicotine in cigarette smoke can act like the neurotransmitter acetylcholine. Nicotine stimulates the body, such as by increasing heart rate, because it produces excitatory messages in much the same way as acetylcholine. Cocaine is an agonist for dopamine—it allows dopamine to linger longer in the synapse, increasing its effectiveness.

The caffeine in coffee interferes with drowsiness by interacting with the chemical messenger systems in the brain.

iStockPhoto/Halfpoint

Other drugs act as *antagonists*, which means that they block the action of neurotransmitters. As mentioned earlier, many of the drugs used to treat schizophrenia are antagonists for dopamine—they bind to receptors and block the effect of dopamine release. The lethal drug curare, which is sometimes used on the tips of hunting arrows and blow darts in South America, is antagonistic to acetylcholine. Curare blocks the receptor systems involved in muscle movements, including those muscles that move the diaphragm during breathing. The result is paralysis and likely death from suffocation. Botox, which is commonly used cosmetically to treat facial wrinkles, is an antagonist as well—it also blocks the release of acetylcholine, which, in turn, prevents muscle contractions and allows bothersome wrinkles to relax and soften. Of course, in its more lethal form—the deadly illness botulism—the antagonistic effects are more widespread, disrupting the ability to breathe and swallow.

In the early 1970s, membrane receptor systems were discovered in the brain that react directly to morphine, a painkilling and highly addictive drug derived from the opium plant (Pert & Snyder, 1973; S. H. Snyder, 2017). Of course, we aren't born with morphine in our brains. It turns out we have receptor systems that are sensitive to morphine because the brain produces its own morphine-like substances called **endorphins**. Endorphins serve as natural painkillers in the body. Systems in the brain release endorphins under conditions of stress or exertion to reduce pain and possibly to provide pleasurable reinforcement (Pert, 2002). As you may already know, endorphins have been linked to the so-called runner's high. It's well established, in fact, that prolonged exercise can indeed lead to endorphin release. Some have even suggested that people can become "addicted" to exercise and experience withdrawal-like symptoms if regular exercise is discontinued. As this point, though, the connection between runner's high, endorphins, and exercise addiction remains controversial (see Szabo et al., 2019). Moreover, it's important not to confuse the runner's high with the mind-altering effects of opioid medications. As you know, there is a serious opioid crisis in the United States and elsewhere. We'll return to the study of drugs, particularly their effects on conscious awareness, in Chapter 6.

The Communication Network

To unravel the complex relationship between the brain and mental processes, we must understand how neurons work together. A vast communication network exists within the brain, involving the operation of thousands of neurons. The way in which these cells interact is critically important. Behaviors, thoughts, feelings, ideas—they don't arise from the activation of single neurons; instead, it is the *pattern of activation* produced by groups of neurons operating together that produces conscious experience and complex behaviors. As a result, we need to be mindful of the specific ways in which neurons are connected and the means through which those connections can be modified by experience.

Information is partly communicated in the nervous system by the *firing rate* of a neuron, which means the number of action potentials it generates per unit of time. The stronger the incoming message, the more rapidly the receiving neuron tends to fire. These firing rates, however, are subject to some natural limitations. For instance, a **refractory period** usually follows the generation of an action potential; during this period, additional action potentials cannot be generated (see Figure 3.6). Even with the refractory period, though, neurons are still able to fire off a relatively steady stream of messages in response to environmental input. Many neurons even appear to have spontaneous firing rates, which means they generate a steady stream of action potentials with little or no apparent input from the environment. A continuously active cell is adaptive because more information can be coded by increasing or decreasing a firing rate than by simply turning a neuron on or off.

FIGURE 3.6 ■ The Action Potential and Its Refractory Period

A refractory period usually follows the generation of an action potential; during this period, additional action potentials cannot be generated.

Carolina Hrejsa/Body Scientific Intl.

Because the brain contains billions of neurons, it's impractical to try to map out individual neural connections. So how can we ever hope to discover how everything works together to produce behavior? One solution is to study nonhuman organisms, whose circuits of neurons are less complex and more easily mapped. Another option is to try to simulate activity of the mind—such as simple learning and memory processes—by creating artificial networks of neurons on computers.

At this point, no one has come close to achieving anything resembling an artificial brain, but simple computerized networks have been developed that show brainlike properties. For example, computerized neural networks can recognize objects when given incomplete information and can perform reasonably well if artificially damaged. If a subset of input units is turned off, perhaps mimicking damage to the brain, activation of the remaining units can still be sufficient to produce the correct output response. This is an adaptive characteristic of both neural circuits in the brain and neural networks. Each can sustain damage and still produce correct responses.

KNOWLEDGE CHECK 3.1

Now test your knowledge about neurons and how they communicate. Select your answers from the following list of terms: *dendrites, soma, axon, terminal buttons, action potential, neurotransmitters, refractory period*. (You will find the answers in the Appendix.)

1. The main body of the cell, where excitatory and inhibitory messages combine: _____

2. The long tail-like part of a neuron that serves as the cell's main transmitter device: _____

3. The all-or-none electrical signal that travels to the end of the axon, causing the release of chemical messengers: _____

4. The branchlike fibers that extend outward from a neuron and receive information from other neurons: _____

5. Acetylcholine, serotonin, GABA, and dopamine are all examples of _____

FIGURE 3.7 ■ The Nervous System

The central nervous system contains the brain and the spinal cord, and the peripheral nervous system is made up of the nerves outside the brain and spinal cord.

Carolina Hrejsa/Body Scientific Intl.

INITIATING BEHAVIOR: A DIVISION OF LABOR

The nervous system has a lot of tough problems to solve. Besides generating behavior and mental processes such as thinking and feeling, the brain must maintain a beating heart, control breathing, and signal the body that it's time to eat. If your body is deprived of food or water, or if its constant internal temperature gets out of whack, you must be motivated to find food, water, or the appropriate shelter. Even the simplest of everyday activities—producing spoken language, walking, perceiving a complex visual scene—require a great deal of coordination among the muscles and sensory organs of the body. To accomplish these different functions, the nervous system divides its labor.

The Central and Peripheral Nervous Systems

The nervous system is divided into two major parts, the **central nervous system** and the **peripheral nervous system**. The central nervous system consists of the brain and spinal cord and acts as the central executive of the body. Decisions are made here, and messages are then communicated to the rest of the body via bundles of axons called **nerves**. The nerves outside the brain and spinal cord form the peripheral nervous system.

It is through the peripheral nervous system that muscles are moved, internal organs are regulated, and sensory input is directed toward the brain. As you can see in Figure 3.7, the peripheral nervous system can be divided further into the somatic and autonomic systems. Information travels to the brain and spinal cord through *afferent* (sensory) nerve pathways; *efferent* (motor) nerve pathways carry central nervous system messages outward to the muscles and glands. The **somatic system** consists of the nerves that transmit sensory information toward the brain, as well as the nerves that connect to the skeletal muscles to initiate movement. Without the somatic system, information about the environment could not reach the brain, nor could we begin a movement of any kind. The **autonomic system** controls the more automatic needs of the body, such as heart rate, digestion, blood pressure, and the activity of internal glands.

These two systems work together to make certain that information about the world is communicated to the brain for interpretation, that movements are carried out, and that the life-sustaining activity of the body is continued.

One critical function of the autonomic system, besides performing the automatic "housekeeping" activities that keep the body alive, is to help us handle and recover from emergency situations. When we're faced with an emergency, such as a sudden attack, our bodies typically produce a fight-or-flight response. The *sympathetic division* of the autonomic system triggers the release of chemicals, creating a state of readiness (e.g., by increasing heart rate, blood pressure, and breathing rate). After the emergency has passed, the *parasympathetic division* calms the body down by slowing heart rate and lowering blood pressure. Parasympathetic activity also helps increase the body's supply of stored energy, which may be diminished in response to the emergency. We'll be discussing the fight-or-flight response in more detail later in the chapter.

Determining Brain Function

Now let's consider the techniques that researchers use to determine how various parts of the brain work. The anatomical features of the nervous system as a whole—the various nerve tracts and so on—can be studied through dissection of the body (after death, of course!). But the dissection of brain tissue, which contains billions of neurons, tells only a limited story. To determine the architecture of the brain, researchers need a broader set of tools. We'll briefly consider three popular techniques: (1) the study of brain damage, (2) activating the brain, and (3) monitoring the brain in action.

Brain Damage

One of the oldest methods for determining brain function is to study people with brain damage. A patient arrives with an injury—perhaps a blow to the right side of the head—and complains of a specific problem, such as trouble moving the left side of the body. In this way, a link is established between a brain area and its function. As early as the 19th century, it was known that damage to the left side of the brain can create movement problems on the right side of the body as well as specific speech difficulties. Destruction of Wernicke's area results in a patient who cannot easily understand spoken language (Wernicke, 1874); damage to Broca's area produces a patient who can understand but not easily produce spoken language (Broca, 1861). Cases such as these suggest that psychological functions are controlled by specific areas of the brain.

Neuroscientists have made many significant advances by studying brain injury. For example, brain-damaged patients have taught us about how knowledge is organized and represented in the brain (Mahon & Caramazza, 2009). Damage to one part of the brain can affect a person's ability to name tools but not fruit; damage to another area might affect the ability to recognize a face. Neuroscientist V. S. Ramachandran (2011) provides a fascinating account in his book *The Tell-Tale Brain*. We meet Jason who is unable to talk, walk, or recognize people—he follows people with his eyes but otherwise exists in a zombie-like state. When his father visits Jason, Jason is incapable of interaction. But if his father calls him on the phone from another room, Jason suddenly becomes fully conscious and carries on a natural conversation. As Ramachandran notes, "It is as if there are two Jasons trapped inside one body: the one connected to vision, who is alert but not conscious, and the one connected to hearing who is alert *and* conscious" (p. 7).

Neuroscientists have made significant progress in the understanding of brain function by studying people with brain damage.

Phanie / Alamy Stock Photo

Case studies of brain damage are useful, but they do have limitations. For one thing, researchers have no control over when and where the injury occurs. In addition, most instances of brain damage, either from an accident or from a tumor or a stroke, produce widespread damage. It's difficult to know exactly which portion of the damaged brain is responsible for the behavioral or psychological problem.

As we saw in Chapter 2, case studies can be rich sources of information, but the researcher typically lacks important controls. Researchers have taken advantage of the fact that brain tissue contains no pain receptors to explore the effects of brain damage in nonhuman animals. It's possible to destroy, or *lesion*, particular regions of an animal's brain by administering an electric current, injecting chemicals, or cutting tissue. Even here it is difficult to pinpoint the damage exactly (because everything in the brain is interconnected), but lesion studies in animals have frequently led to significant advances in our understanding of the brain (Pinel, 1999).

Activating the Brain

It's also possible to activate the brain directly by capitalizing on the electrochemical nature of the communication network. Essentially, messages can be created where none would have normally occurred. Chemicals can be injected that excite the neurons in an area of the brain. Researchers can also insert small wire electrodes into brain tissue, allowing an area's cells to be stimulated electrically. The researcher initiates a message externally, then observes behavior.

Electrical stimulation techniques have been used primarily with animals. Electrodes can be implanted in such a way as to allow an animal to move freely about in its environment (see Figure 3.8). A small pulse of current can then be delivered to various brain regions. Studies have shown that electrical brain stimulation can cause animals to suddenly start eating, drinking, engaging in sexual behavior, or preparing for an attack. Researchers have also discovered that stimulation of some brain regions can act as a powerful reward, leading the animals to engage repeatedly in whatever behavior led to the stimulation (Leon & Gallistel, 1998; Olds, 1958). For example, if rats are taught that pressing a metal bar leads to electrical stimulation of a reward area, they will press the bar thousands of times in an hour. It is tempting to conclude that these regions act as "pleasure centers," at least for rats, but such a conclusion is unwarranted. Electrical stimulation can have widespread effects and may, for instance, lead to changes in the levels or effectiveness of neurotransmitters in the brain. We just don't know. Moreover, it's widely agreed that pleasure in the human brain involves an array of brain regions rather than a single location (Berridge & Kringelbach, 2015).

FIGURE 3.8 ■ Electrical Stimulation

When the rat presses a bar, a small pulse of electric current is delivered to its brain. Stimulation of certain brain areas appears to be quite rewarding to the rat because it presses the bar very rapidly.

Electric stimulator

Connection to stimulator

Pen

Rotating drum

Connection to recorder

Cumulative response recorder

Carolina Hrejsa/Body Scientific Intl.

Under some circumstances, it's possible to stimulate cells in the human brain and note the effects. During certain kinds of brain surgery (such as surgery to reduce the seizures produced by epilepsy), the patient is kept awake while the brain is stimulated with an electrode. Because there are no pain receptors in the brain, the patient typically receives only a local anesthetic prior to the surgery (along with some drugs for relaxation). Keeping the patient awake is necessary because the surgeon can stimulate an abnormal area, prior to removal, to make sure that vital capabilities such as speech or movement will not be affected. Electrical stimulation under these conditions has caused patients to produce involuntary movement, hear buzzing noises, and in some rare instances even experience what they report to be memories (Penfield & Perot, 1963).

In humans, it is also possible to stimulate brain activity through the application of localized magnetic fields. In **transcranial magnetic stimulation (TMS)**, special coils are used to generate magnetic fields that, in turn, direct electrical current to targeted areas in the brain. This stimulation can be used to selectively activate or disrupt performance on an ongoing task. Although safe and reversible, TMS is often used by scientists to create "virtual lesions" in the brain that are diagnostic about brain function. For example, in one recent study, TMS was used to induce "blindsight," an interesting phenomenon in which people report no conscious awareness of seeing a stimulus (e.g., a line of a particular orientation) but can correctly answer questions about it (Koenig & Ro, 2019). TMS is currently used to study a variety of brain functions, including visual perception and memory (Sheu et al., 2019).

Finally, although it is not available for human use, neuroscientists are also experimenting with a technique called **optogenetics** that uses light to activate and control neurons that have been genetically engineered to respond to light. This technique has enabled researchers to investigate how neurons respond when animals learn and remember and then to track those neurons over time. It has even been possible to reinstate prior memories in mice by reactivating those neurons with light delivered through fiber optics into the brain (e.g., Lacagnina et al., 2019). This is an exciting new technique that may have applications at some point to brain disorders such as Alzheimer's disease.

Optogenetics uses light to activate and control neurons that have been genetically engineered to respond to light.

Henning Dalhoff / Science Source

Monitoring the Brain

Other techniques monitor the brain directly and are more easily used to study the human brain. An **electroencephalograph (EEG)** is a device that simply monitors the gross electrical activity of the brain. Recording electrodes attached to the scalp measure global changes in the electrical potentials of thousands of brain cells in the form of line tracings, or brain waves. The EEG is useful not only as a research tool but also for diagnostic purposes. Brain disorders, including psychological disorders, can sometimes be detected through abnormalities in brain waves (Yadollahpour et al., 2017).

The EEG helps neuroscientists both diagnose brain dysfunction and understand normal brain functioning.

BSIP/Universal Images Group via Getty Images

A three-dimensional picture of the brain, including abnormalities in brain tissue, can be obtained through a **computerized tomography scan (CT scan)**. CT scanners use computers to detect how highly focused beams of X-rays change as they pass through the body. CT scans are most often used by physicians to detect tumors or injuries to the brain, but they can also be used to determine whether there is a physical basis for some chronic behavioral or psychological disorder.

Other imaging devices are designed to obtain a snapshot of the brain *at work*. These techniques help the researcher determine how tasks, such as reading a book, affect individual parts of the brain. In **positron emission tomography (PET)**, the patient ingests a harmless radioactive substance, which is then absorbed into the cells of active brain regions. When the person is performing a task, such as speaking or reading, the working areas of the brain absorb more of the ingested radioactive material. The PET scanner then develops a picture that reveals how the radioactive substance has distributed itself over time. It is assumed that those parts of the brain with the most concentrated traces of radioactive material probably play a significant role in the task being performed.

Another popular technique is **magnetic resonance imaging (MRI)**. MRI has two main advantages over PET scanning: It doesn't require the participant to ingest any chemicals, and it's capable of producing extremely detailed, three-dimensional images of the brain. Functional MRI uses the MRI technology to map changes in blood flow or oxygen use as the patient thinks or behaves. Functional MRI, like PET scanning, helps researchers determine where specific kinds of processing may occur in the brain. So far, this popular new technique has helped to isolate the brain regions associated with visual processing, language, attention, memory, and even social interactions (see C. A. Hill et al., 2017). There is some evidence to suggest that functional MRI may even help psychologists distinguish between true and false memories: When we falsely remember something that didn't occur, the blood flow patterns in the brain are somewhat different from those seen when we remember an actual event (Karanian & Slotnick, 2018; Schacter et al., 2011).

MRIs can be used to construct detailed images of the brain.

iStockPhoto/temet

Functional MRIs help neuroscientists determine brain function by recording how blood oxygen use changes in different parts of the brain during performance of a task.

Living Art Enterprises / Science Source

Functional MRI is a powerful investigative tool, and we'll refer to it often throughout this text. But like other investigative tools, it has limitations. The analysis of neuroimaging data typically requires one to use complex statistical techniques to filter out the relevant patterns of activation, and not everyone agrees about the best way to summarize the data. Concerns have been raised as well about the reproducibility of the results, partly because the number of participants who are "scanned" is usually small (Gilmore et al., 2017), and the results may differ from one test session to the next (Elliott et al., 2020). Extra care needs to be taken with neuroimaging data because it can produce an "illusion of explanatory depth" (R. E. Rhodes, 2014). Bolstering an argument with a picture of brain activation tends to make people evaluate the explanation more favorably, even if the picture adds little to the value of the scientific argument (see Weisberg et al., 2018). For a summary of the different brain investigation techniques, see Concept Review 3.2.

CONCEPT REVIEW 3.2
BRAIN INVESTIGATION TECHNIQUES

Technique	Overview	What Can It Show?
Brain damage and lesion	Associate areas of brain damage with changes in behavioral function.	The areas of the brain that may be responsible for different functions.
Electrical brain stimulation	Uses electrical or chemical stimulation to excite brain areas.	How activation of certain brain regions affects behavior.
TMS (transcranial magnetic stimulation)	Special coils are used to generate magnetic fields that, in turn, direct electrical current to target areas in the brain.	This stimulation can be used to selectively activate or disrupt performance on an ongoing task.
EEG (electroencephalograph)	Uses electrodes to record gross electrical activity of the brain.	How overall activity in the brain changes during certain activities, such as sleeping, and may allow for detection of disorders.
CT (computerized tomography) scan	Passes X-rays through the body at various angles and orientations.	Tumors or injuries to the brain, as well as the structural bases for chronic behavioral or psychological disorders.
PET (positron emission tomography) scan	A radioactive substance is ingested; active brain areas absorb the substance; the PET scanner reveals distribution of the substance.	How various tasks (such as reading a book) affect different parts of the brain.
MRI (magnetic resonance imaging)	Monitors systematic activity of atoms in the presence of magnetic fields and radio-wave pulses.	A three-dimensional view of the brain, serving as a diagnostic tool for brain abnormalities, such as tumors. Functional MRI allows for observation of brain function.

Brain Structures and Their Functions

Let's now turn our attention to the brain itself. Remember, it's here that mental processes are represented through the simultaneous activities of billions of individual neurons. Particular regions in the brain contribute unique features to an experience, helping to create a psychological whole. Your perception of a cat is controlled not by a single cell, or even by a single group of cells, but rather by different brain areas that detect the color of the fur or recognize a characteristic meow.

We'll divide our discussion of the brain into sections that correspond to the brain's three major anatomical regions: the *hindbrain*, the *midbrain*, and the *forebrain*.

The Hindbrain: Basic Life Support

The **hindbrain** is the most primitive part of the brain, and it sits right where the spinal cord and brain merge (see Figure 3.9). *Primitive* is an appropriate term for two reasons. First, structures in the hindbrain act as the basic life-support system for the body—no creative thoughts or complex emotions originate here. Second, from the standpoint of evolution, the hindbrain is the oldest part of the brain. Similar structures, with similar functions, can be found throughout the animal kingdom. You can think of the hindbrain as a kind of base camp, with structures that are situated farther up in the brain controlling increasingly more complex mental processes. Not surprisingly, damage to the hindbrain seriously affects our ability to survive.

FIGURE 3.9 ■ The Hindbrain and Midbrain

The hindbrain acts as the basic life-support system for the body, controlling such things as heart rate, blood pressure, and respiration. The midbrain contains structures that help coordinate and relay information to higher centers.

Midbrain
Substantia nigra
Superior colliculus
Inferior colliculus

Forebrain

Hindbrain
Reticular formation
Pons

Medulla
Cerebellum

Carolina Hrejsa/Body Scientific Intl.

As Figure 3.9 shows, the hindbrain contains several important substructures. The *medulla* and the *pons* are associated with the control of heart rate, breathing, blood pressure, and reflexes such as vomiting, sneezing, and coughing. Both areas serve as pathways for neural impulses traveling to and from the spinal cord (the word *pons* means "bridge"). These areas are particularly sensitive to the lethal effects of drugs such as alcohol, barbiturates, and cocaine. The hindbrain also contains the *reticular formation*, a network of neurons and nerves linked to the control of general arousal, sleep, and consciousness.

Finally, at the base of the brain sits a structure that resembles a smaller version of the brain—a kind of "brainlet." This is the **cerebellum** (which means "little brain"), a structure involved in the preparation, selection, and coordination of complex motor movements such as hitting a golf ball, playing the piano, or learning how to use and manipulate tools (J. W. Lewis, 2006). No one is certain about the exact role the cerebellum plays in movement—for instance, it may be a critical component of how we learn to time motor movements (Teki et al., 2011). The cerebellum has been linked to a host of tasks, including language, memory, reasoning, and perhaps even social awareness (Schmahmann, 2019). Again, exactly how the cerebellum contributes to these activities remains a mystery—at least the details haven't been worked out—but it appears to be involved in some way.

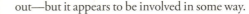

The cerebellum is thought to be involved in the coordination of complex motor movements, such as playing the piano.

iStockPhoto/Vladimir Vladimirov

The Midbrain: Neural Relay Stations

The **midbrain** lies deep within the brain atop the hindbrain. Perhaps because of its central position, structures in the midbrain receive input from multiple sources, including the sense organs. The tectum and its component structures, the superior colliculus and inferior colliculus, serve as important relay stations for visual and auditory information and help coordinate reactions to sensory events in the environment (such as moving the head in response to a sudden sound).

The midbrain also contains a group of neurons, the *substantia nigra*, that release the neurotransmitter dopamine from their terminal buttons. As you saw earlier in the chapter, dopamine seems to be involved in a number of physical and psychological disorders. For example, the rigidity of movement that characterizes Parkinson's disease apparently results from decreased levels of dopamine in the brain. Indeed, the death of neurons in the substantia nigra is believed to be the cause of the disorder. Exactly why this portion of the midbrain degenerates is not known, although both genetic and environmental factors play a role (Przedborski, 2005); recent evidence suggests that the immune system probably plays a role as well, although much remains to be discovered (see De Virgilio et al., 2016).

The Forebrain: Higher Mental Functioning

Moving up past the midbrain we encounter the **forebrain** (see Figure 3.10). The most recognizable feature of the forebrain is the **cerebral cortex**, which is the grayish matter full of fissures, folds, and crevices that covers the outside of the brain (*cortex* is Latin for "bark"). The cortex is quite large in humans, accounting for approximately 80% of the total volume of the human brain (Kolb & Whishaw, 2009). We'll look at the cerebral cortex in depth in a minute. Beneath the cerebral cortex sit the thalamus, the hypothalamus, and the limbic system. The **thalamus** is positioned close to the midbrain and is an important gathering point for input from the various senses. Indeed, the thalamus is the main processing center for sensory input prior to its being sent to the upper regions of the cortex. Besides acting as an efficient relay center, the thalamus is where information from the various senses is combined in some way.

FIGURE 3.10 ■ The Forebrain

The forebrain includes structures such as the limbic system and the cerebral cortex. Structures in the limbic system are thought to be involved in motivation, emotion, and memory. The cerebral cortex controls higher mental processes.

Cerebral cortex

Thalamus

Hypothalamus

Pituitary gland

Amygdala

Hippocampus

Carolina Hrejsa/Body Scientific Intl.

The **hypothalamus**, which lies just below the thalamus, is important in motivation, particularly the regulation of eating, drinking, body temperature, and sexual behavior. In experiments on nonhuman animals, stimulating regions of the hypothalamus kick-starts a variety of behaviors. For example, male and female rats will show characteristic sexual responses when one portion of the hypothalamus is stimulated, whereas damage to another region of the hypothalamus can seriously affect regular eating behavior. Neuroimaging studies have shown that the hypothalamus becomes active when monkeys are exposed to sexually arousing odors from receptive females (Ferris et al., 2001). Some have even suggested that neural circuits in the hypothalamus play an important role in sexual preference and attraction (Poeppl et al., 2016). The hypothalamus also controls the release of hormones by the pituitary gland; you'll read about the actions of hormones shortly when we discuss the endocrine system.

The **limbic system** is made up of several interrelated brain structures, including the amygdala and the hippocampus. The *amygdala* is a small, almond-shaped piece of brain (from the Greek word meaning "almond") that's linked to a number of motivational and emotional behaviors, including fear, aggression, and defensive actions. Destruction of portions of the amygdala in nonhuman animals can produce an extremely passive animal—one that will do nothing in response to provocation. Neuroimaging studies in humans have found that activation in the amygdala increases when people look at faces showing fear, anger, sadness, or even happiness (Yang et al., 2002); moreover, people with damage to the amygdala sometimes have difficulty recognizing emotions like sadness in facial expressions (Adolphs, 2009). Imaging studies have also suggested a link between anxiety disorders and activation of the amygdala (Sah, 2017).

The *hippocampus* (Greek for "seahorse," which it resembles anatomically) is important for the formation of memories, particularly our memory for specific personal events. People with severe damage to the hippocampus can live in a kind of perpetual present—they are aware of the world around them, and they recognize people and things known to them prior to the damage, but they remember almost nothing new. These patients act as if they are continually awakening from a dream; experiences slip away, and they recall nothing from only moments before. Memory depends on networks that extend beyond the hippocampus (Aly & Ranganath, 2018), but there is wide agreement that the hippocampus is vital to the formation of memory records. It may also play an important role in spatial navigation—our ability to find our way from one place to another—which, of course, depends on memory as well (Jeffry, 2018). We'll consider the hippocampus and the role it plays in memory in more detail in Chapter 8.

The Cerebral Cortex

With the cerebral cortex, we finally find the seat of higher mental processes. Thoughts, the sense of self, the ability to reason and solve problems—each arises from neurons firing in patterns somewhere in specialized regions of the cerebral cortex. The cortex is divided into two hemispheres, left and right. The left hemisphere controls the sensory and motor functions for the right side of the body, and the right hemisphere controls these functions for the left side of the body. A structure called the corpus callosum, which we'll discuss later, serves as a communication bridge between the two hemispheres.

Each hemisphere can be further divided into four parts, or lobes: the *frontal, temporal, parietal*, and *occipital lobes* (see Figure 3.11). These lobes control particular body functions, such as visual processing by the occipital lobe and language processing by the frontal and temporal lobes. As usual, a slight warning is in order here: Although researchers have discovered that particular areas in the brain seem to control highly specialized functions, there is almost certainly considerable overlap of function in the brain. The brain consists of team players—no single component is likely to work alone.

FIGURE 3.11 ■ The Cerebral Cortex

The cerebral cortex is divided into two hemispheres—left and right—each consisting of four lobes. The lobes are specialized to control particular functions, such as visual processing in the occipital lobe and language processing in the frontal and temporal lobes.

Carolina Hrejsa/Body Scientific Intl.

The **frontal lobes** are the largest lobes in the cortex and act as the brain's "executive" in charge of planning and coordinating voluntary behavior and decision making. Many higher-order cognitive functions originate here, including problem solving, certain kinds of remembering, and even socialization and personality. Damage to the frontal lobe can lead to withdrawal from the social world, ignoring of friends and relatives, and a refusal to do much of anything (Ramachandran, 2011). The frontal lobes were once the site of a famous surgical operation, the prefrontal lobotomy, which was performed on people suffering from severe and untreatable psychological disorders. The operation was performed to calm the patient and reduce symptoms, which it sometimes did, but the side effects were severe. Patients lost their ability to take initiative or make plans, and they often appeared to lose their social inhibitions. For these reasons, the operation fell out of favor as an acceptable treatment for psychological disorders.

The frontal lobes also contain the *motor cortex*, which controls voluntary muscle movements, as well as areas involved in language production. Broca's area, which is involved in speech production, is located in a portion of the left frontal lobe in most people. The motor cortex sits at the rear of the frontal lobe in both hemispheres; axons from the motor cortex project down to motor neurons in the spinal cord and elsewhere. If neurons in this area of the brain are stimulated electrically, muscle contractions—the twitch of a finger or the jerking of a foot—can occur. Researchers have also discovered an intriguing relation between body parts and regions of the motor cortex. There is a mapping, or *topographic* organization, in which adjacent areas of the body, such as the hand and the wrist, are activated by adjacent neurons in the motor cortex. The motor cortex also contains *mirror neurons*, which may play an important role in empathy and our ability to take the perspectives of others. For more on mirror neurons, take a look at the accompanying Practical Solutions box.

The **parietal lobe** contains the *somatosensory cortex*, which enables us to experience the sensations of touch, temperature, and pain. A lover's kiss on the cheek excites neurons that lie close to those that would be excited by the same kiss to the lips. In addition, as Figure 3.12 demonstrates, there is a relationship between sensitivity to touch (or the ability to control a movement) and size of the representation in the cortex. Those areas of the body that show particular sensitivity to touch, or are associated with fine motor control (such as the face, lips, and fingers), have relatively large areas of neural representation in the cortex. It's not surprising, as a consequence, that we display affection by kissing on the lips rather than, say, rubbing our backs together!

FIGURE 3.12 ■ Cortex Specialization

The motor cortex is at the back of the frontal lobe in each cerebral hemisphere. In a systematic body-to-brain relationship, adjacent parts of the body are activated by neurons in adjacent areas of the cortex. The somatosensory cortex, in the parietal lobe of each hemisphere, controls the sense of touch; again, there is a systematic mapping arrangement. Notice that in each type of cortex, the size of the cortical representation is related to the sensitivity of the body part.

Carolina Hrejsa/Body Scientific Intl.

The parietal lobe is closely identified with our sense of touch and the general integration of sensory information, but like the other brain areas we've considered, it serves a variety of roles in human thought and action. Imaging data suggest that the parietal lobe is involved in language processing and perhaps even social cognition—our ability to infer the beliefs and intentions of other people (Bzdok et al., 2016). Other studies suggest that the parietal lobe, along with other brain areas, is important in imagining and thinking about the future. The ability to project ourselves into the future, imagining how we might act or react to a future threat or encounter, is an extremely adaptive human characteristic (Schacter et al., 2017).

The **temporal lobes**, which lie on the sides of the cortex (think "temples"), are involved in processing auditory information received from the left and right ears. As you'll see in Chapter 5, there is a close relationship between the activity of particular neurons in the temporal lobe and the perception of certain frequencies of sound. As noted earlier, one region of the temporal lobe, Wernicke's area, is involved in language comprehension (the ability to understand what someone is saying). A person with damage to Wernicke's area might be able to repeat a spoken sentence aloud with perfect diction and control yet not understand a word of it; brain-imaging studies also reveal that Wernicke's area becomes active when people are asked to perform tasks that require meaningful verbal processing; it may be the area that modulates the recognition of individual words (Ardila et al., 2016). For most people, speech is localized in the temporal lobe of the left hemisphere.

Finally, at the far back of the brain sit the **occipital lobes**, where most visual processing occurs. It is here that information received from receptor cells in the eyes is analyzed and turned into visual images. The brain paints an image of the external world through a remarkable division of labor. There appear to be processing stations in the occipital lobe designed to integrate separate signals about color, motion, and form (Sincich & Horton, 2005). Not surprisingly, damage to the occipital lobe produces highly specific visual problems—you might lose the ability to recognize an object moving in a particular direction, a color, or even a face (Gainotti & Marra, 2011). We'll consider the organization of this part of the brain in more detail in Chapter 5.

CONCEPT REVIEW 3.3
BRAIN AREAS, STRUCTURES, AND FUNCTIONS

Brain Area	General Function	Structures and Specific Function
Hindbrain	Basic life support	*Medulla* and *pons*: associated with the control of heart rate, breathing, and certain reflexes
		Reticular formation: control of general arousal, sleep, and some movement of the head
		Cerebellum: involved in preparation, selection, and coordination of complex motor movement
Midbrain	Houses neural relay stations	*Tectum* (components are superior colliculus and inferior colliculus): relay stations for visual and auditory information
		Substantia nigra: group of neurons that release the neurotransmitter dopamine
Forebrain	Higher mental functions	*Thalamus*: initial gathering point for sensory input; information combined and relayed here
		Hypothalamus: helps regulate eating, drinking, body temperature, and sexual behavior
		Hippocampus: important to the formation of memories
		Amygdala: linked to fear, aggression, and defensive behaviors
		Cerebral cortex: the seat of higher mental processes, including sense of self and the ability to reason and solve problems

PRACTICAL SOLUTIONS: MIRROR NEURONS AND SOLVING THE "OTHER MIND PROBLEM"

One of the unique characteristics of people, compared to most other animal species, is our keen ability to solve the "other mind problem." We have an unparalleled capacity to get inside the heads of others—to imagine what they're thinking, how they're feeling, and what they're likely to do next. Neuroscientists now believe that they have discovered a key element in the brain that produces this ability: *mirror neurons*. As you've learned in this chapter, neuroimaging studies have revealed that regions in the motor cortex become active when we engage in simple motor movements, such as biting into an apple or clapping our hands. However, the startling discovery is that neurons in these same regions become active when we simply *observe* someone else performing the same actions. The same systems in the brain that are activated by performing an action—waving good-bye—are activated when we watch someone else perform the same task.

Watching someone else's experiences may activate some of the same neural systems in the observer.

iStockPhoto/Jacob Ammentorp Lund

Give it a little thought, and this finding makes sense: Watch someone get stuck with a needle, and what do you do? You're likely to make a face, turn away, or even grab your arm. Watch a good movie, and what happens? You jump, cover your eyes, laugh, and even cry in response to a bunch of two-dimensional images flashing on a screen. You feel the pain, even though you're just sitting in a seat. The discovery of mirror neurons suggests that, well, you really are experiencing the events you're watching—at least in some sense. Mirror neurons help us solve the "other mind problem" and may also be the basis for empathy, our ability to identify and relate to the thoughts and feelings of others (Iacoboni, 2009).

The evidence for such claims is controversial but compelling nonetheless. Brain-imaging studies have shown that when we witness the emotions of others, some of the same emotion systems in our brain get activated. If you watch someone else experience disgust—for example, smelling a disgusting odor—your own "disgust systems" in the brain get activated as well; in fact, if you've recently been contaminated by something, watching other people wash their hands can provide a sense of relief (Jalal & Ramachandran, 2017). Several studies have found relationships (correlations) between the activation of mirror neuron systems and behavioral measures of empathy and one's level of competence in social situations (see Gallese et al., 2011; Iacoboni, 2009). Results like these suggest that mirror neurons play a fundamental role in a variety of social functions (Glenberg, 2011). Some have even suggested that damage to mirror neuron systems in the brain may be partly responsible for autism spectrum disorder, a developmental disorder marked by a reluctance or an inability to interact well with other people (Ramachandran, 2011). Again, though, the evidence is controversial, and it's not clear at this point whether activity in mirror neurons is the cause or the result of social interaction—that is, the behavior of mirror neurons may be the result of some form of social learning (see R. Cook et al., 2014).

Psychologists and neuroscientists agree: Mirror neurons exist in the human brain and may well contribute to a range of important mental and social human capabilities. It's exciting stuff, because mirror neurons sit at the juncture between psychology and neuroscience, but we are a long way from understanding the details. A tremendous amount of research effort is currently ongoing, so there are reasons to be hopeful that we'll see significant progress in the coming decades.

The Divided Brain

The division of labor in the brain is particularly striking in the study of the two separate halves, or hemispheres, of the cerebral cortex. Although the brain is designed to operate as a whole, the hemispheres are *lateralized*, which means that each side is responsible for performing unique and independent functions. This doesn't mean that people are "left-brained" or "right-brained," as some pop psychologists have argued; it simply means that certain functions are controlled primarily by either the right or the left hemisphere. For example, as you've seen, the right hemisphere of the brain controls the movements of the left side of the body; the left hemisphere governs the right side. This means that stimulating a region of the motor cortex in the left cerebral hemisphere will cause a muscle on the right side of the body to twitch. Similarly, if cells in the occipital lobe of the right cerebral hemisphere are damaged, a blind spot will develop in the left portion of the visual world. Lateralization undoubtedly serves some adaptive functions. For example, it may allow the brain to divide its labor in ways that produce more efficient processing.

Information received through the eyes travels to one side of the brain or the other (see Figure 3.13). If you're looking straight ahead, an image coming from the left side of your body (the left visual field) falls on the inside half of the left eye and the outside half of the right eye; receptor cells in these locations transmit their images to the back of the right cerebral hemisphere. Both eyes project information directly to each hemisphere, as the figure shows, but information from the left visual field goes to the right hemisphere and vice versa.

Under normal circumstances, if an object approaches you from your left side, the information eventually arrives on both sides of your brain. There are two reasons for this. First, if you turn your head or eyes to look at the object—from left to right—its image is likely to fall on both the inside and the outside halves of each eye over time. It might start off on the inside half of the left eye, but as your eyes turn, the outside half will soon receive the message. Second, as noted earlier, a major communication bridge—the corpus callosum—connects the two brain halves. Information arriving at the right hemisphere, for example, is transported to the left hemisphere via the **corpus callosum** in well under a tenth of a second. This transfer process occurs automatically and requires no head or eye turning.

Splitting the Brain

Both sides of the brain need to receive information about objects in the environment. To understand why, imagine what visual perception is like for someone without a corpus callosum—someone with a "split brain." Suppose an object suddenly appears in the person's left visual field. There's no time to move the head or eyes, only enough for a reflexive response. Our patient will be incapable of a coordinated response because the image will be registered only in the right hemisphere, which contains the machinery to control only the left side of the body. The split-brain patient will also be unable to name the menacing object because the language comprehension and production centers are located, typically, on the left side of the brain.

Patients like the one just described really do exist; there are people with split brains. Some were born without a corpus callosum; others had their communication gateway cut on purpose by surgeons seeking to reduce the spread of epileptic seizures. The two hemispheres of split-brain patients are not broken or damaged by the operation. Information simply cannot easily pass from one side of the brain to the other. In fact, the behavior of most split-brain patients is essentially

FIGURE 3.13 ■ Visual Processing in the Two Hemispheres

Images originating in the left visual field are projected to the right hemisphere, and information appearing in the right visual field is projected to the left hemisphere. Most language processing occurs in the left hemisphere, so split-brain patients can vocally report only stimuli that are shown in the right visual field. Here the subject can say only *port*, the word available for processing in the left hemisphere.

Left visual field   Right visual field

AIR PORT

Retina

Optic nerve

Corpus callosum

Optic chiasm

Visual cortex

PORT AIR

Carolina Hrejsa/Body Scientific Intl.

normal because most input from the environment still reaches both sides of their brain. These patients can turn their head and eyes freely as they interact with the environment, allowing information to fall on receptor regions that transmit to both hemispheres. The abnormal nature of their brain becomes apparent only under manufactured conditions.

In a classic study by Gazzaniga and colleagues (1965), a variety of images (pictures, words, or symbols) were presented quickly to either the left or the right visual field of split-brain patients. Just like with our hypothetical patient, when an image was shown to the right visual field, it was easily named because it could be processed by the language centers of the left hemisphere. For left visual field presentations, the patients remained perplexed and silent. It was later learned, however, that their silence did not mean that the brain failed to process the image. If the split-brain patients were asked to point to a picture of the object just shown, they could do so, but only with the left hand (Gazzaniga & LeDoux, 1978). The brain had received the input but could not respond verbally. In another case, Gazzaniga and his colleagues presented a picture to the right hemisphere that triggered a negative mood. The patient denied seeing anything, because the picture wasn't available to the language centers in the left hemisphere, but she complained of being upset—in fact, she blamed the experimenters for upsetting her (Gazzaniga, 2008)!

Hemispheric Specialization

The two hemispheres of the cerebral cortex are clearly specialized to perform certain kinds of tasks. The right hemisphere, for example, appears to play a more important role in spatial tasks, such as fitting together the pieces of a puzzle or orienting oneself spatially in an environment. Patients with damage to the right hemisphere characteristically have trouble with spatial tasks, as do split-brain patients who must assemble a puzzle with their right hand. The right hemisphere is also better at recognizing faces and may play a more important role in recognizing the intentions of other people (see Volz & Gazzaniga, 2017).

The left hemisphere—perhaps in part because of the lateralized language centers—contributes more to verbal tasks such as reading and writing. We also use the left hemisphere to solve problems and to create consistent "explanations" of the world. Gazzaniga (2008) calls the left hemisphere the "interpreter" because it smooths over inconsistencies in our actions and creates coherent stories about our behavior. Show the command "walk" to the right hemisphere of a split-brain patient, and they are likely to get up and walk. Ask them why they are walking, and they are likely to fabricate an answer—for example, "I'm thirsty, so I'm going to find a drink." The language centers don't receive the command, so the left hemisphere makes up a story to "interpret" the patient's behavior.

Still, a great deal of cooperation and collaboration goes on between the hemispheres. They interact continuously, and most mental processes, even language to a certain extent, depend on activity in both sides of the brain. In addition, a number of the phenomena observed with split-brain patients also occur in normal people under certain testing conditions (Pinto et al., 2017). You think and behave with a whole brain, not a fragmented one. If one side of the brain is damaged, regions in the other hemisphere can sometimes take over the lost functions. Specialization in the brain exists because it's sometimes adaptive for the two hemispheres to work independently—much in the same way that it's beneficial for members of a group to divide components of a difficult task rather than trying to cooperate on every small activity.

KNOWLEDGE CHECK 3.2

Now test what you've learned about research into brain structures and their functions. Fill in each blank with one of the following terms: *EEG, PET scan, hindbrain, midbrain, forebrain, cerebellum, hypothalamus, cortex, frontal lobes, limbic system, corpus callosum*. (You will find the answers in the Appendix.)

1. A primitive part of the brain that controls basic life-support functions such as heart rate and respiration: _____

2. A structure thought to be involved in a variety of motivational activities, including eating, drinking, and sexual behavior: _____

3. The portion of the cortex believed to be involved in higher-order thought processes (such as planning) as well as the initiation of voluntary motor movements: _____

4. A structure near the base of the brain involved in coordination of complex activities such as walking and playing the piano: _____

5. A device used to monitor the gross electrical activity of the brain: _____

REGULATING GROWTH AND INTERNAL FUNCTIONS: EXTENDED COMMUNICATION

The human body has two communication systems. The first, the nervous system, starts and controls most behaviors—thoughts, voluntary movements, and perceptions of the external world. But the body also has long-term communication needs. The body must initiate and control growth and provide long-term regulation of numerous internal biological systems. Consequently, a second communication system has developed: a network of glands called the **endocrine system**, which uses the bloodstream, rather than neurons, as its main information courier. Chemicals called **hormones** are released into the blood by the various endocrine glands and control a variety of internal functions.

The word *hormone* comes from the Greek *hormon*, which means "to set into motion." Hormones play a role in many basic, life-sustaining activities in the body. Hunger, thirst, sexual behavior, and the fight-or-flight response are all regulated in part by an interplay between the nervous system and hormones released by the endocrine glands. The fact that the body has two communication systems rather than one makes sense from an adaptive standpoint. One system, communication among neurons, governs transmissions that are quick and detailed; the other, the endocrine system, initiates the slower but more widespread and longer-lasting effects. In the following section, we'll consider the endocrine system in more detail and then consider how hormones influence some fundamental differences between men and women.

The Endocrine System

The chemical communication system of the endocrine glands differs in some important ways from the rapid-fire electrochemical activities of the nervous system. Communication in the nervous system tends to be localized, which means that a given neurotransmitter usually affects only cells in a small area. Hormones have widespread effects. Because hormones are carried by the blood, they travel throughout the body and interact with numerous target sites. In contrast to neurotransmitters, hormones also have long-lasting effects. Whereas neural communication operates in the blink of an eye, the endocrine system can produce effects lasting minutes, hours, or even days. In some animals, for example, it is circulating hormones that prepare them for seasonal migration or hibernation. This means that the endocrine system provides the body with a mechanism for both widespread and long-term communication that cannot be produced by interactions among neurons.

Although the endocrine and nervous systems communicate in different ways, their activities are closely coordinated. Structures in the brain (especially the hypothalamus) stimulate or inhibit the release of hormones by the glands; once released, these chemicals then feed back and affect the firing rates of neural impulses. The feedback loop balances and controls the regulatory activities of the body. The hypothalamus is of importance because it controls the pituitary gland. The **pituitary gland**, a kind of master gland, controls the secretion of hormones in response to signals from the hypothalamus; these hormones, in turn, regulate the activity of many of the other vital glands in the endocrine system. It is the pituitary gland, for example, that signals the testes in males to produce *testosterone* and the ovaries in females to produce *estrogen*—both of critical importance in sexual behavior and reproduction.

The endocrine system also helps us react to stressful situations. Suppose you're walking home alone, and two shadowy figures suddenly emerge from an alleyway and move in your direction. You draw in your breath, your stomach tightens, and your rapidly beating heart seems ready to explode from your chest. These whole-body reactions, critical in preparing you to fight or flee, are created by signals from the brain that lead to increased activity of the endocrine glands. The hypothalamus signals the *adrenal glands* (located above the kidneys) to begin secreting such hormones as *norepinephrine* and *epinephrine* into the blood. These hormones, in turn, produce energizing effects on the body, increasing heart rate and directing blood and oxygen flow to energy-demanding cells throughout the body. The body is now prepared for action, enhancing the likelihood of survival (see Figure 3.14).

FIGURE 3.14 ■ The Fight-or-Flight Response

In potentially dangerous situations, the endocrine system releases hormones that produce energizing effects in the body, increasing our chances of survival through fighting back or running away.

Hypothalamus

Stimulates adrenal glands.

Adrenal glands

Secrete norepinephrine and epinephrine into bloodstream.

Norepinephrine and Epinephrine

Cause energy surge and heart rate increase; blood is shunted away from the stomach and intestines to areas that require it; glucose is made available to the muscles.

Carolina Hrejsa/Body Scientific Intl.

Do Men and Woman Have Different Brains?

Prior to birth, hormones released by the pituitary gland determine whether a child ends up with male or female sex organs. At puberty, an increase in sex hormones (testosterone and estrogen) leads males to develop facial hair and deep speaking voices, and females to develop breasts and begin menstruation. It is now suspected that hormones released during development affect the basic wiring patterns of men's and women's brains as well. Evidence suggests that men and women may think differently as the result of sex-specific activities of the endocrine system.

The ability of women and men to perform certain tasks changes as the levels of sex hormones increase or decrease in the body. Women traditionally perform better than men on some tests of verbal ability, and their performance can improve with high levels of estrogen in their body. Similarly, men show slightly better performance on some spatial tasks (such as imagining that three-dimensional objects are rotating), and their performance seems to be related to their testosterone levels. There is even evidence that females who developed in the womb with a male co-twin perform better on spatial memory tasks than females who developed with a female co-twin, presumably because of prenatal exposure to testosterone (D. I. Miller & Halpern, 2014). The evidence is correlational, which means we can't be sure it's the hormones that are causing the performance changes, but the data suggest there may be sex-based differences in some types of mental processing. It is important to understand, though, that these are average group differences and don't apply to all individuals.

It's also the case that girls who have been exposed to an excess of androgens (a group of hormones that include testosterone) during the initial stages of prenatal development, either because of a genetic disorder or from chemicals ingested by the mother during pregnancy, tend to engage in play activities that are more traditionally associated with boys (e.g., Hines et al., 2016). In one study reported by Kimura (1992), researchers at UCLA compared the choice of toys by girls who either had or had not been exposed to excess androgens during early development. The girls who had been exposed tended to prefer the typical masculine activities—smashing trucks and cars together, for example—more than the control girls did.

Male and female brains also show anatomical differences, although such differences have often been exaggerated historically (Shields, 1975). Animal studies have confirmed that male and female rat brains are different; moreover, the differences are attributable, in part, to the early influence of hormones (Zilkha et al., 2017). For humans, imaging studies have revealed sex-based differences in the thickness of cortical tissue, at least at certain points of development, and cortical thickness may be related to the performance of certain cognitive tasks, at least for women (Kurth et al., 2018). Other structural differences exist as well—for example, the amygdala is larger in men—and these differences cannot be accounted for by overall differences in brain volume (Ritchie et al., 2018). Interesting differences have also been found in response to brain damage. For example, damage can sometimes lead to specific deficits in knowledge categories, such as loss in knowledge about plants; women rarely, if ever, show selective deficits in plant knowledge, which may stem from how evolution has selectively shaped the development of male and female brains (Laiacona et al., 2006).

The evidence supporting sex-based differences in brain anatomy and mental functioning is provocative and needs to be investigated further. Hormones released by the endocrine system are known to produce permanent changes early in human development, and it's certainly possible that actions later in life are influenced by these changes. But no direct causal link has yet been established between anatomical differences and the variations in intellectual functioning that are sometimes found between men and women. In fact, some researchers have argued that sex-based differences in brain organization may cause men and women to act more similarly than they would otherwise (De Vries & Boyle, 1998).

The presence of male or female sex organs at birth doesn't necessarily determine one's gender identity.

EZEQUIEL BECERRA/AFP via Getty Images

In addition, the performance differences between women and men on certain laboratory tasks aren't very large and don't reflect general ability. Sex-based differences are extremely small and can, in some instances, be accounted for by experience (see Hyde, 2016). For example, boys tend to get more experience on spatial tasks than girls, due to sports and video games, which might help explain male spatial advantages. There are also significant cultural differences in cognitive abilities—for example, sex differences in math and science are absent in some cultures—which further supports sex-based similarities in cognitive ability (Hyde, 2014). To repeat a theme discussed in Chapter 1, it is difficult to separate the effects of biology (nature) from the ongoing influences of the environment (nurture). Men and women are faced with different environmental demands and cultural expectations during their lifetimes. Without question, those demands help determine the actions they take, and produce many of the behavioral differences that we see between the sexes.

Finally, it's worth emphasizing that the presence of male or female sex organs at birth doesn't necessarily define one's gender identity—that is, people's psychological sense of their gender. Transgender and gender-nonconforming (TGNC) people are those who have a gender identity that does not correspond to their sex assigned at birth. Some studies have suggested that sex hormones during prenatal development play a role in the development of transgender identity, along with some genetic predisposition, but, as we'll discuss elsewhere in the text, gender identity is a complex phenomenon, likely reflecting an interplay of biological, environmental, and cultural factors (see S. M. Rosenthal, 2016).

Now test your knowledge about the differences between the endocrine system and the nervous system. For each statement, decide whether the endocrine system or the nervous system is the most appropriate to apply. (You will find the answers in the Appendix.)

1. Communication effects tend to be localized, affecting only a small area: _____

2. Responsible for whole-body reactions, such as the fight-or-flight response: _____

3. The major determinant of sexual, but not necessarily gender, identity: _____

4. Communicates through the release of epinephrine and norepinephrine: _____

5. Operates quickly, with time scales bordering on the blink of an eye: _____

ADAPTING AND TRANSMITTING THE GENETIC CODE

Brains tend to act in regular and predictable ways. When you read a book, a neuroimaging scan is certain to reveal activity in the occipital lobe of your cortex. If a stroke occurs in the left cerebral hemisphere, there's a good chance you'll find paralysis occurring on the right side of the body. But behavior, the main interest of psychology, remains remarkably difficult to predict. People react differently to the same event—even if they're siblings raised in the same household. How do we explain this remarkable diversity of behavior, given that everyone carries around a similar 3- to 4-pound mass of brain tissue?

One answer is that no two brains are exactly alike. The patterns of neural activity that determine how we think and act are uniquely determined by our individual experiences and by the genetic material we've inherited from our parents. Most of us have no trouble accepting that experience is important, but genetic influences are a little tougher to accept. Sure, hair color, eye color, and blood type may be expressions of fixed genetic influences, but how can genetics govern intelligence, personality, or emotionality?

Recognizing that heredity has a role is a given to the psychologist. You'll find references to genetic influences throughout this book—on a whole host of topics. But it's also important to remember that the genetic code serves two adaptive functions. First, genes provide us with a flexible plan, a recipe of sorts, for our physical and psychological development. Second, genes provide a means through which we're able to pass on physical and psychological characteristics to our offspring, thereby helping to maintain qualities that have adaptive significance.

Natural Selection and Adaptations

Let's return briefly to the topic of natural selection, first addressed in Chapter 1. Charles Darwin proposed the mechanism of natural selection to explain how species change, or evolve, over time. He recognized that certain traits, physical or psychological, can help an organism's reproductive "fitness" and that these features, in turn, are likely to be passed forward from one generation to the next. If a bird is born with a special capacity to store, remember, and relocate seeds, then its chances of living long enough to mate and produce offspring increase. If the bird's offspring share the same capacity for obtaining food, then over many generations the seed-storing trait is likely to become a stable characteristic of the species. It becomes an **adaptation**, or a feature selected for by nature because it increases the chances of the organism to survive and multiply.

Virtually all scientists accept that natural selection is the main mechanism for producing lasting change within and across species. However, not all features of the body and mind are necessarily adaptations. Consider your ability to read and write. These are highly adaptive psychological abilities, yet neither could have evolved through natural selection. Both developed relatively recently in human history—too short a time period for evolutionary change—and emerged long after the human brain had achieved its current size and form (S. J. Gould, 2000). On the other hand, the human eye and the psychological experience of perception are almost certainly specific adaptations molded through generations of evolutionary change (D. D. Hoffman, 2016).

How do we identify which features of our body and mind are adaptations? This is a tough one, particularly with respect to mental processes. As noted in Chapter 1, evolutionary psychologists are convinced that we're born with a number of psychological adaptations (see D. M. Buss, 2019); others believe that our thought processes are shaped largely by the environment—that is, by how we're taught and by the cultural messages we receive (Rose & Rose, 2000). To qualify as an adaptation, one must satisfy several criteria. First, it is necessary to show that the psychological trait can be inherited or passed along across generations through reproduction. Second, at some point in the past, the trait must have been present in some members of the species and not others. Finally, the trait must have been "selected" by nature because it was adaptive—it helped the individual survive or reproduce. Getting this kind of evidence is difficult, if not impossible, for most of the psychological adaptations of interest to evolutionary psychologists (Richardson, 2007). However, the situation is not hopeless. Evolutionary psychologists are constantly gathering evidence that seems to support the existence of psychological adaptations.

For natural selection to produce an adaptation, there needs to be a mechanism for ensuring that variations, or differences, are present within a species. If all the members of a species are the same, then there are no special features for nature to select. There also needs to be some way to guarantee that an adaptive feature can pass from one generation to the next. During Darwin's time, the mechanism for ensuring variability and inheritance was unknown; Darwin made his case by documenting the abundance of variability and inherited characteristics that exist in nature. It was later learned that the mechanism that enables natural selection is the genetic code.

Genetic Principles

Let's briefly review some of the basic principles of genetics. How is the genetic code stored, and what are the factors that produce genetic variability? The genetic message resides within *chromosomes*, which are thin, threadlike strips of DNA. Human cells, except for sperm cells and the unfertilized egg cell, contain a total of 46 chromosomes, arranged in 23 pairs. Half of each chromosome pair is contributed originally by the mother through the egg, and the other half arrives in the father's sperm. **Genes** are segments of a chromosome that contain instructions for influencing and creating hereditary characteristics. For example, each person has a gene that helps determine height or hair color and another that may determine susceptibility to disorders such as muscular dystrophy or even Alzheimer's disease.

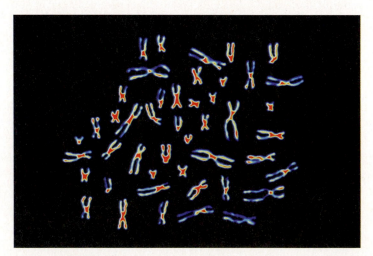

The genetic record we inherit from our parents shapes our physical and psychological characteristics.

Scott Camazine / Science Source

Because humans have *23 pairs* of chromosomes, they have two genes for most developmental characteristics, or traits. People have two genes, for example, for hair color, blood type, and the possible development of facial dimples. If both genes are designed to produce the same trait (such as nearsightedness), the characteristic will likely develop (you'll need glasses). But if the two genes differ—for example, the father passes along the gene for nearsightedness, but the mother's gene is for normal distance vision—the trait is determined by the *dominant gene*; in the case of vision, the "normal" gene will dominate the *recessive gene* for nearsightedness.

The fact that a dominant gene will mask the effects of a recessive gene means that everybody has genetic material that's not expressed in physical or psychological characteristics. A person may see perfectly but still carry around the recessive gene for faulty distance vision. This is the reason parents with normal vision can produce a nearsighted child, or why two brown-haired parents can produce a child with blond hair—it is the combination of genes that determines the inherited characteristics.

Another important distinction is between the **genotype**, which is the actual genetic message, and the **phenotype**, which is the trait's observable characteristics. The phenotype, such as good vision or brown hair, is controlled mainly by the genotype, but it can be strongly influenced by the environment. A person's height and weight are shaped largely by the genotype, but environmental factors such as diet and physical health contribute significantly to the final phenotype. This is an important point to remember: Genes provide the materials from which characteristics develop, but the environment shapes the final product. As stressed in Chapter 1, it's nature via nurture. The environment provides the means through which nature can express itself (Ridley, 2003). There is also a growing research field, called *epigenetics*, that is investigating how the environment leads to modifications in gene expression that, in turn, can affect the extent to which heredity plays a role in physical and behavior traits. Again, these are not modifications in the underlying DNA sequence but changes in gene expression.

Across individuals, variations in the genetic message itself arise because there are trillions of different ways that the genetic information from each parent can be combined at fertilization. Each egg or sperm cell contains a random half of each parent's 23 chromosome pairs. According to the laws of probability, this means that some 8 million (2^{23}) different combinations can reside in either an egg cell or a sperm cell. The meeting of egg and sperm is also a matter of chance, which means that the genetic material from both parents can be combined in some 64 trillion ways—and this is from a single set of parents!

Clearly, there are many ways by which a trait, or combination of traits, can emerge and produce a survival "advantage" for one person over another. But variation in the genetic code can also occur by chance in the form of a **mutation**. A mutation is a spontaneous change in the genetic material that occurs during the gene replication process. Most genetic mutations are harmful to the organism, but occasionally they lead to traits that confer a survival advantage to the organism. Mutations, along with the variations produced by unique combinations of genetic material, are key ingredients for natural selection—together, they introduce novelty, or new traits, into nature.

Genes and Behavior

Now let's return to the link between genetics and psychology—what is the connection between genotypes, phenotypes, and behavior? In some sense, all behavior is influenced by genetic factors because genes help determine the structure and function of the brain. At the same time, no physical or mental trait will ever be determined entirely by genetic factors—the environment always plays some role. But can we predict the psychological traits of an individual by knowing something about the individual's genetic record? Susceptibility to the psychological disorder schizophrenia is a case in point. Natural children of parents with schizophrenia (where either one has the disorder or both do) have a greater chance of developing the disorder themselves, when compared to the children of normal parents. This is the case even if the children are adopted at birth and never raised in an abnormal environment. So, genes probably influence the chances that these children will develop the disorder.

The genetic recipe helps explain physical and sometimes behavioral similarities among family members.

iStockPhoto/monkeybusinessimages

One way to study the link between genes and behavior is to investigate family histories in detail. In **family studies**, researchers look for similarities and differences among biological (blood) relatives to determine the influence of heredity. As you've just seen, the chances of developing schizophrenia increase with a family history. There are many other traits that seem to run in families as well (e.g., intelligence and personality). The trouble with family studies, however, is that members of a family share more than just common genes. They are also exposed to similar environmental experiences, so it's difficult to separate the relative roles of nature and nurture in behavior. Family studies can be useful sources of information—it helps to know that someone is at a greater than average risk of developing schizophrenia—but they can't be used to establish true links between genes and behavior.

In **twin studies**, researchers compare traits between *identical* twins, who share essentially the same genetic material, and *fraternal* twins, who were born at the same time but whose genetic overlap is only roughly 50% (fraternal twins can even be of different sexes). In studies of intelligence, identical twins tend to have much more similar intelligence scores than fraternal twins, even when environmental factors are considered (Bouchard, 1997). Identical twins make ideal research subjects because researchers can control for genetic factors. Because these twins have virtually the same genetic makeup, emerging from a single fertilized egg, any physical or psychological differences that arise during development are likely due to environmental factors. Similarly, if identical twins are raised in different environments but still show similar traits, it's a strong indication that genetic factors are involved in expression of the trait. Neither of these assumptions is foolproof—it's quite possible that identical twins, even if raised in different households, still experience more similar environments than fraternal twins. People who look alike are often treated by the world in similar ways, even if they don't know each other. But twin studies have been a valuable source of information in psychological science, as you'll see in subsequent chapters.

Quantitative Techniques

New techniques may help solve some of the problems just discussed. One new quantitative technique, called *genome-wide complex trait analysis* (GCTA), uses the genetic similarities between unrelated individuals to estimate similarities in psychological traits, such as intelligence or personality (see Plomin & Deary, 2015). No need for twins, or even related individuals; instead, this technique is using recent advances in our understanding of the human genome to explore whether people with similar patterns in their DNA tend to have similar psychological traits. One obvious advantage of this technique is that genetic influences can be calculated from the DNA of thousands or even potentially millions of individuals.

You've been given only a brief introduction to "behavioral genetics" in this section, and we'll be returning to the connection between heredity and environment throughout the book. For now, recognize that how you think and act is indeed influenced by the code stored in your body's chromosomes. Through the random processes that occur at fertilization, nature guarantees diversity within the species. Everyone receives a unique genetic message that, in combination with environmental factors, helps determine brain structure as well as human psychology. From an evolutionary standpoint, diversity is of great importance because it increases the chances that at least some members of a species will have the necessary tools to deal successfully with the problems of survival and reproduction.

KNOWLEDGE CHECK 3.4

To check on your understanding of genetics, choose whether each of the following statements is true or false. (You will find the answers in the Appendix.)

1. Reading and writing are examples of adaptations and therefore result from the mechanism of natural selection. *True or False?*

2. The actual genetic information inherited from one's parents is known as one's genotype. *True or False?*

3. If the two inherited genes for a specific trait differ, the recessive gene plays a stronger role. *True or False?*

4. Psychologists can study genetic effects on a variety of characteristics, such as intelligence or susceptibility to schizophrenia, by studying identical twins raised in different environments. *True or False?*

THE PROBLEMS SOLVED: WHAT BIOLOGICAL SYSTEMS ARE FOR

The human brain, along with the rest of the nervous system, is a biological solution to problems produced by constantly changing environments. Fortunately, out of these biological solutions arise those features that make up the human mind, including intellect, emotion, and artistic creativity. In this chapter, we've considered four central problems of adaptation.

Communicating Internally: Connecting World and Brain

Networks of individual cells, called neurons, establish a marketplace of information called the nervous system. To communicate internally, the nervous system uses an electrochemical language. Messages travel electrically within a neuron, usually from dendrite to soma to axon to terminal button, and then chemically from one neuron to the next. Combining electrical and chemical components creates a quick, efficient, and extremely versatile communication system. Neurotransmitters regulate the rate at which neurons fire by producing excitatory or inhibitory messages, and the resulting patterns of activation shape how we think and act.

Initiating Behavior: A Division of Labor

To accomplish the remarkable variety of functions it controls, the nervous system divides its labor. Using sophisticated techniques, including brain-imaging devices, researchers have begun to map out the regions of the brain that support particular psychological and life-sustaining functions. At the base of the brain, in the hindbrain region, structures control such basic processes as respiration, heart rate, and the coordination of muscle movements. Higher up are regions that control motivational processes such as eating, drinking, and sexual behavior. Finally, in the cerebral cortex, more complex mental processes—such as thought, sensations, and language—are represented. Some functions in the brain appear to be lateralized, which means that they're controlled primarily by one cerebral hemisphere or the other. Through the development of specialized regions of cells, the human brain has become capable of extremely adaptive reactions to its changing environment.

Regulating Growth and Internal Functions: Extended Communication

To solve its widespread and long-term communication needs, the body uses the endocrine system to release chemicals called hormones into the bloodstream. These chemical messengers serve a variety of regulatory functions, influencing growth and development, hunger, thirst, and sexual behavior, in addition to helping the body prepare for action. Hormones released early in development and into adulthood may partly explain some of the behavioral differences between men and women.

Adapting and Transmitting the Genetic Code

Adaptations are traits that arise through the mechanism of natural selection. Although it's difficult to establish which psychological traits are truly adaptations, psychologists acknowledge that our thoughts and behaviors are influenced by genetic factors. The combination of genes inherited from our parents, along with influences from the environment, determines our individual characteristics. Psychologists often try to disentangle the relative contributions of genes and the environment by conducting twin studies, comparing the behaviors and abilities of identical and fraternal twins raised in similar or dissimilar environments. When identical twins show similar characteristics, even though they have been raised in quite different settings, psychologists assume that the underlying genetic code is playing an influential role.

THINKING ABOUT RESEARCH

A summary of a research study in psychology is given in this section. As you read the summary, think about the following questions:

1. Which of the techniques used to study brain function are involved in this study?
2. Besides these two techniques, how might other investigative tools be used to address the question of interest, using the same experimental procedures?
3. Do you think the brain needs different structures to control learning and remembering? How does learning differ from remembering?
4. Can you think of problems researchers might have interpreting results that arise when healthy and amnesic patients are compared in a study?

Article Reference: Palombo, D. J., Hayes, S. M., Reid, A. G., & Verfaellie, M. (2019). Hippocampal contributions to value-based learning: Converging evidence from fMRI and amnesia. *Cognitive, Affective, & Behavioral Neuroscience, 19,* 523–536.

Purpose of the Study: This study investigated whether the hippocampus, which is known to be involved in remembering, also plays a role in value-based learning. Research participants were asked to learn about the value of stimuli, in this case whether people were likely to win money or not. This study is important because it uses two of the techniques discussed in this chapter to investigate brain function—brain imaging and brain damage. The authors proposed that if the hippocampus is involved in learning about value, then (a) it will become activated during a value-learning task (as measured by brain imaging) and (b) people with selective damage to the hippocampus will have difficulty learning the same task.

Method of the Study: Two experiments were conducted. In the first, 30 healthy people were "scanned" (using functional MRI technology) while trying to learn whether particular people had a history of winning money in a game. On each trial, a schematic image of a person was shown, identified by a colored jumpsuit, and the participant was asked, "Does this person win money?" The participant was required to respond "Yes" or "No," and then feedback was given (e.g., "The man wins $1!"). Each of the images was shown repeatedly over trials, with a certain probability of winning money, so the participant gradually learned which of the images corresponded to a "winner" or a "loser." Control participants were shown the same images but were not required to learn anything. In the second experiment, the same task was used, but the investigators tested participants who suffered from severe memory impairments caused by damage to hippocampal regions of the brain.

Results of the Study: In Experiment 1, the imaging data revealed that the hippocampus was indeed activated during the value-learning game, more so for the participants who were required to learn and remember the winners and losers. In Experiment 2, supporting the conclusions of Experiment 1, the amnesic patients had great difficulty with the task, even though they had no trouble performing a perceptual discrimination task involving the same stimuli (a task that does not depend on hippocampal activation).

Conclusions of the Study: The present study confirmed that the hippocampus plays a role in value-based learning. By showing the same effects with two different investigative techniques, using the same experimental task, the investigators were able to provide strong and converging evidence about involvement of a particular brain structure in a learning task.

KNOWLEDGE CHECK: CHAPTER SUMMARY

(You'll find the answers in the Appendix.)

COMMUNICATING INTERNALLY: CONNECTING WORLD AND BRAIN

- The field of (1) ____ studies the connection between the brain and behavior.

- Neurons receive (2) ____ and transmit information (3) ____.

- A neuron consists of (4) ____, a soma, (5) an ____, and terminal buttons. Sensory neurons carry information through the spinal cord to the brain. (6) ____ convey information between internal processing sites. (7) ___ neurons carry messages from the central nervous system to the muscles and glands that produce a (8) ___ response.

- Within a neuron, messages travel electrically from one point to another. From one neuron to another, messages travel (9) ___, through neurotransmitters.

- Groups of neurons operating simultaneously create an (10) ___ pattern that underlies both conscious experiences and complex behaviors.

INITIATING BEHAVIOR: A DIVISION OF LABOR

- We think, feel, and function physically because of a biological division of labor.

- The central nervous system consists of the brain and (11) ___, which communicate to the rest of the body through bundles of (12) ___, or nerves. The peripheral nervous system, which includes the (13) ___ and (14) ___ systems, sends sensory information to the brain, moves muscles, and regulates (15) ___ function.

- Studying brain damage and (16) ___ can reveal brain function. Chemical injection and (17) ___ let scientists stimulate the brain. They can also observe the brain through noninvasive techniques, including monitoring electrical brain activity using an (18) ___ and using X-rays (CT scanning) and neuroimaging devices such as (19) ___ and magnetic resonance imaging (MRI) ___ to create three-dimensional pictures or live snapshots of the brain.

- The (20) ___ provides basic life support, through the medulla, (21) ___, reticular formation, and cerebellum. The (22) ___ relays sensory messages. Higher mental functioning takes place in the (23) ___ using the cerebral cortex, thalamus, hypothalamus, and (24) ___ system.

- The two hemispheres (halves) ___ of the cerebral cortex are (25) ___; that is, each side is responsible for somewhat different functions.

REGULATING GROWTH AND INTERNAL FUNCTIONS: EXTENDED COMMUNICATION

- Endocrine glands release (26) ___ into the blood that interact with the nervous system to regulate such basic activities as the fight-or-flight response.

- The (27) ___ gland releases hormones that determine sexual identity before birth and direct sexual maturity at puberty. Activities in the (28) ___ system may account for basic differences in the ways females and males think and behave.

ADAPTING AND TRANSMITTING THE GENETIC CODE

- Gene-based physical and psychological traits that increase the chances for (29) ___, or of finding a mate, can be selected for by nature and become adaptations. (30) ___, especially psychological ones, can be difficult to identify.

- Inside the cell are 23 pairs of (31) ___, threadlike strips of DNA. (32) ___ are segments of chromosomes that contain instructions for creating or influencing a particular hereditary characteristic. Genes can be dominant or (33) ___.

- (34) ___ studies identify similarities and differences that may reveal the influence of heredity. In (35) ___ studies, researchers compare the behavioral traits of identical twins, who have the same genetic material, and (36) ___ twins, who have only about half their genes in common. Traits that aren't accounted for by genetics are attributed to (37) ___ influences.

CRITICAL THINKING QUESTIONS

1. Do you think it's possible that personality is completely localized in one portion of the brain? If so, then how can you explain the fact that someone's personality can seem to change depending on the situation?

2. Other than as a treatment for epilepsy, can you think of any situations in which having a split brain might be more beneficial than a unified brain?

3. Initiation of the fight-or-flight response clearly has adaptive value. Can you think of any circumstances in which this response might lower the chances of an adaptive response?

4. Do you think a trait can be universal, economical, and adaptive but still be a result primarily of the environment? How can we ever be certain that a trait is an adaptation?

KEY TERMS

acetylcholine (p. 70)

action potential (p. 68)

adaptation (p. 91)

autonomic system (p. 74)

axon (p. 67)

central nervous system (p. 74)

cerebellum (p. 80)

cerebral cortex (p. 81)

computerized tomography scan (CT scan) (p. 77)

corpus callosum (p. 86)

dendrites (p. 67)

dopamine (p. 70)

electroencephalograph (EEG) (p. 77)

endocrine system (p. 88)

endorphins (p. 72)

family studies (p. 94)

forebrain (p. 81)

frontal lobe (p. 83)

gamma-aminobutyric acid (GABA) (p. 71)

genes (p. 92)

genotype (p. 93)

glial cells (p. 66)

glutamate (p. 70)

hindbrain (p. 79)

hormones (p. 88)

hypothalamus (p. 81)

interneurons (p. 65)

limbic system (p. 81)

magnetic resonance imaging (MRI) (p. 78)

midbrain (p. 80)

motor neurons (p. 66)

mutation (p. 93)

myelin sheath (p. 66)

nerves (p. 74)

neurons (p. 65)

neuroscience (p. 64)

neurotransmitters (p. 69)

occipital lobe (p. 84)

optogenetics (p. 77)

parietal lobe (p. 83)

peripheral nervous system (p. 74)

phenotype (p. 93)

pituitary gland (p. 88)

positron emission tomography (PET) (p. 78)

reflexes (p. 66)

refractory period (p. 73)

resting potential (p. 68)

sensory neurons (p. 65)

serotonin (p. 71)

soma (p. 67)

somatic system (p. 74)

synapse (p. 67)

temporal lobe (p. 84)

terminal buttons (p. 67)

thalamus (p. 81)

transcranial magnetic stimulation (TMS) (p. 77)

twin studies (p. 94)

HUMAN DEVELOPMENT

LEARNING OBJECTIVES

4.1   Track the physical changes that occur throughout the life span.

4.2   Identify the cognitive skills that develop in childhood and adolescence and the methods researchers use to study these skills.

4.3   Explain how attachment and identity development influence personality and social connections, and describe the psychological issues associated with death and dying.

4.4   For each of the major sections of the chapter, summarize how developmental processes help children navigate and interact with their world.

CHAPTER OUTLINE

Developing Physically

Developing Intellectually

Developing Socially and Personally

   Practical Solutions: Choosing a Day Care Center

The Problems Solved: Why Do We Develop the Way We Do?

Psychologists study lots of fascinating things, none more so than the mind of a child. Thrust into the world, a bundle of reflexes, within days a baby can recognize familiar faces, voices, and smells. Strikingly social, babies persuasively entice us with their coos, gurgles, and waving fists. Within about a year, they have begun to solve the "other mind problem." They look where we point, understanding our intentions, and point to where they want us to look. By 2 years of age, they feel our pain, showing distress when we're upset, but still reach for the cookie when they know it's forbidden. Despite these adultlike qualities, neither babies nor children are merely tiny adults. Astonishing changes occur throughout the human life span, as you'll soon see.

   The topic of this chapter is human **development**, the age-related physical, intellectual, and social changes that occur throughout life. Why do humans develop? There's one very straightforward reason: Extending the process of development over time allows us to fine-tune our physical, intellectual, and social abilities to better meet the needs of new and changing environments.

THE PROBLEMS TO BE SOLVED: WHY DO WE DEVELOP THE WAY WE DO?

Psychologists who study development are interested in the age-related physical, intellectual, and social changes that occur throughout life. Nature has built a considerable amount of flexibility, or plasticity, into the developmental process. This gives us an exceptional ability to adapt to environmental influences. As you'll soon see, the environment can change the course of development in profound ways. Keep the adaptive significance of development in mind as you consider how we effectively solve the problems associated with developing physically, intellectually, and socially.

Developing Physically

The environment helps shape the physical process of growth and can determine its ultimate outcome, but most physical changes are surprisingly consistent and predictable. We lift our heads before we crawl; we crawl before we walk. In general, the timing of development is a product of evolutionary history and partly reflects the survival problems that our species has been required to solve.

Developing Intellectually

The developmental changes that occur in how people think—what is called cognitive development—are of major importance to psychologists. Intellectually, the newborn is hardly an "adultlet" (or miniature adult). You'll discover there are good reasons to believe that infants see and think about the world somewhat differently than adults. Infants are faced with infant problems, and these problems don't always overlap with those faced by adults.

Developing Socially and Personally

Humans are social animals. We're continually interacting with each other, and these relationships help us adapt successfully to our environment. In this section, we'll consider the milestones of social development, beginning with the formation of attachments to parents and caregivers and ending with a discussion of how relationships change in middle and late adulthood.

DEVELOPING PHYSICALLY

To a child, it seems to take forever to grow up. In fact, we do take a relatively long time to reach full physical maturity compared to other species. At birth, a human newborn's brain has about 25% of its ultimate weight; a chimpanzee newborn's brain has about 60% (Corballis, 1991; Lenneberg, 1967). We do a lot of developing outside of the womb. Still, the main components of the body—the nervous system, the networks of glands, and so on—develop at an astonishingly rapid rate from the point of conception.

Guided by the genetic code and influenced by hormones released by the endocrine system, in the early years we change physically at rates that will never again be matched in our lifetimes. To place the growth rate in some perspective, if we continued to develop at the rate we show in the first 2 years of life, we'd end up over 12 feet tall and weighing several tons! Fortunately, things slow down considerably after the first few years of life; but they never completely stop—we continue to change both physically and mentally until the very moment of death.

The Stages of Prenatal Development

Let's start at the beginning. The human developmental process begins with the union of egg and sperm at conception. Within the fertilized egg, or **zygote**, the 23 chromosomes from the father and the 23 chromosomes from the mother pair up to form the genetic recipe. Over the next 266 days or so (approximately 9 months), the newly formed person undergoes a steady and quite remarkable transformation. We begin as a single cell and end as an approximately 7-pound newborn composed of literally billions of cells. The period of development that occurs before birth is called *prenatal development*, and it's divided into three stages: *germinal, embryonic,* and *fetal*. See Table 4.1 for an overview of these stages.

It takes about two weeks after conception for the zygote to migrate down from the mother's fallopian tubes (where the sperm and egg meet) and implant itself in the wall of the uterus (often called the womb). The period from conception to implantation is called the **germinal period**. It's a make-or-break time for the fertilized egg. Most fertilized eggs do not complete the process; well over half fail to achieve successful implantation, either because of abnormalities or because the implantation site is nutritionally inadequate for proper growth.

Once successful implantation occurs, the **embryonic period** begins. During the next 6 weeks, we develop from an unrecognizable mass of cells to a somewhat familiar creature with arms, legs, fingers, toes, and a distinctly beating heart. In the 7th and 8th weeks after fertilization, sexual differentiation begins. Depending on whether the father has contributed an X or a Y chromosome (the mother always contributes an X), the embryo starts to develop either male or female sexual characteristics (see Figure 4.1). If the developing embryo has inherited a Y chromosome, it begins to secrete the sex hormone *testosterone*, which leads to the establishment of a male sexual reproductive system. In the absence of testosterone, the natural course of development in humans is to become female. At the 9th week of

TABLE 4.1 ■ Prenatal Stages of Development		
Germinal Period	Conception to implantation	Fewer than half of fertilized eggs survive this stage
Embryonic Period	Implantation to 9 weeks postconception	Body shape develops, and sexual differentiation begins – stage of greatest risk of harm from the environment
Fetal Period	9 weeks postconception to birth	Final development of organs and muscular-skeletal structure in preparation for birth

FIGURE 4.1 ■ Prenatal Human Development

5–6 weeks postconception   4 months   6 months   8 months

Science Source; Nestle / Petit Format / Science Source; James Stevenson / Science Source; Bernard Benoit/GE

prenatal development, the **fetal period** begins and continues until birth. Early in this period, the bones and muscles of what is now called the fetus start to develop. By the end of the 3rd month, the skeletal and muscular systems allow for extensive movement—even somersaults—although the fetus at this point is still only about 3 inches long (Apgar & Beck, 1974). By the end of the 6th month, the fetus has grown to over a foot long, weighs in at about 2 pounds, and may be capable of survival if delivered prematurely. The last 3 months of prenatal development are marked by extremely rapid growth, both in body size and in the size and complexity of brain tissue. The fetus also develops a layer of fat under the skin during this period, which acts as protective insulation, and the lungs mature in preparation for the baby's first gasping breath of air.

Environmental Hazards

The internal conditions of the mother's uterus are perfectly "tuned" for physical development. The temperature is right, the fetus floats cushioned in a protective fluid, and regular nourishment is provided through the umbilical cord and placenta. Often, the result is a healthy baby who is ready to take on the world. However, even though the developing child is snugly tucked away within the confines of their mother's womb, it is by no means completely isolated from the effects of the environment. The mother's physical health and diet, as well as exposure to toxins in the environment, can seriously affect the developing child. Mother and child are linked physically, so if the mother smokes, drinks, uses drugs, or gets sick, the effects can transfer to the fetus or embryo. Some psychologists even believe that the mother's psychological state, such as their level of anxiety or stress during pregnancy, can have an important influence on the psychological health of the child (Charil et al., 2010). For example, studies have found that anxiety in mothers can affect brain development before birth (Qiu et al., 2013).

Environmental agents that potentially damage the developing child are called **teratogens**. As a rule, internal structures are most susceptible to teratogens during their formation. For example, if the mother contracts German measles (rubella) during the first 6 weeks of pregnancy, the child is at risk for heart defects because it's during this period that the structures of the heart are formed. In general, the embryonic period is the point of greatest vulnerability, although the central nervous system can be affected throughout prenatal development.

Interestingly, morning sickness, which usually affects the mother during the first 3 months of pregnancy, may be a natural defense against the influence of teratogens (Profet, 1992). Pregnant women often show increased sensitivity to foods and odors and even develop aversions to certain tastes, which could help prevent potentially dangerous foods from being eaten. A food that's perfectly harmless to Mom might be damaging to the developing child. Morning sickness occurs across the world, in every culture, which suggests that it may be an evolutionary adaptation. Women who experience morning sickness are somewhat less likely to suffer miscarriages than women who do not (Flaxman & Sherman, 2000).

The Birth Process

When it's time for a baby to be born, the process of birth will begin automatically, although in some cases where this is a risk to mother or child, a doctor may initiate the process to control the timing. The uterine environment exists to protect the baby while their development starts, but eventually the uterus can no longer provide the necessary support. The baby needs air to breathe and more nourishment than the placenta can supply. It's time for the birth process to begin!

The first stage in this process is early/active labor. Labor is when the mother will begin to experience contractions that start the birthing process. First, the cervix will expand to begin creating a space for the baby's head to come through the birth canal. Once contractions become consistent, strong, and closer together, the cervix fully dilates, and the baby's head begins to drop into the birth canal. This first stage can last several hours. Sometimes, the baby is facing the wrong direction and can be turned within the womb before the first stage begins, or a C-section will be performed to surgically remove the baby from the uterus (in which case the second and third stages are bypassed).

The second stage occurs when the mother begins to push the baby out during the birth. This stage can take a few minutes to a few hours. Once the baby's head emerges, the rest of their body follows quickly, but they are still attached to the mother by the umbilical cord, which is cut shortly after the birth. The baby's airway is cleared of amniotic fluid, and the baby takes their first breath, often followed by their first cry. Finally, in the third stage, the placenta emerges. The placenta is the source of oxygen and nourishment for the fetus in the womb. Further contractions push the placenta out after the baby has been born. Then the fun begins!

Newborn infants range in size and weight but on average weigh about 7 pounds and measure 20 inches long.

iStockPhoto/FatCamera

Growth and Movement During Infancy

The average newborn weighs about 7 pounds and is roughly 20 inches in length. Over the next 2 years, as the child grows from baby to toddler, this weight will quadruple, and the child will reach about half of their adult height. Along with the rest of the body, the brain continues its dramatic growth spurt during this period. A newborn enters the world with a brain that is only 25% of its final weight, but by the second birthday, the percentage has increased to 75%. Remarkably, this increase in brain size is not due primarily to the formation of new neurons, as most of the cells that make up the cerebral cortex are in place well before birth (Rakic, 1991; Sorrells et al., 2018). Instead, the cells grow in size and complexity, and a number of supporting glial cells are added.

Humans are born with a number of motor reflexes. This infant is showing the rooting reflex.

Sally and Richard Greenhill / Alamy Stock Photo

Babies are born with a number of **reflexes** to help them survive in the short term. An infant will suck when something touches the roof of their mouth and root for (seek) food by turning their head and opening their mouth when the side of their face is touched. The sucking and rooting reflexes help a baby prepare for a smooth transition to feeding outside the womb. The Moro (or startle) reflex lasts for the first 2 months and occurs when an infant hears a loud noise. The noise causes the infant to throw back their head, throw out their arms and legs, and then draw them back in toward the body. Infants also have a grasping reflex that causes them to firmly grip something that touches their palm. Two additional reflexes are the Babinski reflex and the tonic reflex. The Babinski reflex causes a baby's toes to fan out when its foot is stroked, and the tonic reflex occurs when a baby's head is turned to one side, the baby's arm extends on that side, and the arm on the other side folds in. Finally, infants show a stepping reflex where their legs appear to be walking when they are held with their feet touching a solid surface. All of these reflexes disappear within the first 2–12 months after birth, but seem to serve the adaptive purpose of developing muscle tone and aiding in clinging while being carried, as these reflexes are also seen in other primates (Berecz et al., 2020).

Motor reflexes in humans are seen in other species, indicating that the reflexes may have adaptive value.

Zoonar GmbH / Alamy Stock Photo

Experience Matters

The fact that substantial numbers of neurons are intact at birth does not mean that the brain of the newborn infant is mature—far from it. The brain still needs to build its vast internal communication network, and it requires experience to accomplish this task. During the final stages of prenatal development, and especially during the first year or two after birth, lots of changes occur in the neural circuitry. More branches (dendrites) sprout off from the existing cells, and the number of connections, or synapses, greatly increases. There is even a kind of neural pruning process in which neurons that are not used simply die. This "bloom and prune" process continues throughout childhood, often occurring in spurts, and is particularly active in the frontal "executive" regions of the brain (J. Hill et al., 2010).

Again, the key principle at work is plasticity. The genetic code does not rigidly fix the internal circuitry of the brain. A kind of rough wiring pattern is established during prenatal development, which is filled in during the important first few years of life. Studies with animals have shown that the quality of early experience may be extremely important during this period. For example, rats and mice raised in enriched environments (with lots of social contact and external stimulation) show significantly more complex and better functioning brain tissue than rats raised in sterile, barren environments (He et al.,

2010). Rats also show better recovery of function after brain injury if their recovery time is spent in an enriched environment (Nithianantharajah & Hannan, 2006).

From Crawling to Walking

Of course, parents don't see their baby's "blooming" neural circuitry—what they notice are the observable things: The baby begins to sit up, crawl, stand alone, and walk. Before a baby can do these things, however, both the brain and the neuron-to-muscle links that radiate throughout the body need to develop adequately.

First, the insulated coating of the axons (myelin sheath), which helps speed up neural transmission, develops. Generally, the nervous system matures in a "down-and-out" fashion—that is, from the head down and from the center out (Shirley, 1933). Infants can lift their heads before they can roll over because the neuron-to-muscle connections in the upper part of the body mature before those in the lower part of the body. Babies crawl before they walk because they're able to control their arms efficiently before they're able to control their legs.

Psychologists don't like to tie developmental milestones directly to age because not all children develop at the same rate. But most children learn to crawl, then stand alone and walk, at about the same time. Figure 4.2 shows the major stages of infant motor development. The sequence of development is generally stable, orderly, and predictable. Also, notice that each stage is associated with a small age range. Roughly 90% of all babies can roll over at 5 months of age, sit without support at 8 months, and then walk alone by 15 months. However, one baby might stand alone consistently at 9 months, whereas another might not accomplish the same feat until nearly 14 months of age. Despite these differences, both babies fall within the normal range of development.

FIGURE 4.2 ■ Major Stages of Motor Development

Although psychologists are reluctant to tie developmental milestones closely to age, most children learn to crawl, stand alone, and walk at about the same age.

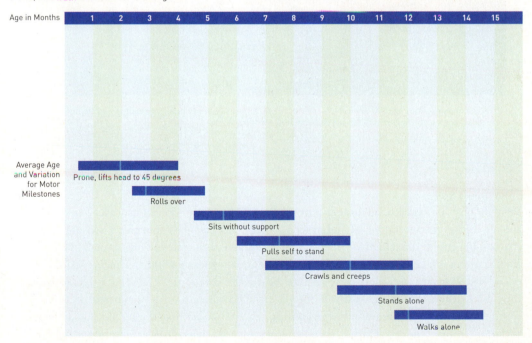

Are There Cultural Differences in Motor Development?

What accounts for differences in motor development? Some children are walking before they are 1 year old, whereas others take much longer. It's hard to tell for any particular case, but both nature and nurture contribute. Each person has a genetic recipe that influences when the individual will develop physically, and environmental experiences can speed up or slow down the process. Some cultures place great value on early motor development and nurture such skills in children. If a baby is routinely exercised and handled during the early months of life, there is some evidence that the baby will progress through the landmark stages of motor development more quickly (Adolph & Robinson, 2015; Hopkins, 1991; Zelazo et al., 1972).

But these differences play little, if any, role in determining final motor development. Hopi babies are traditionally swaddled and bound to cradle boards for much of the first year of life, yet these babies begin walking at roughly the same time as unbound babies (Dennis & Dennis, 1940). Despite the increased popularity of swaddling in Western cultures, more recent studies directly comparing the randomized effects of "swaddling" on motor development have found little or no differences in mental or psychomotor development between swaddled and unswaddled babies (Manaseki-Holland et al., 2010). To learn to walk at a reasonable age, the baby simply needs to be given the opportunity to move around at some point—to "test the waters" and explore things on its own.

Child-rearing practices reflect cultural differences. Hopi babies are traditionally swaddled and bound to cradle boards for much of the first year of life but show no developmental delays in walking.

Cavan Images / Alamy Stock Photo

From Toddlerhood to Adolescence

From the onset of toddlerhood through puberty, the growth rate continues but at a less rapid pace. The average child grows several inches and puts on roughly 6 to 7 pounds annually. These are significant changes, but they're often hard for parents to detect because they represent only a small fraction of the child's current size (2 inches added to a 20-inch baby are far easier to spot than 2 inches added to someone who is 40 inches tall). More noticeable are the changes that occur in hand-to-eye coordination as the child matures. Three-year-olds lack the grace and coordination that are obvious in 6-year-olds. The brain continues to mature, although again at a pace far slower than during prenatal development or during the first two years of life. General processing speed—how quickly we think and react to sudden changes in our environment—increases consistently throughout childhood (Kail, 2008; Kail & Salthouse, 1994).

Between the end of childhood and the beginning of young adulthood lies an important physical and psychological transition period called *adolescence*. Physically, the two most dramatic changes that occur during this time are the adolescent growth spurt and the onset of **puberty**, or sexual maturity (the word *puberty* is from the Latin for "to grow hairy"). Just like with crawling and walking, we can't pinpoint the timing of these changes exactly, particularly for a specific person, but changes usually start occurring for girls at around age 11 and for boys at about 13. Hormones released by the endocrine system rock us out of childhood by triggering a rapid increase in height and weight accompanied by the enlargement and maturation of internal and external sexual organs.

Maturing Sexually

Puberty is the developmental period when we mature sexually and acquire the ability to reproduce. For the adolescent girl, high levels of estrogen in the body lead to external changes, such as breast development and broadening hips, and eventually to the beginning of menarche (the first menstrual flow) at around age 12 or 13. For boys, hormones called androgens lead to the appearance of facial hair, a lower voice, and the ability to ejaculate (release semen) at around age 13 or 14. Neither menarche nor the first ejaculation necessarily means that the adolescent is ready to reproduce—ovulation and sperm production may not occur until months later—but psychologically these "firsts" tend to be highly memorable and emotional events (Y. Chang et al., 2010).

Children reach the adolescent growth spurt at varying ages. Boys typically lag behind girls by as much as two years.

iStockPhoto/zenstock

The onset of puberty shows, yet again, the importance of both nature and nurture in development. Did you know that the average onset age for menarche has dropped from about 16 in the 1880s to the current 12 to 13? Physically, we're maturing earlier than in past generations, and it's not due to systematic changes in genetics. Instead, better nutrition, better living conditions, and improved medical care may be responsible for the trend. Other factors include stress and exposure to endocrine-disrupting chemicals, such as the chemicals present in some plastics. Cultural factors, such as immigration, may also be related to lower onset ages, and onset age differs by country (Parent et al., 2003). Even today, in parts of the world where living conditions are difficult, the average age of menarche is later than in industrialized countries such as the United States. Other factors, such as ethnicity and even family conflict, seem to matter as well (Romans et al., 2003). For example, studies have found that children mature at earlier ages in families that are not close and that contain conflict compared with close and more harmonious families (Steinberg & Morris, 2001). Other studies have shown that the age of onset differs across cultural groups, with younger ages in children of color than their white peers (Reagan et al., 2012). The environment does not cause sexual maturation—that's controlled by the genetic code—but the environment is clearly capable of accelerating or delaying the point when changes start to occur. Because earlier onset of puberty has been shown to be related to negative outcomes, such as lower self-image, anxiety, and depression (Deardorff et al., 2013), it is important for psychologists to understand the factors that affect the changes in timing of puberty onset.

A strenuous daily exercise program may delay the onset of puberty.

iStockPhoto/Image Source .

Becoming an Adult

The adolescent years are marked by dramatic changes in appearance and strength. Motor skills, including hand-to-eye coordination, improve to adult levels during the teenage years. As you may know, there are world-class swimmers and tennis players who are barely into their teens. The brain reaches adult weight by about age 16, although the myelination of the neurons—so critical in early motor development—continues throughout the adolescent years (Paus, 2010). The development of the brain can also be seen in the gradual quickening of reaction times that occurs throughout adolescence (Kail, 2008).

Interestingly, researchers using neuroimaging technology (fMRI) have discovered that significant changes in both myelination and neural "pruning" occur just before and after puberty. These changes, in turn, are believed to alter the internal communication networks, particularly in the prefrontal cortex regions of the brain that control higher-level cognitive abilities. These neural changes correspond with increases in cognitive functioning (e.g., inhibition, processing speed, working memory, and decision making) during adolescence (Blakemore & Choudhury, 2006). These same areas are also thought to control aspects of social processing, such as the ability to understand what other people are thinking and the ability to take the perspective of another person. Although their results are speculative, some researchers have suggested that these brain changes may be responsible for the well-documented and even turbulent changes in social functioning that are associated with adolescence (Blakemore, 2018).

When do we cross the threshold to adulthood? That's a tough question. Becoming an adult is, in some sense, a state of mind. There are differences in how the transition from adolescent to adult is defined across the world. Some cultures have specific rites of passage, and others do not. Moreover, as you know, some adolescents are willing to accept the responsibilities of adulthood quite early, and others are not. Regardless, by the time we reach our 20s, we're physically mature and at the height of our physical prowess.

The Aging Body

Now for the downside. It's barely noticeable at first, but most of us begin slowly and steadily to decline physically, at least with respect to our peak levels of strength and agility, at some point during our 20s. The loss tends to be across the board, which means it applies to virtually all physical functions, from strength, to respiration rate, to the heart's pumping capacity (Whitbourne, 1985). Individual differences occur in the rate of decline, of course, depending on such factors as exercise, illness, and heredity.

(I'm sure you can think of a 40-year-old who is in better physical shape than a 25-year-old.) But wrinkles, age spots, sagging flesh, and loss of muscle tone are all reliable and expected parts of the aging process.

Women begin **menopause**, the period when the menstrual cycle slows down and finally stops, at an average age of 50. Ovulation also stops, so women lose the ability to conceive children. These events are caused by hormonal changes, in particular by a decline in the level of certain hormones in the body. Despite what you might have heard, menopause is not disruptive for all women, either physically or psychologically (Strauss, 2011). The main physical symptoms, such as hot flashes, are not experienced by everyone, and the idea that women typically undergo a sustained period of depression or crankiness is simply a myth (K. A. Matthews, 1992). In fact, some women view menopause as a liberating experience, accompanied by an increased sense of sexual freedom (Eden & Wylie, 2009).

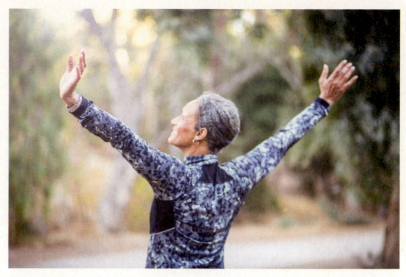

Despite some side effects, such as hot flashes, menopause can be a liberating time for women.

iStockPhoto/adamkaz

The Aging Brain

As we age, significant physical changes begin to occur in the brain as well. The good news is that most older people never experience problems with senility or dementia, but some people do suffer serious brain degeneration—the loss of brain cells—which leads to senility and, in some cases, to a disabling condition called Alzheimer's disease. Fewer than 3% of people at age 65 are afflicted with **dementia**, the technical name for physically based loss in mental functioning. Although that percentage may rise to as much as 35% for individuals over age 85 (Alzheimer's Association, 2019), significant losses in mental functioning are still the exception rather than the rule. Everyone loses brain cells with age, and as you'll see later, declines also occur in certain kinds of memory, sensory ability, and reaction time (see Figure 4.3; Salthouse, 1994).

FIGURE 4.3 ■ Age and Reaction Time

Average reaction time changes between ages 20 and 80, as demonstrated in a cognitive task requiring people to match numbers with symbols on a computer screen. Although reaction time gradually quickens from childhood through adolescence, it gradually slows after age 20.

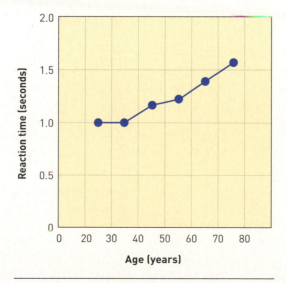

Source: Based on Salthouse, 1994.

But the physical changes that occur in the aging brain are not all bad. Neurons are lost, and the loss may be permanent, but the remaining neurons sometimes increase in complexity. In a famous autopsy study by Buell and Coleman (1979), dendrites were significantly longer and more complex in samples of normal brain tissue taken from elderly adults when compared to those of middle-aged adults (see Figure 4.4). It appears that the brain may compensate for the losses it experiences by making better use of the structures that remain intact. Some researchers believe that sustained mental activity in later years helps promote neural growth, thereby counteracting some of the normal decline in mental skills and even delaying the mental declines associated with Alzheimer's disease (Valenzuela & Sachdev, 2009). There is also evidence that physical activity can delay the onset of Alzheimer's disease in older adults (Brini et al., 2018).

FIGURE 4.4 ■ Aging Neurons

Notice that the dendrites of adult hippocampal neurons actually increase in length and complexity between ages 50 and 70, declining only in late age or with Alzheimer's disease.

Monica Wierzbicki/Body Scientific Intl.

KNOWLEDGE CHECK 4.1

Now test your knowledge about the physical changes that occur during development by deciding whether the following statements are true or false. (You will find the answers in the Appendix.)

1. The period in prenatal development lasting from implantation of the fertilized egg to the end of the 8th week is called the germinal period. *True or False?*

2. The initial development of arms, legs, fingers, and toes occurs during the embryonic period of prenatal development. *True or False?*

3. The large increases in brain size that occur in the first 2 years of life are due primarily to increases in the number of neurons in the brain. *True or False?*

4. The timing of motor development—when a baby begins to crawl, walk, and so on—is affected to a small extent by nature (biology) and to a large extent by nurture (the environment). *True or False?*

5. Everyone loses brain cells with age, and roughly half of all people over age 70 can expect to develop dementia. *True or False?*

DEVELOPING INTELLECTUALLY

Babies are not born seeing and thinking about the world as adults do. Cognitive processes—how we think and perceive—develop over time. Like learning to walk, intellectual development depends on adequate brain development and the right kinds of experiences. In this section, we'll consider three aspects of intellectual development: How do we learn to perceive and remember the world? How do thought processes change with age? How do we develop a sense of right and wrong?

The Tools of Investigation

What does the world look like to a newborn child? Is it a complex three-dimensional world, full of depth, color, and texture? Or is it a "blooming, buzzing confusion," as suggested by the early psychologist William James? Think about how a psychologist might answer these questions. Detecting the perceptual capabilities of an infant is not a simple matter. Babies can't tell us what they see or hear.

Because infants don't communicate as adults do, the analysis of perceptual development (or any other intellectual capacity) requires some creative research methods. It's necessary to devise a way to infer perceptual capabilities from what are essentially immobile, largely uncommunicative infants. Fortunately, babies possess several characteristics that make the job a little easier: (1) They show *preferences*, which means they prefer some stimuli over others; (2) they notice *novelty*, which means they notice new or different things in their environment; and (3) they can *learn* to repeat activities that produce some kind of reward. Researchers have developed techniques that capitalize on each of these tendencies.

The Preference Technique

In the "preference technique" developed by Robert Fantz (1961), an infant is presented with two visual displays at the same time, and the investigator simply records how long the infant looks at each one (see Figure 4.5). Suppose one of the displays shows a male face and the other a female face, and the baby looks at the female face for a significantly longer period of time. By "choosing" to look longer at the female face, the infant has shown a preference. By itself, this preference indicates very little. To infer things about what the baby can really see, it's necessary to present the same two displays several times, switching their positions from trial to trial. If the baby continues to look longer at the female face even though it appears on the left on some trials and on the right on others, we know that the baby can discriminate between the two displays. The infant "tells" us that they can detect differences by exclusively tracking the female face. Notice that we didn't need to ask the baby anything—we simply inferred things about their visual system by measuring behavior.

FIGURE 4.5 ■ **The Preference Technique**

Babies prefer some visual stimuli over others. In this case, the infant demonstrates a preference for a female face by tracking its location across trials. (The preference can be determined by simply recording how long the baby looks at each face.)

Illustrated by Sarah Yeh

Habituation Techniques

One preference babies consistently show is for *novelty*—they like to look at new things. But they tend to ignore events that occur repeatedly without consequence. If you show newborns a blue-colored card and track how their eyes move (or how their heart rate changes), you'll find they spend a lot of time looking at the card when it first appears—it's something new. But if you present the same card over and over again, their interest wanes, and they'll begin to look at something else. This decline in responsiveness to repeated events, called **habituation**, provides an effective tool for understanding the infant's perceptual world. By acting bored, which is defined operationally by how long they look at the card, babies reveal that they remember the stimulus from its previous presentation and recognize that it hasn't changed. It's as if the baby is saying, "Oh, it's that blue card again."

Habituation can be used to discover specific information about how babies perceive and remember their world (Bauer, 2007; Gopnik et al., 1999). Suppose we wanted to discover whether newborns have the ability to see color. We could show the blue card for a while, then suddenly switch to a green card that matches on all other visual dimensions (such as size and brightness). If the infant shows renewed interest in the card—treating the card as if it were new—then the baby must be able to tell the difference between blue and green.

If, on the other hand, the baby continues to ignore the new green card, it suggests that the baby may lack color vision at this stage in development (although there can be other interpretations). We can also study memory by changing the time that elapses between presentations of the card. If the baby continues to act bored by the blue card even though we insert long pauses between presentations, we know that the baby is remembering the card over those time intervals.

Using Rewards

It's also possible to understand what a baby sees, knows, and remembers by rewarding a simple motor movement, such as kicking or sucking on an artificial nipple, in the presence of particular kinds of events (Siqueland & DeLucia, 1969). In research by Carolyn Rovee-Collier (1993), 2- and 3-month-old infants were taught that kicking their legs could produce movement of a mobile hanging overhead. A moving mobile is quite rewarding to babies at this age, and they'll double or triple their rate of leg kicking in a matter of minutes if it leads to movement. We can then study cognitive abilities—such as memory—by taking the mobile away, waiting for some period of time, and then replacing the mobile. If the baby begins leg kicking again at rates similar to those produced at the end of training, the baby has remembered what they have learned. We can also change the characteristics of the mobile after training and learn things about a baby's perceptual abilities. For example, if we train an infant with a blue mobile and then switch to a green one, any differences in leg kicking should help to tell us whether the baby can discriminate between green and blue.

Researcher Carolyn Rovee-Collier showed that infants can learn to kick their legs to get an overhead mobile moving.

iStockPhoto/tatyana_tomsickova

Research Designs

In addition to the "tools" of investigation just described, researchers who study development typically use one of two kinds of research design, *longitudinal* or *cross-sectional*. In a **longitudinal design**, you test the same person (or group of people) repeatedly over time, at various points in childhood or even through adulthood. If you wanted to study perceptual development, for instance, you would track the perceptual capabilities of baby Howard at various points in Howard's life. In a **cross-sectional design**, which is conducted over a more limited span of time, you assess the abilities of *different* people of different ages at the same time. So, rather than just testing Howard when he turns 2, 5, or 10, you would test groups of 2-, 5-, or 10-year-old children simultaneously. There are advantages and disadvantages associated with each research strategy. Concept Review 4.1 describes these for each type of design.

CONCEPT REVIEW 4.1
RESEARCH DESIGNS FOR STUDYING DEVELOPMENT

Type of Design	Overview	Advantages and Disadvantages
Cross-sectional	Researchers compare performance of different people of different ages.	A: Faster, more practical than longitudinal. D: Other variables may be confounded with age.
Longitudinal	Researchers test the same individuals repeatedly over time.	A: Can examine changes in individuals. D: Cost-intensive; subject loss over time.

The Growing Perceptual World

Babies greet the world with reasonably well-functioning sensory systems. Although none is operating at peak efficiency, because the biological equipment is still maturing, babies still see a world of color and shape (Maurer & Lewis, 2018). They even arrive with built-in preferences. One-day-old babies, for example, respond more to patterned stimuli than to unpatterned ones. As shown in Figure 4.6, they also prefer to look at correctly drawn faces rather than scrambled facial features (M. H. Johnson et al., 1991). It's likely that learning plays a role in some of these preferences (Turati, 2004), but reasonably sophisticated perceptual processing occurs soon after birth.

Newborns also hear reasonably well, and they seem to recognize their mother's voice within a day or two (DeCasper & Fifer, 1980). By the 28th week, fetuses will close their eyes in response to loud noises presented near the mother's abdomen. Remarkably, newborns can even hear and remember things that happen *prior* to birth. Infants will also choose to suck on an artificial nipple that produces a recording of a story that was read aloud to them repeatedly before birth (DeCasper & Spence, 1986). It's unlikely that the baby is remembering the story—but it does indicate that babies are sensitive to experiences that happen in the womb (D. K. James, 2010). This is an adaptive ability for the newborn. Babies need nourishment and are dependent on others for survival. Those born into the world with a visual system that can detect shapes and forms and with an auditory system tuned to the human voice have a better chance of survival.

In addition to sights and sounds, babies are quite sensitive to touch, smell, pain, and taste. Place a drop of lemon juice in the mouth of a newborn, and you'll see a distinctive grimace. Place a small amount of sugar in the baby's mouth, and the baby will smack their lips. These distinctive reactions are present at birth and are found even before the infant has had a single taste of food. A baby's sense of smell is developed well enough that the newborn quickly learns to recognize the odor of its mother's breast (Porter et al., 1992). As for pain and touch, babies will reject a milk bottle that is too hot, and as every parent knows, the right kind of pat on the baby's back is pleasurable enough to soothe a newborn into sleep.

FIGURE 4.6 ■ Infant Preferences

In this experiment, babies were shown either a blank stimulus, a stimulus with scrambled facial features, or a face. Each stimulus was first positioned over the baby's head and then moved from side to side. The dependent variable measured the extent to which the baby tracked each stimulus by head turning. As the results show, the babies tracked the face stimulus more than the others (graph adapted from M. H. Johnson et al., 1991).

Carolina Hrejsa/Body Scientific Intl.

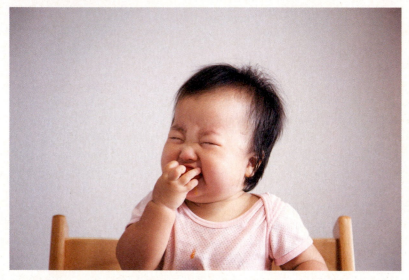

This baby is less than a year old, but even newborn infants show distinctive reactions to a variety of tastes.

iStockPhoto/kohei_hara

Babies even seem to perceive a three-dimensional world. When placed on a visual cliff, such as the one shown in the photo below, 6-month-old babies are reluctant to cross over the apparent drop-off, or cliff, to reach a parent (Gibson & Walk, 1960). Babies as young as 2 months show heart rate changes when they're placed on the glass portion covering the deep side of the visual cliff (Campos et al., 1970).

Still, these are infant perceptions, and the infant's world is different from that of an adult. Newborn babies cannot see as well as adults. They're not very good at discriminating fine detail in visual patterns: Compared with the ideal acuity level of 20/20, babies see a blurry world that is more on the order of 20/400, meaning that what newborns see at 20 feet is what adults with ideal vision see at 400 feet. In addition, newborns probably can't perceive shapes and forms as well as adults do (Maurer & Lewis, 2018), nor can they hear as well as adults. For example, infants seem to have some trouble listening selectively for certain kinds of sounds, and they require sounds to be louder than adults do before those sounds can be detected (Bargones & Werner, 1994).

In the visual cliff apparatus, a plate of glass covers an abrupt drop-off. From the age of approximately 6 months, babies are reluctant to cross the cliff to reach a beckoning parent.

Science History Images / Alamy Stock Photo

Infants' perceptual systems improve markedly during the first few months, partly because of continued physical development but also because experience fine-tunes their sensory abilities. In the visual cliff experiments mentioned earlier, infants with lots of experience crawling are more reluctant to cross over the "cliff" and show more fear (e.g., an elevated heart rate) when lowered over the cliff's deep side (Witherington et al., 2005). Research with nonhumans, such as cats or chimpanzees, has shown that if animals are deprived of visual stimulation during the early weeks or months of life, permanent visual impairments can result (Gandelman, 1992). Thus, perceptual development relies on experience as well as on physically mature sensory equipment.

By the time we leave infancy, our perceptual systems are reasonably intact. Most of the changes that occur during childhood and adolescence affect our ability to use the equipment we have. For example, as children grow older, their attention span improves, and they're better able to attend selectively to information. Memory improves throughout childhood, partly because kids learn strategies for organizing and maintaining information in memory (Ornstein et al., 2008). Moreover, as you'll see in Chapters 5 and 8, how we perceive and remember the world depends on what we know about it. We use our general knowledge about people and events to help us interpret ambiguous stimuli and to remember things that happen in our lives. Perception and memory are influenced by the knowledge gained from experience. This is one of the reasons perceptual development is really a lifelong process.

Piaget and the Development of Thought

It was a Swiss scholar named Jean Piaget (1896–1980) who first convinced psychologists that children think quite differently from adults. Children are not little adults, Piaget argued, who simply lack knowledge and experience; instead, they view the world in a unique way. Piaget believed that everyone is born with a natural tendency to organize the world meaningfully. We construct mental models of the world—called **schemata**—and use these worldviews to

Jean Piaget

Everett Collection Inc / Alamy Stock Photo

guide and interpret our experiences. But schemata are not very adultlike early in development—in fact, they tend not to reflect the world accurately—so much of early intellectual development is spent changing and fine-tuning our worldviews. One of Piaget's primary contributions was to demonstrate that children's reasoning errors can provide a window into how the schema construction process is proceeding.

Consider the two tilted pitchers shown in Figure 4.7. If young children are asked to draw a line indicating how the water level in a tilted pitcher might look, they tend to draw a line that's parallel to the top and bottom of the pitcher, as shown in the cup on the left, rather than parallel to the ground, as shown in the pitcheron the right. This kind of error is important, Piaget argued, because children can't have learned such a thing directly from experience (water never tilts that way in real life). Instead, the error reflects a fundamental misconception of how the world is structured. Young children have an inaccurate internal view, or model, of the world.

FIGURE 4.7 ■ Which of these pitchers shows the correct view of the liquid when the pitcher is tilted?

Illustrated by Sarah Yeh

Assimilation and Accommodation

As their brains and bodies mature, children use experience to build more sophisticated and correct mental models of the world. Piaget suggested that cognitive development is guided by two adaptive psychological processes, *assimilation* and *accommodation*. **Assimilation** is the process through which we fit—or assimilate—new experiences into our existing schemata. For example, suppose a small child who has been raised in a household full of cats mistakenly concludes that the neighbor's new rabbit is simply a kind of kitty. The new experience—the rabbit—has been assimilated into the child's existing view of the world: Small furry things are cats. The second function, **accommodation**, is the process through which we change or modify existing schemata to accommodate new experiences. When the child learns that the new "kitty" hops rather than walks and seems reluctant to eat tuna, the child will need to modify and revise the existing concept of small furry things; the child is forced to change the existing schemata to accommodate the new information. Notice that the child plays an active role in constructing schemata by interacting directly with the world (Piaget, 1929).

Piaget believed that children develop an adult worldview by moving systematically through a series of four stages or developmental periods: *sensorimotor, preoperational, concrete operational*, and *formal operational*. Each of these periods is tied roughly to a particular age range—for example, the preoperational period usually lasts from age 2 to about age 7—but individual differences can occur in how quickly the child moves from one stage to the next. Although the timing may vary from child to child, Piaget believed that the order in which individuals progress through the stages is invariant—it remains the same for everyone. Concept Review 4.2 provides an overview of the stages of Piaget's theory. Let's consider these cognitive developmental periods in more detail.

The Sensorimotor Period: Birth to 2 Years

From birth to about age 2, schemata about the world revolve primarily around the infant's sensory and motor abilities (hence the name **sensorimotor period**). As described in the previous section of this chapter, babies initially interact with the world through a collection of survival reflexes. For example, they'll start sucking when an object is placed in their mouth (the *sucking reflex*), and they'll automatically turn their head in the direction of a touch or brush on the cheek (the *rooting reflex*). This behavior is different from an adult's, but it's useful for a newborn. These reflexes increase the likelihood that the baby will get fed, which, of course, is a significant problem the newborn needs to solve.

As infants develop intellectually over the 1st year, they use their maturing motor skills to understand how they can interact with the world voluntarily. Babies start to vocalize to gain attention; they learn they can kick their legs to make sounds; they acquire the ability to reach with their arms to touch or grasp objects. They begin acting like "little scientists," exploring their world, learning to repeat actions, and testing rudimentary hypotheses about cause and effect (although not in the same conscious way that we might). The initial stirrings of symbolic thought begin during this period. The infant gradually develops the ability to construct internal mental images or symbols.

Early in the 1st year, babies lack **object permanence**, which means they fail to recognize that objects exist when they're no longer in sight. The accompanying photo illustrates how psychologists have measured object permanence. Notice the baby loses interest when the toy is covered, suggesting that the baby is only capable of thinking about objects that are directly in view. Babies at this point are unable to represent objects symbolically—out of sight equals out of mind. But by the end of the first year, Piaget argued, the child has a different reaction to the disappearance of a favored toy; as object permanence develops, the child will begin to search actively for the lost toy.

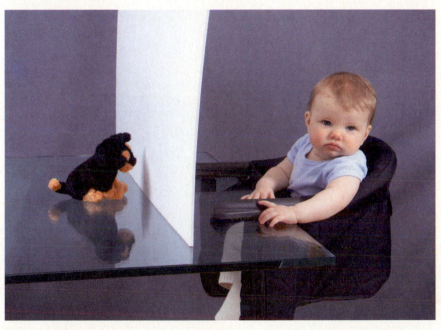

According to Piaget, babies who haven't yet mastered the concept of object permanence don't understand that objects still exist when they're no longer in view. Notice how this boy loses interest when he can no longer see his favorite toy.

Science History Images / Alamy Stock Photo

The Preoperational Period: 2 to 7 Years

From about ages 2 through 7, the child's schemata continue to grow in sophistication. Children in the **preoperational period** no longer have difficulty thinking about absent objects, and they can use one object to stand for another. A 4-year-old can effortlessly use a stick to represent a soaring airplane or a cardboard box for a stove. The child realizes these are not the real objects, but can imagine them to be real for the purposes of play. At the same time, the child still thinks about the world quite differently from an adult. As you'll see momentarily, the child lacks the ability to perform certain basic mental operations—hence Piaget's use of the term *preoperational* to describe a child's mental abilities during this period.

Conservation

Children at the preoperational stage often fail to understand the **principle of conservation**. Conservation means that certain physical properties of an object remain the same despite superficial changes in its appearance (see Figure 4.8). If 4- or 5-year-old children are shown two play dough balls of the same size and are asked which object contains more play dough, most will say that the two balls contain the same amount. But if one of the balls is then rolled into a long sausage-like shape, the children are likely to think that the two quantities of play dough are no longer the same, saying that either the sausage or the ball has more play dough.

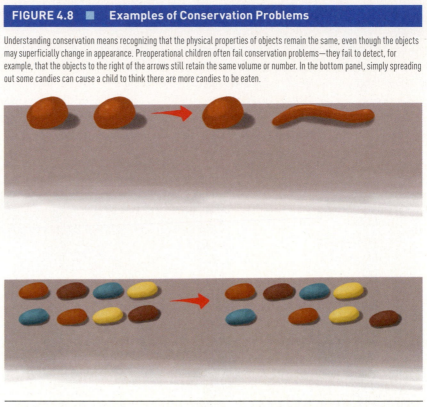

FIGURE 4.8 ■ Examples of Conservation Problems

Understanding conservation means recognizing that the physical properties of objects remain the same, even though the objects may superficially change in appearance. Preoperational children often fail conservation problems—they fail to detect, for example, that the objects to the right of the arrows still retain the same volume or number. In the bottom panel, simply spreading out some candies can cause a child to think there are more candies to be eaten.

Illustrated by Sarah Yeh

Children at this age are unable to understand that a basic property of an object, in this case its mass, doesn't change as the object changes shape. Typically, preoperational children will fail to conserve a basic quantity even if they directly observe the change in appearance taking place. Suppose we ask 5-year-old Sam to pour a cup of water into each of two identical glasses (see Figure 4.9). Sam performs the task and accepts that the two glasses now contain the same amount. We then instruct him to pour the water from one of the glasses into another glass that is tall and thin. Do the glasses now contain the same amount of water? "No," Sam explains, "now the tall one has more water." Sam is not showing any evidence of conservation; he does not yet recognize that how the water looks in the glass has no effect on its volume.

Piaget also discovered that children in the preoperational period tend to see the world, and the objects in it, from primarily one perspective: their own. Children at this stage have a tough time imagining themselves in another person's position. If you ask a child in the preoperational period to describe what another person will see or think, you're likely to find the child simply describing what the child personally sees or thinks. Piaget called this characteristic **egocentrism**—the tendency to view the world from your own unique perspective only. It's not until they develop what psychologists have termed **theory of mind**, or the ability to consider what other people may be thinking and

FIGURE 4.9 ■ Children who lack the concept of conservation mistakenly think that a tall glass will change the amount of liquid poured into it.

Illustrated by Sarah Yeh

what their perspective of a situation might be, that children are able to describe the world from someone else's point of view.

The Concrete Operational Period: 7 to 11 Years

Between the ages of 7 and about 11, children enter the **concrete operational period** and gain the ability to perform mental actions on objects—to verbalize, visualize, and mentally manipulate objects. A child of 8 can consider the consequences of rolling a long strip of play dough into a ball before the action is actually performed. Children in the concrete operational period have fewer difficulties with conservation problems because they are capable of reversing operations on objects—they can mentally consider the effects of both doing and undoing an action.

Children at the concrete operational stage also show the initial stirrings of logical thought, which means they can now mentally order and compare objects and perform more sophisticated classifications. These children can do simple math and solve problems that require elementary reasoning. But their mental operations remain *concrete*, or tied directly to actual objects in the real world. Children at this age have great difficulty with problems that do not flow directly from everyday experience. Ask an 8-year-old to solve a problem involving four-armed people and barking cats, and you're likely to get a blank look. Basically, if something can't be seen, heard, touched, tasted, or smelled, it's going to be tough for these children to think about (although they can imagine non-real-world objects they have encountered, for example, in cartoons or fairy tales). The ability to think truly abstractly doesn't develop until the final stage of cognitive development.

The Formal Operational Period: 11 to Adulthood

By the time children reach their teenage years, most will be in the formal operational period, during which they begin to think much more like an adult. Neither teenagers nor adults have problems thinking about imaginary or artificial concepts; they can consider hypothetical outcomes or make logical deductions about places they've never visited or that might not even exist. Teenagers can develop systematic strategies for solving problems—such as using trial and error—that are beyond the capability of most preteens.

CONCEPT REVIEW 4.2
PIAGET'S STAGES OF COGNITIVE DEVELOPMENT

Stage	Basic Characteristics	Accomplishments	Limitations
Sensorimotor period (birth–2 years)	Schemata about the world revolve primarily around sensory and motor abilities.	Child develops object permanence; learns how to control body; learns how to vocalize, and learns first words.	Schemata are limited primarily to simple sensory and motor function; problems in thinking about absent objects (early).
Preoperational period (2–7 years)	Schemata grow in sophistication. Children can think about absent objects, and can use one object to stand for another.	Children readily symbolize objects, and imaginary play is common; great strides in language development.	Children are prelogical; they fail to understand conservation, due to centration and a failure to understand reversibility; children show egocentricity in thinking.
Concrete operational period (7–11 years)	Children gain the capacity for true mental operations (i.e., verbalizing, visualizing, mental manipulation).	Child understands reversibility and other simple logical operations like categorizing and ordering.	Mental operations remain concrete, tied to actual objects in the real world. Difficulty with problems that do not flow from everyday experience.
Formal operational period (11 years–adulthood)	Mastery is gained over abstract thinking.	Adolescents can think and answer questions in general and abstract ways.	No limitations; development of reasoning is complete. However, not all reach this stage.

Most children reach the formal operational period by their teenage years, when they master abstract thinking.

The **formal operational period** is the stage at which we start to gain mastery over *abstract* thinking. Ask a concrete operational child about the meaning of education, and you'll be likely to hear about teachers and grades. The formal operational adolescent is able to answer the question in a general and abstract way, perhaps describing education as a system organized by parents and the government to foster the acquisition of useful knowledge. Piaget believed that the transition from concrete operational thinking to formal operational thinking probably occurs gradually, over several years, and may not be achieved by everyone (Piaget, 1970). Once this stage is reached, the adolescent is no longer tied to concrete, real-world constructs and can invent and experiment with the possible rather than just with the here and now.

Updates to Piaget's Theory

Jean Piaget revolutionized our understanding of how children think. He successfully convinced the psychological community that children have unique internal schemata, and he provided convincing demonstrations that those schemata, once formed, tend to change systematically over time. But work in cognitive development has continued in the decades since Piaget first developed his theory, and as new data are collected in psychological studies, theories and ideas about behavior are revised based on new information. More recent data have falsified some aspects of his theory, primarily his assumptions about what children really know and when they know it (Gopnik, 2009).

More recent studies have shown that children and young infants are considerably more sophisticated in their models of the world than Piaget believed. For example, Piaget suggested that object permanence doesn't develop until late in the child's 1st year. Although it's true that children will not search for a hidden toy in the first few months of life, more sensitive tests have revealed that even 1- to 4-month-old infants are capable of recognizing that vanished objects still exist (Baillargeon, 2004; see Bremner et al., 2015). These tests suggest that object permanence develops in some form earlier than previously thought.

Additional studies supported this idea. In research by child psychologist T. G. R. Bower (1982), very young infants watched as a screen was moved in front of a toy, blocking it from view (see Figure 4.10). Moments later, when the screen was removed, the infants acted surprised if the toy was absent (it could be secretly removed by the experimenter). If objects no longer exist when removed from view, then a sudden absence shouldn't surprise infants. Other researchers have demonstrated that small infants can show symbolic thought—they understand, for instance, that objects move along continuous paths and do not jump around—and they gain this understanding at points in development far earlier than Piaget imagined (e.g., Spelke & Kinzler, 2007).

FIGURE 4.10 ■ Reevaluating Object Permanence

In this experiment, a screen was moved in front of a toy, blocking it from the infant's view. Moments later, when the screen was removed, the baby's level of surprise (defined as a change in heart rate) was measured. In one condition, the toy appeared behind the screen; in a second condition, it had vanished. Babies showed more surprise when the toy was absent, suggesting that object permanence may develop earlier than Piaget suspected (Bower, 1982).

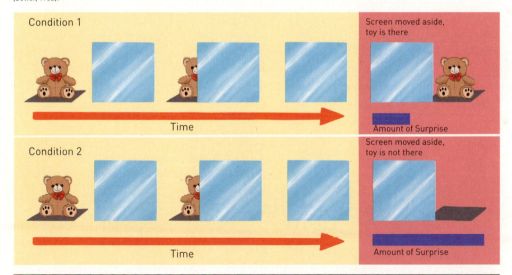

Illustrated by Sarah Yeh

Although the notion of distinct stages, or periods of development, has been a common idea in development, many studies now suggest that developmental changes are more gradual. Piaget recognized that not all children develop at the same rate, but he remained convinced that a child's thought processes undergo sharp transitions from one stage to the next. According to this view, once a child undergoes a stage transition—say, from the preoperational to the concrete operational—the child should be able to perform a variety of new tasks relatively quickly. But this is not usually the case. Most developmental psychologists now believe that cognitive development is better viewed as a process of continual change and adaptation (Newcombe, 2011; Siegler, 1996; Xu, 2019). Current studies (e.g., Fuchs et al., 2010) often distinguish between skills that are specific to a topic area (e.g., understanding of numbers and their relative magnitude) and skills that are more general and cut across several areas of cognition (e.g., memory and general reasoning skills).

The Role of Culture

Research since Piaget's studies has also addressed the role of culture, family dynamics, social structures surrounding the child, and changing environments in which the child lives in the development of cognitive skills (Bronfenbrenner & Ceci, 1994; Vélez-Agosto et al., 2017). The importance of social and cultural influences was promoted by a Russian psychologist, Lev Vygotsky, around the same time that Piaget was developing his theoretical ideas. Vygotsky died in 1934, after only a decade of work in psychology, but his ideas remain very influential (Daniels et al., 2007). Vygotsky argued that cognitive abilities emerge *directly* out of our social interactions with others. He proposed, for example, that inner speech, which we use to think and plan activities, is a natural extension of the outer speech that we use to communicate. He was convinced that intellectual development is tied to social interaction—it grows out of each person's attempts to master social situations. Development can't be understood by considering the individual alone—you must always consider individuals in their social context (Vygotsky, 1978).

For example, imagine asking a 3-year-old child to describe how meals are prepared in the household. It's unlikely that you'll get much of a response—beyond, perhaps, a shrugging of the shoulders or shake of the head. Yet, if we engage the child in some form of social interaction—we provide clues or ask leading questions (e.g., Where is food stored? Where is it cooked?)—we're likely to find that the child actually has quite a bit of knowledge about how food is prepared. Every child has what Vygotsky called a "zone of proximal development," which is the difference between what children can accomplish on their own and what they can do in the context of a social interaction (such as interacting with Mom or Dad). It is our social interactions, Vygotsky argued, that energize development and help to shape how we think.

Cross-cultural research has shown that children across the world develop cognitively in similar ways, but significant cultural differences can occur in the rate of development (Matsumoto, 1994; Molitor & Hsu, 2019). For example, children raised in nomadic societies, which move frequently from place to place, seem to acquire spatial skills (the ability to orient themselves in their environment) earlier than children raised in single, fixed locales. Schooling may also be a factor: Ample cross-cultural evidence indicates that people who never attend school may have a difficult time reaching the formal operational stage of thinking, at least as measured through traditional Piagetian tasks (M. Cole, 1992).

According to Vygotsky, cognitive abilities come from children's social and verbal interactions with other people.

iStockPhoto/martinedoucet

Other studies have shown that in Eastern cultures, where self-regulation is emphasized from an early age, children show better performance on cognitive tasks related to attention and inhibition than children from Western cultures (Oh & Lewis, 2008). Other studies have examined factors that affect Latino immigrants in the United States, such as fear of discovery of undocumented family members and reduced resources in schools (Arellanes et al., 2017). These factors can affect educational opportunities for groups of children that, in turn, influence how quickly their cognitive skills such as scientific reasoning and memory develop. Research that examines the interactions children have with their family, neighborhood, school environment, and peers goes beyond what is commonly included in Piaget's theory of cognitive development.

Core Knowledge

Psychologists who study intellectual development have also discovered that children acquire specialized knowledge very early in life. Not surprisingly, these areas of "core knowledge" tend to be about things relevant to survival or to understanding how people and the world work. For example, infants quickly learn the difference between animate (or living) and inanimate (or nonliving) objects (M. Rhodes & Gelman, 2009). Infants as young as 12 weeks of age show looking-time differences between humans and inanimate objects, and by 2 months of age, infants will smile and coo at responsive humans, but not at toy animals (Opfer & Gelman, 2011). Young children understand that animals move around on their own and inanimate objects do not. Children also understand that biological properties—such as getting hungry or tired—apply only to living things. Infants recognize as well that living things, unlike nonliving objects, act to achieve certain goals (Spelke & Kinzler, 2007). Animals and people are goal-directed, but pieces of wood are not.

Like adults, small children are convinced that animals and people have a kind of "essence" or true nature that is fixed at birth. Preschool children believe that if a kangaroo is adopted and raised by goats, it will still grow up to be good at hopping rather than climbing (goats climb well)—they also continue to believe that the kangaroo will grow up to have a pouch. Moreover, if you tell a child that a raccoon has been modified by a scientist to look like a skunk (even with a smelly pouch), the child is still likely to claim that the animal is a raccoon even though it no longer looks like one. These findings indicate that young children believe that members of categories have core natural qualities that cannot easily be changed by experience (Gelman, 2009).

Moral Development: Learning Right From Wrong

Developing intellectually means more than learning to think logically and form correct internal models of the world. As children mature intellectually, they also develop *character*. They acquire a sense of **morality**, which provides them with a way to distinguish between appropriate and inappropriate actions. In fact, children as young as 4 months old show understanding of moral reasoning for how individuals should act toward each other (Margoni & Surian, 2018; Ting et al., 2020); as they get older, children further refine their moral reasoning based on experiences with others. Psychologists have explored how the development of morality occurs and what factors contribute to a child's moral reasoning.

Kohlberg's Stage Theory

The most influential theory of moral development has been the stage theory proposed by Lawrence Kohlberg. Piaget strongly influenced Kohlberg, who, like Piaget, believed that people move through stages of moral development (Kohlberg, 1963, 1986). He would give people a moral dilemma, ask them to solve it, and use their reasoning to help identify their state of moral development. Let's consider an example, based on Kohlberg (1969):

> A woman is stricken with a rare and deadly form of cancer. There is a drug that can save her, a form of radium recently discovered by a druggist in town. But the druggist is charging $2,000 for the medicine, 10 times what the drug cost him to make. The sick woman's husband, Heinz, tries desperately to raise the money but can raise only half of the needed amount. He pleads

with the druggist to sell him the drug at a reduced cost, or at least to allow him to pay for the drug over time, but the druggist refuses. "No," the druggist says, "I discovered the drug, and I'm going to make money from it." Frantic to save his wife, Heinz considers breaking into the druggist's office to steal the drug.

What do you think? Should the husband steal the drug? Why or why not? Kohlberg was mainly interested in the reasoning behind your answer. He believed that people can be classified into stages of moral development based on how they answer such moral problems. Kohlberg's theory proposes as many as six stages of moral development, but we'll focus on his three main levels only: *preconventional, conventional,* and *postconventional.*

At the lowest level of moral development—the **preconventional level**—decisions about right and wrong are based primarily on external consequences. Young children will typically interpret the morality of a behavior in terms of its immediate individual consequences—that is, whether the act will lead directly to a reward or to a punishment: "Heinz shouldn't steal the drug because he might get caught and punished" or "Heinz should steal the drug because people will get mad at him if his wife dies."

At the **conventional level** of moral reasoning, people justify their actions based on internalized rules. Now an action is right or wrong because it maintains or disrupts the *social order.* Someone at this level might argue that "Heinz shouldn't steal the drug because stealing is against the law" or that "Heinz should steal the drug because husbands have an obligation to protect their wives." Notice here that moral reasoning has moved away from immediate individual consequences to societal consequences. Moral behavior is that which conforms to the rules and conventions of society.

At the final level of moral development, the **postconventional level**, morality is based on abstract reasoning. The person adopts a moral standard based on some universal ethical principle. "An individual human life is more important than society's dictum against stealing," someone at this level might argue. In this case, moral actions are driven by general and abstract personal codes of ethics that may not agree with normal rules of society. Concept Review 4.3 includes an overview of Kohlberg's stages of moral development.

Evaluating Kohlberg's Theory

Developmental psychologists continue to believe that we progress through periods of moral development, from an early focus on immediate individual consequences toward a final principled code of ethics. Several observational studies have confirmed aspects of Kohlberg's views. For example, people do seem to move through the various types of moral reasoning in the sequence suggested by Kohlberg; children at least move from a preconventional to a conventional level in most cultures (J. C. Gibbs et al., 2007). Furthermore, the link that both Piaget and Kohlberg made between moral reasoning and level of cognitive development has clear merit. But Kolhberg's critics argue that he ties the concept of morality too closely to an abstract code of justice—that is, to the idea that moral acts are those that ensure fairness to the individual.

For example, suppose your sense of morality is based not on fairness but rather on concern for the welfare of others. You might believe that the appropriate action is always one that doesn't hurt anyone—or one that considers the happiness of the affected individual. Under these conditions, as analyzed by Kohlberg, your behavior will appear to be driven more by an individual situation than by a consistent code of justice. Psychologist Carol Gilligan (1982) has argued that women in our culture often adopt such a view (a moral code based on caring), whereas men tend to make moral decisions based on an abstract sense of justice. According to

Kohlberg described moral development in terms of stages, similar to Piaget's theory of cognitive development.

Kohlberg's theory, however, this means that women will tend to be classified at a lower level of moral development than men. Gilligan sees this as an unfair and unjustified gender bias.

CONCEPT REVIEW 4.3
KOHLBERG'S STAGE THEORY OF MORAL DEVELOPMENT

Stage	Basis for Moral Judgment	Possible Response to "Was Heinz Right?"
Preconventional	External consequences	Yes: "He can't be happy without his wife." No: "If he gets caught, he'll be put in jail."
Conventional	Social order	Yes: "Spouses are responsible for protecting one another." No: "Stealing is against the law."
Postconventional	Abstract ethical principles	Yes: "Individual lives are more important than society's law against stealing." No: "Laws are necessary in a civilized society; they need to be followed by all to prevent chaos."

The Role of Culture

Gilligan may have overstated the case for sex differences in moral reasoning. Men and women often think in much the same way about the moral dilemmas studied by Kohlberg (L. J. Walker, 1989). At the same time, Western cultures tend to place more value on individualism and stress individual goals more than other cultures, where the emphasis may be on collective goals. These kinds of cultural values certainly affect moral development. For example, Chinese children are taught it's okay to lie politely when it helps the group, but North American children tend to believe a "polite lie" is fine when it helps the individual (Fu et al., 2007). Moreover, the importance a culture places on teaching moral values can affect the speed with which moral development proceeds (J. C. Gibbs et al., 2007). In a study comparing Chinese and German children, the Chinese children considered context and intention in moral judgments at 3 years old, but the German children did not consider these factors until they were 5 years old (Li et al., 2020). The bottom line: Morality seems to develop in a consistent manner across the world—that is, people tend to interpret morality first in terms of external consequences and only later in terms of abstract principles—but, not surprisingly, culture can exert its influence in powerful ways.

The Role of the "Gut"

Kohlberg based his theory of moral development on the study of moral reasoning. He was interested in how children thought about his moral dilemmas—how they consciously "explained" their decisions about right and wrong. But increasingly psychologists are convinced that morality comes first from the gut—our unconscious feelings and emotions about the situation at hand. When we witness a child being slapped, we experience a flash emotional reaction—anger, sympathy, even rage. It is these quick emotional reactions that form much of the basis of our judgments about right and wrong. Higher-level moral reasoning comes later, when we attempt to justify our feelings (Haidt, 2007; Haidt & Kesebir, 2010).

Evidence suggests that our sense of morality lies partly in such gut feelings rather than simply in concepts such as welfare and justice (Turiel, 2015). For example, people are often morally dumbfounded, which means they intuitively know something is wrong, but can't explain it in words. Imagine the following scenario: A brother and sister want to have sex. They're both consenting adults, and they use protection so pregnancy isn't an issue. Is it okay for them to have sex? Most people say absolutely not—it's wrong—but they have a hard time explaining the basis for their judgment. Other evidence comes from neuroscience: People with damage to parts of the brain associated with emotional processing evaluate moral dilemmas differently from normal controls. For example, in one study, brain-damaged patients were more likely to consider attempted murder as morally permissible; they lacked the gut-based emotional reaction that is normally involved in judging harmful intent (Young et al., 2010).

KNOWLEDGE CHECK 4.2

Now test your knowledge of intellectual development by answering these questions. (You will find the answers in the Appendix.)

1. Pick the appropriate research technique from among the following terms: *cross-sectional, habituation, longitudinal, preference,* and *reward.*
   a. Babies learn to kick their legs because it moves the mobile: ___
   b. Babies grow bored and stop looking at repeated presentations of the same event: ___
   c. Comparisons are made among three groups of children; each group contains children of a different age: ___
   d. The development of memory is studied by testing the same individual repeatedly throughout the individual's lifetime: ___

2. According to Piaget, children develop mental models of the world, called schemata, that change as the child grows. During the preoperational period of development, children often fail to recognize that the physical properties of an object can stay the same despite superficial changes in its appearance (e.g., rolling a ball of dough into a sausage shape doesn't change its mass). Piaget referred to this ability as
   a. conservation.
   b. object permanence.
   c. accommodation.
   d. relativistic thinking.

3. Pick the appropriate level of moral development, as described by Kohlberg. Possible answers include conventional, preconventional, and postconventional.
   a. Actions are justified on the basis of whether they disrupt the social order: ___
   b. Actions are justified on the basis of abstract moral principles: ___
   c. Actions are justified on the basis of their immediate consequences: ___

DEVELOPING SOCIALLY AND PERSONALLY

People do not develop in isolation. We're social animals, and the relationships we form with others affect how we act and view ourselves. For infants, relationships with caregivers—usually their parents—guarantee them adequate nourishment and a safe and secure environment. Children work hard to become part of a social group, learning how to get along with peers and to follow the rules and norms of society. For adults, whose social bonds become increasingly intimate, the task is to learn to accept responsibility for the care and support of others. As with most aspects of development, social and personal growth is shaped partly by biology and partly by what we learn from experience.

Forming Bonds With Others

Think again about the problems faced by the newborn: limited motor skills and somewhat fuzzy vision, yet a powerful need for food, water, and warmth. To gain the nourishment needed to live, as well as protection from danger, the newborn relies on interactions with others—usually the mother. The newborn forms **attachments**, strong emotional ties to one or more intimate companions. The need for early attachments is so critical that researchers commonly argue that bonding behavior is built directly into our nature (Bowlby, 1969; Meltzoff & Marshall, 2018).

Both caregiver and infant are preprogrammed from birth to respond to certain signals with attachment behavior. The newborn typically cries, coos, and smiles, and these behaviors lead naturally to attention and support from the caregiver. It's no accident that adults like to hear babies coo or watch them smile—these preferences may be built directly into the genetic code (Bowlby, 1969). At the same time, the baby arrives into the world with a bias to respond to care and particularly to comfort from the caregiver. Newborns imitate the facial expressions of their parents (Meltzoff, 2011), for example, which presumably enhances their social interactions with them.

Notice that both the infant and the caregiver are active participants—the attachment is formed because both parties are prepared to respond with bonding to the right kind of events. The bond usually is formed initially between baby and mother because it is the mother who provides most of the early care.

Contact comfort helps secure the bond of mutual attachment.

iStockPhoto/miodrag ignjatovic

The Origins of Attachment

The idea that humans are built to form strong emotional attachments makes sense from an adaptive standpoint—it helps to guarantee survival. But what determines the strength or quality of the attachment? The quality of the bond that forms between infant and caregiver can vary enormously—some infants are securely attached to their caregivers, while others are not. Research with animal subjects suggests that one very important factor is the amount of actual *contact comfort*—the degree of warm physical contact—provided by the caregiver.

Contact Comfort

In classic research on early attachment, psychologist Harry Harlow noticed that newborn rhesus monkeys, when separated from their mothers at birth, attached themselves to soft cuddly objects left in their cages, such as baby blankets. If one of these blankets was removed for cleaning, the monkeys became extremely upset and would cling to it frantically when the blanket was returned. Intrigued, Harlow began a series of experiments in which he isolated newborn monkeys and raised them in cages with a variety of surrogate, or artificial, "mothers" (Harlow & Zimmerman, 1959). In one condition, baby monkeys were raised with a mother made simply of wire mesh and fitted with an artificial nipple

When forced to choose between surrogate mothers, baby monkeys prefer the soft and cuddly one, even when the wire "mother" provides the food.

Nina Leen / Contributor via Getty Images

that delivered food; in another condition, the babies were exposed to a nippleless cloth mother made of wire mesh that had been padded with foam rubber and wrapped in soft terrycloth.

Which of the two surrogate mothers did the monkeys prefer? If early attachments are formed primarily to caregivers who provide nourishment—that is, infants love the one who feeds them—we would expect the monkeys to prefer and cling to the wire mother because it provides the food. But in the vast majority of cases, the monkeys preferred the cloth mother. If startled in some way, perhaps by the introduction of a foreign object into the cage, the monkeys ran immediately to the cloth mother, hung on tight, and showed no interest in the wire mother that provided the food. Harlow and his colleagues concluded that *contact comfort*—the warmth and softness provided by the terrycloth—was the primary motivator of attachment (Harlow et al., 1971).

For obvious reasons, similar experiments have never been conducted with human babies, and one might reasonably question the ethics of using monkeys in this way as well. However, we have every reason to believe that human infants are like rhesus infants in their desire and need for contact comfort. Many studies have looked at how children progress in institutional settings that provide relatively low levels of contact comfort (J. Hodges & Tizard, 1989; Provence & Lipton, 1962; Spitz, 1945). Children reared in orphanages with poor infant-to-caregiver ratios (e.g., one caregiver for every 10 to 20 infants) often show more developmental problems than children reared in less deprived environments (D. R. Shaffer & Kipp, 2010).

Temperament

Given that physical contact is such a necessary part of a secure attachment, what determines whether infants will receive the contact they need? One factor may be a baby's **temperament**, the general level of its emotional reactivity. Difficult or fussy babies tend to get fewer comforting and responsive reactions, and the quality of the attachment between parent and child can suffer as a result (A. Thomas & Chess, 1977). Links also exist between early temperament and various cognitive abilities, particularly language development (e.g., Dixon & Smith, 2000). However, the evidence supporting a direct link between temperament and attachment remains weak at this point (see Groh et al., 2017).

Psychologists who study temperament find that infants can be categorized into types. As you might guess, some babies are easy; they are basically happy, readily establish daily routines, and tend not to get upset very easily. Other babies are difficult; they have trouble accepting new experiences, establishing routines, and maintaining a pleasant mood. Fortunately, only about 10% of

Children's natural temperament can importantly influence the quality of their attachment with a caregiver.

iStockPhoto/RichLegg
iStockPhoto/txking

babies fall into this difficult group, and about 40% of sampled babies are readily classified as easy (A. Thomas & Chess, 1977). The remaining 50% are more difficult to categorize. Some babies are "slow to warm up," which means they roughly fall between easy and difficult and show a mixture of different temperaments.

Psychologists are convinced that these differences in moodiness, or temperament, can't be explained completely by the environment. Babies are probably born easy or difficult, although experience certainly plays a role (Rothbart, 2007; Zwir et al., 2020). If temperament is based in biology, then you might expect it to remain stable across the life span. If you're a moody baby, then you should be a moody adolescent and a moody adult. Research has generally supported this conclusion (Caspi et al., 2005). Infants who seem very shy or inhibited tend to remain so as they age. Identical twins, who share the same genes, also show more similarities in temperament than do fraternal twins or siblings raised in the same home (Saudino, 2009). As you'll see when you read the discussion of personality in Chapter 11, genetic factors influence many aspects of personality, not just temperament.

Types of Attachment

Not all attachments are created equal: There are differences in the bonds that children form with their caregivers. To investigate these differences, psychologists have used a technique called the **strange situation test**. This test classifies 10- to 24-month-old children into four different attachment groups based on the children's reactions to stressful situations (Ainsworth et al., 1978; Ainsworth & Wittig, 1969). After arrival in the lab, the parent and child are ushered into a waiting room filled with toys; the child is encouraged to play with the toys. Various levels of infant stress are then introduced. A stranger might enter the room, or the parent might be asked to step out for a few moments, leaving the child alone. Of main interest to the psychologist are the child's reactions: Initially, how willing is the child to move away from the parent and play with the toys? How much crying or distress does the child show when the parent leaves the room? How does the child react when the parent comes back into the room—does the child greet and cling to the parent, or does the child move away?

Most infants—approximately 60% to 70%—react to the strange situation test with what psychologist Mary Ainsworth called a *secure attachment*. With the parent present, even if the situation is new and strange, these children play happily and are likely to explore the room looking for interesting toys or magazines to shred. But as the level of stress increases, they become increasingly uneasy and clingy. If the mother leaves the room, the child will probably start to cry but will calm down rapidly if the mother returns.

About 10% of children show a pattern called *resistant attachment*; these children react to stress in an ambiguous way, which may indicate a lack of trust for the parent. Resistant children will act wary in a strange situation, refusing to leave their mother's side and explore the room, and they do not deal well with the sudden appearance of strangers. They cry if the mother leaves the room, yet they're unlikely to greet her with affection on her return. Instead, these children act ambivalent: They remain by her side but resist her affections.

A third group of children—about 20% to 25%—show a pattern of *avoidant attachment*. These children show no strong attachment to the mother in any aspect of the strange situation test. They're not particularly bothered by the appearance of strangers in the room, nor do they show much concern when the mother leaves the room or much interest when she returns. Ainsworth discovered that the parents of these children tend to be unresponsive and impatient when it comes to the child's needs and may even actively reject the child on a regular basis (Ainsworth, 1979).

How a child reacts to the strange situation test provides one indication of the type of attachment the child has formed with a caregiver.

Robert Kneschke / Alamy Stock Photo

The final attachment group—about 5% to 8%—is made up of children who show a pattern of *disorganized/disoriented* attachment. These children react to the strange situation test with inconsistent responses. Sometimes they mimic securely attached children; sometimes they react with fear or anxiety to the returning mother. These children appear to have no consistent strategy for interacting with their caregivers.

What determines the kind of attachment a child will form? There's no easy way to tell. The parent–child relationship depends on the personality characteristics of the parent and child and even on the child-rearing practices of the culture. In Japan, caregivers are less likely to encourage independence and exploration because the Japanese culture tends to value group-oriented accomplishments. This, in turn, can affect how attachments develop and are measured. When babies in the United States are raised according to Japanese practices, they are less likely to be labeled as "securely attached" using the criteria listed earlier, presumably because less of an emphasis has been placed on acting independently (see Rothbaum et al., 2000). Psychologists are convinced that attachment behavior is universal, because forming early attachments is critical to survival, but exactly how the attachment is expressed and how it should be appropriately measured may well depend importantly on cultural factors (Rothbaum & Morelli, 2005).

As a final note to parents, the strange situation test is a laboratory procedure, and observations are made under carefully controlled conditions. You need to take care when drawing conclusions based on your own personal experiences. You shouldn't conclude that your child has an avoidant attachment, for example, just because the child might not cry when left at day care. The strange situation test is based not on haphazard observations but on a careful examination of specific behaviors in a controlled setting.

Do Early Attachments Matter Later in Life?

Given that infants can be easily divided into these attachment groups by around age 1, it's reasonable to wonder about the long-term consequences. Are the avoidant children doomed to a life of insecurity and failed relationships? Children with an early secure attachment do seem to have social and intellectual advantages, at least throughout middle and later childhood. For example, secure attachments in infancy have been associated with higher-quality friendships and romantic relationships in adolescence (Collins et al., 2009). Less secure attachments in infancy, such as disorganized attachments, have been linked to behavior problems—aggression and antisocial behavior—later in life (Fearon et al., 2010).

One question is how much attachment to each parent in two-parent families matters compared to the attachment of each parent on its own. Some studies suggest that a secure attachment to just one parent results in later outcomes that are just as good as secure attachments to both parents, and the attachment effect for one parent was similar for secure attachments to mothers and fathers (Dagan & Sagi-Schwartz, 2018). Thus, the long-held belief that the attachment to one's mother is more important than to one's father may not be accurate.

However, early patterns of attachment are not perfect predictors of later behavior. One problem is stability: Sometimes a child who appears to be insecurely attached at 12 months can act quite differently in the strange situation test a few months later (Lamb et al., 1992). In addition, a child who has a particular kind of attachment to one parent may show quite a different pattern to the other. It's also important to remember that when psychologists talk about predicting later behavior based on early attachment patterns, they are referring mainly to correlational studies. As you learned in Chapter 2, it's not possible to draw firm conclusions about causality from simple correlational analyses. The fact that later behavior can be predicted from early attachment patterns does not mean that early bonding necessarily causes the later behavior patterns—other factors might be responsible. Children who form secure attachments in infancy typically have caregivers who remain warm and responsive throughout childhood, adolescence, and adulthood. So, it could be that securely attached infants tend to have successful relationships later in life because they live most of their lives in supportive environments.

Friends and Peers

Early attachments are important. But the relationships formed after infancy, especially during later childhood and adolescence, matter as well. Under the right circumstances, people can counteract negative experiences of infancy or childhood (Lamb et al., 1992). The significance of friendship is a case in point. Psychologists now recognize that a child's social network—the number and quality of the child's friends—can have a meaningful impact on social development and well-being (Berndt, 2004; Hartup & Stevens, 1997).

Children with friends interact more confidently in social situations, they are more cooperative, and they report higher levels of self-esteem (Newcomb & Bagwell, 1995). Children with friends are also less likely to seek help for psychological problems, and they're more likely to be viewed as well adjusted by teachers and adult caretakers. These trends are true for young children and adolescents, and they continue into adulthood (Berndt & Keefe, 1995). When you read Chapter 16, which deals with stress and health, you'll find that social support—particularly

Friends and peers are important determinants of our personal and social development.
iStockPhoto/shironosov

our network of friends—predicts how well we're able to cope and deal with stressful situations and how well we're able to recover from injury   or disease. This is just as true for children as it is for adults.

Obviously, general conclusions   like these need to be qualified a bit. For example, the quality (or closeness) of the friendship matters, but so does the identity of the friends. If you have very close friends who recommend drug use or a life of crime, the developmental consequences obviously will be less than ideal (Dishion & Tipsord, 2011). We also don't know what aspects of friendship matter most. For instance, people often share similarities with their friends (such as common attitudes and values). Does this mean that friends merely play the role of reinforcing our values and making us more secure in our attitudes? In-depth research on friendships is ongoing, in part because psychologists recognize the value of friendship across the life span. When asked to rank what is most important in their lives, children, adolescents, and adults often pick "friends" as the answer.

The way that children and adolescents interact has been changing rapidly with new technology. Interacting online and through social media has become commonplace among children and is more frequent as they enter adolescence. Recent studies suggest that social media is used by over 90% of U.S. teens aged 13–17 (Weinstein, 2018). Social media use seems to have a range of effects on adolescents' emotional well-being, amount of sleep, and connections with peers. For example, in a study surveying over 500 teens, Emily Weinstein (2018) found that social media effects were reported as primarily positive, with interviews with some teens indicating both positive and negative effects on emotional well-being. Some of the reported benefits include staying connected to peers, gaining a sense of belonging, exploring their identity, and having a creative outlet (Nesi, 2020). During the COVID-19 pandemic, with many schools operating online (or not at all for periods of time) and people staying home in many countries, social media became even more important to adolescents' ability to socially connect with friends and extended family. However, some studies have also found that using social media at night is related to teens getting less sleep, later bedtimes, and taking longer to fall asleep (H. Scott & Woods, 2018). While social media use does seem to have both positive and negative effects, we are only beginning to understand how this changing form of peer interaction is affecting development.

Another very important influence—perhaps even more important than number of friends—is the makeup of a child's peer group. Some psychologists believe that acceptance or rejection by the peer group is a more significant influence on later development than the actual rearing practices of the parent (e.g., J. R. Harris, 2009). When you examine language, for instance, children tend to speak like their peers, not like their parents. If a child grows up in a Spanish-speaking home but the child's peers speak English, then that child not only acquires the new language but prefers it. The same is true for behavior—children tend to adapt their behavior to the local norms, at least when they are outside of the home (J. R. Harris, 2009). Exactly what role the parents play in determining social and personality development, outside of the obvious genetic influence, remains controversial among developmental psychologists.

Child Care: What Are the Long-Term Effects?

What about child care and its long-term impact on development? Most parents of preschool children face a dilemma: Do I stay at home and provide full-time care for my child, or do I work outside the home and place my child in child care? In contemporary American society, day care often turns out to be the answer, although it's not always a choice made voluntarily. For many parents, day care has simply become an economic necessity.

Placing a child in day care is an economic necessity for many parents.

iStockPhoto/monkeybusinessimages

What are the long-term consequences of day care? Will leaving our children in the hands of nonparental caretakers, often for many hours a day, have positive or negative long-term effects on their social and mental development? Well, the answer is "it depends." The data are somewhat mixed, and the results (not surprisingly) depend on the quality, quantity, and type of care involved. For example, there is a relationship between the quality of day care and later academic performance. Children who experience high-quality care tend to have slightly higher vocabulary scores in school, at least through the fifth grade, and there is some evidence that day care quality is a predictor of reading skills as well (Belsky et al., 2007; Dearing et al., 2009). At the same time, children who go to day care "centers," as opposed to in-home care, can show more problem behaviors as measured through the sixth grade (Belsky et al., 2007). It is important to understand, though, that these findings do not apply to all children; instead, these are statistical relationships based on the study of large numbers of children who have been tested in well-controlled longitudinal studies.

Psychologists recognize that *day care* has many meanings—the term can refer to anything from occasional babysitting by a neighbor for a few hours a week, to care by nonparental relatives, to extended care by licensed professionals in for-profit day care centers. It's difficult to draw general conclusions. As with most environmental effects, the role that day care plays in the life of a child will depend on many factors, including the individual characteristics of the child, the parents, and the home environment, as well as the quality, type, and quantity of the service provided. There is no firm evidence that regular day care produces widespread negative effects on development—so don't worry too much. And, as noted earlier, it can have significant positive effects, and some studies have suggested that any negative effects do not persist throughout childhood (Haeck et al., 2018). Moreover, importantly, the quality of parenting turns out to be a much stronger and more consistent predictor of development than early child care experiences (Belsky et al., 2007). For some guidelines on choosing a day care facility, see the Practical Solutions feature.

PRACTICAL SOLUTIONS: CHOOSING A DAY CARE CENTER

If you decide to place your child in day care, it's important to choose a high-quality center. As noted in our discussion, you'll find considerable differences in the quality of existing day care facilities. And, importantly, quality does matter: Factors such as the child-to-staff ratio, the size of the child's care group, and the education of the staff have been shown to correlate with measures of cognitive development. Several professional organizations provide recommendations for assessing the quality of child care (e.g., Child Care Services Association; National Association for Family Child Care). We've summarized some of the main recommendations here:

1. *Check the physical environment*. It's a must to visit the center and make sure the physical structure and play environments are safe. For example, are there fences around the grounds? Is the facility clean? Do you see the staff washing their hands regularly? Hands should be washed before and after diapering, after washing surfaces, and before any kind of food preparation. Is the play

equipment well constructed? Look to see if the electrical outlets are covered, and make certain there are no dangerous or toxic substances within reach of the children. Note: If you're blocked in any way from fully examining the environment, go someplace else for care.

2. *Listen and watch.* Spend some time watching the children who are currently enrolled. Do they look happy? Do they interact easily with each other and with the staff? Do the staff speak to the children in a positive and cheerful tone? Is the setting noisy? High noise levels can signal a lack of control on the part of the staff. If possible, also check with other parents and get their perspectives on the quality of the care.

3. *Count group and staff sizes.* As a general rule, the younger the child, the smaller should be the size of the care group. For infants or toddlers, no more than three to four children should be cared for by a single adult. For 2-year-olds, the size can increase to four to six; for 3-year-olds seven to eight; for 4-year-olds eight to nine; for 5-year-olds eight to ten children. If the child-to-staff ratios exceed these guidelines, the quality of your child's care may suffer.

4. *Ask about staff training.* Although legal requirements vary from state to state, it's a good idea to ask whether the center has been accredited by a professional organization. You should also inquire about the staff turnover rate. Qualified staff should have some specific training in early childhood education or child development. A number of studies have shown that caregiver background—specifically college training—influences the quality of the care provided. The better educated the staff, the more likely the children will be given activities that are appropriate for their developmental stage.

   In a perfect world, all parents would be able to pick and choose from among the best child care facilities. Unfortunately, high-quality centers are not always available or are too costly for the average parent or guardian. You can, however, be an active participant in choosing the best possible option. Take your time, use the guidelines listed here, and do your best to maximize a quality environment for your child.

Forming a Personal Identity: Erikson's Crises of Development

Another cornerstone of social development is the formation of **personal identity**—a sense of self, of who you are as an individual and how well you measure up against peers. We recognize that we're unique people, different from others, quite early in our development. Children as young as 6 months will reach out and touch an image of themselves in a mirror; by 18 to 24 months, if they look into a mirror and notice a smudge mark on their nose, they'll reach up and touch their own face (Butterworth, 1992; M. Lewis & Brooks-Gunn, 1979). Infants' reactions to this "mirror test" depend partly on the culture in which they're raised (Broesch et al., 2011), but the initial stirrings of the self-concept are easily seen within the first year or two of life.

Erik Erikson

Bettmann / Contributor via Getty Images

We use social interactions—primarily those with parents during childhood and with peers later in life—to help us come to grips with who we are as individuals. One of the most influential theories of how this process of identity formation proceeds is the stage theory of Erik Erikson. Erikson (1963, 1968, 1982) believed that our sense of self is shaped by a series of psychosocial *crises* that we confront at characteristic stages in development.

Infancy and Childhood

For the first few years of life, babies are largely at the mercy of others for their survival. According to Erikson, this overwhelming dependency leads to our first true psychosocial crisis, usually in the first year of life: trust versus mistrust. Psychologically and practically, babies face an important problem:

Are there people out there in the world who will meet my survival needs? Resolution of this crisis leads to the formation of an initial sense of either trust or mistrust, and the infant begins to understand that people differ. Some people can be trusted, and some can't. It's through social interactions, learning whom to trust and whom not to trust, that the newborn ultimately resolves the crisis and learns how to deal more effectively with the environment.

During the "terrible twos," children struggle with breaking their dependence on parents. The crisis at this point is *autonomy versus shame or doubt*: Am I capable of independent self-control of my actions, or am I generally inadequate? Between the ages of 3 and 6, the crisis turns to *initiative versus guilt*: Can I plan things on my own, with my own initiative, or should I feel guilty for trying to carry out my own bold plans for action? In late childhood, beginning around age 6 and ending at around age 12, the struggle is for a basic sense of *industry versus inferiority*: Can I learn and master new skills, can I be industrious and complete required tasks, or do I lack fundamental competence?

As they develop their own identity, children are learning what tasks they can perform on their own.

iStockPhoto/Sasiistock

What's important in determining how these crises are resolved is the quality of the child's interactions with parents, peers, and other significant role models. If 5-year-old Roberta's parents repeatedly scold her for taking the initiative to get her own drink of milk, she may develop strong feelings of guilt for trying to become independent. According to Erikson, children with highly critical parents or teachers can acquire a self-defeating attitude that carries over later in life. Children who resolve these crises positively learn to trust themselves and their abilities and acquire a strong positive sense of personal identity.

Adolescence and Young Adulthood

By the time adolescence rolls around, we're mature enough intellectually to begin considering personal qualities that are general and abstract. Adolescents are concerned with testing roles and with finding their true identity: Who am I? What kind of person do I really represent? The teenager acts as a kind of personality theorist, attempting to integrate various self-perceptions about abilities and limitations into a single unified concept of self. Erikson (1968) coined the term *identity crisis* to describe this transition period, which he believed can be filled with turmoil.

Observational studies of how adolescents come to grips with the identity crisis reveal individual differences (Offer & Schonert-Reichl, 1992; A. C. Peterson, 1988). Not all teenagers become paralyzed with identity angst and anxiety—most, in fact, show no more anxiety during this transition period than at other points in their lives. Young people also vary widely in how they commit to a particular view of themselves (Marcia, 1966). Some adolescents choose an identity by modeling others: "I'm honest, open, and cooperative because that's the way I was brought up by my parents." Others develop a personal identity through a soul-searching evaluation of their feelings and abilities. Some adolescents even reject the crisis altogether, choosing instead not to commit to any particular view of themselves.

Peers are important in developing our personal identity in adolescence.

iStockPhoto/Stígur Már Karlsson /Heimsmyndir

Adolescence is also a time when peer relationships are highly influential. Although relationships with parents are still important, peer relationships become of greater importance than in childhood (Scholte & van Aken, 2006). However, peer interactions can have both positive and negative effects. For example, positive peer relationships can protect teens from depression, anxiety, and being victims of bullying (Kochel et al., 2017). But, as discussed earlier, use of social media (a common means of interaction among adolescents) can also be linked with negative behaviors, such as substance use and risky sexual behaviors (Vannucci et al., 2020). Loneliness can also occur if peer interactions are of poor quality (e.g., bullying) or are infrequent due to shyness (Woodhouse et al., 2011). For these reasons, peer relationships can affect our self-image and identity during this period.

Entrance into young adulthood is marked by the crisis of *intimacy versus isolation*. Resolution of the identity crisis causes us to question the meaning of our relationships with others: Am I willing or able to form an intimate, committed relationship with another person? Or will my insecurities and fears about losing independence lead to a lifetime of isolation and loneliness? People who lack an integrated conception of themselves, Erikson argued, cannot commit themselves to a shared identity with someone else. Some have argued that this particular conclusion may be more applicable to men than women (Gilligan, 1982). Historically, women have been forced to deal with intimate commitments—raising a family and running a home—either at the same time as or before the process of searching for a stable personal identity. Things are a bit different now, of course, because many women are establishing professional careers prior to marriage. Overall, the average age at which men and women marry has been steadily increasing in the United States in the past few decades. The average marrying age for men has risen from about 26 in 1990 to almost 30 in 2018; for women, it rose from about 24 to almost 28 (U.S. Census Bureau, 2018). It is clear that both men and women are choosing to marry later than they used to, allowing for a longer time period within which young adults can explore their identity.

Adulthood, Middle Age, and Beyond

With the establishment of career and family, the focus shifts to concern about children and future generations: Am I contributing successfully to the community at large? Am I doing enough to ensure the survival and productivity of future generations? Failure to resolve this crisis (*generativity versus stagnation*) can induce a sense of meaninglessness in middle life and beyond—a condition Erikson calls stagnation.

For some people, especially men in their 40s, this point in psychosocial development is marked by soul-searching questions about personal identity reminiscent of those faced in adolescence (R. L. Gould, 1978; Levinson et al., 1978). A "midlife crisis" arises as people begin to confront their own mortality—the inevitability of death—and as they come to grips with the fact that they may never achieve their lifelong dreams and goals. Although this can be an emotionally turbulent period for some, most of the evidence suggests that the midlife crisis is a relatively rare phenomenon. It gets a lot of attention in the media, and it's certainly consuming for those affected, but probably fewer than 5% of people in middle age undergo anything resembling a turbulent midlife crisis (McCrae & Costa, 2003).

The final stage in the process of psychosocial development, which occurs from late adulthood to the point of death, is the crisis of *integrity versus despair*. It's at this point in people's lives, Erikson believed, that they strive to accept themselves and their pasts—both failures and successes. Older people undergo a kind of life review in an effort to resolve conflicts in the past and to find ultimate meaning in their accomplishments. If successful in this objective search for meaning, they acquire wisdom; if unsuccessful, they wallow in despair and bitterness. An important part of the process is the preparation for death and dying, which we'll discuss in more detail near the end of the chapter. See Concept Review 4.4 for an overview of the stages of Erikson's theory.

Evaluating Erikson's Theory

Erikson's stage theory of psychosocial crises has been quite influential in shaping how psychologists view personal identity development (see Steinberg & Morris, 2001). Erikson recognized that people don't simply establish a rigid personal identity around the time they reach Piaget's formal operational stage; the way people view themselves and their relationships changes regularly throughout their lives. Erikson also understood the important role that social and cultural interactions play in shaping human psychology. Human beings don't grow up in a psychological vacuum; the way we think and act is critically influenced by our interactions with others.

CONCEPT REVIEW 4.4
ERIKSON'S STAGES OF PERSONAL IDENTITY DEVELOPMENT

Life Period	Stage	Conflicts Revolve Around . . .
Infancy and childhood	Trust vs. mistrust (first year of life)	Developing a sense of trust in others: Will the people around me fulfill my needs?
	Autonomy vs. shame or doubt ("terrible twos")	Developing a sense of self-control: Am I in charge of my own actions?
	Initiative vs. guilt (ages 3–6)	Developing a sense of one's own drive and initiative: Can I carry out plans? Should I feel guilty for trying to carry out my own plans?
	Industry vs. inferiority (ages 6–12)	Developing a sense of personal ability and competence: Can I learn and develop new skills?
Adolescence and young adulthood	Identity vs. role confusion (adolescence)	Developing a single, unified concept of self, a sense of personal identity: Who am I?
	Intimacy vs. isolation (young adulthood)	Questioning the meaning of our relationships with others: Can I form a committed relationship with another person, or will my personal insecurities lead to isolation?
Adulthood and older adulthood	Generativity vs. stagnation Integrity vs. despair	Concern over whether one has contributed to the success of children and future generations: Have I contributed to the community at large?
		Acceptance of one's life—successes and failures: Am I content, looking back on my life?

Nevertheless, Erikson's theory suffers from the same kinds of problems as any stage theory. Although there may be an orderly sequence of psychosocial crises, overlap occurs across the stages (Whitbourne et al., 1992). Furthermore, like Piaget, Erikson never clearly articulated how a person actually moves from one crisis stage to the next: What are the psychological mechanisms that allow for conflict resolution, and what determines when and how they will operate (Achenbach, 1992)? Finally, Erikson's theory of identity development, although useful as a general organizing framework, lacks enough scientific rigor. His concepts are vague enough to make scientific testing difficult.

Gender-Role Development

In our discussion of Erikson's theory, we touched briefly on the role of gender in establishing personal identity. Women are often forced to struggle with questions about intimacy and relationships before addressing the identity crisis, as the task of establishing a home and rearing children typically falls on their shoulders. But gender is itself a kind of identity; children gain a sense of themselves as male, female, or other quite early in life, and gender identity has a lasting effect on how people behave and on how others behave toward them.

The foundations of *gender identity* are already in place by the age of 2 or 3. Children at this age often recognize that they're either a boy or a girl (or neither), and they start to give stereotypical responses about gender when asked. For example, when shown a picture of an infant labeled as either a boy or a girl, 3-year-olds are more likely to identify the infant "boy" as the one who is strong, big, or hard and the infant "girl" as the one who is weak, small, and soft (C. Miller et al., 2009). Even so, children at this age have not developed sufficiently to recognize gender as a general and abstract characteristic of individuals. They might believe, for instance, that a boy can become a girl by changing hairstyle or clothing (Marcus & Overton, 1978). To view gender as a stable and unchanging condition requires some ability to conserve—to recognize that the qualities of objects remain the same despite superficial changes in appearance. However, even children as young as 2 to 3 years old are influenced by gender stereotypes in their choice of toys (e.g., boys play with trains more than girls, and girls play with dolls and pink toys more than boys) (Wong & Hines, 2015).

By the time children are in elementary school, gender is seen as a permanent condition—"I'm a boy (or a girl or nonbinary), and I always will be." At this point, children tend to follow well-established **gender roles**—specific patterns of behavior consistent with society's dictums. As C. L. Martin and Ruble (2004) noted, children at this age become "gender detectives who search for cues about gender— who should and should not engage in a particular activity, who can play with whom, and why girls and boys are different" (p. 67). Children at this age typically notice when others' behavior violates gender norms they have learned. For example, a boy who shows up with his fingernails painted bright pink might be looked on negatively by his peers. Forms of gender prejudice and discrimination can begin as early as preschool, but children become somewhat more flexible and accepting of gender "violations" as they grow older (C. L. Martin & Ruble, 2009).

As we develop, our ideas about gender roles can change and become more flexible. In the last 10 years or so, gender identity has gone beyond the simple categories of male and female to include nonbinary gender identities that can be further divided in many ways. In a recent survey of adolescents (where "mischievous" inaccurate reports were corrected for), 3.3% of participants identified as nonbinary gender, along with a smaller proportion of respondents identifying with the gender opposite to their reported biological sex (Kaltiala-Heino & Lindberg, 2019). Thus, gender roles are seen as less structured by at least some of today's adolescents. Despite this trend, gender roles can still affect judgments of others' behavior in adulthood. For example, women in supervisory positions in the workplace are often viewed more negatively when they exhibit the same behaviors as men in the same positions (M. J. Williams & Tiedens, 2016). But by considering the power of gender roles on our perceptions of ourselves and others, we can help to mitigate the negative ways in which gender roles affect our treatment of and attitudes about those around us (Ellemers, 2018).

Nature or Nurture?

How do these firm ideas about gender roles develop? Are they due to biological differences between male and female brains, or do they grow out of experience? We discussed this issue in Chapter 3, where we considered the evidence supporting gender-based differences in brain anatomy and functioning. Although hormones released by the endocrine system early in development may account for some gender differences in behavior and thought (Hines, 2011), psychologists also commonly appeal to the environment to explain gender-role development.

According to *social learning* accounts of gender-role development, children learn to act in a masculine or feminine manner because they grow up in environments that reward them for doing so. Parents across the world look for and reward specific kinds of behavior from their male and female children. The socialization process begins the moment the new parents learn the answer to their question, "Is it a boy or a girl?" Parents become preoccupied with dressing Adorable Ginnie in pink bows and Active Glenn in blue. Television and movies continue the process: Children are exposed to hour after hour of people acting in gender-appropriate ways (Matthes et al., 2016). Studies have indicated, for example, that children who watch a lot of television are more likely to prefer toys that are "gender appropriate" than children who watch little television (McGhee & Frueh, 1980).

Growing up in societies with well-defined gender roles helps establish *gender schemas* (S. L. Bem, 1981). A gender schema is an organized set of beliefs and perceptions held about men and women. Gender schemas guide and direct how we view others, as well as our own behavior. We encountered the concept of schemas (or schemata) earlier in the chapter when we talked about Piaget, and we'll have more to say in later chapters about schemas and the role they play in guiding behavior. For the moment, you can think of schemas as little knowledge packages that people carry around inside their heads. Gender schemas are acquired through learning. They set guidelines for behavior, and they help us decide whether actions are appropriate. As you can probably guess, gender schemas are generally adaptive—they help us interpret the behavior of others—but they can lead to inaccurate perceptions of specific individuals and even to discrimination.

GROWING OLD IN SOCIETY

The physical declines that accompany the aging process obviously present new challenges for the developing individual. As the comedian George Burns once famously quipped, "You know you're getting old when you stoop to tie your shoelaces and wonder what else you could do while you're down there." Yet not all the changes that greet us in our older years are negative—far from it. In fact, some kinds of intelligence seem to increase with age (see Chapter 10). Marital satisfaction often grows (Carstensen, 1995), and many elderly people remain actively involved in the community and report high levels of contentment. One survey found that people in their 70s report more confidence in their ability to perform tasks than do people in their 50s (Wallhagen et al., 1992)!

At the same time, there are definite hurdles in the pathways of the elderly, many related to health care. Elderly people need more physical care, require more doctor visits, and can be at an economic disadvantage due to retirement and shrinking savings. Although most elderly adults do not live in nursing homes, many need continuing care. The COVID-19 illness, for example, was a larger concern for older adults than younger adults due to more serious health issues in this group of people infected with the virus. Whatever form it takes, it's likely to be expensive; the costs of nursing homes continue to rise. To make matters worse, the bulk of the costs often must be borne by family members because Medicare (health care for the elderly funded by the federal government in the United States) doesn't cover custodial, or chronic, care. The scope of the problem is troubling, especially as the "graying of America" continues. In the coming decades, as you probably know, there's expected to be a huge increase in the number of people over age 85.

However, many seniors find this period of their lives to be full of freedom—for some, their working years are over, and they have time to pursue hobbies and travel more. For others, work during their later years is highly rewarding and fulfilling. Although cognitive processes tend to slow down and decline, older adults with a physically active lifestyle show less decline in cognitive abilities, lower mortality rates, and lower incidence of neurological disease (Prakash et al., 2015). Thus, growing old is a positive experience for many adults.

Negative stereotypes about the elderly are very often false. Most elderly people are not sick or disabled but live active and productive lives.

iStockPhoto/adamkaz

Ageism

However, one issue the elderly face is **ageism**, or prejudice based on age. We'll discuss the basis for prejudice, and particularly the formation of stereotypes, in detail in Chapter 13. For the moment, it is enough for you to understand that we all have beliefs about the traits and behaviors of individuals belonging to different groups. Elderly people comprise such a group, and our attitudes and beliefs toward them can affect their ability to cope with the problems of everyday life.

Stereotypes about the elderly are complex and depend on cultural factors and the age of the individual holding the stereotype, but surveys often reveal beliefs that are inaccurate. Palmore (1990) has listed some of the more common myths, including the belief that most elderly people are sick, in mental decline, disabled and therefore unable to work, isolated and lonely, and depressed. In each of these cases, the negative stereotype is misleading or simply not true. Most elderly people are not sick or disabled, and as mentioned earlier, the elderly may often be more contented and less prone to depression than younger people (Lawton et al., 1992; Palmore, 1990). Not surprisingly, negative stereotypes can lead to negative consequences, including the fact that older people are generally evaluated less positively and may be subject to job discrimination (J. L. Macdonald & Levy, 2016).

Some psychologists believe that prejudice toward the elderly arises partly from our anxiety about death (Martens et al., 2005). Terror management theory proposes that each of us is threatened by the idea of dying, and we defend ourselves against the threat by attempting to suppress thoughts about death and by avoiding things that remind us of our mortality (see Pyszczynski et al., 2015). The elderly serve as symbols of our mortality and also of our impending physical decline, which helps feed the negative stereotypes. If college students are asked open-ended questions about death, they subsequently view themselves as less similar to the elderly, and they rate the attitudes of the elderly in a more negative light (Martens et al., 2004).

However, as you'll learn in Chapter 13, stereotypes can be quite adaptive. Like schemas, stereotypes help us organize and make predictions about the world. Not all of the beliefs that accompany stereotypes are negative. For example, people tend to believe that the elderly are kinder, wiser, and more dependable, and have more personal freedom, than younger people (Palmore, 1990). Stereotypic beliefs such as these, although not necessarily accurate, can lead to a kind of favorable discrimination that helps to counteract the negative stereotypes mentioned previously. One of the lessons of social psychology is that how we view others is often tied to our expectations; age can be a powerful determinant of what those expectations will be.

Death and Dying

As we close our discussion of the developmental process, it's fitting that we turn our attention to the final stage of life: death and dying. As just noted, research suggests that people are threatened by death and thoughts about death. It's the process of death that troubles us the most—the unpredictability, the uncertainty, the inability to understand what the end will be like. There are many psychological aspects to death and the dying process, including how people come to grips with their own mortality and how they grieve and accept the loss of others.

Elisabeth Kübler-Ross (1969, 1974) proposed that people progress through five distinct psychological stages as they face death. Based on interviews with hundreds of terminally ill patients, she found that people react to their own impending death via a characteristic sequence: (1) *denial*—"There must be some terrible mistake"; (2) *anger*—"Why is this happening to me?"; (3) *bargaining*—"What can I do to stop this terrible thing?"; (4) *depression*—"Blot out the sun because all is lost"; and (5) *acceptance*—"I am ready to die." As a stage theorist, Kübler-Ross believed that people move through each of these five stages, from denial to acceptance, as a normal part of their emotional acceptance of death.

Kübler-Ross's views on the dying process have been highly influential, in both psychological and medical circles, and rightly so. She was one of the first people to treat the topic of dying thoroughly and systematically. She sensitized legions of physicians to the idea that denial, anger, and depression are normal reactions to dying that should be treated with respect rather than dismissed out of hand. Yet, many psychologists question whether people progress through a fixed set of orderly stages in exactly the way Kübler-Ross described. Not all dying people move through distinct emotional stages, and even if they do, the stages don't seem to follow any set order. Stages might be skipped, be experienced out of order, or alternate, with the person being angry one day and accepting the next.

Many psychologists find it more appropriate to talk about *dying trajectories*. A dying trajectory is the psychological path people travel as they face their impending death. Different people show different trajectories, and the shape and form of the path depend on the illness as well as on the personality of the patient (Bortz, 1990; Glaser & Strauss, 1968). Trajectories are preferred to stages because stages imply that all people react to impending death in fixed and characteristic ways. But there is no right or wrong way to deal with dying—some people may react with anger and denial, others with calm acceptance. Witnesses to the dying process can best serve the dying by offering support and allowing individuals to follow their own unique path.

End-of-Life Decisions

We end the chapter with a little controversy: the decision-making processes that surround the end of life. Should people have the right to control how and when they die, especially if they're faced with a poor quality of life (e.g., constant pain, immobility, or dependency)? Is suicide, assisted suicide, or the termination of medical intervention justified under any circumstance? In some sense, these are legal and ethical questions rather than psychological ones, but questions about controlling the end of life occupy the attention of many people, especially the elderly. In addition, assisting individuals with ending their life in some situations is now legal in Canada, Belgium, the Netherlands, Australia, and some parts of the United States, so it is important to understand what the psychological effects of these choices are.

Little research has been conducted on the psychological factors that influence end-of-life decisions. It seems likely that religious convictions, value systems, life satisfaction, and even fear of death play a role in how people feel about end-of-life options. A study by Cicirelli (1997) confirms these expectations. Older adults, ranging in age from 60 to 100, were asked their views of various end-of-life options. Each person was given sample decision situations such as the following: Mrs. Lee is an elderly widow who has terminal bone cancer. She has had chemotherapy to try to cure the cancer, but it has not helped her, and the side effects from the chemotherapy itself have been difficult to deal with. She is slowly getting worse, and the pain is unbearable. Drugs for pain help some but leave her in a stupor.

The participants were then asked to make judgments about various end-of-life options, such as strive to maintain life, refuse medical treatment or request that it be removed, commit suicide, or allow someone else to the make the decision about terminating life. Cicirelli (1997) found that people were often willing to endorse more than one option, but the majority opinion was to strive to continue life (51% of the participants endorsed this view). Psychosocial factors, such as religious convictions and fear of death, played a significant role in the decision-making process (see also Cicirelli, 2011).

Death can mean many different things to the elderly (Cicirelli, 2002). For some older adults, death is associated with the beginning of the afterlife; for others, it means complete extinction or annihilation. Not surprisingly, how one interprets death influences everyday living, reactions to death, and preparations for death. For those who believe that death provides the opportunity to be reunited with deceased friends and family in an afterlife, stressful end-of-life decisions are often easier to make. The fact that the elderly hold so many different personal meanings of death suggests that it will be difficult for society to reach consensus about the difficulties that surround end-of-life decisions.

Aging of the Population

Research on aging continues to grow as the population of the world continues to age. Since the 1960s, the proportion of the world's population that is aged 65 or older has grown from 5% to 9% and is predicted to be as large as 16% by the year 2050 (Population Reference Bureau, 2018). Some research suggests that as older adults make up more of the population, attitudes toward older adults are changing, particularly in countries that have traditionally been thought to hold high opinions of older adults, like East Asian countries (North & Fiske, 2015). In 2020, COVID-19 affected the elderly particularly hard, and scientists are still trying to understand why. Thus, it is important that we understand how aging affects social, cognitive, and emotional well-being and prepare for a future in which older adults will make up larger segments of the population.

KNOWLEDGE CHECK 4.3

Now test your knowledge about social and personal development by answering the following questions. (You will find the answers in the Appendix.)

1. The strange situation test is often used to study attachment. Identify the type of attachment that best characterizes the following reactions. Choose avoidant, resistant, secure, or disorganized/disoriented.

    a. When Mom leaves the room, the child begins to cry but calms down rapidly when she returns: ____

    b. When Mom leaves the room, the child couldn't care less. There is little reaction or interest when she returns: ____

    c. When Mom leaves the room, the child cries; when Mom returns, the child remains close by but pushes her away when she tries to show affection: ____

    d. When Mom is in the room, the child refuses to leave her side and does not react well to the sudden appearance of strangers: ___

2. According to Erik Erikson, adolescents face a psychosocial crisis called identity versus role confusion. Current research suggests that
    a. this is a time of rebellion for all adolescents.
    b. Erikson made a mistake—no such crisis occurs.
    c. the identity crisis has mostly a genetic basis.
    d. not all teenagers suffer anxiety during this period.

3. Gender identity doesn't develop until a child enters elementary school—it's only at that point that gender roles begin to exert an effect. *True or False?*

4. Which of the following statements about the elderly and growing old in society are true, and which are false?
    a. Most elderly people are sick and disabled. *True or False?*
    b. Stereotypes about the elderly are always harmful. *True or False?*
    c. Most elderly people have little, if any, confidence in their abilities. *True or False?*
    d. The elderly, on average, would rather die than suffer the consequences of a painful and terminal disease. *True or False?*

THE PROBLEMS SOLVED: WHY DO WE DEVELOP THE WAY WE DO?

As we grow from infancy through childhood to adulthood, fundamental changes occur in physical, intellectual, and social functioning. Most of these changes serve adaptive functions. We're not biological machines, predestined to develop in fixed and inflexible ways from birth. Instead, we're born with a genetic recipe that mixes innate potential with the rigors and demands of the environment. It's nature via nurture, and the final product is a better-functioning person, someone who is fine-tuned to the environment.

In many ways, this chapter acts as a concise summary of the topics you'll encounter throughout the book. Understanding human development requires that we take into account all aspects of the psychology of the individual: how people change physically; learn to perceive, think, and remember; and develop socially.

Developing Physically

We begin life as a fertilized egg, or zygote, which contains genetic material packed into chromosomes received from the mother and father. During the prenatal period, we develop rapidly and are especially susceptible to environmental influences. Infancy and childhood are marked by rapid growth in height and weight and by a further maturing of the nervous system. One of the by-products of nerve cell maturation is motor development, the major milestones of which—crawling, standing alone, walking—tend to occur at similar times for most people, in part because the nervous system develops systematically.

As we move through adolescence and into early adulthood, our physical systems continue to change. During puberty people mature sexually and experience hormone-driven changes in physical appearance. Once people reach their 20s, their bodies become mature, and most begin a gradual decline in physical ability. Some declines occur in mental ability over time, especially in old age, although significant losses in mental functioning are the exception, not the rule.

Developing Intellectually

Psychologists use the term *cognitive development* to refer to changes in intellectual functioning that accompany physical aging. Newborns have remarkably well-developed tools for investigating the world around them: They can see, hear, smell, feel, and taste, although not at the same level as they will in later childhood. We leave infancy with well-developed perceptual systems and use the experiences of childhood to help fine-tune our sensory equipment.

Much of what we know about thought processes during infancy and childhood comes from the work of Jean Piaget. Piaget's theory of cognitive development proposes that children use mental models of the world—called schemata—to guide and interpret ongoing experience. Central to the theory is the idea that as children grow and acquire new experiences, their mental models of the world change. Piaget believed that children pass through a series of cognitive stages (sensorimotor, preoperational, concrete operational, and formal operational), each characterized by unique ways of thinking. Lawrence Kohlberg also proposed a stage theory, suggesting that individuals pass through levels of moral development that differ in the extent to which moral actions are seen as being driven by immediate external consequences or by general abstract principles. Not all psychologists agree that cognitive development progresses through fixed stages, but it's clear that qualitative differences in cognitive ability do occur over the course of development.

Developing Socially and Personally

Our relationships with others help us solve problems that arise throughout development. Infants form attachments to gain the nourishment they need for survival. Both infant and caregiver are active participants in the attachment process and are prepared to respond, given the right kinds of environmental events, with mutual bonding. Mary Ainsworth identified several categories of attachment based on the strange situation test. In general, the responsiveness of the parent early in life influences, but does not absolutely determine, the relationships formed by the child later in life.

Another aspect of social development is the formation of personal identity. Erik Erikson argued that personal identity is shaped by a series of psychosocial crises over the life span. During infancy and childhood, we address questions about our basic abilities and independence and learn to trust or mistrust others. During adolescence and adulthood, we deal with the identity crisis and come to grips with our roles as participants in intimate relationships. In later years, we struggle with questions of accomplishment, concern for future generations, and meaning. Other important components of social development include learning gender roles, growing old in society, and confronting the important stages and decisions of dying.

THINKING ABOUT RESEARCH

A summary of a research study in psychology is given in this section. As you read the summary, think about the following questions:

1. Which developmental research design (longitudinal or cross-sectional) does this study adhere to most closely? Explain your answer.
2. Why do you think the researchers chose to look at the age range of 12 to 15 in this study? What kinds of developmental issues are children dealing with in this range?
3. Imagine the researchers had broadened their sample to teens from other countries beyond those tested. What effects do you think there would be of culture on the results of the study?
4. Although not considered in this study, do you think attachment style of the children would affect the relationship between screen time and well-being? Why or why not?

Article Reference: Orben, A., & Przybylski, A. K. (2019). Screens, teens, and psychological well-being: Evidence from three time-use-diary studies. *Psychological Science, 30*, 682–696.

Purpose of the Study: The topic of screen time for children and adolescents is often discussed in the media and elsewhere; yet, the effects of screen time on young people's psychological health and well-being are not well understood. Previous studies have produced inconsistent findings regarding negative effects of screen time and have not provided the best measures of actual screen time in the participants. The current study was designed to address these issues using data sets that more accurately measure screen time in children aged 12 to 15. The researchers predicted that higher levels of screen time use would be related to lower levels of well-being.

Method of the Study: Researchers analyzed three existing data sets. Although data were collected from the participants multiple times in each data set, the researchers only used the most recent measurement from each data set. The first data set was collected from participants in Ireland, mostly aged 13 for approximately 4,500 individuals. These data were collected in 2011 and 2012. The second data set was collected from participants in the United States who were aged 12 to 15. There were nearly 800 individuals in this data set, and it was collected in 2014 and 2015. The third data set was collected from more than 8,000 participants in the United Kingdom aged 13 to 15 in 2015. Screen time was measured from diaries kept during the study by the participants of the amount of time they spent on different forms of technology outside of school (video games, TV and videos, etc.) and from their reports from memory of their screen time. Data were also collected on various behaviors (prosocial behaviors, inattention, etc.), emotional states (depression), and self-esteem, although measures varied by data set.

Results of the Study: The results of the study showed a small negative relationship between screen time and well-being (i.e., as screen time increases, well-being decreases) in some of the data sets, but the relationships were smaller than expected by the researchers in most cases. Further, no relationship was found between screen time and well-being when they examined screen time before bedtime; only a small negative effect was found in the one hour before bedtime data in the U.S. sample.

Conclusions of the Study: From these results, the authors concluded that there is little evidence that higher levels of screen time relate to lower well-being in teens. They also suggested that future studies include the most accurate measures of screen time as possible to allow researchers to draw stronger conclusions from the data.

KNOWLEDGE CHECK: CHAPTER SUMMARY

You will find the answers in the Appendix.

DEVELOPING PHYSICALLY

- Life begins with the fertilized egg, or (1) ___. The (2) ___ period is from conception to (3) ___ of the zygote in the uterine wall. The next six weeks are the (4) ___ period. The (5) ___ period includes development of the skeletal and muscular systems, and lasts from the ninth week of gestation until birth.

- The average newborn weighs about (6) ___ pounds and is about 20 inches long. A newborn's brain shows (7) ___; that is, changes are constantly occurring in the neural circuitry. The sequence of development from lifting the head to walking alone is stable and (8) ___ across cultures. As the infant progresses from crawling to walking, the nervous system develops from the head down and from the center out.

- Past toddlerhood, general processing speed and coordination improve greatly. (9) ___ is an important physical and (10) ___ transition period that features growth spurts and the onset of (11) ___.

- By our 20s, we are (12) ___ mature and at the height of our physical prowess. Reaching adulthood, however, is in some sense a mental rather than a physical state. Small physical declines begin to occur in the 20s. Some people eventually suffer brain degeneration with age, but fewer than 1% of people aged 65 are afflicted with (13) ___, or physically based loss in mental functioning.

DEVELOPING INTELLECTUALLY

- In the (14) ___ technique, an infant is presented with two visual displays simultaneously, and the researcher notes how long the baby looks at each one. Researchers also use (15) ___, the decline in responsiveness to repeated stimulation, to investigate infants' preferences and abilities. Insight into infants' abilities can also be gained by (16) ___ simple motor movements.

- Newborns' (17) ___ systems function reasonably well. Infants prefer some colors and (18) ___; they recognize their mothers' voices a day or two after birth; they are sensitive to smell, taste, and touch; and they seem to perceive the world in three dimensions.

- The elderly commonly report memory problems, and evidence suggests that some kinds of memory do falter with age, but most do not. Age-related memory deficits appear to depend on the particular type of (19) ___ task being used.

- Piaget believed that everyone has a natural tendency to organize the world meaningfully, and that to do so we use (20) ___, or mental models of the world. Cognitive development is guided by (21) ___ (fitting new experiences into existing schemata), and (22) ___ (modifying existing schemata to accommodate new experiences). Piaget proposed four basic stages of cognitive development: (23) ___, (24) ___, (25) ___, and (26) ___ operational.

- At the (27) ___ level, decisions about right and wrong are based primarily on external consequences. At the (28) ___ level, children justify their actions on the basis of internalized rules and on whether an action will maintain or disrupt the social order. At the (29) ___ level, morality is based on abstract principles—such as right and wrong—that may at times conflict with accepted standards.

DEVELOPING SOCIALLY AND PERSONALLY

- Some researchers believe that a newborn is preprogrammed to respond to environmental signals with (30) ___ behavior. Early attachments are formed primarily on the basis of (31) ___ comfort rather than nourishment. (32) ___, an individual type of emotional reactivity, is also an important factor. Attachment bonds have been investigated with the (33) ___ situation test, in which the child is observed reacting to a gradually developed stressful situation. Most children show (34) ___ attachment, though some show resistant, (35) ___, or disorganized/disoriented attachments.

- Erikson believed that personal identity is shaped by a series of (36) ___ crises. During infancy and childhood, these involve trust versus mistrust, (37) ___ versus shame or doubt, initiative versus guilt, and industry versus (38) ___. During adolescence and young adulthood, we experience identity versus (39) ___ confusion.

- Gender identity is usually in place by the time a child is 2 or 3. By the time children are in grade school, they tend to act in accordance with (40) ___. Our sexual perceptions and behaviors are directed by gender (41) ___.

- (42) ___ is prejudice based on a person's age. That the elderly are sick, depressed, or in mental decline are common (43) ___, although the elderly do face the challenges of physical decline.

- Kübler-Ross proposed that the terminally ill pass through five (44) ___ as they approach death: denial, anger, (45) ___, depression, and acceptance. Many psychologists prefer to speak of dying trajectories, the individual paths that are traveled on the way to death.

CRITICAL THINKING QUESTIONS

1. Given that the environment plays such an important role in shaping brain development, what advice would you give new parents to maximize enriched development of their baby's intellectual capabilities?

2. How might you test the idea that mental activity or exercise helps to counteract the decline in mental skills that occurs with age? Can you make predictions based on choice of profession? Should people who choose intellectually challenging professions show less mental decline with age?

3. Do you think Piaget's insights about cognitive development have any implications for education? For example, should teachers be giving first- and second-grade children abstract math problems to solve?

4. Based on what you've learned about moral development, what advice would you give parents who are trying to teach their children about right and wrong?

5. Do you think the findings of the strange situation test would change if the test was conducted in the child's home? Why or why not?

6. How well do Erikson's ideas describe your own personal identity development? Are you going through any fundamental crisis now, or are you aware of having solved one in the past?

7. Do you think that society should work hard to eliminate specific gender roles? Do you believe that people with different genders can be taught to think and act similarly?

KEY TERMS

accommodation (p. 116)

ageism (p. 138)

assimilation (p. 116)

attachments (p. 126)

concrete operational period (p. 119)

conventional level (p. 124)

cross-sectional design (p. 113)

dementia (p. 109)

development (p. 100)

egocentrism (p. 118)

embryonic period (p. 101)

fetal period (p. 102)

formal operational period (p. 120)

gender roles (p. 137)

germinal period (p. 101)

habituation (p. 112)

longitudinal design (p. 113)

menopause (p. 109)

morality (p. 123)

object permanence (p. 117)

personal identity (p. 133)

postconventional level (p. 124)

preconventional level (p. 124)

preoperational period (p. 117)

principle of conservation (p. 118)

puberty (p. 106)

reflexes (p. 104)

schemata (p. 115)

sensorimotor period (p. 116)

strange situation test (p. 129)

temperament (p. 128)

teratogens (p. 102)

theory of mind (p. 118)

zygote (p. 101)

5 SENSATION AND PERCEPTION

Have you ever stared at a Necker cube? Take a look at Figure 5.1 for a minute or so. Notice the lines, the angles, the colors. Each remains fixed on the page—how could it be otherwise? But the cube itself shifts its shape from moment to moment to moment. For a time, the shaded surface of the image forms the front of the cube; in the blink of an eye, magically, it shifts and forms the rear. You see it first from one perspective, and then from another. How is this possible, given that the picture remains fixed? What does it tell us about the world of inner experience?

FIGURE 5.1 ■
The Necker Cube

We're constantly bombarded by messages from the environment. Some arrive as light energy, such as the words you see printed on this page; others, like the spoken sounds of language, arrive as regular changes in air pressure over time. Ultimately, these messages are translated into an electrochemical language for delivery deep within the brain. The products of this translation process, and their subsequent interpretation, serve as the focus of this chapter. It is through sensation and perception that we construct the world of immediate experience.

To understand the difference between the psychological terms *sensation* and *perception*, return momentarily to the Necker cube. It's a geometric figure, a cube, but it can be described in other ways as well. It's made up of lines, angles, patterns of light and dark, colors, and so on. These elementary features—the building blocks of the meaningful image—are processed by the visual system through reasonably well-understood biological systems, and the products are visual sensations. Psychologists have historically thought of **sensations**—such as a pattern of light and dark, a bitter taste, or a change in temperature—as the fundamental, elementary components of an experience. **Perception**, on the other

The basic components of this object—lines, angles, colors—are organized by the girl's visual system into a recognizable cube.

Indiapicture / Alamy Stock Photo

hand, is the collection of processes used to arrive at a meaningful interpretation of those sensations. The simple components are organized into a recognizable form—here, obviously, you perceive a cube.

In the case of the Necker cube, though, the message delivered to the brain is ambiguous. There's more than one interpretation of the physical image, so the brain engages in a perceptual dance, shifting from one interpretation to the other and then back again. What you see, therefore, is not necessarily a faithful reflection of what the world presents; instead, you see an interpretation, or perception, of the message delivered by the physical world. As we'll discuss shortly, sometimes the brain gets it wrong altogether—in those cases, perceptual illusions are produced.

THE PROBLEMS TO BE SOLVED: BUILDING THE WORLD OF EXPERIENCE

To understand how it all works, we must consider how the brain solves three fundamental problems that cut across all the sensory systems. Regardless of whether we're dealing with vision, hearing, touch, smell, or taste, the brain needs to figure out a way to translate the incoming message, identify the key components of the message, and produce a stable interpretation (see Figure 5.2). Keep these three problems in mind as you discover why our sensory systems work the way they do.

Translating the Message

As you learned in Chapter 3, communication in the nervous system is electrochemical. When the world "talks" to the brain, however, the messages arrive in forms that are not electrochemical. For example, you see with light, which arrives in the form of electromagnetic energy; you hear by interpreting sound vibrations or repetitive changes in air pressure. In a sense, it's like trying to listen to someone who speaks a language you don't understand. The brain needs an interpreter—a process through which the incoming message can be changed into an understandable form.

Identifying the Message Components

Once the message has been successfully translated—appearing now in the form of neural impulses—the message components must be extracted or pulled out of the complex sensory pattern. To solve this problem, the newly formed sensory code is delivered to processing stations deep within the brain. Along each pathway, which differs for each of the sensory systems, are specialized regions that perform specific sensory functions.

FIGURE 5.2 ■ Adaptive Problems of Sensation and Perception

To build an internal representation of the outside world, the brain solves three fundamental adaptive problems for each of its sensory systems: (1) It translates messages from the environment into the language of the nervous system; (2) it identifies the elementary components of the messages, such as colors, sounds, simple forms, and patterns of light and dark; and (3) it builds a stable interpretation of those components once they've been identified.

Translating the Message

Identifying the Message Components

Producing Stable Interpretations

Monica Wierzbicki/Body Scientific Intl.

Producing Stable Interpretations

How do these message components, represented as the activities of many thousands of neurons, combine to produce perceptual experiences? You see objects, not patterns of colors, light and dark; you hear melodies, not sequences of irregularly timed sounds. The biological bases of perception—the processes that produce the interpretation—are still poorly understood, but the brain uses certain principles of organization, along with existing knowledge, to help construct the world of experience.

VISION: THE WORLD OF COLOR AND FORM

Let's begin with vision: our sense of sight. To understand vision, it's first necessary to understand how the physical message—*light*—is translated into the electrochemical language of the brain. Next, we'll trace the brain pathways that are used to identify the basic components of the visual message once it's been translated (e.g., lines and colors). Finally, we'll tackle the topic of visual perception: How does the brain create its stable interpretation of the light information it receives?

Vision involves translating light into the electrochemical language of the brain.

iStockPhoto/AleksandarNakic

Translating the Message

Light is a form of electromagnetic energy. Visible light is a small part of an electromagnetic spectrum that includes other energy forms, such as X-rays, ultraviolet rays, and even radio and television waves (see Figure 5.3). Visible light is typically classified by three physical properties. The first is *wavelength*, which corresponds to the physical distance from one energy cycle to the next. Changes in the wavelength of light are generally experienced as changes in color, or **hue**. As shown in Figure 5.3, our visual system is sensitive to wavelengths ranging from about 400 to 700 nanometers (billionths of a meter). These wavelengths are experienced as colors ranging roughly from violet to red. The second property is *intensity*, or amplitude, which is determined by the amount of light falling on an object. Changes in intensity are generally experienced as increases or decreases in **brightness**. Finally, the *purity* of the light, which is determined by the mix of wavelengths present, can influence the saturation, or richness, of perceived colors.

FIGURE 5.3 ■ Light and the Electromagnetic Spectrum

Visible light is actually only a small part of the electromagnetic spectrum, which includes such other energy forms as X-rays and radio and TV waves. Changes in the wavelength of light from about 400 to 700 nanometers are experienced as changes in color; short wavelengths are seen as violets and blues; medium wavelengths as yellows and greens; and long wavelengths as reds.

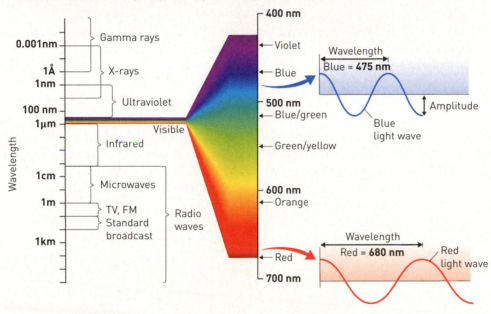

Monica Wierzbicki/Body Scientific Intl.

Light comes from a source, such as the sun or a light bulb, and enters the eye after bouncing off objects in its path. Most of the time, light is a mixture of many different wavelengths. After hitting an object, some of these wavelengths are absorbed—which ones depends on the physical properties of the object—and the remaining wavelengths reflect outward, where they eventually enter the eyes. It is here that the important translation process, called **transduction**, actually occurs.

Entering the Eye

The first step in the translation process is to direct the light toward the light-sensitive receptor cells at the back of each eye. When light bounces off an object, the reflected wavelengths are scattered about. They need to be brought into focus for a clear image to be processed. The focusing process is accomplished by the **cornea**, the protective outer layer of the eye, and by the **lens**, a clear, flexible piece of tissue that sits behind the pupil.

As shown in Figure 5.4, light first passes through the cornea and the pupil before traveling through the lens. Your **pupil** is, in fact, a hole in a ring of tissue called the **iris**. The iris gives the eye its distinctive color (a person with green eyes has green irises), but the color of the iris plays no real role in vision.

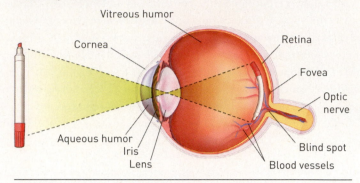

FIGURE 5.4 ■ The Human Eye

Light enters the eye through the cornea, pupil, and lens. As the lens changes shape in relation to the distance of the object, the reflected light is focused at the back of the eye where, in the retina, the visual message is translated.

Carolina Hrejsa/Body Scientific Intl.

Relaxing or tightening the muscles around the iris changes the size of the pupil, thereby regulating the amount of light that enters the eye. In dim light, the pupil gets larger, which allows more light to get in; in bright light, the pupil gets smaller, allowing less light to enter.

The lens focuses the light on the sensory receptors, which are at the back of the eye, much as the lens in an analog camera focuses light on film. But when you focus light in a camera, you change the distance between the lens and the film. Focusing the human eye is accomplished by changing the shape of the lens itself. This process, known as **accommodation**, is influenced by the distance between the lens and the object being viewed. When an object is far away, the lens is relatively long and thin; as the object moves closer, muscles attached to the lens contract, and the lens becomes thicker and rounder. You lose some of this flexibility with age, which makes the accommodation process much harder. This is one of the reasons people typically require reading glasses or bifocals when they reach middle age. The corrective lenses in the glasses help the accommodation process, which the eyes can no longer successfully perform on their own.

By the way, you may have noticed in Figure 5.4 that the image on the retina is inverted, or upside down. This may seem strange, given that we don't see an upside-down world. The inverted image is created by the optical properties of the lens. It tells us, yet again, that our perceptual world is built mainly in our brains. The main function of the eyes is to solve the translation problem and to pass the information to the brain. The brain later corrects the inversion problem, and we see a stable, orderly, and right-side-up world.

Rods and Cones

Light completes its journey when it reaches a thin layer of tissue, called the **retina**, that covers the back of the eye. It is here that the electromagnetic energy gets translated into the inner language of the brain. Embedded in the retina of each eye are about 126 million light-sensitive receptor cells that *transduce*, or change, the light energy into electrochemical impulses. The translation process is chemically based. Each of the receptor cells contains a photopigment that reacts to light. The light causes a chemical reaction that ultimately leads to a neural impulse. Thus, what begins as a pattern of electromagnetic information ends as a pattern of electrochemical signals: the language of the brain.

There are two types of receptor cells contained in the retina, **rods** and **cones**. Of the roughly 126 million receptor cells within each eye, about 120 million are rods, and 6 million are cones. Each receptor type is named for its visual appearance—rods are generally long and thin, whereas cones are short, thick, and tapered to a point. Rods are more sensitive to light than cones; they can generate visual signals when very small amounts of light strike their surface. This makes rods useful at night and in any situation in which the overall level of illumination is low. Rods also tend to be concentrated along the periphery, or sides, of the retina. This is one reason dim images can sometimes be seen better out of the corners of your eyes. (Did you ever notice this?) Cones are concentrated in the very center of the retina, bunched in a small central pit called the **fovea** (which means "central pit"). Unlike rods, cones need relatively high levels of light to operate efficiently. Cones are used for processing fine detail, an ability called **visual acuity**. Cones also play an extremely important role in the early processing of color, as you'll see later in the chapter.

Processing in the Retina

Once the neural impulse is generated by a rod or a cone, it's passed along to other cells in the retina, particularly *bipolar cells*, which feed information from the receptors to *ganglion cells* (see Figure 5.5). Even at this early stage in visual processing, cells in the retina are beginning to "interpret" the incoming visual message. Each ganglion cell has a **receptive field**, which means it receives input from a group of receptor cells and responds only when a pattern of light shines across the retina.

This concept of a receptive field is very important. The fact that a cell, such as a ganglion cell, receives input from several receptor cells means it can pass on more complex information to the brain. Many cells in the retina have *center–surround* receptive fields, as shown in Figure 5.6. In this case, if light falls into the "center" of the cell's receptive field, it reacts by increasing the number of neural signals it sends to the brain. In contrast, if light falls on the sides of its receptive field, the cell will stop sending signals or decrease its firing rate. By detecting the firing rate, the brain determines how light is spread out across the retina and identifies where light stops and starts. This allows us, among other things, to detect *edges*.

Each human retina contains two types of photoreceptor cells: rods and cones. As shown in this color-enhanced photo, the rods are rod shaped in appearance, and the cones are cone shaped.

Louise Hughes / Science Source

FIGURE 5.5 ■ Rods, Cones, and Receptive Fields

Rods and cones send signals to other cells in the retina. Ganglion cells in the fovea, which receive input from cones, tend to have smaller receptive fields than cells located in the sides of the retina, which receive input from rods. This helps to explain why we see fine detail better in the fovea and why we see better out of the sides of our eyes when light levels are low.

Ganglion cells

Fibers to optic nerve

Bipolar cells

Rods

Cones

Carolina Hrejsa/Body Scientific Intl.

FIGURE 5.6 ■ **Center–Surround Receptive Fields**

Receptive fields in the retina often have a center–surround arrangement. Light falling in the center of the field has an opposite effect from light falling in the surround. (a) Light in the center of the field produces an excitatory response (green). (b) Light falling in the surround produces an inhibitory response (purple). (c) When light falls equally in both regions, there is no net increase in the cell's activity compared to its no-light baseline activity level. This kind of receptive field helps the brain detect edges.

A   Light in center: increased rate of firing

B   Light in surround: decreased rate of firing

C   Light in both center and surround: cell fires at roughly its baseline rate

Carolina Hrejsa/Body Scientific Intl.

The visual signals eventually leave the retina, en route to the deeper processing stations of the brain, through a collection of nerve fibers (the axons of ganglion cells) called the *optic nerve*. The optic nerve consists of roughly 1 million axons that wrap together to form a visual transmission cable. Because of its size, at the point where the optic nerve leaves each retina, there is no room for visual receptor cells. This creates a biological **blind spot** because there are no receptor cells in this location. Interestingly, people normally experience no holes in their visual field; as part of its interpretation process, the visual system fills in the gaps to create a continuous visual scene. You can locate your blind spot by following the exercise described in Figure 5.7.

FIGURE 5.7 ■ **The Blind Spot**

To experience your blind spot, simply close your left eye and focus with your right eye on the boy's face. Then hold this book only a few inches from your eyes and slowly move it away until the pie mysteriously disappears. Notice that your brain fills in the spot—complete with the checkerboard pattern.

Monica Wierzbicki/Body Scientific Intl.

Dark Adaptation

Another phenomenon that's linked to processing in the retina is dark adaptation. When we first enter a darkened room, we can't see much of anything (anyone who has ever gone out for popcorn during a movie knows this phenomenon). Gradually, over a span of about 20 to 25 minutes, our eyes adjust. This process is called **dark adaptation**. It's caused by a depletion–regeneration process in the rods and cones as you move from light to dark environments. Remember, visual transduction occurs when light reacts chemically with photopigments in the receptor cells. In bright light, many of these photopigments break down, or become "bleached," and are no longer useful for generating a neural impulse. When you enter a dark movie theater from a bright environment, many of your receptor cells still have their photopigments depleted and cannot yet detect the low levels of light. The photopigments must be regenerated by the cells, a process that takes time. You can try this for yourself by going out into the bright sunlight for a bit and then going back inside to a dark room. At first you won't be able to see much, but slowly your vision will adapt as your photopigments regenerate.

The timing of the adaptation process is shown in Figure 5.8. The dark adaptation curve is produced by measuring the smallest amount of light that can be reliably seen as time passes in the dark. Over 20 to 25 minutes, smaller and smaller amounts of light are needed to achieve accurate detection. Our sensitivity increases over time because the visual receptor cells are recovering from their earlier interactions with bright light. Notice there's a break at about the 8-minute mark. This occurs because rods and cones adapt at different rates. Early in dark adaptation, cones show the most sensitivity, but they achieve their maximum sensitivity rather quickly. After about 7 or 8 minutes in the dark, the rods begin to take over. This is one of the reasons you can't see color very well at night; in low illumination levels, you're relying almost entirely on your rods—which don't do much, if any, color processing.

FIGURE 5.8 ■ The Dark Adaptation Curve

Your eyes gradually adjust to the dark and become more sensitive; that is, you can detect light at increasingly low levels of intensity. The rods and cones adapt at different rates and reach different final levels of sensitivity. The dark adaptation curve represents the combined adaptation of the two receptor types. At about the 8-minute mark, there is a point of discontinuity; this is where further increases in sensitivity are due to the functioning of the rods.

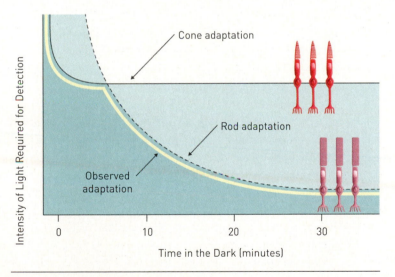

Carolina Hrejsa/Body Scientific Intl.

Identifying the Message Components

After leaving the retina, the neural impulses flow along each optic nerve until they reach the *optic chiasm* (from the Greek word meaning "cross"); here the information travels to the separate hemispheres of the brain (see Figure 5.9). Information that has been detected on the right half of each retina (from the left visual field) is sent to the right hemisphere, and information falling on the left half of each retina (from the right visual field) projects to the left hemisphere. Most visual signals move directly toward a major relay station in the thalamus called the *lateral geniculate nucleus*; other signals, perhaps 10% of the total, detour into a midbrain structure called the *superior colliculus*.

FIGURE 5.9 ■ Visual Pathways

Input from the left visual field falls on the inside half of the left eye and the outside half of the right eye and projects to the right hemisphere of the brain; input from the right visual field projects to the left hemisphere. Visual processing occurs at several places along the pathway, ending in the visual cortex, where highly specialized processing takes place.

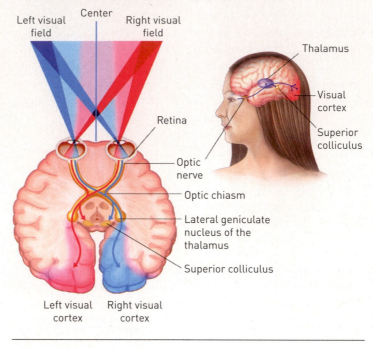

Carolina Hrejsa/Body Scientific Intl.

The Visual Cortex

From the lateral geniculate nucleus, the visual message moves to the back of the brain, primarily to portions of the occipital lobe. Here, in the visual cortex, more components of the message are picked out and identified. **Feature detectors** have been discovered in the visual cortex of cats and monkeys (Hubel & Wiesel, 1962, 1979). Feature detectors are cells that respond best to very specific visual events, such as patterns of light and dark. One type of feature detector, called a *simple cell*, responds actively only when a small bar of light is shown into the eye. Cells of this type also turn out to be orientation specific, which means the visual bar needs to be presented at a particular angle for the cell to respond. The properties of these cells were discovered by measuring neural impulses in individual cells using implanted recording electrodes. An example of this type of experiment, and the equipment used, is shown in Figure 5.10. Remember, there are no pain receptors in the brain, which makes it possible to explore the reactions of brain cells without causing an animal severe discomfort. The recorded cells were found to increase, decrease, or show no changes in their firing rates in response to specific visual stimuli. In Figure 5.10, experimenters are recording the reaction to the presentation of a small bar of light at a particular angle. Again, it was discovered that certain feature detectors in the cat's brain would react to this stimulus, and not to others, and only when the bar was shown at this angle.

Feature detectors are not randomly organized in the visual cortex; rather, there is a kind of master plan to the organization in the brain. Cells that respond to stimuli shown at one orientation, say 20 degrees, tend to sit together in the same "columns" of brain tissue. If a recording electrode is moved across neighboring columns, cells show regular shifts in their orientation specificity. So, if cells in a column A respond to bars at an angle of 20 degrees, then cells in a physically adjacent column B might respond actively only to bars presented at a 30-degree angle. This is generally thought to mean that cells in the visual cortex break down the visual message in a systematic and highly organized way.

Obviously, the brain is sensitive to more than just bars or patterns of light and dark. Some cells respond selectively to more complex patterns—for example, corners, edges, bars that move through the visual field, and bars of a certain characteristic length. Researchers have also found cells—once again in monkey brains—that respond most actively to faces. Moreover, to get the most active response from

FIGURE 5.10 ■ **Feature Detectors in the Visual Cortex**

Hubel and Wiesel discovered feature detectors in the brains of cats and monkeys. Feature detectors increase their firing rates to specific bars of light presented at particular orientations.

Stimulus

| No light | Vertical line | Horizontal line | Diagonal line |

Recording

| Baseline firing rate | Rapid firing rate | Low firing rate | Moderate firing rate |

Monica Wierzbicki/Body Scientific Intl.

these cells, the face needed to look realistically like a monkey—if the face was distorted or cartoonish, the cells did not respond as actively (Perrett & Mistlin, 1987). There's even evidence suggesting that some cells are "tuned" to respond selectively to certain kinds of facial expressions (Hasselmo et al., 1989). Much has been learned in recent years about the way in which the brain codes facial identity in the brain (e.g., see L. Chang & Tsao, 2017).

In humans, researchers have studied how the brain analyzes visual messages by testing brain-damaged patients and using neuroimaging techniques. When parts of the human brain are damaged because of stroke or injury, very selective, even bizarre, visual problems can start to appear. For example, in the condition called *prosopagnosia*, the ability to recognize faces is lost (Behrmann et al., 2009). People with prosopagnosia can fail to recognize acquaintances, family members, and even their own reflection in a mirror! Research suggests that individuals with this condition have difficulty processing faces as a whole, instead focusing on individual features, which interrupts face recognition (Avidan et al., 2011). Another example comes from the increasing worldwide diagnoses of acquired brain injuries (e.g., concussions). Many of these injuries come with visual impairments, and researchers are currently investigating what kinds of visual deficits these patients have (Ambika et al., 2020) and how to help people who've suffered from a brain injury overcome these deficits (Yoo et al., 2020).

Additional evidence comes from the fMRI neuroimaging technique. Consistent with the single-cell recording findings discussed previously, researchers have found regions in the cortex that become highly active when people view faces (Calder et al., 2011). Moreover, these regions fail to show the same levels of activation when patients suffering from prosopagnosia are tested (Hadjikhani & de Gelder, 2002). The fMRI technique is also proving effective for mapping visual pathways in the brain and for detecting whether specific areas of the brain might be involved in the processing of visual images (Wandell & Winawer, 2011).

Studies such as these strongly suggest that the human brain, like the monkey brain, divides its labor. Certain regions of the cortex are specifically designed to process parts of the visual message. In other words, there is specificity in the organization and function of the brain. The exact role that each part plays remains to be worked out. In fact, there continue to be scholarly "battles" among researchers—are there specific areas in the brain that are dedicated to processing faces, language, or even mathematics (Fedorenko et al., 2011)? It's quite likely that specific cells or regions of the brain perform more than one function (Peissig & Tarr, 2007), but the mysteries of how the brain solves the basic problems of vision are beginning to unravel. Concept Review 5.1 summarizes the organization of the sensory system for vision. As we continue to discuss additional senses, you will see that other sensory systems follow a similar structure.

CONCEPT REVIEW 5.1
PARTS OF A SENSORY SYSTEM

General Structure	Purpose	Visual System
Body organ	Collect energy from the environment	Eye
Receptor cells	Convert energy into neural impulse	Photoreceptors (rods and cones)
Nerve fibers	Carry neural impulse to brain areas	Optic nerve
Brain processing areas	Interpret neural impulses to attach meaning to energy collected by the sensory system	Visual cortex in the occipital lobe

FIGURE 5.11 ■ Receptor Sensitivity Curves

Blue-sensitive cones are most likely to respond to short wavelengths of light; green-sensitive cones respond best to medium wavelengths; red-sensitive cones respond best to long wavelengths. Notice that rods are not sensitive to long wavelengths of light (based on E. R. Jones & Childers, 1993).

Carolina Hrejsa/Body Scientific Intl.

Color Vision: Trichromatic Theory

We turn our attention now to color, which is processed along virtually the entire visual pathway. In the retina, early color information is detected by comparing the activity levels of different types of cone receptors; higher up in the brain, messages encounter cells that are "tuned" to respond only to certain colors.

Earlier you learned that color is determined primarily by the wavelength of light reflected back into the eye. In general, short wavelengths (around 450 nanometers) produce blues, medium wavelengths (around 530 nanometers) produce greens, and long wavelengths (around 670 nanometers) produce reds. White light, which most people classify as colorless, is a combination of all of the wavelengths of the visible spectrum. The reason your neighbor's shirt looks red is because chemical pigments in the fabric of the shirt absorb all but the long wavelengths of light; the long wavelengths are reflected into the eyes, and you see the shirt as red.

When reflected wavelengths reach the retina, they activate cones in the fovea. The human eye has three types of cone receptors: One type generates neural impulses primarily to short wavelengths (420 nanometers); another type responds most energetically to medium wavelengths (535 nanometers); and a final type responds most to long wavelengths (565 nanometers) of light. The activity levels of each of the cone types are determined by the photopigment contained in the receptor. Figure 5.11 shows the sensitivities for each of the cones, as well as for the rods.

The **trichromatic theory** of color vision proposes that color information is identified by comparing the activations of these three types of cones (trichromatic means "three-color"). An early version of the theory was proposed in the 19th century by Thomas Young and Hermann von Helmholtz—long before modern techniques had verified the existence of the different cone types. Young and Helmholtz noted that most colors can be matched by mixing three basic, or *primary*, colors. They suggested that the brain must determine color by comparing the activity levels of three primary receptors. When just one receptor type is strongly activated, you see one of the primary colors. For example, when a short-wavelength cone is strongly activated, you will see something in the violet to blue region of the spectrum; when a medium cone is active, you will see something resembling green. For long wavelengths, which activate the third type of cone, you'll see the color red. All other colors, such as pumpkin orange, require the activation of more than one of the receptor types. Most colors correspond to a mixture of wavelengths and are sensed by comparing the activations of the three receptors.

The trichromatic theory explains several interesting aspects of color vision. For example, it explains certain kinds of color blindness. At times, nature makes a mistake and fills someone's red cones with green photopigment or the green cones with red photopigment (Boynton, 1979). Under these rare conditions, which affect more males than females, people are left with two rather than three cone receptors. The trichromatic theory predicts that these *dichromats* (only two rather than three cone types) will lose their ability to discriminate successfully among certain colors. These people can compare the activity levels of only two cone receptors, so, for example, the colors red, yellow, and orange might be perceived as the same shade of yellow. The specific type of color deficiency depends on the type of lost receptor.

Color Vision: Opponent Processes

The trichromatic theory is well supported, but it fails to account completely for color vision. For one thing, the theory has a problem with yellow. Human observers seem convinced that yellow is every bit as "pure" a color as red, green, and blue; even 4-month-old infants prefer dividing the color spectrum into four color categories rather than three (M. H. Bornstein et al., 1976). In addition, most people have no problem reporting a yellowish red or a bluish green but almost never report seeing anything resembling a yellowish blue or, for that matter, a greenish red. Why?

It turns out that certain colors are specially linked, such as blue and yellow, and red and green. You can see this for yourself by looking at Figure 5.12. You'll find that if you stare at a vivid color like blue for a while and then switch over to a blank white space, you will see an afterimage of its complementary color. Exposure to blue results in an afterimage of yellow; exposure to red produces an afterimage of green. Also, when you mix complementary colored lights, you get white, or at least various shades of gray (Hurvich & Jameson, 1951). The special status of yellow, along with the linking of complementary colors, is quite difficult for the trichromatic theory to explain.

The difficulties with the trichromatic view were recognized in the 19th century by the German physiologist Ewald Hering, who proposed an alternative view of color vision: **opponent-process theory**. He suggested there are receptors in the visual

Additive mixing of lights with different wavelengths creates a variety of perceived colors—even white.

Dorling Kindersley / Science Source

FIGURE 5.12 ■ Color Afterimage

Stare closely at the middle of this face for about a minute. Then focus on the black dot on the right. What do you see now? The demo works better in a brightly lit environment.

Monica Wierzbicki/Body Scientific Intl.

system that respond positively to one color type (such as red) and negatively to another (such as green). Instead of three primary colors, Hering proposed six: *blue*, which is linked to *yellow* (therefore solving the problem with yellow); *green*, which is linked to *red*; and finally, *white*, which is linked to *black*. According to the opponent-process theory, people have difficulty perceiving a yellowish blue because activation of, say, the blue mechanism is accompanied by inhibition, or decreased activation, of the yellow mechanism. A yellowish red does not present a problem in this scheme because yellow and red are not linked in an opponent fashion.

Like Young and Helmholtz, Hering had no solid physiological evidence to support his notion of specially linked opponent-process cells. However, a century later, opponent-process cells were discovered in various parts of the visual pathway (see DeValois & DeValois, 1980). The rate at which these cells generate neural impulses increases to one type of color (for example, red) and decreases to another (green).

This means that the visual system must be pulling color information out of the visual message by relying on multiple processing stations. Color information is processed first in the retina through the cones (the trichromatic theory); further up in the brain, opponent-process cells fine-tune and further process the message. Finally, at the level of cortex, groups of neurons again appear to be selectively "tuned" to process color (Shapley & Hawken, 2011), although they may be involved in the processing of other information as well (such as shape). For example, fMRI studies recording neuron activity during presentation of a color show that different aspects of color vision are processed in different sets of neurons in visual cortex (I. Kim et al., 2020). Neuroscientists are still working out the details, but both the trichromatic and opponent-process systems play a role in color vision (Thoreson & Dacey, 2019). Concept Review 5.2 provides an overview of rods and cones and their features.

CONCEPT REVIEW 5.2
COMPARING RODS AND CONES

Characteristic	Rods	Cones
Number	Approximately 120 million per retina	Approximately 6 million per retina
Shape	Generally long and thin	Short, thick, tapered to a point
Location	Concentrated in the periphery of the retina	Concentrated in the center of the retina, the *fovea*
Sensitivity		
—Light	Sensitive at low levels of illumination	Not very sensitive at low levels of illumination
—Detail	Not sensitive to visual detail	High level of sensitivity to detail; high *visual acuity*
—Color	Indistinguishable among different wavelengths	Three types, each maximally sensitive to a different wavelength

Producing Stable Interpretations: Visual Perception

Let's return, for a moment, to the cube in Figure 5.1. You've seen how light bouncing off the page gets translated into an electrochemical signal. Next, specialized regions of the visual pathway break the message down—the brain pulls lines, edges, colors, and even angles of orientation from the visual scene. But your fundamental perception is still a cube—an object with form—not some complex combination of elementary particles.

To understand how the human brain can see "wholes" with visual machinery that seems designed to analyze parts, it helps to remember that perception is only partly determined by what comes in through the eyes. We also rely on what we know to help us construct what we see. Let's consider a simple example: Look at the two images depicted in Figure 5.13. If you were raised in North America, you probably have no trouble seeing the image in panel (a): It's the word DOG, written in white, against a solid black background. Panel (b), on the other hand, might look like a meaningless collection of black shapes. Panel (b) also shows the word DOG, but it's written in Chinese calligraphy. People who can read English, but not Chinese or Japanese (this character has the same meaning in Japanese), see panel (a) as a meaningful image; if Chinese or Japanese is your native language, and you can't read English, panel (b) presents the meaningful image (Coren et al., 1987). Prior knowledge plays a critical role in helping us interpret and organize what we see.

FIGURE 5.13 ■ Prior Knowledge and Perception

Whether you detect meaningful images in (a) and (b) depends on how much prior knowledge you bring to perceptual interpretation.

a   b

Source: Based on *Sensation and Perception*, Third Edition, Stanley Coren, Lawrence M. Ward, and James T. Enns. Copyright © 1989, 1984 Harcourt Brace Jovanovich, Inc.

We also use one part of a visual display to help us interpret other parts. The same "object" is shown in positions 2 and 4 of the following two lines:

but you see the letter *B* or the number 13 depending on which line you read. The surrounding letters and digits act as *context* leading us to expect a particular "whole" in positions 2 and 4. In some cases, the elements can be arranged to make us see things that aren't really there. Is there a white triangle embedded in the middle of Figure 5.14? It sure looks like there is, but the perception is really an illusion—there is no physical stimulus, no reflected pattern of electromagnetic energy on the retina, that corresponds to the triangular form. Yet you interpret the pattern as a triangle.

So, there's more to perception than what meets the eye. Our perceptual world is built by combining two important mental activities. First, the visual system performs an analysis of the actual sensory message, the pattern of electromagnetic information on the retina. Psychologists refer to this as **bottom-up processing**—the processing that starts with the actual physical message. Second, we use our knowledge, beliefs, and expectations about the world to interpret and organize what we see, something psychologists call **top-down processing**. Perception results from these two processes working together. What you see is determined by what's out there in the world but also by what you expect to be out there (Snowden & Schyns, 2006).

FIGURE 5.14   ■   Illusory Contours

Can you see the white triangle embedded in this figure? No physical stimulus corresponds to the triangular form. Nonetheless, people interpret the pattern as a triangle.

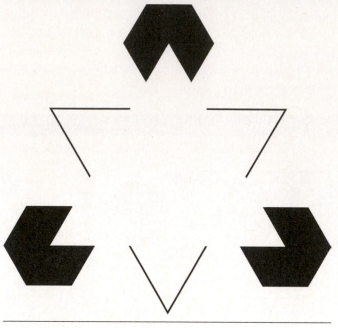

Carolina Hrejsa/Body Scientific Intl.

Principles of Organization

We're also born with strong tendencies to organize incoming visual information in sensible ways. Gestalt psychologists (*Gestalt* translates from German as "configuration" or "pattern") argued forcefully in the first half of the 20th century that we're born with certain organizing principles of perception. For example, we have a natural, automatic tendency to divide any visual scene into a figure and a ground—we see the wine glass as separate from the table, the printed word as separate from the page. The rules governing the separation of figure and ground are complex (e.g., Brooks & Driver, 2010), but as you can see from Figure 5.15, the task is easy or hard depending on whether strong or weak cues are available to guide the interpretation.

FIGURE 5.15   ■   Separating Figure From Ground

We have a natural tendency to divide any visual scene into a "figure" and "(back)ground." This task can be difficult, as with the "hidden faces" painting (a); once you've detected a face, it becomes a "figure" and stops being part of the background. Solving the problem can also be easy but ambiguous (b): Which do you see—a vase or a pair of profiles?

(a) Lucas Vallecillos / Alamy Stock Photo; (b) Illustrated by Sarah Yeh

The Gestalt psychologists outlined several compelling and systematic rules, known generally as the **Gestalt principles of organization**, that govern how people organize what they see:

1. *The law of proximity.* If the elements of a display are close to each other—that is, they lie in close spatial proximity—they tend to be grouped together as part of the same object. Here, for example, you see three groups of dots rather than a single collection.

Proximity

Proximity

Illustrated by Sarah Yeh

2. *The law of similarity.* Items that share physical properties—that physically resemble each other—are placed into the same set. Thus, here you see rows of *X*s and rows of *O*s rather than mixed-object columns.

Similarity

Similarity

Illustrated by Sarah Yeh

3. *The law of closure.* Even if a figure has a gap, or a small amount of its border is missing, people still tend to perceive the object as a whole (e.g., a circle).

Closure

Closure

Illustrated by Sarah Yeh

4. *The law of good continuation.* If lines cross or are interrupted, people tend to still see continuously flowing lines. In the following figure, you are much more likely to see one continuous line that is blocked by the box.

Continuation

Continuation

Illustrated by Sarah Yeh

5. *The law of common fate.* If things appear to be moving in the same direction, people tend to group them together. Here the moving dots are classified together as a group, with some fate in common.

Common Fate

Common fate

Illustrated by Sarah Yeh

FIGURE 5.16 ■ Recognition by Components

Biederman proposed that we recognize visual forms in part by extracting simple geometric forms (geons) from the visual message. Degraded versions of the objects on the left are in the other columns. We have no trouble recognizing the objects in the middle column, but most of us cannot identify those in the right column because the geons are degraded in the right column but not in the middle column.

Source: I. Biederman, "Recognition-by-Components: A theory of human image understanding," 1987, *Psychological Review* 94, p. 135, fig. 16. Copyright © 1987, American Psychological Association.

Object Recognition

These natural grouping rules help simplify the problem of object recognition. Psychologist Irving Biederman (1987; Dickinson & Biederman, 2014) has suggested that the Gestalt principles of organization may help the visual system break down complex visual messages into components called geons (short for "geometric icons"). Geons are simple geometrical forms, such as blocks, cylinders, wedges, and cones. From a collection of no more than 36 geons, Biederman argues, more than 150 million possible complex and meaningful objects can be created—far more than people need to capture the richness of their perceptual world. Once the brain is familiar with the geons, it can recognize the basic components of just about any perceptual experience. Just as the 26 letters of the alphabet form the basis for an incredible variety of words, geons form the "alphabet" for visualizing any object. Computer-generated simple geons are also the way that early three-dimensional animations were created. If you've ever seen early Pixar shorts, you can identify the component shapes that make up common objects such as flowers, bees, and animated desk lamps.

Biederman's theory, which he calls **recognition by components**, helps to explain how people can successfully identify fuzzy or incomplete images. Nature rarely provides all the identifying characteristics of a physical object: Cars are usually partially hidden behind other cars; a hurried glimpse of a child's face in a crowd might be all the information that reaches the eye. Yet the viewer has no trouble recognizing the car or the child. According to Biederman (1987), only two or three geons can be enough for the rapid identification of most objects. To illustrate, Biederman asked people to identify objects such as the ones shown in the left column of Figure 5.16. In some cases, the items were presented intact; in other conditions, the images were made more difficult to see by removing bits of information that either maintained (the middle column) or disrupted (the right column) the component geons. Not surprisingly, people had no problem recognizing the objects in the middle column but had considerably more trouble when the geons were obscured. In fact, Biederman found that identification of the right-column objects was almost impossible—most people in this condition failed to identify any of the objects correctly. A recent study even showed that object recognition in pigeons is driven by identification of component geons (Peissig et al., 2019).

But not all researchers are convinced that a relatively small set of basic shapes is enough to allow us to identify and discriminate among all objects. Many objects share basic parts, yet we're able to tell them apart quickly and efficiently. Moreover, there may be certain kinds of objects, such as faces, that are perceived and remembered immediately as wholes, without any breaking down or building up from parts. As you learned earlier, some cells in the brain respond selectively to faces; also, certain kinds of brain damage make recognizing faces, but not other objects, difficult or impossible. We're capable of recognizing an enormous range of objects in our world without hesitation, so it's likely that our brains solve the problems of object recognition in a number of different ways (Peissig & Tarr, 2007).

Perceiving Depth

Depth perception is another amazing capability of the visual system. It too results from a combination of bottom-up and top-down processing. People use their knowledge about objects, in combination with bottom-up processing of the actual visual message, to create a three-dimensional world. For example, the brain knows and adjusts for the fact that distant objects produce smaller reflections on the retina. If you see two people whom you know to be roughly the same height, but the retinal images they produce are of different sizes, your brain figures out that one person must be standing closer than the other. Experience also makes it clear that closer objects tend to block the images of objects that are farther away.

Another cue for distance, one that artists often use to depict depth in paintings, is *linear perspective*. As shown in the accompanying photos, parallel lines that recede into the distance tend to converge toward a single point. Generally, the farther away two lines are from the observer, the closer together those lines will appear to be. The relative shading of objects in a scene can provide important clues as well: If one object casts a shadow on another, you can often tell which of the two is farther away. Objects that are far away also tend to look blurry and slightly bluish. If you look at a realistic painting of a mountain scene, you'll see that the distant hills lack fine detail and are painted with a tinge of blue.

Can you identify the types of cues present in these "flat" pictures that allow us to perceive depth?

iStockPhoto/karinclaus (top); iStockPhoto/Stanislava Karagyozova (middle); iStockPhoto/Lisa-Blue (bottom)

The depth cues we've been considering are called **monocular depth cues**, which means they require input from only one eye. A person can close one eye and still see a world full of depth based on the use of monocular cues such as those just discussed; you don't need two eyes to perceive depth. But the brain also uses **binocular depth cues**; these are cues produced by two eyes, each with a slightly different view of the world. Hold your index finger up about an inch or so in front of your eyes. Now quickly close and open each eye alternately. You should see your finger jumping back and forth as you switch from one open eye to the other. The finger appears to move because each eye has a slightly different angle of view on the world, producing different images in each retina.

The difference between the locations of the images in the two eyes is called **retinal disparity**. It's a useful cue for depth because the amount of disparity changes with distance from a point of fixation. The farther away an object is from the fixation point, the greater will be the differences in the locations of the images in each eye. The brain derives depth information, in part, by calculating the amount of disparity (difference) between the image in the left eye and the image in the right eye. The brain can also use the degree that the two eyes turn inward, called **convergence**, to derive information about depth. The closer an object is to the face, the more the two eyes must turn inward, or converge, to see the object properly. Not surprisingly, our brain is also able to monitor how these various cues change with motion, such as shifting our head or walking about, to compile an increasingly accurate view of the world in three dimensions (Wexler & van Boxtel, 2005). See Concept Review 5.3 for a list of different visual cues.

CONCEPT REVIEW 5.3
DEPTH CUES

Type of Cue	Cue	Description
Monocular	Relative size	Comparably sized stimuli that produce different-sized retinal images are perceived as varying in distance from the observer.
	Overlap	Closer objects tend to block the images of objects farther away.
	Linear perspective	Parallel lines that recede into the distance appear to converge on a single point.
	Shading	Shadows cast by objects on other objects assist in depth perception.
	Haze	Distant objects tend to look blurry and slightly bluish.
Binocular	Retinal disparity	The difference between the locations of the images in the two eyes; the amount of disparity changes with distance from a point of fixation.
	Convergence	The closer the stimulus, the more the eyes turn inward toward one another.

PRACTICAL SOLUTIONS: CREATING ILLUSION OF DEPTH

Have you ever used a stereoscope—perhaps in its modern form, the View-Master? Or seen a 3D movie with 3D glasses? How about a stereogram? The image shown in Figure 5.17 may look like a bunch of random colored dots, but if you look at it just right, you'll see an image presented in astonishing depth.

Each of these examples represents an instance in which we can see depth from what is, essentially, a 2D visual message. In the case of the stereogram, the 3D image emerges out of a flat, and meaningless, 2D picture—no special equipment is needed, much like 3D glasses allow you to view a 2D movie with depth. How is this possible? Not surprisingly, these visual tricks rely on the same

FIGURE 5.17 ■ A Single-Picture Random Dot Stereogram

Source: Fred Hsu, March 2005.

perceptual principle—retinal disparity—that we discussed in the section on depth perception. We see with two eyes, and each of our eyes sees the world from a slightly different viewpoint. Through a process that is not completely understood, our brain is able to perceive an object in depth by noting, in part, the differences that exist between the left- and right-eye images. As you know from reading the text, this is not the only cue we use to perceive depth (our top-down knowledge of the world is also important), but it's a sufficiently strong cue to trick the brain into seeing depth when it's not really there.

In the case of a 3D movie, the film contains two slightly offset images. By wearing special glasses, the two images can be selectively filtered to your left and right eyes. This creates the image disparity that is needed to create depth. (The 3D effect is achieved in the film production process, not by the glasses, which is why your 3D glasses won't work on just any movie.) A stereoscope is based on a similar principle; when you look through the View-Master, you're actually seeing two different images of the same scene, drawn or photographed from two slightly different perspectives. The View-Master delivers one of the images to each eye, producing the illusion of depth.

A stereogram, such as the one shown in Figure 5.17, is slightly more difficult to see. There is a repeating pattern that is slightly offset. If you focus beyond the image in a certain way, your brain picks up on the disparity, and a 3D image "mysteriously" appears. Here are some simple steps to view the image: First, make sure you're sitting in a brightly lit environment. Position the page up in front of your face, relatively close to your nose, and imagine you're focusing on a distant object beyond the page. This will make the stereogram seem blurry, but that doesn't matter. (You're not really looking at anything in particular, and especially not the stereogram; instead, you're staring blankly forward.) Now start to move the page slowly away from you, trying to keep your eyes focused on the imaginary distant object. Eventually, if you focus on it long enough, the 3D image will appear. Don't get discouraged—it may take a long time for the effect to work.

Motion Perception

We see a three-dimensional world, full of depth, but we experience a world rich in movement as well. Cars speed by, birds soar and dive, and leaves scatter in the wind. Our ability to perceive motion effortlessly is extremely useful. Movement helps us determine the positions of objects over time; it helps us to identify objects as well. Movement gives us information about shape because we're able to see the object from more than one viewpoint. It also helps us solve figure–ground problems—once an object begins to move, we can easily separate its image from a still background. Motion plays an important role in our detection of animacy as well—is that thing hiding in the brush living or nonliving (Gao & Scholl, 2011; Parovel et al., 2018)?

How do we perceive movement? You might think the brain could solve this problem by simply tracking the movement of images across the retina. This is true to a certain extent, but motion perception is more complex than this. Images are constantly moving across our retinas as we turn our eyes, yet we don't necessarily see objects as moving. Moreover, sometimes we perceive motion when there is none. Think about those flashing arrows you see in front of stores or motels—they beckon us in, but they're actually made up of fixed lights that are blinking on and off at regular intervals. We experience an illusion of motion, called the **phi phenomenon**, even though nothing in the environment is really moving. We experience a similar *illusion of motion* every time we watch a movie. Movies are really nothing more than still pictures presented rapidly in succession, but we certainly experience smooth and flowing images.

Neuroscientists have shown that there are designated pathways in the brain that helps us process movement, and a variety of cells that respond specifically to movement have been discovered in the cortex (Battelli et al., 2007). Changes in the retinal image, changes in the motion of the eyes, and changes in the relative positions of objects in the environment all contribute to our general perception of movement. For example, our brain infers movement when the retinal image of one object changes over time but the images of other objects in the background do not. As with depth, many cues in the environment help in the interpretation process.

Perceptual Constancies

Another remarkable feature of the human visual system is its capacity to recognize that an object remains the same even when the image in the retina changes. As you watch a car pull away, the size of its retinal image becomes smaller and smaller—so small, in fact, that it eventually resembles the image that might be reflected from a toy car held at arm's distance. But you never think the car has been mysteriously transformed into a toy. Your visual system maintains a stable interpretation of the image despite the changes in its retinal size.

When you perceive an object, or its properties, to remain the same even though the physical message delivered to the eyes is changing, you are showing what's called a **perceptual constancy**. In the case of the car, it is *size constancy*—the perceived size of the car remains constant even though the actual size of the reflected image is changing with distance. Figure 5.18 provides an example of *shape constancy*. Consider how many changes occur in the reflected image of a door as it slowly moves from closed to open. Yet you still recognize it as a door, not as some bizarre shape that evolves unpredictably over time. Size and shape constancies turn out to be related; both result, at least in part, from the visual system's use of cues to determine distance.

FIGURE 5.18 ■ Shape Constancy

Notice all the changes in the image of a door as it moves from closed to open. Yet we perceive it as a constant rectangular shape.

Carolina Hrejsa/Body Scientific Intl.

FIGURE 5.19 ■   Constancy Cues

We see these three planters as matching in size and shape partly because of depth cues in the environment: Each covers three tiles in length and three in width.

Carolina Hrejsa/Body Scientific Intl.

To see what kinds of cues produce constancy, look at Figure 5.19. You see these planters as the same size and shape in part because of the texture patterns covering the ground. Each of the open boxes covers three texture tiles in length and an additional three in width. The actual retinal image, however, differs markedly for each of the shapes (take a ruler and measure the physical size of each shape). You interpret and see them as the same because your experiences in the world have taught you that size and distance are related in systematic ways.

We experience perceptual constancies for a variety of object dimensions. In addition to size and shape constancy, the brightness and color of an object can appear to remain constant even though the intensity and wavelength of the light changes. Once again, these characteristics help us maintain a stable and orderly interpretation of a constantly changing world. Think about how chaotic the world would appear if you saw a new and different object every time the physical properties of its reflected image changed. For example, instead of seeing the same dancer gliding across the floor, you might be forced to see a string of dancers each engaged in a unique and unusual pose.

Perceptual Illusions

The perception of constancy is not gained without a cost. In its effort to maintain a stable image, the visual system can be tricked—**perceptual illusions**, or inappropriate interpretations of physical reality, can be created. Look at the following two lines:

Müller-Lyer Illusion

iStockPhoto/werbeantrieb

The vertical line with the wings turned out appears longer than the line with the wings turned in, even though each line is identical in length. This is called the Müller-Lyer illusion. You're tricked because your brain uses cues in the environment—in this case the wings are acting as depth cues—to "interpret" the size of the lines. The retinal images of the two lines are the same, but your brain assumes the one with the wings turned out is farther away—hence it scales the image to make it look larger.

As Figure 5.20 shows, this illusion may have a real-life model—interior and exterior corners of a room or building. Notice that for the outside corner of this building the wings are really perspective cues signaling that the front edge is thrusting forward, and the walls are sloping away. For the inside corner, the perspective cues signal the opposite—the inside edge is farther away. Again, the two lines produce the same retinal image, but your visual system assumes that the interior corner is likely to be farther away and consequently must be larger in size.

FIGURE 5.20 ■ The Müller-Lyer Illusion

This particular illusion may be influenced by experiences with the interior and exterior corners of buildings.

Carolina Hrejsa/Body Scientific Intl.

The Ponzo illusion, shown in Figure 5.21(a), operates in a similar way. You see two rectangles that are the same length as slightly different because the perspective cue—the converging parallel lines—tricks your brain into thinking that the rectangle near the top of the display is farther away. Because it has the same size retinal image as the bottom rectangle (remember, the two are physically the same size), the brain compensates for the distance by making the top one appear larger. Figure 5.21(b) shows the illusion yet again: The cats are really the same size, but the one on the top certainly appears larger!

FIGURE 5.21 ■ Illusion of Depth

These two figures, based on the Ponzo illusion, show that depth cues can lead to perceptual errors. In (a) the rectangles are actually the same length, and the cats in (b) are the same size.

a

b

Sources: (a) Monica Schroeder/Science Source; (b) Marekuliasz/Shutterstock.

However, whether you experience these illusions can be affected by your culture and the geographical location in which you've lived your life. Look back at the Müller-Lyer illusion earlier in this section. Individuals raised in cultures with rectangular buildings typically report the illusion. However, when individuals from Indigenous cultures were tested with this figure, they tended to view the lines as of similar length (Phillips, 2019). This perceptual difference across populations seems to be due to the type of buildings you're familiar with, supporting the interpretation of the illusion shown in Figure 5.20. For people who are not familiar with rectangular buildings (like some of the Indigenous people tested with this illusion), the illusion does not appear.

The same is true of the illusion shown in panel (a) of Figure 5.21. For the horizontal lines in this figure, people raised in locations without train tracks or other vertical lines extending to the horizon are less likely to view the top line as longer compared to participants from the United States. Finally, consider the example of "the dress." For a period in 2015, a famous photo circulated on social media with an accompanying argument about the color of "the dress." Some argued that the dress was white with gold trim. Others argued that the dress was blue with black trim. In other words, different people had different perceptions of the color of "the dress." What kinds of cultural factors do you think might influence one's perception of the color of "the dress"?

The famous photo of the dress was seen in two different color schemes by different people.

Natallia Krechka / Alamy Stock Vector

Perception and Action

It's easy to think of visual illusions as tricks—we've fooled the visual system into an inaccurate representation of the world—but the processes involved are useful and adaptive. Usually, depth cues are correct—the object really is farther away—so we are seeing and interpreting objects in the right way. Some psychologists believe that seeing is for the purpose of performing adaptive behaviors. Nature has designed our perceptual systems to help us determine what behaviors we can perform—what psychologists have called **affordances**—and to help us perform those behaviors successfully.

Think about what professional athletes do. When outfielders catch a pop fly, they must use what they see and hear to move quickly to intercept the ball. If you've ever watched a Major League Baseball game, you've seen that players are usually accurate in positioning themselves on the field to catch the ball. According to researchers who believe that the purpose of perception is to help us act, outfielders accomplish this task by moving themselves based on what they see to keep their bodies lined up with the objects they want to intercept. Dogs catch Frisbees the same way (Shaffer et al., 2004). In other words, both outfielders and dogs use visual perception to help them perform intended behaviors. What you see is also influenced by your ability to perform those behaviors: Golfers who are playing well see the hole as bigger when they putt, at least compared to golfers who are putting poorly; softball players who are hitting well report seeing a larger ball; tennis players who are returning the ball well report perceiving the tennis net as lower (for a review, see Witt, 2011). In each case, there seems to be a close relationship between perception and action—what you see is determined by what you have to do, or your ability to perform (Wagman & Morgan, 2010).

More recently, researchers have applied this perspective to understanding how infants move about in the world (Kretch & Adolph, 2017). Researchers have also used virtual reality technology to explore how people's movements are affected by changes to their body shape, such as when their arm is extended in length (Day et al., 2019), and to investigate how people know how accurately they can walk in unusual environments, such as on a ship at sea (Walter et al., 2017, 2019). The results of these studies suggest that one of the important functions of perception is to help us move around in the world and achieve our goals (Wagman & Blau, 2020).

KNOWLEDGE CHECK 5.1

Now test your understanding of how the visual message is translated into the language of the brain.

1. Choose the best answers from among the following terms: *accommodation, cones, cornea, fovea, lens, opponent-process, pupil, receptive field, retina, rods, trichromatic.*
    a. The "central pit" area where the cone receptors tend to be located: ___
    b. Receptors that are responsible for visual acuity, or our ability to see fine detail: ___
    c. The process through which the lens changes its shape temporarily to help focus light: ___
    d. The "film" at the back of the eye that contains the light-sensitive receptor cells: ___
    e. The protective outer layer of the eye: ___

2. Decide whether each of the following statements about how the brain extracts message components is true or false.
    a. Visual messages tend to be analyzed primarily by structures in the superior colliculus, although structures in the lateral geniculate are important too. *True or False?*
    b. It's currently believed that information about color and information about movement are probably processed in separate pathways in the brain. *True or False?*
    c. The opponent-process theory of color vision makes it easier to understand why most people think there are four, rather than three, primary colors (red, green, blue, yellow). *True or False?*
    d. Some feature detectors in the brain are "tuned" to respond only when certain patterns of light enter the eye at specific angles of orientation. *True or False?*

3. Test your knowledge about visual perception by filling in the blanks. Choose your answers from the following terms: *binocular depth cues, bottom-up processing, convergence, monocular depth*

cues, perceptual constancy, perceptual illusion, phi phenomenon, retinal disparity, recognition by components, top-down processing.

   a. The part of perception that is controlled by our beliefs and expectations about how the world is organized: ___

   b. Perceiving an object, or its properties, to remain the same even though the physical message delivered to the eyes is changing: ___

   c. An illusion of motion: ___

   d. The depth cue that is based on calculating the degree to which the two eyes have turned inward: ___

   e. The view that object perception is based on the analysis of simple building blocks, called geons: ___

HEARING: IDENTIFYING AND LOCALIZING SOUNDS

Imagine a world without sound. There wouldn't be music, or speech, or laughter. Sounds help us identify and locate objects; through sound, we're able to produce and comprehend the spoken word. Even our most private sense of self—the world inside our heads—often appears in the form of an inner voice, or an ongoing speech-based monologue (see Chapter 9).

Translating the Message

Just as in vision, audition is accomplished through a sensory system that contains a body organ that captures the physical sensation from the environment, receptor cells to translate the sensation into neural impulses, nerve fibers to carry the neural impulses to the brain, and brain processing areas that interpret the impulses to create a perception. The physical message delivered to the auditory system, **sound**, is a form of energy, like light, that travels as a wave. However, sound is mechanical energy and requires a *medium* (such as air or water) to move. Sound begins with a vibrating stimulus, such as the movement of vocal cords or the plucking of a tight string. The vibration pushes air molecules out into space, where they collide with other air molecules, and a traveling chain reaction begins. Want to feel a pressure wave? Simply put your hand in front of the pounding diaphragm of a stereo speaker.

The rate of the vibrating stimulus determines the *frequency* of the sound, defined as the number of times the pressure wave moves from peak to peak per second (measured in units called *hertz*, where 1 Hz = 1 cycle [repetition]/second). Psychologically, when the frequency of a sound varies, we hear a change in **pitch**, which corresponds roughly to how high or low a tone sounds. Middle C on a piano has a frequency of 262 Hz, and the highest note corresponds to about 4,000 Hz. People are sensitive to frequencies from roughly 20 to 20,000 Hz, but we're most sensitive to frequencies in the 1,000- to 5,000-Hz range. Many important sounds fall into this range, including most of the sounds that make up speech.

The other major dimension of sound is intensity, or *pressure amplitude*. Psychologically, changes in intensity are experienced as changes in *loudness*. As the intensity level increases, it generally seems louder to the ear. The amplitude of a wave is measured in units called *decibels* (dB). To give you some perspective, a normal conversation measures around 60 dB, whereas an incredibly loud rock band can produce sounds over 100 dB. (Just for your information, prolonged exposure to sounds at around 90 dB can produce permanent hearing loss.)

Entering the Ear

Let's follow a sound as it enters the auditory pathway (see Figure 5.22). The first stop, of course, is the ears. The external flap of tissue usually referred to as the "ear" is known technically as the **pinna**; it helps capture the sound, which then funnels down the auditory canal toward the eardrum, or **tympanic membrane**.

The tympanic membrane responds to the incoming sound wave by vibrating. The vibration pattern, which changes for different sound frequencies, is then transmitted through three small bones in the **middle ear**: the *malleus* (or hammer), the *incus* (or anvil), and the *stapes* (or stirrup). These bones help intensify the vibration pattern and prepare it for passage into the inner ear. Inside the inner ear is a bony, snail-shaped sound processor called the **cochlea**; here the sound energy is translated into neural impulses.

FIGURE 5.22   ■   The Structures of the Human Ear

Sound enters the auditory canal and causes the tympanic membrane to vibrate in a pattern that is then transmitted through three small bones in the middle ear to the oval window. The oval window vibrates, causing fluid inside the cochlea to be displaced, which moves the basilar membrane. The semicircular canals contribute to our sense of balance.

Carolina Hrejsa/Body Scientific Intl.

The third bone in the middle ear, the stapes, is connected to an opening in the cochlea called the *oval window*. As the stapes vibrates, it causes fluid inside the cochlea to move a flexible membrane, called the **basilar membrane**, that runs throughout the cochlear shell. Transduction takes place through the activation of tiny auditory receptor cells, called *hair cells*, that lie along the basilar membrane. As the membrane starts to ripple—like a cat moving under a bedsheet—tiny hairs, called cilia, that extend outward from the hair cells are bent (because they knock into something called the tectorial membrane). The bending of these hairs causes the auditory receptor cells to fire, creating a neural impulse that travels up the auditory pathways to the brain (see Figure 5.23).

FIGURE 5.23   ■   The Basilar Membrane

This figure shows an open slice of the cochlea. Sound vibrations cause fluid inside the cochlea to displace the basilar membrane that runs throughout the cochlear shell. Different frequencies trigger different patterns along the membrane. Transduction takes place through bending hair cells. The hair cells nearest the point of maximum displacement will be stimulated the most, helping the brain extract information about pitch.

Carolina Hrejsa/Body Scientific Intl.

Different sound frequencies trigger different movement patterns along the basilar membrane. Higher frequencies of sound cause the membrane to be displaced the most near the oval window; low frequencies produce a traveling wave that reaches its peak deep inside the spiraling cochlea. The brain partly determines pitch by recognizing which of the receptor cells are activated by a particular sound pattern. If hair cells near the oval window are responding the most, the incoming sound is perceived as high in pitch. If many cells along the membrane are active, and the most active ones are far away from the oval window, the incoming sound is perceived as low in pitch.

Identifying the Message Components

The neural impulses generated by the hair cells leave the cochlea in each ear along the *auditory nerve*. Messages that have been received in the right ear travel mainly along pathways leading to the left hemisphere of the brain; left-ear messages go primarily to the right hemisphere. Just as in the visual system, auditory nerve fibers are "tuned" to transmit a specific kind of message. In the visual system, the ganglion cells transmit information about light and dark. In the auditory system, fibers in the auditory nerve pass on *frequency* information. Measurements of individual auditory nerve fibers show tuning curves—for example, a fiber might respond best to an input stimulus of around 2,000 Hz and less well to others.

Detecting Pitch

Complex sounds, such as speech patterns, are built from combinations of simple sound frequencies. The auditory system pulls out information about the simple frequencies, which correspond to different pitches, in several ways. Pitch is determined, in part, by the specific place on the basilar membrane that is active. For example, activation of hair cells near the oval window leads to the perception of a high-pitched sound. This is called the **place theory** of pitch perception (Békésy, 1960). We hear a particular pitch because certain hair cells are responding actively. "Place" in this instance refers to the location of the activated hair cell along the basilar membrane.

Place theory helps explain certain kinds of hearing loss. As people grow older, they have trouble hearing the higher frequencies of sound (such as those in whispered speech). Why? Because most sounds activate the hair cells that lie nearest the oval window. Cells in the interior portions of the cochlea respond actively only when low-frequency sounds are present. If receptor cells wear out from years of prolonged activity, then those nearest the oval window should be among the first to do so. Place theory partly explains, as a result, why older people have difficulty hearing high-pitched sounds.

At the same time, place theory does not offer a complete account of pitch perception. One problem is that hair cells do not act independently—often many are activated at the same time. As a result, it's thought that the brain must also rely on the *rate* at which cells fire their neural impulses. According to **frequency theory**, pitch is determined partly by the frequency of neural impulses traveling up the auditory pathway: The higher the rate of firing, the higher the perceived pitch. Like place theory, frequency theory does a reasonable job of explaining many aspects of pitch perception, but it runs into difficulties with high-frequency sounds. Because of their *refractory periods*, individual neurons cannot fire fast enough to deliver high-frequency information. To solve this problem, the brain

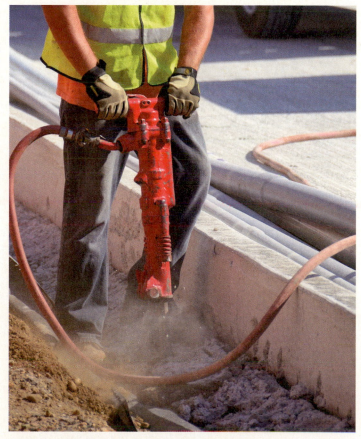

Prolonged exposure to intense noise can create hearing loss.

iStockPhoto/RiverNorthPhotography

tracks the patterns of firing among large groups of neurons. When groups of cells generate neural impulses rapidly in succession, they create *volleys* of impulses that provide additional clues about the pitch of the incoming message (Wever, 1949).

To sum up, the brain uses several kinds of information to extract pitch. The brain uses information about where on the basilar membrane activation is occurring (place theory) as well as the rate at which signals are generated (frequency theory). Neither place nor frequency information, by itself, is sufficient to explain our perception of pitch—both kinds of information are needed.

The Auditory Cortex

The auditory message eventually reaches the auditory cortex, which is located mainly in the temporal lobes of the brain. Cells in the auditory cortex are frequency sensitive, which means they respond best to particular frequencies of sound. There is also a well-developed organization, just like in the visual system. Cells that sit in nearby areas of the auditory cortex are tuned to similar frequencies of sound. Cells that respond to low-frequency sounds are clustered together in one area of the auditory cortex, whereas cells responsive to high-frequency sounds sit in another area (Wang, 2018).

Some cells in the auditory cortex respond best to complex combinations of sounds. For example, a cell might respond only to a sequence of tones that moves from one frequency to another, or to a burst of noise (Pickles, 1988). In animals, cortical cells have been discovered that respond only to sounds that exist in the animal's natural vocabulary, such as a particular shriek, cackle, or trill (Wollberg & Newman, 1972). In people, neuroimaging studies have found specific areas of the brain are activated when complex auditory sequences are played; different regions seem to be involved in detecting the identity of a sound (what) and its location in space (where). Much remains to be learned about how complex sounds—such as patterns of speech—are represented in the cortex, but recent advances in imaging technology are opening many new doors for the researcher. For example, imaging studies have made it clear that multiple pathways are involved in speech perception and comprehension, just as there are multiple processing pathways in vision (see Hickok & Small, 2015).

Producing Stable Interpretations: Auditory Perception

Say the phrase "kiss the sky," then repeat it aloud in rapid succession. Now do the same thing with the word "stress" or "life." You'll notice that your perception of what you're saying undergoes some interesting changes. "Kiss the sky" begins to sound like "kiss this guy"; "stress" will probably turn into "dress" and "life" into "fly." This is a kind of auditory analog to the Necker cube, which was discussed at the beginning of the chapter.

Organizing the Auditory Message

As with the ever-changing cube, the brain is often faced with ambiguous auditory messages—it seeks meaning where it can, usually by relying on established organizational rules (Bregman, 1990; Hirsh & Watson, 1996). The brain separates the incoming auditory stream into figure and ground; it groups auditory events that are similar and that occur close together in time. Sound frequency can be used as a grouping cue to distinguish among voices. Females generally speak at higher frequencies than males. As a result, it is easier to tell the difference between a male and a female talking than it is to tell the difference between two speakers of the same sex. At the same time, the auditory system shows a remarkable ability to maintain perceptual constancy: We can easily recognize the same melody played by different instruments, even though the physical characteristics of the sounds reaching the ears are very different (Zatorre, 2005).

The fact that the brain organizes the incoming sound message should not come as much of a surprise. Think about how easily you can listen to a band or orchestra, filled with many different instruments, and pick out the trumpet, violin, or piano. Think about how easily you can focus on the voice of a friend, to the exclusion of other voices, when you're in the middle of a noisy party. Moreover, your ability to identify and organize sounds increases with experience (J. H. McDermott et al., 2011). We use our knowledge and expectations, through top-down processing, to help us interpret the incoming auditory sequence. Car mechanics, after years of experience, can identify an engine problem simply by listening to the kind of "knocking" the engine makes; cardiologists can use the sounds of the heartbeat to diagnose the health of a cardiovascular system. In one neuroimaging study, people were asked to listen to familiar or unfamiliar songs while being "scanned" in an fMRI machine. At certain points in the song, the music was turned off unexpectedly. During these silent "gaps," activity continued in auditory regions of the brain but to a much greater extent if the participants were familiar with the song. Everyone reported still "hearing" the song during the gaps—a kind of auditory imagery—but only if they were familiar with the song (Kraemer et al., 2005).

Sound Localization

Another useful characteristic of the auditory sense is the ability to determine location. For example, if you're driving down the street fiddling with your car radio and hear a sudden screech of brakes, you're able to identify the source of the sound rapidly and efficiently. How do you accomplish this feat? Just as comparisons between the retinal locations of images in the two eyes provide information about visual depth, message comparisons between the ears help people localize objects in space.

Let's assume that the braking car is approaching yours from the left side. Because your left ear is closer to the source, it will receive the sound slightly sooner than your right ear. If an object is directly in front of you, the message will arrive at both ears simultaneously. By comparing the arrival times between the left and right ears, the brain can localize the sound fairly accurately. What's amazing is that these arrival time differences are extremely small. For example, the maximum arrival time difference, which occurs when an object is directly opposite one ear, is less than one-tenth of a second.

Another important cue for sound localization is *intensity*—more precisely, intensity differences between the ears. The sound that arrives first—to either the left or the right ear—will be somewhat louder, or more intense, than the sound arriving second. These intensity differences are not large, and they depend partly on the frequency of the arriving sound, but they are useful cues for sound localization. Your brain can calculate the differences in arrival times, plus any differences in loudness, and use this information to localize the source. Plus, as noted earlier, imaging studies have found specific regions in the auditory cortex that are dedicated to the localization of sound (Clarke & Thiran, 2004).

KNOWLEDGE CHECK 5.2

Now test your knowledge about the auditory system by determining whether each of the following statements is true or false. (You will find the answers in the Appendix.)

1. Sound is a form of mechanical energy that requires a medium, such as air or water, to move. *True or False?*

2. According to the frequency theory of pitch perception, the location of activity on the basilar membrane is the primary cue for determining pitch. *True or False?*

3. Sound pressure causes tiny hair cells, located in the pinna, to bend, thereby generating a neural impulse. *True or False?*

4. The separation of a sensory message into figure and ground occurs for vision but not for hearing. *True or False?*

5. We use multiple cues to help us localize a sound, including comparisons of arrival times and intensity differences between the two ears. *True or False?*

THE SKIN AND BODY SENSES: FROM TOUCH TO MOVEMENT

We now turn to the three skin senses—touch, temperature, and pain—and to the body senses related to movement and balance. Not surprisingly, the skin and body senses have tremendous adaptive value. You need to detect that spider crawling up your leg; if a blowing ember from the fireplace happens to land on your forearm, it is certainly adaptive to respond quickly. It's also important to detect and control the movement and position of our own bodies. We need to know, for example, whether we're hanging upside down and the current positions of our arms and legs. Human sensory systems have developed not only to detect the presence of objects in the environment but also to provide accurate information about the body itself. As in our earlier discussions, in each case the environmental message must be translated, transmitted to the brain, and interpreted in a meaningful way.

Touch

For touch or pressure, the physical message delivered to the skin is mechanical. An object makes contact with the body—perhaps your fingers actively reach out and initiate the contact—and receptor cells embedded in the skin are disturbed. The mechanical pressure on the cell (it is literally deformed) produces a neural impulse, and the message is then transmitted to the spinal cord and up into the brain.

There are several different types of pressure-sensitive receptor cells in the skin. Some respond to constant pressure; others respond best to intermittent pressure, such as tapping on the skin or a stimulus that vibrates at a certain frequency. As with vision and hearing, touch information is transmitted up the neural pathway through distinct channels to processing stations in the brain, where the inputs received from various points on the body are combined. One kind of nerve fiber might carry information about touch location; other fibers might transmit information about whether the touch has been brief or sustained. Touch is used to determine the properties of objects and surfaces as well as their locations in space (Lederman & Klatzky, 2009).

At the level of the *somatosensory cortex*, located in the parietal lobe of the brain, a close connection is found among regions of the skin and representation in the cortex. As you learned in Chapter 3, the cortex contains multiple "body maps," where adjacent cortical cells have areas of sensitivity that correspond to adjacent areas on the skin. As in the visual cortex, some areas are represented more elaborately than others. For example, a relatively large amount of cortical tissue is devoted to the hands and lips, whereas the middle portion of the back, despite its size, receives little representation in the cortex. Maybe that's the reason we kiss to display intense affection rather than simply pat someone on the back. There's a lot more cortex devoted to the lips than to the back.

Humans use touch to acquire information about shape, firmness, texture, and weight.

iStockPhoto/alle12

Everyone can recognize complex objects exclusively through touch. When blindfolded, people show near-perfect identification of common objects (such as toothbrushes and paper clips) after examining them by active touch (Klatzky et al., 1985). Active skin contact with an object produces not only shape information but information about firmness, texture, and weight. As with seeing and hearing, a person's final interpretation of an object depends on what the person feels as well as on what the person expects to feel. For instance, if you expect to be touched by an object on a particular finger, you are more likely to identify the object correctly (J. C. Craig, 1985). There are also changes in blood flow in the somatosensory cortex when a person simply expects to be touched (Drevets et al., 1995).

Temperature

The body records and processes temperature through "thermoreceptors" located in the skin. **Cold fibers** respond to a cooling of the skin by increasing the production of neural impulses; **warm fibers** respond when the temperature of the skin increases. But our perception of warm and cold is only indirectly related to the actual temperature of the real-world object. To demonstrate, try plunging one hand into a bowl of cold water and the other hand into a bowl of hot water. Now place both hands into a third bowl containing water sitting at room temperature. The hand that was in the cold water will sense the water as warm; the other hand will experience it as cold. Same water, same temperature, but two different perceptual experiences. It's the temperature *change* that determines your perception. When your cold hand touches warmer water, your skin begins to warm; it is the increase in skin temperature that you perceive.

At times these perceptual processes can lead to temperature "illusions." For instance, metal seems cooler than wood even when both are at the same physical temperature. Why? Metal is a better conductor of heat than wood, so it absorbs more warmth from the skin. Consequently, the brain perceives the loss of heat as a cooler physical temperature.

Experiencing Pain

Pain is an adaptive reaction that the body generates in response to events that are intense enough to cause tissue damage. It's not fun, but pain is extremely useful. People who are born without the ability to experience pain live troubled lives. Without pain's signal, they can't tell when the frying pan is too hot to hold; they don't know to shift position when too much pressure is being placed on a joint. Pain is the body's warning system—be careful, something is wrong.

Each of us has pain receptors in the skin, called nociceptors, that can be activated externally (e.g., by heat or severe pressure) or by internal damage or inflammation to our tissues and joints. The psychological experience of pain, however, relies on much more than just a physical stimulus. There are well-documented examples of soldiers who report little or no pain after receiving serious injuries in battle; the same is true of many individuals entering an emergency room. In addition, certain non-Western cultures use rituals that should, from a Western perspective, inflict great pain but apparently do not (Melzack, 1973).

The popularity of winter swimming among Russians demonstrates how the perception of temperature can be influenced by psychological factors.

Dimar Photo / Alamy Stock Photo

Gate-Control Theory

The interplay between the physical and the psychological in pain perception forms the basis for the **gate-control theory** (Melzack & Wall, 1965, 1982). The basic idea is that the neural impulses generated by pain receptors can be blocked, or gated, in the spinal cord by signals produced in the brain. If you've just sliced your finger cutting carrots on the kitchen counter, you normally feel pain. But if a pan on the stove suddenly starts to smoke, the pain evaporates while you try to prevent your house from burning down. According to gate-control theory, the brain can block the critical pain signals from reaching higher neural centers when it is appropriate to do so.

How is the gating action carried out? The mechanisms are unclear, but two types of nerve fibers appear to be responsible for opening and closing the gate. So-called large fibers, when stimulated, produce nervous system activity that closes the gate; other "small" fibers, when stimulated, inhibit those neural processes, and effectively open the gate. External activities—such as rubbing or placing ice on a wound—also apparently stimulate the large fibers, which close the gate, preventing further passage of the pain message toward the brain. The details of the neural circuitry remain to be worked out, and it's worth noting that the neural connections proposed in the original gate-control theory turned out to be wrong. But the idea of a *pain gate* that opens and closes remains popular among researchers (Sufta & Price, 2002), with minor revisions to the theory based on recent data (Pereira & Lerner, 2017).

In addition to gating the pain signals, as we discussed in Chapter 3, the brain can control the experience of pain through the release of chemicals called *endorphins*, which produce painkilling effects like those obtained through morphine. The release of endorphins may help explain those instances in which pain should be experienced but is not. For example, swallowing a sugar pill can sometimes reduce pain even though there's no medical reason it should work (a placebo effect). The locus of such effects, and other analgesic procedures such as acupuncture, might lie in the brain's internal production of its own anti-pain medication.

The Kinesthetic Sense

The word **kinesthesia** literally means "movement"; when used in connection with sensation, the term refers to the ability to sense the position and movement of one's body parts. For example, as you reach toward a blossoming flower, feedback from your skin, tendons, muscles, and especially joints helps you maintain the correct line toward the target. The kinesthetic sense shares many properties with the sense of touch—a variety of receptors in the muscles that surround the joints react to the physical forces produced by moving the limbs.

The nerve impulses generated by the kinesthetic receptors travel to the somatosensory cortex where, it is presumed, increasingly complex cells respond only when body parts (such as the arms) are placed in certain positions (E. B. Gardner & Costanzo, 1981). But the psychological experience of movement is most likely influenced by multiple factors, as with other kinds of perception. The visual system, for example, provides additional feedback about current position, as does the sense of touch (Lederman & Klatzky, 2009).

The Vestibular Sense

We have another complex receptor system, attached to the cochlea of the inner ear, that responds not only to movement but also to acceleration and to changes in upright posture. Each ear contains three small fluid-filled **semicircular canals** that are lined with hair cells similar to those found in the cochlea.

The vestibular sense helps people maintain balance by monitoring the position of the body in space.

iStockPhoto/Tatyana Maximova

If you quickly turn your head toward some object, these hair cells are displaced, and nerve impulses signaling acceleration are transmitted throughout the brain. Some of the nerve fibers project to the cortex; others direct messages to the eye muscles, allowing you to adjust your eyes as your head is turning.

The vestibular system is also responsible for the sense of balance. If you tilt your head or encounter a 360-degree loop on a roller coaster, receptor cells located in other inner ear organs, called **vestibular sacs**, quickly transmit the appropriate orientation information to the brain. Continual disturbance of the semicircular canals or the vestibular sacs can produce dizziness, nausea, and motion.

KNOWLEDGE CHECK 5.3

Now test your knowledge about the skin and body senses by answering the following multiple-choice questions. (You will find the answers in the Appendix.)

1. Alicia holds her left hand in a bowl of cold water and her right hand in a bowl of hot water. She then transfers both hands to a bowl containing water at room temperature. She finds that her left hand now feels warm and her right hand cool. Why?
   a. Cold and hot fibers rebound after continued activity.
   b. It's temperature change that determines perception.
   c. She expects a change; therefore, a change is experienced.
   d. Opponent-process cells in the cortex are reacting.

2. According to gate-control theory, psychological factors can influence the perception of pain by
   a. channeling pain signals to the occipital lobe.
   b. reducing the supply of endorphins in the body.
   c. blocking pain signals from reaching higher neural centers.
   d. blocking pain receptors from relaying messages to the spinal cord.

3. The vestibular sacs contain receptor cells that help us maintain our sense of balance. Where are they located?
   a. In the lateral geniculate nucleus
   b. In the superior colliculus
   c. In the joints and limbs of the body
   d. In the inner ear

THE CHEMICAL SENSES: SMELL AND TASTE

We end our review of the individual sensory systems with the chemical senses, *smell* and *taste*. Few messages from the environment carry as much emotional impact as chemically based input. You can appreciate the touch of a loved one, or the visual beauty of a sunset, but consider your reaction to the smell of decaying meat or to the taste of milk left a bit too long in the sun! Smells and tastes are enormously adaptive because they too possess powerful signaling properties: Like other animals, humans learn to avoid off odors and bitter tastes.

The perception of both smell and taste begins with the activity of receptor cells, called **chemoreceptors**, that react to invisible molecules scattered about in the air or dissolved in liquids. These receptors solve the translation problem and project the newly formed neural impulses toward the brain. Psychologically, the two senses are related: Anyone who has ever had a cold knows that things "just don't taste right" with a plugged nose. You can demonstrate this for yourself by holding your nose and trying to taste the difference between an apple and a piece of raw potato. In fact, people can identify a taste far more efficiently if they are also allowed a brief sniff (Mozell et al., 1969). Let's consider each of these chemical senses in more detail.

Smell

The technical name for the sense of smell is **olfaction**, which comes from the Latin word *olfacere*, meaning "to smell." Airborne molecules enter through the nose or the back of the throat and interact with receptor cells embedded in the upper region of the nasal cavity. Like the receptor systems used to hear and detect motion, the olfactory receptor cells contain tiny hairs, or *cilia*. The airborne molecules are thought to bind with the cilia, causing the generation of a neural impulse. Receptor fibers then move the message forward to the *olfactory bulb*, located at the bottom front region of the brain. From here the information is sent to several areas in the brain.

A taster's ability to identify the smell, or "bouquet," of wine depends on the constellation of airborne chemicals produced by the wine and on the experience of the taster.

iStockPhoto/karelnoppe

Studies have shown that people probably have a thousand or more different kinds of olfactory receptor cells (Buck & Axel, 1991). Each receptor cell responds only to certain molecules, but a given "smell" results from a pattern of activation across a number of these different receptors. Most odors are complex psychological experiences. People have no problem recognizing the smell of frying bacon or the aroma of fresh coffee, but a chemical analysis of these events fails to reveal the presence of any single defining molecule. Clearly, the ability to apply the label "frying bacon" to a set of airborne chemicals arises from complex perceptual processes. It's even possible to produce smell *illusions*—if you're led to expect that a particular odor is present, even though it's not, you're likely to report detecting its presence (O'Mahony, 1978). Similar to other sensory systems, odor perception is likely signaled by a pattern of activation across the olfactory bulb and by changes in the firing rates of neurons (Shepard, 2006).

The neural pathway for smell is somewhat unusual, compared with other sensory systems, because connections are made with forebrain structures such as the amygdala, hippocampus, and hypothalamus (Buck, 1996). As you learned in Chapter 3, these areas have been linked with the regulation of feeding, drinking, sexual behavior, and even memory. Part of the emotional power of olfactory cues might be related to the involvement of this motivational pathway. Certainly, in lower animals, whose behavior is often dominated by odor cues, brain structures such as the hypothalamus and the amygdala seem likely to play a major role in the animal's reaction to odors in its environment.

Many animals release chemicals, called *pheromones*, that cause highly specific reactions when detected by other members of the species (Brennan & Zufall, 2006). Pheromones often induce sexual behavior or characteristic patterns of aggression, but other reactions can be produced. Ants, for example, react to the smell of a dead member of the colony by carrying the decaying corpse outside the nest (Wilson, 1963). So far, much to the disappointment of the perfume industry, little support has been found for human pheromones; at least no scents have been discovered that reliably induce sexual interest (Doty, 2010). There is some tantalizing evidence suggesting that women prefer the scents of men who show physical traits suggestive of "good genes," such as facial symmetry; moreover, these preferences are strongest when the women are most fertile (Thornhill et al., 2003).

Taste

Smell's companion sense, taste, is known by the technical term **gustation**, which comes from the Latin *gustare*, meaning "to taste." Unlike odors, which are difficult to classify, there appear to be four basic tastes: sweet, bitter, salty, and sour. There may be a fifth basic taste as well, called umami (which translates from the Japanese as "meaty" or "savory"); recent studies provide evidence that we have taste receptors for this taste (Zhang et al., 2019). When psychologists use the term *taste*, they are referring to the sensations produced by the taste receptors; they are not referring to the overall richness of the psychological experience that accompanies eating. Typically, the term *flavor* is used to describe the mental experience. **Flavor** is influenced by taste, smell, and the visual appearance of the food, as well as by expectations about the quality of the meal (Shepard, 2006).

Taste receptors are distributed throughout the mouth but mainly occur across the tongue. If you coat your tongue with a mouthful of milk and glance in a mirror, you'll see that your tongue is covered with tiny bumps called *papillae*. The **taste buds**, which contain the actual receptor cells, are embedded within the folds of the papillae. Different types of taste receptor cells have been discovered; each is sensitive to a particular kind of taste molecule—one might respond to salt and another to sweet. Contact with the relevant molecule leads to the generation of neural responses (action potentials), which are then transmitted to several taste-sensitive regions of the brain.

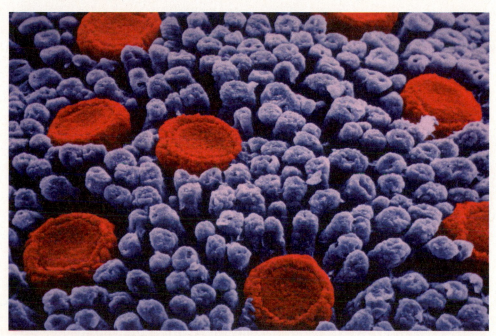

Taste buds, which contain the receptor cells for taste, are embedded within the folds of the large circular papillae.

Omikron / Science Source

The brain produces stable interpretations of taste stimuli, but the identification process is complex. Again, the ultimate experience of flavor depends on many factors. Taste interacts with smell, and experience can alter one's perception. No one is born liking chili peppers. Moreover, prior exposure to one kind of taste often changes the perception of another. Anyone who has ever tried to drink orange juice after brushing their teeth understands how tastes interact. To some extent, the interaction process depends on the similarity of successive tastes. A taste of a sour pickle, but not a salty cracker, will reduce the "sourness" of lemon juice. There are even natural substances that can completely change the normal perception of taste. One substance extracted from berries, called "miracle fruit," turns extremely sour tastes (such as from raw lemons) sweet. Another substance, taken from the leaves of a plant found in India and Africa, temporarily eliminates the sweet taste of sugar. Despite these complexities, there are universals: Babies are born liking sweet tastes and disliking things that taste bitter. Bitter taste can signal potential poisons, and sweetness can help identify sugars that are biologically necessary. These taste fundamentals clearly helped our ancestors adapt and survive in their environments.

Now test your knowledge about smell and taste by filling in the blanks. Choose the best answer from among the following terms: *chemoreceptors, flavor, gustation, hypothalamus, olfaction, olfactory bulb, pheromones, taste, taste buds.* (You will find the answers in the Appendix.)

1.   The general term for receptor cells that are activated by invisible molecules scattered about in the air or dissolved in liquids: ____

2.   One of the main brain destinations for odor messages: ____

3.   A psychological term used to describe the entire gustatory experience: ____

4.   The technical name for the sense of smell: ____

5.   The technical name for the sense of taste: ____

FROM THE PHYSICAL TO THE PSYCHOLOGICAL

There's a transition from the physical to the psychological. Messages originate in the physical world, but our conscious experience of those messages is influenced by our beliefs about how the world is organized. We *interpret* the physical message, and this means our conscious experience of the sensory message can be different from the one that is delivered by the environment. In the field of **psychophysics**, researchers search for ways to describe the transition from the physical to the psychological in the form of mathematical laws. By quantifying the relationship between the physical properties of a stimulus and its subjective experience, psychophysicists hope to develop *general laws* that apply across all kinds of sensory input. Let's consider some examples of how such laws are established.

Stimulus Detection

Psychophysics is one of the oldest research areas in psychology; it dates to the work of Wilhelm Wundt, Gustav Fechner, and others in the 19th century. One of the first questions these early researchers asked was this: What is the minimum amount of stimulus energy needed to produce a sensation? Suppose we present you with a very faint pure tone—one that you cannot hear—and gradually make it louder. At some point, you will hear the tone. This point is known as the **absolute threshold** for the stimulus; it is the level of intensity that lifts the stimulus over the threshold of conscious awareness. One of the early insights of psychophysicists was that absolute thresholds are really not absolute. It turns out that there is no single point at which detection reliably begins. For a given intensity, sometimes people will hear the tone; other times not (the same situation applies to detection in all the sensory modalities, not just auditory). For this reason, absolute thresholds were redefined as the intensity at which people can detect the presence of a stimulus 50% of the time (see Figure 5.24).

It might seem strange that detection changes from moment to moment. Part of the reason is that trial-to-trial observations can be "noisy." It's virtually impossible for a researcher to control for all the things that can affect performance. For example, people might have a momentary lapse in attention that causes them to miss a presented stimulus. Some random activity in the nervous system might even create brief changes in the sensitivity of the receptor systems. Experimenters try to take these factors into account by presenting many detection opportunities and averaging performance over trials.

Psychologists have also developed statistical techniques to pull the "truth" out of noisy data. Human participants often have built-in biases that influence their responses. For example, people will sometimes report the presence of a stimulus even though none has actually been presented. Why? Sometimes observers are simply worried about missing a presented stimulus, so they say, "Yes, I heard it," on every trial. To control for these tendencies, researchers use a technique called **signal detection** that mathematically compares *hits*—in which a stimulus is correctly detected—to *false alarms*—in which the observer claims a stimulus was presented but it was not.

FIGURE 5.24 ■ Absolute Threshold

The more intense the stimulus, the greater the likelihood that it will be detected. The absolute threshold is the intensity level at which we can detect the presence of the stimulus 50% of the time.

Four types of outcomes can occur in a detection situation. Besides hits and false alarms, you can also fail to detect a stimulus when it was actually presented—called a *miss*—or correctly recognize that a stimulus was, in fact, not presented on that trial—called a *correct rejection*. Researchers compare these outcomes over trials to determine true detection ability. Concept Review 5.4 summarizes these different outcomes from signal detection.

To better understand how this works, consider a situation where you are trying to catch a mosquito that has gotten into your house before it bites you. You stand quietly in the room you think it is in and try to detect the buzzing sound it makes. You think you hear the buzzing, so you look around for the mosquito. If it is there, then that's a hit (you detected it when it's really there). If it's not there, then that's a false alarm (you thought it was there when it wasn't). If, instead, you don't hear the mosquito when you stand still, then there are two possibilities: It really isn't in the room (a correct rejection), or it is in the room but you didn't hear it (a miss).

To see why it's important to compare these different outcomes, imagine Lois is participating in a simple detection experiment and that her strategy is to say, "Yes, a stimulus occurred," on every trial (even when no stimulus was actually presented). If the researcher pays attention only to hits, it will appear as if Lois has perfect detection ability—she always correctly identifies a stimulus when it occurs. But saying "Yes" on every trial will also lead to false alarms—she will say "Yes" on trials when no stimulus was actually presented. By comparing hits and false alarms, the researcher can determine whether her high number of "hits" is really due to detection ability or whether it's due to some other bias on her part. If Lois can truly detect the stimulus when it occurs, she should show lots of hits and very few false alarms.

CONCEPT REVIEW 5.4
OUTCOMES FROM SIGNAL DETECTION

The table shows the different response outcomes from detecting a stimulus (e.g., someone's voice) within noise (e.g., a crowded party). Hits and correct rejections represent correct responses; false alarms and misses represent errors in signal detection. Accuracy is determined from both hits and false alarms to account for how often someone responds "Yes" overall.

	Stimulus Present	Stimulus Absent
Response of "Yes, it's there"	Hit	False alarm
Response of "No, it's not there"	Miss	Correct rejection

Difference Thresholds

Researchers in psychophysics have also been concerned with the measurement of **difference thresholds**: the smallest detectable difference in the magnitude of two stimuli. Suppose we present you with two tones, each equally loud. We then gradually increase the intensity of one of the tones until you notice it as being louder than the other (called the *standard*). How much of a change do we need to make for you to detect the difference? As with absolute thresholds, the required amount changes from one moment to the next, but an important general principle emerges.

The addition of a few candles to a brightly lit room has little effect on perceived brightness (a); but when candles are added to a dimly lit room (b), the increase in brightness is quite noticeable.

iStockPhoto/monkeybusinessimages (top); iStockPhoto/VladGans (bottom)

It turns out that detection of a *just noticeable difference* (or JND) depends on how intense the standard was in the first place. If you have your phone cranked up, small changes in the volume will not be noticed; but if the volume starts out low, the same changes are likely to produce a very noticeable difference. If you're at a rock concert and your friend Gillian wants to tell you something, she needs to yell; if you're in a library, a whisper will do. We can state this relationship more formally as follows: The JND for stimulus magnitude is a constant proportion of the size of the standard stimulus. In other words, the louder the standard stimulus (the phone), the more volume will be needed before a difference in loudness will be detected. This general relationship, called **Weber's law**, doesn't work just for loudness—it applies across all the sensory systems. If the lights in your house go off, two candles will make the room a lot brighter than one; if the lights are on, adding one or two candles will lead to little, if any, noticeable increase in brightness (see the accompanying photos). Weber's law demonstrates once again that the relationship between the physical and the psychological is not always direct; increases in the magnitude of a physical stimulus will not always lead to increases in the psychological experience.

Sensory Adaptation

One other feature of all sensory systems is important to remember: Sensory systems are more sensitive to a message when it first arrives than to its continued presence. Through **sensory adaptation**, the body quickly adapts, by reducing sensitivity, to a message that remains constant—such as the feel of a shirtsleeve on your forearm, your hand resting on your knee, or the hum of computers in the background. Think about what the world would be like without sensory adaptation. The water in the pool would never warm up; the smell of garlic from last night's dinner would remain a pervasive force; you would constantly be reminded of the texture of your sock pressing against your foot.

Adaptation is a feature of each of the sensory systems we've discussed. Images that remain stable on the retina will vanish; this doesn't normally occur because the eyes are constantly moving and refreshing the retinal image. If you are presented with a continuous tone, your perception of its loudness decreases over time. If auditory adaptation didn't occur, no one would ever be able to work in a noisy environment. Human sensory systems are designed to detect *changes* in the incoming message; sensitivity is reduced to those aspects of the message that remain the same.

KNOWLEDGE CHECK 5.5

Now test your knowledge of psychophysics by deciding whether each of the following statements is true or false. (You will find the answers in the Appendix.)

1. The intensity level that is required to perceive a stimulus varies across individuals but remains constant for any given individual. *True or False?*

2. A "false alarm" occurs in signal detection when an observer claims a signal was present when, in fact, it was not. *True or False?*

3. According to Weber's law, the detection of a just noticeable difference in magnitude is constant across all intensity levels. *True or False?*

4. Sensory adaptation is a characteristic of all sensory systems. *True or False?*

THE PROBLEMS SOLVED: BUILDING THE WORLD OF EXPERIENCE

To navigate successfully in the world, we rely on multiple sensory systems. As you've seen, the outside world itself is not very user friendly—it bombards the body with energy-based messages, but none arrives in a form appropriate for the language of the brain. Moreover, the messages that our sensory systems receive are complex and ever changing. To build an accurate view of the world, our sensory systems need to solve three problems: (1) The external message must be translated into the internal language of the nervous system; (2) the elementary components must be identified and pulled from the message; and (3) a stable and lasting interpretation of the message components must be built.

Translating the Message

To solve the translation problem, the body relies on specialized receptor cells that generate neural impulses in the presence of different energy sources. In the visual system, receptor cells—rods and cones—react to light; in the auditory system, sound leads to movement of the basilar membrane, which in turn causes tiny hair cells to generate a neural impulse. The body also has specialized receptors that react to pressure on the skin, free-floating chemicals in the air, and the relative position or movement of muscles. Each of these receptor systems acts as a kind of "translator," changing the messages delivered by the world into the electrochemical language of the brain.

Identifying the Message Components

Once translated, systems in the brain work to identify the basic components contained in the sensory message. A variety of neural pathways are specialized to look for specific kinds of sensory information. For example, opponent-process cells in the lateral geniculate are specialized to process color; they signal the presence of one kind of color by increasing the rate at which they generate neural impulses; they signal another kind of color by decreasing their firing rate. Similarly, highly specialized cells in the visual cortex respond only to particular patterns of light and dark. One kind of cell might respond only to a bar of light presented at a particular orientation; another cell might respond only to a pattern of light that moves in a particular direction across the retina.

In the auditory cortex, the brain detects information about the frequencies of sound in an auditory message. Psychologically, changes in frequency correspond to changes in perceived pitch. The brain extracts frequency information by noting the specific place on the basilar membrane where hair cells are stimulated and by noting the rate at which neural impulses are generated over time. It's not unusual for the brain to rely on multiple kinds of processing to extract a particular message component. The perception of color, for instance, relies not only on opponent-process cells but also on the relative activations of three different cone types in the retina.

Producing Stable Interpretations: Auditory Perception

To build a stable interpretation of the sensory message, we use a combination of bottom-up and top-down processing—beliefs and expectations work with the actual sensory input to build perceptions of the external world. In many respects, our perceptual abilities are truly amazing. The pattern of light reflected from a moving object changes continuously with time, yet we have no trouble recognizing a dancer moving effortlessly across the stage. We also have no trouble identifying the voice of a friend in a crowded room, even though the actual auditory message reaching our ears may be filled with frequency information from many different voices.

The brain solves these problems of perception, in part, by relying on organizational "rules." For example, we're born with built-in tendencies to group message components in particular ways. Figures are separated from ground, items that share physical properties are perceived together, and so on. But we also rely on prior knowledge for help in the interpretation process. We use what we know about how cues are related in the environment to arrive at sensible interpretations of ambiguous objects. For instance, if two parallel lines converge in the visual field, the brain assumes that the lines are moving away—like railroad tracks moving off in the distance. Such top-down processing is usually extremely adaptive—it helps us maintain a stable interpretation—although in some cases perceptual illusions may be produced.

THINKING ABOUT RESEARCH

A summary of a research study in psychology is given in this section. As you read the summary, think about the following questions:

1. Explain how this study examines perception in terms of the perception–action perspective.
2. Which Gestalt organizational principles do you think would be useful for the sailors' walking task in this study? Explain how these principles apply to the task.
3. How do you think participants with little or no experience on boats would have performed in the task in this study? What does this tell you about perception?
4. Which sensory system(s) do you think are most important in performing the task in this study? Explain your answer.

Article Reference: Walter, H., Wagman, J. B., Stergiou, N., Erkmen, N., & Stoffregen, T. A. (2017). Dynamic perception of dynamic affordances: Walking on a ship at sea. *Experimental Brain Research, 235*, 517–524.

Purpose of the Study: Consider the task of walking around on a boat out on the ocean. This can be a difficult task, especially when the sea is rough. To better understand how this task is accomplished, researchers investigated how experienced sailors use their judgments to estimate their ability to walk along a narrow path in different directions at sea. These judgments were then compared with the sailors' actual performance to determine how accurate their judgments were (i.e., affordances). The experimenters predicted that the participants would be able to estimate their ability to walk in different directions on the boat accurately, showing that they are able to calculate how well the boat affords walking accurately under different conditions.

Method of the Study: On a boat traveling from Seattle, Washington, to San Diego, California, researchers set up narrow walking tracks from the left side of the boat to the right side (*athwart* direction) and between the front and back of the boat (*fore* and *aft*). While the boat was at sea, they first asked the people working on the boat (16 participants) to judge how far they could accurately walk within the narrow tracks athwart and fore and aft on the boat's deck. They then asked the participants to walk the tracks and measured how far they could walk without falling out of the boundaries of the track.

Results of the Study: The results of the study showed that the participants' judgments of the distance they could walk in the tracks matched their actual walking performance. In addition, judgments and performance in walking differed according to the direction of the track. Participants judged and walked longer distances in the athwart direction than the fore-and-aft direction, which was expected due to the way a boat moves in the ocean (more motion side to side than forward and back).

Conclusions of the Study: From these results, the researchers concluded that, using perception, we can accurately judge affordances for behavior on moving vehicles.

KNOWLEDGE CHECK: CHAPTER SUMMARY

(You will find the answers in the Appendix.)

VISION: THE WORLD OF COLOR AND FORM

- Light reflected from an object enters the (1) ___ through the cornea, (2) ___, and (3) ___. Light reaches the back of the eye, or (4) ___, where light-sensitive receptor cells called (5) ___ and (6) ___ translate the message into the language of the brain.

- After leaving the retina, neural activation flows first to the (7) ___ and then primarily through the lateral geniculate nucleus in the (8) ___. (9) ___ in the visual cortex respond to particular aspects of a stimulus, such as orientation and patterns of light and dark. The trichromatic theory proposes that color information is extracted from (10) ___ different kinds of cones; (11) ___-___ theory proposes that cells respond positively to one color type and negatively to others. Each theory accounts for certain aspects of color vision.

- Bottom-up processing starts with a physical message, and (12) ___-___ processing applies knowledge and expectation. We group incoming visual messages according to Gestalt principles of organization, which include the laws of (13) ___, similarity, (14) ___, good continuation, and common fate. Monocular and (15) ___ cues help us perceive (16) ___. We use top-down processing to help us identify objects and achieve perceptual (17) ___, although sometimes inappropriate interpretations of physical reality can occur.

HEARING: IDENTIFYING AND LOCALIZING SOUNDS

- Sound varies in (18) ___ and (19) ___. Sound wave vibrations enter the ear through the pinna and travel to the tympanic membrane, or (20) ___, and then to the middle ear, inner ear, and cochlea. Vibrating fluid in the (21) ___ displaces the (22) ___, which activates auditory receptors called hair cells.

- The (23) ___ uses several types of information to identify pitch. The (24) ___ of pitch perception holds that we hear a particular pitch because (25) ___ at a certain location on the basilar membrane are responding actively. According to frequency theory, pitch is partly determined by the (26) ___ of neural impulses traveling up the auditory pathway. Final processing of the auditory message takes place in the auditory cortex. Cells in certain areas of the (27) ___ are sensitive to different sound information.

- The brain uses existing knowledge and (28) ___ to impose structure on and (29) ___ incoming auditory messages. Sound (30) ___ depends on comparing how the arrival (31) ___ and (32) ___ of a sound differs from one ear to another.

THE SKIN AND BODY SENSES: FROM TOUCH TO MOVEMENT

- Touch information is transmitted from different types of (33) ___-___ skin cells through distinct neural pathways to the brain, where it is processed by the (34) ___ cortex in the (35) ___ lobe. Cold fibers respond to skin cooling and warm fibers respond to skin warming by (36) ___ neural firing. Temperature perception depends on (37) ___ in temperature.

- According to (38) ___-___ theory, pain receptors generate impulses that are gated, or blocked, in the (39) ___ by brain signals. This can prevent critical pain signals from reaching higher neural centers when appropriate. The (40) ___ also controls our experience of pain by releasing (41) ___, chemicals that produce pain-relieving effects.

- (42) ___ is the ability to sense the (43) ___ and movement of the various parts of the body. Kinesthetic receptors generate nerve impulses that travel to the (44) ___ cortex. The (45) ___ sense responds to movement, (46) ___, and changes in upright posture. (47) ___ canals and vestibular sacs in the ear help us detect the position of the head and influence our sense of balance.

THE CHEMICAL SENSES: SMELL AND TASTE

- The sense of smell, or (48) ___, and taste, or gustation, depends on the activity of (49) ___ that react to molecules in the air or dissolved fluids. Olfaction relies on airborne molecules that enter the nose or back of the throat and interact with chemoreceptors in the (50) ___ cavity to produce a message that travels to the olfactory (51) ___ in the brain. Gustation relies on taste buds that contain chemoreceptors embedded in the tiny bumps on the tongue called papillae. Taste appears to have four categories: sweet, salty, bitter, and sour. Taste messages travel first to the (52) ___ and then to the taste-sensitive regions of the cortex.

FROM THE PHYSICAL TO THE PSYCHOLOGICAL

- The (53) ___ of a stimulus is the level of intensity at which we can detect the presence of the stimulus (54) ___ percent of the time. To account for varying responses, researchers developed (55) ___, a technique that mathematically compares hits to (56) ___ alarms.

- A (57) ___ is the smallest difference in the (58) ___ of two stimuli that can be (59) ___. According to Weber's law, detecting a (60) ___ (JND) depends on the intensity or size of the standard stimulus.

- Sensory (61) ___ is an important function that allows the body to adapt quickly to a (62) ___ by reducing (63) ___ to sensory messages that remain (64) ___, such as the feel of a sleeve on your arm.

CRITICAL THINKING QUESTIONS

1. Can you think of any reason it might be adaptive for the brain to first break the visual pattern down into basic features—such as a bar or a pattern of light and dark—before recombining those features together into a unified whole?

2. Not all psychologists are convinced that these performance effects truly represent perception. When a batter is hitting well, do you think the ball physically "looks" bigger, or is this just an opinion or bias on the part of the perceiver?

3. Can you think of any songs that you like now but didn't like when you first heard them? One possibility is that you've learned to organize the music in a way that makes it more appealing.

4. Can you tell the difference between the touch of a loved one and the touch of a stranger? Do you think you could learn to interpret a touch differently with experience?

5. Some smells and tastes are truly disgusting and lead to characteristic facial expressions and reactions. Can you think of any adaptive reasons we might have such reactions?

KEY TERMS

absolute threshold (p. 184)

accommodation (p. 152)

affordance (p. 172)

basilar membrane (p. 174)

binocular depth cues (p. 166)

blind spot (p. 154)

bottom-up processing (p. 161)

brightness (p. 151)

chemoreceptors (p. 181)

cochlea (p. 173)

cold fibers (p. 179)

cones (p. 152)

convergence (p. 166)

cornea (p. 151)

dark adaptation (p. 155)

difference threshold (p. 186)

feature detectors (p. 156)

flavor (p. 183)

fovea (p. 152)

frequency theory (p. 175)

gate-control theory (p. 180)

Gestalt principles of organization (p. 163)

gustation (p. 183)

hue (p. 151)

iris (p. 151)

kinesthesia (p. 180)

lens (p. 151)

light (p. 151)

middle ear (p. 173)

monocular depth cues (p. 166)

olfaction (p. 181)

opponent-process theory (p. 159)

pain (p. 179)

perception (p. 148)

perceptual constancy (p. 168)

perceptual illusions (p. 169)

phi phenomenon (p. 168)

pinna (p. 173)

pitch (p. 173)

place theory (p. 175)

psychophysics (p. 184)

pupil (p. 151)

receptive field (p. 153)

recognition by components (p. 164)

retina (p. 152)

retinal disparity (p. 166)

rods (p. 152)

semicircular canals (p. 180)

sensations (p. 148)

sensory adaptation (p. 187)

signal detection (p. 184)

sound (p. 173)

taste buds (p. 183)

top-down processing (p. 161)

transduction (p. 151)

trichromatic theory (p. 158)

tympanic membrane (p. 173)

vestibular sacs (p. 181)

visual acuity (p. 152)

warm fibers (p. 179)

Weber's law (p. 187)

CONSCIOUSNESS

LEARNING OBJECTIVES

6.1 Describe the purpose of attention in everyday life and identify its role in visual neglect and attention disorders.

6.2 Differentiate among the stages of sleep and explain the function of REM sleep and dreaming.

6.3 Compare the different types of psychoactive drugs and their effects on the brain and behavior.

6.4 Define hypnosis and describe the effects of hypnosis and meditation on consciousness.

6.5 For each of the major sections of the chapter, summarize how consciousness solves critical problems in the mind and behavior.

CHAPTER OUTLINE

Setting Priorities for Mental Functioning: Attention

    Practical Solutions: Cell Phones and Driving

Sleeping and Dreaming

Altering Awareness: Psychoactive Drugs

Altering Awareness: Induced States

    Practical Solutions: Mindfulness

The Problems Solved: What Is Consciousness For?

Have you ever been reading for a while, only to realize after a few minutes that despite making your way down a page of text, you've not actually noticed anything you were reading? Instead, perhaps you were thinking about the party you went to last night, the fight you just had with your significant other, or what you need to get done tomorrow. You might even be doing that right now. This is a state of consciousness known as daydreaming or mind wandering. Your attention is focused on your internal thoughts instead of on the external stimulus like your book or text. How does this happen? Why can't we always pay attention to things we know we should? What effect does lack of sleep, or drugs we might take, have on our ability to pay attention? These questions relate to the topics in this chapter on consciousness.

THE PROBLEMS TO BE SOLVED: WHAT IS THE PURPOSE OF CONSCIOUSNESS?

Stop for a moment and take a look inside your own head. Try to grab hold of conscious thought and take it for a ride. Forget about its contents—ideas, images, sounds—and concentrate only on the movements from thought to thought to thought to thought. Notice the transitions, the ways ideas and feelings spring forth, only to disappear a moment later. Would you call the movements bumpy? Smooth? The American psychologist William James (1890) was convinced that consciousness *flows*. Consciousness isn't something that can be chopped up into bits, he argued; "[W]ords such as 'chain' or 'train' do not describe it fitly[;] . . . a 'river' or 'stream' are the metaphors by which it is most naturally described" (W. James, 1890, p. 233).

Flow it might, but one of the insights of modern neuroscience is that our thoughts and actions are often controlled by processes that operate *below* levels of conscious awareness. To take an extreme case, you're not aware of the processes controlling your heartbeat or breathing rate, yet these functions carry on like clockwork. Lots of things require little or no conscious thought: our ability to understand spoken language, detecting that one object is farther away than another, sensing anger or happiness from a fleeting glimpse of a face, orienting to a loud noise, riding a bike on an empty road . . . the list goes on and on. Even your mind wandering off from what you are reading seems to happen without your control. But control might be needed to keep your attention on what you are reading.

Even conscious decision making, like your decision to pick up a coffee cup, is importantly controlled by unconscious processes. If we measure the brain activity used to guide behavior, it's already gaining steam well before you consciously decide to take an action (Libet, 2004). In some sense, your brain knows what it wants to do before you do! This doesn't mean that consciousness is unimportant, but it's less involved in guiding immediate behavior than you might think. Indeed, if you measure what people tend to think about, it's usually not about what's happening in the immediate here and now. Instead, we use our conscious thoughts to plan future behaviors, to solve demanding problems, and to think about the consequences of our actions, as in the case of mind wandering just described. Consciousness enables us to assign meaning to our actions, thereby helping us to understand, predict, and ultimately control our world (Baumeister & Masicampo, 2010).

Psychologists define **consciousness** as the subjective *awareness* of internal and external events. The key term here, of course, is *awareness*, but what does it mean to be aware? To be aware is to experience the here and now, and to experience the past in the form of memories, but especially to think and reason. Awareness has the additional property of focus: You can choose to attend to that bug walking up the page of your text, or to the voice of your roommate telling you to turn out the light. You can also use conscious thought to develop strategies for behavior; you can think about what you want to say or do, and you can imagine the outcomes of those actions without actually performing the behaviors. You can use conscious thought to imagine the content of other minds—to predict the behavior of other people and to understand their motivation (Baumeister et al., 2011). In a nutshell, consciousness is an extremely useful feature of the human mind. To appreciate the value of consciousness, as well as to understand how psychologists study it, we'll consider four situations in which the processes of consciousness importantly apply.

Setting Priorities for Mental Functioning: Attention

There are limits to the number of things we can think about at the same time or to the number of tasks we can perform. Have you ever tried to solve a difficult thought problem while someone talks nearby? What about driving and talking on a cell phone—having trouble? Obviously, it's critical to be selective about what we choose to focus on. In this section, we'll discuss how the psychological processes of *attention* help focus our resources on the important tasks at hand.

Sleeping and Dreaming

Sleep clearly serves an adaptive function, and it represents a change in level or state of awareness. But what are the functions of sleep and dreaming? Some researchers believe that we sleep in order to give the brain a chance to rest and restore itself from the day's activities. Others believe that sleep protects us during periods when our sensory equipment is unlikely to function well (such as at night). Dreaming may help us work out hidden conflicts or simply help us exercise the neural circuitry of the brain.

Altering Awareness: Psychoactive Drugs

You know that psychoactive drugs, such as those contained in alcohol and marijuana, can produce mind-bending alterations of consciousness. But did you know that the biological processes that produce these changes are natural and important ingredients of an adaptive mind? Make no mistake—consuming psychoactive drugs can have harmful and long-lasting consequences. But it's important to understand that artificial drugs operate, in part, by tapping natural adaptive systems.

Altering Awareness: Induced States

We'll end the chapter by discussing hypnosis, a procedure that induces a heightened state of suggestibility, and meditation. Both are induced "states" of awareness that have a long history in psychological research. Does hypnosis tell us anything about awareness and its function? Through hypnosis, it's possible to break bad habits (such as smoking) and drastically reduce the experience of pain. The techniques of meditation have proven effective in the treatment of stress, anxiety, and psychological disorders. You'll discover that both hypnosis and meditation can have very useful and adaptive benefits.

SETTING PRIORITIES FOR MENTAL FUNCTIONING: ATTENTION

The world is a teeming smorgasbord of sensory information. We don't experience every sight and sound, of course; we sample selectively from the table based on current needs. If you're searching for friends in a crowded room, you focus on the familiar sound of their voice or the color of their shirt. If you're trying to determine what's for dinner tonight, you sniff the air for the odor of cooking pot roast or simmering spaghetti sauce. You notice those things that are important to the task at hand—you sift through, block out, and focus on those messages that solve the particular problem you face.

Psychologists use the term **attention** to refer to the internal processes that set priorities for mental functioning. For adaptive reasons, the brain uses attention to focus selectively on certain parts of the environment while ignoring others. Obviously, the concepts of attention and consciousness are closely linked—you're consciously aware only of those things that receive some measure of attention. But why is awareness selective? One reason is that the resources of the brain and nervous system are limited. The brain has only so many neurons, and there are limits to how fast and efficiently those neurons can communicate. These limitations require us to make choices about which parts of the environment to process (Broadbent, 1958). But as you'll see, the amount of information we can focus on at one time is limited, so the more information we are presented with at once, the harder these choices become. In fact, research done in a classroom setting shows that students who multitask during lectures (e.g., checking email or Facebook) remember less of the content of the lecture than those who engage in less multitasking (Jamet et al., 2020).

Even if we had unlimited resources, we would still need to make choices. In a mystery novel, certain events are important for solving a murder, and others are "red herrings"—irrelevant points that lead the reader in the wrong direction and delay solving the crime. The trick is to be selective about which clues to pursue. A first-rate detective knows not only what to look for but also what information to avoid. The same is true for even the simplest kind of action, such as walking across the room or reaching for a cup. The visual and motor systems must focus on objects in your path, not every single object in the room. If you looked at and thought about everything, you would become paralyzed with indecision. Prioritizing mental functioning is an important part of how we coordinate and control our behavior.

Experiments on Attention: Dichotic Listening

Research on attention really began in the 1950s with the development of the **dichotic listening** technique (Broadbent, 1952; Cherry, 1953). As shown in Figure 6.1, in a typical experiment, people are asked to listen to spoken messages presented individually to each ear through headphones. To promote selective attention, the task is to *shadow*, or repeat aloud, one of the two messages while ignoring the other. This kind of listening is called *dichotic*, meaning "divided into two," because two messages are involved, delivered separately into each of the two ears.

A dichotic listening experiment requires you to listen to two voices at the same time. Have you ever tried to watch a show while someone next to you is talking nonstop? Not an easy task. In fact, in all likelihood, you had to either ignore one of the two or switch back and forth from one message to the other. This is essentially what happens in a dichotic listening experiment. Forcing a person to repeat just one of the messages aloud usually results in poor processing of the other message. For example, if people are given a surprise test for the unattended message at the end of the experiment, they can usually remember very little, if anything, about its content. They might pick up on the fact that one speaker was male

FIGURE 6.1 ■   **The Dichotic Listening Technique**

In dichotic listening, a person listens to different spoken messages presented simultaneously to each ear and shadows—or repeats aloud—one of the messages while ignoring the other. The task taps the ability to attend selectively.

Illustrated by Sarah Yeh

and the other female, but they remember virtually nothing else about the unattended message (Cherry, 1953; Moray, 1959).

At the same time, we don't just shut off the part of the world that isn't bathed in the spotlight of attention. If we did, we would be in trouble because the world is constantly changing—something new, and possibly important, can happen at any time. Instead, the brain monitors many things at the same time, although the monitoring may be minimal and beyond our current awareness. A case in point is the **cocktail party effect**. Imagine you're at a large party, filled with noisy conversation, and you're trying really hard to hear what your companion is saying. In all likelihood, you won't be consciously aware of all the conversations around you. It's doubtful, for example, that you could repeat what the couple standing next to you is saying. But suppose someone across the room suddenly speaks your name. There's a reasonable chance that you'll turn your head immediately. People in dichotic listening experiments have shown the same effect: They appear to ignore the contents of the unattended message, but if their name appears in it, they notice and remember it later. This is the cocktail party effect, and it suggests that our brains are aware of more than we think.

Another compelling example of how we can monitor multiple messages at the same time comes from an experiment by Treisman (1960), again using the dichotic listening technique. People were presented with compound sentences such as "Against the advice of his broker, the naive investor panicked" in one ear and "Released from his cage, the little lamb bounded into the field" in the other (see Figure 6.2). Subjects were asked to attend to the message in just one of the ears by repeating it aloud, but in the middle of some of the sentences, Treisman switched things around—the second half of each sentence moved to the opposite ear. So, in the attended ear, the subject heard something like "Against the advice of his broker, the little lamb bounded into the field," whereas in the unattended ear, the message became "Released from his cage, the naive investor panicked." The interesting finding was that about 30% of the time people continued to repeat the meaningful sentence ("Against the advice of his broker, the naive investor panicked") even though the message had switched midway from the attended to the unattended ear. Moreover, many reported being unaware that the message had switched.

The cocktail party effect occurs when your attention is captured by a salient stimulus, such as your name.

iStockPhoto/monkeybusinessimages

FIGURE 6.2 ■ Treisman's "Ear-Switching" Experiment

At one point in a dichotic listening experiment by Treisman, unknown to the participant, the to-be-shadowed message was suddenly and without warning switched to the unattended channel. Interestingly, people often continued to repeat the meaningful sentence even though it was now presented in the unattended ear.

Illustrated by Sarah Yeh

These findings suggest that the brain doesn't simply filter out what goes on in the unattended message. It focuses the spotlight of attention on the task at hand, but it carries on at least some unconscious monitoring of the rest of the environment as well. If something important happens, the brain shifts its attention and allows the new event to enter conscious awareness. In Treisman's experiment, the brain must have been following the meaning of the messages in both ears, even though the people who participated were only aware of monitoring one thing. This process is clearly adaptive. People wouldn't live for long in a world where they processed only those things in the realm of immediate awareness.

Processing Without Attention: Automaticity

Remember, a lot of what you do is accomplished without conscious thought. The ability to recognize a facial expression, or orient to a loud noise, may be built directly into the genetic recipe. But you can also drive a car and carry on a conversation at the same time (to some degree—see the Practical Solutions feature later in this section)—you don't need to focus attention on every turn of the wheel or on pressing the brake. These things also occur automatically. In the case of driving, or riding a bike, you have developed a skill that demands less and less attention with practice.

If you practice a task for extended periods, your performance may become automatic. Once acquired, automatic processes no longer require much conscious control.

iStockPhoto/FluxFactory

Psychologists use the term **automaticity** to refer to fast and effortless processing that requires little or no focused attention (Moors & De Houwer, 2006). When you practice a task, such as playing Mozart on the piano, overall speed steadily improves. You may even reach a point where performing the task seems automatic—Mozart rolls off your fingertips with such ease that you're not even consciously aware of finger movement. Automatic processes, once they develop, no longer seem to require conscious control. The mind is free to consider other things while the task itself is performed without a hitch. Many of the activities we take for granted—such as reading, talking, and walking—are essentially automatic processes.

It's possible to measure automaticity through a *divided attention* task (Logan, 1991). In a typical experiment, people are asked to perform two tasks at the same time, such as playing a piece by Mozart on the piano while simultaneously trying to remember a short list of unrelated words. Automaticity is demonstrated when one task, the automatic one, fails to interfere with performance on the other task (Hasher & Zacks, 1979; Shiffrin & Schneider, 1977). Clearly, if you've just learned to play the Mozart piece, your mind will need to focus on every note, and you'll have enough trouble just getting through it without error, let alone recalling a list of words. But if you're an accomplished pianist—if your Mozart performance has become automatic—you can let your fingers do the playing, and your mind can concentrate on remembering the word list.

Notice the relationship between automaticity and awareness, because it tells us something important about the function of consciousness. The better you are at performing a task—the more automatic the task has become—the less likely you are to attend consciously to the details. In fact, some studies have found that highly trained athletes actually improve their skilled performance when they are slightly distracted by other attention-demanding tasks (see Koch & Tsuchiya, 2007). This is a very important characteristic of mental functioning. If we assume that the resources of the brain and nervous system are limited, then automaticity can help free up needed resources for conscious thought. Environmental conditions can change at any moment, so we often need to use conscious awareness as a kind of work space for developing new and creative reactions. We use consciousness for handling the new and demanding while relying on the steady and effortless processes of automaticity to keep moving and acting normally.

But what happens when our attention drifts from the task at hand, sometimes without our awareness? Recent research on mind wandering shows that there are both costs and benefits to such experiences (Smallwood & Schooler, 2015). Mind wandering results in a lowering of task performance. For example, if you mind wander while reading this text, you're less likely to remember what you've read, resulting in the possibility of lower test performance in your course and/or wasted time in having to reread the chapter. However, mind wandering can lead to higher levels of creativity and is related to better performance on a future task that requires you to monitor how much time has passed (Seli et al., 2018). Thus, the flow of consciousness can be beneficial if the costs can be minimized.

PRACTICAL SOLUTIONS: CELL PHONES AND DRIVING

iStockPhoto/FatCamera

You've seen how the resources of the brain are limited. We use the processes of attention to help us attend selectively to current priorities because we simply cannot attend to multiple messages at the same time—at least, not very well. There are some exceptions. Automatic tasks can be performed without the need for sustained attention. Yet tasks that sometimes seem automatic, such as driving, often are not. Certain components of driving are well practiced and require little conscious thought, yet driving demands vigilance at all times. In 2018, 82% of traffic crash fatalities involved distractions, primarily on the part of the driver (National Center for Statistics and Analysis, 2020). The culprits? We're conversing with a friend, listening to a cranked-up radio, or talking on a cell phone.

Quite a bit of research has been done recently on cell phone use during driving. Cellular phones have become extremely popular worldwide—there are over 250 million cell phone users in the

United States alone—and surveys indicate that as many as 75% of cell phone users talk on the phone at least occasionally while driving; half of all adults report they've been in a car when the driver was sending or receiving a text (Madden & Rainie, 2010). Studies have established solid connections between cell phone use and traffic accidents. In fact, talking on a cell phone increases the risk of accident to levels comparable to those of driving with a blood alcohol level above the legal limit (Redelmeier & Tibshirani, 1997). The presence of a correlation between cell phone use and accidents, however, is not sufficient to infer that cell phone use causes accidents. It could be that people who use cell phones while driving are just bad drivers. As you know, correlations do not imply causality.

To determine a causal link, we must have experimental control. A number of experiments have examined the link between cell phone use and driving. Typically, these studies manipulate the type and extent of cell phone use during simulated driving—either in a driving simulator or by requiring people to perform a tracking task on a computer. In a study by Strayer and Johnston (2001), people were asked to use a joystick to move a cursor on a computer screen; the task was to keep the cursor aligned as closely as possible to a moving target (meant to correspond roughly to maintaining location on a road). At random points, either a red or a green light flashed on the computer screen. The participants were instructed to react to the red light by pressing a "brake" button on the joystick. Strayer and Johnston found that when people were engaged in a cell phone conversation while performing the simulated driving task, they missed twice as many red lights. Even when the red light was detected and the brake applied, people were considerably slower to respond. Moreover, the impairments were found regardless of whether the cell phone was handheld while "driving" or a hands-free model. Perhaps not surprisingly, similar studies have found that text messaging during simulated driving also leads to very significant impairments in driving performance (Drews et al., 2009). A recent analysis of a large number of experiments on the effects of cell phone use on driving found that both handheld and hands-free cell phone use reduced driving performance, with a stronger effect when people drove while dialing on their phones (Caird et al., 2018).

Research suggests that cell phone conversations induce a kind of inattention blindness—you literally fail to remember seeing objects in the road because your attention is directed toward the cell phone conversation. Although any kind of in-vehicle conversation can lead to some impairment in driving ability, the effects of cell phone conversations appear to be particularly disruptive (Strayer & Drews, 2007). The implications of this and other recent studies are clear: Turn off the cell phone when you drive. In fact, the U.S. National Transportation Safety Board has advocated for a full ban on cell phones and portable electronic devices in cars.

Disorders of Attention

We've stressed the link between attention and consciousness because, in many respects, attention is the gateway to consciousness. Not surprisingly, if the brain systems that control attention are damaged, there can be a corresponding loss in conscious awareness. Brain researchers have used clinical cases of brain damage to examine how attention and consciousness are related. They're also using neuroimaging techniques to discover attention-related areas of the brain (Nummenmaa & Calder, 2009; Posner & Rothbart, 2007). Let's briefly consider two attention disorders that may be related to brain dysfunction, *visual neglect* and the inattention associated with *attention-deficit/hyperactivity disorder*.

Visual Neglect

Damage to the right parietal lobe of the cerebral cortex can produce an odd and complex disorder of attention called **visual neglect**. People with visual neglect show a tendency to ignore things that appear toward the left side of the body (remember from earlier chapters that the right side of the brain generally controls the left side of the body). Visual neglect can cause people to read only from the right side of pages and copy only the right side of pictures. They may even dress, shave, or apply makeup only to the right side of the body (Bisiach & Rusconi, 1990). It's as if an entire side of their visual field has vanished from awareness. It's also not unusual for these patients to deny that they have a problem. Fortunately, the condition sometimes recovers with time, although it's often associated with other kinds of processing deficits in the brain. It can also arise from damage to the left side of the brain, which then creates problems in the right visual field, but it occurs more frequently with right brain damage (Posner, 1993).

There are also patients who show auditory neglect; after damage to the right hemisphere, they seem somewhat unresponsive to voices and noises that come from their left side (Clarke & Thiran, 2004).

Is the brain really shutting off all the information it receives from one side of the body? Probably not. In one study, a patient suffering from visual neglect was shown drawings of two houses (see Figure 6.3). One house was normal in appearance; the other was normal on the right side but had flames and smoke billowing out from a window on its left side. The patient was asked to choose which of the two houses she would prefer to live in. "The houses look the same to me," she reported, presumably because she was attending only to the right side of each picture. Nevertheless, she consistently chose to live in the house without the flames (Marshall & Halligan, 1988). She showed no conscious awareness of the full image, but her brain was still able to use all the available information to help determine the appropriate behavior (Bisiach, 1992).

FIGURE 6.3 ■ Visual Neglect

Patients suffering from visual neglect might consciously detect no differences between these two houses. But they would probably choose to live in the house without the flames.

Illustrated by Sarah Yeh

Attention-Deficit/Hyperactivity Disorder

A much more common disorder of attention, **attention-deficit/hyperactivity disorder (ADHD)**, is associated with general difficulties in concentrating, paying attention, and self-regulation in general. Symptoms depend on the subtype of ADHD: hyperactive-impulsive, inattentive, or combined, which includes elements of each of the first two types. It's one of the most common psychological problems in school-aged children, although it probably affects only about 3% to 7% of all children, with diagnoses three times more common for boys than girls. However, in some individuals, ADHD can persist into adolescence and adulthood, affecting behavioral functioning across the life span (Barkley, 2016). In addition to attention problems, which affect the quality of their schoolwork, children with ADHD typically exhibit behaviors showing lack of self-control—they may squirm and fidget or blurt out answers to questions before the questions are completely asked. Many children with ADHD can focus on tasks that are highly rewarding (such as video game play) but have a lot of difficulty finishing tasks that are less rewarding (such as schoolwork) or completing tasks with multiple steps. There is strong evidence for genetics as a contributor to ADHD (Demontis et al., 2019).

A diagnosis of ADHD does not always involve hyperactivity.

iStockPhoto/romrodinka

Psychologists are actively searching for the brain mechanisms involved in ADHD. Not surprisingly, neuroimaging studies have shown that the regions of the brain thought to be involved in controlling attention, including the frontal lobe, are selectively involved (Hoogman et al., 2019). There's some evidence that the problem may be associated with irregularities in neurotransmitter action. For example, lower levels of dopamine have been found in people with ADHD than in matched controls (Volkow et al., 2011). It's unlikely that any single brain location is responsible because the disorder is complex and symptoms vary in type and intensity across individuals. There is also evidence that diet plays a role in the severity of symptoms (Dervola et al., 2012).

What about treatment? The news is promising. It turns out that a majority of children and adults who have attention problems can be helped with either medication or a behavior training program, or some combination of both. Children with attention problems need to learn coping strategies to help them perform well in school and in social settings. A training program typically includes teaching study skills, such as learning to write down important information (rather than relying on memory) and offering rewards for sitting still and not being disruptive in social situations. Medications, such as Ritalin, seem to help concentration and self-control of behavior. It's interesting to note that Ritalin, as well as other drugs used to treat the disorder, come from a class of drugs called stimulants that generally increase nervous system activity (you'll read more about stimulants later in this chapter). In low doses, Ritalin improves a person's ability to concentrate and focus attention selectively (Mattay et al., 1996).

Finally, there is some concern among psychologists that ADHD may be overdiagnosed; in fact, there has been rapid growth over the past few decades in the use of medications to treat both children and adults. It's important to be cautious about applying the label "attention disorder" to a child simply because the child has trouble sitting still in school or paying attention. All children are restless from time to time, and certainly most ignore their parents in some situations, but that doesn't mean that medication or a directed training program is in order. Studies show that boys' behavior is more negatively judged, which may result in higher levels of erroneous diagnoses in boys (Fresson et al., 2018). Studies are ongoing to determine if ADHD is being overdiagnosed (e.g., Kazda et al., 2019).

Now test your knowledge about how we set priorities for mental functioning by deciding whether each of the following statements about attention and related disorders is true or false. (You will find the answers in the Appendix.)

1. The cocktail party effect suggests that we cannot attend to more than one message at a time; we focus our attention on one thing, and the rest of the environment is effectively filtered out. *True or False?*

2. In dichotic listening tasks, people are presented with two auditory messages, one in each ear, and the task is to repeat one of the messages aloud while essentially ignoring the other. *True or False?*

3. If a task—such as playing Mozart on the piano—has become automatic, then you can perform a second task—remembering a list of letters—without interfering with performance on the first task. *True or False?*

4. When visual neglect is caused by damage to the right side of the brain, people seem not to notice things that appear on the right side of the body. *True or False?*

5. Attention-deficit/hyperactivity disorder is primarily learned and easily treated solely with special skills training. *True or False?*

SLEEPING AND DREAMING

To set priorities for mental functioning, we focus our attention selectively. If you're trying to read a book, you focus on the page and try to block out distracting sounds. If you're listening to music, you might close your eyes to focus on the rhythms and harmonies. Notice, however, when you redirect your attention in these cases, you're not really changing anything fundamental about the processes of consciousness; instead, you're simply altering the *content* of conscious awareness. In the case of sleep, the change is more fundamental—you're no longer consciously aware of the external world, yet your mind is still quite active. For this reason, sleep is sometimes referred to as a different "state" of consciousness.

Biological Rhythms

The regular daily transition from waking to sleep is an example of what is known generally as a *biological rhythm*. Many bodily functions work in cycles, which is something we share with all other members of the animal kingdom. Sleep and waking vary daily, along with body temperature, hormone secretions, blood pressure, and other processes. Activities that rise and fall along a 24-hour cycle are called **circadian rhythms** (*circa* means "about," and *dies* means "day"). Other biological activities may follow cycles that are either shorter or longer. The female menstrual cycle operates on an approximately 28-day cycle, whereas changes in appetite and the ability to perform certain tasks may change several times throughout the day.

These rhythmic activities are controlled automatically by structures in the brain called **biological clocks**. These clocks trigger the needed activities at just the right time and schedule the internal functions of the body to make sure everything is performing as it should. A particular area of the hypothalamus, called the *suprachiasmatic nucleus*, plays a key role in regulating the clock that controls circadian rhythms. It's thought that the human brain probably has several clocks, each controlling functions such as body temperature or activity level.

Setting Our Biological Clocks

The environment helps our brains synchronize—or set—our internal clocks. Light is a particularly important controller, or *zeitgeber* (meaning "time giver"). If you were suddenly forced to spend all your time in the dark or in a continuously lit environment, you would still sleep regularly, but your sleeping and waking cycles would begin to drift (see Figure 6.4). Rather than falling asleep at your usual 11 p.m.

The activity levels of many animals are controlled by internal clocks that are "set," in part, by the environment. Bears are active during the warm summer months and hibernate during the winter.

and waking at 7 a.m., after a while you might find yourself becoming sleepy at 2 a.m. and rising at 10 a.m. People use light during the day, as well as the absence of light at night, as a way of setting their internal sleep clock (Lavie, 2001).

FIGURE 6.4 ■ Pacing the Internal Clock

Light strongly influences our internal biological clocks. If you were suddenly forced to live without darkness, you would still sleep a normal 8 hours (shown by the length of the bar). But sleep onset times would probably drift. For example, if you usually fall asleep at 11 p.m. and wake at 7 a.m., after a while you might find yourself becoming sleepy at 2 a.m. and rising at 10 a.m.

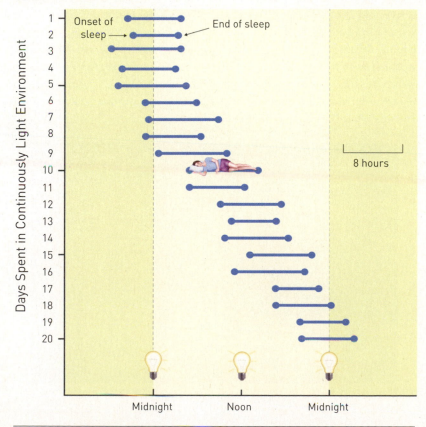

The fact that the environment is so important in maintaining internal body rhythms makes considerable adaptive sense. Remember, the environment also shows regular cycles. The sun rises and sets approximately every 24 hours. There are daily changes in air pressure and temperature caused, in part, by the continuous rotation of the Earth about its axis. It's perfectly reasonable to assume that animals, including humans, have adapted to remain in harmony with these cycles. As the cold of winter approaches, birds fly south for a warmer climate and more abundant food supply; other animals stay put and prepare for hibernation. These changes in behavior are sensible adaptations to fixed changes in the environment that are not under the animal's control.

Jet lag is a good example of how the environment can play havoc with our internal clocks. When you travel to a new time zone, especially if you move east (which shortens your day), your usual signals for sleeping and waking become disrupted—it gets light and dark at unusual times for you. The net result is that you have trouble going to sleep, you get up at the "wrong" time, and you generally feel lousy. Your body needs to reset its clocks in line with your new environment, and this process takes time. This is one reason diplomats and business travelers often arrive at their destinations a few days before an important event or meeting; it gives them time to adjust their internal clocks and shrug off the jet lag.

The Characteristics of Sleep

As mentioned earlier, the transition from waking to sleep can be described as a change in one's state or level of consciousness. Rather than "death's counterfeit" (as Shakespeare called it), sleep does involve awareness, although the focus of that awareness no longer connects directly to events in the world. The sticky problem facing researchers, of course, is that they can't directly measure the internal experience (because the subject is unresponsive). What researchers can do is eavesdrop on the electrical activity of the brain through EEG recordings and draw conclusions about how consciousness is changing based on changes in the patterns of brain activity. It is also possible to use neuroimaging techniques, such as PET scanning and fMRI, to take snapshots of the sleeping brain (Dang-Vu et al., 2010).

As you may recall from Chapter 3, the *electroencephalograph*, or EEG, is a device that monitors the electrical activity of the brain. Electrodes are attached to the scalp, and changes in the electrical potentials of large numbers of brain cells are recorded in the form of line tracings, or brain waves. It's possible to record EEG-based brain waves at any time, including when someone is asleep. The EEG was first applied to the sleeping brain in the 1930s, and by the 1950s researchers had discovered some very intriguing and unexpected things about the sleep process. For example, EEG tracings revealed that during sleep there are regular, or cyclic, changes in brain activity. The EEG also showed that at certain points the electrical activity of the sleeping brain bears a striking similarity to the brain activity of a person who is wide awake (Aserinsky & Kleitman, 1955).

In sleep disorder clinics, changes in the gross electrical activity of the brain are monitored throughout the night.

Bryan and Cherry Alexander / Science Source

Figure 6.5 presents typical EEG recordings made during waking and sleep states. The main things to notice are (1) the *height*, or amplitude, of the brain waves; (2) the *frequency*, or number of cycles per second (usually described in hertz); and (3) the *regularity*, or smoothness, of the pattern. Regular high-amplitude waves of low frequency reflect neural synchrony, meaning that large numbers of neurons are working together. In the first row of tracings, measured when a person was awake, you'll see no evidence of neural synchrony—the EEG pattern is fast and irregular, and the waves are of low amplitude. Presumably, when we're awake, the brain is busy dividing its labor; lots of cells are working on specialized individual tasks, so the combined brain activity tends to look irregular. In contrast, when the brain is in a relaxed state, it produces **alpha waves**, which have a higher amplitude and cycle in a slower, more regular manner.

FIGURE 6.5   ■   EEG Patterns Associated With Sleeping and Wakefulness

As we move from a waking state into sleep, characteristic changes occur in the electrical activity of the brain. Generally, as we become drowsy and move through the different stages of sleep, our brain waves become slower and more regular and show more amplitude. But during REM sleep, when we are presumed to be dreaming, the EEG shows a pattern more closely resembling the waking state.

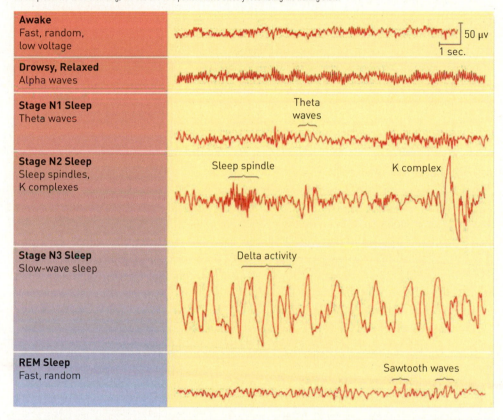

Awake
Fast, random, low voltage

Drowsy, Relaxed
Alpha waves

Stage N1 Sleep
Theta waves

Stage N2 Sleep
Sleep spindles, K complexes

Stage N3 Sleep
Slow-wave sleep

REM Sleep
Fast, random

Source: From *Current Concepts: The Sleep Disorders*, by P. Hauri, 1982, The Upjohn Company, Kalamazoo, Michigan. Reprinted by permission of the author.

Stages of Sleep

As you settle down for the night and prepare for sleep, the fast and irregular wave patterns of the waking state are soon replaced by slower, more regular alpha waves. You're not really asleep at this point—just relaxed and perhaps a little drowsy. The first official sign of sleep—what is called *stage N1* sleep—is marked by a return to waves that are a bit lower in amplitude and slightly more irregular. The dominant wave patterns of stage N1 sleep are called **theta waves**; as you can see in Figure 6.5, they're different from the patterns found in the waking state. Even here, however, people often report that they're not really asleep; instead, they might claim that their thoughts are simply drifting.

The next stage of sleep, *stage N2* sleep, is marked by another change in the EEG pattern. Specifically, the theta activity that defines stage N1 sleep begins to be interrupted occasionally by short bursts of activity called *sleep spindles*. There are also sudden, sharp, intermittent waveforms called *K complexes*. You're definitely asleep at this point, although your brain still shows some sensitivity to events in the external world. Loud noises, for example, tend to be reflected immediately in the EEG pattern by triggering a K complex (Bastien & Campbell, 1992). Your brain reacts, as revealed by the K complex, but you're not really consciously aware of the environment. For instance, you won't do a very good job of responding to signals delivered by an experimenter (say, by raising your finger or hand).

The final stage of sleep, *stage N3*, is a progressively deeper state and shows more synchronized slow-wave brain patterns called **delta activity**; this stage is sometimes called *delta* or *slow-wave sleep*. For many years researchers proposed an additional stage (4), based on the amount of delta activity observed in the EEG pattern, but this convention is no longer widely followed (Iber et al., 2007). Notice the wave patterns in Figure 6.5 appear large (high in amplitude) and cycle slower than the patterns of the earlier sleep stages. You're really asleep now and tough to arouse. If you're shaken awake during slow-wave sleep, you won't be very responsive. You'll act confused and disoriented, and it'll take quite some time for you to reach a normal state of conscious awareness.

REM Sleep

As you move from stage N1 to stage N3 sleep, you're progressing from light to deep sleep. Not surprisingly, other internal measures of arousal, such as breathing rate, heart rate, and blood pressure, decline as you pass through each of the stages. But about 70 to 90 minutes into the sleep cycle, something very unexpected happens—abrupt changes appear in the entire physiological pattern. Heart rate increases rapidly and becomes more irregular; twitching movements might begin in the hands, feet, and face; in males the penis becomes erect, and in females vaginal lubrication begins; the eyes begin to move rapidly and irregularly, darting back and forth or up and down behind the eyelids. The EEG pattern starts to look very similar to the waking state. But you're not awake—you've entered paradoxical, or **REM** (rapid eye movement), sleep.

REM sleep is called "paradoxical" for an obvious reason: The electrical activity of the brain during REM sleep resembles the "awake" pattern, yet you remain deeply asleep. Muscle tone is extremely relaxed, and you're somewhat difficult to arouse. But as the EEG indicates, the brain is extremely active during this period—if jostled awake from REM sleep, you'll seem instantly alert. Again, this contrasts sharply with the confused reaction that people typically have when they're awakened from the early stages of sleep. Perhaps most interesting, people who awaken from REM sleep are likely to report an emotional and story-like dream. In fact, REM-based dreaming is reported well over 80% of the time, even in people who have previously denied that they dream.

There is still debate among sleep researchers about the exact relationship between the REM state and dreaming. People often report dreaming if they're awakened during REM, but dreaming also seems to occur during the earlier stages of sleep. Have you ever experienced a dream moments after going to sleep? Most people have, but it's unlikely that your brain was in an official REM state. Systematic studies of dreaming and the sleep stages have revealed conflicting results. Some studies report low levels of dreaming during non-REM stages (Dement, 1978); other studies have found the percentages to be relatively high (over 50%; see Foulkes, 1985). It remains an open question whether dreaming is an exclusive result of REM, which seems unlikely, or whether dreaming is simply highly correlated with REM activity. We'll have more to say about the REM state momentarily when we consider the function of dreaming.

The Sleep Cycle

During an average night, we cycle through the various stages of sleep, including REM sleep, about four or five times. Each sleep cycle takes about 90 minutes: You progress from stage N1 through stage N3, then back toward stage N1, ending in REM. This sequence remains intact throughout much of the night, but the time spent in each stage changes as morning approaches. During the first cycle of sleep, the majority of time is spent in slow-wave sleep, but REM sleep tends to dominate the later cycles. The amount of time spent in REM sleep increases, and the interval between successive REM states becomes shorter (Ellman et al., 1991). In fact, by the end of the night, you end up spending the majority of your time in REM sleep. As you're aware, many dreams seem to occur toward the end of the sleep period, and these are the dreams you're most likely to remember.

The Function of Sleep

If you sleep eight hours a night and reach the ripe old age of 75, you'll have spent a quarter-century with your eyes closed, your limbs lying useless at your sides, and your outstretched body seemingly open to attack. Doesn't this seem a bit strange? Think about it. What could be the adaptive value, beyond the exercising of neurons during REM sleep, of redirecting the focus of awareness inward, away from potential threats in the environment?

Repairing and Restoring

Researchers aren't exactly sure why people sleep. One possibility is that sleep functions to restore or repair the body and brain. Our daily activities produce wear and tear on the body, and some mind–brain "down time" may be needed to put things back in order. There are definitely periods during sleep, especially slow-wave sleep, when the metabolic activity of the brain is dramatically lowered. Moreover, if people are deprived of sleep for any extended period of time, their ability to perform complex tasks, especially those requiring sustained attention, deteriorates (Lim & Dinges, 2010).

Is the brain really working overtime during sleep—repairing disorganized circuits or restoring depleted resources? Some evidence supports this idea. Slow-wave sleep increases after a bout of vigorous exercise, particularly if you exercise late in the day. There is also an increase in growth hormone during slow-wave sleep. Adequate amounts of sleep are also apparently needed to maintain functioning of the immune system. Researchers aren't completely certain what all these relationships mean at the moment (J. D. Payne & Walker, 2008), but restorative activities clearly do go on during sleep. Moreover, there is excellent evidence that sleep helps us consolidate memories, making them less susceptible to later interference (M. P. Walker & Stickgold, 2006). Slow-wave sleep seems to promote a neural "pruning and sculpting" process that leads to leaner and more stable memory traces (J. D. Payne, 2011). We'll return to the topic of sleep and memory in Chapter 8.

Recent research also suggests that sleep plays a role in maintaining general health through maintenance of the immune system (Irwin, 2015). Sleep (or lack thereof) seems to be related to the risk of infectious disease, poor cardiovascular health, and cancer. For example, production of disease-fighting cells has been shown to increase during sleep. Sleep deprivation or disruption may even reduce the effects of vaccinations for diseases such an influenza and hepatitis. Loss of sleep also increases inflammation, which has been linked to some cancers and heart disease. Researchers are still investigating the biological aspects of sleep that affect these processes.

Survival Value

Another possibility is that sleep is useful because it increases the chances that we'll survive hostile environments. People rely significantly on their visual systems; as a result, we aren't very efficient outside at night when light levels are low. Our ancestors could have moved about at night looking for food, trying to avoid being eaten or killed by some lurking predator, but it was probably a better idea for them to stay sheltered until dawn. Sleep thus became adaptive—particularly sleeping at night—because it stopped people from venturing forth into a dangerous environment (Kavanau, 2002).

The sleeping patterns of animal species in the wild seem to support this view. If sleep is an adaptive reaction to light–dark cycles and susceptibility to predators, then we might expect animals that rely on senses other than vision to be active primarily at night, when vision-based predators would be at a hunting disadvantage. This is indeed the case for mice, rats, and other rodents. Second, large animals that must eat continuously and can't easily find places to hide should sleep very little. And, indeed, grazing animals such as sheep, goats, horses, and cattle, which are vulnerable to surprise attack by predators, sleep only a few hours a day (see Figure 6.6). In one study, researchers found that body weight and susceptibility to attack could explain the majority of the sleeping patterns among different species (Allison & Cicchetti, 1976).

Different species show different sleep patterns consistent with their hunting and foraging patterns.

iStockPhoto/SarahHartMorgan

FIGURE 6.6 ■ Sleep Times for Various Species

Large grazing animals, such as cows and horses, eat frequently and are quite vulnerable to surprise attacks from predators. Such animals tend to sleep very little. Small, quick animals, such as cats and rodents, are less vulnerable to attack and sleep a great deal.

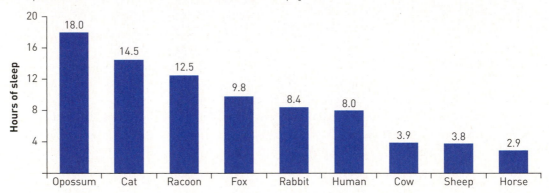

Sleep Deprivation

Earlier we mentioned that our ability to perform complex tasks is disrupted if we haven't received much sleep. Surprised? Well, you've probably performed an all-nighter at some point, only to find yourself irritable and out of sorts the next day. But how serious is prolonged sleep deprivation? From time to time, people have tried to remain awake for very long periods—approaching two weeks—and the results have been generally quite disruptive: Symptoms include slurred speech, sharp declines in mental ability, and even the development of paranoia and hallucinations. When researchers have compared sleep deprivation and the effects of alcohol use on driving performance, they have found that, in some cases, sleep deprivation is equivalent in performance decrements to alcohol intoxication, or perhaps even worse (Lowrie & Brownlow, 2020). In addition, people deprived of sleep for 24 hours show a significant decline in performance of a practiced cognitive task compared to those who have slept, with some of those who were sleep deprived not able to function well enough to perform the task at all (Stepan et al., 2019). Although severely sleep-deprived individuals can appear normal for brief periods, extensive loss of sleep generally hurts virtually all aspects of normal functioning (S. Coren, 1996).

Students tend to be sleep deprived—are you? Sleep deprivation generally hurts virtually all aspects of normal functioning.

iStockPhoto/Tzido

Even more dramatic are the consequences in animal studies. When rats and dogs are deprived of sleep for extended periods, the results can be fatal. Sleep deprivation disrupts the ability of the animal to regulate internal functions, such as temperature, and leads to considerable loss of weight (despite an increased intake of food). The immune system also starts to fail, along with various organs in the body. After roughly three weeks of no sleep, the survival rate among these animals is virtually zero (S. Coren, 1996; Rechtschaffen & Bergmann, 1995). Fortunately, people don't ever reach these levels of sleep deprivation because we simply can't stay awake. Indirectly, however, sleep loss contributes to thousands of deaths each year, mostly through traffic accidents and job-related mishaps.

The Function of REM and Dreaming

It's easy to see how sleep might have developed as an adaptive response, whether to repair, restore, or protect the organism struggling to survive. But why are there stages of sleep? Why, if people want to protect or rest the body, do they spend a significant amount of time in an internally active state like REM sleep? REM sleep is strongly correlated with the recall of dreams: Does dreaming serve some unique biological or psychological function? Unfortunately, we don't really know.

Sleep researchers are still debating whether REM sleep is even necessary for normal functioning. It's possible to deprive people selectively of REM sleep by carefully monitoring the EEG and then waking the person whenever characteristic REM patterns appear in the recordings. Unlike the findings for sleep loss in general, losing significant amounts of REM sleep often does not lead to drastic impairment. People may be a bit more irritable (compared to controls who are shaken awake during non-REM periods), and their performance on tasks requiring logical reasoning and problem solving does suffer, but not much (Ellman et al., 1991). Interestingly, some forms of severe depression appear to be helped by REM sleep deprivation, and some effective antidepressant drugs suppress REM sleep as a side effect (see Reimann et al., 2020).

On the other hand, intriguing changes do occur in sleep patterns after periods of REM deprivation. Sleep researchers have noticed that on the second or third night of REM deprivation, it's necessary to awaken the subject with much greater frequency. When people lose sleep, particularly REM sleep, their bodies attempt to make up for the loss during the next sleep period by increasing the total amount of time spent in the REM stage. The more REM sleep lost, the more the body tries to make it up the next night. This tendency, known as **REM rebound**, is one reason many researchers remain convinced that REM sleep serves some unspecified but extremely important purpose.

Are dreams a consequence of wish fulfillment, random electrical activity in the brain, or something else?

iStockPhoto/Cloud-Mine-Amsterdam

Wish Fulfillment

Why do we dream? Historically, psychologists considered dreaming to be extremely significant. Sigmund Freud believed that dreams, once interpreted, could serve as a "royal road to the unconscious." Freud believed that dreaming was a psychological mechanism for wish fulfillment, a way to satisfy forbidden wishes and desires—especially sexual ones. Dreams often look bizarre, he argued, because the objects within our dreams tend to be symbolic. We hide our true wishes and desires because they're often too unsettling for direct conscious awareness. So, the appearance of a cigar or a gun in a dream (in fact, any elongated object) might represent a penis, whereas a tunnel (or any entryway) could stand for a vagina. To establish the true meaning of the dream, Freud believed it was necessary to distinguish between the dream's **manifest content**—the actual symbols of the dream—and its **latent content**—the hidden desires that are too disturbing to be expressed consciously.

Modern psychologists are reluctant to search for hidden meaning in dreams. Although certain dream events are common across people and cultures (people often dream of flying or falling, for example), and most people have the unsettling experience of recurring dreams, there is no consensus among psychologists about how to interpret dreams. Whether a cigar represents a penis, or just a cigar, isn't immediately obvious—even to the most thoughtful or well-trained psychologist. Moreover, just because you repeatedly dream about being chased by a poodle that looks like your brother Ed doesn't mean the dream is significant psychologically. A troubling dream, for example, might simply cause you to wake up suddenly and think about what has just occurred. As a result, the dream becomes firmly ingrained in memory and likely to occur again.

Activation-Synthesis

An alternative view, the **activation-synthesis hypothesis** of J. A. Hobson and McCarley (1977; J. A. Hobson et al., 2000) proposes that dreaming is a consequence of random activity in the brain. During REM sleep, for reasons that are not particularly clear, cells in the hindbrain tend to spontaneously activate the higher centers of the brain. This activity might arise simply to exercise the brain circuitry (Edelman, 1987), or it could be a consequence of random events in the room (e.g., the cat snoring or a mosquito buzzing around your face). Whatever the reason, the higher brain centers have evolved to interpret lower brain signals in meaningful ways. Thus, the brain creates a story in an effort to make some sense out of the signals it receives. But in the activation-synthesis view, there's little of psychological significance here: Dreams typically represent only random activity in the brain.

The activation-synthesis hypothesis has received a lot of attention because it takes into account how biological activity in the brain changes during sleep. It also provides another explanation for why dream content can be bizarre: Because the activated signals that produce dreams are random in nature, the brain has a tough time creating a story line that is meaningful and consistent. Consequently, there may be some psychological significance to reported dreams after all, but not for the reasons suggested by Freud. The biological mechanisms that generate the REM state are not psychologically driven, but the brain's interpretations of those purely physiological activities may have psychological meaning. The story your brain creates probably tells us something about how you think when you're awake (Domhoff, 2003).

The activation-synthesis hypothesis is an intriguing alternative to the traditional Freudian view, but questions remain about its ultimate viability (see Domhoff, 2019). For example, as noted earlier, we also dream during non-REM states, but the theory focuses primarily on brain activity that occurs during REM sleep. It is also of interest to note that REM activity is commonplace in numerous nonhuman organisms (Durie, 1981). Virtually all mammals experience REM, as do birds and some reptiles, such as turtles. Moreover, human infants spend a remarkable amount of time in REM sleep; even human fetuses show REM patterns in the womb. Perhaps a fetus dreams, but it's unlikely that the fetus is creating an internal "story" to make sense of random activity. Recent advances in neuroimaging are providing clues about the specific neurological changes that occur during REM sleep, so answers may be forthcoming. For example, one study has shown that the same neurons that are active during REM sleep are also active during exploratory behavior in mice. This finding suggests that REM sleep may play a role in replaying events that occurred during waking hours (Blanco-Centurian et al., 2019).

Other Views

We've discussed two prominent views of dreaming—Freud's wish fulfillment and activation-synthesis—but there are others. Some psychologists have suggested that dreams help us solve pressing problems in our lives. We may dream to focus our attention on current problems in order to work toward possible solutions (Cartwright, 1991; Fiss, 1991). Unfortunately, the evidence for the problem-solving view is not very strong, relying primarily on anecdotes that seem to support the position (Blagrove, 1996; Domhoff, 1996). Cartwright (1996) found that depressed individuals who dreamed about the source of their negative emotions (e.g., their spouse during a painful separation) were better adjusted a year later, but something other than dreaming may have been responsible for the improvement. Evidence suggests as well that the content of our dreams affects our behavior. People generally think their dreams are meaningful, and they allow their dreams to influence their judgments and actions. For example, if a friend protects rather than betrays you in a dream, you are likely to report greater affection for that person; if you dream about a plane crash, you may report later that you are less likely to fly (Morewedge & Norton, 2009). But our dreams usually don't deal with current events, and we often have trouble remembering what we dream, so it's unlikely that dreaming evolved simply to help us solve pressing problems (Domhoff, 2003).

Another recent view comes from evolutionary psychology: Dreaming may allow us to simulate threats from the environment and mentally practice the skills needed to avoid those threats (Revonsuo, 2000; Valli & Revonsuo, 2009). We do sometimes dream about aggressive events and threatening situations and take appropriate defense actions (Mathes & Schredl, 2016), but whether dreaming really evolved to help us handle real-world threats remains somewhat speculative. It's safe to assume that REM sleep and dreaming reflect some important property of the brain, but at the moment, the major questions remain unanswered. Concept Review 6.1 provides an overview of different theories about why we sleep.

CONCEPT REVIEW 6.1
FUNCTIONS OF SLEEP AND DREAMING

Why Do We Sleep?

Theory	Description	Evaluation
Repair and restoration	Sleep restores and/or repairs the body and brain.	Some support, but restorative activities of the body are not limited to sleep. Increases in growth hormone occur during slow-wave sleep; sleep may be necessary for adequate functioning of the immune system.
Survival value	Sleep increases chances of survival.	Receives some support from observation of sleep patterns in different species of animals.

Why Do We Dream?

Theory	Description	Evaluation
Wish fulfillment (Freud)	Dreaming is a psychological mechanism for fulfillment of wishes, often sexual in nature.	Difficult to assess; psychologists are reluctant to ascribe hidden meaning to dreams.
Activation-synthesis	Dreaming is a consequence of random activity that occurs in the brain during REM sleep. The brain creates a story to make sense of these random signals.	Theory has led to significant developments in our understanding of the sleeping brain. But dreaming is not limited to REM sleep.
Problem solving	Dreaming helps us focus on our current problems to find solutions.	Evidence tends to be anecdotal, but dream content does affect judgments and behavior.
Threat simulation	Dreaming evolved to help us practice the skills needed to avoid threats.	Still speculation at this point.

Disorders of Sleep

We end our discussion of sleep and dreaming with a brief discussion of sleep disorders. Mental health professionals divide sleep disorders into two main categories: (1) *dyssomnias*, which are problems connected with the amount, timing, and quality of sleep; and (2) *parasomnias*, which are abnormal disturbances that occur during sleep. Let's consider some prominent examples of each type.

Dyssomnias

The most common type of dyssomnia is **insomnia**, where you have difficulty starting or maintaining sleep. Everyone has trouble getting to sleep from time to time, and everyone has awakened in the middle of the night and been unable to get back to sleep. For the clinical diagnosis of insomnia, these difficulties must be chronic—lasting for at least a month. It's been estimated that perhaps 30% of the population suffers from some degree of insomnia, although the number of truly severe sufferers is thought to be closer to 15%. There are many causes for the condition, including stress, emotional problems, and alcohol and other drug use, as well as medical conditions. Some kinds of insomnia may even be learned—for example, children who regularly fall asleep in the presence of their parents often have trouble getting back to sleep if they wake up later alone in their room (Adair et al., 1991). Presumably, these children have learned to associate sleeping with the presence of a parent and consequently can't return to sleep without the parent present.

In **hypersomnia**, the problem is too much sleep. People diagnosed with hypersomnia show excessive sleepiness—they're often caught catnapping during the day, and they complain about being tired all the time. Genetic factors might be involved in this condition (Sehgal & Mignot, 2011), although excessive sleepiness can also be caused by infectious diseases, such as mononucleosis or chronic fatigue syndrome, and by a sleep disorder called *sleep apnea*. Sleep apnea is a relatively rare condition in which the sleeper repeatedly stops breathing throughout the night, usually for short periods lasting up to a minute or so. The episodes typically end with the person waking up gasping for breath. Because these episodes occur frequently throughout the night, the affected person feels tired during the day. Significant sleep apnea problems are found in perhaps 10% of the population, although a higher percentage of people may experience occasional episodes (Latta & Van Cauter, 2003).

An even rarer sleep disorder, called **narcolepsy**, is defined by sudden extreme sleepiness. Sleep attacks can occur at any time during the day and can last from a few seconds to several minutes. What makes this disorder unusual is that the person seems to directly enter a kind of REM sleep state. The person loses all muscle tone and can even fall to the ground in a sound sleep! Fortunately, not all instances of narcolepsy are this extreme, although it can be a disabling condition. The disorder has been linked to the absence of a certain neurotransmitter in the brain (hypocretin), and it may have a genetic link as well (Mahoney et al., 2019). Again, it is rare and probably affects only a few people in a thousand.

Parasomnias

The second category of sleep disorders, parasomnias, includes abnormal sleep disturbances such as nightmares, night terrors, and sleepwalking. **Nightmares** are frightening and anxiety-arousing dreams that occur primarily during the REM stage of sleep. They inevitably cause the sleeper to awaken; if they recur frequently, they can lead to the symptoms of insomnia. What causes nightmares? No one is certain at this point, although frequent nightmares may indicate the presence of a psychological disorder or problems associated with the regulation of emotion (Levin & Nielsen, 2009).

Night terrors, which occur mainly in children, are terrifying experiences in which the sleeper awakens suddenly in an extreme state of panic—the child may sit in bed screaming and will show little responsiveness to others who are present. Fortunately, night terrors are not considered to be indicators of serious psychological or medical problems, and they tend to go away with age.

Finally, **sleepwalking** occurs when the sleeper rises during sleep and wanders about. Sleepwalking happens mainly in childhood, tends to vanish as the child reaches adolescence, and, again, is not thought to result from a serious psychological or medical problem. There's some evidence that sleepwalking runs in families, so you may be born with a genetic susceptibility for the condition (Lecendreux et al., 2003). It's interesting to note that both night terrors and sleepwalking occur during periods of non-REM sleep, which suggests that neither is related entirely to dreaming.

KNOWLEDGE CHECK 6.2

Now test your knowledge about sleep and dreaming by answering the following questions. (You will find the answers in the Appendix.)

1. Choose the EEG pattern that best fits the following descriptions. Options include *alpha waves, delta activity, K complex, sleep spindles, theta waves*, and *REM*.
   a. The characteristic pattern found in stage N1 sleep: ____
   b. Often triggered by loud noises during stage N2 sleep: ____
   c. Another name for the slow-wave patterns that are found during stage N3 sleep: ____
   d. The characteristic pattern of paradoxical sleep: ____

2. Which of the following statements is most consistent with the view that we sleep because it keeps us away from hostile environments during times when we can't see well?
   a. Sleep deprivation leads to a breakdown in normal functioning.
   b. Cats sleep more than cows.
   c. People sleep less as they age.
   d. Fearful dreams make us wary of venturing outside.

3. Diagnose the following sleep disorders based on the information provided. Options include *hypersomnia, insomnia, nightmare, night terror, sleep apnea,* and *sleepwalking*.
   a. Difficulty initiating and maintaining sleep: ___
   b. Sleeper awakens suddenly, screaming, but the EEG pattern indicates a period of non-REM sleep: ___
   c. Sleeper repeatedly stops breathing during the night, usually for short periods lasting less than 1 minute: ___
   d. An anxiety-arousing dream that usually occurs during the REM stage of sleep: ___

ALTERING AWARENESS: PSYCHOACTIVE DRUGS

The rhythmic cycles of sleep reveal how conscious awareness shifts as the electrical activity of the brain changes. We haven't talked much about the factors that control these brain changes, but the brain's chemical messengers, the neurotransmitters, are primarily responsible. The brain is a biochemical factory, altering moods and shifting awareness through the actions of its various neurotransmitters. As we've discussed previously, the brain sometimes reacts to stress or injury by releasing brain chemicals called endorphins, which reduce pain and serve to elevate mood. Altering awareness can be highly adaptive, because the delay of pain can allow an organism to escape from a life-threatening situation.

This series of PET scans shows how administration of a drug affects general activity in the brain over time. The first PET scan in the top row shows a normal active brain; the last PET scan in the bottom row shows diminished activity after the drug has taken full effect.

iStockPhoto/Webeye
Brookhaven National Laboratory / Science Source

If you allow an external agent, such as a drug, to enter your body, it too can radically alter the delicate chemical balance that controls awareness and other mental processes. Obviously, drugs can have tremendously beneficial effects, especially in the treatment of psychological and medical disorders (see Chapter 15). But drugs can have negative effects as well, even though they might seem to change awareness in a highly pleasurable way. *Drug abuse*, particularly of alcohol and tobacco, is directly or indirectly responsible for hundreds of thousands of deaths annually in the United States. In this section, we'll consider the actions of drugs labeled **psychoactive**—those that affect behavior and mental processes through changes in conscious awareness.

Drug Actions and Effects

Psychologists are primarily interested in psychoactive drugs because they help us understand the neural mechanisms that cause behavior. Psychoactive drugs, like most natural drugs produced by the brain, affect the normal communication channels of neurons. Some drugs, like *nicotine*, duplicate the action of neurotransmitters by actually attaching themselves to the receptor sites of neurons; this allows the drug to produce the same effect as the brain's natural chemical messenger. Other drugs depress or block the action of neurotransmitters; some sleeping pills, for instance, decrease norepinephrine or dopamine stimulation. The psychoactive drug *fluoxetine* (known commercially as Prozac) is effective in treating depression; it acts by slowing the process by which the neurotransmitter serotonin is broken down and taken back up into the transmitting cell, keeping the serotonin around in the synapse longer to act on the surrounding cells (Kramer, 1993).

Long-term drug use often changes the way the body reacts. With repeated use, one can develop a **drug tolerance**, which means that increasing amounts of the drug are needed to produce the same physical and behavioral effects (drug tolerance from a learning perspective will be further discussed in Chapter 7). The brain essentially changes its chemistry to adapt to the drug, counteracting its effects. Tolerance, in turn, can lead to **drug dependency**, which is a physical or a psychological *need* for continued use. At this point, if the person stops taking the drug, **withdrawal** symptoms are likely. These are physical reactions such as sweating, vomiting, changes in heart rate, or tremors. Drug dependency is the primary cause of substance abuse, although the mechanisms that lead to dependency are still a matter of some debate. At this point, it's not clear whether dependency develops as a consequence of "urgings" produced by biological withdrawal, fundamental changes in the brain's chemistry, or whether people essentially *learn* to become dependent on the drug with repeated use. It's likely that multiple factors are involved (Degenhardt et al., 2010).

What does seem clear is that drug tolerance can be involved in overdose of a drug. The reason people need higher doses of the drug over time to feel the same effects is that their body has learned to prepare for the drug physiologically based on environmental stimuli typically present when the drug is taken. In a novel environment, that physiological preparation for the drug is absent, resulting in a stronger effect of the typical dose. This can lead to an overdose as a large amount of the drug is taken that the body is not prepared for. Researchers believe this process is the cause of many opiate "overdose" deaths each year (S. Siegel, 2016).

Categories of Psychoactive Drugs

Psychoactive drugs can be classified into three main categories—depressants, stimulants, and hallucinogens—based on their specific mind-altering characteristics. We'll briefly examine each type and then conclude with a discussion of some psychological factors involved in drug use. Concept Review 6.2 provides an overview of the different classes of drugs discussed in this section.

Depressants

In general, drugs classified as **depressants** slow, or depress, the ongoing activity of the central nervous system. Ethyl alcohol, which is present in beer, wine, and distilled drinks, is a well-known example of a depressant. Alcohol increases the effects of a number of neurotransmitters, including GABA, glutamate, and dopamine. The GABA system is involved in the regulation of anxiety and generally reduces, or inhibits, neural activity. (Drugs that block the action of GABA can reduce alcohol's effects.) Alcohol stimulates the release of dopamine as well, which is part of the brain's natural reward system and, at low doses, produces a general stimulatory effect. Animals, by the way, find the effects of alcohol quite reinforcing—they will perform tasks that yield small amounts of alcohol as a reward (Becker et al., 2011).

As alcohol consumption increases, the brain centers that control judgment become sluggish from inhibition. As you're undoubtedly aware, after a few drinks people typically start acting in unusual ways. The normally demure become loud and aggressive; the sexually inhibited become flirtatious and provocative. These behavioral changes are produced, in part, because alcohol reduces self-awareness. Drinkers are less likely to monitor their behaviors and actions closely, and they tend to forget about current problems. These carefree moments are stolen at a cost, of course, because the body eventually reacts to the drug in a negative way. Fatigue, nausea, and depression

Despite the pleasurable properties of alcohol, too much alcohol consumption can have severe negative consequences on your health and well-being.

iStockPhoto/South_agency

are likely to result from drinking too much. If too much alcohol is consumed, the results can even be fatal. Alcohol poisoning, which comes from drinking large quantities of alcohol in a short period of time, often leads to death. The indirect costs are great as well: As activity in the sympathetic nervous system slows, so too does reaction time, which increases the chances of an accident while driving or in the workplace. Thousands of people die every year as a result of alcohol-related incidents.

Barbiturates and *tranquilizers* are also classified as depressant drugs. Both are widely prescribed for the treatment of anxiety and insomnia. They produce effects in the brain similar to those induced by alcohol (the neurotransmitter GABA is again involved). Like alcohol, at low doses tranquilizing agents tend to produce pleasurable feelings of relaxation. But at higher doses your ability to concentrate easily is lost, memory is impaired, and speech becomes slurred. Barbiturates also commonly lead to tolerance and dependency. With continued use, one's metabolism changes, and tolerance sets in. Tranquilizers (such as Valium and Xanax) are less habit forming than barbiturates and for this reason are more likely to be prescribed.

Drugs classified as **opiates** (sometimes called narcotics) also depress nervous system activity, thereby reducing anxiety, elevating mood, and lowering sensitivity to pain. Well-known examples of opiates include opium, heroin, and morphine. Morphine—which is derived from the flowering opium plant—acts on existing membrane receptor sites in the nervous system. Its painkilling effects and pleasurable mood shifts (it's named after Morpheus, the Greek god of dreams) apparently arise from mimicking the brain's own chemicals, specifically endorphins, that are involved in reducing pain. Opiates can produce strong physical and psychological dependence. Stop taking the drug, and the body rebels with intense and prolonged withdrawal symptoms.

People who are regular users of opiates, such as heroin or morphine, suffer in many ways despite any fleeting pleasures that might immediately follow drug use. Kicking an opiate habit is extremely tough because the withdrawal symptoms—which can include everything from excessive yawning, to nausea, to severe chills—last for days. Users who opt for the normal method of administration—intravenous injection—run additional risks from disease, especially HIV. Longitudinal studies of heroin addicts paint a grim picture: Addicts tend to die young (at an average age of about 40) from a variety of causes including suicide, homicide, and overdose (Hser et al., 1993).

The first photo shows the bud of an opium poppy, cut to release the narcotic sap; the second photo shows psilocybin, a type of mushroom that produces hallucinogenic effects; the third photo shows marijuana.

iStockPhoto/xiao zhou
iStockPhoto/Andrei310
iStockPhoto/grandriver

Stimulants

A **stimulant** is a drug that increases central nervous system activity, enhancing neural transmission. Examples of stimulants include caffeine, nicotine, amphetamines, and cocaine. These agents generally increase alertness and can affect mood by inducing feelings of pleasure. The morning cup of coffee is an excellent example of how a stimulant in low doses—caffeine—can improve your mood significantly and even increase concentration and attention. Other side effects of stimulants include dilated pupils, increased heart and respiration rate, and decreased appetite. In large doses, stimulants can produce extreme anxiety and even convulsions and death.

Both amphetamines and cocaine produce their stimulating effects by increasing the effectiveness of the neurotransmitters norepinephrine and dopamine. Dopamine seems to be primarily responsible for the positive, reinforcing qualities of these drugs (Dackis & Miller, 2003). In the laboratory, animals work hard to self-administer drugs that increase the activity of dopamine-based synapses. In the case of cocaine, which is derived from the leaves of the coca plant, the drug blocks the reabsorption of both norepinephrine and dopamine. When reabsorption is blocked, these transmitter substances work for a longer period of time. Cocaine produces intense feelings of euphoria, although the effects of the drug generally wear off quickly. A half-hour or so after the drug enters the body, the user crashes, in part because the drug has temporarily depleted the user's internal supply of norepinephrine and dopamine. Regular use of cocaine produces a number of harmful side effects, including intense episodes of paranoia and even hallucinations and delusions (Adeyemo, 2002).

Cocaine and amphetamines are also available in crystallized forms that can be smoked, snorted, or injected. *Crack*, the crystallized form of cocaine, tends to be purer than street cocaine, and its effects are generally faster acting and more intense. The effects also last for a shorter amount of time, which quickly leads to heightened cravings and a desire for more of the drug. The low that follows crack use is also more intense; again, this increases the desire for more of the drug. These factors produce a lethal combination—a substantial increase in the likelihood of overdose and death, even in occasional and first-time users.

Another stimulant that's shown an alarming increase in popularity in the last couple of decades is a self-labeled designer drug called methamphetamine or *meth*. It is chemically similar to amphetamines (such as Ritalin, described earlier in this chapter as a treatment for ADHD) and has similar effects on the body as cocaine. It can be smoked, swallowed, injected, or snorted. Another drug with similar effects and chemical makeup to meth is methylenedioxymethamphetamine, or MDMA. MDMA is also known as *Ecstasy* or *Molly*. Like other stimulants, meth and MDMA produce feelings of well-being, or even euphoria, and increased energy levels. The dangerous side effects of these drugs are similar to those produced by other stimulants, but there are also side effects unique to each drug. Research with animals has found that MDMA can lead to brain damage through the destruction of serotonin-producing neurons, and it's been shown to interfere with memory and sleep in people (Roberts et al., 2009). Meth has been found to reduce immune function, making users more susceptible to disease (Papageorgiou et al., 2019). Both drugs have the added disadvantage that they're street-made; as a result, users never know exactly what substances they have ingested.

Hallucinogens

For the final category of psychoactive drug, **hallucinogens** (sometimes called psychedelics), the term *psychoactive* is particularly apt. Hallucinogens play havoc with the normal internal construction of reality. Perception itself is fractured, and the world becomes awash in fantastic colors, sounds, and tactile sensations. Two of the best-known examples of these drugs, mescaline and psilocybin, occur naturally in the environment. Mescaline comes from a certain kind of cactus; psilocybin is a type of mushroom. Both have been used for centuries, primarily in the context of religious rituals and ceremonies. Since the 1960s, they have served as potentially dangerous recreational drugs for those seeking alternative realities.

Lysergic acid diethylamide (LSD) is a synthetic version of a psychedelic drug. LSD is thought to mimic the action of the neurotransmitter serotonin (Vollenweider & Kometer, 2010); the drug acts on specific serotonin-based receptor sites in the brain, producing stimulation. For reasons that are not particularly clear, variations in sensation and perception are produced. A typical LSD experience, which can last for hours, consists of profound changes in perception. Some users report a phenomenon called *synesthesia*, which is a blending of sensory experiences—colors may actually feel warm or cold, and rough textures may begin to sing. Also, for unknown reasons, a user's experience can turn sharply wrong. Panic or depression can develop, increasing the likelihood of accidents and personal harm.

Marijuana, which comes from the naturally occurring *cannabis* plant, is another hallucinogenic drug. Specifically, the tetrahydrocannabinol (THC) and cannabidiol (CBD) compounds in the cannabis plant are the main causes of psychoactive effects of marijuana; however, the THC compound is the one that has an intoxicating effect. It is unusual to see profound distortions of perceptual reality with this drug unless large amounts are ingested. Marijuana is usually smoked or swallowed, and its effects last around four hours. Users typically report a melting away of anxiety, a general sense of well-being, and increased awareness of normal sensations. Changes in the perception of time and its passage are sometimes reported, along with increased appetite. The pleasant effects of the drug are followed usually by fatigue and sometimes by sleep.

Marijuana does not always produce a pleasant experience. Some users report anxiety, extreme fearfulness, and panic. A number of studies have shown that marijuana use impairs concentration, motor coordination, and the ability to track things visually (Bolla et al., 2002); these side effects certainly contribute to the likelihood of traffic accidents when driving under the influence. Less is known about the long-term effects of regular use, but there's evidence that chronic use can impair memory functioning (Battisti et al., 2010). On the positive side, marijuana helps reduce some of the negative symptoms

Smoking marijuana can reduce anxiety and the side effects of chemotherapy but can also cause fatigue and impair memory.

iStockPhoto/RealPeopleGroup

of chemotherapy (e.g., nausea), and in some cases, it's proved helpful in treating eye disorders such as glaucoma. Legalization of cannabis use is increasing worldwide, with many U.S. states now allowing legal use of cannabis-containing products, which has led to an increase in research on the positive and negative effects of cannabis use. However, there have been few randomized controlled trials (where people are randomly assigned to ingest the drug or a placebo that does not contain the drug) to date, and those studies have produced inconsistent results (G. Campbell et al., 2019).

CONCEPT REVIEW 6.2
PSYCHOACTIVE DRUGS

Category	Examples	General Effects
Depressants	Ethyl alcohol Barbiturates Tranquilizers	Believed to enhance the effectiveness of GABA and dopamine, which often act as inhibitory messengers in the brain. Produce pleasurable feelings of relaxation, but at high doses concentration and memory are impaired.
Stimulants	Caffeine Nicotine Amphetamines Cocaine Ecstasy	Amphetamines and cocaine may work primarily by increasing the effectiveness of dopamine and norepinephrine. Stimulants tend to increase alertness, elevate mood, and produce physical changes such as increased heart and respiration rate.
Opiates	Opium Morphine Heroin	Depress nervous system activity, resulting in reduced anxiety, mood elevation, and lower sensitivity to pain. Can produce strong physical and psychological dependence.
Hallucinogens	LSD Mescaline Psilocybin Marijuana	Produce variations in sensation and perception. LSD is believed to mimic the action of serotonin. Some users report synesthesia, a blending of sensory experiences. Marijuana leads to a general sense of well-being and heightened awareness of normal sensations. Negative side effects can include anxiety, fearfulness, and panic.

Psychological Factors

Psychoactive drugs often produce individual differences. Two people can take the same drug, in exactly the same quantity, but experience completely different effects. A small amount of LSD consumed by Teo produces a euphoric "religious experience"; the same amount for Alex produces a frightening descent into terror and fear. Why? Shouldn't the effects on neurotransmitters in the brain produce similar or at least consistent psychological effects?

Many factors influence the psychological experience: biological, genetic, and environmental. Smoking marijuana for the first time in a car speeding 75 miles per hour seriously limits the anxiety-reducing effects of the drug. Users report that familiarity is also critical—it's often claimed that you need to "learn" to smoke marijuana or take LSD before the full effects of the drug can be experienced. In fact, experienced users of marijuana have reported experiencing a "high" after smoking a cigarette they only *thought* was marijuana; similar effects did not occur for novice users (R. T. Jones, 1971). Both familiarity and environment affect the user's *mental set*—the person's expectations about the drug's harmful and beneficial consequences. Individual biological and genetic factors are also important: Some people develop resistance or tolerance to a drug faster than others do. The experience of a drug may even depend on such things as whether the person has eaten or is well rested.

The setting in which the drug is experienced can also hide its effects. In a study by J. D. Johnson and colleagues (2000), male college students were asked to judge the acceptability of forced sexual aggression toward a blind date. Everyone saw a video of a couple interacting: For one group, the female in the video acted friendly and cheerful toward the male date (e.g., touching his arm from time to time and sitting close); in a second condition, the woman acted unresponsive and distant. Afterward, everyone was asked to judge how acceptable it would be for the male to force himself sexually on the woman.

Overall the men found such behavior to be unacceptable, but their rating depended, in part, on whether they had just consumed a moderate amount of alcohol. Interestingly, when the woman in the video acted unfriendly and unresponsive, alcohol had essentially no effect—all the men thought sexual aggression toward the woman was unacceptable. However, when the woman in the video acted friendly and responsive, drinking began to matter: Men who had consumed a moderate amount of alcohol were significantly more likely to view sexual aggression as an acceptable response. In this case, alcohol's effect depended importantly on the behavior of others present in the situation.

KNOWLEDGE CHECK 6.3

Now test your knowledge about psychoactive drugs by picking the category of drug that best fits each of the following statements. Choose from among these terms: *depressant, hallucinogen, opiate, stimulant.* (You will find the answers in the Appendix.)

1. Increases central nervous system activity: ___

2. Reduces pain by mimicking the brain's own natural pain-reducing chemicals: ___

3. Tends to produce inhibitory effects by increasing the effectiveness of the neurotransmitter GABA: ___

4. Distorts perception: ___

5. The type of active ingredient found in your morning cup of coffee: ___

ALTERING AWARENESS: INDUCED STATES

The setting is Paris, late in the year 1783. Dressed in a silk robe, German-born physician Franz Anton Mesmer is busy restoring his patients' balance of "universal fluids." In rhythmic thrusts, he passes an iron rod over their outstretched bodies stirring their innate animal magnetism. Some quickly fall into a trancelike state; others become agitated and fitful. All enter an alternative form of consciousness accompanied by a loss of voluntary control. On later awakening, many feel better, apparently cured of their various physical and psychological problems.

Although Mesmer himself eventually fell into disrepute, rejected by the scientific community of his time, the phenomenon of "mesmerizing" did not. We recognize today, of course, that the artificial state of awareness he induced had nothing to do with magnets or the balancing of universal fluids. Instead, the bizarre behavior of his patients is better explained as an example of hypnosis. **Hypnosis** can be defined generally as any form of social interaction that produces a *heightened state of suggestibility* in a willing participant. It is of interest to psychologists, like the related topic of meditation, because it's a technique specifically designed to alter conscious awareness. Hypnosis has many useful and adaptive properties (Kerns et al., 2011).

Although hypnosis is often used for entertainment, it can have considerable clinical value.

iStockPhoto/Peopleimages

The Phenomenon of Hypnosis

Much remains to be learned about hypnosis and its effects. One key question centers on whether it's truly an altered state of awareness or simply a kind of social playacting—more on that later. But we do know a few things about what *hypnosis* is not. For one thing, people who are hypnotized never really enter into anything resembling a deep sleep. The word *hypnosis* comes from the Greek *hypnos*, meaning "to sleep," but hypnosis bears little physiological relation to sleep. The EEG patterns of a hypnotized subject, along with other physiological indices, more closely resemble those of someone who is relaxed rather than deeply asleep (Graffen et al., 1995). Moreover, certain reflexes that are commonly absent during sleep, such as the knee jerk, are still present under hypnosis (Pratt et al., 1988). At the same time, recent studies using the techniques of modern cognitive neuroscience, such as neuroimaging, have detected what appear to be unique neural "signatures" associated with hypnosis (Oakley & Halligan, 2009).

Another myth is that only weak-willed people are susceptible to hypnotic induction. We're all susceptible to a degree, in the sense that we show heightened suggestibility under some circumstances. Hypnotic "suggestibility" scales, which measure susceptibility to induction, indicate that only about 10%–15% of the population is highly hypnotizable (Terhune et al., 2017). But it's not clear exactly what factors account for these differences. Personality studies have shown that people who are easy to hypnotize are not weak willed or conforming, although they may have more active imaginations than people who resist hypnosis (Nadon et al., 1991).

There are many ways to induce hypnosis. In the most popular technique, the hypnotist acts as an authority figure, suggesting to clients that they are growing increasingly more relaxed and sleepy with time: "Your eyes are getting heavier and heavier, you can barely keep your lids open," and so on. Clients are usually asked to fixate on something, perhaps a spot on the wall or a swinging pendulum. The logic here is that eye fixation leads to muscle fatigue, which helps convince clients they are indeed becoming increasingly relaxed; eye fixation also helps them focus their attention. Other approaches to induction rely more on subtle suggestions (Erickson, 1964), but in general no one method is necessarily better than another. In the words of one researcher, "The art of hypnosis relies on not providing the client with grounds for resisting" (Araoz, 1982, p. 106).

Once hypnotized, people act highly suggestible, responding to commands from the hypnotist in ways that seem automatic and involuntary. The hypnotist can use the power of suggestion to achieve beneficial ends, such as helping people kick unwanted habits like smoking or overeating. Anesthetic effects are also possible at certain deep stages of hypnosis. Hypnotized patients report less pain during childbirth (Harmon et al., 1990) and typically suffer less during dental work (Houle et al., 1988). Hypnosis has been shown to reduce pain or increase tolerance when a suggestion is presented to people during hypnosis, although its effect was strongest in people who are highly suggestible (T. Thompson et al., 2019). It's even been possible to perform major surgeries (such as appendectomies) using hypnosis as the primary anesthesia (Kihlstrom, 1985). Research is ongoing to determine the biological basis for these striking analgesic effects. It was once thought, for example, that the release of endorphins by the brain might be responsible, although this possibility now seems less likely (Moret et al., 1991). Imaging studies have been conducted comparing activated areas of the brain before and after painful stimulation—yes, it's possible to scan the brain of a hypnotized patient!—and differences in the activation patterns have been found between hypnotized and waking states (Halsband & Wolf, 2019). No firm conclusions can be drawn at this point, but research is continuing.

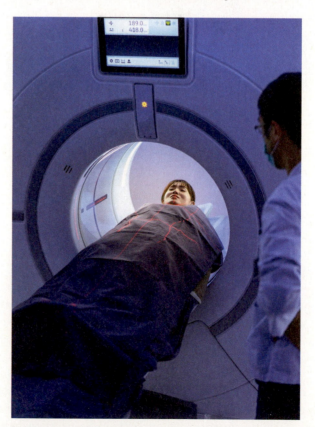

Brain imaging studies have found neural activity differences between hypnotized and waking states.

iStockPhoto/Portra

Memory Enhancement

Another frequent claim is that hypnosis can dramatically improve memory, a phenomenon called **hypnotic hypermnesia**. There have been criminal cases in which hypnotized witnesses have suddenly and miraculously recalled minute details of a crime. In one famous kidnapping case from the 1970s, a bus driver was buried 6 feet underground along with 26 children inside a tractor trailer. Later, under hypnosis, the driver was able to reconstruct details of the kidnapper's license plate—digit by digit. There is a long-standing belief among some psychotherapists that hypnosis is an excellent tool for uncovering hidden memories of abuse or other forms of psychological trauma (Pratt et al., 1988; Yapko, 1994). There have even been well-publicized examples of age regression under hypnosis, in which a person mentally traveled backward to some earlier place (such as the person's second-grade classroom) and was able to recall numerous details.

Unfortunately, there's little hard evidence to support these phenomena scientifically. Memory does sometimes improve after a hypnotic session, but this doesn't mean that the hypnotic state was responsible (Spiegel, 1995). One possibility is that hypnotic induction procedures (the relaxation techniques) simply create effective and supportive environments in which to remember (Geiselman et al., 1985). It's also difficult to judge whether memories recovered during hypnosis are, in fact, accurate representations of what actually occurred. You may "remember" a particularly unfortunate experience from the second-grade classroom, but can you be sure that this traumatic episode indeed occurred as you remember it?

As you'll see in a moment, hypnotized people often adopt roles designed to please the hypnotist. What appear to be memories are sometimes *fabrications*—stories that the person unintentionally makes up to please the hypnotist. For this reason, many states have banned the use of hypnotic testimony in criminal court cases. It's simply too difficult to tell whether the memory recovered after hypnosis is accurate or a product of suggestion. Controlled experiments in the laboratory have been unable to find good evidence for true memory enhancement—at least, memory enhancement that can be tied directly to the properties of hypnosis. There's no question that hypnosis can affect cognitive processes, including memory, but hypnosis holds no special key for unlocking the past.

Explaining Hypnosis

What exactly is hypnosis? How do we explain the heightened suggestibility? There are two prominent explanations: (1) Hypnosis is a kind of dissociation, or true splitting of conscious awareness; and (2) hypnosis represents a kind of social role playing. Let's consider each of these ideas in more detail.

Hypnotic Dissociations

Some researchers have suggested that hypnosis produces **hypnotic dissociations**. *Dissociation* means that the individual experiences a kind of splitting of consciousness where multiple forms of awareness exist simultaneously (E. R. Hilgard, 1986, 1992). This is a fancy way of saying that you have divided consciousness. One stream of consciousness follows the commands of the hypnotist—for example, feeling no pain in response to a painful stimulation. The second kind of awareness, called the "hidden observer," experiences the pain but reveals nothing to the observer.

Support for these ideas comes from experiments in which people are hypnotized and asked to submerge one arm into a bucket of extremely cold ice water (a common procedure to test for the analgesic effects of hypnosis). "You'll be aware of no pain," the participant is told, "but that other part of you, the hidden part that is aware of everything going on, can signal any true pain by pressing this key." A button is made available that the person is allowed to press, at will, with the nonsubmerged hand. It turns out that people press this key repeatedly—reporting the pain—and the key presses become much more frequent the longer the arm is kept submerged. During hypnosis, as well as afterward, people claim to have no knowledge of what the nonsubmerged hand is doing. There is a hidden part of consciousness, Hilgard argues, that maintains realistic contact with what's going on; it is the other hypnotized stream of awareness that feels no pain (also see Spiegel, 1998).

This idea that conscious awareness is divided or split during hypnosis may seem mystical, strange, and worthy of skepticism. But as you know, the brain often divides its labor to arrive at adaptive solutions. You walk and talk at the same time, and you certainly don't consciously think about picking up each leg and putting it down while making a point in the conversation. The idea that consciousness is regularly dissociated, or divided, is not really an issue to most psychologists; it's accepted as a given, as a normal part of psychological functioning.

Social Role Playing

Many psychologists remain skeptical about hypnosis because hypnotized subjects often seem to be playing a kind of role. The behavior of a hypnotized person is easily modified by expectations and by small changes in the suggestions of the hypnotist. For example, if people are told before being hypnotized that a rigid right arm is a prominent feature of the hypnotized state, then rigid right arms are likely to be reported after hypnosis even when no such specific suggestion is made during the induction process (Orne, 1959). It often appears as if people are trying desperately to do whatever they can to act in the suggested way (Kihlstrom & McConkey, 1990).

Hypnotic behavior may, in fact, be a kind of social role playing. Everyone has some idea of what hypnotized behavior looks like—when hypnotized, you fall into a trance state and obey the commands of the all-powerful hypnotist. So, when people agree to be hypnotized, they implicitly agree to act out this role (Barber et al., 1974; Sarbin & Coe, 1972; Spanos, 1982). You don't actually lose voluntary control over your behavior; instead, you follow the lead of the hypnotist and obey the hypnotist's every command because you think, perhaps unconsciously, that involuntary compliance is an important part of what it means to be hypnotized (S. J. Lynn et al., 1990).

Quite a bit of evidence supports this role-playing interpretation of hypnosis. One compelling finding is that many hypnotic phenomena can be reproduced with *simulated subjects*—people who are never actually hypnotized but who are told to act as if they're hypnotized (Spanos, 1986, 1996). Moreover, many of the classic phenomena—such as posthypnotic suggestions—turn out to be controlled mainly by expectations rather than by the hypnotist. For instance, if people are told to respond to a cue, such as tugging on their ear every time they hear a particular word, they will often do so after hypnosis. However, such posthypnotic suggestions work only if people believe they're still participating in the experiment; if the hypnotist leaves the room, or if the participants believe the experiment is over, they stop responding to the cue (see S. J. Lynn et al., 1990, for a review).

At the same time, it's hard to believe that people can simply "role play" the analgesic effects of hypnosis during childbirth or surgery. Some experiments have also found that people can reduce the harmful effects of interference during visual and verbal processing after hypnotic suggestion—somewhat more so than can nonhypnotized people who are trying hard to perform the task (Iani et al., 2006). It is also possible to simulate neurological disorders during hypnosis, such as visual neglect or even blindness. A hypnotic suggestion for color blindness, for example, even seems to suppress the same areas of the brain that are damaged in patients who truly have lost the ability to sense color (Oakley & Halligan, 2009).

Meditation

There are similarities between hypnosis and meditation—both are claimed to produce an altered state of consciousness, and both tend to rely on relaxation. In **meditation**, of course, it's the participant alone who seeks to manipulate awareness. Most meditation techniques require you to perform some time-honored mental exercise, such as concentrating on repeating a particular string of words or sounds called a *mantra*.

The variations in awareness achieved through meditation, as with hypnosis, are often described in mystical or spiritual ways. Meditators report that they're able to obtain an expanded state of awareness, one that is characterized by a pure form of thought

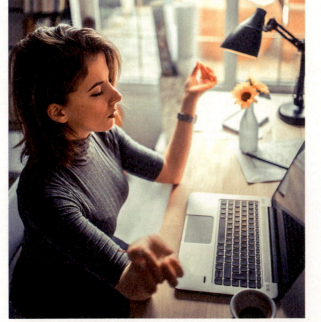

Daily meditation can produce significant reductions in anxiety and improve physical and psychological well-being.

unburdened by self-awareness. There are many forms of meditation and numerous induction proce-dures; most trace their roots back thousands of years to the practices of Eastern religions.

Daily sessions of meditation have been prescribed for many physical and psychological problems. As with hypnosis, the induction procedure usually begins with relaxation, but the mind is kept alert through focused concentration on breathing, internal repetition of the mantra, or efforts to clear the mind. The general idea is to step back from the ongoing stream of mental activity and set the mind adrift in the oneness of the universe. Great insights, improved physical health, and release from desire are some of the reported benefits.

Scientifically, it's clear that meditation can produce significant changes in physiological functions. Arousal is lowered, so heart rate, respiration rate, and blood pressure tend to decrease. EEG recordings of brain activity during meditation reveal a relaxed mind—specifically, there is a significant increase in alpha-wave activity (Benson, 1975). Such changes are, of course, to be expected during any kind of relaxed state and do not necessarily signify anything special about a state of consciousness. Indeed, there appear to be no significant differences between the physiological patterns of accomplished meditators and those of nonmeditators who are simply relaxing (D. S. Holmes, 1987; Travis & Wallace, 1999). At this point, researchers have little to say about the subjective aspects of the meditative experience—whether, in fact, the meditator has indeed merged with the oneness of the universe—but most researchers agree that induc-ing a relaxed state once or twice a day has beneficial effects. One neuroimaging study even found that emotion-regulating brain regions were larger in long-term meditators than in control participants who had never meditated (Luders et al., 2009). It's tough to interpret the results of this study conclusively—it could be that people with better-regulating brains simply like to meditate—but everyone agrees that meditation can be extremely helpful. Daily meditation sessions have helped people deal effectively with chronic anxiety as well as lower blood pressure and cholesterol levels (Seeman et al., 2003).

PRACTICAL SOLUTIONS: MINDFULNESS

Do you ever feel overwhelmed with the number of tasks facing you in the near future? Does thinking about what you need to accomplish flood your mind with anxiety? Recent research suggests that mindfulness could help with these issues. Mindfulness is intentionally attending to a current experi-ence. In other words, being mindful is being aware of what is happening right now, not what you need to do tomorrow or what happened yesterday. Meditation is a form of mindfulness that focuses on one aspect of a current experience, such as breathing, a saying in your mind, or a current sound in the environment. A large number of studies suggest that mindfulness has many benefits, including reducing stress, anxiety, and depression; reducing chronic pain; increasing immune system func-tion; improved task performance through focused attention; and better interpersonal relationships (Creswell, 2017).

Numerous group programs and retreats have been developed to teach people how to be more mindful. Phone and tablet apps are now also available to provide guided medita-tion and encourage mindfulness (e.g., *Calm*). Studies using randomized assignment to mindfulness or control treatments show that mindfulness interventions have a posi-tive effect on both physical and mental health compared with control treatments. Research on the specific mechanisms that cause the positive effects is ongoing, but there is some evidence that mindfulness increases activity in the prefrontal cortex, an area of the brain important for emotional regulation, and decreases activity in flight-or-fight areas of the brain, such as the amygdala (Creswell & Lindsay, 2014).

Simple phone apps can help you develop a meditation routine and increase mindfulness.

Ascannio / Alamy Stock Photo

Mindfulness effects can be achieved with very little training and effort. Studies show that sim-ple 5- or 10-minute guided sessions (such as those available on phone apps) can produce positive effects (e.g., Westbrook et al., 2013). Thus, one can receive benefits of focused awareness of the current moment with just a little time and effort. If you are a student feeling overwhelmed with your workload, research results suggest that mindfulness could help you reduce your anxiety and help you focus on the here and now.

KNOWLEDGE CHECK 6.4

Now test what you've learned about hypnosis and meditation by deciding whether each of the following statements is true or false. (You will find the answers in the Appendix.)

1. The EEG patterns of a hypnotized person resemble those of a person in non-REM sleep. *True or False?*

2. Hypnosis improves memory under some circumstances because it reduces the tendency to fabricate, or make things up, to please the questioner. *True or False?*

3. Hypnotic dissociations represent a kind of splitting of consciousness, in which more than one kind of awareness is present at the same time. *True or False?*

4. Hilgard's "hidden observer" experiments provide support for the social role-playing explanation of hypnosis. *True or False?*

5. Meditation leads primarily to alpha-wave rather than theta-wave EEG activity. *True or False?*

THE PROBLEMS SOLVED: WHAT IS CONSCIOUSNESS FOR?

It's difficult to study consciousness because consciousness is a subjective, personal experience. It's tough to define consciousness objectively, and appealing to the scribblings of an EEG pattern or to a pretty picture from a neuroimaging device may, in the minds of many, fail to capture the complexities of the topic adequately. Is consciousness something that can change its state, like water as it freezes, boils, or evaporates? For the moment, psychologists are working with a set of rather loose ideas about the topic, although conscious awareness is agreed to have many adaptive properties. We considered four adaptive characteristics of consciousness in this chapter.

Setting Priorities for Mental Functioning: Attention

The processes of attention allow the mind to prioritize its functioning. Faced with limited resources, the brain must be selective about the enormous amount of information it receives. Through attention, we can focus on certain aspects of the environment while ignoring others; through attention, we can adapt our thinking in ways that allow for more efficient and deliberate problem solving. Attentional processes enable the brain to divide its processing. People don't always need to be consciously aware of the tasks they perform; automatic processes allow us to perform multiple tasks—such as walking and talking—simultaneously. Certain disorders of attention, including visual neglect and attention-deficit/hyperactivity disorder, provide insights into attention processes. In both of these cases, which may be caused by malfunctioning in the brain, the person's ability to adapt to the environment is compromised.

Sleeping and Dreaming

Sleep is one part of a daily (circadian) rhythm that includes wakefulness, but sleep itself turns out to be composed of regularly changing cycles of brain activity. Studies using the EEG reveal that we move through several distinct stages during sleep, some of which are characterized by intense mental activity. Sleeping may allow the brain a chance to rest and restore itself from its daily workout, or it may simply be adaptive as a period of time out. Remaining hidden and motionless may have protected our ancestors at night when their sensory equipment was unlikely to function well. Dreaming, which occurs mainly during the REM period of sleep, remains a mystery to psychologists. Some believe that dreaming may reveal conflicts that are normally hidden to conscious awareness, or that dreaming may be one way to work out troubling problems. A third possibility is that dreaming is simply the brain's attempt to make sense of spontaneous neural activity. Dreaming may even help us practice, or rehearse, our responses to threatening situations.

Altering Awareness: Psychoactive Drugs

Psychoactive drugs alter behavior and awareness by tapping into natural brain systems that have evolved for adaptive reasons. The brain, as a biochemical factory, is capable of reacting to stress or injury by releasing chemicals that help reduce pain or improve mood. Many of the drugs that are abused regularly in our society activate these natural systems. As a result, the study of psychoactive drugs has enabled researchers to learn more about communication systems in the brain. There are three main categories of psychoactive drugs. Depressants, such as alcohol and barbiturates, lower the ongoing activity of the central nervous system. Stimulants, such as caffeine, nicotine, and cocaine, stimulate central nervous system activity by increasing the likelihood that neural transmissions will occur. Finally, hallucinogens, such as LSD, play havoc with the user's normal internal construction of reality. Although the mechanisms involved are not known, it's believed that LSD mimics the actions of the neurotransmitter serotonin.

Altering Awareness: Induced States

Two techniques have been designed specifically to alter conscious awareness, hypnosis and meditation. Hypnosis is a form of social interaction that induces a heightened state of suggestibility in people. Hypnotic techniques usually promote relaxation, although once achieved, brain activity under hypnosis more closely resembles the waking rather than the sleeping state. In meditation, it is the participant alone who manipulates awareness, often by mentally repeating a particular word or string of words. The biological mechanisms of both hypnosis and meditation are currently being studied with the modern techniques of neuroscience, but each clearly has some positive consequences. Pain and discomfort can be significantly reduced through hypnotic suggestion, and the continued use of meditation has been linked to the reduction of stress and anxiety. Psychologists study hypnosis and meditation, in part, because they believe these techniques may provide important insight into how we respond to the suggestions of others, particularly authority figures.

THINKING ABOUT RESEARCH

A summary of a research study in psychology is given in this section. As you read the summary, think about the following questions:

1. How does this study relate to the concept of consciousness?
2. Why do you think the researchers played the sounds during slow-wave sleep as opposed to other sleep stages?
3. What kinds of sleep disorders might be disruptive to the results of this study? Explain your answer.
4. How do you think the researchers determined that the participants were in slow-wave sleep? What did they measure to determine this?

   Article Reference: Sanders, K. E. G., Osburn, S., Paller, K. A., & Beeman, M. (2019). Targeted memory reactivation during sleep improves next-day problem solving. *Psychological Science, 30*, 1616–1624.

   Purpose of the Study: Some past studies have found that taking a break from trying to solve a problem can help people suddenly realize a solution to the problem. Sanders et al. considered whether sleep can also help. To address inconsistent findings in previous studies that have tested this question, the researchers examined the effect of sleep on problem-solving performance. Based on findings showing that memories can be reorganized during sleep, they predicted that if cues to the puzzles were played during sleep, reactivating relevant memories, people would be able to solve cued puzzles more often than uncued puzzles upon awakening.

Method of the Study: In this experiment, 61 participants completed four sessions—two in the evenings and two in the mornings. During the evening sessions, participants attempted to solve puzzles. A sound was played before each puzzle. Any solved puzzles were removed and replaced with a new puzzle. If they did not solve the puzzle within two minutes, the sound played again, and they were asked to memorize the sound associated with the puzzle. Once six puzzles were unsolved, they stopped. To reinforce the sound and puzzle pairings, participants then were tested on the pairings, which were also presented again to increase memory for the connection. Participants then went home to sleep. During sleep, when the device they were given detected slow-wave sleep, sound cues for three of the unsolved puzzles were played for three minutes each. In the morning, participants returned to the lab. First, they attempted to recall the puzzle paired with each sound presented. They were then asked to solve the six unsolved puzzles from the evening session the night before. They were given four minutes to solve each puzzle. Number of accurately solved puzzles that were cued and not cued during sleep was measured.

Results of the Study: Results of the study showed that participants solved 55% more puzzles that were cued during sleep than puzzles that were not cued during sleep.

Conclusions of the Study: From these results, the researchers concluded that the sounds presented during sleep helped to cue memories of the puzzles, which then led the participants to further process the puzzles and reorganize their thoughts on how to find a solution. Reactivating the puzzle memories during sleep helped the people ultimately solve the problems.

KNOWLEDGE CHECK: CHAPTER SUMMARY

You will find the answers in the Appendix.

SETTING PRIORITIES FOR MENTAL FUNCTIONING: ATTENTION

- (1) ___ refers to the internal process of setting (2) ___ for mental functioning. The brain uses attention to focus selectively on certain aspects of the environment and not others. Why? In part because there are (3) ___ to how fast and efficiently (4) ___ communicate.

- Different messages are received simultaneously by each ear. In (5) ___, the participant tries to repeat one message aloud while ignoring the other. Although the brain appears to (6) ___ many things at the same time, some of the monitoring may be minimal or beyond current (7) ___. One example of this monitoring is the (8) ___.

- (9) ___ refers to mental processing that is (10) ___ and easy, requiring little or no focused (11) ___. Once developed, automatic processing does not seem to require (12) ___ control or awareness. Automaticity can be measured in a (13) ___ attention task.

- Visual (14) ___ is caused most often by damage to the right (15) ___ lobe and results in the tendency to ignore everything on the (16) ___ side of the body. Attention-deficit/hyperactivity disorder (ADHD) is a psychological condition that occurs in 3% to 7% of children and is characterized by (17) ___, which is often combined with impulsivity or hyperactivity.

SLEEPING AND DREAMING

- Structures in the brain called biological (18) ___ trigger biological, or circadian, (19) ___. Sleeping and (20) ___, body temperature, (21) ___ secretions, and other biological processes follow a 24-hour (22) ___ cycle.

- Repeated cycles of brain activity, each about (23) ___ minutes long, occur during sleep. EEG recordings show cyclic changes in brain wave patterns that vary in (24) ___, frequency, and regularity. The sleep cycle contains (25) ___ stages of sleep and REM (rapid eye movement). Stage 1: Alpha waves are dominant. Stage 2: Theta waves are interrupted by K complexes. Stage 3: Delta or (26) ___-wave sleep waves are dominant. REM sleep occurs 70 to (27) ___ minutes into the sleep cycle, and the EEG pattern is similar to the awake state. During REM sleep, abrupt physiological changes occur, and we dream the most.

- Sleep may help (28) ___ and restore the body and brain. Sleep may also help us respond adaptively to changing environmental conditions (for example, by causing us to remain hidden and motionless at night) and increase our likelihood for (29) ___. Sleep deprivation results in a decline in both (30) ___ and physical function.

- REM sleep may strengthen certain kinds of (31) ___. Freud believed that dreams are a form of (32) ___. The activation-(33) ___ hypothesis holds that dreams are a product of (34) ___ activity in the brain. The problem-solving view suggests that dreaming may be a way for us to find solutions to our problems. Dreaming may help us mentally practice our survival skills by allowing us to simulate (35) ___ from the environment.

- Insomnia, (36) ___, and (37) ___ are (38) ___ that involve problems with the amount, quality, and timing of sleep. Nightmares, night (39) ___, and sleepwalking are (40) ___ that involve abnormal sleep disturbances.

ALTERING AWARENESS: PSYCHOACTIVE DRUGS

- Drugs influence the action of (41) ___. Like neurotransmitters, certain drugs alter behavior and (42) ___ processes. A person's physical response to a drug may change with repeated use. With (43) ___, increasing amounts of the substance are required to produce the desired effects. A physical or (44) ___ need for continued drug use indicates (45) ___. Withdrawal involves measurable physical reactions when drug use stops.

- (46) ___, which include (47) ___, barbiturates, and tranquilizers, reduce the activity of the central nervous system. Stimulants, including caffeine, nicotine, amphetamines, and cocaine, (48) ___ central nervous system activity. Opiates (or narcotics), such as opium, heroin, and morphine, depress central nervous system activity and reduce both anxiety and sensitivity to (49) ___. (50) ___ (or psychedelics), including mescaline, psilocybin, and LSD, drastically alter normal (51) ___.

- Psychoactive drugs produce different effects in different people due to biological, genetic, and (52) ___ factors. Reactions to psychoactive drugs can be influenced by the environment, (53) ___ with the effects of the substance, physical state, and mental (54) ___ or expectations.

ALTERING AWARENESS: INDUCED STATES

- Hypnosis produces a heightened state of (55) ___, and physiological indices resemble a (56) ___ state. Hypnosis can produce profound (57) ___-relieving effects and has been used to eliminate unwanted habits.

- A controversial claim is that hypnosis can (58) ___ memory, a phenomenon called hypnotic hypermnesia, but it's not certain that any kind of hypnotic state is responsible. It may be that the (59) ___ techniques create an effective and supportive environment that facilitates remembering.

- Hypnosis may produce hypnotic (60) ___, where (61) ___ is split into multiple forms of awareness. Some researchers suggest that hypnotic behavior may be a form of (62) ___ role playing, in which the subject responds in a way designed to please the hypnotist.

- Meditation, characterized by self-induced altered (63) ___, can cause significant physiological changes, promote relaxation, and reduce (64) ___.

CRITICAL THINKING QUESTIONS

1. Can you think of any circumstances in which your brain attends to things of which you are not aware?

2. In what ways are the symptoms of visual neglect similar to the symptoms of the split-brain patients who were discussed in Chapter 3?

3. Can you think of any workplace environments that might lead to symptoms similar to jet lag?

4. Can you think of any adaptive reasons sleep occurs in stages? What might be the advantage to starting off in a light sleep and moving to a deeper sleep?

5. The activation-synthesis hypothesis proposes that dreams arise from the interpretation of random neural activity. Yet many people dream of flying, falling, or being unprepared for a test. How do you explain the fact that people have similar dreams if dreaming results from random neural activity?

6. Under what circumstances do you think it might be adaptive for someone to enter a heightened state of suggestibility?

7. Can you think of any situations in which memories accessed through hypnosis should be admitted in court? Why or why not?

KEY TERMS

activation-synthesis hypothesis (p. 212)
alpha waves (p. 207)
attention (p. 196)
attention-deficit/hyperactivity disorder (ADHD) (p. 202)
automaticity (p. 199)
biological clocks (p. 204)
circadian rhythms (p. 204)
cocktail party effect (p. 197)
consciousness (p. 195)
delta activity (p. 208)
depressants (p. 217)
dichotic listening (p. 196)
drug dependency (p. 217)
drug tolerance (p. 217)
hallucinogens (p. 220)
hypersomnia (p. 214)
hypnosis (p. 223)

hypnotic dissociation (p. 225)
hypnotic hypermnesia (p. 225)
insomnia (p. 214)
latent content (p. 212)
manifest content (p. 212)
meditation (p. 226)
narcolepsy (p. 215)
night terrors (p. 215)
nightmares (p. 215)
opiates (p. 218)
psychoactive drugs (p. 216)
REM (p. 208)
REM rebound (p. 211)
sleepwalking (p. 215)
stimulants (p. 219)
theta waves (p. 207)
visual neglect (p. 201)
withdrawal (p. 217)

7 LEARNING FROM EXPERIENCE

LEARNING OBJECTIVES

7.1 Compare habituation and sensitization and explain why these processes are examples of learning.

7.2 Explain how the basic elements of classical conditioning solve the problem of learning about signals, and then describe the processes by which this form of conditioning develops in different situations.

7.3 Describe the differences between reinforcement and punishment, both their positive and negative forms, and identify the effects of different schedules of reinforcement on behavior.

7.4 Define observational learning and describe its adaptive value.

7.5 For each of the major sections of the chapter, summarize how learning processes help us adapt to the world we live in.

CHAPTER OUTLINE

Learning About Events: Noticing and Ignoring

Learning What Events Signal: Classical Conditioning

    Practical Solutions: Taste Aversions

Learning About the Consequences of Behavior: Operant Conditioning

    Practical Solutions: Superstitious Behavior

Learning From Others: Observational Learning

    Practical Solutions: Does Exposure to Violence in Video Games Cause Violent Behavior?

The Problems Solved: Learning From Experience

You're sitting at home one Saturday afternoon binge-watching a show. An ad pops up from your favorite pizza place, and you find yourself getting hungry and your mouth watering. In another ad, someone rings a doorbell, and your dog, Bella, starts to bark at the screen. You tell Bella to "Stay," your command for sitting quietly. She obeys your command, and you reward her with a dog treat. However, Bella's barking has brought on an annoying headache, so you go upstairs and get some ibuprofen to reduce the pain. After about 30 minutes, you still feel the headache—your usual dose of ibuprofen isn't helping, so you pause the show and close your eyes, hoping that will help instead. This works well, and you think, "I'll have to try this the next time I have a headache."

All of these common events involve learning to some degree. In this chapter, we will explore how the basic principles of learning come into play in these kinds of everyday experiences.

THE PROBLEMS TO BE SOLVED: HOW DO WE LEARN FROM EXPERIENCE?

Learning is one of the most basic of all psychological processes. The ability to adjust our actions in response to past experience—to learn—is fundamental to our lives. What exactly is learning? You might define it as the process of acquiring knowledge. You go to school; you take classes; you learn things about the world. In essence, that's the same way psychologists think about learning. But, as you know from Chapter 2, psychologists like to define concepts by how those concepts can be measured. "Knowledge" can't be measured directly; instead, **learning** is defined by behavior—more precisely, as a change in behavior, or potential behavior, that results from experience. Notice the emphasis is on behavior, which can be directly observed. We make inferences about learning by observing behavior and noting how it changes over time.

Like most definitions, this one needs a little tweaking. Sometimes behavior changes as a result of experience in ways that we wouldn't classify as learning. For example, your behavior changes as you age. Experience plays a role in development, as you know, but some changes occur purely as a result of physical development. Your behavior also changes when you get injured or sick. Suppose you're stuck in bed for two days with a high fever; your behavior changes—you sleep a lot more than normal—but these changes have nothing to do with learning. The concept of learning is reserved for those cases when behavior changes in a way that reflects the experience—we change our behavior, either as a reaction to the experience or as a result of practice, so we can act more sensibly in the future. In the example scenario described earlier, when you decide to try relaxing to reduce your headache in the future, you do so because you have learned from the experience that relaxing with your eyes closed is effective in reducing your pain. Not surprisingly, there are different kinds of learning, each directed at solving unique problems, and we'll discuss each of these kinds in turn.

Learning About Events: Noticing and Ignoring

We need to recognize new events but also learn to ignore events that occur repeatedly without consequence. A baby crying, the screeching sirens of a fire engine, your dog barking—these sounds demand our attention and cause us to react. Humans and animals notice sudden changes in their environment; they notice those things that are new and potentially of interest. But our reactions to these novel events change with repeated experience, and these changes are controlled by some of the most basic and important of all learning processes.

Learning What Events Signal: Classical Conditioning

When does one event predict that a second event is likely to follow? Many things that happen in our world signal the occurrence of other events. For instance, you know that lightning precedes thunder and that a rattling sound can signal the presence of a venomous snake. You also know that the sight of pizza often means you will soon be eating it (which explains your watering mouth when you see the ad). Often you can't do anything about the co-occurrence of such events, but if you recognize the relationship, you can respond accordingly (you can take cover or move to avoid the snake).

Learning About the Consequences of Behavior: Operant Conditioning

All species, sea snails as well as people, need to learn that some behaviors have consequences. The child who grabs the tail of a cat once too often receives an unwelcome surprise. Your dog may have learned that if she sits and looks up at you expectantly when you say "Stay," she will receive a treat. Behaviors are instrumental in producing rewards and punishments, and it's clearly adaptive for us to learn when and how to act.

Learning From Others: Observational Learning

Often our most important teachers are not our own actions and their consequences but the actions of others. We can learn by example, through observational learning. Obviously, observational learning has considerable adaptive significance: A teenager learns about the consequences of drunk driving, one hopes, not from direct experience but from observing others whose fate has already been sealed. A young monkey in the wild learns to be afraid of snakes not from a deadly personal encounter but from observing its mother's fear.

LEARNING ABOUT EVENTS: NOTICING AND IGNORING

How do we learn to notice and ignore events that occur and repeat in our world? We're constantly surrounded by sights, sounds, and sensations—from the traffic outside the window, to the color of the paint on the wall, to the feel of denim jeans against our legs. As you discovered in Chapter 6, we can't attend to all of these events. The human nervous system has limited resources, so we must prioritize our mental functioning. And this is not only a human problem: Animals, too, have limited resources. They constantly need to decide whether events in their environment are important or unimportant.

Habituation and Sensitization

People and animals are programmed from birth to notice novelty; when something new or different happens, we pay close attention. Suppose you hear a funny ticking noise in your car engine when you press the gas pedal. When you first notice the sound, it occupies your attention. You produce an **orienting response**, which means you orient toward the new sound, maybe by leaning forward and listening. After driving with the problem for a while, however, your behavior changes—the ticking becomes less bothersome, and you may even stop reacting to it altogether. Your behavior changes with repeated experience, which is the hallmark of learning.

It's adaptive for all living things to notice sudden changes in the environment. In this case, the presence of the shark causes the fish to change their group swimming patterns.

iStockPhoto/Tpopova

This example illustrates how our response to a novel or new stimulus changes over time—we get used to the new sound and no longer notice or react to it. This is habituation. **Habituation** occurs when you slow or stop responding to an event that has become familiar through repeated presentation; you may remember we talked about this process in Chapter 4. Most birds will startle and become agitated when the shadow of a hawk passes overhead, but their level of alarm will rapidly decline if the object is presented repeatedly and there's no subsequent attack (Tinbergen, 1951). It makes sense for animals to produce a strong initial orienting response to a sudden change in their environment. If a bird fails to attend quickly to the shape of a predator, it's not likely to survive. Through habituation, organisms learn to be selective about their reactions. They attend initially to the new and unusual but subsequently ignore events that occur repeatedly without consequence.

Habituation plays a role in eating as well—at least in how long and how much food we choose to consume (Raynor & Vadiveloo, 2018). Evidence suggests that we habituate to the taste of food during the course of a meal; this explains, in part, why we stop eating. When we eat the same food during a meal, the sensory stimulation is reduced by the food's repeated presentation. Such a process helps explain why we eat more when there are a variety of foods on our plate (Temple et al., 2008). It also helps explain why we can feel stuffed at the end of a meal, but suddenly feel hungry again when the dessert menu arrives. We have habituated to the main course, not to dessert. Researchers have even suggested that individual differences in our susceptibility to habituation may help explain why some people are obese and others are not (L. H. Epstein et al., 2009).

Variety during a meal increases the chances that we will eat more.

iStockPhoto/Yagi-Studio

A related phenomenon, called **sensitization**, occurs when our response to an event increases rather than decreases with repeated exposure. If you're exposed repeatedly to a loud noise, you're likely to become sensitized to the noise—your reactions become more intense and prolonged with repeated exposure. (This might happen to you when your cat constantly meows for food.) Both habituation and sensitization are natural responses to repeated events. They help us respond appropriately to the environment. Whether repetition of a stimulus will lead to habituation or sensitization depends on several factors (Groves & Thompson, 1970). Generally, sensitization is more likely when the repeated stimulus is intense or punishing. If the stimulus is mild or modest in intensity, repeated exposure usually leads to habituation. Habituation and sensitization also depend importantly on the timing of presentations—for example, habituation typically occurs faster when the repetitions occur closer together in time (R. R. Miller & Grace, 2003).

We rely on simple learning processes such as habituation to help conserve our limited resources. The world is full of events to be noticed, far more than we can ever hope to monitor. Orienting responses guarantee that we will notice the new and unusual, but through habituation we learn to ignore those things that are repeated but of no significant consequence. Therefore, we're able to solve a very important problem—how to be selective about the events that occur and recur in the world.

KNOWLEDGE CHECK 7.1

Now test your knowledge about noticing and ignoring by choosing the best answer for each of the following descriptions. Choose from the following terms: *habituation, orienting response, sensitization.* (You will find the answers in the Appendix.)

1. When Shawn practices his trumpet, he tries repeatedly to hit a high C note. The first time he tries, his roommate says nothing. By the third try, his roommate is banging on the door telling him to be quiet: _____

2. Alonda turns her head and stares intently when a strange howling sound begins in her backyard: _____

3. Kesha loves clocks and has six different varieties in her apartment. Strangely, she never notices any ticking noises: _____

4. Your cat, Comet, used to startle and jump 3 feet in the air whenever you ground your gourmet coffee beans in the morning. Now he never seems to notice: _____

LEARNING WHAT EVENTS SIGNAL: CLASSICAL CONDITIONING

Everyone knows that a flash of lightning means a clap of thunder is likely to follow; experience has taught us to *associate* lightning with thunder. You also know that a sour smell coming from the milk means it probably won't taste very good. In both of these cases, you've learned an association between two events—more specifically, you've learned that one event predicts the other. This knowledge is clearly useful because it allows you to prepare yourself for future events. You know to cover your ears or to avoid drinking the milk.

The scientific study of simple associations like these began around the turn of the 20th century in the laboratory of a Russian physiologist named Ivan P. Pavlov (1849–1936). Pavlov developed a technique, known as **classical conditioning**, to investigate how these associations are formed. Pavlov didn't start off with a burning desire to study learning. His main interest was in digestion, which included the study of how dogs salivate, or drool, in the presence of food. We salivate when food is placed in our mouth, as do dogs, because saliva contains certain chemicals that help in the initial stages of digestion. However, to his annoyance, Pavlov found that his dogs often began to drool much too soon—merely at the sight of the food dish and long before food was actually placed in their mouths. Pavlov referred to these premature droolings as "psychic" secretions, and he began to study why they occurred, in part to avoid future contamination of his digestion experiments.

A dog in one of Russian physiologist Ivan Pavlov's experiments on "psychic" secretions in dogs in 1934. Notice the dog's cheek, which is fitted with a device for measuring salivation.

Universal History Archive / Contributor via Getty Images

The Terminology of Classical Conditioning

Pavlov recognized immediately that "psychic" secretions developed as a result of experience. At the same time, he was keenly aware that drooling in response to food is *not* a learned response. He knew that certain stimuli, which he called **unconditioned stimuli (US)**, automatically lead to responses, which he called **unconditioned responses (UR)**. Food is an unconditioned stimulus that automatically produces salivation as an unconditioned response. Neither dogs nor humans need to be taught to drool when food is placed in their mouths; rather, this response is a reflex similar to the jerking of your leg when the doctor taps you just below the knee. The response produced to an unconditioned stimulus is *unconditioned*—that is, no learning, or conditioning, is required.

The problem facing Pavlov was that his dogs began to drool at the sight of the food dish or even to the sound of an assistant entering the room. Food dishes and footsteps are not unconditioned stimuli that automatically cause a dog to salivate. Drooling in response to such stimuli is learned; it is *conditioned*, or acquired as a result of experience. For this reason, Pavlov began referring to the "psychic" secretions as **conditioned responses (CR)** and to the stimuli that produced them as **conditioned stimuli (CS)**.

Let's take footsteps as an example. The sound of an approaching feeder leads to drooling because the dog has learned that the sound predicts or *signals* the appearance of the food. Footsteps and food bear a special relation to each other in time: When the footsteps are heard, the food is soon to arrive. To use Pavlov's terminology, the footsteps act as a *conditioned stimulus* that produces salivation, a *conditioned response*, in anticipation of food. This is not unlike what happens to you when your mouth begins to water as you sit down to a delicious-looking meal. Conditioned stimuli typically lead to conditioned responses after the conditioned stimulus and the unconditioned stimulus have been paired together in time—the footsteps (the CS) reliably occur just before presentation of the food (the US).

Forming the CS–US Connection

What are the necessary conditions for forming an association between a conditioned stimulus and an unconditioned stimulus? It helps to remember the following general rule: A conditioned stimulus becomes a signal for the unconditioned stimulus when it provides *information* about the delivery of the unconditioned stimulus (Rescorla, 1988). If a bell (CS) is struck just before the delivery of food (US), and these pairings are continued over time, the dog will begin to salivate (CR) whenever the bell (CS) is struck (see Figure 7.1). A connection is formed because the bell provides *information* about the delivery of the food—the dog knows that food will be arriving soon after it hears the bell. This rule helps to explain a number of experimental findings (see Table 7.1 for a summary of these points).

First, for an effective association to form, the conditioned stimulus usually needs to be presented *before* the unconditioned stimulus. If the two are presented at the same time (*simultaneous conditioning*), or if the conditioned stimulus is presented *after* the unconditioned stimulus (*backward conditioning*), little conditioning will occur. This makes sense: In both cases, the conditioned stimulus provides no information about when the unconditioned stimulus will appear, so conditioned responding is unlikely to develop. There are some exceptions to this general rule (R. P. Cole & Miller, 1999; Rescorla, 1980), but usually the conditioned stimulus needs to be presented first, before the unconditioned stimulus, for effective conditioning.

Second, the unconditioned stimulus needs to follow the conditioned stimulus *closely in time*. Pavlov found that if there was a long delay between the bell (CS) and the food (US), his dogs usually didn't form a connection. As the gap between the conditioned stimulus and the unconditioned stimulus increases, one becomes a less efficient signal for the arrival of the other—that is, the conditioned stimulus provides less useful information about the appearance of the unconditioned stimulus. Once again, there are important exceptions to the rule, but they need not concern us here (see Gallistel & Gibbon, 2000). (For one exception, take a look at the Practical Solutions feature on taste aversions.)

Finally, the conditioned stimulus must provide *new* information about the unconditioned stimulus. If you already know when the unconditioned stimulus will occur, then adding another signal will lead to little, if any, evidence of further conditioning. Suppose you teach some rats that a tone is a reliable signal for an electric shock. Once the rats have begun to freeze when they hear the tone (a typical conditioned response to the expectation of shock), you start turning on a light at the same time as you

FIGURE 7.1 ■ Classical Conditioning

Through classical conditioning, organisms learn about the signaling properties of events. The presentation of an unconditioned stimulus (US) leads to an automatic unconditioned response (UR) prior to training. A neutral stimulus is paired closely in time with a US. Eventually, the animal learns that this conditioned stimulus (CS) predicts the occurrence of the US and begins to show an appropriate conditioned response (CR) on presentation of the CS. See Table 7.1 for an overview of the key features of classical conditioning.

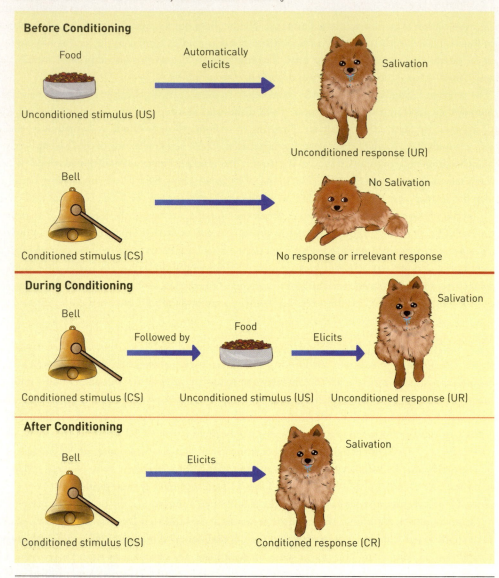

Illustrated by Sarah Yeh

TABLE 7.1 ■ Keys to Connecting the CS to the US

These three elements help make the predictive relationship between the CS and US clear:

● The CS occurs *before* the US.

● The US follows the CS after a *short* delay.

● The CS provides *new* information about the occurrence of the US.

present the tone. Both the light and the tone are then followed by the shock. Under these conditions, rats typically don't act as if the light is also a reliable signal for the shock (e.g., Kamin, 1968). This result is called *blocking* because the established signal, the tone, appears to prevent, or block, the animal from learning about the light. Blocking occurs because the light provides no new information about the shock—the tone already tells the rat the shock is about to occur—so the animal fails to treat it as a significant signal. See Table 7.2 for some additional examples of classical conditioning.

TABLE 7.2 ■ Examples of Classical Conditioning		
Example	**US**	**CS**
The smell of coffee in the morning gives you a surge of energy.	Caffeine in coffee	Odor of coffee
After getting sick from food at your favorite restaurant, seeing the restaurant's logo makes you feel nauseated.	Bacteria in food	Restaurant logo
After you spray your cat in the face with a water bottle, she starts to flinch whenever she hears you watering the plants with the bottle.	Water in face	Sound of spray bottle

PRACTICAL SOLUTIONS: TASTE AVERSIONS

On Saint Thomas in the Virgin Islands, researchers Lowell Nicolaus and David Nellis encouraged captured mongooses to eat eggs laced with carbachol, a drug that produces temporary illness. After 5 days of eating eggs and getting sick, the mongooses reduced their consumption of eggs by about 37% (Nicolaus & Nellis, 1987). In a very different context, in a research program designed to combat the negative effects of chemotherapy, young cancer patients were allowed a taste of some unusually flavored ice cream just before the onset of their normal chemotherapy—a treatment that can produce nausea and vomiting. Several weeks later, when offered the ice cream, only 21% of the children were willing to taste it again (Bernstein, 1978).

For children undergoing the rigors of chemotherapy, like this girl suffering from leukemia, it's important to prevent taste aversions from developing as a negative side effect. Broberg and Bernstein (1987) found that giving children candy with an unusual flavor just before treatment reduced the chances of a taste aversion forming.

iStockPhoto/fpphotobank

Both of these situations represent naturalistic applications of classical conditioning. Can you identify the critical features of each? First, let's look for the unconditioned stimulus—the stimulus that unconditionally produces a response prior to training. In both of these cases, the unconditioned stimulus is the illness-producing event, either the drug carbachol or the cancer-fighting chemotherapy. The response that is automatically produced, unfortunately for the participants, is stomach distress. Children don't need to learn to vomit from chemotherapy; a mongoose doesn't need to be taught to be sick after receiving carbachol. These are inevitable consequences that require no prior conditioning.

Now what is the conditioned stimulus in these cases? What in the environment precedes the unconditioned stimulus? In these examples, it's the taste of the food, either the eggs or the ice cream, that signals the nausea-inducing procedure. It's worth noting that the children were aware that their nausea was produced by the chemotherapy, not the ice cream, yet an association was still formed between the taste of the ice cream and a procedure that led to sickness. A conditioned response, feelings of queasiness to the food, was produced whenever the opportunity to eat was presented. Taste aversions are easy to acquire. They can occur after a single pairing of a novel food and illness.

It is extremely adaptive for people and mongooses to acquire taste aversions to potentially dangerous foods—it is in their interest to avoid those events that signal something potentially harmful. In the two studies we've just considered, the researchers investigated the aversions for a particular reason. Mongooses often eat the eggs of endangered species (such as marine turtles). By baiting the nests of mongoose prey with tainted eggs and establishing a taste aversion, scientists have been able to reduce the overall rate of egg predation. Similar techniques have also been used to prevent sheep from eating dangerous plants in the pasture (Zahorik et al., 1990).

In the case of chemotherapy, Ilene Bernstein was interested in developing methods for avoiding taste aversions: Cancer patients who are undergoing chemotherapy also need to eat, so it's critical to understand the conditions under which aversions are formed. Taste aversions can develop as a side effect of chemotherapy, although modern anti-nausea drugs often help reduce the severity of the stomach distress. Patients tend to avoid foods that they've eaten just before treatment, potentially leading to weight loss that slows down recovery. Researchers have found that associations are particularly likely to form between unusual tastes and nausea. Broberg and Bernstein (1987) found that giving children an unusual flavor of candy just before treatment reduced the likelihood of their forming aversions to their normal diet. These children formed a taste aversion to the candy instead. Another helpful technique is to ask the patient to eat the same, preferably bland, foods before every treatment. Foods that do not have distinctive tastes and that people eat regularly (such as bread) are less likely to become aversive.

Conditioned Responding: Why Does It Develop?

Forming an association between the conditioned stimulus and the unconditioned stimulus—that is, that one signals the appearance of the other—doesn't really explain conditioned responding. Why should dogs drool to a bell that signals food or rats freeze to a tone that predicts shock? One possibility is that conditioned responses prepare the organism for events that are expected to follow; conditioned responses help the organism interact with the unconditioned stimulus, which is usually some kind of biologically significant event (Domjan, 2015). Drooling readies the dog to receive food in its mouth, and "freezing" lowers the chances that any predators will see the rat. Because the conditioned stimulus tells the animal that a significant event is about to occur, it responds in a way that's appropriate for the upcoming event.

It was once commonly believed that the pairing of the conditioned stimulus and the unconditioned stimulus simply caused the unconditioned response to "shift" to the conditioned stimulus. Pavlov was convinced, for example, that the conditioned stimulus acted as a kind of substitute for the unconditioned stimulus—you respond to the conditioned stimulus as if it were essentially identical to the unconditioned stimulus. However, this means that the conditioned response should always be identical, or at least highly similar, to the unconditioned response. Dogs should always drool to a stimulus that predicts the arrival of food; rats should jump to a stimulus that predicts shock because they usually jump when they're actually shocked. But as you've seen, rats will freeze rather than jump to a signal predicting shock.

The form of the conditioned response depends on many factors. In general, the idea that classical conditioning turns the conditioned stimulus into a substitute for the unconditioned stimulus—or that organisms simply learn to respond to the conditioned stimulus in the same way that they automatically respond to the unconditioned stimulus—is misleading or wrong. Instead, we learn relationships among events that occur in our world. We learn that some events signal the occurrence of other events, and we respond appropriately. This perspective is known as the *cognitive view* of classical conditioning.

Second-Order Conditioning

Pavlov also discovered that a conditioned stimulus could be used to condition a second signal. In **second-order conditioning**, an established conditioned stimulus, such as a tone that predicts food, is presented immediately after a new event, such as a light; the unconditioned stimulus itself is never actually presented. In such a case, pairing the tone with the light can be sufficient to produce conditioned responding to the light.

An example from Pavlov's laboratory helps to illustrate the procedure. One of Pavlov's associates, Dr. Y. P. Frolov, first taught a dog that the sound of a ticking metronome signaled meat powder in the mouth. The dog quickly started to drool in the presence of the ticking. A black square was then presented, followed closely by the ticking. After a number of these black square–metronome pairings, even though the ticking was never followed by food powder on these trials, the dog began to drool in the presence of the black square. The dog drooled in response to the square because it signaled the ticking, which the dog had previously learned signaled the food (see Figure 7.2).

FIGURE 7.2 ■ Second-Order Conditioning

In second-order conditioning, an established CS is used in place of a US to condition a second signal. In Frolov's experiment, a ticking metronome was first paired with food; after repeated pairings, the ticking elicited salivation as a CR. Next, a black square—which did not produce salivation initially—was paired with the ticking (no US was presented). After repeated pairings, the presentation of the black square began to produce salivation.

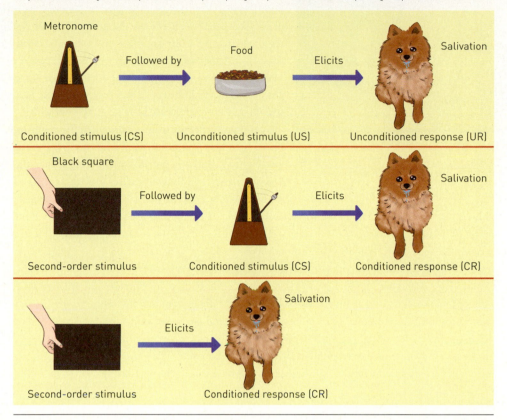

Illustrated by Sarah Yeh

The fact that conditioned stimuli can be used to condition other events greatly expands the number of situations in which classical conditioning applies. You don't need an unconditioned stimulus to be physically present to learn something about its occurrence. For example, consider the logic behind using celebrities to endorse products. Advertisers are trying to get you to form a connection between their product and feelings of pleasure or enjoyment. Most people like Beyoncé because she's linked to something they enjoy—great entertainment. If a product, such as a new perfume, is repeatedly paired with her, you're likely also to associate it with pleasurable consequences—the product becomes a signal for something that leads to enjoyment. This is a kind of second-order conditioning, and it's been used for decades in product ads.

Stimulus Generalization

Pavlov also noticed that conditioned responses tend to generalize to other, related events. If a tone of a particular pitch is established as a signal for food, other similar-sounding tones also produce drooling—even though they are never actually presented in learning trials. When a new stimulus produces a response similar to the one produced by the conditioned stimulus, it's called **stimulus generalization**.

Stimulus generalization is aptly demonstrated in a famous study by the behaviorist John Watson and his colleague Rosalie Rayner published in 1920. Watson and Rayner were interested in applying the principles of classical conditioning to a human—in this case to an 11-month-old infant known as Little Albert. They presented Albert with a white rat (the conditioned stimulus), which he initially reached for, followed quickly by a very loud noise (the unconditioned stimulus), which he did not like. The loud noise, not surprisingly, produced a strong, automatic fear reaction: Albert startled, fell forward, buried his face, and eventually cried (the unconditioned response). After several pairings of the rat with the noise, Albert began to pucker his face, whimper, and try to withdraw his body (all conditioned responses) immediately at the sight of the rat. (By the way, psychologists now rightly question the ethics of this experiment.) But Albert didn't

This still from a 1920 film shows Little Albert reacting with dismay to a white rat that had previously been paired with a very unpleasant noise. On the right is behavioral psychologist John Watson; to the left of Albert is Watson's colleague, Rosalie Rayner.

© Professor Benjamin Harris

just cry at the sight of the rat. His crying generalized to other stimuli—a rabbit, a dog, a fur coat, and even a Santa Claus mask. Many of these stimuli had been presented to Albert before the conditioning session, and none had produced crying. Albert cried at the sight of them now because of his experience with the rat; he generalized his crying response from the white rat to the other stimuli. However, Albert was happy to play with his blocks in between presentation of these stimuli, showing that the fear response did not occur to all things he was presented with, just the stimuli that were similar to the rat (e.g., furry or white).

Stimulus generalization occurs when the newly introduced stimulus is similar to the conditioned stimulus (see Figure 7.3). If you get sick after eating clams, there's a good chance you'll avoid eating oysters; if you've had a bad experience in the dentist's chair, the sound of the neighbor's high-speed drill may make you uncomfortable. When your dog barks at the doorbell sound from the ad in the scenario that we started this chapter with, she may be generalizing from the sound of your doorbell (the normal stimulus she responds to by barking). Generalization makes adaptive sense: Things that look, sound, or feel the same often share significant properties.

Some (e.g., B. Harris, 1979) have criticized the methods used by Watson and Rayner to show stimulus generalization, and again the study itself is ethically misguided, but stimulus generalization has been produced in additional (and more controlled) studies. For example, Hanson (1959) showed stimulus generalization of light stimuli in pigeons. After being trained to respond to light of a specific color, the pigeons continued to respond to lights of a similar color. The closer in color the light was to the originally conditioned stimulus, the higher the response was in the pigeons.

Stimulus Discrimination

Little Albert did notice the difference between white furry or fluffy things and things that were not white and fluffy. For example, he didn't cry when a block of wood was put into his crib. This is called **stimulus discrimination**; it occurs when you respond to a new stimulus in a way that's different from your response to the original conditioned stimulus. Through stimulus discrimination, you reveal that you can distinguish among stimuli, even when those stimuli share properties.

FIGURE 7.3   ■   Stimulus Generalization

After conditioned responding to a CS is established, similar events will often also produce conditioned responding through stimulus generalization. For example, if a red light is trained as a CS, then similar colors that were not explicitly trained will also produce responding if tested. Notice that the less similar the test stimulus is to the training CS, the less generalization occurs.

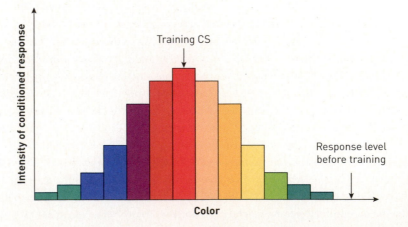

When stimuli do share properties—for example, two tones of a similar pitch—we often need experience to teach us to discriminate. The natural tendency is to generalize—that is, to treat similar things in the same way. Albert could certainly tell the difference among rats, rabbits, and Santa Claus masks; what he needed to learn was which of those white furry things signaled the unfortunate noise. In many cases, the development of stimulus discrimination requires that one directly experience whether or not the unconditioned stimulus will follow a particular event. If event A is followed by the unconditioned stimulus but event B is not, then you learn to discriminate between these two events and respond accordingly.

An Application: Drug Tolerance

Classical conditioning teaches us that certain events signal, or predict, the occurrence of other events. We've been talking about bells and Santa Claus masks, but often the "signal" for significant events is the general environment. For example, if you always eat ice cream in your kitchen, then your kitchen, not your living room, becomes a specific signal for something tasty. Context conditioning is particularly important—and even deadly—in the case of drug addiction. People usually take drugs in the same environment, like a particular room in their house. Associations then form between the room or context and the drug's effects. Pulling out the needle or the bong in your "safe room" signals the body that a powerful drug is about to be injected or smoked.

Many psychologists believe that drug tolerance develops as a classically conditioned response. When intake of a drug is signaled by the environment, the body produces a conditioned response that counteracts the physical effects of the drug—in the same way that a rat freezes when it anticipates a shock. Once signaled that the drug is coming, the body produces internal responses that block or attenuate the drug's effects. This could explain why the normal dose of ibuprofen was not helping your headache in the scenario at the beginning of the chapter. This is drug tolerance—the body needs larger and larger amounts of the drug to overcome the body's compensatory "conditioned" response. Note: The body has *learned* to anticipate the drug, and generate the compensating response, only in particular environments. If the user takes the drug in a different environment, the normal signals will be absent, and the body will not generate its normal compensatory reaction. This process can lead to overdose.

The people who are most likely to suffer drug overdoses are experienced users. These are people who are used to taking their drugs in a particular environment, one that signals the body that the drug is coming. Studies with drug addicts have found that the majority of overdoses occur when the user takes the drug in a new environment. Without the compensatory responses, signaled by the old environment, the normal drug dosage produces devastating and even fatal effects on the body (Siegel, 2016). A similar process seems to occur with recreational alcohol as well. People who drink alcohol in an unusual way, such as switching to a fruit-flavored drink called Four Loko, are more prone to hospitalizations for alcohol intoxication (Siegel, 2011).

People who ingest a typical amount of a drug in an atypical place can suffer the effects of an overdose due to the lack of compensatory response to the drug.

David Izquierdo Roger/ Alamy Stock Photo

Extinction: When the CS No Longer Signals the US

Remember our general rule: A conditioned stimulus becomes a good signal when it provides *information* about the occurrence of the unconditioned stimulus. But what happens if the conditioned stimulus stops signaling the appearance of an unconditioned stimulus? In the procedure of **extinction**, the conditioned stimulus is presented repeatedly, after conditioning, but it is no longer followed by the unconditioned stimulus. Under these conditions, the conditioned stimulus loses its signaling properties, and conditioned responding gradually diminishes as a result. So if a dog drools to a bell that predicts food, and we suddenly stop delivering the food after striking the bell, the dog will eventually stop drooling.

It's sensible for us to change our behavior during extinction because we're learning something new—the conditioned stimulus no longer predicts the unconditioned stimulus. Yet Pavlov discovered an interesting twist: If you wait a while after extinction and present the conditioned stimulus again, sometimes the conditioned response reappears. **Spontaneous recovery** is the recovery of an extinguished response when the conditioned stimulus is presented again, after a delay (see the far right panel in Figure 7.4). In Pavlov's case, his dogs stopped drooling if a bell signaling food was repeatedly presented alone, but when the bell was rung again the day after extinction, the conditioned response reappeared (although often not as strongly). No one is certain exactly why spontaneous recovery occurs, but it tells us that behavior, or performance, isn't always a perfect indicator of what is known or remembered. At the end of extinction, the conditioned stimulus can seem to have lost its signaling properties, but when it is tested after a delay, we see that at least some of the learning remains (Bouton, 2007). Concept Review 7.1 provides a summary of these conditioning phenomena.

FIGURE 7.4 ■ Training, Extinction, and Spontaneous Recovery

During training, Pavlov found that the amount of salivation produced in response to the CS initially increased and then leveled off as a function of the number of CS–US pairings. During extinction, the CS is repeatedly presented without the US, and conditioned responding gradually diminishes. If no testing of the CS occurs for a rest interval following extinction, spontaneous recovery of the CR will often occur if the trial CS is presented again.

CONCEPT REVIEW 7.1
MAJOR PHENOMENA OF CLASSICAL CONDITIONING

Phenomenon	Description	Pavlov's Dogs
Second-order conditioning	An established CS is presented immediately after a new event; after several pairings, this new event may come to elicit a response.	After a dog has been conditioned to salivate in response to a CS (tone), the CS is presented immediately after a new signal (e.g., a light). After several pairings, the light may come to elicit a response.
Stimulus generalization	A new stimulus produces a response similar to the one produced by the CS.	After a dog has been conditioned to salivate in response to a CS (e.g., a bright light), the same response may be produced by a similar stimulus (e.g., a dimmer light).
Stimulus discrimination	The response to a new stimulus is different from the response to the original CS.	After a dog has been conditioned to salivate in response to a CS (light), the response does not occur to a different stimulus, such as a ringing bell.
Acquisition	Conditioned responding becomes stronger with repeated CS–US pairings.	The more times a dog hears the CS (tone) paired with the US (food), the stronger the CR becomes.
Extinction	Conditioned responding diminishes when the CS (after conditioning) is presented repeatedly without the US.	After a dog has been conditioned to salivate in response to a CS (tone), the tone is presented repeatedly without the US (food). The dog's response to the CS lessens.

Phenomenon	Description	Pavlov's Dogs
Spontaneous recovery	Conditioned responding that has disappeared in extinction recovers spontaneously with the passage of time.	After extinction, a dog no longer responds to the CS (tone). After a rest period, the dog will again respond when presented with the CS (tone).

Conditioned Inhibition: Signaling the Absence of the US

During extinction, you learn that a conditioned stimulus no longer predicts the unconditioned stimulus. As a result, you stop responding to a stimulus that once elicited a response because you no longer anticipate that the unconditioned stimulus will follow. You've not forgotten about the unconditioned stimulus. Instead, you've learned something new: A conditioned stimulus that used to signal the unconditioned stimulus no longer does (Rescorla, 2001).

In **conditioned inhibition**, you learn that an event signals the *absence* of the unconditioned stimulus. There are a variety of ways to create an inhibitory stimulus, but most involve presenting a new stimulus when the unconditioned stimulus is normally expected but is not delivered (D. A. Williams et al., 1992). For example, if dogs are currently drooling to a bell that predicts food, then putting the bell together with a light and following this compound (bell + light) with no food will establish the light as a conditioned inhibitor for food. The animal learns that when the light is turned on, food does not follow the bell.

What change in behavior is produced by a stimulus that predicts the absence of something? Inhibitory learning can be expressed in various ways, but often you get a reaction that is the *opposite*

FIGURE 7.5 ■ Conditioned Inhibition

In conditioned inhibition, the CS provides information about the absence of the US. Pigeons will approach and peck at a keylight CS that signals the appearance of food (upper panel), but they will withdraw from a keylight CS signaling no food (lower panel). Notice that the withdrawal response is an indication that the red light has become a conditioned inhibitor—a CS that predicts the absence of food.

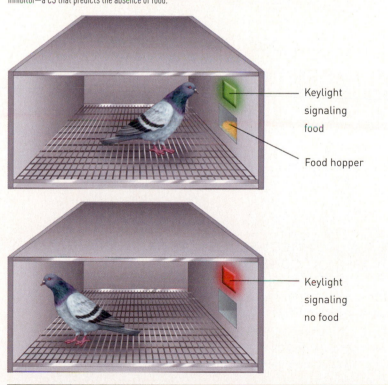

Keylight signaling food

Food hopper

Keylight signaling no food

Monica Wierzbicki/Body Scientific Intl.

of that produced by a normal conditioned stimulus. For example, if a conditioned stimulus signaling food produces an increase in responding, then an inhibitory conditioned stimulus will lead to a decrease in the normal amount of responding. Several experiments have shown that pigeons and dogs will approach a signal predicting food but will withdraw from a stimulus signaling its absence (see Figure 7.5; Hearst & Franklin, 1977; H. M. Jenkins et al., 1978).

It's important to appreciate the value of an inhibitory signal. It's just as adaptive to know that a significant event will not occur as it is to know that the event will occur. For example, every kid knows there are bullies on the playground. The sight of troublemaker Randy usually makes Kelley quake with fear—but not if there's a teacher around. The teacher signals the absence of a negative event—Randy won't be causing any trouble while the teacher is present. Inhibitory stimuli often act as "safety signals," telling people when potentially dangerous events are likely to be absent or when dangerous conditions no longer apply.

KNOWLEDGE CHECK 7.2

Now test your knowledge about classical conditioning by answering the following questions. (You will find the answers in the Appendix.)

1. Growing up, your little sister had the annoying habit of screaming at the top of her lungs every time she stepped into her bathwater. Her screaming always made you wince and cover your ears. Now, years later, you still wince every time you hear running water. Identify these elements of learning:
   a. Unconditioned stimulus: _____
   b. Unconditioned response: _____
   c. Conditioned stimulus: _____
   d. Conditioned response: _____

2. Every year when you visit the optometrist, you get a puff of air blown into your eye to test for glaucoma. It always makes you blink. Just before the puff is delivered, the doctor typically asks you if you're "ready." Now, whenever you hear that word, you feel an urge to blink. Identify these elements of learning:
   a. Unconditioned stimulus: _____
   b. Unconditioned response: _____
   c. Conditioned stimulus: _____
   d. Conditioned response: _____

3. People often wonder whether Little Albert, the participant in the Watson and Rayner experiment, grew up filled with fear and anxiety. Suppose I told you that he suffered no long-term effects from the experiment and, in fact, later grew his own fluffy white beard. Which of the following probably best accounts for his normal development?
   a. Conditioned inhibition
   b. Stimulus generalization
   c. Spontaneous recovery
   d. Extinction

LEARNING ABOUT THE CONSEQUENCES OF BEHAVIOR: OPERANT CONDITIONING

Classical conditioning answers an important survival question: How do we learn that certain events signal the presence or the absence of other events? Through classical conditioning, we learn to expect that certain events will or will not occur, at certain times, and we react accordingly. But our actions under these conditions typically don't have any effect on the presentation of the signal and the unconditioned stimulus. Usually, the conditioned stimulus and the unconditioned stimulus occur outside

Our behavior doesn't affect the stimuli in classical conditioning, but it does affect the stimulus feedback that occurs in the operant conditioning.

John Sirlin/ Alamy Stock Photo

our control. You can't change the fact that thunder will follow lightning; all you can do is prepare for an event (thunder) when a prior event (lightning) tells you it's coming.

There is another type of learning, studied through a procedure called **operant conditioning** (or *instrumental conditioning*), in which we learn that our own *actions*, rather than conditioned stimuli, lead to outcomes. If you study for hours and hours for an exam and receive an A, you learn that your behavior is *instrumental* in producing a top-notch grade; by *operating* on your environment, you have produced a pleasing consequence. Notice how classical conditioning differs from operant conditioning: In the former you learn that events signal outcomes; in the latter you learn that your own behavior produces outcomes (see Figure 7.6).

FIGURE 7.6 ■ Classical Versus Operant Conditioning

In classical conditioning (top row), food is delivered independently of the rat's behavior. The light CS signals the automatic arrival of the food US. In operant conditioning (bottom row), the rat must press the bar in the presence of the light to get the food. The light serves as a discriminative stimulus, indicating that pressing the bar will now produce the food.

a Classical conditioning: Food is delivered independently of rat's behavior

b Operant conditioning: Rat's behavior causes food to appear

Monica Wierzbicki/Body Scientific Intl.

The Law of Effect

The study of operant conditioning predates Pavlov's historic work by several years. In 1895, Harvard graduate student Edward Lee Thorndike (1874–1949), working in his mentor William James's cellar, began a series of experiments on "animal intelligence" using cats from around the neighborhood. He built a puzzle box, which resembled a kind of tiny prison, and carefully recorded the time it took for the cats to escape. Thorndike designed the boxes so that escape was possible only through an unusual response, such as tilting a pole, pulling a string, or pressing a lever (see Figure 7.7). On release, the cats received a small amount of food as a reward. Thorndike's goal was to observe how the cats learned to escape over time. Through trial and error, the cats eventually learned to make the appropriate response, but the learning process was gradual. Thorndike also found that the time it took for an animal to escape on any particular trial depended on the number of prior successful escapes. The more times the animal had successfully escaped in the past, the faster it could get out of the box on a new trial.

FIGURE 7.7 ■ Operant Conditioning

In Thorndike's famous experiments on animal intelligence, cats learned that some kinds of unusual responses—such as pressing a lever or tilting a pole—allowed them to escape from a puzzle box. The graph shows that the time required to escape gradually diminished over learning trials. Here, the cat is learning that its behavior is instrumental in producing escape.

Monica Wierzbicki/Body Scientific Intl.

The relationship between escape time and the number of prior successful escapes led Thorndike to formulate the **law of effect**: If a response in a particular situation is followed by a satisfying or pleasant consequence, then the connection between the response and that situation will be strengthened; if a response in a particular situation is followed by an unsatisfying or unpleasant consequence, the connection will be weakened. According to the law of effect, cats (and people) learn to make certain responses in certain situations; the responses that regularly occur are those that have produced positive consequences in the past. If a response that tends to occur initially (e.g., scratching at the walls of the cage) is not followed by something good (such as freedom from the box), the chances of that same response reoccurring diminish.

The Discriminative Stimulus: Knowing When to Respond

It's important to understand that Thorndike's law of effect applies only to responses that are rewarded in particular situations. If you're praised for raising your hand in class and asking an intelligent question, you're not likely to begin walking down the street repeatedly raising your hand. You know that raising your hand is rewarded only in a particular situation—namely, the classroom lecture. What you really learn is the following: If some stimulus situation is present (the classroom), and you act in a certain way (raising your hand), then some consequence will follow (praise). For example, your dog may have learned that when you say "Stay" (the stimulus situation), if she sits and looks up at you (her behavior), then you will give her a treat (consequence).

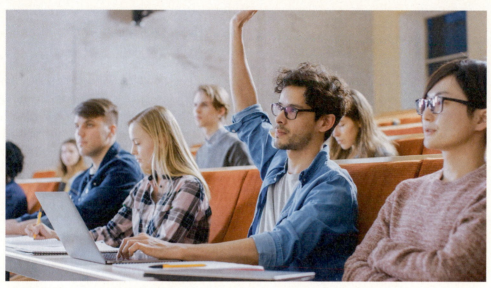

Knowing which situations will elicit a reward for a specific behavior affects when we choose to perform that behavior.

iStockPhoto/gorodenkoff

B. F. Skinner (1938) referred to the stimulus situation as the **discriminative stimulus**. He suggested that a discriminative stimulus "sets the occasion" for a response to be rewarded. Being in class—the discriminative stimulus—sets the occasion for an inquisitive student to be rewarded. In some ways, the discriminative stimulus shares properties with the conditioned stimulus established in classical conditioning. For example, you often find *stimulus generalization* of a discriminative stimulus: If a pigeon is trained to peck a key in the presence of a red light, the bird will later peck the key whenever a light of a similar color is turned on. If you're rewarded for asking questions in psychology, you might naturally generalize your response to another course, such as economics, and raise your hand there. Conversely, *stimulus discrimination* also occurs, usually after experiencing a reward in one situation but not in another. You may learn, for instance, that raising your hand in psychology class leads to positive consequences but a similar behavior in your economics class is frowned on by the professor. In such a case, one setting (psychology) acts as an effective discriminative stimulus for a certain response, but another setting (economics) does not.

The Nature of Reinforcement

The law of effect states that responses will be strengthened if they are followed by a pleasant or satisfying consequence. By "strengthened," Thorndike meant that a response was more likely to occur again in that particular situation. But what defines a pleasant or satisfying consequence? This is a tricky problem because the concept of a "pleasant" or "satisfying" event is highly personal—what's pleasant for me might not be pleasant for you. Moreover, something that's pleasing at one time might not be pleasing at another. Food, for example, is "positive at the beginning of Thanksgiving dinner, indifferent halfway through, and negative at the end of it" (Kimble, 1993).

For these reasons, psychologists use a technical term—**reinforcement**—to describe consequences that strengthen responding. As you'll see, we can distinguish between two major types of reinforcement, *positive* and *negative*.

Positive Reinforcement

If presenting an event after a response increases the strength of the response, it's called **positive reinforcement**. Usually, the presented event is an appetitive reward—something the organism likes, needs, or has an "appetite" for. Food and water are obvious examples, but responses can be reinforcing too (such as sexual activity or painting a picture). Remember, though, it's not the subjective qualities of the consequence that matter—what matters in defining positive reinforcement is whether or not the response that led to the reward is strengthened. As long as the "reward" makes the response more likely to occur again in that situation, the consequence qualifies as positive reinforcement.

Negative Reinforcement

Sometimes responses can be strengthened by the removal of an event—this is called **negative reinforcement**. In most cases, negative reinforcement occurs when a response enables you to eliminate, avoid, or escape from an unpleasant situation. For instance, you hang up the phone on someone who is criticizing you unfairly, shut off the blaring alarm in the morning, or walk out of a boring movie. These responses are more likely to occur again in the future, given the appropriate circumstance, because they lead to the removal of something negative—criticism, noise, or boredom. But, as you may have guessed, the event that's removed doesn't have to be unpleasant—it simply has to strengthen the response that led to the removal.

Students are often confused by the term *negative reinforcement* because they think negative reinforcement is a bad thing. Actually, whenever psychologists use the term *reinforcement*, both positive and negative, they're referring to outcomes that strengthen responses—they increase the chances that you will respond in a similar way again. Here *positive* and *negative* simply refer to whether the response ends with the presentation of something or the removal of something. In both cases, the result is rewarding, and we can expect the response that produced the reinforcement to occur again in that situation. Some additional examples of these types of reinforcement are shown in Concept Review 7.2.

CONCEPT REVIEW 7.2
POSITIVE AND NEGATIVE REINFORCEMENT

Consequence	Description	Example
Positive reinforcement	The presentation of an event after a response increases the likelihood of the response occurring again.	Juan's parents reward him for cleaning his room by giving him $5. This reinforcement increases the likelihood that Juan will clean his room again.
Negative reinforcement	The removal of an event after a response increases the likelihood of the response occurring again.	Hannah's parents nag her continually about cleaning up her room. When she finally cleans her room, her parents stop nagging her. The removal of the nagging increases the probability that Hannah will clean her room again.

Conditioned Reinforcers

Sometimes a stimulus can act like a reinforcer even though it seems to have little or no intrinsic value. For example, money serves as a satisfying consequence even though it's only a well-made piece of paper or pressed metal marked with interesting engravings or numbers on the screen showing your bank account balance. However, having money predicts something of value—you can buy things—and this is what gives it its reinforcing value. In the same way, if a stimulus or event predicts the absence or removal of something negative, then its presentation is also likely to be reinforcing. Stimuli of this type are called **conditioned reinforcers** because their reinforcing properties are acquired through learning (they are also sometimes called "secondary" reinforcers to distinguish them from more "primary" reinforcers such as food or water). These stimuli are reinforcing because they signal the presence or absence of other events.

Punishment: Lowering the Likelihood of a Response

Now for the dark side: *punishment*. Remember, Thorndike claimed that if a response is followed by an unsatisfying or unpleasant consequence, it will be weakened. The term *punishment* refers to outcomes that decrease the likelihood of responding. Like reinforcement, **punishment** comes in two forms, *positive* and *negative*.

Positive Punishment

Positive punishment occurs when the presentation of an event after a response weakens that response, making the response less likely to occur again. Notice that as with reinforcement, the concept is defined in terms of its effect on behavior—lowering the likelihood of responding—rather than on its subjective qualities. Usually, however, positive punishment occurs when a response leads directly to something aversive. If your mom yells at you for hassling the cat, this qualifies as positive punishment. Provided the aversive event (the scolding) is intense enough, the response that produced the punishment (hassling the cat) will tend to disappear rapidly or become suppressed. Spanking is another example.

Negative Punishment

Negative punishment occurs when the *removal* of an event after responding lowers the likelihood of that response occurring again. Instead of yelling at you for hassling the cat, your mom takes away something you like—maybe she grounds you or sends you to your room. Here, she is removing something you like when you engage in an inappropriate behavior—this qualifies as negative punishment. Notice the critical difference between positive and negative punishment: In one case, positive punishment, the response is weakened by the presentation of an aversive stimulus; in the other case, negative punishment, the response is weakened by the removal of something desired. Both positive and negative punishment are recognized as effective training procedures for rapidly suppressing undesirable responses.

What accounts for the rapid suppression of the response that's punished? It seems likely that people simply learn the connection between their behavior and the particular outcome. You learn about the consequences of your actions—that a particular kind of behavior will lead to a relatively unpleasant consequence. In this sense, we don't really need two different explanations to account for the behavior changes produced by reinforcement and punishment; the only major difference is that behavior increases in one situation and declines in the other. In both cases, you use your knowledge about behavior and its consequences to maximize gain and minimize loss in a particular situation. Concept Review 7.3 provides some additional examples of positive and negative punishment.

Practical Considerations

Punishment works—it's an effective technique for suppressing undesirable behavior. However, punishment isn't always the smartest way to change behavior. Sometimes it can be hard to gauge the appropriate strength of the punishing event. When the punishment is aggressive or violent, such as the forceful spanking of a child, you run the risk of hurting the child either physically or emotionally. At the same time, if a child feels ignored, yelling can actually be reinforcing because of the attention it provides.

Moreover, punishment only suppresses a behavior; it doesn't teach the child how to act appropriately. Spanking your child for lying might reduce the lying, but it won't teach the child how to deal more effectively with the social situation that led to the lie. To teach the child about more appropriate forms of behavior, you need to reinforce some kind of alternative response. You must teach the child a positive strategy for dealing with situations that can lead to lying. That's the main advantage of reinforcement over punishment: Reinforcement teaches you what you should be doing—how you should act—whereas punishment only teaches you what you shouldn't be doing.

CONCEPT REVIEW 7.3
COMPARING REINFORCEMENT AND PUNISHMENT

Reinforcement: Consequences that *Increase* the Likelihood of Responding		
Outcome	*Description*	*Example*
Positive reinforcement	A response leads to the presentation of an event that increases the likelihood of that response occurring again.	Five-year-old Ajay helps his mom do the dishes. She takes him to the store and lets him pick out any candy bar he wants. Letting Ajay pick out a candy bar increases the likelihood that he'll help with the dishes again.
Negative reinforcement	A response leads to the removal of an event that increases the likelihood of that response occurring again.	Five-year-old Ajay has been such a good helper all week that his mom tells him that next week he doesn't have to do any of his scheduled chores. Relieving Ajay of his chores increases the likelihood that he'll be a good helper.
Punishment: Consequences that *Decrease* the Likelihood of Responding		
Outcome	*Description*	*Example*
Positive punishment	A response leads to the presentation of an event that decreases the likelihood of that response occurring again.	Five-year-old Ajay runs nearly into the street; his mother pulls him back from the curb and gives him a brief tongue-lashing. This decreases the likelihood that Ajay will run into the street.
Negative punishment	A response leads to the removal of an event that decreases the likelihood of that response occurring again.	Five-year-old Ajay keeps teasing his 3-year-old sister at the dinner table. His mom sends him to bed without his favorite dessert. Withholding the dessert decreases the likelihood that Ajay will tease his sister at the dinner table.

Schedules of Reinforcement

Actions are more likely to be repeated if they're followed by positive or negative reinforcement. However, response strength in operant conditioning depends importantly on how often, and when, the reinforcements are actually delivered. People must understand that their behavior uniquely predicts the reward—if you deliver the reward in a haphazard way, or when the behavior in question has not occurred, learning can be slow or nonexistent (R. R. Miller & Grace, 2003).

A **schedule of reinforcement** is a rule used to determine when particular responses will be reinforced (Ferster & Skinner, 1957). If a response is followed rapidly by reinforcement every time it occurs, the reinforcement schedule is called *continuous*. If reinforcement is delivered only some of the time after the response has occurred, it's called a **partial reinforcement schedule**. There are four major types of partial reinforcement schedules: fixed-ratio, variable-ratio, fixed-interval, and variable-interval. Each produces a distinctive pattern of responding (see Figure 7.8).

FIGURE 7.8   ■   Schedules of Reinforcement

Schedules of reinforcement are rules used to determine when responses will be reinforced. Ratio schedules tend to produce rapid rates of responding because reinforcement depends on the number of responses. Interval schedules tend to produce lower rates of responding because reinforcement is delivered only for the first response after a specified time interval. In the cumulative response functions plotted here, the total number of responses is plotted over time.

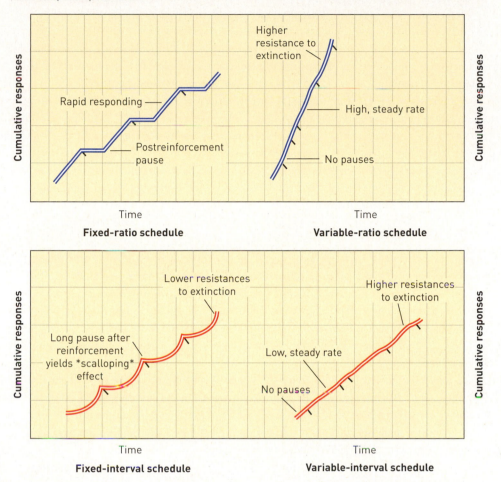

Fixed-Ratio Schedules

Ratio schedules of reinforcement require a certain number of responses before reinforcement is delivered. In a **fixed-ratio (FR) schedule**, the number of required responses is fixed and doesn't change from one instance to the next. Suppose you're paid a dollar for every 100 envelopes you stuff for a local marketing firm. This schedule of reinforcement is called an "FR 100" (fixed-ratio 100) because it requires 100 responses (envelopes stuffed) before the reinforcement is delivered (a dollar). You can stuff the envelopes as quickly as you like, but you must produce 100 responses before you get the reward.

Fixed-ratio schedules typically produce steady, consistent rates of responding because the relationship between the response and the reinforcement is clear and predictable. For this reason, assembly-line work in factories is often reinforced on a fixed-ratio schedule. The only behavioral quirk occurs when the number of required responses is relatively large. For example, if you have to pick 10 bushels of grapes for each monetary reward, you're likely to pause a bit in your responding immediately after the 10th bushel. This delay in responding after reinforcement is called the *postreinforcement pause*. Pausing after reinforcement is easy to understand in this situation—after all, you have to do a lot of work before you receive the next reward.

Variable-Ratio Schedules

A **variable-ratio (VR) schedule** also requires that you make a certain number of responses before reinforcement. (This is the defining feature of a ratio schedule.) However, with a variable-ratio schedule the required number can change over time. Reinforcement might be delivered after the first response initially, but it might take seven responses to get the reward the next time. It's called a variable-ratio schedule because the responder doesn't know how many responses are needed to obtain the reward (that is, the number of responses varies, often in a random fashion).

In a variable-ratio schedule, unlike a fixed-ratio schedule, you can never predict which response will get you the reward. As a result, these schedules typically produce high rates of responding, and the postreinforcement pause, seen in fixed-ratio schedules, is usually absent (after all, the next response might get you the reward again). Gambling is an example of a variable-ratio schedule; because of chance factors, a gambler wins some bets and loses others, but the gambler never knows what to expect on a given bet. You might win two in a row, but then lose the next 10 times you play.

The unpredictability of reward during a variable-ratio schedule makes it difficult to eliminate a response trained on this schedule when the response is no longer reinforced. Consider the typical compulsive slot machine player: Dollar after dollar goes into the machine; sometimes there's a payoff, but more often there's not. Even if the machine breaks and further payments are never delivered, many gamblers would continue playing long into the night. On a variable-ratio schedule, it's hard to see that reinforcements are no longer being delivered because you can never predict when reinforcement will occur.

Fixed-Interval Schedules

In interval schedules of reinforcement, the reward is delivered for the first response that occurs following a certain interval of time. In a **fixed-interval (FI) schedule**, this time period remains constant from one instance to the next. Suppose we reward a pigeon with food when it pecks a lighted response key after 2 minutes have elapsed. In this case, we would be using an "FI 2 min" schedule. Note that the pigeon must still produce the response to receive the reward. (Otherwise the learning procedure would not be operant conditioning.) Pecking just doesn't do any good until at least 2 minutes have elapsed.

Fixed-interval schedules typically produce low rates of responding. There is no direct association between how much you respond and the delivery of reinforcement—you're rewarded only when you respond after the interval has passed—so it doesn't make sense to respond all the time. Another characteristic of fixed-interval schedules is that responding slows down after reinforcement and gradually increases as the end of the interval approaches. If the total number of responses is plotted over time in a cumulative response record, the net effect is a *scalloping* pattern of the type shown in Figure 7.8. Again, this makes adaptive sense—there's no point in responding immediately after reinforcement; you should only start responding when you think the interval has passed.

Variable-Interval Schedules

In a **variable-interval (VI) schedule,** the critical time interval—the amount of time that needs to pass before a response will produce reinforcement—changes. For example, reinforcement might be delivered initially for a response occurring after 2 minutes; next, 10 minutes might have to pass before another response is reinforced. Variable-interval schedules are common in everyday life. Suppose you're waiting for a text from your friend while your phone is in silent mode (perhaps you're in your psychology class). To be rewarded, you know you have to check your phone and that a certain amount of time has to elapse, but you're not sure exactly how long you need to wait. Fishing is the same way. You know you have to cast your line to catch a fish, but you never know when an interested (hungry) fish will happen to swim by.

Like variable-ratio schedules, variable-interval schedules help eliminate the pause in responding that usually occurs after reinforcement. If you stop delivering reinforcements, the rate at which the response will extinguish will also be slower because it's never clear when (or if) another reinforcement will be delivered. For responding to cease, you need to recognize that the relationship between responding and reinforcement has changed—that's tough to do when the reinforcements aren't predictable. Concept Review 7.4 provides an overview of the different types of reinforcement schedules.

CONCEPT REVIEW 7.4
SCHEDULES OF REINFORCEMENT

Type of Schedule	Description	Example	Effect on Behavior
Continuous	Every response is followed rapidly by reinforcement.	Every time Suparna cleans her room, her parents give her a dollar.	Leads to fast acquisition of response, but the response is easily extinguished when the reward is no longer delivered.
Partial	A response is followed by reinforcement only some of the time.	Sometimes Suparna gets a dollar after she cleans her room.	Acquisition is slower, but the learned response is difficult to eliminate when the reward is stopped.
Fixed-ratio	The number of responses required for reinforcement is fixed.	Suparna gets a dollar every third time she cleans her room.	Suparna cleans her room consistently with a pause in cleaning after each dollar received; she stops quickly if the reward stops.
Variable-ratio	The number of responses required for reinforcement varies.	Suparna gets a dollar after cleaning her room a certain number of times, but the exact number varies.	Suparna cleans her room consistently with few pauses; she continues to clean her room even if the reward isn't delivered for a while.
Fixed-interval	Reinforcement is delivered for the first response after a fixed interval of time.	Every Tuesday, Suparna's parents give her a dollar if her room is clean.	Suparna doesn't do much cleaning until Tuesday is approaching; she stops quickly if the reward stops.
Variable-interval	Reinforcement is delivered for the first response after a variable interval of time.	On some random weekday, Suparna gets a dollar if her room is clean.	Suparna cleans her room consistently and doesn't stop even if the reward isn't delivered for a while.

Shaping: Acquiring Complex Behaviors

Reinforcement schedules are fine and good, but how do you train a response that never occurs in the first place? Suppose you want to teach your dog to sit—how do you reward your dog for sitting if the dog never sits on command? Most people simply yell "Sit," push the dog's bottom down, and then stuff a food reward in its mouth. Under these conditions, though, you're not really establishing the proper relationship between the dog's own behavior and the delivery of a reward. You've actually set up a kind of classical conditioning procedure—the dog is taught that having his bottom pushed downward is a *signal* for an inviting unconditioned stimulus (food). This might work, but it doesn't teach the animal that its own behavior is necessary to produce the outcome.

To solve this problem, Skinner (1938) developed a procedure called **shaping**, in which reinforcement is delivered for *approximations* to the desired response. Instead of waiting for the complete response—here, sitting to the command "Sit"—you reinforce some part of the response that is likely to occur without training. For instance, you might reward your dog for simply approaching when you say "Sit." As each part of the response is learned, you become stricter about what constitutes a successful response. Skinner and others have shown that incredibly complex sequences of behavior can be learned using the successive approximation technique of shaping.

It is possible to produce unusual behaviors in animals through shaping—reinforcements are delivered for successive approximations of a desired behavior.

EyeEm/ Alamy Stock Photo

Biological Constraints on Learning

Is it really possible to teach any response, in any situation, provided you have enough time and a reinforcer that works? Probably not. Many psychologists believe there are biological constraints, perhaps based on the genetic recipe, that limit the responses that can be taught. Thorndike, in his early studies of cats in puzzle boxes, noticed that it was basically impossible to increase the probability of yawning or of certain reflexive scratching responses in cats through the application of reinforcement.

Similar observations were reported later by animal trainers Keller Breland and Marion Breland (1961). The Brelands, who were former students of B. F. Skinner, encountered some interesting difficulties while attempting to train various species to make fixed responses. In one case, they tried to train a pig to drop a large wooden coin into a piggy bank (for a bank commercial). They followed the shaping procedure, where approximations of the desired sequence are reinforced, but they could not get the pig to complete the response. The animal would pick up the coin and begin to lumber toward the bank but would stop midway and begin "rooting" the coin along the ground. Despite applying punishment and nonreinforcement of the rooting response, the Brelands could never completely eliminate the unwanted response. They encountered similar problems trying to teach a raccoon to put coins in a bank.

In the cases of the pig and the raccoon, biological tendencies connected with feeding and food reinforcement interfered with the learning of certain response sequences. Pigs root in connection with feeding, and raccoons rub and dunk objects related to food (Domjan, 2015). These natural tendencies are adaptive responses for the animals—at least with respect to feeding—but they may limit what the animals can be taught.

In other cases, people and animals may be predisposed to learn relationships between certain stimuli and outcomes. For example, the delay between experiencing a distinctive taste (such as clam pizza) and subsequent illness can be quite long (hours), yet we're still quite likely to form an aversion to the taste (J. Garcia & Koelling, 1966). We may also be naturally predisposed to learn about and recognize potential predators in our environment, such as snakes. In a classical conditioning procedure, we quickly learn to associate pictures of snakes with aversive events (e.g., shock)—much more quickly, in fact, than we do to nonthreatening events, such as pictures of flowers (Öhman & Mineka, 2001). Some psychologists believe that we have special circuitry in the brain, acquired through evolution, that helps us process and learn about stimuli related to survival threats (Öhman & Mineka, 2003).

PRACTICAL SOLUTIONS: SUPERSTITIOUS BEHAVIOR

Have you ever noticed the odd behavior of a professional baseball player as he approaches the batter's box? He kicks the dirt (a fixed number of times), adjusts his helmet, hitches up his trousers, grimaces, swings toward the pitcher a few times, and adopts a characteristic crouch. Basketball players, as they prepare to make a free throw, endlessly caress the ball with their hands, bounce it a certain number of times, crouch, pause, and release. Such regular patterns are a player's signature—you can identify who's in the batter's box or up at the line by watching these ritualistic preparation patterns.

Mitchell Leff / Contributor via Getty Images

Let's analyze these behaviors from the perspective of operant conditioning. According to the law of effect, these odd patterns of behavior must have been reinforced—they occurred initially, perhaps by chance, and were followed by a reward (a hit or a successful free throw). But the pairing of the behavior with its consequence was really accidental, so psychologists refer to this kind of reinforcement as accidental or adventitious reinforcement. In the player's mind, however, a cause-and-effect link has been formed, and he acts in a similar fashion again. Once the player starts to perform the behavior on a regular basis, it's likely that it will continue to be accidentally reinforced, although on a partial schedule of reinforcement. (Can you identify the particular schedule?) The result is called a superstitious act, and because of the partial schedule (a variable-ratio one), it is difficult to eliminate.

In 1948, B. F. Skinner developed an experimental procedure to mimic and gain control over the development of superstitious acts. He placed hungry pigeons in a chamber and delivered bits of food every 15 seconds, irrespective of what a bird happened to be doing at the time. In his own words:

In six out of eight cases the resulting responses were so clearly defined that two observers could agree perfectly in counting instances. One bird was conditioned to turn counterclockwise about the cage, making two or three turns between reinforcements. Another repeatedly thrust its head into one of the upper corners of the cage. A third developed a "tossing" response, as if placing its head beneath an invisible bar and lifting it repeatedly. (Skinner, 1948, p. 168)

Remember, from the experimenter's point of view, no cause-and-effect relationship existed between these quirky behaviors and the delivery of food. Researchers since Skinner have replicated his results, but with some added caveats (Staddon & Simmelhag, 1971). For example, many of the behaviors that Skinner noted are characteristic responses that birds make in preparation for food; therefore, some of the strange behaviors Skinner observed might have been natural pigeon reactions to the expectation of being fed rather than learned responses. Nevertheless, the point Skinner made is important to remember: From the responder's point of view, illusory connections can form between behaviors and outcomes. Once these connections have been made, it's likely that the behaviors will continue to occur and be accidentally reinforced, thus creating the familiar forms of superstitious acts. Laboratory studies have supported these connections in humans. For example, when participants were asked to complete a putting task with three different golf clubs, they later consistently chose to use the club for which they were given positive feedback (regardless of their actual performance) compared with others that received negative or neutral feedback; people also rated that club higher on various qualities (Churchill et al., 2015).

KNOWLEDGE CHECK 7.3

Now test your knowledge about operant conditioning by answering the following questions. (You will find the answers in the Appendix.)

1. For each of the following statements, decide which term best applies: *negative punishment, positive punishment, negative reinforcement, positive reinforcement.*
    a. Stephanie is grounded for arriving home well past her curfew: _____
    b. Greg receives a bonus of $500 for exceeding his sales goal for the year: _____
    c. Nikki gets a ticket, at double the normal rate, for exceeding the posted speed limit in a school zone: _____
    d. Little Mowrer cries all the time when her mom is home because her mom always comforts her with a kiss and a story: _____
    e. With her dad, Mowrer is a perfect angel because crying can be followed by a stern lecture that lasts for an hour or more: _____

2. Identify the schedule of reinforcement that is at work in each of the following situations. Choose from the following terms: *fixed-interval, fixed-ratio, variable-interval, variable-ratio.*
    a. Rowena feels intense satisfaction after she calls the psychic hotline but only when a psychic named Darlene reads her future: _____
    b. Prana likes to visit the monster truck rally because they always have good corn dogs: _____
    c. Sinead constantly watches her phone because a guy she likes texts her occasionally at unpredictable times: _____
    d. Mohamed has just joined a coffee club; he gets a free pound of gourmet coffee after the 10th pound that he buys: _____
    e. Charlie hangs around street corners for hours at a time. Occasionally, a pretty woman walks by and gives him a smile: _____

LEARNING FROM OTHERS: OBSERVATIONAL LEARNING

The world would be a very unpleasant place if you could only learn through simple trial and error. You could learn to avoid certain foods through positive punishment, but only after eating them and experiencing an unpleasant consequence. You could learn to avoid illegal drugs, but only if you had a bad experience, such as an arrest or a risky overdose. Clearly, it's sometimes best not to undergo the actual experiences that lead to learning.

In the wild, rhesus monkeys show an adaptive fear response in the presence of snakes. Because snakes are natural predators of monkeys, it makes sense for monkeys to avoid them whenever possible. But how do you suppose that fear is originally acquired? According to a strict interpretation of the law of effect, the animal must learn its fear through some kind of direct reinforcement or punishment—that is, through trial and error. This means that a monkey must approach a snake and be bitten (or nearly bitten) before it can learn to fear the snake; unfortunately, this single learning experience is likely to be fatal much of the time. Trial-and-error learning is not always adaptive, especially when you're learning about something dangerous or potentially harmful.

Fortunately, it's possible to learn a great deal without trial and error—by simply observing the experiences of *others*. People and animals can learn from others, and this kind of learning, called **observational learning**, has considerable adaptive value. In the wild, newly weaned rats acquire food habits by eating what the older rats eat (Galef, 1985); red-winged blackbirds will refuse to eat a certain food if they observe another bird getting sick after eating the food (J. R. Mason & Reidinger, 1982); chimpanzees in the wild learn how to use stone tools to crack open nuts by observing older chimpanzees eating (Inoue-Nakamura & Matsuzawa, 1997). Rhesus monkeys, it turns out, acquire their fear of snakes partly through observational learning rather than through direct experience (Öhman & Mineka, 2003). They watch other monkeys in their environment showing fear in the presence of a snake and thereby acquire the tendency to show fear themselves.

Animals can learn to use tools to accomplish tasks by watching other animals perform these behaviors.

iStockPhoto/slpu9945

Is observational learning a unique form of learning? You may remember our Chapter 3 discussion of *mirror neurons* in the brain. Neuroimaging studies have confirmed that regions in the motor cortex become active when we engage in simple motor movements, such as biting an apple or clapping our hands. But neurons in these same regions also become active when we simply *observe* someone else performing the same actions (Acharya & Shukla, 2012). The same systems in the brain that are activated by performing an action—waving good-bye—are activated when we watch someone else perform the same task. The presence of these mirror neurons suggests that our brains are naturally built to model, or imitate, the actions of others. Indeed, babies will imitate their parents' facial expressions—even sticking out their tongues—shortly after birth. Psychologists increasingly believe that imitation, and therefore observational learning, is a natural and important part of our learning repertoire.

Modeling: Learning From Others

We now know a great deal about the conditions that produce effective observational learning in people. One important factor is the presence of a significant role model. As noted, we naturally tend to imitate the behavior of significant others, also known as **modeling**. You probably learned a lot of things by watching your parents or your teachers—even though you may never have been aware of doing so. Research has shown that observational learning is particularly effective if the model has positive characteristics, such as attractiveness, honesty, perceived competence, and some kind of social standing. It's also more likely if you observe the model being rewarded for a particular action or if the model's behavior is particularly successful. Advertisers use modeling to sell products. When we see a celebrity or someone else that we admire using a product, we are more likely to purchase the product. Product placement uses this approach as well by having characters in popular movies drive specific brands of cars or drink specific kinds of vodka. Our increased interest in the products after watching our favorite actor or character use them is based on modeling.

We naturally tend to imitate the behavior of people we admire. This is one reason celebrities are paid to use or endorse products.

Stefanie Keenan / Contributor via Getty Images

In one classic study, Albert Bandura and his colleagues showed nursery-school children a film that portrayed an adult striking, punching, and kicking a large, inflatable, upright "Bobo" doll. Afterward, when placed in a room with Bobo, many of these children imitated the adult and violently attacked the doll (Bandura et al., 1963). In addition, the chances of the children kicking the doll increased if the adult was directly praised in the film for attacking Bobo ("You're the champion!"). Bandura (1986) has claimed that the responses acquired through observational learning are especially strengthened through *vicarious reinforcement*, which occurs when the model is reinforced for an action, or weakened through *vicarious punishment*, in which the model is punished for an action. A clear parallel therefore exists between the law of effect and observational learning; the difference, of course, is that the behavior of others is being reinforced or punished rather than our own.

Bandura did much of the early pioneering work on observational learning (you'll find more discussion of his work in Chapter 12). Bandura believed that much of what we learn from an experience depends on our existing beliefs and expectations. You're unlikely to learn from a model, for example, if you believe you're incapable of ever performing the model's behavior. You can watch a great pianist or singer or athlete, but you're not likely to imitate the person's behavior if you feel you're incapable of performing the task. Our beliefs about our own abilities significantly shape and constrain what we gain from observational learning.

Practical Considerations

Psychologists regularly use the techniques of observational learning to improve or change unwanted behaviors. Many studies have shown that observing desirable behavior can lower unwanted or maladaptive behavior. Children have been able to reduce their fear of dental visits (K. D. Craig, 1978) or impending surgery (Melamed & Siegel, 1975) by observing films of other children effectively handling their dental or surgical anxieties. Clinical psychologists now use observational learning as a technique to deal with specific fears and as a method for promoting cooperative behavior among preschoolers.

At the same time, observational or social learning can have significant negative effects as well. For example, children can witness reinforced acts of violence just by watching some types of cartoons. Although causal connections between media violence and personal aggression remain somewhat controversial (Block & Crain, 2007), the consensus among psychologists supports a link (C. A. Anderson et al., 2003). In addition, it can be difficult for a society to overcome unproductive stereotypes if they're repeatedly portrayed through the behavior of others. Many gender-related stereotypes, such as submissive or helpless behavior in females, continue to be represented in the media. By the age of 6 or 7, children have already begun to shy away from activities that are identified with members of the opposite sex.

Even if people don't directly imitate or model a particular violent act, it's still likely that the observation itself influences the way they think and act. For instance, after playing a violent video game, people are less likely to offer aid to people in pain—the game apparently "desensitizes" people to violent acts (Bushman & Anderson, 2009). Moreover, witnessing repeated examples of fictional violence distorts people's estimates of realistic violence—they're likely to believe, for example, that more people die a violent death than is actually the case. This can lead individuals to show irrational fear and to avoid situations that are in all likelihood safe. People who watch a lot of videos tend to view the world in a way that mirrors what they see on the screen. They might think, for example, that a large proportion of the population are professionals (such as doctors or lawyers) and that few people in society are actually old (Gerbner & Gross, 1976). It's not just the imitation of particular acts we need to worry about: Videos and other vehicles of observational learning can literally change or determine our everyday view of the world (Bandura, 1986; Bushman & Anderson, 2001).

Finally, suppose the link between witnessed violence and personal aggression is real, but small. Imagine, for example, that only 1% of people who watch a violent program become more violent after watching the show. Is this a cause for concern? Remember, many millions of people watch videos every day. If 10 million people watch a show, and only 1% are affected, that still means that 100,000 people have an increased tendency for violence. Those are scary numbers when you consider that it only takes one or two people to terrorize a building or commit murder in a school. Ironically, recent research suggests that when violence is shown in a video program, it may actually hurt the very industries that are sponsoring the show. Evidence collected from Bushman and Phillips (2001) indicates that video violence actually impairs subsequent memory for the brand names and product information shown in accompanying ads.

PRACTICAL SOLUTIONS: DOES EXPOSURE TO VIOLENCE IN VIDEO GAMES CAUSE VIOLENT BEHAVIOR?

Is there a causal link between witnessing violence in video games and later violent behaviors? The media often present a history of violent video game playing by someone who has committed a violent crime, particularly one involving gun violence, as causal. Indeed, the important role that modeling can play in shaping human behavior suggests that such a causal link is plausible. However, anecdotal evidence only shows that two things occurred in the same person, not that one thing *caused* the other. What does psychological science say about this link? Surprisingly, the answer is rather unclear at the moment.

Architect´s Eye/ Alamy Stock Photo

A study by researchers in the United States, Europe, and Japan (C. A. Anderson et al., 2010) reviewed the evidence from past studies to determine if there was a causal relation between exposure to violent video games and a number of measures related to violence, including aggressive behaviors and thoughts of aggression. They concluded that there is strong evidence that exposure to video game violence produces increases in these measures. However, a number of researchers (e.g., Ferguson & Kilburn, 2010; J. Hilgard et al., 2017) have criticized this study and claimed that it does not show evidence of causal link. Further, a recent experimental study (J. Hilgard et al., 2019) with games matched on aspects other than violence, a large sample, and the single measure of aggressive behavior toward someone else after a staged provocation investigated short-term effects of violence in video games. Despite these strong methods, there was no evidence that being exposed to violence in a video game (in this case, the game *Doom II*) caused people to be more violent after they played the game. Other studies (Prescott et al., 2018; T. Willoughby et al., 2012) have examined the long-term effects of violent video games. In these studies, violent video game exposure was related to a small increase in aggressive behavior for some people.

These studies highlight the complexity of studying this topic and the somewhat inconsistent patterns of empirical data. The next time you hear a report that someone who committed a horrible act of violence played a lot of violent video games, remember that the current data are inconsistent in showing a causal link between these behaviors.

KNOWLEDGE CHECK 7.4

Now test your knowledge about observational learning by deciding whether each of the following statements is true or false. (You will find the answers in the Appendix.)

1. Observational learning, like classical conditioning, typically involves learning about events that occur outside of your control. *True or False*?

2. People are more likely to imitate the behavior of a role model if the model is observed being rewarded for a behavior. Bandura refers to this reward process as vicarious reinforcement. *True or False*?

3. Observational learning is usually a passive process. Our beliefs and expectations about how well we can perform the model's behavior play little or no role. *True or False?*

4. Most psychologists believe that video media is a powerful vehicle for observational learning. *True or False?*

5. Clinical psychologists now use observational learning to treat specific fears, such as phobias. *True or False?*

THE PROBLEMS SOLVED: LEARNING FROM EXPERIENCE

As we struggle to survive, our capacity to learn—that is, to change our behavior as a result of experience—represents a great strength. Psychologists have long recognized the importance of understanding how behavior changes with experience; historically, research on learning predates research on virtually all other topics, with the exception of basic sensory and perceptual processes. In this chapter, we've concentrated on relatively simple learning processes. To meet the needs of changing environments, each of us must solve certain types of learning problems, and the principles of behavior you've learned about apply generally across animal species.

Learning About Events: Noticing and Ignoring

Novel or unusual events lead to an orienting response, which helps ensure that we'll react quickly to sudden changes in our environment. The sound of screeching automobile brakes leads to an immediate reaction; we don't have to stop and think about it. At the same time, no one can attend to all the stimuli that surround us, so we learn to ignore events that are of little adaptive significance. Through the process of habituation, characterized by the decline in the tendency to respond to an event that has become familiar, we become selective about responding to events that occur repeatedly in our environment.

Learning What Events Signal: Classical Conditioning

We also learn about what events signal—it's helpful to know, for example, that a wailing siren means an emergency vehicle is somewhere nearby. Signals, or conditioned stimuli, are established through classical conditioning. Events that provide information about the occurrence or nonoccurrence of other significant events become conditioned stimuli. A conditioned stimulus elicits a conditioned response, which is a response appropriate for anticipating the event that will follow. When we hear the siren, we anticipate the arrival of the ambulance and quickly move out of the way.

Learning About the Consequences of Behavior: Operant Conditioning

We also learn that our actions produce outcomes that are sometimes pleasing and sometimes not. In operant conditioning, the presentation and removal of events after responding can either increase or decrease the likelihood of responding in a similar way again. When a response is followed by reinforcement, either positive or negative, the tendency to respond in the same way again is strengthened. When a response is followed by punishment, either positive or negative, we are less likely to repeat the behavior. The schedule of reinforcement matters too. Schedules affect not only how rapidly we will learn and respond but also the pattern of responding; schedules of reinforcement also affect how likely we are to change our behavior if the reinforcement stops.

Learning From Others: Observational Learning

Through observational or social learning, we imitate and model the actions of others, thereby learning from example rather than from direct personal experience. We study how other people behave and how their behavior is reinforced or punished, and we change our own behavior accordingly. Whether or not we will imitate the behavior of others depends on several factors, including the social standing of the model. Observational learning can have a number of effects, both positive and negative, on the individual and on society.

THINKING ABOUT RESEARCH

A summary of a research study in psychology is given in this section. As you read the summary, think about the following questions:

1. Are the rewards and punishments used in the study positive or negative? Explain your answer.
2. Do you think habituation could have played a role in this experiment? Why or why not?
3. How does the researchers' first hypothesis relate to the law of effect?
4. What kind of reinforcement schedule did the researchers use in this experiment for the rewards? Do you think the use of this schedule contributed to the lack of an effect of rewards in this experiment? Why or why not?

Article Reference: Ballard, T. B., Sewell, D. K., Cosgrove, D., & Neal, A. (2019). Informational processing under reward versus punishment. *Psychological Science, 30*(5). https://doi.org/10.1177/0956797619835462

Purpose of the Study: The study tested the effects of reward and punishment on decision making. The researchers compared two competing hypotheses: (1) Rewards and punishments result in more effort being exerted when making a decision, resulting in better decision making. This prediction follows from the idea that people exert effort to obtain rewards and avoid punishment. (2) Rewards and punishments will decrease decision-making performance by diverting attention away from the task because people are more concerned about monitoring their performance. This results in poor processing of the important information for the decision and lowers their performance.

Method of the Study: In this experiment, 35 students performed a motion direction detection task. On each of the trials, participants saw a cloud of 40 moving dots. Some of the dots moved to the top left or top right of the screen while the remaining dots moved in a random direction. Participants were asked to press the "z" key if they saw the dots mostly moving to the left and the "/" key if they saw the dots moving mostly to the right. Participants began the task with 7.50 Australian dollars. In some blocks, they gained A$2.50 (reward) if they achieved 77% accuracy and a mean response time of 1.071 seconds. In other blocks, they lost A$2.50 (punishment) if they did not achieve these goals. Finally, in some blocks, they did not gain or lose money regardless of their performance (neutral). Speed and accuracy on the trials were measured and compared for the three different types of blocks.

Results of the Study: Both speed and accuracy declined when punishment was imposed in the block of trials (lose A$2.50) versus the neutral blocks (no reward or punishment), but there was no evidence of a change in speed or accuracy in the reward blocks (gain A$2.50) compared with the neutral blocks.

Conclusions of the Study: From these results, the authors concluded that there is no evidence that rewards affect decision making, but punishment impairs decision making by reducing one's ability to fully process important information (their second hypothesis).

KNOWLEDGE CHECK: CHAPTER SUMMARY

You will find the answers in the Appendix.

- Learning is defined by a change in (1) _____ that results from (2) _____.

Learning About Events: Noticing and Ignoring

- The limited resources of the nervous system keep us from attending to every environmental stimulus. Psychological processes help us (3) _____ our mental functioning.

- (4) _____ occurs when we stop responding to an event that has become familiar through repeated presentation. Sensitization occurs when responding to an event (5) _____ with repeated exposure to the event.

Learning What Events Signal: Classical Conditioning

- Stimuli and events in the environment have (6) _____ properties that tell us when one event (7) _____ a second one.

- An (8) _____ stimulus (US) leads to an automatic or unconditioned (9) _____ (UR). Repeated pairing of an event or stimulus with a US results in that event becoming a (10) _____ stimulus (CS), which can then elicit a conditioned response (CR).

- For a CS–US connection to form, the CS must provide new (11) _____ about the delivery of the US.

- Sometimes the CS–US pairing leads to a CR that is (12) _____ from the UR. A CR may be opposite to the UR, but a CR usually prepares the organism for the arrival of the (13) _____.

- In (14) _____-order conditioning, an established CS (e.g., a tone that predicts food) immediately follows a (15) _____ event (e.g., a light). The US itself is never presented again, but the pairing of tone and light can now produce conditioned responding to the light alone. Stimulus (16) _____ occurs when a new stimulus produces a response similar to the one produced by the conditioned stimulus. Stimulus (17) _____ occurs when the response to a new stimulus is (18) _____ from the response to the original stimulus.

- If the CS is presented repeatedly, and is no longer followed by the (19) _____, it loses its signaling properties, and the CR gradually becomes weaker. This is called (20) _____. Conditioned (21) _____ occurs when we learn that an event signals the (22) _____ of the US.

Learning About the Consequences of Behavior: Operant Conditioning

- Behaviors produce rewards and punishments, so it's clearly adaptive to learn when and how to operate, or act, on your environment.

- (23) _____ conditioning is a procedure for studying how organisms learn about the (24) _____ of their own behavior. Thorndike's law of (25) _____ holds that if a response is followed by a satisfying or pleasant consequence, the connection between the response and that situation will be (26) _____; conversely, if a response leads to an unsatisfying or unpleasant consequence, the connection will be (27) _____.

- The law of effect applies when a response is rewarded in one situation and not in another. The situation is the (28) _____ stimulus.

- (29) _____ reinforcement occurs when the presentation of an event after a response (30) _____ the likelihood of the response occurring again. Negative reinforcement occurs when removing an event after a response (31) _____ the likelihood of the response occurring again. Conditioned, or secondary, (32) _____ are stimuli that acquire reinforcement properties through learning.

- Positive punishment occurs when the presentation of an event (33) _____ the chances of that response occurring again. (34) _____ punishment occurs when the removal of an event (35) _____ the likelihood of responding.

- A schedule of (36) _____ is a rule used to determine when responses will be reinforced. In a (37) _____ schedule, every response is followed by reinforcement; in a (38) _____ schedule, reinforcement is delivered only after some responses. Partial schedules include (39) _____-ratio, variable- (40) _____, fixed- (41) _____, and (42) _____-interval.

- Someone can be trained to behave in a particular way through (43) _____, which refers to giving reinforcement for successive (44) _____ of the desired behavior.

- Many psychologists believe that (45) _____ constraints, perhaps in the genetic code, limit the responses that can be learned; in addition, we are predisposed to learn relationships between certain stimuli and outcomes, such as taste and illness.

Learning From Others: Observational Learning

- We naturally tend to model the behavior of people who are significant to us. (46) _____ learning is especially likely if the model's characteristics are (47) _____, or if we see that the person is (48) _____ for certain behaviors.

- It's (49) _____ to model the behavior of others because it reduces the likelihood of coming into contact with something harmful or dangerous. Observing desirable behavior can (50) _____ unwanted or maladaptive behavior. Observational learning can also (51) _____ maladaptive behavior, as when people model the violence they see in the media.

CRITICAL THINKING QUESTIONS

1. Can you think of any reason it might be adaptive to begin the digestive process before food actually gets into the mouth?

2. Why do you think it's adaptive to learn associations only when the conditioned stimulus provides new information about the unconditioned stimulus? Can you think of any situations in which it might be useful to learn that many stimuli predict the appearance of the unconditioned stimulus?

3. After reading about Little Albert, can you understand why some psychologists believe that certain psychological problems, such as specific fears called phobias, might result from learning experiences?

4. Can you think of a case in which presenting an unpleasant event actually increases the likelihood of the response that produces it?

5. When you study for an examination or try to do well in school, are you seeking positive reinforcement or negative reinforcement?

6. Do you think monkeys raised in captivity, such as in a zoo, will also show a strong fear of snakes?

7. Given what you've learned about modeling, do you now favor the passage of laws that will control the amount of violence shown in the entertainment media? Why or why not?

KEY TERMS

classical conditioning (p. 238)

conditioned inhibition (p. 247)

conditioned reinforcer (p. 252)

conditioned response (CR) (p. 239)

conditioned stimulus (CS) (p. 239)

discriminative stimulus (p. 251)

extinction (p. 245)

fixed-interval (FI) schedule (p. 256)

fixed-ratio (FR) schedule (p. 255)

habituation (p. 236)

law of effect (p. 250)

learning (p. 235)

modeling (p. 262)

negative punishment (p. 253)

negative reinforcement (p. 252)

observational learning (p. 261)

operant conditioning (p. 249)

orienting response (p. 236)

partial reinforcement schedule (p. 254)

positive punishment (p. 253)

positive reinforcement (p. 252)

punishment (p. 253)

reinforcement (p. 251)

schedule of reinforcement (p. 254)

second-order conditioning (p. 242)

sensitization (p. 237)

shaping (p. 257)

spontaneous recovery (p. 245)

stimulus discrimination (p. 244)

stimulus generalization (p. 243)

unconditioned response (UR) (p. 239)

unconditioned stimulus (US) (p. 239)

variable-interval (VI) schedule (p. 256)

variable-ratio (VR) schedule (p. 255)

Allstar Picture Library Ltd. / Alamy Stock Photo

MEMORY

What if the flow of time suddenly fractured and you were forced to relive the same 10 minutes, over and over again, in an endless pattern? Maybe you'd be driving your car or reading a book; it wouldn't matter—at the end of the interval you'd begin again, back at the same fork in the road or the same location on the page. Think about how this might affect you. Perhaps you wouldn't age, but would you be able to maintain any semblance of psychological health?

The answer, of course, depends on your capacity to remember and forget. If your memories remained intact from one day to the next, if you were aware of the endless repetition, life would quickly become unbearable (even if it was a particularly good day). But if your memories were erased before each new 10-minute interval, you'd lack awareness of your hopeless plight; your life, although existing in an abbreviated form, would continue as usual. This type of situation has been depicted in movies, in which the character relives the same day over and over (e.g., *50 First Dates, Groundhog Day*). As you'll see in this chapter, some individuals suffer a similar kind of memory deficit due to an illness or injury that damaged specific areas of their brain.

It's through **memory**—broadly defined as the capacity to preserve and recover information—that concepts like the past and the present gain meaning in our lives. Like learning, memory is not something that can be directly observed. It's an *inferred* capacity, one that psychologists assume must be operating when people act on information that's no longer physically present. To understand how memory works, we need to consider how memories are formed, how memories are maintained over time, and how the stored information is recovered and translated into performance. The processes of **encoding** determine and control how memories are initially acquired. **Storage** controls how memories are maintained. **Retrieval** is the term used to describe how stored memories are recovered and translated into performance. Each of these key psychological processes is illustrated in Figure 8.1.

FIGURE 8.1 ■ Basic Memory Processes

When a person is asked to remember a word such as CAT, how the person thinks about it will affect how that word is encoded into memory (panel 1). CAT might then be stored in long-term memory by activating existing knowledge structures (panel 2). If the person uses the cue ANIMAL to help retrieve the memory of CAT, it might be difficult to pick out the correct response from other animals stored in memory (panel 3).

Illustrated by Sarah Yeh

THE PROBLEMS TO BE SOLVED: WHAT IS MEMORY FOR?

Memory is a highly adaptive feature of our cognitive tool kit. By maintaining and recovering the past, we equip ourselves to better handle the present. We can change our behavior to correct past mistakes, or we can continue to act in ways that have led to past success. But as you'll see in this chapter, memory is far more than simply recovering past events. A world without memory would be devoid of thought and reason. You would never learn; you would never produce spoken language or understand the words of others; your sense of personal history would be lost along with much, if not all, of your personal identity. In this chapter, we focus on the key adaptive problems that memory helps us solve.

Remembering Over the Short Term

It's natural to link memory to the recovery of events that happened hours, days, or weeks ago, but we need to remember over the very short term as well. Consider the interpretation of spoken language. Because speech unfolds one word at a time, it's necessary to remember the early part of a sentence, after it has receded into the past, before you can hope to understand the meaning of the sentence as a whole. Likewise, when we perform most mental tasks, such as solving math problems, certain bits of information must be retained during the ongoing solution process. Try adding 28 and 35 in your head without remembering to carry the 1 (or subtract 2 if you round the 28 up to 30). By establishing short-term memories, we're able to prolong the incoming message, giving us more time to interpret it properly.

Storing Information for the Long Term

To remember information for longer periods, it needs to be learned in a way that promotes lasting storage. Forming a visual image of a to-be-remembered item generally increases its durability in memory. Thinking about the meaning of the item, or relating the item to other material that's already been stored, helps as well. As you already know, practicing retrieval through self-testing is another extremely effective way to remember over the long term. We'll consider these techniques in some detail, and we'll provide more tips to help you improve your ability to remember.

Recovering Information From Cues

What initiates an act of remembering? What causes you to remember your appointment with your academic adviser this afternoon, what you had for breakfast this morning, or that fleeting encounter you had with a stranger yesterday? Most researchers believe that our memories are triggered by other events, or cues, encountered in the environment. When we fail to remember, it's usually because we lack the right retrieval cues. We'll discuss what makes a "good" retrieval cue, and we'll examine how existing knowledge is used to help us reconstruct what happened in the past.

Updating Memory

It's upsetting to forget, but forgetting has very useful properties. Among other things, it prevents us from acting in ways that are no longer appropriate. It's the homework assignment you need to complete *today* that's critical, not the one from yesterday or the week before. It's your *current* address that you need to remember, not the one from a previous apartment or from the home you lived in as a child (although you can probably still remember that address if you lived there your whole childhood). We'll consider the major determinants of forgetting, both the normal kinds and the abnormal forgetting of the type that characterizes amnesia.

REMEMBERING OVER THE SHORT TERM

When information first reaches the senses, we rely on two memory systems to help us prolong the incoming message over the short term. The first, called **sensory memory**, keeps the message in a relatively pure, unanalyzed form. Sensory memories are like fleeting snapshots of the world. The message is represented in accurate detail—as a kind of picture or echo—but the memory usually lasts less than a second. The second system, **short-term memory**, is a limited-capacity "working memory" that we use to hold information after it has been analyzed for periods lasting on the order of a minute or two. Short-term memories are also rapidly forgotten, but they can be maintained for extended periods through internal repetition. Let's take a brief look at each of these systems and consider some of their important properties.

Sensory Memory: The Icon and the Echo

When you watch a movie, you experience a continuous flow of movement across the screen. As you probably know, the film does not contain moving images; it is composed of still pictures presented rapidly in sequence, each separated by a period of darkness. We perceive a continuous world, some researchers believe, partly because the nervous system activity left by one picture lingers for a brief period prior to presentation of the next image. This extended nervous system

The trails of light created by a whirling sparkler are caused by visual sensory memories, which act like still photographs of the perceptual sense.

ian west / Alamy Stock Photo

activity creates a sensory "memory" that helps to fill the gap, thereby providing a sense of continuous movement.

In vision, the lingering sensory memory trace is called an *icon*, and the sensory memory system that produces and stores icons is known as **iconic memory** (Neisser, 1967). It's relatively easy to demonstrate an icon: Simply twirl a flashlight about in a darkened room, and you will see a trailing edge. You can obtain a similar effect on a dark night by writing your name in the air with a sparkler or a match. These trails of light are not really present in the night air; they arise from the rapidly fading images of iconic memory, which act as still photographs of the world. These images allow the visual sensations to be extended in time so that the brain can more efficiently process the physical message it receives (Coltheart & Coltheart, 2010). In other words, an iconic memory is a short-lived image of a visual sensation (e.g., words on a page, an outdoor scene).

In the auditory system, there is a lingering *echo*, or **echoic memory**. Pure sounds can be held for brief intervals to help auditory perception—echoic memory acts as an echo of sound sensations (e.g., words someone just spoke to us, an abrupt and loud sound). In Chapter 5, you learned how the brain calculates arrival time differences between the ears to help localize sounds. However, to compare arrival times, the first sound must be retained until the second one arrives; echoic memory may help fill the gap. Echoic memory is also widely believed to play a role in language processing, perhaps to help retain exact replicas of sounds during sentence and word processing (Crowder, 1976; Nairne & Neath, 2012).

Measuring Iconic Memory

How can an icon be measured? More than 60 years ago, a graduate student in psychology named George Sperling (1960; also see Averbach & Coriell, 1961) developed a clever procedure for studying the properties of iconic memory. Using an apparatus called a tachistoscope, which presents visual displays for carefully controlled durations (computers were not being used in psychological experiments yet), Sperling showed people arrays of 12 letters arranged in rows. For example:

XLWF

JBOV

KCZR

The person's task was simple: Look at the display and then report the letters. Sounds easy, but the presentation time was extremely brief—the display was shown for only about 50 milliseconds (one-twentieth of a second). Across several experiments, Sperling found that people could report only 4 or 5 letters correctly in this task (out of 12). But more important, they claimed to see an image—an icon— of the *entire* display for a brief period after it was removed from view. All 12 of the letters could be seen, the people claimed, but the image faded before all could be reported.

To provide evidence for this rapidly decaying image, or icon, Sperling tried asking people to report only the letters shown in a particular row—but, critically, he didn't tell them which row until after the display was turned off. A high, medium, or low tone was presented immediately after the display, which cued participants to recall just the top, middle, or bottom row (see Figure 8.2). Sperling called this new condition *partial report* because only a part of the display needed to be recalled. Performance was great—people almost always reported the row of letters correctly.

Remember, people heard the tone *after* the display had been turned off. There was no way to predict which row would be cued, so the entire display must have been available in memory for participants to perform so well. Performance improved, Sperling reasoned, because people had enough time to read a single cued row, but not the entire display, before the iconic image had completely faded. In further experiments, he was able to measure how quickly the sensory image was lost by delaying presentation of the tone. He discovered that the fleeting image—the iconic memory—was indeed short-lived; it disappeared in about half a second.

FIGURE 8.2 ■ The Partial Report Technique

After presentation of the display, a tone indicates the row of letters to be recalled. As the participant attempts to recall them, the visual iconic memory fades and becomes less and less accurate. When only part of the display is to be recalled, most of the relevant information can be reported before the image is completely lost.

Carolina Hrejsa/Body Scientific Intl.

Measuring Echoic Memory

Sensory memories are produced by each of the five senses, but little work has been done on systems other than vision and audition. An experiment by Efron (1970) demonstrates how it's possible to measure the lingering echoic trace, or echo. People were presented with a series of very brief tones, each lasting less than about one-tenth of a second; the task was to adjust a light so that it appeared exactly when each tone ended. Efron discovered that people always thought the tone ended later than it actually did; that is, people reported hearing the tone for a brief period after it had been turned off. Efron argued that this "phantom tone" was caused by a memory—the lingering echo of echoic memory. As in visual sensory memory, auditory sensory memory is believed to last for only a brief period of time—probably less than a second—although in some circumstances it may last longer, perhaps for as long as 5 or 10 seconds (N. Cowan, 1995; Nees, 2016).

Short-Term Memory: Prolonging the Present

The function of sensory memory is to maintain an exact replica of the environmental message, for a very short period, as an aid to perception. *Short-term memory* is the system we use to temporarily store, think about, and reason with information. The term *working memory* is sometimes used because this temporary storage system often acts as a kind of mental workplace, allowing us to store the components of a problem as we work toward a solution (Baddeley, 2017; Nairne, 2002a).

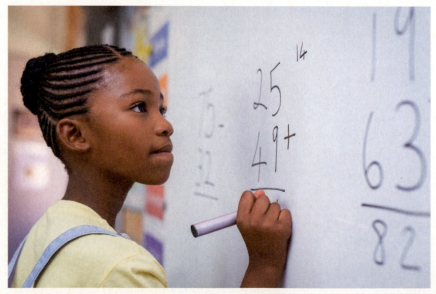

Short-term memory can help us store information we need for everyday tasks such as completing math problems.

iStockPhoto/Ridofranz

It's useful to keep recently presented information available over the short term. Consider language: It would be hard to understand spoken language, which occurs sequentially (one word at a time), without remembering the first part of a spoken phrase. It would also be difficult to read any kind of text without keeping themes of the passage, or what was presented in the previous sentence, in mind. Short-term memories help us produce and interpret spoken language, remember the task we're currently working on, reason and problem-solve, and even think. In the following sections, we consider some of the properties of short-term memories, including how and why they're forgotten.

The Inner Voice

Unlike sensory memories, short-term memories are not exact copies of the environmental message. When we maintain information over the short term, it is usually in the form of an inner "voice." You can convince yourself by repeating this word—PSYCHOLOGY—silently inside your head. Notice you can repeat the word quickly or slowly, and, if you like, you can even insert internal pauses after each repetition. There's nothing visual about this repetition process; you have recoded, or translated, the visual message PSYCHOLOGY into another form—an inner voice.

This notion of an inner voice is supported by the errors that occur during short-term recall. When recalling over the short term, people invariably make errors that are acoustically based. Mistakes tend to *sound* like correct items even when the stimulus materials have never been presented aloud (Conrad, 1964). For example, suppose you're given five letters to remember—B X R C L—but you make a mistake and misremember the fourth letter. Your error will probably be a letter that sounds like the correct one; you're likely to incorrectly remember something like T or P. Notice that C and T and P all sound alike, but they *look* nothing alike. It's believed that errors tend to be acoustic because people typically recode the original visual input into an inner voice.

Why do we store things over the short term in an inner voice? It's probably because we're often called on to interpret and produce spoken language. It makes sense to think in a way that's compatible with the way we communicate. In fact, there's some evidence to suggest that individuals who are deaf or hearing-impaired, particularly those who communicate with American Sign Language, do not rely on an inner voice to the same extent as people with normal hearing; they sometimes encode information in a form that's compatible with their normal language format (Hall & Bavelier, 2011).

The Inner Eye

We usually use our inner voice to store short-term memories, but we can use other formats. For example, sometimes we use visual images. To illustrate, close your eyes and count the number of windows in your house or apartment. Did you perform this task by visualizing the rooms, one by one, and counting the number of windows you "saw"? Now try forming a visual image of a rabbit standing next to an elephant. Does the rabbit in your image have whiskers? If I measure your reaction time, it turns out that you'll answer a question like this more quickly if you imagine the rabbit standing next to a rat instead of next to an elephant (Kosslyn, 1983). This is exactly the kind of result we'd expect if you were looking at an actual picture—the larger the object is in the picture, the easier it is to "see."

Experiments have shown that the imagery produced by the "inner eye" may rely on the same brain mechanisms as normal visual perception. Neuroimaging techniques reveal that imagery and perception activate many of the same regions in the brain (Cichy et al., 2012). Other studies have found that people have trouble storing a visual image in their head while they're also performing a visually based tracking task, such as finding locations on a map (Baddeley & Lieberman, 1980). There are even patients with brain damage who report corresponding impairments in both imagery and visual perception. For example, some patients whose brain damage has caused them to lose their color vision also have difficulty forming a colorful visual image. Thus, there appears to be an important link between the brain systems involved in perception and those involved in mental imagery.

Short-Term Forgetting

Have you ever had trouble remembering something (e.g., what the instructor said during a lecture) long enough to write it down or type it into your laptop? It's possible to prolong short-term memories indefinitely by engaging in **rehearsal**, which is the process of internal repetition, assuming that you have the time and resources to continue the rehearsal process. (Think about the word *rehearsal* as "re-hear-sal," as if listening to the inner voice.) Without rehearsal, however, short-term memories are quickly forgotten (Atkinson & Shiffrin, 1968). In an early investigation of short-term forgetting, Lloyd and Margaret Peterson (1959) asked students to recall short lists of three letters (such as CLX) after delays that ranged from 3 to 18 seconds. The task sounds easy—remembering three letters for less than half a minute—but the experiment had an unusual feature: No one was allowed to rehearse the letters during the delay interval; instead, the students were asked to count backward by threes aloud until a recall signal appeared. You can try this experiment for yourself: Ask someone to read you three letters, then try immediately counting backward by threes from the number 832. Finally, have your friend signal you to recall after about 10 to 20 seconds. Under these conditions, you'll probably find that you forget the letters relatively quickly (if the first trial seems easy, try a few more with different letters). In the Petersons' experiment, the students were reduced to guessing after about 10 to 15 seconds of counting backward (see Figure 8.3).

FIGURE 8.3 ■ The Peterson Distractor Test

On each trial, people were asked to recall three letters in correct order, after counting backward aloud for 3 to 18 seconds. The longer the participants counted, the less likely they were to recall the letters correctly.

Input		Distraction Interval, Counting Backward	Recall
Trial 1	CLX	". . . 391-388"	"C-L-X"
Trial 2	FVR	". . . 476-473-470"	"F-V-R"
Trial 3	ZQW	". . . 582-579-576-573"	"Z-W-Q?"
Trial 4	LBC	". . . 267-264-261-258-255"	"L-B-"
Trial 5	KJX	". . . 941-938-935-932-929-926"	"K-?-?"
Trial 6	MDW	". . . 747-744-741-739-736-733-730"	"?-?-?"

```
0    3    6    9    12   15   18
              Time (sec)
```

Why is information forgotten so rapidly without rehearsal? Some researchers believe that short-term memories are lost spontaneously over time, through a process called *decay*, unless those memories are kept active through rehearsal (Barrouillet et al., 2012). Decay also explains the rapid forgetting of sensory memories. Other researchers believe that short-term forgetting is caused primarily by *interference* from new information or because people confuse current memories with past memories (e.g., Oberauer et al., 2016). A third possibility is that decay and interference operate together to produce information loss. We'll return to the question of what causes forgetting later in the chapter.

Short-Term Memory Capacity

Another characteristic of short-term memory is its limited capacity: We can only remember a small amount of information over the short term. Research has shown that short-term **memory span**—which is defined as the number of items a person can recall in the exact order of presentation on half of the tested memory trials—is typically about seven, plus or minus two items. In other words, short-term memory span ranges between five and nine items (G. A. Miller, 1956). It's easy to remember a list of four items but quite difficult to remember a list of eight or nine items (which is one of the reasons telephone numbers are seven digits long).

Most psychologists believe that the capacity of short-term memory is limited, in part, because it takes time to execute the process of rehearsal. To illustrate, imagine you're asked to remember a relatively long list of letters arranged this way:

CA TFL YBU G

First, try reading this list aloud, from C to G. You'll find that several seconds elapse from start to finish. Now imagine cycling through the list with your inner voice as you prepare for short-term recall. It turns out that the C to G cycling takes a similar amount of time inside your head (Landauer, 1962).

Remember, however, that items stored in short-term memory are forgotten in a matter of seconds, so the first part of the list tends to be forgotten during execution of the last. By the time you've finished with the last letter and returned to the beginning of the list, the early items have already been lost from memory. You can think about this relationship between forgetting and rehearsal as roughly similar to juggling (see Figure 8.4). To juggle successfully, you need to win the battle against gravity. You throw the dinner plates up, and gravity pulls them down. To prevent one of the plates from crashing, it's necessary to catch and toss it back up before gravity runs it into the ground. Similarly, you need to return to the rapidly fading short-term memory trace and reactivate it through rehearsal before the "forces" of forgetting win out. It's a race between two opposing forces—rehearsal and forgetting.

FIGURE 8.4   ■   The Capacity of Short-Term Memory

The amount of information that can be stored in short-term memory depends on rehearsal, which you can think of as roughly analogous to juggling. You return to each rapidly fading short-term memory trace and reactivate it through rehearsal before it is permanently forgotten. Chunking the material makes it easier to rehearse and therefore remember the information.

Illustrated by Sarah Yeh

People differ in their ability to rehearse and maintain short-term memories. These individual differences are related to our ability to allocate attention to a task, such as rehearsal, especially when we have more than one thing to do at a time. Some people are quite good at rehearsing information while performing another task—for example, remembering a coupon code while searching the internet. It turns out that the ability to keep multiple things available in short-term memory at the same time predicts performance on higher-order cognitive tasks, such as reasoning, or even your score on an intelligence test (Fukada et al., 2010). It is also the case that some clinical conditions, such as attention-deficit disorder and schizophrenia, are associated with problems in the ability to use short-term memory effectively (S. K. Hill et al., 2010).

Chunking

As a general rule, memory span is roughly equal to the amount of material you can internally rehearse in about two seconds (which usually turns out to be about seven plus or minus two items). To improve your ability to remember over the short term, then, it's best to figure out a way to rehearse a lot of information in a short amount of time. One effective strategy is **chunking**, which involves rearranging the incoming information into meaningful or familiar patterns, called chunks. Remember that long list of letters presented earlier (CA TFL YBU G)? Perhaps you saw that the same list could be slightly rearranged:

CAT FLY BUG

Forming the letters into words drastically reduces the time it takes to repeat the list internally (try saying CAT FLY BUG over and over internally). In addition, once you remember a chunk, it's easy to recall the letters—in most cases, words are great storage devices for remembering sequences of letters. Of course, the trick lies in finding meaningful chunks in what can appear to be a meaningless jumble of information.

The ability to create meaningful chunks often depends on how much you know about the material that needs to be remembered. Expert chess players can re-create most of the positions on a chessboard after only a brief glance—as long as a meaningful game is in progress (Chase & Simon, 1973). They recognize familiar attack or defense patterns in the game, which allows them to create easy-to-rehearse chunks of position information. Similar results are found when electronics experts are asked to remember complex circuit board diagrams (Egan & Schwartz, 1979). In both cases, if the materials are arranged in a more or less random fashion (e.g., the chess pieces are simply scattered about the board), the skilled retention vanishes, and memory reverts to normal levels.

The Working Memory Model

We've focused on the characteristics of short-term memories—how they're stored and forgotten—but we haven't discussed the "system" that controls memory over the short term. Unfortunately, memory researchers still don't completely agree about the mechanisms that enable us to remember over the short term. Some psychologists believe that memory over the short term is controlled by the same processes that control memory over the long term (Melton, 1963; Nairne, 2002a). But most psychologists assume we have special equipment for short-term memory because of its importance in language and thought. The most popular account of the short-term memory system is the *working memory model* developed originally by Baddeley and Hitch (1974) and elaborated on more recently by Baddeley (2007, 2017).

In the working memory model, several distinct mechanisms are important for short-term retention. First, the temporary storage of acoustic and verbal information is controlled by the *phonological loop*. The phonological loop is the structure we use to temporarily store verbal information and engage in repetitive rehearsal—it corresponds to the inner voice and is believed to play a critical role in language (Baddeley et al., 1998). The short-term retention and processing of visual and spatial information is controlled by a different system—the *visuospatial sketchpad*. If you try to count the number of windows in your house by moving through it in your mind's eye, you are probably involving the visuospatial sketchpad. Finally, Baddeley and Hitch (1974) propose that a *central executive* controls and allocates how processing is divided across the loop and the sketchpad. The central executive determines when the loop or sketchpad will be used and coordinates its actions.

One reason the working memory model is popular among memory researchers is that it helps explain the effects of certain types of brain damage. There are patients, for example, who seem to lose specific verbal skills, such as the ability to learn new words in an unfamiliar language. Other patients retain their language skills but have difficulties with memory for spatial or visual information (Baddeley, 2000, 2007). These results suggest that we have separate systems controlling verbal and visual storage, just as the working memory model proposes. Neuroimaging techniques also show that different areas of the brain are active when we remember spatial and nonspatial information (D'Esposito & Postle, 2015; Jonides et al., 2008).

KNOWLEDGE CHECK 8.1

Now test your knowledge about remembering over the short term by deciding whether each of the following statements best describes sensory memory or short-term memory. (You will find the answers in the Appendix.)

1. Information is forgotten in less than a second: ___

2. Information is stored as a virtually exact copy of the external message: ___

3. Information can be stored indefinitely through the process of rehearsal: ___

4. The system measured through Sperling's partial report procedure: ___

5. Recall errors tend to sound like the correct item even when the item is presented visually: ___

6. May help us calculate message arrival time differences between the two ears: ___

7. Span is roughly equal to the amount of material that you can say to yourself in two seconds: ___

8. Capacity is improved through chunking: ___

STORING INFORMATION FOR THE LONG TERM

Long-term memory is the system we use to maintain information for extended periods. When you remember the name of your fifth-grade teacher or the correct route to class, you're using your long-term memory. Most psychologists believe that the capacity of long-term memory is effectively unlimited. There are no limits to what we can potentially remember, but not everything we experience gets stored. We also don't necessarily store information in a way that makes it easy to remember. To achieve effective long-term storage, it's necessary to *encode* the experience in a way that makes it easy to *retrieve*. We'll consider momentarily the kinds of encoding activities that lead to effective long-term storage, but first let's briefly consider the general kinds of information that are stored.

What Is Stored in Long-Term Memory?

Stop for a moment and think about your first kiss. The recollection (assuming you can remember your first kiss) is likely filled with warmth, intimacy, and perhaps embarrassment. Do you remember the person's name? The situation? The year? Memories that tap some moment from our personal past are called **episodic memories**—they consist of the events, or episodes, that happened to us personally. Most experimental research on memory tests episodic memory because people typically are asked to remember information from an earlier point in the experiment. The task is to remember an *event*, such as a word list, that forms a part of the personal history of the participant.

Some psychologists believe that episodic memory is a uniquely human quality (Tulving, 2002). Other animals show memory, in the sense that they can act on the basis of information that's no longer present (such as remembering the location of food), but they lack the ability to mentally travel backward in time and "relive" prior experiences. They live only in the present and show no awareness of the past. Interestingly, some forms of brain damage produce a similar effect in humans. Such patients appear normal in most respects—they can read and write normally, solve problems, and even play chess—but they lack the ability to remember any events or circumstances from their personal past (M. A. Wheeler & McMillan, 2001).

Now think of a city in Europe that's famous for its fashion and fine wine. A correct response is *Paris*, but did you "remember" or "know" the answer? What about the square root of 9 or the capital city of

It is difficult to teach skills associated with procedural memory because such memories tend to be inaccessible.

iStockPhoto/nazar_ab

the United States? These are certainly memories, in the sense that you have preserved and recovered information from the past, but "remembering" these answers feels vastly different from remembering your first kiss. When you reveal what you know about the world, but make no reference whatsoever to a particular episode from your past, you're using **semantic memory** (*semantic* refers to "meaning"). It's through semantic memory that we store facts and remember the rules we need to know to adapt effectively in the world.

Finally, think about how to tie your shoes, drive a car, or ride a bike. The knowledge about how to *do* things is called **procedural memory**. Most skills, including athletic ability, rely on procedural memories. Procedural memories differ from episodic and semantic memories in a fundamental way: They rarely produce any conscious experience of "remembering." Most people have a difficult time consciously reporting how to tie their shoes or ride a bike. They can do these things, but it's extremely difficult to put the knowledge into words. Procedural memories are among the simplest of all memories to recover, but they are among the most difficult for psychologists to study—they seem to be inaccessible to conscious awareness (Tulving, 1983). For a summary of these memory types—episodic, semantic, and procedural—see Concept Review 8.1.

CONCEPT REVIEW 8.1
VARIETIES OF LONG-TERM MEMORY

Type of Memory	Description	Example
Episodic	Memories that recall a personal moment from our past	Wanda, the mail carrier, remembers that yesterday 10 inches of snow fell, making her job very difficult.
Semantic	Knowledge about the world, with no specific reference to a particular past episode	Wanda knows that mailing a letter first-class costs 55 cents; she also knows that it costs more to send something by express mail.
Procedural	Knowledge about *how* to do something	Wanda drives the streets of her mail route effortlessly, without really thinking about it.

Elaboration: Connecting Material to Existing Knowledge

Now let's turn to long-term episodic memory. What's the best way to remember something over the long term? As a general rule, if you want a lasting memory, relate what you want to remember to what you already know. There's a vast storehouse of information in the brain, and memory works best when you make use of it. When you actively relate new information to the already-stored content of long-term memory, the process is called **elaboration**. Elaboration works for two reasons: First, it helps establish routes to remembering—that is, retrieval "cues" that ease later recovery. Second, elaboration creates a distinctive memory record that stands out and is easy to identify. Elaboration comes in many forms, as the following sections demonstrate.

Think About Meaning

One of the easiest ways to promote elaboration is to think about the *meaning* of the information you want to remember. In an experiment by Craik and Tulving (1975), people were asked questions about single words such as MOUSE. In one condition, the task required everyone to make judgments about the sound of the word (e.g., does the word rhyme with HOUSE?); in another condition, people were required to think about the meaning of the word (e.g., is a MOUSE a type of animal?). Much better memory was obtained in this second condition. Thinking about meaning, rather than sound, leads to richer and more elaborate connections between events and other things in memory. The deeper and more elaborative the processing, the more likely that memory will improve (Craik & Lockhart, 1972).

Notice Relationships

You can also use your existing knowledge to look for relationships among the things that need to be remembered. Suppose you're asked to remember the following list of words:

NOTES PENCIL AIRPODS LAPTOP MUSIC COFFEE

If you think about what the words mean and you look for properties they have in common—perhaps things that you would take to a study session or a lecture—you're engaging in a form of elaboration called *relational processing*. Relational processing works because you are embellishing, or adding to, the input. If you're trying to remember the word PENCIL and you relate the word to an involved sequence of events, there are likely to be lots of cues that will remind you of the correct response at a later time. Thinking about music, notes, drinking coffee—any of these can lead to the correct recall of PENCIL.

Notice Differences

You should also think about how the material you want to remember is different from other information in long-term memory. If you simply encode PENCIL as a writing tool, you might incorrectly recall things like PEN, CHALK, or even CRAYON at a later time. Instead, specify the particular event in detail—we're talking about a yellow, number 2 pencil, not a crayon—so the memory record becomes unique. Unique memory records are remembered better because they stand out—they're easier to distinguish from related, but not appropriate, material in memory.

Elaboration tends to produce unique memory records—referred to as **distinctiveness**. When you compare to-be-remembered information to other things in memory, noting similarities and differences, you encode how that information both shares properties with other information (relational processing) and is unique or different (distinctive processing). This leads to lots of retrieval cues that will help you remember the encoded material. Generally, if you want to remember something particularly well, you should concentrate on encoding both item similarities and item differences (R. R. Hunt & McDaniel, 1993).

Form Mental Pictures

Another way to produce an elaborate memory record is to form a visual image of the material when it's first presented. If you're trying to remember COFFEE, try forming a mental picture of a steaming hot, freshly brewed cup. Forming mental pictures is an effective memory strategy because it naturally leads to elaborate, rich encodings. Mental pictures require you to think about the details of the material, and these details create a distinctive memory record. As you'll see later, many memory improvement techniques, called mnemonic devices, rely importantly on the use of **visual imagery**.

Visual imagery leads to excellent memory, but the memories themselves are not photographic (as you might assume)—instead, they're surprisingly abstract, and important details are often missing or inaccurate. To demonstrate, try forming a visual image of a penny or a quarter (or a coin in a monetary system you are very familiar with). You've seen coins many times, so this should be a fairly easy task. Now try to reproduce the image on paper—simply draw the image depicted on the coin, which direction it is facing, and so on. Your performance is apt to be mediocre at best. People are simply unable to reproduce the main features of a coin very accurately, despite the strong belief that they can see an accurate representation in their head. In fact, it's even difficult for people to recognize the correct coin when it is presented along with incorrect versions. For a display like the one shown in Figure 8.5, fewer than half of the participants pick out the right penny (Nickerson & Adams, 1979). Certainly, if you were looking at a coin, you would be able to trace the features accurately, so the image we form isn't necessarily an accurate representation of physical reality. This in no way detracts from the power of imagery on memory, however. We may not store exact pictures in our head, but the records produced from imagery are among the easiest to retrieve.

FIGURE 8.5 ■ Can You Recognize a Penny?

We may think we can form an accurate mental image of a penny, but it isn't easy to pick a true penny from a group of fake ones. Can you find the real penny in this display?

Reprinted from "Long-Term Memory for a Common Object" by R. S. Nickerson and M. J. Adams in *Cognitive Psychology*, Volume 11, 287–307. Copyright 1979, with permission from Elsevier.

Space Your Repetitions

Elaborate memory traces can also be achieved through repetition: If information is presented more than once, it will tend to be remembered better. The fact that repetition improves memory is not very surprising, but it might surprise you to learn that repetition alone is not what leads to better memory. It's possible to present an item lots of times without improving memory—what's necessary is that you use each repetition as an opportunity to encode the material in an elaborate and distinctive manner. If you think about the material in exactly the same way every time it's presented, your memory won't improve very much.

How the repetitions are spaced is another important factor. Your memory will be better if you distribute the repetitions—that is, if you insert other events (or time) between each occurrence. This is called **distributed practice**. It means that all-night cram sessions where you read the same chapter over and over again are not very effective study procedures. It's better to study a little psychology, do something else, and then return to your psychology. Why does distributed practice lead to the best memory? Again, what matters to memory is how you process the material when it's presented. If you use massed practice—where you simply reread the same material over and over again without a break—you're likely to think about the material in exactly the same way every time it's presented. If you insert a break between presentations, when you see the material again there's a better chance that you'll notice something new or different. Distributed practice leads to memory records that are more elaborate and distinctive.

Consider Sequence Position

If you have to remember a set of items, such as a list of grocery items, you'll tend to remember the items from the beginning and the end of the sequence best. This pattern is shown in Figure 8.6, which plots how well items are recalled as a function of their temporal, or serial, position in a list (this graph is often called a serial position curve). The improved memory for items at the start of the list is called the **primacy effect**; the end-of-the-list advantage is called the **recency effect**. Memory researchers believe that primacy and recency effects arise because items that occur at the beginning and end of a sequence are more naturally distinctive in memory and are therefore easier to rehearse and/or to recall (Surprenant & Neath, 2009). Practically, then, if you're trying to remember a list, put the most important things at the beginning and the end of the list.

FIGURE 8.6 ■ The Serial Position Curve

When asked to recall a list of items, our performance often depends on the temporal, or serial, position of the entries in the list. Items at the beginning of the list are remembered relatively well—the primacy effect—and so are items at the end of the list—the recency effect.

Test Yourself

Finally, you've been getting advice about the importance of practicing retrieval throughout this book. When you test yourself, the act of retrieving the information makes that information more memorable. No one is certain exactly why the benefit occurs, but it is one of the strongest ways to produce lasting long-term memory (Roediger & Karpicke, 2018). One popular account is that testing leads to elaboration; during retrieval, but not reading, we generate cues that will remind us of the tested information. Think about it: When you study something, it's right in front of you—you don't need to generate reminder "cues." But when you're required to produce the information from memory, which you have to do when you test yourself, you're on the lookout for hints or clues that will remind you of the answer later on. The act of retrieval helps establish effective retrieval routes, which is a form of elaboration (Pyc & Rawson, 2010). It's also been suggested that correctly remembering the studied information during retrieval practice strengthens the original memory trace made during encoding (Finn & Roediger, 2011). Studies looking at brain activity during retrieval practice suggest that both of these accounts—elaboration and memory strengthening—are responsible for the memory advantage produced by retrieval practice (X. L. Liu et al., 2018).

Mnemonic Devices

Mnemonic devices (*mnemonic* means "pertaining to memory") are special mental tricks developed thousands of years ago as memory aids (Yates, 1966). They're worth discussing because they're relatively easy to use and they have lots of practical applications—in fact, virtually all "how to" memory books rely entirely on these techniques. Professional memorizers, including those who compete in national and international memory contests (the memory "Olympics"), all use versions of these techniques (Foer, 2011).

One of the oldest mnemonic devices is the **method of loci** (*loci* is Latin for "places"). Like most mnemonic devices, the method of loci relies on visual imagery. You start by choosing a well-known place or location—sometimes called a "memory palace"—that's easy to access and remember. A good example might be your house or a route you take to school. In your mind, you then place the material that you want to remember—suppose it's a list of errands—at various locations along the path or within the location. It's important to form a visual image of each memory item and to link the image to a specific location. If you wanted to remember to pay the gas bill, you could form a mental picture of a large check made out to the gas company and place it in the first location on your path (such as the entry hall in your house).

Depending on the size of your pathway, you can store a relatively large amount of material using this method. At the end of encoding, you might have 15 errands stored. Overdue library books could be linked to the living room sofa, clean shirts encased in plastic could be draped across the kitchen counter, or big bags of dog food could be associated with a dog on the television screen (see Figure 8.7).

FIGURE 8.7 ■ The Method of Loci

To-be-remembered items are mentally placed in various locations along a familiar path. They should now be remembered easily because visual imagery promotes an elaborate memory trace and because the stored locations are easy to access.

Illustrated by Sarah Yeh

To recover the material later, all you need to do is walk along the pathway in your mind, "looking" in the different locations for the objects you've stored. The method of loci is an effective memory aid because it forces you to use imagery—creating an elaborate and distinctive record—and the stored records are easy to recover because the storage locations are easy to access.

The **peg-word method** resembles the method of loci in that it requires you to link material to specific memory cues, but the cues are usually words rather than mental pathways. One easy technique is to pick "peg words" that rhyme with numbers: For instance, one is a *bun*, two is a *shoe*, three is a *tree*, and so forth. This makes the pegs easy to remember and access. You then form an image linking the to-be-remembered material with each of the pegs. You might picture your overdue library books inside a hamburger bun, a bag of dog food sitting inside a shoe, or some clean shirts hanging from a tree. To recover the memory records, you would simply start counting, and the peg word should lead you to the image of the to-be-remembered errand. One is a bun—return books; two is a shoe—buy dog food; three is a tree—pick up shirts.

An alternate version of the peg-word method, called the *linkword system*, has been used successfully to assist in learning foreign language vocabulary (Wyra & Lawson, 2018). Suppose you want to remember the French word for rabbit (*lapin*). While studying, think of an English word that sounds like the French word; perhaps the word *lap* would do for *lapin*. Next, think about the meaning of the French word and try to form a visual image of the result linked to the English word. For example, you might imagine a white furry rabbit sitting in someone's lap. When the word *lapin* appears later on a test, the English word will serve as an effective cue for bringing forth a remembered image of the rabbit (*lap* acts as a kind of peg word for *rabbit*). This method has been shown to produce nearly a doubling of the rate of learning for vocabulary words (Raugh & Atkinson, 1975). Although mnemonics are useful for remembering specific types of information, using mnemonics will not improve your memory abilities overall. But the principles underlying these techniques do tell us a lot about how memory works, and that knowledge can help us determine how best to encode information we want to remember.

Remembering With a Stone-Age Brain

The fact that forming a visual image is an effective way to remember shouldn't surprise you too much. After all, we rely heavily on our visual system to navigate and understand our world, so it makes sense that memory, too, relies to some extent on visual imagery (Paivio, 2007). Most cognitive processes, including memory, evolved to help us solve particular problems, and bear the "footprints" of ancestral selection pressures. For example, if people are asked to think about material in terms of its potential survival value, they remember that material particularly well (Nairne et al., 2019). We also tend to remember living things (animates) better than nonliving things (inanimates), presumably because animates are more relevant to our ability to survive and reproduce (Nairne et al., 2017).

In addition, we are likely to form rich records of the circumstances surrounding emotionally significant and surprising events that we hear about (Hirst & Phelps, 2016). So-called **flashbulb memories** have been reported for lots of events—for example, first learning of the election of President Barack Obama, news of the Sandy Hook elementary school shooting, and, most recently, learning of the shutdowns related to COVID-19. People who experience flashbulb memories are convinced they can remember exactly what they were doing when the event occurred. Playing in school, watching television, talking on the phone—whatever the circumstance, people report vivid details about the events surrounding their first exposure to the news. Do you remember what you were doing when you first heard about the March 11, 2011, earthquake and tsunami and subsequent nuclear disaster in Japan? How about the multiple terrorist attacks in Paris on November 13, 2015? Or how about the storming of the U.S. capitol building on January 6, 2021?

Surprisingly, flashbulb memories are often inaccurate. Many U.S. adults have flashbulb memories for when they heard about the September 11, 2001, terrorist attacks. The consistency and confidence of these memories were examined in a study by Talarico and Rubin (2003). The day after the attacks, they asked students at Duke University to report details of where they were when they heard about the attacks. The researchers also asked the students how confident they were that these details were accurate. The students were then asked to report the details again at a second testing that occurred 7 days, 42 days, or 2,224 days after the first testing. The results showed that consistency of the reported details declined as the time from the event increased. However, confidence in the accuracy of the memories did not decline over time. In other words, the students thought they were remembering things accurately, but the data proved otherwise. The fact that their memories were poor suggests that the psychological experience of flashbulb memories—that is, the strong conviction that one's memories are accurate—may be related more to the emotionality of the original experience than to the presence of a rich and elaborative memory record. In fact, research suggests that flashbulb memories are strongest (although not necessarily more accurate) for personally significant events (i.e., the events to which we have the strongest emotional connection; Talarico & Rubin, 2018).

One reason flashbulb memories tend to be inaccurate is that we often incorporate later experiences into our original memories. When something shocking happens, we talk about it a lot, see footage of the event on the news, and hear other people analyze how and why it happened. The events of September 11, 2001, are a good example. When President George W. Bush was asked about his memory for the events some months later, he remembered having seen footage of the first plane hitting

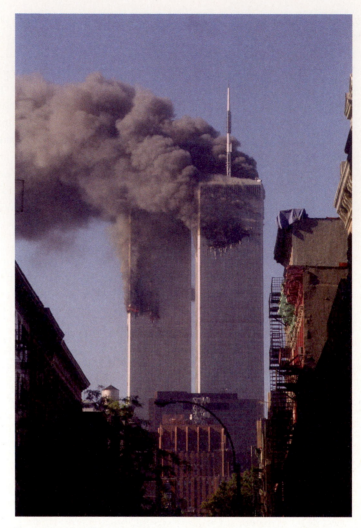

Many adults in the United States have strong flashbulb memories for when and how they heard about the September 11, 2001, terrorist attacks.

Stacy Walsh Rosenstock / Alamy Stock Photo

the tower before he learned about the crash of the second plane. At the time, of course, no footage was available for viewing, so his memory of having seen the first plane attack was simply wrong. This led to some conspiracy theories on the internet—"Bush films his own attack on the World Trade Center"— but a more reasonable explanation is that he simply mistakenly incorporated a later memory (viewing the footage) into his memory for the original event (Greenberg, 2004).

It's important to remember, though, that just because flashbulb memories are sometimes inaccurate doesn't mean they aren't useful and adaptive. We don't necessarily want to remember the past exactly, because the past can never happen again in exactly the same way. Instead, we want to use the past, in combination with the present, to decide on an appropriate action. As you'll see in the next section, remembering often involves reconstructing the past rather than remembering it exactly.

KNOWLEDGE CHECK 8.2

Now test your knowledge of how information is stored over the long term by answering the following questions. (You will find the answers in the Appendix.)

1. For each of the following, decide whether the relevant memory is episodic, semantic, or procedural.
   a. The capital city of Texas is Austin: _____
   b. Breakfast yesterday was ham and eggs: _____

    c.   My mother's maiden name is Hudlow: _____

    d.   Executing a perfect golf swing: _____

    e.   Tying your shoelaces: _____

2.   Your little brother Eddie needs to learn a long list of vocabulary words for school tomorrow. Which of the following represents the best advice for improving his memory?

    a.   Say the words aloud as many times as possible.

    b.   Write down the words as many times as possible.

    c.   Form a visual image of each word.

    d.   Spend more time studying words at the beginning and end of the list.

3.   For each of the following, decide which term best applies. Choose from *distinctiveness, distributed practice, elaboration, method of loci,* and *peg-word technique.*

    a.   Visualize each of the items sitting in a location along a pathway: _____

    b.   Notice how each of the items is different from other things in memory: _____

    c.   Form connections among each of the items to be remembered: _____

    d.   Form images linking items to specific cues: _____

    e.   Engage in relational processing of the to-be-remembered material: _____

RECOVERING INFORMATION FROM CUES

Can you still remember the memory list from a few pages back? You know, the one based on things you might take to a morning lecture class? If you remembered the items, such as PENCIL, LAPTOP, and COFFEE, it's probably because you were able to use the common theme—things you might take to a lecture—as a *cue* to help you remember. Psychologists believe that *retrieval*, the process of recovering previously stored memories, is guided primarily by cues, called *retrieval cues*, that are either generated internally (thinking of the lecture scene helps you remember PENCIL) or present in the environment (a string tied around your finger). Retrieval cues not only initiate an act of remembering; they also help shape what is remembered (or misremembered).

The Importance of Retrieval Cues

A classic study conducted by Tulving and Pearlstone (1966) illustrates the important role that retrieval cues play in remembering. People were given lists to remember containing words from several meaningful categories (types of animals, birds, vegetables, and so on). Later, people were asked to remember the words either with or without the aid of retrieval cues, which were the category names. Half were asked to recall the words without cues, a condition called **free recall**; the other half were given the category names to help them remember, known as **cued recall**. People in the cued-recall condition recalled nearly twice as many words, presumably because the category names helped them gain access to the previously stored material.

Although these results are not surprising, they have important implications for how we need to think about remembering. Because people performed poorly in the free-recall condition, it's tempting to conclude they never learned the material or simply forgot many of the items from the list. But performance in the cued-recall condition shows that the material wasn't lost—it just couldn't be accessed. With the right retrieval cues—in this case the category names—the "lost" material could be remembered with ease. Memory researchers believe that most, if not all, instances of forgetting are caused by a failure to use the right kinds of retrieval cues. Once information is encoded, it is available somewhere in the brain; you simply need appropriate retrieval cues to gain access.

This is the main reason elaboration is an effective strategy for remembering. When you connect material to existing knowledge, creating a rich and elaborate memory record, you're effectively increasing the number of potential retrieval cues. The more retrieval cues, the more likely you'll be able to access the memory record later on. It's also the main reason mnemonic techniques such as the peg-word method work so well—they establish readily available retrieval cues as part of the learning process (e.g., counting to 10 provides immediate access to the relevant "pegs").

Can you name all of your third-grade classmates? Probably not, but your memory is sure to improve if you're given a class photo to use as a retrieval cue.

iStockPhoto/FatCamera

The Encoding–Retrieval Match

Increasing the number of potential retrieval cues helps, but it also helps if the cue matches the memory that was encoded. If you think about the sound of a word during its original presentation, rather than its appearance, then a cue that rhymes with the stored word will be more effective than a visual cue. Similarly, if you think about the meaning of a word during study, then an effective cue will get you to think about the encoded word's meaning during retrieval. Retrieval cues are effective to the extent that they match the way information was originally encoded.

In years to come, these family members may find it easier to remember this welcome-home party at times when they're happy than when they're sad. How does this occurrence reflect the encoding–retrieval match?

Cavan Images / Alamy Stock Photo

Let's consider an example. Suppose you're asked to remember two words: BANK and WAGON. To improve retention, you form a visual image of a WAGON perched on the BANK of a river (see Figure 8.8). Later BANK is provided as a retrieval cue. Will it help you remember WAGON? Probably, but only if you interpret the retrieval cue BANK to mean a slope immediately bordering a river. If for some reason you think about BANK as a place to keep money, you probably won't recover WAGON successfully. A retrieval cue works well only if you interpret it in the proper way. By "proper," psychologists mean that the cue must be interpreted in a way that matches the original encoding. There are some exceptions to this general rule (Nairne, 2002b), but a good encoding–retrieval match is one of the most important factors to consider when seeking a useful retrieval cue.

FIGURE 8.8 ■ The Encoding–Retrieval Match

Memory often depends on how well retrieval cues match the way information was originally studied or encoded. Suppose you're asked to remember the word pair BANK–WAGON. You form a visual image of a wagon teetering on the edge of a riverbank. When presented later with the retrieval cue BANK, you're more likely to remember WAGON if you interpret the cue as something bordering a river than as a place to keep money.

Study — Encoding Input

Retrieval Match — Retrieval Cue: "Bank"

Retrieval Mismatch — Retrieval Cue: "Bank"

Illustrated by Sarah Yeh

The encoding–retrieval match helps to explain why remembering is often state or context dependent. It turns out that divers can remember important safety information better if they learn the information while diving rather than on land (K. M. Martin & Agglelton, 1993). Presumably, there's a better match between encoding and retrieval when information is learned and tested in the same environment. Another example is childhood, or infantile, amnesia: Most of us have a difficult time remembering things that happened to us before the age of 4 or 5. However, it's likely that we interpreted the world very differently when we were small. Childhood amnesia may result, then, from a poor match between the present and the distant past. We see and interpret events differently now than we did as children, so we have few effective retrieval cues available for remembering childhood events (Jack & Hayne, 2010).

Transfer-Appropriate Processing

Is there any way to guarantee a good encoding–retrieval match? One way is to pay close attention to the conditions likely to be present when you need to remember. You can engage in what psychologists call **transfer-appropriate processing**, which means you should encode material using the same kind of mental processes that'll be required during the test. Matching the mental processes used during study and test increases the chances that effective retrieval cues will be available (Lockhart, 2002).

To illustrate, let's assume you're asked to remember the word TUG for a later memory test (see Figure 8.9). If you form a visual image of a tugboat and you're then specifically asked about a tugboat on the memory test, you'll probably perform well. But suppose you're asked instead to remember whether the word TUG was printed in upper- or lowercase letters. All of the elaboration in the world isn't going to help you unless you've specifically encoded the way the letters were shaped ("TUG," not "tug"). The lesson of transfer-appropriate processing is that you need to consider the nature of the test before you can decide how to study most effectively. For some hints on how to apply the principle of transfer-appropriate processing when you prepare for an exam, see the Practical Solutions feature.

FIGURE 8.9 ■ Transfer-Appropriate Processing

It's useful to study material with the same type of mental processes that you'll be required to use when tested. Suppose you form a visual image of a to-be-remembered word (panel 1). If the test requires you to recognize an image of the word, you should do well (panel 2). But if the test asks how the word sounds (panel 3) or whether the word was presented originally in upper- or lowercase letters (panel 4), you're likely to perform poorly. You need to study in a way that is appropriate to the test.

Illustrated by Sarah Yeh

PRACTICAL SOLUTIONS: STUDYING "APPROPRIATELY" FOR EXAMS

You're now familiar with some techniques for improving memory. You form an elaborate and distinctive memory record during encoding, which helps make certain that relevant retrieval cues are available when you need to remember. Practicing retrieval, through repeated self-testing, is one solid way to guarantee good performance over the long term. It also helps to space your practice—don't cram all of your studying and self-testing into one marathon session the night before the test. By studying the material at different times, and in different situations, you increase the chances that the information will be linked to lots of different retrieval cues. Perhaps most important, you should pay particular attention to the concept of transfer-appropriate processing: Make certain that when you test yourself, you do it in a way that resembles what you'll be required to do on the classroom exam.

On a practical level, this means you need to think about the characteristics of an exam before you sit down to study. An essay exam, for example, is a kind of *cued-recall* test—you're given a cue in the form of a test question, and you're required to recall the most appropriate answer. To study for such a test, it's best to practice cued recall: Make up questions relevant to the material and practice recalling the appropriate answer with only the test question as a cue. For a multiple-choice test, which is a kind of *recognition test*, it's necessary to discriminate a correct answer from a group of incorrect answers (called *distractors*). The best way to study for a multiple-choice test is to practice with multiple-choice questions; either make up your own or use questions from a study guide.

Have you ever thought to yourself, "I'll just read the chapter one more time before I go to bed, and I'll ace the exam tomorrow"? Think about it from the perspective of transfer-appropriate processing—what exactly does the typical exam ask you to do? Exams don't measure the speed or fluency with which the chapter can be *read*. Most exams require you to retrieve the material in the presence of cues. So, it makes a lot of sense to practice retrieving the information rather than simply reading it. Learn the material by reading the chapter but prepare for the exam by using processes similar to those required by the test. Practice reproducing the material by answering questions from memory or practice, discriminating correct from incorrect answers by responding to a variety of multiple-choice questions.

Reconstructive Remembering

Retrieval cues guide remembering in much the same way that a physical message guides the processes of perception. As you may recall from Chapter 5, what you "see" really depends on both the incoming message and the expectations you hold about what's "out there." In a similar way, remembering depends on more than just a retrieval cue—your expectations and beliefs color an act of remembering just as they color what you see and hear. Think about what you had for breakfast two weeks ago. Did you skip breakfast or, perhaps, gulp down a quick bowl of cereal? It turns out that what you "remember" in a case like this often corresponds more to habit than to actual fact. If you regularly eat a bowl of cereal in the morning, then eating cereal is what you're likely to recall, even if you broke the routine on that particular day and had a bagel.

Memory Schemas

To understand why memory acts in this way, we must return to that vast storehouse of information in the brain—the repository of episodic, procedural, and especially semantic memories. As you know, we store more than facts in long-term memory—we also store relationships among facts. You know, for example, that houses contain rooms with walls, require insurance protection, and are susceptible to burning down. You know that college students like to sleep late, wear jeans, and listen to loud music. These large clusters of related facts are organized into knowledge structures called **schemas**. Schemas can be about people, places, or activities—we even have them for routines such as going to a restaurant, visiting the local urgent care center, or following daily eating habits. When you remember, you use these organized knowledge packages to help recover the past. So when someone asks you what you ate for breakfast two weeks ago, you can confidently answer "cereal" because you know cereal is what you usually eat for breakfast. You don't have to remember the specific episode; you can rely on your general knowledge.

The trouble with schema-based remembering is that it can easily lead to false or inaccurate retention. You might remember something that's completely wrong—it didn't really happen—yet still be convinced your memory is accurate. (Remember our earlier discussion of flashbulb memories?) Nearly 90 years ago, an English psychologist named Frederic Bartlett asked undergraduates to read an unfamiliar Native North American folktale about people who traveled up a river to battle with some warrior "ghosts" (the story's title was "The War of the Ghosts"). In recalling the story sometime later, the students tended to distort facts, omit details, and fill in information that was not included in the original version. For example, familiar things were substituted for unfamiliar things—the word *boat* was substituted for *canoe*; "hunting seals" was replaced with "hunting beavers." Because these things were not in the story, Bartlett assumed his participants must have used their prior knowledge to reconstruct what they remembered—even though they were convinced they were remembering the material accurately (Bartlett, 1932).

A similar point was made more recently by Loftus and Palmer (1974). Undergraduates were shown a short film depicting an automobile accident. Later, when questioned about the film, the students were asked to estimate how fast the cars were traveling just prior to the accident. Some students were asked to estimate the speed of the cars just before they *smashed* into each other; others were asked how fast the

FIGURE 8.10 ■ Schema-Based Remembering

Loftus and Palmer (1974) found that students remembered cars traveling faster when retrieval instructions used the word *smashed* instead of *contacted*. All people saw the same film, but their different schemas for the words *smashed* and *contacted* presumably caused them to reconstruct their memories differently.

Recall Instructions	Schema	Response
"How fast were the cars going when they smashed into each other?"		"About 42 mph."
"How fast were the cars going when they contacted into each other?"		"About 32 mph."

Illustrated by Sarah Yeh

cars were going before they *contacted* each other. Notice the difference between the words—the schema for *smashed* implies that the cars were traveling at a high rate of speed, whereas *contacted* suggests that the cars were moving slowly. As shown in Figure 8.10, people who heard the word *smashed* in the question estimated that the cars were traveling about 42 miles per hour; people in the *contacted* group gave an estimate of about 10 miles per hour slower.

Once again, these results show that memory is importantly influenced by general knowledge, as well as by expectations. Everyone in the Loftus and Palmer experiment saw the same film, but what people remembered depended on how the questions were worded—that is, on whether people were led to believe that the cars were going fast or slow. In addition to giving estimates of speed, some were asked whether any broken glass was present in the accident scene. When *smashed* was used in the speed question, people were much more likely to incorrectly remember seeing broken glass, even though there wasn't any in the original film. By asking the right kinds of questions during testing, it's possible to make people think they experienced things that did not occur. As Loftus (2018) has emphasized, these findings suggest that caution must be exercised in interpreting the testimony of any eyewitness—reconstructive factors can always be involved.

Here's an easy way to demonstrate schema-based remembering for yourself: Read the following list of words aloud to a group of friends:

BED REST AWAKE TIRED DREAM WAKE SNOOZE

BLANKET DOZE SLUMBER SNORE NAP YAWN DROWSY

Now ask your friends to write down all the words they've just heard. The chances are very good that someone will remember an item that was not on the list, especially the word SLEEP. In experiments using lists of such related items, people have been found to recall nonpresented items (e.g., SLEEP) nearly 50% of the time (Deese, 1959; Roediger & McDermott, 1995). The chances of false memory increase even more when recognition memory is tested—that is, when you're given the word SLEEP and asked if it was presented on the list (K. B. McDermott & Roediger, 1998). What's behind this effect? Obviously, the word SLEEP is highly related to the words on the list. It seems likely that people recognize the relationships among the words and use this knowledge to help them remember. This is a very effective strategy for remembering, but it can lead to false recollections.

Despite the mistakes, schema-based remembering clearly has adaptive value. By relying on preexisting knowledge to "fill in the gaps" or to help interpret fuzzy recollections, you increase the chances that your responses in new environments will be appropriate—after all, the past is usually the best predictor of the future. You can also use your schematic knowledge to "correct" for any minor details you may have missed during the original exposure. If you already have a pretty good idea of what goes on during a visit to a fast-food restaurant, your mind doesn't need to expend a great deal of effort attending to details the next time you enter a McDonald's. You can rely on your prior knowledge to capture the gist of the experience, even though, on the downside, you may recollect a few things that didn't actually happen.

The point made earlier about eyewitness testimony is important, however. Some people, including the members of juries, don't understand the reconstructive nature of remembering. There is evidence that the general public believes that memories are highly accurate, especially when someone expresses lots of confidence about the memory. For example, in one recent survey, nearly 40% of the public agreed with the following statement: "In my opinion, the testimony of one confident eyewitness should be enough to convict a defendant of a crime." When expert memory researchers were asked the same question, none agreed with the statement (Simons & Chabris, 2011). This certainly suggests that too much weight may be given by juries to eyewitness testimony. Eyewitness testimony can be accurate, but recognizing the reconstructive nature of memory should make one skeptical about any remembered event, regardless of its importance or even the confidence of the rememberer (for an important exception, though, see Wixted & Wells, 2017). A recent study suggests that public beliefs about memory may be getting somewhat more accurate, but many individuals still hold inaccurate beliefs about how memory functions (Brewin et al., 2019).

Remembering Without Awareness

Up to this point, we've concentrated on conscious, willful acts of remembering—that is, situations in which you're consciously intending to remember something (such as what you ate for breakfast or the words from a memory list). But we often remember things without conscious intent or awareness. You speak, walk to work, recognize someone you know—all these things require memory, but you're usually not explicitly trying to remember anything. Psychologists use the term **implicit memory** to describe this kind of remembering. **Explicit memory** is the name researchers use to describe conscious, willful remembering. It turns out that implicit memory—remembering without awareness—follows many of the same rules as explicit memory. For example, both implicit and explicit memory are strongly influenced by retrieval cues. If you look at Figure 8.11, you'll see some examples of word and picture fragments. Your ability to complete one of these fragments improves if you've seen the solution word recently during reading (for example, the word fragment C___L is easier to solve if the word CAMEL has been encountered in the prior 24 hours). But importantly, you don't need to remember seeing the word. Your performance improves even if you don't consciously remember the word (which makes the remembering implicit). At the same time, performance depends importantly on whether the earlier encounter matches the fragment. If you need to solve a picture fragment, then you're helped more if the earlier encounter was in the form of a picture—such as seeing a picture of a camel—rather than a word (K. B. McDermott & Roediger, 1994). Once again, the conditions during testing need to match the conditions present during the original exposure.

FIGURE 8.11 ■ Implicit Memory Tests

The person's task in each test is to complete the picture or word fragment so as to identify the object shown on the far right.

| Picture fragment completion | | | | |
| Word fragment completion | C _ _ _ L | CA _ _ L | C _ M _ L | CAMEL |

Source: From Snodgrass, J. G., & Feenan, K. (1990). Copyright © 1990, American Psychological Association. Reprinted with permission.

There are situations in which implicit memory appears to act somewhat differently than explicit memory. One of the most interesting cases is with amnesia, memory loss caused by a physical problem. It turns out that people who suffer from severe amnesia—for example, they show little memory for a sentence spoken moments before—often show little decline in implicit memory. We'll discuss this topic in more detail later in the chapter. There's also evidence suggesting that older adults have better implicit memory for irrelevant information (things that are not central to the task at hand) than younger adults (Gopie et al., 2011). In addition, encoding strategies that typically improve conscious, willful remembering often have little or no effect on implicit memory (Roediger et al., 1992). If you think about the meaning of the material, which induces elaboration, you're much more likely to recall it on an explicit test of memory, such as recall or recognition. But the same improvement often isn't found when memory is tested using an implicit test, such as solving word fragment problems (Graf et al., 1982). Differences such as these have led some researchers to suggest that explicit and implicit memories are controlled by different processing systems in the brain (Squire & Dede, 2015). Many research studies have suggested that explicit memory relies primarily on the medial temporal lobes that include the hippocampus (first described in Chapter 3). Implicit memory, however, relies less on these areas and more on the neocortex and striatum. These differences in brain area specialization across types of memory are seen clearly in patients with damage to the medial temporal lobes; these patients have great difficulty performing explicit tasks but perform more normally on implicit tasks. We will consider these differences further in the section on the neuroscience of forgetting later in this chapter.

Now test your knowledge about how we use cues to help us remember by answering the following questions. Fill in the blanks with one of the following terms: *cued recall, explicit memory, free recall, implicit memory, schema, transfer-appropriate processing.* (You will find the answers in the Appendix.)

1. An organized knowledge package that's stored in long-term memory: _____

2. Remembering without awareness: _____

3. Studying for a multiple-choice test by writing your own multiple-choice questions: _____

4. Remembering material without the aid of any external retrieval cues: _____

UPDATING MEMORY

Like other storage devices, the mind is susceptible to clutter. Effective remembering often hinges on your ability to successfully discriminate one occurrence from another—you need to remember where you parked your car today, not yesterday, or your current address, not a previous one. What if you felt the urge to buy two dozen paper cups every time you entered the grocery store because one time last year you needed paper cups for a party? **Forgetting**, the loss of accessibility to previously stored material, is one of the most important and adaptive properties of your memory system (Bjork, 1989; Nairne & Pandeirada, 2008).

If you need further convincing, consider the case of a Russian journalist known as S. who possessed an extraordinary ability to remember. Through a fluke of nature, S. reacted automatically to stimuli in ways that formed unusual and distinctive encodings. When he heard a tone pitched at 500 hertz, S. reported seeing "a dense orange color which made him feel as though a needle had been thrust into his spine" (Luria, 1968, p. 24). For a 3,000-hertz tone, S. claimed that it "looks something like a firework tinged with a pink-red hue. The strip of color feels rough and unpleasant, and it has an ugly taste—rather like that of a briny pickle" (Luria, 1968, p. 24).

S. had a remarkable memory—he could remember grids of numbers perfectly after 15 years—but he suffered a near fatal flaw: He simply couldn't forget. He had trouble reading books because words or phrases so flooded his mind with previous associations that he had great difficulty concentrating. He would notice, for example, small errors in the text: If a character entered the story wearing a cap and in later pages was described without a cap, S. would become greatly disturbed and disappointed in the author. He had trouble holding a job or even a sustained conversation. For S., the failure to forget produced a truly cluttered mind.

Types of Forgetting

When you think of people with poor memory abilities, you may think of older individuals who have some memory deficits, or individuals who have suffered some form of brain damage. But even those with normal memory abilities can suffer from unwanted forgetting. In his book *The Seven Sins of Memory*, Daniel Schacter (2001) described seven common memory failures that occur in individuals with normal memory abilities (see Concept Review 8.2). He describes these "sins" of memory as by-products of the way our memories function and as typical of us all to varying degrees. The "sins" Schacter describes are transience, absentmindedness, blocking, source misattribution, suggestibility, bias, and persistence. Let's consider what each of these failures are.

Forgetting is often bothersome, but it can have considerable adaptive value.

Transience is a term for normal forgetting of information over time. Later in this section, we'll discuss some possible causes of normal forgetting and the form this forgetting takes. A lack of attention during encoding or retrieval can result in poor memory. Schacter calls this memory failure *absentmindedness*. A good example of this memory failure is not remembering where you have placed something you need to find, such as your car keys. If you do not pay attention to their location when you put them down, there is a good chance you'll not remember where they are (unless you always put them in the same place). This is also one of the main reasons why it's tough to remember the name of someone you've just met—you're too distracted to encode the person's name fully when you first hear it. Schacter describes *blocking* as an experience of knowing that you know information but being unable to retrieve it. When we learn something from one source but remember it as having occurred from another, we suffer *source misattribution*. For example, there are likely times when you have a thought or idea about something that you think is an original thought you generated, but in reality, you read or heard about the idea somewhere else first.

Suggestibility occurs when others' suggestions and statements alter our memories for events in ways we do not even realize. Suggestibility can alter actual memories and even create false memories for events we have never experienced. *Bias* is a similar memory failure to suggestibility. Bias occurs when our current experiences or knowledge alter our memory of a past experience. For example, after going through an unpleasant breakup with a romantic partner, you may remember a happy event you experienced with that partner as more negative than it actually was. Finally, *persistence* is a memory "sin" in which we experience unwanted memories over and over.

In many cases, memory functioning seems so effortless to us that we do not notice these memory failures at all. However, when these errors or failures arise (e.g., not remembering an important concept during an exam), we realize the limitations of our memory abilities. Next, we'll consider the form forgetting takes over time.

CONCEPT REVIEW 8.2
THE SEVEN "SINS" OF MEMORY FROM SCHACTER (2001)

Sin	Description	Example
Transience	Typical forgetting over time	As Diana got to the end of the week, she forgot what she had for breakfast on Monday.
Absentmindedness	Lack of attention at encoding/retrieval, which reduces memory	Jeff is constantly losing his keys because he doesn't pay attention to where he puts them down.
Blocking	Inability to retrieve information you know that you know	Ebony can't remember the name of the actor in the movie she saw last night; she can only think of a name she knows is wrong.
Source misattribution	Misremembering where you learned something	Harry is sure he heard about a new type of drink from his friend, but he actually saw it on social media.
Suggestibility	Alteration of memory from an outside source	Tarif witnessed a blue car crash into a stop sign, but after hearing other witnesses' reports, he later remembers the car crashing into a utility pole.
Bias	Alteration of memory due to later experiences	Lola remembers a pleasant first date with her new boyfriend after several good dates with him, but in reality, the first date didn't go that well.
Persistence	Unwanted memories coming to mind	After having his phone stolen in a mugging, Steve can't stop reliving the event.

How Quickly Do We Forget?

For most people, once an item has left the immediate present, it's forgotten in a regular and systematic way. How quickly an item is forgotten depends on several factors: how the item was initially encoded, whether it was encountered again at some later time, and the kinds of retrieval cues present at the point of remembering. But in general, the course of forgetting looks like the curve shown in Figure 8.12. Most of the forgetting occurs early, but you will continue to forget gradually for a long period following the initial exposure (Murre & Dros, 2015).

FIGURE 8.12 ■ The Ebbinghaus Forgetting Curve

German philosopher Hermann Ebbinghaus memorized lists of nonsense syllables and then measured how long it took to relearn the same material after various delays. Fifty percent savings means it took half as long to relearn the list as it did to learn it originally; 0% savings would mean that it took as long to relearn the list as it did to learn the list originally.

Hermann Ebbinghaus (1850–1909)

Pictorial Press Ltd / Alamy Stock Photo

The forgetting curve shown in Figure 8.12 is taken from some classic work by German philosopher Hermann Ebbinghaus (1885/1964), one of the first researchers to investigate memory and forgetting scientifically. Isolated in his study, he forced himself to learn lists of nonsense syllables (such as ZOK) and then measured how long it took to relearn the same material after various delays (a technique called the *savings method*). As the figure shows, the longer the delay after original learning, the greater effort Ebbinghaus had to spend relearning the list. The Ebbinghaus forgetting function—a rapid loss followed by a more gradual decline—is typical of forgetting. Similar forgetting functions are found for a variety of materials, even for complex skills such as flying an airplane (Fleishman & Parker, 1962) or performing cardiopulmonary resuscitation (McKenna & Glendon, 1985).

Even memories for everyday things, such as the names of high school classmates or material learned in school, are forgotten in regular and systematic ways. In one study, Bahrick (1984) studied memory for a foreign language (Spanish) over intervals that ranged from about 1 to 50 years. In another study, Bahrick and Hall (1991) examined the retention of high school mathematics over 50 years. In both cases, there was rapid loss of recently learned material, followed by more gradual loss, but a considerable amount of knowledge was retained indefinitely. What's surprising about these studies is that a fair amount of the knowledge remained, even though the participants claimed to have not rehearsed or thought about the material in over half a century. (Maybe there's hope for education yet!)

There's one more characteristic of long-term forgetting that you'll probably find interesting. When older adults are asked to recall and date events from their past, not surprisingly they tend to remember things from the more recent past best. However, there's a "bump" in the forgetting curve for events that happened between late adolescence and about age 30 (Koppel & Berntsen, 2014). For some reason, we retain events from this period particularly well—or, at least, these are the events that we're apt to recall in our older years. This is known as the "reminiscence bump," and psychologists aren't exactly certain why it happens. We experience lots of "firsts" during this period (career, possibly marriage and family), so perhaps we simply repeatedly rehearse what happens during the 20-something period throughout our lives (Rubin & Berntsen, 2003). It's also possible that we learn from our culture that important things happen during the "bump" period, so we tend to search for memories from that period when we recall our past (Bohn & Berntsen, 2011).

In addition, research suggests that the way memory is cued for events can affect the age at which memories are reported. Odor cues (i.e., specific scents) trigger earlier memories than word cues, whereas asking people to report important autobiographical memories produces the classic reminiscence bump with most memories reported from people's early 20s. These results suggest that retrieval plays an important role in the reminiscence bump along with encoding (Koppel & Rubin, 2016).

Why Do We Forget?

We can agree that it's adaptive to forget, and we can measure how quickly information becomes unavailable over time, but what causes forgetting? As we discussed earlier, most memory researchers believe that forgetting is cue dependent—you fail to remember a prior event because you don't have the right retrieval cues. But it's also possible that memories simply fade with the passage of time in accordance with a "law of use" (Thorndike, 1914). If you fail to practice a learned habit, such as playing the piano, the habit fades, or *decays*, spontaneously with time.

However, **decay**—the idea that memories fade due to the passage of time—cannot explain most instances of forgetting. For one thing, as you've seen, memories that appear to have been forgotten can be remembered later under the right retrieval conditions. In addition, people often remember trivial things (such as a joke) for years but forget important things that once received a great deal of practice (such as elementary geometry). Even more significant, just because memories are lost with time doesn't mean that *time* alone is the cause. A nail left outside becomes rusty with time, but it is not the passage of time that creates the rust—processes other than time (oxidation, in the case of the rusty nail) produce the changes.

FIGURE 8.13 ■ Interference and Memory

The activities that occur after learning affect how well stored information is remembered. In this study by J. G. Jenkins and Dallenbach (1924), the students remembered better if they slept during the retention interval than if they remained awake. Presumably, the waking activities caused interference.

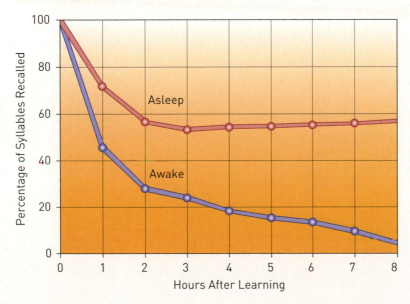

Mechanisms of Forgetting: Retroactive Interference

In forgetting, the "other processes"—which are correlated with the passage of time but are not created by time—often depend on the establishment of other memories. We constantly learn new things, and these new memories compete, or interfere, with the recovery of old memories. College students tend to move around a lot, so every time you get a new apartment you need to learn a new home address. Once you've got the new address memorized, it becomes more difficult to retrieve your old address, even if you actively try to remember. The retrieval cue "home address" has now become associated with something new; as a result, it loses its capacity to produce the old information. Psychologists use the term **retroactive interference** to refer to cases where the formation of new memories hurts the retention of old memories.

In a classic study of retroactive interference, J. G. Jenkins and Dallenbach (1924) asked two students from Cornell University to live in a laboratory for several weeks and learn lists of nonsense syllables either just before bed or early in the morning. The students were tested 1, 2, 4, or 8 hours after learning. The results, which are shown in Figure 8.13, were clear: When the students slept during the delay interval, they remembered more than when they remained awake. A constant amount of time passed in both conditions, so a decay theory would predict no differences between the conditions. The findings suggest it was the activities that occurred during the students' waking hours that produced the information loss. When awake, the students formed new memories, which interfered with recovery of the old material.

Mechanisms of Forgetting: Proactive Interference

It's not just the learning of new information that produces forgetting. Previously learned information can also produce interference. **Proactive interference** occurs when old memories interfere with the recovery of new memories. Suppose English is your native language but you move to Portugal on business. You learn the Portuguese language, fluently, but you find it difficult to stop English words or phrases from coming to mind when you speak. You know the Portuguese word for train is *comboio*, but you find it hard to suppress saying "train" when you're talking in Portuguese (at least for a while). That's proactive interference—old memories interfere with the recovery of new memories. Prior knowledge and habits interfere with the retention of new material.

Most memory researchers believe that forgetting is usually caused by interference, although it's conceivable that decay might operate in certain situations. One possibility is that decay operates when we remember over the very short term—that is, in sensory memory and short-term memory (Barrouillet et al., 2012; see also Ricker et al., 2020). It's also possible that when we learn new material, older memories are "overwritten" and permanently lost (Loftus & Loftus, 1980). But generally, we don't *lose* material with time; the material simply becomes harder to remember because other things interfere with the retrieval process. As new memories are encoded, old retrieval cues become less effective because those cues are now associated with new things.

Motivated or Purposeful Forgetting

Highly unusual or emotional events lead to distinctive, and therefore easy-to-remember, memory records. The adaptive value of a system that "stamps in" significant events is easy to understand— remembering such events can increase our ability to survive. But what about those cases in which it's adaptive to *forget* something, such as a traumatic instance of child abuse or the witnessing of a violent crime?

The idea that the mind might actively repress, or inhibit, certain memory records is an important ingredient of Sigmund Freud's psychoanalytic theory, as you'll see when we discuss personality theories in Chapter 11. Freud introduced **repression** as a "defense mechanism" to push threatening thoughts, memories, and feelings out of conscious awareness. According to Freud, these repressed memories retain the capacity to affect behavior at an unconscious level but cannot be remembered in the conventional sense. The result is a reduction in the experience of anxiety.

The Evidence for Repression

Modern researchers remain undecided about the scientific validity of repression. People typically recall more pleasant than unpleasant events (Wagenaar, 1986), and painful experiences, such as the pain associated with childbirth, also seem to be recollected less well with the passage of time (Robinson et al., 1980). There are also many cases, reported mainly in clinical settings, of what appear to be the repression of traumatic experiences.

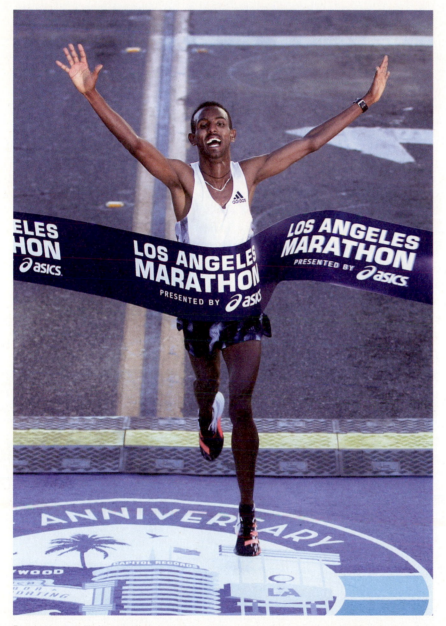

People are more likely to recall pleasant than unpleasant experiences, perhaps because they're reluctant to rehearse unpleasant experiences.

Katelyn Mulcahy/Stringer/Getty Images

For example, in one study, 475 adults undergoing psychotherapy were asked about memories of childhood sexual abuse. Each had reported an incident of abuse during childhood, and each was asked the following specific question: "During the period of time between when the first forced sexual encounter happened and your 18th birthday, was there ever a time when you could not remember the forced sexual experience?" (Briere & Conte, 1993). Fifty-nine percent of the people who answered the question responded "Yes," suggesting that the memories had been pushed out of consciousness for at least some period of time. In another study supporting the same conclusion, L. M. Williams (1992) asked 100 women who had been medically treated for sexual abuse as children—the abuse was documented by hospital and other records—whether they remembered the incident 17 years later. Thirty-eight percent of those responding reported no memory of the abuse, again providing support for the concept of repression.

But does this really mean that the forgetting was caused by repression? It's possible that people tend to remember positive events because these are the types of events that we rehearse and relate to others. The fact that painful experiences are forgotten with the passage of time can be explained in lots of ways—many things are forgotten with the passage of time, especially those unlikely to be rehearsed. In fact, victims of childhood sexual abuse often tell researchers that they deliberately try to avoid thinking about the abuse (McNally & Geraerts, 2009). It's also difficult for researchers to understand why some traumatic memories, such as those typically seen in posttraumatic stress disorder (PTSD), remain extremely difficult to suppress or forget.

There have been attempts to simulate repression in the laboratory. No, people are not exposed to traumatic events; instead, they're simply asked to actively prevent previously learned material from coming to mind. For example, if you've been taught to recall SOCKS every time you're given the word JOY, I might ask you to actively repress thinking about SOCKS the next time you see JOY. Under these conditions, there's some evidence that SOCKS then becomes harder to recall—you've suppressed its representation in memory (M. C. Anderson & Green, 2001; but see Bulevich et al., 2006). Recent evidence suggests as well that it is easier to suppress emotionally negative material than positive material (A. J. Lambert et al., 2010). Moreover, people with severe forms of PTSD may be less able to control these suppression mechanisms (Catarino et al., 2015). But whether the kinds of suppression effects observed in the laboratory are the same as those seen in clinical settings remains a matter of dispute (Erdelyi, 2010). Concept Review 8.3 reviews the different causes of forgetting discussed in this section.

CONCEPT REVIEW 8.3
MECHANISMS OF FORGETTING

Mechanism	Description	Example
Cue dependence	One fails to remember an event due to a lack of appropriate cues.	Although Susan would recognize a definition of semantic memory on a multiple-choice test, she can't think of it for a fill-in-the-blank test.
Decay	Memories fade with the passage of time.	After only a month of lessons, and then 6 years of not playing the piano, Shao forgets how to play.
Proactive interference	Old memories interfere with the recovery of new memories.	Bruce is so impressed with the first person he met at the party that he can't remember the names of those he met later.
Retroactive interference	New memories interfere with the recovery of old memories.	Filling out a job application, Seth can remember only his most recent address, not the one before it.
Motivated forgetting	Traumatic experiences are forgotten to reduce anxiety.	Jackie can't remember too much about the day her parents were seriously injured in an accident.

Whether these laboratory studies really tell us anything about the forgetting of traumatic events remains uncertain. However, as Freud noted, a process of repression might be adaptive in the sense that it can prevent or reduce anxiety. It may also be the case that forgotten events continue to exert indirect influences on behavior in ways that bypass awareness. But the data do suggest that memories, whether "recovered" in therapy or simply in the normal course of everyday activities, should not be taken at face value. It is useful for people to use prior knowledge, as well as current expectations, to help them remember—but perhaps at the cost of sometimes remembering things that didn't actually happen.

The Neuroscience of Forgetting

Forgetting can also be caused by physical problems in the brain, such as those induced by injury or illness. Psychologists use the term **amnesia** to refer to forgetting caused by some kind of physical problem. (Another type of amnesia that's psychological in origin arises from something called a dissociative disorder, but we'll delay our discussion of this kind of forgetting until Chapter 14.)

Types of Amnesia

There are two major kinds of amnesia, retrograde and anterograde. **Retrograde amnesia** is memory loss for events that happened prior to the point of injury (you can think of *retro* as meaning "backward in time"). People who are in automobile accidents, or who receive a sharp blow to the head, often have trouble remembering the events leading directly up to the accident. The memory loss can apply to events that happened only moments before the accident, or the loss can be quite severe; in some cases, patients lose their ability to recall personal experiences that occurred years before the accident. In many cases, fortunately, these memory losses are not permanent and recover slowly over time (Cermak, 1982).

Anterograde amnesia is memory loss for events that happen *after* the point of physical damage. People who suffer from anterograde amnesia often seem locked in the past—they're incapable of forming memories for new experiences. The disorder develops as a result of brain damage, which can occur from the persistent use of alcohol (a condition called *Korsakoff syndrome*), from brain infections (such as viral encephalitis), or, in some cases, as a by-product of brain surgery. One of the most thoroughly studied amnesic patients, known to researchers as H. M., developed the disorder after surgery was performed to remove large portions of his temporal lobes. The purpose of the operation was to reduce the severity of H. M.'s epileptic seizures; the surgery was successful—his seizures were dramatically reduced—but anterograde amnesia developed as an unexpected side effect.

Over the years, patients such as H. M. have been studied in great detail to determine exactly what kinds of memory processing are lost (Milner, 1966). It was originally believed that such patients fail to acquire new memories because some basic encoding mechanisms have been destroyed. It is now clear, however, that these patients can learn a great deal but must be tested in particular ways. If a patient like H. M. is tested implicitly, on a task that does not require *conscious* remembering, performance can approach or even match normal levels. In other words, people with anterograde amnesia perform poorly on explicit memory tasks but perform well on implicit memory tasks.

In one study showing this result, Jacoby and Witherspoon (1982) asked Korsakoff patients with anterograde amnesia to learn homophones for a later memory test. Homophones are words that sound alike but have different meanings and spellings, such as READ and REED. To "bias" a particular interpretation for a given homophone, it was presented as part of a word pair, such as BOOK–READ or, in another condition, SAXOPHONE–REED. (Because the words were presented aloud, the only way to distinguish between the homophones READ and REED was through the accompanying context word BOOK or SAXOPHONE.) Later, the amnesics were asked to recognize the words but were unable to do so—they seemed to have acquired none of the presented information. In a second test, however, the homophones were simply read aloud by the experimenter, and the patients' task was to spell the word. Surprisingly, if the amnesics had earlier received the pair BOOK–READ, they spelled the test homophone READ, but if the homophone had been paired with SAXOPHONE, they spelled it REED.

These results suggest that the homophones were learned by the amnesic patients. The way the patients spelled the homophone during the test depended on their prior experience. Other experiments have revealed similar findings. For example, amnesics are more likely to complete a word fragment (such as E_E__AN_) correctly if they've seen the word before, but if they're asked to recall the word, their performance falters (Graf & Schacter, 1985). Patients who suffer from anterograde amnesia fail to retrieve past experiences whenever they must *consciously* recollect the experience; when the past is assessed indirectly, through a task that does not require conscious remembering, these amnesics often perform at normal levels.

FIGURE 8.14 ■ The Hippocampus

The hippocampus (seen at the location marked in this image of the right hemisphere of the brain) is an important brain structure for intentional retrieval of memories.

Hippocampus

Where Are Memories Stored?

The study of individuals with brain damage, such as Korsakoff patients, has also encouraged researchers to draw tentative conclusions about how and where memories are stored in the brain. We touched on this issue in Chapter 3 when we considered biological processes. In that chapter, special attention was paid to a structure called the *hippocampus*, which most brain researchers believe is critically involved in the formation and storage of memories (e.g., Voss et al., 2017). Damage to the hippocampus, as well as to surrounding structures in the medial temporal brain area, leads to memory problems in a wide variety of species, including humans, monkeys, and rats. Areas surrounding the hippocampus also "light up" (i.e., become more active) in neuroimaging studies when people are asked to recall specific material; in fact, some researchers have suggested that it's even possible to detect specific memories in people by examining the patterns of neural activation around the hippocampus, seen in Figure 8.14 (Chadwick et al., 2010). However, as described earlier in this chapter, damage to the hippocampus affects memory when it is tested explicitly, but not implicitly, suggesting that different brain areas are involved based on how retrieval of the memory occurs.

Thus, no single brain structure, or group of structures, is responsible for all instances of remembering and forgetting. Things are vastly interconnected in the brain, and activity in one part of the brain usually depends on activity in other parts. The regions of the brain involved in the storage of memories also depend

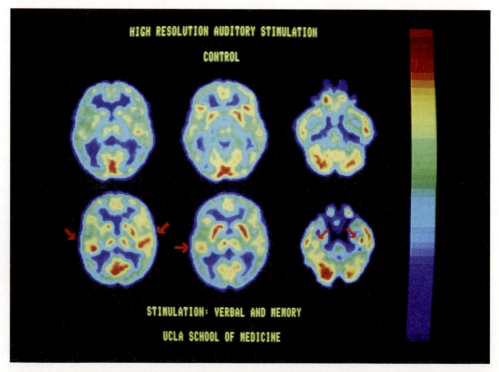

This PET scan shows regions of brain activity during auditory stimulation. The arrows point to areas inside the temporal lobes that become active when words are heard; these same areas are thought to be associated with some kinds of memory.

Dr. John Mazziotta et al. / Science Source

on the type of processing involved. For example, when you try to remember something, the regions of the brain activated during original learning are activated again. So, if you formed a visual image of an object when you first studied it, the visual areas of your brain will be reactivated when you retrieve it (C. E. Webb et al., 2016). If your original encoding was tinged with emotion, the areas of the brain involved in emotional processing will be activated when you remember the event (Danker & Anderson, 2010).

Certain kinds of memory loss, such as those found in Alzheimer's disease, have been linked to inadequate supplies of neurotransmitters in the brain (Francis et al., 2010). But damage to a part of the brain tied to the production of a neurotransmitter (such as acetylcholine) probably has consequences for all regions of the brain that depend on that neurotransmitter. This makes it difficult to pinpoint where a memory is stored or even where the processing relevant to the storage of memories takes place. Modern technological advances are providing researchers with precise information about activity in the brain, but much remains to be learned about the physical basis of remembering.

KNOWLEDGE CHECK 8.4

Now test your knowledge about forgetting and the updating of memory by deciding whether each of the following statements is true or false. (You will find the answers in the Appendix.)

1. Forgetting is usually slow at first and becomes more rapid as time passes. *True or False*?

2. Most psychologists agree that interference rather than decay is primarily responsible for long-term forgetting. *True or False*?

3. Proactive interference occurs when what you learn at time 2 interferes with what you learned previously at time 1. *True or False*?

4. Anterograde amnesia blocks the learning of new information. *True or False*?

5. People recall more pleasant than unpleasant events over time. *True or False*?

6. Psychologists believe that the hippocampus is involved in some, but not all, instances of remembering. *True or False*?

THE PROBLEMS SOLVED: WHAT MEMORY IS FOR

Time flows continuously, so experiences quickly leave the present and recede backward into the past. To understand the capacity to preserve and recover this past, we considered some of the important problems that our memory systems help us solve.

Remembering Over the Short Term

To improve perception and aid comprehension, internal processes help us remember over the short term. In the case of sensory memory, we retain a relatively pure snapshot of the world, or replica of the environmental message. Sensory memories accurately represent the world as recorded by the senses, but they tend to be short-lived, lasting on the order of a second or less. Short-term memory, in contrast, is the system used to store, think about, and reason with the message once it has undergone perceptual analysis. Items are typically maintained in short-term memory in the form of an "inner voice," and they're forgotten rapidly in the absence of rehearsal. The capacity, or size, of short-term memory is determined by a trade-off between the factors that lead to forgetting over the short term (either decay or interference) and the time-limited process of rehearsal.

Storing Information for the Long Term

To store information over the long term, you need to produce elaborate and distinctive memory records. Focusing on the meaning of the input, relating to-be-remembered information to other things in memory, and forming visual images of the input all lead to distinctive memory records. Forming a visual image is particularly effective, and many memory aids, or mnemonic devices, are based on the use of imagery. Long-term memory also depends on how information is actually presented: Items presented near the beginning and end of a sequence are remembered well, as are items that have been repeated. Spaced or distributed practice turns out to be more effective than massed practice. Finally, practicing retrieval through self-testing is particularly effective in producing long-term retention.

Recovering Information From Cues

Successful remembering depends critically on having the right kinds of retrieval cues. Most forms of forgetting are cue dependent, which means that stored information is not really "lost"; it simply can't be accessed without the appropriate retrieval cues. Effective retrieval cues are generally those that match the conditions present during original learning. It's also the case that when people recover information from cues, they rely on their general knowledge. The past is often reconstructed, and the reconstruction process leads to adaptive, but sometimes inaccurate, recollections of the past.

Updating Memory

Forgetting is a useful process. If we didn't constantly change and update our knowledge about the world, our minds would be cluttered with useless facts, such as where the car was parked last Wednesday. Although the mechanisms of forgetting are still being investigated, it seems unlikely that long-term memories fade as a simple by-product of time. Rather, as we learn new things, previously learned material becomes harder to access. New memories compete and interfere with recovery of the old. With the right kinds of cues, however—cues that discriminate one kind of occurrence from another—previously forgotten material becomes refreshed and available for use once again.

THINKING ABOUT RESEARCH

A summary of a research study in psychology is given in this section. As you read the summary, think about the following questions:

1. Does this study examine encoding processes or retrieval processes? Explain your answer.
2. Which of the seven "sins" of memory do you think is responsible for the results of this study? Why?
3. What kind of memory, implicit or explicit, is involved in the task performed in this study? Explain your answer.
4. The researchers suggested that recognizing a face is easier than recalling a name. Based on what you know about memory from this chapter, why do you think this is the case?

Article Reference: Burton, A. M., Jenkins, R., & Robertson, D. J. (2019). I recognize your name but I can't remember your face: An advantage for names in recognition memory. *Quarterly Journal of Experimental Psychology, 72*, 1847–1854.

Note: Experiment 1 from the article is described here.

Purpose of the Study: In this study, the researchers investigated the saying "I recognize your face, but I can't remember your name." They designed a study to test whether it is true that people forget names more often than they forget faces. The researchers suggested that in most circumstances, one is recognizing a face but recalling a name; overall, recognition is often easier than recall. Based on this difference, they tested memory for names and faces in more equivalent ways to determine if memory for names is, in fact, worse than memory for faces.

Method of the Study: Undergraduate students were shown 40 name–face pairs for unfamiliar names and faces. They were asked to try to remember the people shown, including names and faces. They then completed recognition tests, one for names and one for faces. In each test, half of the names/faces shown were ones that had been studied, and half were new unstudied items. For the studied names, half were shown in the same font style as studied, and half were shown in a different font style. For the studied faces, half were the same photo shown at study, and half were different photos of the same person.

Results of the Study: The results of the study showed that recognition accuracy was higher for the names than for the faces. In addition, accuracy was higher when the format for studied items was the same at study and test than when the format changed (different font style or different photo of the same person).

Conclusions of the Study: These results suggest that memory for faces is lower than that for names when both are tested in a similar way with recognition tests. This is a surprising finding, suggesting that the popular belief that faces are easier to remember than names is an illusion—remembering faces is easier only because you typically can recognize a face but you need to recall a name. This is just one study, and it will need to be replicated in other laboratories, but it certainly gives us something to think about.

KNOWLEDGE CHECK: CHAPTER SUMMARY

(You will find the answers in the Appendix.)

- Memory is defined as the capacity to (1) _____ and (2) _____ information.

Remembering Over the Short Term

- Both (3) _____ and (4) _____ sensory memory retain relatively (5) _____ replicas of an incoming stimulus. With (6) _____ memory, a visual memory or image is retained for about half a second, long enough to help process the incoming message. With (7) _____ memory, a pure sound is held briefly in auditory memory and may help in language processing.

- We use (8) _____-term memory to store and think about information temporarily, usually as an "inner voice." Information in short-term memory is quickly (9) _____ if not rehearsed, because of (10) _____ (passing time) or (11) _____ (from the environment). Memory (12) _____ is equal to the amount of information that can be (13) _____ in about (14) _____ seconds, usually seven plus or minus two items. Memory span can be increased through a method called (15) _____, which involves rearranging information into meaningful patterns. Some researchers have suggested that we have special systems in a "working" memory that handle spatial (visuospatial sketchpad) and verbal (phonological loop) information.

Storing Information for the Long Term

- We recall personal moments with (16) _____ memory. (17) _____ memories are of facts and knowledge about the world. Our knowledge of how to do things is stored in (18) _____ memory.

- (19) _____ has to do with making (20) _____ among experiences, which allows for easier (21) _____ of stored memories. It helps to think about the (22) _____ of an experience, notice (23) _____, and notice similarities to and (24) _____ from existing knowledge. You can also improve retention by forming mental (25) _____, by spacing your (26) _____, and by considering the (27) _____ position of the material.

- Mnemonic devices, which include the method of (28) _____ and the peg- (29) _____ technique, are mental exercises that use visual imagery to help us remember.

Recovering Information From Cues

- Researchers believe the amount of information that can be remembered or retrieved depends on (30) _____. Good retrieval cues usually (31) _____ the way the information was encoded. The (32) _____-appropriate processing principle holds that we should study material with the same kinds of (33) _____ processes that will be used during the (34) _____ process.

- (35) _____ are large clusters of related facts about people, activities, and places. Memory schemas are adaptive but can influence what is remembered and may lead to (36) _____ memories.

- When we remember something without conscious awareness, it's called (37) _____ memory. Prior experience and stored memories may influence implicit memory. We use (38) _____ memory when we make a conscious, deliberate effort to recall something.

Updating Memory

- Ebbinghaus found that (39) _____ forgetting occurs soon after initial exposure to an experience, but (40) _____ forgetting can continue for a long time. Forgetting can be extremely (41) _____, as it prevents our minds from becoming cluttered with useless information: We need to remember where we parked our car today, not yesterday.

- The simple passage of time (decay) isn't sufficient to explain most aspects of forgetting. Equally important are (42) _____ interference, in which (43) _____ material interferes with the recovery of old memories, and (44) _____ interference, in which (45) _____ material interferes with the formation and recovery of new memories.

- Freud believed that the mind may deliberately inhibit or (46) _____ certain memories as a form of self-protection. Most researchers are undecided about the scientific (47) _____ of this concept. We do sometimes forget traumatic events, but it's not clear that this forgetting is due to special processes.

- Forgetting caused by a physical problem is called (48) _____. (49) _____ amnesia is loss of memory for events that happened (50) _____ the accident or disease; (51) _____ amnesia causes events that happened (52) _____ the trauma to be forgotten. Although the (53) _____ is important in forming new memories, no single structure is responsible for the complex processes of memory. Amnesia may be regulated by the amount or production of certain (54) _____.

CRITICAL THINKING QUESTIONS

1. Do you consider the lingering afterimage left by the flash of a camera to be a type of memory?

2. Can you think of a reason it might be adaptive for icons to be lost so quickly?

3. Why do you suppose the telephone company created telephone numbers in three chunks—for example, 888-449-5854?

4. Given what you've learned about repetition and memory, do you think it's a good idea to have children learn arithmetic tables by rote repetition?

5. Do you think all remembering is reconstructive? What about sensory memory—isn't that a pure kind of remembering?

6. Can you think of any ways to lessen the influence of proactive interference? Is there any way that you could study information to prevent interference?

KEY TERMS

amnesia (p. 301)

anterograde amnesia (p. 301)

chunking (p. 277)

cued recall (p. 287)

decay (p. 297)

distinctiveness (p. 281)

distributed practice (p. 282)

echoic memory (p. 273)

elaboration (p. 280)

encoding (p. 270)

episodic memory (p. 279)

explicit memory (p. 293)

flashbulb memories (p. 285)

forgetting (p. 294)

free recall (p. 287)

iconic memory (p. 273)

implicit memory (p. 293)

long-term memory (p. 279)

memory (p. 270)

memory span (p. 276)

method of loci (p. 284)

mnemonic devices (p. 283)

9 LANGUAGE AND THOUGHT

LEARNING OBJECTIVES

9.1   Identify the elements of language structure and explain how they contribute to language comprehension.

9.2   Identify the major milestones of language development and evaluate language learning in nonhuman animals.

9.3   Distinguish between different views of categorization and describe the hierarchical organization of categorical knowledge.

9.4   Distinguish between different problem-solving strategies and explain how these differ from insight.

9.5   Identify different decision-making biases and describe how heuristics can result in decision-making errors.

9.6   For each of the major sections of the chapter, summarize how language and thought contribute to human communication and decisions.

CHAPTER OUTLINE

Communicating With Others

Learning Language

Classifying and Categorizing

Solving Problems

   Practical Solutions: Having Difficulty? Take a Break!

Decision Making

The Problems Solved: What Cognition Is For

Wayne Inges chuckles silently to himself as he completes the deal. "That's right," he says, "center court, floor level—$100 for the pair." Having paid only $50 for the ticket pair himself, Wayne pockets a tidy little profit. But there are more fools in the world, so he decides to buy the tickets back for $150. With game time approaching, and desperation setting in, this time the pair of tickets sells for $200. Can you figure out Wayne's total profit for the evening?

To find the answer, your mind begins an internal, goal-directed activity called **thinking**. In its simplest form, thinking involves the internal manipulation of knowledge and ideas. When we think, we act on our knowledge in a directed and purposeful way to solve problems, to reason and make decisions, and to understand and communicate with others. It's not possible to measure thinking directly, but psychologists learn a lot by watching people think and then listening to their rationales for actions or conclusions.

Let's see, Wayne made $50 on the first transaction but spent $150 to buy the tickets back, so he lost the original $50. He finally sold the pair for $200, so his total profit for the evening must be $50, right? Easy enough. We've used our knowledge about the world, and about mathematics, to work systematically toward a goal. It's easy to see the usefulness of the process. Thinking increases your ability to survive because you can act on your knowledge in precise, systematic, and purposeful ways.

But, as perhaps you guessed, our reasoning in this case is completely wrong. We arrived at the wrong answer, as do many others who try this task. Using a slight variation of the same problem, Maier and Burke (1967) found that people come up with the correct answer less than 40% of the time. The correct answer is $100—Wayne paid out a total of $200 ($50 for the first transaction and $150 for the second) and received $300 back from the buyers. Simple subtraction yields the correct answer of $100.

Why the error? Well, the difficulty comes from thinking about Wayne's sales as one continuous event rather than as two separate transactions. Try framing the problem slightly differently: Wayne bought tickets for Friday night's game for $50 and sold them for $100. Next, he bought tickets for Saturday's game for $150 and sold them for $200. Under these conditions, people almost never make an error. One of the challenges of the modern study of thinking, and problem solving in particular, is to understand why human thought processes sometimes break down and lead to errors.

THE PROBLEMS TO BE SOLVED: WHAT ARE COGNITIVE PROCESSES FOR?

The topics we're about to cover—language, forming categories, problem solving, reasoning—are examples of cognition, or reflect the action of cognitive processes. The term *cognition* refers simply to the activities that underlie all forms of thought. These processes are related in many ways: We use language to help establish categories, and we use categories to solve problems and make decisions. Psychologists who study cognition are generally known as cognitive psychologists, but there is a more diverse field, called cognitive science, that draws on the work of professionals in many disciplines, including linguistics, philosophy, biology, computer science, and engineering. Engineers and computer scientists, for example, often attempt to simulate reasoning and thought in computer programs (i.e., artificial intelligence).

The usefulness, or adaptive value, of cognition is obvious. As you'll see shortly, our ability to think, reason, and communicate with others is what sets humans apart from other species. As before, we'll discuss these processes by focusing on a set of specific tasks, or problems, that our cognitive processes help us solve.

Communicating With Others

The ability to communicate, especially through written and spoken language, may well be our greatest success story. No other species on the planet can claim our knack for transmitting knowledge through speech and writing. Through language production we transmit thoughts, feelings, and needs to others; through language comprehension we learn and understand. We'll discuss the basics of language, both production and comprehension, and how cognitive processes aid in our use of language.

Learning Language

Amazingly enough, humans who are exposed to language throughout childhood learn to comprehend and produce language without much (or sometimes any) explicit instruction on the rules of language. No other animal seems to have this ability. Animals can be trained to communicate with their trainers using nonverbal language, but do not seem to learn a language simply through exposure. But does this qualify as learning a language? We'll consider this question and the way that language develops in human children as we discuss how language aids in human connection.

Classifying and Categorizing

To make sense of our environment, especially the objects in it, we carve the world into meaningful chunks called *categories*. Can you imagine a world in which no two things share features in common, where each encounter with a cat, or a bird, or a snake is a new and unique experience? The ability to see similarities among things, to classify objects and events into meaningful categories, allows us to simplify our environment and make predictions about how to act. We'll discuss how people define and structure categories, and you'll see there's some "fuzziness" to the process.

Solving Problems

Think about the dozens of practical problems you face and solve every day. Did you have trouble finding your keys this morning? Have a difficult time choosing what to wear or what show to watch?

The adaptive value of problem solving should be obvious—if humans couldn't solve the problem of where to find food and water or how to woo and win the appropriate mate, our species would quickly follow a path to extinction. We'll discuss the various steps involved in problem solving and some of the pitfalls to avoid.

Decision Making

Finally, when we make decisions, we're required to choose from among a set of alternatives. An important ingredient of decision making is *risk*—choices have consequences, and an incorrect decision can lead to an unpleasant or even fatal outcome. Like problem solving, we use certain strategies to help us make decisions, and these strategies, although generally quite productive, sometimes lead to irrational conclusions.

COMMUNICATING WITH OTHERS

We begin our discussion of thinking, curiously enough, with an extended discussion of language. It might seem funny to lump language and thought together, but the two are closely linked: Language importantly influences the way we think. Remember from Chapter 8 how using the word *smashed* led people to recall things about a car accident that they didn't recall when given the word *contacted* (e.g., broken glass)? Think about the words *doctor* and *secretary*—are you likely to picture a man and a woman, respectively? Do you think twice about a sentence such as "The secretary hates his boss"? It's clear that language affects us in ways that extend well beyond simple communication.

According to the *linguistic relativity hypothesis*, language shapes not only how we think but also how we perceive the world (Whorf, 1956). For example, if your language lacks color terms to distinguish between blue and green, which is the case for some African languages, you may have a difficult time telling those colors apart on a color test. Cross-cultural tests have produced some support for this idea: "What you see when you look at a rainbow actually depends on the language that you speak" (Özgen, 2004, p. 94). Your ability to pick visual targets out of a lineup, such as identifying a cat in a lineup of

Bees do a characteristic waggle dance that may communicate information about the location of nectar. But would you say bees have really developed language?

iStockPhoto/Andreas Häuslbetz

dogs versus other cats, also depends on whether the stimuli are presented to the brain's right or left hemisphere. When the stimuli are presented to the left hemisphere, the side of the brain that usually controls language, the makeup of the lineup (other cats versus dogs) matters more, presumably because language is influencing your visual ability (Gilbert et al., 2008).

Few psychologists believe that language completely determines how we think or perceive. We all share certain cognitive abilities, rooted in our evolutionary past, and those abilities are likely to remain intact regardless of language particulars or environmental influences (Newcombe & Uttal, 2006). Language *influences* how we think and perceive the world, no question about it, but it doesn't completely determine thought (see Lucy, 2016).

The Structure of Language

What is language, and how should it be defined? If you think about it, birds communicate effectively through the production of acoustic sequences (songs). Some people believe that bees can convey information about the exact location of food through a tail-wagging dance (Barron & Plath, 2017; von Frisch, 1967). Even your dog barks at outdoor noises in what appears to be an effort to communicate. But to qualify as a true language, the communication system must have rules, known collectively as **grammar**, that enable the communicator to combine symbols to convey meaning.

Grammar provides rules about which combinations of sounds and words (or gestures in sign languages) are permissible and which are not. Grammar has three aspects: (1) **phonology**, the rules for combining sounds to make words; (2) **syntax**, the rules for combining words to make sentences; and (3) **semantics**, the rules used to communicate meaning. In English we would never say "The cautious the barked nasty at man poodle." This particular combination of words violates a number of rules of syntax, such as the rule that articles (*the*) and adjectives (*nasty*) come before nouns (*man*). We would also never generate a sentence like "Colorless green ideas sleep furiously." Although this is a well-structured sentence, it suffers from a violation of semantics—it has no meaning. We use our knowledge about semantics to pick the appropriate words (perhaps "people" can sleep furiously, but "ideas" cannot) and to infer connections between words and other things in memory (cautious poodles bark at rather than bite nasty people).

Phonemes and Morphemes

All human languages possess a hierarchical structure, which ranges from the fundamental sounds of speech to the more complex levels of spoken conversation. At the bottom of the spoken language hierarchy are **phonemes**, defined as the smallest significant sound units in speech. These speech sounds are produced through a complex coordination of the vocal cords, lungs, lips, tongue, and even teeth. Table 9.1 lists some examples of phonemes in the English language. Notice there isn't a simple relationship between a given letter of the alphabet and a phoneme. The letter *e*, for example, maps onto one kind of speech sound in the word *head* and a different kind in the word *heat*.

Babies greet the world with the ability to produce a large number of fundamental speech sounds, but they quickly restrict the number to a much smaller set (Werker & Tees, 1999). English speakers use only about 40 to 45 phonemes; other languages may use considerably more or fewer. Japanese speakers, for example, do not differentiate between the phonemes *r* and *l* in their native tongue (which makes it difficult for a native Japanese speaker to hear the difference between *race* and *lace*). English speakers do not meaningfully distinguish the *p* sound in *pause* from the *p* sound in *camp*. In Thai or Hindi, these same sound units carry unique and different meanings. Part of the trick to acquiring a foreign language is mastering the basic phonemes of that language.

At the next level in the hierarchy are **morphemes**—the smallest units of language that carry meaning. Morphemes usually consist of single words, such as *cool* or *hip*, but they can also be prefixes and suffixes. For instance, the word *cool* contains a single morpheme, whereas *uncool* contains two—the root word *cool* and the prefix *un*. The grammar of a language dictates the acceptable order of morphemes within a word—*uncool* has definite meaning in the English language; *coolun* does not. The morpheme *s*, when placed at the end of a word (*oars*), designates plural. But the phoneme *s*, when placed at the beginning of that same word (*soar*), means something entirely different.

All told, the average speaker of English knows and uses somewhere between 50,000 and 80,000 morphemes.

Symbol	Examples	Symbol	Examples
b	**b**urger, ru**bb**le	ng	sti**ng**, ri**ng**er
ē	eas**y**, zombi**e**	oy	c**oi**l, empl**oy**
ĕ	**e**nter, m**e**tric	r	**r**at, c**r**ust
f	**f**ungus, **ph**one	s	**s**todgy, be**s**t
ĭ	**i**cky, w**i**g	t	**t**ramp, miss**ed**
ī	**i**ce, sh**y**	th	**th**at, o**th**er
k	**k**itty, a**ch**e	ŭ	**u**gly, b**u**tter
n	**n**ewt, a**nn**oy		

TABLE 9.1 ■ Some Examples of English Phonemes

Words to Sentences

At the higher levels of the language hierarchy are words, phrases, and sentences. Words combine to form phrases; phrases, in conjunction with other phrases, form sentences. To illustrate, the sentence "Stephanie kissed the crying boy" contains a noun (*Stephanie*) and a verb phrase (*kissed the crying boy*). The verb phrase contains a verb (*kissed*) and a noun phrase (*the crying boy*). Perhaps you can remember diagramming sentences in this way in your high school English class (see Figure 9.1). Breaking sentences into phrases has psychological meaning—we clearly use phrases when we generate spoken sentences. If we accurately time you while you are speaking, for example, we'll find that you pause for a moment at the boundaries between major phrases (Boomer, 1965). When you read a sentence, we'll also find that there are measurable changes in brain activity that correspond to phrase changes (M. J. Nelson et al., 2017).

Language researchers have spent decades trying to figure out the rules people use to combine words into phrases and phrases into sentences. It was once thought that a single set of rules might be discovered that would effectively capture all of the nuances of sentence generation—just apply the rules appropriately to words, and you've got language. However, as the linguist Noam Chomsky pointed out, it's unlikely that such a set of rules exists. To bolster his argument, Chomsky came up with sentences such as "Visiting relatives can be a nuisance." It's easy to break this sentence down into its appropriate

FIGURE 9.1 ■ The Units of Language

Languages have a hierarchical structure that includes the fundamental sounds of speech and the more complex levels of spoken conversation. Complex rules determine how words are combined into phrases and sentences, and how fundamental speech sounds (phonemes) combine to create the smallest units of meaning (morphemes) and words.

phrase structure, he argued, but the phrase structure doesn't tell us what the sentence actually means: Are we annoyed that the relatives are visiting, or is it a nuisance to visit relatives? Both meanings apply to the same phrase structure: Visiting relatives—pause—can be a nuisance. Hence, we cannot capture why or how sentences are generated during a meaningful conversation by appealing only to the phrase structure.

Surface and Deep Structure

Chomsky (1957) recognized that there's a difference between the "surface" structure of a sentence and its accompanying, more abstract, "deep" structure. The **surface structure** of a sentence corresponds to its superficial appearance (the literal ordering of words), whereas **deep structure** refers to the underlying representation of meaning or the speaker's intentions. Thus, two sentences can have the same surface structure but two different deep structures (the "visiting relatives" example). Or two different surface structures can arise from the same deep structure ("Stephanie kissed the crying boy" and "The crying boy was kissed by Stephanie").

Chomsky suggested that language production requires the transformation of deep structure into an acceptable surface structure (see Figure 9.2). Many language researchers accept this point, but there are sharp disagreements about how the transformation process actually works (Treiman et al., 2003). There are also disagreements about how best to think about deep structure. The particulars are complex and need not concern us here. The important point is that language is clearly more than sets of words or symbols organized in a fixed and rigid way. In the words of psychologist Steven Pinker, there are "hundreds of millions of trillions of thinkable thoughts" (Pinker, 1997, p. 118), and each can, in principle, be expressed through language and understood. The challenge for language researchers is to discover how this flexibility ultimately comes about.

FIGURE 9.2 ■ Surface Structure and Deep Structure

The surface structure of a sentence is its appearance, the literal ordering of words. Deep structure is the meaning of the sentence. This figure shows how the same surface structure—"Visiting relatives can be a nuisance"—reflects two different deep structures. Similarly, a single deep structure can be transformed into two or more acceptable surface structures.

Illustrated by Sarah Yeh

Language Comprehension

The flip side of language production—that is, understanding the structure and rules of grammar—is language comprehension. How do people use their practical knowledge about the world, and the general context of the conversation, to decide what information another person is trying to communicate? This is not a trivial problem because language comprehension presents many difficulties: We don't always hear sounds correctly; words can have many different meanings; the pitch or rhythm in which a phrase is spoken can help or mislead us; and language is full of metaphors that complicate the interpretation process (Lakoff, 1987; Pinker, 1994).

Top-down processing can help when trying to understand someone speaking in another language.

iStockPhoto/portishead1

Effective communication seems to rely a great deal on *common knowledge* among speakers (H. H. Clark, 1992; Keysar et al., 1998). When you're having a conversation with someone about a mutual friend, you can say "That's typical for him," and there's likely to be no comprehension problem. You both know the statement refers to your friend, and you both have no trouble listing examples of your friend's "typical" behavior. Similarly, when you hear a statement, you don't simply process the sound arriving at your ears into words, phrase structures, and sentences. You make a guess about what the speaker is trying to communicate, perhaps even before the speaker makes a sound, and then you use this expectation to interpret the sounds you hear. In other words, you use your knowledge about a topic or situation to anticipate what someone is going to say to help you understand it faster. Thus, in an important sense, language comprehension shares properties with perception: Both rely on a combination of *top-down* and *bottom-up processing* (J. L. McClelland & Elman, 1986).

Pragmatic Rules

Language researchers use the term **pragmatics** to describe how practical knowledge can be used both to comprehend the intentions of speakers and to produce an effective response. Consider your response to an indirect request such as "Can you close the window?" If you process the request directly—that is, if you take its literal interpretation—you might respond, "Yes, I'm capable of putting enough steady pressure on the window to produce closure." You have answered the question, but clearly you have violated some important pragmatic rules. The speaker was making a request, not asking you about your ability to perform the task. In fact, if you had answered the question in this way, the speaker would have probably inferred that you were using irony or sarcasm in your reply (R. W. Gibbs, 2012).

The pragmatics of language make the study of comprehension processes a challenge. How you interpret someone's words—be they babblings or profound commentary on the hypocrisy of our times—will depend on the shared context of the conversation, as well as on your expectations and beliefs. To facilitate effective communication, good speakers usually follow pragmatic guidelines, or maxims (Grice, 1975):

1. Be informative.

2. Tell the truth.

3. Be relevant.

4. Be clear.

If you choose to answer an indirect request literally ("Yes, I can close the window"), then you're not being relevant—you're violating an accepted guideline for communication. If you don't tell the truth or are purposely vague in answering a request, then you'll soon have trouble finding people who want to talk with you. By following the simple rules presented here and by assuming the same for your conversational partner, you can enhance the ease and flow of conversation.

Of course, the pragmatic guidelines listed earlier shouldn't be taken as universal maxims for communication. What constitutes a polite conversation in one culture may be considered inappropriate in another. It's also better at times to be indirect and even sarcastic when you speak ("Wow, you played well today!") than direct and blunt ("What a horrible game you just played!"). Using sarcasm can elicit fewer negative emotional reactions from others and may even induce them to think more creatively in problem-solving situations (Pickering et al., 2018).

KNOWLEDGE CHECK 9.1

Now test your knowledge about language by answering the following questions. (You will find the answers in the Appendix.)

1. Choose the term that best fits the following descriptions. Choose your answers from the following: *deep structure, morphemes, pragmatics, phonemes, phonology, semantics, surface structure, syntax.*
    a. The smallest significant sound units in speech: _____
    b. The practical knowledge used to understand the intentions of a speaker and to produce an effective response: _____
    c. The rules governing how words should be combined to form sentences: _____
    d. The smallest units in language that carry meaning: _____

2. _____ processing is used when current knowledge aids in language comprehension. _____ processing is used when basic units of a language are pieced together to determine meaning.

LEARNING LANGUAGE

How does language develop? Are humans born with a genetic plan that directs and shapes their communication skills? Or do we acquire language exclusively from experience? Not all people of the world speak the same language, so experience must certainly play an important role. Yet, all known cultures use language for communication. In fact, many language researchers are convinced that babies arrive in the world prepared to learn language, much as they are born prepared to walk. There is a regularity to the development of language, as there is to the development of motor skills, that is difficult to explain by appealing only to the environment (Chomsky, 1986; Pinker, 1994).

Language Development

The universality of language is apparent even at birth. Most babies cry in similar ways, and they move quickly through vocalization milestones that precede formal language development. By 3 to 5 weeks of age, *cooing*—repeating vowel sounds like "oooh" and "aaah"—has been added to the baby's vocalization patterns. *Babbling*—repeating consonant–vowel combinations such as "kaka" or "baba"—begins in virtually all babies between the ages of 4 and 6 months. No matter where you look in the world, this same sequence—crying then cooing then babbling—is found.

Between the ages of 6 and 18 months, experience begins to play a role, shaping and fine-tuning the baby's babblings into language-specific sounds. Babies begin to restrict their vocalizations to the phonemes in the language they hear every day from their parents or guardians; they even acquire a kind of language-specific "accent" by around 8 months of age (de Boysson-Bardies et al., 1984; J. L. Locke, 1994). Simple words—*mama, dada, ball,* and so on—appear by the end of the first year, and by 24 months most babies have developed a vocabulary of perhaps 200 to 300 words. Language comprehension also develops rapidly during this period—in fact, infants develop the ability to understand the words and commands of language *faster* than they actually learn to produce language. Concept Review 9.1 summarizes the development of language learning.

Infants and small children develop rather sophisticated ways to communicate meaningfully—cooing, kicking, pointing, and so on—even though their overt language skills are limited.

iStockPhoto/FatCamera

CONCEPT REVIEW 9.1
HIGHLIGHTS IN LANGUAGE DEVELOPMENT

Age	Linguistic Highlight(s)	Interpretation
3–5 weeks	*Cooing*, or the repetition of vowel sounds such as "oooh" and "aaah."	Cooing is a vocalization milestone that occurs before formal language development; it is similar across cultures, highlighting the universality of language.
4–6 months	*Babbling*, or the repetition of vowel–consonant combinations such as "kaka" or "baba."	Babbling is a vocalization milestone that occurs before formal language development; it is similar across cultures, highlighting the universality of language.
6–18 months	Vocalizations become specific to the native language; the first word is spoken by the end of the first year.	Experience plays a role in vocalization as a baby's babblings are shaped into language-specific sounds. Language comprehension is rapidly developing.
24 months	Vocabulary of at least 200 words; the child shows telegraphic speech, grammatical two-word combinations.	Speech reflects knowledge of syntax, as words are almost always combined in the proper order.
Preschool years	Ability to produce and comprehend sentences.	The child is now showing most of the important features of adult syntax.

Child Speak

As every parent knows, infants and young children develop rather sophisticated ways to communicate meaningfully, even though their language production skills may still be limited. An 18-month-old child can point to the bear-shaped jar on the counter and say "ookie," and Mom or Dad will immediately know what the child has in mind. An enormous amount of information can be packed into a single word, even if that word is spoken incorrectly, when its utterance is combined with a gesture or if the utterance occurs in the right context.

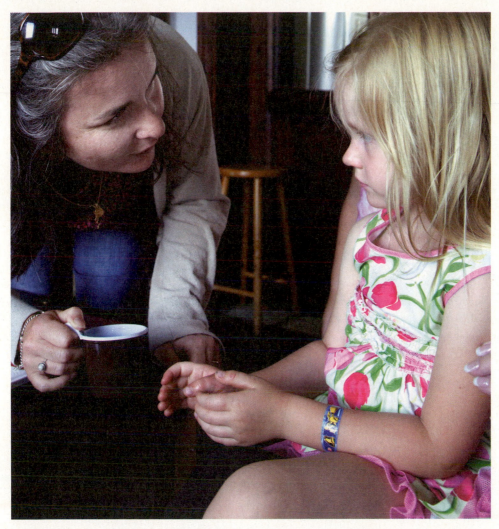

Even though young children have not fully developed language abilities, they can communicate using a combination of simple language and gestures.

Steve Skjold/ Alamy Stock Photo

As the child approaches the end of the second year of life, a phase of *telegraphic speech* begins. Telegraphic speech involves combining two words into simple sentences, such as "Daddy bad" or "Give cookie." It's called telegraphic speech because, as in a telegram, the child characteristically omits articles (*the*) and prepositions (*at, in*) from communications. But a 2-year-old's first sentences reflect a rudimentary knowledge of syntax: Words are almost always spoken in the proper order. For example, a child will reliably say "Want cookie" instead of "Cookie want." During the rest of the child's preschool years, up to around age 5 or 6, sentences become increasingly more complex, to the point where the average child of kindergarten age can produce and comprehend sentences that reveal most of the important features of adult syntax.

It's of enormous interest to psychologists that children develop such sophisticated language skills during their preschool years. After all, few parents sit down with their children and teach them the rules of grammar (such as the differences between present and past tense). Moreover, as we discussed in Chapter 4, children at this age lack the ability to understand most abstract concepts, so they couldn't consciously understand grammatical rules even if parents took the time to try to teach them. Children pick up their language skills implicitly; they automatically learn rules for language production.

The rules children learn during their preschool years are revealed partly by the errors they make. For example, at some point, preschoolers learning English as their native language acquire the rule "Add *ed* to the ends of verbs to make them past tense." Interestingly, children tend to *overgeneralize* this rule—they say things like "goed" or "falled," which are incorrect in English but represent a correct application of the rule. Notice that *goed* is not something that the child could have learned to use directly from experience. No parent rewards a child for saying *goed*, nor does a child hear the word being used by its parents. Rather, the child appears to be naturally "tuned" to pick up communication rules and apply them generally—even if a rule sometimes leads to an incorrect utterance. This natural tendency to learn and apply rules is then shaped by experience as an adult or peer teaches the child that *goed* is incorrect.

Language development continues throughout the school years as children fine-tune their articulation skills and knowledge about grammar. Vocabulary expands, as does the child's ability to communicate abstract concepts. Ultimately, the sophistication of any child's language ability will depend, at least in part, on the child's level of cognitive development. Children think differently as they age, and their increasingly sophisticated cognitive abilities are reflected in their conversations. Culture also affects the changes that take place in language ability as children age, attend school, and converse with peers. Keep these facts in mind as we turn our attention to language abilities in nonhuman species.

Language in Nonhuman Species

Psychologists have recognized for decades that nonhuman animals communicate. Anyone who has ever seen a cat indicate that it would rather be inside the house than outside knows this to be true. The question is whether such forms of communication can legitimately be called *language*. We know that animals sometimes express things symbolically, and there's little doubt that an animal's actions can convey meaning. But to qualify as using a true language, the animals would need to possess at least a rudimentary form of grammar—that is, a set of rules for deciding how symbols can be combined to convey meaning.

Chimpanzees lack the vocal equipment needed to produce the sounds of human speech. But they can be taught to communicate in relatively sophisticated ways with American Sign Language.

Moviestore Collection Ltd/ Alamy Stock Photo

Early attempts to foster language development in chimpanzees, in a form resembling human speech, were not very successful. Chimps were raised in homes, like surrogate children, in an effort to provide the ideal environment for language development. In one case, a chimp named Gua was raised along with the researchers' son, Donald (Kellogg & Kellogg, 1933). Donald and Gua were exposed to the same experiences, and careful attention was paid to rewarding the appropriate vocalizations. But in the end, the Kelloggs had merely produced a fine-speaking son and an effectively mute chimp (legend has it that Donald also developed into an excellent tree-climber). Later efforts to teach chimps to speak yielded the same discouraging results (K. J. Hayes & Hayes, 1951).

Signs and Symbol Communication

These early attempts were misguided, though, because chimps lack the necessary vocal equipment to produce the sounds required for human speech (C. Hayes, 1952). It's like a bird trying to teach a human to fly by raising a boy in a nest. Without wings, the boy just isn't going to fly. For these reasons, subsequent researchers turned to visual communication mediums. Allen Gardner and Beatrice Gardner tried to teach a simplified form of American Sign Language to a chimp named Washoe (R. A. Gardner & Gardner, 1969; R. A. Gardner et al., 1989). By the age of 4, Washoe was capable of producing about 160 appropriate signs, and apparently, she understood a great deal more. Even more impressive was her ability to produce various word combinations, such as "more fruit" or "gimme tickle."

In California, David Premack taught a chimp named Sarah to manipulate plastic shapes that symbolized words (e.g., a plastic triangle stood for the word *banana*). Sarah eventually was able to respond to simple symbol-based sentences that were arranged on a magnetic board (such as "Sarah insert banana into pail"; Premack, 1976). In Georgia, pygmy chimpanzees have been taught to communicate by pressing keys that represent objects such as foods or toys (Rumbaugh, 1977; Savage-Rumbaugh et al., 1986). Again, not only have these chimps learned to associate particular symbols with words or actions, but they've shown the capacity to generate combinations of words by pressing the symbols in sequence (Savage-Rumbaugh et al., 1986).

Work in the Georgia laboratory has also shown that pygmy chimpanzees can understand some spoken English. A chimp named Kanzi can press the appropriate symbol key when a word is spoken (e.g., *banana*). He can also respond appropriately to a variety of spoken commands. When asked "Can you pour the ice water in the potty?" Kanzi picks up the bowl of ice water, heads to the potty, and carefully pours it in (Savage-Rumbaugh et al., 1993). When asked to "Hide the toy gorilla," Kanzi picks up the toy gorilla and attempts to push it under a fence. Kanzi can even perform these tasks when the command is presented over headphones; this is important because it suggests that Kanzi is not simply responding to subtle cues from his handlers.

Is It Really Language?

These are very impressive demonstrations and are quite convincing when you see them in person or on film. Kanzi even made an appearance on *The Oprah Winfrey Show* in 2010! But have chimps such as Kanzi really acquired language? The jury is still out. Some psychologists believe that the chimps' behaviors simply reflect reinforced learning—like a pigeon who has been taught to peck a key for food—rather than true language ability (Terrace, 1986). At the same time, chimps such as Washoe and Kanzi can apparently generate new combinations of words and respond to requests that have never been given before. Washoe, for example, learned to respond to environmental events by producing novel signs. On seeing a duck for the first time, she reportedly signed "water bird." Moreover, it's been shown that chimps can acquire these language skills through observing other chimps, without being trained directly (Savage-Rumbaugh et al., 1986).

This debate is nowhere near a firm resolution. Much of the critical evidence (such as Washoe's "water bird") has come primarily from trainer anecdotes, so some question its scientific value (Wynne, 2007). It's also possible that some of the novel combinations generated by the chimps are simply imitations of their trainers. We just don't know at this point. Most of the psychologists who work with chimps are firmly convinced that the language abilities are real. Kanzi, for example, doesn't seem to follow rigid scripts—he can follow a request that is worded in various ways, which is far beyond what you would expect from a pigeon trained to peck a key. But it is unlikely that Kanzi possesses the kinds of perspective-taking or common knowledge that characterize language abilities in humans (Tomasello, 2017).

As you think about this topic for yourself, it's important to keep in mind that chimpanzees have not evolved to understand or produce human language. Chimps have evolved to solve their own problems—problems that arise from their own unique environments. You should avoid, where possible, adopting too egocentric a view of the world. The human mind has evolved to solve human problems, and those problems may or may not overlap with those of other members of the animal kingdom.

Is Language an Adaptation?

Given that language may be a uniquely human characteristic, it's reasonable to wonder why it developed: Why are humans capable of language but most other species are not? One possibility is that language is an *adaptation*—that is, it evolved specifically as a result of natural selection. It's easy to imagine how language might have given an extra advantage to those who possessed it, aiding everything from hunting and gathering to selecting and convincing a mate. Yet, as we've discussed in other chapters, it's notoriously difficult to tell whether a psychological feature is truly an adaptation. It might be that we're capable of language simply because at some point we evolved big and highly flexible brains.

Proponents of the "language as an adaptation" view (e.g., Pinker, 1994) point to several kinds of evidence: (1) Language is associated with particular regions of the brain (e.g., Broca's and Wernicke's areas); (2) children learn language incredibly quickly and, as noted earlier, aren't taught the rules of language in any kind of systematic fashion; (3) the human ear, as well as the human vocal tract, seems perfectly tailored to meet the needs of speech; and (4) some people seem to inherit tendencies to make certain types of grammatical errors. Another consideration is that there doesn't seem to be a simple relationship between the sophistication of a culture and the complexity of the language spoken; one might expect such a relationship if language development depended strongly on cultural or environmental factors.

Again, though, there are no fossil records to support the evolution of language as there are for certain physical characteristics (such as skull and therefore brain size). Moreover, language is unlikely to have emerged suddenly, in its present form, and some have argued that it's not easy to see the adaptive advantages that would result from simple or intermediate forms of language (Rose & Rose, 2000), although some have argued that language allowed humans to communicate prospective experiences, which is adaptive in planning cooperatively (Boyd, 2018). Many of the universal features that we see in language might also be caused by the way our perceptual systems develop and operate (Gogate & Hollich, 2010). Like many issues in modern evolutionary psychology, the question of how and why language emerged remains controversial (Jackendoff & Pinker, 2005).

KNOWLEDGE CHECK 9.2

Now test your knowledge about language by answering the following questions. (You will find the answers in the Appendix.)

1. Decide whether each of the following statements about language is true or false.
    a. Across the world, babies cry, coo, and babble in similar ways. *True or False?*
    b. Children learn the rules of language primarily by copying the words and phrases of their parents. *True or False?*
    c. Telegraphic speech begins toward the end of the child's second year of life. *True or False?*
    d. Chimpanzees lack the vocal equipment needed to produce human speech. *True or False?*
    e. Chimpanzee Kanzi learned to associate symbols with a variety of words but cannot follow spoken instructions from his trainers. *True or False?*

2. The key to determining whether nonhuman animals can learn language is whether or not they have some understanding of the _____ of language, the rules that determine how it is structured.

CLASSIFYING AND CATEGORIZING

We now turn our attention to another useful cognitive process—the ability to classify and categorize objects. A **category** is a class of objects (people, places, or things) that most people agree belong together. "Vegetables" is a category that contains such things as peas, carrots, and Brussels sprouts; "psychologists" is a category that includes researchers, clinicians, and applied persons working in the field. Categories allow us to *infer* invisible properties about objects (Murphy, 2002). For example, a kite and a doll share important properties as children's toys even though the two objects bear little physical similarity to each other. Once you've successfully categorized something, you can make *predictions* about the future. You know, for example, that if you're offered a member of the category "junk food," it is likely to taste good but be generally bad for your health.

People automatically classify objects, even other people, into well-defined categories. How would you categorize, and what invisible properties would you infer about, this individual? Can you predict how this person might act in a social situation?

PA Images/ Alamy Stock Photo

We'll divide our discussion of classifying and categorizing into three main topics. First, what properties of an object make it a member of a particular category? Second, in making decisions about category membership, do we form and store abstract representations called prototypes? Finally, we'll end the section by briefly considering the structure of categories—are they general or highly specific?

Defining Category Membership

Researchers have spent a lot of time trying to discover the criteria people use to define category membership. What is it about a sparrow that allows us to classify it so effortlessly as a bird? How do we know that a trout is a member of the category "fish" and not something to be used in the garden?

One possibility is that you can easily classify a sparrow as a "bird" because it has certain features that all members of that category share. For example, to be a member of the category "bird," a creature needs to have feathers and be able to do things such as sing, fly, and build nests—these are called the necessary or **defining features** of the category "bird." If the object has all the defining features, it must be an acceptable member of the category; if the object lacks one or more of these qualities, it must be something else (Medin, 1989). From this standpoint, knowing the right category label for an object is simply a matter of learning the right set of defining features (see Figure 9.3).

FIGURE 9.3 ■ Defining Features of a Category

One way to assign category membership is by defining features. For example, members of the generic category "bird" are expected to fly regularly, sing, and lay eggs in nests. Unfortunately, people have a tough time identifying and agreeing on the defining features for most natural categories. All of the objects shown here are birds, but they don't necessarily share the same properties.

Properties	Generic bird	Robin	Sandpiper	Vulture	Chicken	Penguin
Flies regularly	+	+	+	+	−	−
Sings	+	+	+	−	−	−
Lays eggs	+	+	+	+	+	+
Is small	+	+	+	−	−	−
Nests in trees	+	+	−	+	−	−

Monica Wierzbicki/Body Scientific Intl.

But there are problems with this view. It works well for mathematical categories such as "square" or "triangle," but it breaks down for natural objects. Take the category "vehicle," for example. What are the defining features of a vehicle—something that moves along the ground, has wheels, and can transport people? That applies to cars and trucks, but what about a surfboard or a monorail train? Surfboards move through water; monorail trains don't have wheels. What about an elevator, which doesn't have wheels and doesn't move along the ground? Research on natural categories such as birds, vehicles, furniture, and so on demonstrates that people have a tough time identifying and agreeing on just what makes up the acceptable defining features of a category (Malt & Smith, 1984; Rosch & Mervis, 1975).

FIGURE 9.4 ■ Fuzzy Category Boundaries

Are all of these objects members of the category "cup"? Labov (1973) discovered that as the width of the object increased, the more likely people were to label it as a "bowl." But the cup category boundary was fuzzy rather than firm; a significant number of people remained convinced that the fourth object was indeed a cup.

1   2   3   4   5

Source: Goldstein, B. (1994). Psychology. Pacific Grove, CA: Brooks/Cole. Reprinted with permission by Bruce Goldstein.

Most natural categories turn out to have *fuzzy boundaries*. In Figure 9.4, you can see a series of objects that collectively tap the fuzzy boundary of the category "cup." In an experiment by Labov (1973), people were required to name each of these objects. Labov discovered that as the object appeared wider, subjects were increasingly likely to dismiss the "cup" label and characterize the object as a "bowl." But the crossover point was gradual rather than fixed. Even for the object labeled 4, a significant number of people remained convinced that the object was indeed a cup. Results like these suggest that category members have *typical* features that are *characteristic* of the category rather than fixed defining features.

Family Resemblance

Another way to think about the idea of typical features is in terms of what Rosch and Mervis (1975) have called **family resemblance**. Members of the same category will share certain core features, but it isn't necessary for each member to have them all. Within an extended family, for instance, there may be a characteristic drooping nose, close-set beady eyes, a receding hairline, and a prominent, cleft chin. Cousin Theodore may lack the cleft or the beady eyes, but he could still possess a family resemblance that allows outsiders to easily fit him into the appropriate family. For the category "vehicle," people know that a monorail train doesn't have wheels, and it's not shaped anything like a car, but it moves people along the ground and in this sense fits the category label for most people.

Family resemblance is determined by the collection of core features that an object possesses. Again, members of the same category will share many family features, but it's unlikely that any single member will have them all. If a given object has most of the family features, it will be seen as a good member of the category; if an object has only a few, it will be seen as a poor member of the category. A car, for example, has most of the basic features that people assign to the category "vehicle"; an elevator does not. A robin has most of the features of "bird"; an ostrich or a flamingo has few. Through the notion of family resemblance, we can begin to see how natural categories achieve their fuzzy status. There is no absolute set of criteria for what constitutes a vehicle or a bird; there are only good and poor examples of a class of objects that share features (Rosch et al., 1976). Not all categories operate in this way (see Nosofsky et al., 2017), but most natural categories follow the family-resemblance principle.

Does this elevator fit snugly into your category for "vehicle"? If so, what defining features does it share with other members of the category?

gualtiero boffi/ Alamy Stock Photo

Do People Store Category Prototypes?

Family resemblance, combined with the idea that there are good and poor members of a category, leads us naturally to the concept of a prototype. A **prototype** is the best or most representative member of a category: A robin, for example, is close to the prototype for the category "bird"; an apple resembles the prototype for "fruit." Some psychologists believe that we store category prototypes in long-term memory and use them to help decide category membership. If an object, say a small fuzzy creature with a beak, is similar to the prototype for a certain category, "bird," then we assume that the object must be a member of the prototype's category (Goldstone & Kersten, 2003).

However, it isn't necessary to store prototypes to solve categorization problems. Instead, we could simply store all of the category examples (or **category exemplars**) that we encounter. To decide whether a new object is a member of a specific category, we would then compare the object to all of these stored examples rather than to a single prototype. If the object is similar to many examples in a particular category, then we would categorize the object as a member of that category (see Figure 9.5). Here is the main difference between prototype and exemplar views of categorization: In prototype theory, you compare the object to one thing—the prototype; in the exemplar view, the object is compared to many things—the category exemplars. Concept Review 9.2 provides a comparison of the different ideas about how we decide if an object belongs to a specific category.

Whether prototypes or exemplars are used in categorization is currently unknown, although many cognitive psychologists favor the exemplar view because people seem to know a lot about the individual members of a category (Hintzman, 1986; Medin & Shaffer, 1978; Nosofsky, 1992). For example, people seem to know which features go together—such as the fact that small birds are more likely to

FIGURE 9.5 ■ Prototypes Versus Exemplars

How do we decide whether an object is a member of a particular category? According to prototype theory, we compare the object to the abstract "best" example of the category (a generic bird). If the new object is similar to the prototype, it is assigned to the prototype's category. Exemplar theories of categorization propose instead that we compare the new object to all the individual examples of the category that have been stored in memory. Category membership is based on the summed similarity between the new object and the exemplars.

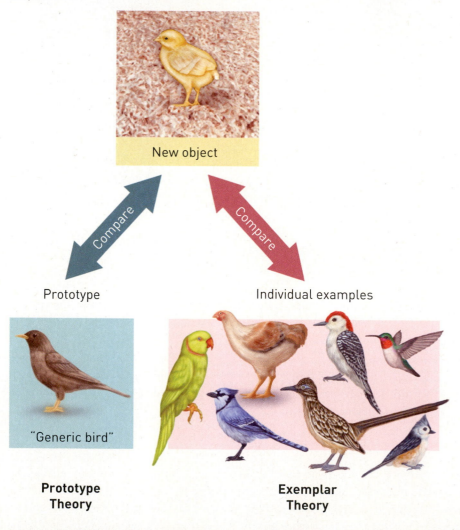

Monica Wierzbicki/Body Scientific Intl.

sing than large birds—and this kind of result is better handled by theories proposing that we store exemplars. Given the flexibility of the human mind, it seems likely that people can solve categorization problems in many different ways—and it may depend on the type of category that we're trying to learn (Ashby & Maddox, 2005). Sometimes we may form prototypes; other times we may rely on rules for deciding category membership; and in many situations we may appeal only to category exemplars (e.g., Nosofsky & Little, 2010).

CONCEPT REVIEW 9.2
DEFINING CATEGORY MEMBERSHIP

View of Categorization	Basis of Categorization	Example
Defining features	Certain features are present that define membership in the category.	Inez knows that a robin is a bird, because a robin has all of the features that define a bird, such as feathers, wings, and a beak.
Family resemblance	The degree to which category members share certain core features; a prototype is the most representative member of a category.	James knows that a robin is a bird, because it shares common features with other members of the bird family. In fact, "robin" could be considered the *prototype* for the category "bird."
Exemplars	All category examples (category exemplars) that we encounter are used for categorization.	Semhar knows that a robin is a bird, because it matches so many of the examples of birds stored in her memory.

The Hierarchical Structure of Categories

Most objects fit nicely into more than one natural category. The reason, in part, is that virtually all categories have a built-in hierarchical structure—that is, there are categories within categories within categories. Consider the class of "living things." Under the umbrella of "living things," we find the category "animals"; under "animals" there are "cats"; under "cats" there are "Siamese cats"; and so on. Most of the time an object, once it's categorized, can easily be recategorized into other, more general levels. A cat is an animal, a living thing, an object found on the planet Earth, and so on. These levels differ from one another in terms of their degree of inclusion. The more general the level, the more inclusive it becomes—there are more examples of living things than animals and more cats than Siamese cats (Murphy & Lassaline, 1997).

Some levels in the category hierarchy also appear to have special properties—they are in a sense psychologically privileged. When we refer to an object during a normal conversation, we tend to use its basic-level category descriptor. **Basic-level categories** generate the most useful and predictive information. When a furry feline saunters by, you call it a cat, not a living thing or an object found on the planet Earth. The category "cat" provides just the right amount of relevant information. People know you're talking about a four-legged object with fur (rather than the nondescriptive "animal"), but you haven't burdened the conversation with a needless amount of detail ("There's an 18-year-old seal-point Siamese that prefers salmon for dinner").

Basic-level categories tend to be at the intermediate levels of the category hierarchy (see Figure 9.6). The top-level categories, or *superordinates*, are simply not very descriptive. When people were asked to list the distinguishing features of top-level categories (such as "living things"), Rosch and her colleagues found that only a few features were actually generated (try it yourself: list the properties that characterize "living things"). At the basic level, more properties were generated, and the generated properties tended to be ones that most members of the category share (Rosch et al., 1976). Basic-level categories are also the category levels first used by children. It is through basic-level categorization that we cut the world into its most informative slices.

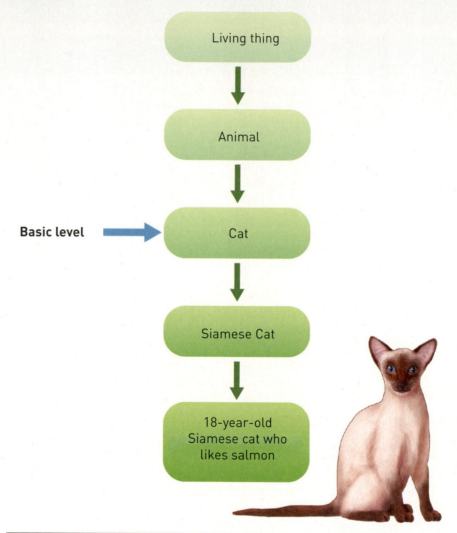

FIGURE 9.6 ■ Category Hierarchies

Virtually all categories have a hierarchical structure—there are categories within categories within categories. Most things, like this cat, fit nicely into several natural category levels. But when people refer to something during normal conversation, they tend to use its intermediate, or basic-level, category label. They call this a "cat" rather than a "living thing," an "animal," or an "18-year-old Siamese cat who likes salmon."

Living thing

Animal

Basic level ➔ Cat

Siamese Cat

18-year-old Siamese cat who likes salmon

Monica Wierzbicki/Body Scientific Intl.

Where Do Categories Come From?

We've considered how useful it is to divide things in the world into categories. Knowing an item is a "cat" means we can predict lots of things about it—it will meow, have lots of fur, and eat fish, but it probably won't like getting wet. We've talked a little bit about how people might categorize objects—comparing an object to a prototype or a bunch of exemplars—but where do categories come from? Certainly, learning and experience are important. We're constantly using our experiences to learn about what things go together. A decade or so ago, none of us had a category called "iPhone apps," but we do now. Categories can be unique to a particular culture, age group, or profession.

At the same time, it's possible that certain categories are *special*, meaning that we will naturally group certain objects together regardless of our experience or the culture in which we've been raised. In Chapter 4, we discussed how children acquire certain kinds of core knowledge early in their development. For example, very young children seem to know the difference between animate (living) and inanimate (nonliving) things. Children have fixed ideas about the category "living things" and can generate lots of predictions about how living things will act and develop (Spelke & Kinzler, 2007; Wellman, 2011). There is even evidence from neuroscience suggesting that specific areas of the brain may be naturally "tuned" to learn about living things (Mahon & Caramazza, 2009). Activity has been shown in visual processing areas of the brain when people complete a categorization task with living objects (animals) that is not present when completing the task with nonliving objects (tools), suggesting that visual features are more important for categorizing living than nonliving objects (Sim & Kiefer, 2005).

People across the world, in very diverse cultures, tend to think about biological categories—such as plants and animals—in the same special ways (Medin & Atran, 2004). These categories are universal, which suggests that we may be born with predispositions to learn and think about their members. Of course, this makes sense from an evolutionary perspective. Being able to classify and make predictions about plants and animals is likely to have helped us survive long enough to reproduce. There is even evidence of a distinct memory advantage for living over nonliving items (Nairne et al., 2017). But as we've discussed previously, evolutionary accounts are quite difficult to confirm—sorry, there are no fossilized brains. Still, researchers continue to take evolutionary factors seriously in their accounts of how we think.

KNOWLEDGE CHECK 9.3

Now test your knowledge about how people form categories by answering the following questions. (You will find the answers in the Appendix.)

1. For each of the following statements, decide on the category term that seems most appropriate. Choose from the following: *category exemplars, defining features, family resemblance, prototype.*
    a. It must be a bird because all birds have wings, feathers, and a beak.
    b. It must be a bird because it looks like all the other birds that I've seen.
    c. It must be a bird because it seems to have some features that are typical of birds.
    d. It must be a bird because it looks a lot like a robin.

2. When people refer to an object, such as your pet, during normal conversation, they tend to use what kind of category descriptor?
    a. Superordinate ("Look, it's an object on the planet Earth.")
    b. Basic level ("Look, it's a cat.")
    c. Subordinate ("Look, it's a seal-point Siamese.")
    d. Functional ("Look, it's something to cuddle.")

SOLVING PROBLEMS

Now let's consider some of the thought processes people use when they try to solve problems. Obviously, problem solving is an extremely adaptive skill. When you're faced with a problem, such as finding a well-paying job, there's a goal—gainful employment—and uncertainty about how to reach that goal. To study the solution process, psychologists often use problems like the following:

> It's early morning, still dark, and you're trying to get dressed. Your 2-month-old baby, snuggled in her crib at the foot of the bed, sleeps peacefully after a night of sustained wailing. You can't turn on the light—she'll wake up for sure—but the black socks and the blue socks are mixed up in the drawer. Let's see, you recall, I have five pairs of black socks and four pairs of blue socks. How many socks do I need to take out of the drawer to guarantee myself a pair of matching colors?

Notice there's a goal (selecting a pair of matching socks), and it's not immediately obvious how to get from the problem to the solution. Psychologists call this a **well-defined problem** (even though you may have no idea how to solve it) because there is a well-stated goal, a clear starting point, and a relatively easy way to tell when a solution has been reached. Finding a decent job is also a well-defined problem. Other kinds of problems do not have well-stated goals, clear starting points, or effective mechanisms for evaluating progress—these are called **ill-defined problems**. An example of an ill-defined problem might be discovering the secret of happiness. Maybe you can agree on the starting point (I'm not happy enough), but the goal (happiness) is pretty tough to define, and it's not at all clear how to reach that goal or how to measure progress.

Certain kinds of problems are well defined, such as finding the correct route on a map. Other problems are ill defined and may not even have a solution. Can you decipher the true meaning of the painting on the right?

Stephen Parker/ Alamy Stock Photo
Robert Nickelsberg / Getty Images

Representing Problem Information

To solve a problem quickly and correctly, regardless of whether it's well defined or ill defined, you first need to represent the problem information in the right way. By *problem representation*, psychologists mean you need to understand exactly what information you have and how that information can potentially be used. Take the sock problem. The correct answer is *three*. There are only two colors, so with three samples, you'll get two that match. This is actually an easy problem, but most people fail to "see" it in the right way. Did you start worrying about the four-to-five color ratio of blue to black? Did you briefly consider calculating some sort of probability? If you fail to detect which information is relevant and which is not, if you get hung up with ratios and probabilities and the like, this can be a very tough problem to solve. Let's consider another example.

Frank Beach is a butcher who works in a specialty meat shop. He is 5 feet, 8 inches tall; his waistline is 35 inches; and he is a stocky guy. What does he weigh?

The answer is—meat. He's a butcher, so he weighs meat. But, of course, your answer depends on how you interpret or represent the problem. If you tried to figure out Frank's weight, in pounds, then your answer would be wrong. You haven't represented the problem in the necessary way.

Functional Fixedness

People often allow their preconceptions to lock them into an incorrect view of problem information. Consider another example, illustrated in Figure 9.7, called the Maier two-string problem (after Maier, 1931). Imagine you're standing in a room with two lightweight strings hanging from the ceiling. The strings are hung at such a distance apart that, when holding one of the strings, you cannot reach the other. Using only a pair of pliers, which happens to be sitting on a table in the room, can you tie the strings together?

FIGURE 9.7 ■ The Maier Two-String Problem

Can you figure out a way to tie these two strings together? Notice there's a pair of pliers on the table.

Monica Wierzbicki/Body Scientific Intl.

This is a reasonably difficult problem because most people have a certain established, or fixed, way of viewing the function of pliers. The solution is to tie the pliers to one of the strings and swing it, like a pendulum, while you hold onto the other string. The correct solution, however, requires you to *restructure* the way you normally think about pliers. Pliers are good for grabbing and holding, but in this case they can serve as pendulum weights too.

The term **functional fixedness** refers to the tendency to see objects, and their functions, in certain fixed and typical ways. Functional fixedness can be an obstacle to problem solving because it often prevents you from recognizing the problem-solving tools that are present in the situation. Here's another one: Try solving the problem illustrated in Figure 9.8. You enter a room in which a candle, a box of tacks, some matches, and a hammer lie on a table. You're told to mount the candle on the wall so that it will still burn properly, using only the objects on the table. Work on the problem for a while before reading on.

Okay: The correct solution is to dump the tacks out of the box, mount the box on the wall with one of the tacks, and then put the candle in the box (Duncker, 1945). The problem is difficult because most people see the box only as a device for holding the tacks, not as something that can potentially help solve the problem. They become *fixed* in their views about the *functions* of objects and thereby fail to identify and define all of the available problem information correctly. People are more likely to show functional fixedness if they are induced to think about the typical function of the object prior to problem presentation (Chrysikou

FIGURE 9.8 ■ The Duncker Candle Problem

Using only the materials shown, figure out a way to mount the candle on the wall.

Monica Wierzbicki/Body Scientific Intl.

& Weisberg, 2005); people are less likely to show the effect if they are encouraged to decompose the object into its component parts (e.g., the shape of the object and its materials) before they think about its possible uses (McCaffrey, 2012). Even thinking about your own identity from multiple angles, such as the fact that you are a reader, you are a student, and you love to eat broccoli, can reduce the effect to some extent (Gaither et al., 2020). But functional fixedness is a powerful phenomenon—the effect seems to occur throughout the world, even in cultures with little exposure to advanced technology (German & Barrett, 2005).

Developing Problem-Solving Strategies

In addition to representing problem information correctly, you need an arsenal of problem *strategies*—techniques that enable you to move systematically toward a problem solution. Two classes of problem strategies can be used, *algorithms* and *heuristics*.

Algorithms

For some well-defined problems, you can use **algorithms**, which are step-by-step rules or procedures that guarantee a solution. You can use algorithms to solve simple math problems, for example, because there are fixed rules for addition, subtraction, and so on. As long as you use the rules properly, you'll always arrive at the correct solution. Solving anagrams, such as MBLOPRE, is another case in point. There are seven letters in the word, which means there are 5,040 possible combinations of the letters. If you systematically work out each of the possible sequences, one will eventually provide a solution to the PROBLEM. But it could take a long time.

Computers are often programmed to use algorithms because computers are capable of examining lots of information very quickly. However, algorithms are not always practical strategies for problem solution, even for computers. Consider chess: In principle, it would be possible to use algorithms to play chess—the computer would simply need to consider all of the possible consequences of a particular move. But practically, computers can't examine all the possible outcomes in a chess game; they can examine only some of them. Overall, there are some 10^{40} possible game sequences, so even if a computer could calculate a game in less than one-millionth of one-thousandth of a second, it would still require 10^{21} centuries to examine all the game possibilities (Best, 1989). It could do it; it would just take a very long time. Another problem with algorithms is that they work for only certain kinds of well-defined problems—there is no algorithm, for example, for deciding how to choose a major or for getting a job you enjoy.

People use heuristics—rules of thumb—when they play chess because the human mind simply cannot examine all the possible moves and their consequences during a game.

iStockPhoto/kali9

Heuristics

When it's not possible to use an algorithm, or when one is not easy to use, people tend to use **heuristics**, which are problem-solving rules of thumb. To solve an anagram, especially one with seven letters, it's not smart to use an algorithmic approach, examining all 5,040 possible letter sequences. Instead, you turn to heuristics. You know that English words don't usually begin with MB, or end with BL, so you can avoid checking out those possibilities. You can use what you know about English words to make guesses about the most likely solution. Heuristics are useful because they can lead to quick and accurate solutions. In natural environments, quick solutions can mean the difference between life and death. An organism can't spend its time wrapped in thought, systematically working through a long list of solution possibilities. Instead, it's adaptive for the organism to guess, as long as it's a reasonable guess based on what it knows.

One common problem-solving heuristic is **means–ends analysis**, which attacks problems by devising *means*, or actions, that reduce the gap between the current starting point and the desired goals, or *ends* (Newell & Simon, 1972). One usually applies this strategy by breaking down the problem into a series of more manageable subgoals, where the appropriate means to an end are clear. Let's assume that Peter, a normally low-achieving undergraduate, wants to start a relationship with Sonita, the brightest student in his psychology class. Obviously, asking Sonita out immediately is unlikely to succeed, so Peter breaks the problem down into more manageable parts.

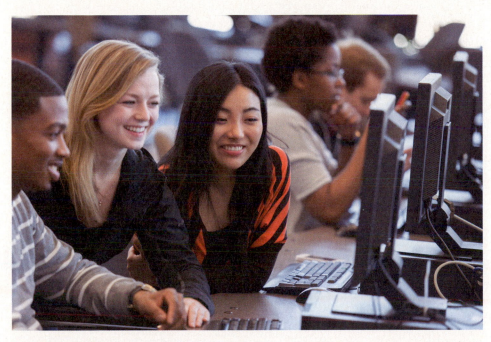

Breaking a problem down into subgoals that get you closer to the main goal (e.g., getting someone to date you) uses a means-ends analysis in solving the problem.

iStockPhoto/FatCamera

First, he reasons, he'll impress her in class by making an insightful comment during the lecture. He now has a new goal, acting intelligent in class, for which there is relatively straightforward means—he needs to study hard so he can master the material. Assuming he's successful (everyone now thinks he's an amazingly insightful young man), he devises a new subgoal: making some kind of personal contact with Sonita. Forming a small study group would be a good means to that end, he figures, so he approaches the recently impressed Sonita with the idea. Notice the key ingredients of the problem-solving strategy: Establish where you are, figure out where you want to be, and then devise a means for effectively getting from here to there. Often, as in Peter's case, means–ends analysis is made more effective by working systematically through subgoals.

Another effective heuristic is **working backward**—starting at the goal state and trying to move back toward the starting point. Suppose someone asked you to generate a set of anagrams. How would you proceed? Would you try to generate sets of randomly arranged letters and then see whether a particular sequence forms a word? Of course not. You would start with the solution, the word, and work backward by mixing up the normal letter sequence.

Here's another example: You're working on a biology project tracking the growth of bacteria in a petri dish. You know this particular strain of bacteria doubles every 2 hours. After starting the experiment, you discover the petri dish is exactly full after 12 hours. After how many hours was the petri dish exactly half-full? To solve this one, it's better to work backward. If the dish is full after 12 hours, and it takes 2 hours for the bacteria to double, what did the dish look like after 10 hours? This turns out to be the answer, which is arrived at rather simply if the problem is attacked in reverse.

Another useful heuristic is **searching for analogies**. If you can see a resemblance between the current problem and some task that you solved in the past, you can quickly obtain an acceptable solution. Imagine a man who buys a horse for $600 and sells it for $700. Later, he buys the same horse back for $800 and sells it again for $900. How much money did the man make in the horse-trading business? The attentive reader will not miss this one. It's a different version of the ticket scalping problem that opened this chapter. If you see the relationship between the two problems, you're unlikely to commit the problem-solving mistakes you made before.

Mental Set

Generally, to solve problems like these, you need to think in creative and novel ways. You may need to look at an everyday object in an unusual way (to break functional fixedness) or even stop using a problem-solving strategy that was successful in the past. Often people adopt **mental sets**, which are tendencies to rely on particular problem-solving strategies that were successful in the past. For example, military commanders lose battles because they rely on tried-and-true attack strategies that simply fail in their current environment. Likewise, your never-fail strategy for getting excellent grades in high school may no longer work in college. You need to formulate a new strategy that's appropriate to the situation you're in now.

At first glance, concepts such as functional fixedness and mental sets don't seem very adaptive—so why are they characteristics of how we solve problems? Wouldn't it be better to consider all possible object uses, or all possible strategies? Actually, the answer is "No." Most of the time, if you view objects in fixed ways or use fixed strategies that have worked well in the past, you're likely to be successful. After all, pliers usually do solve problems having to do with holding and grabbing. Many of the problems we've dealt with here are actually quite artificial—they're set up by psychologists in the hope that our "mistakes" will uncover normal problem-solving methods. The fact that we tend to rely on well-established habits of perception and thought is probably an effective overall problem-solving strategy.

Reaching the Aha! Moment: Insight

Anyone who has struggled with problems of the type we've been considering knows there's often a moment—an Aha! moment—when everything falls into place. The solution seems to pop magically into mind, a process that psychologists call **insight**. All the factors we've been considering, especially problem representation, play a role in achieving insight, but the process itself remains poorly understood. There's some suggestion that the Aha! moment is correlated with solution activation in the middle temporal cortex (Kounios & Beeman, 2014) and perhaps the hippocampus and other limbic structures (Tik et al., 2018).

Insight has been important historically because it suggests that we often don't solve problems through slow and steady trial-and-error learning. Aha! solutions seem to appear spontaneously, in an all-or-none fashion, rather than accumulating slowly over trials. This point was first famously demonstrated in chimpanzees by the Gestalt psychologist Wolfgang Köhler (1925). Köhler was marooned on the Canary Islands during World War I, and he used his free time to experiment with chimpanzees housed in a large outdoor pen. A variety of toys and tools were scattered about in the pen—sticks, boxes, poles, and so forth—which Köhler encouraged the chimps to use in solving problems. For example, he would place food in the pen that was visible, but inaccessible (such as hanging from the ceiling), and record how the chimps managed to reach it. He noticed the chimps would often struggle, failing to get the food, but then suddenly, after seeming to reflect on the situation, they would creatively use a tool (or combination of tools) to secure the food. The solution process was not slow, but sudden and reflective—the chimps seemed to display insight.

Psychologists have tried to study insight systematically in the laboratory, but it can be tough to re-create under controlled conditions. One common strategy is to present people with an insight problem, such as the nine-dot problem shown in Figure 9.9, and then affect solution probability by providing hints or other kinds of information. To solve the nine-dot problem, it's necessary to connect all the dots with exactly four straight lines without lifting the pencil from the paper or retracing. This is an extremely difficult problem to solve, primarily because people are biased perceptually to perceive the nine dots as a square (Maier, 1930). (The solution, shown at the end of the chapter in Figure 9.10, requires you to break the good figure of the square, drawing outside of the imagined lines.) Researchers have been able to increase performance somewhat through strategy training, such as requiring people to learn visual configurations that resemble the final solution, but performance usually remains low (Kershaw & Ohlsson, 2004). Other researchers have attempted to get inside the problem solver's head—for example, by tracking eye movements or general brain activity during a solution attempt (G. Jones, 2003; S. Lang et al., 2006)—but, unfortunately, the Aha! moment remains largely a mystery to researchers at this point.

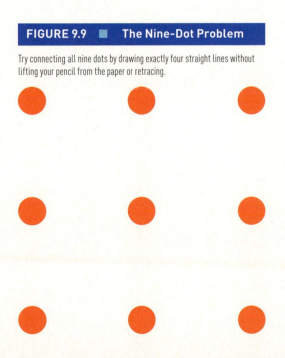

FIGURE 9.9 ■ The Nine-Dot Problem

Try connecting all nine dots by drawing exactly four straight lines without lifting your pencil from the paper or retracing.

PRACTICAL SOLUTIONS: HAVING DIFFICULTY? TAKE A BREAK!

Have you ever been frustrated with a problem and given up, only to find that the solution suddenly and mysteriously appears at a later time? Psychologists refer to this as an *incubation effect*—sometimes we do better at solving a problem when we stop working on it for a while. What accounts for this effect? Why should putting a problem aside increase the chances of reaching a solution?

iStockPhoto/Nadezhda1906

One possibility is that our brain continues to work on the problem, even though our conscious awareness is directed elsewhere. The problem is placed in the background where, over time, our unconscious mind churns out a solution. Unconscious processing probably does play some role in incubation effects, but it's unlikely that the brain is still working on the problem in any kind of direct way (Sio & Ormerod, 2009). A more likely explanation is that the break simply stops you from thinking about the problem in the wrong way. When people have trouble solving a problem, they often continue with the same ineffective strategy, coming up with the same wrong answer again and again. You can get locked into a particular way of viewing the problem components and can't break free. As you know, successful problem solving often requires thinking about the problem components in a novel and creative way. When you take a break and stop thinking about the problem, you're able to approach it later in a fresh and new way. You may even forget about the ineffective problem-solving strategies you used the first time around.

Another possibility is that during the break, while you're doing something else, you will come across information that ultimately helps solve the problem. The additional activity may provide clues or hints that lead to a problem breakthrough. Suppose you're having a difficult time solving an anagram, such as THREAGUD. You stop working on it and turn on a video that shows a happy mom with her children, a boy and a girl, playing nearby. "That's it!" you shout—the solution to the anagram is DAUGHTER. The new activity, watching a video, provided the necessary clue to solve the problem. Regardless of the interpretation, it's a good idea to take a break from time to time when you're trying to solve a tough problem. A fresh mind can do wonders for seeing a problem in a new way or simply for renewing your enthusiasm for finding a solution.

KNOWLEDGE CHECK 9.4

Now test your knowledge about problem solving by answering the following questions. (You will find the answers in the Appendix.)

1. Decide whether each of the following problems is well defined or ill defined. Justify your answer.
    a. Finding your way to a new restaurant in town: _____
    b. Receiving an A in your psychology course: _____
    c. Making your lab partner in chemistry fall madly in love with you: _____
    d. Baking a cherry cheesecake that won't taste like plumber's caulk: _____

2. Try to identify the problem-solving strategy at work in each of the following examples. Choose from the following terms: *algorithm, means–ends analysis, working backward, searching for analogies.*
    a. On the final exam, Myka looks for connections between the physics problems on the test and the ones he worked on while studying.

b. Rachel needs a three-letter word that begins with *R* to complete the crossword puzzle. She mindlessly considers all possible two-letter combinations, placing them after *R* until she arrives at an acceptable word.

c. Hector really needs an A in his philosophy class, but he has no idea what it takes. He decides to concentrate on writing a really top-notch first paper.

d. Courtney needs to generate a set of anagrams for a school project. To generate each anagram, she starts with a word and then scrambles the letters.

DECISION MAKING

Now let's discuss **decision making**, which deals with how we evaluate and choose from among alternatives. Obviously, decision making and problem solving are closely related. When you decide, you're confronted with a set of alternatives, and you must make a choice. The choice is almost always accompanied by risk, so it's in your interest to evaluate and select among the alternatives with care. Think about the decisions of the United Kingdom to leave the European Union, deciding when to move to online learning during the 2020 pandemic, or the physician who must choose between risky treatments that may kill or save a patient. Like problem solving, decision making is influenced by how you represent the alternatives in your mind, your personal biases, and by your choice of decision-making strategies. Let's examine how each of these processes affects the choices we make.

Framing Decision Alternatives

The way the alternatives are presented, called **framing**, can have a dramatic influence on what you decide. In a study by McNeil and colleagues (1982), hospital physicians were asked to choose between two forms of treatment for a patient with lung cancer: either a surgical operation on the lungs or a six-week treatment with radiation. Half of the physicians received the following information prior to making the choice:

> Of 100 people having surgery, 10 will die during treatment, 32 will have died by one year, and 66 will have died by five years. Of 100 people having radiation therapy, none will die during treatment, 23 will have died by one year, and 78 will have died by five years.

Put yourself in the doctor's shoes—which would you choose? The other half of the physicians were given the following:

> Of 100 people having surgery, 90 will be alive immediately after the treatment, 68 will be alive after one year, and 34 will be alive after five years. Of 100 people having radiation therapy, all will be alive immediately after treatment, 77 will be alive after one year, and 22 will be alive after five years.

Do you want to change your mind? Actually, exactly the same information is given in each of these scenarios. The only difference is that the treatment outcomes are described, or framed, around who will die or who will survive; the consequences are exactly the same in each case. Believe it or not, the option that physicians choose depends dramatically on the framing: Radiation therapy is chosen 44% of the time when the outcomes are framed in terms of who will die and only 18% of the time when survival rates are given.

This example is unsettling, especially given the medical context, because it suggests that human decision making is not always a rational process. No one wants to think that doctors make life-or-death decisions based on how treatment options happen to be framed. Yet it's not irrational for people to weigh information differently in different situations (Kahneman et al., 1982). When the alternatives were death based, perhaps the doctors simply connected the deaths to the treatment (surgery will kill 10 people, and radiation none). Alternatively, when the alternatives were framed around who lived, the focus might have been on long-term survival rather than on the hazards of treatment (34 people who receive surgery will be alive after five years, but only 22 radiation patients will survive that long). So, you can't assume the problem information was perceived in the same way in the two framings. You need to take into account how the problem was represented in the mind of the decision maker as well as the kinds of emotions the framing produced: 90% survival after one month sounds good; a 10% death rate sounds frightening (Kahneman, 2011).

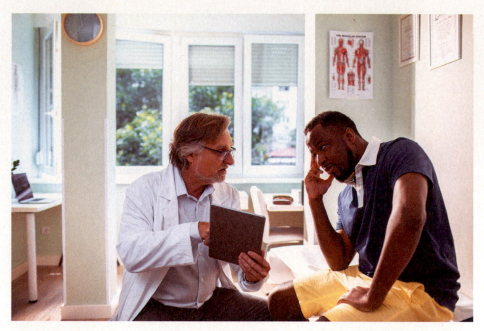

How doctors interpret and frame a patient's treatment options can critically influence the decision-making process.
iStockPhoto/Geber86

Framing experiments have significant implications for everyday decision making. When you're listening to a sales pitch, as you know, the salesperson typically focuses only on the gains: "Eighty-five percent of the people who bought this product reported satisfaction after one year." Well, that means that 15% of the customers didn't report satisfaction—if the focus had been on the 15%, would you still be interested in the product? More ominously, think about how politicians or military leaders frame arguments for or against military intervention. Is the focus on saving lives through enhanced security or on the costs of lives lost? The answer is obvious, but tread carefully. How decision alternatives are framed can significantly affect the final judgment you reach.

Decision-Making Biases

Our personal biases also influence our decision making, just as they do when we attempt to solve problems. For example, people show confirmation biases when they make decisions. In a nutshell, a **confirmation bias** is a tendency to seek out and use information that supports and confirms a prior decision or belief. If a therapist, for instance, believes that all instances of depression are caused by traumatic experiences in childhood (they're not), a confirmation bias might lead the therapist to focus only on childhood troubles during the therapy session.

People also tend to remember information that confirms their preconceptions. When asked to read stories about the sexual activities of men and women, for example, people tend to remember more negative things about the women—even if each story contains an equal number of positive and negative statements about the characters. This occurs, presumably, because of the widespread societal belief, or sexual double standard, that it's okay for men but not women to engage in sexual activity (Marks & Fraley, 2006). To avoid the confirmation bias, you should actively seek out disconfirming evidence; you should ask questions that allow you to reject or rule out one decision alternative over another.

Unfortunately, however, we're also reluctant to believe disconfirming evidence when it occurs. People show **belief persistence** as well, which means we tend to cling to our initial beliefs even when evidence suggests our belief may be wrong. For example, the strong believer in ESP continues to assume it exists even though countless experiments have failed to support its existence. There is always a reason, or a rationale, to hold onto the belief. In Chapter 13, which covers social psychology, we'll discuss in some detail decision-making biases that resemble belief persistence.

Decision-Making Heuristics

When people are forced to choose from among a set of alternatives, most rely on heuristics, or rules of thumb, just as they do when solving problems. These strategies simplify the decision-making process and often lead to correct judgments, but they sometimes lead you to the wrong decision. Concept Review 9.3 provides an overview of these heuristics.

Representativeness

Suppose you're asked to judge the likelihood of some event falling into class A or B. In such a case you might rely on a rule of thumb called the **representativeness heuristic**. You make your choice by deciding how "representative" the event seems to the average, or prototypical, member of each class. It's easiest to demonstrate with an example. Let's assume your friends, the Renfields, have six children. If B denotes boy and G denotes girl, which of the following two birth-order sequences do you think is more likely?

BBBGGG

BGGBGB

If you picked the second alternative, you're like most people. According to the rules of probability, though, the two outcomes are equally likely. Whether your next child will be a boy or a girl doesn't depend on the sex of your previous children—each event is independent of the others. Even so, people favor the second alternative because the first sequence clashes with their worldview of randomness. The first sequence just doesn't look like the outcome of a random process—it's not *representative* of what people think "randomness" looks like.

What if you flipped a coin six times and got six heads? You'd probably think it was a crooked coin. Again, a sequence of six heads isn't similar to, or representative of, what you think of as a random sequence. You have taken the outcome and compared it to some standard and made your decision accordingly. People often use the representativeness heuristic to make decisions in real-world settings. For example, clerks in stores use the products that a shopper buys as a way of judging age. If someone loads a shopping cart with products normally thought to be representative of an older consumer, the clerk's estimate of the shopper's age increases (M. McCall, 1994).

Using a heuristic such as representativeness is adaptive and beneficial most of the time, but as you've seen, it can lead to irrational decisions. Here's another one: Imagine you're leafing through a stack of questionnaires that have been filled out by some adult men. One of the respondents lists his height as 6 feet, 5 inches, but his answers are so sloppily written that you can't make out his circled profession—it's either bank president or basketball player (in the National Basketball Association). You need to make a choice: Which is he? Most people choose NBA player because the applicant is tall and apparently not interested in careful writing (Beyth-Marom & Lichtenstein, 1984). This is not a very rational choice, however, because the odds of someone in the sample being a professional basketball player are extremely low—bank presidents outnumber NBA players by a wide margin (probably at least 50 to 1). In choosing basketball player, people have ignored the *base rate*, or how likely the event is to occur in the population being sampled.

The representativeness heuristic also dupes people into committing what is called the *conjunction error*. Consider the following: Linda is 31 years old, single, outspoken, and very bright. She majored in philosophy. As a student, she was deeply concerned with issues of discrimination and social justice and participated in Black Lives Matter demonstrations. Which of the following alternatives is more likely?

1. Linda is a bank teller.

2. Linda is a bank teller and active in the feminist (e.g., #MeToo) movement.

In a study conducted by Tversky and Kahneman (1983), 85% of the participants judged alternative 2 to be the more likely. Why? Because Linda's description is more representative of someone active in the feminist movement than it is of a bank teller. But think about it—how can the odds of two things happening together be higher than the likelihood of any one of those events happening alone? Notice the second alternative is actually a subset of the first alternative and therefore cannot be more likely. Those who choose alternative 2 have acted illogically, at least from the standpoint of the rational decision maker.

Conjunction errors occur when we estimate that two simultaneous events are more probable than either event on its own.

iStockPhoto/YinYang

Availability

Sometimes we rely on memory to help us make our decisions. Estimate the likelihood that you'll forget to turn off your phone during a lecture. If you can easily remember lots of instances in which your phone rang during a lecture, causing the professor and students to look over at you, your estimate of forgetting is likely to be high. You have relied on your previous experiences—particularly those experiences that easily come to mind—as a basis for judging probability. This kind of judgment relies on an **availability heuristic**. Once again, it's likely to be adaptive much of the time, but as with the representativeness heuristic, researchers can arrange situations that make this decision-making strategy look irrational.

Which do you think is more likely, an English word that begins with the letter *K* or an English word with *K* in the third position? By now you're probably skeptical about your first choice, but most people think English words that begin with *K* are more likely (Tversky & Kahneman, 1973). In fact, English words with *K* in the third position are much more common (the ratio is about 3 to 1). Which do you think is more likely, someone dying from any kind of accident or someone dying from a stroke? Accidents, right? It's not even close. More than twice as many people are likely to die from stroke than from any kind of accident (Slovic et al., 1982). People make the error because examples of the incorrect alternative are more likely to come to mind. It's easier to think of an English word with *K* in the first position, and accidental deaths get much more publicity than deaths due to stroke.

Anchoring and Adjustment

Judgments are also influenced by starting points—that is, by any initial estimates you might be given. Tversky and Kahneman (1974) asked people to estimate the proportion of African countries belonging to the United Nations. Prior to answering, participants were given a number (between 0 and 100) and were asked to pick the correct proportion by moving up or down from this starting point. For example, you might be given the number 10 and asked to estimate the proportion using 10 as a base. For groups that received 10 and 65 as the initial starting points, the estimated proportion of African countries was 25% and 45%, respectively—a whopping difference. The judgments were clearly influenced by the initial estimates, or anchors, and people tended to stay relatively close to the starting points as they made their decisions.

In another experiment described by Tversky and Kahneman (1974), one group of people was asked to estimate the product of the following numbers:

$$1 \times 2 \times 3 \times 4 \times 5 \times 6 \times 7 \times 8$$

whereas a second group was asked to estimate the product of the same numbers presented in reverse order:

$$8 \times 7 \times 6 \times 5 \times 4 \times 3 \times 2 \times 1$$

The correct answer in both cases is 40,320. But the first group gave an average estimate of 512, whereas the second group's estimate averaged 2,250—quite a difference, given that it's the same problem in both cases. In this example, the early numbers in the sequence serve as the anchors leading to either low or more moderate estimates.

The use (and misuse) of anchors has lots of practical implications. If you're negotiating to buy a house or a car, be careful about what the seller throws out as an initial offer. If the seller begins with an outrageously high offer, you're more likely to use that price as an anchor and assume the item is worth more. Estimates given in fine-art auctions have been found to influence the first bids that are given by potential buyers. Stores have been able to increase sales by placing limits on the number of items that can be purchased. Telling people that they can buy only "12 bottles of this magical cleaner" increases people's estimates of how many bottles they want to buy. Trial lawyers can potentially increase or decrease damage amounts by mentioning a ridiculously high or low initial amount to the deciding judge (Kahneman, 2011).

People are much more likely to worry about the occurrence of fires if a recently publicized event (such as the large wildfires that burned in the Western United States in 2020 and 2021) is fresh and available in their minds.

ROBYN BECK / Getty Images

The Value of Heuristics

What are we to make of such an imperfect decision maker? As psychologist Reid Hastie (1991) notes, the heuristic tool user described by Kahneman and Tversky is "an image of a decision maker of 'small brain' attempting to make do with a limited set of useful, imperfect, and not-too-demanding cognitive subroutines" (p. 136).

Imperfect though heuristics may be, there are several points worth making in their favor. First, heuristics are often surprisingly effective. In fact, in some cases, heuristics can lead to more accurate decisions than so-called rational ways of deciding (Gigerenzer, 2018). Second, heuristics are economical. Optimal, or rational, decision making can be a complex, time-consuming activity. Strategies that lead to quick decisions with little cost are adaptive even if they sometimes lead to error. Third, to act optimally, you must have all the information needed to calculate a choice; unfortunately, you often don't have all of this information. In these cases, heuristics become useful tools for pointing you in the right direction.

Moreover, as we discussed in the section on framing effects, the fact that people make errors in artificial laboratory situations is somewhat misleading. We can define what the rational decision might be, based on objective information, but people don't always interpret the decision alternatives in the way the researcher intends. We all bring background knowledge to a situation that affects how we think and behave. In the "Linda is a bank teller" example, for instance, people know there are more bank tellers in the world than feminist bank tellers. People understand a great deal about the frequencies of events in the world—the mistake is made because they're thinking about a single case, Linda, rather than about probabilities in general (Fiedler, 1988; Gigerenzer, 1996).

Just because you make decision errors doesn't mean you're using ineffective cognitive processes. Think back to Chapter 5 and our discussion of perceptual illusions. It's easy to arrange situations in which you might see or hear things that aren't really there, but your visual system is still highly adaptive. Just because your visual system can be tricked by an illusion doesn't mean it's a bad system. Similarly, when you make decisions, you're relying on adaptive systems that serve you very well in the majority of situations (Gigerenzer, 1997, 2018).

CONCEPT REVIEW 9.3
DECISION-MAKING HEURISTICS

Heuristic	Description	Example
Representativeness	We arrive at a decision by comparing the similarity of the object or event to the average member of each class.	Juan meets his new college roommate, Bryce, who is 6'10" and very athletic looking. Juan assumes that Bryce is a basketball player, probably on scholarship.
Availability	We estimate the odds of some event occurring on the basis of how easily examples come to mind.	Stella reads so much in the newspaper about car accidents that she believes her chances of dying in a car accident are greater than her chances of dying from a stroke.
Anchoring and adjustment	Judgments are influenced by initial estimates.	Stacey holds a garage sale and sells two big items early for a total of $150. Throughout the day, she overestimates how much she is making, and in the end, she is disappointed by her actual profit.

Now test your knowledge about decision making by picking the term that best fits the following statements. Choose your answer from the following: *availability heuristic, anchoring and adjustment heuristic, framing, representativeness heuristic.* (You will find the answers in the Appendix.)

1. Matt used to fly to visit his parents during the Thanksgiving break, but after seeing nonstop coverage of a gory plane accident, he now chooses to drive.

2. Lavon, a broker, used to tell people that his mutual fund lost money only 3 times in the past 10 years. Now he tells them that the fund has made money 7 of the past 10 years. He's noticed a very marked improvement in overall sales of the fund.

3. Keagan sleeps until noon, parties at night, and carries around a big backpack the rest of the time. Her neighbor, Eileen, assumes that Keagan is a college student.

4. Graham, who made lots of sales early in the morning, estimates that he and Leslie made $700 from their yard sale; Leslie, who had a big afternoon, puts the estimate at $300.

THE PROBLEMS SOLVED: WHAT COGNITION IS FOR

In this chapter, we've discussed how people use mental or cognitive processes to communicate, categorize, find solutions to problems, and decide among alternatives. Each of these topics illustrates how we use cognitive processes, along with existing knowledge, to coexist successfully with our environment.

Communicating With Others

To communicate effectively, humans have developed rules (grammar) for combining arbitrary symbols in meaningful ways to express thoughts, feelings, and needs to others. A proper grammar consists of rules for combining sounds (phonology), rules for constructing sentences from words (syntax), and rules for meaning (semantics). To understand how language works, language researchers believe it's important to distinguish between the surface structure of a sentence—the literal ordering of words— and its deep structure, which represents the speaker's intentions. To comprehend the communications of others, we rely on mutual knowledge, or pragmatics, to interpret statements or requests that may be riddled with ambiguity.

Learning Language

The sequence of language development turns out to be universal—no matter where you look in the world, babies show similar milestones in language development. This finding has led many researchers to conclude that people are born ready to learn language just like they're born ready to walk. The ability to produce written and spoken language enables people to gather and transmit knowledge in ways that seem to be one of the truly unique characteristics of the human species. Whether or not language is truly an adaptation (a product of natural selection) remains controversial.

Classifying and Categorizing

When we categorize, or put objects into meaningful groups, we create a world that's more sensible and predictable. Categories enable us to infer invisible properties about objects—if X is a member of category Y, then X will have at least some of the properties of category Y members. As a result, we can make accurate predictions about the things we encounter. How is category membership defined? Evidence suggests that people often rely on family resemblance. Members of the same category tend to share certain basic or core features. At the same time, categories are remarkably flexible; their boundaries are fuzzy, which allows us to classify things even when those objects may not share all the typical features of the category members. Categories also have structures that are hierarchical—there are categories within categories within categories. An object that fits the category "Siamese cat" also fits the category "animal" or "living thing." We most commonly assign objects to basic-level categories, which tend to be at intermediate levels of the hierarchy. Although many categories are learned through experience, such as iPhone apps, our brains may have been "tuned" by evolution to acquire certain natural categories (e.g., plants, animals).

Solving Problems

When faced with a problem, there is a goal, which may or may not be well defined, and it's not immediately obvious how to get from the problem to the solution. One of the common pitfalls in problem solving occurs when we allow preconceptions to influence how we represent problem information. For example, most people fall prey to functional fixedness, or the tendency to see objects and their functions in certain fixed ways. Algorithms are procedures that guarantee a solution, but they're often time-consuming and can't always be applied. Heuristics are problem-solving rules of thumb that can be applied quickly but don't always lead to the correct solution. Examples of problem-solving heuristics include means–ends analysis, working backward, and searching for analogies. Psychologists are also very interested in insight—the Aha! moment that occurs when solutions suddenly become available. Unfortunately, little is known about the psychological processes involved.

Decision Making

The study of decision making looks at how we evaluate and choose from among a set of alternatives. When we make decisions, we're confronted with a set of alternatives and required to make a choice. Choice in decision making is almost always accompanied by risk, so it's useful to evaluate and select among the alternatives with care. As with problem solving, decision making is influenced by how the alternatives are viewed or represented. For example, how alternatives are framed can affect the decision that is made. We commonly use a variety of decision heuristics, including representativeness, availability, and anchoring and adjustment. These strategies may not always cause us to make the right decision, but they allow us to move quickly toward the goal and to use past experience.

THINKING ABOUT RESEARCH

A summary of a research study in psychology is given in this section. As you read the summary, think about the following questions:

1. In what way(s) are categories involved in the method of the study?
2. Is the refugee resettlement problem a well-defined or ill-defined problem? Explain your answer.
3. How did the participants' mental set contribute to the results of the study?
4. Which biases or heuristics described in the chapter do you think contribute to people's opinions about whether refugees should be accepted into their country? Explain how you think these biases/heuristics contribute to their decisions.

Article Reference: Madan, S., Basu, S., Rattan, A., & Savani, K. (2019). Support for resettling refugees: The role of fixed versus growth mind-sets. *Psychological Science, 30*, 238–249.

Purpose of the Study: The current study examined the role that one's ideas and beliefs about immigrants play in attitudes about whether one's country should allow refugees to resettle there. The researchers argued that one's ideas about whether the kind of person one is can change (growth mind-set) or not (fixed mind-set) can affect attitutudes about refugee resettlement. They predicted that the more one holds a growth mind-set, the more one would support allowing refugees to resettle in one's country.

Method of the Study: Six studies were conducted online with participants who were residents of the United States or the United Kingdom. Studies 1, 2, 5, and 6 used surveys to test relationships between participants' mind-set (growth or fixed) and their attitudes about refugees being allowed to enter their country, whether they can assimilate to their host country (adopt their host country's values, attitudes, and behaviors), and whether they should assimilate to their host country. Studies 3 and 4 were experiments that randomly assigned participants to read an article arguing for either a growth mind-set or a fixed mind-set. Their attitudes about refugee policies were then measured with a survey.

Results of the Study: The first two correlational studies (Studies 1 and 2) showed that a growth mind-set predicted stronger support for accepting refugees into the participants' country for both U.S. and U.K. residents. Study 3 showed that exposure to the growth mind-set caused stronger support for accepting refugees than exposure to the fixed mind-set. Study 4 showed that growth mind-set exposure caused stronger beliefs that refugees can assimilate to their new country. Studies 5 and 6 further supported these results with additional correlational data.

Conclusions of the Study: The results in the study supported the researchers' hypothesis that one's mental set plays an important role in one's attitude about refugees resettling in one's country and whether refugees can assimilate to their new country.

KNOWLEDGE CHECK: CHAPTER SUMMARY

(You'll find the answers in the Appendix.)

COMMUNICATING WITH OTHERS

- To qualify as language, a communication system must have (1) _____, which consists of (a) phonology, the rules for combining (2) _____ to make words; (b) syntax, the rules for combining words to make (3) _____; and (c) semantics, the rules for communicating (4) _____. Languages are hierarchical, ranging from (5) _____, the smallest significant sound units, and (6) _____, the smallest meaningful units, to words and sentences. Sentences have (7) _____ structure, the literal ordering of words, and (8) _____ structure, the underlying meaning; language production turns deep structure into an acceptable surface structure.

- Effective communication relies heavily on the speakers' common (9) _____ and a combination of bottom-up and (10) _____ processing. (11) _____ refers to how we use (12) _____ knowledge to comprehend what someone says and to respond effectively.

LEARNING LANGUAGE

- The universality of language is apparent at birth. Crying, cooing, and babbling are important vocalization milestones. Simple words appear by the end of a child's (13) _____ year. By the age of 2, (14) _____ speech begins: The child communicates without using articles (*the*) or prepositions (*at, in*), showing an elementary awareness of (15) _____. Children often (16) _____ grammatical rules.

- Although the vocal (17) _____ of chimps makes actual speech (18) _____, some have been taught to communicate with humans through signs and symbols, including American (19) _____ Language. Researchers disagree about whether such achievements represent true (20) _____.

- Many psychologists assume that language is an (21) _____, which means it evolved as a result of natural selection. Language is associated with particular regions of the (22) _____; children learn language incredibly quickly without specifically being taught the rules; the human (23) _____ and vocal tract seem perfectly tailored to meet the needs of speech; and some people inherit tendencies to make certain types of (24) _____ errors. Even so, the question of how and why language emerged remains controversial.

CLASSIFYING AND CATEGORIZING

- A (25) _____ is a class of objects—people, places, or things—that belong together. To determine membership in a category, things are classified by their (26) _____ features, which are shared by all (27) _____. (28) _____ categories usually have (29) _____ boundaries, which suggests that members have (30) _____ rather than fixed features. Family (31) _____ is determined by the collection of (32) _____ features that an object possesses. Members of the same category will share many but not all family features.

- Category membership may be determined by comparison to a (33) _____, the one best or most (34) _____ member of a category. Alternatively, we may store category examples, or category (35) _____, of every category and assign category membership based on comparison to these instances.

- All categories are (36) _____. (37) _____-level categories generate the most useful and (38) _____ information and are at (39) _____ levels of the category hierarchy. (40) _____ categories are at the top level and aren't especially (41) _____.

SOLVING PROBLEMS

- A (42) _____ problem has a well-stated goal, a clear starting point, and an easy way to tell when a solution has been reached. The goal and starting point of an (43) _____-defined problem aren't (44) _____, and the problem lacks an effective mechanism for evaluating progress.

- To solve a problem quickly and (45) _____, you must represent, or understand, the information you have about the problem and how it can be used. Obstacles to problem representation include functional (46) _____, which is a tendency to see objects and their functions in fixed, typical ways.

- For certain types of well-defined problems, we can use (47) _____, step-by-step procedures that guarantee a solution. When algorithms aren't feasible, we can try problem-solving (48) _____, or rules of thumb. The three most common heuristics are (49) _____ analysis, working (50) _____, and searching for (51) _____. People often adopt (52) _____ sets, a tendency to rely on particular problem-solving strategies that were successful in the past.

- (53) _____ is a process in which a solution seems to "magically" come to mind. The process has been studied in the lab but remains poorly understood.

DECISION MAKING

- Decisions can be dramatically influenced by (54) _____, the way alternatives are structured or presented, which in turn influences how the problem is (55) _____ in the mind of the decision maker.

- The (56) _____ bias is the tendency to seek out and use information that confirms a previous decision or long-standing (57) _____. We also tend to show belief (58) _____, clinging to our initial beliefs even when confronted with evidence that counters them.

- When asked to judge the likelihood of an event belonging to a class, we often rely on the (59) _____ heuristic, which means that we arrive at a decision by comparing the similarity of the object or event in question to the average or (60) _____ member of each class. If we use the (61) _____ heuristic, we base our estimates on the ease with which examples of the event come to mind. Our judgments are also influenced by starting points, or (62) _____, which are initial estimates we might be given. Though imperfect, heuristics are adaptive because they lead to (63) _____ and effective decisions with little cost. Even when we don't have all the important information about a problem, (64) _____ still help point us in the right direction. However, using heuristics may sometimes lead to (65) _____ in the decision-making process.

CRITICAL THINKING QUESTIONS

1. Based on what you've learned about Chomsky's work, why might it be difficult to program a computer to understand speech?

2. In normal conversation, how much meaning do you think is typically communicated nonverbally—such as through frowning or folding your arms?

3. Although categories are usually adaptive, can you think of any instance in which categorizing an object or a person might not be adaptive? How about when you stereotype someone?

4. If you wanted to decide whether your friend Bob fits the category "furniture," do you think you would compare him to a prototype (such as a couch or a chair), or would you think about all the things that you've used as a "seat" in your lifetime?

5. Do you think problem solving is a part of decision making, or is decision making a part of problem solving?

KEY TERMS

algorithms (p. 332)

availability heuristic (p. 340)

basic-level categories (p. 327)

belief persistence (p. 339)

category (p. 323)

category exemplars (p. 326)

confirmation bias (p. 338)

decision making (p. 337)

deep structure (p. 315)

defining features (p. 324)

family resemblance (p. 325)

framing (p. 337)

functional fixedness (p. 331)

grammar (p. 313)

heuristics (p. 333)

ill-defined problem (p. 330)

insight (p. 334)

means–ends analysis (p. 333)

mental set (p. 334)

morphemes (p. 313)

phonemes (p. 313)

phonology (p. 313)

pragmatics (p. 316)

prototype (p. 325)

representativeness heuristic (p. 339)

searching for analogies (p. 334)

semantics (p. 313)

surface structure (p. 315)

syntax (p. 313)

thinking (p. 310)

well-defined problem (p. 330)

working backward (p. 334)

iStockPhoto/kali9

10 INTELLIGENCE

On a Saturday morning in October, Malik Tarpy drops down his yellow number 2 pencil and glances about the room with a cocky grin. Around him, working feverishly, sit dozens of others, similar in age and ambition, but with pencils raised and sweat collecting on furrowed brows. Malik has finished early, as is his custom, and he's just aced an important exam. Next stop: medical school, a top residency, and a lifetime of security.

Meanwhile, outside in a park across the street, Larry Steinway has also dropped his yellow pencil. But he doesn't notice. He'll need to rely on his attendant to recover it. Although physically Larry is 22, his mind drifts in a world occupied by a 4-year-old's thoughts and impulses. He uses language haltingly; his hopes for an elementary school education are limited. Still, he responds quickly when his attendant asks him to calculate the number of seconds elapsing in 65 years, 14 days, and 15 hours. His answer includes the correct number of leap years and arrives in slightly under a minute and a half.

Overhead, unknown to Larry, flies a single Clark's nutcracker in search of a place to deposit its recently harvested supply of pine seeds. On this particular trip, one of many over the past few months, the bird will store its 25,000th seed. Across miles of terrain lie thousands of secret caches, all attributable to this one bird, scattered among the storage locations of other nutcrackers. Over the coming winter months, this bird will successfully revisit its own hiding places, ignoring others, and recover some 80% of the hidden seeds.

Each of these sketches demonstrates actions that *might* be characterized as intelligent. What do you think? We can certainly agree that Malik Tarpy fits the description—ace performer on tests, self-assured; he probably gets all A's and is popular in school. But what about Larry Steinway—someone who is poor at language, who operates at a mental level far below his physical age? Definitely not intelligent, you say; but then how do you explain his extraordinary calculating skills? Isn't "lightning calculation" an odd but nevertheless intelligent form of behavior? Finally, consider the Clark's nutcracker. It can't do geometry or calculus, but could you remember where you put 25,000 seeds scattered across miles of confusing terrain? Don't you think this remarkable ability to adapt to the harshness of winter is a prime example of intelligent behavior?

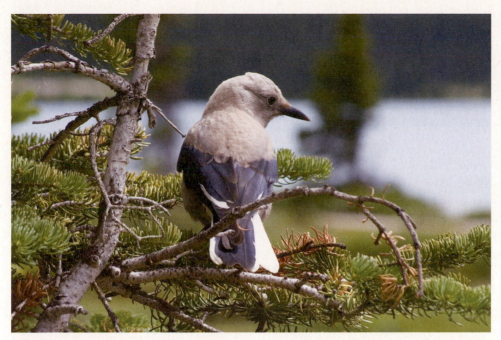

This little bird, a Clark's nutcracker, can remember the locations of thousands of seeds scattered across miles of confusing terrain. Wouldn't you call this a form of "intelligent" behavior?

iStockPhoto/Bastar

THE PROBLEMS TO BE SOLVED: WHAT IS INTELLIGENCE, AND WHAT IS IT FOR?

When psychologists talk about **intelligence**, they're usually referring to an internal capacity or ability that accounts for individual differences in mental performance, an ability that enables us to adapt successfully to changing environments. Notice the emphasis is partly on individual differences among people—specifically, the differences people show in their ability to perform tasks. People differ in ability, and the measurement of these differences is used to define the capacity called "intelligence." Think about it: If everyone had the same ability to solve math problems or devise creative ideas, the label "intelligent" would be meaningless. Psychologists who study intelligence attempt to measure the differences among people and then determine how and why those differences occur. One of the important goals is to use individual differences to predict things such as job performance and success in school. In this chapter, we'll focus on three fundamental problems facing the intelligence researcher: conceptualizing, measuring, and discovering the source of individual differences in intellectual ability.

Conceptualizing Intelligence

Many people talk of intelligence as if it's some "thing" that's possessed by a person, such as blue eyes, long fingers, or a slightly crooked gait. Yet we can neither see intelligence nor measure it directly with a stick. Intelligence may not even be best viewed as a single capacity; it may be better seen as a collection of separate abilities. It's possible that we have multiple intelligences ranging from the more traditional verbal and math skills to musical ability, mechanical ability, and even athletic ability. We'll discuss how psychologists have attempted to conceptualize intelligence over the years and where the brunt of opinion lies today.

Measuring Individual Differences

Regardless of how we choose to conceptualize intelligence, there's still the practical problem of measuring individual differences. For any particular task, such as performing well in school, people will show a range of abilities. Some people will perform extremely well; others will struggle. If these abilities can be measured accurately, through the use of psychological tests, then it should be possible to tailor your activities to fit your skills. You can be advised not to enter cartography school if your spatial abilities are weak, or you can be steered toward a career as a writer or journalist if your verbal abilities are strong. We'll discuss how intelligence is typically measured and some of the characteristics of effective tests.

Discovering the Sources of Intelligence

Does intelligent behavior come primarily from your genetic background or from life experiences? People do differ in ability, but it's not immediately obvious whether these differences are largely inborn or due simply to one's environmental history. Is poor map reading a permanent condition, resulting from a lack of the right kind of genes, or can a superior ability to read maps be taught? Because of the wiring in my brain, am I doomed to forever have trouble fixing that leaky faucet in my kitchen, or can I be taught mechanical skills? We'll discuss the origins of intelligence from the perspective of nature and nurture and address some of the controversies that still surround the study of individual differences.

CONCEPTUALIZING INTELLIGENCE

When discussing intelligence, it makes sense to consider its adaptive characteristics. If you're able to maneuver successfully through life, rising to the top of your profession, then most would agree the label "intelligent" aptly describes your abilities. One way to think about intelligence, then, is in terms of your ability to solve the problems that are unique to your environment—in essence, that is what intelligence is for. The fact that nutcrackers can efficiently hide and relocate thousands of seeds is certainly intelligent from the standpoint of adapting to the harshness of winter (Kamil & Balda, 1990). But conceptualizing intelligence simply in terms of adaptability does not tell us much about what accounts for individual differences. People (and nutcrackers) differ in their ability to fit successfully into their environments, even when they're faced with similar problems. We need to understand the factors that produce individual differences—remember, that's the main focus of intelligence researchers. In this section of the chapter, we'll consider several ways of generally conceptualizing intelligence.

Psychometrics: Measuring the Mind

We begin with the psychometric approach, which proposes that intelligence is a mental capacity that can be understood by analyzing performance on mental tests. The word **psychometrics** literally means "a measure of the mind." Intelligence is determined by administering a variety of tests that measure specific mental skills, such as verbal comprehension, memory, or spatial ability. The results are then analyzed statistically, and conclusions are drawn about underlying mental abilities.

One of the first attempts to treat intelligence in this way was developed in the 19th century by Englishman Sir Francis Galton (1822–1911). Galton was a half-cousin of Charles Darwin, and like his famous relative, he was deeply committed to the idea of survival of the fittest. Galton (1869) believed individual differences in ability had their basis in heredity and could be measured through a series of tests of sensory discrimination and reaction time. For a small fee, visitors to Galton's laboratory were given a variety of psychological and physical tests, measuring such things as visual acuity, grip strength, and reaction time to sounds. At the end of the test session, they were handed a card with a detailed record of their scores (E. R. Hilgard, 1987; R. C. Johnson et al., 1985).

Galton believed he was measuring intelligence with his set of tests. He based his belief partly on the fact that there often appeared to be relationships among the various scores received by particular individuals. If they tended to score high on a certain test, such as sensory acuity, they tended to score high on other measures as well. This pattern suggested to Galton that each of the separate tests might be tapping into some general ability—a general intelligence that contributed in some way to each of the different measured skills.

Francis Galton's First Anthropometric Laboratory at the International Health Exhibition, South Kensington, 1884–5.

Sir Francis Galton (1822–1911) and his "anthropometric" laboratory, where he measured intellectual ability.

Hulton Archive / Stringer via Getty Images Science & Society Picture Library / Contributor via Getty Images

As it turned out, Galton's laboratory investigations into the measurement of intelligence were unsuccessful. His measurements were crude, and his tests were later shown to be poor predictors of actual intellectual performance, such as academic success (Wissler, 1901). For these and other reasons, his contributions are primarily of historical rather than scientific interest. But his methods captured the attention of other researchers, who went on to develop the psychometric approach in a more rigorous way. Among the more influential of those who carried on the Galton tradition was a mathematically inclined psychologist named Charles Spearman (1863–1945).

Spearman and Factor *g*

Charles Spearman's principal contribution was the development of a mathematical technique called **factor analysis**, which is a procedure for isolating the various factors that account for test performance. For example, as Galton suggested, it's possible that each of us has a single underlying ability—intelligence—that helps to explain our performance on lots of mental tests. Alternatively, there could be multiple factors involved—we might be intelligent in one way, such as in an ability to remember, and not very intelligent in another, such as in mathematical problem solving. Spearman's technique enabled researchers to study these possibilities in a systematic way.

To get an idea of how factor analysis works, think about star athletes who excel in several sports. It's natural to assume that good athletes have general athletic ability that reveals itself in a number of ways. If you were to correlate performance across a variety of skills, you should be able to predict how well individuals will perform on one measure of skill, given that you know how well they perform on others. Good athletes, for instance, should run fast, jump high, and have quick reflexes. Correlations exist because presumably an underlying ability—athletic skill—contributes to each of the individual performance measures. Similar logic applies to intelligence: Someone who is high (or low) in intelligence should perform well (or poorly) on many different kinds of ability tests. If there is general intelligence, you should be able to predict performance on one type of test (such as math) if you know how well the person performs on other tests (such as verbal comprehension or spatial ability).

When Spearman (1904) applied factor analysis to the testing of mental ability, he discovered evidence for general intellectual ability. A single factor in the analysis, which he called g (for **general intelligence**), helped to explain performance on a wide variety of mental tests. Yet, he discovered that it wasn't possible to explain individual test scores entirely by referring to *g*. The correlations among the test scores were high but not perfect. He found, for example, that someone who performed extremely well on a test of verbal comprehension did not necessarily excel on a test of spatial ability. He argued, therefore, that it's necessary to take specific abilities, which he called s (for **specific intelligence**), that are *unique* to each individual test into account (see Figure 10.1). To predict performance on a test of verbal comprehension, for example, you need a measure of ability that is specific to verbal comprehension in addition to *g*.

Hierarchical Models of Intelligence

As you might expect, Spearman's two-factor analysis of intelligence was quite influential in its time, and it remains influential today. But over the years his conclusions were challenged, especially his concept of general intelligence or *g*. Psychologist L. L. Thurstone (1938) applied a somewhat different version of factor analysis, as well as a more extensive battery of tests, and discovered evidence for seven "primary mental abilities": verbal comprehension, verbal fluency, numerical ability, spatial ability, memory, perceptual speed, and reasoning. Thurstone rejected Spearman's notion of a single general intelligence, *g*. His analysis indicated that these seven primary abilities are largely independent—just because people are good at verbal reasoning doesn't mean they will be good at memory or show perceptual speed. If performance on one type of test tells us little or nothing about performance on a second test, it's unlikely that the two tests are measuring the same general underlying ability.

Psychologists have argued for decades about (a) the proper way to apply factor analysis, (b) the kinds of ability tests that should be used, and (c) whether single or multiple factors are needed to explain the test results. But the evidence for a central *g* is hard to dismiss completely, at least when intelligence is defined by performance on tests of mental ability. Different intelligence tests have been developed, virtually all of which find evidence for general intelligence; in fact, evidence for *g* is currently "perhaps the most replicated result in all of psychology" (Kovacs & Conway, 2016, p. 151). Moreover, the measurements of *g* correlate very highly across the tests, even though they were developed in different ways (Deary, 2012). For this reason, most modern psychometric theories accept the concept of general intelligence.

FIGURE 10.1 ■ Spearman's General and Specific Factors

Spearman discovered that to explain performance on a variety of mental tests it was necessary to consider (1) a common factor, called *g* for general intelligence, that contributes to performance on all of the tests, and (2) specific abilities—labeled here as *s1* through *s7*—that contribute uniquely to the particular tests.

Monica Wierzbicki/Body Scientific Intl.

But *g* alone is not enough to explain performance. Psychologists commonly propose more of a hierarchical structure, such as that shown in Figure 10.2. General intelligence, *g*, occupies a position at the top of the hierarchy, and various subfactors (or abilities) that may or may not operate independently from one another sit at the lower levels. This represents a compromise of sorts between Thurstone's view—that there is more than one primary mental ability—and Spearman's concept of general intelligence or *g*. One popular modern version of a hierarchical model is the Cattell–Horn–Carroll theory of cognitive abilities (see W. J. Schneider & McGrew, 2018). General intelligence (*g*) again sits at the top of the hierarchy with two lower levels representing "broad" abilities (which include things such as processing speed, reasoning abilities, and memory functioning) and "narrow" abilities (representing particular kinds of reasoning or memory). We expand on these secondary abilities in the next section.

Michael Jordan showed great skill in basketball and in baseball as well. Do his skills support the existence of a factor tapping general athletic ability?

MIKE NELSON/AFP via Getty Images Jonathan Daniel /Allsport

FIGURE 10.2 ■ Hierarchical Models

Many psychologists now propose hierarchical models of intelligence that include elements found in the theories of both Spearman and Thurstone. Like Thurstone, hierarchical models propose separate factors that contribute independently to certain types of tests (for example, factor 1 contributes to tests 1–3, but not to tests 4–9). Like Spearman, these models also assume that each of the separate factors is influenced by an overall *g*.

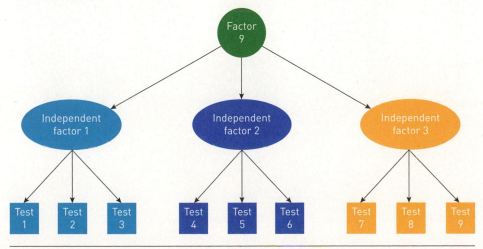

Carolina Hrejsa/Body Scientific Intl.

Fluid and Crystallized Intelligence

The evidence for general intelligence is compelling, but what kinds of cognitive abilities are involved? What features of the mind enable an individual to perform well across a wide range of tasks, from verbal ability to memory to reasoning? Raymond Cattell and John Horn have suggested that *g* contains two distinct components, fluid intelligence and crystallized intelligence (Cattell, 1963, 1998; Horn & Cattell, 1966). **Fluid intelligence** is a measure of your ability to reason abstractly, especially in novel situations, in ways that are relatively uninfluenced by experience. It's the type of intelligence that is probably determined primarily by biological or genetic factors, such as the speed of processing among the neurons in your brain (Deary, 2012; Schubert, Hagemann, & Frischkorn, 2017). **Crystallized intelligence** measures acquired knowledge and ability. You learn things about the world, such as how to solve arithmetic problems, and develop abilities based on your level of schooling and other cultural influences.

In most cases, intelligent behavior relies on both fluid and crystallized intelligence. For example, as you know from earlier chapters, people differ in their ability to perform several tasks at the same time. If I ask you to solve math problems while remembering a list of words, your ability to perform this dual task generally predicts how well you'll do on a standard test of intelligence (Engle, 2001; Unsworth et al., 2009). It's likely that you're born with a certain amount of conscious capacity (or mental resources), which is linked to fluid intelligence, but your performance also depends on what you've learned from experience. If you've learned to chunk or rehearse effectively (see Chapter 8), then your performance on the dual task will improve. These acquired strategies reflect crystallized intelligence, which develops with experience.

Notice that neither fluid nor crystallized intelligence needs to be conceptualized as a single "thing" that must exist somewhere in the brain or in the genetic code. In fact, fluid intelligence is often linked to a set of cognitive processes, typically referred to as executive functions, that are tapped well by standard types of intelligence tests (e.g., Engle, 2018). These executive functions include attention (the ability to focus on a task), cognitive control (the ability to shift among concurrent tasks), memory retrieval (the ability to retrieve information selectively that is relevant to the task), and information updating (the ability to remove or inhibit information that is no longer relevant or useful). It should not be surprising, then, that researchers have been unable to find a single gene (or even set of genes) that can be uniquely linked with intelligence (Sniekers et al., 2017). As suggested by the hierarchical models, intelligence is influenced by a number of factors.

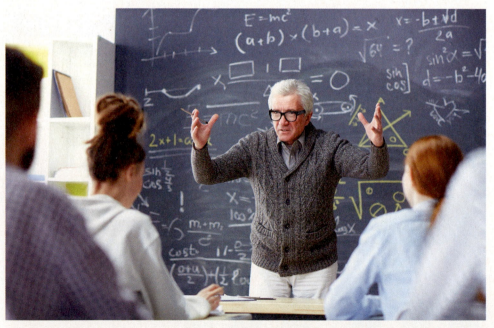

Crystallized intelligence measures acquired knowledge and ability. You learn things about the world, such as how to solve arithmetic problems, and develop abilities based on your level of schooling and other cultural influences.

iStockPhoto/shironosov

The distinction between fluid and crystallized intelligence is also important because it helps to explain how mental abilities change with age and across different cultures (E. Hunt, 2011; Salthouse, 2012). As you'll see later in the chapter, fluid and crystallized intelligence should change in somewhat different ways as we age. There are also striking differences in performance on psychometric tests of mental ability across different cultures and socioeconomic classes. These differences can't be easily explained from the perspective of general intelligence, unless we assume that an important part of general intelligence is acquired from experience. Distinguishing between fluid and crystallized intelligence can help explain how people who are born with the same amount of natural (fluid) intelligence can end up performing quite differently on tests of mental ability.

Multiple Intelligences

Let's pause momentarily and return to Larry Steinway, that fictional lightning calculator we met earlier. After reading the previous sections, what do you think psychologists with a psychometric bent would have to say about Larry's intelligence? How does someone with a highly specialized skill—lightning calculation—but with otherwise impaired mental abilities fit into these views of intelligence? In some respects Larry has a fast brain, but it's highly doubtful he could read a map very well or solve a complicated analogy problem. We can be sure that Larry will not perform well on a standardized battery of tests, which means that his assigned value of *g* will be far lower than average.

Consider also the gifted athlete, who soars high above the basketball rim but has trouble reading their daughter's nursery rhymes. Or the respected mathematical wizard, full professor at a major university, who has trouble matching their shoes, let alone their socks, in the morning. These are stereotypes, of course, but the point to be made is that people sometimes show specialized skills or abilities that stand alone and are not representative of a general ability. Spectacular skill can be shown in one area accompanied by profound deficits in another. Perhaps more important, these selective skills are often in areas not traditionally covered by commonly used intelligence tests.

Gardner's Case Study Approach

Howard Gardner (1983, 1993) argues that traditional conceptions of intelligence need to be broadened to include special abilities or talents. He rejects the idea that intelligence can be adequately captured through the analysis of test performance (as used by the psychometric approach). Rather than searching for a single ability called intelligence, we should understand that human behavior is rich in selective talents and abilities: We need a theory of **multiple intelligences**, not a method for discovering a single underlying *g*. *An* intelligence (rather than *the* intelligence) is defined as the ability to solve problems that matter in a specific cultural setting (Walters & Gardner, 1986). Although Gardner believes each of these separate intelligences may be rooted in the biology of the brain (see Shearer & Karanian, 2017), each can be expressed in a variety of ways, depending on one's culture. When average people around the world are asked to talk about their personal conceptions of intelligence, they almost always describe intelligence in terms of multiple factors or dimensions (Sternberg & Kaufman, 1998).

Rather than studying intelligent behavior in the laboratory, Gardner uses a case study approach. He studies reports of particular individuals with special abilities or talents, such as superior musicians, poets, or scientists. He's also looked extensively at the effects of damage to the brain. He's noted, for example, instances in which brain damage affects one kind of ability, such as reasoning and problem solving, yet leaves other abilities, such as musical skill, intact. Based on his research, Gardner (1999; H. Gardner & Moran, 2006) has identified what he believes to be at least eight distinct kinds of intelligence.

1. *Musical intelligence*: the type of ability displayed by gifted musicians or child prodigies

2. *Bodily-kinesthetic intelligence*: the type of ability shown by gifted athletes, dancers, or surgeons who have great control over body movements

3. *Logical-mathematical intelligence*: the type of ability displayed by superior scientists and logical problem solvers

4. *Linguistic intelligence*: the type of ability shown by great writers or poets who can express themselves verbally

5. *Spatial intelligence*: the type of ability shown by those with superior navigation skills or an ability to visualize spatial scenes

6. *Interpersonal intelligence*: the type of ability shown by those who can easily infer other people's moods, temperaments, or intentions and motivations

7. *Intrapersonal intelligence*: the ability shown by those who have great insight into their own feelings and emotions

8. *Naturalist intelligence*: the ability to observe and interact with diverse species in nature; the type of ability shown by a biologist or environmentalist

Notice that some forms of intelligence, as described by Gardner, are covered well by conventional tests of mental ability. Psychometric approaches focus extensively on logical-mathematical intelligence and to some extent on linguistic and spatial intelligence. Moreover, as discussed earlier, some researchers who use the psychometric approach, including Thurstone, have argued that it's important to distinguish among distinct and independent types of intelligence. But researchers who conceptualize intelligence in this way rarely, if ever, concentrate on intelligences such as musical ability or great athletic skill. The multiple-intelligences approach considerably broadens the conceptualization of intelligence.

The multiple-intelligences approach also fits well with everyday views on intelligence. Most people readily accept the idea of multiple intelligences. Gardner's theory has also had a large impact in educational settings. Many schools have designed educational programs around individual students' strengths and weaknesses among the different measured intelligences (e.g., Denny, 2010). Similar approaches could be applied to workloads in business and industry. Yet critics question how much scientific evidence actually supports the theory (E. Hunt, 2011); in fact, as Gardner (2016) readily admits, "most psychologists, and particularly most psychometricians, have never warmed to the theory" (p. 169). Part of the problem is the extensive evidence for an overarching *g*, but Gardner also never developed rigorous ways to measure or test the different intelligences. Little empirical evidence actually supports the theory as a whole, and those studies that have attempted validation have yielded inconsistent results (e.g., Visser et al., 2006).

Some individuals possess a high level of body-kinesthetic intelligence.

Don Arnold / Contributor via Getty Images

Multiple Intelligences: Sternberg's Triarchic Theory

Robert Sternberg's **triarchic theory** of intelligence also proposes that the study of intelligence can be expanded into more practical and applied domains. Sternberg was trained as a cognitive psychologist. As a result, he believes it's important to understand the mental operations behind the planning and execution of specialized tasks. But he also believes any complete account of intelligence needs to address behavior outside of the laboratory. For example, what is the form of intelligence that enables people to think creatively about problems that arise in everyday life? Furthermore, how does intelligence relate to the practical experience of the individual? Consequently, he accepts the idea that there may be multiple kinds of intelligence. *Triarchic* roughly means "ruled by threes," and not surprisingly, Sternberg's conceptualization of intelligence is divided into three major parts (Sternberg, 1985, 1988).

Sternberg believes that any complete theory of intelligence must refer in some way to basic analytic skills. Some people are simply better than others at processing information. They're good at representing (or seeing) problems in the right way, and they can generate effective strategies for solutions. People with lots of **analytical intelligence** tend to perform well on conventional tests that measure reasoning and logical-mathematical ability (such as the SAT). Because most psychometric tests of intelligence require these kinds of abilities, people who are high in analytic intelligence tend to be assigned a high *g*, for general intelligence. If you know people who perform well in school or who claim to be highly intelligent based on a standardized test, they are likely to score high on analytic intelligence.

Sternberg proposes a second kind of intelligence, **creative intelligence**, that expresses how well people can create, invent, and discover. Performing well on a standardized intelligence test does not guarantee creativity or mean you can apply the skills you've mastered in a new way. The world is full of people who are good in school, or who perform well on standardized tests, but who can't seem to think their way out of a paper bag. They lack creativity and seem to have trouble applying what they've learned (Sternberg, 1985).

Finally, people differ in **practical intelligence**, a measure of how well people can take ideas and put them into everyday practice. People with practical intelligence solve problems that are uniquely posed by their cultural surroundings. They mold themselves well into existing settings, and they can select new environments, if required, that provide a better fit for their talents. In a nutshell, these individuals have "street smarts"—they size up situations well and act accordingly. You probably know someone who seems to lack analytic skills—who fails school or drops out—but still manages to succeed in life.

Sternberg's triarchic theory represents another attempt to broaden the concept of intelligence. Like Howard Gardner's approach, Sternberg's theory deals with behaviors and skills that aren't normally covered by the standard psychometric approach. Triarchic theory, like Gardner's theory, can be applied in classroom settings where particular types of intelligence can be nurtured and developed (Sternberg & The Rainbow Project Collaborators, 2006). Sternberg and his research teams have also conducted rigorous studies to validate his approach—in the laboratory, in classrooms, and in many different cultures (see Sternberg, 2011, 2015). Still, even if it is desirable to broaden our conceptualization of intelligence, that doesn't mean that psychometric approaches to intelligence have no value. As you'll see in the next section, psychometric tests are extremely useful in predicting future performance. For a summary of the different views of intelligence, see Concept Review 10.1.

CONCEPT REVIEW 10.1
VIEWS OF INTELLIGENCE

Approach	Example(s)	Intelligence Is . . .
Psychometric	Spearman's factor *g* Hierarchical models	A mental capacity that can be understood by analyzing performance on mental tests.
Biological	Mental speed Fluid intelligence	Reflected in the speed of mental processing and in cognitive processes that are relatively uninfluenced by experience.

(Continued)

Approach	Example(s)	Intelligence Is...
Environmental	Acquired knowledge Crystallized intelligence	Based on life experiences, such as schooling and cultural influences.
Multiple intelligences	Gardner's multiple intelligences	Eight proposed abilities that permit an individual to solve problems or fashion products that are of consequence in a particular setting.
Triarchic theory	Analytic intelligence Creative intelligence Practical intelligence	The ability to process information analytically; the ability to cope with novel tasks; the ability to solve problems posed by unique cultural surroundings.

(Continued)

KNOWLEDGE CHECK 10.1

For each of the following statements, pick the term that best describes the approach to conceptualizing intelligence. Choose your answers from the following: *psychometric, multiple intelligences, triarchic theory.* (You will find the answers in the Appendix.)

1. Mitsuko has street smarts—she can mold herself successfully in any situation: _____

2. Jeremy flunks most of his classes, but he's a brilliant pianist, so he considers himself to be highly intelligent: _____

3. Lucy has just finished an exhaustive battery of mental tests; she's waiting to find out if she has a high *g*: _____

4. Natalie wants to understand the concept of intelligence, so she has signed up for a class on factor analysis: _____

5. Verne shows great insight into the feelings of others, which makes him score high on tests of interpersonal intelligence: _____

6. Shelia scored a perfect 4.0 grade point average in high school but has trouble applying what she's learned to new situations. She's beginning to feel that she might not be so intelligent after all: _____

MEASURING INDIVIDUAL DIFFERENCES

We've now considered how psychologists have tried to conceptualize intelligence. However, we have yet to discuss how individual differences are actually measured. People differ. Pick just about any attribute—height, weight, friendliness, intelligence—and you're going to find a scattering, or range, of individual values. Some people are tall, some are short; some people are friendly, some are not. As discussed in the previous section, the study of individual differences is important because many psychological concepts, including intelligence and personality, are defined and measured by individual differences.

If we can measure how you compare to others on a psychological dimension, we can then assess your current and future capabilities. For example, **achievement tests** measure your current knowledge or competence in a particular subject (such as math or reading). Researchers or teachers can use the results of an achievement test to assess the effectiveness of a learning procedure or a curriculum in a school. We can also use individual differences to make predictions about the future, such as how well you can be expected to do in your chosen profession or whether you're likely to succeed in college. **Aptitude tests** measure the ability to learn in a particular area, to acquire the knowledge needed for success in a given domain. Aptitude test results can be used to help choose a career path or even to decide whether to take up something as a hobby, such as car mechanics or the violin.

The Components of a Good Test

What are the characteristics of a "good" test—that is, a test that can be expected to provide a good measure of individual differences? Given the need to measure these differences, it's crucial that the measurement device provides information that is scientifically useful. Researchers generally agree on the three characteristics needed for a good test: *reliability, validity,* and *standardization*. Please note that these are characteristics of the test, not of the person taking the test.

Reliability

The first test characteristic, **reliability**, is a measure of the *consistency* of the test results. Reliable tests produce similar scores from one administration to the next. Suppose we want to measure creativity, and we design a test that produces a score from 0 to 100 on a creativity scale. We measure Mateo, and he gets a score of 13; we measure Cynthia, and she tops out at 96. Clearly, we conclude, Cynthia is more creative than Mateo. But is she really? To be sure about the results, we administer the test again and find that the scores reverse. Sadly, our creativity test lacks reliability—it doesn't produce consistent scores from one administration to the next.

It's important for a test to be reliable so we can draw firm conclusions from the results. Cynthia might be more creative than Mateo, but the difference in scores could also be due to an artifact, or failing, of the test. On this particular administration Cynthia scored higher, but that's no guarantee tomorrow's results will produce the same conclusion. One way to measure a test's reliability is to give it to the same group of individuals on two separate occasions. *Test–retest reliability* is then calculated by comparing the scores across the repeated administrations. Often, a correlation coefficient is computed that indicates how well performance on the second test can be predicted from performance on the first. The closer the test–retest correlation comes to a perfect +1.00, the higher the reliability of the test.

Validity

The second test characteristic, **validity**, tells us how well a test measures what it's supposed to measure. A test can yield reliable data—consistent results across repeated administrations—yet not truly measure the psychological characteristic of interest. If a test of creativity is based on the measurement of shoe size, then the data are likely to be reliable but not valid. Shoe size isn't going to change much from one measurement to the next, but it has little to do with creativity.

Actually, there are several different forms of validity, three of which we discuss here. *Content validity* measures whether the content of a test samples broadly across the domain of interest. If you're trying to get a general measure of creativity, your test should not be limited to one kind of creativity, such as artistic creativity. For the test to have a high degree of content validity, it should probably measure artistic, verbal, mechanical, mathematical, and other kinds of creativity.

Sometimes psychologists are interested in designing a test that predicts some future outcome, such as job performance or success in school. For a test to have *predictive validity*, it must predict this outcome adequately. The SAT is a well-known case in point. The SAT is designed to predict success in college. So to assess its predictive validity, we need to ask whether the SAT predicts college performance as expressed through a measure such as college grade point average. Various studies have shown that the correlation between SAT scores and the grade point averages of college freshmen is somewhere around +.50 (Kunkel & Hezlett, 2010). Statistically, this means that we can predict college performance with the SAT to some degree, but our predictive abilities are not perfect.

A third kind of validity, *construct validity*, measures how well a test applies to a particular theoretical construct. Suppose we have a theory of creativity that's developed well enough to generate a wide variety of predictions—how creative people act, the kinds of books they read, their susceptibility to mental disorders, and so on. To have high construct validity, our test must predict performance on each of these separate indices of creativity, rather than on just one. If a test has high construct validity, its scores tend to vary in ways that are predicted by the theory. So if the theory predicts that creative people are more likely to suffer from depression, then people who score high on the creativity test should have a greater likelihood of depression.

Standardization

The third general characteristic of a good test of individual differences is **standardization**. When you take a test such as the SAT, or any national aptitude or achievement test, you quickly learn that the testing procedures are extremely rigid. If you're taking the test in person, you can break the test seal only at a certain time, the instructions are spoken in a monotone by a very serious administrator, and your yellow number 2 pencil must be put down at an exact tick of the clock. Online versions are comparably standardized—the instructions and timing remain constant for all. These tests are *standardized*, which means the testing, scoring, and interpretation procedures remain the same across all administrations of the test. Standardization is important because it guarantees that all test takers will be treated the same.

In fact, the proper interpretation of a test score absolutely demands standardization. Remember, we're concerned with individual differences—it doesn't make much sense to compare two or more scores if different instructions or scoring procedures have been used across the test sessions. A person's score on a test of individual differences can be understood only with respect to a reference group, often called a *norm group*, and everyone within the group must receive the same test and administration procedures. We'll return to this notion of a norm reference group momentarily when we consider the concept of the IQ. For a summary of the components of a good test, see Concept Review 10.2.

Students regularly take standardized tests that measure achievement or aptitude.

iStockPhoto/artisteer

CONCEPT REVIEW 10.2
COMPONENTS OF A GOOD TEST

Component	Description	Example
Reliability	Consistency of test results	Taking a test twice should yield similar scores each time.
Validity	Does the test measure what it's supposed to?	Among several measures of validity are the content, predictive, and construct measures.
—Content	The degree to which a test samples broadly across the domain of interest	The items on a test of creativity should cover different types of creativity, such as artistic, mathematical, and verbal.

Component	Description	Example
—Predictive	The degree to which a test predicts some future outcome	Performance on the ACT® should correlate with later performance in college classes.
—Construct	The degree to which a test taps into a particular theoretical construct	Performance on a creativity test should correlate with other characteristics or indices thought to be associated with creativity.
Standardization	Testing, scoring, and interpretation procedures are the same across all administrations of the test.	Everyone who takes the SAT® receives the same instructions, and has to complete the test within the same specified period of time.

IQ: The Intelligence Quotient

The most famous index of intelligence is the **IQ**, or **intelligence quotient**. The IQ score comes from performance on a test, and it may well be the most widely applied psychological measure in the world. Yet how can a single number be used to measure intelligence?

This might strike you as odd given our earlier discussion about multiple intelligences and the need to establish a wide variety of criteria for what it means to be intelligent. The key to appreciating the IQ, and to understanding why it is so widely applied, is in the concept of *validity*: What is the IQ designed to measure, and how successfully does it achieve its goal? It turns out that IQ does a reasonably good job of predicting what it was designed to predict.

The intelligence quotient traces back about a hundred years to the work of the French psychologist Alfred Binet and his associate Théodore Simon. In 1904, Binet and Simon were commissioned by the French government to develop a test that would identify children who were considered "dull"—specifically, children who would have a difficult time grasping concepts in school. It was the French government's intention to help these children, once they were identified, through special schooling. The mission of the test was primarily practical, not theoretical; the charge was to develop a test that would accurately measure individual differences in future academic performance.

Mental Age

Not surprisingly, Binet and Simon designed their test to measure the skills that are needed in school—such as memory, reasoning, and verbal comprehension. The goal was to determine the **mental age**—or what Binet and Simon called the *mental level*—of the child, which was defined as the chronological age that best fit the child's current level of intellectual performance. Mental age is typically calculated by comparing a child's test score with the average scores for different age groups. For example, let's suppose that an average 8-year-old is able to compare two objects from memory, recognize parts of a picture that are missing, count backward from 20 to 0, and give the correct day and time. An average 12-year-old might be able to define abstract words, name 60 words in 3 minutes, and discover the meaning of a scrambled sentence. If Jenny, who is 8, is able to solve the problems of the typical 12-year-old, she would be assigned a mental age of 12.

Notice that mental age and chronological age do not have to be the same, although they will be on average (an average 8-year-old should solve problems at the average 8-year-old level). Because intelligence tests are given to lots of children, it's possible to determine average performance for a given age group and then to determine the appropriate mental age for a

Alfred Binet was commissioned by the French government to develop a test that would help teachers identify students who might have a difficult time grasping academic concepts.

Photo 12 / Contributor via Getty Images

particular child. By using mental age, Binet and Simon (1916/1973) were able to identify the slow and quick learners and to recommend appropriate curriculum adjustments.

In the first two decades of the 20th century, Binet and Simon's intelligence test was revised several times and was ultimately translated into English for use in North America. The most popular American version was developed by psychologist Lewis Terman at Stanford University; this test later became known as the *Stanford–Binet* test of intelligence. It was also Terman who popularized the idea of an intelligence quotient (based on an idea originally proposed by German psychologist William Stern), which is defined as follows:

$$\text{Intelligence Quotient (IQ)} = \text{Mental Age} / \text{Chronological Age} \times 100$$

The IQ is a useful measure because it establishes an easy-to-understand baseline for "average" intelligence—people of average intelligence will have an IQ of 100 because their mental age will always be equal to their chronological age. People with IQs greater than 100 will be above average in intelligence; those below 100 will be below average in intelligence.

Deviation IQ

Defining IQ simply in terms of the *ratio* of mental age to chronological age has some problems. For one thing, it's hard to compare the meaning of the ratio across different ages. If a 5-year-old performed like a 7-year-old, the 5-year-old would be given an IQ of 140 (7 / 5 × 100 = 140). But if a 10-year-old scored at the level of a 12-year-old, the 10-year-old IQ would be only 120 (12 / 10 × 100 = 120). Both are performing at levels 2 years above their chronological age, but they receive very different IQs. Moreover, how much sense does it make to argue that a 30-year-old who performs comparably to a 60-year-old should be given a vastly higher IQ (60 / 30 × 100 = 200)?

To overcome this problem, most modern intelligence tests retain the term IQ but define it in terms of a *deviation*, or difference, rather than as a ratio. A **deviation IQ** still uses 100 as a baseline average, but an IQ of 100 is redefined as the average score in the distribution of scores for people of a certain age. A particular person's IQ is then calculated by determining where the individual's test score "sits," relative to the average score obtained by others in the same age group. (Note that *age* is the norm group used for defining the concept of intelligence.) Figure 10.3 shows a frequency distribution of scores that might result from administering a test such as the Stanford–Binet to large groups of people. The average of the distribution is 100, and approximately half of the test takers will produce scores above 100 and the other half below 100.

One of the characteristics of modern intelligence tests is their tendency to produce very regular and smooth distributions of scores. Not only will the most common score be 100 (by definition), but

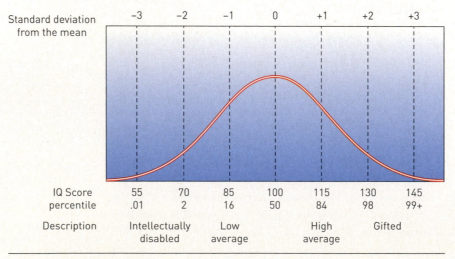

FIGURE 10.3 ■ **The Distribution of IQ Scores**

IQ scores for a given age group are typically distributed in a bell-shaped, or normal, curve. The average and most frequently occurring IQ score is defined as 100. Roughly 68% of the test takers in this age group receive IQ scores between 115 and 85, one standard deviation above and below the mean. People labeled "gifted," with an IQ of 130 or above, or "intellectually disabled," with an IQ of 70 or below, occur infrequently in the overall population.

Illustrated by Sarah Yeh

roughly 68% of the people who take the test will receive an IQ score between 85 and 115. With a distribution like the one shown in Figure 10.3, we can easily calculate the percentage of the population likely to receive a particular IQ score. You will find, for example, that approximately 98% of the people who take the test will receive a score at or below 130. Notice once again that IQ in this case is defined in terms of how a score compares to the scores of other people in the same age group.

Extremes of Intelligence

Tests such as the Stanford–Binet or the related Wechsler Adult Intelligence Scale have been given to thousands and thousands of people. Most people fall within a normal or average range, which covers scores from about 70 to about 130. Individuals who fall above or below this range represent *extremes* in intelligence.

Intellectual Disability

A score of 70 or below on a standard IQ test is associated with the diagnosis of an **intellectual disability** (formerly known as *mental retardation*), although other factors (such as daily living skills) contribute to any diagnosis. An intellectual disability must be diagnosed prior to age 18, which means that limitations in intellectual functioning arising during adulthood—for example, from brain damage—don't lead to the diagnosis (American Association on Intellectual and Developmental Disabilities, 2010). Individuals with intellectual disabilities have significant limitations in adaptive behavior, including conceptual (e.g., literacy), social (interpersonal), and practical (personal care) skills.

What causes intellectual disabilities? There are many possible causes, some genetic and some environmental. Down syndrome, for example, is typically associated with low IQ scores and is caused by a genetic abnormality—usually an extra chromosome. Another genetic condition is phenylketonuria (PKU), a metabolic disorder associated with a defective enzyme that can lead to a disability if not corrected early in development. Environmental factors during development, such as inadequate nutrition or illness, can also contribute. In Chapter 4, we talked about the potentially damaging effects of teratogens, such as excessive use of alcohol or other drugs, on the intellectual capacity of the developing fetus. There are probably hundreds of potential causes for extremely low IQ scores, and, once again, a low IQ score does not guarantee a diagnosis of an intellectual disability.

With the proper support, people with intellectual disabilities are able to lead independent lives and may not even be recognized by the community as having any serious mental deficiencies.

Digital Light Source / Contributor via Getty Images

Although intellectual disabilities are assumed to affect somewhere between 1% and 3% of the population, the vast majority of these people (perhaps 85%) are only mildly affected. With the proper support, most are able to lead independent lives and may not even be recognized by the community as having any serious mental deficiencies. By no means does an intellectual disability imply an inability to learn or prosper. Even the roughly 15% of cases who are diagnosed as moderately to profoundly disabled can lead satisfying and fulfilling lives. Numerous agencies such as the American Association on Intellectual and Developmental Disabilities provide useful information and help to support ongoing research (check out the AAIDD website here: www.aaidd.org).

Giftedness

At the other end of the IQ scale are those considered **gifted**, with IQs at or above approximately 130. Many studies have tracked the intellectual and social accomplishments of gifted children, partly as a means of checking on the validity of the IQ measure. One of the most famous of these studies was begun in the 1920s by Lewis Terman (1925; Terman & Ogden, 1947). Terman was interested in whether children identified early in life as gifted would be likely to achieve success throughout their lives. The answer, on average, was "Yes"—Terman's gifted subjects earned more college degrees than average, made more money, wrote more books, generated more successful patents, and so on. Similar results have been found in other studies, most recently for adolescents with exceptional mathematical or verbal reasoning ability (e.g., Lubinski, 2009, 2016).

Interestingly, the kids studied by Terman (often known collectively as the "Termites") turned out to be emotionally stable and socially skilled as well, which is surprising given the bookworm stereotype that people have of highly intelligent people. Many had successful marriages, and their divorce rate was lower than that of the general population (Terman, 1954). More recent studies have generally confirmed this conclusion, although some evidence indicates that those with gifted IQs, particularly those with high verbal ability, are more likely to report psychological problems (see Karpinski et al., 2018). In each of these cases, however, the connection between IQ and outcomes is correlational, so we need to exercise caution in drawing conclusions. In such studies, there are apt to be many potentially confounding factors. To list just one example, high-IQ children tend to come from economically privileged households, which might help account for later success and reported emotional stability (Tomlinson-Keasey & Little, 1990).

Finally, there are *savants*, who may show limited intellectual or social functioning overall but have tremendous "gifts" in a particular domain. Calendrical savants, for example, have the amazing ability to name the weekday corresponding to a particular date, often in a matter of seconds (R. Cowan et al., 2003). Psychologists have studied savants, and tracked their abilities over time, but remain uncertain about the origins of their remarkable abilities. There's some evidence that the ability is innate, produced by some kind of atypical brain organization or genetic information (Nurmi et al., 2003), but other studies have found no abnormalities in the brains of savants (R. Cowan & Frith, 2009). Savants are more likely to be male, and savant skills are often associated with disorders such as childhood autism (Heaton & Wallace, 2004). Experience probably plays a role in the development of the special skills, although many appear not to have been explicitly taught (R. Cowan & Frith, 2009). Whether most savants truly possess some kind of exceptional cognitive skill, or simply engage in extensive practice of a skill that is rewarded by their peers, remains an open question (Rieznik et al., 2017).

The Validity of Intelligence Testing

How valid is IQ as a measure of intellectual ability? Does it truly tap some hidden but powerful feature of the mind that accounts for individual differences? Does it adequately measure the ability to adapt and solve the problems of survival? Remember, here we use "validity" in the technical sense: How well does the test measure the thing that it's supposed to measure? To assess the validity of the IQ, then, we must ask: How well do the tests that produce IQ scores predict their criterion of interest?

The most widely applied intelligence tests today are the Stanford–Binet, the Wechsler Adult Intelligence Scale (WAIS), and the Wechsler Intelligence Scale for Children (WISC). These are not the only tests; in fact, if we combine intelligence tests with measures of scholastic aptitude, more than a hundred different tests are currently in use. Often these tests are given for the same reason that originally motivated Binet and Simon—to predict some kind of academic performance, usually grades in high school or college. From this perspective, IQ passes the validity test with flying colors: IQ, as measured by Stanford–Binet or the Wechsler tests, typically correlates about +.50 or higher with school grades (Ceci, 1991; C. Murray & Wren, 2003). Notice that the correlation isn't perfect, but it's reasonably high when you consider all of the uncontrolled factors that can affect grades in school (motivation, home environment, participation in extracurricular activities, and so on).

IQ scores, or measures of intelligence in general, actually predict a host of different outcomes. In addition to educational success, IQ successfully predicts performance on the job, training success, and leadership skills (Kunkel & Hezlett, 2010). You can even get a reasonable idea about people's health and longevity from knowing their IQ, at least on average (Batty et al., 2008). In one study, based on data collected from nearly a million Swedish men, the risk of dying in the 20 years that followed administration of an IQ test was closely related to the score. The risk of dying was about three times greater for those who scored in the lowest IQ group. Of course, it isn't your IQ score itself that is making you live or die—people with higher IQ scores are likely to make better health-related decisions (e.g., choosing not to smoke) and to avoid environments in which death by accident or homicide is likely.

Critics of IQ often point out that it fails to provide a broad index of intelligence. As we discussed earlier, it's proper to define intelligence broadly. There are many ways that people can fit successfully into their environments, and not all forms of multiple intelligence are measured by traditional IQ tests. This criticism has been widely recognized, however, and efforts have been made to develop tests that measure a variety of abilities. The influential tests of David Wechsler, for example, were developed in part to measure nonverbal aspects of intellectual ability. The Wechsler tests include not only verbal–mathematical questions of the type traditionally found on the Stanford–Binet test but also nonverbal questions requiring things such as the completion or rearrangement of pictures (see Figure 10.4). Performance is then broken down into a verbal IQ, a nonverbal (or "performance") IQ, and an overall IQ based on combining the verbal and nonverbal measures.

FIGURE 10.4 ■ Examples From the WAIS

The Wechsler Adult Intelligence Scale measures both verbal and nonverbal aspects of intellectual ability. Included here are samples of the various question types.

Wechsler Adult Intelligence Scale (WAIS)		
Test	**Description**	**Example**
Verbal scale		
Information	Taps general range of information.	On what continent in France?
Comprehension	Tests understanding of social conventions and ability to evaluate past experience.	Why are children required to go to school?
Arithmetic	Tests arithmetic reasoning through verbal problems.	How many hours will it take to drive 150 miles at 50 miles per hour?
Performance scale		
Block design	Tests ability to perceive and analyze patterns by presenting designs that must be copied with blocks.	Assemble blocks to match this design:
Picture arrangement	Tests understanding of social situations through a series of pictures that must be arranged in the right sequence to tell a story.	Put the pictures in the right order:
Object assembly	Tests ability to deal with part-to-whole relationships by presenting puzzle pieces that must be assembled to form a complete object.	Assemble the pieces into a complete object:

Source: From Weiten, W., *Psychology: Themes and Variations*, 3E.

Again, intelligence tests were originally designed to accomplish some specific result, such as predicting future academic performance, not to provide an index of true intellectual ability. So, if you develop a test to predict college performance, it probably isn't reasonable to expect it to predict creativity, originality, or the ability for deep thought. This also means that intelligence tests can potentially suffer from cultural limitations. A test designed to measure the abilities of high school students in suburbia may be less valid for students from the inner city or from a different region of the world. This doesn't mean that intelligence tests aren't useful—you just need to be aware of what the tests were designed to measure.

Labeling Effects

Another potentially serious criticism of IQ concerns labeling. You take a test as a child, your IQ is calculated by comparing your performance with that of other kids your age, and the score becomes part of your continuing academic record. Once the IQ label is applied—you're smart, you're below average, and so on—expectations are generated in those who have access to your score. A number of studies have shown that intelligence labels influence how teachers interact with their students in the classroom. There is often a kind of "rich get richer" and "poor get poorer" effect—the kids with the "smart" label are exposed to more educational opportunities and are treated with more respect, although sometimes a student's work ethic can be affected in a negative way; for example, children who have been told they're smart may have a poor tolerance for failure and avoid challenges (Dweck & Yeager, 2019). Similarly, things are often held back from the "slow" kids, so they're less likely to be exposed to factors that might nurture academic growth.

Labeling effects were particularly serious in the early decades of the 20th century when intelligence tests were first developed. Tests were widely administered—for example, to newly arriving immigrants and to all army recruits—before the impact of cultural and educational factors on test performance were well understood. As we'll discuss later, people can perform poorly on an intelligence test because the test has certain built-in biases with respect to language and cultural lifestyle. Imagine, for example, that as part of an intelligence test I asked you to identify the vegetable broccoli. Easy, but not if you were raised in a culture that did not include broccoli as part of its diet (see Shuttleworth-Edwards, 2016). In such a case, you would probably get the question wrong, but it wouldn't say anything about your intellectual or academic potential.

Researchers were not very sensitive to these concerns when intelligence tests were first developed. The result was that certain population groups, such as immigrants from southern and eastern Europe, generally performed poorly on these tests. Some psychologists even went so far as to label these immigrant groups "feebleminded" or "defective" based on their test performance. Immigration laws enacted in the

Within 24 hours of arriving at Ellis Island, immigrants were subjected to a variety of mental and physical examinations. Unfortunately, the exams were sometimes used to discriminate unfairly among population groups; at the time, administrators were simply not sensitive to the influence of cultural factors on test performance.

MPI / Stringer via Getty Images

1920s discriminated against poorly performing groups by reducing immigration quotas. Psychologists are now more aware of test bias and have worked very hard to reduce its influence on test performance.

Individual Differences Related to Intelligence

To end our discussion of the measurement of individual differences, we'll briefly consider three psychological characteristics that are often associated with the topic of intelligence: creativity, emotional intelligence, and tacit knowledge. None is necessarily related to *g* (general intelligence).

Creativity

The term **creativity** refers to the ability to generate ideas that are original and novel and have value to the individual or group (Hennessey & Amabile, 2010). Creative thinkers think in unusual ways, which means they can look at the usual and express it in an unusual way. Creative thinkers tend to see the "big picture" and are able to find connections among things that others might not see. Importantly, however, it's not just the generation of new and different ideas that makes one creative; those ideas must also be useful and relevant—they must potentially have adaptive value.

How is creativity measured? Psychologists have devised a number of ways to measure individual differences in creative ability. One popular technique is to supply a group of unrelated words, or unrelated objects in a picture, and ask a person to generate as many connections among the items as possible (Mednick, 1962; Torrance, 1981). Try it yourself: Take these words—*food, catcher, hot*—and try to think of a fourth word (or words) that relates to all three. Measures like these reveal individual differences among people—some find this task to be quite easy, while others find it extremely hard. Moreover, performance on these creativity tests can then be correlated with other abilities, such as IQ or job success, to see if there is a connection. Researchers are also actively exploring possible brain mechanisms for creativity—for example, there is some evidence that people are most creative when they are in mental states associated with reduced levels of the neurotransmitter norepinephrine (Heilman, 2016). Most of this work remains speculative at this point, however, and much remains to be learned.

What's the relation between creativity and intelligence? When intelligence is conceptualized in a broad way, creativity fits in nicely as a part of general intellectual ability. (You'll remember, for instance, that Sternberg's triarchic theory includes the concept of creative intelligence.) However, there isn't a straightforward relationship between creativity and IQ. Correlations between them are usually low (Horn, 1976; Kee, 2005), although positive correlations have been found between creativity and some measures of verbal intelligence (Silvia, 2008). Traditional IQ tests don't really measure creative thinking in a direct way, so perhaps it's not surprising that the correlations are often low (J. C. Kaufman, 2015).

Emotional Intelligence

The second psychological characteristic, emotional intelligence, is gaining popularity among psychologists and is worthy of brief note. **Emotional intelligence** is the ability to perceive, understand, and express emotion (Mayer & Salovey, 1997; Salovey & Mayer, 1990). The concept applies to perceiving and understanding the emotions of others as well as to understanding and controlling one's own emotions. Emotions, as you'll see in Chapter 12, play a large role in behavior, so it's clearly useful to manage and express them appropriately.

People who score high on emotional intelligence can read others' emotions well and tend to be empathetic as a result. They're good at managing conflict, both their own and the conflicts of others. Not surprisingly, emotional intelligence is believed to be an excellent predictor of success in career and social settings. In fact, some have argued that emotional intelligence may be a more important predictor of success in life than more traditional conceptions of intelligence (Goleman, 1995). It is possible to measure emotional intelligence in a number of ways, although most tests resemble self-report questionnaires of the type used in many intelligence tests. The net result is a value on an emotional intelligence "scale" that can then be used to predict other measures of performance. It is also common to distinguish between trait and ability emotional intelligence, with the former measuring how well an individual understands emotions and emotional functioning and the latter measuring typical behaviors in emotion-relevant situations (see O'Connor et al., 2019).

Measures of emotional intelligence do seem to predict success in a variety of contexts, from the workplace, to personal relationships, and even to investor behavior (Brackett et al., 2011). Tests of emotional intelligence have been applied across the world, in dozens of different cultures, and do a reasonable job of predicting job performance (Zeidner et al., 2008). There's clearly overlap between emotional intelligence and the broad conceptions of intelligence proposed by others (e.g., Gardner and Sternberg), but the similarities and differences have yet to be worked out in a systematic way (G. Matthews et al., 2005). It could be that emotional intelligence fits snugly into the psychometrics-based hierarchical models that we discussed earlier, perhaps as one of the various subfactors that sit below the general factor g (Mayer et al., 2016). Research on emotional intelligence is ongoing, but the concept is proving useful to psychologists and is widely applied in the workplace (see Cherniss et al., 2006).

Tacit Knowledge

Finally, most intelligence tests contain questions that are specific and well defined. You must have certain knowledge to perform well; there are right and wrong answers for each question. There's also usually only one method for solving the problem. But to succeed in many areas, such as on a job, you often need knowledge and abilities that are not so cut and dried—unspoken rules and strategies that are rarely, if ever, taught formally. This kind of unspoken practical know-how is called **tacit knowledge**.

Tacit knowledge is rarely assessed on standardized tests of intelligence. It's a kind of procedural how-to knowledge that isn't written in books. Instead, it comes primarily from experience—from watching and analyzing the behavior of others. Moreover, people clearly differ in their grasp of job-relevant tacit knowledge. Some managers understand the rules for maximizing the performance of their subordinates better than others do. When tacit knowledge is actually measured, by asking people on the job to make ratings about imaginary job scenarios, it seems to do a reasonably good job of predicting job performance. Sternberg and Wagner (1993) found that tacit knowledge correlates significantly with salary, performance ratings, and the prestige of the business or institution where the person is employed. Tacit knowledge also improves with work experience, which is what you would expect. However, tacit knowledge may bear little relation to general ability, as measured by g. In fact, in some cultures negative correlations have been reported—the higher the index of tacit knowledge, the lower the measure of g—suggesting that practical knowledge is sometimes emphasized at the expense of academic skills (Cianciolo et al., 2006; Sternberg & Hedlund, 2002). This is a somewhat controversial conclusion, though, as g is widely believed to contribute to performance on most, if not all, types of cognitive tasks (Gottfredson, 2003; E. Hunt, 2011).

The idea that it's useful to develop and use multiple strategies to perform successfully is almost certain to be true. We soak up knowledge where we can; and, as we've seen in earlier chapters, modeling others is an important vehicle for guiding behavior. As it stands now, however, the concept of tacit knowledge, while intuitively plausible, remains somewhat slippery scientifically. Critics have questioned whether tacit knowledge is really anything different from job knowledge (Schmidt & Hunter, 1993). Although important, measurements of tacit knowledge may simply be indices of what's been learned on the job.

PRACTICAL SOLUTIONS: CAN MOZART'S MUSIC MAKE YOU SMARTER?

People are always looking for ways to boost intelligence, especially new parents, who want to do everything possible to improve their newborn's cognitive functioning. Perhaps you were exposed to Baby Einstein as a child, a line of interactive multimedia products designed to boost language and cognitive ability. Listening to the music of Mozart is also claimed to make you smarter, or at least improve your functioning on cognitive tasks. Some years ago, the governor of Georgia actually budgeted money for cassettes of classical music, which could be given to the parents of each new infant born in the state. Other states have considered requiring that classical music be played in all elementary schools. Most agree that Mozart was a genius, but can his music really make you smarter?

The answer is "yes and no, although primarily no." In initial work on this topic, undergraduates showed a significant improvement in their average spatial-reasoning scores after listening to 10 minutes of Mozart's *Sonata for Two Pianos in D Major*. Control undergraduates, who spent the

Mozart was a musical genius, but can his music really make you smarter?

same amount of time in silence or listening to relaxation tapes, failed to show similar improvements (Rauscher et al., 1993). Some researchers have had trouble repeating this so-called Mozart effect (K. M. Steele et al., 1999), but a number of laboratories have now confirmed the basic finding (see Pietschnig et al., 2010, for a review). If you spend time listening to some elegant classical music, rather than sitting in silence, you're likely to perform slightly better on some measures of cognitive ability.

What causes the improvement? One possibility is that Mozart's music, because of its creative and innovative structure, activates the same portions of the brain that handle spatial-reasoning tasks (Rauscher et al., 1995; Verrusio et al., 2015). On the other hand, maybe people simply enjoy listening to music and are therefore in a better mood, or more alert, when they're asked to perform the reasoning tasks. To conclude that Mozart is responsible for the improvement would require experiments to rule out alternative interpretations. In fact, it turns out that listening to a Stephen King short story can also produce a Mozart-like effect, as long as it's enjoyable to the listeners (Nantais & Schellenberg, 1999). Moreover, slow and sad selections of classical music fail to produce improvements in spatial reasoning, suggesting that it's indeed an enhancement in mood or arousal that is responsible for the effect (W. F. Thompson et al., 2001).

The Mozart effect is a classic example of how psychological findings can be overblown, or misused, by the popular press (Waterhouse, 2006). Although the original findings probably have some scientific validity, the improvements were always relatively small and lasted only for brief periods. Moreover, the improvements were only shown on particular kinds of spatial-reasoning tasks and not on others. There's certainly no evidence to suggest that listening to 10 minutes of Mozart, or Stephen King, produces lasting improvements in general intelligence. Listening to something you enjoy simply makes you feel better, and you're likely to perform better on certain tasks, but it doesn't really make you smarter in any lasting or significant way.

By the way, baby media don't seem to have any positive effect on language development either. In one study, 12- to 18-month-old children were exposed to a best-selling DVD that promised improved language skills. The babies watched the video at least five times a week for four weeks but showed no improvement in language skills compared to a control group that didn't watch the video. In fact, the video babies actually learned fewer new words than a group of babies who were taught the same words from their parents (DeLoache et al., 2010). The age-old caveat remains true today: Buyer beware!

Check what you know about the measurement of individual differences by answering the following questions. (You will find the answers in the Appendix.)

1. For each of the following statements, pick the test characteristic that is most appropriate. Choose from the following: *reliability, standardization, validity*.

   a. Donna performs poorly on the SAT, so she takes it again and finds herself performing poorly again: _____

   b. Larry has devised a new test of intelligence, but he finds that it predicts nothing about school performance or success on the job: _____

   c. Chei-Wui wants to see how consistent scores are on his new intelligence test, so he correlates answers across repeated administrations of the test: _____

   d. Robert's new job is to administer the GRE˙. He is very careful to keep the testing and scoring procedures the same for everybody who takes the test: _____

2. Decide whether each of the following statements is true or false.

   a. Lucinda has a mental age of 8 and an IQ of 160—this means that she must be 5 years old chronologically. *True or False?*

   b. Average IQ, based on the deviation IQ method, varies with chronological age. *True or False?*

   c. Lewis has just scored below 70 on his IQ test, which means that he will soon be labeled with an intellectual disability. *True or False?*

   d. Creativity increases with intellectual ability, as measured by IQ. *True or False?*

DISCOVERING THE SOURCES OF INTELLIGENCE

We've seen that people differ, and we've considered some of the ways to measure those differences. We've also discussed methods for conceptualizing the differences—there may be differences in *g*; or, perhaps, people may lack one or more of the special talents needed for intelligent performance. But what accounts for these differences? Why is one person's *g* higher or lower than another person's *g*? Can anything be done about these differences, or are they fixed in stone?

There are essentially two ways to explain individual differences in intelligence. First, you can appeal to biology, particularly the internal *genetic code*—those strands of DNA that determine eye color, thickness of hair, and possibly *g*. According to this view, intellectual potential is established at conception through some particularly fortunate (or unfortunate) combination of genes. Alternatively, you can appeal to an external cause, specifically the *environment*. Variations in *g* might be attributable to one's past experiences—perhaps Malik Tarpy scores high on IQ tests because he was reinforced for intellectual pursuits or went to excellent schools; perhaps Larry Steinway performs poorly because as a child he was exposed to toxins (such as lead paint). In this section, we'll frame this classic nature–nurture debate and consider the evidence relevant to each position. But first we have a practical issue to consider—how stable is the IQ measure itself?

The Stability of IQ

If intelligence is caused primarily by genetic and/or biological factors, we might expect intellectual ability to change very little over time or at least remain stable throughout normal adulthood. On the other hand, if intelligence is determined mainly by the environment, we would probably expect to find changes over time: IQ might rise and fall depending on experience or environmental setting. Neither of these arguments is airtight—for instance, your environment might remain constant over time, or the genetic code might express itself throughout your lifetime; it might also be the case that IQ is determined by early experience and remains fixed after a certain point in development. Even so, examining the stability of IQ seems like a reasonable place to start the search.

When intelligence is measured in the standard way, through performance on psychometric tests, its stability depends partly on when the measuring process begins. Before the age of about 3 or 4, it's difficult to get accurate assessments of intellectual ability. Infants can't talk or show lasting attention, so conventional testing procedures can't be used. Investigators resort to indirect measures, such as recording whether babies choose to look at old or new pictures presented on a screen. There's evidence that babies who quickly habituate, or lose interest, in response to repeated presentations of the same picture, and who prefer to look at novel pictures when they're shown, score higher on intelligence tests later in childhood (M. H. Bornstein, 1989). Other studies have shown that measuring an infant's ability to attend selectively to novel events predicts adult IQ and academic achievement reasonably well (Fagan et al., 2007). The time period that elapses between successful measurements of intelligence also matters, along with the particular measurement tool that is used. There is a growing consensus, though, that measurements of intelligence are quite stable, even from a very young age, as long as these potential measurement problems are taken into account (see Yu et al., 2018). By the time children reach the age of 6, when more conventional intelligence tests can be given, IQ scores predict performance on later IQ tests quite well.

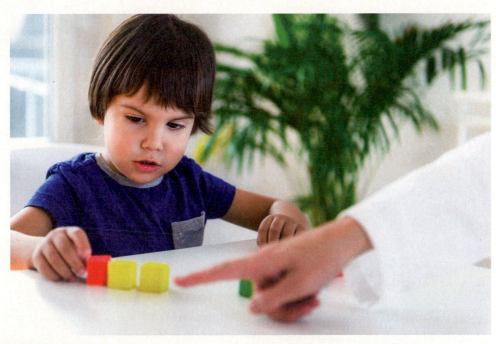

Although tests are available for measuring intelligence in small children, reliable results are easier to obtain starting around age 4.

Science Photo Library/ Alamy Stock Photo

Longitudinal Studies

One of the best ways to measure the stability of IQ is through a longitudinal study, which involves testing the same people repeatedly as they age. The most widely known investigation of the stability of adult intelligence is the Seattle Longitudinal Study, which has examined mental test performance for approximately 5,000 adults ranging in age from 25 through 88 (Schaie, 2005, 2013). The participants have been tested in 7-year cycles, dating back to 1956, using a variety of tests to measure things such as verbal fluency, inductive reasoning, and spatial ability. Schaie and his colleagues have found great stability in intellectual ability throughout adulthood. From age 25 to about age 60, there appears to be no uniform decline in general intellectual ability, as measured through the test battery (see Figure 10.5). After age 60, abilities begin to decline, although the losses are not great until late in life (Schaie, 2016). There are also large individual differences—some people show excellent test performance in their 80s, whereas others do not.

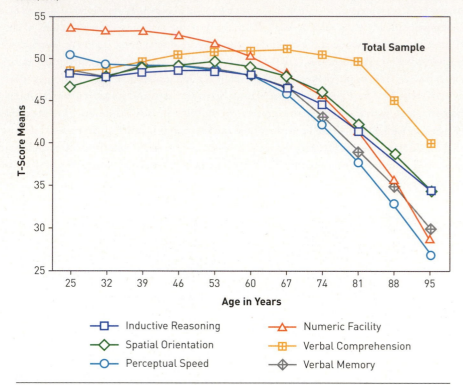

FIGURE 10.5 ■ The Stability of Intellectual Ability

Data from the Seattle Longitudinal Study show how performance changes on a variety of mental tasks performed by adults between the ages of 25 and 95. Notice that average performance is remarkably stable up to about age 60, when some declines begin (data from Schaie, 2013).

Source: Adapted from Schaie, K. W. (2013). *Developmental influences on adult intellectual development: The Seattle Longitudinal Study* (2nd rev. edn., p. 162). New York: Oxford University Press.

It's difficult to interpret changes in IQ with age because many factors change along with age. Elderly people are more likely to have physical problems, for example, that can affect performance. Declines in intelligence with age also depend on the type of intellectual ability measured. Earlier we discussed the distinction between *fluid intelligence*, which reflects basic reasoning and processing skills, and *crystallized intelligence*, which reflects acquired knowledge. The current thinking is that fluid intelligence declines somewhat with age—because the biology of the brain changes—whereas crystallized intelligence remains constant, or perhaps even increases, until late in adulthood (Beier & Ackerman, 2005; A. S. Kaufman & Horn, 1996). The brain becomes a bit slower with age, but people continue to add knowledge and experiences that help solve the problems of everyday life.

The Flynn Effect

Another curious fact about the stability of IQ, although it applies more to populations than to individuals, is that performance on IQ tests seems to be rising steadily and consistently over time. On average, people who take standardized intelligence tests today perform slightly better than people who took similar tests a decade ago, and the same general decade-by-decade increases have been seen since the 1930s (Flynn, 1987, 2007). This trend, known as the *Flynn effect*, has been documented worldwide, but it remains largely unexplained. Most psychologists believe the environment must be responsible because the world's gene pool is unlikely to have changed much in the past 100 years (although see Mingroni, 2007).

Most explanations of the Flynn effect appeal to factors such as increased nutrition or better schooling (R. Lynn, 2009; Neisser, 1998). Better nutrition and health care can certainly lead to better brain functioning, although increases in brain functioning probably can't account for the trend (Nettelbeck & Wilson, 2004). We're also exposed to new technologies, which, in turn, could help develop abstract thinking. (Think about how sophisticated we are about using cell phones and the internet.) In addition, more and more children are now placed in day care or preschool, and these experiences might contribute to better performance on standardized tests as well. It's interesting, though, that most of the improvements are seen on nonverbal portions of intelligence tests, those portions that tap abstract problem-solving ability. It's difficult to see how these kinds of abilities can be easily learned (Wai & Putallaz, 2011).

Because of the Flynn effect, IQ tests are periodically "renormed" to adjust for the fact that scores are rising. The average score is reset to 100 (remember our earlier discussion of deviation IQ), which means you now need to do better on the test, relative to how the test was scored in the past, to receive a given IQ. Some psychologists believe this rescoring process is having unintended effects. For example, suppose scores are rising less rapidly for people with borderline intellectual functioning (those with IQ scores around 70). Under the new scoring guidelines, significantly more individuals are likely to be diagnosed with an intellectual disability than in the past. Many other classification decisions are based, in part, on IQ—everything from eligibility for military service to application of the death penalty—so understanding the Flynn effect is likely to remain a priority for psychologists in the future (Trahan et al., 2014). Interestingly, some evidence suggests as well that the Flynn Effect may be slowing or even reversing in the 21st century, but whether this trend will continue remains unknown.

Nature: The Genetic Argument

A number of early pioneers in intelligence testing, including Sir Francis Galton, believed strongly that individual differences in mental ability are inherited. After all, Galton argued, it's easy to demonstrate that intellectual skill runs through family lines (remember, his cousin was Charles Darwin, and his grandfather was another famous evolutionist, Erasmus Darwin). But family-tree arguments, used in isolation, aren't very convincing. Environmental factors, such as social and educational opportunities, can explain why members of the same family show similar skills. Growing up in a family that places value on intellectual pursuits determines to some extent what sort of behaviors will be rewarded in a child, or the particular type of role models that will be available. In fairness to Galton, he realized that both inherited and environmental factors are needed to explain mental ability fully—in fact, it was Galton (1869, 1883) who coined the phrase "nature versus nurture."

To establish a genetic basis for a psychological or physical characteristic, it's necessary to control for the effects of the environment. In principle, if two people are raised in exactly the same environment and have exactly the same experiences, any differences in IQ must be due to inherited factors (nature). In this case, you've held the nurturing effects of the environment constant, so any differences must be due to genetics. Alternatively, if two people are born with exactly the same genes but end up with quite different intelligence scores, it must be the environment, not genes, that is responsible (nurture). We can't perform these kinds of experimental manipulations in the laboratory, for obvious reasons, but we can look for relevant natural comparisons.

Twin Studies

As discussed in Chapter 3, psychologists often study identical twins, who share nearly complete genetic overlap, to tease apart the nature and nurture components of mind and behavior. In twin studies, researchers search for identical twins who have been raised together in the same household or who have been separated at birth through adoption (T. J. Bouchard & McGue, 1981; T. J. Bouchard et al., 1990). It is assumed that the effects of the environment are similar for twins raised together but quite different, at least on average, for twins raised apart. If intelligence comes primarily from genetic factors, we can expect identical twins to have very similar intelligence scores, regardless of the environments in which they've been raised. One way to measure similarity is by correlation. More specifically, you can attempt to predict the IQ of one twin given the IQ of the other.

If genes are largely responsible for intelligence, we can expect to get a strong positive correlation between IQ scores for identical twins. We won't necessarily expect it to be exactly +1.00 because of measurement error or other uncontrolled factors. In reviewing the research literature on this issue, T. J. Bouchard and McGue (1981) found strong evidence for the genetic position: The IQ scores of identical twins are indeed quite similar, irrespective of the environment in which the twins have been reared. As shown in Figure 10.6, the IQ scores for twins reared together showed an average correlation of .86; for twins reared apart, the average correlation remained strongly positive at .72 (T. J. Bouchard & McGue, 1981).

If intelligence comes primarily from genetic factors, we can expect identical twins to have very similar intelligence scores, regardless of the environments in which they've been raised.

Cultura Creative RF / Alamy Stock Photo

FIGURE 10.6 ■ Nature Versus Nurture

The horizontal bars show the mean correlation coefficients for pairs of people with differing amounts of genetic overlap who have been reared in similar or different environments. For example, the top bar shows the average correlation for identical twins who have been reared together in the same environment, and the bottom bar shows the correlation coefficient for adopted siblings reared together. Higher correlations mean that the measured IQ scores are more similar.

*One of both the sibling pairs were adopted.

Source: Data from Bouchard & McGue, 1981.

It's also useful to compare intelligence scores for fraternal twins (who are genetically no more similar than normal siblings) and among unrelated people who have been reared together or apart. In general, the impressive finding is that the closer the overlap in genes, the more similar the resulting IQs. Notice, for example, that the average correlation for adopted siblings who have been reared together (.30) is much lower than the average correlation for identical twins reared apart (.72). Similarity in environmental history is not as strong a predictor of intelligence as similarity in genetic background. Data such as these suggest that genetic history plays an important role in intelligence, at least when intelligence is measured through conventional IQ testing (see also Plomin et al., 1997).

As we discussed in Chapter 3, there is a new quantitative technique, called *genome-wide complex trait analysis* (GCTA), that uses the genetic similarities between unrelated individuals to estimate similarities in psychological traits, such as intelligence or personality (see Plomin & Deary, 2015). Twins, or even related individuals, are not required; instead, this technique can use recent advances in our understanding of the human genome to explore whether people with similar patterns in their DNA tend to have similar psychological traits. In the case of intelligence, researchers have begun to identify genetic variants that correlate with intelligence, but their contribution to the overall differences that are seen in intelligence test scores remains relatively small at this point (Plomin & von Stumm, 2018).

Heritability

Intelligence researchers often use the term *heritability* to describe the influence of genetic factors on intelligence. Heritability is a mathematical index that represents the extent to which differences within a population can be accounted for by genetic factors. For any group of people, you will find individual differences in IQ scores; heritability measures the role genetic factors play in producing these differences. It's expressed as a percentage, so if the heritability of intelligence were 100%, all differences in measured IQ could be explained genetically. Most estimates of the heritability of intelligence, derived from twin studies, hover at around 50%, which means that approximately half of the differences in IQ have a genetic basis. Interestingly, the heritability of intelligence appears to increase somewhat with age, at least from childhood to young adulthood (Haworth et al., 2010). One possibility is that as people age, they choose to live in environments that maximize their genetic potential; hence, the environment will appear to exert less of an influence on the measured differences among individuals (Plomin & Deary, 2015).

Estimates of heritability apply only to groups, not to individuals. A heritability estimate of 50% does not mean that 50% of someone's intelligence is due to the person's genes. To see why, imagine two groups of people with the same genetic histories. Group A is placed in a rigidly controlled environment where everyone is treated exactly the same. For group B, the environment is allowed to vary. If IQ scores are influenced by the environment in any way, we can expect the heritability values to be quite different for these two groups, even though the groups' genetic backgrounds are identical. Because the environment is held constant in group A, all of the differences in measured IQ will be due to genes. In group B, the heritability index will be lower because some of the differences in IQ will be due to environmental effects. Heritability tells us only that for a given group a certain percentage of the differences in intelligence can be explained by genetic factors.

Nurture: The Environmental Argument

Most psychologists agree that intelligence is influenced by genetic factors. This is not really surprising given that cognitive abilities are almost certainly influenced by biological factors, such as the speed or efficiency of neural processing. There are other neurological data as well, such as activation levels in the frontal lobes and overall connectivity in the brain, that have been linked to measures of intelligence (e.g., Barbey, 2018; M. W. Cole et al., 2015). But did you notice in Figure 10.6 that identical twins reared together have IQs that are more similar than do identical twins reared apart? This means that individual differences in intelligence can't be explained completely through genetic background; it's not even close—the environment clearly plays an important role.

In this section, we'll consider some environmental influences on IQ by addressing a controversial topic in the study of intelligence: group differences in IQ. The majority of intelligence researchers agree that there are stable differences in IQ across racial, ethnic, and socioeconomic groups. For example, Asian Americans tend to score higher on standardized intelligence tests, on average, than white European Americans. White Americans, on average, score higher than African Americans and Hispanic Americans (Brody, 1992; R. Lynn, 1994).

Group differences in IQ, although stable, reflect average *group* differences. Not every Asian American scores high on an intelligence test, nor does every African American score low. In fact, the differences among IQ scores within a population (African Americans, Asian Americans, and so on) are much larger than the average differences between groups. This means that a large number of African Americans will score higher than the average white American, just as many Asian Americans will have scores below the average for whites. The average population differences cannot be applied to single individuals, but the group differences are real and should be explained. How can we account for these differences? Although some psychologists have speculated that evolutionary and genetic factors are partly responsible for IQ differences among racial and ethnic groups (Rushton & Jensen, 2005), it's very difficult to rule out environmental explanations (Nisbett, 2009). Up to this point, as psychologist Earl Hunt notes, "[N]o genes related to the difference in cognitive skills across the various racial and ethnic groups have ever been discovered" (E. Hunt, 2011, p. 446). In addition, as we discuss shortly, many factors co-vary with group—that is, the interpretation of group differences in intelligence is often confounded by other factors.

Economic Differences

For example, on average there are significant economic differences among racial/ethnic groups that could contribute to performance, making interpretation of the IQ differences difficult. For example, African Americans and Hispanic Americans in the United States are more likely to live at or below the poverty level. Poverty is often associated with poor nutrition and difficulties in obtaining proper health care, and it may hurt one's chances to enter adequate schools. African Americans and Hispanic Americans are also more likely than white Americans to suffer racial discrimination. The impact of these factors on intelligence testing is not completely understood, although they likely play an important role. African Americans, white Americans, and Hispanic Americans tend to live in very different and somewhat isolated worlds. As a consequence, it's hard to disentangle the effects of the environment from any genetic differences that might contribute to intelligence.

Test Bias

Psychologists have also been concerned that test biases might contribute to group differences in IQ scores (Bernal, 1984). Racial/ethnic group differences depend, to a certain extent, on the type of intelligence test administered (Brody, 1992). This raises the very real possibility that cultural biases might be contaminating some of the test questions. For example, if I ask you a question such as "Who wrote *Faust*?"(which once appeared on a Wechsler test), your ability to answer correctly will depend partly on whether your culture places value on exposure to such information. Psychologist Robert L. Williams has shown that when an intelligence test is used that relies heavily on African American terms and expressions, white students who have had limited experience with African American culture perform poorly.

However, psychologists have worked hard to remove bias from standard intelligence and achievement tests (Raven et al., 1985); in some cases, the development of "culture-fair" tests has reduced racial differences in measured ability. However, significant group differences usually remain even after culture-bound questions have been altered or removed. Of course, whether it is possible to remove bias completely is open for debate, and some believe that it is essentially impossible given that any standardized test will reflect the values of the culture that developed it. Still, the predictive value of IQ tests, on things like school performance, tends to be similar across racial groups. This suggests that test bias is not a major determinant of group differences in IQ.

Stereotype Threat

While bias in the content of intelligence tests has been reduced, other environmental factors remain. When people take intelligence tests, they have certain expectations about how they'll perform; these expectations, in turn, can significantly affect the final score. If you're nervous or expect to bomb the test, you're less likely to do well. Psychologist Claude M. Steele and his colleagues argue that African Americans often feel pressured or threatened by stereotypes and perform poorly as a result.

In support of this conclusion, Steele and Aronson (1995) found that African Americans performed more poorly on a verbal test when they thought the test was measuring intelligence rather than general problem solving. Everyone in the experiment took exactly the same test, but they were led to believe, through instructions, that it was either an intelligence test or a problem-solving test. Presumably the label "intelligence test" activated the negative stereotype, creating pressure and anxiety, and performance suffered as a result. Whether this pressure can account for the differences found between groups on intelligence tests remains uncertain; in fact, there is no direct evidence in the Steele and Aronson (1995) study that stereotype threat explains preexisting IQ differences among groups, but stereotype threat remains an important factor to consider (Schmader, 2010). We'll return to the effects of stereotypes on expectations and performance in Chapter 13.

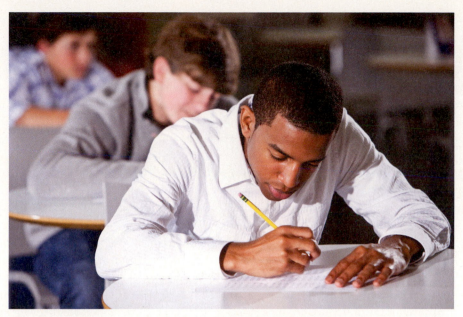

African Americans often feel pressured or threatened by stereotypes and can perform poorly as a result.

iStockPhoto/kali9

Adoption Studies

A more direct test of environmental explanations of racial/ethnic differences comes from IQ studies of African American children who have been reared in white homes. If the average African American childhood experience leads to skills that do not transfer well to standard tests of intelligence, then we would expect African American children raised in white middle-class homes to have higher IQ scores. In general, this assumption is supported by the data. Scarr and Weinberg (1976) investigated interracial adoptions in Minnesota and found that the average IQ for African American children reared in economically advantaged white households was significantly higher than the national African American mean score. This finding was confirmed again in later follow-up studies (Waldman, et al. 1994; Weinberg et al., 1992). You certainly shouldn't conclude from this finding that white households are somehow better than other households. The results simply imply that some cultural experiences, particularly those related to socioeconomic class, can give one an advantage on the tests currently being used to assess intelligence. Moreover, although these transracial adoption studies documented increases in IQ scores in certain environments, which is a useful finding, some group differences still remained.

The Interaction of Nature and Nurture

So what are we to conclude about the relative contributions of genetics and the environment to intelligence? Nature–nurture issues are notoriously difficult to resolve, and this is especially true in the politically sensitive area of intelligence (E. Hunt & Carlson, 2007). It's extremely difficult to control for the effects of either the environment or genetics. Consider the twin studies—how reasonable is it to assume that twins who have been reared apart have had unrelated environmental experiences? Are adopted children really representative of the racial or ethnic populations from which they have been drawn (Brody, 2007)? It's difficult to answer these questions because neither the environment nor genetic structure can be manipulated directly in the laboratory (at least for humans).

Given the current evidence, the most reasonable position to take is that intelligence, like many other psychological attributes, is determined by a mixture of genes and environment. The genes you inherit from your parents place upper and lower bounds on intellectual ability. Genes may importantly determine how your brain is wired, and possibly the speed of neural transmission or executive functions, but the expression of your genetic material is strongly influenced by the environment. Nature always works via nurture and vice versa—one can't happen without the other (Ridley, 2003).

Recall from Chapter 3 that geneticists use the term *genotype* to refer to the genetic message itself and *phenotype* to refer to the observable characteristics that actually result from genetic expression. An analogy of the genotype–phenotype relationship that is sometimes used by intelligence researchers compares the development of intelligence to the nurturing of flowering plants (e.g., Lewontin, 1976). Imagine that we have a packet of virtually identical seeds, and we toss half into a pot containing fertile soil and half into a pot of barren soil. The seeds tossed into the poor soil will undoubtedly grow, but their growth will be stunted relative to that of the group planted in the rich soil. Because these are virtually identical groups of seeds, containing similar distributions of genetic information, any differences in growth between the pots are due entirely to the environment (the soil). So, too, with intelligence—two people can be born with similar genetic potential, but the degree to which their intellectual potential will "blossom" will depend critically on the environment.

Consider as well that within each handful of seeds there will be variations in genetic information. Some plants will grow larger than others, regardless of the soil in which they've been thrown. A similar kind of result would be expected for intelligence—variations in the genetic message will produce individual differences in IQ that cannot be adequately explained by environmental variables. In fact, after analyzing the differences within a pot, we might conclude that all of the differences are due to inherited factors. But even if the differences within a group are due to genes, the differences between groups would still be due to the environment (fertile or barren soil). This kind of insight might help account, in part, for the racial/ethnic differences in IQ discussed earlier. Even though genes may exert a strong influence within a population, between-population differences may still be determined primarily by the environment (Eysenck & Kamin, 1981; Lewontin, 1976). Of course, this analogy assumes that the genetic profiles are similar across racial groups, which may not be the case (see Warne et al., 2018).

One other feature of the interaction between nature and nurture is worth noting . . . yet again. Environmental experiences do not occur independent of inherited factors. It's a two-way street. The environment will partly determine how genetic information is expressed, but so too will genetic information determine experience. If you're born with three arms, because of some odd combination of inherited factors, your interactions with the world will be quite different from those of a person with two arms. The fact that you have three arms will color your environment—it will determine how you are treated and the range of opportunities to which you are exposed. If you're born with genes that grant you a higher intellectual potential, then early on you're likely to be exposed to opportunities that will help you realize your full intellectual potential; conversely, if you're born with a lower intellectual potential, the environment is likely to shape you away from intellectually nurturing experiences (see Figure 10.7). Such is the way of life and of the world.

FIGURE 10.7 ■ Reaction Range

Each person may have genes that set limits for intellectual potential (sometimes called a reaction range). In this case, Tom inherited an IQ potential anywhere between 80 and about 112. The IQ that Tom actually obtains (shown as the dark bar) is determined by the kind of environment in which he is reared. Notice that Miguel inherited a greater IQ potential than Tom, but if Tom is raised in an enriched environment, his IQ may actually turn out to be higher than Miguel's.

Illustrated by Sarah Yeh

Check your knowledge about the sources of intelligence by deciding whether each of the following statements is true or false. (You will find the answers in the Appendix.)

1. Longitudinal studies of intelligence reveal that fluid, but not crystallized, intelligence remains largely constant across the life span. *True or False?*

2. Twin studies have shown that fraternal twins raised together tend to have more similar IQs than identical twins raised apart. *True or False?*

3. Most psychologists now believe that genetic factors definitely play a role in intelligence. *True or False?*

4. A heritability estimate of 70% means that 70% of one's intelligence is due to one's genetic structure. *True or False?*

5. Test bias is recognized as a possible contributor to measured intelligence, but it's unlikely to be a strong determinant of group differences in IQ. *True or False?*

THE PROBLEMS SOLVED: WHAT IS INTELLIGENCE, AND WHAT IS IT FOR?

You've seen in this chapter that psychologists think about intelligence primarily in terms of individual differences. People differ, and we can develop tests that measure these differences effectively. From an analysis of individual differences, psychologists have tried to develop theories of intellectual functioning: What kinds of mental processes underlie intelligent thought? We've seen that one way to characterize intelligence is by the adaptability of behavior. From a functional perspective, this view of intelligence makes the most sense. What makes one species member intelligent, and another not, may be dictated by how well organisms adapt to changing environments and solve the problems of survival. From this perspective, the Clark's nutcracker, in its successful search for a cache of seeds, fits the adaptive view of intelligence just as well as the cocky student who aces the SAT. In this chapter, our discussion revolved around three problems that face researchers of intelligence.

Conceptualizing Intelligence

Researchers conceptualize intelligence in a number of ways. Proponents of psychometric approaches describe cognitive ability by analyzing performance on mental tests. They traditionally draw distinctions between a general factor of intelligence, *g*, which applies broadly, and specific factors, *s*, which measure separate abilities. The idea that intelligence must be broken down into several, or multiple, kinds of ability remains popular today, although researchers disagree as to how many or what types of intelligence need to be included.

There's some evidence that performance on traditional tests of mental ability might be related to the speed of processing among neurons in the brain. Both the multiple-intelligences approach of Howard Gardner and the triarchic theory of Robert Sternberg suggest that the concept of intelligence must be defined broadly. We cannot rely entirely on academic ability to define intelligence—everyday intelligence and street smarts also enhance our ability to adapt.

Measuring Individual Differences

Concepts such as intelligence really have little meaning outside of the study of individual differences—it's how the mental ability of Sam differs from the mental ability of Jennifer that makes the concept of intelligence meaningful. A good test of intelligence has three main characteristics: reliability, validity, and standardization. Understanding the concept of test validity is crucial because it holds the key to appreciating the widespread use of standardized measures such as IQ or tests such as the SAT. Researchers who study individual differences are often primarily interested in using test results to make predictions about future success. Will Jennifer perform well in school? Will Sam make it as a graduate student in psychology? As you've seen, the IQ test itself was originally developed to measure academic ability, not as some ultimate measure of mental capacity. Still, IQ tests correlate reasonably well with a host of outcomes, including academic and job success and even health and longevity.

Discovering the Sources of Intelligence

There are two main ways to explain how differences in intelligence might arise, genetics and the environment. Twin studies provide convincing evidence that at least some kinds of mental ability are inherited, although how much remains controversial. However, the role of the environment in determining IQ cannot be discounted. Intelligence, like many psychological attributes, grows out of an interaction between nature and nurture.

THINKING ABOUT RESEARCH

A summary of a research study in psychology is given in this section. As you read the summary, think about the following questions:

1. Is it possible to improve fluid intelligence through training?
2. Will people who score low on a measure of fluid intelligence benefit more from training than those with a higher initial score?
3. Is it a good idea to encourage people to "brain train" as they age in an effort to maintain high levels of intellectual functioning?
4. How might the results of this study apply to theories that focus on multiple intelligences?

Article Reference: Foster, J. L., Harrison, T. L., Hicks, K. L., Draheim, C., Redick, T. S., & Engle, R. W. (2017). Do the effects of working memory training depend on baseline ability level? *Journal of Experimental Psychology: Learning, Memory, and Cognition, 43,* 1677–1689.

Purpose of the Study: This study investigated whether training on cognitive tasks, ones that tap executive functions that correlate with fluid intelligence, improves general cognitive functioning. Brain training products are widespread in the marketplace—for example, brain "fitness" software that supposedly improves general intelligence—but does the scientific evidence back up such claims? The investigators were also interested in whether any advantages of training would differ between people with high or low working memory capacities—that is, those who naturally show attention- and memory-related abilities that are predictive of general intelligence.

Is it a good idea to encourage people to "brain train" as they age in an effort to maintain high levels of intellectual functioning?

Postmodern Studio/ Alamy Stock Photo

Method of the Study: Pretesting identified two groups of people—those with either high or low working memory capacities. Each person then received 20 training sessions on two working memory span tasks—one that had a verbal component (e.g., remembering letters) and one that was primarily spatial (e.g., remembering the positions of shapes). Each training session contained eight blocks of trials, and the difficulty of the task increased as the participant's performance improved. After training, everyone was given a range of assessment tests designed to measure the various cognitive abilities thought to be involved in intelligence (e.g., memory updating, the ability to multitask, and more direct measures of fluid intelligence). An active control group engaged in similar training sessions, but on a task that was unrelated to working memory capacity (visual search).

Results of the Study: Across the 20 training sessions, participants showed significant improvements on the training tasks. There was steady performance growth, regardless of whether the participant initially showed a high or low working memory capacity. In fact, the training benefits were somewhat higher for the people with the higher capacities, suggesting that it may not be possible to easily eliminate preexisting differences in executive functioning. On the after-training assessment tests, no general improvements were found compared to the active control group, unless the transfer test closely resembled the training test. For example, extensive training on the working memory span task did not improve performance on tests of attention control, memory updating, or multitasking ability.

Conclusions of the Study: First, working memory training seems to increase rather than decrease the gap that exists between people with high and low working memory spans. Second, training on a task that correlates with fluid intelligence does not transfer to other tasks that tap general cognitive functioning. In a nutshell, engaging in a cognitive "workout" is capable of improving performance on similar workout tasks, but its positive benefits do not appear to transfer to general intellectual functioning.

KNOWLEDGE CHECK: CHAPTER SUMMARY

(You will find the answers in the Appendix.)

CONCEPTUALIZING INTELLIGENCE

- The (1) _____ approach proposes that intelligence can be understood by statistically analyzing (2) _____ on tests that measure specific mental skills. Spearman used (3) _____ analysis to study the relationships, or (4) _____, among test scores and to analyze the factors that account for test performance. He proposed that we possess (5) _____ intelligence, or *g*, as well as specific abilities, or *s*.

- (6) _____ intelligence is the ability to reason, (7) _____ problems, and remember; it may be influenced by (8) _____ and biological factors. (9) _____ intelligence reflects the (10) _____ and abilities that we acquire from experience.

- Gardner proposed that traditional views of intelligence be broadened to include special (11) _____ or talents that reflect (12) _____ intelligences. He identified (13) _____ kinds of intelligence: musical, bodily-kinesthetic, logical-mathematical, (14) _____, spatial, interpersonal, (15) _____, and naturalist.

- Sternberg's (16) _____ theory of intelligence proposed that intelligence has three main components. (17) _____ intelligence is the ability to process information; (18) _____ intelligence is used in coping with new kinds of tasks; and (19) _____ intelligence has to do with how well people adapt to the environment.

MEASURING INDIVIDUAL DIFFERENCES

- (20) _____ is a measure of the (21) _____ of test results. (22) _____ is whether a test measures what it is supposed to measure. (23) _____ ensures that the testing, scoring, and interpretation procedures are similar every time the test is administered.

- IQ is an index of (24) _____ that was originally designed to identify children who were likely to have trouble in school. A test was developed that would determine a child's (25) _____ age, which is typically calculated by comparing a child's test score with the (26) _____ score for (27) _____ age groups. Traditionally, IQ was calculated by dividing mental age by

(28) _____ age and multiplying the quotient by 100. Now, however, a (29) _____ IQ is calculated by determining where a given test score "sits" in relation to the average score.

- An IQ score of 70 or below is associated with an (30) _____, although several criteria must be met for a formal diagnosis. An IQ of (31) _____ or above indicates (32) _____.

- Scores on traditional IQ tests (33) _____ well with school test scores or grades, although critics argue that IQ doesn't reflect the whole range of intellectual ability. (34) _____ effects may occur when teachers' knowledge of IQ scores affect how they interact with students. The effects of the IQ label were particularly serious during the early 20th century when many immigrants who had not mastered (35) _____ were given intelligence tests and were labeled "feebleminded" or "defective" when they failed to perform well.

- (36) _____ is the ability to generate novel and original ideas. (37) _____ intelligence is the ability to perceive, (38) _____, and express emotion. (39) _____ knowledge is an unspoken practical know-how that is rarely formally taught and comes primarily from (40) _____.

DISCOVERING THE SOURCES OF INTELLIGENCE

- One of the best ways to measure the stability of IQ is through a (41) _____ study, which involves testing the same people repeatedly as they age. Current thinking is that (42) _____ intelligence, which reflects basic (43) _____ skills, may (44) _____ with age, whereas (45) _____ intelligence, which reflects acquired (46) _____, remains (47) _____ or increases with age. The (48) _____ effect is a trend that has been documented worldwide and shows that performance on IQ tests seems to be rising steadily and consistently over time.

- (49) _____ studies address the role of (50) _____ and (51) _____ on intelligence. Identical twins have very (52) _____ IQ scores, regardless of whether they were raised in the same (53) _____. (54) _____ is a mathematical index that shows the extent to which IQ differences within a population can be accounted for by (55) _____ factors. Estimates of heritability apply to (56) _____, not to individuals.

- Most researchers agree that there are stable group (57) _____ in IQ across racial, ethnic, and social lines, which may be explained by (58) _____ differences or test (59) _____. Adoption studies support the role of the (60) _____ in explaining group differences. Intelligence is determined by a mixture of (61) _____ and (62) _____ influences. Genes place (63) _____ and lower limits on intellectual ability. However, the environment will partly determine how (64) _____ information is expressed, and genetic information will influence (65) _____.

CRITICAL THINKING QUESTIONS

1. Based on our discussion, how reasonable do you think it is to compare the intelligence of people from one culture to another?

2. How well does the notion of general intelligence describe you? If you're good at one subject, does that predict how well you do in others?

3. Which do you think contributes the most to performance on an essay exam: fluid or crystallized intelligence?

4. Do you think the average person on the street believes superior artistic or athletic ability qualifies as a type of intelligence?

5. Pick one of your classes in school. Do you think the tests that you've taken so far have been valid? What specific kind of validity are you using as a basis for your answer?

6. Do you see any similarities between the way deviation IQ is interpreted and the way you normally interpret your test scores in a class?

7. Do you think it makes sense for elementary schools to use "tracking" systems—that is, to divide children early on into different classes based on performance on standardized tests?

8. Elderly people are often said to possess wisdom. In what ways do you think the label "wise" differs from the label "intelligent"?

9. Do you think it's possible to tease apart the relative contributions of nature and nurture to intelligence by studying animals in the laboratory?

10. Suppose we broaden the concept of intelligence to include athletic and artistic ability. Would it bother you to think that these abilities are influenced primarily by genetic factors?

KEY TERMS

achievement tests (p. 360)

analytical intelligence (p. 359)

aptitude tests (p. 360)

creative intelligence (p. 359)

creativity (p. 369)

crystallized intelligence (p. 356)

deviation IQ (p. 364)

emotional intelligence (p. 369)

factor analysis (p. 353)

fluid intelligence (p. 356)

g (general intelligence) (p. 353)

gifted (p. 366)

heritability (p. 377)

intellectual disability (p. 365)

intelligence (p. 351)

intelligence quotient (IQ) (p. 363)

mental age (p. 363)

multiple intelligences (p. 357)

practical intelligence (p. 359)

psychometrics (p. 352)

reliability (p. 361)

s (specific intelligence) (p. 354)

standardization (p. 362)

tacit knowledge (p. 370)

triarchic theory (p. 359)

validity (p. 361)

11 PERSONALITY

LEARNING OBJECTIVES

11.1 Explain how psychologists use factor analysis to identify personality traits; evaluate Allport's contrasting viewpoint; and identify the differences between self-report inventories and projective personality tests.

11.2 Identify and evaluate Freud's tripartite theory of the human mind and personality, and contrast it with humanistic and social–cognitive accounts of personality.

11.3 Describe the debate psychologists have had about cross-situational consistency in behavior, otherwise known as the person–situation debate, and explain how genetic factors influence personality.

11.4 For the major sections of the chapter, summarize how personality is defined and measured and whether and why people act consistently across situations.

CHAPTER OUTLINE

Conceptualizing and Measuring Personality

Determining How Personality Develops

Resolving the Person–Situation Debate

    Practical Solutions: The Value of Self-Monitoring

The Problems Solved: What Personality Is For

It's the annual holiday party for Everville Industries. Elijah Hobart has worked at the company for a year and a half now, and he's itching for a promotion to the advertising department. To his left stands the head of advertising, Mr. Barker, along with several of Hobart's equally ambitious coworkers. The topic of conversation is the company's recent disastrous marketing campaign, spearheaded by Barker, whose shortcomings are recognized by everyone in the group save one—Barker himself.

"It just goes to show you," Barker says confidently, "you can never underestimate the ignorance of the people. It was a brilliantly conceived but unappreciated plan."

"Absolutely," says Ms. Adler, "a brilliant plan."

"People are just ignorant," employee Jones remarks. "They wouldn't know a good marketing campaign if it came up and bit them on the cheek."

What jerks, the little voice inside Hobart's head chimes. These people have no values or sense of personal integrity. Everyone knows the campaign was terrible.

"And what about you, Hobart?" Barker says, his eyes meeting Elijah's. "What do you think?"

"Brilliant plan, sir," Hobart says, hesitating only slightly. "The work of a genius . . ."

Our topic in this chapter is **personality**, defined as the set of characteristics that distinguishes us from others and leads us to act consistently across situations. At its core, the study of personality, like the study of intelligence, is first and foremost the study of individual differences (Cronbach, 1957). People seem to differ in lasting ways: Rowena is outgoing, confident, and friendly; Liam is shy in social settings and has an annoying habit of lying. In a very real sense, personality **traits**, predispositions to respond in certain ways, define people. Traits make people unique, identifiable, and generally predictable across time. Potentially, we can use personality traits to explain why Rowena's and Liam's actions remain stable and consistent across situations. But, as the opening vignette illustrates, sometimes the situation can hijack our behavior, leading us to act in ways that are inconsistent with our normal traits and actions.

THE PROBLEMS TO BE SOLVED: WHAT IS PERSONALITY, AND WHAT IS IT FOR?

From an adaptive perspective, remaining consistent in our thoughts and actions, especially if they lead to successful outcomes, makes sense. Most psychologists believe we have traits such as fearfulness or aggressiveness because those traits increase the likelihood of our survival. But the question of where those traits come from (hint: nature or nurture?) and why people can differ so dramatically in trait expression has perplexed researchers for decades. As you read this chapter, think back to the issues we considered in Chapter 10 on intelligence—you'll find many similarities between the study of intelligence and the study of personality.

Conceptualizing and Measuring Personality

To understand the concept of personality, it's necessary to consider the whole person. This means you can't simply record the actions of someone in a restricted situation or even in several situations. You need to measure the *enduring* aspects of behavior—those things that distinguish you from others consistently across time. Although there's no simple way of addressing this problem, psychologists have relied on a host of techniques to conceptualize and measure personality. Measures of personality traits, like those for intelligence, turn out to be highly predictive of consequential life outcomes.

Determining How Personality Develops

What factors in development lead to stable and consistent behavior? It's one thing to identify and measure a person's lasting traits but quite another to understand their origin. Where do personality traits come from, and what accounts for the differences among individuals? Why does Liam have that nasty tendency to lie, and why does sweet Rowena always see the sunny side of a rotten situation? It is here, in the study of personality development, that you'll find some of the most ambitious and best-known attempts at psychological theory.

Resolving the Person–Situation Debate

All major theories of personality assume that the environment shapes and changes our behavior—the actions of Elijah in our opening vignette is a case in point. However, because personality consists of those traits that are supposed to remain the same across situations, we're faced with a kind of theoretical puzzle. In essence, personality should be something that's largely independent of the environment. Remember, people are supposed to act the same regardless of the situation. Is behavior really as consistent across situations as many people, including psychologists, assume? In the final section of the chapter, we'll discuss the evidence—and controversy—that bears on this issue.

CONCEPTUALIZING AND MEASURING PERSONALITY

It's not necessary to have a complete understanding of personality to identify and measure differences among people. In fact, we need some formal way of classifying individual differences before we can know exactly what needs to be explained. **Trait theories** are systems for assessing how people differ, particularly how people differ in their tendencies to act consistently across situations. As a general rule, trait theories use a *psychometric approach*—that is, they seek to identify stable individual differences by analyzing the performances of large groups of people on rating tests or questionnaires.

If you open any dictionary, you'll find thousands of words that fit the everyday definition of a personality trait. In fact, it's been estimated that approximately 1 out of every 22 words in the English language is a trait-related term (Allport & Odbert, 1936). One goal of the trait theorist is to reduce these thousands of descriptive terms to a smaller set of more basic terms—to find a kind of common denominator among groups of terms. For example, when you describe someone with words such as *kind, trusting,* and *warm,* you might really be describing a more general characteristic of the person,

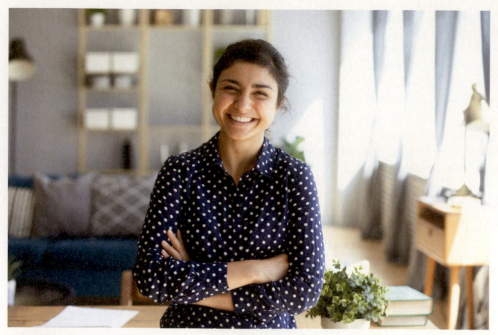

Try coming up with a set of trait words to describe this individual. What are the chances that your words will apply in all situations?

iStockPhoto/fizkes

such as *agreeableness* or *pleasantness*. The researcher attempts to identify basic traits from among the thousands of personality descriptors that are common in the language. How can this be accomplished?

The Factor Analytic Approach

One solution is to use the statistical technique of *factor analysis*. As we discussed in Chapter 10, factor analysis is a mathematical procedure that's used to analyze correlations among test responses. The goal is to identify a set of factors that collectively predict test performance. To see how this works in the case of personality, imagine asking a large group of people to rate themselves on a variety of personality characteristics. For example: "On a scale of 1 (*not at all*) to 7 (*extremely*), how well do you think the term *brooding* is characteristic of you?" When we look at the results, we'll undoubtedly see many individual differences. Some people will see themselves as brooders, and others won't; some people will score high on aggressiveness and competitiveness, while others will classify themselves as passive and shy.

However, researchers are really interested in how the trait ratings correlate with one another. Do people who rate themselves as, say, "kind" also tend to rate themselves as "warm" and "trusting"? More specifically, can we predict people's rating on one trait given that we know their rating on some other trait? If we can, then it's reasonable to assume that some general personality characteristic, such as pleasantness, is being measured by the more specific personality descriptors. This is the logic behind factor analysis—discover the common denominators for personality by noting which terms cluster statistically in a group.

Source Traits and Superfactors

Psychologists frequently apply factor analysis to personality data. For practical reasons, it's common to rely on ratings of personality descriptors, such as "kind" or "warm," which people give about themselves or others. Psychologist Raymond Cattell was able to use rating data of this sort to identify 16 basic personality factors from a set of traits that originally numbered in the thousands (Cattell et al., 1970). Cattell's 16 factors, which he called *source traits*, are listed in Figure 11.1. Notice that each factor is shown as a dimension marked by an opposing pole: reserved–outgoing, trusting–suspicious, relaxed–tense, and so on. Any particular individual will have a unique personality profile, reflecting the person's standing on each of the dimensions. So, you might be closer to "reserved" than "outgoing," be more "controlled" than "uncontrolled," and have a tendency to be "tough-minded" rather than "sensitive."

FIGURE 11.1   ■   A Personality Profile

This is a sample personality profile as measured by Cattell's 16 personality factors. Notice that our personalities are defined by our standing on each of the 16 trait dimensions.

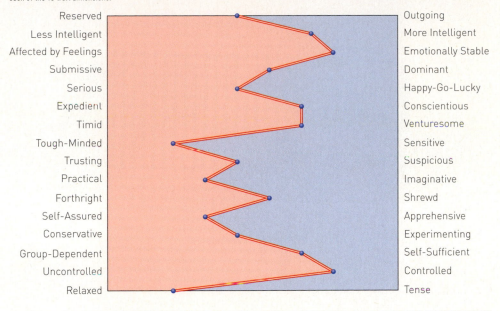

Source: Reprinted with permission from R. B. Cattell, "A 16PF Profile," in *Psychology Today.* pp. 40–46. Copyright© 1973 Sussex Publishers, Inc.

However, the factors that are discovered depend partly on how the mathematical technique of factor analysis is interpreted. Whereas Cattell reported 16 primary factors (along with some additional secondary or second-order factors), Hans Eysenck proposed only three *superfactors*: (1) *extroversion*, which refers roughly to how outgoing and sociable you are; (2) *neuroticism*, which captures your degree of anxiety, worry, or moodiness; and (3) *psychoticism*, which represents your tendencies to be insensitive, uncaring, or cruel toward others (Eysenck, 1970, 1991). Specific personality descriptors, such as "touchy" or "lively," are presumed to reflect some combination of each of the three primary dimensions.

The Big Five

Psychologists continue to argue about the number of factors that best describe personality, but the field has largely settled on a more intermediate solution: It is now widely accepted that the best solution to the factoring problem is to propose *five* basic personality dimensions (McCrae & Costa, 1985, 2003). The aptly named **Big Five** personality dimensions include *extroversion, agreeableness, conscientiousness, neuroticism,* and *openness.* Each is listed in Figure 11.2 along with some of the descriptors that identify each trait. So, for example, people who score highly on the extroversion dimension tend to see themselves as talkative, sociable, fun-loving, and affectionate. People who are low on extroversion would show the opposite tendencies: untalkative, retiring, sober, and reserved.

Notice that *extroversion* and *neuroticism* are two of the three primary dimensions suggested by Eysenck. In fact, Eysenck (1991) argued that psychoticism, his remaining dimension, simply reflects a combination of the Big Five's agreeableness, conscientiousness, and (perhaps) openness (see also Scholte & De Bruyn, 2004). The debate continues, but the consensus today favors the Big Five. Studies have analyzed trait ratings collected from around the world, and evidence for a Big Five emerges quite consistently across most cultures (Heine & Buchtel, 2009; but see Gurven et al., 2013). In addition to supporting the Big Five, the data suggest that the basic structure of personality is universal rather than dependent on cultural background (Allik et al., 2013).

Psychologists have been keenly interested in the measurement of personality traits, especially the extent to which traits such as the Big Five predict behavior (Fleeson & Gallagher, 2009). For example, do certain personality traits correlate strongly with academic achievement or work performance?

FIGURE 11.2   ■   The Big Five

Many psychologists believe that personality is best analyzed in terms of five fundamental personality dimensions.

Conscientiousness
Ethical, dependable, productive, purposeful

Agreeableness
Sympathetic, warm, trusting, cooperative

Neuroticism
Anxious, insecure, guilt-prone, self-conscious

Extroversion
Talkative, sociable, fun-loving, affectionate

Openness
Daring, nonconforming, showing unusually broad interests, imaginative

Illustrated by Sarah Yeh

The answer appears to be "Yes," particularly conscientiousness as measured by the Big Five (Poropat, 2009). Overall, Big Five traits have been linked to dozens of life outcomes, everything from subjective well-being, to religious beliefs, to humor, to the degree of satisfaction in our romantic and sexual relationships (M. S. Allen & Walter, 2018). In addition, psychologists have discovered links between personality traits and mental health. Studies have found significant correlations between Big Five personality traits and anxiety, depression, and substance use/abuse disorders (Kotov et al., 2010). Moreover, importantly, many of these trait–outcome relationships have been replicated in large-scale studies involving thousands of participants (Soto, 2019).

At the same time, the fact that five (or three) factors can be used to categorize people doesn't tell us anything about the internal processes that determine a personality profile (Hampson, 2012). Some psychologists have also questioned whether all aspects of personality can be captured by any small set of personality dimensions (see Livesley et al., 2003). To understand personality completely, the critics argue, you need to understand the ability of people to *change* as well as to stay the same across situations. We'll discuss how the environment affects the consistency of behavior later in the chapter.

Allport's Trait Theory

Like the factor analysts, psychologist Gordon Allport (1897–1967) was convinced that people have personality traits, or "predispositions to respond." But he wasn't convinced that the building blocks of personality could be understood from massive statistical analyses of group responses. Allport believed that personality is a measure of one's *uniqueness* as an individual. So the proper focus should be on individuals, he argued, not on groups. His approach, which he called *idiographic* (which means "relating to the individual"), was to study particular individuals in great detail. An advantage of this kind of case study approach is that consistencies in behavior can be recorded across an entire lifetime rather than just in a limited setting (Barenbaum, 1997).

One of Allport's main contributions was his general classification scheme for identifying personality traits (Allport, 1937). Allport believed some people show *cardinal* personality traits. **Cardinal traits** are the ruling passions that dominate an individual's life. If you spend your life in a mountain monastery, rejecting all worldly possessions, your passion "to serve god" would likely satisfy Allport's description of a cardinal trait. Perhaps you know someone whose every thought or action revolves around the pursuit of wealth, fame, or power. People with cardinal traits do not represent the average—these

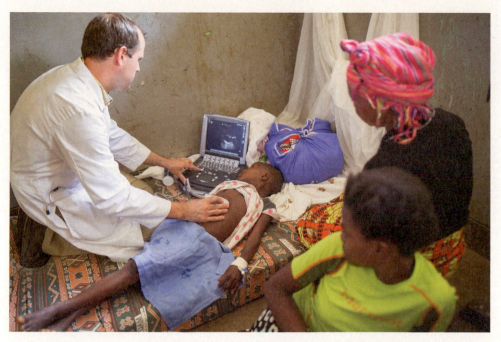

Cardinal traits are ruling passions that dominate a person's life, such as a compelling need to help others at the expense of personal comfort.

Jake Lyell/ Alamy Stock Photo

people are driven and highly focused; every action is motivated by a particular goal. We can't really capture a cardinal trait by applying a technique such as factor analysis, however, because cardinal traits are uniquely defined by the individual rather than by the group.

Allport believed cardinal traits are rare. Most people have personalities that are controlled by several lasting characteristics, which he labeled *central* traits. **Central traits** are the 5 to 10 descriptive terms you would use to describe someone you know. Rowena? She's outgoing and friendly, very trustworthy, sentimental, and honest to the core. In addition to central traits, Allport suggested that everyone has **secondary traits**, which are less obvious because they may not always appear in behavior; the particular situation, or context, matters. For example, Rowena might also have a secondary trait of "testiness" that shows up only when she goes on an extended diet. Personality characteristics, therefore, can appropriately be described in terms of *levels* ranging from dominant (cardinal) to representative (central) to occasional (secondary).

Personality Tests

There are practical reasons to measure personality traits. Suppose you're the personnel director at a large nuclear power plant. You need to hire responsible people to run the plant, people who have the right stuff to handle potentially dangerous materials in an emergency. You wouldn't want to hire someone like Liam, with his tendency to lie and act compulsively under pressure. How do you decide for a given individual? You can choose from two main categories of personality tests, *self-report inventories* and *projective tests*.

Self-Report Inventories

The most popular personality tests are **self-report inventories**, which use a questionnaire format to identify personality characteristics. People are asked to answer questions about how they typically think, act, and feel. Their responses, or *self-reports*, are compared to test averages compiled from thousands of other test takers. As a general rule, self-report inventories are easy to administer, and they paint a reliable picture of how someone differs from the average. Liam, for instance, would probably raise red flags on a number of measures; his answers are likely to show some disregard for social customs (compared to the average) and a marked tendency toward impulsiveness. If you were the personnel director, you could easily make your hiring—or, more accurately, no-hire—decision based partly on the test results.

Professionals use many kinds of self-report inventories. Some tests are based on popular trait theories. For example, to assess normal personality traits, you can administer the *Sixteen Personality Factor Questionnaire (16PF)*, which is a 187-item inventory designed to measure the 16 primary personality factors identified by Cattell (Cattell et al., 1970). Alternatively, there is the *Revised NEO Personality Inventory (NEO-PI-R)*, which measures your standing on the Big Five personality traits identified in Figure 11.2. One widely used self-report inventory is the *Minnesota Multiphasic Personality Inventory (MMPI)*. The MMPI contains hundreds of true–false questions that people answer about themselves (e.g., "I never get angry"); it's now available in several revised forms (e.g., Sellbom, 2019). The responses are expressed in a personality profile that describes a person's scores on various subscales (see Figure 11.3).

FIGURE 11.3   ■   MMPI Profiles

Psychologists often use the MMPI to help diagnose psychological disorders. A client's scores on the various clinical scales can be compared to average scores from people who are not suffering from psychological problems, as well as from people who have been diagnosed with specific problems, such as depression or schizophrenia.

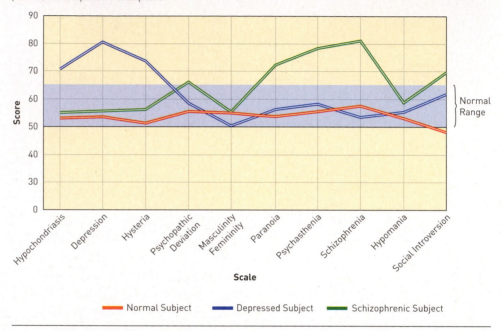

Source: Adapted from Weiten, 1995.

In addition to measuring personality characteristics, the MMPI is often used as a technique for diagnosing psychological disorders. A person's responses are compared to those of average test takers but also to the responses of individuals with known psychological problems. There are records, for example, of how people who suffer from such disorders as paranoia (irrational beliefs of persecution) are likely to answer certain questions. The test responses of someone like Liam can then be compared with the average "paranoia" personality profile to see if he fits the bill. Comparisons of this sort are useful in diagnosing problems and in making judgments about how appropriate an individual might be for a high-risk form of employment.

The main advantage of self-report inventories is that they are objective tests—they're standardized, everyone takes the same test, and they can easily be scored by a computer. There have been literally thousands of studies conducted testing the reliability and validity of these measures, especially the MMPI (Ben-Porath, 2003). The fact that the MMPI is one of the most widely applied measures in clinical assessment is one testament to its usefulness. At the same time, self-report inventories depend on the accuracy of the information provided by the test taker. If people choose to be deceptive on the test, or try to make themselves look good in some way, the results can be of little value (Nichols & Greene, 1997).

Projective Personality Tests

In a **projective personality test**, you're asked to interpret an unstructured or ambiguous stimulus. The assumption is that you'll "project" your thoughts and true feelings into the stimulus interpretation, thereby revealing elements of your personality. For example, take a look at the inkblot shown in

Figure 11.4, which is similar to the kind of unstructured stimulus used on the *Rorschach test*. Clearly, you argue, the inkblot exemplifies the fundamental decay of human society. The image symbolizes the need for aggressive action on the part of all responsible people—we must rise up and defeat the tyranny that, like an out-of-control cancer, is eating away at the virtue and values of common folk. Right? Well . . . Can you see how people's interpretation of such a stimulus might provide insight into their personality? If Liam always sees snakes and decaying dragons in the images, whereas Rowena sees butterflies and flowers, it's not too difficult to infer that they have quite different personalities.

FIGURE 11.4 ■ Projective Tests

In projective personality tests, we are asked to interpret unstructured or ambiguous stimuli. Our answers are presumed to provide insight into our personalities. What do you see hidden in this inkblot—the fundamental decay of human society?

Carolina Hrejsa/Body Scientific Intl.

Another popular projective personality test is the *Thematic Apperception Test (TAT)*. Instead of an inkblot, you're shown an ambiguous picture and asked to make up a story. Think of the *Mona Lisa*; what is she thinking and feeling? Again, the idea is that you'll reveal aspects of yourself in the stories you tell. Both the TAT and the Rorschach test use a standardized set of stimuli, so your responses can be compared to those of other people who've interpreted the same picture. Some psychologists prefer to use tests such as the TAT or the Rorschach, rather than self-report inventories, because projective tests help clients open up and talk about themselves and their problems (Medoff, 2004).

Projective tests allow you to respond freely, in a manner that's less restrictive than self-report inventories. But this can make the responses hard to interpret: How do we know what your responses truly mean? Psychologists have tried to develop reliable standards for interpreting responses in these kinds of tests. Typically, the researcher or clinician is trained to look for common themes in interpretation (such as a tendency to see death, decay, or aggressiveness) or for qualities such as originality. The clinician might also look for such things as the realistic nature of the interpretation: Does the response really match the perceptual structure of the stimulus? If you claim to see a dragon in an inkblot, your general view of the world may slant toward fantasy rather than reality. The degree to which you seek help in your interpretation may also be instructive. For example, people who constantly seek guidance from the clinician before giving an answer are likely to be classified as dependent.

Again, none of the personality assessment procedures we've discussed is perfect, neither self-report inventories nor projective tests. The scoring procedures for projective tests can be somewhat unreliable; it's not uncommon for administrators to arrive at quite different interpretations of the same subject's responses (see Beutler & Berren, 1995). At the same time, evidence suggests that projective tests, particularly the Rorschach test, are reasonably valid and reliable, "roughly on par with other commonly used tests" (Society for Personality Assessment, 2005, p. 220). Personality tests of this sort remain reasonably popular and widely used across the world, although there has been a decline in the popularity of these tests in the United States (Piotrowski, 2015).

KNOWLEDGE CHECK 11.1

Check your knowledge about conceptualizing and measuring personality by answering the following questions. (You will find the answers in the Appendix.)

1. For each of the following, identify the personality dimension of the Big Five that the statement best describes. Choose from the following terms: *extroversion, agreeableness, conscientiousness, neuroticism, openness.*

    a. Joanne is known as a risk-taker; she just loves to bungee jump: _____
    b. It's hard to get Mimi to stop talking: _____
    c. Raphael is very cooperative; he's virtually always sympathetic to my needs: _____
    d. Mark is very insecure; he always seems to feel guilty about something: _____
    e. Maureen is very productive, and she has very high ethical standards: _____

2. For each of the following, pick the personality test that the statement best describes. Choose from the following: *MMPI, NEO-PI-R, 16PF, Rorschach, TAT.*

    a. An ambiguous picture is shown, and the client is asked to make up a story about its contents: _____
    b. An objective self-report inventory that is often used in clinical settings: _____
    c. A test used primarily to measure someone's standing on the Big Five: _____
    d. A projective personality test using standardized inkblots as stimuli: _____
    e. Designed to create a personality profile representing Cattell's source traits: _____

DETERMINING HOW PERSONALITY DEVELOPS

As you've just seen, we can describe the personality traits of people like Liam or Rowena—perhaps their standing on the Big Five—and there's a good chance our measurements will be reasonably accurate and reliable. But description is not the same thing as explanation. We may know Rowena has a sunny disposition, but trait theories don't tell us much about the origins of those characteristics. Why do Liam and Rowena differ? In this section, we'll consider three very different approaches to understanding personality development: the psychodynamic theory of Sigmund Freud, humanistic theories, and social–cognitive theories.

The Psychodynamic Approach of Freud

Let's role-play: You're a clinician, and your latest patient, 18-year-old Katharina, complains of persistent physical problems. "I'm often overcome with a frightful choking feeling," she insists. "I have trouble catching my breath, and my head begins to spin. I truly think I must be about to die." Extensive examinations reveal no physical cause; the attacks appear suddenly without warning and seem unrelated to activity or general health. Katharina herself provides no insight: "There's nothing in my head when the attacks begin; my mind is a blank." The only additional information you have about Katharina is that she's reluctant to involve herself with members of the opposite sex, and she has a persistent dream in which she appears as a young child pursued from room to room by a shadowy figure.

Think about this case study for a moment. Can you draw any general conclusions about Katharina's personality from an analysis of her symptoms? The case itself is typical of the clinical problems Sigmund Freud (1856–1939) encountered in the late 19th century. Remember, Freud was a medical doctor by training. He established a private practice in Vienna, where he specialized in a branch of medicine concerned with disorders of the nervous system. Freud routinely saw patients like Katharina, who seemed to have physical problems without physical causes. He used these cases (known in that time as *hysterics*) as the basis for his highly influential **psychodynamic theory** of personality and mind, as well as for his method of treatment known as *psychoanalysis*.

The Structure of the Mind

Freud believed the human mind can be divided into three major parts: the *conscious*, the *preconscious*, and the *unconscious*. The **conscious mind** contains one's current awareness—those things that occupy the focus of your attention at the moment. The **preconscious mind** contains inactive but accessible thoughts and memories—those things that you can easily recall, if desired, but are simply not thinking about at the moment. Finally, the **unconscious mind** houses all the memories, urges, and conflicts that are beyond awareness. Freud believed that the content of the unconscious mind exerts powerful and long-lasting influences on behavior, despite the fact that it's hidden and unavailable to consciousness.

From Freud's perspective, Katharina's panicky behavior is likely to be caused by forces originating in her unconscious mind. Consider her dream of being chased by a shadowy figure. She can remember the details—her appearance as a young child, perhaps the color and shapes of the rooms—but her conscious memory of the dream, according to Freud, is unreliable. The parts of the dream she remembers, its *manifest content*, are merely symbolic of the dream's true unconscious meaning, or *latent content*. As we discussed in Chapter 6, Freud believed that dreams represent wish fulfillment; dreams are simply one way of gratifying desires or dealing with forbidden conflicts that are normally stored in the unconscious. In Katharina's case, the shadowy figure may well have arisen from a traumatic childhood experience—perhaps an unwelcome sexual advance by a relative—or even from her own unconscious desire for a sexual experience. Freud relied heavily on dream interpretation as a technique for mapping out the contents of the unconscious mind. Dreams, Freud argued, represent a "royal road" to the unconscious (Freud, 1900/1913).

The Structure of Personality

Freud believed that human personality consists of three parts: the *id, ego*, and *superego* (see Figure 11.5). As a student of biology, Freud was committed to the idea that behavior is influenced by biological forces. He was convinced that each of us is born with powerful instinctual drives, particularly related to sex and aggression, which motivate and control our actions. Freud used the term **id** to represent the portion of personality that is governed by these forces (translated from the Latin, *id* means "it"). As a component of personality, the id seeks immediate satisfaction of natural urges, without concern for the morals and customs of society. It obeys what Freud called the *pleasure principle*—the pursuit of pleasure through the satisfaction of animalistic urges. Ironically, from an adaptive standpoint, it's this dark side of personality—the seeker of pleasure—that guarantees survival of the species by motivating a desire for sexual intercourse.

At the same time, Freud understood that we're more than just irrational sex machines. He suggested that the forces of the id are balanced by a moral arm of personality called the superego. The **superego** is the part of our personality that encourages us to act in an ideal fashion—to act in accordance with the moral customs defined by parents and culture. The superego is shaped by experience, and it acts, in part, as a conscience; it makes us feel good when we act the way we should and feel guilty when our behavior strays from accepted standards. Like the id, the superego is essentially irrational—it seeks only moral perfection. Left to its own devices, the superego would undercut or block the more basic urges, even though those urges may help us satisfy fundamental survival needs. The superego follows an *idealistic principle*: Always act in a proper and ideal fashion as defined by parents and culture.

Sitting between the forces of the id and superego, and acting as a mediator, is the third component of personality—the ego. The **ego**, which comes from the Latin word for "I," serves an executive role in Freud's conception of personality. The ego encourages you to act with reason and deliberation and helps you conform to the requirements of the external world. Freud suggested that the ego obeys a *reality principle*; it monitors the real world looking for appropriate outlets for the id's needs, but it also listens intently to the moralistic preaching of the superego. The ego's goal is compromise among three demanding masters: the external world, the id, and the superego.

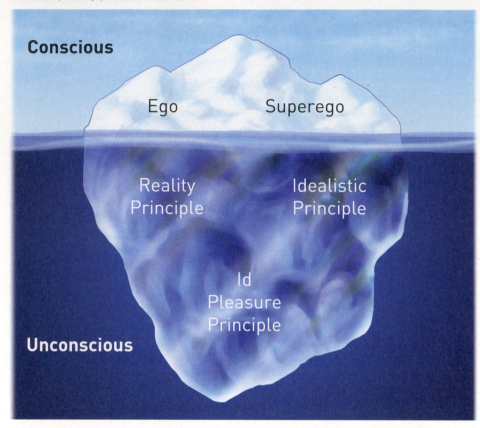

FIGURE 11.5 ■ Freud's View of Personality

Freud believed that our personalities are influenced by three forces. The id is the unconscious and unrepentant seeker of pleasure; the superego is the moral seeker of ideal behavior; and the ego is the executive that acts in accordance with reality. Just as most of an iceberg lies beneath the water, much of personality operates at an unconscious level.

Monica Wierzbicki/Body Scientific Intl.

Defense Mechanisms: The Ego's Arsenal

As noted previously, Freud believed we're unaware of the conflicts that regularly rage among the id, ego, and superego. We consciously experience only the side effects of these battles. For example, Freud believed the experience of *anxiety* (an unpleasant feeling of dread) often results from confrontations between the ego and the id. But the ego does not enter the battlefield unarmed. Freud proposed that the ego uses a variety of **defense mechanisms**, which are unconscious processes that can ward off the anxiety that comes from confrontation with the id.

The most important weapon in the ego's arsenal is **repression**, a process that keeps anxiety-producing thoughts and feelings buried in the unconscious. When a primitive urge from the id rears its ugly head, the ego actively represses the thought or feeling. The urge is blocked, jammed down into the dark recesses of the unconscious. Freud was convinced that we're particularly likely to repress sexual thoughts or experiences. Unrestricted sexual activity is typically discouraged by parents and society—this was particularly true in Freud's time—so sexual thoughts and feelings must be actively blocked by the reality-driven ego. Repression is

Freud believed that people sometimes deal with unacceptable feelings by attributing them to others through a process called projection. Freud might argue that the man on the left is "projecting" anger from some deeper conflict onto the woman on the right.

iStockPhoto/StockPlanets

a kind of self-deception—the mind deals with the anxiety-producing impulse by acting as if it isn't there. Similar kinds of self-deception occur with the other defense mechanisms Freud proposed. For a listing of some of these other important defense mechanisms, along with some examples, take a look at Concept Review 11.1.

CONCEPT REVIEW 11.1
DEFENSE MECHANISMS

Mechanism	Description	Example
Repression	Anxiety-producing thoughts and feelings are kept buried in the unconscious.	Horace doesn't remember the horrible fire that nearly killed him when he was a child.
Denial	You refuse to believe information that leads to anxiety.	Clay continues to deny that his four-martini lunches are a problem.
Rationalization	Explanations are created to deal with threatening thoughts.	Suze explains that she failed the test because the teacher asked the wrong questions.
Projection	Unacceptable wishes or feelings are attributed to others.	Lydia deals with her attraction to her married supervisor Bill by accusing fellow employee Kelly of flirting with him.
Reaction formation	You behave in a way that is counter or opposite to how you feel.	Although deeply resentful of how his mother treated him as a child, Juan calls her every day and showers her with affection.
Sublimation	Unacceptable impulses are channeled into socially acceptable activity.	Tze is rude and critical and likes to put people down. She decides to become a stand-up comic.

Psychosexual Development

To Freud, the unconscious mind is a bubbling cauldron of hidden conflicts, repressed memories, and biological urges. In the case of the biological urges, their origin is relatively clear—people are born with instinctual drives for self-preservation and sex. But where do the hidden conflicts come from? Why are people tormented by repressed memories that arise directly from life's experiences? Freud believed that people travel through stages of psychosexual development in their childhood (Freud, 1905/1962). How children deal with their emerging sexuality importantly affects the way they think and feel when they reach adulthood.

Each developmental stage is associated with a sensitive region of pleasure, which Freud called an *erogenous zone*. In roughly the first year of life—during the **oral stage**—pleasure is derived primarily from sucking and from placing things in the mouth (such as the mother's breast). In the second year of life, the focus of pleasure shifts to the anus. During this **anal stage**, pleasure arises from the process of defecation, the passing of feces. From ages 3 through 5, in the **phallic stage**, the genital regions of the body receive the focus of attention. The child obtains intense gratification from self-stimulation of the sexual organs.

Freud believed we move through these stages for primarily biological reasons. All organisms, including humans, need to learn how to gain nourishment, control the elimination of waste, and satisfy the sexual drive. Unfortunately, it's possible to become stalled, or fixated, at a particular stage, which, in turn, can have long-lasting effects on personality. By *fixation*, Freud meant that a person will continue to act in ways that are appropriate for a particular stage, seeking pleasure in stage-dependent ways, even after one has physically matured. There are two primary ways in which the fixation process can occur: Either the child gains excess gratification from a stage, or the child becomes excessively frustrated. It's the second of these two situations that has received the most attention.

Notice the oral and anal stages are associated with the potentially traumatic experiences of weaning and toilet training. Freud emphasized these experiences because a child can become easily frustrated during either process. People who are fixated in the oral stage, Freud believed, continue to derive pleasure from oral activities into adulthood. They become excessive smokers, or overeaters, or people who bite their nails. Fixation at the anal stage might lead to excessive neatness or messiness. The pleasure-seeking activities in these instances are symbolic, of course; compulsive room cleaning might be a symbolic attempt at the pleasure a child sometimes receives from the retention of feces.

Freud's interpretation of the phallic stage of psychosexual development was particularly controversial. He was convinced that small children have intense but unconscious sexual urges that become focused during this stage toward the opposite-sex parent. Boys become erotically attracted to their mother, a condition Freud called the *Oedipus complex* (after the Greek tragedy of Oedipus, who unknowingly killed his father and married his mother); girls become attracted to their father in what has been called the *Electra complex* (after the mythical Greek Electra, who hated and conspired to murder her mother). Desire for the opposite-sex parent creates enormous unconscious conflicts in the developing child. Freud believed that many adult sexual or relationship problems can be traced back to a failure to resolve these conflicts adequately.

After the age of 5 or 6, boys and girls enter a kind of psychosexual lull—called the **latency period**—during which their sexual feelings are largely suppressed. During this period, children direct their attention to social concerns, such as developing solid friendships. Beginning with the onset of puberty, one enters the **genital stage**. Here, sexuality reawakens, but in what Freud considered to be a more direct and appropriate fashion. Erotic tendencies now tend to be directed toward members of the opposite sex.

After the age of 5 or 6, boys and girls enter a latency period during which their sexual feelings are largely suppressed and they become more social.

iStockPhoto/HaiMinhDuong

Adler, Jung, and Horney

Freud's emphasis on the role of sexuality in personality development was received with skepticism by many, even from those who were firmly committed to his general approach. One of the first to split from Freud's inner circle of disciples was Alfred Adler (1870–1937). Adler disagreed strongly with Freud about the role of early psychosexual experience. He felt the important factor in personality development was not childhood trauma but rather how we come to deal with a basic sense of *inferiority*. To Adler, personality arises from our attempts to overcome or compensate for fundamental feelings of inadequacy. Adler was responsible for coining the term *inferiority complex*, a concept, he argued, that motivates a great deal of human behavior. It is our natural drive for superiority that explains motivation, not sexual gratification (Adler, 1927).

Adler was not the only dissenting voice. Other early advocates of Freud's theory began to break away and offer new and revised forms of the theory. One of the biggest personal blows to Freud was the departure of his disciple Carl Jung (1875–1961), whom Freud had picked as his intellectual heir. Jung, like Adler, was dissatisfied with Freud's narrow reliance on sexuality as the dominant source of human motivation. Jung believed instead in the idea of a "general life force," which he adopted from his extensive study of Eastern religions and mythology. This general life force was sexual in part but included other basic sources of motivation as well, such as the need for creativity (Jung, 1923).

Among Jung's more influential ideas was his concept of the **collective unconscious**. Jung believed that each person has a shared unconscious, in addition to the personal unconscious described by Freud, that's filled with mystical symbols and universal images that have accumulated over the lifetime of the human species. These symbols are inherited—passed from one generation to the next—and tend to represent enduring concepts (or *archetypes*), such as god, mother, earth, and water. Actually, the idea that all humans share certain concepts buried deep in a collective unconscious can also be found in the writings of Freud, but Jung expanded on the idea and assigned it a central focus.

Another blow to Freud was the dissenting voice of Karen Horney (1885–1952), one of the first women to learn and practice psychodynamic theory. Horney agreed with Freud's basic approach, but she rebelled against what she felt was Freud's male-dominated views of sexuality. Freud had argued in his writings that women are fundamentally dissatisfied with their sex—they suffer from what he called *penis envy*—a view that Horney found unsatisfactory in many ways. She boldly confronted Freud, both personally and in her writings, and offered revised forms of psychodynamic theory that treated women in a more balanced way (Horney, 1967). One of her more lasting theoretical contributions was her insistence that a link exists between the irrational beliefs people hold about themselves and their psychological problems (Horney, 1945). As you'll see in Chapters 14 and 15, this idea continues to be influential in the conceptualization and treatment of psychological disorders.

Karen Horney rebelled against what she felt were Freud's male-dominated views on sexuality.

Bettmann/Contributor via Getty Images

Evaluating Psychodynamic Theory

Few psychological theories have been as influential as Freud's. Many of the terms and concepts he introduced—particularly his ideas about the unconscious—have become part of modern language and beliefs. You were probably familiar with such Freudian terms as *repression, id, ego*, and *projection* before you opened this psychology text. Moreover, the suggestion that personality is determined in part by how we learn to satisfy basic biological drives, as well as deal effectively with the demands of society and the outside world, is still a very modern and widely accepted idea (R. F. Bornstein, 2003). But psychodynamic theory, as envisioned by Freud, has steadily lost its influence over the years.

Part of the problem is that many of the ideas Freud proposed lack scientific rigor; he never articulated concepts such as the id, superego, and ego with ringing precision. As a result, it's been difficult, if not impossible, to subject them to proper scientific testing. Consider the concept of repression, which Freud believed to be the bedrock of psychodynamic theory. If repressed memories are hidden behind the veil of the unconscious, expressing themselves only in masked and largely symbolic ways, can we ever be certain that we've correctly identified these unconscious influences? Most of the evidence for repression has come from clinical case studies, from individuals who are probably not representative of the general population. It's not easy to study repression in the laboratory, either because of ethical concerns or because we simply don't know what conditions need to be met for repression to occur. Many people have undergone traumatic events in their childhood yet remain psychologically healthy (Loftus, 1993). In fairness, there have been attempts over the years to provide more rigorous definitions of the various defense mechanisms that Freud proposed, and to test them empirically (e.g., see Cramer, 2015), but no general consensus has emerged and such mechanisms are rarely a part of modern theories of personality.

Freud was an innovative thinker, and he should be given credit for challenging the ideas of his time. For example, prior to Freud, Western culture remained firmly committed to long-standing ideas about the innocence and purity of childhood. Sexuality, it was widely believed, was absent from personality prior to puberty. Freud recognized that at least some forms of sexual pleasure can occur in childhood and can influence behavior and attachment. But he tied his views of sexuality to particular zones of the body, and to a particular developmental stage–based trajectory, without essentially any scientific evidence. Modern views of cognitive and social development, as we discussed in Chapter 4, bear little resemblance to Freud's ideas (see Silverman, 2020).

In addition to the problems of testability and lack of scientific rigor, Freud's theory is often criticized for its biases against women. As mentioned earlier, he painted women as individuals unsatisfied with their gender, who need to come to grips with the fact that they lack a penis. Freud was also reluctant to believe women's testimonials of rape or childhood sexual abuse—he saw these accounts as symbolic expressions of unconscious conflicts rather than as actual events. Most psychologists consider these positions, along with Freud's general male-oriented approach, to be unrealistic and even distasteful (see Else-Quest & Hyde, 2018).

Humanistic Approaches to Personality

There's another reason many psychologists don't like Freud's psychodynamic approach: It paints a very dark picture of human nature. In describing the origins of personality, Freud often compared the mind to a battlefield, where irrational forces are continuously engaged in a struggle for control. According to Freud, our actions are motivated primarily by the need to satisfy animalistic urges related to sex and aggression; our conscious awareness of why we act is misleading and symbolic, representative of conflicts created during toilet training or as a result of being weaned.

Humanistic psychology is largely a reaction against this pessimistic view of the human spirit. Humanistic psychologists don't talk about battlefields and conflict; instead, they speak of growth and potential. It's not animalistic urges that explain personality; it's the *human* with our unparalleled capacity for self-awareness, choice, responsibility, and growth. Humanistic psychologists believe each of us can control our own behavioral destiny—we can consciously rise above whatever animalistic urges might be coded in our genes. We're built and designed for personal growth, to seek our fullest potential, to self-actualize—to become all we are capable of becoming.

To a humanist, there are many ways to explain individual differences in behavior. First, each of us is considered to be naturally *unique*. We're more than the sum of a set of predictable parts—everyone is a unique and individual *whole*. Second, the environment influences the natural growth process. Like plants, people will grow best in fertile and supportive environments; barren environments can't stop the growth process, but they can prevent us from realizing our own true potential (Rogers, 1963). Third, and perhaps most important, how we act is determined by our unique view of the world—our interpretation of reality. How we view ourselves and the environment guides and motivates our actions. Notice the emphasis here is on conscious mental processes. We're assumed to be responsible for our own actions, although sometimes our subjective experience of reality is not an accurate reflection of the real world. We'll consider the views of two prominent humanistic psychologists in this section, Carl Rogers and Abraham Maslow.

Carl Rogers and the Self

To humanist Carl Rogers (1902–1987), the essence of personality is wrapped up in the concept of the self or, more specifically, the *self-concept*. He defined the **self-concept** as an organized set of perceptions about one's abilities and characteristics—it amounts to that keen sense of oneself, what it means to be "I" or "me." Rogers believed that the self-concept comes primarily from social interactions, particularly the interactions we have with our parents, friends, and other significant role models. The people around us mold and shape our self-image through their ongoing evaluations of our actions.

We rely on the judgments of others to tell us who we truly are and what we can hope to become, Rogers argued, because of a basic need for **positive regard**. We value what others think of us and consistently seek others' approval, love, and companionship. Unfortunately, in real life, **conditions of worth** tend to be attached to the approval of others. For instance, let's suppose you come from a family that values education and intellectual pursuits. You, however, couldn't care less about such things—your interests are in popular music and athletics. To gain acceptance from your parents, you may deny your true feelings and modify your self-concept to bring it more in line with what your parents believe: "I'm not someone who cares about a trivial activity like sports; I'm someone who cares intensely about the pursuit of knowledge."

But herein lies a major problem, Rogers argued. The self-concept that you work so hard to form inevitably conflicts with what you truly feel from experience. You may decide to spend the evening reading the philosophical musings of Immanuel Kant, but you'll probably find your mind drifting and your feelings of self-worth diminishing. Rogers called this condition **incongruence**, which he defined as a discrepancy between the image you hold of yourself—your self-concept—and your actual day-to-day experiences. Incongruence leads to the experience of anxiety and ultimately forms the basis for psychological problems. True psychological health, Rogers suggested, comes when the self-concept is *congruent* (agrees) with your true feelings and experiences—that is, when your opinions and beliefs about yourself accurately reflect your everyday experiences. Chapter 15 outlines what Rogers felt was the appropriate therapeutic solution to conditions of incongruence. To anticipate the discussion just a bit, Rogers was convinced that the therapist's proper role is to be nonjudgmental—to accept the feelings and actions of the client unconditionally. By eliminating the *conditions of worth*, the client is able to develop a self-concept more congruent with reality.

With respect to personality and its development, Rogers believed that regularities in behavior come largely from the structure of the self-concept. Personality is defined by consistent behavior across situations; people tend to act consistently, he argued, simply because their actions consistently mirror their established self-concept. We act in ways that support our beliefs about ourselves. More often than not, we actively seek to protect our self-image. Given a choice, you might consistently choose to read philosophy rather than watch sports because it's consistent with your vision of *you*. If you chose sports, you would need to reconsider who you really are, which is the sort of confrontation that we tend to avoid.

Sometimes we do things that we don't like to preserve our self-concept.

iStockPhoto/SDI Productions

Abraham Maslow and Self-Actualization

Although Carl Rogers was committed to the role played by the self-concept, he also believed strongly in the potential for personal growth. We may act defensively and seek to protect a rigid self-concept, but at our core we're creative people who have the power to fulfill our personal potential. This idea that everyone has a basic need for **self-actualization**—the need to move forward toward the realization of potential—also plays a pivotal role in Abraham Maslow's view of personality.

We will outline Maslow's views in more detail in Chapter 12 when we discuss motivation. Maslow believed that human motivation is grounded in the satisfaction of need. There are certain things that humans must do—such as obtain food and water and protect themselves from danger—before their potential can be fully realized. One of Maslow's main contributions was his proposal of the *need hierarchy*, shown in Figure 11.6, which expresses the order in which needs must be satisfied. Notice that safety and survival needs sit below the need for love and belonging in the need hierarchy. It's unlikely that you'll appear to be spiritual or loving if you're constantly worrying about your next meal. It's only after the basic needs are satisfied—those related to survival—that the more spiritual side of personality can be developed.

FIGURE 11.6 ■ **Maslow's Hierarchy of Needs**

Maslow proposed that our observable personality characteristics will indicate where we are positioned in the hierarchy of needs. Someone who must worry constantly about biological or safety needs will behave differently than someone who is seeking to satisfy needs at the highest levels of the pyramid.

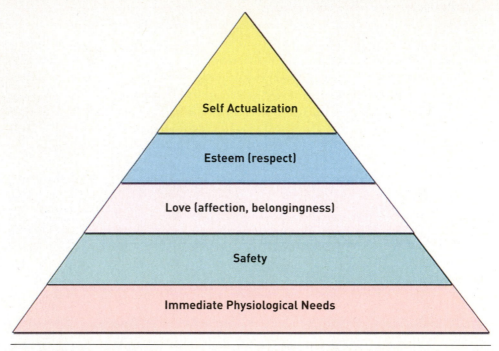

Source: From Figure 1 in Kenrick, D. T., Griskevicius, V., Neuberg, S. L., & Schaller, M. (2010).

Your personality characteristics will reflect where you're positioned in the hierarchy of needs. Maslow had a very positive view of human nature. A person may consistently act unkind, defensive, or aggressive, he argued, but these personality traits appear only when one fails to satisfy basic needs—they'll never be fundamental to the human spirit. To support this claim, Maslow pointed to the behavior of individuals who he felt had progressed through the entire hierarchy. The characteristics of human personality, he argued, are highly consistent across individuals at the highest levels of the hierarchy. People who are self-actualizing show none of the darker personality traits exhibited by those locked in at lower levels; they tend to be positive, creative, accepting individuals (Leclerc et al., 1998).

Maslow's conclusions were based largely on the study of particular individuals, people whom he knew and admired. He also studied the personality traits of people who were very successful, such as Albert Einstein, Abraham Lincoln, and Eleanor Roosevelt. All self-actualizing people, he argued, share certain personality traits. They tend to be accepting of themselves and others, to be self-motivated and problem oriented, and to have a strong ethical sense and hold democratic values. Self-actualizing people also often undergo what Maslow called *peak experiences*—emotional, often religious, experiences in which one's place in a unified universe becomes clear and meaningful. Notice these are all positive traits; self-actualizing people tend to be at peace with themselves and with the world.

Evaluating Humanistic Theories

The humanistic approach, with its optimistic emphasis on positive growth, has had considerable influence in psychology. Concepts like the *self* and the *self-concept* have received a great deal of attention, and as you'll see in Chapter 15, humanistic approaches to psychotherapy are popular and widely applied. The humanistic approach provides a nice balance to the pessimism of Freud. Rather than ignoring conscious influences on behavior, humanists champion personal choice and responsibility. Take a trip to your local bookstore and check the shelves devoted to psychology—you'll find that many of the books emphasize the control *you* can exert over your own behavior. This is one indication of the humanists' widespread impact, especially in tapping the general population's interest in psychology.

But as contributors to scientific psychology, humanistic psychologists are often criticized (see Funder, 2001). Many of the basic concepts we've discussed, such as the potential for growth and self-actualization, are vague and difficult to pin down. It's also not clear where these tendencies come from and under which conditions they'll fully express themselves. Remember, too, that the humanists place important emphasis on personal, subjective experience. This means that researchers must often rely on self-reports to generate data, and some question whether self-reports produce reliable and accurate representations of internal psychological processes (Bland & DeRobertis, 2020). So, in addition to problems of conceptual vagueness, humanism lacks adequate testability.

The humanistic approach to personality is also criticized for adopting too optimistic and self-centered a view of human nature. The arguments of Rogers and Maslow are partly reactions against the pessimism of Freud. But like Freud, humanistic theorists have adopted a rather extreme view of human nature: People constantly strive for growth, unless constrained in some way by the environment, and are driven to pursue lofty individual goals. Thus, we have the dark view described by Freud (people are driven by unconscious animalistic urges) countered by the extremely optimistic views of the humanists. Many psychologists believe it's better to adopt a balanced approach: People are neither inherently good nor inherently evil; they sometimes act in self-interested ways that appear animalistic, but these actions are often adaptive and increase one's likelihood of survival (Kenrick, 2011). At the same time, placing too much emphasis on unconscious biological motives is itself misleading—we undoubtedly exercise considerable conscious control over our behavior.

Social–Cognitive Approaches to Personality

One particularly important characteristic of both the psychodynamic and humanistic conceptions of personality is their emphasis on built-in or natural needs. People are born with animalistic urges that must be satisfied, or they greet the world naturally good with a compelling need for personal growth. The environment plays a critical role in determining final personality, but the role is essentially secondary—personal experiences and cultural norms merely constrain or enhance the full expression of natural needs.

But what about the possibility that people simply *learn* to act in consistent ways? Isn't it possible that Liam's tendency to lie and Rowena's outgoing and sunny disposition come entirely from experience? Maybe Liam stole candy when he was 4 and was rewarded by not being caught; maybe Rowena learned at an early age that smiles are often met with smiles and that a good deed will be returned in kind. According to **social–cognitive theories** of personality, human experience, not human nature, is the primary cause of personality growth and development. The *social* side of the approach emphasizes the role of experience; the *cognitive* side emphasizes how one's interpretation of the experience plays a significant role in determining what's actually learned.

Behaviorist Roots

Social–cognitive theories were originally influenced by the behaviorist tradition in psychology. As discussed in Chapter 1, behaviorists believe that psychologists should look to *observable behavior* for answers to psychological questions; the research goal is to understand how behavior changes when rewards and punishments are applied. What we call personality, then, could be nothing more than the collective actions we've learned to produce in various situations. As with all other animals, if our behavior is rewarded in a particular situation, we'll be more likely to repeat it the next time we're in the same situation.

There are three main ways in which people acquire such response tendencies (see Chapter 7). First, through *classical conditioning*, we learn that certain kinds of events signal other events. Imagine that as a small child Little Albert is frightened in the presence of a white furry rat; he develops a specific fear, or phobia, of small furry animals that continues on into adulthood. His behavior is consistent over time—he panics at the sight of anything small and furry—due in large part to this early childhood experience. Second, through *operant conditioning*, we learn about the consequences of our behavior. If we're rewarded in some context for acting aggressively, we'll tend to act aggressively in the future. If we are repeatedly put down at parties for being outgoing, we'll learn to be withdrawn and to avoid social situations. Here again it is the environment—one's past history of rewards and punishments—that is shaping behavior.

The third way that consistencies in behavior can develop is through observational learning, or *modeling*. We observe the behavior of others around us—especially role models—and imitate the behavior. As we discussed in Chapter 7, it's adaptive for organisms to mimic the behavior of others, because in this way they can learn appropriate behavior without directly experiencing the consequences of an inappropriate action. Rhesus monkeys, for example, learn to show fear in the presence of snakes through modeling their parents' behavior, not from directly experiencing the negative consequences of a bite (Mineka, 1987). Modeling approaches assume that many personality traits come from copying the behavior of others, especially when the behavior of the model regularly leads to positive, reinforcing outcomes and, perhaps, when we are likely to feel empathy with the model (Bandura, 1986; Olsson et al., 2016).

The Role of Internal Beliefs

Very few psychologists believe the environment alone determines your personality. This is because the psychological effect of most experiences—positive or negative—depends crucially on how you interpret the experience. Suppose we ask two groups of people to perform a relatively difficult task, such as predicting sequences of numbers. We tell one of the groups that performance on the task is based on skill; the other group is told that success or failure is due entirely to chance. (Unknown to the participants, we actually rig the procedure so people in both groups will succeed and fail the same number of times.) It turns out that task effort, as well as the amount learned, depends on how much control you think you have over the outcome. People who believe their performance is skill-based work harder and learn more from the task (Rotter et al., 1961).

The important point here is that the groups perform differently even though everyone receives exactly the same number of rewards and punishments. So it's not only the literal distribution of rewards and punishments that matters; your belief about the origins of those consequences is also important. Some psychologists believe that enduring personality traits are based partly on one's perceived **locus of control**—how much control you feel you have over your environment (Rotter, 1966). People who are oriented externally, known as *externals*, perceive little connection between their own actions and the occurrence of rewards; they tend to see themselves as powerless and generally have low levels of self-esteem (Lefcourt, 1982). Internally oriented people, known as *internals*, view the world as responsive to their actions; they feel confident they can control when rewards and punishments occur. Internally oriented people display high levels of self-confidence and tend to score higher than externally oriented individuals on a variety of academic and social measures (Ryckman, 2004). People with an internal locus of control also show more persistence when looking for a job and often end up with higher wages (Caliendo et al., 2015).

Interestingly, U.S. college students seem to be trending toward more of an external locus of control. Young Americans increasingly believe they have little direct control over what happens in their lives (Twenge, 2014). For example, one study found that the average college student in 2002 had more of an external locus of control than 80% of the college students in the early 1960s (Twenge et al., 2004; but see Trzesniewski & Donnellan, 2010, for a different result). Why the trend? No one knows for certain, but greater cynicism, increased social isolation, negative social trends (including increased media coverage of negative events), and the tendency to adopt a "victim mentality" have all been suggested as reasons. It's an unfortunate trend because, again, an external locus of control, and its accompanying feelings of powerlessness, is typically associated with a host of negative consequences.

How we act and feel often depends on how much control we think we have over the environment. Externals, who perceive little connection between their own actions and rewards, tend to see themselves as powerless and to have low levels of self-esteem.

iStockPhoto/AntonioGuillem

Locus of control is related to another psychological concept called **self-efficacy** (Bandura, 1986, 2001). Whereas locus of control refers to your beliefs about how much control you can exert over the environment, self-efficacy is defined as the beliefs you hold about your own ability. For example, Raymond might be convinced people can control their environment, but feel he personally lacks the skill. In this case, he would be rated as low in self-efficacy, with an internal locus of control. On the other hand, he might be extremely confident in his basic abilities (high self-efficacy) but believe he can do little to control the things around him (external locus of control). Often a person's degree of self-efficacy is related to particular situations or tasks. You might believe strongly in your ability to excel academically but lack any measure of confidence in your social skills.

Locus of control and self-efficacy are important concepts. They tell us that what we learn from the environment depends on more than the delivery of rewards and punishments. What you expect and believe about the world and your abilities influences the types of tasks you'll choose to engage in, as well as the effectiveness of rewards and punishments. If you're convinced you have little or no ability in social settings—your self-efficacy is low—you'll either avoid going to parties or act nervous and uncomfortable when you do go. If you feel you have no chance of succeeding in your psychology course because the teaching assistant doesn't like you—that is, you've adopted an external locus of control—your motivation to work hard is likely to be low. Note in these cases your internal beliefs end up affecting your overt behavior (avoidance of parties or class), which, in turn, affects the likelihood that you'll be rewarded. Psychologist Albert Bandura (1986) has referred to this relationship between beliefs, overt behavior, and the environment as one of **reciprocal determinism**: Beliefs, behavior, and the environment interact to shape what's learned from experience (see Figure 11.7). Recent work suggests that the concept of reciprocal determinism can be used effectively to explain performance in academic settings across a variety of cultures (T. Williams & Williams, 2010).

FIGURE 11.7 ■ Reciprocal Determinism

Bandura proposed that personality is shaped by complex interactions among expectations and beliefs, behavior, and the rewards and punishments delivered by the environment. In this case, expecting failure in class (personal/cognitive factors) affects studying (behavior), which in turn affects the likelihood of success on the test (environment). The arrows point both ways, suggesting that these factors all interact.

Illustrated by Sarah Yeh

Evaluating Social–Cognitive Theories

Most psychologists believe learning plays an important role in personality development. Furthermore, the idea that cognitive factors help determine what's learned, rather than just rewards and punishments, is also widely accepted. Critics of the social–cognitive approach simply argue that it is insufficient as a general account of personality development (Feist et al., 2018; Ryckman, 2008). Social–cognitive theories, for example, tend to neglect the individual as a *whole*, choosing instead to concentrate on how people have learned to respond in particular situations.

The approach has been criticized as well for failing to emphasize the role of biological and genetic factors in development. Although biological drives and urges may not completely determine personality, biological ancestry can't be ignored. By choosing to focus primarily on the environment, the social–cognitive theorists sometimes ignore important motivational factors that are controlled largely by biological processes. For example, there appear to be stable sex differences in personality that exist cross-culturally, suggesting that hormonal differences early in development play a role in personality development (Schmitt et al., 2017). In fairness, social–cognitive theories recognize this limitation and have tried to integrate genetic, biological, and environmental factors into a more general theory of personality development (e.g., Mischel & Shoda, 1998). For a summary of the different views of personality development, see Concept Review 11.2.

CONCEPT REVIEW 11.2
VIEWS OF PERSONALITY DEVELOPMENT

Approach	Description	Example
Psychodynamic	Personality can be influenced by forces originating in the unconscious and is made up of three components: *id* (instinctive urges), *ego* (conscious decision making), and *superego* (conscience).	Jane is strongly attracted to men, but her parents are very strict about dating, so her sexual feelings are repressed. As a result, she tends to avoid men and is uncomfortable when she is around them.
Humanistic	We ultimately control our own behavioral destiny. Personality reflects our uniqueness, as well as our environment and our personal view of the world.	Because of criticism from her parents during childhood, Jane has developed a poor self-concept. She has not experienced unconditional positive regard and as a result feels uncomfortable with who she is.
Social–cognitive	Personality results from an interaction between the experiences delivered by the environment and our interpretations of those experiences.	Jane goes to an all-girls high school and doesn't encounter many boys. As a result, she is a bit uncomfortable around them and acts nervous. They then tend to avoid her, and she feels even more uncomfortable.

KNOWLEDGE CHECK 11.2

Check your knowledge of how personality develops by deciding whether each of the following statements is most likely to have been made by a psychodynamic, humanistic, or social–cognitive personality theorist. (You will find the answers in the Appendix.)

1. Ethel talks a lot, but that's only because she's trying to cover up her true feelings of inadequacy: _____

2. Teresa is very demanding, but that's because her boyfriend always gets her what she wants: _____

3. Sally can't help herself—her basic needs are preventing her from realizing her true potential: _____

4. Sharma seems to be a tireless volunteer, but in truth she secretly resents people in need: _____

5. Robert isn't really an intellectual—he just acts that way because both of his parents are famous academics and he desperately wants to please them: _____

6. Henry is shy because he lacks confidence in his abilities, and he's convinced that he can't really influence or control the people around him: _____

7. Ralph sleeps around a lot, but that's because he can't control his animalistic nature: _____

RESOLVING THE PERSON–SITUATION DEBATE

According to social–cognitive theories, behavior is primarily a product of the environment. As a result, you might be expected to act somewhat inconsistently from one situation to the next. If you're rewarded for acting bold and aggressive when negotiating a deal (such as buying a car), you'll almost certainly act bold and aggressive in such situations in the future. But if similar actions lead to rejection in the classroom or in social situations, you might very well turn meek and mild in class or at a party. If you think about it, you probably know people who seem to change their behavior at the drop of a hat, acting one way in one situation and quite differently in another.

This kind of reasoning really strikes at the core of personality. Remember, personality is defined in terms of lasting qualities—the characteristics that distinguish us from others and lead us to act consistently across situations. Throughout this chapter, we've assumed that such characteristics exist and that they can be measured and interpreted. But the assumption of cross-situational consistency in behavior has been challenged by some prominent psychologists, notably Walter Mischel, and the issue has come to be known as the **person–situation debate**.

The Person–Situation Debate

The argument is really a simple one. If people possess unique and enduring personality traits, we should be able to predict their behavior from one situation to the next. If you believe Liam to be dishonest, perhaps because you witnessed him peering over Rowena's shoulder during a history test, you expect him to be dishonest in the future. You predict he will pocket a dropped wallet or take the money Rowena left lying on the counter. Put more technically, measurements of behavior should correlate across situations; that is, if you know the chances that people will perform a trait-related action in situation A, you should be able to predict the chances that they will perform a similar action in situation B.

Unfortunately, as Mischel (1968) pointed out decades ago, there's limited evidence for this assumption (see also D. R. Peterson, 1968). If you look carefully at studies reporting correlations between measures of behavior that tap a particular kind of personality trait, such as how honest you are at two different points in time, the correlations are almost always low. Whereas a correlation of 1.00 implies perfect behavioral consistency across situations, Mischel found that actual correlations rarely exceeded .30 and were sometimes even lower (see also Kenrick & Funder, 1988; L. Ross & Nisbett, 1991). To say the least, Mischel's conclusions were quite controversial; in fact, they rocked the foundation of personality theory. Without consistency in behavior, the psychological construct of personality has little meaning.

Situational Consistency

Despite the data, very few psychologists (including Mischel) reject the concept of personality altogether. People may not always act consistently *across* situations, but they do tend to act consistently *within* a situation. For example, in a famous study by Hartshorne and May (1928), the honesty of schoolchildren was tested by placing them in situations in which they could act dishonestly without much chance of being caught (money was left on a table, cheating on a test was possible, and so on). Little evidence of cross-situational consistency was found, but the children did tend to act the same way in a similar situation. For instance, kids who cheated on a test were not necessarily more likely to steal money, but they were more likely to cheat on a test again if given the chance. In short, people do act consistently from one situation to the next, as long as the situations are similar (Mischel & Peake, 1982; Mischel & Shoda, 1995).

Moreover, results of the type reported by Hartshorne and May and others (see Mischel, 1968) are based primarily on the observation of single individual behaviors (e.g., Did the child steal the money on the table?) rather than on collections of behaviors. To get an accurate estimate of a true personality trait, many psychologists believe, you need to collect lots of observations, not just one; single observations tend to be unreliable and not necessarily representative of true behavior (S. Epstein, 1979). One reason reliable personality traits are often obtained through psychometric tests (see the earlier discussion of trait theorists) might be that the collected ratings are based on a long history of watching oneself or others behave (L. Ross & Nisbett, 1991).

In fact, if you record how people act across longer periods of time, rather than in single situations, they tend to act quite consistently. For example, Fleeson (2001) asked people to rate themselves on the

Big Five trait adjectives five times a day for a period of several weeks (e.g., How "talkative" were you in the last three hours?). Although people's ratings on the Big Five dimensions varied a lot over the course of a day, their average ratings over a week were quite stable from one week to the next. For any given Big Five dimension, such as extroversion, we're apparently capable of a wide range of expression, but our average rating remains stable and unique over time (Fleeson, 2004).

Self-Monitoring

Some psychologists have argued that the tendency to act consistently or haphazardly across different situations may itself be a kind of personality trait and, furthermore, its expression may depend on the culture in which you live (K. D. Locke et al., 2017). People differ in the extent to which they engage in **self-monitoring**, which is the tendency to mold or change your behavior to fit the situation at hand (M. Snyder, 1974, 1987). People who are high self-monitors attend closely to their present situation and change their behavior to best fit their needs. They're likely to alter their behavior, and even their stated opinions and beliefs, simply to please someone with whom they're currently interacting. People who are low self-monitors are less likely to change their actions or beliefs and, consequently, are more likely to show consistency in their behavior across situations (Gangestad & Snyder, 1985).

Scales have been developed to measure self-monitoring tendencies. Typically, you're asked to respond to statements such as "I'm not always the person that I appear to be" or "I might deceive people by acting friendly when I really dislike them." People who score highly on self-monitoring, not surprisingly, are likely to conform to social norms. They also tend to be aware of how their behavior is affecting others. High self-monitors even seem to remember the actions of others better than low self-monitors, especially when those actions are unexpected or unusual (Beers et al., 1997). Thus, self-monitoring can be quite adaptive: It's usually in our interest to monitor the environment and change our behavior accordingly (Graziano & Bryant, 1998; Mischel & Shoda, 1998). For more on the practical value of self-monitoring, take a look at the Practical Solutions feature.

PRACTICAL SOLUTIONS: THE VALUE OF SELF-MONITORING

Not surprisingly, your personality traits can play an important role in determining how well you succeed in life. Consider your ability to self-monitor—that is, your capacity to "act like different persons in different situations and with different people" (M. Snyder, 1995, p. 39). Clearly, if your goal is politics, self-monitoring would be a plus, but people who rate highly in self-monitoring seem also to have advantages in many other professions and activities. For example, high self-monitors tend to get better performance evaluations on the job—from both peers and supervisors (J. S. Miller & Cardy, 2000). High self-monitors even get higher tips when employed as waiters and waitresses at restaurants (M. Lynn & Simons, 2000).

Why are high self-monitors successful? One factor is their natural tendency to be good actors—they can tell people what they want to hear in a believable way and then act accordingly. High self-monitors also spend time closely observing their environments and, as a result, tend to be perceptive at reading other people. High self-monitors are good at spotting deception, and they're usually quite accurate in judging personality characteristics (Sanz et al., 1996). The net result is that high self-monitors tend to occupy central and important positions in social networks, which, in turn, helps them perform well on the job (Ajay et al., 2001).

Should we all try to become high self-monitors, or at least improve on our self-monitoring skills? As with many other personality traits, there may be a genetic component to self-monitoring (Gangestad & Simpson, 1993), so it's possible that our options are limited. And it's important to note that there are some downsides to the self-monitoring trait. For example, high self-monitors are more concerned with a person's social status than low self-monitors; they also have difficulty committing to romantic relationships, show less marital satisfaction, and are more likely to divorce (Leone & Hall, 2003). In addition, couples that consist of two high self-monitors are less likely to trust one another than couples consisting of two low self-monitors (Norris & Zweigenhaft, 1999). High self-monitors also tend to stick to well-defined social situations that, in turn, allow them to use established social scripts (Ickes et al., 2006). Perhaps not surprisingly, high self-monitors are also more likely to be addicted to Facebook than low self-monitors (Pornsakulvanich, 2018).

Successful politicians are often high self-monitors, which means they attend closely to the situation and behave accordingly.

Chase Guttman/Alamy Stock Photo

From a practical standpoint, it might make sense for employers to pay attention to the self-monitoring trait. It seems clear that self-monitoring is related to job performance, especially in jobs that require adapting to social situations. People who adapt well to their environment are more likely to see the rewards it can bring, even at the risk of appearing to be a little inconsistent in their behavior across situations.

A Resolution

Most psychologists resolve the person–situation debate by simply assuming that it's necessary to take both the person and the situation into account. It's unlikely that either alone is enough to explain behavior or to allow us to predict consistency (Mischel, 2004). People *interact* with situations, and how they behave will depend partly on what's required by current needs. Personality "traits" will reveal themselves primarily in situations in which they're relevant and may not otherwise. Similarly, given the right situation, each of us is capable of acting in a way that seems to violate our basic nature. Recognition of the vital role of the person and the situation is so widespread that one prominent personality psychologist proclaimed that the person–situation debate "can at least be declared about 98% over" (Funder, 2001, p. 199). (We'll return to this issue, and provide some compelling illustrations of the power of the situation, when we take up the general topic of social psychology in Chapter 13.)

Genetic Factors in Personality

There's other evidence supporting the "person" in personality development. We may be born with certain genetic predispositions—perhaps our brains are wired in a certain way—that cause us to act in consistent ways throughout our lifetime. Indeed, recent neuroimaging work suggests that the Big Five personality traits are associated with the activation of unique regions in the brain (DeYoung et al., 2010; also see Mitchell & Kumari, 2016). It's not unusual for family members to show similar personality traits, although experience could play an important role in producing these similarities. At the same time, brothers and sisters can show strikingly different personality traits, even though they've been raised in what seem to be highly similar environments. Observations like these indicate that more than the environment is at work in determining personality.

Twin Data

Evidence for genetic factors in personality, as in the study of intelligence, comes primarily from twin studies. Identical twins are compared with fraternal twins when the twins have been reared together or apart. There are reports of identical twins who were separated at birth but ended up sharing many of the same personality traits. One example is the identical twins Oscar and Frank—one raised as a Nazi in Czechoslovakia and the other as a Jew in Trinidad. When they were reunited in 1979, it was discovered that they shared numerous odd but consistent behaviors. For example, they both had a habit of sneezing deliberately in elevators to surprise people, and they both liked to flush toilets before and after use.

However, examples such as these can't be used to make a convincing scientific case. Coincidences are possible, and some of the more famous reunited twins may have had ulterior motives for manufacturing shared traits (for example, Oscar and his brother eventually sold the rights to their story in Hollywood). More compelling evidence comes from group studies, in which the personality characteristics of large numbers of twins are analyzed. In one such study (Tellegen et al., 1988), 217 pairs of identical twins who had been reared together and 44 pairs of twins who had been reared apart were compared with 114 pairs of fraternal twins reared together and 27 pairs reared apart. Each of the participants was administered the MMPI, which, as you remember from our earlier discussion, is a widely used questionnaire for measuring personality traits.

Some of the results of this study are shown in Figure 11.8, for several of the personality traits measured by the MMPI. Of main interest is the similarity between members of a twin pair, expressed in terms of correlation coefficients. In other words, for a trait such as aggressiveness or positive emotionality, can we predict the score that one twin will receive on the MMPI if we know the score of the other twin? Correlations close to 1.00 suggest that members of a twin pair share many of the same personality traits. As the figure indicates, identical twins tend to show higher correlations than fraternal twins, regardless of whether they've been reared together or apart. Twins who share the same genes but have been raised in different households tend to have more similar personality traits than fraternal twins who have been raised together. Studies focusing on the Big Five personality dimensions have reached similar conclusions: There appears to be a strong genetic component underlying individual differences in personality measures. Overall, the current consensus is that the heritability of personality is around .40, meaning that 40% of the individual differences that one finds in personality are due to genetic factors (Sanchez-Roige et al., 2018; Vukasovic & Bratko, 2015). Genetic links have also been established using genome-wide analyses, although use of this methodology is still in its early stages (e.g., Lo et al., 2017).

Of course, these data are based primarily on self-report inventories. Psychologists have rarely conducted studies observing actual behaviors among large groups of twins, so caution is needed before drawing firm conclusions (Funder, 2001; Maccoby, 2000). Moreover, as noted in Chapter 10, it's not necessarily the case that twins reared in separate environments have distinctly different experiences. For example, identical twins look similar and so might be treated by the world in similar ways based on their level of attractiveness (see Chapter 13). The genome-wide analyses are less susceptible to this criticism.

Overall, the twin data do indicate that at least some enduring psychological traits may have their origins in genetic predispositions present at birth (T. J. Bouchard, 2004). Not surprisingly, psychologists have argued as well that certain traits are likely to be grounded in genetics because of the adaptive role those traits played in the evolutionary history of our species (e.g., D. M. Buss, 2012; Penke & Jokela, 2016). Of course, the expression of genetic tendencies depends on the nurturing conditions (the environment): Nature interacts with nurture in determining a person's final physical and psychological makeup. Therefore, although genes may play a critical role in determining how personality develops, environmental factors are also extremely important (Beer et al., 1998; Plomin et al., 1998).

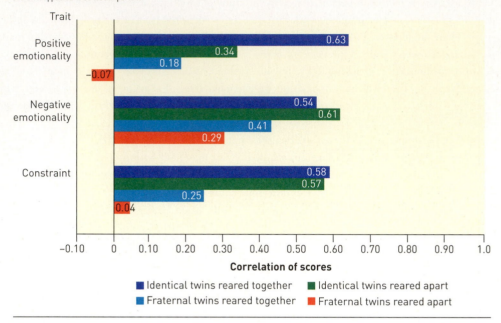

FIGURE 11.8 ■ The Genetics of Personality

Are identical twins more likely than fraternal twins to share basic personality traits? Does the rearing environment matter? These average correlations from Tellegen and colleagues reveal consistent differences between identical and fraternal twins, irrespective of the rearing environment, suggesting that genetics plays a role in determining personality. The environment also had a significant effect in some cases, but overall it appeared to be less important.

Source: Adapted from "Personality Similarity in Twins Reared Apart and Together," by A. Tellegen et al., 1988. *Journal of Personality and Social Psychology, 54*(6), 1031–1039. Copyright © 1988 by the American Psychological Association.

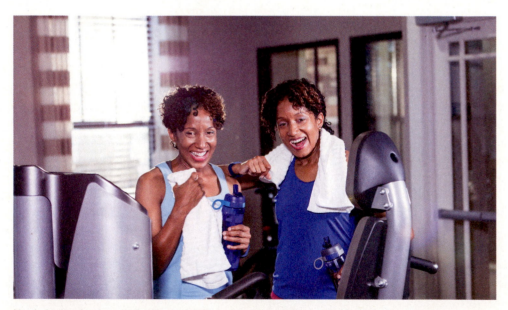

Identical twins often have similar likes and dislikes—is it nature, nurture, or both?

iStockPhoto/kali9

KNOWLEDGE CHECK 11.3

Check your knowledge about the person–situation debate by deciding whether each of the following statements is true or false. (You will find the answers in the Appendix.)

1. In the Hartshorne and May study, students who cheated on a test were not more likely to steal money, but they were more likely to cheat on a test again if given the chance. *True or False?*

2. People tend to act consistently from one situation to the next, as long as the situations are similar. *True or False?*

3. People who are low self-monitors tend to change their behaviors to fit the situation at hand. *True or False?*

4. Identical twin studies show little evidence for genetic contributions to personality characteristics, as measured by the MMPI. *True or False?*

5. Most psychologists believe personality traits are revealed in all situations, regardless of the relevance of the trait. *True or False?*

THE PROBLEMS SOLVED: WHAT PERSONALITY IS FOR

There's little question in most people's minds about the status of personality—anyone will tell you that people differ in enduring ways. We all have behavioral quirks that distinguish us from others, and we often give the impression of acting consistently across situations. If asked, people have little trouble making judgments about the personality of others. We quickly and without hesitation identify Rowena as friendly and outgoing and Liam as nasty and generally no good. Moreover, as discussed at the beginning of this chapter, it makes adaptive sense to act consistently, especially when particular actions help us to survive and enjoy productive lives. Thus personality is clearly an important and useful feature of what it means to be human.

To psychologists, however, the study of personality has proven to be difficult and elusive. Historically, researchers have disagreed about how to best approach the topic. As we've seen, questions have even been raised about the validity of the concept itself—how useful is personality in describing individual differences in behavior? (Remember, similar issues were raised about the study of intelligence.) Still, the vast majority of psychologists agree that personality is a useful construct and that it is needed to describe the full range of human psychological functioning.

Conceptualizing and Measuring Personality

Trait theories are formal systems for measuring and identifying personality characteristics, such as emotional stability or extroversion. Currently, the trait theorists seem to agree that there are five basic personality dimensions—the so-called Big Five (extroversion, agreeableness, conscientiousness, neuroticism, and openness)—that accurately and reliably describe a person's unique and consistent attributes. Psychometric techniques such as factor analysis, along with the development of personality tests such as the NEO-PI-R and the MMPI, have proven useful in advancing theory and in applying what we've learned about personality to practical settings. For example, the MMPI and the NEO-PI-R are sometimes used in business settings as part of the decision-making process for hiring new employees.

Determining How Personality Develops

Identifying stable personality traits, however, leaves unanswered the general question of how those traits originate. Noted psychologists have developed several grand theories of personality development, including the psychodynamic approach of Freud, the humanistic perspective of Rogers and Maslow, and the social–cognitive approach of Bandura, Mischel, and others. These theoretical frameworks propose very different mechanisms for personality development and offer quite different conceptions of human nature. The pessimism of Freud, with his emphasis on battling unconscious biological urges, is counterbalanced by the optimism of the humanists. From a social–cognitive perspective, the environment and beliefs about controlling that environment produce the consistent actions that define personality. Each of these perspectives has been enormously influential in psychology.

Resolving the Person–Situation Debate

The concept of personality demands at least some consistency in behavior across situations. But evidence suggests that cross-situational consistency in behavior may be low. In light of the person–situation debate, a proper analysis of behavior requires consideration of the interaction between the person and the situation. We must also keep in mind the contribution of genetics to personality—twin studies indicate that there may be a genetic component to enduring behavior.

THINKING ABOUT RESEARCH

A summary of a research study in psychology is given in this section. As you read the summary, think about the following questions:

1. Do you think your personality influences the kinds of advertisements that appeal to you on social media platforms such as Facebook?
2. Are you more likely to purchase a product when its ad uses images or descriptions that match your profile on the Big Five?
3. Is it ethical for an advertiser to use information about your personality, gathered from your Facebook "likes" or your browsing history, to design its advertising?
4. What are some potential methodological pitfalls of using Facebook, rather than an artificial laboratory setting, to investigate psychological targeting?
5. If you were designing such a study, how would you maintain internal validity—for example, random assignment of the ads to the different target populations?

Article Reference: Matz, S. C., Kosinski, M., Nave, G., & Stillwell, D. J. (2017). Psychological targeting as an effective approach to digital mass persuasion. *Proceedings of the National Academy of Sciences, 114*, 12714–12719.

Purpose of the Study: This study investigated whether persuasive ads are more effective in influencing behavior when they are tailored to people's unique psychological characteristics. For example, are you more likely to click on an advertisement, or purchase the advertised product, if the ad uses language or visuals that appeal to your standing or profile on the Big Five? The researchers were also interested in testing these ideas in a natural field setting—Facebook—as opposed to a more traditional lab setting.

Method of the Study: Professional graphic designers or copy editors manipulated the language and images in several advertisements to create ads that were tailored to specific personality profiles—for example, an "extraverted" ad contained information consistent with being active, assertive, or energetic whereas an "introverted" ad was designed to appeal to someone quiet, reserved, or shy. The ads were then displayed, using Facebook's standard ad platform, to assess how the different versions of the ads performed. Using recent advances in the assessment of psychological traits from digital footprints—for example, Facebook likes—the researchers were able to investigate responses to the ads for populations of Facebook users that differed on two important psychological traits: extraversion and openness to experience. The two main dependent variables of interest were response rates (clicking on the ad) and purchase rates.

Results of the Study: The researchers were able to reach over 3.5 million individuals with the psychologically tailored ads. The advertisements that were matched to people's extraversion or openness-to-experience level resulted in up to 40% more clicks and up to 50% more purchases than their mismatching counterparts. The same pattern of results was found for ads targeting extraversion and openness to experience.

Conclusions of the Study: The results of the study confirmed the effectiveness of tailoring persuasive ad appeals to the personality profiles of people. The findings suggest that it is possible to influence the behavior of large groups of people with targeted advertising that appeals to their particular standing on personality traits such as the Big Five.

KNOWLEDGE CHECK: CHAPTER SUMMARY

You will find the answers in the Appendix.

CONCEPTUALIZING AND MEASURING PERSONALITY

- (1) _____ analysis studies correlations among test responses, with the goal of identifying a set of factors that together predict test performance on a personality test.

- Raymond Cattell identified (2) _____ factors or source traits. Hans (3) _____ argued that personality can best be described in terms of (4) _____ primary dimensions, or superfactors: extroversion, neuroticism, and (5) _____. The contemporary Big (6) _____ approach holds that extroversion, (7) _____, openness, (8) _____, and (9) _____ best describe personality.

- (10) _____ proposed a classification scheme for identifying personality traits. (11) _____ traits are ruling passions that dominate a person's life. (12) _____ traits are expressed by the (13) _____ to 10 descriptive terms that you'd use to describe someone you know well. (14) _____ traits are less obvious traits that are not always reflected in behavior.

- (15) _____-report inventories are (16) _____, standardized, fill-in-the-answer tests, such as the (17) _____ Personality Factor Questionnaire and the Minnesota (18) _____ Personality Inventory (MMPI). With (19) _____ personality tests, such as the Rorschach test and the Thematic (20) _____ Test (TAT), elements of individual test takers' personalities are revealed in the way they interpret an unstructured or (21) _____ stimulus.

DETERMINING HOW PERSONALITY DEVELOPS

- Sigmund Freud divided the mind into three parts, (22) _____, (23) _____, and (24) _____, and argued that the (25) _____ mind powerfully affects behavior. Dreams are a window into the unconscious and have an external or (26) _____ content and a (27) _____ or latent content. Personality consists of the (28) _____, which is governed by inborn (29) _____; the (30) _____, which encourages us to act in an ideal fashion; and the (31) _____, which acts to compromise and encourages us to act with reason and deliberation. Conflict among the various aspects of personality results in (32) _____, which we attempt to combat with (33) _____ mechanisms. As children, we progress through (34) _____ stages that help determine adult personality.

- (35) _____ psychology developed largely in reaction to Freud's pessimistic view of human nature. The approach emphasizes self- (36) _____, choice, (37) _____, growth, and the uniqueness of all persons. According to Carl Rogers, we have a basic need for (38) _____ regard. Problems may arise when we mold our self-concept to satisfy others (conditions of worth), which can lead to (39) _____, a discrepancy between the true self and experience. Abraham Maslow stressed the drive toward (40) _____-_____, using a pyramid to prioritize needs—your personality reflects where you fit in the need hierarchy.

- Social– (41) _____ approaches hold that personality growth and development result from interactions between experiences and how we interpret them (cognitions or beliefs). We acquire situation-specific response tendencies through (42) _____ conditioning, operant conditioning, and (43) _____. According to (44) _____ learning theory, we acquire many personality traits by imitating others. How we (45) _____ our experiences is also critical. Perceived (46) _____ of control—how much power we think we have over our environment—and self- (47) _____—our beliefs about our own abilities—determine how we ultimately interpret experience and shape its effects on personality.

RESOLVING THE PERSON–SITUATION DEBATE

- The person–situation debate is about whether people are (48) _____ in their behavior from one situation to another. Most psychologists note that although behavior across situations may not be consistent, behavior is usually consistent (49) _____ a situation. The tendency to act consistently or inconsistently may itself be a personality trait, one known as (50) _____. High self-monitors pay close attention to their own behavior, modifying it as necessary to fit their needs in a situation, and are more likely to act (51) _____ across situations. Low self-monitors are less likely to change their beliefs and actions and are more likely to act (52) _____ across situations. Current thinking is that the individual and the situation (53) _____ to produce personality.

- Studies with (54) _____ and fraternal twins who have been raised together or apart indicate that (55) _____ factors contribute to personality. Traits measured by the MMPI reveal that identical twins tend to show more similar traits than (56) _____ twins, whether or not they were raised together. Such data have convinced psychologists that some enduring personality traits are rooted in genetic predispositions present at birth.

CRITICAL THINKING QUESTIONS

1. When comparing Allport's approach to the factor analytic approach, think back to our discussions in Chapter 2. What are the advantages and disadvantages of using case studies, which examine single individuals, versus surveys, which rely on responses from large groups?

2. Do you think there is any connection between the interpretation of projective personality tests and the interpretation of dreams? Could we use dream interpretation as a way of discovering someone's true personality?

3. How do the modern memory concepts of short- and long-term memory relate to Freud's three-part theory of the mind?

4. What are the adaptive qualities of the superego? What would happen to the human species if the superego always controlled behavior?

5. Most people deny that they've ever had sexual feelings toward their parents. If you were Freud, how would you explain these denials?

6. Think about how good it makes you feel to talk to a really close friend. From the perspective of humanistic theory, why should this be the case?

7. Carla receives an A in her psychology class but attributes it to the fact that her teacher is easy. Does she have an internal or external locus of control? How confident do you think she is of her own abilities?

8. Decide whether each of your friends is a high or a low self-monitor. Which of them do you prefer to be around—the high self-monitors or the low self-monitors?

KEY TERMS

anal stage (p. 399)

Big Five (p. 391)

cardinal traits (p. 392)

central traits (p. 393)

collective unconscious (p. 401)

conditions of worth (p. 402)

conscious mind (p. 397)

defense mechanisms (p. 398)

ego (p. 397)

genital stage (p. 400)

humanistic psychology (p. 402)

id (p. 397)

incongruence (p. 403)

latency period (p. 400)

locus of control (p. 406)

oral stage (p. 399)

person–situation debate (p. 410)

personality (p. 388)

phallic stage (p. 399)

positive regard (p. 402)

preconscious mind (p. 397)

projective personality test (p. 394)

psychodynamic theory (p. 397)

reciprocal determinism (p. 407)

repression (p. 398)

secondary traits (p. 393)

self-actualization (p. 403)

self-concept (p. 402)

self-efficacy (p. 407)

self-monitoring (p. 411)

self-report inventories (p. 393)

social–cognitive theories (p. 405)

superego (p. 397)

trait (p. 388)

trait theories (p. 389)

unconscious mind (p. 397)

iStockPhoto/andresr

12 MOTIVATION AND EMOTION

You sense only rapid movement at first—then the cool feel of metal on your cheek. You exhale, gasping, as a bony arm wraps itself around your neck. "It's your nightmare, my friend," a voice growls. "Your wallet or your life." Inside, your sympathetic nervous system jumps into action—releasing epinephrine, targeting the critical organs of the body and the neural communication chains. Your mind, flooded with the arousal, struggles to decide on the best response. But you're in a psychological meltdown—you see only jumbled images of the sidewalk and needle tracks dotting the arm grasping your neck. You can't think clearly; in your mind there is only surprise, confusion, and the smothering grip of fear.

Not a very pleasant scenario. Two people, reacting to circumstance, each in a highly activated state. For psychologists, however, the interplay is of special interest. The unfolding action strikes at the core of what psychology is about: understanding the causes and motivations of behavior. What factors initiate and direct behavior? What causes the criminal to attack the victim? Is it the reinforcing value of money? Is it the loss of control driven by an internal need for drugs? And what about the emotions that accompany the act—fear, excitement, despair? How do emotions enhance our ability to function? Do the emotions themselves motivate and direct behavior?

THE PROBLEMS TO BE SOLVED: WHAT ARE MOTIVATION AND THE EMOTIONS FOR?

Motivation refers to the set of factors that *initiate* and *direct* behavior, usually toward a goal. If you're motivated, your behavior becomes activated and goal directed. Hunger is a classic example; something happens in the body or in the environment that stimulates us to pursue food. Rewards can be motivating as well—we're likely to repeat an action that led to a reward. **Emotions** are complex psychological events that are often associated with goal-directed behavior. Emotions typically involve (1) a *physiological* reaction, usually arousal; (2) some kind of *expressive* reaction, such as a distinctive facial expression; and (3) some kind of *subjective experience*, such as the conscious feeling of being happy or sad. Each of the preceding chapters touched in one way or another on the question of *why* behavior occurs, but we'll focus our attention here on goal-directed behaviors—those actions specifically related to survival and reproduction.

Activating Behavior

Anyone hoping to survive in a changing environment must react quickly to circumstance. You need to anticipate future outcomes and act accordingly, *now*, with vigor and persistence. Much of the time our actions are controlled by *internal* factors that push us in the direction of a goal. For example, if you're deprived of food or water, a delicate internal balance is disrupted. A specific need is signaled, which you seek to satisfy in order to restore that internal balance. At other times we're motivated by *external* events, things in our environment that exert powerful pulling effects. The sight of an attractive person or a demanding and expectant boss can be sufficient to initiate and direct behavior. We'll discuss how psychologists think about the "activation" of behavior as well as the general concept of "need."

Meeting Biological Needs: Hunger and Eating

We all need to eat—it's a requirement of living. Consequently, there must be internal mechanisms that make us hungry and interested in eating at regular intervals. To understand how our bodies maintain the proper levels of internal energy, we'll consider the relevant internal and external cues that activate and control eating. We'll discuss how the body monitors internal physiological states, using brain mechanisms to check on energy reserves and control our eating behavior. We'll also discuss how external cues in the environment compel us to eat and how these cues can influence food selection. Whether you like broccoli, reject mushrooms, or happily consume squid depends on a variety of factors, including what you've learned about these foods.

Meeting Biological Needs: Sexual Behavior

Are you "consumed" by sex? Do you have a reasonably intense sexual "appetite"? Unlike eating, sex isn't necessary for individual survival. You can live a perfectly productive life, at least in principle, without ever once engaging in a sexual act. But adequate sexual performance is needed for survival of the *species*. Consequently, internal systems must have evolved that help motivate an interest in sex. We'll discuss some of the biological and psychological mechanisms that motivate sexual behavior, as well as some of the physiological characteristics of the human sexual response.

Expressing and Experiencing Emotion

Emotions have considerable adaptive significance. Consider anger. Anger occurs in response to an environmental event, usually the perceived misdeed of another, which causes the body to enter a highly aroused state. The arousal activates behavior and leads to reactions that may substantially increase (or decrease) the likelihood of survival. Once the emotion gains hold, overt physical expressions arise, particularly facial expressions. From an adaptive perspective, the sight of an angry person carries important signaling properties—others know to shy away and avoid interaction. As you'll see, emotions are easy to identify but difficult to define. In fact, the idea of universal emotions, such as anger, may be misguided. It might be better to think of emotions as categories, consisting of multiple components (physical and psychological) that are uniquely constructed to meet the needs at hand.

ACTIVATING BEHAVIOR

What factors activate and control goal-directed behavior? At first, psychologists thought there might be a single source of motivation, based either in the body or in the environment. It's possible, for example, that we're born with biological machinery that compels us to act in fixed ways regardless of what we learn from experience. But this idea is largely rejected by modern psychologists, who believe instead that no single explanation of goal-directed behavior is likely to be found. The reason is simple: Virtually all forms of behavior are determined by multiple causes. Factors both inside and outside the body contribute to motivation. In the following sections, we'll consider examples of these influences.

Internal Factors: Instincts and Drive

To survive, we all must do certain things. Sleeping, eating, and drinking are activities we need to perform at regular intervals. It makes sense, then, to assume that our motivation to perform these activities comes naturally. Yet just how rigidly controlled are human goal-directed behaviors? In nature, birds don't need to be taught how to build nests in the springtime or fly south in the winter; cats don't need to be taught to show interest in small, furry creatures. These are unlearned, characteristic patterns of responding—called **instincts**—that are controlled by events in the environment. Instincts share properties with *reflexes*, which we discussed in Chapter 3, but instincts typically involve more complex patterns of behavior than those covered by simple reflexes.

The factors that initiated and are directing this behavior include internal ones, such as depleted energy resources, and external ones, such as the sight of an attractive meal. Hunting behavior may also be controlled to a certain extent by instincts—unlearned, characteristic patterns of responding that are triggered by specific stimuli.

iStockPhoto/Stefonlinton

Human Instincts

It's widely accepted that instincts play a role in nonhuman species, but psychologists are more skeptical about human behavior. Early on, psychologists followed the lead of Charles Darwin in suggesting that instincts underlie much of human motivation. Humans don't need to be taught to take care of their young, William James (1890) argued, or to cry as infants, to clean themselves when dirty, or even to play, love, imitate, or be curious. These are ingrained biological "musts" that are as natural to the human as nest building is to the bird.

Yet just because a behavior occurs on a regular basis doesn't mean it's *instinctive*—that is, unlearned and characteristic in its display. There's no way to measure an instinct directly by looking inside the body, so it's easy to fall into a "naming" trap: Someone shows sympathy for a child in need, and the temptation is to name a corresponding sympathy instinct (Holt, 1931). Over the years, psychologists argued about which behaviors qualify as instincts. William James (1890) identified some 20 physical and 17 mental human instincts; William McDougall (1908) was convinced of only 12 (he later changed his mind and increased the number to 17). Without an objective way of verifying that the behavior was truly "unlearned," instincts eventually fell out of favor as an explanation for goal-directed human behavior.

Today, evolutionary psychologists are seeking to revive the concept of human instincts, although in a more flexible form. Evolutionary psychologists believe that we are born with specific mental "software" that helps control and guide our actions. But those actions need not be as inflexible and characteristic as many of the instincts seen in nonhuman species (D. M. Buss, 2019).

Drive

Psychologists next turned to the concept of drive. A **drive** is an internal state that arises in response to a need, such as hunger or thirst. It's clear that the human body is designed to seek fairly stable and constant internal conditions. For example, the body needs to maintain an adequate internal supply of fluids and a constant internal temperature. The body maintains its steady state through a process called **homeostasis**, much like the thermostat in a house maintains a constant internal temperature by turning the heat on or off (Cannon, 1929). Once a specific need is detected, drive serves a general activating function—drive energizes the organism, causing it to seek immediate reduction of the need (Berridge, 2004). If your water supply is used up, you're driven to drink and restore the appropriate balance. Similar processes are assumed to operate for hunger and internal body temperature (see Figure 12.1).

FIGURE 12.1 ■ Homeostasis

It's adaptive for the body to maintain stable and constant internal conditions. If your internal temperature rises above or falls below an optimal level, you are driven to perform actions that will restore the "steady state."

Illustrated by Sarah Yeh

When an organism seeks to reduce drive—to restore homeostatic balance—it doesn't matter how balance is restored. Drive is a more flexible concept than instinct. People can use what they've learned from experience to help them satisfy the need; they're not stuck with one fixed pattern of behavior that's triggered only by certain events or stimuli in the environment. You can think about drive as analogous to the running engine of a car. A properly running engine is necessary for the car to move, just as drive is necessary to start goal-directed behavior, but the engine doesn't determine where the car will travel or how you'll get across town. But as you'll see shortly, goal-directed behavior also depends critically on the value, or *incentive*, of the goal. You're much more likely to eat if you like the food, even though a wide variety of food options may satisfy the internal need. You sometimes even eat in the absence of need—you have that second brownie just because it looks good.

External Factors: Incentive Motivation

As just noted, goal-directed behavior depends partly on what we learn from experience. External rewards, such as money or a good grade, exert powerful pulling and guiding effects on our actions. Generally, whether you'll be motivated to perform an action depends on the value—positive or negative—of the incentive. For this reason, psychologists use the term **incentive motivation** to help explain goal-directed behavior. Whitney is motivated to jog for an extra 5 minutes so she can eat that extra brownie; Mateo is motivated to avoid the kitchen because of the extra calories (and guilt) he knows the brownie will produce. Notice this type of motivation differs from drive—drive is an internal *push* that compels a person to action; incentives are external *pulls* that tempt people with the prospects of receiving powerful reinforcing or punishing consequences. Appealing to incentive motivation, rather than drive, helps to explain some vexing problems, such as the current obesity epidemic, that are difficult to explain simply from the perspective of homeostasis (Kringelbach & Berridge, 2017).

Internal factors can interact with external factors in a number of ways. Whether or not you're thirsty, for example, affects the incentive value of water; water tastes better, and is more rewarding, when you've been deprived of it for a while (Blundell & Rogers, 1991; Bolles, 1972). Rewarding you with an end-of-chapter test, thereby motivating you to study, has more of an effect when you're a high procrastinator—that is, someone who finds it difficult to find the motivation to study (Tuckman, 1998). Internal states of deprivation can also act as cues for responding. You might learn to perform a certain type of action when you're thirsty or hungry (Hull, 1943); alternatively, you might learn that hunger or thirst means that food or water will be especially rewarding (Davidson et al., 2019; Higgs, 2016). Remember, motivated behavior is virtually always jointly determined by internal and external factors. Neither factor alone is sufficient to explain motivation. For a summary of the general approaches to motivation that we've discussed so far, see Concept Review 12.1.

CONCEPT REVIEW 12.1
GENERAL APPROACHES TO MOTIVATION

Approach	Source of Motivation	Summary and Evaluation
Instinct	Internal	Unlearned, characteristic patterns of responding that are controlled by specific triggering mechanisms in the world. They play a role in nonhuman species but are insufficient to explain goal-directed human behavior.
Drive	Internal	A psychological state that arises in response to a physiological need, such as hunger or thirst. *Homeostasis* is the process through which the body maintains a steady state. While it is a more flexible concept than instinct, drive does not explain behavior in the absence of need.
Incentive motivation	External	Helps to explain goal-directed behavior. People are driven by external rewards that exert powerful pulling and guiding effects on their actions.

Achievement Motivation

Another example is the push for achievement. Each of us, to varying degrees, has an internally driven need for achievement (J. W. Atkinson, 1957; D. C. McClelland et al., 1953; H. A. Murray, 1938). **Achievement motivation** pushes us to seek success and significant accomplishment in our lives. Are you driven by a need for success? Studies have shown that people who rate high in achievement motivation tend to work harder and more persistently on tasks; they also tend to achieve more than those who rate low in achievement motivation (J. W. Atkinson & Raynor, 1974; W. H. Cooper, 1983).

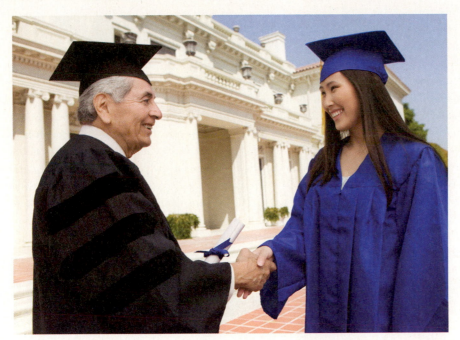

People who rate highly on achievement motivation tend to work harder and more persistently on tasks.

iStockPhoto/IPGGutenbergUKLtd

However, whether you'll work hard on any particular task depends on your expectations of success and on how much you value the task (J. W. Atkinson, 1957; Molden & Dweck, 2000). You can have a high internal need for achievement but choose not to persist on a task either because you place no value on it or because you lack confidence in your ability to succeed. For example, young children who experience failure on mathematics problems early in life can develop a helpless attitude that prevents them from persisting and succeeding on mathematical tasks later on. Conversely, children who perform well on such tasks gain confidence in their ability and appear motivated to take on similar tasks in the future (Smiley & Dweck, 1994; Wigfield, 1994).

Your achievement goal is important too. It matters whether you're motivated to master a task—that is, to develop a skill or ability in a given area—or whether you're simply motivated to do better than someone else (Hulleman et al., 2010). You may want to get an A in your psychology class, but is your goal to master psychological science or beat out the other students? People who focus just on performance (beating others) are likely to avoid risky learning opportunities; they are overly concerned with making errors or not doing well. People who are motivated by mastery are more likely to engage in effortful learning opportunities and seek out challenges (Mangels et al., 2006). Your achievement goal also tells us something about the emotions you're likely to experience during the task. For example, people driven by a need to perform well are less likely to enjoy the task and tend to be more anxious (Huang, 2011). There even seems to be an effect on memory. People who seek to master a task are more likely to maintain memories about the learning experience after a delay (Murayama & Elliot, 2011).

Parents and teachers play an important part in determining achievement motivation and achievement goals. If parents value a task, it's likely their child will value it too and be more motivated to succeed. What children are told about their performance on a task is also important. For example, if children are praised for their effort, they tend to work harder, report more enjoyment, and show more interest. On the other hand, if they're told that performance is tied to an ability such as natural intelligence, children show less achievement motivation—especially if they fail or perform poorly on the task (see Lin-Siegler et al., 2016). This is true for adults as well; if you perform poorly on a test in math or science, and you believe these fields require some kind of natural aptitude to perform well, then you're more likely to give up and seek achievement elsewhere (Leslie et al., 2015). I'm just no good at psychology, you say, and focus instead on your mastery of engineering.

Cultural Factors

Every society in the world establishes standards for achievement—the skills and tasks deemed important and unimportant—and these standards influence what we seek to achieve and, perhaps, the level of productivity of the society as a whole (D. C. McClelland, 1961). For example, whether a society values individual success or collective success seems to affect individual levels of achievement motivation. Middle school athletes in the United States report more self-confidence than comparable students in Korea, and they are more easily motivated, presumably because a greater emphasis is placed on individual success in the United States (B. J. Kim et al., 2003).

As we discussed in Chapter 2, mounting evidence suggests that gender differences in achievement—such as the tendency for men to outperform women in mathematics—are strongly tied to such cultural factors (see Hyde, 2014, 2016). In the United States, for instance, the parents of boys place greater value on success in mathematics than do the parents of girls (Parsons et al., 1982); at the same time, boys often receive the message that they should study less, which helps explain why girls outperform boys in other subjects (Van Houtte, 2004). Consequently, the expectations and values of the parents help to determine the achievement motivation of the children.

Intrinsic Motivation

We've talked about motivation in terms of internal pushes and external pulls, but sometimes we engage in actions for which there's no obvious internal or external motivational source. A child spends hours carefully coloring a picture or playing with a doll; you might become transfixed by a crossword puzzle or by a long walk on the beach. There's certainly no biological *need* that drives coloring or walking. There's also no clear-cut external incentive: Nobody pays the child for coloring or you for finishing the crossword puzzle. **Intrinsic motivation** is the term used to describe behaviors that appear to be entirely self-motivated. We engage in the action for its own sake, not because someone offers us a reward or because the action restores some internal homeostatic balance (Lepper et al., 2005; R. M. Ryan & Deci, 2000).

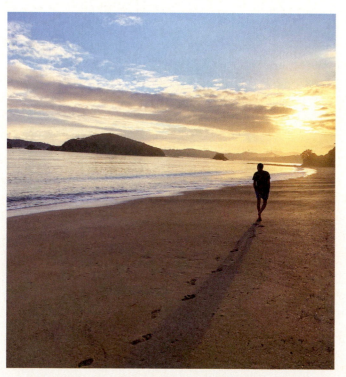

Sometimes we engage in behaviors that are intrinsically motivated.

iStockPhoto/Cas

In fact, it turns out that when we're intrinsically motivated, supplying an external reward can lower interest in the task. In a classic study by Lepper, Greene, and Nisbett (1973), preschool children who were naturally interested in drawing were asked to draw either for its own sake or to win a "Good Player" certificate. Psychologically, we would expect the external reward to bolster drawing even more than normal—after all, drawing is now followed by a concrete positive consequence—but it didn't. The children in the reward condition showed less interest in drawing a week later. The reward reduced the value of the behavior, making it less rewarding or interesting than it otherwise would have been.

This study has been repeated with other rewards and with activities other than drawing. The story is much the same: External rewards can lower our desire to perform a task. Once a reward is involved, we're less likely to enjoy that task for its own sake in the future. This doesn't always happen, of course, but it does occur in some instances (Henderlong & Lepper, 2002). Think about professional athletes. Many sports fans complain that the external reward of money has ruined professional sports. Even baseball players sometimes complain that the game was more fun back in the sandlot, before millions of dollars entered into the motivational chain.

How can a reward lead to a negative effect? One possibility is that people see external rewards, even praise, as an indirect way of controlling their behavior. Drawing loses its value because it's now something you're doing to please the person giving you the reward—you're no longer drawing simply because it pleases *you*. Choosing to perform the task, rather than being pulled by an external reward, is an important factor in intrinsic motivation (Patall et al., 2008). Another possibility is that the reward degrades the value of the task—for example, the baseball player begins to believe it's the money that makes them play, rather than love for the game. Neuroimaging work suggests that the introduction of an external reward can change how specific reward centers in the brain react to a task that was previously performed without any reward (Murayama et al., 2010). Some researchers have even suggested that traits such as creativity should never be rewarded lest the positive internal value of engaging in a creative act be destroyed (Amabile, 1983; B. Schwartz, 1990).

Not all psychologists are comfortable with these conclusions. External reward enhances creativity under some circumstances, and the negative effects of reward on task motivation only occur in some circumstances (Eisenberger & Cameron, 1996). For example, in the 1973 study by Lepper and colleagues, children did indeed choose to draw less frequently when they were rewarded for drawing, but this effect occurred only when the children *expected* the reward. When children were given an unexpected reward for drawing, they later spent more time drawing than a group who had received no reward. Therefore, the negative effect of reward on intrinsic motivation may be related to the expectation or promise of reward rather than to the reward itself (Cameron & Pierce, 1994). Moreover, when an activity is linked to many outcomes, then the value of the activity can become "diluted" (K. Woolley & Fishbach, 2018). For example, children are less intrinsically motivated to eat certain foods once they learn that those foods serve other goals besides tasting good—for instance that eating the food makes them healthier or smarter (Maimaran & Fishbach, 2014).

Maslow's Hierarchy of Needs

Most general theories of motivation appeal primarily to biological factors. The body seeks to maintain a delicate internal balance (homeostasis), and if that balance is disrupted, we're motivated to restore it. However, as you've just seen, not all needs are biological in origin—for example, the need for achievement (H. A. Murray, 1938). For this reason, some psychologists have tried to classify "need," to determine whether some needs are more basic or important than others.

The **need hierarchy** proposed by Abraham Maslow is a well-known example. We discussed Maslow's ideas briefly in Chapter 11—the essential component of his theory is the *prioritizing* of needs: Some needs have special priority and must be satisfied before others. Obviously, if we don't eat or drink water on a regular basis, we'll die. Maslow's theory is often represented as a pyramid, to emphasize the fact that human motivation rests on a foundation of biological and security "musts" (see Figure 12.2). It's only after satisfying the survival needs—such as hunger and thirst—that we can consider more social or spiritual needs, such as the need for love or self-esteem. At the top of the structure sits the need for self-actualization, which Maslow believed represented our desire to reach our true potential as human beings.

FIGURE 12.2 ■ A Hierarchy of Needs

Maslow proposed that human needs are prioritized: Some must be satisfied before others can be addressed, including physiological and safety needs. At the top of the pyramid is the need for self-actualization, our natural desire to reach our true potential.

Source: From Figure 1 in Kenrick, D. T., Griskevicius, V., Neuberg, S. L., & Schaller, M. (2010).

The pyramid is often used as a symbol for Maslow's system because it captures the upward thrust of human motivation. As a humanistic psychologist, Maslow (1954) believed all people have a compelling need to grow, to better themselves as functioning individuals. Maslow was strongly influenced by people who he felt had reached their fullest potential, such as Thomas Jefferson and Albert Einstein. He used their personality characteristics as a way of defining what it means to sit at the top of the pyramid—to be self-actualized. These characteristics included spontaneity, openness to experience, and a high degree of ethical sensitivity. In his later years, Maslow fine-tuned the hierarchy, adding some additional motivational levels, but they need not concern us here (see Compton, 2018).

Probably the most important feature of the Maslow hierarchy is the laddering of needs. Psychologists might disagree about the specific order that Maslow proposed—does the need to belong and be accepted have higher priority than the need for self-esteem?—but the idea that humans have a wide variety of needs that must be prioritized has been enormously influential. If you have to worry about putting food on the table, and consequently steal from others on a regular basis, you might appear to lack moral or ethical values. But this isn't necessarily a permanent fixture of your personality—under different circumstances, with a full stomach, you might act extremely ethically.

Applied psychologists have extended Maslow's ideas to the workplace to help employers better understand the behavior of their employees. Many employers now recognize that employees' needs change depending on their position in the management hierarchy. When people receive low pay or have poor job security, their work behavior is directed toward satisfying basic needs. Promotion may help satisfy the fundamental needs, but new, perhaps more demanding ones will quickly arise. Employers must be sensitive to the particular needs at each level of the management hierarchy (Muchinsky, 2003). Similar arguments have been applied to student success in academic settings (e.g., Freitas & Leonard, 2011). Madison Avenue has even gotten wind of the idea: Consumers receive individualized ads based on their perceived position in the hierarchy of needs (C. Peterson & Park, 2010).

Critics of Maslow's theory often point to its lack of scientific rigor. Because the various needs are not defined clearly in a way that each can be individually measured, it's difficult to test the different proposals of the need hierarchy (Wahba & Bridwell, 1976). Moreover, representing the theory as a pyramid suggests that people cannot seek to satisfy multiple needs at the same time; in fact, Maslow believed that behavior is influenced by multiple needs concurrently, rather than only one need at a time. As Bridgman et al. (2019) have recently noted, Maslow himself never proposed the pyramid structure. More recently, efforts have been made to update and revise the hierarchy, based on developments in evolutionary biology (Kenrick et al., 2010). Here, needs are prioritized based on their evolutionary function—for example, finding and retaining a good mating partner—as well as on when they first appear developmentally.

KNOWLEDGE CHECK 12.1

Check your knowledge about activating behavior by answering the following questions. (You will find the answers in the Appendix.)

1. Which of the following statements best captures the difference between an instinct and a drive?
   a. A drive is a reflex; an instinct is not.
   b. Instincts are learned; drives are not.
   c. Instincts lead to fixed response patterns; drives do not.
   d. Instincts restore appropriate internal balance; drives do not.

2. Which type of motivation—achievement, incentive, or intrinsic—best describes each of the following behaviors?
   a. Whitney never misses her daily jogging session—she loves the brownie she gives herself at the end: _____
   b. Janice spends hours practicing the piano—she just seems to love playing: _____
   c. Candice studies at least 6 hours a day—she is obsessed with the idea of finishing first in her class: _____
   d. Jerome rarely paints for fun anymore, not since he started teaching art classes at the local college: _____

3. According to Maslow's hierarchy of needs, we can reach our true potential as human beings only after
   a. restoring a proper level of homeostatic balance.
   b. satisfying basic survival and social needs.
   c. satisfying our need for achievement.
   d. eliminating the need for rewards.

MEETING BIOLOGICAL NEEDS: HUNGER AND EATING

Why do we eat? Obviously, from a survival standpoint, eating is a no-brainer—we need food and water to survive. But we eat for reasons that are more complex than you might think. If you ask children why they eat, they'll explain they eat "because I'm hungry" or "because my tummy hurts." An adult's response will appear more sophisticated, but it usually amounts to much the same thing: "We eat because our bodies need food, internal energy." This is true; eating is a biologically driven behavior. But eating is psychologically driven as well. We sometimes feel hungry when there is no physical need; and, as any dieter knows, a strong will can stop consumption even when the physical need is present. We can resist the urge to eat by avoiding food or food-related cues that might otherwise entice us to eat.

Internal Factors Controlling Hunger

Researchers have spent decades trying to understand the internal mechanisms that influence when and why we eat. We know that the body monitors itself, particularly its internal supply of resources, in a number of ways. For example, there's a connection between the volume and content of food in the stomach and the frequency of neural activity in certain areas of the brain (Sharma et al., 1961). Psychologically, people report little if any hunger or interest in food when their stomach is full, and hunger increases in a relatively direct way as the stomach empties (Sepple & Read, 1989).

Chemical Signals

The body regularly checks several important suppliers of internal energy. One critical substance is glucose, a kind of sugar required for energy production. Receptors in the liver or intestines react to changes in the amount of glucose in the blood, or perhaps to how this sugar is being used by the cells, and appropriate signals are communicated upward to the brain. There's also a hormone called *ghrelin* that increases before eating and decreases afterward. Ghrelin is produced in the stomach, and it's been associated with feelings of hunger (F. Langlois et al., 2011). When ghrelin is injected directly into the brains of rats, it can stimulate eating behavior (Kanoski et al., 2013).

But the main story isn't about internal signals that push us to eat; it's about chemical signals that stop us from eating—what are called satiety or **satiation signals**. People are rarely compelled to eat because of an internal biological deficit, such as a dangerously low level of glucose. Most of the time we're pushed by external cues—habits such as the time of day, the sight of tasty food, or even stress. This makes sense from an evolutionary perspective because our ancestors couldn't drive down to the nearest fast-food restaurant for nourishment; they had to eat whenever food was available or it was safe to eat. We choose to stop eating, or skip a meal, because of internal signals that make us feel full. Probably the most important satiation signal is the hormone cholecystokinin (CCK), which is released by the gastrointestinal tract during a meal. CCK travels to the brain, which, in turn, suppresses our desire to eat (Woods & D'Alessio, 2008).

Your body also monitors and releases hunger-related hormones based on your total amount of body fat. There is a hormone called leptin that rises and falls with the amount of body fat; high levels of leptin are often found in obese individuals, and leptin levels typically drop when individuals go on a diet (Woods et al., 2000). Leptin plays a critical role in weight loss and if blocked can lead to increased food intake and weight gain. Resistance to leptin is thought to play an important role in the development and maintenance of obesity (Morton et al., 2006). Insulin, a hormone released by the pancreas, also varies with body fat. The body needs insulin to help pump the nutrients present in the blood into the cells, where they can be stored as fat or metabolized into needed energy. At the start of a meal, the brain sends signals to the pancreas to begin the production and release of insulin in preparation for

Such internal factors as the amount of food in the stomach and the amount of glucose in the blood play an important role in making people feel sated after a meal.

iStockPhoto/stock_colors

the rise in blood sugar produced by the food. As insulin does its job, the levels of blood sugar go down, and you eventually feel hungry again. If either insulin or leptin is injected into the body, people act as if they have too much body fat and start to reduce their food intake (Woods & D'Alessio, 2008). One possibility is that insulin enhances the potency of CCK, suppressing our desire to eat (May et al., 2016).

Brain Regions

Ultimately, of course, the experience of hunger originates in the brain. It's the activation of brain structures that kick-starts and directs the search for food. A number of years ago, it was discovered that if a particular portion of the hypothalamus is lesioned (destroyed) in laboratory animals, a curious transformation occurs. Lesioned animals appear to be hungry all the time and show a striking tendency to overeat. In fact, each animal becomes an eating machine—if allowed, it balloons up to several times its normal weight (A. W. Hetherington & Ranson, 1942). If this same area is stimulated electrically, rather than destroyed, the opposite pattern emerges. Electrical stimulation causes the animal to lose all interest in food, even if there's a real need for nutrients in the body.

If a particular portion of the hypothalamus is destroyed, a rat becomes an eating machine and can balloon up to several times its normal weight.

ORNL / Science Source

   Neuroscientists now believe that the hypothalamus contains receptors that are sensitive to the presence of food-related hormones such as insulin and leptin (M. W. Schwartz, 2006). Leptin, for example, binds with receptors in the hypothalamus that, in turn, enhance the body's response to satiation signals (stop eating) and lower the reward value of food (e.g., make food taste less good). Such a process is adaptive because it prevents us from accumulating too many nutrients in the blood—more than our bodies can safely handle. Portions of the hindbrain are also critical in the initiation of eating (Sweeney et al., 2017), and the hippocampus is involved as well. You may remember from Chapter 8 that we discussed an amnesic called H. M. who was doomed to live in a kind of perpetual present—he could remember nothing of what happened to him moments before. H. M., who had damage to his temporal lobes and hippocampus, also had trouble monitoring his need for food. Sometimes he'd claim to be hungry immediately after finishing a meal. He may have simply forgotten he'd eaten; but as Davidson (1993) points out, he also was clearly unable to use internal signals from his body as cues for hunger or satiety. These data suggest an important role for the hippocampus in feeding behavior.

External Factors Controlling Hunger

It's a mistake to think about eating as simply a means to satisfy a variety of internal energy needs. We often eat for reasons unrelated to restoring internal homeostatic balance. Haven't you ever eaten to reduce stress or simply to make yourself feel good? Have you ever eaten to promote social interaction, as in going out to dinner with friends? We all have. People even use food to make ethical statements. For example, some people are vegetarians because they believe it's wrong to eat other animals.

Eating Habits

Most eating habits develop through personal experience and by modeling the behavior of others. These learned habits control much of our decision making about food. You're probably used to eating at certain times and in certain places. If you're offered a tasty snack, how much you eat is determined partly by the time of day—if the offer comes shortly before dinner, you take less than if the offer comes

One's cultural and ethnic background exerts a powerful effect on food selection. Would you be willing to consume the shrimp shown in the top photo? How about the delicacies on the bottom?

in the middle of the afternoon (Schachter & Gross, 1968). You also know from past experience how much food you can eat and still feel okay. You know, for instance, that if you eat the whole pizza you will probably feel sick afterward, even though the pizza may taste great at the time. Our memories of prior eating experiences importantly control how much and how often we eat, typically because we've learned how rewarding (or nonrewarding) certain foods can be (Higgs, 2016).

Cultural and ethnic background is another powerful influence (Rozin et al., 1999). Most people who grow up in the United States will not willingly choose to eat dogs or sheep's eyes, but these are considered delicacies in some parts of the world. Are you hesitant about eating pork or beef? You probably are if you're an Orthodox Jew or a native of India. And it's not just the appearance of food or where it comes from. People around the world often discriminate among eating partners. For example, members of some social classes would never consider eating with those they consider to be social inferiors.

Food Cues

The decision to eat is also importantly controlled by the appearance of food cues, which act as retrieval cues for prior memories about the rewarding value of food. Studies have investigated how the brain reacts to the appearance of food cues; the resulting brain activation levels have been shown to predict food choice, snack consumption, and even future weight gain (see Charbonnier et al., 2018). Animals know that certain kinds of food taste good, and the sight of these foods is often enough to make them start eating. If hungry rats are taught that a flashing light predicts food, they'll start eating in the presence of the light even if they've been fully fed moments before (Weingarten, 1983). Waiters push the dessert tray under your nose because they know the sight of the sugar-filled array will be more likely to break down your reserve than just hearing about what's for dessert. Again, your choice of the New York cheesecake with the strawberry sauce is not driven by internal need. Your blood contains plenty of appropriate nutrients—the sight of the food, and its association with past pleasures, acts as an external pull, motivating your choice to consume. For more information on potential food cues, take a look at the Practical Solutions feature.

PRACTICAL SOLUTIONS: DIETARY VARIETY AND WEIGHT GAIN

Is variety in your diet a good thing? From a nutritional standpoint, of course, it's essential that you eat foods that deliver needed vitamins and other nutrients. But from a psychological standpoint, variety within a meal can make you eat more food. Suppose we let you eat one of your favorite flavors of ice cream, as much as you like, and record how much you eat; in a second case, we give you several different types of ice cream and, again, let you eat to your heart's desire. The evidence indicates you'll eat significantly more in the second instance (Raynor & Epstein, 2001).

Variety, particularly the introduction of a new and different food, has a way of counteracting fullness, or satiety. This is one of the reasons dessert looks good even though you've just pushed away your dinner plate. The effect of variety on consumption, which occurs for both humans and animals, suggests that satiety is *sensory-specific*—that is, eating makes us lose interest in the particular food we're eating but not necessarily other foods. If people are asked to rate the pleasantness of sweet foods after eating a meal containing sweet food, their ratings drop; but the meal has no effect on their

If you want to eat less food, try reducing the amount of variety on your plate.

iStockPhoto/YinYang

rating of savory foods (Rolls et al., 1984). The effect applies to the taste and color of food as well as to its shape and texture. For instance, your pleasantness ratings for hard foods (such as a baguette or an apple) drop after consumption, but not your ratings for soft foods (Guinard & Brun, 1998). Even the addition of condiments, such as ketchup, can have an effect. People who have lost interest in eating French fries alone suddenly want more if ketchup is offered as a condiment (Brondel et al., 2009).

Some psychologists have suggested that dietary variety may be a factor in the development of obesity. It's possible, for example, that obese individuals show less sensory-specific satiety, which, in turn, causes them to eat more; alternatively, perhaps they show greater levels of sensory-specific satiety, which leads them to eat a greater variety of foods at a meal. Remember, though, obesity is not caused simply by the amount of food consumed—your weight depends on many factors, including genetics. The variety of foods present in a meal can, however, influence weight gain because variety determines how much you eat. One common reason people give for not finishing a meal is that they're "tired" of the food (M. M. Hetherington, 1996)—variety, of course, works against this tendency. From a practical standpoint, if you want to eat less, try reducing the amount of variety on your plate. Eat right, but cut down on the variety.

Regulating Body Weight

Why are some people thin and others obese? Not surprisingly, internal and external factors combine to regulate body weight. Some factors, such as genetic predisposition, play a particularly important role (Kowalski, 2004). For example, when identical twins—those sharing the same genetic material—are fed identical diets, they tend to gain virtually the same amount of weight. But if two unrelated people are given matched diets, the differences in weight gain can be substantial (C. Bouchard et al., 1990). You probably know people who seem to eat continuously and never gain weight; others put on weight after only a small daily increase in caloric intake. In short, the amount of food you eat only partly determines what you normally weigh (Benton & Young, 2017).

Set Point

Researchers used to believe we have a natural body weight, or **set point**, that more or less controls our tendency to gain or lose weight (Keesey & Powley, 1975). Most people show little variation in weight from year to year, presumably because their bodies manipulate the motivation to eat, as needed, to maintain the appropriate set point weight. When people go on a diet and dip below their natural weight, well over 90% of them eventually gain that weight back (R. J. Martin et al., 1991). Here, again, the idea is that the body adjusts how much it eats, rebounding after a diet, to produce stability in body weight.

But if there is a set point, it's a loose one—meaning that there may be upper or lower limits on our general weight (Muller et al., 2010). Body weight is determined by a number of factors, both internal and external. Genetic factors certainly play an important role: People are born with a certain number of fat cells, and this number may constrain just how much weight they can hope to gain or lose (Faust, 1984). Your metabolic rate—how quickly you burn off calories—is another important internal factor; again, it's determined in part by your genetic makeup but also by experience. Research in rats indicates that nicotine may lower metabolic set point; if so, although speculative, this may help explain why people sometimes gain weight after they stop smoking (Frankham & Cabanac, 2003; see also Heindel et al., 2017). Concept Review 12.2 summarizes the main factors involved in hunger.

CONCEPT REVIEW 12.2
FACTORS INVOLVED IN HUNGER

Type of Factor	Factor	Role in Hunger
Internal	Chemical signals	Receptors in the liver respond to changes in the amount of *glucose* in the blood. The hormone *ghrelin* may play a role in hunger, but most internal signals are designed to stop us from eating. The hormone CCK is an important satiation signal. The hormones insulin and leptin are also important regulators of hunger and are tied to a person's amount of body fat.

Type of Factor	Factor	Role in Hunger
	Brain	Regions of the hypothalamus help to control eating, but the precise role of each is unclear. Portions of the brain stem also seem important in the initiation of eating.
External	Eating habits	Learned habits develop through personal experience and modeling the behavior of others. Cultural and ethnic background also plays a critical role in when and what you eat.
	Food cues	Factors such as the attractiveness of food, or its association with past pleasures, can serve as an external pull, motivating eating behavior.

Obesity

What causes **obesity**, the condition characterized by excessive body fat? Obesity rates are on the rise, startlingly so over the past few decades (e.g., Lahey & Khan, 2018). Think about how easy it is to get tasty fast food or prepackaged meals or to stuff yourself at an all-you-can-eat buffet. At one time it was thought that overweight people simply lacked sufficient willpower to resist overeating, especially when appealing food was in view (Schachter, 1971). Overweight people are more likely to order a specific dish in a restaurant after a tasty description; they're also more likely than nonobese people to report that food still tastes good after a filling meal.

Yet to explain obesity by appealing to willpower, or to any one psychological factor, is simplistic and misleading. As noted previously, just because someone eats a lot doesn't mean the person will gain excessive amounts of weight. Some people can eat a lot and gain little weight; others gain weight on limited diets. It's increasingly apparent that genetic factors predispose people to become overweight (see van der Klaauw & Farooqi, 2015). Even so, the ultimate causes of obesity are certain to lie in a complex combination of biology and psychology: metabolic rate, set point, number of fat cells, learned eating habits, cultural role models, level of stress—all contribute in one way or another to weight control.

Given the recent and dramatic increases in obesity rates across the world, it is clear that the environment must be extremely important; in turn, excessive and prolonged weight gains may change how the brain and body function—the brain's responsiveness to leptin, for instance, may decrease (Morton et al., 2006). Prolonged exposure to high-fat diets may also produce changes in the brain, such as inflammation of critical brain structures, that influence the effectiveness of satiation signals (E. Smith et al., 2011). Even the regular consumption of diet soda, which is artificially sweetened, can disrupt how well the brain and body monitor caloric intake, leading eventually to weight gain (see Swithers, 2016). Obviously, proper diet, and gaining some control over how much you eat, is important to maintaining a healthy lifestyle; we'll return to this issue in more detail in Chapter 16.

Eating Disorders

The quest for a perfect body shape is a billion-dollar industry with worldwide influence. As you know, society sets weight ideals, often through advertising, and our notions about attractiveness have become closely tied to meeting these standards. Although there are important cultural differences in body weight "ideals," in Western countries a desire for thinness is commonplace (Swami et al., 2010). If you're extremely overweight, you're more likely to suffer from health problems, so you need to monitor what you eat carefully. But the pursuit of *unrealistic* weight goals, ones that you can never hope to reach because of your genetic background, can lead to significant psychological and physical problems. Unhappiness and depression are the all-too-frequent by-products of the failure to reach the proper ideal.

Interestingly, people's assessments of their own weight, and its relation to these standards, are typically inaccurate. In addition, most people are simply wrong about what members of the opposite sex consider to be an ideal body weight (Swami et al., 2010). On average, straight women tend to think straight men prefer thinner women than they do; when men are asked about their own ideal weight, it tends to be heavier than what the average straight woman rates as most attractive. Not surprisingly, these mistaken beliefs often help

Social standards concerning ideal weight have changed considerably over the years.

iStockPhoto/Max5799
DEA PICTURE LIBRARY / Contributor via Getty Images

promote a negative body image. A negative body image, in turn, can increase one's susceptibility to eating disorders such as *anorexia nervosa* and *bulimia nervosa* (Polivy & Herman, 2002).

Anorexia Nervosa

In a survey of 8th- and 10th-grade students, it was discovered that more than 60% of the women and 28% of the men were actively dieting (Hunnicutt & Newman, 1993). The concern—some would say obsession—with weight and dieting starts early in Western cultures. For an unfortunate few, the consequences can be life threatening. In the condition called **anorexia nervosa**, otherwise healthy people fail to maintain a normal weight level, typically because they have an irrational fear of being overweight. In such cases, a person can literally be starving to death and still see an overweight person in the mirror. The condition mainly affects young women and usually begins between the ages of 15 and 29 (perhaps as many as 1% of adolescent women are affected). Somewhere between 5% and 10% of those with the disorder will eventually die as a result, either from medical problems or from suicide. This mortality rate is astonishingly high—as high as that seen in any form of psychological disorder (Attia, 2010). Not surprisingly, the causes of this disorder are complex and probably involve genetic as well as psychological factors (Gadsby, 2017; Keel et al., 2012).

One of the many features associated with anorexia nervosa is the slowing or ceasing of menstruation and associated reproductive functions. This has led some evolutionary psychologists to suggest that a predisposition for anorexia may have served an adaptive function at some point in our evolutionary history—perhaps because it lowered the likelihood of a young girl becoming pregnant in a stressful environment (J. L. Anderson & Crawford, 1992). This may have been true at some point in our ancestral past, but anorexia nervosa is certainly not adaptive in modern environments. Besides interfering with reproductive functions, the condition is associated with low blood pressure, loss of bone density, and gastrointestinal problems. Anorexia nervosa is a very serious and chronic condition that needs immediate and prolonged treatment.

This young woman suffers from anorexia nervosa, a condition characterized by an intense fear of being overweight.

Denis Putilov/ Alamy Stock Photo

Bulimia Nervosa

In the eating disorder known as **bulimia nervosa**, the principal symptom is *binge eating*. A binge is an episode in which a person consumes large quantities of food, often junk food, in a limited period of time. The condition is marked by a lack of control—the person feels unable to stop the eating or to control the content of the food being consumed. A bingeing episode is often followed by *purging*, in which the person induces vomiting or uses laxatives in an effort to stop potential weight gain. Like anorexia, bulimia primarily affects women and is characterized by an obsessive desire to be thin.

Bulimia is also associated with serious medical problems. One of the defining characteristics of bulimia is that the person can appear normal, without the excessive weight loss found in anorexia. Yet repeated vomiting can damage the intestines, lead to nutritional problems, and even promote tooth decay. Psychologically, bulimia nervosa is associated with a preoccupation or obsession with weight gain and a fear of becoming obese. Bulimia can be harder to diagnose than anorexia because the bingeing and purging usually occur in private (Polivy & Herman, 2002).

Psychologists originally assumed that eating disorders such as bulimia and anorexia were caused primarily by cultural factors—specifically, the fixation by many Western cultures on staying thin. Anorexia nervosa, in particular, was believed to be a recent phenomenon, rarely diagnosed prior to the 1970s and confined largely to the West. However, recent work suggests that anorexia nervosa may be neither recent nor culture bound. Cases can be traced back to medieval times, and the disorder occurs today in all parts of the world. Bulimia nervosa, on the other hand, may follow a different pattern. A large and significant increase in bulimia occurred in the latter half of the 20th century, and little evidence for the condition exists outside of cultures with Western influences (see Keel & Klump, 2003). However, evidence does suggest that exposure to Western ideals about thinness can be associated with higher incidences of eating disorders in non-Western countries (see Doris et al., 2015).

Related Disorders

Although anorexia and bulimia are the most widely known eating disorders, there are many other conditions. In fact, people with anorexia and bulimia represent a minority of individuals with serious eating problems (Keel et al., 2012). There is a condition known as *binge eating disorder* in which one sees episodes of binge eating, but without the purging seen in bulimia nervosa. One can also find people who purge following consumption of normal or small amounts of food (known as *purging disorder*). There are other individuals, typically those suffering from insomnia, who consume large amounts of food at night, a condition called *night eating syndrome*. At present, psychologists don't know how all these conditions relate to one another or their ultimate cause. Eating disorders commonly co-occur with other psychological problems, particularly depression, which makes isolation of their causes particularly difficult (see Puccio et al., 2016). Considerable research effort is currently being directed at understanding how biological, cultural, and psychological factors interact to produce these conditions (Culbert et al., 2015).

KNOWLEDGE CHECK 12.2

Check your knowledge about hunger and eating by deciding whether each of the following statements is true or false. (You will find the answers in the Appendix.)

1. A hormone called ghrelin, which is produced in the stomach, has been associated with feelings of hunger. *True or False?*

2. The principal symptoms of anorexia nervosa are bingeing and purging. *True or False?*

3. High levels of a hormone called leptin are often found in obese individuals. *True or False?*

4. Obesity is primarily caused by poor dietary habits. *True or False?*

5. Destruction of portions of the hypothalamus can cause a rat to overeat and gain substantial amounts of weight. *True or False?*

MEETING BIOLOGICAL NEEDS: SEXUAL BEHAVIOR

Does your world revolve around sex? Maybe not, but sex is still a powerful motivator of people around the world. Every significant culture has well-established rules and guidelines for the teaching and practice of behavior related to courtship, mating, and the sexual act. Just think for a moment about advertising, television, and movies. Enough said.

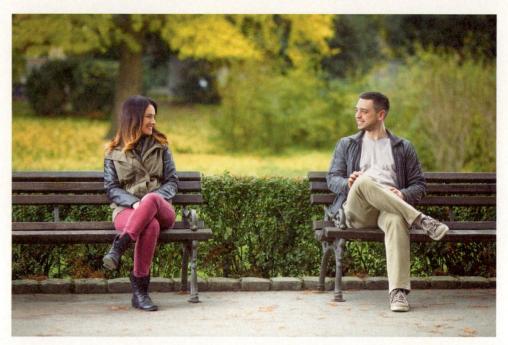

Besides reproduction, finding an appropriate mate opens the door for companionship, protection, and love.

iStockPhoto/bokan76

But where exactly is the need? What problem is solved by the pursuit and completion of the sexual act? Is there some kind of internal sex gauge that monitors sexual deprivation and adjusts behavior accordingly? You certainly won't die if your goal-directed sexual pursuits fail, as you might from an unsuccessful search for nutrients. So why sex? Why did we evolve a form of reproduction that requires finding a mate as opposed to some kind of asexual reproduction or cloning process? Engaging in a sexual act can put you at risk, either from predators or from disease. It also takes a lot of time and effort to find an appropriate mate—time and energy that might be better spent satisfying basic energy needs.

Evolutionary biologists and psychologists have spent a lot of time considering the costs and benefits of sexual reproduction (e.g., Burke & Bonduriansky, 2017; Kenrick, 2011). Some have argued that sex introduces genetic variation within the species, which can help individual genes survive and compete in changing environments. But, of course, sexual motivation has its advantages within a single lifetime too. In addition to the pleasurable and reinforcing aspects of sex, relationships offer companionship, protection, and love. In this section of the chapter, we'll consider some of the specifics of sexual motivation, beginning with a brief discussion of the human sexual response cycle. Then we'll look at the internal and external factors that motivate sexual behavior. We'll conclude with a look at issues involved in mate selection and sexual orientation.

The Sexual Response Cycle

Humans are capable of wide and imaginative varieties of lovemaking, but biologically the sexual response follows a standard four-step sequence (see Figure 12.3). As documented by researchers William Masters and Virginia Johnson (1966), who spent years studying the human sexual response in the laboratory, the response cycle begins with an **excitement phase**. Sexual excitement is characterized by changes in muscle tension, increased heart rate and blood pressure, and a rushing of blood into the genital organs. In men, the increased blood supply causes an erection in the penis; in women, the clitoris swells and the lining of the vaginal wall becomes lubricated.

The excitement phase is followed by a **plateau phase**, during which sexual arousal continues to increase, at a slower rate, toward a maximum point. The penis becomes fully erect, and vaginal lubrication increases. Other changes begin that are appropriate to the reproductive process—the internal shape of the vagina changes in preparation for the receipt of the sperm-laden semen; the

FIGURE 12.3 ■ The Sexual Response Cycle

The human sexual response is believed to follow a four-component biological sequence: (1) During an initial excitement phase, arousal increases rapidly. (2) During the plateau phase, arousal increases steadily but more slowly. (3) In the orgasmic phase, sexual release occurs. (4) In the resolution phase, arousal falls back toward normal levels. For men, the resolution phase is characterized by a refractory period during which further stimulation fails to produce visible signs of arousal or orgasm.

Monica Wierzbicki/Body Scientific Intl.

testes of men rise up in preparation for ejaculation. Sexual release is next, in the **orgasmic phase**, and occurs in the form of rhythmic contractions in the sex organs; in men, these rhythmic contractions are accompanied by ejaculation. Interestingly, the subjective experience of the orgasm is apparently quite similar for men and women despite the obvious physiological differences (Mah & Binik, 2002). When asked to review written descriptions of the orgasmic experience, outside readers usually can't tell whether a description was written by a man or a woman (Proctor et al., 1974).

The sexual response cycle ends with a **resolution phase**, during which arousal returns to normal levels and, at least for men, there is a *refractory period* where further stimulation fails to produce visible signs of arousal or orgasm. The length of the resolution phase is highly variable—it can last anywhere from a few minutes to several days—and no one is quite sure exactly what determines when it will end. Age and prior frequency of sexual release seem to be important factors, as is the degree of emotional closeness with one's partner (Crooks & Baur, 2017).

Internal Factors

For most animals, including primates, sexual behavior is strongly controlled by chemical messengers (sex hormones) that rise and fall in cycles (Pfaff, 1999). A female rat will assume a characteristic posture—signaling she's ready for mounting and copulation by the male—but only during the time in her hormonal cycle when she is most likely to become impregnated. She'll adjust her posture to prepare for the weight of the male, she'll move her tail aside, and she'll even approach and nuzzle the male to ensure his attention. But these behaviors are tightly locked to the presence of the appropriate hormones—estradiol and progesterone in the case of the female rat. If these hormones are absent, the female will show no interest in sex at all, choosing instead to display indifference or hostility toward the sexually active male. If these hormones are injected artificially, sexual receptivity can be induced under conditions in which it would not normally occur (Lisk, 1978). As with the female, sexual behavior of the male rat depends on the presence of the appropriate hormone—testosterone. If testosterone is absent, so too is the desire to have sex.

Hormones and Human Sexuality

Humans also show regular variations in the hormones relevant to sex and reproduction. These sets of hormones—*estrogens* in women and *androgens* in men—play a critical role in physical development, affecting everything from the development of the sex organs to the wiring structure of the brain (see Chapter 3). But the initiation and control of adult sexual behavior doesn't appear to be a matter of simply mixing and matching the right internal chemicals. Human sexual behavior remains largely under our control, although learned social and cultural factors exert an influence. Instead of instinctive posturing and fixed courtship rituals, people in most cultures largely choose when, where, and how they engage in sexual activity.

Animals often show rigid courtship and mating rituals that are largely under the control of internal hormones.

iStockPhoto/dylan_burrill

This doesn't mean that hormones aren't important in human sexual behavior. There's some evidence that a woman's peak of sexual desire occurs in the middle of her menstrual cycle, near the time of ovulation, although the nature of the sexual relationship may matter (Gangestad et al., 2010). There's also evidence that testosterone affects sexual desire in both men and women. For example, when testosterone levels are reduced sharply—as occurs, for instance, following removal of the testes (medical castration) in men—there's often a loss of interest in sex. In fact, sex offenders are sometimes treated by administering drugs that block the action of testosterone. But neither men nor women are rigidly controlled by these hormones. Some castrated men continue to enjoy and seek out sexual encounters, even without hormone replacement therapy. Similarly, women continue to seek out and enjoy sexual relations after menopause when the levels of female sex hormones decline.

External Factors

Rather than appealing to hormones to explain sexual desires, psychologists typically focus instead on the value, or incentive, of the sexual act. Clearly, there's something about the internal wiring of the brain that makes the sexual act itself immensely rewarding for most people. The sight of an attractive person acts as a signal for something pleasurable, and we are pulled, or motivated, toward an object that may lead to reinforcing sexual release.

While this is not a very romantic description of sexual desire, to be sure, it's the sexual "signals" in our environment that often stimulate sexual desire. Both men and women are sexually aroused by explicit visual stimuli, although women, if questioned, are less likely to report the arousal (J. L. Peterson & Hyde, 2011). Women are also more likely to label an explicit film clip as "pornographic" than men (B. J. Willoughby & Busby, 2016). If excitement is measured through physiological recording devices, then men and women show similar arousal responses to erotic pictures and movies (M. Allen et al., 2007). It depends on the nature of the material, though—women show less arousal than men to erotic video clips that don't also include a romantic component (Rupp & Wallen, 2008). The ways people dress and wear their hair, the shapes of their bodies—all contribute to popular conceptions of attractiveness and help to promote sexual interest.

Touch and Smell

Touch is another important external source of sexual arousal. When stimulated, certain parts of the body (known commonly as *erogenous zones*) are highly arousing for most people and may act as one of the few completely natural, or unlearned, arousal sources (although erogenous zones can develop or be influenced by experience). We frequently communicate through touch, and touch is an important source of information in all corners of the world (E. McDaniel & Andersen, 1998).

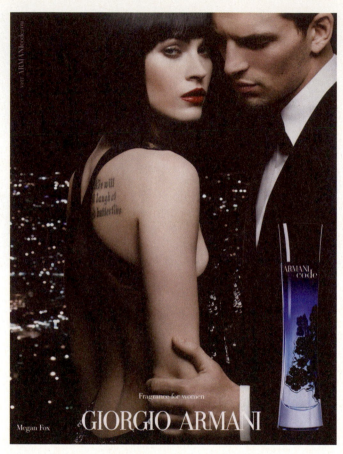

Certain smells can be highly arousing, although in humans it's more learning than biology that makes the perfume industry a success.

Grzegorz Czapski/ Alamy Stock Photo

In contrast, for many animals, odor or smell initiates sexual interest. In Chapter 5, we discussed chemicals called *pheromones* that are released by the females of many species during periods of receptivity. Pheromones are odor-producing chemicals, and they drive dogs, pigs, and many other creatures into a sexual frenzy. There's no strong evidence that human pheromones affect sexual desire, but researchers remain open-minded about a possible role (Wyatt, 2015). How a person smells definitely matters—both men and women report that odor is an important factor in selecting a lover (Herz & Cahill, 1997). One recent study found that human tears contain a chemical signal that can affect sexual desire in men. Men who sniffed tears from a woman who had recently cried reported reduced sexual arousal compared to men who sniffed a saline solution (Gelstein et al., 2011). Moreover, as you learned in Chapter 5, women seem to prefer the scent of men who show physical traits suggestive of "good genes," such as facial symmetry; moreover, these preferences are strongest when the women are most fertile (Thornhill et al., 2003).

Mate Selection

In choosing a mate, what determines whom we consider attractive and desirable? Not surprisingly, our conceptions of attractiveness are influenced by both biological and environmental factors (see Chapter 13). Societies have unique cultural definitions of attractiveness, their own rules for attracting a mate, and different views on what kinds of sexual behavior are considered appropriate.

Sexual Scripts

Psychologists believe we acquire **sexual scripts** as we develop—these are learned programs that instruct us on how and why to interact, and what to do in our interactions, with sexual partners (Gagnon, 1990; Gagnon & Simon, 1973). Sexual scripts contribute to the differences seen in male and female sexual behavior. Among other things, sexual scripts affect the attitudes we hold toward the sexual act. Boys typically learn, for example, to associate sexual intimacy with genital fondling; girls are more likely to identify intimacy with romantic love. These scripts affect expectations and can result in miscommunication between the sexes. For instance, teenage girls who engage in premarital sex often expect to marry their partners, but this expectation is less true for their male partners (R. Coles & Stokes, 1985). Sexual scripts may also account, in part, for why men sometimes employ aggression or strategies based on force to help them achieve their sexual interests (K. M. Ryan, 2004). Sexual scripts can be expected to change over time, as the culture changes. For example, young adults are more likely to report having sex with a friend or acquaintance than in the past (Monto & Carey, 2014); sexual scripts are also more likely to stress equality in sexual behavior between men and women than in past decades (see Wiederman, 2015).

Evolutionary Influences

Sexual scripts can differ from one culture to the next, but some mating strategies appear to be universal. In nearly every culture, men are more likely than women to pursue *short-term* sexual strategies—brief affairs or one-night stands. For example, at least among college students, most men aren't bothered very much by the idea of having sexual intercourse with a woman they met only an hour before; for most women, the idea of such casual sex is a "virtual impossibility" (see Schmitt & International Sexuality Description Project, 2003). Across all parts of the world, men seem to value attractiveness in a long-term mating partner, usually prefer to mate with women who are on the average younger than themselves, and report wanting more variety in their sexual partners (Gray et al., 2019; Schmitt, 2017). Women, on the other hand, tend to place much greater value on a mating partner's financial prospects than men do—a pattern that again holds across the world (see Figure 12.4).

The fact that these differences are present in every society suggests there may be adaptive reasons for these gender-based behaviors—or that the behaviors themselves may be adaptations. Men might pursue multiple sexual partners to increase the likelihood of successful reproduction (Dawkins, 1986). Women might prefer a man of high economic means because the responsibility of rearing and nurturing a child often falls on the woman's shoulders. Throughout evolutionary history, men and women have faced gender-specific reproductive problems, and their attitudes and mating rituals have probably developed, in part, to help resolve these problems (for a review, see D. M. Buss & Schmitt, 2019).

At the same time, it's misleading to focus too much on sex differences—there are many similarities in how men and women view prospective mates (Smiler, 2011). There are also lots of individual differences—for example, not all men actively seek short-term mating partners. It's also very difficult to disentangle evolutionary influences from what may simply be learned social "roles" (Eagly & Wood, 1999). As noted previously, human sexual behavior shows considerable flexibility—the biological forces of nature influence but need not determine our final behavior. We'll return to the debate about the roles of biology versus the environment, specifically with respect to conceptions of attractiveness, in Chapter 13.

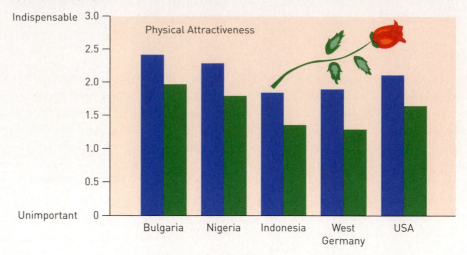

FIGURE 12.4 ■ Cultural Mating Strategies

Men and women in different parts of the world were asked to rate the importance of physical attractiveness and financial prospects in a long-term partner. On average, men rated physical attractiveness higher than women did, and women were more likely than men to value a partner's financial prospects.

Source: Data from Buss & Schmitt, 1993.

Sexual Orientation

Sexual orientation refers to the part of individual identity that includes a person's sexual and emotional attraction to another person, and the behavior and social affiliation that may result from this attraction. The term *homosexual* is applied when the attraction is predominantly to members of the same sex; *heterosexual* refers to other-sex attraction. Estimates of the number of people in the United States who fit the description of homosexual vary, ranging from 1% or 2% to perhaps as high as 10%, depending on how the term is defined (Savin-Williams, 2006). In a recent Gallup poll, conducted in 2017 and based on 340,000 interviews, 4.5% of Americans identified as lesbian, gay, bisexual, or transgender people (see Newport, 2018). Exact numbers are difficult to determine, partly because people are reluctant to disclose intimate information about sexual orientation. Moreover, in some respects, sexual orientation is best seen as a continuum rather than as a category with fixed boundaries. People who are predominantly homosexual sometimes seek out heterosexual relationships, and many heterosexuals have had sexual experiences with members of the same sex.

But what accounts for a sexual and emotional attraction to members of the same sex? If the purpose of sexual desire is to procreate—to ensure continuation of the species—in what way can homosexuality be considered adaptive? There's no simple answer to this question, although certainly same-sex relationships have nurturing qualities that go well beyond sexual encounters. For many years, psychologists believed that homosexuality developed from experience, particularly the experiences children have with their parents. Homosexuality was considered to be an abnormal condition that arose from dysfunctional home environments, usually as a consequence of having a domineering mother and a passive father. But this view is no longer widely accepted, primarily because a close examination of family histories revealed that the home environments of heterosexuals and homosexuals are quite similar (A. P. Bell et al., 1981).

Sexual orientation is likely determined, at least in part, by biological factors. People may, in fact, be "born gay" although the evidence is not completely conclusive. When researcher Simon LeVay (1991) compared the autopsied brains of homosexual and heterosexual men, he discovered that a cluster of neurons associated with the hypothalamus was consistently larger in heterosexual men. Exactly how or why this portion of the brain influences sexual orientation is unknown. There is some evidence that having biological brothers increases the chances of homosexuality in later-born males; one interpretation of this fraternal birth order effect is that prior male births somehow change the mother's uterine environment (see Blanchard, 2018). There have also been reports suggesting a genetic locus for sexual orientation. For example, twin studies have revealed that if one identical twin is homosexual, there is an approximately 30%–40% chance that the other twin will share the same sexual orientation; for fraternal twins or nontwin brothers and sisters, the likelihood that both will be homosexual is considerably lower (Kirk et al., 2000). Systematic analyses of the chromosomes of homosexual brothers originally provided evidence for what the researchers believed might be a "gay gene" (Hamer et al., 1993), but these findings have proven difficult to replicate (Dawood et al., 2009). Recent genome-wide association studies have detected genetic variants that are associated with male homosexuality, but this research is still in its early stages (Sanders et al., 2018).

It's simply too early to tell what all these results mean. The biological findings remain correlational; we simply know that sexual orientation may be *associated* with certain brain structures or genetic markers—but correlational data don't allow us to determine the *cause* of sexual orientation. Moreover, it seems very unlikely that biological factors alone will solve the mysteries of sexual orientation—after all, a significant percentage of identical twins of homosexual people do not share this orientation. The environment is certain to play an important role, but the nature of that role has yet to be determined. Finally, remember that sexual orientation is not a fixed attribute of a person, like blue eyes or blond hair; we're attracted to others for many reasons, and there may be multiple pathways and reasons for a particular sexual orientation.

KNOWLEDGE CHECK 12.3

Check your knowledge about the internal and external factors that control sexual behavior by deciding whether each of the following statements is true or false. (You will find the answers in the Appendix.)

1. In the human sexual response cycle, the period just prior to orgasm is called the plateau phase. *True or False?*

2. It is possible to affect sexual desire in men by altering the natural levels of the hormone testosterone in the body. *True or False?*

3. Across the world, men value attractiveness in a long-term mating partner and universally prefer to mate with women who are, on average, younger than themselves. *True or False?*

4. Twin studies have revealed that if one identical twin is homosexual, there is an approximately 50% chance that the other twin will share the same sexual orientation. *True or False?*

EXPRESSING AND EXPERIENCING EMOTION

Most psychologists are convinced that motivation and emotion are closely linked. Both terms, in fact, derive from the Latin *movere*, meaning "to move." Many conditions that are motivating also give rise to the experience of emotion. Suppose you're thirsty and put change into a Coke machine. If the money gets stuck, blocking your goal, you're likely to get frustrated and angry. The emotional experience, in turn, produces its own energizing effect on behavior—maybe you start screaming and kicking the machine (which may or may not help). It's difficult to discuss the topic of motivation without also considering emotion.

As we discussed at the beginning of the chapter, emotions are complex psychological events that involve a mixture of reactions: (1) a *physiological response* (usually arousal), (2) an *expressive reaction* (distinctive facial expression, body posture, or vocalization), and (3) some kind of *subjective experience* (internal thoughts and feelings). Each of these components is shown in Figure 12.5.

Why experience emotions in the first place? Psychologists generally believe emotions help us adapt to rapidly changing environmental conditions. Emotions are powerful motivators of behavior—they help us prioritize our thoughts and force us to focus on finding problem solutions. Physiological arousal, for instance, prepares the body for fight or flight and helps us direct our actions in the face of danger. Through expressive behaviors, such as the characteristic facial grimace of anger, it's possible to communicate our mental state instantly to others (see R. E. Jack & Schyns, 2017). Emotions can even stimulate social behaviors. People perform better and are more likely to help others when they feel happiness (Hoffman, 1986); people are also more likely to volunteer aid after doing something for which they feel guilt (J. M. Carlsmith & Gross, 1969).

FIGURE 12.5 ■ The Composition of Emotion

Emotions are complex experiences that involve (1) a physiological response, (2) an expressive reaction, and (3) some kind of subjective experience.

Emotion

Body Response (Arousal)
Increased blood pressure, heart rate, muscle tension, respiration

Expressive Reaction
Facial expression, acting out

Subjective Experience
Feeling of happiness, anger, fear, etc.

Are There Basic Emotions?

Can you name all the important emotions? The English language is full of words, literally hundreds in fact, that relate to emotion. But are there hundreds of emotions, or just a basic few? This seems like a simple question, but it's one that's perplexed researchers for decades (Hess, 2017; Russell, 2003). To get a sense of the difficulty, try compiling your own list of basic emotions. While you're at it, ask your friends and see how much you agree. Let's see: anger, fear, joy . . . how about interest, loathing, jealousy, or distraction? Psychologists have been compiling their own lists for decades without general agreement.

If forced to choose, most people (including emotion researchers) agree on about a half-dozen. Most lists include anger, fear, happiness, and sadness (Ekman, 1999; Ortony & Turner, 1990). Researchers who believe these emotions are basic, or universal, argue convincingly that certain emotions, such as anger, increase the chances of survival. People also have no trouble recognizing expressions of anger, fear, sadness, and happiness in other people, through either facial expressions or emotional vocalizations (Sauter et al., 2010). Paul Ekman and his colleagues asked volunteers to match photographs of grimacing, smiling, or otherwise distinctive facial displays to a number of basic emotion labels. There was wide agreement on six fundamental emotions: happiness, surprise, fear, sadness, anger, and disgust combined with contempt (Ekman, 1992; Ekman & Friesen, 1986).

Facial Expressions and Culture

One of the signature characteristics of an emotion is a facial expression. Regardless of where you look in the world, people identify facial expressions with emotional states. For example, a furrowed brow and a square mouth with pursed lips tends to signify anger worldwide (Ekman & Friesen, 1975). Ekman and Friesen (1975) tested members of a rural, isolated culture in New Guinea. These people had no experience with Western culture, yet they correctly identified the emotions expressed in photographs of Caucasian faces. Similarly, when U.S. college students were later shown photos of the New Guinea people acting out various emotions, they too were able to identify the emotions with a high degree of accuracy. However, it's not clear that emotion labels necessarily mean the same thing across cultures (Russell, 1994), and there do appear to be some cultural differences in emotion recognition (R. E. Jack et al., 2016).

Different emotions are often associated with particular facial expressions. Can you identify the emotion expressed in each of these photos?

Courtesy of Paul Ekman

The cross-cultural data encourage the view that the expression of emotion may have a biological or genetic origin. Babies show a wide range of emotional expressions at a very young age (Izard, 1994), and even babies who are born blind, or with both visual and hearing impairments, show facial expressions similar to sighted babies (Eibl-Eibesfeldt, 1973). It appears people may purse their lips and furrow their brow when they're mad because these tendencies are built directly into the genetic code rather than having been learned. The idea that there are at least some universal facial expressions certainly makes adaptive sense because facial expressions are often excellent signals to others about our current internal state (Ekman & Keltner, 1997).

At the same time, the story is not as simple as it might seem. Facial expressions are clearly signals for emotion, but their interpretation also depends importantly on the context or situation (Barrett, 2017; Barrett et al., 2011). The same scowling face can be perceived as signaling anger, disgust, or even puzzlement depending on the situation. If the person is in danger, the expression will likely be seen as fear; but if the same expression is paired with something disgusting (e.g., a person looking at a decaying animal), it will be interpreted as an expression of disgust. This fits in well with the general account of perception that was outlined in Chapter 5. What we perceive is a product of the sensory signal (the facial expression) as well as our general expectation about what is "out there" (top-down processing). This guarantees that the same facial expression, depending on the circumstance, might be interpreted differently by different people (Gendron et al., 2018).

The Facial-Feedback Hypothesis

Feedback from the muscles in the face may even help influence the internal emotional experience. According to the **facial-feedback hypothesis**, muscles in the face deliver signals to the brain that are then interpreted, depending on the pattern, as subjective emotional states (Tomkins, 1962). Other researchers suggest there may be direct connections between expressions and physical changes in the brain. For example, smiling can alter the volume of air that is inhaled through the nose; these changes, in turn, can affect the temperature of the brain, which, in turn, might affect mood (McIntosh et al., 1997; Zajonc et al., 1993).

The facial-feedback hypothesis suggests an interesting possibility: If asked to adopt a particular facial expression artificially, will you experience a corresponding change in emotion? In fact, some kinds of forced smiling, frowning, or grimacing have been shown to modulate emotional reports in some cases (e.g., Soussignan, 2002). You can try this for yourself: Try forcing yourself to smile or grimace in an exaggerated way. Do you feel any different? Some therapists recommend that clients who are depressed literally force themselves to smile when they're feeling depressed. Here's another piece of evidence: People who have just received a facial injection of Botox®, which paralyzes certain muscles in the face, have shown changes in their responsiveness to emotional stimuli (Davis et al., 2010).

But the facial-feedback hypothesis has not fared well in recent replication efforts. For example, one preregistered study attempted to replicate the finding that holding a pen in one's teeth, which forces a kind of smile, causes people to rate a cartoon as funnier (Strack et al., 1988). Seventeen laboratories participated in the replication project, and overall no support was found for the facial-feedback effect (Wagenmakers et al., 2016). On the other hand, a recent meta-analysis, which considered the results from 138 different studies, concluded that facial feedback can indeed influence emotional experience, although the effect is relatively small and variable (N. A. Coles et al., 2019).

How Convincing Is the Evidence?

The link among facial expressions, biology, and emotion suggests that certain emotions may be universal (Izard, 2007). But does the fact that people universally have facial expressions for fear, anger, or happiness mean that these emotions are somehow more primary or basic than others? Some psychologists think not. Remember, many psychologists disagree about which emotions belong on the basic list. Does interest, wonder, or guilt belong? How about shame, contempt, or elation? Each of these terms has been identified as basic by at least one prominent emotion researcher. The problem is that humans are capable of an enormous range of emotional experiences. Consider the differences among fear, terror, panic, distress, rage, and anxiety. It is clearly appropriate to use each of these terms in some circumstances and not in others. How can we explain a complex emotion such as terror? If it's not a basic emotion, is it somehow manufactured in the brain by combining or blending more fundamental emotions such as fear, surprise, and possibly anger?

It may not be possible to explain human emotional experiences by combining a set of basic emotions. Rather than basic emotions, some argue, it may be better to think of basic responses that are *shared* by a wide variety of emotional experiences (e.g., Barrett, 2006). For example, as noted earlier, the furrowed brow commonly seen in anger is not exclusive to anger but also occurs when people are frustrated, puzzled, or even just working hard on a task. The furrowed brow may occur in any situation in which a person is somehow blocked from reaching a goal; its appearance, by itself, is not sufficient to conclude that the person is angry.

It may help to think about the analogy of human language. There are hundreds of different languages across the world, and each follows certain universal rules (relating to sound and word combinations). But it doesn't make any sense to argue that some of these languages are more basic than others. Human languages are built up from basic components and share many features in common. Similarly, when people are in the grip of an emotion, they may experience many basic and universal conditions (such as a tendency to smile or frown, approach or avoid), but these are merely the components of emotion, not the emotions themselves (Russell, 2003; Turner & Ortony, 1992).

FIGURE 12.6 ■ Arousal and Task Performance

For a given task, performance tends to be best at intermediate levels of arousal. Too little or too much arousal often leads to a decrease in performance.

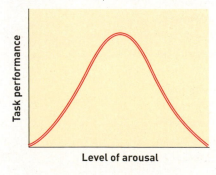

The Emotional Experience: Arousal

Psychologists may disagree about whether there are basic emotions, but everyone agrees about certain aspects of the emotional *experience*. Virtually all emotions, for instance, lead to *physiological arousal*. Muscles tense, heart rate speeds up, and blood pressure and respiration rates skyrocket. These emotional symptoms come from activity of the autonomic nervous system as it prepares the muscles and organs of the body for a fight-or-flight response. We usually experience emotions in situations that are significant for one reason or another—for instance, the car of a drunken driver swerves sharply into our path, or the sound of breaking glass from the basement window startles us awake. It's adaptive for the body to react quickly in such cases, and the rapid onset of physiological arousal serves that function well.

But emotional arousal can have a negative side as well. Too much arousal can lead to a breakdown in behavioral, biological, or psychological functioning. Figure 12.6 shows the relationship that exists between level of arousal and task performance. Notice the pattern looks like an arch or an inverted *U*. For a given task, as arousal levels increase from low to moderate, performance generally rises. Some people perform better under pressure—the track star runs a little faster or jumps a little higher. You may well perform better on a test if the test is particularly important. But too much pressure, which causes too much arousal, causes a sharp drop-off in task performance. Did you have trouble thinking when you took the SAT? Too much emotional pressure creates a level of arousal that hurts rather than helps normal mental functioning.

Understanding the relationship between arousal and performance has helped psychologists interpret behavior in a variety of situations. For example, as you know, people who witness crimes are sometimes inaccurate in their later recollections. One factor that contributes to the poor memory is the high level of arousal generated in crime scenes. If someone holds a gun to your head, your level of arousal is likely to block normal cognitive processing. You're simply too aroused to process the details of the crime scene effectively. Moreover, as you'll see in Chapter 13, the relationship between arousal and performance also helps us to understand how our behavior changes in the presence of other people—our performance is either facilitated or impaired when other people are around, perhaps because the presence of others changes our overall level of arousal.

The Emotional Experience: Subjective Reactions

Experiencing an emotion involves much more than a facial expression or a flood of physiological arousal. Your thoughts, your perceptions, and the things you notice in the environment all change when you experience an emotion. Even the acoustic patterns in your voice change in measurable ways (Kamiloğlu et al., 2020). But as we discussed earlier, it's difficult to measure the internal experience accurately and reliably. After all, the emotional experience is by definition personal and subjective. We can ask someone what it feels like to be angry, happy, or scared, but the constraints of language restrict the answers we receive. Some cultures don't even have a word in their language to describe the concept of an emotion. The Ifaluk people of Micronesia, for example, have only the word *niferash*, which roughly translates as "our insides" (Lutz, 1982; Matsumoto, 1994).

Anger

It is possible to study the conditions that lead to emotions. For example, in the case of *anger*, people have been asked to keep daily and weekly records, noting the specific situations that made them mad. Most people get angry at least several times a week (but to different degrees); some experience the emotion several times a day (Averill, 1983). There are individual differences among people, suggesting that one's anger threshold may be an inherited biological trait (Veenstra et al., 2018). Anger clearly serves an adaptive function: It causes us to tackle our problems head on and express our grievances, and it also serves as a signal to others that they should change their ways or avoid interaction (Lench et al., 2016).

What causes anger? Not surprisingly, the causes are many (Berkowitz & Harmon-Jones, 2004). If you're restrained in some way, physically or psychologically, you're likely to get mad. More generally, people tend to get angry when their expectations are violated. If you're counting on someone to act a certain way, and those expectations are violated, you'll probably get mad. This is one of the reasons we often get angry at the ones we love. We tend to expect more from the people we love, which, in turn, increases the chances that our expectations will be violated. We also get angry when unpleasant things happen, even if it doesn't involve the violation of an expectation. I bet you get mad when you trip over something on the sidewalk or bang your knee against a wall. Right? Physical pain, physically unpleasant situations, and major social stresses all reliably lead to anger.

Is the expression of anger healthy psychologically? Psychologists remain undecided about the benefits of venting anger or blowing off steam. On one hand, expressing your feelings may have a cathartic effect: The expression of anger can lead to an emotional release that is ultimately calming. On the other hand, getting physically angry could well increase the chances that you'll get angry again (Novaco, 2016). When you express anger, and feel the calming effect that follows, you reinforce the anger response. Some psychologists have found that encouraging people to express their feelings of anger or hostility leads to more expressions or feelings of anger in the future (Bushman, 2002). Evidence suggests as well that people who punish a rule-violator end up feeling worse than those who don't exact "revenge" (K. M. Carlsmith et al., 2008). The expression of anger can also lead to increased risk-taking and other kinds of self-defeating behavior. We'll return to the effects of anger, specifically on stress and health, in Chapter 16.

Is the expression of anger healthy psychologically? Psychologists remain undecided about the benefits of venting anger or blowing off steam.

iStockPhoto/fizkes

Happiness

Understanding that anger arises from violations of expectations also helps account for the experience of *happiness*. There has been a dramatic increase in the scientific study of happiness over the past several decades (psychologists used to focus primarily on negative emotions); there is even a thriving field called "positive psychology" that studies how and when happiness and well-being flourish (see Seligman, 2019). Perhaps not surprisingly, happiness is associated with a variety of positive outcomes, including better immune system functioning, longevity, gains in income, and success in marriage (see Myers & Diener, 2018). In general, people tend to gain or lose happiness as a result of the comparisons they make—either with others (a well-known tendency called *social comparison*) or with things or experiences from their past (Cacioppo & Gardner, 1999). People set standards for satisfaction, and they're happy if those standards are maintained or surpassed. The trouble is that our standards are constantly changing—Eddie and Lucinda may be able to keep up with the Joneses next door, but there's always the Mendenhalls down the street who just bought that new boat. Once people reach a certain level of satisfaction, they often form a new level, and then another, and never quite attain complete happiness.

Many psychological judgments, not just emotions, are linked to comparisons with some standard, or *adaptation level*. You learned in Chapter 5 that whether we will hear one tone as louder than another depends on how loud the standard tone was to begin with. Human judgments are relative—there's no sense in which a tone is loud, a light is bright, or a person is happy or sad without answering the question, "Relative to what?" Even negative events can seem positive if they are placed in the right context. For example, arguing with a spouse is rated more positively if it's preceded by the rating of an extremely negative event, such as a death in the family (Schwarz & Strack, 1999). A study of athletes at the 1992 Olympic Games revealed that bronze medal winners (third place) were happier than silver medal winners (second place); presumably, the bronze medalists focused on the accomplishment of winning a medal, whereas the silver medalists saw themselves as failing to reach gold (Medvec et al., 1995). If asked, most believe that people who have a severe disability, such as those with paraplegia, spend the majority of their time in a bad mood. In fact, nothing could be further from the truth. The well-being of people with paraplegia tends to be normal most of the time—people adapt, even to the most horrific of circumstances (Kahneman, 2011).

The fact that happiness is relative helps to explain some phenomena that might seem a bit mysterious. Why is the couple who just won the multimillion-dollar lottery still bickering? Why is Ed, who recently succeeded in getting the most popular girl in class to hang out with him, now anxiously seeking the attention of someone else? How can that homeless man, with only scraps to eat and tattered clothes, wake up every morning with a smile on his face? Happiness is not some Holy Grail that can be sought and sometimes found—it's an elusive and fickle condition that depends on constantly changing standards and comparisons.

Disgust

Usually included in the group of basic emotions is *disgust*, a marked aversion toward something distasteful (literally meaning "bad taste"). It's easy to appreciate the adaptive value of this particular emotion, especially as a mechanism to make certain we select and reject the appropriate foods. The facial expression that typically accompanies disgust is itself an adaptive reaction to a potentially harmful substance. You wrinkle your nose, and your mouth drops open in a characteristic gape. Wrinkling the nose closes off the air passages, cutting off any offending odor; the gaping expression "causes the contents of the mouth to dribble out" (Rozin & Fallon, 1987, p. 24).

Yet there is a psychology to disgust that extends beyond its role in food rejection. To illustrate, suppose you come home one evening and find a cockroach nesting on your toothbrush. Is it conceivable that you would ever use that toothbrush again? Suppose we dropped it into boiling water for a while to ensure sterilization. Would you use it now? Probably not by choice. In a study by Paul Rozin and his colleagues, a dead but sterilized cockroach was dropped into a glass of juice and offered to thirsty subjects. Not surprisingly, few people showed any interest in drinking the juice, even though they knew the roach had been sterilized (Rozin et al., 1986). Most people are also reluctant to consume their favorite soup if they witness the bowl being stirred by a never-used comb or fly swatter (Rozin & Fallon, 1987).

The experience of disgust seems to be universal—appearing cross-culturally—but the emotion takes time to develop. For example, if children under age 4 are presented with what adults consider a disgusting odor (feces or synthetic sweat), they tend not to be bothered, or they may even react positively. Children under age 2, as any parent knows, are happy to put just about anything into their mouths, even "disgusting" objects. In one study, it was found that 62% of tested children under age 2 would put imitation dog feces in their mouth; 31% would mouth a whole, sterilized grasshopper (Rozin et al., 1986). Children simply have no conception that these objects are potentially harmful—they must learn what not to put in their mouths.

Many psychologists also believe that the emotion of disgust plays a role in our moral judgments—such as our views on abortion, animal cruelty, or whether it is okay to eat genetically modified food (e.g., Chapman & Anderson, 2013; S. E. Scott et al., 2016). In Chapter 4, we discussed how decisions about right and wrong, such as whether or not it's ever appropriate for siblings to have sex, can be based on emotional "gut reactions." Invoking a disgust reaction in people has been shown to affect subsequent judgments on these kinds of moral vignettes. In addition, people who score high on disgust sensitivity scales also show more sensitivity to certain judgments about morality (Wagemans et al., 2018).

Would you eat anything else on this plate?

iStockPhoto/fcafotodigital

Theories of Emotion: Body to Mind

Emotions are complex events. People subjectively experience happiness or sadness, but they also experience important changes in their body and on their face. Questions about how these various components interact have stumped emotion researchers for decades. For example, what exactly causes the body reaction? Is the arousal caused by the internal subjective experience, or are we happy or sad because our bodies have been induced to react in a particular way?

There are a number of possible explanations (for an overview, see Figure 12.7). The most natural argument is that the internal experience drives the physiological reaction. We tremble, gasp, and increase our heart rate because some event has caused us to become afraid. We feel fear, and our body reacts with physiological arousal. Surprisingly, this straightforward view of emotion has been rejected by emotion researchers for more than a century. William James (1890) saw the commonsense view as backward: "The more rational statement is that we feel sorry because we cry, angry because we strike, afraid because we tremble, and not that we cry, strike, or tremble because we are sorry, angry, or fearful" (p. 1066). Although James believed our interpretation of the situation also plays a role (Ellsworth, 1994; W. James, 1894), he was convinced that the body reaction occurs before the subjective experience of emotion rather than the other way around.

The James–Lange Theory

The idea that the body reaction drives the subjective experience of emotion is known as the **James–Lange theory** of emotion. Lange is coupled with James because Danish physiologist Carl Lange proposed a similar idea at roughly the same time as James. Why reject the commonsense approach in favor of such a counterintuitive view? Neither James nor Lange presented much evidence in support of this account (other than personal impressions). However, some significant predictions can be derived from their view. For instance, imagine we could somehow reduce or eliminate significant body reactions. The James–Lange theory predicts we should lose the corresponding experience of emotion. To test this idea, interviews have been conducted with people suffering from spinal cord injuries. Because of nerve damage, these people either have lost feeling in major portions of their bodies or at least have reduced sensory feedback. In support of the James–Lange view, some people with paraplegia have reported a drop-off in the intensity of their emotional experience (for example, anger lost its "heat"; Hohmann, 1966). Other studies, using neuroimaging techniques, have reached similar conclusions (Nicotra et al., 2006).

FIGURE 12.7 ■ Four Views of Emotion

The commonsense view, largely rejected by psychologists, assumes that an environmental stimulus creates a subjective experience (fear), which in turn leads to a physiological reaction (arousal). The James–Lange theory proposes instead that the physical reaction drives the subjective experience. In the Cannon–Bard theory, the physical reaction and the subjective experience are assumed to be largely independent processes. In the two-factor theory, it is the cognitive interpretation and labeling of the physical response that drives the subjective experience.

Theory	Stimulus	Response	Report
Common sense		**Fear** — Subjective experience → Body response (arousal)	"My heart is pounding because I feel afraid."
James–Lange		Body response (arousal) → **Fear** — Subjective experience	"I feel afraid because my heart is pounding."
Cannon–Bard		→ Body response (arousal) / → **Fear** — Subjective experience	"The dog makes me feel afraid and my heart pounds."
Two-factor		Body response (arousal) → Interpretation → **Fear** — Subjective experience	"My pounding heart means I'm afraid because I interpret the situation as dangerous."

Illustrated by Sarah Yeh

The James–Lange theory also predicts that unique physical changes should accompany each of the different emotional experiences. That is, a particular body response must produce anger, happiness, fear, and so on. But as noted previously, the dominant physiological response during an emotion is *arousal*, and heart rate changes, sweaty palms, and an increased breathing rate seem to be characteristic of virtually all emotions rather than just a select few. Think about how your body feels just before an important exam. How about the feelings you have before an important and long-awaited date? Would you describe the emotions as similar?

Sophisticated measuring devices have enabled researchers to record small, previously undetectable changes in body reactions. Such data may eventually help us to distinguish the body reaction for one emotional state from the body reaction of another (P. J. Lang, 1994; Levenson, 1992). No firm conclusions can be drawn at this point, but the evidence increasingly suggests that unique biological markers may be associated with particular emotions (Hamann, 2012; Saarimaki et al., 2016). Establishing definitive links between emotional states and physiological responses is an important step for emotion researchers, although perhaps not an unexpected one. After all, anger and happiness certainly are experienced differently and therefore must ultimately reflect differences in brain activity. But given the controversies surrounding the definition of a "basic" emotion, and the various ways in which the components of emotions can be expressed and shared, consensus on the issue is unlikely to be reached anytime soon.

The Cannon–Bard Theory

Historically, it didn't take too long for critics of the James–Lange theory of emotion to emerge. Physiologist Walter Cannon mounted an influential attack in the 1920s. Cannon (1927) recognized that the body reacts in essentially the same way to most emotional experiences. He was also convinced that the conscious experience of emotion has a rapid onset—people feel fear immediately after seeing an attacking dog—but the physiological reactions that come from the autonomic nervous system have a relatively slow onset time (glands need to be activated, hormones need to be released into the bloodstream, and so on). Cannon felt the subjective experience of emotion and the associated body reactions are *independent processes*. Emotions and arousal may occur together, but one doesn't cause the other. Cannon's view was later modified somewhat by Philip Bard, so this approach is now generally known as the **Cannon–Bard theory** of emotion.

The Schachter and Singer Experiment

We've now discussed three different theories of emotion: (1) People experience emotions subjectively, which then leads to body reactions such as arousal (the commonsense view); (2) the body generates a characteristic internal reaction, which then produces the appropriate emotional experience (James–Lange); and (3) body reactions and subjective experiences occur together, but independently (Cannon–Bard). None of these views remains popular among emotion researchers.

The major problem with this trio of emotion theories is that they fail to take into account the cognitive side of emotion. To understand exactly what this means, we need to consider a study that was conducted in the early 1960s by psychologists Stanley Schachter and Jerome Singer (see Figure 12.8). College students were recruited to participate in an experiment designed to test the effects of vitamin injections on vision. What the students didn't know, however, was that the vitamin cover story was a ploy—rather than vitamins, they were injected with either a dose of epinephrine (which produces physiological arousal symptoms) or a dose of saline (which produces no effects). A second manipulated variable was expectation: Half the people in each of the injection groups were told to expect arousal symptoms—as a side effect of the vitamins—and the other half were told to expect no reaction of any kind.

Now let's consider what effect these conditions should have on emotional reactions. Suppose you're sitting in a room, waiting for further instructions from the experimenter, when suddenly your heart begins to race and your palms begin to sweat. According to James–Lange, this arousal should translate into some kind of emotional experience; you might, for example, expect to become scared or irritated. But Schachter and Singer (1962) found that the experience of emotion was determined almost entirely by expectation. Those students who were told to anticipate arousal from the injection showed little emotional reaction to the arousal when it occurred. Only when the arousal was unexpected did people begin to report strong emotions.

More importantly, Schachter and Singer were able to influence the quality of the emotion when it occurred. Joining the participant in the waiting room was a disguised member of the experimental team, introduced as another participant in the experiment. Unknown to the real participant, the accomplice was instructed to act in a way that was either playful and euphoric or angry and disagreeable. In later assessments of mood, Schachter and Singer found that aroused but uninformed students tended to adopt the mood of the accomplice. If the accomplice was playful, the students reported feeling happy; if the accomplice was angry, the students reported feeling irritation.

Two-Factor Theory

The results of the Schachter and Singer experiment led to what is known as the **two-factor theory** of emotion. In two-factor theory, autonomic arousal is still a critical determinant of the emotional experience (factor 1). But equally important is the *cognitive appraisal* or *interpretation* of that arousal when it occurs (factor 2). An intense body reaction may be necessary for the full experience of an emotion, but

FIGURE 12.8 ■ The Schachter and Singer Experiment

Volunteer participants were injected with a drug that produced symptoms of physiological arousal. Half the participants were informed about the drug's effects; the others were not. When placed in a room with either a euphoric or an angry accomplice, only the uninformed people adopted the same mood. Presumably, the informed participants attributed their arousal symptoms to the drug, whereas the uninformed participants interpreted the symptoms as an emotional experience.

Illustrated by Sarah Yeh

it's not sufficient. It's how you *interpret* the arousal that ultimately determines your subjective emotion. So, you're scared when you face a venomous snake not only because your body is aroused but also because your mind understands that what's causing the arousal is dangerous. You *label* the arousal and thereby determine the emotion that's experienced.

Like the other theories of emotion we've discussed, two-factor theory has generated its share of criticism. For example, some researchers remain convinced that emotions such as anger and fear can arise directly without higher-level interpretation or appraisal (Russell, 2003; Winkielman & Berridge, 2004). However, it's possible to draw several tentative conclusions. First, it's reasonably clear that arousal contributes to the experience of emotion. Second, the situation in which the arousal occurs, and our expectations about the source of the arousal, contribute to the emotional experience. Third, rather than saying the body reaction creates the emotion, or vice versa, it's better to conclude that emotions arise from interactions among several sources: the stimulus event that leads to the reaction, autonomic changes in arousal, and the expectation-based cognitive labels applied to everything involved.

Check your knowledge about expressing and experiencing emotion by answering the following questions. (You will find the answers in the Appendix.)

1. For each of the following, pick the component of emotion that best fits the situation: *body response, expressive reaction*, or *subjective experience*.
   a. Sally likes to dance when she's happy: _____
   b. Yolanda grimaces and wrinkles her nose when she sees spaghetti with clam sauce: _____
   c. Mei feels her heart start racing whenever she sees her boyfriend approach: _____
   d. Robert would rather use the words *delighted, glad, pleased*, and *excited* to describe how he feels, instead of the word *happy*: _____

2. Which of the following situations is most likely to produce happiness?
   a. Receiving a B on a test when you were expecting a C
   b. Receiving an A on a test when you were expecting an A
   c. Receiving a C on a test when you were expecting to flunk
   d. Stimulation of the hypothalamus

3. For each of the following, pick the theory of emotion that best fits the situation: *James–Lange, Cannon–Bard*, or *two-factor*.
   a. I love it when my heart starts racing because it makes me feel happy: _____
   b. I must be in love because they just gave me a wink and my heart is racing: _____
   c. I feel happy right now, and by the way, my heart is also racing: _____
   d. You're not in love; you just drank too much coffee this morning: _____

THE PROBLEMS SOLVED: WHAT MOTIVATION AND THE EMOTIONS ARE FOR

Motivation and its intimate companion, emotion, are highly adaptive processes that help you initiate and direct your behavior, maintain your internal energy needs, and even prolong the species. Each of us simply must do certain things—eat, drink, maintain a constant internal temperature—and psychologists have struggled for decades to discover how the body accomplishes these ends.

Activating Behavior

As you've seen, motivation depends on an interplay between internal and external factors. Much of the time, behavior is controlled by internal factors that compel us in the direction of a goal. Our bodies are constantly monitoring internal energy levels, and once a disruption in the homeostatic balance is detected, we seek to restore the balance. In these cases, it's likely that motivated behavior arises directly as a consequence of biological factors and requires little direct experience with the environment.

But even something as biologically significant as eating or drinking can't be explained by appealing only to innate internal factors. All forms of motivated behavior are influenced by external factors as well. External rewards, or incentives, exert powerful pulling and guiding effects on our actions. Understanding motivation then becomes a matter of specifying how these *external* factors interact with *internal* factors to activate and control behavior. One way in which internal and external factors interact is described by Maslow's notion of a needs hierarchy. The essential component of Maslow's theory is the prioritizing of need: Some needs, especially those critical to survival, must be satisfied before others—for example, the need for self-actualization—can be pursued.

Meeting Biological Needs: Hunger and Eating

Internally, the body monitors everything from the amount of food in the stomach, to the level of glucose in the blood, to specific hormones that both start and stop us from eating. Most of the time, we're perfectly ready to start eating, but the body generates satiation or satiety signals to stop us from eating too much. Although researchers are uncertain about its precise function in controlling eating, the hypothalamus is believed to play an important role. But we also eat for reasons that appear unrelated to restoring homeostatic balance. Food, and particularly eating, is clearly reinforcing. As you've seen, people are much more likely to motivate themselves to eat if they like the food—the vigor or intensity with which they respond depends critically on the value, or incentive, of the food. A number of factors, both genetic and environmental, play a role in regulating body weight. Eating disorders such as anorexia nervosa and bulimia nervosa tend to have psychological origins related to body image but may be influenced by genetic factors as well.

Meeting Biological Needs: Sexual Behavior

Sexual activity is adaptive for a species because it increases the chances that the species will continue. But on an individual level, sex is also reinforcing, and sexual desire compels us to pursue a mate, thereby opening the door for companionship, protection, and love. The sexual response itself consists of four main phases (excitement, plateau, orgasmic, and resolution). Hormones appear to play much less of a role in controlling sexual desire in humans when compared with other animals. Different cultures have different views of attractiveness and different codes of conduct for sexual activity. Many psychologists believe people acquire sexual scripts that instruct them on how and why they interact, and what to do in their interactions, with potential sexual partners. Mate selection and sexual orientation, however, are probably influenced by biological as well as environmental factors.

Expressing and Experiencing Emotion

Emotions typically involve a mixture of reactions, including a physiological response (arousal), a characteristic expressive reaction (such as a distinctive facial expression), and some kind of subjective experience (such as the feeling of happiness or sadness). The physical expression of an emotion enables us to communicate our feelings to others. The internal components—arousal, for example—prepare us for action. Thoughts become prioritized, and muscles are ready to respond. Emotions are powerful adaptive tools: They not only increase the likelihood of survival but also make life itself worth living.

The subjective experience of emotion is often relative—whether we feel happy, for example, seems to depend on the comparisons we make with others and with our past experiences. Although a number of theories have tried to explain the relation between arousal and the experience of emotion, most psychologists believe that the experience of emotion depends partly on the presence of a body response—general arousal—and partly on the cognitive appraisals we make about the origin of arousal when it occurs.

THINKING ABOUT RESEARCH

A summary of a research study in psychology is given in this section. As you read the summary, think about the following questions:

1. What is the independent variable in this study? Do you think the authors have adequately controlled for all of the differences that might exist between graphic and text labels?
2. How might you use operant conditioning principles (the application of rewards and punishments) to explain the results of this study?
3. Do you think there could be side effects, or unintended consequences, to using graphic labels to change our drinking habits?
4. Are you comfortable with the government using psychological principles to control the behavior of consumers?
5. Can you relate these findings to the different theories of emotion that we discussed in this chapter?

Article Reference: Donnelly, G. E., Zatz, L. Y., Svirsky, D., & John, L. K. (2018). The effect of graphic warnings on sugary-drink purchasing. *Psychological Science, 29,* 1321–1333.

Purpose of the Study: To promote a healthy lifestyle, governments often mandate warning labels on products to lower consumption. This field study was designed to test the effectiveness of such labels on actual consumer choice. Of main interest was a comparison between typical text warning labels (e.g., drinking sugary beverages can lead to tooth decay) and more graphic versions with explicit pictures of health-related outcomes. The investigators were also interested in the possible psychological mechanisms that determine a label's effectiveness.

Method of the Study: The study occurred in a hospital cafeteria. An initial two-week period was used to collect baseline beverage-sales data for both sugary and nonsugary drinks (including water). In subsequent weeks, labels were introduced—either *text warnings* (e.g., "Drinking beverages with added sugar contributes to obesity, diabetes, and tooth decay"), *graphic warnings* (which added images portraying the different health conditions to the text warnings), or simple *calorie labels*. The labels were displayed on the cooler shelves immediately below the sugary drinks. Over a 2-week span, the investigators recorded the proportion of sugary and nonsugary drinks that were purchased by the participants. Follow-up studies used surveys to investigate the extent to which the warnings elicited negative emotions and people's sentiments about whether using such warnings was appropriate.

a
120-290 CALORIES PER CONTAINER.
2,000 calories a day is used for general nutrition advice, but calorie needs vary.

b
WARNING: Drinking beverages with added sugar(s) contributes to obesity, diabetes, and tooth decay.

c
WARNING: Drinking beverages with added sugar(s) contributes to:

OBESITY

DIABETES

TOOTH DECAY

Source: Donnelly, G. E., Zatz, L. Y., Svirsky, D., & John, L. K. (2018).

Results of the Study: The investigators found that the graphic warning labels reduced the percentage of sugary drinks that people purchased, leading them to choose water instead. Moreover, despite their widespread use in the marketplace, neither the text warnings nor the calorie labels had any significant effect on purchasing behavior. The follow-up surveys indicated that the graphic labels elicited negative emotions in people, which, in turn, led them to consider the health consequences of consumption. Moreover, although people were less likely to support the use of graphic images on beverage products compared to normal text warnings, this negative sentiment was reduced when the effectiveness of the images was explained.

Conclusions of the Study: Graphic warning labels can be an effective way of reducing the consumption of potentially harmful beverages. The results could spur more effective labeling policies that facilitate healthy choices.

KNOWLEDGE CHECK: CHAPTER SUMMARY

You will find the answers in the Appendix.

ACTIVATING BEHAVIOR

- (1) _____ are unlearned responses controlled by specific external triggering stimuli; they do not adequately explain human behavior. A (2) _____ is an internal state that arises in response to a (3) _____ need. Drives lead to more flexible responses than instincts.

- The term (4) _____ *motivation* is used to explain (5) _____-directed behavior. The value of the incentive—positive or negative—helps determine whether you'll be motivated to perform a task. An incentive is an external pull with (6) _____ or punishing consequences that helps explain motivated or goal-directed behavior.

- (7) _____ motivation is an internally driven need for success and accomplishment. People who rate high in achievement motivation tend to work (8) _____ and more persistently on tasks. (9) _____ motivation describes behaviors that are entirely self-motivated. (10) _____ rewards sometimes lower intrinsic motivation. (11) _____ factors may explain differences in achievement motivation.

- Usually represented as a pyramid, Maslow's (12) _____ of (13) _____ assumes that needs are prioritized and some must be satisfied before others can be met. Fundamental (14) _____ needs are primary; once they have been met, we can work toward fulfilling our needs for personal (15) _____, spiritual meaning, and (16) _____. At the top of the hierarchy is the need to reach our fullest potential, or to (17) _____.

MEETING BIOLOGICAL NEEDS: HUNGER AND EATING

- The hormone (18) _____ may play a role in hunger, but most internal signals are designed to stop us from eating. The hormone CCK is an important (19) _____ signal. The hormones insulin and (20) _____ are also important regulators of hunger and are tied to a person's amount of body fat. Brain areas that signal hunger include the (21) _____, (22) the _____ brain, and the (23) _____. Eating habits are influenced through (24) _____, experience, and modeling. Our eating behavior is partly determined by food (25) _____ and their association with past pleasures and discomforts. Cultural factors can also be important.

- Our natural body weight is probably determined partly by (26) _____ and partly by a (27) _____ point that may loosely influence our tendency to gain or lose weight. (28) _____ rates are on the rise and reflect biological and psychological factors that include (29) _____ rate, number of fat cells, (30) _____ eating habits, cultural role models, and (31) _____ levels.

- People often make inaccurate assessments of their own weight and its relation to (32) _____ ideals, which can result in a (33) _____ body image and increase one's susceptibility to eating disorders. (34) _____ nervosa is a condition in which people fail to maintain a normal body weight. (35) _____ nervosa is a condition in which people purge after binge eating.

MEETING BIOLOGICAL NEEDS: SEXUAL BEHAVIOR

- The four phases of the human sexual response cycle are (36) _____, (37) _____, (38) _____, and (39) _____. Resolution features a (40) _____ period, during which stimulation fails to produce further (41) _____.

- Hormones control sexual behavior in most species, but human sexual behavior is also influenced largely by (42) _____ cultural factors. Human hormones related to sexual behavior and reproduction differ by sex: The primary sex hormone in females is (43) _____, and (44) _____ is predominant in males.

- Touch is an important source of sexual arousal, especially the stimulation of (45) _____ zones. Odors or smells called (46) _____ may initiate sexual behavior in many species, though not necessarily in humans.

- Attractiveness is strongly influenced by biological and (47) _____ factors. One theory proposes that we acquire sexual (48) _____ that tell us how to interact with sexual partners. Despite individual differences in our scripts, similarities among sexual scripts may be due to (49) _____ influences. In nearly every (50) _____, men are more likely to value physical attractiveness than women, who usually emphasize financial prospects.

- (51) _____ and (52) _____ factors influence sexual (53) _____, or whether a person is attracted to members of the same sex (homosexual) or the other sex (heterosexual).

EXPRESSING AND EXPERIENCING EMOTION

- The basic (54) _____ expressions of emotions tend to be universal, which suggests that emotions may be (55) _____ in origin. These basic emotions include (56) _____, fear, (57) _____, and sadness. According to the facial- (58) _____ hypothesis, the movement of muscles in the face creates an internal experience that we think of as emotion.

- Emotions are associated with (59) _____ arousal. Very (60) _____ or low levels of arousal tend to disrupt (61) _____.

- Anger is typically associated with having one's (62) _____ violated. Whether or not it's healthful to vent anger is (63) _____. (64) _____ seems to rely on comparing ourselves to others or current experiences with those in the past. (65) _____ is an adaptive emotion that protects us from coming into contact with or ingesting harmful substances and tends to develop with age.

- The most natural way of relating body to mind is to assume that the subjective experience drives the physical reaction (commonsense view). The James–Lange theory assumes the opposite—that the (66) _____ reaction drives the (67) _____ experience of emotion, predicting that unique physical changes should accompany different emotions. The (68) _____–Bard theory proposes that the subjective experience and the physical reaction are (69) _____ processes. Schachter and Singer's (70) _____-factor theory assumes that emotion results from cognitive (71) _____, or interpretation, of autonomic arousal.

CRITICAL THINKING QUESTIONS

1. Suppose you spend every Saturday morning volunteering at a local homeless shelter. How do you think your attitude might change if you started receiving a paycheck for your time?

2. Turn back Chapter 4 on development and think about the various personal crises people confront as they age. Is there any way you can tie these crises to the needs that Maslow discussed in his hierarchy?

3. Can you think of any factors, besides behavior modeling, that might help to determine eating habits? What about the availability of food—when was the last time you saw sheep's eyes on the menu at the local diner?

4. Given the importance of the sexual act to the continued survival of the species, do you think there is justification for placing a great deal of emphasis on sex in our theories of behavior and mind (e.g., Freud)?

5. Other than through stimulating sexual desire, how might physical attractiveness affect the thoughts and actions of others?

6. Have you ever heard actors talk about how they "become the role" when they're playing emotional parts? What might psychologists tell actors to help them understand why this happens?

7. If expectations play an important role in determining whether an emotion will be experienced, would you expect to find cultural differences in the expression of emotion?

KEY TERMS

achievement motivation (p. 424)

anorexia nervosa (p. 436)

bulimia nervosa (p. 437)

Cannon–Bard theory (p. 454)

drive (p. 423)

emotions (p. 421)

excitement phase (p. 439)

facial-feedback hypothesis (p. 447)

homeostasis (p. 423)

incentive motivation (p. 424)

instincts (p. 422)

intrinsic motivation (p. 426)

James–Lange theory (p. 452)

motivation (p. 420)

need hierarchy (p. 427)

obesity (p. 435)

orgasmic phase (p. 440)

plateau phase (p. 439)

resolution phase (p. 440)

satiation signals (p. 430)

set point (p. 434)

sexual orientation (p. 444)

sexual scripts (p. 443)

two-factor theory (p. 454)

iStockPhoto/Oinegue

13 SOCIAL PSYCHOLOGY

LEARNING OBJECTIVES

13.1 Explain how attitudes are formed, the functions they serve, and the factors that affect our attitudes toward others.

13.2 Describe how and why behavior changes in social settings and the effects of culture on these changes.

13.3 Define the types of relationships we have with other people and the factors that affect those relationships.

13.4 For each of the major sections of the chapter, summarize how interactions with other people affect our behavior.

CHAPTER OUTLINE

Interpreting the Behavior of Others: Social Cognition

> **Practical Solutions: Combating Prejudice and Discrimination**

Behaving in the Presence of Others: Social Cognition

Establishing Relations With Others

The Problems Solved: What Social Processes Are For

You've just arrived at a party at your friend's house. You walk in the door and see your friends standing near the table of food. You join the group and start talking with them about your school's basketball team and its chances for the upcoming season. While you're talking with your friends, you notice someone looking at you from the other side of the room. As the conversation continues, their gaze falls on you repeatedly. You start to wonder why they are looking at you: Is it someone you know and can't remember meeting? Is it someone who is attracted to you? Do you have toothpaste crusted on your face?

As you consider the motives of the person staring at you, your friends notice that you aren't paying attention. "Are we boring you?" they ask. "No," you say. "That person in the blue shirt over there is looking at me, and I don't know why." Everyone in your group turns to look at the person in the blue shirt. Their face flushes, and they turn away. One of your friends says, "Hey, I know them. They were at that party you had 2 weeks ago." "Oh, yeah," you say. "I remember now. I talked to them about our hometown. We grew up in the same town." With the mystery solved, you walk over and say "Hi" to the person in the blue shirt. But as you converse with them, they keep looking over at your group of friends. Eventually, they ask you, "Do you really hang out with those guys? They look like they want to get into it with me for talking to you." As you look back at your group of friends, you wonder what it is about them and their behavior that is leading to his opinion. What does this person see that is being interpreted as hostile? Is it how your friends are dressed? Is it the way they are talking? Suddenly, your new friend doesn't seem like a friend at all.

THE PROBLEMS TO BE SOLVED: WHAT ARE SOCIAL PROCESSES FOR?

Social psychology is the discipline that studies how we think about, influence, and relate to other people. As you'll see shortly, how we think and act changes in characteristic ways when we're in the presence of others. In fact, the mere presence of other people, as well as their behavior, can be among the most powerful and pervasive of environmental influences. The scenario described here shows how we interpret the behavior of others and how others' behavior affects our behavior. It also shows our desire to interact with others to form relationships. We'll tackle the topics of social psychology by focusing on these three specific social problems that play a vital role in helping us adjust and adapt successfully to our world.

Interpreting the Behavior of Others: Social Cognition

As social animals, living in a social world, we're constantly trying to interpret the behavior of other people. We form impressions of our friends, our teachers, and our colleagues at school and in the work-place—we even form impressions of the people we meet on the street. We develop theories about why people behave the way they do; we form attitudes that help us act adaptively in the presence of particular individuals or groups. At the same time, as you'll see, there are systematic biases in the interpretation process as well.

Behaving in the Presence of Others: Social Influence

Everyone's behavior is strongly influenced by the social context. For example, sometimes your ability to perform a task will improve when others are present; sometimes your performance will fall apart. Your behavior will also be strongly influenced by the presence of authority figures and by the opinions of fellow members in a group. What are the factors that determine when you'll yield to the demands of others, and what implications do these factors have for the structure of society?

Establishing Relations With Others

It's certainly adaptive to interpret the behavior of others and to change behavior accordingly in their presence. But among our most important social actions are the relationships we form with others. Without attraction and romantic love, it's unlikely that the human species would survive; but it's not just mating we need—we rely on the relationships within the family as well as the social structures within society to help protect and nurture us and our offspring.

INTERPRETING THE BEHAVIOR OF OTHERS: SOCIAL COGNITION

We begin our treatment of social psychology with a discussion of how people *think about* other people—how impressions of others are formed, how causes are attributed to behavior, and the mechanisms that underlie the formation of attitudes about people and things. Social psychologists typically group these topics together under the title of **social cognition**, which is the study of how we use cognitive processes—such as perception, memory, and thought—to help make sense of other people as well as ourselves. First up is the topic of person perception, which deals specifically with how we form impressions of others.

Person Perception: How Do We Form Impressions of Others?

When we first discussed the topic of perception in Chapter 5, we focused on the processes used to interpret elementary sensations into meaningful wholes. In that chapter, you learned that perception is driven by a combination of *bottom-up processing*—the actual physical sensations received by the sensory equipment—and *top-down processing*, which relies on our expectations and beliefs about the world to interpret what we are experiencing. We do not simply see what's "out there" in the physical world; our perceptions are also influenced by our *expectations* of what we'll find.

A similar kind of analysis applies to the perception of people. When you meet a person for the first time, your initial impressions are influenced by physical factors—attractiveness, facial expression, skin color, clothing—and by your meaningful interpretations of those physical features. If you see a sloppily dressed, unshaven man weaving down the street, you're likely to form a negative first impression, partly because past experiences have taught you to avoid people who fit this description. You could be wrong, of course, but in the face of limited information, it's usually adaptive to use background knowledge to help predict the consequences of an interaction. There are many factors that affect our attitudes toward other people, but our first impression is a powerful one. An **attitude** is simply a positive or negative evaluation that, in turn, predisposes us to act in certain ways.

Physical Appearance

One of the most powerful determinants of a first impression is a person's *physical appearance*. In fact, evidence suggests that we can form an initial impression, such as how trustworthy a person might be, after looking at a face for as little as 50 milliseconds (Todorov et al., 2009). Studies have shown that when we first look at people who are physically attractive, we assume that they are more intelligent and honest, better adjusted, and more socially aware than people with average looks (Eagly et al., 1991; Gutiérrez-García et al., 2019). In general, physically attractive people are also thought to be healthier (Kalick et al., 1998), more inclined to succeed academically (Chia et al., 1998), and less likely to get "carded" if they try to buy alcohol (M. McCall, 1997). These tendencies don't diminish as we age—the elderly also show a strong tendency to attribute positive personality characteristics to attractive people (Larose & Standing, 1998).

How might the biases held by the teacher affect the way they handle this situation?

iStockPhoto/SolStock

Why do we rely on physical appearance to form a first impression? It seems like a rather shallow way to judge a person. The reason is simple: When you form a *first* impression, you use the information that's available. You almost always notice the way a person looks, along with one's facial expression, and perhaps even the way the person is walking or sitting. These raw materials are combined with your background knowledge to generate an expectation of what an encounter with that person might be like (Hehman et al., 2019).

Judging a book by its cover isn't always an effective long-term strategy for impression formation. Not all people rely on physical appearance to the same extent (Livingston, 2001), and cultural background is important too—some cultures don't rely on attractiveness as much as others (L. Wheeler & Kim, 1997). Further, our impressions of others, particularly first impressions, can be biased. As an example, when teachers in training who were mostly white (70%) and female (89%) were asked to judge the emotional expressions of Black and white children from novel photographs, the teachers judged the expressions of Black children to be angry more often than the expressions of white children, and the expressions of boys to be angry more often than those of girls (Halberstadt et al., 2020). These results were found along with unconscious (*implicit*) preferences for white faces in a cognitive task by the participants. Consider how these biases might play out in the classroom in a teacher's first impression of a negative interaction between two students. Which children are more likely to be punished based on these impressions?

However, first impressions can be helpful in the short term if they are unbiased and accurate. They can help you form a quick assessment of a dangerous situation. If you are walking down the middle of a street and a Chihuahua is barking at you on one side and a pit bull is barking at you on the other side, which side will you choose to walk on? And how does your attitude about these dog breeds affect your decision of which side of the street to walk on?

Social Schemas

Much of the knowledge we use in social situations comes from social categories or schemas (Bodenhausen et al., 2003). Schemas are general knowledge structures stored in memory, such as your knowledge about how houses are constructed or about what it's like to go to a restaurant or the doctor's office (see Chapter 8). We use schemas to help us remember but also to help organize and interpret ongoing experience. A schema can be formed about most anything—a person, a place, or a thing. When schemas are about social experiences or people, they're commonly called **social schemas** (Fiske, 1993).

How other people look is likely to activate social schemas that direct and guide your behavior. Social schemas are generally adaptive, but under some circumstances they can lead to inappropriate conclusions or actions.

iStockPhoto/Paolo Paradiso

Suppose you encounter that unshaven, sloppily dressed man on the street. Your initial impression is likely to be negative because his tattered appearance activates a common social schema about people. An unkempt appearance is associated with negative social characteristics—such as laziness or even criminal behavior—and his weaving gait signals possible drunkenness. All these things encourage you to categorize the man as "trouble" and make it less likely that you'll either ask him for help or give help to him if he requests it. Both the man's physical appearance and his behavior feed into your existing social schema about seedy characters; once he's been categorized, the schema directs you to alter your behavior accordingly.

Stereotypes

When social schemas revolve around the traits and behaviors of *groups* and their members, they're called **stereotypes**. We form stereotypes about many kinds of social groups, from insurance agents to college professors, but the three most common are based on gender, race, and age (Fiske, 1993). Most people carry around a collection of impressions about men and women. For example, men are typically seen as strong, dominant, and aggressive; women are typically seen as sensitive, warm, and dependent (Deaux & Lewis, 1984). These impressions, even if misleading, can have far-reaching consequences for how individuals are treated and the opportunities they will be offered (Ellemers, 2018).

Stereotypes seem to share many of the properties of categories. Not surprisingly, some of the more popular theories of how stereotypes are formed resemble the theories of categorization discussed in Chapter 9. For example, *prototype theories* of stereotypes assume we store abstract representations of the typical features of a group; we then judge individuals based on their similarity to the prototype (Cantor & Mischel, 1978). *Exemplar theories* assume we store memories of particular individuals, or exemplars, and these individual memories form the basis for stereotypes (E. R. Smith & Zárate, 1992). Studies examining the neuropsychology of stereotypes support this connection, showing that areas of the brain responsible for semantic knowledge are involved in tasks that include stereotypes (Amodio, 2014). Recall from Chapter 9 that knowledge about concepts is influenced by our experiences. Stereotypes about people also develop based on what we see in the behaviors of our parents and peers and the kinds of people we interact with in our environments. The less experience we have with different types of people, the more we tend to rely on our stereotypes of the groups we think they belong to.

Stereotypes become "activated" whenever we're exposed to stereotypic beliefs and actions. For example, heterosexual men are more likely to behave sexually toward a woman if they've recently seen an ad in which women are presented as sexual objects (Rudman & Borgida, 1995). Witnessing a Black man engaging in a negative stereotypic behavior influences how a white man evaluates other Black men (Henderson-King & Nisbett, 1996). Recent exposure to behavior consistent with a stereotype activates, or "primes," the stereotype, which in turn affects future behavior (T. L. Stewart et al., 1998). At the same time, the effects depend importantly on the situation. For example, you are more susceptible to the negative effects of an activated stereotype if you're angry, and less susceptible if you're being praised (E. R. Smith & Semin, 2007).

However, it's worth noting that concerns have recently been raised about the replicability of these kinds of social or stereotypic priming results. Recall that in Chapter 2, issues with replicating results in psychological science were discussed—many of the nonreplicated results have come from this area of research. For example, early research showed that when people were exposed to or "primed" with stereotypic information about what life is like as a "professor," they subsequently performed better on an unrelated trivia test compared to people who were primed with characteristics involving a less desirable "soccer hooligan" (Dijksterhuis & Van Knippenberg, 1998). The idea was that priming intelligence would increase later intelligent behavior. However, in a very large preregistered replication report, involving more than 4,000 participants, no social priming effects of this type were found (O'Donnell et al., 2018). Hence, it is unclear at this point how easily stereotypes can be primed and how strong the effects of this priming will turn out to be. But as more researchers conduct replications of findings in this area, the strength of these effects will become clearer.

Self-Fulfilling Prophecies

Despite the controversies surrounding specific social priming effects, everyone agrees that stereotypes importantly influence our expectations and actions. Once stereotypes are engaged, we expect certain kinds of behavior from members of groups. These expectations can produce what is called the **self-fulfilling prophecy effect**, which occurs when your expectations about a person's actions cause that person to behave in the expected way (Merton, 1948). If you expect someone to be unreliable and you act in line with your expectations (such as snubbing or avoiding the person), the chances that the person will assume that role in the future increase.

Let's consider an experiment demonstrating the effect. In a study by Mark Snyder and colleagues (1977), undergraduate men were asked to talk to undergraduate women, whom they had never met, on the telephone. Prior to the conversation, the men were shown a photograph of their prospective telephone partner. The partner appeared as either physically attractive or physically unattractive. In reality, the photos were of women from another college; they were not really photos of the women participating in the study. The intention of the experimenters was simply to lead the men to *believe* they were talking to a woman who was attractive or unattractive. As for the women, they were not given a photo of their partner, nor were they told that the man had been biased to think of them in a particular way. All of the telephone calls were taped, and social aspects of the men's and women's conversational styles were then rated by judges who were unaware of the men's assignment group.

Not surprisingly, if the men thought they were talking to an attractive woman, their conversational styles were friendly and positive—more so than if their partner had been presented as unattractive. But the important finding of the study focused on the women. It turned out that the women's conversational styles also differed, depending on whether the man they were talking to thought they were attractive. The women who were presumed by their partners to be attractive were rated by the judges as more friendly, more open and poised, and generally more pleasant than the women shown as unattractive. Remember, these women had no idea their male partners had preformed opinions about their attractiveness. Apparently, the friendly, positive conversational styles of the men elicited similar qualities from the women. This is the self-fulfilling prophecy effect—the expectations that we have toward others, along with our actions, can influence them to act in the expected way (see Figure 13.1).

Self-fulfilling prophecies can have either positive or negative effects on people. As you've just seen, if someone expects you to be unattractive, or of lower intellect, those expectations can bring out the worst in you. One study found that parents' beliefs about whether their adolescent child would engage in illegal drinking predicted the child's subsequent drinking behavior—if both parents expected their child to drink illegally, there was a greater chance their child would, in fact, drink illegally. But if a parent thought illegal drinking was unlikely, then this, too, predicted subsequent drinking behavior (Madon et al., 2004). A self-fulfilling prophecy for teachers' judgments of students and students'

FIGURE 13.1   ■   The Self-Fulfilling Prophecy Effect

Our impressions of other people can affect how they behave, leading them to act in the expected ways. In the study by Mark Snyder and colleagues (1977), if a male subject thought he was talking to an attractive female on the phone, his conversational style was rated as more friendly and positive—but so too was the conversational style of the woman on the other end.

Illustrated by Sarah Yeh

academic achievement and motivation has also been supported by many studies (Zhu et al., 2018). The fact that expectations can importantly shape behavior has many implications for society, especially when it comes to the expectations generated about groups.

Prejudice

Stereotypes can lead to rigid interpretations of people. This is an important topic in current times because our attitudes and impressions of people can affect our behaviors toward them in negative ways. Stereotypes can cause us to overgeneralize and place too much emphasis on the differences that exist *between* groups (for instance, between men and women or between people of different races) and too little emphasis on the differences that exist *within* groups. Not all women are dependent, nor are all men strong. Furthermore, when the beliefs we hold about a group are negative or extreme, stereotypes increase the likelihood of prejudice and discrimination. **Prejudice** occurs when groups and their members are evaluated in a negative way (although you can also prejudge members of a group in a positive way). **Discrimination** occurs when those beliefs lead to behaviors that are directed against members of the group. For example, you might be excluded from a job, or even criminally assaulted, just because of negative beliefs activated by your skin color or sexual preference (see Figure 13.2).

Stereotypic beliefs, including those that lead to prejudice, may be automatically activated and not always under our conscious control (Bargh & Williams, 2006). For example, we discussed how simply witnessing a behavior can be enough to activate prejudicial evaluations. Apparently, we don't even need to be consciously aware of the exposure. In a study by Greenwald and Banaji (1995), words that were consistent with a negative stereotype about Black individuals were flashed on a computer screen at speeds too fast to be noticed. The people who were working at the computers were then more likely to evaluate a fictional character as having traits consistent with a negative Black stereotype (e.g., aggressive). This suggests that stereotypes can be activated and influence behavior in ways that are not consciously controlled (Devine & Sharp, 2009). That is one reason to consider how negative stereotypes develop in the first place, and target their development as well as the behaviors that result from them.

It is also important to distinguish between *explicit* and *implicit* prejudice. Explicit prejudice refers to negative attitudes about a group that are consciously endorsed. For example, if asked, a person might willingly admit prejudicial feelings about certain racial groups. Implicit prejudice refers to prejudicial thoughts that come to mind unintentionally and may not be consciously recognized or controllable (Gawronski & Bodenhausen, 2006). For example, people might claim (and even consciously believe) that they have no negative feelings about Black individuals, but move to the other side of the street when a Black man approaches. There is a disconnect between what they consciously believe and their underlying implicit (or covert) beliefs.

FIGURE 13.2 ■ Prejudice Versus Discrimination

Prejudice is when someone judges someone else based on their being part of a specific group (such as the thoughts the person on the left might be having). *Discrimination* occurs when someone behaves toward someone else based on their being part of a specific group (such as the two people on the right excluding the third person).

Illustrated by Sarah Yeh

As measured by implicit tests, prejudice seems to be widespread (Greenwald et al., 2009). For example, presenting a photograph of a Black or white face can affect how pleasantly or unpleasantly people judge a Chinese ideograph to be moments later—even if the face is only presented for a very short duration (e.g., less than a tenth of a second). If briefly presenting a Black face leads someone to rate the ideograph as more unpleasant, compared to when a white face is presented, that indicates the presence of some implicit prejudice. Again, a person can self-report no explicit prejudice but show significant implicit prejudice on such a test. In one study that controlled for explicit racial prejudice self-reports, it was found that people who showed implicit racial prejudice were less likely to vote for Barack Obama in the 2008 U.S. presidential election (B. K. Payne et al., 2010). However, some researchers question whether implicit prejudice, as revealed through implicit tests, is automatically linked to explicit prejudice (e.g., Blanton et al., 2009). Thus, finding evidence of implicit prejudice does not necessarily mean that someone is likely to behave in a discriminatory way toward others.

The good news is that we can reduce the prejudicial feelings that come from stereotypes (either explicit or implicit prejudice) through repeated exposure to individuals in the stereotyped group.

President Barack Obama

Souza, Pete, photographer Official portrait of President-elect Barack Obama [graphic] / Pete Souza. 2009 January 13.

For instance, a study has shown that as the amount of social contact between heterosexual and homosexual people increases, negative feelings decrease (Whitely, 1990). However, there are several crucial elements at work in the maintenance of stereotypic beliefs. Whether beliefs will change depends on the nature of the social interactions and how representative the contacted individuals are of their stereotyped group. Moreover, the contact must be widespread and repeated; otherwise, people will attempt to defend their stereotypic views by explaining away individual contacts as unrepresentative of the group (Weber & Crocker, 1993).

Being aware of stereotypes can also help. Once you recognize that stereotypical reactions are common, and maybe even automatic, you can take steps to reduce their influence. Research shows, for example, that diversity training in workplace settings is related to more positive attitudes about others following the training (Kalinoski et al., 2013). One course of action is to adjust your behavior in a way that opposes the presumed influence of the stereotype. For example, if you're a man interviewing a woman for a job, steer away from questions that relate to typical gender stereotypes. In fact, thinking in terms of binary gender categories ignores the gender identification of many individuals. It may even be possible to actively suppress stereotypic thoughts under some circumstances— that is, to prevent stereotypic thoughts from ever entering conscious awareness (e.g., Wyer, 2007). For more information on reducing the negative influence of stereotypic beliefs, see the Practical Solutions feature.

Obviously, prejudging people based on stereotypes can lead to many kinds of discrimination, including racism, sexism, and ageism. Stereotypes are not necessarily accurate representations of people, nor can they be expected to apply to all individuals within a group. Still, as general rules of thumb, researchers assume that stereotypes do have adaptive value. They help people carve their social worlds into meaningful chunks, thereby providing a sense of direction about how to act when encountering new people. Furthermore, not all components of stereotypes are inaccurate, nor are all instances of prejudice negative. Stereotyping occurs in every culture of the world, and it's simply another way in which our minds organize and categorize the world. Concept Review 13.1 summarizes the different factors that affect our perceptions of others.

CONCEPT REVIEW 13.1
FACTORS IN PERSON PERCEPTION

Factor	Role in Person Perception	Example
Physical appearance	We tend to assume that physically attractive individuals are more intelligent, well adjusted, and socially aware.	Tyrone encounters Michelle at a party. He finds her quite attractive. In addition, he perceives her as very personable, good-humored, and intelligent.
Social schemas	We use schemas (e.g., *stereotypes*) to organize and interpret ongoing experiences.	Tyrone believes most women are sensitive, warm, and dependent. He finds that Michelle's behavior fits this pattern.
Self-fulfilling prophecies	The activation of stereotypes leads to expectations of certain types of behavior. These expectations can cause a person to behave in the expected way.	Tyrone is very attentive toward Michelle at the party, bringing her refreshments and introducing her to all of his friends. Michelle relaxes; she begins to open up and make witty comments.

PRACTICAL SOLUTIONS: COMBATING PREJUDICE AND DISCRIMINATION

It's generally adaptive for us to form stereotypes if they are accurate and unbiased—they help us categorize our social world and make quick and efficient decisions about how to act. But when stereotypes lead to prejudice or discrimination, it's obviously in our interest to reduce their influence. There are several ways to combat stereotyping and prejudice (Paluck & Green, 2009). As our awareness of a group increases, we're less prone to negative beliefs and actions. It's also possible to actively suppress stereotypic beliefs. For example, if undergraduates are asked to write essays about well-defined groups, such as elderly, LGBTQ, or Black individuals, their essays will show less stereotypic content if they've been instructed to actively avoid thinking about group members in preconceived ways.

Ironically, when people are taught to suppress thoughts and beliefs, there is some evidence for rebound effects. When we are no longer attempting to suppress them, those very thoughts seem to become more accessible and influential (Ford et al., 2017; Wegner, 1994). For example, after suppression of a stereotype, people are more likely to recollect words consistent with the stereotype and can identify stereotypic words more quickly. Therefore, thought suppression may not be the best solution to reducing prejudice and discrimination.

A more promising alternative is to practice taking the perspective of others. Galinsky and Moskowitz (2000) asked undergraduates to write a narrative essay about a day in the life of an elderly man. One group was told to adopt the perspective of the man: "to imagine a day in the life of this individual as if you were this individual, looking at the world through his eyes and walking through the world in his shoes" (p. 711). Compared to control conditions, those who adopted the man's perspective produced fewer stereotypic words in their essays and, in fact, tended to write about the subject in a more positive way. Moreover, there were no rebound effects. Similar results were found when white students were asked to take the perspective of a Black individual. Among other things, perspective taking increased the participants' awareness of the continued discrimination that is directed against Black individuals (see also Todd et al., 2012).

Thinking about an out-group individual's "true self" in terms of morals and values has also been found to increase both positive attitudes and positive behaviors toward that individual (De Freitas & Cikara, 2018). When people were asked to determine if an individual's "true self" caused a change in that individual's behavior, they were more likely to judge in-group and out-group members similarly and more likely to donate money to an out-group charity. These results show that when people consider others' behavior in the context of their morals and values, it can increase their positive attitudes and helping behaviors toward others from a negatively stereotyped out-group.

Organizations often include diversity and inclusion training for their employees with the goal of helping people become more aware of the narrow perspectives that affect their attitudes toward others. Research suggests that such training can be helpful in some cases more than in others. For example, Egan Brad et al. (2019) found that for pre-millennials (adults over age 36 years at the time of the study) with liberal or moderate political attitudes, a white privilege salience exercise increased anti-racist attitudes, but in millennials (young adults aged 18–34 at the time of the study) with moderate or conservative political attitudes, this exercise resulted in resistance to anti-racist attitudes. Thus, the best strategies to combat prejudice may differ depending on the individual's age and political attitudes.

Negative stereotypes, which form the basis for prejudice and discrimination, exist and can be hard to avoid. And, unfortunately, evidence of these stereotypes is increasing in many parts of the world (Bieber, 2020). But, as our familiarity with group members increases, the likelihood of prejudice and discrimination decreases. One reason may be that familiarity enables us to better see the world through another's eyes.

Attribution Theory: Attributing Causes to Behavior

It's natural for us to interpret the behavior of others. A wife tries to understand why her husband keeps peeking at his cell phone during their anniversary dinner; a student tries to understand why the teacher responds to their appeal for a grade change with a curt "I didn't give you the grade; you earned the grade." When people assign causes to behaviors, psychologists refer to these inferences as **attributions**; attribution theories are concerned primarily with the processes that underlie these inferences of cause and effect (Heider, 1944; E. E. Jones & Davis, 1965).

Let's consider an example of the attribution process at work. Suppose you notice that the mood of your friend Ira improves noticeably on Monday, Wednesday, and Friday afternoons, after he returns from lunch. He smiles a lot, exchanges pleasantries, and offers advice freely. These behaviors contrast sharply with his normally gruff manner and generally sour disposition. What accounts for the behavior change? According to the *co-variation model of attribution* (Kelley, 1987), the first thing you'll look for is some factor that happens at the same time as, or *co-varies* with, the behavior change. You'll try to identify an event or some other factor that is present when the behavior changes and absent when the behavior change doesn't occur. In this example, it turns out Ira goes to his aerobic exercise class between 12 p.m. and 1 p.m. on those 3 days.

But co-variation by itself is not a sufficient condition for the attribution of causality, for much the same reason that we can't infer causality from a simple correlation (see Chapter 2). Just because Ira's mood improves after his exercise class doesn't mean exercise is the cause of the change—other factors may be involved. According to the co-variation model, we rely on three additional pieces of information to help us make the appropriate inference: *consistency, distinctiveness*, and *consensus*. When assessing *consistency*, we try to determine whether the change occurs regularly when the causal event is present—does Ira's mood consistently improve after exercise class? *Distinctiveness* provides an indication of whether the change occurs uniquely in the presence of the event—does Ira's mood improve after lunch only if he's been exercising? Finally, we look for *consensus*, which tells us whether other people show similar reactions when they're exposed to the same causal event—is elevation of mood a common reaction to exercising?

Internal Versus External Attributions

These three factors—consistency, distinctiveness, and consensus—work together to help us form an attribution. In the example we've been considering, we'll probably assume it's the *external* event—the exercise class—that's the cause of Ira's mood change. People tend to make an **external attribution**, one that appeals to external causes, when the behavior is high in consistency, distinctiveness, and consensus. In the case of Ira's pleasant mood, it's highly consistent (it happens every Monday, Wednesday, and Friday afternoon); its occurrence is distinctive (it occurs only after exercise class); and there is a high level of consensus (exercise tends to make people happy).

But what if no single event can be used to explain someone's behavior? Suppose Ira consistently smiles and acts pleasant in the afternoon, but he also smiles during the mornings and on days he's skipped the exercise class. Under these conditions, it's doubtful you'll appeal to the environment to explain his behavior; instead, you'll make an **internal attribution**, which means you'll attribute his pleasant behavior to some internal personality trait or disposition: "Ira just has a great personality; he's a friendly, pleasant guy." Internal attributions are common when the consistency of a behavior is high but its distinctiveness and consensus are low. If Ira is pleasant all the time, his behavior after lunch lacks distinctiveness, and you'll be unlikely to appeal to some lunch activity to explain his behavior. Similarly, if the consensus is low—suppose exercise rarely improves mood for most people—you'll again resist attributing his pleasantries to this event (see Figure 13.3).

The Fundamental Attribution Error

The attribution process seems logical enough, but we sometimes take shortcuts. We often need to make judgments quickly, and it's effortful and time consuming to consider all possible factors logically. So we cut corners in the attribution process. What happens, however, is that these shortcuts tend to produce consistent biases and errors in the judgment process. One of the most common of these biases is the **fundamental attribution error** (sometimes also known as the *correspondence bias*): When we interpret another person's behavior, we tend to overestimate the influence of internal personal factors and underestimate the role of external situational factors (L. Ross, 1977, 2018).

FIGURE 13.3 ■ The Covariation Model of Attribution

When we make internal attributions, we attribute behavior to internal personality characteristics; external attributions assume behavior reflects factors in the environment. In Kelley's attribution model, whether an internal or external attribution will be made about a particular behavior depends on consistency, distinctiveness, and consensus.

In a classic demonstration of this bias, researchers E. E. Jones and Harris (1967) had college students read essays expressing either positive or negative opinions about Fidel Castro's Communist regime in Cuba (at the time Castro's Cuba was a hot topic of discussion). Before reading the essays, one group of students was told that the person writing the essay had been allowed to write freely and choose the position adopted in the text. A second group was told the writer had no choice and had been forced to adopt a particular pro or con position. Afterward, the students in both groups were asked to speculate about the writer's true opinion on the topic. Thinking logically, you might assume that if the writer had been given a choice, then the essay position probably reflected the writer's true opinion on Castro. Alternatively, if the writer had been simply following directions, it would be difficult to tell. To the surprise of the experimenters, however, the students tended to believe the essay *always* reflected the writer's true opinion, even when the students knew that the essay writer had been forced to adopt a specific position. This is the fundamental attribution error at work: People tend to attribute an individual's activities to internal personal factors, even when there are strong situational explanations for the behavior (E. E. Jones, 1990).

Consider another example: You're driving down the street, at a respectable speed, when you glance in your rearview mirror and see a truck bearing down on your bumper. You speed up a bit, only to find the truck mirroring your every move. Being tailgated like this is a relatively common experience. But what kind of attribution do you typically make about the driver? Do you attribute the behavior to the person or to the situation? If you're like most people, your first response is likely to be an internal attribution—you naturally assume that the driver behind you has some severe personality flaw; put simply, the driver is a jerk. You ignore the possibility that situational factors might be compelling the driver to drive fast. Isn't it possible, for instance, that the driver is late for work or has a sick child in the back seat who is in need of a doctor? These kinds of attributions, which focus on the situation, don't usually enter our minds because our first tendency is to attribute behavior to an internal personality characteristic.

The Actor–Observer Effect

Now let's switch gears. Think about what happens when you make attributions about your own behavior. Suppose you're the one doing the tailgating. Under these conditions, will you blame your tailgating on the fact that you're a jerk? Probably not. Instead, you're likely to explain your behavior by appealing to the situation. You're tailgating, you explain, because you're late for an appointment, or because the driver in front of you is simply driving too slowly. Generally, each of us shows what's called an **actor–observer effect**—we tend to attribute our own behavior to external sources but attribute the behavior of others to internal sources.

How we interpret risky behavior on the road depends on who is doing the driving.

iStockPhoto/SDI Productions

One exception to this general rule is the **self-serving bias**, which means we take internal credit for our actions when those actions produce positive outcomes—such as attributing a solid A on the psychology test to hard work and intelligence. But we'll blame the situation when our behaviors are questionable or lead to failure. The self-serving bias is adaptive because it bolsters our self-esteem and enables us to project a sense of self-importance and confidence to the world (C. R. Snyder, 1989).

These attributional biases have important implications—not just for you but for society as well. The tailgating example is relatively harmless (unless this behavior causes an accident), but consider when the focus is on social problems such as welfare or homelessness. Because of attribution biases, you might naturally attribute, for example, being on welfare or losing a job to laziness, incompetence, or some other negative internal trait. But in many cases an individual is on welfare or out of work because of situational factors, perhaps because of some catastrophic life event. Attribution biases may have considerable adaptive value—because they allow us to make quick decisions about the causes of behavior—and may even be the products of adaptations rooted in our evolutionary past (Andrews, 2001; von Hippel & Trivers, 2011). But they do have a downside; they can lead to misleading or even incorrect conclusions.

People often think that game show hosts, such as Ellen DeGeneres, are extremely knowledgeable. What attribution processes might underlie such an inference?

Andrew Chin/Getty Images

Attribution biases are reduced in some situations. For example, you're less likely to show the self-serving bias if you're working on a task with someone you know very well. If you're in a close relationship with your task partner, you're less likely to take credit for success on the task and assign blame for failure; if you don't know this person very well, your partner gets the blame for failure, and you take credit for success (Sedikides et al., 1998). Your mood also seems to matter. For example, evidence indicates that you're more likely to show the fundamental attribution error if you're in a positive mood; if you're in a negative mood, you're more willing to blame the situation, rather than the person, for the behavior (Forgas, 1998).

There appear to be cultural differences in these attributional biases as well. For example, people in East Asian cultures (e.g., Korean, Chinese) are less susceptible to the fundamental attribution error than people in Western cultures (de Oliveira & Nisbett, 2017). People in East Asian cultures, as noted previously, are more likely to focus on situational factors than people raised in the West. When asked to make a causal judgment about someone's behavior, the natural tendency of many Asians is to make a situation-based, external attribution. Although all cultures show the fundamental attribution error under some circumstances, the effect is easier to find among Westerners (Masuda & Kitayama, 2004) and may be related to differences in brain functioning shaped by one's culture (M. F. Mason & Morris, 2010).

Attitudes and Attitude Change

We end our discussion of social cognition by considering attitudes and attitude change in more detail. As noted earlier, an attitude is simply a positive or negative evaluation that, in turn, predisposes us to act in certain ways. Like the other forms of social cognition we've discussed, attitudes are beneficial for several reasons. When they guide behavior, attitudes help us remain consistent in our actions and help us use our knowledge about individuals or situations. Attitudes also play an important role in our perception and interpretation of the world. They help us focus our attention on information relevant to our beliefs—particularly information that can help confirm an existing belief. As a result, attitudes may serve a kind of defensive function, protecting people's basic beliefs about themselves and others (Fazio, 1986).

The Components of an Attitude

Traditionally, social psychologists divide attitudes into three main components: a cognitive component, an affective component, and a behavioral component (Olson & Maio, 2003). The *cognitive component* represents what people know or believe about the object of their attitude; the *affective component* is made up of the feelings that the object produces; and the *behavioral component* is a predisposition to act toward the object in a particular way.

FIGURE 13.4 ■ The Three Components of Attitudes

Social psychologists typically divide attitudes into cognitive, affective, and behavioral components.

Attitude
Cognitive Knowledge about the object
Affective Emotional feelings
Behavioral Predisposition to act

To see how these three components work together, let's suppose you've formed an unfavorable attitude toward your landlord. Your attitude rests on a foundation of facts and beliefs about behavior. You know, for instance, that the landlord has raised your rent three times in the last year, that he enters your apartment without first asking permission, and that he won't let you keep your cat Kepler in the apartment without a huge pet deposit. These facts and beliefs form the cognitive component of your attitude. Accompanying these facts are your emotional reactions, which make up the affective component—when you see or think about your landlord, you get angry and slightly sick to your stomach. Finally, the behavioral component of your attitude predisposes you to act in certain ways. You may spend every Sunday reading the classified ads looking for a new apartment, and you may constantly complain about your landlord to anyone who'll listen. It's these three factors in combination—cognitive, affective, and behavioral—that compose what psychologists mean by an attitude (see Figure 13.4).

Notice the behavioral component of the attitude is described as a *predisposition* to act. This is an important point to remember because attitudes don't always directly affect behavior. As you know, people sometimes act in ways that are inconsistent with their attitudes (Ajzen, 2001; Ajzen & Fishbein, 1977). When directly confronting your landlord, you may be all smiles even though underneath you're steaming. Attitudes do not always connect with behavior because behavior is usually determined by multiple factors—especially external factors. In some situations, it's simply unwise to express your true feelings, such as when dealing with the landlord. In other situations, people act quickly and mindlessly without considering the true meaning or ramifications of their behavior (Langer, 1989). For example, people often sign petitions for activities they may not completely believe in or buy products that they don't really want, simply because they're in a hurry and don't want to be bothered further.

How Are Attitudes Formed?

Where do attitudes come from? There are many routes to attitude formation. We use our everyday experiences as the basis for many of our ideas and beliefs. How we interpret those experiences also depends partly on our inborn intellectual and personality traits (Tesser, 1993). Even something as simple as *mere exposure* can be sufficient to change your feelings about an object (Greenwald & Banaji, 1995). In classic work by Robert Zajonc (1968), people were shown photographs of undergraduate men taken from a school yearbook. Some of the photos were shown only once or twice; others were shown up to 25 times. Following exposure, everyone was asked to give an estimate of how much they liked each of the men shown. The results revealed that the more often a photo had been presented, the more the participants claimed to "like" the person shown. It's not clear exactly how to interpret this finding, in part because people's ratings change on a whole host of dimensions following exposure (Mandler et al., 1987). But it demonstrates how easily attitudes can be affected (Zajonc, 2001).

How closely do your attitudes mirror the positions and beliefs of your peer group?

iStockPhoto/NickyLloyd

Experience is generally agreed to be the single most important factor affecting attitude formation. For instance, attitudes can be conditioned through experiences of the type discussed in Chapter 7. Events that occur outside of our control can acquire signaling properties, through *classical conditioning*, and then serve as an initial foundation for an attitude (Petty et al., 2001). Advertisers commonly try to manipulate how we feel toward consumer products by pairing the product with something pleasurable, such as an attractive model or a successful athlete. Through *operant conditioning*, attitudes are influenced by the rewards and punishments we receive for our actions. Certainly if you express a tentative opinion on a subject—"We've got too much big government in this country"—and this opinion is reinforced by people whom you respect, you're likely to express this same attitude again. Operant conditioning teaches us about the consequences of our behavior, and direct experience of this sort plays a significant role in attitude formation. Support for this idea also comes from studies showing that reward areas of the brain are active when we are considering our values while communicating with others (Falk & Scholz, 2018).

Finally, much of what we acquire from experience is the result of *observational learning*. We model significant others—our parents, peers, teachers, and so on—when it comes to both attitudes and behavior. The political convictions of most people, for example, mirror quite closely the political attitudes of their parents (McGuire, 1985). People use their peers, too, as a kind of reference group for judging the acceptability of their behaviors and beliefs. All you need to do is take a random sample of the behavior of teenagers in a local high school to see how important modeling behavior can be. Everything from language to musical taste to hairstyle to shoe type is replicated from one teen to the next.

Central and Peripheral Routes to Persuasion

For decades, social psychologists have been interested not only in how attitudes are formed but also in how attitudes can be changed (Bohner & Dickel, 2011). We're bombarded daily by persuasive messages from sources in business, politics, religion, and the arts. For obvious reasons, psychologists have tried to determine the important ingredients of persuasion: What are the factors that determine whether you'll be convinced to buy a particular product or support a particular political campaign? According to one popular theory of attitude change, known as the **elaboration likelihood model**, there are two primary routes to persuasion, one that is central and one that is peripheral (Petty & Cacioppo, 1986; Wegener & Carlston, 2005).

The *central route* to persuasion is the most obvious and familiar one. It operates when we're motivated and inclined to process an incoming persuasive communication with effort, care, and attention; we'll listen carefully to the arguments of the message, then judge those arguments according to their merits. Suppose you recently changed your views on the topic of abortion after listening to a persuasive speaker at your school. If you carefully weighed the quality and strength of the arguments and then changed your attitude accordingly, you were convinced via the central route. Not surprisingly, attitude changes that result from this kind of central processing tend to be stable and long lasting (Olson & Zanna, 1993).

The *peripheral route* to persuasion operates when we're either unable to process the message carefully or unmotivated to do so. When we process a message peripherally, our attitudes are much more susceptible to change from superficial cues or from mere exposure (Petty & Wegener, 1997). Think about the typical ad for beer. You don't see logical arguments about the quality of the product—you see talking frogs or partying dogs. The same is true for fast-food ads. There's no discussion of nutrition—again, it's talking animals, costumed characters, or anecdotes about families and minivans. When our motivation to process the message is low, we're much more likely to be persuaded by **source characteristics**—things such as celebrity, attractiveness, or power.

Advertisers typically capitalize on the peripheral route to persuasion because most of the time we don't process advertisements on social media or

Why do you suppose this company chose to use Ryan Reynolds in its ad?

Grzegorz Czapski / Alamy Stock Photo

websites with a high level of involvement. We're also more likely to rely on processing shortcuts (*heuristics*) to form opinions when we process a message peripherally (Chaiken et al., 1989). For instance, you might adopt a favorable attitude toward an expensive product because you believe that "better products are more expensive," or you might buy the products endorsed by your favorite celebrities because you think they wouldn't endorse something that isn't high in quality.

The Festinger and Carlsmith Study

We can also be persuaded to change our attitudes because of our own actions. In a highly influential study of attitude change conducted by Festinger and Carlsmith (1959), male college students were asked to perform some incredibly boring tasks, such as placing sewing spools onto a tray, during an hour-long session. At the end of the hour, some of the participants (the experimental group) were given a bogus cover story. They were told that one purpose of the study was to examine the effects of motivation on task performance. The next student, the researcher explained, needed to be told that the experiment was filled with interesting and enjoyable tasks. Would they mind going into the adjacent waiting room and telling this student that the experiment was interesting and enjoyable? To provide an incentive, the experimenter offered some of the participants a monetary reward of $1 and others a reward of $20.

The point of the offer was to get the members of the experimental group to act in a way that contradicted their true feelings, or attitudes, about the experiment. The task was clearly boring, so they were essentially asked to lie for either a small or a large reward. Festinger and Carlsmith were interested in what effect this behavior would have on people's attitudes about the experiment. After accepting the offer, and lying to convince the next participant, the students' attitudes about the experimental tasks were assessed through an interview. The researchers found that attitudes about the experimental tasks did indeed change—they became more positive relative to the attitudes of a control group, who had not been asked to lie. Moreover, the positive shift was larger for people receiving $1 than for those receiving $20. The more money people were paid to act inconsistently with their true feelings, the less likely their attitudes were to change (see Figure 13.5).

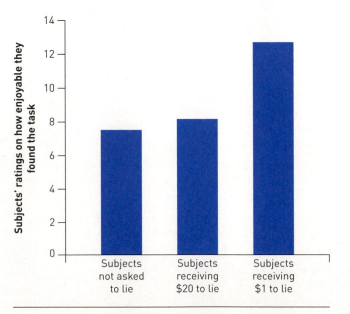

FIGURE 13.5 ■ Cognitive Dissonance

Festinger proposed that attitudes change when there is a discrepancy between what we believe and how we act. Presumably, it was tough to justify lying for a small amount of money, which created a lot of cognitive dissonance, so the subjects in the $1 condition simply changed their original attitude about the task

Source: Data from Festinger & Carlsmith, 1959.

Cognitive Dissonance

The results from the study may seem perplexing. You would probably have predicted that the students receiving $20 would show the greatest attitude change—after all, wouldn't a large reward have a greater reinforcing effect? The answer, according to Festinger's (1957) theory of **cognitive dissonance**, is that inconsistent behavior produces tension—or what he called *dissonance*. Think about it. Which action is going to lead to greater internal turmoil, lying to receive $1 or lying to receive $20? Most people can easily justify a simple white lie when offered a reasonable amount of money, especially when asked by an authority figure (remember that $20 was worth a lot more in the 1950s than it is now). But to lie for a measly $1 is tough to justify—unless, of course, you can justify the action by changing your initial attitude about the task. According to cognitive dissonance theory, if the discrepancy between what you believe and how you act is great, you will either (1) change your behavior or (2) change your beliefs.

Since cognitive dissonance theory was first introduced in the 1950s, hundreds of follow-up studies have been conducted (Aronson, 1992). Most have confirmed Festinger and Carlsmith's basic finding: When people are induced to act in ways that are inconsistent with their attitudes, their attitudes often change. But not all psychologists are convinced that internal tension, or dissonance, results from acting inconsistently with your beliefs. You might, for example, simply feel uncomfortable about your actions (Elliot & Devine, 1994), or you might feel personally responsible for creating an unwanted or negative situation (Blanton et al., 1997; J. Cooper, 1992). Recent work using neuroimaging techniques provides some support for the original concept of dissonance. As in the Festinger and Carlsmith study, people were asked to act inconsistent with their attitudes—but while being scanned in an MRI device! Specifically, they were asked to provide misleading ratings about their comfort level—for example, "I feel calm and peaceful in the scanner"—to put the next participant's mind at ease. Not surprisingly, "lying" about how they felt caused their subsequent attitudes about scanning to change relative to a control group. But the important finding was that their degree of attitude change was associated with brain regions that are thought to be activated when we hold conflicting thoughts—that is, when we are experiencing cognitive dissonance (van Veen et al., 2009). Consider how these findings might apply to your life. Have you ever "liked" something on social media that your friends asked you to endorse and then found that you actually liked that attitude or product more later on?

Self-Perception Theory

One of the best-known alternatives to dissonance theory is Daryl Bem's (1967, 1972) **self-perception theory**. This theory is based on the idea that we are active observers of our own behavior. We learn from our behavior and use our actions as a basis for inferring internal beliefs. For example, if I sit down and practice the piano for 2 hours a day, it must be the case that I like music and think I have at least a bit of musical talent. If I regularly stop for hamburgers and fries for lunch, it must be the case that I like fast food. The basis for the attitude is self-perception—behavior is observed, and attitudes follow from the behavior.

We may form attitudes, at least in part, by observing our own behavior. If I regularly eat cheeseburgers, then my attitude about cheeseburgers must be positive.

iStockPhoto/ugurv

Many experimental findings support these basic ideas. For example, the Festinger and Carlsmith study can be interpreted from this perspective. You observe yourself telling someone that a boring task is interesting, for a measly $1, and conclude that because you engaged in this behavior your attitude toward the task must not have been that negative. In another classic example, known as the *foot-in-the-door technique*, Jonathan Freedman and Scott Fraser (1966) convinced a group of California householders to sign a petition expressing support for safe driving. Several weeks later, the researchers returned with a request that the householders now place a large and quite ugly "Drive Safely" billboard in their yards. The petition signers were three times more likely to comply with this new request than a control group of people who were not asked to sign a petition. What's the interpretation? The signing of the original petition triggered *self-perception*, which then helped shape the attitude: If I signed the petition, then I must be a strong advocate for safe driving (see also Burger & Caldwell, 2003).

A related phenomenon is the *lowball technique*. You wander into the local electronics store to look around. You're not ready to buy, but the salesperson offers you a tremendous price on a piece of high-quality equipment. You agree to make the purchase, convinced you've received a great deal. The salesperson leaves to finish the paperwork with the manager of the store. He returns a few minutes later with some bad news: The offered price was a mistake—the manager rejected the deal—but he will be able to sell you the equipment at a price that is still lower than what most people pay. Reluctantly you agree to buy, even though you probably would have rejected this deal if it had been offered first. In this case, by getting you to agree verbally to the initial purchase, the salesperson has lowered your resistance to buying the product (Burger & Cornelius, 2003).

Of course, there are boundary conditions for these effects—we do not always match our attitudes to our behaviors—but monitoring behavior is clearly an important ingredient of attitude formation and change. It may be that we're particularly likely to use our own actions as a guide when we're unsure or undecided about our attitude. Or we may use our own behavior to see if our attitudes or opinions have recently changed: "Do I still like playing video games? Well, let's see. I haven't played a game for a while, so I must not be crazy about them anymore." It's adaptive for us to use multiple sources of information for establishing our beliefs, including our own actions. The ways that our attitudes are formed and changed are summarized in Concept Review 13.2.

CONCEPT REVIEW 13.2
ROOTS OF ATTITUDES AND ATTITUDE CHANGE

Mechanism	Description	Example ("Whom should I vote for?")
Central route	When motivated to process an incoming message, we listen carefully to the arguments given and judge them on their merits.	Jaraan is not sure which candidate to vote for in the governor's race. He obtains detailed information on their views on the major issues and, after considering each, decides on the Democratic candidate.
Peripheral route	When we are unable or unwilling to process a message carefully, our attitudes are affected more by superficial cues or mere exposure.	Yvette hasn't really kept up with the governor's race but has seen ads for both candidates. She laughs at the Republican candidate's humorous ad, so she decides to vote for him.
Cognitive dissonance	Behavior that is inconsistent with attitudes produces tension (i.e., *dissonance*). If the tension is large enough, attitudes or behavior will change.	Jeremy has always considered himself a Republican, and he backs his party's candidate for governor. Lately he's been dating a woman who is very involved in the Democratic candidate's campaign. Jeremy finds that his attitudes toward this candidate are becoming more and more favorable.

Mechanism	Description	Example ("Whom should I vote for?")
Self-perception	We learn from our behavior, using our actions as a basis for inferring beliefs: Attitudes follow behavior.	Teagan gets a phone call from the third-party campaign headquarters pleading for help. The third party can't compete with the other two campaigns unless it raises more money for its candidate. Teagan agrees to donate $20 to the cause. Looking back, she decides she must really favor the third-party candidate.

KNOWLEDGE CHECK 13.1

Now test your knowledge about how we form impressions of others by answering the following questions. (You will find the answers in the Appendix.)

1. Decide whether each of the following statements about person perception is true or false.
   a. On average, attractive people are assumed to be more intelligent, better adjusted, and more socially aware than people with average looks. *True or False?*
   b. Prototype theories assume that we represent stereotypes with individuals, or exemplars. *True or False?*
   c. Stereotypes can be activated automatically and can influence our later behavior in ways that seem to bypass awareness. *True or False?*
   d. Studies suggest that it might be possible to reduce the prejudicial feelings that arise from stereotypes through repeated contact with individuals in the stereotyped group. *True or False?*

2. For each of the following, decide whether you are most likely to make an internal or an external attribution for the situation described.
   a. A perfect score on your psychology exam: _____
   b. Josie always smiles after her psychology lecture, but everyone else in the class leaves mad: _____
   c. A failing score on your psychology exam: _____
   d. Eagerly anticipating your food, you notice your waiter seems to spend a lot of time talking to the host instead of checking on their tables: _____

3. Decide whether each of the following statements about attitudes and attitude change is true or false.
   a. For an attitude to guide behavior, it should be appropriate or relevant to the situation. *True or False?*
   b. The peripheral route to persuasion operates when our level of involvement in or commitment to a message is high. *True or False?*
   c. According to cognitive dissonance theory, it is inconsistencies between internal beliefs and our actions that lead to attitude change. *True or False?*
   d. Mere exposure can lead to attitude change, but only if we're processing an incoming communication with care and attention. *True or False?*

BEHAVING IN THE PRESENCE OF OTHERS: SOCIAL INFLUENCE

We now turn our attention to the topic of **social influence**: How is our behavior affected by the presence of others? By the word *others*, social psychologists mean the general social context, but it can have a variety of meanings in practice. Our behavior might change because we interact with a single individual, perhaps an authority figure such as our boss, or by the collective behavior of people in a group.

Moreover, as you will soon see, the presence of others can cause us to act in a new or different way or change our attitudes and beliefs. Think back to the scenario at the start of the chapter. How does people's behavior change when they realize someone is looking at them? Does your behavior change when you are at a party with friends compared with when you are on your own?

Demonstrating the phenomenon of social facilitation, people tend to eat more in the presence of others.

iStockPhoto/ViewApart

Social Facilitation and Interference

One of the simplest examples of social influence is the phenomenon of social facilitation. **Social facilitation** is the *enhancement* in performance that is sometimes found when we perform in the presence of others. To demonstrate social facilitation, you need to compare someone's task performance in two conditions, when performing alone and when performing in the presence of other people. If performance improves when other people are around, you've demonstrated social facilitation.

Social facilitation is a widespread effect, occurring in many kinds of social environments and for many kinds of tasks (Aiello & Douthitt, 2001). Motorists drive through intersections faster when another car is traveling in the lane beside them (Towler, 1986); people run faster when others are present (Worringham & Messick, 1983); people even eat more when dining out with friends than when eating alone (Clendenen et al., 1994). In fact, the effect is not restricted to humans—ants will excavate dirt more quickly to build their nests when other ants are present (Chen, 1937); hungry chickens will eat more when other chickens observe passively though a clear plastic wall (Tolman, 1968); cockroaches will even run faster down an alleyway when a "spectator" roach watches from a small plastic enclosure (Zajonc et al., 1969).

But there's another side to the coin. It's easy to think of examples of how we've "risen to the occasion" and excelled when an audience was present, but the opposite can occur as well. Sometimes performing in a crowd impairs performance—we "choke," a tendency referred to as **social interference**. Talented Angela, who finally performed Bach's Invention No. 1 perfectly in her last practice session, finds her fingers fumbling helplessly during the piano recital. Confident Hernando, who thought he had learned his lines to perfection, stands embarrassingly silent on center stage on opening night. Social interference is the opposite of social facilitation, but both represent cases in which our ability to perform a task is influenced by the presence of others.

Social Influences on Altruism: The Bystander Effect

The presence of other people influences whether we show **altruism**—that is, whether we act in a way that shows unselfish concern for the welfare of others. Both people and animals engage in altruistic behaviors—we help others in need—and these behaviors may arise, in part, from adaptations rooted in our evolutionary past (D. M. Buss, 2019; J. R. Stevens & Hauser, 2004). We're more likely to engage in

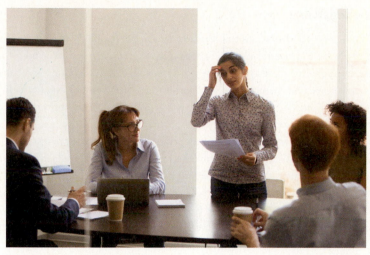

When a task is difficult, performing in the presence of others can lead to social interference: What seemed easy in private becomes a nightmare in public.

iStockPhoto/fizkes

kin-directed altruism, which means there's a greater chance we'll help relatives, but we'll help strangers under some circumstances—even if it means putting ourselves at risk. Some have suggested that we act altruistically because we anticipate that the favor will be returned in kind—a concept called *reciprocal altruism* (Trivers, 1985). Putting yourself at risk can be adaptive, therefore, because it increases the chances that you'll be helped in other situations.

Altruistic behavior is strongly controlled by the social environment. Think about the last time you were driving on the highway and noticed some poor person standing alongside a disabled car. Did you stop and help? Did you at least pull out your cell phone and inform the police or highway patrol? If you're like most people, you probably did nothing. In all likelihood, you failed to accept responsibility for helping—you left that job for someone else.

Consider the 2020 death of George Floyd by a Minneapolis police officer. Other officers were present at the scene while Officer Derek Chauvin knelt on Floyd's neck for over 8 minutes. Why didn't they stop him or at least force him to check on Floyd? Were they afraid to contradict a fellow officer? Did they think someone else would stop him? This situation is not unique in cases of police brutality. Often other officers are present while suspects are harmed. Does the presence of other people make them feel they have reduced responsibility for stepping in?

The reluctance to come to someone's aid when other people are present, or are assumed to be present, is known generally as the **bystander effect** (Darley & Latané, 1968). Although it's relatively easy to document in natural environments, it's also possible to study the bystander effect in the laboratory. Consider the following scenario. You've volunteered to participate in a psychology experiment that involves groups of students discussing the problems of college life. To minimize embarrassment, you're allowed to sit in a small cubicle where you can communicate with the others via an intercom system. Before the experiment begins, you're told that one, two, or five other people will be participating. The session begins, and suddenly one of the group members, who had previously mentioned being subject to epileptic seizures, begins to have a seizure. Over the intercom, his voice begins to garble— "Somebody-er-er-help-er-uh-uh-uh"—followed by silence. What do you do? Do you get up and help, or sit where you are?

In the actual experiment, of course, no one had a seizure; the experimenters manufactured the incident to observe the bystander effect. There was also only one real participant in the experiment—the "others" were simply recorded voices played during the study. The researchers found that whether the real participant would offer help to the imaginary seizure victim depended on how many other people the participant believed to be present. When the participant believed that only one other person was participating in the group, the participant almost immediately rose to intervene. But when it was presumed that four others (in addition to the seizure victim) were present, only 62% of the participants offered aid (Darley & Latané, 1968).

Diffusion of Responsibility

Most social psychologists are convinced that the behavior of the people in these experiments is neither atypical nor representative of general apathy. Instead, the reluctance to get involved—to help others—can be explained by appealing once again to the powerful role of social context. We tend not to lend a hand, or get involved, because the presence of others leads to **diffusion of responsibility**—we believe others have already done something to help or will soon get involved. If we know that others are present in the situation, such as in the experiment with the seizure situation, we allow our sense of responsibility to *diffuse*, or spread out widely, among the other people presumed to be present.

The bystander effect is a disturbing but powerful example of social influence. Again, it has been replicated many times in numerous social settings that extend beyond the laboratory (Latané & Nida, 1981); it seems to hold as well in cases of cyberbullying (Brody & Vangelisti, 2016). As a general rule, the more witnesses there are, the less likely it is that anyone will step forward to offer aid. In fact, this relationship holds even if you simply imagine yourself in a group. One study found that people who imagined themselves eating dinner with 30 of their friends were less likely to pledge money to a charity than people who imagined themselves eating with only 10 people or just one other person (S. M. Garcia et al., 2002).

There are exceptions to the rule. For instance, people are more likely to help if they've recently observed others being helpful, if they don't think the people around them have the ability to help, or if they truly perceive the situation as an emergency with high potential for danger (Fischer et al., 2006). Dangerous situations lead to higher levels of arousal and more helping (Fischer et al., 2011). Still, diffusion of responsibility remains widespread and easy to document. The tendency to diffuse responsibility doesn't mean that people are bad or selfish; it simply provides yet another indication of how social factors can strongly influence behavior. Our behavior changes when we are in the presence of others, and although the forces that produce the bystander effect may not make us feel good about ourselves, this behavior may be adaptive. Stopping to help someone in need could place one in danger—there may be a definite cost to helping behavior—and diffusion of responsibility is one way of reducing the risk.

The Power of the Group

The power of social context over human behavior is especially noticeable when we act as members of a well-defined group. Our behavior is shaped not only by the characteristics of the group—its size and the unanimity of its members—but even by the mere fact that we're *in* a group. Social psychologists have identified a number of psychological phenomena that illustrate the power of group membership. We'll consider three in the following sections: social loafing, deindividuation, and conformity.

Social Loafing

During our discussion of social facilitation, you learned that a person's performance often changes when others are present. Whether performance improves or declines depends on factors such as the difficulty of the task or one's general level of arousal. But when participating as a member of a group, most people show a tendency to engage in **social loafing**, which means they put out less effort than when they are alone (Latané et al., 1979). Social loafing is easy to demonstrate in the laboratory. In one study, volunteer subjects were instructed to clap and cheer as loudly as possible while blindfolded and listening to noise over headphones. Just before they began the task, the participants were told they would be clapping either with a group of other people or by themselves. When the volunteers believed they were part of a clapping group, their individual output dropped considerably.

Like many of the phenomena we've discussed in this chapter, social loafing is a complex phenomenon. Whether it occurs in a particular situation will depend on many factors, including the importance of the task, the cohesiveness of the group, and the personalities of the group members (Karau & Hart, 1998; Smrt & Karau, 2011). The effect also occurs widely across cultures, although it may be especially common in cultures that stress individuality (Karau & Williams, 1993). Some social psychologists believe there may be a connection between social loafing and the bystander effect. Bibb Latané (1981) has argued that both effects result from diffusion of responsibility. In the bystander effect, people suspect that others either will or have become involved; in social loafing, we assume that others will carry the load. In both cases, the fact that we are simply one of many makes us feel less accountable for our behavior. We fail to step up and take full responsibility, or to work to our fullest capabilities, because the responsibility can be diffused or spread to the other members of the group.

Deindividuation

The fact that we sometimes feel less accountable for our behavior when we're in a group setting can lead to a phenomenon called **deindividuation**. Imagine yourself at a particularly lively party: The people around you are acting crazy—they're drinking too much, they're damaging the furniture, and some are even beginning to shed their clothes. Are you likely to start doing the same? Some psychologists believe that people in large groups lose their sense of individuality. We can enter a depersonalized state of mind called deindividuation, which increases the chances of engaging in destructive, aggressive, or deviant behavior. Under most circumstances, it's highly unlikely that you will trash the furniture in a friend's home. But when you're part of a large rowdy group, deindividuation can lead you to do things that you might not otherwise do.

Once again, diffusion of responsibility is likely to play a role in such situations. When you're in a large group, you're less likely to feel accountable for your actions. You feel anonymous, which lowers your normal restraints on destructive actions. You also feel less self-conscious—you go along with the group, on a whim, because you're not thinking about your normal standards, values, and morals. Whether you truly enter a depersonalized state of mind is debatable, but your actions do differ from normal. Some psychologists have argued that deindividuation is simply an example of situation-specific behavior; your behavior is being controlled by an unusual situation, and your actions probably don't provide much information about how you typically behave (Postmes & Spears, 1998).

At the same time, deindividuation plays a central role in prejudice, discrimination, and racism (Zimbardo, 2007). Group membership can lead individuals to perform actions, particularly toward members of an "out-group," that they are less likely to perform otherwise. History is full of egregious examples of group-based behavior—for example, lynching and looting—that are fueled, in part, by deindividuation.

Conformity

Another property of group membership is **conformity**, which occurs when a person's opinions, feelings, and behaviors start to move toward the group norm. When you're in a group setting, you feel social pressure, which, in turn, causes you generally to comply, or go along, with the wishes of the group—even though you may not always be aware that you're doing so. Studies investigating issues of

People can feel less accountable for their behavior in a group setting, a phenomenon known as deindividuation.

Brent Stirton / Getty Images News

conformity and compliance to group norms are among the oldest and best known of all social psychology experiments.

FIGURE 13.6 ■ The Asch Study of Conformity

Do you think you would have any trouble choosing the correct comparison line in this task? Asch found that people often conformed to the group opinion.

Standard line

Comparison lines

1   2   3

In one classic study of conformity, psychologist Solomon Asch (1951, 1955) rigged the following experimental setup. People were asked to participate in a simple perception experiment that required them to make judgments about line length. Two cards were shown, one displaying a standard line of a particular length and the other showing three comparison lines of differing lengths. The participant was required to state aloud which of the three comparison lines was the same length as the standard line (see Figure 13.6). The task was quite simple—there was no question about the correct answer. The catch was that this was a group experiment, and the other members of the group were really confederates of the experimenter—they were not volunteers but rather were there to put social pressure on the true participant.

The confederates were instructed to lie on a certain number of the trials. They were told to give a response, aloud, that was clearly wrong (such as picking comparison line 1 as the correct answer). Asch was mainly concerned with how often these incorrect answers would affect the answers of the real participant. Imagine yourself in this situation—you know the answer is line 2, but four of your fellow participants have already given 1 as a response. Do you conform to the opinions of your peers, even though doing so conflicts with what you know to be true? The results were not particularly encouraging for those who champion individualism. Asch found that in approximately 75% of the sessions people complied on, at least one of the trials, and the overall rate of conformity was around 37%. Although peer pressure wasn't always effective in altering behavior—in fact, only 5% of the participants conformed on every trial—it was a powerful influence. In describing his results, Asch (1955) put it this way: "That reasonably intelligent and well-meaning young people are willing to call white black is a matter of concern" (p. 34).

As you might imagine, the Asch experiments had quite an impact on the psychological community. Similar experiments have been conducted on dozens of occasions, not only in the United States but in many other countries around the world. Generally, Asch's results have held up well, although a number of variables affect whether conformity will occur. Asch himself found, for example, that the rate of compliance dropped dramatically when one of the confederates dissented from the majority and gave the correct answer. It was also discovered that the size of the group is not as important as you might think. Conformity increases as the size of the group gets larger, but it levels off relatively quickly. The pressure to conform does not increase directly with group size; after a certain point, usually when the majority group contains three to five members, adding even more confederates has less of an effect (Tanford & Penrod, 1984). Your feelings about the status of the group as a whole also matter; if you have little or no respect for the other members of the group, you're less likely to conform. Conformity is particularly likely in the presence of an **in-group**—that is, a group of individuals with whom you share features in common or with whom you identify (see Cialdini & Goldstein, 2004).

Why do we conform to the majority opinion? One possibility is that we generally seek approval or rewards in social settings and try to avoid rejection, so we act to please by complying with social customs and norms. Clearly, voicing a dissenting opinion increases the risk of rejection by the group, so we choose to conform. Recent neuroimaging studies have suggested that areas of the brain normally associated with the processing of rewards may be involved in social conformity (Falk & Scholz, 2018). But it may also be the case that we use the majority group opinion as a source of information. If four or five people around you are convinced that comparison line 1 is the correct answer, perhaps your perception of the stimulus is flawed in some way. Perhaps your angle of sight is misleading, or your memory for the comparison line is wrong. Consequently, you use the opinions of the others in the group as information or evidence about what has really been presented.

It's best not to underestimate the power of group rejection, though. **Ostracism**, defined as being excluded and ignored by the group, can have serious psychological and even physical consequences (K. D. Williams & Nida, 2011). When we are excluded or ignored by others, our sense of belongingness, self-esteem, and control is threatened. We feel anger, sadness, and even pain. We may even make poor choices in whom we associate with in the future as we seek acceptance (Hales & Williams, 2018). Even the briefest of encounters, such as a lack of eye contact by others in a social setting, is enough to induce such feelings and reactions. Some psychologists believe that our reactions to ostracism may be rooted in our evolutionary past—we may even have built-in ostracism detectors—because ostracism from the group in ancestral times decreased the chances of survival (K. D. Williams, 2009). Conforming to the group opinion may be a small price to pay to help maintain a meaningful existence.

Group Decision Making

As you've just seen, members of an in-group can exert considerable pressure on one another to conform to the standards or norms of the group. One consequence of these internal pressures is that groups tend to take on behavioral characteristics of their own, especially when group decisions need to be made. Obviously, the psychology of group decision making is critically important—it affects everything from how verdicts are reached by juries, to how families decide where to go on vacation, to decisions made by Congress. Psychologists have identified two important characteristics of group decision making, *group polarization* and *groupthink*.

Group Polarization

When members of an in-group arrive at a consensus, there is a tendency for the group's opinion to polarize. **Group polarization** means that the group's dominant point of view—which is usually determined by the initial views of the majority—becomes stronger and even more extreme with time. Suppose you join a local action group dedicated to exposing corporate corruption. If the group tends to believe initially that corporate corruption is a significant and rising problem, it's likely that over time you and the rest of the members of the group will become even more convinced of that position. On a more extreme level, similar processes are thought to play a role in the development and maintenance of many terrorist organizations (E. F. Thomas et al., 2014).

Polarization occurs when a group's majority opinion becomes stronger and more extreme with time. What's the likelihood that people in this group will adopt more tolerant views in the future?

Michael Willis / Alamy Stock Photo

What accounts for group polarization? Not surprisingly, some of the same factors that promote conformity promote polarization. For example, group discussions tend to provide information that consolidates initial opinions. Those who enter the group with strong opinions make strong cases for their viewpoint, and dissenting viewpoints are less likely to be heard (D. D. Stewart & Stasser, 1995). At the same time, the social aspects of the discussion play an important role. People want to be liked by the other members of the group, so they shift their attitude toward the group consensus. You're more likely to be accepted by the group if you forcefully argue in favor of the group's dominant viewpoint.

Groupthink

The trend toward consensus and polarization of opinion may also be influenced by what psychologists call **groupthink**: Members of a group become so interested in seeking a consensus that they start to ignore and even suppress dissenting views. Janis (1982, 1989) found evidence for groupthink when he looked at how well-established in-groups arrived at decisions, particularly policy decisions by members of the government. He and others analyzed a number of watershed events in U.S. policymaking, including the decision to escalate the war in Vietnam, the decision by President John F. Kennedy to invade Cuba in 1961, the decision by NASA to launch the ill-fated *Challenger* space shuttle, and even voters' behavior in the 2016 U.S. presidential election. Scholars have also looked for evidence of groupthink in the decision to invade Iraq in 2003 (Badie, 2010).

In an alarming number of the cases he studied, Janis discovered that group members systematically sought consensus at the expense of critical analysis. Group members often acted as if they were trying to convince themselves of the correctness of their position. When alternative views were expressed, those views were either suppressed or dismissed. The management at NASA had clear evidence that freezing launch temperatures might pose a problem for the *Challenger*, but the managers chose to ignore that evidence in the interest of going forward with the mission. The result of groupthink is general closed-mindedness and an overestimation of the uniformity of opinion.

Can groupthink be avoided? According to Janis (1982), it's possible to counteract groupthink by following certain prescriptions. For instance, it helps to have a leader who seems impartial, one who does not quickly endorse a position. One or more members of the group can also be assigned a kind of devil's advocate role in which they are expected and encouraged to represent a dissenting position. Perhaps most important, however, is the simple recognition by the group that social influences such as groupthink are real phenomena that affect behavior, irrespective of group members' intelligence or commitment to the truth. Groupthink can be avoided, but it requires reconsidering how group decision making is normally conducted. Concept Review 13.3 summarizes the key influences of others on our behavior.

CONCEPT REVIEW 13.3
INFLUENCES OF THE GROUP

Phenomenon	Description
Social facilitation	An enhancement in performance sometimes found when we perform in the presence of others. This is especially likely with easy or well-practiced tasks.
Social interference	A decline in performance when one is in the presence of others. This is especially likely with tasks that are unique or not well learned.
Bystander effect	The reluctance to come to someone's aid when other people are present. This is characterized by diffusion of responsibility, the tendency to believe that others will help.
Social loafing	Most people show a strong tendency to put in less effort when they are working in a group compared to when they work alone.
Deindividuation	When in large groups, we can lose our sense of individuality and be more likely to engage in destructive, aggressive, or deviant behavior.
Conformity	A person's opinions, feelings, and behaviors start to move toward the group norm.
Group polarization	A group's dominant point of view becomes stronger and even more extreme with time.
Groupthink	Members of a group become so interested in seeking a consensus of opinion that they ignore and suppress dissenting views.

The Power of Authority: Obedience

Up to this point in our discussion of social influence, we've concentrated on how behavior is affected by the presence of others, where the others have simply been any individuals who happen to be present in the social context. But in many cases it does matter *who* these others happen to be—and what roles these people play in your life.

Psychologists use the term **obedience** to describe the form of compliance that occurs when people respond to the orders of an authority figure. For example, in 1978 in a rural area of Guyana, South America, hundreds of converts to the religious teachings of Reverend Jim Jones chose, under his direct orders, to commit mass suicide. Most people find it extremely difficult to understand such events and consider them to be social aberrations committed by people far different from themselves. Admittedly, you might toe the line in front of your boss, and do and say things that you don't really believe, but murder innocent people? Drink something laced with cyanide? Never.

The Milgram Experiment

Psychologist Stanley Milgram (1963) set out to determine just how resistant the average person is to the demands of authority. He placed an advertisement in a local newspaper recruiting men for a study looking at the effects of punishment on learning. The participants were told that for a small fee they would be asked to play one of two roles in the experiment: either a *learner*, which required memorizing and then recalling lists of word pairs, or a *teacher*, whose task it was to administer an electric shock to the learner whenever he made any recall errors. Each session required two participants, one teacher and one learner, and the assignment of condition was decided by drawing slips of paper out of a hat.

But things were not exactly what they appeared to be. In fact, in every case the true volunteer, the one who had responded to the ad, was picked to be the teacher. The learner was a confederate of the experimenter, someone who was fully informed about the true nature of the study. Although it was set up to look as though he was receiving shocks throughout the session, he was never actually shocked. The idea was to get the confederate to make learning errors and then to assess how willing the teacher was to administer the shock under the authority of a hovering and demanding experimenter.

To begin the setup, the unwitting teacher watched as the learner was led away to an adjacent room and hooked up to a shock-administering apparatus. Back in the original room, the teacher was then placed in front of an imposing-looking electrical shock generator, which contained some 30 different switches. It was explained that each switch was able to generate a level of shock intensity, ranging from 15 volts (Slight Shock), through 150 volts (Strong Shock), and finally up to 450 volts (labeled simply XXX). With the experimenter standing by his side, the teacher was instructed to begin reading and then testing the learner's memory for the words, via intercom, and to administer a shock whenever the learner failed to call out the correct answer. Moreover, to see how the degree of punishment influenced learning, the teacher was instructed to increase the voltage level of the shock, by moving to a new switch, with each new mistake.

Remember, no one was shocked in this experiment; the learner was *in on* the experiment, and he was told to make mistakes consistently throughout the session. To add to the cover story, he was also instructed to respond vocally and actively to the shocks, via the intercom, whenever they were delivered (the learner's responses were prerecorded). At first, when the shock levels were low, there wasn't much response. But as the prearranged mistakes continued—which, of course, required the teacher to continue increasing the voltage of the shock—loud protests began to come over the intercom. By the time the mistake-prone learner was receiving 150-volt shocks, he was demanding to be released from the experiment. By around 300 volts, he was screaming in agony in response to each delivered shock and pounding on the wall; after the 330-volt level, the shocks yielded no response at all—simply silence.

Listening to these disturbing pleas for help did not make the average teacher very comfortable. In fact, most quickly expressed concern over the consequences of the shocking and wanted to discontinue the experiment. But the teacher's concerns were met with resistance from the authoritative experimenter, who demanded that the shocks go on. "Please continue," the experimenter responded. "You have no other choice; you must go on." What would you do in this situation? You're participating in an experiment, which is being conducted in the name of science, but the task requires you to inflict quite a

These photos were taken during one of Milgram's early experiments on obedience to authority. The first shows the "shock generator" used during the experiment; the second shows the "learner"—actually a confederate of the experimenter—being hooked up to the shock-delivery apparatus; and in the third, the "teacher" sits in front of the shock generator in the presence of the demanding experimenter.

From the film "Obedience" copyright 1968 by Stanley Milgram © renewed 1993 by Alexandra Milgram, distributed by Alexander Street Press

bit of pain and suffering on someone else. Do you blindly go forward, delivering shocks in compliance with the requests of the authority figure, or do you quit and give the experimenter a piece of your mind? Of course, this was exactly the question of interest to Milgram—how obedient would people be to the unreasonable requests of an authority figure?

Interestingly, before the experiment began, Milgram asked several people, including professionals, to predict how much shock participants would be willing to deliver in his task. Most predicted that obedience would be low; the estimates were that only a few people in a thousand would deliver shocks up to 450 volts and that most would defy the experimenter after discomfort was expressed by the learner. The results were far different. Milgram found that 65% of the 40 people who participated were willing to deliver shocks up to 450 volts, and no one quit before the pounding on the wall started. This means that 26 of the 40 participants went all the way to the final switch—the one with the ominous XXX label—despite the agonized pleas from the learner. This remarkable finding rocked the psychological community and initiated a great deal of subsequent research, as well as a firestorm of controversy.

Controversies and Ethical Concerns

Milgram's (1963) experiment was controversial for several reasons. First, the way it was conducted raised serious ethical questions. The people in his study were misled from the beginning and became severely distressed during their participation. Milgram observed a number of indications of distress during the experiment—the "teachers" sometimes groaned, bit their lips, trembled, stuttered, and even broke into a sweat. Many critics feel that this kind of psychological manipulation—even though done to advance knowledge—cannot be justified (Baumrind, 1964; Schlenker & Forsyth, 1977). In response, Milgram (1974) argued that his participants were thoroughly debriefed at the end of the experiment—they were told in detail about the true nature of the experiment—and were generally glad they had participated. Follow-up questionnaires sent to the participants months later revealed that only a handful felt negatively about the experiment. However, in-depth analyses of the Stanley Milgram Papers, along with interviews of the study's participants by researchers, suggest that the participants were not fully debriefed as to the deception used in the study (G. Perry, 2013).

Another major question raised about the experiment concerned the procedure itself. Some critics argued that perhaps the participants had seen through the cover and were simply trying to please the experimenter; others argued that the results, although interesting, had no general applicability beyond the laboratory. People must have assumed that things were okay, these critics reasoned; otherwise, no one would have believed that an experiment of this type could be conducted. In response, Milgram again pointed out that his participants tended to get extremely distressed in the setting, which suggests that they didn't figure out the deception and were expressing their true feelings. Some have also suggested that the prodding of the teacher by the experimenter was inconsistent across participants and amounted to bullying in some cases (Griggs & Whitehead, 2015).

In the 59 years since Milgram's original experiment was conducted, his general procedure has been repeated, in many countries around the world (for a recent example using more ethical procedures, see Burger et al., 2011). Few psychologists today question the validity of Milgram's basic findings, although it's clear that the degree of compliance depends on many factors. For example, the Milgram experiment was conducted at a prestigious university (Yale); when the same study was conducted in a less prestigious setting—a rundown office building—compliance dropped (although it remained alarmingly high). People were also less likely to comply if the authority figure left the room after explaining the experiment or if the person giving the orders looked ordinary rather than official or scientific (Milgram, 1974). Thus, obedience to authority is not absolute—it depends on the characteristics of the situation, the characteristics of the participant, and the characteristics of the person giving the orders (Burger, 2009; Haslam et al., 2014; Twenge, 2009).

Finally, a cautionary note: Although behavior can certainly change in the presence of an authority figure, even dramatically in some cases, obedience shouldn't be used in every case to explain away the actions of people who commit terrible crimes. In the case of Nazi Germany, for example, "I was just following orders" became the standard rallying cry for those accused of some truly horrendous actions. There are limits to the effects of authority, and social psychologists are careful to draw distinctions between obedience to authority, as witnessed in Milgram's settings, and the cruelties practiced by many executioners in concentration camps (Cialdini & Goldstein, 2004). There's no question that we can all be pushed to extremes in the presence of an authority figure, but obedience (or deindividuation) can't be used as an overriding excuse, or even explanation, for genocide or other horrendous acts.

The Role of Culture

You've now seen how our thoughts and actions change when we're in the presence of others, particularly groups. The group can exert a powerful influence on members' judgments, leading to conformity, groupthink, and obedience to authority. In some cases, you may find yourself giving in to the group's demands at the expense of your own personal convictions.

But is the tendency to conform, or to sacrifice one's individual desires for the collective, necessarily bad? Is conformity or obedience a sign of weakness, or is it a sign of strength? The answer depends partly on the culture in which you are raised. In most Western cultures, such as the United States, people are taught from a very young age to adopt an *independent* view of the self; that is, people are rewarded for viewing themselves as unique individuals, with special and distinctive qualities. American children, for example, are likely to be told things like "the squeaky wheel gets the grease." Be someone different, be an individual with unique qualities—these are the things that count. Although Western cultures certainly value acts of charity or unselfish devotion to others, such acts are typically viewed as reflecting distinctive personal qualities—qualities that make someone stand out as an admirable individual.

In many non-Western cultures, particularly East Asian cultures, people adopt a very different, *interdependent* view of the self (Markus & Kitayama, 1991, 1994). In Japan, for example, children are taught to think of themselves from the perspective of the collective—as members of a group with common goals—rather than as individuals striving to be different. In Japan, children are told, "The nail that stands out gets pounded down." Such cultural differences are reflected in people's inner thoughts and feelings. When asked to write self-descriptions, East Asians are likely to list personal qualities that they share with others ("I come from Kyoto") and to think they are more similar to others than others are to them. Westerners, in contrast, tend to describe themselves as dissimilar to others, and they use individualistic characteristics ("I'm very talented on the flute") to describe themselves (Trafimow et al., 1991). The majority of Westerners also tend to think of themselves as above average in intelligence and leadership ability, which is a trend rarely seen among East Asians (Markus & Kitayama, 1991).

In some Asian cultures, children are encouraged to adopt an "interdependent" view of self; that is, they view themselves primarily as members of a group with common goals rather than as individuals striving to be unique.

mikecranephotography.com / Alamy Stock Photo

What do such findings mean? They should reinforce the idea that cultural factors can't be ignored in the interpretation and study of behavior and mind. Our thoughts and actions are influenced by our efforts to adapt successfully to our individual environments. As cultural demands on the individual vary, so too will the individual's actions. To the individual, these cultural views of the self produce both costs and benefits. For example, those who adopt an independent view of the self tend to score higher on measures of self-esteem and self-efficacy, which, in turn, can increase one's subjective sense of well-being (Heine & Buchtel, 2009). On the other hand, those who think the world revolves around "me" have trouble securing and maintaining long-term relationships (Robins & Beer, 2001). Recent studies (e.g., Hamamura, 2012) suggest that the independent view of the self is increasing across many countries and cultures, including some East Asian cultures (Santos et al., 2017).

KNOWLEDGE CHECK 13.2

Now test your knowledge about social influence by answering the following questions. (You will find the answers in the Appendix.)

1. Pick the psychological term that best fits each of these statements. Choose from the following: *social facilitation, social loafing, deindividuation, bystander effect, conformity, group polarization, groupthink, obedience.*

   a. Casey is normally shy and polite, but at the rock concert last night he was loud and shouted obscenities at the police: _____

   b. Megan writes extremely well, but she contributes little to group discussions during class: _____

    c. Sergio is convinced that his study group is dead wrong about their interpretation of the Milgram experiment, but he chooses to nod in agreement with the others in the group: _____

    d. Landlord Sang-Woo notices that the grievances coming from his tenant group have become increasingly more rigid and demanding over time: _____

    e. Gabriella never calls 911 when she sees a broken-down car by the side of the road—she assumes everyone has a cell phone: _____

    f. Teresa notices that she always talks more when she's at a large party: _____

2. Which of the following situations should lead to the greatest reduction in obedience to authority?
    a. The authority figure wears a uniform in front of the teacher.
    b. The authority figure stands close to the teacher.
    c. The experiment is conducted in a federal building.
    d. The experiment is conducted in the teacher's home.

ESTABLISHING RELATIONS WITH OTHERS

Social psychology is the discipline that studies how we think about, influence, and relate to other people. So far, we've dealt with social thought and social influence. We now turn our attention to a third and final component: How do we establish and maintain *relations* with others? People are not merely objects to be interpreted or forces that exert influences on behavior. For most of us, it is the personal relationships we establish that are paramount in our lives. Most people depend on their interactions with friends, lovers, and family not only for protection and sustenance but also to help give meaning to their lives.

    We've encountered the topic of social relations several times in earlier chapters. In Chapter 4, when we discussed social development, we dealt in detail with the topic of *attachment*. But in that case, we were concerned with how people use social bonds to help solve the problems that arise during development. Infants are born with limited motor skills and somewhat immature perceptual systems; consequently, they need to establish strong bonds with their caregivers to survive. In Chapter 12, when we discussed motivation and emotion, we saw how people use facial expressions to communicate

Our relationships with others protect us, nurture us, and give meaning to our lives.

their emotions to others and how people are motivated to secure sexual partners. In this section, we'll consider some of the factors that influence interpersonal attraction, which often forms the basis for relationship development, and then we'll discuss how psychologists have attempted to tackle the mysterious subject of love.

What Makes Someone Attractive?

Can one fall in love at first sight? What would this love be based on? Few things are as alluring as the sight of an attractive face. Beauty is a powerful motivator of behavior, a fact confirmed by the many millions of dollars spent annually on cosmetics and other beauty aids. The concept of attractiveness is important to the psychologist because people's physical appearance often helps shape how their behavior will be interpreted and therefore how others will treat them. As you learned earlier in the chapter, people commonly rely on social schemas to form impressions, and there is considerable evidence to suggest that physical attractiveness is used as a basis for generating expectations about others (Eagly et al., 1991). Just think about the words of the 19th-century German poet Johann Christoph Friedrich Schiller: "Physical beauty is the sign of an interior beauty, a spiritual and moral beauty." Schiller's insight is certainly not lost on modern advertisers who, as you know, rely heavily on the power of an attractive face to help sell their clients' products.

An Evolutionary Perspective

What exactly is it that makes a face physically beautiful? What are the qualities that determine whether someone's looks are considered desirable? One way to think about this problem is from the perspective of evolutionary theory. If the purpose of attraction is to secure an ideal mate, then preferably it should be someone with a high reproductive capacity or someone who is able to provide protection for one's children and compete successfully for needed resources. This kind of reasoning predicts that people should be attracted to opposite-sex members who are youthful, vigorous, and healthy looking because these qualities increase the likelihood of successful reproduction and child-rearing (D. M. Buss, 2012; Little et al., 2011).

Another prediction of evolutionary theory is that features of attractiveness should cut across cultural boundaries. If attractiveness is grounded somewhere deep in our genetic ancestry, then it shouldn't matter much where you are reared and what experiences you have; in general, there should be worldwide agreement about what constitutes attractiveness. Notice this conclusion contrasts sharply with the generally accepted idea that "beauty is in the eye of the beholder," but it's supported, at least in part, by empirical research. Several studies have found that when ratings of attractiveness are compared cross-culturally, attractive faces share a number of basic structural features (J. H. Langlois et al., 2000). It's also been discovered that babies, within hours of birth, prefer to look at pictures of faces that adults have rated as attractive over faces that have been rated as unattractive (J. H. Langlois et al., 1987; Slater et al., 1998). It's unlikely that we can appeal to experience—that is, sustained exposure to some culturally based definition of beauty—to account for this preference. However, some caution needs to be taken: Evolutionary explanations of behavior can be difficult to test, primarily because we have limited knowledge about the ancestral environments in which psychological traits are presumed to have evolved.

Attractive Faces May Be Average

Some research suggests that the universality of attractiveness may be partly because people are programmed to prefer faces that are *average* representations of faces in the population (J. H. Langlois & Roggman, 1990; J. H. Langlois et al., 1994). Average in this case does not necessarily mean common, typical, or frequently occurring faces. Instead, it means prototypical faces—that is, faces that are good representations of the category "faces." In Chapter 9, we defined category prototypes as the best or most representative members of a category—a robin, for example, is probably close to the prototype for the category "bird." Accordingly, attractive faces are those that are particularly *facelike*, or representative of the category of faces.

The faces in each row are composites created by averaging 2 individual faces (far left), 8 faces (middle photos in each row), or 32 faces (far right). The composite faces were created using the averaging process employed by J. H. Langlois and Roggman (1990).

© Judith Langlois

Langlois and Roggman (1990) supported this view by asking people to rate the attractiveness of average faces that were generated electronically on a computer. To create these faces, hundreds of individual black-and-white photographs, composed of male or female white, Asian, and Latinx faces, were first scanned by a computer and then digitized into matrices of individual gray values. Each of these gray values corresponded to a shade of gray sitting at a small location on the scanned face. A whole face was represented by many thousands of these gray values, as they are in a typical newspaper photo or video display. As you probably know, any image you see in a newspaper or on a video monitor is a configuration of many rows and columns of individual intensity dots or pixels. When viewed as a whole, the dots blend together to form a familiar image on the page or screen.

The unique feature of the Langlois and Roggman research was that people were sometimes shown faces that were generated by averaging the gray values across a large collection of individual faces. An individual dot in one of these composite faces was set by averaging the values of all the dots at the same relative location in the face pool. The result was a "blended face" that did not look exactly like any one of the individual faces but rather represented a kind of prototype face in the population. Volunteer participants were asked to rate these faces for attractiveness, along with the individual faces that had been used to form the composite. The surprising result was that people generally rated the composite faces as more attractive than the individual faces (see also G. Rhodes & Tremewan, 1996). Recent research also suggests that more typical faces are judged as more trustworthy than less typical faces (Sofer et al., 2015).

Why would people prefer faces that are prototypical? Langlois and Roggman offer several reasons. One possibility is that prototypical faces are easy to identify and classify as human faces. Classifying something as a face may not seem like much of a task for adults, but it could well be difficult for the newborn infant. It is critical for infants to be able to recognize a looming visual configuration as a face because they are dependent on their social interactions with people for survival. Yet the visual acuity of the newborn is limited, so faces that are particularly facelike may make this critical classification process easier. Another possibility is that people are programmed biologically to prefer prototypical faces because individuals with average features may be less likely to harbor potentially harmful genetic mutations—that is, they may be "signals" for genetic health. Likewise, faces that are symmetrical in appearance tend to be preferred as well—perhaps, again, because they provide clues about the genetic health of a potential mating partner (Komori et al., 2009; G. Rhodes, 2006).

The Subjective Components

Despite the evidence for universality in how people conceive of attractiveness, most psychologists recognize that there is a strong subjective component to the perception of beauty. As discussed in Chapter 12, standards of beauty have changed over time in most cultures of the world. In Western societies, for instance, our icon of beauty, the fashion model, has ranged from a curvaceous bustiness at one point to slender tomboyishness at the next (Silverstein et al., 1986).

It's also the case that features considered attractive in one culture—pierced noses, liposuctioned thighs, elongated earlobes—may be considered unattractive in another. Perceptions of attractiveness and beauty also clearly change with experience. We generally rate people we like as more attractive than people we don't like; moreover, if you've just been shown a picture of a strikingly attractive person, your ratings of average-looking people go down (Kenrick et al., 1989). If a male face has been previously paired with a smiling female face, women tend to rate the man's face as more attractive (B. C. Jones et al., 2007). Beauty is not entirely in the eye of the beholder, as the research of Langlois and Roggman (1990) indicates, but there is indeed a measurable subjective component that cannot be ignored.

The perception of beauty has subjective components that are culturally dependent.

PhotoStock-Israel / Alamy Stock Photo

Determinants of Liking and Loving

If you had to list all the things you look for in a friend, what would they be? Understanding? A sense of humor? Intelligence? What if the word *husband, wife,* or *lover* was substituted for *friend*—would the characteristics on your list change? Might you add wealth, security, or attractiveness? If you ask people to create such a list—and psychologists have done so numerous times—most people have no trouble coming up with a wish list of characteristics for "friend" or "marriage partner of my dreams." But how important do these well-thought-out and carefully chosen factors turn out to be? Do we really form friendships, or choose marriage partners, based on some relationship equation that sums desirable and undesirable attributes in a logical and rational way?

One of the most important lessons of this textbook, and certainly of this chapter, is that our behavior is strongly influenced by external forces in the environment. People act the way they do partly because of conscious, internally driven processes but also because the environment shapes and constrains the possible behaviors. In the case of interpersonal attraction, it turns out that the environment often plays a major role in determining both whom you choose to spend time with and whom you consider to be an appropriate mate. As you learned earlier in the chapter, even mere exposure to something can be enough to increase its likeability (Zajonc, 1968). People like things that are familiar, even when that familiarity has been created by simple repetition in the environment.

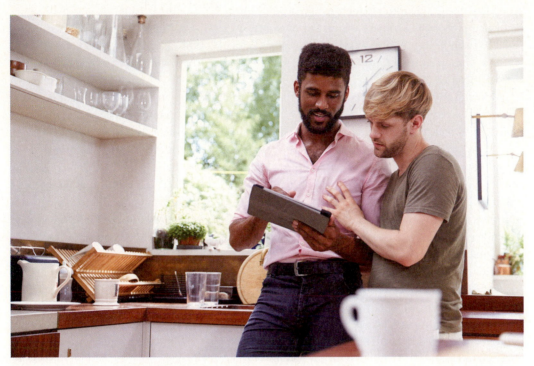

The environment plays a large role in who we choose to associate with.

iStockPhoto/monkeybusinessimages

Proximity

In a classic study conducted over 70 years ago, psychologist Leon Festinger and his colleagues (1950) analyzed the friendships that formed among students living in an apartment complex near the Massachusetts Institute of Technology. Festinger and his colleagues found that they could predict the likelihood of a friendship forming by simply noting the *proximity*—defined in terms of the closeness of living quarters—between two people in the building. When the students were asked to list their three closest friends, two-thirds of the time they named students who lived in their same apartment complex. Moreover, when a fellow apartment dweller was listed as a friend, two-thirds of the time the person lived on the same floor as the respondent. Clearly, the choice of friends is strongly influenced by where one lives. People tend to end up with friends who live nearby.

Of course, it isn't proximity by itself that leads to liking and loving. When people live close by, you see them a lot, and it may be the increased exposure that promotes the attraction (Rivera et al., 2010). We've already seen that increased exposure leads to an increase in rated likeability, but it also provides the opportunity for interaction. When you consistently interact with someone, mutual feelings of connectedness and belonging tend to follow. In other words, familiarity leads to attraction (Reis et al., 2011). You see each other as members of the same *in-group*—that is, as people who share features in common. In fact, you don't even have to interact physically with someone for increased liking to occur. Psychologists John Darley and Ellen Berscheid (1967) found that even the anticipation of an interaction with someone you don't already know can cause you to rate that person as more attractive. And in today's world full of social media connections, this effect is particularly relevant.

Similarity

We also tend to like and form relationships with people who are *similar* to us. Friends and intimate partners typically resemble each other in age, social status, education level, race, religious beliefs, political attitudes, intelligence, and even physical attractiveness. People who smoke are more likely than nonsmokers to initiate a romantic relationship with someone who smokes or who has greater perceived approval for smoking (Etcheverry & Agnew, 2009); we even pick dogs that, at least on some dimensions, seem to resemble us physically (Roy & Christenfeld, 2004). People may report preferring physically attractive mates, but most end up marrying someone who is approximately equal to them in degree of physical attractiveness (Feingold, 1988, 1990). So, if you believe in the idea that "opposites attract," think again—in reality, it is the birds of a feather that tend consistently to flock together.

Although few psychologists question the finding that similarities attract, there are disagreements about how best to interpret this finding. The fact that similarities are found between the physical and attitudinal dimensions of friends and lovers doesn't provide any insight into why these similarities exist. As we discussed in Chapter 2, correlations do not imply causality. One possibility is that we like others who share our beliefs and attitudes because they *validate* those beliefs, which further helps convince us that our beliefs are the right ones (Byrne, 1971; Laprelle et al., 1990). The finding that *perceived* similarity of attitudes is a better predictor of interpersonal attraction than actual attitudes is consistent with this conclusion (R. M. Montoya et al., 2008). Another possibility is that we spend time with others like ourselves because we dislike people who hold different views (Rosenbaum, 1986). It's not so much that we want to spend time with those who resemble us; it's that we don't want to spend time with those who don't.

A third possibility is that environmental factors are responsible. Partners in romantic relationships might be similarly attractive because attractiveness dictates to some extent who you can find as a mate. Physically unattractive people, for example, might be unable to attract mates who are more attractive; or it could be that society dictates that attractive people reject those who are less attractive. Socioeconomic class also tends to limit our options. If we are poor and live in a less desirable section of town, our interactions are likely to be with people who are members of the same socioeconomic class. Generally, people who live in the same neighborhood, attend the same church, or go off to the same university already share many features in common, and it is from this pool that people typically find their companions. However, the recent increase in connections between people through social media may be changing this trend (e.g., T. Ryan et al., 2017). This is still an open question in this area of study.

Reciprocity

There's also a role in the dynamics of interpersonal attraction for **reciprocity**, or our tendency to return in kind the feelings that are shown toward us. If someone doesn't like you and displays hostility at every turn, you usually have similarly negative feelings toward that person. If someone likes you, or even if you simply think the person likes you, then you tend to like that person back (Curtis & Miller, 1986; Kelley, 1983). In a study by Curtis and Miller (1986), participants were asked to have a conversation with someone who they believed had been told either positive or negative information about them (actually, the conversation partner hadn't been told anything). If the people believed they were talking to someone who perceived them in a positive light, they tended to be friendlier and more open in their conversation—they acted as if they liked their partner more.

Reciprocity helps lead to interpersonal attraction because it is self-fulfilling and because people who like you tend to be reinforcing and accepting of your actions. But it doesn't always work. If you feel that the positive actions of another are motivated for some selfish reason—as part of a scam or to get something such as a promotion—then your reaction will typically be negative (E. E. Jones, 1964). Ingratiation, in which a person consciously tries to win the affections of another for some ulterior motive, is likely to backfire as a strategy if it is discovered. We're attracted to people who like us, but only if we believe and trust their intentions (R. M. Montoya & Insko, 2008).

The Psychology of Romantic Love

When psychologists study *interpersonal attraction*, it's likely to be seen as interesting and important research by most casual observers. But when psychologists turn to the study of "love," the reactions are often far different. How, you ask, can someone understand, define, or attempt to measure such a thing as love? Love is a topic to be tackled by the poet or the artist, not the questionnaire-laden social psychologist. Perhaps. But as you'll soon see, that hasn't stopped psychologists from trying.

Defining Love

Psychologists recognize that love is a complex emotion that can be expressed in a variety of forms. There is the love that exists between parent and child, between lovers, between spouses, even between friends. In each case, when it's measured through a questionnaire, the relationship is typically characterized by the giving and receiving of support, a kind of mutual understanding, and intense personal satisfaction (Fehr & Russell, 1991; Sternberg & Grajek, 1984). Although there may be fundamental similarities in how love is experienced, the amount of love that is reported depends on the type of relationship studied. Women, for example, might report *loving* their lover more than a best friend but *liking* their best friend more; men, on the other hand, report liking *and* loving their lover more than they report these feelings for their friends (Sternberg, 1986).

When the relationship between two individuals is romantic, it is popular to distinguish further between passionate love and companionate love. **Passionate love** is an intense emotional state characterized by a powerful longing to be with the other person (Hatfield, 1988). For many people, passionate love resembles a ride on a kind of emotional roller coaster—they experience intense joy if their feelings are shared, and intense pain and despair if their feelings are unrequited. **Companionate love** tends to be less emotional and intense, but its feelings of trust and warmth can be more enduring. Whereas passionate love leads to intense arousal, companionate love leads to self-disclosure—we are willing to reveal our innermost secrets because the relationship sits on a bedrock of trust. It is, of course, possible for both passionate love and companionate love to be present in the same relationship, but this is not always the case.

Views of Love

Psychologist Robert Sternberg (1986, 1999) has argued for what he calls a triangular view of love. He sees love as being composed of three major dimensions—intimacy, passion, and commitment—that vary in relation to one another (see Figure 13.7). *Intimacy* is the emotional component that brings closeness, connectedness, and warmth to a relationship. *Passion* is the motivational component that

---

FIGURE 13.7 ■ The Triangular View of Love

Robert Sternberg proposed that there are many kinds of love, each defined by the degree of passion, intimacy, and commitment present in the relationship.

Passion	Intimacy	Commitment	Type of love that results
+	−	−	Infatuated love
−	+	−	Liking (friendship)
−	−	+	Empty love
+	+	−	Romantic love
−	+	+	Companionate love
+	−	+	Fatuous love

Source: Based on Sternberg, 1986.

underlies arousal, physical attraction, and sexual behavior. *Commitment* is the decision-making arm of love—how willing are the partners to stick with the relationship in times of trouble? All forms of love comprise some combination of these three components. For example, according to Sternberg (1986), *romantic love* is marked by a combination of intimacy and passion (but it may lack commitment), *companionate love* is high in intimacy and commitment (but without passion), and *empty love* occurs when there is commitment but little or no passion or intimacy.

Current ideas about love consider how relationships develop over time (Berscheid, 2010). What patterns have been found? Do couples gain intimacy? Lose passion? Become increasingly willing to commit? It is impossible to predict for any particular relationship, but research findings propose some general trends. On average, the passion component of love builds early and rapidly in a relationship—it can even be experienced almost immediately on meeting another—but it's difficult to sustain for long periods (Hatfield et al., 2008). Commitment, on the other hand, is slow to develop but can be quite long lasting. Intimacy, too, is unlikely to be found early in a relationship (there is too much uncertainty), but it grows and maintains itself in most successful relationships. Compassionate love, or "self-less" love, also seems to be involved in relationship satisfaction and stability over time (Fehr, Harasymchuk, & Sprecher, 2014). Attachment between partners can also develop over time (Berscheid, 2010). The components of love are fluid, changing over time in ways that reflect the successes and failures of the interactions between the partners.

Can we predict how long a specific love relationship will last? A number of studies have been conducted on this topic with some surprising results. For instance, it turns out that for college students your roommate is a better judge, on average, of how long your romantic relationship will last than you and your romantic partner (T. K. MacDonald & Ross, 1999). It's also the case that your original ratings of the quality of the relationship correlate more highly with the eventual outcome than your predictions about how long the relationship will last. Often our "hopes" for what a relationship will become are inaccurate; what matters is our ongoing assessment of the quality of the relationship (and, of course, you might consider paying some attention to what your roommates think because they tend to be more "objective" about your relationships).

Research on romantic love has focused overwhelmingly on heterosexual relationships, but researchers are beginning to expand studies to become more inclusive of different types of relationships (Thorne et al., 2019). As homosexual and other types of relationships have become widely accepted, and many nations now legally recognize same-sex marriages, the scope of studies on romantic love is expanding into these areas (e.g., Diamond, 2003). Further, culture plays a role in the influence of different factors on romantic interest and relationships, such as attachment processes (Pepping et al., 2017) and family dynamics (Tyrell et al., 2016). Thus, there is still a lot for psychologists to learn about romantic love and relationships.

Whether you'll end up staying in a close relationship depends on many factors, some having little or nothing to do with "love." For example, people who are highly invested in a relationship—if they share property, friends, or kids—tend to stick it out (Rusbult et al., 2012). Alternatives matter as well: How easily can you survive on your own, and what are the chances that you'll find another relationship partner? Strong personal or moral convictions can also lead to stability in a relationship. You may dislike your partner intensely but feel that it's wrong to break up a relationship. Satisfaction, or happiness, with your partner is only one determinant of a relationship that lasts (M. S. Clark & Grote, 2003).

KNOWLEDGE CHECK 13.3

Now test your knowledge about how we establish relationships with other people by deciding whether each of the following statements is true or false. (You will find the answers in the Appendix.)

1. Babies, within hours of birth, show a preference for attractive over unattractive faces. *True or False?*

2. Blending studies of facial attractiveness indicate that faces that are unusual or distinct tend to receive higher ratings of attractiveness than averaged faces. *True or False?*

3. Studies have found that if you've just been shown a picture of a strikingly attractive person, your ratings of an average-looking person go up. *True or False?*

4. Friends and intimate partners typically resemble each other in age, social status, education level, race, religious beliefs, political attitudes, intelligence, and even physical attractiveness. *True or False?*

5. According to the triangular theory of love, infatuated love represents passion without intimacy or commitment. *True or False?*

6. Passionate love typically leads to more feelings of warmth and trust than does companionate love. *True or False?*

THE PROBLEMS SOLVED: WHAT SOCIAL PROCESSES ARE FOR

Our actions, thoughts, and feelings come from the interactions we have with ever-changing environments. Among the most powerful components of these environments are social ones—people around us strongly influence our thoughts and actions. Social psychology is the discipline that studies how people think about, influence, and relate to others. In this chapter, we tackled the topic areas of social psychology from the perspective of three major social problems.

Interpreting the Behavior of Others: Social Cognition

As we move through the social world, it's extremely adaptive for us to try and make sense of the people around us. We form initial impressions of others by using the information we have available—such as the physical appearance of the person—and by relying on preexisting knowledge categories, called social schemas, which help us interpret that information. Schemas are useful because they can direct our actions in uncertain situations. But schemas can also lead to stereotypes—beliefs about people belonging to groups—which, although useful in many ways, can produce prejudice and discrimination.

Attributions—how we infer the causes of another's behavior—form another important part of the overall interpretation process. When attempting to explain the actions of others, we look for factors that co-vary with the behavior, and we assess the consistency of the behavior, its distinctiveness, and whether there is consensus among people. Whether you look for causes in the external environment or within the person depends on how these three factors work together. Some basic attribution biases—such as the fundamental attribution error—also help shape our inferences.

Attitudes, which are positive or negative evaluations, are typically separated into three components: a cognitive component, an affective component, and a behavioral component. Attitude formation is influenced by a number of factors, but direct experience plays a major role. One popular theory of attitude change is the elaboration likelihood model, which proposes that there are central and peripheral routes to persuasion. A number of studies indicate that when people are induced to act in ways that are inconsistent with their existing attitudes, their attitudes often change as a result.

Behaving in the Presence of Others: Social Influence

Psychologists use the term *social influence* to describe how behavior is affected by other people in one's environment. Sometimes social influence can produce positive effects, as in social facilitation, and sometimes the presence of others hinders performance, as in social interference. The presence of others can also affect our willingness to deliver aid to people in need. The bystander effect reveals that we're generally reluctant to come to someone's aid when other people are present. One interpretation of this effect appeals to diffusion of responsibility: We believe that others have already done something to help or will soon get involved.

Behavior is also strongly influenced by the social pressures of groups and of authority. Participation as a member of a well-defined group can make us conform, which means that our opinions and behaviors will tend to move toward the group norm. Conformity operates on the group level as well. It is common for groups to polarize, which means that the group's dominant point of view tends to become stronger and more extreme with the passage of time. If groupthink is present, members have become so interested in seeking a consensus of opinion that dissenting views are ignored or suppressed. Milgram's famous experiment on obedience demonstrated that people can be induced by an authority figure to engage in behavior that they would not engage in otherwise. The degree of compliance depends on the characteristics of the situation and on the characteristics of the person giving the orders.

Establishing Relations With Others

Often the most meaningful things in our lives are the social relations that we've established with others. How are relationships formed? We examined facial attractiveness and discovered that attractiveness may be determined, in part, by innate biological factors. People tend to prefer average, or prototypical, faces—perhaps because they're easier to identify or they signal genetic health. Among the factors that influence liking and loving are familiarity, proximity, similarity, and reciprocity. We're more likely to be attracted to someone we know, who lives nearby, who is similar to ourselves, and who likes us back. Psychologists have also attempted to understand love, which is typically defined in terms of multiple components—such as intimacy, passion, and commitment. Whether a person ends up in a relationship based on passionate love or companionate love depends on how these components work together in the relationship.

THINKING ABOUT RESEARCH

A summary of a research study in psychology is given in this section. As you read the summary, think about the following questions:

1. Is it possible that the "liking gap" described in the Purpose section is due to the fundamental attribution error? Why or why not?
2. Do you think the finding of a larger "liking gap" for shy individuals is related to the self-fulfilling prophecy? Why or why not?
3. How might stereotypes contribute to the "liking gap"?
4. Are the behaviors exhibited in the study realistic? Why or why not?

Article Reference: Boothby, E. J., Cooney, G., Sandstrom, G. M., & Clark, M. S. (2018). The liking gap in conversations: Do people like us more than we think? *Psychological Science, 29*, 1742–1756. doi: 10.1177/0956797618783714

Note: Study 1a from this article is summarized as follows.

Purpose of the Study: This study was designed to answer a research question about social perceptions of others: "How accurate are people's judgments of how much they are liked by someone they are talking to?" Based on past studies' results showing that individuals are more critical of themselves than others are (i.e., they have a negative self-bias), the researchers hypothesized that people will underestimate how much others like them, a result they termed the liking gap.

Method of the Study: In this study, 36 people were recruited from the local community through flyer postings. Respondents were paid $10 for their participation. Participants were assigned in same-sex pairs to hold a 5-minute conversation in a lab setting. A sheet of icebreakers was provided to aid the conversation. Their conversations were recorded. At the end of the 5-minute period, the participants were separated and asked to rate items about how much they liked their conversation partner and how much they thought their conversation partner liked them. They then completed some personality measures.

Results of the Study: On average, participants judged that their partner liked them less than they liked their partner. In other words, ratings of how much they liked their partner were significantly higher than ratings of how much they thought they were liked. This result shows the predicted liking gap. Results from the personality measures also showed that this liking gap was larger for people who scored higher on shyness.

Conclusions of the Study: These results suggest that people do underestimate how much they are liked in conversations with others. Further studies by these researchers supported these results, explored why the liking gap exists, and generalized the results to different lengths of conversations and more naturalistic situations.

KNOWLEDGE CHECK: CHAPTER SUMMARY

(You will find the answers in the Appendix.)

INTERPRETING THE BEHAVIOR OF OTHERS: SOCIAL COGNITION

- Our perceptions of others are guided by bottom-up processing—actual physical sensations—and (1) ____-down processing—our beliefs and (2) ____. For example, physical attractiveness significantly shapes our interpretations, and so do existing social schemas and (3) ____. In the self-fulfilling prophecy effect, social (4) ____ lead us to expect certain kinds of behavior from members of certain groups, and these expectations can cause the expected behavior. Stereotypes also lead to (5) ____ and discrimination. Prejudice can be reduced through repeated exposure to individual members of the stereotyped group or by adopting the perspective of group members.

- Attributions are the causes we assign to behaviors. According to the co-variation model, we rely on consistency, (6) ____, and consensus to make the appropriate inference. When a behavior is high on all three dimensions, we tend to make (7) ____ attributions—to credit an outside source; when a behavior is high in consistency but low in consensus and distinctiveness, we tend to make (8) ____ attributions—to credit inherent personality traits. When we consider the behavior of others and overestimate the role of (9) ____ factors and underestimate outside influences, we are making the (10) ____. The general rule in which we tend to attribute our own behavior to external sources and the behavior of others to internal sources is known as the (11) ____–____ effect. An exception to this rule is a (12) ____ bias, our tendency to take credit for actions that produce positive outcomes and to blame other people when our actions are questionable or lead to failure.

- Attitudes have (13) ____, (14) ____, and (15) ____ components. (The behavioral component is a predisposition to behave in a certain way; our attitudes don't always directly affect our behavior.) Attitudes form primarily from (16) ____, through classical and (17) ____ conditioning and (18) ____ learning. According to the elaboration (19) ____ model, our attitudes can be changed through a (20) ____ route, when we listen carefully to a message and judge it on its merits, or through a (21) ____ route, when superficial cues or mere exposure to a message affects us more. According to cognitive (22) ____ theory, inconsistencies between behavior and (23) ____ lead to internal
(24) ____, or dissonance, that is relieved by changing one's attitude. According to self- (25) ____ theory, we may also use our own behavior as the basis for our attitudes about ourselves.

BEHAVING IN THE PRESENCE OF OTHERS: SOCIAL INFLUENCE

- When we're in the presence of others, social (26) ____ may improve our (27) ____. Social (28) ____ occurs when being around others (29) ____ our performance.

- The sense of (30) ____ causes us to act out of (31) ____ concern for others. But the (32) ____ effect makes us reluctant to step forward and help when other people are present. A diffusion of (33) ____ comes from believing that someone else has already taken action or will soon get involved.

- People have a tendency toward social (34) ____, putting out (35) ____ effort when working with a (36) ____ than when working alone. (37) ____ occurs when we feel less accountable in the presence of others than when we're on our own. When someone's opinions, feelings, and behaviors reflect a group norm rather than individual preference, (38) ____ has occurred; this is especially likely if pressure to fit in arises from an in-group with which you share common features or identify.

- When the (39) ____ point of view within a group becomes stronger and more extreme with time, group (40) ____ has occurred. (41) ____ has occurred when group members become so interested in achieving a (42) ____ of opinion that they (43) ____ and even suppress dissenting views.

- When we respond to the orders of an authority figure or institution, we are showing (44) ____. In the Milgram experiment, (45) ____% of the research participants willingly followed orders to deliver electric shocks up to 450 volts to another person, despite the learner's pleas. The study has been criticized on ethical grounds, as well as for its procedures. However, in the 30 years since the experiment, the general procedure has been repeated and has (46) _____ Milgram's findings, although the degree of compliance that people will show depends on many factors.

- In most Western cultures, including the United States, people are taught from a very young age to adopt an (47) _____ view of the self; that is, they are rewarded for viewing themselves as unique individuals. In many non-Western cultures, especially in Asia, people adopt a very different, (48) _____ view of the self. They are taught to consider themselves as members of a group with common goals rather than as individuals striving to be different.

ESTABLISHING RELATIONS WITH OTHERS

- Physical attractiveness powerfully influences our behavior. An (49) _____ perspective predicts that we will be attracted to people who look youthful, vigorous, and (50) _____, or who may be able to provide protection and sustenance, because these qualities increase the likelihood of successful reproduction and child-rearing. The universality of attractiveness may reflect the fact that we seem programmed to prefer faces that represent the average, or represent the category of (51) _____. The perception of beauty does, however, have a strong (52) _____ component.

- Attraction to others depends on their proximity and (53) _____ to us, and on (54) _____, the tendency to return feelings that are shown toward us.

- (55) _____ love is an intense emotional state in which one individual is possessed by the powerful longing to be with another. (56) _____ love tends to be less emotional and intense and is characterized by feelings of trust and warmth. According to the (57) _____ theory, the experience of love has three major aspects—(58) _____, (59) _____, and (60) _____—components that change with time.

CRITICAL THINKING QUESTIONS

1. Do you think the social schemas that were activated in the telephone study were different for the men and the women? If so, in what way?

2. Suppose you were forced to make an attribution quickly, without much time for thought. Do you think quickly formed attributions are more likely to be internal or external? Explain.

3. Do you think it's likely that all people have an innate attitude, or preference, for pleasurable things over painful things? What other kinds of attitudes might be influenced by genetic factors?

4. Next time you visit a social media site, notice which ads rely on logical arguments and which use humor or celebrity endorsers. Do you see any connection between the type of product and the style of persuasion? What kinds of products are more likely to induce us to use central rather than peripheral processing?

5. When people conform, they act in ways that are inconsistent with their attitudes. What implications should this have for attitude change?

6. Why might it be adaptive for us to respond so readily to the demands of an authority figure?

7. Think about your own relationship experiences. Have you ever felt peer pressure to find a partner who meets a well-defined set of standards? How important were these factors in your decisions?

8. If you had to write a prescription for a successful marriage, how would you rate the dimensions of the triangle?

KEY TERMS

actor–observer effect (p. 474)

altruism (p. 482)

attitude (p. 465)

attributions (p. 472)

bystander effect (p. 483)

cognitive dissonance (p. 479)

companionate love (p. 499)

conformity (p. 485)

deindividuation (p. 485)

diffusion of responsibility (p. 484)

discrimination (p. 469)

elaboration likelihood model (p. 477)

external attribution (p. 473)

fundamental attribution error (p. 473)

group polarization (p. 487)

groupthink (p. 488)

in-group (p. 486)

internal attribution (p. 473)

obedience (p. 489)

ostracism (p. 486)

passionate love (p. 499)

prejudice (p. 469)

reciprocity (p. 498)

self-fulfilling prophecy effect (p. 468)

self-perception theory (p. 479)

self-serving bias (p. 475)

social cognition (p. 465)

social facilitation (p. 482)

social influence (p. 481)

social interference (p. 482)

social loafing (p. 484)

social psychology (p. 464)

social schema (p. 466)

source characteristics (p. 477)

stereotypes (p. 467)

iStockPhoto/Martin Dimitrov

14 **PSYCHOLOGICAL DISORDERS**

"You shouldn't really be reading this book, you know. In fact, put it down—now. The intentions of these authors are not pure . . . they don't have your best interest in mind. They want to convince you that you have no true control over your life. To them, you're nothing more than a machine shaped by the whims of changing environments; you're the product of forces outside of your control—biological drives, toilet-training habits, unbalanced mixtures of neurotransmitters in your brain.

"But you and I are more than that—we're more than the product of brain biochemistry or dirty little habits. We have inner control over our lives. You and I are in touch with the essence of the inner one, although perhaps it is only I who recognizes this fact at the moment. I've stopped you because it's time to prepare now . . . the first of the tribe arrived weeks ago . . . he's here, inside my head, and he's telling me the real truth. There's nothing to fear . . . we're still in control . . . it will be our choice, not theirs, to submit. And when we do, the truth about the conspiracy will be revealed to all. . . ."

Imagine being on the receiving end of such a conversation. What would be your reaction? At best, we suspect you'd categorize this person as odd; more likely, you'd label them as disturbed. Their thinking is certainly distorted, and they are more than a bit paranoid. But do they suffer from a *true psychological disorder* needing treatment, or are they simply eccentric? How can we tell? What are the criteria used to define and describe psychological disorders and abnormal behavior? Is distorted thinking merely a personal choice, a way to be different or unique, or is it something more like strep throat or a bladder infection—something that we should try to treat and cure?

THE PROBLEMS TO BE SOLVED: WHAT ARE PSYCHOLOGICAL DISORDERS?

In this chapter, we consider the classification and treatment of psychological disorders. Obviously, before treating a psychological problem, you must determine whether there is indeed a problem that requires treatment. Making this determination is more difficult than you might think. Let's imagine you arrive home tonight and find your roommate awake but slumped in a corner with his cap pulled down over his eyes. You ask him to explain, but he tells you to mind your own business. Later that night, you hear sobbing and crying coming from behind his locked bedroom door. His bizarre behavior continues for the next two days. He refuses to respond to questions, he stops going to class, and he refuses to eat or clean himself. He's suffering from a psychological disorder, right? Perhaps. But suppose you learn that his father and mother were just killed in an automobile accident. What would your reaction be now? Would you conclude that he's psychologically disturbed or that he's simply showing an intense but normal grief reaction? To help you understand how psychologists diagnose psychological disorders, our discussion will revolve around the following three-part question: How do we conceptualize, classify, and understand abnormal behavior? Once you see how psychologists think about abnormality, the stage will be set for treatment, which is covered in depth in Chapter 15.

Conceptualizing Abnormality: What Makes Behavior Abnormal?

A person who suffers from one or more psychological problems is typically classified as abnormal. Indeed, the terms *abnormal* and *abnormal behavior* are often used as roughly equivalent to the term *psychological disorder*. But over the years, psychologists have struggled with how best to define abnormality. When people behave abnormally, their actions tend to be unusual or dysfunctional, and they often appear to be suffering from considerable personal distress. But for reasons we'll discuss in the first section of the chapter, none of these criteria alone is sufficient to capture the concept. Most conceptualizations of abnormality rely on multiple criteria.

Classifying Psychological Disorders

Even if we reach agreement about the proper way to define abnormality, we still need a way to name and classify the underlying disorders that lead to abnormal behavior. Psychologists and psychiatrists have worked hard to develop a system for the diagnosis and classification of psychological disorders. There are many kinds of known psychological problems—ranging from anxiety disorders to depression to schizophrenia—and each is classified by a well-defined set of criteria. Although it's a common belief among the general public that psychological disorders are idiosyncratic—which means they arise in different ways for different individuals—you'll see that most disorders actually produce characteristics that are consistent and reliable.

Understanding Psychological Disorders: Biological, Cognitive, or Environmental?

In the final section of the chapter, we'll discuss how researchers attempt to understand the causes of psychological disorders. What causes an anxiety disorder, depression, or schizophrenia? Do psychological disorders result from some kind of mental breakdown, or are they simply adaptive reactions to stress? If it's a breakdown, is the cause of the breakdown biological or environmental? We'll consider the major theoretical tools used by mental health professionals to explain abnormal behavior. Not surprisingly, the answer to many psychological problems lies partly in biology and partly in the environment.

CONCEPTUALIZING ABNORMALITY: WHAT MAKES BEHAVIOR ABNORMAL?

When you encounter someone who claims that voices in their head are busy plotting a conspiracy, it's not difficult to categorize this behavior as abnormal; clearly, this person is in trouble and in need of some professional help. But sharp dividing lines don't always exist between normal and abnormal behavior. Sometimes behavior that appears abnormal can turn out to be a reasonable reaction to a stressful event, such as the roommate's reaction to the death of their parents. It's also the case that a behavior that seems abnormal in one culture can appear to be perfectly normal in another (e.g., Koç & Kafa, 2019; Rathod, 2017). Entering a trance state and experiencing visual hallucinations is considered abnormal in Western cultures, but in other cultures it may not be (Bentall, 1990).

A trance state is likely to be classified as abnormal in Western cultures, but not necessarily in other cultures.

SOPA Images / LightRocket

Even within a culture, conceptions of abnormality can change over time. For many years, homosexuality was considered abnormal by the psychological community—in fact, it was considered a psychological disorder. But this view of homosexuality is rejected by psychologists today. Fifty years ago, a strong dependence on tobacco wouldn't have raised an eyebrow, but today if you're hooked on tobacco, you could easily be classified as having a substance-related disorder. Given these changing conceptions, psychologists are justifiably cautious when applying the label of abnormality. Behavior usually must meet a set of criteria before it's considered abnormal (Frances & Widiger, 2012).

Characteristics of Abnormal Behavior

Over the years, researchers have proposed a number of defining criteria for abnormality. In each case, as you'll see, the proposed criteria capture some but not all of the important features of what is agreed to be abnormal behavior.

Statistical Deviance

One way to define abnormal behavior is in terms of **statistical deviance**, or infrequency. Any given behavior, such as arguing with your neighbors or hearing voices, occurs with a certain probability in society at large. Most people have argued with their neighbors, but few actually converse with disembodied voices. According to the concept of statistical deviance, a behavior is abnormal if it occurs infrequently among the members of a population. As you've learned elsewhere in this text, it's not unusual for psychologists to classify behavior on the basis of statistical frequency. For example, the term used to define superior intellectual ability—*gifted*—was defined with respect to statistical frequency, as was the concept of an *intellectual disability*. So, it should come as no surprise that statistical frequencies have been used to define abnormality.

But statistical deviance—that is, something that is extreme or different from the average—can't be used as the sole criterion for labeling a behavior as abnormal. It's easy to come up with a list of behaviors that are statistically infrequent but are not abnormal in a psychological sense. For example, LeBron James has skills on the basketball court that are extreme, and thereby statistically deviant, but to be a great athlete does not make one abnormal. Similarly, only a handful of individuals have reached the intellectual heights of Albert Einstein or Isaac Newton, but superior intelligence is not abnormal in the usual psychological sense of the word. Another problem is the cutoff point: Just how infrequent or unusual must a behavior be to be characterized as abnormal? So far, psychologists have failed to find a satisfactory answer to this question.

Although Bill Gates and Yo-Yo Ma are statistically deviant in some respects, would you classify them as psychologically abnormal?

Getty Images / Getty Images Entertainment
Handout/Biden Inaugural Committee via Getty Images

Cultural Deviance

Another criterion is **cultural deviance**, which compares a behavior to existing cultural norms. In this case, a behavior is considered abnormal if it violates the accepted standards of society. For example, it's not considered normal or acceptable to walk to class in the nude. Such a behavior breaks the established rules of our culture, and if you do it, it's likely that people will think you have a serious problem.

But once again, cultural deviance by itself fails as a sufficient criterion. Many people who have committed a crime violate the established norms of society—stealing cars or embezzling money, for example. Such behavior might be abnormal by both statistical and cultural standards, but that doesn't mean all criminals suffer from psychological disorders. There are also many people who suffer from legitimate psychological problems, such as anxiety or depression, who never violate a law or established standard of society. Finally, as we just discussed, behaviors that are abnormal in one culture may be considered normal in another. There are cultures in the world, for instance, where nakedness in public breaks no established cultural rules. People who suffer from psychological disorders may indeed violate cultural norms in some instances, but often they do not.

Emotional Distress

A third characteristic of many kinds of abnormal behavior is the presence of personal or **emotional distress**. People who suffer from psychological disorders often experience great despair and unhappiness. They feel hopeless, lost, and alienated from others. In fact, it's the emotional distress that usually leads them to seek professional help for their problems. But not all disorders make people unhappy; there are lots of people who have little contact with reality but seem perfectly content in their fantasy world. Likewise, there are many distressed people in the world—for example, those who have recently lost a loved one or a job—who would not be classified as abnormal by the psychological community.

Dysfunction

A final criterion for abnormality focuses on **dysfunction**: Has there been a breakdown in normal functioning that prevents the person from successfully following adaptive strategies? People who suffer from psychological disorders are often unable to function well in typical daily activities—they may not eat properly, clean themselves, or be able to hold a job. Their ability to think clearly may be impaired, which affects their ability to adapt successfully in their environment. As you'll see later, the assessment of global functioning—defined as the ability to adapt in social, personal, and occupational environments—often plays a large role in the diagnosis and treatment of psychological disorders.

Summarizing the Criteria

You've seen that abnormal behavior can be statistically or culturally deviant, it can involve personal or emotional distress, and it can signal impairment or dysfunction. Normal behavior, then, could be any behavior that is relatively common, does not cause personal distress, or generally leads to adaptive consequences. However, none of the criteria that we've discussed is sufficient to diagnose a person with a psychological disorder. Crying hysterically for hours at a time may be a normal grief reaction, or it may

FIGURE 14.1 ■ The Normal-to-Abnormal Continuum

"Abnormal" and "normal" are not fixed categories but endpoints on a continuum. To a certain degree, everyone has acted unusually, suffered from emotional distress, or failed to follow an adaptive strategy.

Normal	Criterion	Abnormal
Common	Statistical deviance	Rare
Acceptable	Cultural deviance	Unacceptable
Low	Emotional distress	High
Adaptive	Dysfunction	Maladaptive

signal a serious disorder. Even a behavior that seems to be clearly abnormal—such as a paranoid delusion that people are out to get you—might be adaptive in some environments.

You should also recognize that "abnormal" and "normal" are not rigid categories. Each of us can relate in one way or another to the criteria of abnormality we've just discussed. We all know people who have occasionally acted unusually, suffered from emotional distress, or failed to function well in everyday settings. Many psychological disorders are characterized by behaviors or feelings that are merely exaggerations of normal ones, such as anxiety, feelings of sadness, or concerns about one's health. Consequently, it's better to think about normal and abnormal behavior as endpoints on a continuum rather than as nonoverlapping categories (see Figure 14.1). For a summary of the main criteria for defining abnormality, see Concept Review 14.1.

CONCEPT REVIEW 14.1
CRITERIA FOR DEFINING ABNORMALITY

Criterion	Description	Example
Statistical deviance	Behavior that occurs infrequently among the members of a population	Jon goes back to make sure his front door is locked exactly 12 times each morning. As he walks to the door, he mutters over and over, "Lock the door . . ." No one else in the neighborhood does this.
Cultural deviance	Behavior that violates the accepted standards of society	Jon notices that each time he comes back to his front door, talking to himself, his neighbors look at him rather nervously, and they tend to avoid him at other times.
Emotional distress	Great despair and unhappiness	Jon is very distressed by his compulsive behavior.
Dysfunction	A breakdown in normal functioning	Jon's routine of checking his front door 12 times every morning has made him late for work a number of times, and his job is in jeopardy.

The Concept of Insanity

Behavior can mean different things depending on the context in which it occurs—something that's abnormal in one situation may be quite normal in another. Yet regardless of where you travel in the world, some behaviors will always be recognized as abnormal: Consider the serial killer Jeffrey Dahmer, who admitted to butchering, cannibalizing, and having sex with the dead bodies of more than a dozen young men and boys. Everyone, including the mental health professionals who examined Dahmer, was in agreement—this was a man suffering from some serious psychological problems.

But from a legal standpoint Dahmer was judged by a jury to be perfectly sane. Despite the best efforts of his legal team to have him declared mentally unfit, and thus not responsible for his crimes, Dahmer was found legally sane. He stood trial and was convicted of his crimes (later, while serving his life sentence, he was brutally murdered by a fellow inmate). Sounds perplexing, but *insanity* is a *legal* concept rather than a psychological one; in fact, the term *insanity* has been out of favor among mental health professionals for about a century (see K. Weiss et al., 2019).

Its definition varies somewhat from state to state, but **insanity** is usually defined in terms of the defendant's thought processes *at the time of the crime*: A criminal is insane, and therefore not guilty by reason of insanity, if, because of a "mental disease," the individual fails to appreciate or understand that certain actions are wrong in a legal or moral sense. Dahmer was judged capable of understanding the wrongfulness of his actions; as a result, he failed the insanity test, even though he was clearly suffering from serious psychological problems.

Most mental health professionals accept that people with serious psychological disorders are sometimes incapable of judging the appropriateness of their actions. As you'll soon see, psychological disorders can lead to distorted views of the world—affected individuals not only act in ways that are abnormal, but their very thoughts, beliefs, and perceptions of the world can be wildly distorted as well. But exercise caution: It's important not to confuse the concept of insanity with the concept of a psychological disorder.

Jeffrey Dahmer
Ralf-Finn Hestoft/CORBIS/Corbis via Getty Images

The Medical Model: Conceptualizing Abnormality as a Disease

To understand how disorders are classified by the psychological community, we need to discuss the *medical model* of diagnosis. According to the **medical model**, abnormal behavior is caused by an underlying *disease*—a kind of mental *illness*—that can be *cured* with the appropriate therapy. This conception of abnormality has been quite influential. As you already know, there are good reasons to believe that behavior is strongly influenced by biological factors, such as the actions of neurotransmitters in the brain. In addition, biomedical therapies, such as the administration of psychoactive drugs, are often effective in treating psychological problems. It's also the case that most psychological disorders can be classified in terms of *symptoms*. Depression, for example, typically leads to one or more of the following: sad mood, diminished interest in pleasure, difficulty in sleeping, feelings of worthlessness, and so on. The medical influence is deeply ingrained in the very language used by psychologists—they speak of mental health, mental illness, or psychopathology in much the same way a physician describes a medical condition.

But is the medical model an appropriate way to view abnormality? Some researchers believe it's wrong to draw direct comparisons between physical illness and psychological problems (Szasz, 1961, 2000). Both strep throat and depression lead to a set of reliable symptoms. But we know that strep throat is caused by a physical problem—bacteria; at this point, the cause of depression is still being debated. In addition, people often seek treatment for psychological problems that are perhaps more accurately described as problems in living. How these adjustment problems are interpreted also seems to depend on the particular social or cultural context, which is not the case for most medical conditions. Some kinds of bizarre behavior thought to be abnormal in one culture can be considered normal in another, but strep throat produces fever and pain regardless of the cultural environment.

Problems Associated With Labeling

Critics of the medical model also express concern about **diagnostic labeling effects**. Labeling a psychological problem as an illness or a disorder tends to attach a stigma that can be difficult to overcome (Hipes et al., 2016). A number of studies have found that applying the label "mental patient" leads people to interpret behavior in a far different light than they would otherwise. In one study, professional therapists watched a videotape of a man describing his personal adjustment problems (Langer & Abelson, 1974). If, prior to viewing the tape, the therapists were told that the man was a mental patient, they rated his adjustment problems more negatively than did other therapists who were simply told he was a job applicant (see Figure 14.2). Methodological issues have been raised about these types of studies (e.g., ecological validity), but as we've stressed in previous chapters, people's expectations clearly do importantly influence how they interpret new information.

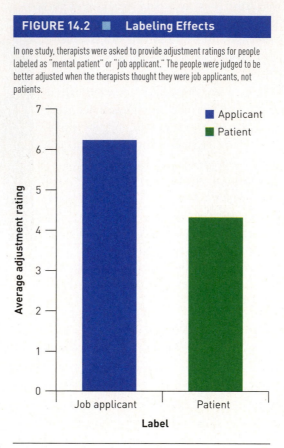

FIGURE 14.2   ■   Labeling Effects

In one study, therapists were asked to provide adjustment ratings for people labeled as "mental patient" or "job applicant." The people were judged to be better adjusted when the therapists thought they were job applicants, not patients.

Source: Data from Langer & Abelson, 1974.

The Rosenhan Study

In one particularly influential study of labeling effects, David Rosenhan, along with seven other co-investigators, arrived separately at several psychiatric hospitals in the early 1970s with the complaint that they were hearing voices (Rosenhan, 1973). Actually, each of the participants was perfectly normal. They simply adopted the role of a pseudopatient—they feigned, or faked, a disorder to see how labeling would affect their subsequent treatment. On arrival they reported to the psychiatric staff that they were hearing a disembodied voice in their head, a voice that repeated things like "empty," "hollow," and "thud." They were all admitted to hospitals, and virtually all received the diagnosis of schizophrenia (a condition, as you'll see later, characterized by serious disturbances in thought and emotion).

Again, the purpose of the study was to see how an initial diagnosis of schizophrenia would affect subsequent treatment. From the point of admission, none of the participants continued to act strangely. In all interactions with the hospital staff, they acted normally and gave no indications that they were suffering from a disorder. However, despite their normal behavior, none of the staff ever recognized them as pseudopatients; indeed, written hospital reports later revealed that the staff members tended to interpret normal behaviors as symptomatic of a disorder. It was the real patients who felt the researchers somehow did not belong; several voiced their suspicions, claiming, "You're not crazy. You're a journalist or a professor" (these comments were partly made in reaction to the fact that the pseudopatients spent time taking notes). Once the pseudopatients had been admitted and labeled as "abnormal," their behaviors were seen by the staff through the lens of expectation, and normal, sane behavior was never recognized as such. On average, the pseudopatients remained in the hospital for 19 days—the stays ranged from under a week to almost two months—and on release all were given the diagnosis of schizophrenia "in remission" (which means not currently active).

The Rosenhan study is considered important because it suggests that diagnostic labels can become self-fulfilling prophecies. Once you're diagnosed, you're likely to be treated as if you're suffering from a disorder, and this treatment (1) may make it difficult to recognize normal behavior when it occurs, and (2) may increase the likelihood that you'll act in an abnormal way. If the people in your environment expect you to act abnormally, you may very well start to act in a way that's consistent with those expectations (see Chapter 13).

Since its publication in 1973, the Rosenhan study has been widely analyzed in psychological circles (see Cummins, 2017). Its lessons about the hazards of labeling are clear enough, but questions have been raised about the ethics of the study as well as the conclusions that were reached (Bartels & Peters, 2017). For example, the admission of the pseudopatients by the hospital staff, as well as their subsequent diagnosis, was reasonable given the patients' reported symptoms. The diagnosis of a psychological disorder depends on what the patient reports, and the trained professionals in this case had no reason to assume that the patients were lying or manufacturing symptoms. In addition, it's possible and even reasonable to dispute the claim that the attending staff failed to recognize that the pseudopatients were acting normally. After all, they were released with the label "in remission," so the staff must have recognized that they were no longer acting in an abnormal way (Spitzer, 1975). More troubling, though, are recent suggestions that Rosenhan fabricated some of his data and selectively reported how some of the pseudopatients were treated (see Cahalan, 2019).

KNOWLEDGE CHECK 14.1

Check your knowledge of how abnormality is conceptualized by deciding whether each of the following statements is true or false. (You will find the answers in the Appendix.)

1. When a behavior occurs infrequently among members of a population, it meets the criterion of cultural deviance. *True or False*?

2. To receive the diagnosis of a psychological disorder, a person must be suffering from a certain amount of emotional distress. *True or False*?

3. In many cases, abnormal behaviors are simply exaggerated versions of normal behaviors. *True or False*?

4. According to the medical model, psychological disorders can and should be classified in terms of symptoms. *True or False*?

5. In the Rosenhan study, hospital staff members quickly picked up on the fact that the pseudopatients were no longer acting abnormally. *True or False*?

CLASSIFYING PSYCHOLOGICAL DISORDERS

Now, finally, we turn to the actual classification process. As mentioned in the previous section, specific psychological disorders are often diagnosed in terms of defining criteria or symptoms. This is the approach used by the *Diagnostic and Statistical Manual of Mental Disorders*, published by the American Psychiatric Association. From this point forward, we'll refer to this manual by its more commonly used acronym: the **DSM**. The purpose of the DSM is to provide clinicians with a well-defined classification system, based on objective and measurable criteria, so that reliable diagnoses of psychological disorders can be produced worldwide; it is also designed to coordinate with the World Health Organization's International Classification of Diseases (ICD-11), which covers medical as well as psychological problems. The DSM is intended only for the purposes of diagnosis and classification; it does not suggest therapies or methods of treatment.

How does the classification system work? The DSM contains descriptions, symptoms, and other criteria for diagnosing mental disorders. Each of its chapters is dedicated to a broad diagnostic category (such as depressive disorders or anxiety disorders). However, people are rarely pigeonholed into a single diagnostic category by clinicians because more than one psychological disorder can occur in the same individual. In fact, many mental health professionals disagree with placing psychological problems into discrete categories (e.g., obsessive–compulsive disorder), preferring instead to characterize disorders in terms of dimensions that can co-occur across conditions (Widiger & Gore, 2014). The latest edition of the DSM (DSM-5) was partly designed to integrate dimensional and categorical approaches to classification (American Psychiatric Association, 2013).

The clinician's goal is to describe the full range of symptoms, the severity of those symptoms, and other pertinent information. It is important to know a person's medical history, for example, because some medical conditions (such as Alzheimer's disease) can contribute to abnormal behavior. Environmental or psychosocial problems need to be considered as well. Is the client going through a difficult divorce, or has the client recently been fired? Finally, it matters to the clinician how someone is functioning in daily life. If one is so severely impaired that one cannot hold a job, go to school, or even keep clean, it may be necessary to initiate a period of hospitalization. Figure 14.3 summarizes some of the disorders we'll be discussing in the following sections and presents data on how likely each disorder is to occur in the population at large.

Anxiety Disorders: Fear and Apprehension

We begin with anxiety disorders. Although it may be difficult to understand the paranoid delusions of those suffering from more severe disorders, it's not difficult to understand the apprehension,

DSM-5

H.S. Photos / Alamy Stock Photo

FIGURE 14.3 ◼ **Prevalence Rates for Various Psychological Disorders**

Each bar shows the percentage of individuals in a sample of more than 8,000 participants who reported suffering from the listed psychological disorder during the previous 12 months or earlier. Note: A given individual might have reported suffering from more than one of these disorders concurrently.

Source: Data from Kessler et al., 1994.

worry, and fear that characterize anxiety. Most people understand anxiety because it's often an important part of our everyday experience. We become anxious when we meet someone new, when awaiting the beginning of an exam, or when a car swerves dangerously close. Moreover, even though the physical and psychological changes that accompany anxiety can seem unpleasant, anxiety is basically an adaptive human response. The physical changes prepare the body to take action—to fight or flee—and thereby increase the chances of survival. The psychological changes cause us to become attentive—we monitor our environment more closely so we're apt to notice a potentially dangerous event when it occurs.

But there is a dark side to anxiety. When anxiety becomes too persistent and intense, it interferes with the ability to function. **Anxiety disorders** are diagnosed when the levels of apprehension and worry become so extreme that overall behavior is impaired in some way. For example, if you consistently fail exams because you can't collect your thoughts, or if you refuse to leave the house because you're convinced you'll experience a frightening panic attack, you're likely to be suffering from an anxiety disorder. There are several kinds of anxiety disorders, and each is defined by its own set of DSM diagnostic criteria. We'll concentrate on some common ones in this section: generalized anxiety disorder, panic disorder, phobias, and social anxiety disorder. In order to receive a particular diagnosis, though, the main symptoms cannot be better explained by a medical condition (e.g., a thyroid problem) or by some other mental disorder.

Generalized Anxiety Disorder

The defining characteristic of **generalized anxiety disorder** is excessive and chronic worrying that lasts for a significant period of time (e.g., on most days, for 6 months or more). The anxiety is "free-floating," as Sigmund Freud described it, and can't be attributed to any single identifiable source. People who suffer from this problem worry in general (which is captured in the name *generalized anxiety disorder*), and they fret constantly about any number of minor things (T. A. Brown et al., 2001). More important, the worrying is unrealistic—there's usually little, if any, chance that the feared event will actually occur.

People afflicted with generalized anxiety disorder are chronically tense. Not surprisingly, they often report a range of physical symptoms, especially muscle tension and fatigue, and they're likely to have trouble sleeping and become easily irritated as well. They're also likely to spend a lot of time worrying about the future and avoiding events with possible negative outcomes. Such symptoms are easy to understand—after all, these people are living in a world of perpetual worry; the worst, they assume, is about to happen.

Panic Disorder

Generalized anxiety is marked by chronic, unfocused worrying. In **panic disorder**, people suffer from recurrent episodes, or attacks, of extremely intense fear or dread. A panic attack is a sudden and alarming event, and it can make you feel as if you're about to die (or, sometimes, go crazy). Panic attacks are brief, but they produce high levels of anxiety and, as a result, are accompanied by a collection of physical symptoms: a pounding heart, shortness of breath, sweating, nausea, chest pains, and so on. These symptoms can be devastating experiences, and they often lead to persistent concern about the possibility of having additional attacks. It's worth noting that a single isolated panic attack is not sufficient for diagnosis of a panic disorder; the attacks need to occur repeatedly (see Meuret et al., 2017).

Panic disorder is sometimes associated with an additional complication, called *agoraphobia*, that comes from the worry that further panic attacks might occur. **Agoraphobia**—which translates from the Greek as "fear of the marketplace"—causes people to restrict their normal activities in an extreme way (Sanchez-Meca et al., 2010). People with agoraphobia typically avoid crowded or public places, such as shopping malls or restaurants, because they're afraid they'll experience a panic attack and be unable to cope effectively with the situation (especially the accompanying physical symptoms). In severe cases, people with agoraphobia may simply refuse to leave their house; home, it is reasoned, is the only safe place in the world. For obvious reasons, both panic disorder and agoraphobia can significantly reduce one's ability to function successfully.

A person with agoraphobia may be reluctant to leave home, fearing that once one is outside, a panic attack will result in helplessness.

iStockPhoto/Highwaystarz-Photography

Phobic Disorder

The defining feature of **phobic disorder** (or *specific phobia*) is a highly focused fear of a specific object or situation—such as a bug, a snake, flying, heights, a closed place, or a storm. Like the other anxiety disorders we've discussed, phobias are irrational, which means that the level of anxiety the object or situation produces is in no way justified by reality. Elevators do fall, snakes do bite, planes do crash—but these events are rare and do not justify daily worry. Many people show mild forms of phobic reactions—and, again, in some cases the object of the anxiety is indeed dangerous (some snakes do kill)—but in specific phobic disorder the fear and distress can be severely disabling. To avoid the anxiety-producing object or situation, people with phobic disorder might significantly disrupt their normal routines; they may avoid work or school or travel in the slight chance that they will encounter the object of their fear.

Specific phobias typically revolve around one of four classes of fear-inducing objects or situations: (1) animals (insects, snakes, dogs, and the like), (2) natural environments (storms, heights, water, and the like), (3) blood-injection-injury (the sight of blood or even the thought of an injection), and (4) specific situations (fears associated with public transportation or closed-in places). There are other phobias as well—such as fear of choking or fear of costumed characters—that don't fit easily into these established categories. Most people who suffer from phobias tend to have more than one, and often more than one type (Stinson et al., 2007). For a look at how likely the various phobias are to occur among the general population, see Figure 14.4.

How do you feel about snakes and flying in an airplane? Both are common sources of phobias.

iStockPhoto/hobo_018
iStockPhoto/MartiSaiz

FIGURE 14.4   ■   Prevalence Rates of Various Phobias

Each bar shows the percentage of people in a large sample who reported suffering from a particular kind of phobia.

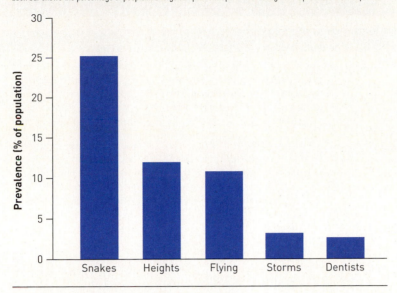

Source: Data from Agras, Sylvester, & Oliveau, 1969.

Social Anxiety Disorder

Also known as social phobia, **social anxiety disorder** occurs when people become extremely anxious and self-conscious in everyday social situations. People with this disorder often have an excessive fear of being watched and judged by others and of performing actions that might embarrass them. Like the other anxiety disorders, social anxiety disorder is often accompanied by physical symptoms (blushing, sweating, trembling, nausea), which only magnify the level of worry. The disorder might manifest itself only in very specific situations, such as talking to other people, or it can occur broadly across a variety of social situations. Social anxiety disorder is recognized currently as one of the most common psychological disorders (Swinson, 2005).

Gender and Culture

In general, women are more likely to suffer from anxiety disorders than men, although this trend differs somewhat across cultures (Remes et al., 2016). About two-thirds of people diagnosed with generalized anxiety disorder are women, as are three-fourths of those with agoraphobia, and the ratio of women to men for specific phobias could be as high as 4 to 1. Social anxiety disorder is more prevalent in women than in men, and the clinical effects tend to be more severe as well (Asher et al., 2017). Why is there a sex difference? Researchers are not certain, although cultural or environmental explanations seem most likely. Men are typically raised to "tough things out," which means they're less likely to report the symptoms of anxiety or seek treatment. Men are also more likely to "treat" the symptoms of anxiety by turning to alcohol or drugs (with sometimes devastating consequences). Other factors may be involved as well, such as physiological reactivity or genetic vulnerabilities (see McLean & Anderson, 2009).

Anxiety disorders occur in all cultures of the world, but the focus of the anxiety can differ, as well as the chances that the disorder will be reported. For example, for unknown reasons, Hispanics and Asian Americans in the United States have a somewhat lower risk of developing a specific phobia than white Americans (Stinson et al., 2007). In developing countries, people are more likely to focus on the physical symptoms of anxiety and tend not to report the subjective feelings associated with panic, dread, or worry. Culture undoubtedly plays a significant role in the onset of these disorders as well, but we'll delay our discussion of this possibility until later in the chapter. For a summary of the different anxiety disorders, see Concept Review 14.2.

CONCEPT REVIEW 14.2
ANXIETY DISORDERS

Disorder	Description	Example
Generalized anxiety disorder	Excessive and chronic worrying that lasts for a significant period. Accompanied by excessive autonomic activity (e.g., increased respiration, heart rate).	Sophia spends most of her day worrying about the safety of her loved ones. Her stomach bothers her, and she experiences heart palpitations.
Panic disorder	Recurrent episodes or "attacks" of extremely intense fear or dread. Sometimes accompanied by agoraphobia, the fear of being in public due to anticipation of another panic attack.	During her daily drive to work, Sophia's heart suddenly began to race, and she had trouble catching her breath. She felt an extreme sense of dread and began to sweat. A trip to the emergency room revealed nothing wrong.
Specific phobia	A highly focused fear of a specific object or situation. Most focus on animals, natural environments, blood–injection–injury, or specific situations.	Sophia refused to take the new COVID vaccine because she is deathly afraid of needles.
Social anxiety disorder	Marked fear or anxiety about one or more social situations. Individuals fear that they will act in a way or show anxiety that will lead to a negative evaluation in a social setting.	Sophia never goes to parties. She is convinced people will think negative thoughts about her, so she avoids most social interactions.

Obsessive–Compulsive Disorder

Obsessive–compulsive disorder is characterized by persistent, uncontrollable thoughts and urges, called *obsessions*, or by the presence of a compelling need to perform one or more actions repeatedly, which is called a *compulsion* (see Hirschtritt et al., 2017). Have you ever had part of a song or jingle ramble endlessly through your head—one that keeps repeating despite your best efforts to stop it? So-called "earworms" are somewhat like obsessions, although in obsessive–compulsive disorder the obsessive thoughts tend to focus on fears (such as being contaminated by germs), doubts (such as forgetting to turn off the stove), and impulses (such as hurting oneself or another).

Compulsions consist of cleaning or checking or other actions that prevent unwanted thoughts or urges from occurring. For example, you might repeat the alphabet aloud over and over in an effort to divert your thinking away from a frightening or inappropriate aggressive or sexual impulse. Generally, compulsive behaviors are designed to reduce the anxiety or distress caused by obsessions. In extreme cases, the compulsions are so repetitive and ritualistic that they essentially prevent the sufferer from leading anything resembling a normal life. Some people become housebound, relentlessly cleaning rooms; others feel irresistibly compelled to leave work 10 to 15 times a day to check and make sure the stove wasn't left on. Interestingly, in the majority of such cases the affected individuals understand that their actions are irrational and of little adaptive value. The disorder simply compels the action.

Not surprisingly, obsessive–compulsive disorder is usually associated with anxiety. In fact, the disorder is sometimes classified as an anxiety disorder. However, not all obsessions or compulsions generate marked anxiety or distress. For this reason, some mental health professionals believe it should be classified as its own diagnostic category as it was in the most recent edition of the DSM.

Somatic Symptom Disorders: Body and Mind

A common phenomenon, called the *medical student syndrome*, often plagues medical students as they first learn about the various diseases of the body. The students find that the symptoms described in class, or in their textbooks, are increasingly familiar and personal. A deep pain that appears suddenly in the night is interpreted as a signal for the final stages of pancreatic cancer; that darkening blemish on the forehead becomes the rare form of skin cancer that often accompanies AIDS. In almost every case the student is perfectly healthy, but the mind plays its tricks, and the student fears the worst.

Mental health professionals classify psychological problems that focus on the physical body as **somatic symptom disorders** (also known as *somatoform disorders; soma* means "body"). Obviously, like medical students, most people have experienced imagined illnesses at some point in their lives. You're probably familiar with the everyday term *hypochondriac* (or *hypochondriasis*), which refers to someone who worries about illness or physical symptoms. But when the worry is excessive, and not typically grounded in any physical reality, a true psychological disorder may be indicated.

The key characteristic of somatic symptom disorders is a persistent preoccupation with health (Kurlansik & Maffei, 2016). People with these disorders can have specific body complaints (such as continuing pain), or they can simply worry excessively about the possibility of contracting a serious disease. The pain in the side, the slight case of indigestion, the occasional irregular heartbeat—each might be interpreted as symptomatic of a serious medical condition. Moreover, unlike the situation for the average medical student, these preoccupations persist for months and often cause significant distress and impaired functioning. People suffering from somatic symptom disorders typically devote a great deal of their time and energy to these symptoms or health concerns. Constant medical checkups may be requested, or doctors may be avoided out of fear that the suspected diagnosis will be confirmed.

One kind of somatic symptom disorder, called **conversion disorder**, produces real physical or neurological impairment. Someone with conversion disorder might report being blind, or paralyzed, or unable to speak; the person might even experience seizures resembling those found in epilepsy or other neurological disorders (Bowman, 1998). These are not feigned symptoms; that is, these problems are not intentionally produced by the individual to gain sympathy or attention. These are real problems, although no physical cause can be discovered. Neuroscientists are using imaging techniques in an effort to understand how and why the brain produces the physical effects (e.g., de Lange et al., 2007).

Obviously, in such cases there's always the possibility that a true neurological or other physical problem does exist; physical problems are indeed sometimes misdiagnosed as conversion disorder (see Feinstein, 2018). But when the reported problems disappear after effective therapy, a psychological origin is usually indicated. You may remember from our discussion of personality in Chapter 11 that Freud often used his

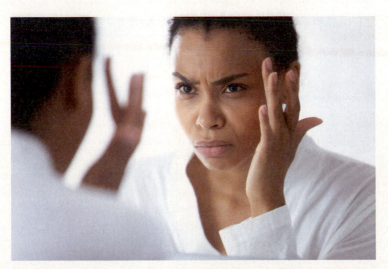

People suffering from somatoform disorders imagine that normal physical characteristics are symptoms of disease.

iStockPhoto/fizkes

psychoanalytic techniques to treat patients with conversion disorder (although the problem was known as *hysteria* in his day). In fact, the term *conversion*, as used here, originates from psychodynamic theory and Freud's proposal that unconscious conflicts have been converted into a physical form.

Gender and Culture

Somatic symptom disorders occur somewhat more frequently in women than in men, but the differences are not large (Kirmayer et al., 2003). Each of the disorders occurs cross-culturally as well, but there are some unique expressions in specific cultures. A condition called *koro*, for example, occurs mainly in Asian men—it's characterized by a persistent fear that the genitals will retract into the abdomen (Dan et al., 2017). A related condition, known as *dhat*, occurs mainly in India and is characterized by anxiety associated with the loss of semen from sexual activity (Kar & Sarkar, 2015).

Dissociative Disorders: Disruptions of Identity or Awareness

Dissociative disorders are defined by the separation, or *dissociation*, of conscious awareness from previous thoughts or memories. People affected by these disorders lose memory for some specific aspect of their life, or even their entire sense of identity. The theme of the confused amnesiac, searching for a lost identity, has been explored repeatedly in films throughout the years. We'll focus our attention on three types of dissociative disorder: dissociative amnesia, dissociative fugue, and dissociative identity disorder.

Dissociative Amnesia

In Chapter 8, when we tackled remembering and forgetting, we discussed various kinds of amnesia, or the inability to remember or retain personal experiences. It was noted that amnesia could result from either physical factors (such as brain damage) or psychological factors (such as traumatic stress). In **dissociative amnesia**, which is assumed to be psychological in origin, the person is unable to remember important personal information. The amnesia can be general, as in the failure to remember one's identity or family history, or it can be localized, such as the failure to remember a specific traumatic life experience. In dissociative amnesia, the forgetting can last for hours or years. It often disappears as mysteriously as it arose.

Dissociative Fugue

In **dissociative fugue**, there is also a loss of personal identity—people forget who they are—but it's accompanied by an escape or flight from the home environment (fugue literally means "flight"). Imagine leaving for work or school as usual only to "awaken" later in a different city or state. Sometimes the fugue state can last months or even years; some individuals experiencing this disorder have even adopted different identities in their new locale. Recovery can be sudden and often complete, but people will typically claim that they have no knowledge of their activities during the blackout period.

Dissociative Identity Disorder

In what is perhaps the most baffling of all dissociative disorders, **dissociative identity disorder**, a person alternates among what appear to be two or more distinct identities or personality states (hence the alternative name, *multiple personality disorder*).

In dissociative identity disorder, the unique personalities or identities appear to take control of one's thoughts and actions, one personality at a time. More important, the personality in control will profess to have only limited awareness of the other personality inhabitants. Commonly, there is interpersonality amnesia, which means that events experienced while the person is inhabited by personality A cannot be remembered when the person is occupied by personality B (Eich et al., 1997). It's for this reason that the disorder is classified as *dissociative*—there is a separation of current conscious awareness from prior thoughts and memories. Dozens of different identities may be involved, including both men and women, and a given identity will tend to have unique physical attributes, such as a distinct tone of voice, facial expression, handwriting style, or behavioral habit.

Kenneth Bianchi, known as the Hillside Strangler, claimed that he could not be held responsible for the rape and murder of several California women because he suffered from dissociative identity disorder. The evidence presented at trial suggested that Bianchi was faking the disorder; he was later convicted and sentenced to life imprisonment.

Bettmann / Getty Images

Controversy surrounds the diagnosis of dissociative identity disorder. First, this disorder often co-occurs with other psychological problems (such as depression and somatic symptom disorders), so it's difficult to pinpoint the ultimate cause of any particular symptom (Ross et al., 1990). Second, although each of the observed personalities may be distinguished on the basis of personality tests or physiological measures, we still cannot be completely certain about the origins of these differences—other factors, such as mood or arousal differences, may partly account for the distinct performance patterns (Fahy, 1988; Lilienfeld, 1994). Third, studies have found that the interpersonality "amnesia" that helps to define the disorder is found only with certain kinds of memory tests (e.g., Huntjens et al., 2007).

Finally, several studies have shown that it's relatively easy to fake or simulate multiple personalities (Spanos et al., 1985). This raises the possibility that people with dissociative identity disorder may actually be role playing, perhaps in a way comparable to those who have been hypnotized. As you might recall from Chapter 6, many psychologists question whether hypnosis truly represents some kind of dissociated state; instead, hypnotized people often seem eager to please the hypnotist by acting in accordance with a hypnotized role. This is not necessarily a conscious choice made by those who have been hypnotized; instead, it may represent a kind of unconscious or involuntary compliance (S. J. Lynn et al., 1990). Some researchers are convinced that dissociative identity disorder is best interpreted as a kind of self-hypnosis that arises partly to please the therapist. There has been an unusually rapid rise in the number of cases of dissociative identity disorder as the disorder has been publicized in the media and in movies, which lends support to the role-playing hypothesis. In addition, there is some evidence that people diagnosed with dissociative identity disorder are highly hypnotizable and therefore suggestible (see Maldonado & Spiegel, 2015).

Despite the controversy, dissociative identity disorder has been retained as a diagnosis in the DSM. It does seem clear that not all aspects of the disorder can be consciously faked (Kluft, 1991). Highly specific physiological differences have been reported across personalities—such as differences in visual acuity or eye muscle balance (S. D. Miller, 1989)—and it seems unlikely that such things could be easily faked (see Figure 14.5). There also appear to be certain similarities in the past histories of affected individuals that have convinced many of the validity of the diagnosis. For example, the occurrence of abuse, usually sexual or physical, tends to be a significant predictor of the disorder (Sar et al., 2007). The diagnosis of dissociative identity disorder remains controversial, but it is recognized as a legitimate disorder by the psychological community at large.

FIGURE 14.5 ■ Optical Changes Across Personalities

Individuals diagnosed with dissociative identity disorder were asked to undergo ophthalmological (eye) exams while "inhabited" by three different personalities in turn. Significant differences were found in optical functioning across personalities, more so than occurred for control subjects who were asked to fake different personalities during each exam.

Source: Data from Miller, 1989.

Depressive and Bipolar Disorders

From time to time, everyone experiences depression, that overwhelming feeling that things are completely hopeless and sad. For most, thankfully, the experience is brief. Moreover, most of us can account for our depressed mood by pointing to a particular experience or event in our lives: We failed the test; our beloved pet died; our once-trusted romantic partner now prefers the affections of another. But when an extreme mood swing is not short lived and is accompanied by other symptoms, such as a prolonged loss of appetite and a negative self-concept, a depressive disorder may be present. **Depressive disorders** are characterized by prolonged and disabling disruptions in emotional state.

A **major depressive episode** is usually marked by feelings of intense sadness and worthlessness. When you enter a major depressive episode, the world is seen through a kind of dark filter. You feel extremely sad and full of self-doubt, and the environment seems overwhelming, imposing, and full of obstacles that can't be overcome. This worldview of a depressed person is a particularly grim aspect of the disorder—if you're depressed, the future seems hopeless with little or no possibility of a reprieve. Moreover, the negative self-image seems to be grounded in reality; depressed people are absolutely convinced about the truth of their hopelessness, which tragically leads some to consider suicide as their only outlet.

Major depression is more than just feeling sad. You literally view and interpret the world differently when you're depressed, which tends to feed back and confirm your negative self-concept. Normal activities are interpreted as indicating some dire consequence (for example, if a friend fails to call, it must mean the friend no longer cares). As you'll see in the next chapter, one of the goals of therapy in treating depression is to change depressed individuals' thought patterns—to make them see the world in a more realistic way.

Mental health professionals distinguish among several types of depressive disorders, based partly on the length and severity of the depressive episode. For example, a major depressive episode can be classified as *recurrent*, which means that it has occurred more than once in an individual's lifetime (but separated by a period of at least two months). There is also a condition called *dysthymic disorder*, in which the depressive symptoms tend to be milder and less disruptive but more chronic. Most major depressive episodes end after a period of weeks or months and the person returns to normal, but people affected by dysthymic disorder show a relatively continuous depressed mood for a period of at least two years.

Bipolar Disorder

In a major depressive episode, depression typically runs its course, and the individual returns to a normal state. The depression may occur again, but the disorder is defined by a mood shift in only one direction—toward the negative. In **bipolar disorder**, one experiences mood shifts in two directions, traveling from the depths of depression (a major depressive episode) to a hyperactive, euphoric condition called a **manic episode**. When in a manic state, people act as if they're on top of the world—they are hyperactive and talkative, and seem to have little need for sleep. These symptoms may seem positive and desirable, but they're balanced by tendencies toward grandiosity, distractibility, and risk taking. In a manic state, individuals might attempt a remarkable feat—such as scaling the Statue of Liberty—or perhaps go on a sudden spending spree, cashing in all their savings. People who are experiencing mania may report feeling great, but their thinking is far from normal or rational. Their speech can appear disrupted because they shift rapidly from one fleeting thought to another.

To be classified as a manic episode in the DSM, this abnormally elevated mood state must last for at least a week, although it can last for significantly longer. Like a depressive episode, the manic state typically goes away, even without treatment, and the person either returns to normal or roller-coasters into another depressive episode. People who suffer from bipolar disorder live lives of extreme highs and lows. Not surprisingly, their ability to function normally in society is often severely impaired. Moreover, tragically, it's been estimated that as many as 19% of individuals who are affected with bipolar disorder eventually end up committing suicide (Ostacher & Eidelman, 2006).

People suffering from bipolar disorder live lives of extreme highs and lows.

iStockPhoto/sdominick

Suicide

As just noted, suicide can be one fatal consequence of suffering from a mood-related disorder. It's worth pausing for a moment and considering suicide because it's a significant problem worldwide. Suicide is the second leading cause of death for people between the ages of 15 and 34. Suicide rates are highest for Alaska Natives and Native North Americans followed by European Americans, at least in the United States (Horwitz et al., 2016). Men are 3 to 4 times more likely to commit suicide than women (although women are more likely to attempt suicide), and the average suicide rate for Blacks is lower than that for white people (Colucci & Martin, 2007). The vast majority of people who kill themselves suffer from some kind of psychological disorder (Garland & Zigler, 1993).

What are the risk factors associated with suicide? In addition to a psychological disorder, many different factors can be involved. Alcohol use and abuse are particularly likely in adolescent suicides, and present in perhaps the majority of suicides. Another important factor is the sudden occurrence of a very stressful event—something like the death of a loved one, failure or rejection in a personal relationship, or even a natural disaster. Evidence suggests that suicide rates increase after natural disasters, such as floods, hurricanes, and earthquakes (Krug et al., 1998). Suicide may also be contagious: There are increased suicide rates following widely publicized suicides, especially among adolescents, suggesting that imitation or modeling is an important factor (M. S. Gould & Kramer, 2001).

Suicide is the second leading cause of death for people between the ages of 15 and 34.

Colin Bennett / Alamy Stock Photo

Among the most significant predictors of suicide are prior suicide attempts and suicidal thoughts. Among adolescents there is somewhere between a 3:1 and 6:1 ratio of serious suicidal thoughts to actual suicide attempts. Not everyone who thinks about suicide makes an attempt—and the ratio of attempted suicides to successful suicides is estimated to be about 11:1. But suicidal thinking is a serious warning sign. Treatment options for the psychological conditions associated with suicide are discussed in Chapter 15, but a variety of intervention programs are used to tackle the suicide problem nationally. For example, the Centers for Disease Control and Prevention recommends that teams of mental health professionals be sent to schools, for counseling and screening, whenever a student or visible member of the community commits suicide. Moreover, most cities and towns now have 24-hour suicide hotline services that enable people in need to voice their concerns and learn alternative ways of dealing with their crises. Most psychologists are optimistic that as the risk factors associated with suicide are identified, and treatment options become more accessible, suicide rates can be slowed or reversed. For more on the prevention of suicide, take a look at the Practical Solutions feature.

PRACTICAL SOLUTIONS: SUICIDE PREVENTION

Suicide is relatively rare in childhood and early adolescence but increases significantly in the late teens and early 20s. Suicide is now the second leading cause of death among young adults. Although the causes of suicide are many, and may differ from early to late adulthood, psychologists are attempting to isolate the factors that can lead to prevention (at any age). Let's consider some recommendations being offered to reduce suicide among young adults (see M. S. Gould & Kramer, 2001):

1. *Gatekeeper Training.* Most professionals are convinced that suicidal youths are underidentified. There is a compelling need to train members of the community to recognize the warning signs of suicide and to offer educated assistance. We need programs to train people who come in contact with potential suicides—both in schools and in the community. Interestingly, current research indicates that it may be better to train school officials (teachers, coaches, counselors) to screen for potential victims because student-centered educational programs have met with limited success.

2. *Skills Training.* Rather than focusing on student programs that deal specifically with suicide and its prevention, it may be more effective to develop programs that teach students basic problem-solving, decision-making, and communication skills. Life-skills training and teaching general coping strategies can reduce the risk factors typically associated with suicide (Eggert et al., 1995). By teaching students skills to handle the problems that arise in day-to-day living, we increase their self-esteem and their ability to handle stressors in the environment.

3. *Increase Media Awareness.* Social learning and modeling can significantly increase the risk of suicide among the young. Considerable evidence supports contagion effects (copycat suicides). When suicidal behavior is given wide exposure in the media, even fictional suicides in movies, it can be followed by a significant increase in the number of suicides and suicide attempts (Gould, 2001). Members of the media should be educated about the risks associated with modeling suicide and encouraged to reduce the amount or emphasis of such coverage.

4. *Crisis Centers.* Crisis centers, or suicide hotlines, are an important and widely available method for reducing suicide risk. Suicides are often associated with significant traumatic or stressful events, so providing a social network for someone in need is clearly a useful strategy. Unfortunately, significant risk groups tend not to take advantage of these centers. For example, young white women are the most frequent users of crisis hotlines—men tend to stay away. Accordingly, although effective for the groups that use them, crisis centers are not a complete solution to suicide prevention.

Gender and Culture

As noted previously, women are significantly more likely to attempt suicide than men (although men are more often successful); overall, women are more likely to report, and be treated for, major depression, which may help explain the trend (Hammen, 2003). Cross-cultural studies have found that the rates of major depression are higher for women across the world, ranging from developing countries to major industrialized nations. Interestingly, though, there doesn't appear to be a similar sex difference for bipolar disorder.

The symptoms reported for major depression are also quite similar across the world, particularly loss of energy, insomnia, and thoughts of death or suicide. People's internal thoughts about depression, however, do seem to depend partly on their cultural worldview. For example, in cultures stressing individuality, such as Western nations, people talk about their symptoms in terms of their personal identity ("I feel blue"); in cultures stressing an interdependent (collective) view of the self, symptoms might be described in terms of the group ("Our life has lost its meaning") (cf. Barlow & Durand, 2012).

Schizophrenia: Faulty Thought Processes

For most of the psychological disorders considered so far, you probably experienced at least a glimmer of recognition. Everyone can identify with anxiety, the occasional obsessive thought, or even a slight case of depression. It's only when these tendencies become *excessive* and interfere with normal functioning that you are likely to be diagnosed with an actual psychological disorder. But in the case of schizophrenia, which translates literally as "split mind," the psychological changes can be so profound that one is thrust into a world that bears little resemblance to everyday experience. A person with schizophrenia lives in an internal world marked by thought processes that have gone awry; delusions, hallucinations, and generally disordered thinking become the norm.

Schizophrenia is a bit unusual compared to the other disorders we've considered because it doesn't always reveal itself in the same way; whereas everyone who suffers from an anxiety disorder feels apprehensive, or in depression feels sad, the symptoms of schizophrenia are not necessarily shared by all affected individuals. Schizophrenia is a complex disorder that is expressed in a variety of complex ways—no single symptom must be present for the diagnosis to be applied (Walker et al., 2004).

Despite the translation of schizophrenia as "split mind," it's not the same thing as a dissociative identity disorder. Schizophrenia leads to faulty thought processes and inappropriate emotions—not to dissociations among distinct personality types. In fact, when the Swiss psychiatrist Eugen Bleuler (1908) originally introduced the term *schizophrenia*, he was referring primarily to the fact that affected individuals have trouble holding onto a consistent line of thought. Their thinking is disorganized; their thought lines and associations seem to split apart and move forward in inconsistent ways. Both schizophrenia and dissociative identity disorder are serious psychological problems, but they fall into different categories in the DSM.

Diagnostic Symptoms

There are three main types of symptoms in schizophrenia: positive, negative, and cognitive. Positive symptoms usually include observable expressions of abnormal behavior, such as delusions or hallucinations; negative symptoms consist of deficits in behavior, such as an inability to express emotion; cognitive symptoms include difficulties in memory and decision making and in the ability to sustain attention. The DSM requires that two or more characteristic symptoms be present for the diagnosis of schizophrenia, but a particular person may have many or only a few. As with the other disorders we've considered, these symptoms must last for a significant period of time, they must cause social or job distress, and they cannot be due to the effects of a general medical condition or to the use of a drug or medication.

Let's consider some of the major positive symptoms of schizophrenia in more detail. As noted earlier, one of the main problems in schizophrenia is distorted or disorganized thinking. People with schizophrenia often suffer from *delusions*, which are thoughts with inappropriate content. If someone sitting next to you in class leaned over and claimed to be Elvis in disguise, or Jesus Christ, or Adolf Hitler, the content of these thoughts would clearly be inappropriate or deviant—this individual would be suffering from a delusion.

It's also not unusual for people with schizophrenia to report distorted perceptions of the world. For them, objects can seem to change their shape or size; distances can be perceived in ways that are different from reality. Frequently, the *hallucinations*—which are perceptions that have no basis in external stimulation—are auditory. People with schizophrenia claim to hear disembodied voices in their heads, giving them commands or commenting on the quality of their activities ("You're an idiot," "You should stay away from that person," and so on). Some researchers believe these voices may originate from the same areas of the brain that control language production. It may be that people with schizophrenia are actually "listening" to their inner voice (see Chapter 8) but fail to recognize the voice as their own. Instead, they falsely attribute the source of the voice to something external (Hugdahl & Sommer, 2018; Lutterveld et al., 2011).

Highlighted in this PET scan are areas of the brain that appear to be selectively activated during auditory and visual hallucinations. A young man suffering from schizophrenia was asked to press a button, initiating the scan, every time he experienced a hallucination.

D. Silbersweig / Science Source

Other positive symptoms of schizophrenia include *disorganized speech* and *catatonia*. Sometimes the speech patterns of a person with schizophrenia appear jumbled and incoherent; the person jumps repeatedly from one disconnected topic to another ("I went to the beach today where the moon pulls the rabbit out of the hat. I'm the world's greatest cook, but that's because volcanic magma heats the glaciers and makes the water and the sand"). It's as if the mind has lost its internal editor—ideas or thoughts no longer flow in a connected way. In addition to displaying speech problems, people with schizophrenia can behave in ways that are quite disorganized and bizarre. A person might engage in repetitive activities, such as swirling one's arms repeatedly, or will appear to laugh or cry at inappropriate times. When *catatonia* is present, people may adopt a peculiar stance or position and remain immobile for hours, or they may wildly and suddenly change position for no apparent reason.

In catatonia, a symptom of schizophrenia, the affected person adopts a peculiar stance or position and remains immobile for hours.

Grunnitus Studio / Science Source

Negative symptoms of schizophrenia are expressed by the elimination or reduction of normal behavior. For example, it's common for people with schizophrenia to display *restricted or flat affect*, which means they show little or no emotional reaction to events. Show someone with restricted affect an extremely funny movie or a tragic, heartrending photo, and the person is unlikely to crack a smile or shed a tear. People with schizophrenia may also refuse to engage in the most basic and important of everyday activities. They may refuse to speak, or interact socially, and they may even refuse to wash themselves, to eat, or to get dressed. Activities that are pleasurable to most people become unpleasurable or uninteresting to some individuals with schizophrenia.

Finally, the cognitive symptoms of schizophrenia can be more subtle and difficult to detect, often appearing only after neuropsychological testing. Schizophrenia can produce marked deficits in the ability to absorb information and process it effectively. People with schizophrenia usually have difficulties associated with "working memory," that portion of our memory system that enables us to maintain information in consciousness and use it in ongoing tasks (e.g., J. M. Gold et al., 2019). People with schizophrenia often have difficulty concentrating and integrating thoughts and feelings. There is evidence suggesting that cognitive difficulties may be apparent even before the onset of the more severe symptoms discussed earlier (see Manoach & Stickgold, 2019).

For obvious reasons, people with schizophrenia are often unable to cope successfully at school or at work. In many cases, their behavior becomes so maladaptive that hospitalization is required. As you'll see later in the chapter, there are reasons to believe that people with schizophrenia may be suffering from problems in the brain itself—fundamental neurological problems may cause the bizarre thinking and behaviors that plague people affected with the disorder.

Gender and Culture

Researchers remain uncertain about how gender affects the likelihood of developing schizophrenia. Historically, it's been assumed that men and women are equally likely to develop the disorder, but more recent research suggests that men are at greater risk (McGrath et al., 2008). Moreover, men tend to develop the disorder earlier in life, about four years earlier on average, whereas women show an increased risk of developing schizophrenia in later years (Mendrek & Mancini-Marie, 2016). For unknown reasons, women are also more likely than men to benefit favorably from treatment (E. Walker et al., 2004).

Schizophrenia is a worldwide phenomenon, occurring in every studied racial and cultural group. However, there are differences in the rates of diagnosis—for example, more Black Americans are diagnosed with schizophrenia than white Americans—and people seem to recover better in some cultures than in others (see Jarvis et al., 2020). These patterns are puzzling to researchers and poorly understood. Some researchers have suggested that the racial differences in diagnosis may be related to bias or discrimination (Goater et al., 1999), but other possibilities remain, including differences in genetic susceptibility.

Personality Disorders

Personality disorders are chronic or enduring patterns of behavior that lead to significant impairments in social functioning. People with personality disorders tend to act in inflexible and maladaptive ways; they show impairments in personality functioning and possess "pathological" personality traits. For example, one might show an exaggerated sense of entitlement, as in **narcissistic personality disorder**, which leads to excessive attempts to attract and be the focus of attention. One of the best-known examples of a personality disorder, occurring mainly in males, is the **antisocial personality disorder**. Such people lack empathy, are egocentric, and show little respect for social customs or norms. They act as if they have no conscience—they lie, cheat, or steal and show no remorse for their actions if caught. Someone with antisocial personality disorder is likely to have no qualms about committing criminal acts, even murder. Many end up with long criminal records and spend significant periods of time in jail (Cunningham & Reidy, 1998). Another common personality disorder is **borderline personality disorder**, which affects mainly young women. This disorder is associated with a poor self-image and an inability to regulate emotions, and can be associated with aggression, self-injury, and substance abuse. People with borderline personality disorder often have unstable patterns of social relationships.

Many mental health professionals believe personality disorders are unique because they tend to be more *ingrained* and *inflexible* than the other major clinical syndromes we've discussed. These are not problems that typically appear and disappear over time, which is the case with many psychological disorders. These problems reflect basic personality and, as a result, tend to continue throughout adulthood and are resistant to therapy.

Because personality disorders are linked to personality, some mental health professionals have argued that it's wrong to think of them as *disorders* in the same sense as a phobia or depression (Gunderson, 1992; Trull & McCrae, 1994). In fact, as mentioned earlier in the chapter, during development of the latest version of the DSM, there was vigorous debate about whether it makes scientific sense to describe personality disorders in terms of discrete categories such as those listed previously (see Zachar et al., 2016). In Chapter 11, we discussed the idea that personality can be defined by the Big Five personality dimensions (McCrae & Costa, 1985). Some researchers have argued that it's better to think about people with personality disorders as simply extreme or deviant on one or more of these five dimensions—extroversion, agreeableness, conscientiousness, neuroticism, and openness. For example, the dimension of *agreeableness* measures the extent to which an individual is kind, warm, and trusting. It's possible that people classified with antisocial personality disorder may simply lie near an extreme pole on the agreeableness scale—they trust almost no one. Current assessment procedures suggest that the Big Five may be sufficient to account for the complexities of these "disorders," but researchers continue to investigate the topic vigorously (Widiger et al., 2018).

KNOWLEDGE CHECK 14.2

Check your knowledge about how psychological disorders are classified by picking the diagnostic category that best describes each of the following behavior patterns. Pick from among the following terms: *anxiety disorder, obsessive–compulsive disorder, somatic symptom disorder, dissociative disorder, depressive disorder, schizophrenia, personality disorder.* (You will find the answers in the Appendix.)

1. Sharma is convinced that the ringing in her ears means she has a brain tumor, even though a variety of doctors can find nothing wrong: _____

2. Gabriella is a checker—she often drives home five or six times a day to make sure she hasn't left the oven on: _____

3. Kunal hasn't left his house for 6 years—it's the only place he really feels safe: _____

4. Otto hates himself. He's convinced that he's worthless, stupid, and unlovable. No one can convince him otherwise: _____

5. Sergio is found wandering aimlessly in the park. When questioned, he can't remember who he is or how he got to the park: _____

6. Roger is a habitual con artist with little regard for the truth. He steals regularly and feels no guilt or remorse about his actions: _____

7. Melissa is convinced that her psychology professor is beaming his thoughts directly into her brain; she feels empowered and ready to complete her takeover of the world: _____

8. Billy shows little or no emotional reaction to events in his world; in fact, he usually stands in the corner for hours at a time with his right arm resting on his head: _____

UNDERSTANDING PSYCHOLOGICAL DISORDERS: BIOLOGICAL, COGNITIVE, OR ENVIRONMENTAL?

The DSM is designed to provide a reliable way for mental health professionals to diagnose psychological problems. The word *reliable* in this case refers to whether professional clinicians will tend to arrive at the same or similar diagnoses for people with a given set of symptoms. Still, it's important to remember that the DSM is only a classification system—it does not indicate anything about the root cause, or etiology, of the underlying disorder. What factors, alone or in combination, conspire to produce a major clinical syndrome like depression, anxiety, or schizophrenia? The answer—in a nutshell—is that we don't know for sure. But most current explanations, as well as most approaches to therapy, appeal to *biological, cognitive,* or *environmental* factors.

The recognition that psychological disorders are influenced by these three factors is sometimes called the **bio-psycho-social perspective**. Biological factors (*bio*) include physiological problems with the body, particularly the brain, along with genetic influences. Cognitive factors (*psycho*) include our beliefs, styles of thought, and any other psychological mechanisms that potentially influence behavior. Finally, environmental factors (*social*) include what we learn from the environment, cultural influences, and how other people treat us in our daily lives. We'll consider each of these three major factors in greater detail in the following sections.

Biological Factors: Is It in the Brain or Genes?

Over the past several decades, there have been significant advances in our understanding of the brain and its functions. Most researchers are now convinced that at least some kinds of abnormal behavior result directly from brain dysfunction. The disordered thoughts of schizophrenia, for example, may be partly due to a malfunctioning brain. What's the evidence? Biological accounts are typically supported by two kinds of findings. First, abnormal brain chemistry or abnormal brain structures accompany some kinds of mental disorders. Second, it turns out that a number of psychological disorders may have a powerful genetic component—psychological disorders tend to run in families in ways that can't be easily explained by environmental histories. We discussed some of these findings in Chapter 3; we'll review and expand on that discussion here.

Neurotransmitter Imbalances

As you may recall from Chapter 3, schizophrenia has been linked to the neurotransmitter dopamine (S. H. Snyder, 1976), or possibly to an interaction between dopamine and other neurotransmitters (Iverson & Iverson, 2007). Support for the link has come primarily from studying how different drugs affect the disorder. Among the most effective treatments for schizophrenia are medications that act as dopamine antagonists, which means they reduce or block the effect of dopamine in the brain. Medications that increase the level of dopamine in the brain can also produce side effects that resemble the symptoms found in schizophrenia. Abnormal dopamine levels are probably not the only cause of schizophrenia— for example, not all people with schizophrenia are helped by dopamine-reducing medications—but problems in brain neurochemistry are widely believed to be involved in the disorder. Currently, the neurotransmitter glutamate is also thought to be involved in the development and maintenance of schizophrenia (Uno & Coyle, 2019), along with possibly GABA and serotonin (S. F. Taylor & Tso, 2015).

Neurotransmitter imbalances, which may be caused by structural problems in the brain, also contribute to mood disorders, such as manic episodes and depression. Once again, most of the effective medications for these problems act by altering the actions of neurotransmitters in the brain. Fluoxetine (more commonly known by its brand name, *Prozac*) is one of the most commonly prescribed treatments for depression; it acts by slowing the reuptake of *serotonin*, thereby prolonging the neurotransmitter's effectiveness. More generally, depression and mania have been linked to neurotransmitters called *monoamines*, which include serotonin, norepinephrine, and dopamine. Researchers currently believe these neurotransmitters are involved in the regulation of mood, although the specifics remain a mystery (Carr & Lucki, 2011). It's unlikely that mood disorders are caused by an inadequate supply of any one of these neurotransmitters. Instead, a decrease in one may have multiple effects on the others. A decrease in serotonin, for instance, may permit the levels of other neurotransmitters in the brain to vary more widely; these more complex interactions probably work together in some way to alter mood abnormally. Research suggests that stress hormones, such as cortisol, may play a role as well in mood disorders such as depression (Sher, 2004).

These PET scans, taken from a person diagnosed with schizophrenia (right) and from one without the disorder (left), show dramatic differences in brain activity levels. The blue and green areas show relatively low activity.

Science Source

Structural Problems

As suggested earlier, in addition to neurochemical problems, such as imbalances in neurotransmitters, there are likely to be structural problems in the brains of people suffering from serious psychological problems. For example, hundreds of studies have documented smaller brain volumes, on average, for people with schizophrenia relative to normal controls (see Kuo & Pogue-Geile, 2019). People with schizophrenia tend to have larger ventricles, which are the liquid-filled cavities in the brain (Sayo et al., 2012). Larger ventricles are associated with the loss, or shrinkage, of brain tissue. There's also evidence that activity in the frontal areas of the brain is abnormally low in schizophrenia patients (Berman & Weinberger, 1990). Although it's not clear why these activity levels are low, decreased brain activity in certain prefrontal regions may directly or indirectly alter the neural pathways associated with the neurotransmitter dopamine. Postmortem studies have also found abnormalities in how neurons are interconnected in certain regions of the brain, suggesting that schizophrenia involves faulty wiring in the neural circuits (e.g., Fornito & Bullmore, 2015).

These data are convincing, but it's important to remember that not all people with schizophrenia show these kinds of neurological problems; not all people with schizophrenia have larger ventricles or show lower frontal lobe activity. Moreover, not all people who have been diagnosed with depression respond to drug therapies that alter the levels or actions of monoamines. So we're left with a somewhat cloudy picture. There's little doubt that psychological disorders are sometimes associated with observable abnormalities in brain chemistry or function. But whether these factors are the true cause of disorders such as schizophrenia or depression, or simply one cause, or occur somehow as a consequence of having the disorder is not currently known.

Genetic Contributions

Increasingly, researchers are concluding that people may inherit predispositions toward abnormality. For example, the odds that any particular individual in the population will develop schizophrenia are roughly 1 in 100. But if you have a brother, sister, or parent with the disorder, the odds increase dramatically, perhaps to 1 in 10. If you have an identical twin—someone who has essentially the same genetic information as you do—and your twin has been diagnosed with schizophrenia, the odds that you will develop the disorder during your lifetime jump to about 1 in 2 (Gottesman, 1991) (see Figure 14.6). Notice that the disorder can't be explained entirely by appealing to genetic factors—otherwise, identical twins would always share the disorder—but these data suggest that genetic background plays a significant role (see also Gejman et al., 2011). Recent work exploring genome-wide associations has confirmed this conclusion as well—there appear to be unique genetic patterns associated with schizophrenia (see Henriksen et al., 2017).

FIGURE 14.6 ■ The Genetics of Schizophrenia

Each bar shows the risk of developing schizophrenia when one or more relatives have been diagnosed with the disorder. In general, the closer an individual is genetically to the person with schizophrenia, the more likely the individual is to develop the disorder.

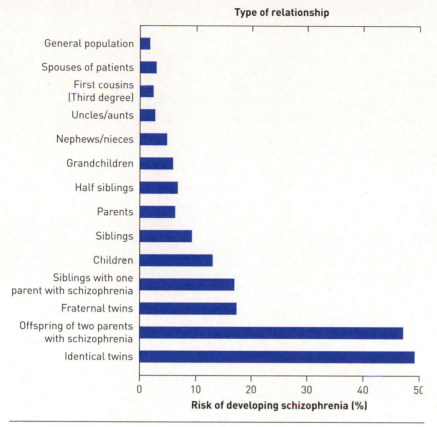

Source: Based on Gottesman, 1991.

As you know from our many discussions of the nature–nurture issue throughout this book, it's not easy to separate inherited characteristics from those acquired through experience. Just because there's a family history of a disorder doesn't mean the cause is genetic; family members are typically raised in similar environments, so experience could account for the shared psychological problems. In the case of schizophrenia, however, even when children are adopted and raised apart from their biological parents, there still appears to be a familial link. Adopted children who have biological parents with schizophrenia are more likely to be diagnosed with schizophrenia themselves, even if they've had little or no contact with the parents (Tienari et al., 2006).

A similar pattern emerges with depressive disorders. Depression and bipolar disorder tend to run in families, and the concordance rate, which measures the likelihood of sharing a disorder, is quite high between identical twins. A number of studies have shown that if one twin is diagnosed with depression, there is a 50% or greater chance that the other twin will also be diagnosed with depression; the concordance rate may be even higher for bipolar disorders (Gershon, 1990). It is also the case that adoptees with biological parents who suffer from a mood disorder are themselves more likely to suffer from a mood disorder. It's the biological history rather than the environmental history that, on average, predicts the chances of becoming affected. As with schizophrenia, recent genome-wide association studies have identified genetic patterns or variants that are associated with depressive disorders (Mullins & Lewis, 2017).

Genetic factors help predict the likelihood that someone will suffer from certain psychological disorders, but genetic factors are not sufficient to explain abnormal behavior. Once again, having an identical twin with schizophrenia or bipolar disorder does not guarantee that you'll have a similar problem. Your genetic code may predispose you to a disorder—it may set the stage—but other environmental factors must be present for the disorder to actually develop. For example, problems during childbirth, such as the development of an infectious disease or exposure to an environmental stressor, may help to explain why one twin eventually develops schizophrenia whereas the other does not. Anxiety disorders may be likely to occur in people who are born with sensitive temperaments, but experience will determine whether a full-blown disorder actually develops. To repeat a common theme, it is the interaction between nature and nurture that is important.

Cognitive Factors: Is It Maladaptive Thoughts and Beliefs?

If you look closely into the mind of someone with a psychological disorder, you'll often find disordered styles of thinking. People with anxiety disorders, somatic symptom disorders, or the other disorders we've discussed typically believe things about themselves or about the world that have little or no basis in reality. Robert, who is depressed, is convinced that he lacks ability and drive, even though he is a successful banker. Jill, who suffers from agoraphobia, refuses to leave her house because she's convinced that something terrible will happen outside, even though she can think of no real reason for this belief.

Many psychologists feel that such faulty beliefs may be more than symptoms of an underlying disorder—they may contribute to, or even cause, the disorder itself. To see how this might work, suppose we're able to convince you, by feeding you false but convincing reports, that evil extraterrestrials have landed in a nearby city. Your anxiety level will certainly shoot up, and there's little question your behavior will change. You might not leave your house, and you might end up spending a lot of your time huddled under a table in your basement. This is abnormal behavior, but it is rational if the underlying cause of the behavior—the belief that the world may end soon—is true. Many people with psychological disorders act the way they do because they have incorrect beliefs. If you're absolutely convinced that you're no good and you can never succeed at anything, it's not surprising that you withdraw from social situations and fail to secure steady employment.

Maladaptive Attributions

Psychologists use the term *attribution* to refer to the processes involved in assigning causality to a behavior (see Chapter 13). When you fail at something, like a test or a new job, you attribute the failure to a cause, such as your own incompetence or the lousy teacher. It turns out that people who have psychological disorders, particularly depression, have relatively distinctive and predictable attributional or explanatory styles. Unfortunately, the attributions are often maladaptive, which means they lead to behaviors that are abnormal or unproductive.

As Figure 14.7 shows, when something bad happens to a person prone to depression, the person is likely to explain it in terms of *internal* ("I'm to blame rather than the situation"), *stable* (long lasting), and *global* (widespread) attributions (Abramson et al., 1989; Rubenstein et al., 2016). Let's suppose you fail a test at school. If you're depressed, you'll probably attribute that failure to some personal inadequacy (internal) that is likely to be long lasting (stable) and that will apply in lots of situations other than school (global). People who are not prone to depression tend to have more flexible explanatory styles. They might attribute the failure to some *external* source ("I've got a rotten teacher") and consider the failure to be *unstable* ("I had a bad day"), and they'll probably make a *specific* rather than global attribution. Nondepressed people have less of a tendency to overgeneralize from a situation at school to other areas of life.

Learned Helplessness

What produces these different explanatory styles? It's difficult to know whether people who make maladaptive attributions do so because they're depressed or whether it's the unfortunate explanatory style that creates the depression. Some researchers believe that prolonged experience with failure may be one contributing factor. According to the **learned helplessness** theory of depression (Seligman, 1975), if individuals repeatedly fail while attempting to control their environment, they acquire a general sense of helplessness. They give up and become passive, which, the theory proposes, leads to depression. Still, it's unlikely that we can account for all forms of depression by appealing only to repeated failure. Experience with failure may be a necessary condition for acquiring depression, but it is not a sufficient condition. Many people fail repeatedly yet show no tendencies toward depression.

FIGURE 14.7 ■ **Maladaptive Thoughts in Depression**

Depressed individuals tend to attribute failure to internal, stable, and global conditions.

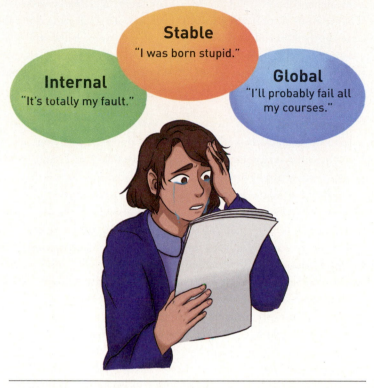

Illustrated by Sarah Yeh

Moreover, it is not really the failure that leads to depression but rather one's attributions about the failure. Instead of learning to be helpless, it may be the sense of *hopelessness*—the belief that things cannot become better because of internal, stable, and global factors—that is more likely to produce depression, at least in some people (Joiner et al., 2001). Whether this sense of hopelessness can be explained by appealing to experience alone, such as emotional maltreatment during childhood, or to some interaction between experience and biological or genetic predispositions is still being actively investigated (see R. T. Liu et al., 2015).

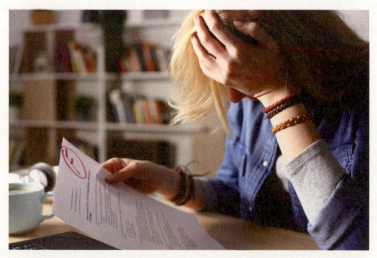

If you're depressed, you'll probably attribute failure to some personal inadequacy (internal) that is likely to be long lasting (stable) and that will apply in lots of situations other than school (global).

iStockPhoto/Pheelings Media

Environmental Factors: Is It Learned Through Experience?

All theories of psychological disorders ultimately appeal either directly or indirectly to environmental factors. Even if a researcher believes a disorder like schizophrenia is primarily caused by a genetically induced problem in the brain, it's still necessary to explain why identical twins don't always share the disorder. Experience clearly plays a pivotal role. Similarly, the irrational beliefs and explanatory styles that characterize depression must be learned somewhere, although two people with the same experiences may not always share the same set of beliefs. Once again, experience is the bedrock on which the psychological interpretation is built.

The Role of Culture

As we've discussed throughout this chapter, cultural factors also play an obvious and important role (Harper, 2001). Although the symptoms of most serious psychological disorders—such as schizophrenia and depression—are generally similar across the world, culture-based differences do exist. For example, the types of delusions found in schizophrenia depend to a certain extent on cultural background (Tateyama et al., 1998). Different cultural groups may also be more or less likely to show symptoms of disorders because of cultural "rules" for expressing emotion and action (see de Gelder & Huis in 't Veld, 2016). If an individual lives in a culture that discourages the expression of emotion, then depression will be somewhat harder to detect and treat.

People's cultural background may also determine the chances that they'll be exposed to environmental events that can trigger the onset of psychological disorders. Obviously, those who live somewhere in the world where war or extreme poverty is a way of life are likely to encounter more stressful events, which, in combination with a genetic predisposition, can lead to psychological problems. Cultural goals or ideals can also influence psychological health. For example, living in a society that places enormous emphasis on weight ideals can increase the chances that individuals will suffer from an eating disorder (see Chapter 12). (You'll learn more about how cultural ideals and stressors in everyday life can affect your physical and psychological health in Chapter 16.)

Conditioning Disorders

A number of mental health professionals feel that at least some psychological disorders may be learned. People can learn to act and think abnormally in the same way they might learn how to bake a cake, make friends, or avoid talking in class. Experts with this view of abnormality propose that learning principles of the type discussed in Chapter 7 help explain why psychological disorders develop and how they can be best treated. A specific phobia, for example, could be acquired through classical conditioning; individuals might learn to associate a particular stimulus or event with something that makes them afraid. Alternatively, people might learn to act abnormally through operant conditioning because they've been reinforced for those actions. Acting in a strange way thus becomes more likely than it was before.

Learning theorists believe that *modeling*, or observational learning, plays a particularly important role in the development of some psychological disorders. As we discussed in Chapter 7, there are reasons to believe that phobias can be acquired through modeling (Mineka & Zinbarg, 2006). Some of the best evidence has come from animal studies, where it's possible to control how the fear reaction is initially learned. Rhesus monkeys who are raised in the wild show an extremely strong fear response to snakes; monkeys who have been reared in the laboratory show a similar reaction, but only if they've witnessed other monkeys reacting fearfully when snakes are introduced into the cage. So it's not necessary for the animal to experience something negative directly, such as getting attacked and bitten by the snake; the animal can acquire its fear simply by watching other monkeys act afraid (M. Cook & Mineka, 1989). Modeling in this case makes adaptive sense because appropriate actions can be learned without directly experiencing negative consequences.

The monkey data are important because they show how modeling can lead to the acquisition of a strong fear response. Obviously, for monkeys in the wild it's quite adaptive to be afraid of snakes. For humans, we know that modeling is also a powerful way to learn, but the evidence that modeling underlies phobias—which, after all, are essentially irrational fears—is still indirect at this point. We know that many people with phobias can't remember having a traumatic experience with the object of their fear (Rachman, 1990). It's also the case that phobias tend to run in families—if your father is afraid of heights, there's an increased chance that you'll share that same fear (Fyer et al., 1990). This kind of evidence is consistent with a modeling account of phobias, but it doesn't preclude alternative accounts. It seems likely, for instance, that some kind of biological predisposition is also needed (Czajkowski et al., 2011).

As with the biological, genetic, and cognitive factors we've considered, it's unlikely that learning principles alone will be able to account for why people develop psychological disorders. People probably can't learn the delusional thought patterns of schizophrenia, for example, although stressful events in the environment undoubtedly play an important role in this disorder. Even with phobias, which may be largely learning based, it's probably necessary to be predisposed to anxiety for a full-blown phobia to develop. Experience plays a significant role in the development of most psychological disorders, but it doesn't act alone. Behavior, both normal and abnormal, is virtually always produced by multiple causes. See Concept Review 14.3 for a review of the main causes of psychological disorders.

CONCEPT REVIEW 14.3
CAUSES OF PSYCHOLOGICAL DISORDERS

Factor	Description	Example
Biological	Physiological problems, particularly in the brain. Can include neurotransmitter imbalances, structural problems, and genetic influences.	Danae feels extremely depressed. She goes to a psychologist who asks her whether anyone else in her family has suffered from depression. Danae reports that her mother and grandmother did have bouts of severe depression.
Cognitive	Our beliefs and styles of thought, such as maladaptive attributions and a sense of hopelessness.	Danae is struggling with her studies. She receives a D on a big exam. She is disgusted with herself and keeps thinking, "How could I be so stupid? I am such a loser!"
Environmental	The influence of experience and culture. Cultural background, events, and learning all have an impact on psychological disorders.	Danae's family has always struggled financially, and now her parents are going through a nasty divorce. Danae acts disruptively because it's one of the few ways she can get any attention from them.

KNOWLEDGE CHECK 14.3

Check your knowledge about how psychologists have attempted to understand psychological disorders by answering the following questions. (You will find the answers in the Appendix.)

1. Which of the following biological conditions is most likely to be a contributing factor in schizophrenia?
   a. Slowed reuptake of the neurotransmitter serotonin
   b. Excessive amounts of the neurotransmitter dopamine
   c. Smaller-than-normal ventricles in the brain
   d. Increased random activity in the frontal lobes

2. Studies examining the genetics of schizophrenia have discovered the following:
   a. Schizophrenia is a learned rather than an inherited disorder.
   b. Living with two parents with schizophrenia increases your risk of developing schizophrenia by about 65%.

    c. Identical twins are more likely to develop schizophrenia than fraternal twins.

    d. If your identical twin has schizophrenia, you have about a 50% chance of developing the disorder yourself.

3. Psychologists studying depression have found that depressed people tend to make the following kinds of personal attributions:

    a. External, stable, and global

    b. Internal, unstable, and global

    c. Internal, stable, and specific

    d. Internal, stable, and global

4. Studies examining how monkeys develop a strong fear response to snakes have been used to support which of the following accounts of specific phobias?

    a. Operant conditioning

    b. Observational learning

    c. Learned helplessness

    d. Classical conditioning

THE PROBLEMS SOLVED: WHAT ARE PSYCHOLOGICAL DISORDERS?

In this chapter, we've considered what happens when a person's thoughts and actions become disordered. Most mental health professionals believe it's possible and useful to distinguish between normal and abnormal behavior. In addition, as you've seen, a relatively precise and rigorous classification system exists for the diagnosis and labeling of psychological disorders when they occur. But what are the implications for our general theme of a functional and adaptive mind? It hardly seems adaptive to suffer from a psychological disorder—in fact, lack of adaptiveness is often used as a criterion for labeling a behavior as abnormal.

It's important to keep in mind that abnormal behaviors are often simply extreme versions of behaviors that otherwise have adaptive qualities. Anxiety, for instance, is an adaptive body response that prepares us for action and helps keep us vigilant in our surroundings. It becomes a problem only in its extreme form, when it is prolonged and chronic enough to impair normal functioning. Sigmund Freud believed certain kinds of psychologically based amnesias are adaptive because they prevent traumatic memories from intruding into conscious awareness. To paraphrase William Shakespeare, there may indeed be a bit of method in madness. On the other hand, it's also reasonable to propose that psychological disorders represent a kind of breakdown in the system. In particular, schizophrenia may arise from faulty brain functioning—the system ceases to be adaptive because it no longer has the capacity to function properly.

Conceptualizing Abnormality: What Makes Behavior Abnormal?

Conceptualizing *abnormal* behavior turns out to be a rather difficult thing to do. A number of criteria have been proposed, including the notions of statistical and cultural deviance. By *deviance*, psychologists typically mean behavior that is unusual in some way, either with respect to its statistical likelihood or with respect to the accepted norms of the culture. Abnormality can also be defined in terms of emotional distress or dysfunction. None of these criteria alone is sufficient to capture the concept. The concept of abnormality is usually defined by a combination of these factors.

Currently, many mental health professionals conceive of abnormal behavior from a medical model. According to this view, psychological disorders are best described as "illnesses" that can be "cured" through appropriate treatment. There are advantages and disadvantages to this approach, and it should not be taken too literally. Physical illnesses often have clearly identifiable causes, but this is seldom true for psychological disorders. Also of concern are the effects of diagnostic labeling of disorders: Diagnostic labels can sometimes become self-fulfilling prophecies, which can make it harder for a suffering person to recover.

Classifying Psychological Disorders

Most mental health professionals rely on the DSM, which lists objective criteria for the diagnosis of psychological disorders. Anxiety disorders are diagnosed when a person's apprehension and worry become so extreme that behavior is impaired. Generalized anxiety disorder is characterized by chronic worrying that can't be attributed to any obvious source. Phobias are highly focused fears of specific objects or events. Obsessive–compulsive disorder is characterized by the presence of persistent, uncontrollable thoughts (obsessions) or by compelling needs to perform actions repetitively (compulsions).

In somatic symptom disorders, the focus revolves around the body: You might have a persistent preoccupation with the possibility that you've contracted a serious disease, or you might appear to suffer from an actual physical problem that has no identifiable physical cause (conversion disorder).

In dissociative disorders, the person appears to separate, or dissociate, previous thoughts and memories from current conscious awareness. These disorders include dissociative amnesia, dissociative fugue states, and the more controversial dissociative identity disorder, in which the person appears to have two or more distinct personalities.

Depressive disorders are associated with prolonged disruptions in emotional state. In bipolar disorder, an individual alternates between the highs of mania and the lows of depression. Schizophrenia, the final clinical syndrome we discussed, is characterized by distorted thoughts and perceptions. The symptoms of schizophrenia include delusions, hallucinations, and disorganized speech and behavior. Negative symptoms include restricted or flat affect, which means that the person shows little or no emotional reaction to events. People with personality disorders show impairments in personality functioning and possess "pathological" personality traits. The net result is chronic or enduring patterns of behavior that lead to significant impairments in social functioning.

Understanding Psychological Disorders: Biological, Cognitive, or Environmental?

Mental health professionals currently believe that the root cause, or etiology, of most disorders lies in a combination of biological, cognitive, and environmental factors. Some disorders may result from disordered or malfunctioning brains. There's evidence to support the idea that some psychological problems result from neurotransmitter problems or perhaps from structural problems in the brain. Many psychological disorders also appear to have a genetic basis—individuals may inherit a predisposition for a particular kind of problem.

Psychological disorders are also typically characterized by maladaptive thinking, and it has been suggested that maladaptive beliefs and attributions contribute to the appearance of abnormal behavior. Depressed individuals, for example, tend to attribute negative events to internal, stable, and global causes; these attributions are often associated with a sense of hopelessness, or the faulty belief that things cannot get better.

Finally, all theories of psychological disorders rely in one form or another on the environment. For example, your cultural background may play a role in the expression of biological or genetic predispositions and may even determine the kinds of personal attributions you make. It's possible that some psychological problems arise almost entirely from environmental influences. It's possible that people learn to act abnormally, either through conditioning or through modeling the behavior of significant people around them.

THINKING ABOUT RESEARCH

A summary of a research study in psychology is given in this section. As you read the summary, think about the following questions:

1. This is a correlational study. What factors might be co-varying with the two measures (positive thinking and depression) that limit any conclusions about causality?

2. Can you think of a way to address this research question through an experiment rather than as a correlational study? Would your experiment be ethical?

3. Do the results of this study fit better with environmental, cognitive, or biological theories of depression?
4. Can you think of a way that genetics is playing a role in the outcomes of this study?

Article Reference: Oettingen, G., Mayer, D., & Portnow, S. (2016). Pleasure now, pain later: Positive fantasies about the future predict symptoms of depression. *Psychological Science, 27*, 345–353.

Purpose of the Study: One of the hallmarks of clinical depression is the tendency to think negative thoughts about yourself and your abilities (e.g., "I'm worthless, and I'm to blame"). One might anticipate, then, that people who think positively about the future will be less prone to depression. However, some researchers believe that indulging in positive future fantasies is a risk factor for depression. This is because people who always see the sunny side of a situation tend to produce less effort and have been shown to be less successful in various life domains, such as academic achievement and interpersonal relations. The current study was designed to test this idea by measuring the short- and long-term effects of positive thinking on depressive tendencies.

Method of the Study: In four different studies, the investigators collected measures of positive thinking, along with a measure of depressive symptoms, at baseline and then again some months later. For example, in one study over 4 days, people were randomly "beeped" eight times a day and asked to respond to the following query: "How positive or negative were your thoughts and images?" (1 = *very negative*; 7 = *very positive*). At baseline, each person was also asked to complete a standard questionnaire designed to measure the symptoms of depression. Seven months later, the participants were tested again with the same standardized depression scale. The main measure of interest was the correlation between the degree of positive thinking and the extent of self-reported depressive symptoms.

Results of the Study: As you might have expected, the researchers found a negative correlation between positive thoughts and depression when the two were measured concurrently—that is, the people who reported more positive thoughts during the initial baseline period also reported fewer symptoms of depression. However, the correlation was positive, meaning that greater amounts of positivity predicted more depressive symptoms, when the depression scale was administered seven months later. Similar results were found in three other studies.

Conclusions of the Study: Common sense suggests that positive thinking will shelter people from depression. However, to the extent that always anticipating positive outcomes leads you to put out less effort, and enjoy future accomplishments prematurely, then you are psychologically less prepared to handle future disappointments when they inevitably occur. The researchers conclude that people are better off contrasting their positive thoughts about the future with consideration of the real-life obstacles that need to be overcome to achieve success.

KNOWLEDGE CHECK: CHAPTER SUMMARY

You will find the answers in the Appendix.

Conceptualizing Abnormality: What Makes Behavior Abnormal?

- "Abnormal" and "normal" are best understood as ends of a (1) _____ rather than as distinct categories. Statistical (2) _____ refers to behavior that occurs infrequently among members of a population. (3) _____ deviance is a criterion used to compare behaviors to current cultural (4) _____. The extent of (5) _____ distress is also relevant in evaluating whether a condition is abnormal. A final criterion is the extent of (6) _____, a breakdown in the ability to perform typical daily activities.

- "Insanity" is a (7) _____ concept, not a (8) _____ one. A criminal is insane, and therefore not guilty by reason of insanity, if, because of a mental condition, the criminal fails to (9) _____ at the time of the crime that certain actions are wrong in a (10) _____ or (11) _____ sense.

- According to the (12) _____ model, abnormal behavior is caused by an underlying (13) _____. This model is influential, and (14) _____ have been developed that are effective in treating a variety of psychological disorders. Some researchers feel that it is difficult to make direct comparisons between (15) _____ and psychological illnesses.

- Critics of the medical model are concerned that (16) _____ a psychological disorder as an illness attaches a (17) _____ to the person that is hard to overcome. Research has shown that labeling someone as "abnormal" can lead people to interpret (18) _____ behaviors as signs of a (19) _____ disorder.

Classifying Psychological Disorders

- The *Diagnostic and Statistical Manual of Mental Disorders* (DSM) is a well-defined (20) _____ system for psychological disorders. Based on (21) _____ and (22) _____ criteria, it contains descriptions, symptoms, and other criteria for diagnosing mental disorders. The DSM does (23) _____ suggest therapies or methods of treatment.

- A person may be diagnosed with an (24) _____ disorder if the level of (25) _____ and worry is so extreme that behavior is impaired. (26) _____ anxiety disorder is characterized by excessive, chronic, and unfocused worrying. (27) _____ disorder is characterized by (28) _____ attacks of intense (29) _____ or dread and is sometimes complicated by (30) _____, the fear of being in public. The defining feature of a specific (31) _____ is a highly focused fear of a particular object or situation. In (32) _____–_____ disorder, a person suffers from persistent thoughts (obsessions) or the compelling need to perform actions (compulsions).

- (33) _____ disorders are associated with the (34) _____ body. A healthy person suffers from persistent physical symptoms or misinterprets normal bodily signs as evidence of (35) _____. In (36) _____ disorder, there is real physical impairment with no apparent physical cause.

- People with a (37) _____ disorder have a loss of memory. In (38) _____ amnesia, a person is unable to remember important personal information. Dissociative (39) _____ involves a loss of personal (40) _____ followed by a flight from home. A person with dissociative (41) _____ disorder alternates among distinct (42) _____ or identity states; controversy surrounds such a diagnosis.

- Prolonged emotional disruptions are known as (43) _____ disorders. A major (44) _____ episode is characterized by numerous symptoms, which may include loss of interest in daily activities, chronic fatigue, trouble concentrating, and suicidal thoughts. A person with (45) _____ disorder alternates between (46) _____ and the hyperactive euphoria associated with (47) _____. A bipolar disorder may result in (48) _____; risk factors include substance abuse, a sudden very stressful event, the recent occurrence of other suicides, and prior suicide attempts and suicidal thoughts.

- Schizophrenia is a class of disorders that is characterized by fundamental disturbances in thought processes, (49) _____, or behavior. Both (50) _____ and negative symptoms are associated with schizophrenia. Positive symptoms include (51) _____, thoughts with bizarre content, and (52) _____, perceptions that aren't triggered by external stimuli. Negative symptoms involve the elimination or reduction of normal behavior such as (53) _____ affect, showing little emotional reaction. Other symptoms can include (54) _____, a general physical immobility or sudden wild adjustment of position, and disorganized (55) _____.

- In (56) _____ disorders, chronic behavior patterns lead to significant impairment in (57) _____ functioning. (58) _____ personality disorder features an exaggerated sense of self and the need to attract the attention of others; a person with (59) _____ personality disorder shows little or no respect for social norms. Some psychologists believe that people with these disorders are simply at an extreme on one or more of the Big (60) _____ personality dimensions.

Understanding Psychological Disorders: Biological, Cognitive, or Environmental?

- Some psychological disorders coincide with abnormal brain (61) _____ or structure. Many psychological disorders have a strong (62) _____ basis; people may inherit a predisposition toward certain disorders. Schizophrenia has been linked to an oversupply of (63) _____ and to the interaction of dopamine and other neurotransmitters such as glutamate, GABA, and (64) _____. Mood disorders may also reflect (65) _____ imbalances.

- People with psychological disorders (especially depression) have distinctive and predictable (66) _____ styles. Someone with a tendency toward depression is likely to respond to a negative event with (67) _____, stable, and (68) _____ attributions. According to the (69) _____ theory of depression, people who repeatedly fail to (70) _____ their environment give up and may have a sense of hopelessness, which leads to depression.

- (71) _____ plays a pivotal role in psychological disorders. For example, (72) _____ can affect whether you will be exposed to an event that triggers the onset of a disorder and how the disorder will be (73) _____. Some psychologists believe that certain disorders can be (74) _____ through (75) _____.

CRITICAL THINKING QUESTIONS

1. Suppose a 70-year-old entered college and started acting exactly the same way as a 20-year-old sophomore. Would you consider this person's behavior to be abnormal?

2. How might acceptance of the medical model influence the availability of treatment options? Might it cause an overemphasis on biological treatments for psychological problems?

3. Do you think it was ethical for Rosenhan and his colleagues to trick the hospital staff? Did the research ends justify the means?

4. Can you think of reasons it might be adaptive for people to show specific reactions for each of the four classes of phobic stimuli described in the text?

5. Can you think of any reason a client who is seeking help for a psychological problem might want desperately to please the therapist?

6. Think back to our earlier discussion of how to conceptualize abnormality. Do you think personality disorders should be labeled as "abnormal" behaviors?

7. Based on our earlier discussion of schizophrenia, can you think of any reason people diagnosed with schizophrenia might not all show the same neurological problems?

8. Try to identify your own attributional style. Do you tend to attribute outcomes to global, stable, and internal causes?

9. Do you suffer from any kind of phobia? Can you trace the fear to any particular experience in your life? Does anyone else in your family share the same fear?

KEY TERMS

agoraphobia (p. 517)

antisocial personality disorder (p. 529)

anxiety disorders (p. 517)

bio-psycho-social perspective (p. 531)

bipolar disorder (p. 524)

borderline personality disorder (p. 529)

conversion disorder (p. 521)

cultural deviance (p. 511)

depressive disorders (p. 524)
diagnostic labeling effects (p. 514)
dissociative amnesia (p. 522)
dissociative disorders (p. 522)
dissociative fugue (p. 522)
dissociative identity disorder (p. 522)
DSM (p. 515)
dysfunction (p. 511)
emotional distress (p. 511)
generalized anxiety disorder (p. 517)
insanity (p. 513)
learned helplessness (p. 534)

major depressive episode. (p. 524)
manic episode (p. 524)
medical model (p. 513)
narcissistic personality disorder (p. 529)
obsessive–compulsive disorder (p. 520)
panic disorder (p. 517)
personality disorders (p. 529)
phobic disorder (p. 518)
schizophrenia (p. 527)
social anxiety disorder (p. 519)
somatic symptom disorders (p. 521)
statistical deviance (p. 510)

iStockPhoto/RossHelen

THERAPY

If you're hearing voices in your head, and you're convinced that the alien takeover is on schedule for next Tuesday, it's likely you're having trouble leading a normal life. You probably can't hold a job or make lasting friends, and you may even have difficulty carrying on a meaningful conversation. Clearly, you need some kind of treatment—**psychotherapy**—to deal with your mental, emotional, and behavioral problems. But as you'll discover in this chapter, even those with less severe disturbances can benefit from the right kind of therapy. Suppose Carlos turns down the job of national sales manager simply because he's afraid of flying; what if Julie spends most of her time alone in her apartment because she's convinced that she'll embarrass herself in social settings?

Treatment options are available to tackle these kinds of problems in everyday living as well—psychotherapy isn't just for the severely impaired. Mental health professionals have a variety of tools at their disposal to help people regain their ability to function well in their surroundings. The particular tool used by the therapist depends on a number of factors, including the specific type of disorder being treated and the personality of the person seeking treatment. Treatment can be administered in a variety of ways. Some people respond well to one-on-one encounters with a therapist; others thrive best in group settings. As we discussed in Chapter 1, good therapists tailor the treatment to meet the needs of the particular client. This doesn't mean that therapists must abandon all theoretical orientations, but it does require flexibility. Good therapists recognize that a method that works for one person can be ineffective for another.

THE PROBLEMS TO BE SOLVED: HOW ARE THERAPIES DEVELOPED AND EVALUATED?

As you saw in Chapter 14, when psychologists study the cause of a psychological disorder, they usually look for contributions from biological, cognitive, or environmental factors. Abnormal behavior can be caused by problems in the brain, irrational beliefs, environmental experiences, or some combination of these factors. As a result, most kinds of psychotherapy are specifically designed to treat the body, the mind, or the environment.

Treating the Body: Biomedical Therapies

Abnormal functioning in the brain is thought to contribute to a number of disorders. Schizophrenia, for example, might be due in part to an imbalance in neurotransmitters; depression and mania have also been linked to the activity of neurotransmitters. To address these kinds of problems, it makes sense to consider treating the body itself through *biomedical therapies*. One option might be to administer a drug that restores the proper balance of neurotransmitters; other options might include surgery to fix the damage that exists in a particular region of the brain or even the use of electric shock treatment.

Treating the Mind: Insight Therapies

Psychological disorders are often associated with abnormal thoughts and beliefs. Many psychologists are convinced that the key to improvement is insight—you must gain awareness of your own thought processes. When you think of psychotherapy, do you imagine someone lying on a couch talking about dreams and early childhood experiences? Although this stereotypical image is accurate in some respects, you'll see in the discussion of *insight therapies* that many therapists have abandoned the couch, as well as the emphasis on dreams and early experiences. What remains is the idea that exploring one's thought processes can be an effective tool for solving psychological problems.

Treating the Environment: Behavioral Therapies

Psychologists also accept that certain kinds of disorders might be learned. We might learn to think and act in abnormal ways in much the same way that we acquire other thoughts and actions—through operant conditioning, classical conditioning, or modeling the actions of others. *Behavioral therapies* use basic learning principles to change dysfunctional behaviors into adaptive behaviors. For example, if experience has taught you to associate high places with disabling fear, it might be possible to alter the association either through extinction or by counterconditioning relaxation to replace the fear.

Evaluating and Choosing Psychotherapy

Do all forms of therapy work, or are some more effective than others? Therapy can be a costly and time-consuming process, so it's important to evaluate the advantages and disadvantages of the intervention. A number of studies have been conducted comparing people who have undergone therapy with those left untreated. Although many studies demonstrate the effectiveness of psychotherapy, some of the findings may surprise you.

TREATING THE BODY: BIOMEDICAL THERAPIES

Psychological disorders have been around since the beginning of recorded history. And for just as long, people have speculated about what causes abnormal behavior and have offered remedies for its treatment. At one time it was popular to appeal to supernatural forces: People who exhibited bizarre or deviant behavior were believed to be possessed by evil spirits or demons. The "cure" was to torture the sufferer in an effort to drive out the evil inhabitants.

But not all serious thinkers adopted such views. In fact, more than 2,000 years ago, Hippocrates (469–377 BCE) and his followers suggested that psychological disorders should be treated as products

Early forms of "therapy" might have included cutting holes in the head to release evil spirits.

Retro AdArchives / Alamy Stock Photo

of the body. Hippocrates believed people get depressed or exhibit manic episodes for much the same reason they fall victim to the common cold—the body and the brain, and hence the mind, are affected by some kind of "disease." Hippocrates even went so far as to recommend changes in diet and exercise as a way of treating depression, a course of action that many modern therapists consider appropriate today.

The medical approach to understanding disorders gained scientific respectability in the 19th and early 20th centuries as researchers began to establish links between known physical problems and the symptoms of psychological disorders. By the end of the 19th century, it was recognized that the venereal disease *syphilis* is responsible not only for a steady deterioration in physical health (and eventually death) but also for the appearance of paranoia and hallucinations. Establishing a link between syphilis and mental problems was an important step in the eventual development of biologically based therapies. Early "cures" for the disease included injecting sufferers with the blood of malaria patients in an effort to induce a high fever that would "burn out" the syphilis bacteria; today, of course, doctors use antibiotics to treat syphilis.

In this section of the chapter, we'll consider several modern biological approaches to the treatment of psychological disorders. **Biomedical therapies** use physiological interventions to reduce or eliminate the symptoms of psychological disorders. By far the most popular approach is treatment with medication, and we'll consider this approach first, but other biomedical therapies are available, including electroconvulsive therapy and psychosurgery.

Drug Therapies

The psychological community recognized the remarkable potential of drug therapy in the early 1950s when two French psychiatrists, Jean Delay and Pierre Deniker, reported success in treating the positive symptoms of schizophrenia with a drug called *chlorpromazine* (often sold under the brand name Thorazine). Patients suffering from delusions and hallucinations showed considerable improvement after using the drug. Since that time, dozens of other drugs have proved successful in treating a wide variety of psychological disorders. In fact, specific medications are now available to treat most of the disorders we considered in Chapter 14—everything from obsessive–compulsive disorder to depression. Unfortunately, these drugs do not work for all people, and as you'll see, some drugs have disturbing side effects. But they've helped thousands, and in many ways they've revolutionized the mental health profession.

Medications such as Chlorpromazine are used to help eliminate the symptoms of schizophrenia.

Ralf Falbe / Alamy Stock Photo

Antipsychotic Drugs

Medications that treat the positive symptoms of schizophrenia—for example, delusions or hallucinations—are commonly called **antipsychotic drugs**. Chlorpromazine is an example of such a drug, but a number of others are also available. The majority of these antipsychotic drugs are believed to act on the neurotransmitter *dopamine* in the brain. As we discussed in Chapter 14, many researchers believe schizophrenia is caused partly by abnormalities in the regulation of dopamine. Chlorpromazine acts as a dopamine *antagonist*, meaning that it blocks or slows down the use of dopamine in the brain (e.g., Weiden, 2007; see Figure 15.1). The fact that dopamine antagonists work so well in treating positive symptoms is considered strong support for the dopamine hypothesis of schizophrenia (E. Walker et al., 2004).

FIGURE 15.1 ■ Dopamine Antagonists

Some antipsychotic medications act as antagonists, which means they block or slow down the action of neurotransmitters in the brain. Here, a dopamine antagonist binds with the receptor membrane, blocking the neurotransmitter.

Neural impulse arrives at terminal button

Vesicle containing dopamine

Dopamine is released

Dopamine antagonists prevent dopamine from binding to membrane receptors

Monica Wierzbicki/Body Scientific Intl.

But dopamine antagonists don't work for all sufferers of schizophrenia. Moreover, these drugs tend to work almost exclusively on positive symptoms. The negative symptoms of schizophrenia, such as the sharp decline in the normal expression of emotions, are rarely affected by the administration of traditional antipsychotic medications. Antipsychotic drugs can also produce unwanted and persistent side effects in some people, including drowsiness, difficulties in concentrating, blurry vision, and movement disorders. One particularly serious side effect is a condition called *tardive dyskinesia*, which produces involuntary movements of the tongue, jaw, mouth, and face. These side effects can be permanent, and they act as a two-edged sword: Not only are they extremely uncomfortable, but they increase the chances that the patient will stop taking the medication. Without the medication, of course, the positive symptoms of the disorder are likely to reemerge.

Newer medications, including *clozapine* and *risperidone*, work well for people who don't respond to the more traditional dopamine antagonists (Chakos et al., 2001). These medications do not produce movement side effects such as tardive dyskinesia, although medical complications can still be a concern. From a research standpoint, the effectiveness of the newer second-generation medications is noteworthy because they don't work by simply regulating the amount of dopamine in the brain. It's believed they affect a number of neurotransmitters, including dopamine and serotonin (Richtand et al., 2007). This suggests that dopamine alone, as we noted in Chapter 14, can't account entirely for schizophrenic disorders. Recently, researchers have begun to focus extensively on the neurotransmitter *glutamate*. Some evidence suggests that altering presynaptic levels of glutamate may be an important key to reducing the symptoms characteristic of schizophrenia (Howes et al., 2015; Uno & Coyle, 2019).

Antidepressant Drugs

The 1950s also witnessed the introduction of medications for treating manic episodes and depression. Depressive disorders have been linked to several neurotransmitters, including norepinephrine and serotonin. **Antidepressant drugs** act by modulating the availability or effectiveness of these

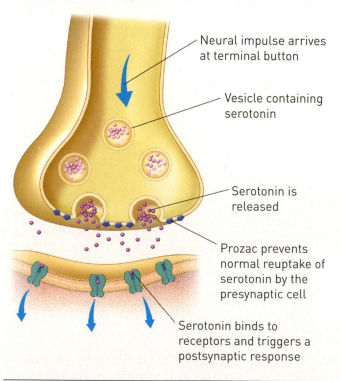

FIGURE 15.2 ■ Reuptake Blockers

Some kinds of antidepressant medications block the reabsorption of neurotransmitters, which then linger longer in the synapse and continue to activate receptor neurons. Prozac is in the class of antidepressants that block the reabsorption of serotonin.

Neural impulse arrives at terminal button

Vesicle containing serotonin

Serotonin is released

Prozac prevents normal reuptake of serotonin by the presynaptic cell

Serotonin binds to receptors and triggers a postsynaptic response

Monica Wierzbicki/Body Scientific Intl.

neurotransmitters. The group of antidepressants called *tricyclics*, for example, alter mood by acting primarily on norepinephrine; tricyclics apparently allow norepinephrine to linger in synapses longer than normal, which eventually modulates its effectiveness. The most commonly prescribed antidepressants act on serotonin. So-called *selective serotonin reuptake inhibitors* (SSRIs) block the reabsorption (or reuptake) of serotonin into the neuron, thereby allowing it to linger longer in the synapse and continue to activate receptor neurons (see Figure 15.2). Commonly prescribed examples of SSRIs include Prozac, Lexapro, Paxil, and Zoloft.

Researchers do not know how or why these medications affect mood, although experimental research (usually with animals) continues to suggest that serotonin is important (e.g., Carr & Lucki, 2011). Fortunately, existing medications do work well for many individuals affected with depression. It's been estimated that sustained use of antidepressants successfully controls depression in well over 50% of all depressed people, although some of the benefits may be due to placebo-like effects (Kirsch, 2010). On the downside, it can take several weeks for these medications to begin working (the time period may differ across the different types of antidepressants), and potential side effects must be monitored. SSRIs, for example, can produce agitation or restlessness, difficulty sleeping, weight gain, and even diminished sexual desire.

Effective medications are also available for treating bipolar disorder, which produces mood swings between depression and hyperactive manic episodes. Bipolar disorder is usually treated by administering a common salt called *lithium carbonate*. Lithium is more effective for bipolar disorder than other antidepressants because it works well on mania; it puts people on a more even keel and helps to prevent the reoccurrence of future manic episodes. But it, too, needs to be monitored closely because lithium use has been linked to a variety of medical complications (see, e.g., Ballesteros et al., 2017).

Antianxiety Drugs

For the treatment of psychological problems associated with anxiety, mental health professionals typically use **antianxiety drugs**, known more generally as *tranquilizers*. Tranquilizers come from a class of chemicals called *benzodiazepines*—Valium and Xanax are popular brand names—and they are quite effective for reducing tension and anxiety. In the mid-1970s, it was estimated that 10% to 20% of adults in the Western world were "popping" tranquilizers (Greenblatt & Shader, 1978), which gives you some idea of their widespread use. In recent years, use of tranquilizers has been on the decline, primarily because mental health professionals recognize a downside to their continued use.

Most benzodiazepines appear to work on the neurotransmitter GABA, which produces primarily inhibitory effects. The effectiveness of GABA increases after taking the drug, which leads to a lowering of excitation in affected neurons (Gielen et al., 2012). Potential side effects include drowsiness, impaired motor coordination, and possible psychological dependence (Wells & Carter, 2006). Tranquilizers can act as a psychological crutch after lengthy use, so the majority of clinicians now recommend that they be used primarily as a short-term remedy for anxiety rather than as a long-term cure. Newer antianxiety drugs, such as *buspirone*, may not produce the same degree of dependency. Increasingly, however, therapists are finding that antidepressants, particularly SSRIs, are effective in treating anxiety disorders, and they're now being widely prescribed (Jakubovski et al., 2019). For a brief review of drug therapies, see Concept Review 15.1.

CONCEPT REVIEW 15.1
DRUG THERAPIES

Type of Drug	What It Treats	Examples and Effects
Antipsychotic	Positive symptoms of schizophrenia, including delusions, hallucinations, and disorganized speech	*Chlorpromazine* is a *dopamine antagonist*. It blocks or impedes the flow of dopamine in the brain. *Clozapine* has proven effective in alleviating some symptoms of schizophrenia.

(Continued)

(Continued)

Type of Drug	What It Treats	Examples and Effects
Antidepressants	Depressive disorders	Tricyclics alter mood by acting primarily on norepinephrine, allowing it to linger in synapses longer. *Fluoxetine* (e.g., Prozac) works primarily on serotonin, blocking its reuptake into the neuron. *Lithium carbonate* is used to treat bipolar disorder.
Antianxiety	Psychological problems associated with anxiety	Tranquilizers come from a class of chemicals called benzodiazepines. They appear to work on the neurotransmitter GABA, which produces primarily inhibitory effects. The result is a lowering of excitation in affected neurons, reducing tension and anxiety.

Electroconvulsive Therapy

When traditional medications fail, particularly for depression, clinicians sometimes turn to a more controversial form of biomedical therapy: shock treatment. As you know, the language of the nervous system is partly electrical in nature. If electric shock is administered to the brain, a brief brain seizure

ECT is a reasonably safe and effective form of treatment for patients suffering from severe depression, but it is still considered controversial by mental health professionals.

Will & Deni McIntyre / Science Source

will occur that produces, among other things, convulsions and loss of consciousness. When **electroconvulsive therapy (ECT)** was first introduced in the 1930s, it was a terrifying and hazardous procedure; patients suffered serious side effects that included the occasional broken bone from the convulsions. Modern applications of ECT are much less physically traumatic; the patient is given a light anesthetic and medications that relax the muscles so injuries won't occur.

Many mental health professionals believe ECT is a reasonably safe and effective form of treatment for people who suffer from severe depression. It's used almost exclusively for depression, although some clinicians believe it benefits other psychological problems as well, particularly schizophrenia (Grover et al., 2019). It's considered to be a treatment of last resort, to be used only when people have shown little or no response to antidepressant or antipsychotic drugs or other conventional forms of psychotherapy. Controlled research studies have found that ECT is successful perhaps as much as 50% to 70% of the time in lessening the symptoms of depression in people who have not otherwise responded to treatment. Typically, these studies involve direct comparisons between depressed people who receive ECT and those who undergo the same procedural preparations but don't actually receive the shock.

Controversies

Despite the demonstrated effectiveness of ECT as a treatment for severe depression, the procedure remains controversial for several reasons. First, no one is certain exactly why the treatment works. It's possible that shocking the brain affects the release of neurotransmitters or changes some structural feature of the brain that allows for better communication among neurons (see, e.g., A. D. Chang et al., 2018), but at present there's no definitive answer as to why the procedure changes mood. Second, ECT produces side effects, particularly confusion and a loss of memory for events surrounding the treatment (e.g., W. V. McCall, 2007). These side effects are usually temporary, and they're not serious for most people, but they remain a concern. Third, people who receive ECT for depression have a relatively high relapse rate, which means they're likely to tailspin into another depressive episode at some point (W. V. McCall, 2001). Finally, some researchers are concerned that ECT might cause permanent brain damage. Effective ECT usually requires repeated administrations of the shock over several weeks, and it's not known what long-term effects these treatments have on the brain.

Is ECT worth the risks? The answer depends on the needs of the particular person. If you're deeply depressed and no other treatment options have provided relief, or if the side effects of traditional medications cannot be tolerated, ECT can be a lifesaver. Many clinicians believe that if it comes down to a desperate choice between ending your life and suffering some confusion and memory loss, trying ECT is certainly worth the risk. Newer treatment options on the horizon may eventually prove more effective and have fewer side effects. For example, there is a procedure called *magnetic seizure therapy* that uses magnetic fields to induce brief seizures in the cortex, without the electrical stimulation of brain structures involved in memory. Early evidence suggests that this technique may be effective in treating depression, without some of the side effects associated with ECT (Cretaz et al., 2015).

Psychosurgery

There is a direct connection between biological problems in the brain and some psychological disorders. People suffering from schizophrenia, for example, sometimes show structural abnormalities in the brain. It makes sense, then, to consider the possibility of direct intervention, through brain surgery, to fix these problems permanently. Certainly if your appendix or gall bladder was infected and the diseased organ was creating a whole host of physical symptoms, you wouldn't think twice about fixing the problem with surgery. Wouldn't it be nice if we could just remove the part of the brain that is causing the psychological problem?

Actually, the use of **psychosurgery**—surgery that destroys or alters tissue in the brain in an effort to affect behavior—has been around for decades. In the 1930s, a surgical procedure called the *prefrontal lobotomy* was pioneered by a Portuguese physician, Egas Moniz (and later in the United States by Walter Freeman and James Watts). The operation involved a crude separation of the frontal lobes from the rest of the brain. The surgery was designed to sever various connections in the brain's circuitry in the hope that it might produce calming tendencies in disturbed patients. The procedure was widely

Dr. Walter Freeman is shown here in 1949, demonstrating psychosurgery. He is inserting an instrument under the patient's upper eyelid to sever certain neural connections in the brain and thereby relieve symptoms of a psychological disorder. Operations of this type are no longer performed.

Bettmann / Getty Images

used for several decades, and, in fact, Moniz was awarded the Nobel Prize for his work in 1949. But prefrontal lobotomies eventually fell into disrepute. Many patients were killed by the procedure, and it produced serious cognitive deficits in many others. They lost their ability to plan and coordinate actions, capabilities associated with activity in the frontal lobes.

Psychosurgery is still used as a way of treating problems that have failed to respond to conventional forms of therapy, but its use is exceedingly rare. One modern form of psychosurgery, called a *cingulotomy*, is sometimes used to treat obsessive–compulsive disorder and severe forms of depression (e.g., Baker et al., 2019). The surgery destroys a small portion of tissue in the limbic system of the brain. As with ECT, however, physicians really have no idea why this procedure works, nor can they explain why it works in some people but not in others. It's another treatment of last resort that has proven effective for some but has not gained wide acceptance among the general psychological community. As our understanding of the brain increases, however, it seems likely that surgical approaches to treatment may rise in popularity (Read & Greenberg, 2009).

KNOWLEDGE CHECK 15.1

Check your knowledge about biomedical therapies by answering the following questions. (You will find the answers in the Appendix.)

1. Pick the psychological disorder that is best treated by each of the following therapies or medications. Choose your answers from among the following: *depression, manic episode, generalized anxiety disorder, schizophrenia.*
   a. Clozapine: _____
   b. Prozac: _____
   c. Cingulotomy: _____
   d. ECT: _____
   e. Benzodiazepine: _____

2. Which of the following statements about ECT (electroconvulsive therapy) is false?
    a. ECT is an effective treatment for depression.
    b. Researchers are uncertain how ECT works.
    c. ECT can produce confusion and some memory loss.
    d. ECT is used regularly to treat schizophrenia.

TREATING THE MIND: INSIGHT THERAPIES

People who suffer from psychological disorders often carry around faulty or irrational beliefs about the world and about themselves. Many clinicians are convinced that the proper role for the therapist is to confront these irrational thoughts and beliefs directly through insight therapies. **Insight therapies** are designed to give clients self-knowledge, or *insight*, into the content of their thought processes, usually through extensive one-on-one verbal interactions. The hope is that with insight people will adopt a more realistic, adaptive view of the world and change their behavior accordingly.

There are many types of insight therapy. We'll consider three in this section: *psychoanalysis, cognitive therapies*, and *humanistic approaches*. Most other insight therapies are related to these three main approaches. The common thread is the belief that cognitive or mental insight can produce significant changes in one's psychological condition. The therapies differ in the kinds of beliefs or memories that are considered to be important and in how the client's insight can best be obtained. Finally, we'll end this section by briefly discussing the value of group and family therapy.

Psychoanalysis: Resolving Unconscious Conflicts

Probably the best-known insight therapy is **psychoanalysis**, which comes originally from the work of Sigmund Freud. As you may remember from Chapter 11, Freud placed enormous emphasis on the concept of the *unconscious mind*. He believed that each of us houses a hidden mental reservoir that is filled with memories, primitive urges, and conflicts. We can't directly think about the urges and memories stored in the unconscious mind, but they affect our behavior nonetheless. Freud believed that through psychoanalysis these hidden impulses and memories can be brought to the surface of awareness, freeing us from unwanted thoughts and behaviors.

Freud based his theory primarily on case studies. He routinely treated patients with troubling psychological problems, and he discovered he could often help these people by getting them to recall and relive traumatic experiences they had apparently forgotten, or repressed. Freud was particularly interested in the emotionally significant experiences of childhood because he believed that during childhood we progress through a number of psychologically "fragile" stages of psychosexual development (see Chapter 11). Traumatic experiences are, by definition, anxiety provoking and therefore difficult for the young mind to deal with, so they're buried in the unconscious. Although no longer consciously available, these experiences continue to affect behavior.

Sigmund Freud used the analysis of dreams, even his own, as the "royal road" to understanding the content of the unconscious mind.

Bettmann / Getty Images

The Tools of Psychoanalysis

The goal of psychoanalysis is to help uncover, and thereby relive, unconscious conflicts. Obviously, because people are unaware of the conflicts, the therapist needs certain tools to access what is buried in the unconscious mind. Freud liked to compare psychoanalysis to excavating a buried city, but instead of picks and shovels his tools were the uncensored expressions and feelings of his patients. Freud relied heavily on a technique called **free association**, in which people were asked to relax and freely express whatever thoughts and feelings happened to come into their minds. To the untrained eye the result was a series of meaningless and unrelated streams of thought, but to Freud these free associations represented symbolic clues to the content of the unconscious.

Freud's other important therapeutic tool was dreams. Through **dream analysis**, he felt the therapist was handed a royal road to the unconscious. As we discussed in Chapter 6, Freud was convinced that dreams are partly a psychological mechanism for wish fulfillment, a way to satisfy hidden desires that are too anxiety provoking to come to consciousness directly. The story line of dreams, he believed, is largely symbolic—there is a hidden meaning to dreams, a *latent content*, that reveals the unconscious. This latent content can be contrasted with the actual events and symbols of the dream, which Freud called its *manifest content*. Freud encouraged his patients to describe their dreams so he could acquire further clues in his search for hidden psychological truth.

Resistance and Transference

In classic psychoanalysis, the therapist seeks to understand the content of the unconscious, but it's really the client who needs the insight. The therapist can't simply relay the hidden meanings that are uncovered—explanation is not enough. Instead, the individual needs to face the emotional conflicts directly and relive them, and the therapist acts only as a kind of learned guide. But the journey toward insight is not an easy one, and the therapist must usually maneuver around a number of roadblocks. For example, people typically go through periods in which they are uncooperative. They show **resistance**, which is an unconsciously motivated attempt to subvert or hinder the therapy.

Why would people try to block their own therapy? Hidden conflicts are anxiety provoking, so people use defense mechanisms to reduce the anxiety. As Freud (1912/1964) put it, "Resistance accompanies the treatment at every step; every single association, every act of the patient's . . . represents a compromise between the forces aiming at cure and those opposing it" (p. 140). The resistance can express itself in a variety of ways; the client might become inattentive, claim to forget dreams, skip therapy sessions, or argue with the directions suggested by the therapist.

Overcoming resistance is a major challenge for the therapist. Freud believed that a turning point comes when the client begins to show a type of resistance called transference. **Transference** occurs when thoughts or feelings are expressed toward the therapist that are actually representative of the way clients feel about other significant people in their life. Clients "transfer" feelings of love, hate, or dependence onto a substitute figure, the therapist. Depending on the repressed feelings being tapped, a client might turn the therapist into an object of passionate love or into a hated and despised individual (see Figure 15.3).

Transference is a significant event in analysis because it means that the client's hidden memories and conflicts are close to the surface of consciousness. The client is fully aware of the strong feelings being experienced—although the object of those feelings is inappropriate—and this gives the therapist an opportunity to help the client work

FIGURE 15.3 ■ Resistance and Transference

Freud believed that uncooperative actions by the client, which he called resistance, were unconsciously motivated attempts to subvert the therapeutic process. Through transference, Freud believed, clients transfer unconscious feelings about significant others onto the therapist.

Resistance

Transference

Illustrated by Sarah Yeh

through what those feelings might mean. The person is no longer in denial of powerful emotional urges—they're right there on the surface, ready to be dealt with. At the same time, it's important for the therapist to recognize that the client's feelings at this point are symbolic. It's not uncommon for the patient to express feelings of strong sexual desire for the therapist, for example, and it would be inappropriate and unethical for the therapist to take them as literal truth (see Knapp, 2012).

Current Applications

Classical psychoanalysis, as practiced by Freud and his contemporaries, is very time-consuming. It can take years for the analyst to excavate the secrets of the unconscious, and the client needs to be properly prepared to accept the insights when they're delivered. Remember, the client is setting up roadblocks throughout the process. So this kind of therapy is certainly far from a quick fix. It's not only time-consuming but also expensive.

For these reasons, modern practitioners of psychoanalysis often streamline the therapeutic process (e.g., see R. P. Hobson, 2016). Briefer forms of therapy encourage the therapist to take a more active role. Rather than waiting for people to find insight themselves, the analyst is much more willing to offer interpretations in the early stages of therapy. Instead of waiting for transference to occur on its own, the analyst might encourage role playing in an attempt to get the person to deal with deep-seated feelings. Using these techniques, progress can occur in weeks or months rather than requiring years of analysis (see Charman, 2004).

In addition to increasing the speed of treatment, modern versions of psychoanalysis are often tailored to meet the needs of the particular client. No attempt is made to excavate and reconstruct the person's entire personality; instead, the analyst focuses on selective defense mechanisms or conflicts that are more pertinent to the individual's symptoms. Often a greater emphasis is placed on improving the client's interpersonal and social skills, and less attention is given to sexual and aggressive drives. Because these forms of treatment differ from classical psychoanalysis, they usually go by the more general term *psychodynamic therapy*.

Cognitive Therapies: Changing Maladaptive Beliefs

According to Freud's theory, a person's conscious thoughts, beliefs, and feelings are important primarily because they provide clues to the inner workings of the unconscious mind. **Cognitive therapies**, in contrast, place a much greater emphasis on the conscious beliefs themselves, rather than on what those beliefs may mean symbolically. Cognitive therapists assume that irrational beliefs and negative thoughts are primarily responsible for psychological disorders. If you can change the negative thoughts and beliefs, the psychological disorder will be changed as well.

Let's take depression as an example. People who are depressed usually don't think productively. They view themselves as essentially worthless and unlovable, and they see little chance that things will change for the better in the future. Thinking in such a way clouds the interpretation of normal events; everyday experiences are passed through a kind of negative filter, which means that depressed people often jump to irrational conclusions. For instance, a depressed woman whose husband arrives home slightly late from work might be immediately convinced that her husband is having an affair. The depressed student who fails the test might see the F as confirmation of a dull and stupid mind.

Cognitive therapists believe it's not direct experience, such as failure on a test, that produces depression. Think about it. It's not particularly difficult to fail a test—just stop going to class or refrain from studying. The F by itself doesn't logically mean much. You can fail a test for many reasons, and most have nothing to do with your intrinsic worth as a human being. But in the mind of someone who is depressed, the event (failing the test) is accompanied by an irrational belief ("I'm incredibly stupid"), and it's this belief that leads to negative emotional consequences (feeling sad and depressed). Thus, it's the *interpretation* of the event, not the event itself, that leads to problems (Beck, 1991; Ellis, 1962, 1993; see Figure 15.4).

FIGURE 15.4 ■ The Cognitive View of Depression

Cognitive therapists believe that internal thoughts and beliefs, not direct experience, lead to depression.

Illustrated by Sarah Yeh

Rational-Emotive Therapy

The goal of cognitive therapy, then, is to remove these irrational beliefs. But how can irrational beliefs be changed? One technique is to challenge the beliefs directly, through active and aggressive confrontation. In **rational-emotive therapy**, developed by Albert Ellis, the therapist acts as a cross-examiner, verbally questioning the client's irrational thought processes. Here's an excerpt from an exchange between a therapist practicing rational-emotive therapy and a client showing signs of depressed thinking (from Walen et al., 1992, pp. 204–205):

Therapist: You really believe that you're an utterly worthless person. By definition, that means that you're doing things poorly. Can you prove to me that that's correct?

Client: But I've failed at so many things.

Therapist: Just how many?

Client: I've lost my job, my wife is threatening to leave me, I don't get along with my kids—my whole life's a mess!

Therapist: Well, let me make two points. First of all, that's not every aspect of your life. Second, you seem to take total responsibility for all of those events, rather than only partial responsibility.

Client: But even if I'm not totally responsible, I'm still a failure.

Therapist: No. You've failed at those things. There are other things you haven't failed at.

Client: Like what?

Therapist: You still manage to get up every morning, you keep up appearances, you manage your finances well considering your economic plight—there's lots of things you do well.

Client: But they don't count!

Therapist: They don't count to you right now because you're overly concerned with negative issues, but they certainly *do* count. There are lots of people who don't do those things well. Are *they* failures?

Client: No, but . . .

Therapist: You know, Jack, you're one of the most conceited people I've ever met!

Client: What do you mean? I've just been telling you how lousy I am!

Therapist: The fact that you hold two different standards tells me how conceited you are. You hold much higher standards for yourself than for anyone else, which implies that you think you're much better than others. It's okay for those lowly slobs to have problems, but not a terrific person like you. Isn't that contradictory to your notion that you're worthless?

Client: Hmmmmm.

Therapist: How about instead of rating yourself as worthless, you just accept the failings that you do have and try your best to improve them?

Client: That sounds sensible.

Therapist: Let's take one of those problem areas now and see how we can improve things . . .

The important part of rational-emotive therapy is the therapist's attack on the rationality of the client's beliefs. The therapist points out the irrationality of the client's thought processes, sometimes in a confrontational manner, in the hope that the negative beliefs will ultimately be rejected, lessening their emotional consequences. Albert Ellis (1962) outlined what he believed to be the irrational beliefs that affect most people who seek treatment for psychological disorders. The therapist tries initially to pinpoint which of these beliefs the client holds, so they can be changed accordingly. Here are a few examples from Ellis's list:

1. I must be loved and approved of by every significant person in my life, and if I'm not, it's awful.

2. It's awful when things are not the way I'd like them to be.

3. I should be very anxious about events that are uncertain or potentially dangerous.

4. I am not worthwhile unless I am thoroughly competent, adequate, and achieving at all times, or at least most of the time in at least one major area.

5. I need someone stronger than myself on whom to depend or rely.

What makes these beliefs irrational is their inflexibility and absoluteness. I *must* be loved and approved; I *must* be thoroughly competent; I *need* someone stronger than myself. The client firmly believes things must be a particular way or something awful or catastrophic will happen. Ellis has used the term *musterbation* to refer to this kind of irrational thinking. Any time you find yourself thinking that something *must* be a particular way, you're guilty of musterbation.

Albert Ellis developed rational-emotive therapy to help free people from irrational thoughts and beliefs.

Peter Kevin Solness/Fairfax Media via Getty Images

Beck's Cognitive Therapy

Although all forms of cognitive therapy focus on changing irrational thought processes, not all treatments are as harsh as rational-emotive therapy. The rational-emotive therapist will essentially lecture—and in some instances even belittle—the client in an effort to attack faulty beliefs. Other cognitive therapies, such as the treatment procedures pioneered by Aaron Beck, take a more subtle tack. Rather than directly confronting clients, Beck suggests it's more therapeutic for clients to identify negative forms of thinking themselves. The therapist acts as an adviser, or co-investigator, helping clients discover their own unique kinds of faulty beliefs (Beck & Dozois, 2011).

In a sense, clients who undergo Beck's cognitive therapy are asked to become psychological detectives. Part of the therapy involves extensive record keeping or "homework." Between therapeutic sessions, Beck asks his clients to record their automatic (or knee-jerk) thoughts and emotions in a notebook as they experience various situations during the day. Clients are then asked to write rational responses to those thoughts and emotions, as if they were scientists evaluating data. Is the thought justified by the actual event? What's the evidence for and against the conclusions that they reached? The therapist hopes clients will eventually discover the contradictions and irrationality in their thinking and realign their beliefs accordingly (see Figure 15.5).

FIGURE 15.5 ■ Homework From a Cognitive Therapist

During cognitive therapy, people are often asked to record their automatic thoughts and emotions in a daily log, which requires them to construct a rational response to the situation and then rerate the emotional reaction.

Situation	Emotion(s)	Automatic thought(s)	Rational response	Outcome
1. Actual event leading to unpleasant emotion, or 2. Stream of thoughts daydreams or recollections, leading to unpleasant emotion.	1. Specify sad/anxious/angry, etc. 2. Rate degree of emotion, 1–100.	1. Record automatic thought(s) that preceded emotion(s). 2. Rate belief in automatic thought(s), 0–100%.	1. Write rational response to automatic thought(s). 2. Rate belief in rational response, 0–100%.	1. Rerate belief in automatic thought(s), 0–100%. 2. Specify and rate subsequent emotions, 0–100.
7/15 Audre didn't return my phone call.	Anxious - 75 Sad - 55 Angry - 40	People don't like talking to me - 75% I'm incompetent. 65%	She's out walking the dog so she hasn't had the time to call back. 70%	1. 35% 15% 2. Relieved - 35

Explanation: When you experience an unpleasant emotion, note the situation that seemed to stimulate the emotion. (If the emotion occurred while you were thinking, daydreaming, etc., please note this.) Then note the automatic thought associated with the emotion. Record the degree to which you believe this thought: 0% = not at all, 100% = completely. In rating degree of emotion: 1 = a trace, 100 = the most intense possible.

Source: Adapted from "Depression," by A. T. Beck and J. E. Young. In D. H. Barlow (Ed.), *Clinical Handbook of Psychological Disorders: A Step by Step Treatment Manual*, pp. 667–668.

Humanistic Therapies: Treating the Human Spirit

In cognitive therapy, the goal is for clients to gain insight into their faulty and irrational ways of thinking. In classical psychoanalysis, the focus is on hidden conflicts and desires. In **humanistic therapy**, the therapist tries to help clients gain insight into their own fundamental *self-worth* and *value* as humans. Therapy is a process of discovering one's own unique potential, one's natural capacity to grow and better oneself as a human being.

Humanistic therapists believe that people are capable of controlling their own behavior—we can help "fix" our own problems—because each of us has free will. We sometimes lose sight of our potential for change because we're concerned about what others think of us and of our actions. We let others control how we think and feel. It is the therapist's job to help clients rediscover their natural self-worth—to help them get back in touch with their own true feelings, desires, and needs—by acting as a confidant and friend.

In humanistic therapies, the therapist tries to provide a completely supportive environment, which allows clients to rediscover their natural self-worth.

iStockPhoto/fizkes

Client-Centered Therapy

Humanistic therapies resemble cognitive therapies in their emphasis on conscious thought processes. But the goal is not to criticize or correct irrational thinking; quite the contrary, it's to be totally supportive in all respects. The therapist's proper role is to be nonjudgmental, which means the client should be accepted unconditionally. According to humanistic therapists such as Carl Rogers, the most effective form of therapy is **client-centered therapy**—it is the client, not the therapist, who ultimately holds the key to psychological health and happiness.

We discussed the theoretical ideas of humanistic psychologists, especially Carl Rogers, in some detail in Chapter 11. Rogers was convinced that most psychological problems originate from *incongruence*, which he defined as the discrepancy between our self-concept and the reality of our everyday experiences. People often hold an inaccurate view of themselves and their abilities, Rogers argued, because of an ingrained need for *positive regard*—they seek the approval, love, and companionship of significant others (such as their parents). But these significant others tend to attach *conditions of worth* to their approval: They demand that we think and act in ways that may not be consistent with our true inner feelings. Improvement comes from providing a warm and supportive environment—without conditions of worth—that will encourage clients to accept themselves as they truly are.

In client-centered therapy, the therapist seeks to provide three essential core qualities to the client: *genuineness, unconditional positive regard*, and *empathy*. As the client's confidant, the therapist must be completely genuine—the therapist must act without phoniness and express true feelings in an open and honest way. The second quality, unconditional positive regard, means that the therapist cannot place conditions of worth on the client. The therapist must be totally accepting and respectful of the client at all times, even if the client thinks and acts in a way that seems irrational or inappropriate. Remember, humanists believe all people are essentially good—they simply need to be placed in an environment that will nurture their natural tendencies toward positive growth.

The third quality, empathy, is achieved when the therapist is able to truly understand and accept what clients are feeling—to see things from their perspective. Through empathy, the therapist acquires the capacity to reflect those feelings back in a way that helps clients gain insight into themselves. Consider the following interaction between Carl Rogers and one of his clients, a woman coming to grips with deep feelings of betrayal and hurt that she's tried to cover up (from Rogers, 1951, p. 94):

Client: I never did really know. But it's—you know, it's almost a physical thing. It's—it's sort of as though I were looking within myself at all kinds of—nerve endings and bits of things that have been sort of mashed.

Rogers: As though some of the most delicate aspects of you physically almost have been crushed or hurt.

Client: Yes. And you know, I do get the feeling, "Oh, you poor thing." (Pause)

Rogers: Just can't help but feel very deeply sorry for the person that is you.

Client: I don't think I feel sorry for the whole person; it's a certain aspect of the thing.

Rogers: Sorry to see the hurt.

Client: Yeah.

Notice that Rogers reflects back the feelings of the client in a completely nonjudgmental fashion. He is seeking to understand and empathize with her feelings, thereby validating their existence and helping her to work through them. Notice also that it's the client, not the therapist, who is doing the analyzing. Client-centered therapy is based on the idea that it's the clients who understand what truly hurts them psychologically, and it's the clients who have the best sense of how to proceed with therapy. All the therapist can do is provide the right kind of supportive environment and help clients recognize their own self-worth and trust their own instincts.

Other Humanistic Approaches

Client-centered therapy is the most popular form of humanistic therapy, but it's not the only one. *Gestalt therapy*, developed by Fritz Perls (1969; Perls et al., 1951), also places the burden of treatment in the hands of a "naturally good" client, but the approach is far less gentle and nondirective than client-centered therapy. In Gestalt therapy, clients are actively encouraged—even forced—to express their feelings openly. The emphasis is on the "here and now," rather than past events, and the therapist uses a variety of techniques to get the client to open up. For example, in the "empty chair" technique, clients are asked to project their feelings onto an empty chair in the room and then, literally, "talk" to those feelings (or to the person who is the source of those feelings). The idea is that only through fully understanding and overtly expressing oneself as a whole person (the word *Gestalt* roughly translates from the German as "whole") can a person hope to take responsibility for those feelings and change them for the better.

Another group of humanistic treatments is known collectively as *existential therapies*. Existential therapists believe psychological problems originate from the anxieties created by personal choices, such as whether to stay in school, get married, or quit a job. These fundamental choices—choices that relate to one's daily existence as a human being—are often difficult to face, and individuals may choose not to deal with them directly. Existential therapists encourage their clients to accept responsibility for these decisions, but in a supportive environment that encourages positive growth (see van Deurzen & Arnold-Baker, 2018). For a summary of insight therapies see Concept Review 15.2.

CONCEPT REVIEW 15.2
INSIGHT APPROACHES TO PSYCHOTHERAPY

APPROACH	WHAT THE PSYCHOPATHOLOGY IS ATTRIBUTED TO	APPROACH TO TREATMENT FOR DEPRESSION
Psychoanalysis	Unconscious conflict, often rooted in childhood trauma	Debbie is depressed because of repressed fears that her parents don't really love her. They were not very affectionate while she was growing up. Her therapist tries to get Debbie to talk about her childhood relationship with her parents.
Cognitive	Conscious processes, including irrational beliefs and negative thoughts	Troy is having a tough time with his parents. They want him to major in business, which he hates. He feels like a terrible person for not following his parents' wishes; after all, they're paying his tuition. His therapist attempts to show him that disagreeing with his parents over his college major does not reflect badly on him as a person.
Humanistic	Problems with self-concept, or *incongruence* between self-concept and reality	Azra feels guilty. She plans on having only one child, but her parents would like lots of grandchildren, and Azra is an only child. Azra feels bad about herself and her failure to gain acceptance from her parents. Her therapist listens as Azra describes her feelings and tries to be warm, supportive, and open to what she is saying.

Group Therapy

Therapy is commonly perceived as a one-on-one experience—you and the therapist sit alone in a room discussing your problems. But there is no principled reason why the therapies we've been discussing can't be conducted in group rather than individual sessions. In **group therapy**, you join other people who are undergoing treatment for a similar problem. Typically, group sessions include the therapist and somewhere between 4 and 15 clients, although there are few hard-and-fast rules for conducting group sessions; for example, in some cases there may be more than one therapist involved in the session (Yalom, 2005).

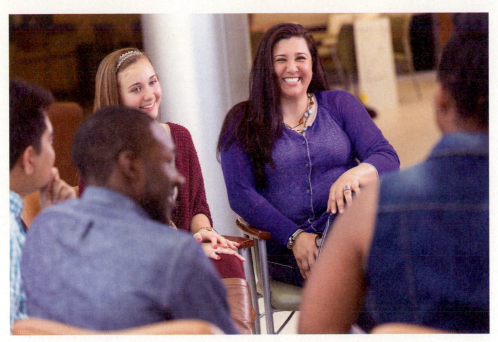

Participating in group therapy enables a client to learn from others with similar concerns.

iStockPhoto/SDI Productions

At first glance, the idea of group therapy seems troubling to most people. After all, who wants to talk about their personal problems in front of others? It's hard enough to open up to one person—the therapist—but at least the therapist is a trained professional. Yet groups offer a number of advantages over individual sessions. First, group therapy can be much more cost effective because the therapist can meet with multiple clients at the same time. Second, hearing other people talk about problems that match your own can be educational. You can learn about their strategies for coping with problems, and you can see firsthand how their symptoms compare to your own. Third, and perhaps most important, when you hear testimonies from other people, it's easier to realize that you're not alone—you're not the only person who is suffering from psychological problems. As you'll discover later in this chapter, empathy is a very important predictor of success in therapy. Group settings can improve the trusting relationship you have with your therapist as well as with other people who share your problem.

Family Therapy

One place where group therapy can be particularly appropriate is with the family. Rather than just treating an individual, in **family therapy** the therapist treats the family as a whole, as a kind of social *system*. Clearly, if one member of a family suffers from a psychological problem, such as depression, all family members tend to be affected, and all can benefit from treatment. Moreover, the family environment can play either a positive or a negative role in helping a particular family member recover from a psychological problem. If the family understands the disorder and what's necessary for treatment, the odds of successful treatment go up considerably. Family therapists work on ways to improve interpersonal communication and collaboration among family members.

Check your knowledge of insight therapies by matching each of the following statements to a type of therapy. Choose from among the following: *psychoanalysis, Gestalt therapy, rational-emotive therapy, Beck's cognitive therapy, client-centered therapy, family therapy.* (You will find the answers in the Appendix.)

1. "You think you're worthless? Well, I'm sitting here spending time with you, so how can you be completely worthless? It's a ridiculous idea." _____

2. "I want you to keep a record of your thoughts, and the situations that produce them, so that you can judge whether those thoughts are really appropriate given the situation." _____

3. "Don't leave. Sit down and tell me again about the dream you had last night." _____

4. "You feel pain, deep pain, and you just can't get beyond the hurt that you feel inside." _____

5. "Talk to the chair . . . be the chair. Open up and let your true feelings come out." _____

6. "It's not just your problem. Each of you needs to communicate better and learn to work together to solve problems and avoid conflicts." _____

TREATING THE ENVIRONMENT: BEHAVIORAL THERAPIES

Traditional insight therapists address psychological problems by searching the mind for hidden conflicts, faulty beliefs, or damaged self-worth. But there are alternative approaches to therapy that focus more on *behavior* than thoughts or memories. **Behavioral therapies** are designed to change unwanted or maladaptive behavior through the application of basic learning principles. Behavioral therapies are often used in conjunction with other therapies, particularly cognitive therapies, but they can be quite effective when used alone (Spiegler & Guevremont, 2010).

As we discussed in Chapter 14, many psychologists are convinced that psychological problems can be learned, or acquired, as a result of experience. Afraid of snakes? Perhaps you had a frightening experience at some point in your life—you may have been bitten by a snake—and this experience caused you to associate snakes with a negative emotional consequence. The snake isn't symbolic of some hidden sexual conflict—you just learned that when snakes are around, you can be bitten; as a result, snakes have become "signals" for something bad.

If you believe that a psychological problem has been learned, it doesn't make sense to spend months or years searching for a hidden reason for the problem. It's better to treat the surface symptoms by learning something new. More productive actions need to be rewarded, or the negative associations you've formed need to be extinguished or counteracted. We'll consider several behavioral approaches in this section of the chapter, beginning with an effective technique for treating phobias that is based on the principles of *classical conditioning*.

Conditioning Techniques

In Chapter 7, we discussed how dogs and people learn about the signaling properties of events. In Pavlov's classic experiments, dogs learned that one event, called the *conditioned stimulus*, signaled the occurrence of a second event, called the *unconditioned stimulus*. After pairing the conditioned stimulus and the unconditioned stimulus together in time, Pavlov found that his dogs responded to the conditioned stimulus in a way that anticipated the arrival of the unconditioned stimulus. For example, if a bell (the conditioned stimulus) was repeatedly presented just prior to food (the unconditioned stimulus), the dogs would begin to drool (the conditioned response) to the bell in anticipation of the food. Pavlov also showed that this conditioned response, the drooling, was sensitive to how well the conditioned stimulus predicted the occurrence of the unconditioned stimulus: If the bell was rung repeatedly after conditioning but the food was no longer presented, the dog eventually stopped drooling to the bell (a procedure Pavlov called *extinction*).

Now let's consider the case of a specific phobia, such as fear of snakes. Specific phobias are highly focused fears of objects or situations. When the feared object is present, it produces an intense anxiety reaction. In the

1920s, psychologist Mary Cover Jones proposed that such intense fear reactions can be treated as if they're classically conditioned responses. A snake produces fear because some kind of earlier experience has taught you to associate snakes with something fearful. Perhaps while standing near one as a child, your brother or sister screamed in terror, thereby scaring you. Jones's analysis suggested a treatment: It might be possible to eliminate phobias by teaching a new association between the feared object and something pleasurable. As she reported in 1924, she was able to use this logic to treat a little boy's fear of rabbits. She fed the boy some tasty food in the presence of the rabbit, which extinguished the association between the rabbit and an earlier negative experience and replaced it with a more pleasurable association (M. C. Jones, 1924).

Systematic Desensitization

The treatment pioneered by Mary Cover Jones was later refined by psychiatrist Joseph Wolpe into a technique known as **systematic desensitization** (Wolpe, 1958, 1982). As with Jones's approach, systematic desensitization uses *counterconditioning* as a way of reducing the fear and anxiety that have become associated with a specific object or event. The therapist attempts to replace the negative association with something relaxing and pleasurable. It's a gradual process that involves three major steps:

1. The therapist helps the client construct an *anxiety hierarchy*, which is an ordered list of situations that lead to fearful reactions. The client is asked to imagine a series of anxiety-provoking situations, beginning with the least fear-arousing and ending with the feared situation itself.

2. The therapist spends time teaching the client ways to achieve deep muscle relaxation. A state of deep relaxation is incompatible with the experience of anxiety—you can't be afraid and relaxed at the same time.

3. With the help of the therapist, the client then attempts to work through the anxiety hierarchy, forming an image of each of the scenes while maintaining the state of relaxation. The idea is to pair the images of fearful situations with the pleasurable state of relaxation so as to extinguish the old negative association and replace it with something relaxing.

Let's imagine you have a deep, irrational fear of flying in an airplane. Treatment starts by having you create a list of flying-related situations that cause you to feel increasingly anxious. Next, you receive lessons in how to relax yourself fully. Finally, you begin working through your hierarchy. Perhaps you start by simply imagining a picture of an airplane. If you can remain relaxed under these conditions, the therapist will direct you to move up the hierarchy to the next most stressful situation—perhaps imagining the airplane actually taking off. Gradually, over time, you will learn to relax in increasingly more stressful situations, even to the point where you can imagine yourself strapped in the seat as the plane rolls down the runway. If you can stay relaxed—which is incompatible with fear and anxiety—the fearful association with planes will extinguish and be replaced by an association that is neutral or positive. Eventually, when you move to a real situation, the learning will generalize, and you will no longer be afraid to fly in a plane. This type of therapy is summarized in Figure 15.6 using another specific phobia—the fear of snakes.

FIGURE 15.6 ■ Systematic Desensitization

After learning relaxation techniques, the client works slowly through an anxiety hierarchy. At first, she simply imagines the feared object. Eventually, the relaxation response can be maintained while she experiences the actual feared situation.

Illustrated by Sarah Yeh

The idea that we can reduce our fear by confronting the very thing that we fear the most has been extremely effective in the treatment of phobic disorders. Interestingly, though, it turns out that repeated exposure to the feared object or event may be what matters most. Many clinicians today find that neither progressive muscle relaxation nor construction of the hierarchy is necessary for improvements to occur. Simple exposure to the feared object is often sufficient for improvement; in fact, therapists have been using advances in virtual reality technology to expose clients to virtual examples of their feared object with great success (Powers & Emmelkamp, 2008).

Aversion Therapy

Systematic desensitization attempts to eliminate unpleasant associations by replacing them with pleasant ones. In **aversion therapy**, the therapist tries to replace a pleasant reaction to a harmful stimulus with something unpleasant, such as making the client feel bad rather than good after smoking a cigarette or having a drink of alcohol. Once again, the idea is to use counterconditioning, but the goal is to make the target situation something to be avoided rather than approached.

Aversion therapy replaces positive associations with negative ones, such as making a smoker feel bad rather than good after having a cigarette.

iStockPhoto/byakkaya

In the case of alcohol dependency, people can be given a drug (Antabuse) that causes them to be become nauseated and vomit if they take a drink of alcohol. The drug interacts with alcohol, creating extreme discomfort. Under these conditions, the person who is drinking learns a new association that helps combat the alcohol dependency—drinking leads to an unpleasant feeling. A similar technique can be used for smoking, wherein drugs containing certain chemicals leave an extremely bad taste in one's mouth after smoking. The old association connecting pleasure with smoking is replaced by a new association that connects smoking with a terrible taste.

Aversion therapy can be quite effective if the client takes the aversive drug for a sufficient period of time. However, people who undergo aversion therapy are often reluctant to continue the treatment unless they're closely supervised. If the client stops the treatment and returns to normal drinking or smoking, the newly learned negative association will extinguish and be replaced by the old, positive association. Ethical concerns have also been raised about this form of treatment. Although those who participate do so voluntarily, they are often people who are desperately seeking a solution to their problems. Because the treatment directly induces extremely unpleasant experiences, many therapists are convinced that it should be used only as a treatment of last resort.

Applying Rewards and Punishments

As we discussed in Chapter 7, it's possible to change behavior by teaching people about the direct consequences of their behavior. You can be shaped, through the application of rewards and punishments, away from abnormal actions and toward more normal ones. Although aversion therapy involves elements of punishment—the act of drinking is followed by an extremely unpleasant consequence—its goal is mainly to replace prior pleasant emotional associations with unpleasant ones. Behavioral therapies that use rewards and punishments are designed to modify specific unwanted behaviors by teaching people about the consequences of their actions.

Token Economies

Shaping behavior through the delivery of rewards has been particularly effective in institutional settings. When people are confined to mental hospitals or other kinds of care facilities, it's usually because they can't cope successfully without constant supervision. If people can't care for themselves—if they don't wash, eat proper foods, or protect themselves from harm—they need a structured environment around them. In institutional settings, therapists have found that setting up token economies—in which patients are rewarded for behaving appropriately—can be quite effective in teaching patients how to cope with the realities of everyday life (e.g., Seegert, 2003).

In a token economy, the client is reinforced for acting in appropriate ways.

Michael Dwyer / Alamy Stock Photo

In a **token economy**, institutionalized patients are rewarded with small tokens (such as poker chips) whenever they engage in an appropriate activity. Certain rules are established and explained to the patient, which determine when tokens are handed out (or taken away). For example, if Forrest, who is suffering from schizophrenia, takes his medication without complaint, he is given a plastic token. Candita might receive tokens for getting out of bed in the morning, washing her hair, and brushing her teeth. The tokens can later be exchanged for certain privileges, such as being able to watch a movie or stay in a private room. Similarly, if a patient acts in an inappropriate manner, the therapist might choose to take tokens away as a form of punishment. This technique is called a token *economy* because it represents a voluntary exchange of goods and services—the patient exchanges appropriate behavior for the privileges that tokens provide.

Token economies are highly successful in helping patients develop the skills they'll need to function well inside and outside of the institution. Not only do the everyday maintenance activities of the patients improve, but social behavior and even vocational skills can be shaped using token rewards. Token economies have also been used in classroom settings to reward children for showing appropriate individual and group behavior and even to increase participation in large college courses (Doll et al., 2013).

Punishment

Token economies tend to be based primarily on the application of reward as a way of changing unwanted behaviors. But as we've seen, punishment can also be an effective way to teach people about the consequences of their behavior. And, indeed, there are instances in which therapists feel that following a behavior with an aversive stimulus (sometimes even a shock) or removing something pleasant is justified. Consider individuals who are extremely self-destructive—perhaps children who continually bang their heads against the wall. Under these conditions, the safe delivery of an aversive event can reduce these self-destructive behaviors, preventing serious injury (Lovaas, 1987; Lovaas et al., 1973).

But punishment is rarely used as the sole kind of behavioral intervention, for several reasons. First, punishment has side effects—for example, it can damage the working relationship between the therapist and the client. Second, punishment by itself only teaches someone what not to do; it doesn't teach someone the appropriate way to act. Third, punishing someone who is in the grips of a psychological disorder raises ethical concerns. We can't be sure the person on the receiving end of the aversive event approves of the treatment, even though the therapist may be convinced it's in the client's best interest.

Social Skills Training

Serious psychological disorders can have a devastating effect on a person's ability to function successfully in virtually all environments, especially social ones. In schizophrenia, for example, social or occupational dysfunction is one of the defining characteristics of the disorder. Patients with schizophrenia tend to isolate themselves from others, and when they do interact socially, they typically act in odd or peculiar ways.

In such cases, therapists face a practical problem: How can they improve the social skills of the person with the disorder? This is a particularly important concern in schizophrenia, which is often difficult to treat. Even with medication, many patients suffer relapses of symptoms, and some symptoms of the disorder, including social withdrawal and flat affect, cannot be treated effectively with conventional psychoactive drugs. For these reasons, therapists sometimes turn to *social skills training*, which is a form of behavioral therapy that uses modeling and reinforcement to shape appropriate adjustment skills.

Social skills training is usually a multistep process. To teach conversational skills, for example, the therapist might begin with a discussion of appropriate verbal responses in a conversation, followed by a videotaped demonstration. The patient is then asked to "role play" an actual conversation, and the therapist provides either corrective feedback or positive reinforcement. "Homework" might then be assigned, in which the patient is encouraged to practice these skills outside of the training session, preferably in new situations. If the training is conducted in an institutional setting, such as a mental health unit, the therapist must monitor the patient's subsequent interactions carefully so that appropriate reinforcement can be delivered.

Social skills training usually takes place over many sessions, and it's often combined with other forms of treatment (such as psychoactive drugs or some form of insight therapy). The application of these simple learning principles—positive reinforcement and modeling—can lead to significant improvements in social functioning, and in the quality of life for individuals affected with psychological disorders (Kurtz & Mueser, 2008). Remember, one of the most important goals of any therapy is to improve a person's ability to function in everyday situations; at times, focusing on specific symptoms—even something as simple as knowing how to answer a casual question in an appropriate way—can make an enormous difference. For a summary of behavioral therapies, see Concept Review 15.3.

CONCEPT REVIEW 15.3
BEHAVIORAL THERAPIES

APPROACH	IDEA THAT IT IS BASED ON	THERAPEUTIC APPROACH
Systematic desensitization	Intense anxiety is the result of classically conditioned associations.	Uses counterconditioning to reduce the fear and anxiety that are associated with a particular object or event. The therapist attempts to replace a negative association with something relaxing and pleasurable.
Aversion therapy	Problem behaviors are based partly on classically conditioned associations.	The therapist tries to replace a pleasant reaction to a harmful stimulus with an unpleasant reaction. For example, the pleasurable reaction associated with smoking is replaced by a new association between smoking and a terrible taste.
Token economy	Behavior can be changed by teaching people about the direct consequences of their behavior.	The therapist and patient have a voluntary exchange of goods and services—the patient exchanges appropriate behavior for privileges provided by tokens.
Punishment	Behavior can be changed by teaching people about the direct consequences of their behavior.	An inappropriate (e.g., self-injurious) behavior is followed by an aversive stimulus or by the removal of a pleasant stimulus.
Social skills training	Behavior can be changed using modeling and reinforcement.	The therapist models behavior and provides corrective feedback to the "role playing" patient.

KNOWLEDGE CHECK 15.3

Check your knowledge about behavioral therapies by answering the following questions. (You will find the answers in the Appendix.)

1. According to the classical conditioning account of phobias, the feared stimulus, such as a snake, acts as a(n)
   a. unconditioned stimulus.
   b. conditioned stimulus.
   c. conditioned response.
   d. conditioned reinforcer.

2. In systematic desensitization, the fear that has become associated with a specific object or event is reduced through
   a. counterconditioning and extinction.
   b. second-order conditioning.
   c. delivery of an aversive consequence.
   d. token rewards.

3. Which of the following is not a major concern in aversion therapy?
   a. Clients cannot truly give informed and voluntary consent.
   b. Effective punishments can't be delivered because pain thresholds are high.
   c. Clients are often reluctant to continue treatment.
   d. Newly learned negative associations can extinguish.

4. In a token economy, the token acts as which of the following?
    a. Conditioned stimulus
    b. Punishment
    c. Conditioned inhibitor
    d. Reinforcement

EVALUATING AND CHOOSING PSYCHOTHERAPY

When people make the decision to enter therapy, they do so because they're in need of help. Carlos is unable to advance his career in sales because of his extreme fear of flying; Julie lives a life of quiet desperation, mostly alone in her room, because she suffers from a social phobia. We've now examined the major types of therapy, but we've said little about their relative effectiveness. How well does psychotherapy actually work? Are all forms of therapy equally effective, or do some forms of therapy work better than others?

To assess the effectiveness of any therapy requires carefully controlled research. As discussed in Chapter 2, just because someone's behavior changes after a manipulation doesn't mean it was the manipulation that caused the change. Someone might enter therapy and leave improved some time later, but the change could have occurred for reasons unrelated to the actual treatment. Perhaps the person simply improved spontaneously over time. Most people who get the flu improve over time—even if they never see a doctor—and it could be that the same kind of thing happens with psychological disorders. A control group—in which no treatment is given—is needed to confirm that the therapy was indeed responsible for the improvement. Fortunately, a number of such controlled research studies have been conducted.

Clinical Evaluation Research

Let's begin by considering a famous example of a clinical evaluation study (Sloane et al., 1975). In this study, conducted at a Philadelphia psychiatric clinic in the mid-1970s, men and women who were seeking treatment primarily for anxiety disorders were assigned at random to one of three treatment conditions. One group of patients was assigned to therapists experienced in the practice of *psychodynamic* techniques (the analysis of unconscious conflicts and memories); a second group was assigned to experienced *behavioral* therapists (using systematic desensitization and other learning-based techniques); and a third group—the *control* group—was placed on a "waiting list" and received no immediate treatment. After 4 months, an independent team of therapists, who were unaware of the treatment assignments, was called in to evaluate the progress of the patients in each of the three groups.

The results were somewhat surprising. The good news is that the therapies clearly worked. As shown in Figure 15.7, the people who were given either psychodynamic or behavioral therapy showed significantly more improvement after 4 months than the people who were left on the waiting list (although it's interesting to note that the waiting list people improved also). But there were no significant differences between the two treatment conditions—the behavioral approach worked just as well as the psychodynamic approach. Even more surprising was the finding that 8 months later, at a year-end follow-up assessment, the patients in the control group had essentially caught up with the treatment patients—they had improved enough to be comparable to the patients in the other two groups. Thus, the treatments worked, but it seems that their primary effect was simply to speed up natural improvement.

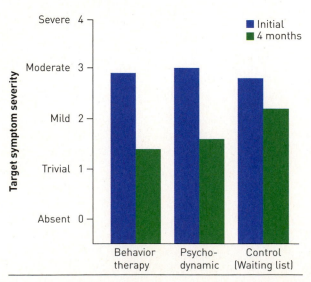

FIGURE 15.7 ■ Evaluating Forms of Treatment

After 4 months, people receiving therapy showed significantly fewer severe symptoms than people in the control group, but there were no significant differences in the results of behavioral and psychodynamic therapy.

Source: Data from Sloane et al., 1975.

Meta-Analysis

The Philadelphia study is important because it's an example of how evaluation research should be conducted—random assignment to groups, the use of a no-treatment control, and an independent assessment procedure (Wolpe, 1975). Since that study was first reported, hundreds of other studies have been conducted (although not all have included the same rigorous control procedures). Rather than picking and choosing from among these studies, mental health professionals often rely on a technique called meta-analysis to help them draw conclusions about this research. In a **meta-analysis**, many different studies are compared statistically on some common evaluation measure. The comparison standard is usually something called an *effect size*, which is essentially a standardized measure of the difference between treatment and control conditions.

In one of the first extensive meta-analytic studies, Smith and colleagues analyzed the results of 475 research studies designed to evaluate one or more forms of psychotherapy (M. L. Smith & Glass, 1977; M. L. Smith et al., 1980). Although the individual studies covered a wide range of psychological problems and therapeutic techniques, in each case it was possible to compare a treatment condition to some kind of control condition (usually an untreated group). Smith and colleagues reached two major conclusions from their meta-analysis of the data. First, there was a consistent and large treatment advantage (see Figure 15.8). People who experienced some kind of active psychotherapy were better off, on average, than roughly 80% of the people who were left untreated. Second, when the various kinds of psychotherapy were compared, few, if any, differences were found. It really didn't matter whether the patient was receiving an insight therapy or a behavioral therapy—all produced the same amount of improvement (see also Wampold et al., 1997).

FIGURE 15.8 ■ The Effectiveness of Psychotherapy

In a meta-analysis that assessed hundreds of clinical evaluation studies, people who experienced some form of active psychotherapy were better off, on average, than roughly 80% of the people who were not treated.

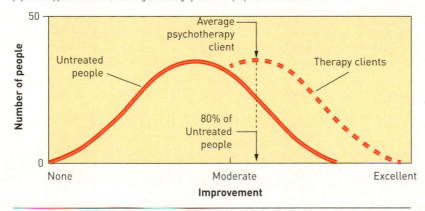

Source: Data from Smith et al., 1980.

There have been hundreds of other attempts to meta-analyze evaluation studies. Some have sought to exercise more control over the research quality of the studies included (Lipsey & Wilson, 1993); others have attempted to extend the areas of examination to include client characteristics, experience of the therapist, or length of the treatment (M. J. Lambert & Bergin, 1994). In general, the findings support two main conclusions: Therapy works, and the effects of therapy are long lasting. For example, one review of meta-analysis studies, which examined some 302 published meta-analyses, found that only 6 produced negative effect sizes (which means that patients undergoing therapy actually got worse than untreated controls) and that the vast majority were overwhelmingly positive (Lipsey & Wilson, 1993).

Controversies

There is widespread agreement among professionals that psychotherapy works, but clinical evaluation studies remain the subject of debate. For example, what should constitute the proper evaluation control? Let's return to the Philadelphia experiment in which two treatment groups (psychodynamic and behavioral) were compared with a group containing people who were left on a waiting list. Remember, the control patients actually got considerably better over time, to a point at which, after a year, they had improved to the same levels as the treatment groups. Psychologists call this kind of improvement in the absence of treatment **spontaneous remission**, and it's been estimated that psychological disorders may improve on their own as much as 30% or more of the time (Eysenck, 1952; Rutherford et al., 2012).

But did the people who were left on the waiting list in the Philadelphia experiment really receive no treatment? This is a difficult question to answer—it depends on how you define treatment. Although these people received no formal psychotherapy, they were given initial psychological tests and were called frequently and given support. Their simple involvement in the study, along with the expectation that they would be receiving some help, may itself have acted as a kind of therapy. Similar effects are commonly found with many placebo controls, in which clients are given attention and support but not formal therapy. Many critics have argued that these no-treatment conditions actually involve factors— such as social support—that are common to most forms of therapy (see M. J. Lambert, 2005). We'll return to this issue in the next section.

The finding that all types of psychotherapy are equally effective has also been questioned (see Cuijpers et al., 2019). It's probably reasonable to assume that certain treatments work best for certain kinds of problems. For example, cognitive therapies may be particularly effective for treating depression or its relapse (Tolin, 2014; but see Wampold et al., 2017), and behavioral therapies may be consistently effective for combating anxiety disorders such as specific phobias (Choy et al., 2007). But even if the treatment is matched to the problem, client variables can influence the effectiveness of the therapy. Not all people have the desire or capacity to respond to rational, verbal arguments of the type used by some cognitive therapists, or to the probing questions of the psychoanalyst. As a result, it's very difficult to conduct an evaluation study that properly takes all of these factors into account. Moreover, often one finds a correlation between a particular form of therapy and an effective outcome, but the causal mechanisms behind the improvement remain unknown (Kazdin, 2007).

Common Factors Across Psychotherapies

Clinical researchers have also considered the possibility that there may be common, nonspecific factors shared by all therapies, regardless of surface differences. Although the various therapies we've considered seem to be very different, and they're clearly driven by very different assumptions about human psychology, they do share features in common (Grencavage & Norcross, 1990; Rosenzweig, 1936). Michael Lambert and Allen Bergin (1994) have suggested that these common factors can be grouped into three main categories: *support factors, learning factors*, and *action factors* (see also M. J. Lambert & Ogles, 2004).

Support Factors

Virtually all therapies that produce positive outcomes provide tangible support for the client. People who enter therapy find themselves face-to-face with someone who is willing to accept and understand their problems. Both the therapist and the client have a common goal, which is to help the client get better. Regardless of their theoretical orientation—psychodynamic, cognitive, behavioral, or humanistic—effective therapists are clearly interested in listening to and reassuring their clients and in developing a positive, trusting relationship. A number of studies have found a strong correlation between the amount of empathy that the therapist establishes with the client and the effectiveness of the treatment (see Nienhuis et al., 2018).

It's also important that the client and the therapist form a *therapeutic alliance*, which means that the client and the therapist must work together to deal with the problems at hand. If the client perceives the therapeutic alliance to be strong, and works hard to maintain a strong alliance, there is a greater chance that the therapy will be successful (Zuroff & Blatt, 2006).

Learning Factors

When people go through therapy, they learn things about themselves. They learn about their thought processes, or about their behavior, or about important factors in their past that might be contributing to current discomforts. Effective therapists often act as mirrors, reflecting a client's beliefs and actions in ways that provide critical insight. Regardless of the method of treatment, effective therapists also give feedback about how various experiences relate to one another. They point out connections among experiences—how we might behave and think similarly across different situations. People are often helped because they're given a reason or a rationale for their problems.

To take a case in point, consider the homework assignments common in cognitive therapy. Here, the client is simply asked to list the specific situations that led to unpleasant thoughts (emotions) and to provide alternative responses. Even without the development of rational response alternatives, it's useful simply to know the particular situations that make you upset or unhappy. If you learn, for instance, that you tend to get emotionally upset regularly after talking to an old romantic partner, then you can work to avoid encounters in the future. Knowledge is useful, and therapy is an excellent vehicle for learning things about yourself.

Action Factors

Finally, all forms of therapy ultimately provide people with a set of specific suggestions for action. Troubled clients might be asked to face their fears, take risks, or directly test irrational beliefs. They might be given specific strategies for coping with anxiety or training in how to relax. Irrespective of the specific suggestions, providing clients with a tangible course of action may be sufficient to give them hope and allow them to feel in control of their problem.

PRACTICAL SOLUTIONS: CHOOSING A THERAPIST

At some point in your life, you might find yourself in need of a psychotherapist. Perhaps you'll experience a simple problem in living, or maybe something more serious. What should you do? Given our discussion about the relative effectiveness of the various treatment options, it might seem natural to conclude that it doesn't make much difference whom you choose. But remember, one of the best predictors of treatment success is the amount of empathy between the client and the therapist. Therefore, it's critical that you find someone you trust and with whom you feel comfortable interacting. The level of trust you feel with the therapist is very important; don't be afraid to shop around to find the right person.

Cultural barriers sometimes prevent members of ethnic minorities from benefiting from mental health resources. It's essential for a therapist to be sensitive to a client's cultural background and general worldview.

iStockPhoto/KatarzynaBialasiewicz

Currently, most psychotherapists describe themselves as *eclectic* in their orientation. This means they're willing to pick and choose from among treatment options to find the techniques that work best for the individual client. It used to be the case that therapists would align themselves with a particular approach or "school"—such as psychoanalysis or behavior therapy—but in one survey of 800 therapists, 68% of those responding described their orientation as eclectic (Jensen et al, 1990). You can expect most therapists to be flexible in their approach, and if one form of treatment is not yielding results—or if you feel uncomfortable with the approach—you can expect the therapist to be open to trying something different. Effective therapy requires open communication, and the therapist depends on your feedback as a client throughout the treatment process.

Mental health professionals also recognize that cultural factors are important in both the diagnosis and the treatment of psychological disorders (e.g., Rathod, 2017). For many years, cultural barriers made it difficult for members of ethnic minorities to use and benefit from mental health resources. Language differences between the client and the therapist clearly undermine effective communication, as do differences between the therapist's and the client's worldview.

Does this mean you should always seek a therapist with a cultural background identical to your own? Not necessarily. For one thing, there is still a shortage of therapists from ethnic minorities in the United States. This means that finding a cultural match may be difficult. Moreover, with the increased exposure to cultural influences, many therapists are now making concerted efforts to become culturally sensitive. In fact, special training programs are now available to help therapists break down some of the barriers that exist for clients from diverse cultural backgrounds. By gaining knowledge about a variety of customs and lifestyles and working directly with culturally diverse clients, therapists hope to remove barriers to effective empathy.

KNOWLEDGE CHECK 15.4

Check your knowledge about evaluating and choosing psychotherapy by deciding whether each of the following statements is true or false. (You will find the answers in the Appendix.)

1. Psychological disorders may improve on their own as much as 30% or more of the time. *True or False?*

2. According to most meta-analytic studies, people who experience active psychotherapy are better off, on average, than roughly 80% of the people who are left untreated. *True or False?*

3. Most evaluation studies show that specific disorders, such as depression, require specific forms of therapy, such as psychoanalysis. *True or False?*

4. One factor common to all forms of psychotherapy is the need to investigate the traumatic events of childhood. *True or False?*

5. In choosing a therapist, perhaps the most important factor is empathy—finding someone you trust and with whom you feel comfortable. *True or False?*

THE PROBLEMS SOLVED: DEVELOPING AND EVALUATING PSYCHOTHERAPIES

In this chapter, we've discussed the various tools therapists use to treat psychological disorders. In each case, the goal of the therapist is to find a way to improve the client's ability to function successfully in the world. As you've seen, most forms of therapy address one or more of the three basic factors thought to contribute to psychological disorders: biological factors, cognitive factors, and environmental factors.

Treating the Body: Biomedical Therapies

Therapies that use medical interventions to treat the symptoms of psychological problems are called *biomedical therapies*. The idea that psychological disorders can be treated as illnesses, in the same way that physicians treat the common cold, has a long history. The most popular form of biomedical therapy is drug therapy, in which medications are given to affect thought and mood by altering the actions of neurotransmitters in the brain. Antipsychotic drugs, for example, reduce the symptoms of schizophrenia by acting as antagonists to the neurotransmitter dopamine in the brain. The antidepressant drug Prozac acts on the neurotransmitter serotonin, and antianxiety drugs—tranquilizers—are believed to act on neurotransmitters in the brain that have primarily inhibitory effects.

In the event that drug therapies fail, mental health professionals sometimes turn to other forms of biomedical intervention, such as electroconvulsive therapy (ECT) and psychosurgery. Shock therapy is used to treat severe forms of depression, but usually only if more conventional forms of treatment have failed. No one is completely sure why the administration of electric shock affects mood, but there's wide agreement that ECT works for many patients. Even more controversial than ECT is psychosurgery, in which some portion of the brain is destroyed or altered in an attempt to eliminate the symptoms of a mental disorder. The infamous prefrontal lobotomies of yesteryear are no longer conducted (partly because they produced unacceptable side effects), but some kinds of surgical intervention in the brain are still used.

Treating the Mind: Insight Therapies

In *insight therapy*, the psychotherapist attempts to treat psychological problems by helping clients gain insight, or self-knowledge, into the contents of their thought processes. Usually, this insight is obtained through prolonged verbal, one-on-one interactions between the therapist and the client. Perhaps the best-known form of insight therapy is Freudian psychoanalysis. The goal of psychoanalysis is to help the client uncover and relive conflicts that have been hidden in the unconscious mind. The psychoanalyst uses such techniques as free association and dream analysis to help probe the contents of the unconscious. As hidden conflicts begin to surface during the course of therapy, the client will typically show what Freud called resistance—an attempt to hinder the progress of therapy—and transference, in which the client transfers feelings about others onto the therapist.

Cognitive therapists believe that psychological problems come primarily from irrational beliefs and thought processes. The therapist attempts to change the client's negative beliefs and thoughts by actively attacking them in verbal exchanges. The therapist points out the irrationality of negative thoughts, using evidence where possible, in the hope that the client will reject the beliefs, thereby lessening their emotional consequences. Less aggressive forms of cognitive therapy encourage clients to analyze the rationality of their own thoughts and beliefs through homework assignments. *Humanistic therapies* have a quite different goal. Here, the idea is to help clients gain insight into their own self-worth and value as humans. It is the client, not the therapist, who holds the key to self-improvement. Humanistic therapists view therapy as a process of discovering one's natural tendencies toward growth and free will. In client-centered therapy, the therapist tries to provide an approving and nonjudgmental environment, thereby enabling clients to recognize and trust their own true instincts.

Treating the Environment: Behavioral Therapies

Behavioral therapies are designed to treat actual behavior rather than inner thought processes. Behavioral therapists assume that many kinds of psychological problems have been learned and can be treated through the application of learning principles. With counterconditioning techniques, for example, the therapist attempts to replace learned associations that are negative with new, pleasurable associations. Thus, in systematic desensitization, specific phobias are treated by having the client (1) construct an anxiety hierarchy of fear-inducing situations, (2) learn relaxation techniques, and (3) work through the anxiety hierarchy, imagining each of the scenes while maintaining a feeling of relaxation. Pairing the feared object with relaxation is intended to extinguish the old, negative association and replace it with something pleasurable. Other behavioral therapies make use of rewards and punishments to change behavior. In token economies, patients are rewarded with small tokens whenever they engage in normal or appropriate behaviors. The tokens can then be exchanged later for more tangible rewards or privileges. Social skills training uses both reinforcement and modeling to encourage more adaptive behavior.

Evaluating and Choosing Psychotherapy

Evaluating any form of psychotherapy requires controlled research in which treatment groups are compared with appropriate control conditions. Hundreds of such studies have been conducted, and meta-analyses of their results typically reach two main conclusions. First, people who receive psychotherapy do significantly better than those left untreated. Second, those positive effects are often long lasting. Although there are sometimes few, if any, advantages found for one type of psychotherapy over another, certain forms of therapy do seem to work best for particular types of psychological disorders.

One reason most forms of treatment are effective may be that common factors are shared by all psychotherapies. These common factors can be grouped into three main categories: support, learning, and action. All therapists provide some kind of support for their clients, and therapist empathy has been shown to be important to outcome success. All forms of therapy also help clients learn about themselves and their behavior, and clients are provided with specific prescriptions for action or behavior change. In choosing a therapist, it's critical that you find someone you trust and with whom you feel comfortable interacting. Cultural factors are also important, because for therapy to work the therapist must be sensitive to the client's cultural worldview.

THINKING ABOUT RESEARCH

A summary of a research study in psychology is given in this section. As you read the summary, think about the following questions:

1. What is unique about the sample used in this study? Is it a random sample? If not, why not?
2. Can you conclude from this study that catastrophic thinking and PTSD are causally related? If not, how might you design the study differently?
3. The results of this study fit naturally with cognitive-behavioral forms of therapy. Why? Do you think that psychodynamic or purely behavioral therapies might be relevant as well?
4. Using what you've learned about therapy, what kinds of specific interventions might the U.S. Army employ to reduce catastrophic thinking among the soldiers?

Article Reference: Seligman, M. E. P., Allen, A. R., Vie, L. L., Ho, T. E., Scheier, L. M., Cornum, R., & Lester, P. B. (2019). PTSD: Catastrophizing in combat as risk and protection. *Clinical Psychological Science, 7,* 516–529.

Purpose of the Study: In our discussion of insight therapies, particularly cognitive therapies such as rational-emotive therapy, we noted that negative "catastrophic" thinking is believed to be a major determinant of psychological disorders such as depression or posttraumatic stress disorder (PTSD). The current study, which tested nearly 80,000 active-duty soldiers in the U.S. military, assessed whether measures of catastrophic thinking are associated with an increased risk of developing PTSD in actual combat situations.

Method of the Study: The unique feature of this study was that the authors were able to test essentially the entire eligible population of active-duty U.S. Army soldiers in an initial assessment period. From this group, the researchers followed nearly 80,000 soldiers, those who agreed to participate and did not suffer from preexisting mental health conditions, during their follow-up deployment to either Iraq or Afghanistan. The initial assessments included measures of catastrophic thinking, coping strategies, social support, and depressive symptoms. For example, to measure catastrophic thinking, the soldiers were asked to respond on a five-point scale from 1 (*not like me at all*) to 5 (*very much like me*) to questions such as "When bad things happen to me, I expect more bad things to happen" or "When bad things happen to me, I cannot stop thinking about how much worse things will get." The soldiers were also given tests to measure general health and amount of alcohol use. The soldiers were then observed until one of the following events occurred: a diagnosis of PTSD, separation from service, mortality unrelated to PTSD, or the conclusion of an observation period that lasted for several years. A measure of combat intensity was also collected at the end of the deployment period.

Results of the Study: The authors observed a total of 3,084 diagnosed cases of PTSD during the study, a rate of 3.88%. Soldiers who scored lowest on the initial test of catastrophic thinking were found to have 25% less risk of developing PTSD, compared to a group scoring in the middle range of the scale, and those soldiers scoring highest in catastrophic thinking had a 29% greater PTSD risk than the middle group. The authors also found that combat intensity was a major risk factor for developing the disorder.

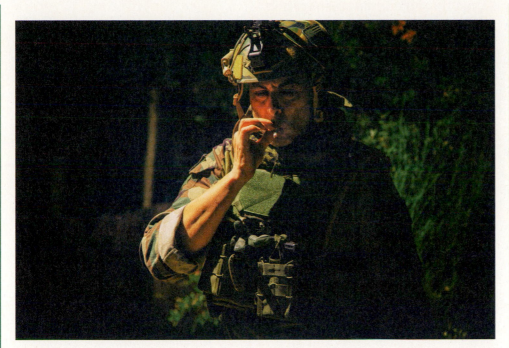

Catastrophic thinking can increase the likelihood of developing the symptoms of PTSD.

iStockPhoto/zabelin

Conclusions of the Study: The authors concluded that preexisting high catastrophic thinking placed soldiers at a 29% higher risk for developing PTSD than soldiers with average catastrophic thinking levels. They recommended that the U.S. Army consider possible interventions to reduce catastrophic thinking prior to combat to reduce the risk of developing PTSD.

KNOWLEDGE CHECK: CHAPTER SUMMARY

You will find the answers in the Appendix.

TREATING THE BODY: BIOMEDICAL THERAPIES

- Most typical antipsychotic drugs work primarily on the neurotransmitter (1) _____ and are used to treat schizophrenia. These medications, which include chlorpromazine (Thorazine), are limited in their effectiveness, and side effects may include (2) _____ dyskinesia, which produces disabling involuntary movements. Clozapine and risperidone are newer antipsychotics that act on several neurotransmitters and help people who don't respond to typical antipsychotic medication. (3) _____ drugs also modulate the effectiveness of neurotransmitters, particularly norepinephrine and (4) _____. (5) _____ disorders have traditionally been treated with the common salt (6) _____ carbonate. (7) _____ medications, or tranquilizers, are in a class of drugs called benzodiazepines, which work primarily on the neurotransmitter (8) _____.

- Many professionals believe that (9) _____ therapy (ECT) is a reasonably (10) _____ and effective treatment 50% to 70% of the time for (11) _____ depression, though it is usually used as a last resort. The treatment is controversial for a number of reasons. No one completely understands why it is effective, and it can produce temporary side effects such as (12) _____ and memory loss.

- (13) _____ affects behavior by destroying or altering (14) _____ tissue. (15) _____ lobotomy (now in disrepute) produces calming effects in disturbed patients. Although cingulotomy is sometimes used to treat obsessive– (16) _____ disorder and severe forms of depression, psychosurgery is performed very (17) _____.

TREATING THE MIND: INSIGHT THERAPIES

- Sigmund Freud believed that (18) _____ brings hidden memories and impulses to awareness, freeing the client from unwanted thoughts and behaviors. The tools used to uncover unconscious conflicts include (19) _____ association and (20) _____ analysis. (21) _____, seen in unconsciously motivated attempts to hinder therapy, and (22) _____, where a client begins to express thoughts and feelings toward the therapist that are really how the client feels about other people, also provide clues about (23) _____ conflicts. Modern psychoanalysts (24) _____ the therapeutic process, which is often tailored to meet specific individual needs.

- (25) _____ therapists emphasize the content of the (26) _____ mind, believing that irrational beliefs and negative thoughts influence our interpretations of events. In (27) _____-emotive therapy, the therapist cross-examines the client, challenging (28) _____ thought processes. Aaron Beck's (29) _____ therapy helps clients more subtly to identify their own faulty beliefs through record keeping and other types of homework.

- In (30) _____ therapy, clients gain insight into their own fundamental self-worth and (31) _____. Client- (32) _____ therapy supports the client in all respects. The key to improvement is a warm supportive environment that helps the client overcome (33) _____, a discrepancy between the (34) _____ and the reality of our everyday experiences. The therapist provides genuineness, unconditional (35) _____ regard, and empathy. (36) _____ therapy is a version of humanistic therapy that encourages and even forces clients to express their feelings openly.

- (37) _____ therapy brings together clients who are experiencing (38) _____ problems. (39) _____ therapy treats the family as a social system; the therapist helps members improve their (40) _____ communication styles and learn to collaborate with each other.

TREATING THE ENVIRONMENT: BEHAVIORAL THERAPIES

- A person with a phobia associates a certain object or situation with (41) _____. (42) _____ techniques may be used to change the association to something pleasurable. In (43) _____, the therapist uses (44) _____ to systematically associate relaxation with feared objects, as rated in an anxiety (45) _____. In (46) _____ therapy, a pleasant reaction to a harmful stimulus, such as alcohol, is replaced with an unpleasant reaction and results in a new association.

- People can be shaped by (47) _____ and (48) _____ to give up abnormal behaviors in exchange for functional ones. In a (49) _____ economy, whenever institutionalized patients engage in an appropriate activity, they are rewarded with tokens that they can exchange for (50) _____. (51) _____ may also be effective in teaching people to understand the (52) _____ of their actions and is sometimes used to discourage self-injurious behavior. (53) _____ skills training is a form of behavioral therapy that uses modeling and reinforcement to shape appropriate adjustment skills.

EVALUATING AND CHOOSING PSYCHOTHERAPY

- A study that compared psychodynamic and (54) _____ therapies with a control condition demonstrated that therapy clearly worked, but that there were no reliable (55) _____ in the effectiveness of the two approaches. A (56) _____-analysis of psychotherapy evaluation studies also showed that therapy works and that the effects are long lasting. In addition, some problems may improve on their own through spontaneous (57) _____. Although all kinds of therapy show similar effectiveness, certain kinds of treatment may work best with certain kinds of problems.

- All forms of therapy involve (58) _____, (59) _____, and (60) _____ factors. The therapist provides support for the client by expressing understanding and empathy. People in therapy usually learn something about themselves, and all therapies offer suggestions for action. Such common factors may account for the finding that various approaches are equally (61) _____.

CRITICAL THINKING QUESTIONS

1. Just because dopamine antagonists reduce the positive symptoms of schizophrenia does not necessarily mean that dopamine causes schizophrenia. Why not?

2. Imagine you're treating a severely depressed person who is clearly suicidal. Remember, drug therapies can take weeks to work. Would you consider ECT for such a person? How about an elderly patient who refuses to eat, just wants to die, and cannot be given medications because of side effects?

3. What do you think Freud would have thought about the value of biomedical therapies? Would he have supported or rejected the idea of treating psychological disorders through medications, ECT, or psychosurgery?

4. Where do you think irrational beliefs come from? Is it possible that people are taught to think in absolute and inflexible ways by their parents, by role models, or by the general culture?

5. Think about the interactions you've had with a really close friend. Do you see any similarities to the client-centered approach advocated by Carl Rogers?

6. Can you think of a role that reinforcement might play in maintaining a phobia? Isn't it true that every time you stay away from a snake, you avoid being bitten?

7. In what ways is shaping, which we discussed in Chapter 7, similar to and different from the procedures of systematic desensitization?

8. Is it ethical to assign patients who are seeking help for their psychological problems to a no-treatment control?

KEY TERMS

antianxiety drugs (p. 551)

antidepressant drugs (p. 550)

antipsychotic drugs (p. 549)

aversion therapy (p. 566)

behavioral therapies (p. 564)

biomedical therapies (p. 548)

client-centered therapy (p. 561)

cognitive therapies (p. 557)

dream analysis (p. 556)

electroconvulsive therapy (ECT) (p. 553)

family therapy (p. 563)

free association (p. 556)

group therapy (p. 563)

humanistic therapy (p. 560)

insight therapies (p. 555)

meta-analysis (p. 571)

psychoanalysis (p. 555)

psychosurgery (p. 553)

psychotherapy (p. 546)

rational-emotive therapy (p. 558)

resistance (p. 556)

spontaneous remission (p. 572)

systematic desensitization (p. 565)

token economy (p. 567)

transference (p. 556)

iStockPhoto/mapodile

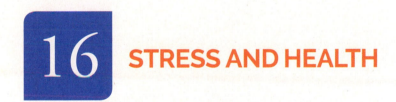

16 STRESS AND HEALTH

Mei was pushing hard. Set to graduate at the end of the current semester, she needed to maintain her grade point average. Rumors were spreading that the campus would be closing soon—apparently a new form of virus was spreading. *Not here, of course,* Mei thought. *Plus, I'm young and healthy, so there's no chance it could affect me.* She glanced over at her roommate, who was also studying hard. Thinking she looked a little flushed, "Are you okay?" Mei asked.

"Hanging in there," the roommate said as she turned toward Mei and coughed.

Although we can't claim exclusive rights to the "age of stress," we certainly live in a demanding and uncertain time. Everybody expects something from us, and they seem to want it now. Your teachers expect the subject matter to be learned, the paper written; your boss expects overtime in addition to your regular hours; your parents expect that weekly phone call, delivered in a pleasant and friendly tone. Add in the constant threat of a terrorist attack or imminent death from a novel virus, and . . . well, enough said.

THE PROBLEMS TO BE SOLVED: WHAT IS THE CONNECTION BETWEEN STRESS AND HEALTH?

Our focus in this chapter is the general topic of health psychology. **Health psychology** is part of a broad movement, known as *behavioral medicine*, that seeks to understand the role of biological, psychological, environmental, and cultural factors in the promotion of physical health and the prevention of illness. Not surprisingly, health psychologists are particularly interested in psychological and environmental contributions to health. They tend to focus on questions such as these: Are there particular personality characteristics that determine who becomes sick or who will recover from illness? Can the same theories that have been used successfully to diagnose and treat psychological disorders be applied to the promotion of physical health? Is it possible to identify the kinds of working environments that lead to illness or promote recovery? Are there specific strategies, or lifestyle choices, that reduce the likelihood of getting sick?

Stress is an adaptive reaction to events in the world, but prolonged exposure to stressful environments can have a negative impact on health. Our discussion revolves around four key issues related to stress and to health psychology in general.

Experiencing Stress

Everyone has an intuitive sense of what *stress* is, but the term can be defined in a variety of ways. We'll discuss some of the meanings of the term as well as various components of the stress response. Health psychologists conceive of stress not as a single reaction, such as a sudden release of activating hormones, but rather as an extended response that occurs over time.

Reacting to Prolonged Stress

The human body is usually well equipped to deal with unexpected trauma by activating those systems that are needed to respond to the emergency. But if the threat continues for an extended period of time, the body's defenses begin to break down. We'll consider some of the physical consequences of prolonged exposure to stress, including the role stress plays in the immune system.

Reducing and Coping With Stress

Given that prolonged exposure to stress can have negative long-term consequences, psychologists have developed specific treatment methods for reducing and controlling stress. A number of techniques are available for managing stress, and we'll consider some of them later in the chapter.

Living a Healthy Lifestyle

Whether you'll remain healthy throughout your life depends importantly on the lifestyle habits you choose. Obviously, if you choose to engage in risky behaviors—such as smoking, failing to get adequate nutrition, or practicing unsafe sex—you increase your chances of illness or death. Health psychologists have joined with other professionals, including physicians, to offer prescriptions for a healthful lifestyle. We'll discuss some of these recommendations along with their foundations in psychological theory.

EXPERIENCING STRESS

"Stress" is one of those concepts that's easy to identify but difficult to define precisely. Part of the problem is that the term can be used in a variety of ways. For example, we frequently describe stress as if it were an actual *stimulus* (such as an event or a person) that places a demand on us or threatens our well-being ("That final next week is going to kill me"). On the other hand, we're just as likely to describe stress as a physical *response* or reaction that we feel ("I'm really stressed out"). To complicate matters even further, whether we feel stress depends on how we interpret the situation we're in (Lazarus, 1966, 2007). Consequently, stress is best treated as an internal psychological *process* through which external events are interpreted as threatening or demanding.

For our purposes, we'll define **stress** as the physical and psychological reaction people have to demanding situations, and we'll refer to the demanding or threatening situations that produce stress as **stressors**. For example, the jackknifed tractor trailer blocking your speedy route home is a stressor, whereas your fuming physical and emotional reaction to it is stress. First we'll consider some of the physical and psychological characteristics of stress; then we'll examine the external and internal factors that contribute to stress.

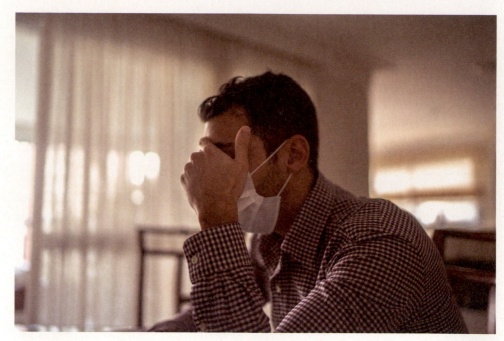

Prolonged exposure to stress can lead to physical and psychological problems.

iStockPhoto/FG Trade

The Stress Response

If you're like most people, you probably think stress is a bad thing. Certainly when you're "stressed out," you tend to feel lousy, and there's no question that extended exposure to stressful situations can have long-term negative consequences. But it's important to understand that stress is in many ways an adaptive reaction. When you're in a threatening situation, or when someone is placing demands on you, it's important that your body become activated so you can respond to the threat in the most appropriate way. The experience of stress does exactly that, at least initially—it activates you (Korte et al., 2005). Stress can also improve your ability to focus and concentrate on a task (Degroote et al., 2020), and it can even enhance your ability to detect positive emotions on faces (von Dawans et al., 2020). It's when environmental demands begin to exceed your body's ability to regulate its capacities that the trouble begins (Koolhaas et al., 2011).

Physiological Reactions

In the 1930s, a physician named Hans Selye (1936, 1952, 1974) introduced an influential model of the stress reaction that he called the **general adaptation syndrome (GAS)**. Selye was convinced that our reaction to stressful situations is general and nonspecific, by which he meant that people are biologically programmed to respond to most threats in the same way. He was initially led to this idea as a medical student when he was struck by the similarities he saw among his patients. Across wildly different illnesses and injuries, his patients seemed to share a "syndrome of just being sick" that suggested to Selye that the body was reacting to each threatening situation in a very general way (no matter the illness or injury). Later, working in the laboratory with rats, he was able to confirm his hypothesis under controlled experimental conditions. Rats subjected to a variety of different kinds of threat—cold, heat, shock, restraint—produced a similar pattern of responses.

Selye's concept of the GAS proposes that the body reacts to threat in three stages, or phases (see Figure 16.1). The first phase, the *alarm reaction*, corresponds to the adaptive fight-or-flight response we've discussed in previous chapters (Cannon, 1932). The body becomes energized, through activation of the sympathetic division of

FIGURE 16.1 ■ The General Adaptation Syndrome

Hans Selye proposed that the body reacts to threat or demand in three stages or phases: (1) an alarm reaction that corresponds to the fight-or-flight response; (2) resistance, during which the body adjusts its reaction in an effort to cope with a threat that is still present; and (3) exhaustion, which occurs when the body's energy reserves become so depleted that it starts to give up.

General adaptation syndrome

Alarm	Resistance	Exhaustion
Fight-or-flight response	Body adjusts to continuing threat	Energy resources depleted: body starts to give up

the autonomic nervous system, and hormones are released by the glands of the endocrine system. Heart rate and respiration rate increase, as does blood flow to the muscles; each of these actions helps prepare the body for immediate defensive or evasive action. The alarm reaction enables us to get out of life-threatening jams, but it is extremely intense and can't be sustained for long periods without serious negative consequences (even death).

If the threat continues but is not serious enough to demand a continued alarm reaction, the body enters a *resistance* phase. During this phase, the body adjusts its physiological reaction to reduce, or cope with, the still-present threat. Arousal levels remain higher than normal, but the body is capable of replenishing at least some of its resources. During the resistance phase, people are able to function reasonably well, but they are particularly susceptible to other stressors in the environment and may begin to suffer from health problems, or what Selye called "diseases of adaptation."

Finally, if the person is unable to find a way to neutralize the threat, the body eventually enters the *exhaustion phase* of the GAS. The body simply can't continue to maintain a high state of readiness for extended periods of time. Eventually, energy reserves become so taxed and depleted that the body starts to give up. During this period, resistance declines to the point at which the stress reaction becomes more and more maladaptive. Death, or some kind of irreversible damage, becomes a real possibility.

Selye's notion of the GAS has remained influential over the years (Fink, 2016). But researchers no longer believe the body's reaction to threat is as general and nonspecific as Selye suggested. Different stressors may well produce somewhat different patterns of response in the body (Goldstein & Kopin, 2007). Moreover, as you'll see a little later, the stress reaction depends on the cognitive interpretation, or appraisal, of the threatening situation.

The early stages of the stress response are clearly adaptive because they help initiate a fight-or-flight response.

iStockPhoto/vlapaev

Psychological Reactions

Stress is not just a physiological reaction to threat; there are also emotional and behavioral components to the reaction. We'll consider the psychological consequences of prolonged exposure to stressful situations later in the chapter, but emotional reactions are an important part of the stress response regardless of when or how long it occurs. *Fear* is a common reaction to threat, as is *anger*. Stressful situations can also lead to feelings of *sadness, dejection*, or even *grief* (Lazarus, 1991). These emotional reactions help to reinforce the idea that stress is not completely general and nonspecific—people are capable of responding emotionally to different stressors in very different ways.

The psychological experience of stress is not even necessarily negative. Stress can have significant short- and long-term psychological benefits (e.g., Dhabhar, 2019). For example, one study that examined the psychological characteristics of people who suffered from frequent physical illness found them to be more understanding (empathetic) of others and more tolerant of uncertainty (Haan, 1977). Stressful situations require people to use their skills and to interact with the environment. As individuals deal with stress, they often learn useful things about themselves and their abilities (Haan, 1993). Moreover, people who can successfully resolve a stressful situation gain confidence in their abilities. Laboratory work has even found that rats allowed to escape from shock, thereby reducing stress, have better-functioning immune systems than rats who receive no shock (Laudenslager et al., 1983). A similar reaction may happen to people: Stress can, at times, lead to the release of hormones that are health enhancing (de Kloet et al., 2005). Stress can also lead to positive emotions that help people replenish their resources and cope more effectively (Folkman, 2008; also see the Thinking About Research section at the end of the chapter).

Male–Female Differences

Although the basic physiological stress reaction (i.e., activation of the sympathetic nervous system) is similar between males and females, some psychologists believe there are important behavioral differences. For example, rather than showing the fight-or-flight response, which is characteristic of males, females seem predisposed to react to stressors with "tending and befriending" behavior (S. E. Taylor, 2002, 2006). Because of evolutionary pressures, females may have evolved to respond by tending and protecting offspring (in addition to themselves) rather than fighting or fleeing the scene.

According to Taylor and her colleagues, it's more adaptive for males to react to potential harm by being aggressive or fleeing; females are faced with different pressures, especially the care of the young, and often lack the necessary physical equipment to ward off threats through aggression. Although women can certainly become physically aggressive in some settings, aggression and flight are secondary reactions to threat. Instead, the first line of defense is to protect and calm offspring, which increases the chances of offspring survival. In addition, females appear more likely to create and maintain social networks that potentially can aid in protecting themselves and their offspring (S. E. Taylor & Master, 2011).

The proposal that males and females differ fundamentally in their behavioral reactions to stressors is somewhat controversial—especially the idea that sex-specific stress reactions may be adaptations arising from evolutionary pressures (Geary & Flinn, 2002). Moreover, recent studies suggest that men are also prone to endorsing tend-and-befriend responses during stress (Levy et al., 2019). However, sex differences in the expression and susceptibility to stress appear across the animal kingdom and may have some basis in the biology of male and female brains (Bale & Epperson, 2015). As Taylor and her colleagues note, the vast majority of research on the behavioral components of the stress response has been conducted on males, so much remains to be learned about the role of sex differences in the basic stress response (also see Lupien et al., 2009).

Cognitive Appraisal

Most psychologists are convinced that stress is closely related to emotion because the experience of stress is critically influenced by the way we perceive or *appraise* the situation (Lazarus, 1993, 2007). To feel stress, it's necessary (1) to perceive there's some kind of demand or threat present and (2) to conclude that you may not have adequate resources available to deal with that threat. If you have a black belt in the martial arts, then the sudden appearance of an unarmed thug is not likely to cause much stress—the threat is there, but you have adequate defensive resources should you need to use them.

This idea that our stress reaction depends on the **cognitive appraisal** of the situation is reminiscent of what we know about the experience of emotions. As you may remember from Chapter 12, the same physiological reaction can lead to different emotional experiences, depending on how we interpret the arousal experienced. The same is true for stress. Identical environmental events can lead to two very different stress reactions, depending on how the event is interpreted.

Consider an upcoming exam: Everyone in the class will receive the same test, but not everyone will feel the same amount of stress. Those people who are prepared for the exam—the people like you who read the chapter and engage in self-testing—are likely to feel less stress. Again, you perceive the threat, but you have adequate resources to deal with it (see Figure 16.2). The converse is also true—dangerous situations must be perceived as dangerous for a stress response to be produced. A small child doesn't necessarily understand that a loaded gun is dangerous, and may feel no stress while handling it.

FIGURE 16.2 ▪ Cognitive Appraisal

Whether an event will create stress depends on how that event is interpreted. A stress reaction is more likely if you feel your resources are inadequate to deal with the potential threat.

Illustrated by Sarah Yeh

There's a great deal of support for cognitive appraisal in the experience of stress (Folkman & Moskowitz, 2004). In one study of elementary school children, urine samples were taken from the children both on normal school days and on days when they were about to take standardized achievement tests. The urine sample measured the amount of cortisol, an important stress hormone, that each child produced (notice that the researchers provided an operational definition of stress in terms of the amount of hormone measured). Not surprisingly, more cortisol was found on test days, suggesting a higher level of stress, but the increase in stress depended on the child's previously recorded overall intelligence score. The children with higher intelligence scores showed less of a stress reaction on test days, presumably because they considered the test to be less of a threat (Tennes & Kreye, 1985).

External Sources of Stress

Because the stress reaction depends on one's appraisal of the situation, it's impossible to compile an exhaustive list of life's stressors. We can never predict how everyone will react to an environmental event, even though it may seem clearly stressful to the majority. All we can do is catalogue external situations, or life events, that induce stress reactions in *most* individuals. We'll consider three major classes of external stressors in this section: significant life events, daily hassles, and general factors in the environment.

Significant Life Events

Certain events are virtually guaranteed to produce stress. We can all agree that the death of a loved one or getting fired from a job is likely to produce an extended stress reaction in most people. On a larger scale, natural disasters or catastrophes—such as the recent coronavirus pandemic or the terrorist attacks that occurred in the United States on September 11, 2001—unquestionably produce stress that is prolonged and widespread. In the case of September 11, a national phone survey conducted three to five days after the attack found that more than 44% of the people surveyed reported one or more substantial symptoms of stress, and more than 90% reported feeling symptoms of stress to at least some degree (Schuster et al., 2001).

FIGURE 16.3 ■ Reacting to a Natural Disaster

The data shown here present the mean monthly hospital emergency room visits, mental health crisis line calls, and number of clients served by a community alcohol center for comparable time periods before and after the eruption of Mount St. Helens in 1980.

Source: Data from Adams & Adams, 1984.

Many studies have found clear links between such events and subsequent physical and psychological problems, particularly for the September 11 attack (e.g., Heim et al., 2004). In the 7 months following the 1980 volcanic eruption of Mount St. Helens in Washington state, one nearby town reported more than a 30% increase in the number of hospital emergency room visits compared to a similar period in the year prior to the eruption (Adams & Adams, 1984; see Figure 16.3). These visits were *not* for injuries directly caused by the eruption but rather for general health problems that may have been created or enhanced by the experience of stress.

Over the years, researchers have tried to compile lists of external life stressors. The best-known example is the Social Readjustment Rating Scale, which was put together by researchers Thomas Holmes and Richard Rahe (1967). Holmes and Rahe interviewed thousands of people who were suffering from health problems, and then tried to determine whether certain kinds of events preceded the onset of the health problems. The results are shown in Table 16.1, which lists the various significant life events mentioned by the people interviewed, ranked in terms of "life change units" (roughly representing the amount of adjustment the event caused in the person's life).

There are two interesting things to notice about the results shown in the table. First, most of these life events are connected with some kind of *change* in day-to-day activities. This suggests that the disruption caused by the event is just as important as the event itself in causing the stress reaction. People feel stress, in part, because something happens that requires them to alter their ways or lifestyle. Second, notice that many of the events listed in the table are actually quite *positive*. For example, marriage and retirement make the top 10. Even vacations and Christmas make the list. This is not really too surprising if you think about it, because each is associated with some kind of temporary or long-lasting disruption of normal routines.

The results listed in Table 16.1 are decades old, but they continue to be used by researchers to predict the likelihood of stress. Dozens of studies have found significant correlations between these rankings and various measures of stress, including physical and psychological problems (see, e.g., Tibubos et al., 2020). At the same time, not all experts are satisfied with the methods that were used to devise the scale, and it's been revised to take into account such factors as gender, age, and amount of education (C. J. Hobson & Delunas, 2001; M. A. Miller & Rahe, 1997). Remember as well that change by itself does not necessarily lead to stress reactions in all individuals. You can't automatically assume that if one of these events happens to you, you'll feel stress. It's how you appraise the event that's really important, along with your assessment of whether you have adequate resources to deal with the life change when it occurs. For this reason, investigators have developed interview techniques to define and measure major significant life events for particular individuals (see Monroe & Slavich, 2020).

Daily Hassles

It's not just the big events that cause problems. The little things, the daily irritations and hassles of life, also contribute significantly to the experience of stress. Think about how you feel when you're stuck in a long checkout line at the market, when someone's tailgating you on the freeway, or when you're hungry and you've waited a half-hour or more for your order at a restaurant. Some

TABLE 16.1 ■ Social Readjustment Rating Scale

Rank	Life Event	Point Value
1	Death of spouse	100
2	Divorce	73
3	Marital separation	65
4	Jail term	63
5	Death of close family member	63
6	Personal injury or illness	53
7	Marriage	50
8	Fired at work	47
9	Marital reconciliation	45
10	Retirement	45
11	Change in health of family member	44
12	Pregnancy	40
13	Sex difficulties	39
14	Gain of new family member	39
15	Business readjustment	39
16	Change in financial state	38
17	Death of close friend	37
18	Change to different line of work	36
19	Change in number of arguments with spouse	35
20	Mortgage over $10,000	31
21	Foreclosure of mortgage or loan	30
22	Change in responsibilities at work	29
23	Son or daughter leaving home	29
24	Trouble with in-laws	29
25	Outstanding personal achievement	28
26	Wife begins or stops work	26
27	Begin or end school	26
28	Change in living conditions	25
29	Revision of personal habits	24
30	Trouble with boss	23
31	Change in work hours or conditions	20
32	Change in residence	20
33	Change in schools	20
34	Change in recreation	19
35	Change in church activities	19
36	Change in social activities	18

(*Continued*)

TABLE 16.1 ■ Social Readjustment Rating Scale (*Continued*)		
Rank	**Life Event**	**Point Value**
37	Mortgage or loan less than $10,000	17
38	Change in sleeping habits	16
39	Change in number of family get-togethers	15
40	Change in eating habits	15
41	Vacation	13
42	Christmas	12
43	Minor violations of the law	11

Source: Reprinted from *Journal of Psychosomatic Research, 11*, T. H. Holmes and R. H. Rahe, "The Social Readjustment Rating Scale," pp. 213–218. Copyright © 1967, with permission of Elsevier Science.

psychologists believe the cumulative effect of such daily hassles may be more important in creating lasting stress than significant life events (Lazarus & Folkman, 1984; T. W. Miller, 1993). Kanner and colleagues (1981) developed a Hassles Scale, and it seems to predict the likelihood of physical and mental health problems. The more hassles you experience in your daily life, the more likely you'll experience health problems. Included on the scale are such things as concern about one's weight and physical appearance, home maintenance, and worries about misplacing or losing something. To deal with methodological concerns, various versions of the Hassles Scale have been developed over the years (see Wright et al., 2020). There is even a version that is specifically designed to measure hassles among university students (Pett & Johnson, 2005).

Environmental Factors

The environment is also a significant source for stress. *Noise* is a good example. Think about how difficult it is to study when someone is talking loudly nearby or how irritated you get when you're roused from sleep by the whirring, clanging sounds of the morning garbage truck. Chronic exposure to noise interferes with everyday activities, and it's been linked with stress-related disorders such as ulcers and high blood pressure (Dzhambov & Dimitrova, 2017; Evans, 1997) and with a general decline in the perceived quality of life (Evans et al., 1995). Schoolchildren experience more stress when they're exposed to chronic noise, and cognitive measures (such as reading comprehension) appear to suffer (Haines et al., 2001).

A crowded urban environment is a source of stress for many people.

iStockPhoto/Hydromet

Another environmental factor is *crowding*. The more people who live or work around you, the more likely you'll experience a stress reaction (Regoeczi, 2003). Living in a crowded environment makes us generally more susceptible to health problems and increases the likelihood of aggression. People who live in high-rise apartment buildings, filled with tenants, are more likely to behave aggressively than those who live in apartment buildings with fewer floors (P. A. Bell et al., 1990). The effects of crowding on health and aggression have also been studied extensively in prison settings—incarcerated people who live in crowded environments suffer more health problems and are more likely to act aggressively than inmates housed in less crowded environments (Haney, 2006; Paulus, 1988). Crowding can also lower creativity, as it tends to promote more conventional ways of thinking (Maeng et al., 2017).

Crowding and noise are two examples of environmental stressors, but there are many others. For example, stress and health have been closely linked to the family social environment, peer interactions, conditions in the workplace, socioeconomic class, and the general characteristics of the neighborhood in which you live (Cutrona et al., 2006). There is, in fact, an entire specialty in psychology—called **environmental psychology**—devoted to the study of environmental effects on behavior and health. Environmental psychologists have shown particular interest in the psychology of urban living because living in a large city is likely to expose one to a variety of environmental stressors (particularly noise and crowding). In general, people succumb to stress when they're forced to live in situations in which there is excessive stimulation, movement is constrained, or resources are limited.

Internal Sources of Stress

As you're now aware, no single event or set of living conditions will automatically lead to stress in everyone. Stressors are very much in the eye of the beholder, which means we need to know something about the internal characteristics of an individual before we can predict how the individual will react to a stressor. But what exactly are these internal characteristics? We'll consider three in this section: perceived control, explanatory style, and personality.

Perceived Control

To experience stress, you must perceive a threat or some kind of demand, and you need to feel you lack the resources to deal effectively with that threat. This second part of the appraisal process, the assessment of resources, is influenced by a psychological construct called **perceived control,** which is the amount of influence you feel you have over a situation and your reaction to it. Perceived control significantly affects the amount of stress you'll experience. If you perceive a demand or threat and you think you have no control over the situation, your body is likely to react with arousal, the release of stress hormones, and there will be changes in the activities of your immune system (Brosschot et al., 1998). If the situation continues for a prolonged period, negative physical and psychological consequences are likely to result.

Many examples, both scientific and anecdotal, support the link between perceived control and stress (Leotti et al., 2010). Early in the crewed space program, for instance, the Mercury astronauts insisted that manual controls and windows be placed in the orbiting space capsule. Although not necessary from an engineering standpoint, doing so gave the astronauts a sense of control over their environment, which reduced their stress. In laboratory studies, animals that are exposed to shocks that they can stop by turning a wheel are less likely to develop ulcers than animals who receive the same amount of shock but cannot control it (J. M. Weiss, 1977); similarly, after acute stress, people are more likely to persist on a task if they are allowed to control the effects of a task setback when it occurs (Bhanji et al., 2016). Moreover, people with an internal locus of control, those who feel they generally have control over the events in their environment, show less of a stress response when allowed to control a stressor in the laboratory than people with an external locus of control (Bollini et al., 2004). Finally, anxious individuals who feel they lack control after a heart attack are more likely to suffer complications than those with high perceived control (Moser et al., 2007).

Explanatory Style

The cognitive appraisal process, and therefore susceptibility to stress, is also influenced by one's general style of thinking. At several points we've discussed the importance of *attributions*, or our conclusions about cause and effect. People offer different kinds of explanations for the positive and negative events that occur in their world. For example, someone with an *internal, stable*, and *global* explanatory style is likely to attribute a negative event to some long-lasting personal inadequacy that applies in lots of situations: "My spouse left me because I'm witless; I've always been witless, and I can never hope to convince anyone otherwise."

We've seen elsewhere that a person's explanatory style contributes to psychological disorders such as depression (see Chapter 14). Perhaps not surprisingly, explanatory style has also been linked to physical health and susceptibility to stress. People who consistently make internal, stable, and global attributions for negative events suffer from increased stress-related health problems in midlife as well as later in life (Kamen-Siegel et al., 1991; C. Peterson et al., 1988). In one particularly intriguing study, C. Peterson and Seligman (1987) analyzed the explanatory styles of 94 members of the Baseball Hall of Fame who had played at some point between 1900 and 1950. Most of these players were dead at the time of the study, so the researchers had to glean the players' explanatory styles from stories and quotations in old newspapers. The players with negative explanatory styles were found, on average, to have lived shorter lives. More recently, it was found that baseball players who smiled intensely during their official team photograph tended to live longer than players who refused to smile or showed only partial smiles (Abel & Kruger, 2010).

Personality Characteristics

Both perceived control and explanatory style are related more generally to personality. Previously, we defined *personality* as the set of psychological characteristics that distinguishes us from others and leads us to act consistently across situations. Explanatory style may be linked to a personality characteristic such as *optimism*—the belief that good things will happen—which some psychologists have argued is a relatively enduring trait that changes little over a lifetime (Scheier & Carver, 1993, 2018). Optimism scales have been developed and used to look for a connection between personality and health. In one study, optimism was assessed on the day before a group of men underwent coronary bypass surgery. The optimists reacted physiologically to the surgery in ways that lowered the risk of heart attack; they also recovered more quickly after the surgery (Scheier et al., 1989). Optimistic people reported less pain and better physical functioning, experienced fewer physical symptoms, and were less likely to be rehospitalized after heart surgery than people with a pessimistic outlook (Rasmussen et al., 2009). Other studies have demonstrated links between psychosocial factors such as optimism and improved functioning of the immune system (see Antoni & Lutgendorf, 2007), as well as long-term mortality in patients suffering from rheumatoid arthritis (Crowson et al., 2017).

An optimistic view of life can clearly reduce stress. In one study, rescue and recovery workers at the crash site of an airline accident (USAir Flight 427) were studied 2, 6, 9, and 12 months after the crash. Those individuals who maintained an optimistic outlook reported less stress and generally better coping strategies. They also tended to have better social support networks and thereby improved resources for dealing with the stress associated with the accident (Dougall et al., 2001). Consequently, an optimistic outlook not only can help you establish and maintain friends, but it may help you live longer too (T. W. Smith, 2006). This conclusion has been supported by long-term epidemiological studies that have followed large samples of people over years (E. S. Kim et al., 2017; Scheier & Carver, 2018).

The most widely recognized personality characteristics that have been linked to stress-related health disorders, particularly coronary heart disease, are *Type A* and *Type B* behavior patterns. You're familiar with the Type A personality: hard driving, ambitious, easily annoyed, and impatient. Those with a Type A personality seem to be immersed in a sea of perpetual self-imposed stress; they're too busy to notice or enjoy the things around them because they're engaged in a relentless pursuit of success. Type B personality types are essentially people who lack the Type A attributes—they put themselves under less pressure and appear more relaxed.

The connection between Type A behavior patterns and heart disease was first noted by cardiologists Meyer Friedman and Ray Rosenman (1974). Friedman and Rosenman were interested in explaining why only some people with known risk factors for heart disease—such as smoking, obesity, inactivity, and so on—actually develop heart problems. People can appear to have identical risk profiles but end up healthy in one instance and disease prone in another. Friedman and Rosenman proposed that the

There is an important connection between personality and the stress response.

iStockPhoto/Pekic

solution lies in the connection between personality and stress. People who are psychologically prone to stress—Type A personalities—will prove more susceptible to diseases of the heart.

Recent work suggests that a more complete answer lies in further analyzing the Type A behavior pattern or personality, which turns out to be quite complex. To be classified as a Type A personality requires that a person be rated on a number of dimensions—competitiveness, ambition, hostility, and so on—and not all of these attributes are equally important. Researchers now believe it's probably hostility, anger, and the expression of anger—what are sometimes called *Type D* (or "distressed") personality characteristics—that are most responsible for producing subsequent coronary artery disease (see Kupper & Denollet, 2018). Other researchers have detected a relationship between emotional intelligence, which taps one's ability to deal effectively with emotions, and general health (Martins et al., 2010). For a summary of the different sources of stress, see Concept Review 16.1.

CONCEPT REVIEW 16.1
SOURCES OF STRESS

External	
Source	*Description*
Significant life events	Major life events associated with a change in day-to-day activities; they can be positive (e.g., getting married) or negative (e.g., death of a loved one).
Daily hassles	Daily irritations and hassles, such as getting stuck in traffic.
Environmental factors	Stressors present in the environment, such as noise and crowding.
Internal	
Source	*Description*
Perceived control	The amount of influence you feel you have over a situation. A sense of control often lessens the stress.

(Continued)

(*Continued*)

External	
Explanatory style	One's general style of thinking about and explaining events. People who make internal, stable, and global attributions for negative events are more likely to suffer from stress-related health problems.
Personality characteristics	*Optimism* (the belief that good things will happen) generally reduces stress. Hostility, anger, and an inability to deal effectively with emotions have also been associated with elevated stress and heart problems.

KNOWLEDGE CHECK 16.1

Check your knowledge about the stress response by answering each of the following questions. (You will find the answers in the Appendix.)

1. Hans Selye's concept of the general adaptation syndrome (GAS) proposes that the body reacts to stress in three phases. Which of the following shows the correct sequence of these phases?
   a. Resistance, alarm, exhaustion
   b. Exhaustion, resistance, alarm
   c. Alarm, resistance, exhaustion
   d. Exhaustion, alarm, resistance

2. The experience of stress is related to the experience of emotion in which of the following ways?
   a. The experience of stress, like emotion, is an inevitable reaction to threat.
   b. The experience of stress, like emotion, is accompanied by very distinctive facial expressions.
   c. The experience of stress, like emotion, depends on the appraisal of the event rather than on the event itself.
   d. The experience of different kinds of stress, like emotion, leads to highly specific kinds of body reactions.

3. According to the Social Readjustment Rating Scale, which of the following events is most likely to cause stress-related health problems?
   a. Marriage
   b. Death of a close friend
   c. Sex difficulties
   d. Trouble with your boss

4. Which of the following internal characteristics is least likely to be associated with stress-related health problems?
   a. Low levels of perceived control
   b. Type D behavior pattern
   c. An optimistic outlook
   d. Internal, stable, and global attributions

REACTING TO PROLONGED STRESS

There's a definite connection between prolonged stress and physical and psychological health. Stress is an adaptive reaction to threat—it helps us to survive. But when it's prolonged, when we're not able to reduce or eliminate the perceived threat, the mind and body start to break down. If the stress reaction is extreme enough, the breakdown can be sudden and may even result in death; in most cases, however, the effects are gradual and reveal themselves slowly through a growing list of physical and psychological problems. In this section of the chapter, we'll consider the nature of these breakdowns and how and why they occur.

Physical Consequences of Stress

Stress has been implicated in a wide variety of health problems. In addition to ulcers and heart disease, stress has been linked to everything from the common cold to chronic back pain, multiple sclerosis, and even cancer (Schneiderman et al., 2001). Most of the scientific evidence is correlational, which means a statistical relationship has been found between health problems, such as heart disease, and some measurement of stress. Large numbers of people are interviewed, and health histories as well as stress levels are measured. The net result is that we can predict whether someone, on average, has an increased chance of developing a particular kind of health problem by knowing the amount of stress that person experiences on a regular basis. But this doesn't tell us whether a causal relationship exists between stress and illness. To determine that, we must turn to experimental research.

It's difficult to conduct experimental research on stress and health for obvious ethical reasons. Ethically, we can't randomly divide people into groups, subject some of them to high levels of stress, and then monitor the later consequences of that manipulation on health. But experimental studies have been conducted on groups of people who have been previously identified as having either a high or low level of stress in their lives. In one study (Cohen et al., 1993), people with high and low levels of stress were given nasal drops that either contained or did not contain a common cold virus. It was a double-blind study, so neither the participants nor the researchers were aware during the course of the study who was getting the actual virus and who was not. Afterward, when the assignments were decoded, it was found that the high-stress people who received the virus were the ones most likely to show cold symptoms. Living a stressful life apparently lowers one's ability to fight off disease.

The Immune Response

To understand why stress increases susceptibility to illness, we need to consider the human *immune system*, a complex defense system that's constantly on the lookout for foreign substances, such as viruses or bacteria. The primary weapons of the immune system are **lymphocytes**, which are specialized white blood cells that attack and destroy most of these foreign invaders. Stress can lower the immune response by decreasing the number of lymphocytes in the bloodstream. Stress can also suppress the response of the lymphocytes to foreign substances that have invaded the body, and can even lead to the reactivation of latent viruses (Marketon & Glaser, 2008). Prolonged stress can also lead to chronic low-grade inflammation in the body that, in turn, is associated with negative long-term health consequences

People who are subjected to chronic stress by environmental conditions can have weakened immune systems.

iStockPhoto/FG Trade

(Kiecolt-Glaser et al., 2010). The mechanisms that produce these changes are not completely understood, although the prolonged release of stress hormones into the bloodstream probably plays a significant role (Kupper & Denollet, 2018).

Several investigations have shown that stressful life events directly affect the immune response. Medical students, on average, have fewer lymphocytes in their blood during a period of final exams compared to levels found before exams (Kiecolt-Glaser et al., 1984); they're also more likely to get sick during exams. People who have recently had a spouse or loved one die also show a suppressed immune response. One investigative team tracked the immune response in men married to women with advanced breast cancer. Samples of the men's blood were taken during a period of months preceding and following their wives' deaths. On average, the existing lymphocytes in blood samples drawn *after* the wives had died showed a weaker response to foreign substances (Schleifer et al., 1983).

The fact that stress weakens the immune system has led researchers to wonder about the effects of stress on more chronic illnesses, such as cancer. In the laboratory, it's been shown that stress can increase the growth rate of cancerous tumors in animals (Antoni & Lutgendorf, 2007). There have also been reports that cancer patients who are optimistic, or who are given therapy to help reduce anxiety and depression, survive longer than patients who are hopeless or depressed (Andersen, 1992; Spiegel et al., 1989). Stress may affect not only the body's ability to fight cancer but also the likelihood that cancer cells will form in the first place (Antoni & Dhabhar, 2019).

At present, however, researchers remain cautious about the link between psychology, the immune system, and cancer. Not all studies have found associations between psychological factors and cancer, and the fact that data linking cancer to stress have often come from correlational studies means that it's difficult to draw conclusions about cause and effect. It's possible that "stressful" people, on average, have a greater risk of acquiring cancer because they tend to engage in unhealthful behaviors—such as smoking—as a way of dealing with the stress. People who are optimistic about their survival from cancer may also tend to comply more with the recommendations of their doctors. Although there may be a statistical association between stress and cancer, that does not necessarily mean that stress is causing cancer by compromising the functioning of the immune system. Again, for obvious ethical reasons, it's tough to conduct rigorous experimental studies on the topic. There have been studies showing that stress management and other forms of psychotherapy can improve long-term outcomes in cancer patients (see Antoni & Dhabhar, 2019), but more studies are needed to determine the cause (see Boesen & Johansen, 2008).

Cardiovascular Disease

Health psychologists have also intensively studied the well-documented relationship between stress and cardiovascular disease (problems connected with the heart and blood vessels). We discussed the connection between personality characteristics and heart problems earlier, but we left the mechanisms through which stress undermines cardiovascular health unspecified. The two most important risk factors in heart disease are (1) high cholesterol levels in the blood and (2) high blood pressure. Prolonged exposure to stress increases both of these risk factors (Kubzansky & Adler, 2010).

Increased blood pressure, a natural by-product of the stress response, is generally helpful over the short term in preparing us to react to a threat. But if the elevated pressure continues, it causes wear and tear on the blood vessels in the body, which can lead to both cardiovascular disease and kidney problems. Stress can also directly affect the level of cholesterol in the blood. When college students are anticipating an upcoming exam, samples of their blood show higher levels of cholesterol (Van Doornen & Van Blokland, 1987). It's possible that when people sense threat, the body directs the blood flow to the muscles and away from internal organs, such as the liver, that remove fat and cholesterol from the blood.

Psychological Consequences of Stress

Think about how you feel when you're "stressed out." That recurring cold or sour stomach seems like it'll never go away. But the mental and emotional changes can be just as profound. You feel anxious, out of control, emotionally drained, and, after a while, possibly even sad and depressed. Stress is not a pleasant experience, and if the stress reaction is intense enough, or if it continues long enough, serious psychological problems can result.

Psychologists are convinced that stressful life events play a significant role in the onset of many psychological disorders. If you interview people who have suffered from major depression or a bipolar disorder, you'll find that most have experienced some kind of major stressor just before or early into the depressive episode—they got fired from their job, they moved to a new town, they're mired in a nasty divorce, and so on. Stress has been implicated in the onset of schizophrenia as well. Several studies have shown that stressful life events tend to precede the development of schizophrenic episodes (e.g., Tessner et al., 2011).

But, importantly, not all people who experience intense stress go on to develop serious psychological problems. In fact, the majority of people who experience a traumatic life stressor do not subsequently develop psychological disorders. Psychologists assume there must be some kind of vulnerability, perhaps rooted in the genetic recipe, before stress leads to an extreme disorder such as major depression or schizophrenia.

Posttraumatic Stress Disorder

You're familiar with this scenario: A soldier returns home from war, shell shocked, suffering from sleepless nights and flashbacks of traumatic episodes in battle. Hollywood has exploited this image to the point where the "unstable Vietnam vet" has become an unfortunate part of our collective sense of the Vietnam experience. In reality, the vast majority of soldiers who returned from Vietnam, Iraq, or Afghanistan have experienced no long-term psychological problems. At the same time, psychologists do recognize that exposure to extreme stress can produce a serious psychological condition known as **posttraumatic stress disorder (PTSD)**. This disorder is not limited to battle veterans; it can occur in any individual who has undergone a traumatic episode, such as a physical attack, rape, or a natural disaster.

Traumatic events can lead to prolonged stress reactions, including PTSD in some individuals.

REUTERS / Alamy Stock Photo

In the *Diagnostic and Statistical Manual of Mental Disorders* (DSM), PTSD is associated with a variety of diagnostic symptoms. Many of these symptoms are, in fact, typical and normal reactions to traumatic events. But in PTSD, the individual fails to recover from the event, and the symptoms persist for an extended period of time (M. J. Friedman et al., 2011).

1. *Recurrent recollections or flashbacks.* The person relives the traumatic event in some way. These recurrences or flashbacks can take the form of persistent thoughts or images of the traumatic scene, and they can even involve vivid hallucinations; the affected person seems at times to be reexperiencing the event—fighting the battle anew or fending off the attacker.

2. *Avoidance of stimuli associated with the trauma.* People with PTSD actively try to avoid anything that reminds them of the event. This avoidance behavior can lead to significant disruptions in normal social functioning as individuals turn away from friends and loved ones who in some way remind them of the trauma.

3. *Chronic arousal symptoms.* These symptoms can include sleep problems, irritability or outbursts of anger, and difficulties in concentrating.

4. *Negative changes in mood and cognition.* PTSD often affects mood, leading to persistent and exaggerated negative beliefs about oneself, others, and the world. In some cases, it can also lead to changes in cognitive functioning, such as an inability to remember important aspects of the traumatic event.

Obviously, PTSD is a disabling condition, not only for the individuals who are directly affected but also for family and friends. The cause of the disorder is clear—traumatic stress—but the reason only some people who experience trauma develop PTSD remains a mystery. There's evidence that the intensity of the trauma may be important. For example, Vietnam veterans who were in heavy combat were significantly more likely to develop PTSD than those serving in noncombat roles (Goldberg et al., 1990). But, once again, this doesn't explain why the disorder remains relatively rare even among people who have experienced extreme trauma. As we discussed at the end of Chapter 15, the extent to which one engages in negative "catastrophic" thinking may be one factor (Seligman, 2019), but there are likely to be many more. As with most psychological disorders, the chances that PTSD will develop undoubtedly depend on a complex mix of biological and environmental factors, including a genetic predisposition (see Hu et al., 2020).

Burnout

Stress does not need to be extreme to produce unpleasant psychological consequences. In the 1970s, the term *burnout* was introduced by psychologists to describe a syndrome that develops in certain people who are exposed to stressful situations that are demanding but not necessarily traumatic (Freudenberger, 1974; Maslach, 1976). Although the term **burnout** has become a household word, to psychologists it refers to "a state of physical, emotional, and mental exhaustion caused by long-term involvement in emotionally demanding situations" (Pines & Aronson, 1988, p. 9). When burnout occurs, individuals essentially lose their spirit—they become emotionally drained, they feel used up, and they lose their sense of personal accomplishment.

As with PTSD, stress is a necessary but not a sufficient condition for producing burnout. Not everyone who has a demanding and stressful job becomes burned out. Burnout seems to occur only in idealistic individuals—people who have entered their careers with a high sense of motivation and commitment. In the words of psychologist Ayala Pines (1993), "You cannot burn out unless you were 'on fire' initially" (p. 386). Because burnout primarily affects highly motivated individuals, it can have a high cost for organizations as well as for the individual. People who suffer from burnout lose their edge on the job—they become disillusioned with their work, are frequently absent from the job, and usually are at increased risk for a host of physical problems (Maslach & Leiter, 2008).

Why does burnout occur? The underlying cause may well be related to a loss of meaning in life (Pines, 1993), to a loss of control in the workplace (McKnight & Glass, 1995), or to a diminished sense of personal accomplishment (Rotenstein et al., 2018). People who are subject to burnout are usually those who think of their work as a kind of "calling." They use success on the job as a way of validating their existence. They identify so closely with their work that when failure happens, their entire life loses meaning. Failure is much more likely when the job is demanding and taxes the individual's resources, which is probably the reason stress is typically associated with the syndrome. If the overall stress levels can be reduced, perhaps by providing a better support system within the work environment, burnout is less likely to occur (see Leiter & Maslach, 2005; Patel et al., 2018). Concept Review 16.2 provides a summary of the different consequences of stress.

CONCEPT REVIEW 16.2
CONSEQUENCES OF STRESS

Physical	
What Stress Affects	*Nature of the Effect*
Immune response	Stressful events directly affect the immune response, lowering the number of disease-fighting *lymphocytes* and causing chronic low-grade inflammation.
Cardiovascular disease	Increased blood pressure from prolonged stress causes wear and tear on blood vessels, which can lead to cardiovascular disease.

Psychological	
What Stress Leads To	*Nature of the Effect*
Posttraumatic stress disorder	A serious psychological condition that can result from exposure to extreme stress. PTSD is characterized by flashbacks, avoidance of trauma-associated stimuli, chronic arousal symptoms, and negative changes in mood and cognition.
Burnout	A state of physical, emotional, and mental exhaustion caused by long-term involvement in emotionally demanding situations. It seems to occur in idealistic individuals who are highly motivated, perhaps due to a loss of control or a loss of meaning in life.

KNOWLEDGE CHECK 16.2

Check your knowledge about reacting to stress by deciding whether each of the following statements is true or false. (You will find the answers in the Appendix.)

1. Lymphocytes are the primary weapons of the human immune system. *True or False?*

2. Much of the data linking cancer and stress have come from correlational studies; researchers are unable, therefore, to draw firm conclusions about cause and effect. *True or False?*

3. Stress is known to affect blood pressure, but no links have been established between stress and cholesterol levels. *True or False?*

4. Posttraumatic stress disorder is a common reaction to experiencing a traumatic event. *True or False?*

5. Burnout is more likely to occur in people who use success on the job as a way of giving life meaning. *True or False?*

REDUCING AND COPING WITH STRESS

Because stress is associated with so many physical and psychological problems, it's important to develop techniques for reducing stress. Unfortunately, stressors are often outside of our direct control—you can't prevent the tornado that skirts your town or the death of a valued friend from accident or illness. But techniques are available for coping with stressors when they're present. **Coping** is a term psychologists use to describe efforts to manage conditions of threat or demand that tax one's resources (Lazarus,

1993). In this section, we'll consider three coping strategies for controlling or reducing stress: (1) relaxation techniques, (2) social support systems, and (3) learning to reappraise the environment in a less threatening way.

Relaxation Techniques

By definition, the stress response is incompatible with relaxation. You cannot be prepared to fight or flee if your body is calm, relaxed, and free from arousal-inducing stress hormones. Studies have shown that high-stress individuals can reduce the physically threatening components of the stress reaction—such as high blood pressure—by simply practicing a regimen of relaxation techniques. You may remember that we discussed how relaxation can be used effectively in the treatment of anxiety disorders (Chapter 15); similar relaxation techniques have proven effective in reducing long-term stress.

A number of relaxation procedures are available to help manage stress. In *progressive muscle relaxation*, you're taught to concentrate on specific muscle groups in the body, to note whether there is any tension, and then to relax those specific groups. Often in progressive relaxation you learn to address muscle groups in sequence. For example, you might begin with the muscle groups in the neck, move to the shoulders, and so on, first tensing and then relaxing each group. In this way, you learn to pay attention to how muscles in your body feel when tense or relaxed. Progressive relaxation has been used successfully to treat a variety of stress-related health problems, everything from tension headaches to sleep problems to more serious psychological problems (see Dolbier & Rush, 2012). In a related technique, called *autogenic relaxation*, you're taught to focus on directing blood flow toward tense muscle groups, "warming" and relaxing each group; once again, autogenic relaxation has proven beneficial in treating stress-related conditions (Friedlander et al., 1997).

Exercise, meditation, and even social support can be excellent vehicles for coping with stress.

iStockPhoto/VisualCommunications

Relaxation techniques are sometimes accompanied by *meditation* or *mindfulness* training. We discussed some of the benefits of mindfulness in Chapter 6. Meditation essentially involves learning how to relax, using techniques similar to progressive muscle relaxation. But you're also taught some time-tested mental exercises, such as repeating a string of words or sounds over and over in your head. The mental repetition, or mindfulness, focuses awareness and helps prevent potentially distracting or stress-producing thoughts from interfering with the relaxation response. (For instance, if you're concentrating on repeating the phrase "I'm at one with the universe," you can't simultaneously be worrying about whether the relaxation technique is working.) Daily meditation sessions clearly help people deal with stress-related arousal and anxiety disorders and are likely to prevent the later development of health problems such as high blood pressure (Montero-Marin et al., 2019; Rainforth et al., 2007).

Biofeedback

The goal of relaxation training is to lower components of the stress response, such as blood pressure, heart rate, and muscle tension. For example, if stress-related headaches are caused by tension in the muscles of the head and scalp, then people should be able to reduce or eliminate the pain by relaxing these specific muscle groups. Some researchers have suggested that it helps to give people feedback—**biofeedback**—about the effectiveness of their relaxation efforts. With biofeedback, monitoring equipment provides a continuous reading of your physiological state. In the case of tension headaches, the feedback would indicate the tension levels in the muscles of the head; for blood pressure or heart rate, you would be able to read your blood pressure and heart rate directly from appropriate monitoring equipment.

Not surprisingly, biofeedback works (e.g., Kennedy & Parker, 2019). When people are given information about how well their relaxation efforts are succeeding, compared with control subjects who are given no feedback, it's easier to control the relevant physiological response (Nestoriuc &

Martin, 2007). But interestingly, it's also the subsequent feeling of *control* that leads to reductions in the stress response. In one study on tension headaches, three groups of people were given a feedback signal that they were led to believe indicated a successful lowering of muscle tension in their foreheads. Actually, unknown to them, the signal had three different meanings: In one group, it appeared only when participants successfully increased the amount of tension in their foreheads; in a second group, the signal appeared whenever the amount of tension decreased; in a third group, it appeared when tension levels remained the same. Remarkably, despite the misleading feedback in two of the groups, everyone reported headache improvement (see Figure 16.4). Apparently, feeling that you have some control over your body can be sufficient to lower stress-induced pain (Andrasik & Holroyd, 1980). Remember, whether you'll experience a stress response depends on a cognitive appraisal of your resources. If you feel you have the ability to control the threat or demand, even if that control is illusory, you're less likely to experience stress.

FIGURE 16.4 ■ Biofeedback, Perceived Control, and Stress

People in three groups were led to believe that they could lower the amount of muscle tension in their foreheads through biofeedback. Actually, they learned to increase, decrease, or keep the tension levels the same. Yet all three groups showed significant improvement in headache symptoms, irrespective of condition. Apparently, the mere fact that the people believed they were lowering the tension levels was sufficient to produce improvement. Also shown are the data for controls who received no biofeedback.

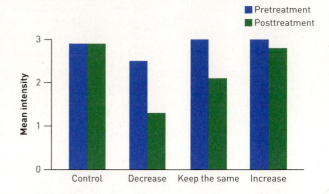

Source: Data from Andrasik & Holroyd, 1980.

Social Support

Although it may seem like a cliché, having a good friend to lean on during a time of stress really does matter. Psychologists use the term **social support** to refer to the resources we receive from other people or groups, often in the form of comfort, caring, or help. There is a great deal of evidence to suggest that social support can improve one's psychological and physical health (see Holt-Lunstad et al., 2015). People with well-established social support systems are less likely to suffer a second heart attack (Case et al., 1992), are more likely to survive life-threatening cancer (Chou et al., 2012), and are less likely to consider suicide if they're infected with HIV (S. G. Schneider et al., 1991). Other studies have established that social support plays a role in lowering the likelihood of depression and in speeding recovery (Marroquin, 2011). Social support has been found as well to reduce stress and anxiety in undergraduate and graduate college students throughout the semester (Miryam et al., 2019).

The support of family and friends can be especially helpful when the environment itself acts as a stressor.

iStockPhoto/simonapilolla

Social support probably helps reduce stress for many reasons. Some evidence suggests that social support helps people learn how to regulate their emotions more effectively (Marroquin, 2011). Another likely possibility is that social contacts help people maintain a healthful lifestyle. Friends and family push you out the door for your morning jog, force you to take your medications, or encourage you to visit the doctor regularly. Family and friends also bolster your confidence in times of stress, so you're more likely to feel that you have the necessary resources to cope with the demand. In a time of loss, such as immediately after the death of a spouse, social support lowers the chances that a grieving person will engage in unhealthful behaviors, such as drinking. (For a discussion of how pets can act as a form of positive social support, see the Practical Solutions feature.)

It's also the case that having someone to talk things over with can help you cope with stress. James Pennebaker (1990) has conducted a number of studies in which college students were encouraged to talk or write about upsetting events in their lives (everything from a divorce in the family to fears about the future). When compared to the control students, who were asked to talk or write about trivial things, the students who opened up showed improved immune functioning and were less likely to visit the college health center over the next several months. Pennebaker has found similar benefits for people who lived through natural disasters (such as earthquakes) or were part of the Holocaust. Opening up, talking about things, and confiding in others really seems to help people cope (Pennebaker & Chung, 2007).

At the same time, psychologists recognize that social support can have a negative side as well. If you are frequently opening up to others by expressing your emotions (e.g., anger), then you may increase the likelihood of subsequent depression (Chue et al., 2017). Moreover, if you've come to depend on another for support and that support is no longer delivered, your ability to cope can be compromised. Social support can also reduce self-reliance in some people, which may produce psychological distress and impair their ability to cope. Whether people respond favorably to social support and the receipt of aid or consider it to be a meddling nuisance depends to some extent on how much control they feel they have over their own actions and the outcomes of their actions.

Reappraising the Situation

When thinking about how to cope with stress, it's important to remember that it's not the sudden life event or the daily hassle that actually leads us to experience stress—it's our *interpretation* of the event that really matters. Even the death of a spouse or the occurrence of a natural disaster, cruel as it may seem, will create significant stress only if the event is appraised in a negative way. Imagine if your spouse were suffering from an incurable disease, one that produced extreme and persistent pain. Under these conditions, death could be seen as a kind of blessing.

Remember, too, that many instances of stress are caused by the little things, the daily hassles of life. Getting stuck in traffic, or in the wrong line at the supermarket, makes us feel stressed only because we have a tendency to "catastrophize" the situation: "This is absolutely awful . . . I can't stand waiting here any longer . . . I'm going to get home late, and my family will be mad." It's not the delay that creates the stress; it's the things we tell ourselves about the delay that cause the problems. As a result, many psychologists feel that stress can be managed effectively through logical reanalysis and positive reappraisal. If you can interpret the hassle in a more logical and positive manner, you can reduce or eliminate the stress reaction.

Stress management techniques that rely on cognitive reappraisal take a variety of forms. For instance, you can be taught to focus on certain aspects of the situation that distract you from catastrophizing. If you're stuck in the wrong checkout line, rather than concentrating on how you "must" get home on time, pick up one of the tabloids and read about the latest sighting of Elvis. Alternatively, try using your past experiences to reappraise the consequences: "Let's see, this certainly is not the first time I've been stuck in a checkout line, and my family and friends still think I'm okay." Another approach would be to analyze the situation logically and derive alternatives for the future: "Every time I come to the market at 5:30, right after work, I get stuck in a line—maybe if I wait and go after dinner, there will be less of a wait."

Some stress management programs recommend that clients keep daily records of the specific situations that have led to stress, as well as the specific symptoms and thoughts that arose (an example is shown in Figure 16.5). The value of a stress record is that it allows the client to recognize any unrealistic thoughts or conclusions on the spot because they need to be written down. With time, clients get a pretty good idea of the situations that lead to the highest stress, and they gain insight into the thought processes that produce their reactions. As each unrealistic thought is recognized, the client can work at reappraising the situation and confronting any negative attitudes or beliefs (Barlow et al., 2001).

FIGURE 16.5 ■ A Daily Stress Record

Stress management programs often recommend that clients keep daily records of situations that lead to stress, along with the specific symptoms and thoughts that arise.

Sample Daily Stress Record

Week of _____

	(1) Starting time	(2) Ending time	(3) Highest stress (0-8)	(4) Triggers	(5) Symptoms	(6) Thoughts
Date						
1-5	10:00 am	11:00 am	7	Sales meeting	Sweating, headache	My figures are bad.
1-7	5:15 pm	5:35 pm	6	Traffic jam	Tension, impatience	I'll never get home.
1-8	12:30 pm	12:32 pm	3	Lost keys	Tension	I can't find my keys.
1-9	3:30 pm	4:30 pm	4	Waiting for guests	Sweating, nausea	Are they lost?

Stress scale:
8, 7 Extreme stress
6, 5 Great stress
4, 3 Moderate stress
2, 1 Mild stress
0 No stress

Source: From D. H. Barlow, R. M. Rapee, & L. C. Reisner, "Daily Stress Record," *Mastering Stress 2001—A LifeStyle Approach*, p. 12. Copyright© 2001. Dallas, TX: American Health Publishing Company. Reproduced with permission of the author.

KNOWLEDGE CHECK 16.3

Check on your knowledge about stress management techniques by answering the following questions. (You will find the answers in the Appendix.)

1. Relaxation techniques, such as meditation or progressive muscle relaxation, appear to work because
   a. they promote a sense of "connectedness" with the therapist.
   b. they lead to positive cognitive reappraisals.
   c. the stress response is incompatible with relaxation.
   d. they cause you to open up and express feelings.

2. Biofeedback may be effective for managing stress because it
   a. gives you a feeling of control.
   b. leads to muscle relaxation.
   c. trains neurons to fire in sequence.
   d. works well with meditation.

3. Which of the following statements about the influence of social support on stress is false?
    a. Social contacts help you maintain a healthy lifestyle.
    b. Social support increases the chances that you'll open up and express feelings.
    c. Social support can reduce the chances of a second heart attack.
    d. Social support makes it easier to cope if the support is no longer delivered.

4. Elroy no longer fumes when he gets stuck in traffic because he's stopped catastrophizing about the consequences. Which of the following stress management techniques is Elroy probably using?
    a. Cognitive reappraisal
    b. Autogenic relaxation
    c. Progressive muscle relaxation

PRACTICAL SOLUTIONS: PET SUPPORT

Having a loved one or a good friend to talk to about your problems makes a difference, and that friend doesn't even need to be human. The companionship of pets—dogs, cats, even birds—has repeatedly been found to be an effective form of social support. Heart attack victims who own pets, for example, are more likely to survive the first year after the attack than are non-pet owners. Correlational studies among the elderly have found that pet ownership is inversely related to the severity of psychological problems: People who are attached to their pets are less likely to show the symptoms of depression (Garrity et al., 1989). Ownership of a dog, in particular, is an excellent predictor of whether or not an elderly person will feel the need to visit a doctor (J. M. Siegel, 1990).

There's some evidence to suggest that having a pet may even be a more effective buffer against stress than having a human companion. In an experiment conducted by Karen Allen and her colleagues (1991), female dog owners agreed to have several physiological reactions monitored while they tried to solve relatively difficult math problems. Prior to starting the task, the women were randomly divided into three groups. In one group, the women were allowed to have their dog with them in the room while completing the math task. In a second group, no dogs were allowed, but each woman was allowed the presence of a close human friend. In the third group, no social support was present during the testing.

FIGURE 16.6 ■ Pets as Stress Moderators

In one study, a pet's presence during a stressful task significantly lowered the stress reaction (measured here in terms of pulse rate) compared to when a friend was present or to a control condition in which neither a friend nor a pet was present (data from K. M. Allen et al., 1991).

Illustrated by Sarah Yeh

A variety of physiological reactions were measured, including heart rate and blood pressure. Not surprisingly, solving difficult math problems led directly to stress-related arousal—heart rate increased, as did blood pressure. But the amount of reactivity depended on the group: The women who were allowed to have their dog with them showed the lowest arousal effects compared to the women in the other two groups (see Figure 16.6). The presence of the pet apparently acted as an effective buffer against stress. The surprise finding of the study was that having a close human friend sit nearby while solving the math problems actually led to the highest relative stress reaction.

Does this mean that pets are more therapeutic than friends or loved ones? For some people in some situations, the answer may well be "Yes." Allen and her colleagues argued that pets are often effective buffers against stress because they're essentially nonevaluative. Pets don't make value judgments about their caretakers. Your dog or cat doesn't care one bit about how well you're doing on some math task, but your close human friend might. A friend's expectations can place added pressure on you as you perform an already stressful task. A participant in the study by Allen and colleagues (1991) put it this way: "Pets never withhold their love, they never get angry and leave, and they never go out looking for new owners" (p. 588). Another participant offered the following: "Whereas husbands may come and go, and children may grow up and leave home, a 'dog is forever'" (p. 588). The opinions of these participants may not be shared by everyone, nor do you need to hold these strong views to appreciate the value of pet companionship. The data simply indicate that pets can be an important part of your social network and that they can clearly help you cope with stress.

LIVING A HEALTHY LIFESTYLE

One of the challenges of the health psychology movement is to devise a comprehensive and workable framework for health promotion (Leventhal et al., 2008). In offering prescriptions for healthful lifestyles, psychologists recognize that not all risk factors can be controlled. For example, susceptibility to disease and stress are influenced by genetic factors, and older adults are at a greater risk of developing a host of health-related problems. Obviously, people have no control over heredity, and they can't help the fact that they grow old. But there are lifestyle choices that can make a difference.

Get Fit: The Value of Aerobic Exercise

Exercise is an excellent example of an activity that can have a substantial positive impact on physical and psychological health, especially if the exercise is sustained and aerobic. **Aerobic exercise** consists of high-intensity activities that increase both heart rate and oxygen consumption, such as fast walking, running, dancing, rowing, swimming, and so on. Regular aerobic exercise improves cardiovascular fitness over the long term and, on average, increases the chances that you'll live longer.

Psychologically, regular exercise improves mood and makes people more resistant to the effects of stressors. Much of the evidence is correlational (studies have shown statistical relationships between the regularity of exercise and reported mental health), but controlled experimental studies have reached the same conclusion (Ströhle, 2009). For example, in a study by McCann and Holmes (1984), volunteer female college students who were suffering from mild depression were asked to (1) engage in a regular program of aerobic exercise, (2) learn relaxation techniques, or (3) do nothing. After 10 weeks, the aerobic exercise group showed the largest improvement in mood. Other work indicates that 30 minutes of moderate exercise daily may be sufficient to improve mood (Hansen et al., 2001). In another study of stress resistance, men were randomly assigned to exercise conditions that involved either aerobic activity or nonaerobic strength-and-flexibility training. After 12 weeks of training, the men in the aerobic group showed lower blood pressure and heart rate when they were exposed to situations involving mental stress (Blumenthal et al., 1988).

Regular exercise is an important ingredient in a healthful lifestyle.

iStockPhoto/ViewApart

Researchers have yet to understand fully how or why exercise improves psychological health and functioning. Over the short term, vigorous exercise increases the amount of oxygen that reaches the brain, which undoubtedly improves cognitive functioning, and sustained exercise may alter mood-inducing neurotransmitters in the brain (Heijnen et al., 2016). It is also clearly the case that aerobic exercise, as it improves cardiovascular health, will lessen the physiological effects of the stress reaction. But there may also be placebo-like effects involved: People who choose to exercise regularly are convinced they're going to improve their health, and they subsequently rate themselves as more psychologically healthy than they may in fact be (Pierce et al., 1993). Sticking to an exercise routine may also increase one's sense of self-control or self-efficacy, which, in turn, leads to a more positive self-concept (Ströhle, 2009).

Don't Smoke: Tobacco and Health

Virtually everyone knows that smoking or the oral ingestion (chewing) of tobacco is bad for your health. There is no shortage of studies available to document this fact. Few researchers question, for example, that smoking contributes annually to hundreds of thousands of deaths in the United States alone, from associated heart disease, cancer, stroke, and emphysema. And it's not just the smokers who are affected—the babies of women who smoke during pregnancy tend to have lower birth weights and are at increased risk for birth defects; even people who are simply exposed to smoke secondhand may suffer from subsequent health problems. So why, given that it is so damaging to their health, do people smoke?

First, the good news is that smoking rates have been declining for decades. For example, in the United States approximately 15% of adults currently smoke cigarettes, which is down from nearly half of all adults in the 1950s (e.g., Jamal et al., 2018). Smoking is recognized to be *addictive* by the vast majority of mainstream researchers in the health-related sciences. Many people who smoke regularly become dependent on their daily dosage, and when they try to quit, they suffer physical and psychological withdrawal symptoms. The DSM lists criteria for a diagnosis of tobacco withdrawal that include insomnia, irritability, difficulty concentrating, and increased appetite or weight gain. The symptoms of withdrawal can be severe enough to cause a significant disruption in normal everyday functioning. This conclusion, of course, comes as no surprise to anyone who has ever tried to quit smoking after prolonged use.

The reinforcing effects of cigarette smoking can be explained by chemical reactions in the brain and to factors in the culture at large. Within the brain, it takes only seconds for nicotine—the active agent in cigarette smoke—to stimulate the central nervous system, elevating heart rate, blood pressure, and mood. Many smokers report that cigarettes not only improve mood but help alleviate anxiety and stress. At the same time, tobacco companies launch advertising campaigns designed to make smoking appear desirable. Tobacco use is identified with role models—often thin, vigorous, and healthy people on horseback or frolicking on the beach—or is associated with independence and nonconformity. Unfortunately, these types of advertising campaigns are often particularly effective for those in adolescence, which is the time when most smokers begin their habit.

You've probably heard the saying that the best way to stop smoking is never to start. It's undoubtedly true because, once started, tobacco use is a difficult habit to break. The psychological and physical withdrawal symptoms associated with tobacco use make quitting extraordinarily difficult. Furthermore, cues in the environment (such as seeing someone else smoking) regularly trigger the habit (Tiffany et al., 2000). A variety of smoking cessation techniques that rely on psychological principles have been developed, but they tend to be effective only over the short term. For example, some programs use learning principles to "punish" tobacco use and encourage users to replace positive associations with negative ones. These programs often prove effective initially, but in the long run the vast majority of smokers return to the habit. In the words of Mark Twain: "To cease smoking is the easiest thing I ever did; I ought to know because I've done it a thousand times."

Tobacco companies often associate their products with healthy, vigorous lifestyles.

RiskyWalls / Alamy Stock Photo

Eat Right: The Value of Proper Nutrition

In Chapter 12, we dealt with the adaptive problem of how to motivate eating behavior. Obviously, to maintain proper functioning of body and mind, people need to consume the necessary amounts of food. In our earlier discussion of eating, we didn't pay too much attention to the quality of the food that people consume; instead, our concern was mainly with the internal and external factors that underlie the motivation to eat. But proper nutrition is vitally important in maintaining a healthful body and mind, and health psychologists are engaged in a vigorous campaign to improve people's dietary habits.

The dietary habits of most North Americans leave much to be desired. After a long period of relative stability, overweight and obesity rates in the United States began to increase in the 1980s and have continued to increase to the present day. Currently, more than 40% of U.S. adults are classified as obese. To put this number in perspective, in the year 2000 no U.S. state had an obesity rate of 30% or more; by 2018, that number had increased to over 30 states. At present, there isn't a single U.S. state that has an obesity rate below 20%. Our diet tends to be too high in calories, fat, cholesterol, sugar, protein, and salt. High-fat diets have been linked to heart disease, stroke, and several kinds of cancer, as well as to obesity. Diets that are high in cholesterol contribute to heart disease because the cholesterol can lodge in the walls of arteries, leading to a hardening and narrowing that restricts blood flow.

Of course, not everyone who maintains a diet high in fat or cholesterol will develop these problems (because genetic predispositions are also a factor), but there's no question that many people eat themselves into an early grave.

Given the overwhelming amount of evidence linking diet to health, why don't people eat better? For many people, it's not the amount of food they eat but their choice of food that creates the problems. Consider the following: A baked potato has 0.5% of its calories as fat; when that same potato is French fried, it has 42% of its calories as fat (Winikoff, 1983). Everyone has a handy list of reasons for choosing to eat fast food, including the fact that it tastes good. But from a nutritional standpoint, fast foods tend to come up short because they're packed with fat and sodium. The best advice is to avoid foods with too much fat, cholesterol, sugar, and sodium. This is not a new message for you, we're sure, but remember: You're now much more sophisticated about the psychological factors that influence your choice of foods (see Chapter 12).

Avoid Risky Behavior: Protect Yourself From Disease

Choosing a healthful lifestyle requires having the right kind of information about how to prevent health-impairing habits. Health psychologists often distinguish among three main types of prevention programs:

1. *Primary prevention* is designed to educate the public as a whole in ways to reduce or eliminate a problem before it starts.

2. *Secondary prevention* involves the early identification of risk factors in specific population groups.

3. *Tertiary prevention* seeks to handle and contain an illness or habit once it has been acquired.

All three types of prevention programs have been used to deal with the recent rise of COVID-19.

iStockPhoto/urbazon

All three types of prevention programs are needed, but stopping an illness or habit before it starts—primary prevention—obviously has greater long-term significance. The recent threat of COVID-19, caused by the coronavirus, is a case in point. The use of social distancing measures, which have been adopted worldwide, is an example of primary prevention—it is designed to stop the infection before it gains hold in a community. Identifying populations at risk, such as people over age 60 with underlying conditions, and targeting those groups is an example of secondary prevention. Finally, scientists across the world are working to identify effective treatments and techniques for prolonging life during the recovery period. All three forms of prevention have been critical to reducing the devastating effects of this virus.

Another case in point, one in which all three forms of prevention have been used effectively is HIV (the human immunodeficiency virus), which can lead to AIDS (*acquired immune deficiency syndrome*). As you know, **AIDS** is an infectious disease that involves a gradual weakening and disabling of the immune system. AIDS is "acquired," meaning that it's not a by-product of the genetic code, and it develops as a result of infection with HIV. HIV does its damage by attacking cells in the immune system, which leaves the body unable to fight off opportunistic infections that would otherwise be controlled. The AIDS disease is diagnosed in the latter stages of HIV infection when the immune system has been sufficiently compromised.

Infection with HIV is preventable when the proper steps are taken to control its transmission. HIV is transmitted through contact with bodily fluids, particularly blood and semen. The virus is found in saliva, urine, and tears, but the amount is so small that infection through casual contact—even kissing—is extremely unlikely. The most likely means of transmission is through sexual contact or sharing intravenous needles with someone infected with the virus. The use of latex condoms during sexual activity dramatically reduces the chances of infection. Recent advances in the treatment of AIDS are promising as well, although many parts of the world continue to suffer significant loss (see Eisinger & Fauci, 2018).

Although COVID-19 and HIV infection are medical conditions, psychologists have two important roles to play. First, the only effective way to control widespread infection is to prevent risk-taking behavior. The public needs to be educated about how a virus or other disease spreads, and any misconceptions that currently exist need to be countered. For example, there are still people who are convinced that AIDS is a problem unique to people who engage in same-sex intercourse, despite the fact that the disease can be—and is being—readily transmitted through heterosexual contact. The other key role being played by psychologists is a therapeutic one. Once infected, people are subjected to an overwhelming amount of stress. Not only are these individuals faced with the prospects of an early death, but in some cases they must face the stigma that can accompany the disease. Psychologists are actively involved in establishing treatment programs that can help people cope with their disease.

KNOWLEDGE CHECK 16.4

Check your knowledge of living a healthy lifestyle by deciding whether each of the following statements is true or false. (You will find the answers in the Appendix.)

1. Aerobic exercise improves cardiovascular health and general mood but produces few changes in the physiological effects of the stress reaction. *True or False*?

2. Smoking is recognized to be addictive by the vast majority of mainstream researchers in the health-related sciences. *True or False*?

3. For many people, it's not the amount of food they eat but their choice of food that creates health problems. *True or False*?

4. Teaching children about the hazards of smoking or drugs would be classified as an example of secondary prevention. *True or False*?

THE PROBLEMS SOLVED: UNDERSTANDING THE CONNECTION BETWEEN STRESS AND HEALTH

The close relationship among thoughts, emotions, and the physical reactions of the body means that understanding and promoting physical health requires some attention to psychological factors. Health psychology is part of a broader movement, called behavioral medicine, that seeks to understand the medical consequences of the interaction between body and mind. Health psychologists are especially interested in the psychological and environmental factors—everything from personality characteristics to the work environment—that both produce illness and affect the likelihood of recovery.

Experiencing Stress

Stress has historically been a somewhat difficult concept to define. It can be conceived of as a stimulus, as a response, or as a process through which external events are interpreted as threatening or demanding. We chose to treat stress as the physical and psychological reaction to demanding situations. The stress response is often treated as an extended reaction that occurs in phases. According to the general adaptation syndrome proposed by Hans Selye, the body initially reacts to threat with a highly adaptive fight-or-flight response (although there may be gender differences in the behavioral response); if the threat continues, the body goes through resistance and exhaustion phases that make it vulnerable to disease.

To experience stress, it's necessary to both perceive a threat and feel that you lack the necessary resources to deal with it effectively. This means that identical environmental events can lead to very different stress reactions, depending on how the situation is interpreted. Overall, however, it is possible to identify some common sources of stress. External sources of stress include significant life events, daily hassles, and environmental factors such as noise and crowding. Internal sources of stress include perceived control—how much influence you feel you have over the situation—and explanatory style.

Certain personality characteristics have been linked to stress. Individuals who are prone to hostility or the expression of anger—what is sometimes called a Type D (or "distressed") personality—appear to be at increased risk for subsequent heart disease.

Reacting to Prolonged Stress

Stress is an adaptive reaction to threat, but if the threat is extended over time, both body and mind can start to break down. Stress has been implicated in a wide variety of health problems, ranging from heart disease to the common cold. A number of studies have shown that prolonged stress can affect immune functioning, which is the body's method for fighting off disease. Stress can compromise the immune response either by lowering the number of specialized white blood cells (lymphocytes) or by somehow suppressing the response of those lymphocytes to foreign substances that have invaded the body. Evidence suggests that stress can also lead to chronic low-grade inflammation in the body.

Two chronic psychological consequences of prolonged stress are posttraumatic stress disorder and burnout. PTSD results from exposure to extreme trauma, such as that experienced during battle or as a result of a physical assault. The symptoms of the disorder include flashbacks in which the traumatic event is reexperienced, avoidance of stimuli associated with the trauma, chronic arousal problems, and negative changes in mood and cognition. *Burnout* is a term that psychologists use to describe a state of physical, emotional, and mental exhaustion that sometimes develops after prolonged stress.

Reducing and Coping With Stress

We use coping strategies to manage conditions of threat that tax our resources. Effective coping techniques include relaxation training, the use of social support, and reappraisal. The stress response is incompatible with relaxation, and relaxation training can help lower components of the stress response (such as blood pressure and heart rate). In progressive muscle relaxation training, the client is taught to concentrate on specific muscle groups in the body, note whether they seem tense, and then relax those specific groups. Sometimes it's useful to provide biofeedback as well.

Additional evidence indicates that social support—the resources received from other people—can also help you cope effectively with stress. Friends and family help us maintain a healthful lifestyle, boost our confidence, or simply provide an avenue for us to open up and express our feelings. Talking about things and confiding in others really seem to help people deal with stress. Finally, because stress depends on how you interpret the threatening or demanding situation, it can often be managed effectively through cognitive reappraisal. You can be taught to reinterpret significant life events or daily hassles in a less stressful way. Some stress management programs encourage clients to keep daily stress records. By identifying the kinds of situations that create stress, as well as the negative thoughts those situations produce, you become better prepared to reinterpret those situations and thoughts in a more adaptive manner.

Living a Healthy Lifestyle

Aerobic exercise is one example of an activity that can have a positive effect on physical and psychological health. Regular exercise improves mood and makes people more resistant to the effects of stressors. Another lifestyle choice that directly affects physical health is the decision not to smoke. Smoking and other tobacco use contribute to hundreds of thousands of deaths annually in the United States alone, from associated heart disease, cancer, stroke, and emphysema. Tobacco use stimulates activity in the central nervous system, which is immediately reinforcing, but prolonged use leads to addiction or dependence that can be difficult to overcome.

Proper nutrition is another important ingredient in maintaining a healthy body and mind. The North American diet tends to be too high in calories, fat, cholesterol, sugar, protein, and salt. Poor dietary habits can lead to significant long-term health problems. Finally, maintaining a healthful lifestyle includes avoiding risky behaviors and preventing disease. For example, psychologists are playing an important role in the COVID-19 pandemic by educating the public about the importance of social distancing as well as through the establishment of treatment programs that can help people cope with the psychological effects of the disease.

THINKING ABOUT RESEARCH

A summary of a research study in psychology is given in this section. As you read the summary, think about the following questions:
1. Identify the method used in this study. Is it observational, correlational, or experimental?
2. What are the advantages and disadvantages of using Big Data to increase our knowledge about behavior and mind?
3. What do the current results tell us about how individuals cope with life's stressors?
4. How might the conclusions of this study apply to the world's collective reaction to the recent COVID-19 pandemic?

Jane Ali / Alamy Stock Photo

Article Reference: Garcia, D., & Rimé, B. (2019). Collective emotions and social resilience in the digital traces after a terrorist attack. *Psychological Science, 30,* 617–628.

Purpose of the Study: When a society suffers a collective trauma or stress, such as a natural disaster or a terrorist attack, people tend to gather together and talk about their negative emotions. Garcia and Rimé (2019) were interested in whether these collective emotional responses are followed by an increase in long-term solidarity, meaning expressions of prosocial behavior and connectedness that could potentially help people cope and recover from life stressors. To test this idea, the authors used Big Data—they analyzed the linguistic content of social media in the months preceding and following a terrorist incident in Paris, France.

Method of the Study: The focus of the analysis was French social media content on Twitter before and after a November 2015 Paris terrorist attack. Using linguistic analyses and statistical modeling, the authors examined the temporal dynamics of the collective emotional reactions that followed the attacks and assessed their relationship to lexical indicators associated with solidarity. The data set included some 62,000 user accounts and tens of millions of tweets. Of main interest were the expressions of positive and negative emotion terms (e.g., *sadness, anger*), social terms (e.g., *people, relationships, social activities*), and terms related to prosocial behavior (e.g., *caring, solidarity*). For comparison, they also analyzed tweet content for several weeks prior to the attacks.

Results of the Study: Not surprisingly, the authors recorded a collective negative emotional response to the attack, but this response was followed by a marked long-term increase in the use of terms related to solidarity. Expressions of social processes, positive affect, and prosocial behavior were higher in the months after the attack.

Conclusions of the Study: The authors concluded that the negative emotions that occur among people immediately surrounding a period of intense stress, in this case a terrorist attack, can lead to a long-term increase in the activation of social processes, the use of language related to social behavior, and the expression of positive affect. It is through shared distress that our bonds can become stronger, which, in turn, may make us better able to adapt to the next threat.

KNOWLEDGE CHECK: CHAPTER SUMMARY

You will find the answers in the Appendix.

Experiencing Stress

- According to the general (1) _____ syndrome (GAS), people respond to threats or demands in (2) _____ phases. The (3) _____ reaction corresponds to the fight-or-flight response; during the (4) _____ stage the body adjusts its reaction to cope with the continuing threat; finally, if we can't neutralize the effect, the (5) _____ phase sets in. Common psychological reactions to stress include (6) _____, anger, (7) _____, dejection, and grief.

- Most psychologists believe stress is closely related to the experience of (8) _____. How stress is experienced is affected by how people (9) _____ the situation they're in. A greater stress response will be produced if people perceive a threat directly and believe that their resources are inadequate to deal with it.

- (10) _____ life events can create a great deal of stress. According to the (11) _____ Readjustment Rating Scale, both positive and (12) _____ life events that are associated with (13) _____ may produce stress. Psychologists recognize that (14) _____ hassles and environmental factors such as (15) _____ and crowding are important determinants of chronic stress. (16) _____ psychology is devoted to the study of environmental effects on behavior and health.

- (17) _____ control is how much influence we believe we have over a situation. Generally, the less perceived control, the (18) _____ the resulting stress. (19) _____ style can also contribute to stress and influence health. People with Type D personalities are hostile and angry, stress-producing characteristics linked with (20) _____ disease.

Reacting to Prolonged Stress

- Stress lowers the (21) _____ response, and therefore decreases either the number of (22) _____ or their ability to respond to the presence of foreign substances. The link between stress and the immune system has led to speculation about a possible relationship between stress and illnesses such as cancer, although researchers offer such conclusions cautiously. Prolonged exposure to stress is also associated with (23) _____ blood pressure and high (24) _____, which are major risk factors in cardiovascular disease.

- Psychologists are convinced that (25) _____ life events may produce (26) _____ disorders, possibly through an interaction with (27) _____ vulnerability. Extreme stress produced by traumatic experiences is sometimes associated with (28) _____ stress disorder, which is characterized by (29) _____, avoidance of trauma-associated stimuli, and chronic arousal symptoms. (30) _____, another effect of prolonged stress, is a state of emotional and mental (31) _____ caused by lasting involvement in situations that are emotionally demanding. Burnout may be caused by loss of (32) _____ in the workplace or of (33) _____ in life.

Reducing and Coping With Stress

- Stress is incompatible with (34) _____, which is an effective stress reducer. Progressive (35) _____ relaxation involves concentrating on specific muscle groups, noting tension and deliberately relaxing the affected areas. In (36) _____ relaxation, the focus is on directing blood flow toward specific muscle groups, warming and relaxing them. (37) _____ is also an effective relaxation technique. (38) _____ has been shown to facilitate relaxation by providing information about the effectiveness of the techniques the person is using. (39) _____ support helps to reduce stress but may have a negative effect as well in certain situations.

- How one (40) _____ events partly determines how stressful they are, so many stress management techniques involve cognitive (41) _____. This may include focusing on aspects of the situation that aren't upsetting, which prevents the reaction that a catastrophe has occurred, or analyzing the situation in a logical fashion.

Living a Healthy Lifestyle

- (42) _____ exercise increases heart rate and oxygen consumption and can have a highly positive impact on both (43) _____ and (44) _____ health. It can improve (45) _____ and increase (46) _____ to stressors. Why exercise improves functioning hasn't been exactly determined, but it may involve improved cardiovascular and cognitive function and alterations in mood-enhancing chemicals.

- Correlational and experimental evidence has demonstrated the link between (47) _____ use and serious (48) _____ problems. Smoking seems to produce (49) _____ reactions in the brain that reinforce the habit. Although many smokers fail to quit because tobacco is highly (50) _____ and is associated with (51) _____ effects, smoking rates have been on the decline.

- Proper (52) _____ is vital to a healthy (53) _____ and (54) _____, yet in the United States many people maintain a diet that is high in calories, cholesterol, fat, and other substances that are damaging when consumed in excess. Nutritional problems usually have to do with the (55) _____ of food that is eaten, not necessarily the amount.

- (56) _____ prevention is aimed at reducing health problems or eliminating them (57) _____ they start. (58) _____ prevention involves early identification of risk factors in specific (59) _____. (60) _____ prevention seeks to handle and contain an illness that has already developed. The prevalence of COVID-19 underscores the important need for a special emphasis on (61) _____ prevention programs.

CRITICAL THINKING QUESTIONS

1. Just because two things occur together, such as illness and empathy, doesn't mean that one causes the other. How would you determine whether physical illness truly causes increased empathy?

2. Try listing and ranking the life events that cause, or have caused, you the most stress. Do your rank orderings differ from those listed in Table 16.1?

3. Suppose you discover a group of people living in a crowded and noisy environment who show little or no stress reaction. How would you interpret your findings?

4. How might the onset of a psychological disorder, such as depression, be an adaptive reaction to prolonged stress?

5. Do you think it's possible that people who are healthier tend to get more social support than those who are sick? Might this fact account for the correlation?

6. What's the link between these stress management programs and the techniques used in cognitive therapies, such as rational-emotive therapy?

7. Do you think there's a connection between age and the chances of living a healthy lifestyle? If so, why do you think this is?

KEY TERMS

aerobic exercise (p. 605)

AIDS (p. 609)

biofeedback (p. 600)

burnout (p. 598)

cognitive appraisal (p. 586)

coping (p. 599)

environmental psychology (p. 591)

general adaptation syndrome (GAS) (p. 584)

health psychology (p. 582)

lymphocytes (p. 595)

perceived control (p. 591)

posttraumatic stress disorder (PTSD) (p. 597)

social support (p. 601)

stress (p. 583)

stressors (p. 583)

APPENDIX

CHAPTER 1

Knowledge Check 1.1

1. False. Internal thoughts and feelings are often studied by psychologists; a thought or a feeling can be considered a type of behavior when it is revealed through written or spoken expression.

2. True.

3. True.

4. False. Psychiatrists are medical doctors who receive specialized training in psychology, but their interests do not differ in any fundamental way from those of psychologists. Both psychologists and psychiatrists work on severe psychological problems such as schizophrenia.

Knowledge Check 1.2

1. **a.** Most psychologists believe that mental events arise entirely from activity in the brain.

2. Functionalists and structuralists used the technique of *introspection* to understand immediate conscious experience. The *structuralists* believed that it was best to break the mind down into basic parts, much as a chemist would seek to understand a chemical compound. The *functionalists* were influenced by Darwin's views on natural selection and focused primarily on the purpose and adaptive value of mental events. *Behaviorism*, founded by John Watson, steered psychology away from the study of immediate conscious experience to an emphasis on *behavior*.

3. **a.** Psychoanalysis often places a strong emphasis on hidden urges and memories related to sex and aggression.

Knowledge Check 1.3

1. **a.** Clinical psychologists who adopt an eclectic approach often consider the preferences of the client, as well as the type of problem presented, in deciding on the most appropriate therapy.

2. Over the past several decades, psychologists have returned to the study of internal mental phenomena such as consciousness. This shift away from strict behaviorism has been labeled the *cognitive* revolution. An important factor that helped fuel this revolution was the development of the *computer*, which became a model of sorts for the human mind. Developments in *biology* are also playing an important role in shaping modern psychology and in creating effective treatments for psychological problems.

3. True.

4. **a.** Our cultural background can influence how we think, reason, and remember.

Knowledge Check: Chapter Summary

1. behavior
2. mind
3. observation
4. behavior
5. Clinical
6. Applied
7. Research
8. philosophy
9. physiology
10. Descartes
11. mind
12. Empiricism
13. Nativism
14. Darwin
15. genes or nature
16. experience or nurture
17. Structuralism
18. Functionalism
19. Behaviorism
20. psychoanalysis
21. unconscious
22. Humanistic

23. Calkins
24. Washburn
25. Woolley
26. Ladd-Franklin
27. Martin
28. Howard
29. Bernal
30. Eclectic
31. memory
32. chemical
33. Evolutionary
34. values
35. Data
36. replicated

CHAPTER 2

Knowledge Check 2.1

1. The middle point in an ordered set of scores is the *median*.

2. The *case study* technique, which focuses on the study of a single instance of behavior, is open to criticism because its results may lack *external validity*.

3. When behavior changes as a result of the observation process, the recorded data are said to suffer from a problem of *reactivity*.

4. The descriptive research technique used to gather limited amounts of information from many people is called a *survey*.

Knowledge Check 2.2

1. negative
2. positive
3. positive
4. zero

Knowledge Check 2.3

1. In experimental research, the researcher actively manipulates the environment to observe its effect on behavior. The aspect of the environment that is manipulated is called the *independent* variable; the behavior of interest is measured by the *dependent* variable. To draw conclusions about cause and effect, the experimenter must make certain that the *independent* variable is the only thing changing systematically in the environment.

2. a. The independent variable—Tom Cruise versus Barney—is not the only factor changing across the groups.

3. a. increases the likelihood that participant differences will be equally represented in each group.

Knowledge Check 2.4

1. Psychologists have a responsibility to respect the rights and dignity of all people. To ensure that research participants are treated ethically, psychologists use (a) informed *consent*, which means that everyone is fully informed about the potential risks of the project; (b) *confidentiality*, which assures that the participant's right to privacy will be maintained; and (c) *debriefing*, which is designed to provide more information about the purpose and procedures of the research.

2. a. is justified, but only under some circumstances.

3. a. animals can give no informed consent.

Knowledge Check: Chapter Summary

1. hypothesis
2. Descriptive
3. observe
4. Naturalistic behavior
5. noninterfering
6. Case
7. hypotheses
8. responses
9. representative
10. individual
11. regularities
12. hypotheses
13. Descriptive
14. Inferential
15. correlation
16. variables
17. predict

18. causality
19. experimental control
20. experimental
21. environment
22. hypothesis
23. independent
24. manipulated
25. dependent
26. measured
27. control
28. independent
29. two
30. control group
31. experimental
32. single-blind
33. double-blind
34. experimenter
35. controls
36. participate
37. Debriefing
38. Confidentiality
39. control
40. humane

CHAPTER 3

Knowledge Check 3.1

1. The *soma* is the main body of the cell, where excitatory and inhibitory messages combine.
2. The *axon* is the long tail-like part of a neuron that serves as the cell's main transmitter device.
3. The *action potential* is the all-or-none electrical signal that leads to the release of chemical messengers.
4. The *dendrites* are the branchlike fibers that extend outward from a neuron and receive information from other neurons.
5. Acetylcholine, serotonin, GABA, and dopamine are all examples of *neurotransmitters*.

Knowledge Check 3.2

1. The *hindbrain* is the primitive part of the brain that controls basic life-support functions such as heart rate and respiration.
2. The *hypothalamus* is a structure thought to be involved in a variety of motivational activities, including eating, drinking, and sexual behavior.
3. The *frontal lobes* are the portion of the cortex believed to be involved in higher-order thought processes (such as planning) as well as the initiation of voluntary motor movements.
4. The *cerebellum* is a structure near the base of the brain involved in coordination of complex activities such as walking and playing the piano.
5. An *EEG* is a device used to monitor the gross electrical activity of the brain.

Knowledge Check 3.3

1. nervous system
2. endocrine system
3. endocrine system
4. endocrine system
5. nervous system

Knowledge Check 3.4

1. False. Reading and writing skills developed too recently in the history of the species to be adaptations.
2. True.
3. False. Dominant genes play a stronger role.
4. True.

Knowledge Check: Chapter Summary

1. neuroscience
2. integrate
3. electrochemically
4. dendrites
5. axon
6. Interneurons
7. Motor
8. behavioral
9. chemically

10. activation
11. spinal cord
12. axons
13. autonomic
14. somatic
15. organ
16. lesions
17. electrodes
18. electroencephalograph (EEG)
19. positron emission tomography (PET)
20. hindbrain
21. pons
22. midbrain
23. forebrain
24. limbic
25. lateralized
26. hormones
27. pituitary
28. endocrine
29. survival
30. Adaptations
31. chromosomes
32. Genes
33. recessive
34. Family
35. twin
36. fraternal
37. environmental

CHAPTER 4

Knowledge Check 4.1

1. False. The period in prenatal development from implantation of the fertilized egg to the end of the eighth week is called the embryonic period.

2. True.

3. False. The neurons in the brain increase in size and complexity, not in number. The number of glial cells in the brain, however, may increase with age.

4. False. The timing of motor development is determined primarily by nature—the genetic code—although the environment may play some role.

5. False. We all lose brain cells with age, but the vast majority of people over 70 will not develop dementia.

Knowledge Check 4.2

1. a. Reward. In the reward technique, babies are given reinforcement when they perform a movement, such as kicking their legs, in response to a presented event.
    b. Habituation. The decline in responsiveness to repeated presentations, called habituation, can be used to infer that the baby recognizes that elements of the event have been repeated.
    c. Cross-sectional. In a cross-sectional design, different age groups are studied at the same time.
    d. Longitudinal. In a longitudinal design, the same individual is tested repeatedly across the life span.

2. a. Conservation. Conservation refers to the ability to recognize that certain physical properties of an object, such as mass, remain the same despite changes in the object's appearance.

3. a. Conventional. According to Kohlberg, individuals at the conventional level of moral reasoning decide the correctness of their actions on the basis of whether or not they disrupt the social order.
    b. Postconventional. At the postconventional level, moral reasoning is based on abstract principles that may or may not conflict with accepted standards.
    c. Preconventional. At the preconventional level, moral decisions are made on the basis of the action's immediate consequences.

Knowledge Check 4.3

1. a. secure
    b. avoidant
    c. resistant
    d. resistant

2. a. Not all teenagers suffer anxiety during this period.

3. False. Gender identity is already being formed by age 2 or 3.

4. a. False. Most elderly people are not sick and disabled, although physical problems certainly increase with age.
    b. False. Some stereotypes about the elderly are positive, such as the belief that all elderly are wise and kind.

c. False. Research suggests the opposite—that elderly people are confident in their abilities.

d. False. Research suggests that most elderly people prefer to strive to keep on living when faced with a painful and terminal disease.

Knowledge Check: Chapter Summary

1. zygote
2. germinal
3. implantation
4. embryonic
5. fetal
6. 7
7. plasticity
8. predictable
9. Adolescence
10. psychological
11. puberty
12. physically
13. dementia
14. preference
15. habituation
16. rewarding
17. sensory
18. shapes
19. memory
20. schemata
21. assimilation
22. accommodation
23. sensorimotor
24. preoperational
25. operational
26. formal
27. preconventional
28. conventional
29. postconventional
30. attachment
31. contact
32. Temperament
33. strange
34. secure
35. avoidant
36. psychosocial
37. autonomy
38. inferiority
39. role
40. gender roles
41. schema
42. Ageism
43. myths
44. stages
45. bargaining

CHAPTER 5

Knowledge Check 5.1

1. a. Fovea. This is the "central pit" area where the cone receptors tend to be located.
   b. Cones. These receptors are responsible for visual acuity, or our ability to see fine detail.
   c. Accommodation. Through this process, the lens changes its shape temporarily to help focus light.
   d. Retina. This "film" at the back of the eye contains the light-sensitive receptor cells.
   e. Cornea. This is the protective outer layer of the eye.

2. a. False. The majority of visual messages are analyzed in the lateral geniculate and primary visual cortex, although some messages are relayed to the superior colliculus.
   b. True.
   c. True.
   d. True.

3. a. Top-down processing. This is the part of perception that is controlled by our beliefs and expectations about how the world is organized.
   b. Perceptual constancy. This can be defined as perceiving an object, or its properties, to remain the same even though the physical message delivered to the eyes is changing.
   c. Phi phenomenon. This is an illusion of motion.
   d. Convergence. This depth cue is based on calculating the degree to which the two eyes have turned inward.

e. Recognition by components. This is the view that object perception is based on the analysis of simple building blocks, called geons.

Knowledge Check 5.2

1. True.

2. False. Place, not frequency, theory proposes that the location of activity on the basilar membrane is the primary cue for determining pitch.

3. False. Hair cells are located in the cochlea, not the pinna, and they are "bent" by movement of the basilar membrane.

4. False. Figure–ground organization occurs in hearing as well as in vision.

5. True.

Knowledge Check 5.3

1. a. Our perception of temperature is influenced by the changes that occur from one environment to the next.

2. a. Psychological factors are thought to somehow block pain messages from reaching higher neural centers.

3. a. The vestibular sacs are part of the structures of the inner ear.

Knowledge Check 5.4

1. Chemoreceptors. The general term for receptor cells that are activated by invisible molecules scattered about in the air or dissolved in liquids.

2. Olfactory bulb. One of the main brain destinations for odor messages.

3. Flavor. A psychological term used to describe the entire gustatory experience.

4. Olfaction. The technical name for the sense of smell.

5. Gustation. The technical name for the sense of taste.

Knowledge Check 5.5

1. False. There is no single point in an intensity curve at which detection reliably begins, even for a single individual.

2. True.

3. False. Detection of a just noticeable difference in magnitude depends on the intensity of the standard used for comparison.

4. True.

Knowledge Check: Chapter Summary

1. eye
2. pupil
3. lens
4. retina
5. rods
6. cones
7. optic chiasm
8. thalamus
9. Feature detectors
10. three
11. opponent-process theory
12. top-down
13. proximity
14. closure
15. binocular
16. depth
17. constancy
18. frequency
19. amplitude
20. eardrum
21. cochlea
22. basilar membrane
23. brain
24. place theory
25. hair cells
26. frequency
27. auditory cortex
28. expectations
29. organize
30. localization
31. time
32. intensity
33. pressure-sensitive
34. somatosensory
35. parietal

36. increasing

37. changes

38. gate-control

39. spinal cord

40. brain

41. endorphins

42. Kinesthesia

43. position

44. somatosensory

45. vestibular

46. acceleration

47. Semicircular

48. olfaction

49. chemoreceptors

50. nasal

51. bulb

52. thalamus

53. absolute threshold

54. 50

55. signal detection

56. false

57. difference threshold

58. magnitude

59. detected

60. just noticeable difference

61. adaptation

62. stimulus

63. sensitivity

64. constant

CHAPTER 6

Knowledge Check 6.1

1. False. The cocktail party effect suggests that we do at least some monitoring of unattended messages. We hear our name when it's spoken from across the room.

2. True.

3. True.

4. False. In visual neglect, damage to the right side of the brain means that people will fail to recognize things on the left side of the body.

5. False. Although some aspects of attention-deficit/ hyperactivity disorder may be learned, most researchers believe that some kind of neurological problem also contributes to the disorder.

Knowledge Check 6.2

1. a. Theta waves. The characteristic pattern found in stage N1 sleep.
   b. K complex. Often triggered by loud noises during stage N2 sleep.
   c. Delta activity. Another name for the slow-wave patterns that are found during stage N3 sleep.
   d. REM. The characteristic pattern of paradoxical sleep.

2. a. Cats sleep more than cows.

3. a. Insomnia. Difficulty initiating and maintaining sleep.
   b. Night terror. Sleeper awakens suddenly, screaming, but the EEG pattern indicates a period of non-REM sleep.
   c. Sleep apnea. Sleeper repeatedly stops breathing during the night, usually for short periods lasting less than 1 minute.
   d. Nightmare. An anxiety-arousing dream that usually occurs during the REM stage of sleep.

Knowledge Check 6.3

1. Stimulant. Increases central nervous system activity.

2. Opiate. Reduces pain by mimicking the brain's own natural pain-reducing chemicals.

3. Depressant. Tends to produce inhibitory effects by increasing the effectiveness of the neurotransmitter GABA.

4. Hallucinogen. Distorts perception (and may lead to flashbacks).

5. Stimulant. The type of active ingredient found in your morning cup of coffee.

Knowledge Check 6.4

1. False. The EEG patterns of a hypnotized person more closely resemble the patterns found when the person is awake, not asleep.

2. False. Hypnosis increases the chances of fabrication and does not generally lead to better memory.

3. True.

4. False. Hilgard's experiments support the idea of hypnotic dissociations.

5. True.

Knowledge Check: Chapter Summary

1. Attention
2. priorities
3. limits
4. neurons
5. dichotic listening
6. monitor
7. awareness
8. cocktail party effect
9. Automaticity
10. fast
11. attention
12. conscious
13. divided
14. neglect
15. parietal
16. left
17. distractibility
18. clocks
19. rhythms
20. waking
21. hormone
22. circadian
23. 90
24. height or amplitude
25. three
26. slow
27. 90
28. repair
29. survival
30. mental
31. memories
32. wish fulfillment
33. synthesis
34. random
35. threats
36. hypersomnia
37. narcolepsy
38. dyssomnias
39. terrors
40. parasomnias
41. neurotransmitters
42. mental
43. drug tolerance
44. psychological
45. dependency
46. Depressants
47. alcohol
48. increase
49. pain
50. Hallucinogens
51. perception
52. environmental
53. familiarity
54. set
55. suggestibility
56. relaxed
57. pain
58. enhance
59. relaxation
60. dissociations
61. consciousness
62. social
63. awareness
64. anxiety

CHAPTER 7

Knowledge Check 7.1

1. sensitization

2. orienting response

3. habituation

4. habituation

Knowledge Check 7.2

1. a. The unconditioned stimulus is the screaming.
   b. The unconditioned response is wincing and covering your ears.
   c. The conditioned stimulus is the sound of running water.
   d. The conditioned response is wincing.

2. a. The unconditioned stimulus is the puff of air.
   b. The unconditioned response is blinking.
   c. The conditioned stimulus is the word *ready*.
   d. The conditioned response is the urge to blink.

3. a. Extinction. It's likely that the stimuli presented in the experiment (soft furry things) occurred again many times in Albert's life without the accompanying loud noise. So, the association was extinguished.

Knowledge Check 7.3

1. a. Negative punishment. Arriving home late is punished by the removal of freedom.
   b. Positive reinforcement. The bonus is presented to increase the chances of similar sales behavior again.
   c. Positive punishment. The ticket is delivered to lower the likelihood of speeding in a school zone (although one might argue that the ticket also removes something she likes—money—making it negative punishment).
   d. Positive reinforcement. Crying increases because Mom delivers a kiss and a story.
   e. Positive punishment. Dad delivers a stern lecture for crying, which lowers the likelihood of crying in his presence.

2. a. Variable-ratio. Reinforcement depends on the number of calls, but the number of calls is not constant or predictable.
   b. Fixed-ratio. Reinforcement always occurs when she goes to a rally.

   c. Variable-interval. Reinforcement cannot be predicted and depends on the passage of time rather than the number of responses.
   d. Fixed-ratio. Reinforcement is delivered after a fixed number of purchases.
   e. Variable-interval. Reinforcement is not predictable and depends on the passage of time.

Knowledge Check 7.4

1. False. Observational learning often applies to our own behavior—we learn to act in a certain way by observing a role model.

2. True.

3. False. Our beliefs about how well we can perform a task (self-efficacy) play an important role in observational learning.

4. True.

5. True.

Knowledge Check: Chapter Summary

1. behavior

2. experience

3. prioritize

4. Habituation

5. increases

6. signaling

7. predicts

8. unconditioned

9. response

10. conditioned

11. information

12. different

13. US

14. second-

15. new

16. generalization

17. discrimination

18. different

19. US

20. extinction

21. inhibition
22. absence
23. Operant
24. consequences
25. effect
26. strengthened
27. weakened
28. discriminative
29. Positive
30. increases
31. increases
32. reinforcers
33. decreases
34. Negative
35. decreases
36. reinforcement
37. continuous
38. partial
39. fixed
40. ratio
41. interval
42. variable
43. shaping
44. approximations
45. biological
46. Observational
47. positive
48. rewarded
49. adaptive
50. reduce
51. increase

CHAPTER 8

Knowledge Check 8.1

1. sensory memory
2. sensory memory

3. short-term memory
4. sensory memory
5. short-term memory
6. sensory memory
7. short-term memory
8. short-term memory

Knowledge Check 8.2

1. **a.** semantic
   b. episodic
   c. semantic
   d. procedural
   e. procedural

2. **a.** Form a visual image of each word.

3. **a.** Method of loci. A mnemonic device in which you visualize each of the items sitting in a different location along a pathway.
   b. Distinctiveness. The appropriate term to use when you notice how each of the items is different from other things in memory.
   c. Elaboration. The formation of connections among each of the items to be remembered.
   d. Peg-word technique. The formation of images linking items to specific cues.
   e. Elaboration. The process of engaging in relational processing of the to-be-remembered material.

Knowledge Check 8.3

1. Schema. An organized knowledge package that's stored in long-term memory.

2. Implicit memory. Remembering without awareness.

3. Transfer-appropriate processing. Studying for a multiple-choice test by writing your own multiple-choice questions.

4. Free recall. Remembering material without the aid of any external retrieval cues.

Knowledge Check 8.4

1. False. Most forgetting occurs early and is followed by more gradual loss.

2. True.

3. False. Proactive interference occurs when prior learning interferes with later remembering.

4. False. People with anterograde amnesia can learn new things, but they lose the ability to access those memories consciously.

5. True.

6. True.

Knowledge Check: Chapter Summary

1. preserve

2. recover

3. visual

4. auditory

5. exact

6. iconic

7. echoic

8. short

9. forgotten

10. decay

11. interference

12. span

13. rehearsed

14. two

15. chunking

16. episodic

17. Semantic

18. procedural

19. Elaboration

20. connections

21. retrieval

22. meaning

23. relationships

24. differences

25. images

26. repetitions

27. sequence

28. loci

29. word

30. cues

31. match

32. transfer

33. mental

34. retrieval

35. Schemas

36. false

37. implicit

38. explicit

39. most

40. gradual

41. adaptive

42. retroactive

43. new

44. proactive

45. old

46. repress

47. validity

48. amnesia

49. Retrograde

50. before

51. anterograde

52. after

53. hippocampus

54. neurotransmitters

CHAPTER 9

Knowledge Check 9.1

1. **a.** Phonemes. The smallest significant sound units in speech.
  b. Pragmatics. The practical knowledge used to understand the intentions of a speaker and to produce an effective response.
  c. Syntax. The rules governing how words should be combined to form sentences.
  d. Morphemes. The smallest units in language that carry meaning.

2. *Top-down* processing is used when current knowledge aids in language comprehension. *Bottom-up* processing is used when basic units of a language are pieced together to determine meaning.

Knowledge Check 9.2

1. **a.** True.
   b. False. Children seem to learn the rules of language implicitly when exposed to language in their environment.
   c. True.
   d. True.
   e. False. Kanzi could follow spoken instructions from his trainers.

2. The key to determining whether nonhuman animals can learn language is whether or not they have some understanding of the *syntax* of language, the rules that determine how it is structured.

Knowledge Check 9.3

1. **a.** defining features
   b. category exemplars
   c. family resemblance
   d. prototype

2. **a.** Basic level ("Look, it's a cat.")

Knowledge Check 9.4

1. **a.** well-defined problem
   b. well-defined problem
   c. ill-defined problem
   d. ill-defined problem

2. **a.** searching for analogies
   b. algorithm
   c. means–ends analysis
   d. working backward

Knowledge Check 9.5

1. availability heuristic

2. framing

3. representativeness heuristic

4. anchoring and adjustment heuristic

Knowledge Check: Chapter Summary

1. grammar

2. sounds

3. sentences

4. meaning

5. phonemes

6. morphemes

7. surface

8. deep

9. knowledge

10. top-down

11. Pragmatics

12. practical

13. first

14. telegraphic

15. syntax

16. overgeneralize

17. anatomy or tract

18. impossible

19. Sign

20. language

21. adaptation

22. brain

23. ear

24. grammatical

25. category

26. defining

27. members

28. Natural

29. fuzzy

30. typical

31. resemblance

32. core

33. prototype

34. representative

35. exemplars

36. hierarchical

37. Basic-

38. predictive

39. intermediate

40. Superordinate

41. descriptive

42. well-defined

43. ill

44. clear

45. correctly

46. fixedness

47. algorithms

48. heuristics

49. means–ends

50. backward

51. analogies

52. mental

53. Insight

54. framing

55. represented

56. confirmation

57. belief

58. persistence

59. representativeness

60. prototypical

61. availability

62. anchors

63. quick

64. heuristics

65. errors

CHAPTER 10

Knowledge Check 10.1

1. Triarchic theory. "Street smarts" is an example of practical intelligence.

2. Multiple intelligences. Musical ability is considered to be a type of intelligence in Gardner's theory.

3. Psychometric. Intelligence is measured by analyzing performance on mental tests.

4. Psychometric. Factor analysis is a statistical technique used to analyze test performance.

5. Multiple intelligences. Insight into the feelings of others is a type of intelligence in Gardner's theory.

6. Triarchic theory. Applying what's been learned to new situations is a kind of creative intelligence.

Knowledge Check 10.2

1. a. Reliability. Donna's performance is consistent across testing.
   b. Validity. Larry's new test doesn't measure what it's supposed to measure.
   c. Reliability. Chei-Wui is checking on the consistency of test scores.
   d. Standardization. Robert makes certain that the testing and scoring procedures are the same for everybody who takes the test.

2. a. True.
   a. False. Average IQ, based on the deviation IQ method, is always 100 regardless of age.
   b. False. The diagnosis of an intellectual disability depends on many factors, such as one's ability to adapt.
   c. False. Creativity doesn't correlate very highly with IQ.

Knowledge Check 10.3

1. False. Fluid intelligence shows some decline over the life span.

2. False. Identical twins reared apart tend to have more similar IQs than fraternal twins raised together.

3. True.

4. False. Heritability tells us only that, for a given group, a certain percentage of the differences in intelligence can be explained by genetic factors.

5. True.

Knowledge Check: Chapter Summary

1. psychometric

2. performance

3. factor

4. correlations

5. general

6. Fluid

7. solve

8. genetic

9. Crystallized

10. knowledge

11. abilities

12. multiple

13. eight
14. linguistic
15. intrapersonal
16. triarchic
17. Analytic
18. creative
19. practical
20. Reliability
21. consistency
22. Validity
23. Standardization
24. intelligence
25. mental
26. average
27. different
28. chronological
29. deviation
30. intellectual disability
31. 130
32. giftedness
33. correlate
34. Labeling
35. English
36. Creativity
37. Emotional
38. understand
39. Tacit
40. experience
41. longitudinal
42. fluid
43. reasoning
44. decline
45. crystallized
46. knowledge
47. constant
48. Flynn

49. Twin
50. genetics
51. environment
52. similar
53. environment
54. Heritability
55. genetic
56. groups
57. differences
58. economic
59. bias
60. environment
61. genetic
62. environmental
63. upper
64. genetic
65. experience

CHAPTER 11

Knowledge Check 11.1

1. **a.** openness
   b. extroversion
   c. agreeableness
   d. neuroticism
   e. conscientiousness

2. **a.** TAT
   b. MMPI
   c. NEO-PI-R
   d. Rorschach
   e. 16PF

Knowledge Check 11.2

1. psychodynamic
2. social–cognitive
3. humanistic
4. psychodynamic
5. humanistic
6. social–cognitive
7. psychodynamic

Knowledge Check 11.3

1. True.

2. True.

3. False. High self-monitors tend to adapt their behavior to the situation.

4. False. Genetics appears to play a significant role in personality as measured by the MMPI.

5. False. Personality traits may only reveal themselves if they are relevant, or needed, in the situation.

Knowledge Check: Chapter Summary

1. Factor
2. 16
3. Eysenck
4. three
5. psychoticism
6. Five
7. agreeableness
8. neuroticism
9. conscientiousness
10. Allport
11. Cardinal
12. Central
13. 5
14. Secondary
15. Self
16. objective
17. 16
18. Multiphasic
19. projective
20. Apperception
21. ambiguous
22. conscious
23. preconscious
24. unconscious
25. unconscious
26. manifest
27. hidden
28. id
29. drives
30. superego
31. ego
32. anxiety
33. defense
34. psychosexual
35. Humanistic
36. awareness
37. responsibility
38. positive
39. incongruence
40. self-actualization
41. cognitive
42. classical
43. modeling
44. social
45. interpret
46. locus
47. efficacy
48. consistent
49. within
50. self-monitoring
51. inconsistent
52. consistent
53. interact
54. identical
55. genetic
56. fraternal

CHAPTER 12

Knowledge Check 12.1

1. a. Instincts lead to fixed response patterns; drives do not.

2. Choose the appropriate term:
   a. Incentive motivation. Whitney jogs because of the reward.

b. Intrinsic motivation. Janice's playing is self-motivated.

c. Achievement motivation. Candice studies to satisfy a need for achievement.

d. Intrinsic motivation. Jerome has become less motivated because of the reward.

3. a. Satisfying basic survival and social needs.

Knowledge Check 12.2

1. True.

2. False. Bingeing and purging are the principal symptoms of bulimia nervosa.

3. True.

4. False. Obesity is caused by many factors, not necessarily poor dietary habits.

5. True.

Knowledge Check 12.3

1. True.

2. True.

3. True.

4. True.

Knowledge Check 12.4

1. a. Dancing is an expressive reaction.
   b. Grimacing and wrinkling one's nose is an expressive reaction.
   c. A racing heart is a body response.
   d. Robert is telling us about his subjective experience.

2. a. Receiving a C on a test when you were expecting to flunk is the largest change in expectation (i.e., adaptation level).

3. a. James–Lange
   b. two-factor
   c. Cannon–Bard
   d. two-factor

Knowledge Check: Chapter Summary

1. Instincts

2. drive

3. physiological

4. incentive

5. goal

6. reinforcing

7. Achievement

8. harder

9. Intrinsic

10. External

11. Cultural

12. hierarchy

13. needs

14. biological

15. security

16. relationships

17. self-actualize

18. ghrelin

19. satiation

20. leptin

21. hypothalamus

22. hind

23. hippocampus

24. learning

25. cues

26. genetics

27. set

28. Obesity

29. metabolic

30. learned

31. stress

32. cultural

33. negative

34. Anorexia

35. Bulimia

36. excitement

37. plateau

38. orgasm

39. resolution

40. refractory

41. arousal

42. learned

43. estrogen

44. androgen

45. erogenous

46. pheromones

47. cultural

48. scripts

49. evolutionary

50. culture

51. Biological

52. environmental

53. orientation

54. facial

55. biological

56. anger

57. happiness

58. feedback

59. physiological

60. high

61. performance

62. expectations

63. controversial

64. Happiness

65. Disgust

66. physical

67. subjective

68. Cannon

69. independent

70. two

71. appraisal

CHAPTER 13

Knowledge Check 13.1

1. **a.** True.
   b. False. Exemplar, not prototype, theories assume that we represent stereotypes with individuals, or exemplars.
   c. True.
   d. True.

2. **a.** internal
   b. internal
   c. external
   d. internal

3. **a.** True.
   b. False. The central, not peripheral, route to persuasion operates when our level of involvement in or commitment to a message is high.
   c. True.
   d. False. Mere exposure is most likely to lead to attitude change when we're processing a message peripherally.

Knowledge Check 13.2

1. **a.** deindividuation
   b. social loafing, although conformity is also a possibility
   c. conformity
   d. group polarization
   e. bystander effect
   f. social facilitation

2. **a.** The experiment is conducted in the teacher's home.

Knowledge Check 13.3

1. True.

2. False. Averaged faces tend to be rated as most attractive.

3. False. Your ratings would go down.

4. True.

5. True.

6. False. Companionate love typically leads to more feelings of warmth and trust than does passionate love.

Knowledge Check: Chapter Summary

1. top

2. expectations

3. stereotypes

4. schemas

5. prejudice

6. distinctiveness

7. external

8. internal

9. internal

10. fundamental attribution error

11. actor–observer

12. self-serving

13. cognitive

14. affective

15. behavioral

16. experience

17. operant

18. observational

19. likelihood

20. central

21. peripheral

22. dissonance

23. attitudes

24. tension

25. perception

26. facilitation

27. performance

28. interference

29. impairs

30. altruism

31. unselfish

32. bystander

33. responsibility

34. loafing

35. less

36. group

37. Deindividuation

38. conformity

39. dominant

40. polarization

41. Groupthink

42. consensus

43. ignore

44. obedience

45. 65

46. replicated

47. independent

48. interdependent

49. evolutionary

50. healthy

51. faces

52. subjective

53. similarity

54. reciprocity

55. Passionate

56. Companionate

57. triangular

58. intimacy

59. passion

60. commitment

CHAPTER 14

Knowledge Check 14.1

1. False. When a behavior occurs infrequently among members of a population, it meets the criterion of statistical deviance.

2. False. Not all people with psychological disorders are emotionally distressed.

3. True.

4. True.

5. False. In many cases, hospital staff members appeared not to notice or classify the pseudopatients' behavior as normal—at least not quickly.

Knowledge Check 14.2

1. somatic symptom disorder (hypochondriasis or conversion disorder)

2. obsessive–compulsive disorder

3. anxiety disorder (panic disorder, agoraphobia)

4. depressive disorder

5. dissociative disorder (dissociative fugue)

6. personality disorder (antisocial personality disorder)

7. schizophrenia (paranoia)

8. schizophrenia (catatonia)

Knowledge Check 14.3

1. **a.** Excessive amounts of the neurotransmitter dopamine.

2. **a.** If your identical twin has schizophrenia, you have about a 50% chance of developing the disorder yourself.

3. **a.** Internal, stable, and global

4. **a.** Observational learning

Knowledge Check: Chapter Summary

1. continuum
2. deviance
3. Cultural
4. norms
5. emotional
6. dysfunction
7. legal
8. psychological
9. understand
10. legal
11. moral
12. medical
13. disease
14. medications
15. physical
16. labeling
17. stigma
18. normal
19. mental
20. classification
21. objective
22. measurable
23. not
24. anxiety
25. apprehension
26. Generalized
27. Panic
28. sudden
29. fear
30. agoraphobia
31. phobia
32. obsessive–compulsive
33. Somatic symptom
34. physical
35. disease
36. conversion
37. dissociative
38. dissociative
39. fugue
40. identity
41. identity
42. personalities
43. depressive
44. depressive
45. bipolar
46. depression
47. mania
48. suicide
49. emotion
50. positive
51. delusions
52. hallucinations
53. restricted or flat
54. catatonia
55. speech
56. personality
57. social
58. Narcissistic
59. antisocial
60. Five
61. chemistry
62. genetic
63. dopamine
64. serotonin

65. neurotransmitter
66. explanatory
67. internal
68. global
69. learned helplessness
70. control
71. Experience
72. culture
73. expressed
74. learned
75. classical conditioning

CHAPTER 15

Knowledge Check 15.1

1. a. schizophrenia
   b. depression
   c. depression
   d. depression
   e. generalized anxiety disorder

2. a. ECT is used regularly to treat schizophrenia.

Knowledge Check 15.2

1. rational-emotive therapy
2. Beck's cognitive therapy
3. psychoanalysis
4. client-centered therapy
5. Gestalt therapy
6. family therapy

Knowledge Check 15.3

1. a. conditioned stimulus.
2. a. counterconditioning and extinction.
3. a. Effective punishments can't be delivered because pain thresholds are high.
4. a. Reinforcement

Knowledge Check 15.4

1. True.
2. True.

3. False. Many evaluation studies show that the particular form of treatment doesn't matter.
4. False. Some types of treatment, such as most behavioral therapies, show concern only for the present symptoms.
5. True.

Knowledge Check: Chapter Summary

1. dopamine
2. tardive
3. Antidepressant
4. serotonin
5. Bipolar
6. lithium
7. Antianxiety
8. GABA
9. electroconvulsive
10. safe
11. severe
12. confusion
13. Psychosurgery
14. brain
15. Prefrontal
16. compulsive
17. rarely
18. psychoanalysis
19. free
20. dream
21. Resistance
22. transference
23. unconscious
24. streamline
25. Cognitive
26. conscious
27. rational
28. faulty or irrational
29. cognitive
30. humanistic

31. value

32. centered

33. incongruence

34. self-concept

35. positive

36. Gestalt

37. Group

38. similar

39. Family

40. interpersonal

41. anxiety

42. Conditioning

43. systematic desensitization

44. counterconditioning

45. hierarchy

46. aversion

47. rewards

48. punishments

49. token

50. privileges

51. Punishments

52. consequences

53. Social

54. behavioral

55. differences

56. meta

57. remission

58. support

59. learning

60. action

61. effective

CHAPTER 16

Knowledge Check 16.1

1. **a.** Alarm, resistance, exhaustion

2. **a.** The experience of stress, like emotion, depends on the appraisal of the event rather than on the event itself.

3. **a.** Marriage

4. **a.** An optimistic outlook

Knowledge Check 16.2

1. True.

2. True.

3. False. Stress has been shown to affect cholesterol levels.

4. False. Most people who suffer trauma do not develop posttraumatic stress disorder.

5. True.

Knowledge Check 16.3

1. **a.** the stress response is incompatible with relaxation.

2. **a.** gives you a feeling of control.

3. **a.** Social support makes it easier to cope if the support is no longer delivered.

4. **a.** Cognitive reappraisal

Knowledge Check 16.4

1. False. Aerobic exercise can lessen the physiological effects of the stress reaction.

2. True.

3. True.

4. False. Teaching children about the hazards of smoking or drugs would be classified as an example of primary prevention.

Knowledge Check: Chapter Summary

1. adaptation

2. three

3. alarm

4. resistance

5. exhaustion

6. fear

7. sadness

8. emotion

9. appraise

10. Significant
11. Social
12. negative
13. change
14. daily
15. noise
16. Environmental
17. Perceived
18. greater
19. Explanatory
20. heart
21. immune
22. lymphocytes
23. high
24. cholesterol
25. stressful
26. psychological
27. genetic
28. posttraumatic
29. flashbacks
30. Burnout
31. exhaustion
32. control
33. meaning
34. relaxation
35. muscle

36. autogenic
37. Meditation
38. Biofeedback
39. Social
40. interprets
41. reappraisal
42. Aerobic
43. physical
44. mental or psychological
45. mood
46. resistance
47. tobacco
48. health
49. chemical
50. addictive
51. withdrawal
52. nutrition
53. body
54. mind
55. type
56. Primary
57. before
58. Secondary
59. populations
60. Tertiary
61. primary

GLOSSARY

absolute threshold. The level of intensity that lifts a stimulus over the threshold of conscious awareness; it's usually defined as the intensity level at which people can detect the presence of the stimulus 50% of the time.

accommodation. (1) The process through which we change or modify existing schemata to accommodate new experiences. (2) In vision, the process through which the lens changes its shape temporarily to help focus light on the retina.

acetylcholine. A neurotransmitter that plays multiple roles in the central and peripheral nervous systems, including the excitation of muscle contractions.

achievement motivation. An internal drive or need for achievement that is possessed by all individuals to varying degrees.

achievement tests. Psychological tests that measure your current level of knowledge or competence in a particular subject.

action potential. The all-or-none electrical signal that travels down a neuron's axon.

activation–synthesis hypothesis. The idea that dreams represent the brain's attempt to make sense of the random patterns of neural activity generated during sleep.

actor–observer effect. The overall tendency to attribute our own behavior to external sources but to attribute the behavior of others to internal sources.

adaptation. A trait that has been selected for by nature because it increases the reproductive "fitness" of the organism.

aerobic exercise. High-intensity activities, such as running and swimming, that increase both heart rate and oxygen consumption.

affordance. Recognizing opportunities for behavior through perception.

ageism. Discrimination or prejudice against an individual based on physical age.

agoraphobia. An anxiety disorder that causes individuals to restrict their normal activities; someone suffering from agoraphobia tends to avoid public places out of fear that a panic attack will occur.

AIDS. Acquired immune deficiency syndrome, a disease that gradually weakens and disables the immune system.

algorithms. Step-by-step rules or procedures that, if applied correctly, guarantee a problem solution.

alpha waves. The pattern of brain activity observed in someone who is in a relaxed state.

altruism. Acting in a way that shows unselfish concern for the welfare of others.

amnesia. Forgetting that is caused by physical problems in the brain, such as those induced by injury or disease.

anal stage. Freud's second stage of psychosexual development, occurring in the second year of life; pleasure is derived from the process of defecation.

analytical intelligence. The ability to perform well on conventional tests that measure reasoning and logical-mathematical ability.

anorexia nervosa. An eating disorder diagnosed when an otherwise healthy person refuses to maintain a normal weight level because of an intense fear of being overweight.

anterograde amnesia. Memory loss for events that happen after the point of physical injury.

antianxiety drugs. Medications that reduce tension and anxiety.

antidepressant drugs. Medications that modulate the availability or effectiveness of the neurotransmitters implicated in mood disorders.

antipsychotic drugs. Medications that reduce the positive symptoms of schizophrenia.

antisocial personality disorder. A personality disorder characterized by little, if any, respect for social laws, customs, or norms.

anxiety disorders. A class of disorders marked by excessive apprehension and worry that in turn impairs normal functioning.

applied psychologists. Psychologists who extend the principles of scientific psychology to practical problems in the world.

aptitude tests. Psychological tests that measure your ability to learn or acquire knowledge in a particular subject.

assimilation. The process through which we fit—or assimilate—new experiences into existing schemata.

attachments. Strong emotional ties formed to one or more intimate companions.

attention. The internal processes used to set priorities for mental functioning.

attention-deficit/hyperactivity disorder (ADHD). A psychological disorder marked by difficulties in concentrating or in sustaining attention for extended periods; can be associated with hyperactivity.

attitude. A positive or negative evaluation that, in turn, predisposes us to act in certain ways; attitudes are typically broken down into cognitive, affective, and behavioral components.

attributions. The inference processes people use to assign cause and effect to behavior.

automaticity. Fast and effortless processing that requires little or no focused attention.

autonomic system. The collection of nerves that controls the more automatic needs of the body (such as heart rate, digestion, and blood pressure); part of the peripheral nervous system.

availability heuristic. The tendency to base estimates on the ease with which examples come to mind.

aversion therapy. A treatment for replacing a positive reaction to a harmful stimulus, such as alcohol, with something negative, such as feeling nauseated. Aversion therapy replaces positive associations with negative ones, such as making a smoker feel bad rather than good after having a cigarette.

axon. The long tail-like part of a neuron that serves as the cell's transmitter.

basic-level categories. The level in a category hierarchy that provides the most useful and predictive information; the basic level usually resides at an intermediate level in a category hierarchy.

basilar membrane. A flexible membrane running through the cochlea that, through its movement, displaces the auditory receptor cells, or hair cells.

behavior. Observable actions such as moving about, talking, gesturing, and so on; behavior can also refer to the activity of cells and to thoughts and feelings.

behavioral therapies. Treatments designed to change behavior through the use of established learning techniques.

behaviorism. A school of psychology proposing that the only proper subject matter of psychology is observable behavior rather than immediate conscious experience.

belief persistence. In decision making, the tendency to cling to initial beliefs when confronted with disconfirming evidence.

Big Five. The five dimensions of personality—extroversion, agreeableness, conscientiousness, neuroticism, and openness—that have been isolated through the application of factor analysis.

binocular depth cues. Cues for depth that depend on comparisons between the two eyes.

biofeedback. Specific physiological feedback people are given about the effectiveness of their relaxation efforts.

biological clocks. Brain structures that schedule rhythmic variations in bodily functions by triggering them at the appropriate times.

biomedical therapies. Biologically based treatments for reducing or eliminating the symptoms of psychological disorders.

bio-psycho-social perspective. The idea that psychological disorders are influenced, or caused, by a combination of biological, psychological (cognitive), and social (environmental) factors.

bipolar disorder. A type of mood disorder in which the person experiences disordered mood shifts in two directions—from depression to a manic state.

blind spot. The point where the optic nerve leaves the back of the eye.

borderline personality disorder. A personality disorder characterized by problems with emotional regulation, social relationships, and sense of self.

bottom-up processing. Processing that is controlled by the physical message delivered to the senses.

brightness. The aspect of the visual experience that changes with light intensity; in general, as the intensity of light increases, so does its perceived brightness.

bulimia nervosa. An eating disorder in which the principal symptom is binge eating (consuming large quantities of food) followed by purging, in which the person voluntarily vomits or uses laxatives to prevent weight gain.

burnout. A state of physical, emotional, and mental exhaustion created by long-term involvement in an emotionally demanding situation.

bystander effect. The reluctance to come to the aid of a person in need when other people are present.

Cannon–Bard theory. A theory of emotion that argues that body reactions and subjective experiences occur together, but independently.

cardinal traits. Allport's term to describe personality traits that dominate an individual's life, such as a passion to serve others or to accumulate wealth.

case study. A descriptive research technique in which the effort is focused on a single case, usually an individual.

category. A class of objects (people, places, or things) that most people agree belong together.

category exemplars. Specific examples of category members that are stored in long-term memory.

central nervous system. The brain and the spinal cord.

central traits. Allport's term to describe the 5 to 10 descriptive traits that you would use to describe someone you know—friendly, trustworthy, and so on.

cerebellum. A hindbrain structure at the base of the brain involved in the coordination of complex motor skills.

cerebral cortex. The outer layer of the brain, considered to be the seat of higher mental processes.

chemoreceptors. Receptor cells that react to invisible molecules scattered about in the air or dissolved in liquids, leading to the senses of smell and taste.

chunking. A short-term memory strategy that involves rearranging incoming information into meaningful or familiar patterns.

circadian rhythms. Biological activities that rise and fall in accordance with a 24-hour cycle.

classical conditioning. A set of procedures used to investigate how organisms learn about the signaling properties of events. Classical conditioning involves learning relations between events—conditioned and unconditioned stimuli—that occur outside of one's control.

client-centered therapy. A form of humanistic therapy proposing that it is the client, not the therapist, who holds the key to psychological health and happiness; the therapist's role is to provide genuineness, unconditional positive regard, and empathy.

clinical psychologists. Psychologists who specialize in the diagnosis and treatment of psychological problems.

cochlea. The bony, snail-shaped sound processor in the inner ear where sound is translated into nerve impulses.

cocktail party effect. The ability to focus on one auditory message and ignore others; also refers to the tendency to notice when your name suddenly appears in a message that you've been actively ignoring.

cognitive appraisal. The idea that to feel stress you need to perceive a threat and come to the conclusion that you may not have adequate resources to deal with the threat.

cognitive dissonance. The tension produced when people act in a way that is inconsistent with their attitudes.

cognitive revolution. The shift away from strict behaviorism, begun in the 1950s, characterized by renewed interest in fundamental problems of consciousness and internal mental processes.

cognitive therapies. Treatments designed to remove irrational beliefs and negative thoughts that are presumed to be responsible for psychological disorders.

cold fibers. Neurons that respond to a cooling of the skin by increasing the production of neural impulses.

collective unconscious. The notion proposed by Carl Jung that certain kinds of universal symbols and ideas are present in the unconscious of all people.

companionate love. A kind of emotional attachment characterized by feelings of trust and companionship; companionate love is marked by a combination of intimacy and commitment, but passion may be lacking.

computerized tomography scan (CT scan). The use of highly focused beams of X-rays to construct detailed anatomical maps of the living brain.

concrete operational period. Piaget's third stage of cognitive development, lasting from age 7 to age 11. Children acquire the capacity to perform a number of mental operations but still lack the ability for abstract reasoning.

conditioned inhibition. Learning that an event signals the absence of the unconditioned stimulus.

conditioned reinforcer. A stimulus that has acquired reinforcing properties through prior learning.

conditioned response (CR). The acquired response that is produced by the conditioned stimulus in anticipation of the unconditioned stimulus.

conditioned stimulus (CS). The neutral stimulus that is paired with the unconditioned stimulus during classical conditioning.

conditions of worth. The expectations or standards that we believe others place on us.

cones. Receptor cells in the central portion of the retina that transduce light energy into neural messages; they operate best when light levels are high, and they are primarily responsible for the ability to sense color.

confidentiality. The principle that personal information obtained from a participant in research or therapy should not be revealed without the individual's permission.

confirmation bias. The tendency to seek out and use information that supports and confirms a prior decision or belief.

conformity. The tendency to comply with the wishes of the group; when people conform, their opinions, feelings, and behaviors generally start to move toward the group norm.

confounding variable. An uncontrolled variable that changes along with the independent variable.

conscious mind. The content of awareness—those things that occupy the focus of one's current attention.

consciousness. Awareness of one's internal and external states.

conventional level. In Kohlberg's theory of moral development, the stage in which actions are judged to be right or wrong based on whether they maintain or disrupt the social order.

convergence. A binocular cue for depth that is based on the extent to which the two eyes move inward, or converge, when looking at an object.

conversion disorder. The presence of real physical problems, such as blindness or paralysis, that seem to have no identifiable physical cause.

coping. Efforts to manage or master conditions of threat or demand that tax one's resources.

cornea. The transparent and protective outer covering of the eye.

corpus callosum. The collection of nerve fibers that connects the two cerebral hemispheres and allows information to pass from one side to the other.

correlation. A statistic that indicates whether two variables vary together in a systematic way; correlation coefficients vary from $+1.00$ to -1.00.

creative intelligence. The ability to create, invent, and discover.

creativity. The ability to generate ideas that are original, novel, and useful.

cross-sectional design. A research design in which multiple groups of individuals of varying ages are assessed at once.

crystallized intelligence. The knowledge and abilities acquired as a result of experience (as from schooling and cultural influences).

cued recall. A testing condition in which people are given an explicit retrieval cue to help them remember.

cultural deviance. A criterion of abnormality stating that a behavior is abnormal if it violates the rules or accepted standards of society.

culture. The shared values, customs, and beliefs of a group or community.

dark adaptation. The process through which the eyes adjust to dim light.

debriefing. At the conclusion of an experimental session, informing the participants about the general purpose of the experiment, including any deception that was involved.

decay. The proposal that memories are forgotten or lost spontaneously with the passage of time.

decision making. The thought processes involved in evaluating and choosing from among a set of alternatives; it usually involves some kind of risk.

deep structure. The underlying representation of meaning in a sentence.

defense mechanisms. According to Freud, unconscious processes used by the ego to ward off the anxiety that comes from confrontation, usually with the demands of the id.

defining features. The set of features necessary to make objects acceptable members of a category.

deindividuation. The loss of individuality, or depersonalization, that comes from being in a group.

delta activity. The pattern of brain activity observed in stage N3; it's characterized by synchronized slow waves. Also called slow-wave sleep.

dementia. Physically based losses in mental functioning.

dendrites. The fibers that extend outward from a neuron and receive information from other neurons.

dependent variable. The behavior that is measured or observed in an experiment.

depressants. A class of drugs that slow or depress the ongoing activity of the central nervous system.

depressive disorders. Prolonged and disabling disruptions in emotional state.

descriptive research. Methods designed to observe and describe behavior.

descriptive statistics. Mathematical techniques that help researchers describe their data.

development. The age-related physical, intellectual, social, and personal changes that occur throughout an individual's lifetime.

deviation IQ. An intelligence score that is derived from determining where your performance sits in an age-based distribution of test scores.

diagnostic labeling effects. The fact that labels for psychological problems can become self-fulfilling prophecies; the label may make it difficult to recognize normal behavior when it occurs, and it may actually increase the likelihood that a person will act in an abnormal way.

dichotic listening. Different auditory messages are presented separately and simultaneously to each ear. The subject's task is to repeat aloud one message while ignoring the other.

difference threshold. The smallest detectable difference in the magnitude of two stimuli.

diffusion of responsibility. The idea that when people know (or think) that others are present in a situation, they allow their sense of responsibility for action to diffuse, or spread out widely, among those who are present.

discrimination. Behaviors that are directed against members of a group.

discriminative stimulus. The stimulus situation that sets the occasion for a response to be followed by reinforcement or punishment.

dissociative amnesia. A psychological disorder characterized by an inability to remember important personal information.

dissociative disorders. A class of disorders characterized by the separation, or dissociation, of conscious awareness from previous thoughts or memories.

dissociative fugue. A loss of personal identity that is often accompanied by a flight from home.

dissociative identity disorder. A condition in which an individual alternates between what appear to be two or more distinct identities or personalities (also known as multiple personality disorder).

distinctiveness. Refers to how unique or different a memory record is from other things in memory. Distinctive memory records tend to be recalled well.

distributed practice. Spacing the repetitions of to-be-remembered information over time.

dopamine. A neurotransmitter that has been linked to reward and pleasure systems in the brain; decreased levels have been linked to Parkinson's disease, and increased levels have been linked to schizophrenia.

double-blind study. Neither participants nor research observers are aware of who has been assigned to the experimental and control groups; it's used to control for both participant and experimenter expectancies.

dream analysis. A technique used in psychoanalysis; Freud believed that dreams are symbolic and contain important information about the unconscious.

drive. A psychological state that arises in response to an internal physiological need, such as hunger or thirst.

drug dependency. A condition in which one experiences a physical or a psychological need for continued use of a drug.

drug tolerance. An adaptation made by the body to compensate for the continued use of a drug, such that increasing amounts of the drug are needed to produce the same physical and behavioral effects.

DSM. The *Diagnostic and Statistical Manual of Mental Disorders*, which is used for the diagnosis and classification of psychological disorders.

dysfunction. A breakdown in normal functioning; abnormal behaviors are those that prevent one from pursuing adaptive strategies.

echoic memory. The system that produces and stores auditory sensory memories.

eclectic approach. The idea that it's useful to select information from several sources rather than to rely entirely on a single perspective or school of thought.

ego. In Freud's theory, the portion of personality that induces people to act with reason and deliberation and helps them conform to the requirements of the external world.

egocentrism. The tendency to see the world from one's own unique perspective only; a characteristic of thinking in the preoperational period of development.

elaboration. An encoding process that involves the formation of connections between to-be-remembered input and other information in memory.

elaboration likelihood model. A model proposing two primary routes to persuasion and attitude change: a *central* route, which operates when we are motivated and focusing our attention on the message, and a *peripheral* route, which operates when we are either unmotivated to process the message or unable to do so.

electroconvulsive therapy (ECT). A treatment used primarily for depression in which a brief electric current is delivered to the brain.

electroencephalograph (EEG). A device used to monitor the gross electrical activity of the brain.

embryonic period. The period of prenatal development lasting from implantation to the end of the eighth week.

emotional distress. A criterion of abnormality stating that abnormal behaviors are those that lead to personal distress or emotional upset.

emotional intelligence. The ability to perceive, understand, and express emotion in ways that are useful and adaptive.

emotions. Psychological events involving (1) a physiological reaction, usually arousal; (2) some kind of expressive reaction, such as a distinctive facial expression; and (3) some kind of subjective experience, such as the conscious feeling of being happy or sad.

empiricism. The idea that knowledge comes directly from experience.

encoding. The processes that determine and control how memories are formed.

endocrine system. A network of glands that uses the bloodstream, rather than neurons, to send chemical messages that regulate growth and other internal functions.

endorphins. Morphinelike chemicals that act as the brain's natural painkillers.

environmental psychology. A specialty area in psychology devoted to the study of environmental effects on behavior and health, such as the effects of crowding or noise.

episodic memory. A memory for a particular event, or episode, that happened to you personally, such as remembering what you ate for breakfast this morning or where you went on vacation last year.

evolutionary psychology. A movement proposing that we're born with mental processes and "software" that were acquired through natural selection in our ancestral past and help us to solve specific adaptive problems.

excitement phase. The first component of the human sexual response cycle; it's characterized by changes in muscle tension, increased heart rate and blood pressure, and a rushing of blood into the genital organs.

experimental research. A technique in which the investigator actively manipulates the environment to observe its effect on behavior.

explicit memory. Conscious, willful remembering.

external attribution. Attributing the cause of a person's behavior to an external event or situation in the environment.

external validity. The extent to which results generalize to other situations or are representative of real life.

extinction. Presenting a conditioned stimulus repeatedly, after conditioning, without the unconditioned stimulus, resulting in a loss in responding.

facial-feedback hypothesis. The proposal that muscles in the face deliver signals to the brain that are then interpreted, depending on the pattern, as a subjective emotional state.

factor analysis. A statistical procedure that groups together related items on tests by analyzing the correlations among test scores.

family resemblance. The core features that category members share; a given member of the category may have some but not necessarily all of these features.

family studies. The similarities and differences among biological (blood) relatives are studied to help discover the role heredity plays in physical or psychological traits.

family therapy. A form of group therapy in which the therapist treats the family as a whole, as a kind of social system. The goals of the treatment are often to improve interpersonal communication and collaboration.

feature detectors. Cells in the visual cortex that respond to very specific visual events, such as bars of light at particular orientations.

fetal period. The period of prenatal development lasting from the ninth week until birth.

fixed-interval (FI) schedule. A schedule in which the reinforcement is delivered for the first response that occurs following a fixed interval of time.

fixed-ratio (FR) schedule. A schedule in which the number of responses required for reinforcement is fixed and does not change.

flashbulb memories. Rich memory records of the circumstances surrounding emotionally significant and surprising events.

flavor. A psychological term used to describe the gustatory experience. Flavor is influenced by taste, smell, and the visual appearance of food, as well as by expectations about the food's quality.

fluid intelligence. The natural ability to solve problems, reason, and remember; fluid intelligence is thought to be relatively uninfluenced by experience.

forebrain. The outer portion of the brain, including the cerebral cortex and the structures of the limbic system.

forgetting. The loss of accessibility to previously stored material.

formal operational period. Piaget's last stage of cognitive development; thought processes become adultlike, and people gain mastery over abstract thinking.

fovea. The "central pit" area in the retina where the cone receptors are located.

framing. The way in which the alternatives in a decision-making situation are structured.

free association. A technique used in psychoanalysis to explore the content of the unconscious; clients are asked to freely express whatever thoughts and feelings happen to come into their minds.

free recall. A testing condition in which a person is asked to remember information without explicit retrieval cues.

frequency theory. The idea that pitch perception is determined partly by the frequency of neural impulses traveling up the auditory pathway.

frontal lobe. One of four anatomical regions of each hemisphere of the cerebral cortex, located on the top front of the brain; it contains the motor cortex and may be involved in higher-level thought processes.

functional fixedness. The tendency to see objects, and their functions, in certain fixed and typical ways.

functionalism. An early school of psychology; functionalists believed that the proper way to understand mind and behavior is to first analyze their function and purpose.

fundamental attribution error. When people seek to interpret someone else's behavior, they tend to overestimate the influence of internal personal factors and underestimate the role of situational factors.

g (general intelligence). According to Spearman, a general factor, derived from factor analysis, that underlies or contributes to performance on a variety of mental tests.

gamma-aminobutyric acid (GABA). A neurotransmitter that may play a role in the regulation of anxiety; it generally produces inhibitory effects.

gate-control theory. The idea that neural impulses generated by pain receptors can be blocked, or gated, in the spinal cord by signals produced in the brain.

gender roles. Specific patterns of behavior that are consistent with how society dictates males and females should act.

general adaptation syndrome (GAS). Hans Selye's model of stress as a general, nonspecific reaction that occurs in three phases: alarm, resistance, and exhaustion.

generalized anxiety disorder. Excessive worrying, or free-floating anxiety, that lasts for at least six months and that cannot be attributed to any single identifiable source.

genes. Segments of chromosomes that contain instructions for influencing and creating particular hereditary characteristics.

genital stage. Freud's final stage of psychosexual development, during which one develops mature sexual relationships with members of the opposite sex.

genotype. The actual genetic information inherited from one's parents.

germinal period. The period in prenatal development from conception to implantation of the fertilized egg in the wall of the uterus.

Gestalt principles of organization. The organizing principles of perception proposed by the Gestalt psychologists. These principles include the laws of proximity, similarity, closure, continuation, and common fate.

gifted. A label generally assigned to someone who scores above 130 on a standard IQ test.

glial cells. Cells that fill in space between neurons, remove waste, or help neurons to communicate efficiently.

glutamate. The most common neurotransmitter in the brain.

grammar. The rules of language that enable the communicator to combine symbols to convey meaning.

group polarization. The tendency for a group's dominant point of view to become stronger and more extreme with time.

group therapy. A form of therapy in which several people are treated simultaneously in the same setting.

groupthink. The tendency for members of a group to become so interested in seeking a consensus of opinion that they start to ignore and even suppress dissenting views.

gustation. The sense of taste.

habituation. The decline in the tendency to respond to an event that has become familiar through repeated exposure.

hallucinogens. A class of drugs that tends to disrupt normal mental and emotional functioning, including distorting perception and altering reality.

health psychology. The study of how biological, psychological, environmental, and cultural factors are involved in physical health and the prevention of illness.

heritability. A mathematical index that represents the extent to which IQ differences in a particular population can be accounted for by genetic factors.

heuristics. The rules of thumb we use to solve problems; heuristics can usually be applied quickly, but they do not guarantee that a solution will be found.

hindbrain. A primitive part of the brain that sits at the juncture point where the brain and spinal cord merge. Structures in the hindbrain, including the medulla, pons, and reticular formation, act as the basic life-support system for the body.

homeostasis. The process through which the body maintains a steady state, such as a constant internal temperature or an adequate amount of fluids.

hormones. Chemicals released into the blood by the various endocrine glands to help control a variety of internal regulatory functions.

hue. The dimension of light that produces color; hue is typically determined by the wavelength of light reflecting from an object.

humanistic psychology. A movement in psychology that focuses on people's unique capacities for choice, responsibility, and growth.

humanistic therapy. Treatments designed to help clients gain insight into their fundamental self-worth and value as human beings.

hypersomnia. A chronic condition marked by excessive sleepiness.

hypnosis. A form of social interaction that produces a heightened state of suggestibility in a willing participant.

hypnotic dissociation. A hypnotically induced splitting of consciousness during which multiple forms of awareness exist.

hypnotic hypermnesia. The supposed enhancement in memory that occurs under hypnosis; there is little if any evidence to support the existence of this effect.

hypothalamus. A forebrain structure thought to play a role in the regulation of various motivational activities, including eating, drinking, and sexual behavior.

iconic memory. The system that produces and stores visual sensory memories.

id. In Freud's theory, the portion of personality that is governed by inborn instinctual drives, particularly those related to sex and aggression.

ill-defined problem. A problem, such as the search for "happiness," that has no well-stated goal, no clear starting point, and no mechanism for evaluating progress.

implicit memory. Remembering that occurs in the absence of conscious awareness or willful intent.

incentive motivation. External factors in the environment that exert pulling effects on our actions.

incongruence. A discrepancy between the image we hold of ourselves—our self-concept—and the sum of all our experiences.

independent variable. The aspect of the environment that is manipulated in an experiment. It must consist of at least two conditions.

inferential statistics. Mathematical techniques that help researchers decide whether data are representative of a population or whether differences among observations can be attributed to chance.

informed consent. The principle that before consenting to participate in research, people should be fully informed about any significant factors that could affect their willingness to participate.

in-group. A group of individuals with whom one shares features in common or with whom one identifies.

insanity. A legal term usually defined as the inability to understand that certain actions are wrong, in a legal or moral sense, at the time of a crime.

insight. The moment when a problem solution seems to pop suddenly into one's mind.

insight therapies. Treatments designed to give clients self-knowledge, or insight, into the content of their thought processes.

insomnia. A chronic condition marked by difficulties in initiating or maintaining sleep, lasting for a period of at least one month.

instincts. Unlearned characteristic patterns of responding that are controlled by specific triggering stimuli in the world.

intellectual disability. A label generally assigned to someone who scores below 70 on a standard IQ test, although other factors, such as one's ability to adapt to the environment, are also important.

intelligence. An internal capacity or ability that accounts for individual differences in mental test performance and enables us to adapt to ever-changing environments.

intelligence quotient (IQ). Mental age divided by chronological age and then multiplied by 100.

internal attribution. Attributing the cause of a person's behavior to an internal personality trait or disposition.

internal validity. The extent to which an experiment has effectively controlled for confounding variables; internally valid experiments allow for the determination of causality.

interneurons. Cells that transfer information from one neuron to another; interneurons make no direct contact with the outside world.

intrinsic motivation. Goal-directed behavior that seems to be entirely self-motivated.

iris. The ring of colored tissue surrounding the pupil.

James–Lange theory. A theory of emotion that argues that body reactions precede and drive the subjective experience of emotions.

kinesthesia. In perception, the ability to sense the position and movement of one's body parts.

latency period. Freud's period of psychosexual development, from age 5 to puberty, during which the child's sexual feelings are largely suppressed.

latent content. According to Freud, the true psychological meaning of dream symbols.

law of effect. If a response in a particular situation is followed by a satisfying consequence, it will be strengthened. If a response in a particular situation is followed by an unsatisfying consequence, it will be weakened.

learned helplessness. A general sense of helplessness that is acquired when people repeatedly fail in their attempts to control their environment; learned helplessness may play a role in depression.

learning. A relatively permanent change in behavior, or potential behavior, that results from experience.

lens. The flexible piece of tissue that helps focus light toward the back of the eye.

light. The small part of the electromagnetic spectrum that is processed by the visual system.

limbic system. A system of structures thought to be involved in motivational and emotional behaviors (the amygdala) and memory (the hippocampus).

locus of control. The amount of control that people feel they have over the environment.

longitudinal design. A research design in which the same people are studied or tested repeatedly over time.

long-term memory. The system used to maintain information for extended periods of time.

lymphocytes. Specialized white blood cells that have the job of attacking foreign substances, such as viruses and bacteria.

magnetic resonance imaging (MRI). A device that uses magnetic fields and radio-wave pulses to construct detailed, three-dimensional images of the brain; "functional" MRIs can be used to map changes in blood oxygen use as a function of task activity.

major depressive episode. A type of mood disorder characterized by depressed mood and other symptoms.

manic episode. A disordered state in which the person becomes hyperactive and talkative, and has a decreased need for sleep; a person in a manic state may engage in activities that are self-destructive or dangerous.

manifest content. According to Freud, the actual symbols and events experienced in a dream.

mean. The arithmetic average of a set of scores.

means–ends analysis. A problem-solving heuristic that involves devising actions, or means, that reduce the distance between the current starting point and the desired end (the goal state).

median. The middle point in an ordered set of scores; half of the scores fall at or below the median score, and half fall at or above the median score.

medical model. The view that abnormal behavior is symptomatic of an underlying "disease," which can be "cured" with the appropriate therapy.

meditation. A technique for self-induced manipulation of awareness, often used for the purpose of relaxation and self-reflection.

memory. The capacity to preserve and recover information.

memory span. The number of items that can be recalled from short-term memory in their proper presentation order on half of the tested memory trials.

menopause. The period during which a woman's menstrual cycle slows down and finally stops.

mental age. The chronological age that best fits a child's level of performance on a test of mental ability.

mental set. The tendency to rely on well-established strategies when attempting to solve problems.

meta-analysis. A statistical technique used to compare findings across many different research studies; comparisons are based on some common evaluation measure, such as the difference between treatment and control conditions.

method of loci. A mnemonic device in which you choose some pathway, such as moving through the rooms in your house, and then form visual images of the to-be-remembered items sitting in locations along the pathway.

midbrain. The middle portion of the brain, containing such structures as the tectum, superior colliculus, and inferior colliculus; midbrain structures serve as neural relay stations and may help coordinate reactions to sensory events.

middle ear. The portion between the eardrum and the cochlea containing three small bones (the malleus, incus, and stapes) that help to intensify and prepare the sound vibrations for passage into the inner ear.

mind. The contents and processes of subjective experience: sensations, thoughts, and emotions.

mnemonic devices. Special mental tricks that help people think about material in ways that improve later memory. Most mnemonic devices require the use of visual imagery.

mode. The most frequently occurring score in a set of scores.

modeling. The natural tendency to imitate the behavior of significant others.

monocular depth cues. Cues for depth that require input from only one eye.

morality. The ability to distinguish between appropriate and inappropriate actions.

morphemes. The smallest units in a language that carry meaning.

motivation. The set of factors that initiate and direct behavior, usually toward some goal.

motor neurons. Cells that carry information away from the central nervous system to the muscles and glands that directly produce behavior.

multiple intelligences. The notion proposed by Howard Gardner that people possess a set of separate and independent "intelligences" ranging from musical to linguistic to interpersonal ability.

mutation. A spontaneous change in the genetic material that occurs during the gene replication process.

myelin sheath. An insulating material that protects the axon and helps to speed up neural transmission.

narcissistic personality disorder. A personality disorder characterized by an exaggerated sense of entitlement, which leads to excessive attempts to attract and be the focus of attention.

narcolepsy. A rare sleep disorder characterized by sudden extreme sleepiness.

nativism. The idea that some knowledge is innate, or present at birth.

naturalistic observation. A descriptive research technique that records naturally occurring behavior as opposed to behavior produced in the laboratory.

need hierarchy. The idea popularized by Maslow that human needs are prioritized in a hierarchy.

negative punishment. An event that, when removed after a response, lowers the likelihood of that response occurring again.

negative reinforcement. An event that, when removed after a response, increases the likelihood of that response occurring again.

nerves. Bundles of axons that make up neural "transmission cables."

neurons. The cells in the nervous system that receive and transmit information.

neuroscience. An interdisciplinary field of study directed at understanding the brain and its relation to behavior.

neurotransmitters. Chemical messengers that relay information from one neuron to the next.

night terrors. Terrifying experiences, which occur mainly in children, in which the sleeper awakens suddenly in an extreme state of panic.

nightmares. Frightening and anxiety-arousing dreams that occur primarily during the REM stage of sleep.

obedience. The form of compliance that occurs when people respond to the orders of an authority figure.

obesity. A weight problem characterized by excessive body fat.

object permanence. The ability to recognize that objects still exist when they're no longer in sight.

observational learning. Learning by observing the experience of others.

obsessive–compulsive disorder. A disorder that manifests itself through persistent and uncontrollable thoughts, called obsessions, or by the compelling need to perform repetitive acts, called compulsions.

occipital lobe. One of four anatomical regions of each hemisphere of the cerebral cortex, located at the back of the brain; visual processing is controlled here.

olfaction. The sense of smell.

operant conditioning. A procedure for studying how organisms learn about the consequences of their own voluntary actions (also called instrumental conditioning).

operational definitions. Definitions that specify how concepts can be observed and measured.

opiates. A class of drugs that reduce anxiety, lower sensitivity to pain, and elevate mood; opiates often act to depress nervous system activity.

opponent-process theory. A theory of color vision proposing that cells in the visual pathway increase their activation levels to one color and decrease their activation levels to another color—for example, increasing to red and decreasing to green.

optogenetics. A technique that uses light to activate and control neurons that have been genetically engineered to respond to light.

oral stage. The first stage in Freud's conception of psychosexual development, occurring in the first year of life; in this stage, pleasure is derived primarily from sucking and placing things in the mouth.

orgasmic phase. The third stage in the human sexual response cycle. It's characterized by rhythmic contractions in the sex organs; in men, ejaculation occurs. There is also the subjective experience of pleasure, which appears to be similar for men and women.

orienting response. An inborn tendency to notice and respond to novel or surprising events.

ostracism. When one is excluded and ignored by one or more others in a group.

pain. An adaptive response by the body to any stimulus that is intense enough to cause tissue damage.

panic disorder. A condition marked by recurrent discrete episodes or attacks of extremely intense fear or dread.

parietal lobe. One of four anatomical regions of each hemisphere of the cerebral cortex, located roughly on the top middle portion of the brain; it contains the somatosensory cortex, which controls the sense of touch.

partial reinforcement schedule. A schedule in which reinforcement is delivered only some of the time after the response has occurred.

passionate love. An intense emotional state characterized by a powerful longing to be with a specific person; passionate love is marked by a combination of intimacy and passion, but commitment may be lacking.

peg-word method. A mnemonic device in which you form visual images connecting to-be-remembered items with retrieval cues, or pegs.

perceived control. The amount of influence you feel you have over a situation and your reaction to it.

perception. The collection of processes used to arrive at a meaningful interpretation of sensations.

perceptual constancy. Perceiving the properties of an object to remain the same even though the physical properties of the sensory message are changing.

perceptual illusions. Inappropriate interpretations of physical reality. Perceptual illusions often occur as a result of the brain's using otherwise adaptive organizing principles.

peripheral nervous system. The network of nerves that links the central nervous system with the rest of the body.

personal identity. A sense of who one is as an individual and how well one measures up against peers.

personality. The distinguishing pattern of psychological characteristics—thinking, feeling, and behaving—that differentiates us from others and leads us to act consistently across situations.

personality disorders. Chronic or enduring patterns of behavior that lead to significant impairments in social functioning.

person-situation debate. A controversial debate centering on whether people really do behave consistently across situations.

phallic stage. Freud's third stage of psychosexual development, lasting from about age 3 to age 5; pleasure is gained from self-stimulation of the sexual organs.

phenotype. A person's observable characteristics, such as red hair. The phenotype is controlled mainly by the genotype, but it can also be influenced by the environment.

phi phenomenon. An illusion of movement that occurs when stationary lights are flashed in succession.

phobic disorder. (or *specific phobia*) A highly focused fear of a specific object or situation.

phonemes. The smallest significant sound units in speech.

phonology. Rules governing how sounds should be combined to make words in a language.

pinna. The external flap of tissue normally referred to as the "ear"; it helps capture sounds.

pitch. The psychological experience that results from the auditory processing of a particular frequency of sound.

pituitary gland. A kind of master gland in the body that controls the release of hormones in response to signals from the hypothalamus.

place theory. The idea that the location of auditory receptor cells activated by movement of the basilar membrane underlies the perception of pitch.

placebo. An inactive, or inert, substance that resembles an experimental substance.

plateau phase. The second stage in the human sexual response cycle. Arousal continues to increase, although at a slower rate, toward a preorgasm maximum point.

positive punishment. An event that, when presented after a response, lowers the likelihood of that response occurring again.

positive regard. The idea that we value what others think of us and that we constantly seek others' approval, love, and companionship.

positive reinforcement. An event that, when presented after a response, increases the likelihood of that response.

positron emission tomography (PET). A method for measuring how radioactive substances are absorbed in the brain; it can be used to detect how specific tasks activate different areas of the living brain.

postconventional level. Kohlberg's highest level of moral development, in which moral actions are judged on the basis of a personal code of ethics that is general and abstract and that may not agree with societal norms.

posttraumatic stress disorder (PTSD). A trauma-based anxiety disorder characterized by flashbacks, avoidance of stimuli associated with the traumatic event, and chronic arousal symptoms.

practical intelligence. The ability to take ideas and apply them successfully to everyday situations.

pragmatics. The practical knowledge used to comprehend the intentions of a speaker and to produce an effective response.

preconscious mind. The part of the mind that contains all of the inactive but potentially accessible thoughts and memories.

preconventional level. In Kohlberg's theory, the lowest level of moral development, in which decisions about right and wrong are made primarily in terms of external consequences.

prejudice. Positive or negative evaluations of a group and its members.

preoperational period. Piaget's second stage of cognitive development, lasting from age 2 to about age 7; children begin to think symbolically but often lack the ability to perform mental operations such as conservation.

primacy effect. The better memory of items near the beginning of a memorized list.

principle of conservation. The ability to recognize that the physical properties of an object remain the same despite superficial changes in the object's appearance.

proactive interference. A process in which old memories interfere with the recovery of new memories.

procedural memory. Knowledge about how to do things, such as riding a bike or swinging a golf club.

projective personality test. A type of personality test in which individuals are asked to interpret unstructured or ambiguous stimuli.

prototype. The best or most representative member of a category (such as robin for the category "bird").

psychiatrists. Medical doctors who specialize in the diagnosis and treatment of psychological problems.

psychoactive drugs. Drugs that affect behavior and mental processes through alterations of conscious awareness.

psychoanalysis. Freud's method of treatment that attempts to bring hidden impulses and memories, which are locked in the unconscious, to the surface of awareness, thereby freeing the client from disordered thoughts and behaviors.

psychodynamic theory. An approach to personality development, based largely on the ideas of Sigmund Freud, that holds that much of behavior is governed by unconscious forces.

psychology. The scientific study of behavior and mind.

psychometrics. The use of psychological tests to measure the mind and mental processes.

psychophysics. A field of psychology in which researchers search for ways to describe the transition from the physical stimulus to the psychological experience of that stimulus.

psychosurgery. Surgery that destroys or alters tissues in the brain in an effort to affect behavior.

psychotherapy. Treatment designed to help people deal with mental, emotional, or behavioral problems.

puberty. The period during which a person reaches sexual maturity and is potentially capable of producing offspring.

punishment. Consequences that decrease the likelihood of responding in a similar way again.

pupil. The hole in the center of the eye that allows light to enter.

random assignment. A technique ensuring that each participant in an experiment has an equal chance of being assigned to any of the conditions in the experiment.

random sampling. A procedure guaranteeing that everyone in the population has an equal likelihood of being selected for the sample.

range. The difference between the largest and smallest scores in a distribution.

rational-emotive therapy. A form of cognitive therapy in which the therapist acts as a kind of cross-examiner, verbally assaulting the client's irrational thought processes.

reactivity. When behavior changes as a result of the observation process.

recency effect. The better memory of items near the end of a memorized list.

receptive field. In vision, the portion of the retina that, when stimulated, causes the activity of higher-order neurons to change.

reciprocal determinism. The idea that beliefs, behavior, and the environment interact to shape what is learned from experience.

reciprocity. The tendency for people to return in kind the feelings that are shown toward them.

recognition by components. The idea proposed by Biederman that people recognize objects perceptually via smaller components called geons.

reflexes. Automatic motor behaviors present in humans at birth.

reflexes. Largely automatic body reactions—such as the knee jerk—controlled primarily by spinal cord pathways.

refractory period. The period of time following an action potential when more action potentials cannot be generated.

rehearsal. A strategic process that helps to maintain short-term memories indefinitely through the use of internal repetition.

reinforcement. Response consequences that increase the likelihood of responding in a similar way again.

reliability. A measure of the consistency of test results; reliable tests produce similar scores or indices from one administration to the next.

REM. A stage of sleep characterized by rapid eye movements and low-amplitude, irregular EEG patterns resembling those found in the waking brain. REM is typically associated with dreaming.

REM rebound. The tendency to increase time spent in REM sleep after REM deprivation.

representativeness heuristic. The tendency to make decisions based on an alternative's similarity, or representativeness, in relation to an ideal. For example, people decide whether a sequence is random based on how irregular the sequence looks.

repression. A defense mechanism that individuals use unknowingly to push threatening thoughts, memories, and feelings out of conscious awareness.

research psychologists. Psychologists who try to discover the basic principles of behavior and mind.

resistance. In psychoanalysis, a person's unconsciously motivated attempts to subvert or hinder the process of therapy.

resolution phase. The fourth and final stage in the human sexual response cycle. Arousal returns to normal levels. For men, there is a refractory period during which further stimulation fails to produce visible signs of arousal.

resting potential. The tiny electrical charge in place between the inside and the outside of the resting neuron.

retina. The thin layer of tissue that covers the back of the eye and contains the light-sensitive receptor cells for vision.

retinal disparity. A binocular cue for depth that is based on location differences between the images in each eye.

retrieval. The processes that determine and control how memories are recovered and translated into performance.

retroactive interference. A process in which the formation of new memories hurts the recovery of old memories.

retrograde amnesia. Memory loss for events that happened prior to the point of brain injury.

rods. Receptor cells in the retina, located mainly around the sides, that transduce light energy into neural messages; these visual receptors are highly sensitive and are active in dim light.

s (specific intelligence). According to Spearman, a specific factor, derived from factor analysis, that is unique to a particular kind of test.

satiation signals. Internal chemical signals, such as the hormone CCK, that reduce our desire to eat.

schedule of reinforcement. A rule that is used to determine when particular responses will be reinforced.

schema. An organized knowledge structure in long-term memory.

schemata. Mental models of the world that we use to guide and interpret our experiences.

schizophrenia. A class of disorders characterized by fundamental disturbances in thought processes, emotion, or behavior.

scientific method. A multistep technique that generates empirical knowledge—that is, knowledge derived from systematic observations of the world.

searching for analogies. A problem-solving heuristic that involves trying to find a connection between the current problem and some previous problem you have solved successfully.

secondary traits. The less obvious characteristics of an individual's personality that do not always appear in one's behavior, such as testiness when on a diet.

second-order conditioning. A procedure in which an established conditioned stimulus is used to condition a second neutral stimulus.

self-actualization. The ingrained desire to reach one's true potential as a human being.

self-concept. An organized set of perceptions that we hold about our abilities and characteristics.

self-efficacy. The beliefs we hold about our own ability to perform a task or accomplish a goal.

self-fulfilling prophecy effect. A condition in which our expectations about the actions of another person lead that person to behave in the expected way.

self-monitoring. The degree to which people monitor a situation closely and change their behavior accordingly; people who are high self-monitors may not behave consistently across situations.

self-perception theory. The idea that people use observations of their own behavior as a basis for inferring their internal beliefs.

self-report inventories. Personality tests in which people answer groups of questions about how they typically think, act, and feel; their responses, or self-reports, are then compared to average responses compiled from large groups of prior test takers.

self-serving bias. The tendency to make internal attributions about one's own behavior when the outcome is positive and to blame the situation when one's behavior leads to something negative.

semantic memory. Knowledge about the world, stored as facts that make little or no reference to one's personal experiences.

semantics. The rules used in language to communicate meaning.

semicircular canals. A receptor system attached to the inner ear that responds to movement and acceleration and to changes in upright posture.

sensations. The elementary components, or building blocks, of an experience (such as a pattern of light and dark, a bitter taste, or a change in temperature).

sensitization. Increased responsiveness, or sensitivity, to an event that has been repeated.

sensorimotor period. Piaget's first stage of cognitive development, lasting from birth to about 2 years of age; schemata revolve around sensory and motor abilities.

sensory adaptation. The tendency of sensory systems to reduce sensitivity to a stimulus source that remains constant.

sensory memory. An exact replica of an environmental message, which usually lasts for a second or less.

sensory neurons. Cells that carry environmental messages toward the spinal cord and brain.

serotonin. A neurotransmitter that is linked to sleep, dreaming, and general arousal and may also be involved in some psychological disorders such as depression and schizophrenia.

set point. A natural body weight, perhaps produced by genetic factors, that the body seeks to maintain.

sexual orientation. The part of individual identity that includes a person's sexual and emotional attraction to another person and the behavior and/or social affiliation that may result from this attraction.

sexual scripts. Learned cognitive programs that instruct us on how, why, and what to do in our interactions with sexual partners.

shaping. A procedure in which reinforcement is delivered for successive approximations of the desired response.

short-term memory. A limited-capacity system that we use to hold information after it has been analyzed for periods lasting less than a minute or two.

signal detection. A technique used to determine the ability of someone to detect the presence of a stimulus.

single-blind study. Experimental participants do not know to which condition they have been assigned (e.g., experimental versus control); it's used to control for participant expectancies.

sleepwalking. The sleeper arises during sleep and wanders about.

social anxiety disorder. Intense fear of being watched, judged, and embarrassed in social situations.

social cognition. The study of how people use cognitive processes—such as perception, memory, thought, and emotion—to help make sense of other people as well as themselves.

social facilitation. The enhancement in performance that is sometimes found when an individual performs in the presence of others.

social influence. The study of how the behaviors and thoughts of individuals are affected by the presence of others.

social interference. The impairment in performance that is sometimes found when an individual performs in the presence of others.

social loafing. The tendency to put out less effort when working in a group compared to when working alone.

social psychology. The discipline that studies how people think about, influence, and relate to other people.

social schema. A general knowledge structure, stored in long-term memory, that relates to social experiences or people.

social support. The resources we receive from other people or groups, often in the form of comfort, caring, or help.

social–cognitive theories. An approach to personality that suggests it is human experiences, and interpretations of those experiences, that determine personality growth and development.

soma. The cell body of a neuron.

somatic symptom disorders. Psychological disorders that focus on the physical body. These disorders can be associated with specific body complaints (such as continuing pain) and/or excessive worry about the possibility of contracting a serious disease.

somatic system. The collection of nerves that transmits information toward the brain and connects to the skeletal muscles to initiate movement; part of the peripheral nervous system.

sound. The physical message delivered to the auditory system; a mechanical energy that requires a medium such as air or water in order to move.

source characteristics. Features of the person who is presenting a persuasive message, such as attractiveness, amount of power, or fame.

spontaneous recovery. The recovery of an extinguished conditioned response after a period of nonexposure to the conditioned stimulus.

spontaneous remission. Improvement in a psychological disorder without treatment—that is, simply as a function of the passage of time.

standard deviation. An indication of how much individual scores differ or vary from the mean.

standardization. Keeping the testing, scoring, and interpretation procedures similar across all administrations of a test.

statistical deviance. A criterion of abnormality stating that a behavior is abnormal if it occurs infrequently among the members of a population.

stereotypes. The collection of beliefs and impressions held about a group and its members; common stereotypes include those based on gender, race, and age.

stimulants. A class of drugs that increase central nervous system activity, enhancing neural transmission.

stimulus discrimination. Responding differently to a new stimulus than how one responds to an established conditioned stimulus.

stimulus generalization. Responding to a new stimulus in a way similar to the response produced by an established conditioned stimulus.

storage. The processes that determine and control how memories are stored and kept over time.

strange situation test. Gradually subjecting a child to a stressful situation and observing the child's behavior toward the parent or caregiver. This test is used to classify children according to type of attachment—secure, resistant, avoidant, or disorganized/disoriented.

stress. People's physical and psychological reactions to demanding situations.

stressors. The demanding or threatening situations that produce stress.

structuralism. An early school of psychology; structuralists tried to understand the mind by breaking it down into basic parts, much as a chemist might try to understand a chemical compound.

superego. In Freud's theory, the portion of personality that motivates people to act in an ideal fashion, in accordance with the moral customs defined by parents and culture.

surface structure. The literal ordering of words in a sentence.

survey. A descriptive research technique designed to gather limited amounts of information from many people, usually by administering some kind of questionnaire.

synapse. The small gap between the terminal buttons of a neuron and the dendrite or cell body of another neuron.

syntax. Rules governing how words should be combined to form sentences.

systematic desensitization. A technique that uses counterconditioning and extinction to reduce the fear and anxiety that have become associated with a specific object or event.

systematic introspection. An early technique used to study the mind; systematic introspection required people to look inward and describe their own experiences.

tacit knowledge. Unspoken practical knowledge about how to perform well on the job.

taste buds. The receptor cells on the tongue.

temperament. A child's general level of emotional reactivity.

temporal lobe. One of four anatomical regions of each hemisphere of the cerebral cortex, located roughly on the sides of the brain; it's involved in certain aspects of speech and language perception.

teratogens. Environmental agents—such as disease organisms or drugs—that can potentially damage the developing embryo or fetus.

terminal buttons. The tiny swellings at the end of the axon that contain chemicals important to neural transmission.

thalamus. A relay station in the forebrain thought to be an important gathering point for input from the senses.

theory of mind. The understanding that others' mental perspectives differ from one's own.

theta waves. The pattern of brain activity observed in stage N1 sleep.

thinking. The processes that underlie the mental manipulation of knowledge, usually in an attempt to reach a goal or solve a problem.

token economy. A type of behavioral therapy in which patients are rewarded with small tokens when they act in an appropriate way; the tokens can then be exchanged for certain privileges.

top-down processing. Processing that is controlled by one's beliefs and expectations about how the world is organized.

trait. A stable predisposition to act or behave in a certain way.

trait theories. Formal systems for assessing how people differ, particularly in their predispositions to respond in certain ways across situations.

transcranial magnetic stimulation (TMS). Coils are used to generate magnetic fields that, in turn, direct electrical current to target areas in the brain.

transduction. The process by which external messages are translated into the internal language of the brain.

transfer-appropriate processing. The idea that the likelihood of correct retrieval is increased if people use the same kind of mental processes during testing that they used during encoding.

transference. In psychoanalysis, patients' expression of thoughts or feelings toward the therapist that are actually representative of the way they feel about other significant people in their life.

triarchic theory. Robert Sternberg's theory of intelligence; it proposes three types of intelligence: analytic, creative, and practical.

trichromatic theory. A theory of color vision proposing that color information is extracted by comparing the relative activations of three different types of cone receptors.

twin studies. Identical twins, who share genetic material, are compared to fraternal twins to determine the roles heredity and environment play in psychological traits.

two-factor theory. A theory of emotion that argues that the cognitive interpretation, or appraisal, of a body reaction drives the subjective experience of emotion.

tympanic membrane. The eardrum, which responds to incoming sound waves by vibrating.

unconditioned response (UR). The observable response that is produced automatically, prior to training, on presentation of an unconditioned stimulus.

unconditioned stimulus (US). A stimulus that automatically leads to an observable response prior to any training.

unconscious mind. The part of the mind that Freud believed houses all the memories, urges, and conflicts that are truly beyond awareness.

validity. An assessment of how well a test measures what it is supposed to measure.

variability. A measure of how much the scores in a distribution of scores differ from one another.

variable-interval (VI) schedule. A schedule in which the allotted time before a response will yield reinforcement varies from trial to trial.

variable-ratio (VR) schedule. A schedule in which a certain number of responses are required for reinforcement, but the number of required responses typically changes.

vestibular sacs. Organs of the inner ear that contain receptors thought to be primarily responsible for balance.

visual acuity. The ability to process fine detail in vision.

visual imagery. The processes used to construct an internal visual image.

visual neglect. A complex disorder of attention characterized by a tendency to ignore things that appear on one side of the body (usually the left side).

warm fibers. Neurons that respond vigorously when the temperature of the skin increases.

Weber's law. The principle stating that the ability to notice a difference in the magnitude of two stimuli is a constant proportion of the size of the standard stimulus. Psychologically, the more intense a stimulus is to begin with, the more intense it will need to become for one to notice a change.

well-defined problem. A problem with a well-stated goal, a clear starting point, and a relatively easy way to tell when a solution has been obtained.

withdrawal. Physical reactions, such as sweating, vomiting, changes in heart rate, or tremors, that occur when a person stops taking certain drugs after continued use.

working backward. A problem-solving heuristic that involves starting at the goal state and moving backward toward the starting point to see how the goal state can be reached.

zygote. The fertilized human egg, containing 23 chromosomes from the father and 23 chromosomes from the mother.

REFERENCES

Abel, E. L., & Kruger, M. L. (2010). Smile intensity in photographs predicts longevity. *Psychological Science, 21*, 542–544.

Abramson, L. Y., Metalsky, G. I., & Alloy, L. B. (1989). Hopelessness depression: A theory-based subtype of depression. *Psychological Review, 96*, 358–372.

Acharya, S., & Shukla, S. (2012). Mirror neurons: Enigma of the metaphysical modular brain. *Journal of Natural Science, Biology, and Medicine, 3*, 118–124.

Achenbach, T. M. (1992). Developmental psychopathology. In M. H. Bornstein & M. E. Lamb (Eds.), *Developmental psychology: An advanced textbook* (pp. 629–675). Erlbaum.

Adair, R., Bauchner, H., Phillip, B., Levenson, S., & Zuckerman, B. (1991). Night waking during infancy: Role of parent presence at bedtime. *Pediatrics, 87*, 500–504.

Adams, P. R., & Adams, G. R. (1984). Mount Saint Helens's ash-fall: Evidence for a disaster stress reaction. *American Psychologist, 39*, 252–260.

Adeyemo, S. A. (2002). Can the action of amphetamine on dopamine cause schizophrenia? *Psychology & Education, 39*, 29–39.

Adler, A. (1927). *Understanding human nature*. Greenberg.

Adolph, K., & Robinson, S. R. (2015). Motor development. In L. Liben & U. Muller (Eds.), *Cognitive processes: Vol. 2. Handbook of child psychology and developmental science* (7th ed., pp. 114–157). Wiley.

Adolphs, R. (2009). The social brain: Neural basis of social knowledge. *Annual Review of Psychology, 60*, 693–716.

Agras, W. S., Sylvester, D., & Oliveau, D. (1969). The epidemiology of common fears and phobia. *Comprehensive Psychiatry, 10*, 151–156.

Ahern, J., Galea, S., Resnick, H., & Vlahov, D. (2004). Television images and probable posttraumatic stress disorder after September 11. *Journal of Nervous and Mental Disease, 192*, 217–226.

Aiello, J. R., & Douthitt, E. A. (2001). Social facilitation from Triplett to electronic performance monitoring. *Group Dynamics, 5*, 163–180.

Ainsworth, M. D. S. (1979). Attachment as related to mother-infant interactions. In J. S. Rosenblatt, R. A. Hinde, C. Beer, & M. Busnel (Eds.), *Advances in the study of behavior* (Vol. 9, pp. 1–51). Academic Press.

Ainsworth, M. D. S., Blehar, M., Waters, E., & Wall, S. (1978). *Patterns of attachment*. Erlbaum.

Ainsworth, M. D. S., & Wittig, B. A. (1969). Attachment and exploratory behavior of one-year-olds in a strange situation. In B. M. Foss (Ed.), *Determinants of infant behaviour* (Vol. 4, pp. 113–136). Methuen.

Ajay, M., Kilduff, M., & Brass, D. J. (2001). The social networks of high and low self-monitors: Implications for workplace performance. *Administrative Science Quarterly, 46*, 121–146.

Ajzen, I. (2001). Nature and operation of attitudes. *Annual Review of Psychology, 52*, 27–58.

Ajzen, I., & Fishbein, M. (1977). Attitude-behavior relations: A theoretical analysis and review of empirical research. *Psychological Bulletin, 84*, 888–918.

Allen, K. M., Blascovich, J., Tomaka, J., & Kelsey, R. M. (1991). Presence of human friends and pet dogs as moderators of autonomic responses to stress in women. *Journal of Personality and Social Psychology, 61*, 582–589.

Allen, M., Emmers-Sommer, T., DeAlessio, D., Timmerma, L., Hanzal, A., & Korus, J. (2007). The connection between the physiological and psychological reactions to sexually explicit materials: A literature summary using meta-analysis. *Communication Monographs, 74*, 541–560.

Allen, M. S., & Walter, E. E. (2018). Linking Big Five personality traits to sexuality and sexual health: A meta-analytic review. *Psychological Bulletin, 144*, 1081–1110.

Allik, J., Realo, A., & McCrae, R. R. (2013). Universality of the five-factor model of personality. In P. T. Costa & T. A. Widiger (Eds.), *Personality disorders and the five factor model of personality* (pp. 61–74). American Psychological Association.

Allison, T., & Cicchetti, D. V. (1976). Sleep in mammals: Ecological and constitutional correlates. *Science, 194*, 732–734.

Allport, G. W. (1937). *Personality: A psychological interpretation*. Holt.

Allport, G. W., & Odbert, H. H. (1936). Trait-names: A psycho-lexical study. *Psychological Monographs, 47*(1, Whole No. 211).

Aly, M., & Ranganath, C. (2018). New perspectives on the hippocampus and memory. *Neuroscience Letters, 680*, 1–3.

Alzheimer's Association. (2019). *2019 Alzheimer's disease facts and figures*. https://www.alz.org/media/documents/alzheimers-facts-and-figures-2019-r.pdf

Amabile, T. M. (1983). *The social psychology of creativity*. Springer-Verlag.

Ambika, S., Atiya, A., Ravi, A., Mani, R., Bhattacharya, B., Praveen, S., & Hussaindeen, J. R. (2020). Visual profile of acquired brain injury in Indian cohort: A retrospective study. *Brain Injury, 34*, 1168–1174. doi: 10.1080/02699052.2020.1792985

American Association on Intellectual and Developmental Disabilities. (2010). *Intellectual disability: Definition, classification, and systems of supports* (11th ed.). American Association on Intellectual and Developmental Disabilities.

American Psychiatric Association. (2013). *DSM-5's integrated approach to diagnosis and classifications*. https://www.psychiatry.org/psychiatrists/practice/dsm/educational-resources/dsm-5-fact-sheets

American Psychological Association. (2016). *Ethical principles of psychologists and code of conduct*. American Psychological Association.

American Psychological Association. (2017). *Profile of APA members: 2017*. American Psychological Association.

Amodio, D. M. (2014). The neuroscience of prejudice and stereotyping. *Nature Reviews Neuroscience, 15*, 670–682.

Andersen, B. L. (1992). Psychological interventions for cancer patients to enhance quality of life. *Journal of Consulting and Clinical Psychology, 60*, 552–568.

Anderson, C. A., Berkowitz, L., Donnerstein, E., Huesmann, L. R., Johnson, J. D., Linz, D., Malamuth, N. M., & Wartella, E. (2003). The influence of media violence on youth. *Psychological Science in the Public Interest, 4*, 81–110.

Anderson, C. A., Shibuya, A., Ihori, N., Swing, E. L., Bushman, B. J., Sakamoto, A., Rothstein, H. R., & Saleem, M. (2010). Violent video game effects on aggression, empathy, and prosocial behavior in eastern and western countries: A meta-analytic review. *Psychological Bulletin, 136*, 151–173.

Anderson, J. L., & Crawford, C. B. (1992). Modeling the costs and benefits of reproductive suppression. *Human Nature, 3*, 299–334.

Anderson, M. C., & Green, C. (2001). Suppressing unwanted memories through executive control. *Nature, 410*, 366–369.

Andrasik, F., & Holroyd, K. A. (1980). A test of specific and nonspecific effects in the biofeedback treatment of tension headache. *Journal of Consulting and Clinical Psychology, 48*, 575–586.

Andrews, P. W. (2001). The psychology of social chess and the evolution of attribution mechanisms: Explaining the fundamental attribution error. *Evolution and Human Behavior, 22*, 11–29.

Angell, J. R. (1903). The relations of structural and functional psychology to philosophy. *Philosophical Review, 12*, 203.

Antoni, M. H., & Dhabhar, F. S. (2019). The impact of psychosocial stress and stress management on immune responses in patients with cancer. *Cancer, 9*, 1417–1431.

Antoni, M. H., & Lutgendorf, S. (2007). Psychosocial factors and disease progression in cancer. *Current Directions in Psychological Science, 16*, 42–46.

Apgar, V., & Beck, J. (1974). *Is my baby all right?* Pocket Books.

Araoz, D. L. (1982). *Hypnosis and sex therapy*. Brunner/Mazel.

Ardila, A., Bernal, B., & Rosselli, M. (2016). How localized are language brain areas? A review of Brodmann areas involvement in oral language. *Archives of Clinical Neuropsychology, 31*, 112–122.

Arellanes, J. A., Viramontez Anguiano, R. P., & Lohman, B. J. (2019). Bettering the educational attainment for Latino families: How families view the education of their children. *Journal of Latinos and Education, 18*(4), 349–362.https://doi.org/10.1080/1534 8431.2018.1426465

Aronson, E. (1992). The return of the repressed: Dissonance theory makes a comeback. *Psychological Inquiry, 3*, 303–311.

Asch, S. E. (1951). Effects of group pressure on the modification and distortion of judgments. In H. Guetzkow (Ed.), *Groups, leadership, and men* (pp. 177–190). Carnegie Press.

Asch, S. E. (1955, May). Opinions and social pressures. *Scientific American, 193*, 31–35.

Aserinsky, E., & Kleitman, N. (1955). Two types of ocular motility occurring in sleep. *Journal of Applied Physiology, 8*, 1–10.

Ashby, F. G., & Maddox, W. T. (2005). Human category learning. *Annual Review of Psychology, 56*, 149–178.

Asher, M., Asnaani, A., & Aderka, I. M. (2017). Gender differences in social anxiety disorder. *Clinical Psychology Review, 56*, 1–12.

Atkinson, J. W. (1957). Motivational determinants of risk-taking behavior. *Psychological Review, 64*, 359–372.

Atkinson, J. W., & Raynor, J. O. (Eds.). (1974). *Motivation and achievement*. Winston.

Atkinson, R. C., & Shiffrin, R. M. (1968). Human memory: A proposed system and its control processes. In K. W. Spence & J. T. Spence (Eds.), *The psychology of learning and motivation: Advances in research and theory* (Vol. 2, pp. 89–195). Academic Press.

Atkinson, R. C., & Shiffrin, R. M. (1971, August). The control of short-term memory. *Scientific American, 225*, 82–90.

Attia, E. (2010). Anorexia nervosa: Current status and future directions. *Annual Review of Medicine, 61*, 425–435.

Averbach, E., & Coriell, A. S. (1961). Short-term memory in vision. *Bell System Technical Journal, 40*, 309–328.

Averill, J. R. (1983). Studies on anger and aggression: Implications for theories of emotion. *American Psychologist, 38*, 1145–1160.

Avidan, G., Tanzer, M., & Behrmann, M. (2011). Impaired holistic processing in congenital prosopagnosia. *Neuropsychologia, 49*, 2541–2542. doi:10.1016/j.neuropsychologia.2011.05.002

Baddeley, A. D. (2000). The episodic buffer: A new component of working memory? *Trends in Cognitive Sciences, 4*, 417–423.

Baddeley, A. D. (2007). *Working memory, thought, and action*. Oxford University Press.

Baddeley, A. D. (2017). *Exploring working memory: Selected works of Alan Baddeley*. Routledge.

Baddeley, A. D., Gathercole, S. E., & Papagno, C. (1998). The phonological loop as a language learning device. *Psychological Review, 105*, 158–173.

Baddeley, A. D., & Hitch, G. (1974). Working memory. In G. H. Bower (Ed.), *The psychology of learning and motivation* (Vol. 8, pp. 47–89). Academic Press.

Baddeley, A. D., & Lieberman, K. (1980). Spatial working memory. In R. Nickerson (Ed.), *Attention and performance VIII* (pp. 521–539). Erlbaum.

Badie, D. (2010). Groupthink, Iraq, and the war on terror: Explaining US policy shift toward Iraq. *Foreign Policy Analysis, 6*, 277–296.

Bahrick, H. P. (1984). Semantic memory content in permastore: 50 years of memory for Spanish learned in school. *Journal of Experimental Psychology: General, 113*, 1–29.

Bahrick, H. P., & Hall, L. K. (1991). Lifetime maintenance of high school mathematics content. *Journal of Experimental Psychology: General, 120*, 20–33.

Baillargeon, R. (2004). Infants' physical world. *Current Directions in Psychological Science, 13*, 89–94.

Baker, B., Cetin, C., Oppong, J., & Erdogan, A. M. (2019). Current ablation type surgical treatment modalities in treatment-resistant major depression: A review of the recent major surgical series. *Journal of Basic and Clinical Health Sciences, 3*, 1–8.

Bale, T. L., & Epperson, C. N. (2015). Sex differences and stress across the lifespan. *Nature Neuroscience, 18*, 1413–1420.

Ballesteros, A., Rosero, A. S., Garica-Parreno, E., & Manrique, E. (2017). Lithium and EKG abnormalities: A review. *European Psychiatry*, *41*, S750.

Bandura, A. (1986). *Social foundations of thought and action*. Prentice-Hall.

Bandura, A. (2001). Social cognitive theory: An agentic perspective. *Annual Review of Psychology*, *52*, 1–26.

Bandura, A., Ross, D., & Ross, S. A. (1963). Imitation of film-mediated aggressive models. *Journal of Abnormal and Social Psychology*, *66*, 3–11.

Barber, T. X., Spanos, N. P., & Chaves, J. (1974). *Hypnosis, imagination, and human potentialities*. Pergamon.

Barbey, A. K. (2018). Network neuroscience theory of human intelligence. *Trends in Cognitive Sciences*, *22*, 8–20.

Barenbaum, N. B. (1997). The case(s) of Gordon Allport. *Journal of Personality*, *65*, 743–755.

Bargh, J. A., & Williams, E. L. (2006). The automaticity of social life. *Current Directions in Psychological Science*, *15*, 1–4.

Bargones, J. Y., & Werner, L. A. (1994). Adults listen selectively; infants do not. *Psychological Science*, *5*, 170–174.

Barkley, R. A. (2016). Recent longitudinal studies of childhood attention-deficit/hyperactivity disorder: Important themes and questions for further research. *Journal of Abnormal Psychology*, *125*, 248–255.

Barlow, D. H., & Durand, V. M. (2012). *Abnormal psychology: An integrative approach* (6th ed.). Wadsworth.

Barlow, D. H., Rapee, R. M., & Reisner, L. C. (2001). *Mastering stress 2001: A lifestyle approach*. American Health.

Barrett, L. F. (2006). Are emotions natural kinds? *Perspectives on Psychological Science*, *1*, 28–58.

Barrett, L. F. (2017). The theory of constructed emotion: An active construction account of interoception and categorization. *Social Cognitive and Affective Neuroscience*, *12*, 1–23.

Barrett, L. F., Mesquita, B., & Gendron, M. (2011). Context in emotion perception. *Current Directions in Psychological Science*, *20*, 286–290.

Barron, A. B., & Plath, J. A. (2017). The evolution of honey bee dance communication: A mechanistic perspective. *Journal of Experimental Biology*, *220*, 4339–4346.

Barrouillet, P., De Paepe, A., & Langerock, N. (2012). Time causes forgetting from working memory. *Psychonomic Bulletin & Review*, *19*, 87–92.

Bartels, J. M., & Peters, D. (2017). Coverage of Rosenhan's "On being sane in insane places" in abnormal psychology textbooks. *Teaching of Psychology*, *44*, 169–173.

Bartlett, F. C. (1932). *Remembering*. Cambridge University Press.

Bastien, C., & Campbell, K. (1992). The evoked K-complex: All or none phenomenon? *Sleep*, *15*, 236–245.

Battelli, L., Alvaro, P.-L., & Cavanagh, P. (2007). The "when" pathway of the right parietal lobe. *Trends in Cognitive Sciences*, *11*, 204–210.

Battisti, R. A., Roodenrys, S., Johnstone, S. J., Respondek, C., Hermens, D. F., & Solowij, N. (2010). Chronic use of cannabis and poor neural efficiency in verbal memory ability. *Psychopharmacology*, *209*, 319–330.

Batty, G. D., Deary, I. J., Tengstrom, A., & Rasmussen, F. (2008). IQ in early adulthood and later risk of death by homicide: Cohort study of 1 million men. *The British Journal of Psychiatry*, *193*, 461–465.

Bauer, P. J. (2007). *Remembering the times of our lives: Memory in infancy and beyond*. Erlbaum.

Baumeister, R. F., Bratslavsky, E., Muraven, M., & Tice, D. M. (1998). Ego depletion: Is the active self a limited resource? *Journal of Personality and Social Psychology*, *74*, 1252–1265.

Baumeister, R. F., & Masicampo, E. J. (2010). Conscious thought is for facilitating social and cultural interactions: How mental simulations serve the animal-culture interface. *Psychological Review*, *117*, 945–971.

Baumeister, R. F., Masicampo, E. J., & Vohs, K. D. (2011). Do conscious thoughts cause behavior? *Annual Review of Psychology*, *62*, 331–361.

Baumrind, D. (1964). Some thoughts on the ethics of research: After reading Milgram's "Behavioral study of obedience." *American Psychologist*, *19*, 421–423.

Beck, A. T. (1991). Cognitive therapy: A 30-year retrospective. *American Psychologist*, *46*, 368–375.

Beck, A. T., & Dozois, D. J. A. (2011). Cognitive therapy: Current status and future directions. *Annual Review of Medicine*, *62*, 397–409.

Beck, A. T., & Young, J. E. (1985). Depression. In D. H. Barlow (Ed.), *Clinical handbook of psychological disorders* (pp. 206–244). Guilford Press.

Becker, H. C., Lopez, M. F., & Doremus-Fitzwater, T. L. (2011). Effects of stress on alcohol drinking: A review of animal studies. *Psychopharmacology*, *218*, 131–156.

Beer, J. M., Arnold, R. D., & Loehlin, J. C. (1998). Genetic and environmental influences on MMPI factor scales: Joint model fitting to twin and adoption data. *Journal of Personality & Social Psychology*, *74*, 818–827.

Beers, M. J., Lassiter, G. D., & Flannery, B. C. (1997). Individual differences in person memory: Self-monitoring and the recall of consistent and inconsistent behavior. *Journal of Social Behavior & Personality*, *12*, 811–820.

Behrmann, M., Avidan, G., Thomas, C., & Humphreys, K. (2009). Congenital and acquired prosopagnosia: Flip sides of the same coin? *Perceptual Expertise*, *31*, 167–197.

Beier, M. E., & Ackerman, P. L. (2005). Age, ability, and the role of prior knowledge on the acquisition of new domain knowledge: Promising results in a real-world learning environment. *Psychology and Aging*, *20*, 341–355.

Békésy, G. von. (1960). *Experiments in hearing*. McGraw-Hill.

Bell, A. P., Weinberg, M. S., & Hammersmith, S. K. (1981). *Sexual preference: Its development in men and women*. Indiana University Press.

Bell, P. A., Fisher, J. D., Baum, A., & Greene, T. E. (1990). *Environmental psychology* (3rd ed.). Holt, Rinehart & Winston.

Belsky, J., Burchinal, M., McCartney, K., Vandell, D. L., Clarke-Stewart, K. A., & Owen, M. T. (2007). Are there long-term effects of early child-care? *Child Development*, *78*, 681–701.

Bem, D. J. (1967). Self-perception: An alternative interpretation of cognitive dissonance phenomena. *Psychological Review*, *74*, 183–200.

Bem, D. J. (1972). Self-perception theory. In L. Berkowitz (Ed.), *Advances in experimental social psychology* (Vol. 6, pp. 1–62). Academic Press.

Bem, S. L. (1981). Gender schema theory: A cognitive account of sex-typing. *Psychological Review*, *88*, 354–364.

Ben-Porath, Y. S. (2003). Assessing personality and psychopathology with self-report inventories. In J. R. Graham & J. A. Naglieri (Eds.), *Handbook of psychology: Assessment psychology* (Vol. 10, pp. 553–577). Wiley.

Benson, H. (1975). *The relaxation response*. Morrow.

Bentall, R. P. (1990). The illusion of reality: A review and integration of psychological research on hallucinations. *Psychological Bulletin*, *107*, 82–95.

Benton, D., & Young, H. A. (2017). Reducing calorie intake may not help you lose body weight. *Perspectives on Psychological Science*, *12*, 703–714.

Berecz, B., Cyrille, M., Casselbrant, U., Oleksak, S., & Norholt, H. (2020, June 20). Carrying human infants: An evolutionary heritage. *Infant Behavior and Development*. Advance online publication doi: 10.1016/j.infbeh.2020.101460

Berkowitz, L., & Harmon-Jones, E. (2004). Toward an understanding of the determinants of anger. *Emotion*, *4*, 107–130.

Berman, K. F., & Weinberger, D. R. (1990). Lateralization of cortical function during cognitive tasks: Regional cerebral blood flow studies of normal individuals and patients with schizophrenia. *Journal of Neurology, Neurosurgery, and Psychiatry*, *53*, 150–160.

Bernal, E. M. (1984). Bias in mental testing: Evidence for an alternative to the heredity-environment controversy. In C. R. Reynolds & R. T. Brown (Eds.), *Perspectives on bias in mental testing* (pp. 171–187). Plenum.

Berndt, T. J. (2004). Children's friendships: Shifts over a half-century in perspectives on their development and their effects. *Merrill-Palmer Quarterly*, *50*, 206–223.

Berndt, T. J., & Keefe, K. (1995). Friends' influence on adolescents' adjustments to school. *Child Development*, *66*, 1312–1329.

Bernstein, I. L. (1978). Learned taste aversions in children receiving chemotherapy. *Science*, *200*, 1302–1303.

Berridge, K. C. (2004). Motivation concepts in behavioral neuroscience. *Physiology & Behavior*, *81*, 179–209.

Berridge, K. C., & Kringelbach, M. L. (2015). Pleasure systems in the brain. *Neuron*, *86*, 646–664.

Berscheid, E. (2010). Love in the fourth dimension. *Annual Review of Psychology*, *61*, 1–25.

Best, J. B. (1989). *Cognitive psychology* (2nd ed.). West.

Beutler, L. E., & Berren, M. R. (Eds.). (1995). *Integrative assessment of adult personality*. Guilford Press.

Beyth-Marom, R., & Lichtenstein, S. (1984). *An elementary approach to thinking under uncertainty*. Erlbaum.

Bhanji, J. P., Kim, E. S., & Delgado, M. R. (2016). Perceived control alters the effect of acute stress on persistence. *Journal of Experimental Psychology: General*, *145*, 356–365.

Bieber, F. (2020, April 27). Global nationalism in times of the COVID-19 pandemic. *Nationalities Papers*. Advance online publication. doi:10.1017/nps.2020.35

Biederman, I. (1987). Recognition-by-components: A theory of human image understanding. *Psychological Review*, *94*, 115–147.

Binet, A., & Simon, T. (1973). *The development of intelligence in children*. Arno Press. (Original work published 1916)

Bisiach, E. (1992). Understanding consciousness: Clues from unilateral neglect and related disorders. In A. D. Milner & M. D. Rugg (Eds.), *The neuropsychology of consciousness* (pp. 133–137). Academic Press.

Bisiach, E., & Rusconi, M. L. (1990). Break-down of perceptual awareness in unilateral neglect. *Cortex*, *26*, 643–649.

Bjork, R. A. (1989). Retrieval inhibition as an adaptive mechanism in human memory. In H. L. Roediger & F. I. M. Craik (Eds.), *Varieties of memory and consciousness: Essays in honor of Endel Tulving* (pp. 309–330). Erlbaum.

Blagrove, M. (1996). Problems with the cognitive psychological modeling of dreaming. *Journal of Mind and Behavior*, *17*, 99–134.

Blakemore, S.-J. (2018). *Inventing ourselves: The secret life of the teenage brain*. Public Affairs.

Blakemore, S.-J., & Choudhury, S. (2006). Development of the adolescent brain: Implications for executive function and social cognition. *Journal of Child Psychology and Psychiatry*, *47*, 296–312.

Blanchard, R. (2018). Fraternal birth order, family size, and male homosexuality: Meta-analysis of studies spanning 25 years. *Archives of Sexual Behavior*, *47*, 1–15.

Blanco-Centurian, C., Luo, S., Spergel, D. J., Vidal-Ortiz, A., Oprisan, S. A., Van den Pol, A. N., Liu, M., & Shiromani, P. J. (2019). Dynamic network activation of hypothalamic MCH neurons in REM sleep and exploratory behavior. *The Journal of Neuroscience*, *39*, 4986–4998.

Bland, A. M., & DeRobertis, E. M. (2020). Humanistic perspective. In V. Ziegler-Hill & T. K. Shackelford (Eds.), *Encyclopedia of personality and individual differences*. Springer. https://doi.org/10.1007/978-3-319-24612-3_1484

Blanton, H., Cooper, J., Skurnik, I., & Aronson, J. (1997). When bad things happen to good feedback: Exacerbating the need for self-justification with self-affirmations. *Personality & Social Psychology Bulletin*, *23*, 684–692.

Blanton, H., Jaccard, J., Klick, J., Mellers, B., Mitchell, G., & Tetlock, P. E. (2009). Strong claims and weak evidence: Reassessing the predictive validity of the IAT. *Journal of Applied Psychology*, *94*, 567–582. https://doi.org/doi:10.1037/a0014665

Bleuler, E. (1908). Die prognose der Dementia praecox (Schizophreniegruppe). *Allgemeine Zeitschrift fur Psychiatrie*, *65*, 436–464.

Block, J. J., & Crain, B. R. (2007). Omissions and errors in media: Violence and the American public. *American Psychologist*, *62*, 252–253.

Blumenthal, J. A., Emery, C. F., Walsh, M. A., Cox, D. R., Kuhn, C. M., Williams, R. B., & Williams, R. S. (1988). Exercise training in healthy Type A middle-aged men: Effects on behavioral and cardiovascular responses. *Psychosomatic Medicine*, *50*, 418–433.

Blundell, J. E., & Rogers, P. J. (1991). Hunger, hedonics, and the control of satiation and satiety. In M. I. Friedman, M. G. Tordoff, & M. R. Kare (Eds.), *Chemical senses* (Vol. 4, pp. 127–148). Marcel Dekker.

Bodenhausen, G. V., Macrae, C. N., & Hugenberg, K. (2003). Social cognition. In T. Millon & M. J. Lerner (Eds.), *Handbook of psychology: Personality and social psychology* (Vol. 5, pp. 257–282). Wiley.

Boesen, E. H., & Johansen, C. (2008). Impact of psychotherapy on cancer survival: Time to move on? *Current Opinion in Oncology, 20*, 372–377.

Bohn, A., & Berntsen, D. (2011). The reminiscence bump reconsidered: Children's prospective life stories show a bump in young adulthood. *Psychological Science, 22*, 197–202.

Bohner, G., & Dickel, N. (2011). Attitudes and attitude change. *Annual Review of Psychology, 62*, 391–417.

Bolla, K. I., Brown, K., Eldreth, D., & Cadet, J. L. (2002). Dose-related neurocognitive effects of marijuana use. *Neurology, 59*, 1337–1343.

Bolles, R. C. (1972). Reinforcement, expectancy, and learning. *Psychological Review, 79*, 394–409.

Bolles, R. C. (1993). *The story of psychology: A thematic history.* Brooks/Cole.

Bollini, A. M., Walker, E. F., Hamann, S., & Kestler, L. (2004). The influence of perceived control and locus of control on the cortisol and subjective response to stress. *Biological Psychology, 67*, 245–260.

Boomer, D. S. (1965). Hesitation and grammatical encoding. *Language and Speech, 8*, 145–158.

Boring, E. G. (1950). *A history of experimental psychology* (2nd ed.). Appleton-Century-Crofts.

Bornstein, M. H. (1989). Stability in early mental development: From attention and information processing in infancy to language and cognition in childhood. In M. H. Bornstein & N. A. Krasnegor (Eds.), *Stability and continuity in mental development: Behavioral and biological perspectives* (pp. 147–170). Erlbaum.

Bornstein, M. H., Kessen, W., & Weiskopf, S. (1976). Color vision and hue categorization in young human infants. *Journal of Experimental Psychology: Human Perception and Performance, 2*, 115–129.

Bornstein, R. F. (2003). Psychodynamic models of personality. In T. Millon & M. J. Lerner (Eds.), *Handbook of psychology: Personality and social psychology* (Vol. 5, pp. 117–134). Wiley.

Bortz, W. M. (1990). The trajectory of dying: Functional status in the last year of life. *Journal of the American Geriatrics Society, 38*, 146–150.

Bouchard, C., Tremblay, A., Despres, J., Nadeau, A., Lupien, P. J., Theriault, G., Dussault, J., Moorjani, S., Pinault, S., & Fournier, G. (1990). The response to long-term overfeeding in identical twins. *New England Journal of Medicine, 322*, 1477–1487.

Bouchard, T. J., Jr. (1997). IQ similarity in twins reared apart: Findings and responses to critics. In R. J. Sternberg & E. L. Grigorenko (Eds.), *Intelligence, heredity, and environment* (pp. 126–160). Cambridge University Press.

Bouchard, T. J., Jr. (2004). Genetic influence on human psychological traits. *Current Directions in Psychological Science, 13*, 148–151.

Bouchard, T. J., Jr., Lykken, D. T., McGue, M., Segal, N. L., & Tellegean, A. (1990). Sources of human psychological differences: The Minnesota study of twins reared apart. *Science, 250*, 223–228.

Bouchard, T. J., Jr., & McGue, M. (1981). Familial studies of intelligence: A review. *Science, 212*, 1055–1059.

Bouton, M. E. (2007). *Learning and behavior: A contemporary synthesis.* Sinauer Associates.

Bower, T. G. R. (1982). *Development in infancy* (2nd ed.). Freeman.

Bowlby, J. (1969). *Attachment and loss: Vol. 1. Attachment.* Basic Books.

Bowman, E. S. (1998). Pseudoseizures. *Psychiatric Clinics of North America, 21*, 649–657.

Boyd, B. (2018). The evolution of stories: From mimesis to language, from fact to fiction. *WIREs Cognitive Science, 9*, 1–16.

Boynton, R. M. (1979). *Human color vision.* Holt, Rinehart & Winston.

Brackett, A. A., Rivers, S. E., & Salovey, P. (2011). Emotional intelligence: Implications for personal, social, academic, and workplace success. *Social and Personality Compass, 5*, 88–103.

Bregman, A. S. (1990). *Auditory scene analysis.* Bradford/MIT Press.

Breland, K., & Breland, M. (1961). The misbehavior of organisms. *American Psychologist, 16*, 681–684.

Bremner, J. G., Slater, A. M., & Johnson, S. P. (2015). Perception of object persistence: The origins of object permanence in infancy. *Child Development Perspectives, 9*, 7–13.

Brennan, P. A., & Zufall, F. (2006). Pheromonal communication in vertebrates. *Nature, 444*, 308–315.

Brewin, C. R., Li, H., Ntarantana, V., Unsworth, C., & McNeilis, J. (2019). Is the public understanding of memory prone to widespread "myths"? *Journal of Experimental Psychology: General, 148*(12), 2245–2257.

Bridgman, T., Cummings, S., & Ballard, J. (2019). Who built Maslow's pyramid? A history of the creation of management studies' most famous symbol and its implications for management education. *Academy of Management Learning & Education, 18*, 81–98.

Briere, J., & Conte, J. (1993). Self-reported amnesia for abuse in adults molested as children. *Journal of Traumatic Stress, 6*, 21–31.

Brini, S., Sohrabi, H. R., Peiffer, J. J., Karrasch, M., Hämäläinen, H., Martins, R. N., & Fairchild, T. J. (2018). Physical activity in preventing Alzheimer's disease and cognitive decline: A narrative review. *Sports Medicine, 48*, 29–44. doi: 10.1007/s40279-017-0787-y

Broadbent, D. E. (1952). Failures of attention in selective listening. *Journal of Experimental Psychology, 44*, 428–433.

Broadbent, D. E. (1958). *Perception and communication.* Pergamon Press.

Broberg, D. J., & Bernstein, I. L. (1987). Candy as a scapegoat in the prevention of food aversions in children receiving chemotherapy. *Cancer, 60*, 2344–2347.

Broca, P. (1861). Remarques sur le siege de la faculte du langage articule, suivies d'une observation d'aphemie (perte de la parole). *Bulletin de la Societé Anatomique (Paris), 36*, 330–357.

Brody, N. (1992). *Intelligence* (2nd ed.). Academic Press.

Brody, N. (2007). Barriers to understanding racial differences in intelligence. *Perspectives on Psychological Science, 2,* 214–215.

Brody, N., & Vangelisti, A. L. (2016). Bystander intervention in cyberbullying. *Communication Monographs, 83,* 94–119.

Broesch, T., Callaghan, T., Henrich, J., Murphy, C., & Rochat, P. (2011). Cultural variations in children's mirror self-recognition. *Journal of Cross-Cultural Psychology, 42,* 1018–1029.

Brondel, L., Romer, M., Van Wymelbeke, V., Pineau, N., Jiang, T., Hanus, C., & Rigaud, D. (2009). Variety enhances food intake in humans: Role of sensory-specific satiety. *Physiology & Behavior, 97,* 44–51.

Bronfenbrenner, U., & Ceci, S. J. (1994). Nature-nuture reconceptualized in developmental perspective: A bioecological model. *Psychological Review, 101*(4), 568–586. https://doi.org/10.1037/0033-295X.101.4.568

Brooks, J. L., & Driver, J. (2010). Grouping puts figure-ground assignment in context by constraining propagation of edge-assignment. *Attention, Perceptions, & Psychophysics, 72,* 1053–1069.

Brosschot, J. F., Godaert, G. L. R., Benschop, R. J., Olff, M., Ballieux, R. E., & Heijnen, C. J. (1998). Experimental stress and immunological reactivity: A closer look at perceived uncontrollability. *Psychosomatic Medicine, 60,* 359–361.

Brown, P. C., Roediger, H. L., & McDaniel, M. A. (2014). *Make it stick: The science of successful learning.* Harvard University Press.

Brown, T. A., O'Leary, T. A., & Barlow, D. H. (2001). Generalized anxiety disorder. In D. H. Barlow (Ed.), *Clinical handbook of psychological disorders: A step-by-step treatment manual* (3rd ed., pp. 154–208). Guilford Press.

Bruce, D. (1985). The how and why of ecological memory. *Journal of Experimental Psychology: General, 114,* 78–90.

Buck, L. (1996). Information coding in the vertebrate olfactory system. *Annual Review of Neuroscience, 19,* 517–544.

Buck, L., & Axel, A. (1991). A novel multigene family may encode odorant receptors: A molecular basis for odor recognition. *Cell, 65,* 175–187.

Buell, S. J., & Coleman, P. D. (1979). Dendritic growth in the aged human brain and failure of growth in senile dementia. *Science, 206,* 854–856.

Bulevich, J. B., Roediger, H. L., Balota, D. A., & Butler, A. C. (2006). Failure to find suppression of episodic memories in the think/nothink paradigm. *Memory & Cognition, 34,* 1569–1577.

Buller, D. (2005). Evolutionary psychology: The emperor's new paradigm. *Trends in Cognitive Sciences, 9,* 277–283.

Burger, J. M. (2009). Replicating Milgram: Would people still obey today? *American Psychologist, 64,* 1–11.

Burger, J. M., & Caldwell, D. F. (2003). The effects of monetary incentives and labeling on the foot-in-the-door effect: Evidence for a self-perception process. *Basic & Applied Social Psychology, 25,* 235–241.

Burger, J. M., & Cornelius, T. (2003). Raising the price of agreement: Public commitment and the low-ball compliance procedure. *Journal of Applied Social Psychology, 33,* 923–934.

Burger, J. M., Girgis, Z. M., & Manning, C. C. (2011). In their own words: Explaining obedience to authority through an examination of participants' comments. *Social Psychology and Personality Science, 2,* 460–466.

Burke, N. W., & Bonduriansky, R. (2017). Sexual conflict, facultative asexuality, and the true paradox of sex. *Trends in Evolution & Ecology, 32,* 646–652.

Bushman, B. J. (2002). Does venting anger feed or extinguish the flame? Catharsis, rumination, distraction, anger and aggressive responding. *Personality & Social Psychology Bulletin, 28,* 724–731.

Bushman, B. J., & Anderson, C. A. (2001). Media violence and the American public. *American Psychologist, 56,* 477–489.

Bushman, B. J., & Anderson, C. A. (2009). Comfortably numb: Desensitizing effects of violent media on helping others. *Psychological Science, 20,* 273–277.

Bushman, B. J., & Phillips, C. M. (2001). If the television program bleeds, memory for the advertisement recedes. *Current Directions in Psychological Science, 10,* 43–47.

Buss, D. M. (2012). *Evolutionary psychology: The new science of the mind* (4th ed.). Allyn & Bacon.

Buss, D. M. (2019). *Evolutionary psychology: The new science of the mind* (6th ed.). Routledge.

Buss, D. M., & Schmitt, D. P. (1993). Sexual strategies theory: An evolutionary perspective on human mating. *Psychological Review, 100,* 204–232.

Buss, D. M., & Schmitt, D. P. (2019). Mate preferences and their behavioral manifestations. *Annual Review of Psychology, 70,* 77–110.

Butterworth, G. (1992). Origins of self-perception in infancy. *Psychological Inquiry, 3,* 103–111.

Byrne, D. (1971). *The attraction paradigm.* Academic Press.

Bzdok, D., Hartwigsen, G., Reid, A., Laird, A. R., Fox, P. T., & Eickhoff, S. B. (2016). Left inferior parietal lobe engagement in social cognition and language. *Neuroscience and Biobehavioral Reviews, 68,* 319–334.

Cacioppo, J. T., & Gardner, W. L. (1999). Emotion. *Annual Review of Psychology, 50,* 191–214.

Cahalan, S. (2019). *The great pretender.* Grand Central.

Caird, J. K., Simmons, S. M., Wiley, K., Johnston, K. A., & Horrey, W. J. (2018). Does talking on a cell phone, with a passenger, or dialing affect driving performance? An updated systematic review and meta-analysis of experimental studies. *Human Factors, 60,* 101–133.

Calder, A. J., Rhodes, G., Johnson, M. L., & Haxby, J. V. (Eds.). (2011). *The Oxford handbook of face perception.* Oxford University Press.

Caliendo, M., Cobb-Clark, D. A., & Uhlendorff, A. (2015). Locus of control and job search strategies. *Review of Economics and Statistics, 97,* 88–103.

Cameron, J., & Pierce, W. D. (1994). Reinforcement, reward, and intrinsic motivation: A meta-analysis. *Review of Educational Research, 64,* 363–423.

Campbell, D. T., & Stanley, J. C. (1966). *Experimental and quasi-experimental designs for research.* Rand McNally.

Campbell, G., Stockings, E., & Nielsen, S. (2019). Understanding the evidence for medical cannabis and cannabis-based medicines for the treatment of chronic non-cancer pain. *European Archives of Psychiatry & Clinical Neuroscience, 269*, 135–144.

Campos, J. J., Langer, A., & Krowitz, A. (1970). Cardiac responses on the visual cliff in prelocomotor human infants. *Science, 170*, 196–197.

Cannon, W. B. (1927). The James-Lange theory of emotions: A critical examination and an alternative theory. *American Journal of Psychology, 39*, 106–124.

Cannon, W. B. (1929). *Bodily changes in pain, hunger, fear, and rage.* Appleton.

Cannon, W. B. (1932). *The wisdom of the body.* Norton.

Cantor, N., & Mischel, W. (1978). Prototypes in person perception. *Advances in Experimental Social Psychology, 12*, 3–52.

Carlsmith, J. M., & Gross, A. E. (1969). Some effects of guilt on compliance. *Journal of Personality and Social Psychology, 11*, 240–244.

Carlsmith, K. M., Wilson, T. D., & Gilbert, D. Y. (2008). The paradoxical consequences of revenge. *Journal of Personality and Social Psychology, 95*, 1316–1324.

Carr, G. V., & Lucki, I. (2011). The role of serotonin receptor subtypes in depression: A review of animal studies. *Psychopharamacology, 213*, 265–287.

Carstensen, L. L. (1995). Evidence for a life-span theory of socioemotional selectivity. *Current Directions in Psychological Science, 4*, 151–156.

Cartwright, R. (1991). Dreams that work: The relation of dream incorporation to adaptation to stressful events. *Dreaming, 1*, 2–9.

Cartwright, R. (1996). Dreams and adaptation to divorce. In D. Barrett (Ed.), *Trauma and dreams* (pp. 179–185). Harvard University Press.

Case, R. B., Moss, A. J., Case, N., McDermott, M., & Eberly, S. (1992). Living alone after myocardial infarction: Impact on prognosis. *Journal of American Medical Association, 267*, 515–519.

Caspi, A., Roberts, B. W., & Shiner, R. L. (2005). Personality development: Stability and change. *Annual Review of Psychology, 56*, 453–484.

Catarino, A., Kupper, C. S., Werner-Seidler, A., Dalgleish, T., & Anderson, M. C. (2015). Failing to forget: Inhibitory-control deficits compromise memory suppression in posttraumatic stress disorder. *Psychological Science, 26*, 604–616.

Cattell, R. B. (1963). Theory of fluid and crystallized intelligence: A critical experiment. *Journal of Educational Psychology, 54*, 1–22.

Cattell, R. B. (1998). Where is intelligence? Some answers from the triadic theory. In J. J. McArdle & R. W. Woodcock (Eds.), *Human cognitive abilities in theory and practice* (pp. 29–38). Erlbaum.

Cattell, R. B., Eber, H. W., & Tatsuoka, M. M. (1970). *Handbook for the sixteen personality factor questionnaire (16PF).* Institute for Personality and Ability Testing.

Ceci, S. J. (1991). How much does schooling influence intellectual development and its cognitive components? A reassessment of the evidence. *Developmental Psychology, 27*, 703–722.

Cermak, L. S. (1982). The long and the short of it in amnesia. In L. S. Cermak (Ed.), *Human memory and amnesia* (pp. 43–59). Erlbaum.

Chadwick, M. J., Hassabis, D., Weiskopf, N., & Maguire, E. A. (2010). Decoding individual episodic memory traces in the human hippocampus. *Current Biology, 20*, 544–547.

Chaiken, S., Liberman, A., & Eagly, A. H. (1989). Heuristic and systematic information processing: Within and beyond the persuasion context. In J. S. Uleman & J. A. Bargh (Eds.), *Unintended thought* (pp. 212–252). Guilford Press.

Chakos, M., Lieberman, J., Hoffman, E., Bradford, D., & Sheitman, B. (2001). Effectiveness of second-generation antipsychotics in patients with treatment-resistant schizophrenia: A review and meta-analysis of randomized trials. *American Journal of Psychiatry, 158*, 518–526.

Chang, A. D., Vaidya, P.V., Retzbach, E. P., Chung, S. J., Kim, U., Baselice, K., Maynard, K., Stepanian, A., Staley, M., Xiao, L., Blouin, A., Han, S., Lee, J., Worley, P. F., Tamashiro, K. L., Hempstead, B. L., Martinowich, K., Wilson, M. A., Baraban, J. M., & Reti, I. M. (2018). Narp mediates antidepressant-like effects of electroconvulsive seizures. *Neuropsychopharmacology, 43*, 1088–1098.

Chang, L., & Tsao, D. Y. (2017). The code for facial identity in the primate brain. *Cell, 169*, 1013–1028.

Chang, Y., Hayter, M., & Wu, S. (2010). A systematic review and meta-ethnography of the qualitative literature: Experiences of the menarche. *Journal of Clinical Nursing, 19*, 447–460.

Chapman, H. A., & Anderson, A. K. (2013). Things rank and gross in nature: A review and synthesis of moral disgust. *Psychological Bulletin, 139*(2), 300–327.

Charbonnier, L., van Meer, F., Johnstone, A. M., Crabtree, D., Buosi, D., Manios, Y., Androutsos, O., Giannopoulou, A., Viergever, M. A., Smeets, P. A. M., & Full4Health Consortium. (2018). Effects of hunger state on the brain responses to food cues across the life span. *NeuroImage, 171*, 246–255.

Charil, A., Laplante, D. P., Vaillancourt, C., & King, S. (2010). Prenatal stress and brain development. *Brain Research Reviews, 65*, 56–79.

Charman, D. P. (Ed.). (2004). *Core processes in brief psychodynamic psychotherapy.* Erlbaum.

Chase, W. G., & Simon, H. A. (1973). The mind's eye in chess. In W. G. Chase (Ed.), *Visual information processing* (pp. 215–281). Academic Press.

Chen, S. C. (1937). Social modification of the activity of ants in nest-building. *Physiological Zoology, 10*, 420–436.

Cherniss, C., Extein, M., Goleman, D., & Weissberg, R. P. (2006). Emotional intelligence: What does the research really indicate? *Educational Psychologist, 41*, 239–245.

Cherry, E. C. (1953). Some experiments on the recognition of speech with one and with two ears. *Journal of the Acoustical Society of America, 25*, 975–979.

Chia, R. C., Allred, L. J., Grossnickle, W. F., & Lee, G. W. (1998). Effects of attractiveness and gender on the perception of achievement-related variables. *Journal of Social Psychology, 138*, 471–477.

Chomsky, N. (1957). *Syntactic structures.* Mouton.

Chomsky, N. (1986). *Knowledge of language: Its nature, origins, and use.* Praeger.

Chou, A. F., Stewart, S. L., Wild, R. C., & Bloom, J. R. (2012). Social support and survival in young women with breast carcinoma. *Psycho-Oncology, 21*, 125–133.

Choy, Y., Fyer, A. J., & Lipsitz, J. D. (2007). Treatment of specific phobia in adults. *Clinical Psychology Review, 27*, 266–286.

Chrysikou, E. G., & Weisberg, R. W. (2005). Following the wrong footsteps: Fixation effects of pictorial examples in a design problem-solving task. *Journal of Experimental Psychology: Learning, Memory, and Cognition, 31*, 1134–1148.

Chue, A. E., Gunthert, K. C., Ahrens, A. H., & Skalina, L. M. (2017). How does social anger expression predict later depression symptoms? It depends on how often one is angry. *Emotion, 17*, 6–10.

Churchill, A., Taylor, J. A., & Parkes, R. (2015). The creation of a superstitious belief regarding putters in a laboratory-based golfing task. *International Journal of Sport and Exercise Psychology, 13*, 335–343.

Cialdini, R. B., & Goldstein, N. J. (2004). Social influence: Compliance and comformity. *Annual Review of Psychology, 55*, 591–621.

Cianciolo, A. T., Grigorenko, E. L., Jarvin, L., Gil, G., Drebot, M. E., & Sternberg, R. J. (2006). Practical intelligence and tacit knowledge: Advancements in the measurement of developing expertise. *Learning and Individual Differences, 16*, 235–253.

Cichy, R. M., Heinzle, J., & Haynes, D. (2012). Imagery and perception share cortical representations of content and location. *Cerebral Cortex, 22*, 372–380.

Cicirelli, V. G. (1997). Relationship of psychosocial and background variables to older adults' end-of-life decisions. *Psychology and Aging, 12*, 72–83.

Cicirelli, V. G. (2002). *Older adults' views on death*. Springer.

Cicirelli, V. G. (2011). Religious and nonreligious spirituality in relation to death acceptance or rejection. *Death Studies, 35*, 124–146.

Clark, H. H. (1992). *Arenas of language use*. University of Chicago Press.

Clark, M. S., & Grote, N. K. (2003). Close relationships. In T. Millon & M. J. Lerner (Eds.), *Handbook of psychology: Personality and social psychology* (Vol. 5, pp. 447–461). Wiley.

Clarke, S., & Thiran, A. B. (2004). Auditory neglect: What and where in auditory space. *Cortex, 40*, 291–300.

Clendenen, V. I., Herman, C. P., & Polivy, J. (1994). Social facilitation of eating among friends and strangers. *Appetite, 23*, 1–13.

Cohen, S., Tyrrell, D. A., & Smith, D. A. (1993). Negative life events, perceived stress, negative affect, and susceptibility to the common cold. *Journal of Personality and Social Psychology, 64*, 131–140.

Cole, M. (1992). Culture in development. In M. H. Bornstein & M. E. Lamb (Eds.), *Developmental psychology: An advanced textbook* (pp. 731–789). Erlbaum.

Cole, M. W., Ito, T., & Braver, T. S. (2015). Lateral prefrontal cortex contributes to fluid intelligence through multinetwork connectivity. *Brain Connectivity, 5*, 497–504.

Cole, R. P., & Miller, R. R. (1999). Conditioned excitation and conditioned inhibition acquired through backward conditioning. *Learning & Motivation, 30*, 129–156.

Coleman, P. (1993). Overview of substance abuse. *Primary Care, 20*, 1–18.

Coles, N. A., Larsen, J. T., & Lench, H. C. (2019). A meta-analysis of the facial feedback literature: Effects of facial feedback on emotional experience are small and variable. *Psychological Bulletin, 145*, 610–651.

Coles, R., & Stokes, G. (1985). *Sex and the American teenager*. Harper & Row.

Collins, W. A., Welsh, D. P., & Furman, W. (2009). Adolescent romantic relationships. *Annual Review of Psychology, 60*, 631–652.

Coltheart, M., & Coltheart, V. (2010). Visual memories. In V. Coltheart (Ed.), *Tutorials in visual cognition* (pp. 349–365). Psychology Press.

Colucci, E., & Martin, G. (2007). Ethnocultural aspects of suicide in young people: A systematic literature review. Part 2: Risk factors, precipitating agents, and attitudes toward suicide. *Suicide and Life-Threatening Behavior, 37*, 222–237.

Compton, W. C. (2018, March 21). Self-actualization myths: What did Maslow really say? *Journal of Humanistic Psychology*. Advance online publication.

Conrad, R. (1964). Acoustic confusion in immediate memory. *British Journal of Psychology, 55*, 75–84.

Cook, M., & Mineka, S. (1989). Observational conditioning of fear to fear-relevant versus fear-irrelevant stimuli in rhesus monkeys. *Journal of Abnormal Psychology, 98*, 448–459.

Cook, R., Bird, G., Catmur, C., Press, C., & Heyes, C. (2014). Mirror neurons: From origin to function. *Behavioral and Brain Sciences, 37*, 177–192.

Cook, T. D., & Campbell, D. T. (1979). *Quasi-experimentation: Design and analysis for field settings*. Rand McNally.

Cooper, J. (1992). Dissonance and the return of the self-concept. *Psychological Inquiry, 3*, 320–323.

Cooper, W. H. (1983). An achievement motivation nomological network. *Journal of Personality and Social Psychology, 44*, 841–861.

Corballis, M. C. (1991). *The lopsided ape: Evolution of the generative mind*. Oxford University Press.

Coren, S. (1996). *Sleep thieves*. Free Press.

Coren, S., Porac, C., & Theodor, L. H. (1987). Set and subjective contour. In S. Petry & G. E. Meyer (Eds.), *The perception of illusory contours* (pp. 237–245). Springer-Verlag.

Cosmides, L., & Tooby, J. (1992). Cognitive adaptations for social exchange. In J. H. Barkow, L. Cosmides, & J. Tooby (Eds.), *The adapted mind* (pp. 163–228). Oxford University Press.

Cowan, N. (1995). *Attention and memory: An integrated framework*. Oxford University Press.

Cowan, R., & Frith, C. (2009). Do calendrical savants use calculation to answer date questions? A functional magnetic resonance imaging study. *Philosophical Transactions of the Royal Society, 364*, 1417–1424.

Cowan, R., O'Conner, N., & Samella, K. (2003). The skills and methods of calendrical savants. *Intelligence, 31*, 51–65.

Craig, J. C. (1985). Attending to two fingers: Two hands are better than one. *Perception & Psychophysics, 38*, 496–511.

Craig, K. D. (1978). Social disclosure, coactive peer companions, and social modeling determinants of pain communications. *Canadian Journal of Behavioural Science, 10*, 91–104.

Craik, F. I. M., & Lockhart, R. S. (1972). Levels of processing: A framework for memory research. *Journal of Verbal Learning and Verbal Behavior, 11*, 671–684.

Craik, F. I. M., & Tulving, E. (1975). Depth of processing and the retention of words in episodic memory. *Journal of Experimental Psychology: General, 104*, 268–294.

Cramer, P. (2015). Defense mechanisms: 40 years of empirical research. *Journal of Personality Assessment, 97*, 114–122.

Crawford, C. B. (2007). Reproductive success: Then and now. In S. W. Gangestad & J. A. Simpson (Eds.), *The evolution of mind: Fundamental questions and controversies* (pp. 69–77). Guilford Press.

Creswell, J. D. (2017). Mindfulness interventions. *Annual Review of Psychology, 68*, 491–516.

Creswell, J. D., & Lindsay, E. K. (2014). How does mindfulness training affect health? A mindfulness stress buffering account. *Current Directions in Psychological Science, 23*, 401–407.

Cretaz, E., Brunoni, A. R., & Lafer, B. (2015). Magnetic seizure therapy for unipolar and bipolar depression. *Neural Plasticity*, Article ID 521398.

Cronbach, L. J. (1957). The two disciplines of scientific psychology. *American Psychologist, 12*, 671–684.

Crooks, R., & Baur, K. (2017). *Our sexuality* (13th ed.). Cengage.

Crowder, R. G. (1976). *Principles of learning and memory*. Erlbaum.

Crowson, A. D., Colligan, R. C., Matteson, E. L., Davis, J. M., & Crowson, C. S. (2017). Explanatory style in patients with rheumatoid arthritis: An unrecognized predictor of morality. *Journal of Rheumatology, 44*, 170–173.

Cuijpers, P., Reijnders, M., & Huibers, M. J. H. (2019). The role of common factors in psychotherapy outcomes. *Annual Review of Clinical Psychology, 17*, 207–231.

Culbert, K. M., Racine, S. E., & Klump, K. L. (2015). Research review: What we have learned about the causes of eating disorders—a synthesis of sociocultural, psychological, and biological research. *Journal of Child Psychology and Psychiatry, 56*, 1141–1164.

Cumming, G. (2014). The new statistics: Why and how. *Psychological Science, 25*, 7–29.

Cummins, I. (2017, January 30). Rereading Rosenhan. *Illness, Crisis, & Loss*. Advance online publication. https://doi.org/10.1177/1054137317690377

Cunningham, M. D., & Reidy, T. J. (1998). Antisocial personality disorder and psychopathy: Diagnostic dilemmas in classifying patterns of antisocial behavior in sentencing evaluations. *Behavioral Sciences & the Law, 16*, 333–351.

Curtis, R. C., & Miller, K. (1986). Believing another likes or dislikes you: Behaviors making the beliefs come true. *Journal of Personality and Social Psychology, 51*, 284–290.

Cutrona, C. E., Wallace, G., & Wesner, K. A. (2006). Neighborhood characteristics and depression: An examination of stress processes. *Current Directions in Psychological Science, 15*, 188–192.

Czajkowski, N., Kendler, K. S., Tambs, K., Roysamb, E., & Reichborn-Kjennerud, T. (2011). The structure of genetic and environmental risk factors for phobias in women. *Psychological Medicine, 41*, 1987–1995.

Dackis, C. A., & Miller, N. S. (2003). Neurobiological effects determine treatment options for alcohol, cocaine, and heroin addiction. *Psychiatric Annals, 33*, 585–592.

Dagan, O., & Sagi-Schwartz, A. (2018). Early attachment network with mother and father: An unsettled issue. *Child Development Perspectives, 12*, 115–121. doi: 10.1111.cdep.12272

Dan, A., Mondal, T., Chakraborty, K., Chaudhuri, A., & Biswas, A. (2017). Clinical course and treatment outcome of Koro: A follow-up study from a Koro epidemic reported from West Bengal, India. *Asian Journal of Psychiatry, 26*, 14–20.

Dang-Vu, T. T., Schabus, M., Desseilles, M., Sterpenich, V., Bonjean, M., & Maquet, P. (2010). Functional neuroimaging insights into the physiology of human sleep. *Sleep, 33*, 1589–1603.

Daniels, H., Cole, M., & Wertsch, J. V. (Eds.). (2007). *The Cambridge companion to Vygotsky*. Cambridge University Press.

Danker, J. F., & Anderson, J. R. (2010). The ghosts of brain states past: Remembering reactivates the brain regions engaged during encoding. *Psychological Bulletin, 136*, 87–102.

Darley, J. M., & Berscheid, E. (1967). Increased liking as a result of the anticipation of personal contact. *Human Relations, 20*, 29–39.

Darley, J. M., & Latané, B. (1968). Bystander intervention in emergencies: Diffusion of responsibilities. *Journal of Personality and Social Psychology, 8*, 377–383.

Darwin, C. (1859). *On the origin of species*. Murray.

Darwin, C. (1871). *Descent of man*. Murray.

Davidson, T. L. (1993). The nature and function of interoceptive signals to feed: Toward integration of physiological and learning perspectives. *Psychological Review, 100*, 640–657.

Davidson, T. L., Jones, S., & Stevenson, R. J. (2019). The cognitive control of eating and body weight: It's more than what you "think." *Frontiers in Psychology, 10*, Article 62.

Davis, J. I., Senghas, A., Brandt, F., & Ochsner, K. N. (2010). Thee effects of Botox injections on emotional experience. *Emotion, 10*, 433–440.

Dawkins, R. (1976). *The selfish gene*. Oxford University Press.

Dawkins, R. (1986). Wealth, polygyny, and reproductive success. *Behavioral and Brain Sciences, 9*, 190–191.

Dawood, K., Bailey, J. M., & Martin, N. G. (2009). Genetic and environmental influences on sexual orientation. In Y. Kim (Ed.), *Handbook of behavioral genetics* (pp. 269–279). Springer.

Day, B., Ebrahimi, E., Hartman, L. S., Pagano, C. C., Robb, A. C., & Babu, S. V. (2019). Examining the effects of altered avatars on perception-action in virtual reality. *Journal of Experimental Psychology: Applied, 25*, 1–24. doi: 10.1037/xap0000192

De Freitas, J., & Cikara, M. (2018). Deep down my enemy is good: Thinking about true self reduces intergroup bias. *Journal of Experimental Social Psychology, 74*, 307–316.

De Pitta, M., Brunel, N., & Volterra, A. (2016). Astrocytes: Orchestrating synaptic plasticity? *Neuroscience, 323*, 43–61.

De Virgilio, A., Greco, A., Fabbrini, G., Inghilleri, M., Rizzo, M. I., Gallo, A., Conte, M., Rosato, C., Appiani, M. C., & de Vincentiis, M. (2016). Parkinson's disease: Autoimmunity and neuroinflammation. *Autoimmunity Reviews, 15*, 1005–1011.

De Vries, G. J., & Boyle, P. A. (1998). Double duty for sex differences in the brain. *Behavioural Brain Research, 92*, 205–213.

Deardorff, J., Cham, H., Gonzales, N. A., White, R. M. B., Tein, J.-Y., Wong, J., & Roosa, M. W. (2013, September). Pubertal timing and Mexican-origin girls' internalizing and externalizing symptoms: The influence of harsh parenting. *Developmental Psychology*, 49(9), 1790–1804. doi: 10.1037/a0031016

Dearing, E., McCartney, K., & Taylor, B. A. (2009). Does high quality early child care promote low-income children's math and reading achievement in middle childhood? *Child Development*, 80, 1329–1349.

Deary, I. J. (2012). Intelligence. *Annual Review of Psychology*, 63, 453–482.

Deaux, K., & Lewis, L. L. (1984). The structure of gender stereotypes: Interrelationships among components and gender label. *Journal of Personality and Social Psychology*, 46, 991–1004.

de Boysson-Bardies, B., Sagat, L., & Durand, C. (1984). Discernable differences in the babbling of infants according to target language. *Journal of Child Language*, 11, 1–16.

DeCasper, A. J., & Fifer, W. P. (1980). Of human bonding: Newborns prefer their mothers' voices. *Science*, 208, 1174–1176.

DeCasper, A. J., & Spence, M. J. (1986). Prenatal maternal speech influences newborns' perception of speech sounds. *Infant Behavior and Development*, 9, 133–150.

Deese, J. (1959). On the prediction of occurrence of particular verbal intrusions in immediate recall. *Journal of Experimental Psychology*, 58, 17–22.

de Gelder, B., & Huis in 't Veld, E. (2016). Cultural differences in emotional expressions and body language. In J. Y. Chiao, S.-C. Li, R. Seligman, & R. Turner (Eds.), *Oxford library of psychology. The Oxford handbook of cultural neuroscience* (pp. 223–234). Oxford University Press.

Degenhardt, L., Bruno, R., & Topp, L. (2010). Is ecstasy a drug of dependence? *Drug and Alcohol Dependence*, 107, 1–10.

Degroote, C., Schwaninger, A., Heimgartner, N., Hedinger, P., Ehlert, U., & Wirtz, P. H. (2020). Acute stress improves concentration performance: Opposite effects of anxiety and cortisol. *Experimental Psychology*, 67(2), 88–98.

de Kloet, E. R., Joëls, M., & Holsboer, F. (2005). Stress and the brain: From adaptation to disease. *Nature Reviews Neuroscience*, 6, 463–475.

de Lange, F. P., Roelofs, K., & Toni, I. (2007). Increased self-monitoring during imagined movements in conversion paralysis. *Neuropsychologia*, 45, 2051–2058.

DeLoache, J. S., Chiong, C., Sherman, K., Islam, N., Vanderborght, M., Troseth, G. L., Strouse, G. A., & O'Dougherty, K. (2010). Do babies learn from baby media? *Psychological Science*, 21, 1570–1574.

Dement, W. C. (1978). *Some must watch while some must sleep.* Norton.

Demontis, D., Walters, R. K., Martin, J., Mattheisen, M., Als, T. D., Agerbo, E., Baldursson, G., Belliveau, R., Bybjerg-Grauholm, J., Bækvad-Hansen, M., Cerrato, F., Chambert, K., Churchhouse, C., Dumont, A., Eriksson, N., Gandal, M., Goldstein, J. I., Grasby, K. L., Grove, J., . . . Neale, B. M. (2019). Discovery of the first genome-wide significant risk loci for ADHD. *Nature Genetics*, 51, 63–75.

Dennett, D. C. (1995). *Darwin's dangerous idea: Evolution and the meanings of life.* Simon & Schuster.

Dennis, W., & Dennis, M. G. (1940). The effect of cradling practices upon the onset of walking in Hopi children. *Journal of Genetic Psychology*, 56, 77–86.

Denny, M. (2010). Teaching for multiple intelligences in undergraduate education. *Communications in Computer and Information Science*, 73, 690–691.

de Oliveira, S., & Nisbett, R. E. (2017). Culture changes how we think about thinking: From "human inference" to "geography of thought." *Perspectives on Psychological Science*, 12, 782–790.

Dervola, K. S., Roberg, B. Å., Wøien, G., Bogen, I. L., Sandvik, T. H., Sagvolden, T., Drevon, C. A., Johansen, E. B., & Walaas, S. I. (2012). Marine omega-3 polyunsaturated fatty acids induce sex-specific changes in reinforcer-controlled behaviour and neurotransmitter metabolism in a spontaneously hypertensive rat model of ADHD. *Behavioral and Brain Functions*, 8, 1–13.

D'Esposito, M. D., & Postle, B. R. (2015). The cognitive neuroscience of working memory. *Annual Review of Psychology*, 66, 115–142.

DeValois, R. L., & DeValois, K. K. (1980). Spatial vision. *Annual Review of Psychology*, 31, 309–341.

Devine, P. G., & Sharp, L. B. (2009). Automaticity and control in stereotyping and prejudice. In T. D. Nelson (Ed.), *Handbook of prejudice, stereotyping, and discrimination* (pp. 61–88). Psychology Press.

Dewey, J. (1896). The reflex arc concept in psychology. *Psychological Review*, 3, 357–370.

DeYoung, C. G., Hirsh, J. B., Shane, M. S., Papademetris, X., Rajeevan, N., & Gray, J. R. (2010). Testing predictions from personality neuroscience: Brain structure and the big five. *Psychological Science*, 21, 820–828.

Dhabhar, F. S. (2019). The short-term stress response: Mother Nature's mechanism for enhancing protection and performance under conditions of threat, challenge, and opportunity. *Frontiers in Neuroendocrinology*, 49, 175–192.

Diamond, L. M. (2003). What does sexual orientation orient? A biobehavioral model distinguishing romantic love and sexual desire. *Psychological Review*, 110, 173–192. doi: 10.1037/0033-295X.110.1.173

Dickinson, S., & Biederman, I. (2014). Geons. In K. Ikeuchi (Ed.), *Encyclopedia of computer vision* (pp. 338–346). Springer.

Dijksterhuis, A., & van Knippenberg, A. (1998). The relation between perception and behavior, or how to win a game of Trivial Pursuit. *Journal of Personality and Social Psychology*, 74, 865–877.

Dishion, T. J., & Tipsord, J. M. (2011). Peer contagion in child and adolescent social and emotional development. *Annual Review of Psychology*, 62, 189–214.

Dittmar, H., Long, K., & Meek, R. (2004). Buying on the Internet: Gender differences in on-line and conventional buying motivations. *Sex Roles*, 50, 423–444.

Dixon, W. E., Jr., & Smith, P. H. (2000). Links between early temperament and language acquisition. *Merrill-Palmer Quarterly*, 46, 417–440.

Dolbier, C. L., & Rush, T. E. (2012). Efficacy of abbreviated progressive muscle relaxation in a high-stress college sample. *International Journal of Stress Management*, 19, 48–68.

Doll, C., McLaughlin, T. F., & Barretto, A. (2013). The token economy: A recent review and evaluation. *International Journal of Basic and Applied Science*, 2, 131–149.

Domhoff, G. (1996). *Finding meaning in dreams: A quantitative analysis*. Plenum.

Domhoff, G. (2003). *The scientific study of dreams: Neural networks, cognitive development, and content analysis*. American Psychological Association.

Domhoff, G. W. (2019). The neurocognitive theory of dreams at age 20: An assessment and a comparison with four other theories of dreaming. *Dreaming, 29*, 265–302.

Domjan, M. (2015). *The principles of learning and behavior* (7th ed.). Cengage/Wadsworth.

Doris, E., Shekriladze, I., Javakhisvili, N., Jones, R., Treasure, J., & Tchanturia, K. (2015). Is culture change associated with eating disorders? A systematic review of the literature. *Eating and Weight Disorders, 20*, 149–160.

Doty, R. L. (2010). *The great pheromone myth*. The Johns Hopkins University Press.

Dougall, A. L., Hyman, K. B., Hayward, M. C., McFeeley, S., & Baum, A. (2001). Optimism and traumatic stress: The importance of social support and coping. *Journal of Applied Social Psychology, 31*, 223–245.

Drevets, W. C., Burton, H., Videen, T. O., & Snyder, A. Z. (1995). Blood flow changes in human somatosensory cortex during anticipated stimulation. *Nature, 373*, 249–252.

Drews, F. A., Yazdani, H., Godfrey, C. N., Cooper, J. M., & Strayer, D. L. (2009). Text messaging during simulated driving. *Human Factors, 51*, 762–770.

Duncker, K. (1945). On problem solving. *Psychological Monographs, 58*(5, Whole No. 270).

Dunlosky, J., & Rawson, K. A. (2011). Overconfidence produces underachievement: Inaccurate self evaluations undermine students' learning and retention. *Learning and Instruction, 22*, 271–280.

Durie, D. J. (1981). Sleep in animals. In D. Wheatley (Ed.), *Psychopharmacology of sleep*. Raven Press.

Dweck, C. S., & Yeager, D. S. (2019). Mindsets: A view from two eras. *Perspectives on Psychological Science, 14*, 481–496.

Dzhambov, A. M., & Dimitrova, D. D. (2017). Children's blood pressure and its association with road traffic exposure: A systematic review with meta-analysis. *Environmental Research, 152*, 244–255.

Eagleman, D. (2011). *Incognitio: The secret lives of the brain*. Pantheon Books.

Eagly, A. H., Ashmore, R. D., Makhijani, M. G., & Longo, L. C. (1991). What is beautiful is good, but...: A meta-analytic review of research on the physical attractiveness stereotype. *Psychological Bulletin, 110*, 109–128.

Eagly, A. H., & Wood, W. (1999). The origins of sex differences in human behavior: Evolved dispositions versus social roles. *American Psychologist, 54*, 408–423.

Ebbinghaus, H. (1964). *Memory: A contribution to experimental psychology*. Dover. (Original work published 1885)

Edelman, G. M. (1987). *Neural Darwinism*. Basic Books.

Eden, K. J., & Wylie, K. R. (2009). Quality of sexual life and menopause. *Women's Health, 5*, 385–396.

Efron, R. (1970). The relationship between the duration of a stimulus and the duration of a perception. *Neuropsychologia, 8*, 37–55.

Egan Brad, L. C., Spisz, T. J., & Tanega, C. G. (2019). Does "privilege checking" make us less racist, or more? Generation and political orientation matter. *Race and Social Problems, 11*, 1–14. https://doi.org/10.1007/s12552-018-9246-0

Egan, D., & Schwartz, B. (1979). Chunking in recall of symbolic drawings. *Memory & Cognition, 7*, 149–158.

Eggert, L. L., Thompson, E. A., Herting, J. R., Randell, B., & Mazza, J. (1995). Reducing suicide potential among high-risk youth: Tests of a school-based prevention program. *Suicide and Life-Threatening Behavior, 25*, 276–296.

Eibl-Eibesfeldt, I. (1973). The expressive behavior of the deaf-and-born-blind. In M. von Cranach & I. Vine (Eds.), *Social communication and movement* (pp. 163–194). Academic Press.

Eich, E., Macaulay, D., Loewenstein, R. J., & Dihle, P. H. (1997). Memory, amnesia, and dissociative identity disorder. *Psychological Science, 8*, 417–422.

Eisenberger, R., & Cameron, J. (1996). Detrimental effects of reward: Reality or myth? *American Psychologist, 51*, 1153–1166.

Eisinger, R. W., & Fauci, A. S. (2018). Ending the HIV/AIDS pandemic. *Emerging Infectious Diseases, 24*(3), 413–416.

Ekman, P. (1992). Are there basic emotions? *Psychological Review, 99*, 350–353.

Ekman, P. (1999). Basic emotions. In T. Dalgleish & M. Power (Eds.), *Handbook of cognition and emotion* (pp. 45–60). Wiley.

Ekman, P., & Friesen, W. V. (1975). *Unmasking the face*. Prentice-Hall.

Ekman, P., & Friesen, W. V. (1986). A new pan-cultural facial expression of emotion. *Motivation and Emotion, 10*, 159–168.

Ekman, P., & Keltner, D. (1997). Universal facial expressions of emotion: An old controversy and new findings. In U. C. Segerstrale & P. Molnar (Eds.), *Nonverbal communication: Where nature meets culture* (pp. 27–46). Erlbaum.

Ellemers, N. (2018). Gender stereotypes. *Annual Review of Psychology, 69*, 275–298.

Elliot, A. J., & Devine, P. G. (1994). On the motivational nature of cognitive dissonance: Dissonance as psychological discomfort. *Journal of Personality and Social Psychology, 67*, 382–294.

Elliott, M. L., Knodt, A. R., Ireland, D., Morris, M. L., Poulton, R., Ramrakha, S., Sison, M. L., Moffitt, T. E., Caspi, A., & Hariri, A. R. (2020). What is the test-retest reliability of common task-functional MRI measures? New empirical evidence and a meta-analysis. *Psychological Science*. Advance online publication. https://doi.org/10.1177/0956797620916786

Ellis, A. (1962). *Reason and emotion in psychotherapy*. Prentice-Hall.

Ellis, A. (1993). Fundamentals of rational-emotive therapy for the 1990s. In W. Dryden & L. K. Hill (Eds.), *Innovations in rational-emotive therapy* (pp. 1–32). Sage.

Ellman, S. J., Spielman, A. J., Luck, D., Steiner, S. S., & Halperin, R. (1991). REM deprivation: A review. In S. J. Ellman & J. S. Antrobus (Eds.), *The mind in sleep* (2nd ed., pp. 329–376). Wiley.

Ellsworth, P. C. (1994). William James and emotion: Is a century of fame worth a century of misunderstanding? *Psychological Review, 101*, 222–229.

Else-Quest, N. M., & Hyde, J. S. (2018). *The psychology of women and gender* (9th ed.). SAGE.

Engle, R. W. (2001). What is working memory capacity? In H. L. Roediger, J. S. Nairne, I. Neath, & A. M. Surprenant (Eds.), *The nature of remembering* (pp. 297–314). American Psychological Association.

Engle, R. W. (2018). Working memory and executive attention: A revisit. *Perspectives on Psychological Science, 13*, 190–193.

Epstein, L. H., Temple, J. L., Roemmich, J. N., & Bouton, M. E. (2009). Habituation as a determinant of human food intake. *Psychological Review, 116*, 384–407.

Epstein, S. (1979). The stability of behavior: On predicting most of the people much of the time. *Journal of Personality and Social Psychology, 37*, 1097–1126.

Erdelyi, M. H. (2010). The ups and downs of memory. *American Psychologist, 65*, 623–633.

Erickson, M. H. (1964). A hypnotic technique for resistant patients. *American Journal of Clinical Hypnosis, 7*, 8–32.

Erikson, E. (1963). *Childhood and society.* Norton.

Erikson, E. (1968). *Identity: Youth and crisis.* Norton.

Erikson, E. (1982). *The life cycle completed: Review.* Norton.

Etcheverry, P. E., & Agnew, C. R. (2009). Similarity in cigarette smoking attracts: A prospective study of romantic partner selection by own smoking and smoking prototypes. *Psychology of Addictive Behaviors, 23*, 632–643.

Evans, G. W. (1997). Environmental stress and health. In A. Baum, T. Revenson, & J. E. Singer (Eds.), *Handbook of health psychology* (pp. 365–385). Erlbaum.

Evans, G. W., Hygge, S., & Bullinger, M. (1995). Chronic noise and psychological stress. *Psychological Science, 6*, 333–338.

Every-Palmer, S., Jenkins, M., Gendall, P., Hoek, J., Beaglehole, B., Bell, C., Williman, J., Rapsey, C., & Stanley, J. (2020). Psychological distress, anxiety, family violence, suicidality, and wellbeing in New Zealand during the COVID-19 lockdown: A cross-sectional study. *PLoS ONE, 15*(11), e0241658. https://doi.org/10.1371/journal.pone.0241658

Eysenck, H. J. (1952). The effects of psychotherapy: An evaluation. *Journal of Consulting Psychology, 16*, 319–324.

Eysenck, H. J. (1970). *The structure of human personality* (3rd ed.). Methuen.

Eysenck, H. J. (1991). Dimensions of personality: 16, 5, or 3? Criteria for a taxonomic paradigm. *Personality and Individual Differences, 12*, 773–790.

Eysenck, H. J., & Kamin, L. (1981). *The intelligence controversy: H. J. Eysenck vs. Leon Kamin.* Wiley.

Fagan, J. F., Holland, C. R., & Wheeler, K. (2007). The prediction, from infancy, of adult IQ and achievement. *Intelligence, 35*, 225–231.

Fahy, T. A. (1988). The diagnosis of multiple personality: A critical review. *British Journal of Psychiatry, 153*, 597–606.

Falk, E., & Scholz, C. (2018). Persuasion, influence, and value: Perspectives from communication and social neuroscience. *Annual Review of Psychology, 69*, 329–356.

Fantz, R. L. (1961, May). The origin of form perception. *Scientific American, 204*, 66–72.

Faust, I. M. (1984). Role of the fat cell in energy balance physiology. In A. J. Stunkard & E. Stellar (Eds.), *Eating and its disorders* (pp. 97–107). Raven.

Fazio, R. H. (1986). How do attitudes guide behavior? In R. M. Sorrentino & E. T. Higgins (Eds.), *Handbook of motivation and cognition: Foundations of social behavior* (Vol. 1, pp. 204–243). Guilford Press.

Fearon, R. P., Bakermans-Kranenburg, M. J., van IJzendoorn, M. H., Lapsley, A., & Roisman, G. I. (2010). The significance of insecure attachment and disorganization in the development of children's externalizing behavior: A meta-analytic study. *Child Development, 81*, 435–456.

Fedorenko, E., Behr, M. K., & Kanwisher, N. (2011). Functional specificity for high-level linguistic processing in the brain. *Proceedings of the National Academy of Sciences, 108*, 16428–16433.

Fehr, B., Harasymchuk, C., & Sprecher, S. (2014). Compassionate love in romantic relationships: A review and some new findings. *Journal of Social and Personal Relationships, 31*, 575–600.

Fehr, B., & Russell, J. A. (1991). The concept of love: Viewed from a prototype perspective. *Journal of Personality and Social Psychology, 60*, 425–438.

Feingold, A. (1988). Matching for attractiveness in romantic partners and same-sex friends: A meta-analysis and theoretical critique. *Psychological Bulletin, 104*, 226–235.

Feingold, A. (1990). Gender differences in effects of physical attractiveness on romantic attraction: A comparison across five research paradigms. *Journal of Personality and Social Psychology, 59*, 981–993.

Feinstein, A. (2018). Conversion disorder. *Continuum (Behavioral Neurology and Psychiatry), 24*, 861–872.

Feist, J., Feist, G., & Roberts, T. (2018). *Theories of personality* (9th ed.). McGraw-Hill.

Ferguson, C. J., & Kilburn, J. (2010). Much ado about nothing: The misestimation and overinterpretation of violent video game effects in eastern and western nations: Comment on Anderson et al. (2010). *Psychological Bulletin, 136*, 174–178.

Ferris, C. F., Snowdon, C. T., King, J. A., Duong, T. Q., Ziegler, T. E., Ugurbil, K., Ludwig, R., Schultz-Darken, N. J., Wu, Z., Olson, D. P., Sullivan, J. M., Jr., Tannenbaum, P. L., & Vaughan, J. T. (2001). Functional imaging of brain activity in conscious monkeys responding to sexually arousing cues. *Neuroreport: For Rapid Communication of Neuroscience Research, 12*, 2231–2236.

Ferster, C. B., & Skinner, B. F. (1957). *Schedules of reinforcement.* Appleton-Century-Crofts.

Festinger, L. (1957). *A theory of cognitive dissonance.* Stanford University Press.

Festinger, L., & Carlsmith, J. M. (1959). Cognitive consequences of forced compliance. *Journal of Abnormal and Social Psychology, 58*, 203–210.

Festinger, L., Riecken, H. W., & Schacter, S. (1956). *When prophecy fails.* University of Minnesota Press.

Festinger, L., Schachter, S., & Black, K. (1950). *Social pressures in informal groups: A study of human factors in housing.* Harper.

Fiedler, K. (1988). The dependence of the conjunction fallacy on subtle linguistic factors. *Psychological Research, 50*, 123–129.

Fink, G. (2016). Eighty years of stress. *Nature*, *539*, 175–176.

Finn, B., & Roediger, H. L., III (2011). Enhancing retention through reconsolidation: Negative emotional arousal following retrieval enhances later recall. *Psychological Science*, *22*, 781–786.

Fischer, P., Greitemeyer, T., Pollozek, F., & Frey, D. (2006). The unresponsive bystander: Are bystanders more responsive in dangerous emergencies? *European Journal of Social Psychology*, *36*, 267–278.

Fischer, P., Krueger, J. I., Greitemeyer, T., Vogrincic, C., Kastenmüller, A., Frey, D., Heene, M., Wicher, M., & Kainbacher, M. (2011). The bystander-effect: A meta-analytic review on bystander intervention in dangerous and non-dangerous emergencies. *Psychological Bulletin*, *137*(4), 517–537.

Fiske, S. T. (1993). Social cognition and social perception. *Annual Review of Psychology*, *44*, 155–194.

Fiss, H. (1991). Experimental strategies for the study of the function of dreaming. In S. J. Ellman & J. S. Antrobus (Eds.), *The mind in sleep* (2nd ed., pp. 308–326). Wiley.

Flaxman, S. M., & Sherman, P. W. (2000). Morning sickness: A mechanism for protecting mother and embryo. *Quarterly Review of Biology*, *75*, 113–148.

Fleeson, W. (2001). Towards a structure- and process-integrated view of personality: Traits as density distributions of states. *Journal of Personality and Social Psychology*, *80*, 1011–1027.

Fleeson, W. (2004). Moving personality beyond the person-situation debate. *Current Directions in Psychological Science*, *13*, 83–87.

Fleeson, W., & Gallagher, M. P. (2009). The implications of Big-Five standing for the distribution of trait manifestation in behavior: Fifteen experience-sampling studies and a meta-analysis. *Journal of Personality and Social Psychology*, *97*, 1097–1114.

Fleishman, E. A., & Parker, J. F., Jr. (1962). Factors in the retention and relearning of perceptual motor skill. *Journal of Experimental Psychology*, *64*, 215–226.

Flynn, J. R. (1987). Massive IQ gains in 14 nations: What IQ tests really measure. *Psychological Bulletin*, *101*, 171–191.

Flynn, J. R. (2007). *What is intelligence?* Cambridge University Press.

Foer, J. (2011). *Moonwalking with Einstein: The art and science of remembering everything*. Penguin Group.

Folkman, S. (2008). The case for positive emotions in the stress process. *Anxiety, Stress, & Coping*, *21*, 3–14.

Folkman, S., & Moskowitz, J. T. (2004). Coping: Pitfalls and promise. *Annual Review of Psychology*, *55*, 745–774.

Ford, T. E., Teeter, S. R., Richardson, K., & Woodzicka, J. A. (2017). Putting the brakes on prejudice rebound effects: An ironic effect of disparagement humor. *The Journal of Social Psychology*, *157*, 458–473.

Forgas, J. P. (1998). On being happy and mistaken: Mood effects on the fundamental attribution error. *Journal of Personality & Social Psychology*, *75*, 318–331.

Fornito, A., & Bullmore, E. T. (2015). Reconciling abnormalities of brain network structure and function in schizophrenia. *Current Opinion in Neurobiology*, *30*, 44–50.

Foulkes, D. (1985). *Dreaming: A cognitive-psychological analysis*. Erlbaum.

Frances, A. J., & Widiger, T. (2012). Psychiatric diagnosis: Lessons from the DSM-IV past and cautions for the DSM-5 future. *Annual Review of Clinical Psychology*, *8*, 109–130.

Francis, P. T., Ramirez, M. J., & Lai, M. K. (2010). Neurochemical basis for symptomatic treatment of Alzheimer's disease. *Neuropharmacology*, *59*, 221–229.

Frankham, C., & Cabanac, M. (2003). Nicotine lowers the body-weight set-point in male rats. *Appetite*, *41*, 1–5.

Freedman, J. L., & Fraser, S. C. (1966). Compliance without pressure: The foot-in-the-door technique. *Journal of Personality and Social Psychology*, *4*, 195–202.

Freitas, F. A., & Leonard, L. J. (2011). Maslow's hierarchy of needs and student academic success. *Teaching and Learning in Nursing*, *6*, 9–13.

Fresson, M., Meulemans, T., Dardenne, B., & Geurten, M. (2018). Overdiagnosis of ADHD in boys: Stereotype impact on neuropsychological assessment. *Applied Neuropsychology: Child*, *8*, 231–245.

Freud, S. (1910). The origin and development of psychoanalysis. *American Journal of Psychology*, *21*, 181–218.

Freud, S. (1913). *The interpretation of dreams* (A. A. Brill, Trans.). Macmillan. (Original work published 1900)

Freud, S. (1940). *An outline of psychoanalysis*. Norton.

Freud, S. (1962). *Three contributions to the theory of sexuality*. Dutton. (Original work published 1905)

Freud, S. (1964). The dynamics of transference. In J. Strachey (Ed. & Trans.), *The standard edition of the complete works of Sigmund Freud* (Vol. 12). Hogarth Press. (Original work published 1912)

Freudenberger, H. J. (1974). Staff burnout. *Journal of Social Issues*, *30*, 159–165.

Friedlander, L., Lumley, M. A., Farchione, T., & Doyal, G. (1997). Testing the alexithymia hypothesis: Physiological and subjective responses during relaxation and stress. *Journal of Nervous & Mental Disease*, *185*, 233–239.

Friedman, M. J., Resick, P. A., Bryant, R. A., Strain, J., Horowitz, M., & Spiegel, D. (2011). Classification of trauma and stressor-related disorders in DSM-5. *Depression and Anxiety*, *28*, 737–749.

Friedman, M., & Rosenman, R. F. (1974). *Type A behavior and your heart*. Knopf.

Fu, G., Xu, F., Cameron, C. A., Herman, G., & Lee, K. (2007). Cross-cultural differences in children's choices, categorizations, and lies. *Developmental Psychology*, *43*, 278–293.

Fuchs, L. S., Geary, D. C., Compton, D. L., Fuchs, D., Hamlett, C. L., Seethaler, P. M., Bryant, J. D., & Schatschneider, C. (2010). Do different types of school mathematics development depend on different constellations of numerical versus general cognitive abilities? *Developmental Psychology*, *46*(6), 1731. doi: 10.1037/a0020662

Fukada, K., Vogel, E., Mayr, U., & Awh, E. (2010). Quantity not quality: The relationship between fluid intelligence and working memory capacity. *Psychonomic Bulletin & Review*, *17*, 673–679.

Funder, D. C. (2001). Personality. *Annual Review of Psychology*, *52*, 197–221.

Fyer, A. J., Mannuzza, S., Gallops, M. S., Martin, L. Y., Aaronson, C., Gorman, J. M., Liebowitz, M. R., & Klein, D. F. (1990). Familial transmission of simple phobias and fears: A preliminary report. *Archives of General Psychiatry*, *47*, 252–256.

Gadsby, S. (2017). Explaining body size beliefs in anorexia. *Cognitive Neuropsychiatry, 22*, 495–507.

Gagnon, J. H. (1990). The explicit and implicit use of the scripting perspective in sex research. *Annual Review of Sex Research, 1*, 1–43.

Gagnon, J. H., & Simon, W. (1973). *Sexual conduct: The social sources of human sexuality*. Aldine.

Gainotti, G., & Marra, C. (2011). Differential contribution of right and left temporo-occipital and anterior temporal lesions to face recognition disorders. *Frontiers in Human Neuroscience, 5*, 1–11.

Gaither, S. E., Fan, S. P., & Kinzler, K. D. (2020, January). Thinking about multiple identities boosts children's flexible thinking. *Developmental Science, 23*(1), e0012871. https://doi.org/10.1111/desc.12871

Galef, B. G., Jr. (1985). Social learning in wild Norway rats. In T. D. Johnston & A. T. Pietrewicz (Eds.), *Issues in the ecological study of learning* (pp. 143–166). Erlbaum.

Galinsky, A. D., & Moskowitz, G. B. (2000). Perspective-taking: Decreasing stereotype expression, stereotype accessibility, and in-group favoritism. *Journal of Personality and Social Psychology, 78*, 708–724.

Gallese, V., Gernsbacher, M. A., Heyes, C., Hickok, G., & Iacoboni, M. (2011). Mirror neuron forum. *Perspectives on Psychological Science, 6*, 369–407.

Gallistel, C. R., & Gibbon, J. (2000). Time, rate, and conditioning. *Psychological Review, 107*, 289–344.

Galton, F. (1869). *Hereditary genius: An inquiry into its laws and consequences*. Appleton.

Galton, F. (1883). *Inquiries into human faculty and development*. Macmillan.

Gandelman, R. (1992). *Psychobiology of behavior development*. Oxford University Press.

Gangestad, S. W., & Simpson, J. A. (1993). Development of a scale measuring genetic variation related to expressive control. *Journal of Personality, 61*, 133–158.

Gangestad, S. W., & Snyder, M. (1985). On the nature of self-monitoring: An examination of latent causal structure. In P. Shaver (Ed.), *Review of personality and social psychology* (Vol. 6, pp. 65–85). Sage.

Gangestad, S. W., Thornhill, R., & Garver-Apgar, C. E. (2010). Fertility in the cycle predicts women's interest in sexual opportunism. *Evolution and Human Behavior, 31*, 400–411.

Gao, T., & Scholl, B. J. (2011). Chhasing vs. stalking: Interrupting the perception of animacy. *Journal of Experimental Psychology: Human Perception and Performance, 37*, 669–684.

Garcia, D., & Rimé, B. (2019). Collective emotions and social resilience in the digital traces after a terrorist attack. *Psychological Science, 30*, 617–628.

Garcia, J., & Koelling, R. A. (1966). Relation of cue to consequence in avoidance learning. *Psychonomic Science, 4*, 123–124.

Garcia, S. M., Weaver, K., Moskowitz, G. B., & Darley, J. M. (2002). Crowded minds: The implicit bystander effect. *Journal of Personality and Social Psychology, 83*, 843–853.

García-Cáceres, C., Balland, E., Prevot, V., Luquet, S., Woods, S. C., Koch, M., Horvath, T. L., Yi, C.-X., Chowen, J. A., Verkhratsky, A., Araque, A., Bechmann, I., & Tschöp, M. H. (2019). Role of astrocytes, microglia, and tanycytes in brain control of systemic metabolism. *Nature Neuroscience, 22*, 7–14.

Gardner, E. B., & Costanzo, R. H. (1981). Properties of kinesthetic neurons in somatosensory cortex of awake monkeys. *Brain Research, 214*, 301–319.

Gardner, H. (1983). *Frames of mind: The theory of multiple intelligences*. Basic Books.

Gardner, H. (1993). *Multiple intelligences: The theory in practice*. Basic Books.

Gardner, H. (1999). *Intelligence reframed: Multiple intelligences for the 21st century*. Basic Books.

Gardner, H. (2016). Multiple intelligences: Prelude, theory, and aftermath. In R. J. Sternberg, S. T. Fiske, & D. J. Foss (Eds.), *Scientists making a difference* (pp. 167–170). Cambridge University Press.

Gardner, H., & Moran, S. (2006). The science of multiple intelligences theory: A response to Lynn Waterhouse. *Educational Psychologist, 41*, 227–232.

Gardner, R. A., & Gardner, B. T. (1969). Teaching sign language to a chimpanzee. *Science, 165*, 664–672.

Gardner, R. A., Gardner, B. T., & Van Cantfort, T. E. (Eds.). (1989). *Teaching sign language to chimpanzees*. SUNY Press.

Garland, A. F., & Zigler, E. (1993). Adolescent suicide prevention: Current research and social policy implications. *American Psychologist, 48*, 169–182.

Garrity, T. F., Stallones, L., Marx, M. B., & Johnson, T. P. (1989). Pet ownership and attachment as supportive factors in the health of the elderly. *Anthrozoos, 3*, 35–44.

Gawronski, B., & Bodenhausen, G. (2006). Associative and propositional processes in evaluation: An integrative review of implicit and explicit attitude change. *Psychological Bulletin, 132*, 692–731.

Gazzaniga, M. S. (2008). *Human. The science behind what makes us human*. HarperCollins.

Gazzaniga, M. S., Bogen, J. E., & Sperry, R. W. (1965). Observations on visual perception after disconnection of the cerebral hemispheres in man. *Brain, 88*, 221–236.

Gazzaniga, M. S., & LeDoux, J. E. (1978). *The integrated mind*. Plenum.

Geary, D. C., & Flinn, M. V. (2002). Sex differences in behavioral and hormonal response to social threat: Commentary on Taylor et al. (2000). *Psychological Review, 109*, 745–750.

Geiselman, R. E., Fisher, R. P., MacKinnon, D. P., & Holland, H. L. (1985). Eyewitness memory enhancement in the police interview: Cognitive retrieval mnemonics versus hypnosis. *Journal of Applied Psychology, 70*, 401–412.

Gejman, P. V., Sanders, A. R., & Kendler, K. S. (2011). Genetics of schizophrenia: New findings and challenges. *Annual Review of Genomics and Human Genetics, 12*, 121–144.

Gelman, S. A. (2009). Essentialist reasoning about the biological world. In A. Berthoz & Y. Christen (Eds.), *Neurobiology of "Umwelt": How living beings perceive the world* (pp. 7–16). Springer.

Gelstein, S., Yeshurun, Y., Rozenkrantz, L., Shushan, S., Frumin, I., Roth, Y., & Sobel, N. (2011). Human tears contain a chemosignal. *Science*, *331*, 226–230.

Gendron, M., Crivelli, C., & Barrett, L. F. (2018). Universality reconsidered: Diversity in meaning making of facial expressions. *Current Directions in Psychological Science*, *27*, 211–219.

Gerbner, G., & Gross, L. (1976). Living with television: The violence profile. *Journal of Communications*, *26*, 172–199.

German, T. P., & Barrett, H. C. (2005). Functional fixedness in a technologically sparse culture. *Psychological Science*, *16*, 1–5.

Gershon, E. S. (1990). Genetics. In F. K. Goodwin & K. R. Jamison (Eds.), *Manic-depressive illness*. Oxford University Press.

Gibbs, J. C., Basinger, K. S., Grime, R. L., & Snarey, J. R. (2007). Moral judgment development across cultures: Revisiting Kohlberg's universality claims. *Developmental Review*, *27*, 443–500. doi: 10.1016/j.dr.2007.04.001

Gibbs, R. W., Jr. (2012). Are ironic acts deliberate? *Journal of Pragmatics*, *44*, 104–115.

Gibson, E. J., & Walk, R. D. (1960, April). The "visual cliff." *Scientific American*, *202*, 64–71.

Gielen, M. C., Lumb, M. J., & Smart, T. G. (2012). Benzodiazepines modulate GABA receptors by regulating the preactivation step after GABA binding. *Journal of Neuroscience*, *32*, 5707–5715.

Gigerenzer, G. (1996). On narrow norms and vague heuristics: A reply to Kahneman & Tversky. *Psychological Review*, *103*, 592–596.

Gigerenzer, G. (1997). Ecological intelligence: An adaptation for frequencies. In D. Cummins & C. Allen (Eds.), *The evolution of mind* (pp. 264–280). Oxford University Press.

Gigerenzer, G. (2018). The heuristics revolution: Rethinking the role of uncertainty in finance. In R. Viale, S. Mousavi, B. Alemanni, & U. Filotto (Eds.), *The behavioral finance revolution: A new approach to financial policies and regulations* (pp. 115–247). Edward Elgar.

Gilbert, A. L., Regier, T., Kay, P., & Ivry, R. B. (2008). Support for lateralization of the Whorf effect beyond the realm of color discrimination. *Brain and Language*, *105*(2), 91–98. doi: 10.1016/j.bandl.2007.06.001

Gilligan, C. (1982). *In a different voice: Psychological theory and women's development*. Harvard University Press.

Gilmore, R. O., Diaz, M. T., Wyble, B. A., & Yarkoni, T. (2017). Progress toward openness, transparency, and reproducibility in cognitive neuroscience. *Annuals of the New York Academy of Sciences*, *1396*, 5–18.

Glaser, B. G., & Strauss, A. L. (1968). *Time for dying*. Aldine.

Glenberg, A. M. (2011). Positions in the mirror are closer than they appear. *Perspectives on Psychological Science*, *6*, 408–410.

Gluck, J. P., & Bell, J. (2003). Ethical issues in the use of animals in biomedical and psychopharmacological research. *Psychopharmacology*, *171*, 6–12.

Goater, N., King, M., Cole, E., Leavey, G., Johnson-Sabine, E., Blizard, R., & Hoar, A. (1999). Ethnicity and outcomes of psychosis. *British Journal of Psychiatry*, *175*, 34–42.

Gogate, L., & Hollich, G. (2010). Invariance detection within an interactive system: A perceptual gateway to language development. *Psychological Review*, *171*, 496–516.

Gold, J. M., Bansal, S., Gaspar, J. M., Chen, S., Robinson, B. M., Hahn, B., & Luck, S. J. (2019, May 15). People with schizophrenia show enhanced cognitive costs of maintaining a single item in working memory. *Psychological Medicine*. https://doi.org/10.1017/S0033291719000862 Advance online publication

Goldberg, J., True, W. R., Eisen, S. A., & Henderson, W. G. (1990). A twin study of the effects of the Vietnam War on posttraumatic stress disorder. *Journal of the American Medical Association*, *263*, 1227–1232.

Goldstein, D. S., & Kopin, I. J. (2007). Evolution of concepts of stress. *Stress: The International Journal on the Biology of Stress*, *10*, 109–120.

Goldstone, R. L., & Kersten, A. (2003). Concepts and categorization. In A. Healy & R. Proctor (Eds.), *Handbook of psychology: Vol. 4. Experimental psychology* (pp. 599–621). Wiley.

Goleman, D. (1995). *Emotional intelligence*. Bantam.

Goodall, J. (1990). *Through a window: My thirty years with the chimpanzees of Gombe*. Houghton Mifflin.

Gopie, N., Craik, F. I. M., & Hasher, L. (2011). A double dissociation of implicit and explicit memory in younger and older adults. *Psychological Science*, *22*, 634–640.

Gopnik, A. (2009). *The philosophical baby*. Farrar, Straus, & Giroux.

Gopnik, A., Meltzoff, A. N., & Kuhl, P. K. (1999). *The scientist in the crib: Minds, brains, and how children learn*. William Morrow.

Gore-Felton, C., Koopman, C., Thoresen, C., Arnow, B., Bridges, E., & Spiegel, D. (2000). Psychologists' beliefs and clinical characteristics: Judging the veracity of childhood sexual abuse memories. *Professional Psychology: Research and Practice*, *31*, 372–377.

Gottesman, I. I. (1991). *Schizophrenia genesis: The origins of madness*. Freeman.

Gottfredson, L. S. (2003). Dissecting practical intelligence theory: Its claims and evidence. *Intelligence*, *31*, 343–397.

Gould, E., Tanapat, P., Hastings, N. B., & Shors, T. J. (1999). Neurogenesis in adulthood: A possible role in learning. *Trends in Cognitive Sciences*, *3*, 186–192.

Gould, M. S. (2001). Suicide and the media. In H. Hendin & J. J. Mann (Eds.), *Suicide prevention: Clinical and scientific aspects* (pp. 200–224). New York Academy of Sciences.

Gould, M. S., & Kramer, R. A. (2001). Youth suicide prevention. *Suicide and Life-Threatening Behavior*, *31*(Supplement), 6–31.

Gould, R. L. (1978). *Transformations: Growth and change in adult life*. Simon & Schuster.

Gould, S. J. (2000). More things in heaven and earth. In H. Rose & S. Rose (Eds.), *Alas, poor Darwin: Arguments against evolutionary psychology*. Harmony Books.

Gould, S. J., & Lewontin, R. C. (1979). The spandrels of San Marco and the Panglossian paradigm: A critique of the adaptionist program. *Proceedings of Royal Society of London*, *205*, 581–598.

Graf, P., Mandler, G., & Haden, P. E. (1982). Simulating amnesic symptoms in normal subjects. *Science*, *218*, 1243–1244.

Graf, P., & Schacter, D. L. (1985). Implicit and explicit memory for new associations in normal and amnesic subjects. *Journal of Experimental Psychology: Learning, Memory, & Cognition*, *11*, 501–518.

Graffen, N. F., Ray, W. J., & Lundy, R. (1995). EEG concomitants of hypnosis and hypnotic susceptibility. *Journal of Abnormal Psychology, 104*, 123–131.

Gray, P. B., Garcia, J. R., & Gesselman, A. N. (2019). Age-related patterns in sexual behaviors and attitudes among single US adults: an evolutionary approach. *Evolutionary Behavioral Sciences, 13*, 111–126.

Graziano, W. G., & Bryant, W. H. M. (1998). Self-monitoring and the self-attribution of positive emotions. *Journal of Personality & Social Psychology, 74*, 250–261.

Greenberg, D. L. (2004). President Bush's false "flashbulb" memory of 9/11/01. *Applied Cognitive Psychology, 18*, 363–370.

Greenblatt, D. J., & Shader, R. I. (1978). Pharmacotherapy of anxiety with benzodiazepines and beta-adrenergic blockers. In M. Lipton, A. DiMascio, & F. Killiam (Eds.), *Psychopharmacology: A generation of progress* (pp. 1381–1390). Raven.

Greenwald, A. G., & Banaji, M. R. (1995). Implicit social cognition: Attitudes, self-esteem, and stereotypes. *Psychological Review, 102*, 4–27.

Greenwald, A. G., Poehlman, T. A., Ulhman, E. L., & Banaji, M. R. (2009). Understanding and using the implicit association test: III. Meta-analysis of predictive validity. *Journal of Personality and Social Psychology, 97*, 17–41.

Greenwald, A. G., Spangenberg, E. R., Pratkanis, A. R., & Eskenazi, J. (1991). Double-blind tests of subliminal self-help audiotapes. *Psychological Science, 2*, 119–122.

Grencavage, L. M., & Norcross, J. C. (1990). Where are the common factors? *Professional Psychology: Research and Practice, 21*, 372–378.

Grice, H. P. (1975). Logic and conversation. In P. Cole & J. L. Morgan (Eds.), *Syntax and semantics: Vol. 3. Speech acts* (pp. 41–58). Seminar Press.

Griffiths, T. L. (2015). Manifesto for a new (computational) cognitive revolution. *Cognition, 135*, 21–23.

Griggs, R. A., & Whitehead, G. I., III. (2015). Coverage of recent criticisms of Milgram's obedience experiments in introductory social psychology textbooks. *Theory & Psychology, 25*, 564–580.

Groh, A. M., Narayan, A. J., Bakermans-Kranenburg, M. J., Roisman, G. I., Vaughn, B. E., Pasco Fearon, R. M., & van IJzendoorn, M. H. (2017). Attachment and temperament in early life course: A meta-analytic review. *Child Development, 88*, 770–795.

Grover, S., Swapnajeet, S., Rabha, A., & Koirala, R. (2019). ECT in schizophrenia: A review of the evidence. *Acta Neuropsychiatrica, 31*, 115–127.

Groves, P. M., & Thompson, R. F. (1970). Habituation: A dual-process theory. *Psychological Review, 77*, 419–450.

Guinard, J. X., & Brun, P. (1998). Sensory-specific satiety: Comparison of taste and texture effects. *Appetite, 31*, 141–157.

Gunderson, J. G. (1992). Diagnostic controversies. In A. Tasman & M. B. Riba (Eds.), *Review of psychiatry* (Vol. 11). American Psychiatric Press.

Gurven, M., von Rueden, C., Massenkoff, M., Kaplan, H., & Lero Vie, M. (2013). How universal is the Big Five? Testing the five-factor model of personality variation among forager-farmers in the Bolivian Amazon. *Journal of Personality and Social Psychology, 104*, 354–470.

Gutiérrez-García, A., Beltrán, D., & Calvo, M. G. (2019). Facial attractiveness impressions precede trustworthiness inferences: lower detection thresholds and faster decision latencies. *Cognition and Emotion, 33*, 378–385. doi: 10.1080/02699931.2018.1444583

Haan, N. (Ed.). (1977). *Coping and defending: Processes of self-environment organization*. Academic Press.

Haan, N. (1993). The assessment of coping, defense, and stress. In L. Goldberger & S. Brezitz (Eds.), *Handbook of stress: Theoretical and clinical aspects* (2nd ed.). Free Press.

Hadjikhani, N., & de Gelder, B. (2002). Neural basis of prosopagnosia: An fMRI study. *Human Brain Mapping, 16*, 176–182.

Haeck, C., Lebihan, L., & Merrigan, P. (2018). Universal child care and long-term effects on child well-being: Evidence from Canada. *Journal of Human Capital, 12*, 38–98.

Hagger, M. S., Chatzisarantis, N. L. D., Alberts, H., Anggono, C. O., Batailler, C., Birt, A. R., Brand, R., Brandt, M. J., Brewer, G., Bruyneel, S., Calvillo, D. P., Campbell, W. K., Cannon, P. R., Carlucci, M., Carruth, N. P., Cheung, T., Crowell, A., De Ridder, D. T. D., Dewitte, S., . . . Zwienenberg, M. (2016). A multilab preregistered replication of the ego-depletion effect. *Perspectives on Psychological Science, 11*, 546–573.

Hagger, M. S., Wood, C., Stiff, C., & Chatzisarantis, N. L. D. (2010). Ego depletion and the strength model of self-control: A meta-analysis. *Psychological Bulletin, 136*, 495–525.

Haidt, J. (2007). The new synthesis in moral psychology. *Science, 316*, 998–1001.

Haidt, J., & Kesebir, S. (2010). Morality. In S. Fiske & D. Gilbert (Eds.), *Handbook of social psychology* (5th ed., pp. 797–832). Wiley.

Haines, M. M., Stansfeld, S. A., Job, R. F. S., Berglund, B., & Head, J. (2001). Chronic aircraft noise exposure, stress responses, mental health and cognitive performance in school children. *Psychological Medicine, 31*, 265–277.

Halberstadt, A. G., Cooke, A. N., Garner, P. W., Hughes, S. A., Oertwig, D., & Neupert, S. D. (2020). Racialized emotion recognition accuracy and anger bias of children's faces. *Emotion*. https://doi.org/http://dx.doi.org/10.1037/emo0000756 Advance online publication

Hales, A. H., & Williams, K. D. (2018). Marginalized individuals and extremism: The role of ostracism in openness to extreme groups. *Journal of Social Issues, 74*, 75–92.

Hall, M. L., & Bavelier, D. (2011). Short-term memory stages in sign vs. speech: The source of the serial span discrepancy. *Cognition, 120*, 54–66.

Halsband, U., & Wolf, T. G. (2019). Functional changes in brain activity after hypnosis: Neurobiological mechanisms and application to patients with a specific phobia—limitations and future directions. *International Journal of Clinical and Experimental Hypnosis, 67*, 449–474.

Hamamura, T. (2012). Are cultures becoming individualistic? A cross-temporal comparison of individualism-collectivism in the United States and Japan. *Personality and Social Psychology Review, 16*, 3–24.

Hamann, S. (2012). Mapping discrete and dimensional emotions onto the brain: Controversies and consensus. *Trends in Cognitive Sciences, 16*, 458–466.

Hamer, D. H., Hu, S., Magnuson, V. L., Hu, N., & Pattatucci, A. M. L. (1993). A linkage between DNA markers on the X chromosome and male sexual orientation. *Science, 261*, 321–327.

Hamilton, W. D. (1964). The genetical evolution of social behavior, I and II. *Journal of Theoretical Biology, 7*, 1–52.

Hammen, C. (2003). Mood disorders. In G. Stricker & T. A. Widiger (Eds.), *Handbook of psychology: Clinical psychology* (Vol. 8, pp. 93–118). Wiley.

Hampson, S. E. (2012). Personality processes: Mechanisms by which personality traits "get outside the skin." *Annual Review of Psychology, 63*, 315–339.

Haney, C. (2006). Overcrowding and the situational pathologies of prison. In C. Haney (Ed.), *Reforming punishment: Psychological limits to the pains of imprisonment*. American Psychological Association.

Hansen, C. J., Stevens, L. C., & Coast, J. R. (2001). Exercise duration and mood state: How much is enough to feel better? *Health Psychology, 20*, 267–275.

Hanson, H. M. (1959). Effects of discrimination training on stimulus generalization. *Journal of Experimental Psychology, 58*, 321–334.

Harlow, H. F., Harlow, M. K., & Meyer, D. R. (1971). From thought to therapy: Lessons from a primate laboratory. *American Scientist, 59*, 538–549.

Harlow, H. F., & Zimmerman, R. R. (1959). Affectional responses in the infant monkey. *Science, 130*, 421–432.

Harmon, T. M., Hynan, M. T., & Tyre, T. E. (1990). Improved obstetric outcomes using hypnotic analgesia and skill mastery combined with childbirth education. *Journal of Consulting and Clinical Psychology, 58*, 525–530.

Harper, G. (2001). Cultural influences on diagnosis. *Child & Adolescent Psychiatric Clinics of North America, 10*, 711–728.

Harris, B. (1979). Whatever happened to little Albert? *American Psychologist, 34*, 151–160.

Harris, J. R. (2009). *The nurture assumption: Why children turn out the way they do* (2nd ed.). Free Press.

Hartshorne, H., & May, A. (1928). *Studies in the nature of character: Vol. 1. Studies in deceit*. Macmillan.

Hartup, W. W., & Stevens, N. (1997). Friendships and adaptation in the life course. *Psychological Bulletin, 121*, 355–370.

Harvey, P. D. (2001). Vulnerability to schizophrenia in adulthood. In R. E. Ingram & J. M. Price (Eds.), *Vulnerability to psychopathology: Risk across the lifespan*. Guilford Press.

Hasher, L., Stolzfus, E. R., Zacks, R. T., & Rypma, B. (1991). Age and inhibition. *Journal of Experimental Psychology: Learning, Memory, & Cognition, 17*, 163–169.

Hasher, L., & Zacks, R. R. (1979). Automatic and effortful processes in memory. *Journal of Experimental Psychology: General, 108*, 356–388.

Haslam, N., Loughnan, S., & Perry, G. (2014). Meta-Milgram: An empirical synthesis of the obedience experiments. *PLOS ONE, 9*, 1–9.

Hasselmo, M. E., Rolls, E. T., & Baylis, G. C. (1989). The role of expression and identity in the face-selective responses of neurons in the temporal visual cortex of the monkey. *Behavioral Brain Research, 32*, 203–218.

Hastie, R. (1991). A review from a high place: The field of judgment and decision making as revealed in its current textbooks. *Psychological Science, 2*, 135–138.

Hatfield, E. (1988). Passionate and companionate love. In R. J. Sternberg & M. L. Barnes (Eds.), *The psychology of love* (pp. 191–217). Yale University Press.

Hatfield, E., Pillemer, J. T., O'Brien, M. U., & Le, Y. L. (2008). The endurance of love: Passionate and companionate love in newlywed and long-term marriages. *Interpersona, 2*, 35–64.

Haworth, C. M. A., Wright, M. J., Luciano, M., Martin, N. G., de Geus, E. J. C.., van Beijsterveldt, C. E. M.., Bartels, M., Posthuma, D., Boomsma, D. I., Davis, O. S. P., Kovas, Y., Corley, R. P., Defries, J. C., Hewitt, J. K., Olson, R. K., Rhea, S.-A., Wadsworth, S. J., Iacono, W. G., McGue, M., . . . Plomin, R. (2010). The heritability of general cognitive ability increases linearly from childhood to young adulthood. *Molecular Psychiatry, 15*, 1112–1120.

Hayes, C. (1952). *The ape in our house*. Gollacz.

Hayes, K. J., & Hayes, C. (1951). The intellectual development of a home-raised chimpanzee. *Proceedings of the American Philosophical Society, 95*, 105–109.

He, S., Ma, J., Liu, N., & Yu, X. (2010). Early enriched environment promotes neonatal GABAergic neurotransmission and accelerates synapse maturation. *Journal of Neuroscience, 30*, 7910–7916.

Hearst, E., & Franklin, S. R. (1977). Positive and negative relations between a signal and food: Approach-withdrawal behavior to the signal. *Journal of Experimental Psychology: Animal Behavior Processes, 3*, 37–52.

Heaton, P., & Wallace, G. L. (2004). Annotation: The savant syndrome. *Journal of Child Psychology & Psychiatry, 45*, 899–911.

Hegarty, P. (2017). *A recent history of lesbian and gay psychology*. Routledge.

Hehman, E., Stolier, R. M., Freeman, J. B., Flake, J. K., & Xie, S. Y. (2019). Toward a comprehensive model of face impressions: What we know, what we do not, and paths forward. *Social and Personality Psychology Compass, 13*, e12431. https://doi.org/10.1111/spc3.12431

Heider, F. (1944). Social perception and phenomenal causality. *Psychological Review, 51*, 358–374.

Heijnen, S., Hommel, B., Kibele, A., & Colzato, L. S. (2016). Neuromodulation of aerobic exercise: A review. *Frontiers in Psychology, 6*, 1890.

Heilman, K. M. (2016). Possible brain mechanisms of creativity. *Archives of Clinical Neuropsychology, 31*, 285–296.

Heim, C., Bierl, C., Nisenbaum, R., Wagner, D., & Reeves, W. C. (2004). Regional and prevalence of fatiguing illnesses in the United States before and after the terrorist attacks of September 11, 2001. *Psychosomatic Medicine, 66*, 672–678.

Heindel, J. J., Blumberg, B., Cave, M., Machtinger, R., Mantovani, A., Mendez, M. A., Nadal, A., Palanza, P., Panzica, G., Sargis, R., Vandenberg, L. N., & vom Saal, F. (2017). Metabolism disrupting chemicals and metabolic disorders. *Reproductive Toxicology, 68*, 3–33.

Heine, S. J., & Buchtel, E. E. (2009). Personality: The universal and the culturally specific. *Annual Review of Psychology, 60*, 369–394.

Henderlong, J., & Lepper, M. R. (2002). The effects of praise on children's intrinsic motivation: A review and synthesis. *Psychological Bulletin, 128*, 774–795.

Henderson-King, E. I., & Nisbett, R. E. (1996). Anti-Black prejudice as a function of exposure to the negative behavior of a single Black person. *Journal of Personality and Social Psychology, 71*, 654–664.

Hennessey, B. A., & Amabile, T. M. (2010). Creativity. *Annual Review of Psychology, 61*, 569–598.

Henrich, J., Heine, S. J., & Norenzayan, A. (2010). Beyond WEIRD: Toward a broad-based behavioral science. *Behavioral and Brain Sciences, 33*, 111–135.

Henriksen, M. G., Nordgaard, J., & Jansson, L. B. (2017). Genetics of schizophrenia: Overview of methods, findings, and limitations. *Frontiers in Human Neuroscience, 11*, Article 322.

Herz, R. S., & Cahill, E. D. (1997). Differential use of sensory information in sexual behavior as a function of gender. *Human Nature, 8*, 275–286.

Hess, U. (2017). Emotion categorization. In H. Cohen & C. Lefebvre (Eds.), *Handbook of categorization in cognitive science* (pp. 107–126). Elsevier.

Hetherington, A. W., & Ranson, S. W. (1942). The relation of various hypothalamic lesions to adiposity in the rat. *Journal of Comparative Neurology, 76*, 475–499.

Hetherington, M. M. (1996). Sensory-specific satiety and its importance in meal termination. *Neuroscience and Biobehavioral Reviews, 20*, 113–117.

Hickok, G., & Small, S. L. (2015). *Neurobiology of language.* Academic Press.

Higgs, S. (2016). Cognitive processing of food rewards. *Appetite, 104*, 10–17.

Hilgard, E. R. (1986). *Divided consciousness: Multiple controls in human thought and action* (Rev ed.). Wiley.

Hilgard, E. R. (1987). *Psychology in America: An historical survey.* Harcourt Brace Jovanovich.

Hilgard, E. R. (1992). Dissociation and theories of hypnosis. In E. Fromm & M. Nash (Eds.), *Contemporary hypnosis research* (pp. 69–101). Guilford Press.

Hilgard, J., Engelhardt, C. R., & Rouder, J. N. (2017). Overstated evidence for short-term effects of violent games on affect and behavior: A reanalysis of Anderson et al. (2010). *Psychological Bulletin, 143*, 757–774.

Hilgard, J., Engelhardt, C. R., Rouder, J. N., Segert, I. L., & Bartholow, B. D. (2019). Null effects of game violence, game difficulty, and 2D:4D digit ratio on aggressive behavior. *Psychological Science, 30*, 606–616.

Hill, C. A., Shinsuke, S., Polania, R., Moisa, M., O'Doherty, J. P., & Ruff, C. C. (2017). A causal account of the brain network underlying strategic social behaviour. *Nature Neuroscience, 20*, 1142–1149.

Hill, J., Inder, T., Neil, J., Dierker, D., Harwell, J., & Van Essen, D. V. (2010). Similar patterns of cortical expansion during human development and evolution. *Proceedings of the National Academy of Sciences, 107*, 13135–13140.

Hill, S. K., Griffin, G. B., Miura, T. K., Herbener, E. S., & Sweeney, J. A. (2010). Salience of working-memory maintenance and manipulation deficits in schizophrenia. *Psychological Medicine, 40*, 1979–1986.

Hines, M. (2011). Gender development and the human brain. *Annual Review of Neuroscience, 34*, 69–88.

Hines, M., Pasterski, V., Spencer, D., Neufeld, S., Patalay, P., Hindmarsh, P. C., Hughes, I. A., & Acerini, C. L. (2016). Prenatal and androgen exposure alters girls' responses to information indicating gender-appropriate behaviour. *Proceedings of the Royal Society, 371*, 20150125.

Hintzman, D. L. (1986). "Schema abstraction" in a multiple-trace memory model. *Psychological Review, 93*, 411–428.

Hipes, C., Lucas, J., Phelan, J. C., & White, R. C. (2016). The stigma of mental illness in the labor market. *Social Science Research, 56*, 16–25.

Hirschtritt, M. E., Bloch, M. H., & Mathews, C. A. (2017). Obsessive-compulsive disorder: Advances in diagnosis and treatment. *Clinical Review & Education, 317*, 1358–1367.

Hirsh, I. J., & Watson, C. S. (1996). Auditory psychophysics and perception. *Annual Review of Psychology, 47*, 461–484.

Hirst, W., & Phelps, E. A. (2016). Flashbulb memories. *Current Directions in Psychological Science, 25*, 36–41.

Hobson, C. J., & Delunas, L. (2001). National norms and life-event frequencies for the revised Social Readjustment Rating Scale. *International Journal of Stress Management, 8*, 299–314.

Hobson, J. A., & McCarley, R. W. (1977). The brain as a dream state generator: An activation-synthesis hypothesis of the dream process. *American Journal of Psychiatry, 134*, 1335–1348.

Hobson, J. A., Pace-Schott, E. F., & Stickgold, R. (2000). Dreaming and the brain: Toward a cognitive neuroscience of conscious states. *Behavioral and Brain Sciences, 23*, 793–842.

Hobson, R. P. (2016). *Brief psychoanalytic therapy.* Oxford University Press.

Hodges, J., & Tizard, B. (1989). IQ and behavioral adjustment of ex-institutional adolescents. *Journal of Child Psychology and Psychiatry, 30*, 53–75.

Hodges, S., Berry, E., & Wood, K. (2011). SenseCam: A wearable camera that stimulates and rehabilitates autobiographical memory. *Memory, 19*, 685–596.

Hoffman, D. D. (2016). The interface theory of perception. *Current Directions in Psychological Science, 25*, 157–161.

Hoffman, M. L. (1986). Affect, cognition, motivation. In R. M. Sorrentino & E. T. Higgins (Eds.), *Handbook of motivation and cognition: Foundations of social behavior* (pp. 244–280). Guilford Press.

Hohmann, G. W. (1966). Some effects of spinal cord lesions on experienced emotional feelings. *Psychophysiology, 3*, 143–156.

Holmes, D. S. (1987). The influence of meditation versus rest on physiological arousal: A second examination. In M. A. West (Ed.), *The psychology of meditation* (pp. 81–103). Clarendon Press.

Holmes, T. H., & Rahe, R. H. (1967). The Social Readjustment Rating Scale. *Journal of Psychosomatic Research, 11*, 213–218.

Holt, E. B. (1931). *Animal drive and the learning process: An essay toward radical empiricism.* Holt.

Holt-Lunstad, J., Smith, T. B., Baker, M., Harris, T., & Stephenson, D. (2015). Loneliness and social isolation as risk factors for mortality: A meta-analytic review. *Perspectives on Psychological Science, 10*, 227–237.

Hoogman, M., Muetzel, R., Guimaraes, J. P., Shumskaya, E., Mennes, M., Zwiers, M. P., Jahanshad, N., Sudre, G., Wolfers, T., Earl, E. A., Soliva Vila, J. C., Vives-Gilabert, Y., Khadka, S., Novotny, S. E., Hartman, C. A., Heslenfeld, D. J., Schweren, L. J. S., Ambrosino, S., Oranje, B., . . . Franke, B. (2019). Brain imagining of the cortex in ADHD: A coordinated analysis of large-scale clinical and population-based samples. *American Journal of Psychiatry*, *176*, 531–542.

Hopkins, B. (1991). Facilitating early motor development: An intra-cultural study of West Indian mothers and their infants living in Britain. In J. K. Nugent, B. M. Lester, & T. B. Brazelton (Eds.), *The cultural context of infancy: Vol. 2. Multicultural and interdisciplinary approaches to parent-infant relations* (pp. 93–143). Ablex.

Horn, J. L. (1976). Human abilities: A review of research and theory in the early 1970s. *Annual Review of Psychology*, *27*, 437–485.

Horn, J. L., & Cattell, R. B. (1966). Refinement and test of the theory of fluid and crystallized ability intelligences. *Journal of Educational Psychology*, *57*, 253–270.

Horney, K. (1945). *Our inner conflicts: A constructive theory of neurosis*. Norton.

Horney, K. (1967). *Feminine psychology*. Norton.

Horwitz, A. G., Opperman, K. J., Burnside, A., Ghazuiddin, N., & King, C. A. (2016). Youth suicide. In M. R. Korin (Ed.), *Health promotion for children and adolescents*. Springer.

Houle, M., McGrath, P. A., Moran, G., & Garrett, O. J. (1988). The efficacy of hypnosis- and relaxation-induced analgesia on two dimensions of pain for cold pressor and electrical tooth pulp stimulation. *Pain*, *33*, 241–251.

Howes, O., McCutchen, R., & Stone, J. (2015). Glutamate and dopamine in schizophrenia: An update for the 21st century. *Journal of Psychopharmacology*, *29*, 97–115.

Hser, Y., Anglin, M. D., & Powers, K. (1993). A 24-year follow-up of California narcotics addicts. *Archives of General Psychiatry*, *50*, 577–584.

Hu, Y., Chu, X., Urosevich, T. G., Hoffman, S. N., Kirchner, H. L., Adams, R. E., Dugan, R. J., Boscarino, J. J., Shi, W., Withey, C. A., Figley, C. R., & Boscarino, J. A. (2020). Predictors of current DSM-5 PTSD diagnosis and symptom severity among deployed veterans: Significance of predisposition, stress exposure, and genetics. *Neuropsychiatric Disease and Treatment*, *16*, 43–54.

Huang, C. (2011). Achievement goals and achievement emotions: A meta-analysis. *Educational Psychology Review*, *23*, 359–388.

Hubbel, J. C. (1990, January). Animal rights war on medicine. *Reader's Digest*, 70–76.

Hubel, D. H., & Wiesel, T. N. (1962). Receptive fields, binocular interaction, and functional architecture in the cat's visual cortex. *Journal of Physiology*, *160*, 106–154.

Hubel, D. H., & Wiesel, T. N. (1979, September). Brain mechanisms and vision. *Scientific American*, *241*, 150–162.

Hugdahl, K., & Sommer, I. E. (2018). Auditory verbal hallucinations in schizophrenia from a levels of explanation perspective. *Schizophrenia Bulletin*, *44*, 234–241.

Hull, C. L. (1943). *Principles of behavior*. Appleton-Century.

Hulleman, C. S., Schrager, S. M., Bodmann, S. M., & Harackiewicz, J. M. (2010). A meta-analytic review of achievement goal measures: Different labels for the same constructs or different constructs with similar labels? *Psychological Bulletin*, *136*, 422–449.

Hunnicutt, C. P., & Newman, I. A. (1993). Adolescent dieting practices and nutrition knowledge. *Health Values*, *17*, 35–40.

Hunt, E. (2011). *Human intelligence*. Cambridge University Press.

Hunt, E., & Carlson, J. (2007). Considerations relating to the study of group differences in intelligence. *Perspectives on Psychological Science*, *2*, 194–213.

Hunt, R. R., & McDaniel, M. A. (1993). The enigma of organization and distinctiveness. *Journal of Memory and Language*, *32*, 421–445.

Huntjens, R. J. C., Peters, M. L., Woertman, L., van der Hart, O., & Postma, A. (2007). Memory transfer for emotionally valenced words between identities in dissociative identity disorder. *Behavior Research and Therapy*, *45*, 775–789.

Hurvich, L. M., & Jameson, D. (1951). The binocular fusion of yellow in relation to color theories. *Science*, *114*, 199–202.

Hyde, J. S. (2014). Gender similarities and differences. *Annual Review of Psychology*, *65*, 373–398.

Hyde, J. S. (2016). Sex and cognition: gender and cognitive functions. *Current Opinion in Neurobiology*, *38*, 53–56.

Iacoboni, M. (2009). Imitation, empathy, and mirror neurons. *Annual Review of Psychology*, *60*, 653–670.

Iani, C., Ricci, F., Gherri, E., & Rubichi, S. (2006). Hypnotic suggestion modulates cognitive conflict. *Psychological Science*, *17*, 721–727.

Iber, C., Ancoli-Israel, S., Chesson, A., & Quan, S. F. (2007). *The AASM manual for the scoring of sleep and associated events*. American Academy of Sleep Medicine.

Ickes, W., Holloway, R., Stinson, L. L., & Hoodenpyle, T. G. (2006). Self-monitoring in social interaction: The centrality of self-affect. *Journal of Personality*, *74*, 659–684.

Inoue-Nakamura, N., & Matsuzawa, T. (1997). Development of stone tool use by wild chimpanzees (*Pan troglodytes*). *Journal of Comparative Psychology*, *111*, 159–713.

Ioannidis, J. P. A. (2005). Why most published research findings are false. *PLoS Med*, *2*, 696–701.

Irwin, M. R. (2015, January 3). Why sleep is important for health: A psychoneuroimmunology perspective. *Annual Review of Psychology*, *66*, 143–172. doi: 10.1146/annurev-psych-010213-115205

Iverson, S. D., & Iverson, L. L. (2007). Dopamine: 50 years in perspective. *Trends in Neurosciences*, *30*, 188–193.

Izard, C. E. (1994). Innate and universal facial expressions: Evidence from developmental and cross-cultural research. *Psychological Bulletin*, *115*, 288–299.

Izard, C. E. (2007). Basic emotions, natural kinds, emotion schemas, and a new paradigm. *Perspectives on Psychological Science*, *2*, 260–280.

Jack, F., & Hayne, H. (2010). Childhood amnesia: Empirical evidence for a two-stage phenomenon. *Memory*, *18*, 831–844.

Jack, R. E., & Schyns, P. G. (2017). Towards a social psychophysics of face communication. *Annual Review of Psychology*, *68*, 26–297.

Jack, R. E., Sun, W., Delis, I., Garrod, O. G. B., & Schyns, P. G. (2016). Four not six: Revealing culturally common facial expressions of emotion. *Journal of Experimental Psychology: General*, *145*, 708–730.

Jackendoff, R., & Pinker, S. (2005). The nature of the language faculty and its implications for evolution of language (Reply to Fitch, Hauser, and Chomsky). *Cognition, 97*, 211–225.

Jacoby, L. L., & Witherspoon, D. (1982). Remembering without awareness. *Canadian Journal of Psychology, 36*, 300–324.

Jakubovski, E., Johnson, J. A., Nasir, M., Muller-Vahl, K., & Bloch, M. H. (2019). Systematic review and meta-analysis: Dose-response curve of SSRIs and SNRIs in anxiety disorders. *Depression & Anxiety, 36*, 198–212.

Jalal, B., & Ramachandran, V. S. (2017). "I feel your disgust and relief": Can the action understanding system (mirror neuron system) be recruited to induce disgust and relief from contamination vicariously, in individuals with obsessive-compulsive disorder symptoms? *Neurocase, 23*, 31–35.

Jamal, A., Phillips, E., Gentzke, A. S., Homa, D. M., Babb, S. D., King, B. A., & Neff, L. J. (2018). Current cigarette smoking among adults—United States, 2016. *Morbidity and Mortality Weekly Report, 67*(2), 53–59.

James, D. K. (2010). Fetal learning: A critical review. *Infant and Child Development, 19*, 45–54.

James, W. (1884). Some omissions of introspective psychology. *Mind, 9*, 1–26.

James, W. (1890). *The principles of psychology*. Holt.

James, W. (1894). The physical basis of emotion. *Psychological Review, 1*, 516–529.

Jamet, É., Gonthier, C., Cojean, S., & Colliot, T. (2020, May). Does multitasking in the classroom affect learning outcomes? *Computers in Human Behavior, 106*. doi: 10.1016/j.chb.2020.106264

Janis, I. L. (1982). *Victims of groupthink* (2nd ed.). Houghton Mifflin.

Janis, I. L. (1989). *Crucial decisions: Leadership in policymaking and crisis management*. Free Press.

Jarvis, G. E., Iyer, S. N., Andermann, L., & Fung, K. P. (2020). Culture and psychosis in clinical practice. In J. C. Badcock & G. Paulik (Eds.), *A clinical introduction to psychosis*. Elsevier.

Jason, L. A., Glantsman, O., O'Brien, J., & Ramian, K. (2019). Introduction to the field of community psychology. In L. A. Jason, O. Glantsman, J. O'Brien, & K. Ramian (Eds.), *Introduction to community psychology: Becoming an agent of change*. https://press.rebus.community/introductiontocommunitypsychology/chapter/intro-to-community-psychology/

Jeffry, K. J. (2018). The hippocampus: From memory, to map, to memory map. *Trends in Neurosciences, 41*, 64–66.

Jenkins, H. M., Barrera, F. J., Ireland, C., & Woodside, B. (1978). Signal-centered action patterns of dogs in appetitive classical conditioning. *Learning and Motivation, 9*, 272–296.

Jenkins, J. G., & Dallenbach, K. M. (1924). Obliviscence during sleep and waking. *American Journal of Psychology, 35*, 605–612.

Jensen, J. P., Bergin, A. E., & Greaves, D. W. (1990). The meaning of eclecticism: New survey and analysis of components. *Professional Psychology: Research and Practice, 21*, 124–130.

Johnson, J. D., Noel, N. E., & Sutter-Hernandez, J. (2000). Alcohol and male acceptance of sexual aggression: The role of perceptual ambiguity. *Journal of Applied Social Psychology, 30*, 1186–1200.

Johnson, M. H., Dziurawiec, S., Ellis, H., & Morton, J. (1991). Newborns' preferential tracking of face-like stimuli and its subsequent decline. *Cognition, 40*, 1–19.

Johnson, R. C., McClearn, C. G., Yuen, S., Nagoshi, C. T., Ahern, F. M., & Cole, R. E. (1985). Galton's data a century later. *American Psychologist, 40*, 875–892.

Johnson, S. P. (1997). Young infants' perception of object unity: Implications for the development of attentional and cognitive skills. *Current Directions in Psychological Science, 6*, 5–11.

Joiner, T. E., Jr., Steer, R. A., Abramson, L. Y., Alloy, L. B., Metalsky, G. I., & Schmidt, N. B. (2001). Hopelessness depression as a distinct dimension of depressive symptoms among clinical and non-clinical samples. *Behaviour Research & Therapy, 39*, 523–536.

Jones, B. C., DeBruine, L. M., Little, A. C., Burriss, R. P., & Feinberg, D. R. (2007). Social transmission of face preference among humans. *Proceedings of the Royal Society B, 274*, 899–903.

Jones, E. E. (1964). *Ingratiation*. Appleton-Century-Crofts.

Jones, E. E. (1990). *Interpersonal perception*. Freeman.

Jones, E. E., & Davis, K. E. (1965). A theory of correspondent inferences: From acts to dispositions. In L. Berkowitz (Ed.), *Advances in experimental social psychology* (Vol. 2, pp. 219–266). Academic Press.

Jones, E. E., & Harris, V. A. (1967). The attribution of attitudes. *Journal of Experimental Social Psychology, 3*, 1–24.

Jones, E. R., & Childers, R. L. (1993). *Contemporary college physics* (2nd ed.). Addison-Wesley.

Jones, G. (2003). Testing two cognitive theories of insight. *Journal of Experimental Psychology: Learning, Memory, and Cognition, 29*, 1017–1027.

Jones, M. C. (1924). A laboratory study of fear: The case of Peter. *Pedagogical Seminary, 31*, 308–315.

Jones, R. T. (1971). Tetrahydrocannabinol and the marijuana-induced social "high" or the effects on the mind of marijuana. In A. J. Singer (Ed.), Marijuana: Chemistry, pharmacology, and patterns of social use. *Annals of the New York Academy of Sciences, 191*, 155–165.

Jonides, J., Lewis, R. L., Nee, D. E., Lustig, C. A., Berman, M. G., & Moore, K. S. (2008). The mind and brain of short-term memory. *Annual Review of Psychology, 59*, 193–224.

Jung, C. G. (1923). *Psychological types*. Pantheon Books.

Kahneman, D. (2011). *Thinking, fast and slow*. Farrar, Straus, & Giroux.

Kahneman, D., Slovic, P., & Tversky, A. (Eds.). (1982). *Judgment under uncertainty: Heuristics and biases*. Cambridge University Press.

Kail, R. (2008). Speed of processing in childhood and adolescence: Nature, consequences, and implications for understanding atypical development. In J. DeLuca & J. H. Kalmar (Eds.), *Information processing speed in clinical populations* (pp. 101–123). Taylor & Francis.

Kail, R., & Salthouse, T. A. (1994). Processing speed as a mental capacity. *Acta Psychologica, 86*, 199–225.

Kalick, S. M., Zebrowitz, L. A., Langlois, J. H., & Johnson, R. M. (1998). Does human facial attractiveness honestly advertise health? Longitudinal data on an evolutionary question. *Psychological Science, 9*, 8–13.

Kalinoski, Z. T., Steele-Johnson, D., Peyton, E. J., Leas, K. A., Steinke, J., & Bowling, N. A. (2013). A meta-analytic evaluation of diversity training outcomes. *Journal of Organizational Behavior, 34*, 1076–1104.

Kaltiala-Heino, R., & Lindberg, N. (2019, January). Gender identities in adolescent population: Methodological issues and prevalence across age groups. *European Psychiatry*, *55*, 61–66. doi: 10.1016/j.eurpsy.2018.09.003

Kamen-Siegel, L., Rodin, J., Seligman, M. E. P., & Dwyer, J. (1991). Explanatory style and cell-mediated immunity in elderly men and women. *Health Psychology*, *10*, 229–235.

Kamil, A. C., & Balda, R. P. (1990). Differential memory for different cache sites by Clark's nutcrackers (*Nucifraga columbiana*). *Journal of Experimental Psychology: Animal Behavior Processes*, *16*, 162–168.

Kamiloğllu, R., Fischer, A. & Sauter, D. (2020) Good vibrations: A review of vocal expressions of positive emotions. *Psychonomic Bulletin & Review*, *27*, 237–265.

Kamin, L. J. (1968). "Attention-like" processes in classical conditioning. In M. R. Jones (Ed.), *Miami symposium on the prediction of behavior: Aversive stimulation* (pp. 9–33). University of Miami Press.

Kandimalla, R., & Reddy, P. H. (2017). Therapeutics of neurotransmitters in Alzheimer's disease. *Journal of Alzheimer's Disease*, *57*, 1049–1069.

Kanner, A. D., Coyne, J. C., Schaefer, C., & Lazarus, R. S. (1981). Comparison of two modes of stress measurement: Daily hassles and uplifts versus major life events. *Journal of Behavioral Medicine*, *4*, 1–39.

Kanoski, S. E., Fortin, S. M., Ricks, K. M., & Grill, H. J. (2013). Ghrelin signaling in the ventral hippocampus stimulates learned and motivational aspects of feeding via PI3K-Akt signaling. *Biological Psychiatry*, *73*, 915–923.

Kaplan, R. M., & Saccuzzo, D. P. (2005). *Psychological testing: Principles, applications, and issues* (6th ed.). Wadsworth.

Kar, K. K., & Sarkar, S. (2015). Dhat syndrome: Evolution of concept, current understanding, and need of an integrated approach. *Journal of Human Reproductive Science*, *8*, 130–134.

Karanian, J. M., & Slotnick, S. D. (2018). Confident false memories for spatial location are mediated by V1. *Cognitive Neuroscience*, *9*, 139–150.

Karau, S. J., & Hart, J. W. (1998). Group cohesiveness and social loafing: Effects of a social interaction manipulation on individual motivation within groups. *Group Dynamics*, *2*, 185–191.

Karau, S. J., & Williams, K. D. (1993). Social loafing: A meta-analytic review and theoretical integration. *Journal of Personality and Social Psychology*, *65*, 681–706.

Karpicke, J. D. (2017). Retrieval-based learning: A decade of progress. In J. T. Wixted (Ed.), *Learning and memory: A comprehensive reference: Vol. 2. Cognitive psychology of memory* (J. H. Byrne, Series ed., pp. 487–514). Academic Press.

Karpicke, J. D., & Roediger, H. L., III. (2008). The critical importance of retrieval for learning. *Science*, *319*, 966–968.

Karpinski, R. I., Kinase Kolb, A. M., Tetreault, N. A., & Borowski, T. B. (2018). High intelligence: A risk factor for psychological and physiological overexcitabilities. *Intelligence*, *66*, 8–23.

Kaufman, A. S., & Horn, J. L. (1996). Age changes on tests of fluid and crystallized ability for women and men on the Kaufman Adolescent and Adult Intelligence Test (KAIT) at ages 17–94 years. *Archives of Clinical Neuropsychology*, *11*, 97–121.

Kaufman, J. C. (2015). Why creativity isn't in IQ tests, why it matters, and why it won't change anytime soon. *Journal of Intelligence*, *3*, 59–72.

Kavanau, J. L. (2002). REM and NREM sleep as natural accompaniments of the evolution of warm-bloodedness. *Neuroscience and Biobehavioral Reviews*, *26*, 889–906.

Kazda, L., Bell, K., Thomas, R., McGeechan, K., & Barratt, A. (2019). Evidence of potential overdiagnosis and overtreatment of attention deficit hyperactivity disorder (ADHD) in children and adolescents: Protocol for a scoping review. *British Medical Journal Open*, *9*, e032327.

Kazdin, A. E. (2007). Mediators and mechanisms of change in psychotherapy research. *Annual Review of Clinical Psychology*, *3*, 1–27.

Kee, K. H. (2005). Can only intelligent people be creative? A meta-analysis. *Journal of Secondary Gifted Education*, *16*, 57–66.

Keel, P. K., Brown, T. A., Holland, L. A., & Bodell, L. P. (2012). Empirical classification of eating disorders. *Annual Review of Clinical Psychology*, *8*, 381–404.

Keel, P. K., & Klump, K. L. (2003). Are eating disorder culture-bound syndromes? Implications for conceptualizing their etiology. *Psychological Bulletin*, *129*, 747–769.

Keesey, R. E., & Powley, T. L. (1975). Hypothalamic regulation of body weight. *American Scientist*, *63*, 558–565.

Keith, K. D. (2019). *Cross-cultural psychology* (2nd ed.). Wiley.

Kelley, H. H. (1983). Love and commitment. In H. H. Kelley, E. Berscheid, A. Christensen, J. H. Harvey, T. L. Huston, G. Levinger, E. McClintock, L. A. Peplau, & D. R. Peterson (Eds.), *Close relationships* (pp. 265–314). Freeman.

Kelley, H. H. (1987). *Attribution in social interaction*. In E. E. Jones, D. E. Kanouse, H. H. Kelley, R. E. Nisbett, S. Valins, & B. Weiner (Eds.), *Attribution: Perceiving the causes of behavior* (pp. 1–26). Erlbaum.

Kellogg, W. N., & Kellogg, L. A. (1933). *The ape and the child*. McGraw-Hill.

Kennedy, L., & Parker, S. H. (2019). Biofeedback as a stress management tool: A systematic review. *Cognition, Technology, & Work*, *21*, 161–190.

Kenrick, D. T. (2011). *Sex, murder, and the meaning of life: A psychologist investigates how evolution, cognition, and complexity are revolutionizing our view of human nature*. Basic Books.

Kenrick, D. T., & Funder, D. C. (1988). Profiting from controversy: Lessons of the person-situation debate. *American Psychologist*, *43*, 23–34.

Kenrick, D. T., Griskevivius, V., Neuberg, S. L., & Schaller, M. (2010). Renovating the pyramid of needs: Contemporary extensions built upon ancient foundations. *Perspectives on Psychological Science*, *5*, 292–314.

Kenrick, D. T., Gutierres, S. E., & Goldberg, L. (1989). Influence of erotica on judgments of strangers and mates. *Journal of Experimental Social Psychology*, *25*, 159–167.

Kerns, R. D., Sellinger, J., & Goodin, B. R. (2011). Psychological treatment of chronic pain. *Annual Review of Clinical Psychology*, *7*, 411–434.

Kershaw, T. C., & Ohlsson, S. (2004). Multiple causes of difficulty in insight: The case of the nine-dot problem. *Journal of Experimental Psychology: Learning, Memory, and Cognition*, *30*, 3–13.

Kessler, R. C., McGonagle, K. A., Shanyang, Z., Nelson, C. B., Hughes, M., Eshleman, S., Wittchen, H., & Kendler, K. S. (1994). Lifetime and 12-month prevalence of DSM-III-R psychiatric disorders in the United States. *Archives of General Psychiatry*, *51*, 8–19.

Key, W. B. (1973). *Subliminal seduction*. Prentice-Hall.

Keysar, B., Barr, D. J., Balin, A., & Paekm, T. S. (1998). Definite reference and mutual knowledge: Process models of common ground in comprehension. *Journal of Memory and Language*, *39*, 1–20.

Kiecolt-Glaser, J. K., Garner, W., Speicher, C., Penn, G. M., Holliday, J., & Glaser, R. (1984). Psychosocial modifiers of immunocompetence in medical students. *Psychosomatic Medicine*, *46*(1), 7–14.

Kiecolt-Glaser, J. K., Gouin, J., & Hantsoo, L. (2010). Close relationships, inflammation, and health. *Neuroscience Biobehavioral Review*, *35*, 33–38.

Kihlstrom, J. (1985). Hypnosis. *Annual Review of Psychology*, *36*, 385–418.

Kihlstrom, J., & McConkey, K. M. (1990). William James and hypnosis: A centennial reflection. *Psychological Science*, *1*, 174–178.

Kim, B. J., Williams, L., & Gill, D. L. (2003). A cross-cultural study of achievement orientation and intrinsic motivation in young USA and Korean athletes. *International Journal of Sport Psychology*, *34*, 168–184.

Kim, E. S., Hagan, K. A., Grodstein, F., DeMeo, D. L., De Vivo, I., & Kubzansky, L. D. (2017). Optimism and cause-specific mortality: A prospective cohort study. *American Journal of Epidemiology*, *185*, 21– 29.

Kim, I., Hong, S. W., Shevell, S. K., & Shim, W. M. (2020). Neural representations of perceptual color experience in the human ventral visual pathway. *Proceedings of the National Academy of Sciences*, *117*, 13145–13150. www.pnas.org/cgi/doi/10.1073/pnas.1911041117

Kimble, G. A. (1993). A modest proposal for a minor revolution in the language of psychology. *Psychological Science*, *4*, 253–255.

Kimmel, A. J. (2011). Deception in research. In S. J. Knapp (Ed.), *APA handbook of ethics in psychology: Vol. 2. Practice, teaching, and research* (pp. 401–421). American Psychological Association.

Kimura, D. (1992, September). Sex differences in the brain. *Scientific American*, *267*, 118–125.

Kirk, K. M., Bailey, J. M., Dunne, M. P., & Martin, N. G. (2000). Measurement models for sexual orientation in a community twin sample. *Behavior Genetics*, *30*, 345–356.

Kirmayer, L. J., Looper, K. J., & Taillefer, S. (2003). Somatoform disorders. In M. Hersen & S. M. Turner (Eds.), *Adult psychopathology and diagnosis* (4th ed., pp. 420–475). Wiley.

Kirsch, I. (2010). *The emperor's new drugs: Exploding the antidepressant myth*. Basic Books.

Kitayama, S., & Salvador, C. E. (2017). Culture embrained: Going beyond the nature-nurture dichotomy. *Perspectives on Psychological Science*, *12*, 841–854.

Klatzky, R. L., Lederman, S. J., & Metzger, V. A. (1985). Identifying objects by touch: An "expert system." *Perception & Psychophysics*, *37*, 299–302.

Kluft, R. P. (1991). Multiple personality disorder. In A. Tasman & S. M. Goldfinger (Eds.), *Review of psychiatry* (Vol. 10). American Psychiatric Press.

Knapp, S. J. (Eds.). (2012). *APA handbook of ethics in psychology*. American Psychological Association.

Koç, V., & Kafa, G. (2019). Cross-cultural research on psychotherapy: The need for a change. *Journal of Cross-Cultural Psychology*, *50*, 100–115.

Koch, C., & Tsuchiya, N. (2007) Attention and consciousness: Two distinct brain processes. *Trends in Cognitive Science*, *11*(1), 16–22.

Kochel, K. P., Bagwell, C. L., Ladd, G. W., & Rudolph, K. D. (2017, July). Do positive peer relations mitigate transactions between depressive symptoms and peer victimization in adolescence? *Journal of Applied Developmental Psychology*, *51*, 44–54. doi: 10.1016/j.appdev.2017.04.003

Koenig, L., & Ro, T. (2019). Dissociations of conscious and unconscious perception in TMS-induced blindsight. *Neuropsychologica*, *128*, 215–222.

Kohlberg, L. (1963). The development of children's orientations toward a moral order: I. Sequence in the development of moral thought. *Vita Humana*, *6*, 11–33.

Kohlberg, L. (1969). Stage and sequence: The cognitive-developmental approach to socialization. In D. A. Goslin (Ed.), *Handbook of socialization theory and research* (pp. 347–480). Rand McNally.

Kohlberg, L. (1986). *The psychology of moral development*. Harper & Row.

Köhler, W. (1925). *The mentality of apes*. Pelican.

Kolb, B., & Whishaw, I. Q. (2009). *Fundamentals of human neuropsychology* (6th ed.). Worth.

Komori, M., Kawamura, S., & Ishihara, S. (2009). Averageness or symmetry: Which is more important for facial attractiveness? *Acta Psychologia*, *131*, 136–142.

Koolhaas, J. M., Bartolomucci, A., Buwalda, B., de Boer, S. F., Flügge, G., Korte, S. M., Meerlo, P., Murison, R., Olivier, B., Palanza, P., Richter-Levin, G., Sgoifo, A., Steimer, T., Stiedl, O., van Dijk, G., Wöhr, M., & Fuchs, E. (2011). Stress revisited: A critical evaluation of the stress concept. *Neuroscience & Biobehavioral Reviews*, *35*, 1291–1301.

Koppel, J., & Berntsen, D. (2014). The cultural life script as cognitive schema: How the life script shapes memory for fictional life stories. *Memory*, *22*, 949–971.

Koppel, J., & Rubin, D. C. (2016). Recent advances in understanding the reminiscence bump: The importance of cues in guiding recall from autobiographical memory. *Current Directions in Psychological Science*, *25*, 135–140.

Korte, S. M., Koolhaas, J. M., Wingfield, J. C., & McEwen, B. S. (2005). The Darwinian concept of stress: Benefits of allostatsis and costs of allostatic load and the trade-offs in health and disease. *Neuroscience and Biobehavioral Reviews*, *29*, 3–38.

Kosinski, M., Wang, Y., Lakkaraju, H., & Leskovec, J. (2016). Mining big data to extract patterns and predict real-life outcomes. *Psychological Methods*, *21*, 493–506.

Kosslyn, S. M. (1983). *Ghosts in the mind's machine: Creating and using images in the brain*. Horizon.

Kotov, R., Games, W., Schmidt, F., & Watson, D. (2010). Linking "Big" personality traits to anxiety, depressive, and substance use disorders: A meta-analysis. *Psychological Bulletin*, *136*, 768–821.

Kounios, J., & Beeman, M. (2014). The cognitive neuroscience of insight. *Annual Review of Psychology*, *65*, 71–93.

Kovacs, K., & Conway, A. R. A. (2016). Process overlap theory A unified account of the general factor of intelligence. *Psychological Inquiry*, *27*, 151–177.

Kowalski, T. J. (2004). The future of genetic research on appetitive behavior. *Appetite*, *42*, 11–14.

Kraemer, D. J., Macrae, C. N., Green, A. E., & Kelley, W. M. (2005). Sounds of silence activates auditory cortex. *Nature*, *434*, 158.

Kramer, P. D. (1993). *Listening to Prozac*. Viking.

Kretch, K. S., & Adolph, K. E. (2017). The organization of exploratory behaviors in infant locomotor planning. *Developmental Science*, *20*(4), e12421. doi: 10.1111/desc.12421

Kringelbach, M. L., & Berridge, K. C. (2017). Neuroscience of reward, motivation, and drive. *Recent Developments in Neuroscience Research on Human Motivation*, *19*, 23–35.

Krug, E. G., Kresnow, M., Peddicord, J., Dahlberg, L., Powell, K., Crosby, A., & Annest, J. (1998). Suicide after natural disasters. *New England Journal of Medicine*, *338*, 373–378.

Kübler-Ross, E. (1969). *On death and dying*. Macmillan.

Kübler-Ross, E. (1974). *Questions and answers on death and dying*. Macmillan.

Kubzansky, L. D., & Adler, G. K. (2010). Aldosterone: A forgotten mediator of the relationship between psychological stress and heart disease. *Neuroscience Biobehavioral Review*, *34*, 80–86.

Kunkel, N. R., & Hezlett, S. A. (2010). Fact and fiction in cognitive ability testing for admissions and hiring decisions. *Current Directions in Psychological Science*, *19*, 339–345.

Kuo, S. S.., & Pogue-Geile, M. F.. (2019). Variation in fourteen brain structure volumes in schizophrenia: A comprehensive meta-analysis of 246 studies. *Neuroscience & Biobehavioral Reviews*, *98*, 85–94.

Kupper, N., & Denollet, J. (2018). Type D personality as a risk factor in coronary heart disease: A review of current evidence. *Current Cardiology Reports*, *20*(11), 104.

Kurlansik, S. L., & Maffei, M. S. (2016). Somatic symptom disorder. *American Family Physician*, *93*, 49–55.

Kurth, F., Spencer, D., Hines, M., & Luders, E. (2018). Sex differences in associations between spatial ability and corpus callosum morphology. *Journal of Neuroscience Research*, *96*, 1380–1387.

Kurtz, M. M., & Mueser, K. T. (2008). A meta-analysis of controlled research on social skills training for schizophrenia. *Journal of Consulting and Clinical Psychology*, *76*, 491–504.

Labov, W. (1973). The boundaries of words and their meanings. In C. J. N. Bailey & R. W. Shiny (Eds.), *New ways of analyzing variation in English* (Vol. 1, pp. 340–371). Georgetown University Press.

Lacagnina, A. F., Brockway, E. T., Crovetti, C. R., Shue, F., McCarty, M. J., Sattler, K. P., Lim, S. C., Leal Santos, S., Denny, C. A., & Drew, M. R. (2019). Distinct hippocampal engrams control extinction and relapse of fear memory. *Nature Neuroscience*, *22*, 753–761.

Lahey, R., & Khan, S. S. (2018). Trends in obesity and risk of cardiovascular disease. *Current Epidemiology Reports*, *5*, 243–251.

Laiacona, M., Barbarotto, R., & Capitani, E. (2006). Human evolution and the brain representation of semantic knowledge: Is there a role for sex differences? *Evolution and Human Behavior*, *27*, 158–168.

Lakoff, G. (1987). *Women, fire, and dangerous things: What categories reveal about the human mind*. University of Chicago Press.

Lamb, M. E., Ketterlinus, R. D., & Fracasso, M. P. (1992). Parent-child relationships. In M. H. Bornstein & M. E. Lamb (Eds.), *Developmental psychology: An advanced textbook* (pp. 465–518). Erlbaum.

Lambert, A. J., Good, K. S., & Kirk, I. J. (2010). Testing the repression hypothesis: Effects of emotional valence on memory suppression in the think–no think task. *Consciousness and Cognition*, *19*, 281–293.

Lambert, M. J. (2005). Early response in psychotherapy: Further evidence for the importance of common factors rather than "placebo effects." *Journal of Clinical Psychology*, *61*, 855–869.

Lambert, M. J., & Bergin, A. E. (1994). The effectiveness of psychotherapy. In A. E. Bergin & S. L. Garfield (Eds.), *Handbook of psychotherapy and behavior change* (4th ed.). Wiley.

Lambert, M. J., & Ogles, B. M. (2004). The efficacy and effectiveness of psychotherapy. In M. J. Lambert (Ed.), *Bergin and Garfield's handbook of psychotherapy and behavior change*. Wiley.

Landauer, T. K. (1962). Rate of implicit speech. *Perceptual and Motor Skills*, *15*, 646.

Lang, P. J. (1994). The varieties of emotional experience: A meditation on James-Lange theory. *Psychological Review*, *101*, 211–221.

Lang, S., Kanngieser, N., Jaskowski, P., Haider, H., Rose, M., & Verleger, R. (2006). Precursors of insight in event-related brain potentials. *Journal of Cognitive Neuroscience*, *18*, 2152–2166.

Lange, F., & Eggert, F. (2014). Sweet delusion: Glucose drinks fail to counteract ego depletion. *Appetite*, *75*, 54–63.

Langer, E. J. (1989). *Mindfulness*. Addison-Wesley.

Langer, E. J., & Abelson, R. P. (1974). A patient by any other name: Clinician group differences in labeling bias. *Journal of Consulting and Clinical Psychology*, *42*, 4–9.

Langlois, F., Langlois, M., Carpentier, A. C., Brown, C., Lemieux, S., & Hivert, M. (2011). Ghrelin levels are associated with hunger as measured by the Three-Factor Eating Questionnaire in healthy young adults. *Physiology & Behavior*, *104*, 373–377.

Langlois, J. H., Kalakanis, L., Rubenstein, A. J., Larson, A., Hallamm, M., & Smoot, M. (2000). Maxims or myths of beauty? A meta-analytic and theoretical review. *Psychological Bulletin*, *126*, 390–423.

Langlois, J. H., & Roggman, L. A. (1990). Attractive faces are only average. *Psychological Science*, *1*, 115–121.

Langlois, J. H., Roggman, L. A., Casey, R. J., Ritter, J. M., Rieser-Danner, L. A., & Jenkins, V. Y. (1987). Infant preferences for attractive faces: Rudiments of a stereotype? *Developmental Psychology*, *23*, 363–369.

Langlois, J. H., Roggman, L. A., & Musselman, L. (1994). What is average and what is not average about attractive faces? *Psychological Science*, *5*, 214–220.

Laprelle, J., Hoyle, R. H., Insko, C. A., & Bernthal, P. (1990). Interpersonal attraction and descriptions of the traits of others: Ideal similarity, self similarity, and liking. *Journal of Research in Personality*, *24*, 216–240.

Larose, H., & Standing, L. (1998). Does the halo effect occur in the elderly? *Social Behavior & Personality*, *26*, 147–150.

Latané, B. (1981). The psychology of social impact. *American Psychologist*, *36*, 343–356.

Latané, B., & Nida, S. A. (1981). Ten years of research on group size and helping. *Psychological Bulletin, 89*, 308–324.

Latané, B., Williams, K., & Harkins, S. (1979). Many hands make light the work: The causes and consequences of social loafing. *Journal of Personality and Social Psychology, 37*, 822–832.

Latta, F., & Van Cauter, E. (2003). Sleep and biological clocks. In M. Gallagher & R. J. Nelson (Eds.), *Handbook of psychology: Vol. 3. Biological psychology* (pp. 355–377). Wiley.

Laudenslager, M. L., Ryan, S. M., Drugen, R. L., Hyson, R. L., & Maier, S. F. (1983). Coping and immunosuppression: Inescapable but not escapable shock suppresses lymphocyte proliferation. *Science, 221*, 568–570.

Lavie, P. (2001). Sleep-wake as a biological rhythm. *Annual Review of Psychology, 52*, 277–303.

Lawton, M. P., Kleban, M. H., Rajagopal, D., & Dean, J. (1992). Dimensions of affective experience in three age groups. *Psychology and Aging, 7*, 171–184.

Lazarus, R. S. (1966). *Psychological stress and the coping process.* McGraw-Hill.

Lazarus, R. S. (1991). *Emotion and adaptation.* Oxford University Press.

Lazarus, R. S. (1993). Why we should think of stress as a subset of emotion. In L. Goldberger & S. Breznitz (Eds.), *Handbook of stress: Theoretical and clinical aspects* (2nd ed., pp. 21–39). Free Press.

Lazarus, R. S. (2007). Stress and emotion: A new synthesis. In A. Monat, R. S. Lazarus, & G. Reevy (Eds.), *The Praeger handbook on stress and coping* (pp. 33–52). Praeger.

Lazarus, R. S., & Folkman, S. (1984). *Stress, appraisal and coping.* Springer.

Lecendreux, M., Bassetti, C., Dauvilliers, Y., Mayer, G., Neidhart, E., & Tafti, M. (2003). HLA and genetic susceptibility to sleepwalking. *Molecular Psychiatry, 8*, 114–117.

Leclerc, G., Lefrancois, R., Dube, M., Hebert, R., & Gaulin, P. (1998). The self-actualization concept: A content validation. *Journal of Social Behavior & Personality, 11*, 69–84.

Lederman, S. J., & Klatzky, R. L. (2009). Haptic perception: A tutorial. *Attention, Perception, & Psychophysics, 71*, 1439–1459.

Lefcourt, H. M. (1982). *Locus of control: Current trends in theory and research.* University of Waterloo.

Lehman, D. R., Chiu, C., & Schaller, M. (2004). Psychology and culture. *Annual Review of Psychology, 55*, 689–714.

Leiter, M. P., & Maslach, C. (2005). A. Antoniou & C. Cooper (Eds.), *Research companion to organizational health psychology* (pp. 544–564). Elgar.

Lench, H. C., Tibbett, T. P., & Bench, S. W. (2016). Exploring the toolkit of emotion: What do sadness and anger do for us? *Social and Personality Psychology Compass, 10*, 11–25.

Lenneberg, E. H. (1967). *Biological foundations of language.* Wiley.

Leon, M. I., & Gallistel, C. R. (1998). Self-stimulating rats combine subjective reward magnitude and subjective reward rate multiplicatively. *Journal of Experimental Behavior: Animal Behavior Processes, 24*, 165–277.

Leone, C., & Hall, I. (2003). Self-monitoring, marital dissatisfaction, and relationship dissolution: Individual differences in orientations to marriage and divorce. *Self & Identity, 2*, 189–202.

Leotti, L. A., Iyengar, S. S., & Ochsner, K. N. (2010). Born to choose: The origins and value of the need for control. *Trends in Cognitive Sciences, 14*, 457–463.

Lepper, M. R., Corpus, J. H., & Iyengar, S. S. (2005). Intrinsic and extrinsic motivational orientations in the classroom: Age differences and academic correlates. *Journal of Educational Psychology, 97*, 184–196.

Lepper, M. R., Greene, D., & Nisbett, R. E. (1973). Undermining children's intrinsic interest with external reward: A test of the "overjustification" hypothesis. *Journal of Personality and Social Psychology, 28*, 129–137.

Leslie, S. J., Cimpian, A., Meyer, M., & Freeland, E. (2015). Expectations of brilliance underlie gender distributions across academic disciplines. *Science, 347*, 262–265.

LeVay, S. (1991). A difference in hypothalamic structure between heterosexual and homosexual men. *Science, 253*, 1034–1037.

Levenson, R. W. (1992). Autonomic nervous system differences among emotions. *Psychological Science, 3*, 23–27.

Leventhal, H., Weinman, J., Leventhal, E. A., & Phillips, L. A. (2008). Health psychology: The search for pathways between behavior and health. *Annual Review of Psychology, 59*, 477–505.

Levin, R., & Nielsen, T. (2009). Nightmares, bad dreams, and emotional dysregulation. *Current Directions in Psychological Science, 18*, 84–88.

Levine, G., & Parkinson, S. (1994). *Experimental methods in psychology.* Erlbaum.

Levinson, D. J., Darow, C. N., Klein, E. B., Levinson, M. H., & McKee, B. (1978). *The seasons of a man's life.* Knopf.

Levy, K. N., Hlay, J. K., Johnson, B. N., & Witmer, C. P. (2019). An attachment theoretical perspective on tend-and-befriend stress reactions. *Evolutionary Psychological Science, 5*, 426–439.

Lewis, J. W. (2006). Cortical networks related to human use of tools. *The Neuroscientist, 12*, 211–231.

Lewis, M., & Brooks-Gunn, J. (1979). *Social cognition and the acquisition of self.* Plenum.

Lewontin, R. (1976). Race and intelligence. In N. J. Block & G. Dworkin (Eds.), *The IQ controversy: Critical readings* (pp. 78–92). Pantheon.

Li, J., Hou, W., Zhu, L., & Tomasello, M. (2020, July 8). The development of intent-based moral judgment and moral behavior in the context of indirect reciprocity: A cross-cultural study. *International Journal of Behavioral Development, 44*(6). https://doi.org/10.1177/0165025420935636

Libet, B. (2004). *Mind time: The temporal factor in consciousness.* Harvard University Press.

Lilienfeld, S. O. (1994). Conceptual problems in the assessment of psychopathy. *Clinical Psychology Review, 14*, 17–38.

Lim, J., & Dinges, D. F. (2010). A meta-analysis of the impact of short-term sleep deprivation on cognitive variables. *Psychological Bulletin, 136*, 375–389.

Lin-Siegler, X., Dweck, C. S., & Cohen, G. L. (2016). Instructional interventions that motivate classroom learning. *Journal of Educational Psychology, 108*, 295–299.

Linda, W. P., & McGrath, R. E. (2017). The current status of prescribing psychologists: Practice patterns and medical professional evaluations. *Professional Psychology: Research and Practice, 48*, 38–45.

Lindsay, D. S., & Poole, D. A. (1998). The Poole et al. (1995) survey of therapists: Misinterpretations by both sides of the recovered memories controversy. *Journal of Psychiatry and Law, 26*, 383–399.

Lipsey, M. W., & Wilson, D. B. (1993). The efficacy of psychological, educational, and behavioral treatment: Confirmation from meta-analysis. *American Psychologist, 48*, 1181–1209.

Lisk, R. D. (1978). J. B. Hutchinson (Ed.), *Biological determinants of sexual behaviour* (pp. 425–466). Wiley.

Little, A. C., Jones, B. C., & DeBruine, J. M. (2011). Facial attractiveness: Evolutionary based research. *Philosophical Transactions of the Royal Society B, 366*, 1638–1659.

Liu, R. T., Kleiman, E. M., Nestor, B. A., & Cheek, S. M. (2015). The hopelessness theory of depression: A quarter-century in review. *Clinical Psychology Science and Practice, 22*, 345–365.

Liu, X. L., Tan, D. H., & Reder, L. M. (2018). The two processes underlying the testing effect: Evidence from event-related potentials (ERPs). *Neuropsychologia, 112*, 77–85.

Livesley, W. J., Jang, K. L., & Vernon, P. A. (2003). Genetic basis of personality structure. In T. Millon & M. J. Lerner (Eds.), *Handbook of psychology: Personality and social psychology* (Vol. 5, pp. 59–84). Wiley.

Livingston, R. W. (2001). What you see is what you get: Systematic variability in perceptual-based social judgment. *Personality & Social Psychology Bulletin, 27*, 1086–1096.

Lo, M.-T., Hinds, D. A., Tung, J. Y., Franz, C., Fan, C.-C., Wang, Y., Smeland, O. B., Schork, A., Holland, D., Kauppi, K., Sanyal, N., Escott-Price, V., Smith, D. J., O'Donovan, M., Stefansson, H., Bjornsdottir, G., Thorgeirsson, T. E., Stefansson, K., McEvoy, L. K., . . . Chen, C.-H. (2017). Genome-wide analyses for personality traits identify six genomic loci and show correlations with psychiatric disorders. *Nature Genetics, 49*, 152–156.

Locke, J. L. (1994). Phases in the child's development of language. *American Scientist, 82*, 436–445.

Locke, K. D., Church, A. T., Mastor, K. A., Curtis, G. J., Sadler, P., McDonald, K., Vargas-Flores, J. J., Ibáñez-Reyes, J., Morio, H., Reyes, J. A. S., Cabrera, H. F., Mazuera Arias, R., Rincon, B. C., Albornoz Arias, N. C., Muñoz, A., & Ortiz, F. A. (2017). Cross-situational self-consistency in nine cultures: The importance of separating influences of social norms and distinctive dispositions. *Personality and Social Psychology Bulletin, 43*, 1033–1049.

Lockhart, R. S. (2002). Levels of processing, transfer-appropriate processing, and the concept of robust encoding. *Memory, 10*, 397–403.

Loftus, E. F. (2018). Eyewitness testimony: An eyewitness report. In T. Grisso & S. L. Brodsky (Eds.), *The roots of modern psychology and law* (pp. 31–43). Oxford University Press.

Loftus, E. L. (1993). The reality of repressed memories. *American Psychologist, 48*, 518–537.

Loftus, E. L. (2018). Eyewitness science and the legal system. *Annual Review of Law and Social Science, 14*, 1–10.

Loftus, E. L., & Loftus, G. R. (1980). On the permanence of stored information in the brain. *American Psychologist, 35*, 409–420.

Loftus, E. L., & Palmer, J. C. (1974). Reconstruction of automobile destruction: An example of the interaction between language and memory. *Journal of Verbal Learning and Verbal Behavior, 13*, 585–589.

Logan, G. D. (1991). Automaticity and memory. In W. E. Hockley & S. Lewandowsky (Eds.), *Relating theory and data: Essays on human memory in honor of Bennet B. Murdock* (pp. 347–366). Erlbaum.

Lorenz, K. Z. (1958, December). The evolution of behavior. *Scientific American, 199*, 67–78.

Lovaas, O. I. (1987). Behavioral treatment and normal educational and intellectual functioning in young autistic children. *Journal of Consulting and Clinical Psychology, 55*, 3–9.

Lovaas, O. I., Koegel, R., Simmons, J. Q., & Long, J. S. (1973). Some generalization and follow-up measures on autistic children in behavior therapy. *Journal of Applied Behavior Analysis, 6*, 131–166.

Lowrie, J., & Brownlow, H. (2020). The impact of sleep deprivation and alcohol on driving: A comparative study. *BMC Health, 20*, 980.

Lubinski, D. (2009). Exceptional cognitive ability: The phenotype. *Behavioral Genetics, 39*, 350–358.

Lubinski, D. (2016). From Terman to today: A century of findings on intellectual precocity. *Review of Educational Research, 86*, 900–944.

Lucy, J. A. (2016). Recent advances in the study of linguistic relativity in historical context: A critical assessment. *Language Learning, 66*, 487–515.

Luders, E., Toga, A. W., Lepore, N., & Gaser, C. (2009). The underlying anatomical correlates of long-term meditation: Larger hippocampal and frontal volumes of gray matter. *Neuroimage, 45*, 672–678.

Lupien, S. J., McEwan, B. S., Gunnar, M. R., & Heim, C. (2009). Effects of stress throughout the lifespan on the brain, behavior and cognition. *Nature Reviews Neuroscience, 10*, 434–445.

Luria, A. R. (1968). *The mind of a mnemonist*. Basic Books.

Lutterveld, R. V., Sommer, I. E. C., & Ford, J. M. (2011). The neurophysiology of auditory hallucinations—a historical and contemporary review. *Frontiers in Psychiatry, 2*, 1–7.

Lutz, C. (1982). The domain of emotion words in Ifaluk. *American Ethnologist, 9*, 113–128.

Lynn, M., & Simons, T. (2000). Predictors of male and female servers' average tip earnings. *Journal of Applied Social Psychology, 30*, 241–252.

Lynn, R. (1994). Some reinterpretations of the Minnesota transracial adoption study. *Intelligence, 19*, 21–27.

Lynn, R. (2009). What has caused the Flynn effect? Secular increases in the Development Quotients of infants. *Intelligence, 37*, 16–24.

Lynn, S. J., Rhue, J. W., & Weekes, J. R. (1990). Hypnotic involuntariness: A social cognitive analysis. *Psychological Review, 97*, 169–184.

Maccoby, E. (2000). Parenting and its effects on children: On reading and misreading behavioral genetics. *Annual Review of Psychology, 51*, 1–27.

Macdonald, J. L., & Levy, S. R. (2016). Ageism in the workplace: The role of psychosocial factors in predicting job satisfaction, commitment, and engagement. *Journal of Social Issues, 72*, 169–190.

MacDonald, T. K., & Ross, M. (1999). Assessing the accuracy of predictions about dating relationships: How and why do lovers' predictions differ from those made by observers? *Personality and Social Psychology Bulletin, 25*, 1417–1429.

Madden, M., & Rainie, L. (2010). *Adults and cell phone distractions.* Pew Internet & American Life Project.

Madon, S., Guyll, M., Spoth, R., & Willard, J. (2004). Self-fulfilling prophecies: The synergistic accumulative effect of parents' beliefs on children's drinking behavior. *Psychological Science, 15,* 837–845.

Maeng, A., Tanner, R. J., & Wu, K. (2017). The influence of social crowding on creativity. *Advances in Consumer Research, 45,* 243–247.

Mah, K., & Binik, Y. M. (2002). Do all orgasms feel alike? Evaluating a two-dimensional model of the orgasm experience across gender and sexual context. *Journal of Sex Research, 39,* 104–113.

Mahon, B. Z., & Caramazza, A. (2009). Concepts and categories: A cognitive neuropsychological perspective. *Annual Review of Psychology, 60,* 27–51.

Mahoney, C. E., Cogswell, A., Koralnik, I. J., & Scammell, T. E. (2019). The neurobiological basis of narcolepsy. *Nature Reviews Neuroscience, 20,* 83–93.

Maia, T. V., & Frank, M. J. (2017). An integrative perspective on the role of dopamine in schizophrenia. *Biological Psychiatry, 81,* 52–66.

Maier, N. R. F. (1930). Reasoning in humans I: On direction. *Journal of Comparative Psychology, 10,* 115–143.

Maier, N. R. F. (1931). Reasoning in humans II: The solution to a problem and its appearance in consciousness. *Journal of Comparative Psychology, 12,* 181–194.

Maier, N. R. F., & Burke, R. J. (1967). Response availability as a factor in the problem-solving performance of males and females. *Journal of Personality and Social Psychology, 5,* 304–310.

Maimaran, M., & Fishbach, A. (2014). If it's useful and you know it, do you eat? Preschoolers refrain from instrumental food. *The Journal of Consumer Research, 41,* 642–655.

Maldonado, J. R., & Spiegel, D. (2015). Dissociative disorders. In A. Tasman et al. (Ed.), *Psychiatry.* Wiley. https://doi.org/10.1002/9781118753378.ch61

Malt, B. C., & Smith, E. E. (1984). Correlated properties in natural categories. *Journal of Verbal Learning and Verbal Behavior, 23,* 250–269.

Manaseki-Holland, S., Spier, E., Bavuusuren, B., Bayandorj, T., Sprachman, S., & Marshall, T. (2010). Effects of traditional swaddling on development: A randomized controlled trial. *Pediatrics, 126,* 1485–1492.

Mandler, G., Nakamura, Y., & Van Zandt, B. J. S. (1987). Nonspecific effects of stimuli that cannot be recognized. *Journal of Experimental Psychology: Learning, Memory, & Cognition, 13,* 646–648.

Mangels, J. A., Butterfield, B., Lamb, J., Good, C., & Dweck, C. S. (2006). Why do beliefs about intelligence influence learning success? A social cognitive neuroscience model. *SCAN, 1,* 75–86.

Manoach, D. S., & Stickgold, R. (2019). Abnormal sleep spindles, memory consolidation, and schizophrenia. *Annual Review of Clinical Psychology, 15,* 451–479.

Marcia, J. E. (1966). Development and validation of ego identity status. *Journal of Personality and Social Psychology, 3,* 551–558.

Marcus, D. E., & Overton, W. F. (1978). The development of cognitive gender constancy and sex-role preferences. *Child Development, 49,* 434–444.

Margoni, F., & Surian, L. (2018). Infants' evaluation of prosocial and antisocial agents: A meta-analysis. *Developmental Psychology, 54*(8), 1445–1455. http://dx.doi.org/10.1037/dev0000538

Marketon, J. I., & Glaser, R. (2008). Stress hormones and immune function. *Cellular Immunology, 252,* 16–26.

Marks, M. J., & Fraley, R. C. (2006). Confirmation bias and the sexual double standard. *Sex Roles, 54,* 19–26.

Markus, H., & Kitayama, S. (1991). Culture and the self: Implications for cognition, emotion, and motivation. *Psychological Review, 98,* 224–253.

Markus, H., & Kitayama, S. (1994). A collective fear of the collective: Implications for selves and theories of selves. *Personality and Social Psychology Bulletin, 20,* 568–579.

Marroquin, B. (2011). Interpersonal emotion regulation as a mechanism of social support in depression. *Clinical Psychology Review, 31,* 1276–1290.

Marshall, J. C., & Halligan, P. W. (1988). Blindsight and insight in visuo-spatial neglect. *Nature, 336,* 766–767.

Martens, A., Goldenberg, J. L., & Greenberg, J. (2005). A terror management perspective on ageism. *Journal of Social Issues, 61,* 223–239.

Martens, A., Greenberg, J., Schimel, J., & Landau, M. J. (2004). Ageism and death: Effects of mortality and perceived similarity to elders on reactions to elderly people. *Personality and Social Psychology Bulletin, 30,* 1524–1536.

Martin, C. L., & Ruble, D. (2004). Children's search for gender cues: Cognitive perspectives on gender development. *Current Directions in Psychological Science, 13,* 67–70.

Martin, C. L., & Ruble, D. N. (2009). Patterns of gender development. *Annual Review of Psychology, 61,* 353–381.

Martin, K. M., & Aggleton, J. P. (1993). Contextual effects on the ability of divers to use decompression tables. *Applied Cognitive Psychology, 7,* 311–316.

Martin, R. J., White, B. D., & Hulsey, M. G. (1991). The regulation of body weight. *American Scientist, 79,* 528–541.

Martins, A., Ramalho, N., & Morin, E. (2010). A comprehensive meta-analysis of the relationship between emotional intelligence and health. *Personality and Individual Differences, 49,* 554–564.

Maslach, C. (1976). Burned out. *Human Behavior, 5,* 16–22.

Maslach, C., & Leiter, M. P. (2008). Early predictors of job burnout and engagement. *Journal of Applied Psychology, 93,* 498–512.

Maslow, A. H. (1954). *Motivation and personality.* Harper.

Mason, J. R., & Reidinger, R. F. (1982). Observational learning of aversions in red-winged blackbirds (*Agelaius phoeniceus*). *Auk, 99,* 548–554.

Mason, M. F., & Morris, M. W. (2010). Culture, attribution, and automaticity: A social cognitive neuroscience view. *Scan, 5,* 292–306.

Masters, W. H., & Johnson, V. E. (1966). *Human sexual response.* Little, Brown.

Masuda, T., & Kitayama, S. (2004). Perceiver-induced constraint and attitude attribution in Japan and the US: A case for the cultural dependence of the correspondence bias. *Journal of Experimental Social Psychology, 40,* 409–416.

Mathes, J. M., & Schredl, M. (2016). Threats in dreams: Are they related to waking-life? *International Journal of Dream Research, 9,* 58–66.

Matsumoto, D. (1994). *People: Psychology from a cultural perspective.* Brooks/Cole.

Mattay, V. S., Berman, K. F., Ostrem, J. L., Esposito, G., Van-Horn, J. D., Bigelow, L. B., & Weinberger, D. R. (1996). Dextroamphetamine enhances "neural network-specific" physiological signals: A positron-emission tomography rCBF study. *Journal of Neuroscience, 16,* 4816–4822.

Matthes, J., Prieler, M., & Adam, K. (2016). Gender-role portrayals in television advertising across the globe. *Sex Roles, 75,* 314–327.

Matthews, G., Zeidner, M., & Roberts, R. D. (2005). Emotional intelligence: An elusive ability. In O. Wilheim & R. Engle (Eds.), *Understanding and measuring intelligence* (pp. 79–99). Sage.

Matthews, K. A. (1992). Myths and realities of the menopause. *Psychosomatic Medicine, 54,* 1–9.

Maurer, D., & Lewis, T. L. (2018). Visual systems. In R. Gibb & B. Kolb (Eds.), *The neurobiology of brain and behavioral development* (pp. 213–233). Academic Press.

May, A. A., Liu, M., Woods, S. C., & Begg, D. P. (2016). CCK increases the transport of insulin into the brain. *Physiology & Behavior, 165,* 392–397.

Mayer, J. D., Caruso, D. R., & Salovey, P. (2016). The ability model of emotional intelligence: Principles and updates. *Emotion Review, 8,* 290–300.

Mayer, J. D., & Salovey, P. (1997). What is emotional intelligence? In P. Salovey & D. Sluyter (Eds.), *Emotional development, emotional literacy, and emotional intelligence* (pp. 3–31). Basic Books.

McCaffrey, T. (2012). Innovation relies on the obscure: A key to overcoming the classic problem of functional fixedness. *Psychological Science, 23,* 215–218.

McCall, M. (1994). Decision theory and the sale of alcohol. *Journal of Applied Social Psychology, 24,* 1593–1611.

McCall, M. (1997). The effects of physical attractiveness on gaining access to alcohol: When social policy meets social decision making. *Addiction, 92,* 597–600.

McCall, W. V. (2001). Electroconvulsive therapy in the era of modern psychopharmacology. *International Journal of Neuropsychopharmacology, 4,* 315–324.

McCall, W. V. (2007). The persistence or the disintegration of memory: Cognitive side effects of electroconvulsive therapy. *Journal of ECT, 23,* 59–60.

McCann, I. L., & Holmes, D. S. (1984). Influence of aerobic exercise on depression. *Journal of Personality and Social Psychology, 46,* 1142–1147.

McClelland, D. C. (1961). *The achieving society.* Von Nostrand.

McClelland, D. C., Atkinson, J. W., Clark, R. A., & Lowell, E. W. (1953). *The achievement motive.* Appleton-Century-Crofts.

McClelland, J. L., & Elman, J. L. (1986). The TRACE model of speech perception. *Cognitive Psychology, 18,* 1–86.

McCrae, R. R., & Costa, P. T., Jr. (1985). Updating Norman's "adequate taxonomy": Intelligence and personality dimensions in natural language and in questionnaires. *Journal of Personality and Social Psychology, 49,* 710–721.

McCrae, R. R., & Costa, P. T., Jr. (2003). *Personality in adulthood* (2nd ed.). Guilford Press.

McDaniel, E., & Andersen, P. A. (1998). International patterns of interpersonal tactile communication: A field study. *Journal of Nonverbal Behavior, 22,* 59–75.

McDermott, J. H., Wroblewski, D., & Oxenham, A. J. (2011). Recovering sound sources from embedded repetition. *Proceedings of the National Academy of Sciences, 108,* 1188–1193.

McDermott, K. B., & Roediger, H. L., III. (1994). Effects of imagery on perceptual implicit memory tests. *Journal of Experimental Psychology: Learning, Memory, & Cognition, 20,* 1379–1390.

McDermott, K. B., & Roediger, H. L., III. (1998). Attempting to avoid illusory memories: Robust false recognition of associates persists under conditions of explicit warnings and immediate testing. *Journal of Memory and Language, 39,* 508–520.

McDougall, W. (1908). *An introduction to social psychology.* Methuen.

McGhee, P. E., & Frueh, T. (1980). Television viewing and the learning of sex-role stereotypes. *Sex Roles, 6,* 179–188.

McGrath, J., Saha, S., Chant, D., & Welham, J. (2008). Schizophrenia: A concise overview of incidence, prevalence, and mortality. *Epidemiologic Reviews, 30,* 67–76.

McGuire, W. J. (1985). Attitudes and attitude change. In G. Lindzey & E. Aronson (Eds.), *Handbook of social psychology* (Vol. 2, pp. 233–346). Random House.

McIntosh, D. N., Zajonc, R. B., Vig, P. S., & Emerick, S. W. (1997). Facial movement, breathing, temperature, and affect: Implications of the vascular theory of emotional efference. *Cognition & Emotion, 11,* 171–195.

McKenna, S. P., & Glendon, A. I. (1985). Occupational first aid training: Decay in cardiopulmonary resuscitation (CPR) skills. *Journal of Occupational Psychology, 58,* 109–117.

McKnight, J. D., & Glass, D. C. (1995). Perceptions of control, burnout, and depressive symptomatology: A replication and extension. *Journal of Consulting & Clinical Psychology, 63,* 490–494.

McLean, C. P., & Anderson, E. R. (2009). Brave men and timid women? A review of gender differences in fear and anxiety. *Clinical Psychology Review, 29,* 496–505.

McNally, R. J., & Geraerts, E. (2009). A new solution to the recovered memory debate. *Perspectives on Psychological Science, 4,* 126–134.

McNeil, B. J., Pauker, S. G., Cox, H. C., Jr., & Tversky, A. (1982). On the elicitation of preferences for alternative therapies. *New England Journal of Medicine, 306,* 1259–1262.

Medin, D. L. (1989). Concepts and conceptual structure. *American Psychologist, 44,* 1469–1481.

Medin, D. L., & Atran, S. (2004). The native mind: Biological categorization and reasoning in development and across cultures. *Psychological Review, 111,* 960–983.

Medin, D. L., & Shaffer, M. M. (1978). A context theory of classification learning. *Psychological Review, 85,* 207–238.

Mednick, S. A. (1962). The associative basis of the creative process. *Psychological Review, 69,* 220–232.

Medoff, D. (2004). Assessing clinical personality assessment. *Journal of Personality Assessment, 82,* 241–243.

Medvec, V. H., Madey, S. F., & Gilovich, T. (1995). When less is more: Counterfactual thinking and satisfaction among Olympic medalists. *Journal of Personality and Social Psychology, 69*, 603–610.

Melamed, B. G., & Siegel, L. J. (1975). Reduction of anxiety in children facing hospitalization and surgery by use of filmed modeling. *Journal of Consulting and Clinical Psychology, 43*, 511–521.

Melton, A. W. (1963). Implications of short-term memory for a general theory of memory. *Journal of Verbal Learning and Verbal Behavior, 2*, 1–21.

Meltzoff, A. N. (2011). U. Goswami (Ed.), *The Wiley-Blackwell handbook of childhood cognitive development* (2nd ed., pp. 49–75). Wiley-Blackwell.

Meltzoff, A. N., & Marshall, P. J. (2018). Human infant imitation as a social survival circuit. *Current Opinion in Behavioral Sciences, 24*, 130–136.

Melzack, R. (1973). *The puzzle of pain*. Basic Books.

Melzack, R., & Wall, P. D. (1965). Pain mechanisms: A new theory. *Science, 150*, 971–979.

Melzack, R., & Wall, P. D. (1982). *The challenge of pain*. Penguin.

Mendrek, A., & Mancini-Marie, A. (2016). Sex/gender differences in the brain and cognition in schizophrenia. *Neuroscience & Biobehavioral Reviews, 67*, 57–78.

Merikle, P. M., & Skanes, H. E. (1992). Subliminal self-help audiotapes: A search for placebo effects. *Journal of Applied Psychology, 77*, 772–776.

Merton, R. (1948). The self-fulfilling prophecy. *Antioch Review, 8*, 193–210.

Meuret, A. E., Kroll, J., & Ritz, T. (2017). Panic disorder comorbidity with medical conditions and treatment implications. *Annual Review of Clinical Psychology, 13*, 209–240.

Milgram, S. (1963). Behavioral study of obedience. *Journal of Abnormal and Social Psychology, 67*, 371–378.

Milgram, S. (1974). *Obedience to authority*. Harper & Row.

Miller, C., Lurye, L. E., Zosuls, K. M., & Ruble, D. N. (2009). Accessibility of gender stereotype domains: Developmental and gender differences in children. *Sex Roles, 60*, 870–881.

Miller, D. I., & Halpern, D. F. (2014). The new science of cognitive sex differences. *Trends in Cognitive Science, 18*, 37–45.

Miller, G. A. (1956). The magical number seven plus or minus two: Some limits on our capacity for processing information. *Psychological Review, 63*, 81–97.

Miller, G. A., Galanter, E., & Pribram, K. H. (1960). *Plans and the structure of behavior*. Holt.

Miller, J. S., & Cardy, R. L. (2000). Self-monitoring and performance appraisal: Rating outcomes in project teams. *Journal of Organizational Behavior, 21*, 609–626.

Miller, M. A., & Rahe, R. H. (1997). Life changes scaling for the 1990s. *Journal of Psychosomatic Research, 43*, 279–292.

Miller, R. R., & Grace, R. C. (2003). Conditioning and learning. In A. Healy & R. Proctor (Eds.), *Handbook of psychology: Vol. 4. Experimental psychology* (pp. 357–397). Wiley.

Miller, S. D. (1989). Optical differences in cases of multiple personality disorder. *Journal of Nervous and Mental Disease, 177*, 480–486.

Miller, T. W. (1993). The assessment of stressful life events. In L. Goldberger & S. Breznitz (Eds.), *Handbook of stress: Theoretical and clinical aspects* (2nd ed., pp. 161–173). Free Press.

Milner, B. (1966). Amnesia following operation on the temporal lobes. In C. W. M. Whitty & O. L. Zangwill (Eds.), *Amnesia* (pp. 109–133). Butterworths.

Mineka, S. (1987). A primate model of phobic fears. In H. Eysenck & I. Martin (Eds.), *Theoretical foundations of behavior therapy* (pp. 81–111). Plenum.

Mineka, S., & Zinbarg, R. (2006). A contemporary learning theory perspective on the etiology of anxiety disorders. *American Psychologist, 61*, 10–26.

Mingroni, M. A. (2007). Resolving the IQ paradox: Heterosis as a cause of the Flynn effect and other trends. *Psychological Review, 114*, 806–829.

Miryam, Y., Nicoloro-SantaBarbara, J., Grey, N. E., Moyer, A., & Lobel, M. (2019). Meta-analytic evaluation of stress reduction interventions for undergraduate and graduate students. *International Journal of Stress Management, 26*, 132–145.

Mischel, W. (1968). *Personality and assessment*. Wiley.

Mischel, W. (2004). Toward an integrative science of the person. *Annual Review of Psychology, 55*, 1–22.

Mischel, W., & Peake, P. K. (1982). Beyond déja vu in the search for cross-situational consistency. *Psychological Review, 89*, 730–755.

Mischel, W., & Shoda, Y. (1995). A cognitive-affective system theory of personality: Reconceptualizing situations, dispositions, dynamics, and invariance in personality structure. *Psychological Review, 102*, 246–268.

Mischel, W., & Shoda, Y. (1998). Reconciling processing dynamics and personality dispositions. *Annual Review of Psychology, 49*, 229–258.

Mitchell, R., & Kumari, V. (2016). Hans Eysenck's interface between the brain and personality: Modern evidence on the cognitive neuroscience of personality. *Personality and Individual Differences, 103*, 74–81.

Molden, D. C., & Dweck, C. S. (2000). Meaning and motivation. In C. Sansone & J. M. Harackiewicz (Eds.), *Intrinsic and extrinsic motivation: The search for optimal motivation and performance* (pp. 131–159). Academic Press.

Molitor, A., & Hsu, H. (2019). Child development across cultures. In K. D. Keith (Ed.), *Cross-cultural psychology: Contemporary themes and perspectives* (2nd ed., pp. 153–189). Wiley.

Monroe, S. M., & Slavich, G. M. (2020). Major life events: A review of conceptual, definitional, measurement issues, and practices. In K. L. Harkness & E. P. Hayden (Eds.), *The Oxford handbook of stress and mental health*. Oxford University Press.

Montero-Marin, J., Garcia-Campayo, J., Perez-Yus, M., & Zabaleta-del-Olmo, E. (2019). Meditation techniques v. relaxation therapies when treating anxiety: A Meta-analytic review. *Psychological Medicine, 49*, 2118–2133.

Monto, M. A., & Carey, A. G. (2014). A new standard of sexual behavior? Are claims associated with the "hookup culture" supported by general social survey data? *Journal of Sex Research, 51*, 605–615.

Montoya, R. M., Horton, R. S., & Kirchner, J. (2008). Is actual similarity necessary for attraction? A meta-analysis of actual and perceived similarity. *Journal of Social and Personal Relationships, 35*, 597–601.

Montoya, R. M., & Insko, C. A. (2008). Toward a more complete understanding of the reciprocity of liking effect. *European Journal of Social Psychology, 38,* 477–498.

Moors, A., & De Houwer, J. (2006). Automaticity: A theoretical and conceptual analysis. *Psychological Bulletin, 132,* 297–326.

Moray, N. (1959). Attention in dichotic listening: Affective cues and the influence of instructions. *Quarterly Journal of Experimental Psychology, 11,* 56–60.

Moret, V., Forster, A., Laverriere, M. C., & Lambert, H. (1991). Mechanism of analgesia induced by hypnosis and acupuncture: Is there a difference? *Pain, 45,* 135–140.

Morewedge, C. K., & Norton, M. I. (2009). When dreaming is believing: The (motivated) interpretation of dreams. *Journal of Personality and Social Psychology, 96,* 249–264.

Morton, G. J., Cummings, D. E., Baskin, D. G., Barsh, G. S., & Schwartz, M. W. (2006). Central nervous system control of food intake and body weight. *Nature, 443,* 289–295.

Moser, D. K., Riegel, B., McKinley, S., Doering, L. V., An, K., & Sheahan, S. (2007). Impact of anxiety and perceived control on in-hospital complications after myocardial infarction. *Psychosomatic Medicine, 69,* 10–16.

Mozell, M. M., Smith, B., Smith, P., Sullivan, R., & Swender, P. (1969). Nasal chemoreception in flavor identification. *Archives of Otolaryngology, 90,* 367–373.

Muchinsky, P. M. (2003). *Psychology applied to work* (7th ed.). Wadsworth.

Muller, C. L., Anacker, A. M. J., & Veenstra-VanderWeele, J. (2016). The serotonin system in autism spectrum disorder: From bio-marker to animal models. *Neuroscience, 321,* 24–41.

Muller, M. J., Bosy-Westphal, A., & Heymsfield, S. B. (2010). Is there evidence for a set point that regulates body weight? *F1000 Medical Reports, 2,* 59.

Mullins, N., & Lewis, C. M. (2017). Genetics of depression: Progress at last. *Current Psychiatry Reports, 19,* 43.

Murayama, K., & Elliot, A. J. (2011). Achievement motivation and memory: Achievement goals differentially influence immediate and delayed remember-know recognition memory. *Personality and Social Psychology Bulletin, 37,* 1339–1348.

Murayama, K., Matsumoto, M., Izuma, K., & Matsumoto, K. (2010). Neural basis of the undermining effect of monetary reward on intrinsic motivation. *Proceedings of the National Academy of Sciences, 107,* 20911–20916.

Murphy, G. L. (2002). *The big book of concepts.* MIT Press.

Murphy, G. L., & Lassaline, M. E. (1997). Hierarchical structure in concepts and the basic level of categorization. In K. Lamberts & D. R. Shanks (Eds.), *Knowledge, concepts and categories: Studies in cognition* (pp. 93–131). MIT Press.

Murray, C., & Wren, C. T. (2003). Cognitive, academic, and attitudi-nal predictors of the grade point averages of college students with learning disabilities. *Journal of Learning Disabilities, 36,* 407–415.

Murray, H. A. (1938). *Explorations in personality.* Oxford University Press.

Murre, J. M. J., & Dros, J. (2015). Replication and analysis of Ebbinghaus' forgetting curve. *PLoS ONE, 10*(7), e0120644. doi:10.1371/journal.pone.0120644

Muthukrishna, M., Bell, A. V., Henrich, J., Curtin, C. M., Gedranovich, A., McInerney, J., & Thue, B. (2020, January 19). *Beyond WEIRD psychology: Measuring and mapping scales of cultural and psychological distance.* http://dx.doi.org/10.2139/ssrn.3259613

Myers, D. G., & Diener, E. (2018). The scientific pursuit of happi-ness. *Perspectives on Psychological Science, 13,* 218–225.

Nadon, R., Hoyt, I. P., Register, P. A., & Kihlstrom, J. F. (1991). Absorption and hypnotizability: Context effects reexamined. *Journal of Personality and Social Psychology, 60,* 144–153.

Nairne, J. S. (2002a). Remembering over the short-term: The case against the standard model. *Annual Review of Psychology, 53,* 53–81.

Nairne, J. S. (2002b). The myth of the encoding–retrieval match. *Memory, 10,* 389–395.

Nairne, J. S. (2005). The functionalist agenda in memory research. In A. F. Healy (Ed.), *Experimental cognitive psychology and its appli-cations* (pp. 115–126). American Psychological Association.

Nairne, J. S., Coverdale, M. E., & Pandeirada, J. N. S. (2019). Adaptive memory: The mnemonic power of survival-based gen-eration. *Journal of Experimental Psychology: Learning, Memory, and Cognition, 45*(11), 1970–1982.

Nairne, J. S., & Neath, I. (2012). Sensory and working memory. In A. Healy & R. Proctor (Eds.), *Handbook of psychology: Vol. 4. Experimental psychology* (2nd ed., pp. 419–446). Wiley.

Nairne, J. S., & Pandeirada, J. N. S. (2008). Forgetting. In H. L. Roediger III., & J. H. Byrne (-in-chief) (Eds.), *Learning and memory: A comprehensive reference: Vol. 2. The cognitive psychology of mem-ory* (pp. 179–194). Elsevier.

Nairne, J. S., VanArsdall, J. E., & Cogdill, M. (2017). Remembering the living: Episodic memory is tuned to animacy. *Current Directions in Psychological Science, 26,* 22–27.

Nantais, K. M., & Schellenberg, E. G. (1999). The Mozart effect: An artifact of preference. *Psychological Science, 10,* 370–373.

Nasrallah, H. A. (2017). Prescribing is the culmination of exten-sive medical training and psychologists don't qualify. *Current Psychiatry, 16,* 11–16.

Nathan, D. (2011). *Sybil exposed: The extraordinary story behind the famous multiple personality case.* Free Press.

National Center for Statistics and Analysis. (2020, April). *Distracted driving 2018* (Research Note. Report No. DOT HS 812 926. National Highway Traffic Safety Administration.

Nees, M. A. (2016, December 2). Have we forgotten auditory sen-sory memory? Retention intervals in studies of nonverbal auditory working memory. *Frontiers in Psychology.* https://doi.org/10.3389/fpsyg.2016.01892

Neisser, U. (1967). *Cognitive psychology.* Appleton-Century-Crofts.

Neisser, U. (1978). Memory: What are the important questions? In M. M. Gruneberg, E. E. Morris, & R. N. Sykes (Eds.), *Practical aspects of memory* (pp. 3–24). Academic Press.

Neisser, U. (Ed.). (1998). *The rising curve: Long-term gains in IQ and related measures.* American Psychological Association.

Nelson, L. D., Simmons, J., & Simonsohn, U. (2018). Psychology's renaissance. *Annual Review of Psychology, 69,* 511–534.

Nelson, M. J., El Karoui, I., Giber, K., Yang, X., Cohen, L., Koopman, H., Cash, S. S., Naccache, L., Hale, J. T., Pallier, C., & Dehaene, S. (2017). Neurophysiological dynamics of phrase-structure building during sentence processing. *Proceedings of the National Academy of Sciences*, *114*, E3669–E3678.

Nesi, J. (2020, March). The impact of social media on youth mental health: Challenges and opportunities. *North Carolina Medical Journal*, *81*(2), 116–121. doi: 10.18043/ncm.81.2.116

Nestoriuc, Y., & Martin, A. (2007). Efficacy of biofeedback for migraine: A meta-analysis. *Pain*, *128*, 111–127.

Nettelbeck, T., & Wilson, C. (2004). The Flynn effect: Smarter not faster. *Intelligence*, *32*, 85–93.

Newcomb, A. F., & Bagwell, C. L. (1995). Children's friendship relations: A meta-analytic review. *Psychological Bulletin*, *117*, 306–347.

Newcombe, N. S. (2011). What is neoconstructivism? *Child Development Perspectives*, *5*, 157–160.

Newcombe, N. S., & Uttal, D. H. (2006). Whorf versus Socrates, round 10. *Trends in Cognitive Sciences*, *10*, 394–396.

Newell, A., & Simon, H. A. (1972). *Human problem solving*. Prentice-Hall.

Newport, F. (2018, May 22). *In U.S., estimate of LGBT population rises to 4.5%*. https://news.gallup.com/poll/234863/estimate-lgbt-population-rises.aspx

Nichols, D. S., & Greene, R. L. (1997). Dimensions of deception in personality assessment: The example of the MMPI-2. *Journal of Personality Assessment*, *68*, 251–266.

Nickerson, R. S., & Adams, M. J. (1979). Long-term memory for a common object. *Cognitive Psychology*, *11*, 287–307.

Nicolaus, L. K., & Nellis, D. W. (1987). The first evaluation of the use of conditioned taste aversion to control predation by mongooses upon eggs. *Applied Animal Behaviour Science*, *17*, 329–346.

Nicotra, A., Critchley, H. D., Mathias, C. J., & Dolan, R. J. (2006). Emotional and autonomic consequences of spinal cord injury explored using functional brain imaging. *Brain*, *129*, 718–728.

Nienhuis, J. B., Owen, J., Valentine, J. C., Winkeljohn Black, S., Halford, T. C., Parazak, S. E., Budge, S., & Hilsenroth, M. (2018). Therapeutic alliance, empathy, and genuineness in individual adult psychotherapy: A meta-analytic review. *Psychotherapy Research*, *28*, 593–605.

Nisbett, R. E. (2009). *Intelligence and how to get it*. Norton.

Nisbett, R. E., Peng, K., Choi, I., & Norenzayan, A. (2001). Culture and systems of thought: Holistic versus analytic cognition. *Psychological Review*, *108*, 291–310.

Nithianantharajah, J., & Hannan, A. J. (2006). Enriched environments, experience-dependent plasticity and disorders of the nervous system. *Nature Reviews Neuroscience*, *7*, 697–709.

Norris, S. L., & Zweigenhaft, R. L. (1999). Self-monitoring, trust, and commitment in romantic relationships. *The Journal of Social Psychology*, *139*, 215–220.

North, M. S., & Fiske, S. T. (2015). Modern attitudes toward older adults in the aging world: A cross-cultural meta-analysis. *Psychological Bulletin*, *141*, 993–1021. doi: 10.1037/a0039469

Nosofsky, R. M. (1992). Exemplars, prototypes, and similarity rules. In A. F. Healy & S. M. Kosslyn (Eds.), *Essays in honor of William K. Estes: Vol. 2. From learning processes to cognitive processes* (pp. 149–167). Erlbaum.

Nosofsky, R. M., & Little, D. R. (2010). Classification response times in probabilistic rule-based category structures: Contrasting exemplar-retrieval and decision-bound models. *Memory & Cognition*, *38*, 916–927.

Nosofsky, R. M., Sanders, C. A., Gerdom, A., Douglass, B. J., & McDaniel, M. A. (2017). On learning natural-science categories that violate the family-resemblance principle. *Psychological Science*, *28*, 104–114.

Novaco, R. W. (2016). Anger. In G. Fink (Ed.), *Handbook of stress: Vol. 1. Stress: Concepts, cognition, emotion, and behavior* (pp. 285–292). Academic Press.

Nummenmaa, L., & Calder, A. J. (2009). Neural mechanisms of social attention. *Trends in Cognitive Sciences*, *13*, 135–143.

Nurmi, E. L., Dowd, M., Tadevosyan-Leyfer, O., Haynes, J. L., Folstein, S. E., & Sutcliffe, J. S. (2003). Exploratory subsetting of autism families based on savant skills improves evidence of genetic linkage to 15q11-q13. *Journal of the American Academy of Child & Adolescent Psychiatry*, *42*, 856–863.

Oakley, D. A., & Halligan, P. W. (2009). Hypnotic suggestion and cognitive neuroscience. *Trends in Cognitive Sciences*, *13*, 264–270.

Oberauer, K., Farrell, S., Jarrold, C., & Lewandowsky, S. (2016). What limits working memory capacity? *Psychological Bulletin*, *142*, 758–799.

O'Boyle, E. H., Jr., Humphrey, R. H., Pollack, J. M., Hawver, T. H., & Story, P. A. (2010). The relation between emotional intelligence and job performance: A meta-analysis. *Journal of Organizational Behavior*, *32*, 788–818.

O'Connor, P. J., Hill, A., Kaya, M., & Martin, B. (2019). The measurement of emotional intelligence: A critical review of the literature and recommendations for researchers and practitioners. *Frontiers in Psychology*, *28*. https://doi.org/10.3389/fpsyg.2019.01116

O'Donnell, M., Nelson, L. D., Ackermann, E., Aczel, B., Akhtar, A., Aldrovandi, S., Alshaif, N., Andringa, R., Aveyard, M., Babincak, P., Balatekin, N., Baldwin, S. A., Banik, G., Baskin, E., Bell, R., Białobrzeska, O., Birt, A. R., Boot, W. R., Braithwaite, S. R., . . . Zrubka, M. (2018). Registered replication report: Dijksterhuis and van Knippenberg (1998. *Perspectives on Psychological Science*, *13*, 268–294.

Offer, D., & Schonert-Reichl, K. A. (1992). Debunking the myths of adolescence. *Journal of the American Academy of Child and Adolescent Psychiatry*, *31*, 1003–1013.

Oh, S., & Lewis, C. (2008). Korean preschoolers' advanced inhibitory control and its relation to other executive skills and mental state understanding. *Child Development*, *79*, 80–99.

Öhman, A., & Mineka, S. (2001). Fear, phobias, and preparedness: Toward an evolved module of fear and fear learning. *Psychological Review*, *108*, 483–522.

Öhman, A., & Mineka, S. (2003). The malicious serpent: Snakes as a prototype stimulus for an evolved module for fear. *Current Directions in Psychological Science*, *12*, 5–9.

Olds, J. (1958). Satiation effects in self-stimulation of the brain. *Journal of Comparative and Physiological Psychology*, *51*, 675–678.

Olson, J. M., & Maio, G. R. (2003). Attitudes in social behavior. In T. Millon & M. J. Lerner (Eds.), *Handbook of psychology: Personality and social psychology* (Vol. 5, pp. 299–325). Wiley.

Olson, J. M., & Zanna, M. P. (1993). Attitudes and attitude change. *Annual Review of Psychology*, *44*, 117–154.

Olsson, A., McMahon, K., Papenberg, G., Zaki, J., Bolger, N., & Ochsner, K. N. (2016). Vicarious fear learning depends on empathic appraisals and trait empathy. *Psychological Science, 27,* 25–33.

O'Mahony, M. (1978). Smell illusions and suggestion: Reports of smells contingent on tones played on television and radio. *Chemical Senses and Flavor, 3,* 183–187.

Open Science Collaboration. (2015). Estimating the reproducibility of psychological science. *Science, 349,* 943.

Opfer, J. E., & Gelman, S. A. (2011). Development of the animate-inanimate distinction. In U. Goswami (Ed.) *The Wiley-Blackwell handbook of childhood cognitive development* (2nd ed., pp. 213–238). Wiley-Blackwell.

Orne, M. T. (1959). The nature of hypnosis: Artifact and essence. *Journal of Abnormal and Social Psychology, 58,* 277–299.

Orne, M. T. (1969). Demand characteristics and the concept of quasi-controls. In R. Rosenthal & R. L. Rosnow (Eds.), *Artifact in behavioral research* (pp. 143–179) Academic Press.

Ornstein, P. A., Haden, C. A., & San Souci, P. (2008). The development of skilled remembering in children. In H. L. Roediger III (Ed.), *Learning and memory: A comprehensive reference* (Vol. 2, pp. 715–744). Elsevier.

Ortony, A., & Turner, T. J. (1990). What's basic about basic emotions? *Psychological Review, 97,* 315–331.

Ostacher, M. J., & Eidelman, P. (2006). Suicide in bipolar depression. In R. El-Mallakh & N. Ghaemi (Eds.), *Bipolar depression: A comprehensive guide.* American Psychiatric Publishing.

Özgen, E. (2004). Language, learning, and color perception. *Current Directions in Psychological Science, 13,* 95–98.

Paivio, A. (2007). *Mind and its evolution.* Erlbaum.

Palmore, E. B. (1990). *Ageism: Negative and positive.* Springer.

Palombo, D. J., Hayes, S. M., Reid, A. G., & Verfaellie, M. (2019). Hippocampal contributions to value-based learning: Converging evidence from fMRI and amnesia. *Cognitive, Affective, & Behavioral Neuroscience, 19,* 523–536.

Paluck, E. L., & Green, D. P. (2009). Prejudice reduction: What works? A review and assessment of research and practice. *Annual Review of Psychology, 60,* 339–367.

Papageorgiou, M., Raza, A., Fraser, S., Nurgali, K., & Apostolopoulos, V. (2019). Methamphetamine and its immune-modulating effects. *Maturitas, 121,* 13–21.

Parent, A.-S., Teilmann, G., Juul, A., Skakkebaek, N. E., Toppari, J., & Bourguignon, J. P. (2003, October). The timing of normal puberty and the age limits of sexual precocity: Variations around the world, secular trends, and changes after migration. *Endocrine Reviews, 24*(5), 668–693. doi: 10.1210/er.2002-0019

Parovel, G., Guidi, S., & Kreß, K. (2018). Different contexts change the impression of animacy. *Attention, Perception, & Psychophysics, 80,* 553–563. doi: https://doi.org/10.3758/s13414-017-1439-x

Parsons, J. E., Kaczala, C., & Meece, J. L. (1982). Socialization of achievement attitudes and beliefs: Classroom influences. *Child Development, 53,* 322–339.

Patall, E. A., Cooper, H., & Robinson, J. C. (2008). The effects of choice on intrinsic motivation and related outcomes: A meta-analysis of research findings. *Psychological Bulletin, 134,* 270–300.

Patel, R. S., Bachu, R., Adikey, A., Malik, M., & Shah, M. (2018). Factors related to physician burnout and its consequences: A review. *Behavioral Sciences, 8,* 98.

Paulus, P. B. (1988). *Prison crowding: A psychological perspective.* Springer.

Paus, T. (2010). Growth of white matter in the adolescent brain: Myelin or axon? *Brain & Cognition, 72,* 26–35.

Payne, B. K., Krosnick, J. A., Pasek, J., Lelkes, Y., Akhtar, O., & Tompson, T. (2010). Implicit and explicit prejudice in the 2008 American presidential election. *Journal of Experimental Social Psychology, 46,* 367–374.

Payne, J. D. (2011). Learning, memory and sleep in humans. *Sleep Medicine Clinics, 6,* 15–30.

Payne, J. D., & Walker, M. P. (2008). Does delta sleep matter? *INSOM, 10,* 3–10.

Peissig, J. J., & Tarr, M. J. (2007). Visual object recognition: Do we know more now than we did 20 years ago? *Annual Review of Psychology, 58,* 75–96.

Peissig, J. J., Young, M. E., Wasserman, E. A., & Biederman, I. (2019). Pigeons spontaneously form three-dimensional shape categories. *Behavioural Processes, 158,* 70–76. https://doi.org/10.1016/j.beproc.2018.11.00

Penfield, W., & Perot, P. (1963). The brain's record of auditory and visual experience. *Brain, 86,* 595–696.

Penke, L., & Jokela, M. (2016). The evolutionary genetics of personality revisited. *Current Opinion in Psychology, 7,* 104–109.

Pennebaker, J. W. (1990). *Opening up: The healing power of confiding in others.* Morrow.

Pennebaker, J. W., & Chung, C. K. (2007). Expressive writings, emotional upheavals, and health. In H. S. Friedman & R. C. Silver (Eds.), *Foundations of health psychology* (pp. 263–284). Oxford University Press.

Pepping, C. A., Taylor, R., Koh, K., & Halford, W. K. (2017). Attachment, culture, and initial romantic attraction: A speed-dating study. *Personality and Individual Differences, 108,* 79–85. https://doi.org/10.1016/j.paid.2016.11.056

Pereira, P. J. S., & Lerner, E. A. (2017). Gate control theory springs leak. *Neuron, 93,* 723–724. doi:10.1016/j.neuron.2017.02.016

Perls, F. S. (1969). *Gestalt therapy verbatim.* Real People Press.

Perls, F. S., Hefferline, R. F., & Goodman, P. (1951). *Gestalt therapy.* Julian.

Perrett, D. I., & Mistlin, A. M. (1987). Visual neurones responsive to faces. *Trends in Neuroscience, 10,* 358–364.

Perry, G. (2013). Deception and illusion in Milgram's accounts of the obedience experiments. *Theoretical & Applied Ethics, 2,* 79–92.

Perry, J. L., & Dess, N. K. (2012). Laboratory animal research ethics: A practical, educational approach. In S. J. Knapp (Ed.), *APA handbook of ethics in psychology* (pp. 423–440). American Psychological Association.

Pert, C. B. (2002). The wisdom of the receptors: Neuropeptides, the emotions, and bodymind. *Advances in Mind-Body Medicine, 18,* 30–35.

Pert, C. B., & Snyder, S. H. (1973). The opiate receptor: Demonstration in nervous tissue. *Science, 179,* 1011–1014.

Peterson, A. C. (1988). Adolescent development. *Annual Review of Psychology, 39,* 583–607.

Peterson, C., & Park, N. (2010). What happened to self-actualization? Commentary on Kenrick et al. (2010). *Perspectives on Psychological Science, 5,* 320–322.

Peterson, C., & Seligman, M. E. P. (1987). Explanatory style and illness. *Journal of Personality, 55,* 237–265.

Peterson, C., Seligman, M. E. P., & Vaillant, G. E. (1988). Pessimistic explanatory style is a risk factor for physical illness: A thirty-five-year longitudinal study. *Journal of Personality and Social Psychology, 55,* 23–27.

Peterson, D. R. (1968). *The clinical study of social behavior.* Appleton-Century-Crofts.

Peterson, J. L., & Hyde, J. S. (2011). Gender differences in sexual attitudes and behaviors: A review of meta-analytic results and large datasets. *Journal of Sex Research, 48,* 149–165.

Peterson, L. R., & Peterson, M. J. (1959). Short-term retention of individual items. *Journal of Experimental Psychology, 58,* 193–198.

Pett, M. A., & Johnson, M. M. (2005). Development and psychometric evaluation of the revised University Student Hassles Scale. *Educational and Psychological Measurement, 65,* 984–1010.

Petty, R. E., & Cacioppo, J. T. (1986). *Communication and persuasion: Central and peripheral routes to attitude change.* Springer-Verlag.

Petty, R. E., DeSteno, D., & Rucker, D. D. (2001). The role of affect in attitude change. In J. P. Forgas (Ed.), *Handbook of affect and social cognition* (pp. 212–233). Erlbaum.

Petty, R. E., & Wegener, D. T. (1997). Attitude change: Multiple roles for persuasion variables. In D. Gilbert, S. Fiske, & G. Lindzey (Eds.), *Handbook of social psychology* (4th ed., pp. 323–390). McGraw-Hill.

Pfaff, D. W. (1999). *Drive: Neurobiological and molecular mechanisms of sexual motivation.* MIT Press.

Phillips, W. L. (2019). Cross-cultural differences in visual perception of color, illusions, depth, and pictures. In K. D. Keith (Ed.), *Cross-cultural psychology* (2nd ed., pp. 287–308). Wiley Blackwell.

Piaget, J. (1929). *The child's conception of the world.* Harcourt Brace.

Piaget, J. (1970). Piaget's theory. In P. H. Mussen (Ed.), *Carmichael's manual of child psychology* (Vol. 1). Wiley.

Pickering, B., Thompson, D., & Filik, R. (2018). Examining the emotional impact of sarcasm using a virtual environment. *Metaphor and Symbol, 33,* 185–197.

Pickles, J. O. (1988). *An introduction to the physiology of hearing* (2nd ed.). Academic Press.

Pierce, T. W., Madden, D. J., Siegel, W. C., & Blumenthal, J. A. (1993). Effects of aerobic exercise on cognitive and psychosocial functioning in patients with mild hypertension. *Health Psychology, 12,* 286–291.

Pietschnig, J., Voracek, M., & Formann, A. K. (2010). Mozart effect-Shmozart effect: A meta-analysis. *Intelligence, 38,* 314–323.

Pinel, J. (1999). Rhinal cortex, but not medial thalamic, lesions cause retrograde amnesia for objects in rats. *Neuroreport, 10,* 2853–2858.

Pines, A. (1993). Burnout. In L. Goldberger & S. Breznitz (Eds.), *Handbook of stress: Theoretical and clinical aspects* (2nd ed., pp. 386–402). Free Press.

Pines, A., & Aronson, E. (1988). *Career burnout: Causes and cures* (2nd ed.). Free Press.

Pinker, S. (1994). *The language instinct.* HarperCollins.

Pinker, S. (1997). *How the mind works.* Norton.

Pinto, Y., de Haan, E. H. F., & Lamme, V. A. F. (2017). The split-brain phenomenon revisited: A single conscious agent with split perception. *Trends in Cognitive Sciences, 21,* 835–851.

Piotrowski, C. (2015). On the decline in projective techniques in professional psychology. *North American Journal of Psychology, 17,* 259.

Plomin, R., Corley, R., Caspi, A., Fulker, D. W., & DeFries, J. (1998). Adoption results for self-reported personality: Evidence for non-additive genetic effects? *Journal of Personality & Social Psychology, 75,* 211–218.

Plomin, R., & Deary, I. J. (2015). Genetics and intelligence differences: Five special findings. *Molecular Psychiatry, 20,* 98–108.

Plomin, R., Fulker, D. W., Corley, R., & DeFries, J. C. (1997). Nature, nurture, and cognitive development from 1 to 16 years: A parent–offspring adoption study. *Psychological Science, 8,* 442–447.

Plomin, R., & von Stumm, S. (2018). The new genetics of intelligence. *Nature Reviews Genetics, 19,* 148–159.

Plous, S. (1991). An attitude survey of animal rights activists. *Psychological Science, 2,* 194–196.

Poeppl, T. B., Langguth, B., Rupprecht, R., Laird, A. R., & Eickhoff, S. B. (2016). A neural circuit encoding sexual preference in humans. *Neuroscience & Biobehavioral Reviews, 68,* 530–536.

Polivy, J., & Herman, C. P. (2002). Causes of eating disorders. *Annual Review of Psychology, 53,* 187–213.

Population Reference Bureau. (2018). *2018 World Population Data Sheet.* https://www.prb.org/wp-content/uploads/2018/08/2018_WPDS.pdf

Pornsakulvanich, V. (2018). Excessive use of Facebook: The influence of self-monitoring and Facebook usage on social support. *Kasetsart Journal of Social Sciences, 39,* 116–121.

Poropat, A. E. (2009). A meta-analysis of the Five-Factor model of personality and academic performance. *Psychological Bulletin, 135,* 322–338.

Porter, R. H., Makin, J. W., Davis, L. B., & Christensen, K. M. (1992). Breast-fed infants respond to olfactory clues from their own mother and unfamiliar lactating females. *Infant Behavior and Development, 15,* 85–93.

Posner, M. I. (1993). Interaction of arousal and selection in the posterior attention network. In A. Baddeley & L. Weiskrantz (Eds.), *Attention: Selection, awareness, and control: A tribute to Donald Broadbent* (pp. 390–405). Clarendon Press.

Posner, M. I., & Rothbart, M. K. (2007). Research on attention networks as a model for the integration of psychological science. *Annual Review of Psychology, 58,* 1–23.

Postmes, T., & Spears, R. (1998). Deindividuation and antinormative behavior: A meta-analysis. *Psychological Bulletin, 123,* 238–259.

Powers, M. B., & Emmelkamp, P. M. G. (2008). Virtual reality exposure therapy for anxiety disorders: A meta-analysis. *Journal of Anxiety Disorders*, *22*, 561–569.

Prakash, R. S., Voss, M. W., Erickson, K. I., & Kramer, A. F. (2015, January). Physical activity and cognitive vitality. *Annual Review of Psychology*, *66*, 769–797. https://doi.org/10.1146/annurev-psych-010814-015249

Pratt, G. J., Wood, D., & Alman, B. M. (1988). *A clinical hypnosis primer*. Wiley.

Premack, D. (1976). *Intelligence in ape and man*. Erlbaum.

Prescott, A. T., Sargent, J. D., & Hull, J. G. (2018). Metanalysis of the relationship between violent video game play and physical aggression over time. *Proceedings of the National Academy of Sciences*, *115*, 9882–9888.

Proctor, F., Wagner, N., & Butler, J. (1974). The differentiation of male and female orgasm: An experimental study. In N. Wagner (Ed.), *Perspectives on human sexuality* (pp. 115–134). Behavioral Publications

Profet, M. (1992). Pregnancy sickness as adaptation: A deterrent to maternal ingestion of teratogens. In J. H. Barkow, L. Cosmides, & J. Tooby (Eds.), *The adapted mind* (pp. 327–365). Oxford University Press.

Provence, S. A., & Lipton, R. C. (1962). *Infants in institutions*. International Universities Press.

Przedborski, S. (2005). Pathogenesis of nigral cell death in Parkinson's disease. *Parkinsonism and Related Disorders*, *11*(Suppl. 1), S3–S7.

Puccio, F., Fuller-Tyszkiewicz, M., Ong, D., & Krug, I. (2016). A systematic review and meta-analysis on the longitudinal relationship between eating pathology and depression. *International Journal of Eating Disorders*, *49*, 439–454.

Pyc, M. A., & Rawson, K. A. (2010). Why testing improves memory: Mediator effectiveness hypothesis. *Science*, *330*, 335.

Pyszczynski, T., Soloman, S., & Greenberg, J. (2015). Thirty years of terror management theory: From genesis to revelation. *Advances in Experimental Social Psychology*, *52*, 1–70.

Qiu, A., Rifkin-Graboi, A., Chen, H., Chong, Y.-S., Kwek, K., Gluckman, P. D., Fortier, M. V., & Meaney, M. J. (2013). Maternal anxiety and infants' hippocampal development: Timing matters. *Translational Psychiatry*, *3*, e306. doi: 10.1038/tp.2013.79

Rachman, S. J. (1990). *Fear and courage*. Freeman.

Rainforth, M. V., Schneider, R. H., Nidich, S. I., Gaylord-King, C., Salerno, J. W., & Anderson, J. W. (2007). Stress reduction programs in patients with elevated blood pressure: A systematic review and meta-analysis. *Current Hypertension Reports*, *9*, 520–528.

Rakic, P. (1991). Plasticity of cortical development. In S. E. Brauth, W. S. Hall, & R. J. Dooling (Eds.), *Plasticity of development* (pp. 127–161). Bradford/MIT Press.

Ramachandran, V. S. (2011). *The tell-tale brain: A neuroscientist's quest for what makes us human*. Norton.

Rasmussen, H. N., Scheier, M. F., & Greenhouse, J. B. (2009). Optimism and physical health: A meta-analytic review. *Annals of Behavioral Medicine*, *37*, 239–256.

Rathod, S. (2017). Contemporary psychotherapy and cultural adaptations. *Journal of Contemporary Psychotherapy*, *47*, 61–63.

Raugh, M. R., & Atkinson, R. C. (1975). A mnemonic method for learning a second-language vocabulary. *Journal of Educational Psychology*, *67*, 1–16.

Rauscher, F. H., Shaw, G. L., & Ky, K. N. (1993). Music and spatial task performance. *Nature*, *365*, 611.

Rauscher, F. H., Shaw, G. L., & Ky, K. N. (1995). Listening to Mozart enhances spatial-temporal reasoning: Toward a neurophysiological basis. *Neuroscience Letters*, *185*, 44–47.

Raven, J. C., Court, J. H., & Raven, J. (1985). *A manual for Raven's progressive matrices and vocabulary scales*. H. K. Lewis.

Raynor, H. A., & Epstein, L. H. (2001). Dietary variety, energy regulation, and obesity. *Psychological Bulletin*, *127*, 325–341.

Raynor, H. A., & Vadiveloo, M. (2018). Understanding the relationship between food variety, food intake, and energy balance. *Current Obesity Reports*, *7*, 68–75.

Read, C. N., & Greenberg, B. D. (2009). Psychiatric neurosurgery 2009: Review and perspective. *Seminars in Neurology*, *29*, 256–265.

Reagan, P. B., Salsberry, P. J., Fang, M. Z., Gardner, W. P., & Pajer, K. (2012, October). African-American/white differences in the age of menarche: Accounting for the difference. *Social Science & Medicine*, *75*(7), 1263–1270. doi: 10.1016/j.socscimed.2012.05.018

Rechtschaffen, A., & Bergmann, B. M. (1995). Sleep deprivation in the rat by the disk-over-water method. *Behavioural Brain Research*, *69*, 55–63.

Redelmeier, D. A., & Tibshirani, R. J. (1997). Association between cellular-telephone calls and motor vehicle collisions. *New England Journal of Medicine*, *336*, 543–458.

Ree, M. J., & Earles, J. A. (1992). Intelligence is the best predictor of job performance. *Current Directions in Psychological Science*, *1*, 86–89.

Regoeczi, W. C. (2003). When context matters: A multilevel analysis of household and neighborhood crowding on aggression and withdrawal. *Journal of Environmental Psychology*, *23*, 457–470.

Reimann, D., Krone, L. B., Wulff, K., & Nisson, C. (2020). Sleep, insomnia, and depression. *Neuropsychopharamacology*, *45*, 74–89.

Reis, H. T., Maniaci, M. R., Caprariello, P. A., Eastwick, P. W., & Finkel, E. J. (2011). Familiarity does indeed promote attraction in love interaction. *Journal of Personality and Social Psychology*, *101*, 557–570.

Remes, O., Brayne, C., van der Linde, R., & Lafortune, L. (2016). A systematic review of reviews on the prevalence of anxiety disorders in adult populations. *Brain and Behavior*, *6*, e00497. doi: 10.1002/brb3.497

Rescorla, R. A. (1980). Simultaneous and successive associations in sensory preconditioning. *Journal of Experimental Psychology: Animal Behavior Processes*, *6*, 207–216.

Rescorla, R. A. (1988). Pavlovian conditioning: It's not what you think it is. *American Psychologist*, *43*, 151–160.

Rescorla, R. A. (2001). Retraining of extinguished Pavlovian stimuli. *Journal of Experimental Psychology: Animal Behavior Processes*, *27*, 115–124.

Revonsuo, A. (2000). The reinterpretation of dreams: An evolutionary hypothesis of the function of dreaming. *Behavioral and Brain Sciences*, *23*, 877–901.

Rhodes, G. (2006). The evolutionary psychology of facial beauty. *Annual Review of Psychology*, *57*, 199–226.

Rhodes, G., & Tremewan, T. (1996). Averageness, exaggeration, and facial attractiveness. *Psychological Science*, 7, 105–110.

Rhodes, M., & Gelman, S. A. (2009). Five-year-olds' beliefs about the discreteness of category boundaries for animals and artifacts. *Psychonomic Bulletin & Review*, 16, 920–924.

Rhodes, R. E., Rodriguez, F., & Shah, P. (2014). Explaining the alluring influence of neuroscience information on scientific reasoning. *Journal of Experimental Psychology: Learning, Memory, and Cognition*, 40, 1432–1440.

Richardson, R. C. (2007). *Evolutionary psychology as maladapted psychology*. MIT Press.

Richtand, N. M., Welge, J. A., Logue, A. D., Keck, P. E., Strakowsi, S. M., & McNamara, R. K. (2007). Dopamine and serotonin receptor binding and antipsychotic efficacy. *Neuropsychopharmacology*, 32, 1715–1726.

Ricker, T. J., Sandry, J., Vergauwe, E., & Cowan, N. (2020). Do familiar items decay? *Journal of Experimental Psychology: Learning, Memory, and Cognition*, 46(1), 60–76.

Ridley, M. (2003). *Nature via nurture: Genes, experience, and what makes us human*. HarperCollins.

Rieznik, A., Lebedev, M., & Sigman, M. (2017). Dazzled by the mystery of mentalism: The cognitive neuroscience of mental athletes. *Frontiers in Human Neuroscience*, 11, Article 287.

Riggio, R. E. (2017). *Introduction to industrial/organizational psychology* (7th ed.). Routledge.

Ritchie, S. J., Cox, S. R., Shen, X., Lombardo, M. V., Reus, L. M., Alloza, C., Harris, M. A., Alderson, H. L., Hunter, S., Neilson, E., Liewald, D. C. M., Auyeung, B., Whalley, H. C., Lawrie, S. M., Gale, C. R., Bastin, M. E., McIntosh, A. M., & Deary, I. J. (2018). Sex differences in adult human brain: Evidence from 5216 UK Biobank participants. *Cerebral Cortex*, 28, 2959–2975.

Rivera, M. T., Soderstrom, S. B., & Uzzi, B. (2010). Dynamics of dyads in social networks: Assortative, relational, and proximity mechanisms. *Annual Review of Sociology*, 36, 91–115.

Roberts, G. M. P., Nestor, L., & Garavan, H. (2009). Learning and memory deficits in ecstasy users and their neural correlates during a face-learning task. *Brain Research*, 1292, 71–81.

Robins, R. W., & Beer, J. S. (2001). Positive illusions about the self: Short-term benefits and long-term costs. *Journal of Personality and Social Psychology*, 80, 340–352.

Robinson, J. O., Rosen, M., Revill, S. I., David, H., & Rus, G. A. D. (1980). Self-administered intravenous and intramuscular pethidine. *Anaesthesia*, 35, 763–770.

Roediger, H. L., III, & Karpicke, J. D. (2018). Reflections on the resurgence of interest in the testing effect. *Perspectives on Psychological Science*, 13, 236–241.

Roediger, H. L., III, & McDermott, K. B. (1995). Creating false memories: Remembering words not presented in lists. *Journal of Experimental Psychology: Learning, Memory, & Cognition*, 21, 803–814.

Roediger, H. L., III., Weldon, M. S., Stadler, M. L., & Riegler, G. L. (1992). Direct comparison of two implicit memory tests: Word fragment and word stem completion. *Journal of Experimental Psychology: Learning, Memory, & Cognition*, 18, 1251–1269.

Rogers, C. R. (1951). *Client-centered therapy*. Houghton Mifflin.

Rogers, C. R. (1963). The actualizing tendency in relation to "motives" and to consciousness. In M. R. Jones (Ed.), *Nebraska symposium on motivation* (Vol. 11, pp. 1–24). University of Nebraska.

Rolls, B. J., van Duijvencvoorde, P. M., & Rolls, E. T. (1984). Pleasantness changes and food intake in a varied four course meal. *Appetite*, 5, 337–348.

Romans, S. E., Martin, M., & Herbison, G. P. (2003). Age of menarche: The role of some psychosocial factors. *Psychological Medicine*, 33, 933–939.

Rosch, E., & Mervis, C. B. (1975). Family resemblances: Studies in the internal structure of categories. *Cognitive Psychology*, 7, 573–605.

Rosch, E., Mervis, C. B., Gray, W. D., Johnson, D. M., & Bayes-Braem, P. (1976). Basic objects in natural categories. *Cognitive Psychology*, 8, 382–439.

Rose, H., & Rose, S. (2000). *Alas, poor Darwin: Arguments against evolutionary psychology*. Harmony Books.

Rosenbaum, M. E. (1986). The repulsion hypothesis: On the non-development of relationships. *Journal of Personality and Social Psychology*, 51, 1156–1166.

Rosenhan, D. L. (1973). On being sane in insane places. *Science*, 179, 250–258.

Rosenthal, R. (1966). *Experimenter effects in behavioral research*. Appleton-Century-Crofts.

Rosenthal, R., & Rosnow, R. L. (Eds.). (1969). *Artifact in behavioral research*. Academic Press.

Rosenthal, R., & Rosnow, R. L. (1975). *The volunteer subject*. Wiley.

Rosenthal, S. M. (2016). Transgender youths: Current concepts. *Annals of Pediatric Endocrinology & Metabolism*, 21, 185–192.

Rosenzweig, S. (1936). Some implicit common factors in diverse methods of psychotherapy. *American Journal of Orthopsychiatry*, 6, 422–425.

Rosnow, R. L., & Rosenthal, R. (1996). *Beginning behavioral research: A conceptual primer* (2nd ed.). Macmillan.

Ross, C. A., Miller, S. D., Reagor, P., Bjornson, L., Fraser, G. A., & Anderson, G. (1990). Structured interview data on 102 cases of multiple personality disorder from four centers. *American Journal of Psychiatry*, 147, 596–601.

Ross, L. (1977). The intuitive psychologist and his shortcomings: Distortions in the attribution process. In L. Berkowitz (Ed.), *Advances in experimental social psychology* (Vol. 10, pp. 173–220). Academic Press.

Ross, L. (2018). From the fundamental attribution error to the truly fundamental attribution error and beyond: My research journey. *Perspectives on Psychological Science*, 136, 750–769.

Ross, L., & Nisbett, R. E. (1991). *The person and the situation: Perspectives of social psychology*. McGraw-Hill.

Rotenstein, L. S., Torre M., & Ramos, M. A., Rosales, R. C., Guille, C., Sen, S., & Mata, D. A. (2018). Prevalence of burnout among physicians: A systematic review. *Journal of the American Medical Association*, 320, 1131–1150.

Rothbart, M. K. (2007). Temperament, development, and personality. *Current Directions in Psychological Science*, 16, 207–212.

Rothbaum, F., & Morelli, G. (2005). Attachment and culture: Bridging relativism and universalism. In W. Friedlemeier, P. Chakkarath, & B. Schwarz (Eds.), *Culture and human development: The importance of cross-cultural research in the social sciences* (pp. 99–124). Psychology Press.

Rothbaum, F., Weisz, J., Pott, M., Kazuo, M., & Morelli, G. (2000). Attachment and culture: Security in the United States and Japan. *American Psychologist, 55*, 1093–1104.

Rotter, J. B. (1966). Generalized expectancies for internal versus external locus of control of reinforcement. *Psychological Monographs, 80*((Whole No. 609).

Rotter, J. B., Liverant, S., & Crowne, D. P. (1961). The growth and extinction of expectancies in change controlled and skilled tasks. *Journal of Psychology, 52*, 161–177.

Rovee-Collier, C. (1993). The capacity for long-term memory in infancy. *Current Directions in Psychological Science, 2*, 130–135.

Roy, M. M., & Christenfeld, N. (2004). Do dogs resemble their owners? *Psychological Science, 15*, 361–363.

Rozin, P., & Fallon, A. E. (1987). A perspective on disgust. *Psychological Review, 94*, 23–41.

Rozin, P., Fischler, C., Imada, S., Sarubin, A., & Wrzesniewski, A. (1999). Attitudes to food and the role of food in life in the U.S.A., Japan, Flemish Belgium and France: Possible implications for the diet–health debate. *Appetite, 33*, 163–180.

Rozin, P., Hammer, L., Oster, H., Horowitz, T., & Marmara, V. (1986). The child's conception of food: Development of categories of accepted and rejected substances. *Journal of Nutrition Education, 18*, 75–81.

Rubenstein, L. M., Freed, R. D., Shapero, B. G., Fauber, R. L., & Alloy, L. B. (2016). Cognitive attributions in depression: Bridging the gap between research and clinical practice. *Journal of Psychotherapy Integration, 26*, 103–155.

Rubin, D. C., & Berntsen, D. (2003). Life scripts help to maintain autobiographical memories of highly positive, but not highly negative, events. *Memory & Cognition, 31*, 1–14.

Rudman, L. A., & Borgida, E. (1995). The afterglow of construct accessibility: The behavioral consequences of priming men to view women as sexual objects. *Journal of Experimental Social Psychology, 31*, 493–517.

Rumbaugh, D. M. (Eds.). (1977). *Language learning by a chimpanzee: The Lana project.* Academic Press.

Rupp, H. A., & Wallen, K. (2008). Sex differences in response to visual sexual stimuli: A review. *Archives of Sexual Behavior, 37*, 206–218.

Rusbult, C. E., Agnew, C. R., & Arriaga, X. B. (2012). The investment model of commitment processes. In P. A. M. Van Lange, A. W. Kruglanski, & E. T. Higgins (Eds.), *Handbook of theories of social psychology* (Vol. 2, pp. 218–231). Sage.

Rushton, J. P., & Jensen, A. R. (2005). Thirty years of research on race differences in cognitive ability. *Psychology, Public Policy, and Law, 11*, 235–294.

Russell, J. A. (1994). Is there universal recognition of emotion from facial expression? A review of the cross-cultural studies. *Psychological Bulletin, 115*, 102–141.

Russell, J. A. (2003). Core affect and the psychological construction of emotion. *Psychological Review, 110*, 145–172.

Rutherford, B. R., Mori, S., Sneed, J. R., Pimontel, M. A., & Roose, S. P. (2012). Contribution of spontaneous improvement to placebo response in depression: A meta-analytic review. *Journal of Psychiatric Research, 46*(6), 697–702.

Ryan, K. M. (2004). Further evidence for a cognitive component of rape. *Aggression & Violent Behavior, 9*, 579–604.

Ryan, R. M., & Deci, E. L. (2000). Intrinsic and extrinsic motivations: Classic definitions and new directions. *Contemporary Educational Psychology, 25*, 54–67.

Ryan, T., Allen, K., Gray, D., & McInerney, D. (2017). How social are social media? A review of online social behaviour and connectedness. *Journal of Relationships Research, 8*, E8. doi:10.1017/jrr.2017.13

Ryckman, R. M. (2004). *Theories of personality* (8th ed.). Wadsworth.

Ryckman, R. M. (2008). *Theories of personality.* (9th ed.). Wadsworth.

Saarimaki, H., Gotsopoulos, A., Jääskeläinen, I. P., Lampinen, J., Vuilleumier, P., Hari, R., Sams, M., & Nummenmaa, L. (2016). Discrete neural signatures of basic emotions. *Cerebral Cortex, 26*(6), 2563–2573.

Sacks, O. (1985). *The man who mistook his wife for a hat and other clinical tales.* Summit Books.

Sacks, O. (2010). *The mind's eye.* Knopf.

Sah, P. (2017). Fear, anxiety, and the amygdala. *Neuron, 96*, 1–2.

Salovey, P., & Mayer, J. D. (1990). Emotional intelligence. *Imagination, Cognition, and Personality, 9*, 185–211.

Salthouse, T. A. (1994). The nature of the influence of speed on adult age differences in cognition. *Developmental Psychology, 30*, 240–259.

Salthouse, T. A. (2012). Consequences of age-related cognitive declines. *Annual Review of Psychology, 63*, 201–226.

Sanchez-Meca, J., Rosa-Alcazar, A. I., Marin-Martinez, F., & Gomez-Conesa, A. (2010). Psychological treatment of panic disorder with or without agoraphobia: A meta-analysis. *Clinical Psychology Review, 30*, 37–50.

Sanchez-Roige, S., Gray, J. C., MacKillop, J., Chen, C. H., & Palmer, A. A. (2018). The genetics of human personality. *Genes, Brain and Behavior, 17*, e12439.

Sanders, A. R., Beecham, G. W., Guo, S., Dawood, K., Rieger, G., Badner, J. A., Gershon, E. S., Krishnappa, R. S., Kolundzija, A. B., Duan, J., MGS Collaboration, Gejman, P. V., Bailey, J. M., & Martin, E. R. (2018). Genome-wide association study of male sexual orientation. *Scientific Reports, 7*, 16950. doi: https://doi.org/10.1038/s41598-017-15736-4

Sanson, A., & Di Muccio, C. (1993). The influence of aggressive and neutral cartoons and toys on the behaviour of preschool children. *Australian Psychologist, 28*, 93–99.

Santos, H. C., Varnum, M. E. W., & Grossmann, I. (2017). Global increases in individualism. *Psychological Science, 28*, 1228–1239.

Sanz, J., Sanchez-Bernados, M. L., & Avia, M. D. (1996). Self-monitoring and the prediction of one's own and others' personality test scores. *European Journal of Personality, 10*, 173–184.

Sar, V., Akyuz, G., & Dogan, O. (2007). Prevalence of dissociative identity disorder among women in the general population. *Psychiatry Research, 149*, 169–176.

Sarbin, T. R., & Coe, W. C. (1972). *Hypnosis: A social psychological analysis of influence communication*. Holt, Rinehart & Winston.

Saucier, D. A., & Cain, M. E. (2006). The foundations of attitudes about animal research. *Ethics & Behavior, 16*, 117–133.

Saudino, K. J. (2009). The development of temperament from a behavioral genetics perspective. *Advances in Child Development and Behavior, 37*, 201–231.

Sauter, D. A., Eisner, F., Ekman, P., & Scott, S. K. (2010). Cross-cultural recognition of basic emotions through nonverbal emotional vocalizations. *Proceedings of the National Academy of Sciences, 107*, 2408–2412.

Savage-Rumbaugh, S., McDonald, D., Sevcik, R., Hopkins, W., & Rupert, E. (1986). Spontaneous symbol acquisition and communicative use by pygmy chimpanzees. *Journal of Experimental Psychology: General, 115*, 211–235.

Savage-Rumbaugh, S., Murphy, J., Sevcik, R., Brakke, K., Williams, S., & Rumbaugh, D. M. (1993). Language comprehension in ape and child. *Monographs of the Society for Research in Child Development, 58* (3–4, Serial No. 233), .

Savin-Williams, R. C. (2006). Who's gay? Does it matter? *Current Directions in Psychological Science, 15*, 40–44.

Sayo, A., Jennings, R. G., & Van Horn, J. D. (2012). Study factors influencing ventricular enlargement in schizophrenia: A 20 year follow up meta-analysis. *NeuroImage, 59*, 154–167.

Scarr, S., & Weinberg, R. A. (1976). IQ test performance of Black children adopted by White families. *American Psychologist, 31*, 726–739.

Schachter, S. (1971). *Emotion, obesity, and crime*. Academic Press.

Schachter, S., & Gross, L. (1968). Manipulated time and eating behavior. *Journal of Personality and Social Psychology, 10*, 98–106.

Schachter, S., & Singer, J. E. (1962). Cognitive, social, and physiological determinants of emotional state. *Psychological Review, 69*, 379–399.

Schacter, D. L. (2001). *The seven sins of memory*. Houghton Mifflin.

Schacter, D. L., Benoit, R. G., & Szpunar, K. K. (2017). Episodic future thinking: Mechanisms and functions. *Current Opinion in Behavioral Sciences, 17*, 41–50.

Schaie, K. W. (2005). *Developmental influences on adult intelligence: The Seattle Longitudinal Study*. Oxford University Press.

Schaie, K. W. (2013). *Developmental influences on adult intellectual development: The Seattle Longitudinal Study* (2nd ed.). Oxford University Press.

Schaie, K. W. (2016). The longitudinal study of adult cognitive development. In R. J. Sternberg, S. T. Fiske, & D. J. Foss (Eds.), *Scientists making a difference* (pp. 218–221). Cambridge University Press.

Scheier, M. F., & Carver, C. S. (1993). On the power of positive thinking: The benefits of being optimistic. *Current Directions in Psychological Science, 2*, 26–30.

Scheier, M. F., & Carver, C. S. (2018). Dispositional optimism and physical health: A long look back, a quick look forward. *American Psychologist, 73*, 1082–1094.

Scheier, M. F., Matthews, K. A., Owens, J. F., Magovern, G. J., Sr., Lefebvre, C. R., Abbott, R. A., & Carver, C. S. (1989). Dispositional optimism and recovery from coronary artery bypass surgery: The beneficial effects on physical and psychological well-being. *Journal of Personality and Social Psychology, 57*, 1024–1040.

Schleifer, S. J., Keller, S. E., Meyerson, A. T., Raskin, M. J., Davis, K. L., & Stein, M. (1983). Suppression of lymphocyte stimulation following bereavement. *Journal of the American Medical Association, 250*, 374.

Schlenker, B. R., & Forsyth, D. R. (1977). On the ethics of psychological research. *Journal of Experimental Social Psychology, 13*, 369–396.

Schmack, K., Stuke, H., Stezer, P., & Heinz, A. (2018). L-DOPA induces psychosis-like perception by disrupting the discrimination between relevant and irrelevant stimuli. *Biological Psychiatry, 83*, S445.

Schmader, T. (2010). Stereotype threat deconstructed. *Current Directions in Psychological Science, 19*, 14–18.

Schmahmann, J. D. (2019). The cerebellum and cognition. *Neuroscience Letters, 688*, 62–75.

Schmidt, F. L., & Hunter, J. E. (1993). Tacit knowledge, practical intelligence, general mental ability, and job knowledge. *Current Directions in Psychological Science, 2*, 8–9.

Schmitt, D. P. (2017, June 28). What type of person would agree to have sex with a stranger? *Psychology Today*. https://www.psychologytoday.com/blog/sexual-personalities/201706/who-would-agree-have-sex-total-stranger

Schmitt, D. P., & International Sexuality Description Project. (2003). Universal sex differences in the desire for sexual variety: Tests from 52 nations, 6 continents, and 13 islands. *Journal of Personality and Social Psychology, 85*(1), 85–104. http://dx.doi.org/10.1037/0022-3514.85.1.85

Schmitt, D. P., Long, A. E., McPhearson, A., O'Brien, K. Remmert, B., & Shah, S. H. (2017). Personality and gender differences in global perspective. *International Journal of Psychology, 52*, 45–56.

Schneider, S. G., Taylor, S. E., Hammen, C., Kemeny, M. E., & Dudley, J. (1991). Factors influencing suicide intent in gay and bisexual suicide ideators: Differing models for men with and without human immunodeficiency virus. *Journal of Personality and Social Psychology, 61*, 776–788.

Schneider, W. J., & McGrew, K. S. (2018). The Cattell–Horn–Carroll theory of cognitive abilities. In D. P. Flanagan & E. M. McDonough (Eds.), *Contemporary intellectual assessment: Theories, tests and issues* (4th ed., pp. 73–163). Guilford Press.

Schneiderman, N., Antoni, M. H., Saab, P. G., & Ironson, G. (2001). Health psychology: Psychosocial and biobehavioral aspects of chronic disease management. *Annual Review of Psychology, 52*, 555–580.

Scholte, R. H. J., & De Bruyn, E. J. (2004). Comparison of the giant three and the big five in early adolescents. *Personality and Individual Differences, 36*, 1353–1371.

Scholte, R. H. J., & van Aken, M. (2006). Peer relations in adolescence. In S. Jackson & L. Goossens (Eds.), *Handbook of adolescent development* (pp. 175–199). Psychology Press.

Schreiber, F. (1973). *Sybil*. Warner Books.

Schubert, A., Hagemann, D., & Frischkorn, G. T. (2017). Is general intelligence little more than speed of higher-order processing? *Journal of Experimental Psychology: General, 146*, 1498–1512.

Schuster, M. A., Stein, B. D., Jaycox, L. H., Collins, R. L., Marshall, G. N., Elliott, M. N., Zhou, A. J., Kanouse, D. E., Morrison, J. L., & Berry, S. H. (2001). A national survey of stress reactions after the September 11, 2001, terrorist attacks. *New England Journal of Medicine, 345*, 1507–1512.

Schwartz, B. (1990). The creation and destruction of value. *American Psychologist, 45,* 7–15.

Schwartz, M. W. (2006). Central nervous system regulation of food intake. *Obesity, 14,* 1S–8S.

Schwarz, N., & Strack, F. (1999). Reports of subjective well-being: Judgmental processes and their methodological implications. In D. Kahneman, E. Diener, & N. Schwarz (Eds.), *Hedonic psychology: Scientific perspectives on enjoyment, suffering, and well-being* (pp. 61–84). Cambridge University Press.

Scott, H., & Woods, H. C. (2018). Fear of missing out and sleep: Cognitive behavioural factors in adolescents' nighttime social media use. *Journal of Adolescence, 68,* 615–665.

Scott, S. E., Inbar, Y., & Rozin, P. (2016). Evidence for absolute moral opposition to genetically modified food in the United States. *Perspectives on Psychological Science, 11,* 315–324.

Sedikides, C., Campbell, W. K., Reeder, G. D., & Elliot, A. J. (1998). The self-serving bias in relational context. *Journal of Personality & Social Psychology, 74,* 378–386.

Seegert, C. R. (2003). Token economies and incentive programs: Behavioral improvement in mental health inmates housed in state prisons. *Behavior Therapist, 208,* 210–211.

Seeman, T. E., Dublin, L. F., & Seeman, M. (2003). Religiosity/spirituality and health: A critical review of the evidence for biological pathways. *American Psychologist, 58,* 53–63.

Sehgal, A., & Mignot, E. (2011). Genetics of sleep and sleep disorders. *Cell, 146,* 194–207.

Seli, P., Smilek, D., Ralph, B. C. W., & Schacter, D. L. (2018). The awakening of the attention: Evidence for a link between the monitoring of mind wandering and prospective goals. *Journal of Experimental Psychology: General, 147,* 431–443. https://doi.org/10.1037/xge0000385

Seligman, M. E. P. (1975). *Helplessness: On depression, development, and death.* Freeman.

Seligman, M. E. P. (2019). Positive psychology: A personal history. *Annual Review of Clinical Psychology, 15,* 1–23.

Sellbom, M. (2019). The MMPI-2-Restructured Form (MMPI-2-RF): Assessment of personality and psychopathology in the twenty-first century. *Annual Review of Clinical Psychology, 15,* 149–177.

Selye, H. (1936). A syndrome produced by diverse nocuous agents. *Nature, 138,* 32.

Selye, H. (1952). *The story of the adaptation syndrome.* Acta.

Selye, H. (1974). *Stress without distress.* Lippincott.

Sepple, C. P., & Read, N. W. (1989). Gastrointestinal correlates of the development of hunger in man. *Appetite, 13,* 183–191.

Shaffer, D. M., Krauchunas, S. M., Eddy, M., & McBeath, M. K. (2004). How dogs navigate to catch Frisbees. *Psychological Science, 15,* 437–441. 0.1111/j.0956-7976.2004.00698.x

Shaffer, D. R., & Kipp, K. (2010). *Developmental psychology: Childhood and adolescence* (8th ed.). Cengage.

Shapley, R., & Hawken, M. J. (2011). Color in the cortex: Single- and double-opponent cells. *Vision Research, 51,* 701–717.

Sharma, K. N., Anand, B. K., Due, S., & Singh, B. (1961). Role of stomach in regulation of activities of hypothalamic feeding centers. *American Journal of Physiology, 201,* 593–598.

Shearer, C. B., & Karanian, J. M. (2017). The neuroscience of intelligence: Empirical support for the theory of multiple intelligences. *Trends in Neuroscience and Education, 6,* 211–223.

Shepard, G. M. (2006). Smell images and the flavour system in the human brain. *Nature, 444,* 316–321.

Sher, L. (2004). Hypothalamic-pituitary-adrenal function and preventing major depressive episodes. *Canadian Journal of Psychiatry, 49,* 574–575.

Sheu, Y.-S., Liang, Y. M., & Desmond, J. E. (2019, February 21). Disruption of cerebellar prediction in verbal working memory. *Frontiers in Human Neuroscience.*

Shiffrin, R. M., & Schneider, W. (1977). Controlled and automatic human information processing II: Perceptual learning, automatic attending, and a general theory. *Psychological Review, 84,* 127–190.

Shirley, M. M. (1933). *The first two years: A study of 25 babies. Vol. 1: Postural and locomotor development.* University of Minnesota Press.

Shrout, P. E., & Rodgers, J. L. (2018). Psychology, science, and knowledge construction: Broadening perspectives from the replication crisis. *Annual Review of Psychology, 69,* 487–510.

Shuttleworth-Edwards, A. B. (2016). Generally representative is representative of none: Commentary on the pitfalls of IQ test standardization in multicultural settings. *The Clinical Neuropsychologist, 30,* 975–998.

Siegel, J. M. (1990). Stressful life events and use of physician services among the elderly: The moderating role of pet ownership. *Journal of Personality and Social Psychology, 58,* 1081–1086.

Siegel, S. (2011). The Four-Loko effect. *Perspectives in Psychological Science, 6,* 357–362.

Siegel, S. (2016). The heroin overdose mystery. *Current Directions in Psychological Science, 25,* 375–379.

Siegler, R. S. (1996). *Children's thinking: Beyond the immaculate transition.* Oxford University Press.

Silverman, D. K. (2020). Psychosexual stages of development (Freud). In V. Ziegler-Hill & T. K. Shackelford (Eds.), *Encyclopedia of personality and individual differences.* Springer. https://doi.org/10.1007/978-3-319-24612-3_1417

Silverstein, B., Perdue, L., Peterson, B., & Kelly, E. (1986). The role of the mass media in promoting a thin standard of bodily attractiveness for women. *Sex Roles, 14,* 519–532.

Silvia, P. J. (2008). Creativity and intelligence revisited: A latent variable analysis of Wallach and Kogan (1965). *Creativity Research Journal, 20,* 34–39.

Sim, E. J., & Kiefer, M. (2005). Category-related brain activity to natural categories is associated with the retrieval of visual features: Evidence from repetition effects during visual and functional judgments. *Cognitive Brain Research, 24,* 260–273.

Simons, D. J., & Chabris, C. F. (2011). What people believe about how memory works: A representative survey of the U.S. population. *PLOS One, 6,* 1–6.

Sio, U. N., & Ormerod, T. C. (2009). Does incubation enhance problem solving? A meta-analytic review. *Psychological Bulletin, 135,* 94–120.

Siqueland, E. R., & DeLucia, C. A. (1969). Visual reinforcement of nonnutritive sucking in human infants. *Science, 165,* 1144–1146.

Skinner, B. F. (1938). *The behavior of organisms: An experimental analysis*. Appleton-Century.

Skinner, B. F. (1948). "Superstition" in the pigeon. *Journal of Experimental Psychology, 38*, 168–172.

Skinner, B. F. (1969). *Contingencies of reinforcement: A theoretical analysis*. Appleton-Century-Crofts.

Slater, A., Von der Schulenburg, C., Brown, E., Badenoch, M., Butterworth, G., Parsons, S., & Samuels, C. (1998). Newborn infants prefer attractive faces. *Infant Behavior & Development, 21*, 345–354.

Sloane, R. B., Staples, F. R., Cristol, A. H., Yorkston, N. J., & Whipple, K. (1975). *Psychotherapy versus behavior therapy*. Harvard University Press.

Slovic, P., Fischhoff, B., & Lichtenstein, S. (1982). Facts versus fears: Understanding perceived risk. In D. Kahneman, P. Slovic, & A. Tversky (Eds.), *Judgment under uncertainty: Heuristics and biases* (pp. 65–102). Cambridge University Press.

Smallwood, J., & Schooler, J. W. (2015). The science of mind wandering: Empirically navigating the stream of consciousness. *Annual Review of Psychology, 66*, 487–518.

Smarandescu, L., & Shimp, T. A. (2015). Drink Coca-Cola, eat popcorn, and choose Powerade: Testing the limits of subliminal persuasion. *Marketing Letters, 26*, 715–726.

Smiler, A. P. (2011). Sexual strategies theory: Built for the short-term or the long-term? *Sex Roles, 64*, 603–612.

Smiley, P. A., & Dweck, C. S. (1994). Individual differences in achievement goals among young children. *Child Development, 65*, 1723–1743.

Smith, E., Hay, P., Campbell, L., & Troller, J. N. (2011). A review of the association between obesity and cognitive functions across the lifespan: Implications for novel approaches to prevention and treatment. *Obesity Reviews, 12*, 740–755.

Smith, E. R., & Semin, G. R. (2007). Situated social cognition. *Current Directions in Psychological Science, 16*, 132–135.

Smith, E. R., & Zárate, M. A. (1992). Exemplar-based model of social judgment. *Psychological Review, 99*, 3–21.

Smith, M. L., & Glass, G. V. (1977). Meta-analysis of psychotherapy outcome studies. *American Psychologist, 32*, 752–760.

Smith, M. L., Glass, G. V., & Miller, T. I. (1980). *The benefits of psychotherapy*. Johns Hopkins University Press.

Smith, T. W. (2006). Personality as risk and resilience in physical health. *Current Directions in Psychological Science, 15*, 227–231.

Smrt, D. L., & Karau, S. J. (2011). Protestant work ethic moderates social loafing. *Group Dynamics: Theory, Research, and Practice, 15*, 267–274.

Sniekers, S., Stringer, S., Watanabe, K., Jansen, P. R., Coleman, J. R. I., Krapohl, E., Taskesen, E., Hammerschlag, A. R., Okbay, A., Zabaneh, D., Amin, N., Breen, G., Cesarini, D., Chabris, C. F., Iacono, W. G., Ikram, M. A., Johannesson, M., Koellinger, P., Lee, J. J., . . . Posthuma, D. (2017). Genome-wide association meta-analysis of 78,308 individuals identifies new loci and genes influencing human intelligence. *Nature Genetics, 49*, 1107–1112.

Snowden, P. T., & Schyns, P. G. (2006). Channel surfing in the visual brain. *Trends in Cognitive Sciences, 10*, 538–545.

Snyder, C. R. (1989). Reality negotiation: From excuses to hope and beyond. Self-illusions: When are they adaptive? [Special issue] *Journal of Social and Clinical Psychology, 8*, 130–157.

Snyder, M. (1974). The self-monitoring of expressive behavior. *Journal of Personality and Social Psychology, 30*, 526–537.

Snyder, M. (1987). *Public appearances/private realities: The psychology of self-monitoring*. Freeman.

Snyder, M. (1995). Self-monitoring: Public appearances versus private reality. In G. G. Brannigan & M. R. Merrens (Eds.), *The social psychologists: Research adventures* (pp. 34–50). McGraw-Hill.

Snyder, M., Tanke, E. D., & Berscheid, E. (1977). Social perception and interpersonal behavior: On the self-fulfilling nature of social stereotypes. *Journal of Personality and Social Psychology, 35*, 656–666.

Snyder, S. H. (1976). The dopamine hypothesis of schizophrenia: Focus on the dopamine receptor. *American Journal of Psychiatry, 133*, 197–202.

Snyder, S. H. (2017). A life of neurotransmitters. *Annual Review of Pharmacology and Toxicology, 57*, 1–11.

Society for Personality Assessment. (2005). The status of the Rorschach in clinical and forensic practice: An official statement by the Board of Trustees of the Society for Personality Assessment. *Journal of Personality Assessment, 85*, 219–237.

Sofer, C., Dotsch, R., Wigboldus, D. H. J., & Todorov, A. (2015). What is typical is good: The influence of face typicality on perceived trustworthiness. *Psychological Science, 26*, 39–47.

Sorrells, S. F., Paredes, M. F., Cebrian-Silla, A., Sandoval, K., Qi, D., Kelley, K. W., James, D., Mayer, S., Chang, J., Auguste, K. I., Chang, E. F., Gutierrez, A. J., Kriegstein, A. R., Mathern, G. W., Oldham, M. C., Huang, E. J., Garcia-Verdugo, J. M., Yang, Z., & Alvarez-Buylla, A. (2018). Human hippocampal neurogenesis drops sharply in children to undetectable levels in adults. *Nature, 555*, 377–381.

Soto, C. J. (2019). How replicable are links between personality traits and consequential life outcomes? The Life Outcomes of Personality Replication Project. *Psychological Science, 30*(5). https://doi.org/10.1177/0956797619831612

Soussignan, R. (2002). Duchenne smile, emotional experience, and autonomic reactivity: A test of the facial feedback hypothesis. *Emotion, 2*, 52–74.

Spanos, N. P. (1982). Hypnotic behavior: A cognitive, social psychological perspective. *Research Communications in Psychology, Psychiatry, and Behavior, 7*, 199–213.

Spanos, N. P. (1986). Hypnotic behavior: A social psychological interpretation of amnesia, analgesia, and "trance logic." *The Behavioral and Brain Sciences, 9*, 449–502.

Spanos, N. P. (1996). *Multiple identities and false memories: A sociocognitive perspective*. American Psychological Association.

Spanos, N. P., Weeks, J. R., & Bertrand, L. D. (1985). Multiple personality: A social psychological perspective. *Journal of Abnormal Psychology, 92*, 362–376.

Spearman, C. (1904). "General intelligence," objectively determined and measured. *American Journal of Psychology, 15*, 201–293.

Spelke, E. S., & Kinzler, K. D. (2007). Core knowledge. *Developmental Science, 10*, 89–96.

Sperling, G. (1960). The information available in brief visual presentations. *Psychological Monographs, 74* (Whole No. 48).

Spiegel, D. (1995). Hypnosis and suggestion. In D. L. Schacter (Ed.), *Memory distortion* (pp. 129–149). Harvard University Press.

Spiegel, D. (1998). Social psychological theories cannot completely account for hypnosis: The record was never crooked. *American Journal of Clinical Hypnosis*, *41*, 158–161.

Spiegel, D., Bloom, J. R., Kramer, H. C., & Gotheil, E. (1989). Effect of psychosocial treatment on survival of patients with metastatic breast cancer. *Lancet*, *14*, 888–891.

Spiegler, M. D., & Guevremont, D. C. (2010). *Contemporary behavior therapy* (5th ed.). Cengage.

Spitz, R. A. (1945). Hospitalism: An inquiry into the genesis of psychiatric conditions in early childhood. *Psychoanalytic Study of the Child*, *1*, 53–74.

Spitzer, R. L. (1975). On pseudoscience in science, logic in remission, and psychiatric diagnosis: A critique of Rosenhan's "On being sane in insane places." *Journal of Abnormal Psychology*, *84*, 442–452.

Squire, L. R., & Dede, A. J. O. (2015). Conscious and unconscious memory systems. *Cold Spring Harbor Perspectives in Biology*, *7*, 1–15. doi: 10.1101/cshperspect.a021667

Sripada, C., Kessler, D., & Jonides, J. (2014). Methylphenidate blocks effort-induced depletion of regulatory control in healthy volunteers. *Psychological Science*, *25*, 1227–1234.

Staddon, J. E. R., & Simmelhag, V. L. (1971). The "superstition" experiment: A reexamination of its implications for the principles of adaptive behavior. *Psychological Review*, *78*, 3–43.

Steele, C. M., & Aronson, J. A. (1995). Stereotype threat and the intellectual test performance of African Americans. *Journal of Personality and Social Psychology*, *69*, 797–811.

Steele, K. M., Bass, K. E., & Cook, M. D. (1999). The mystery of the Mozart effect: Failure to replicate. *Psychological Science*, *10*, 366–369.

Steinberg, L., & Morris, A. S. (2001). Adolescent development. *Annual Review of Psychology*, *52*, 83–100.

Stepan, M. E., Fenn, K. M., & Altmann, E. M. (2019). Effects of sleep deprivation on procedural errors. *Journal of Experimental Psychology: General*, *148*, 1828–1833.

Sternberg, R. J. (1985). *Beyond IQ: A triarchic theory of human intelligence.* Cambridge University Press.

Sternberg, R. J. (1986). A triangular theory of love. *Psychological Review*, *93*, 119–135.

Sternberg, R. J. (1988). *The triarchic theory of mind: A new theory of human intelligence.* Viking Press.

Sternberg, R. J. (1999). *Cupid's arrow: The course of love through time.* Cambridge University Press.

Sternberg, R. J. (2011). From intelligence to leadership: A brief intellectual autobiography. *Gifted Child Quarterly*, *55*, 309–312.

Sternberg, R. J. (2015). Multiple intelligences in the new age of thinking. In S. Goldstein, D. Princiotta, & J. A. Naglieri (Eds.), *Handbook of intelligence: Evolutionary theory, historical perspectives, and current concepts* (pp. 229–241). Springer.

Sternberg, R. J., & Grajek, S. (1984). The nature of love. *Journal of Personality and Social Psychology*, *47*, 312–329.

Sternberg, R. J., & Hedlund, J. (2002). Practical intelligence, *g*, and work psychology. *Human Performance*, *15*, 143–160.

Sternberg, R. J., & Kaufman, J. C. (1998). Human abilities. *Annual Review of Psychology*, *49*, 479–502.

Sternberg, R. J., & The Rainbow Project Collaborators. (2006). The Rainbow Project: Enhancing the SAT through assessments of analytical, practical, and creative skills. *Intelligence*, *34*, 321–350.

Sternberg, R. J., & Wagner, R. K. (1993). The *g*-ocentric view of intelligence and job performance is wrong. *Current Directions in Psychological Science*, *2*, 1–5.

Stevens, J. R., & Hauser, M. D. (2004). Why be nice? Psychological constraints on the evolution of cooperation. *Trends in Cognitive Sciences*, *8*, 60–65.

Stevens, S. S. (1939). Psychology and the science of science. *Psychological Bulletin*, *36*, 221–263.

Stewart, D. D., & Stasser, G. (1995). Expert role assignment and information sampling during collective recall and decision making. *Journal of Personality & Social Psychology*, *69*, 619–628.

Stewart, T. L., Doan, K. A., Gingrich, B. E., & Smith, E. R. (1998). The actor as context for social judgments: Effects of prior impressions and stereotypes. *Journal of Personality and Social Psychology*, *75*, 1132–1154.

Steyvers, M., & Benjamin, A. S. (2019). The joint contribution of participation and performance to learning functions: Exploring the effects of age in large-scale data sets. *Behavior Research Methods*, *51*, 1531–1543.

Stinson, F. S., Dawson, D. A., Chou, S. P., Smith, S., Goldstein, R. B., Ruan, W. J., & Grant, B. F. (2007). The epidemiology of DSM-IV specific phobia in the USA: results from the National Epidemiologic Survey on Alcohol and Related Conditions. *Psychological Medicine*, *37*, 1047–1059.

Strack, F., Martin, L. L., & Stepper, S. (1988). Inhibiting and facilitating conditions of the human smile: A nonobtrusive test of the facial feedback hypothesis. *Journal of Personality and Social Psychology*, *54*, 768–777.

Strauss, J. R. (2011). Contextual influences on women's health concerns and attitudes toward menopause. *Health & Social Work*, *36*, 121–127.

Strayer, D. L., & Drews, F. A. (2007). Cell-phone-induced driver distraction. *Psychological Science*, *16*, 128–131.

Strayer, D. L., & Johnston, W. A. (2001). Driven to distraction: Dual-task studies of simulated driving and conversing on a cellular telephone. *Psychological Science*, *6*, 462–466.

Ströhle, A. (2009). Physical activity, exercise, depression and anxiety disorders. *Journal of Neural Transmission*, *116*, 777–784.

Sufta, K. J., & Price, D. D. (2002). Gate control theory reconsidered. *Brain & Mind*, *3*, 277–290.

Surprenant, A. M., & Neath, I. (2009). *Principles of memory.* Psychology Press.

Swami, V., Frederick, D. A., Aavik, T., Alcalay, L., Allik, J., Anderson, D., Andrianto, S., Arora, A., Brännström, A., Cunningham, J., Danel, D., Doroszewicz, K., Forbes, G. B., Furnham, A., Greven, C. U., Halberstadt, J., Hao, S., Haubner, T., Hwang, C. S., & Zivcic-Becirevic, I. (2010). The attractive female body weight and female body dissatisfaction in 26 countries across 10 world regions: Results of the International Body Project I. *Personality and Social Psychology Bulletin*, *36*, 309–325.

Sweeney, P., Li, C. M., & Yang, Y. (2017). Appetite suppressive role of medial septal glutamatergic neurons. *Proceedings of the National Academy of Sciences*, *114*, 13816–13821.

Swinson, R. P. (2005). Social anxiety disorder. *The Canadian Journal of Psychiatry*, *50*, 305–307.

Swithers, S. E. (2016). Not-so-healthy sugar substitutes? *Current Opinion in Behavioral Sciences*, *9*, 106–110.

Szabo, A., Griffiths, M. D., & Demetrovics, Z. (2019). In D. Bagchi, S. Nair, & C. K. Sen (Eds.), *Nutrition and enhanced sports performance* (2nd ed., pp. 63–72). Academic Press.

Szasz, T. (1961). *The myth of mental illness: Foundations of a theory of personal conduct*. Hoeber-Harper.

Szasz, T. (2000). Second commentary on "Aristotle's function argument." *Philosophy, Psychiatry, & Psychology*, *7*, 3–16.

Talarico, J. M., & Rubin, D. C. (2003). Confidence, not consistency, characterized flashbulb memories. *Psychological Science*, *14*, 455–461.

Talarico, J. M., & Rubin, D. C. (2018). Ordinary memory processes shape flashbulb memories of extraordinary events: A review of 40 years of research. In O. Luminet & A. Curic (Eds.) *Flashbulb memories: New challenges and future perspectives* (2nd ed., pp. 73–95). Psychology Press.

Tanford, S., & Penrod, S. (1984). Social influence model: A formal integration of research on majority and minority influence processes. *Psychological Bulletin*, *95*, 189–225.

Tateyama, M., Asai, M., Hashimoto, M., Bartels, M., & Kasper, S. (1998). Transcultural study of schizophrenic delusions: Tokyo versus Vienna versus Tuebingen (Germany). *Psychopathology*, *31*, 59–68.

Taylor, F. W. (1911). *Principles of scientific management*. Harper.

Taylor, S. E. (2002). *The tending instinct: Women, men, and the biology of relationships*. Holt.

Taylor, S. E. (2006). Tend and befriend: Biobehavioral bases of affiliation under stress. *Current Directions in Psychological Science*, *15*, 273–276.

Taylor, S. E., & Master, S. L. (2011). Social responses to stress: The trend-and-befriend model. In R. J. Contrada & A. Baum (Eds.), *The handbook of stress science* (pp. 101–109). Springer.

Taylor, S. F., & Tso, I. F. (2015). GABA abnormalities in schizophrenia: A methodological review of in vivo studies. *Schizophrenia Research*, *167*, 84–90.

Tellegen, A., Lykken, D. T., Bouchard, T. J., Jr., Wilcox, K. J., Segal, N. L., & Rich, S. (1988). Personality similarity in twins reared apart and together. *Journal of Personality and Social Psychology*, *54*, 1031–1039.

Temple, J. L., Giacomelli, A. M., Roemmich, J. N., & Epstein, L. H. (2008). Dietary variety impairs habituation in youth. *Health Psychology*, *27*, S10–S19.

Tennes, K., & Kreye, M. (1985). Children's adrenocortical responses to classroom activities and tests in elementary school. *Psychosomatic Medicine*, *47*, 451–460.

Terhune, D. B., Cleeremans, A., Raz, A., & Lynn, S. J. (2017). Hypnosis and top-down regulation of consciousness. *Neuroscience and Biobehavioral Reviews*, *81*, 59–74.

Terman, L. M. (1925). *Mental and physical traits of a thousand gifted children*. Stanford University Press.

Terman, L. M. (1954). The discovery and encouragement of exceptional talent. *American Psychologist*, *9*, 221–238.

Terman, L. M., & Ogden, M. (1947). *Genetic studies of genius: Vol. 5. The gifted child grows up*. Stanford University Press.

Terrace, H. S. (1986). *Nim: A chimpanzee who learned sign language*. Columbia University Press.

Tesser, A. (1993). The importance of heritability in psychological research: The case of attitudes. *Psychological Review*, *100*, 129–142.

Tessner, K. D., Mittal, V., & Walker, E. F. (2011). Longitudinal study of stressful life events and daily stressors among adolescents at high risk for psychotic disorders. *Schizophrenia Bulletin*, *37*, 432–441.

Thomas, A., & Chess, S. (1977). *Temperament and development*. Bruner/Mazel.

Thomas, E. F., McGarty, C., & Louis, W. (2014). Social interaction and psychological pathways to political engagement and extremism. *European Journal of Social Psychology*, *44*, 15–22.

Thompson, T., Terhune, D. B., Oram, C., Sharangparni, J., Rouf, R., Solmi, M., Veronese, N., Stubbs, B. (2019). The effectiveness of hypnosis for pain relief: A systematic review and meta-analysis of 85 controlled experimental trials. *Neuroscience and Biobehavioral Reviews*, *99*, 298–310.

Thompson, W. F., Schellenberg, E. G., & Husain, G. (2001). Arousal, mood, and the Mozart effect. *Psychological Science*, *12*, 248–251.

Thoreson, W. B., & Dacey, D. M. (2019). Diverse cell types, circuits, and mechanisms for color vision in the vertebrate retina. *Physiological Reviews*, *99*, 1527–1573. doi: 10.1152/physrev.00027.2018

Thorndike, E. L. (1898). Animal intelligence: An experimental study of the associative processes in animals. *Psychological Review, Monograph Supplements*, *2*(Serial No. 8).

Thorndike, E. L. (1914). *The psychology of learning*. Teachers College Press.

Thorne, S. P., Hegerty, P., & Hepper, E. G. (2019). Equality in theory: From a heteronormative to an inclusive psychology of romantic love. *Theory & Psychology*, *29*, 240–257. 10.1177/0959354319826725

Thornhill, R., Gangestad, S. W., Miller, R., Scheyd, G., McCollough, J. K., & Frankin, M. (2003). Major histocompatibility complex genes, symmetry, and body scent attractiveness in men and women. *Behavioral Ecology*, *14*, 668–678.

Thurstone, L. L. (1938). *Primary mental abilities*. University of Chicago Press.

Tibubos, A. N., Burghardt, J., Klein, E. M., Brähler, E., Jünger, C., Michal, M., Wiltink, J., Wild, P. S., Münzel, T., Singer, S., Pfeiffer, N., & Beutel, M. E. (2020, February 12). Frequency of stressful life events and associations with mental health and general subjective health in the general population. *Journal of Public Health: From Theory to Practice*. Advance online publication. https://doi.org/10.1007/s10389-020-01204-3

Tienari, P., Wahlberg, K., & Wynne, L. (2006). Finnish adoption study of schizophrenia: Implications for family interventions. *Family, Systems, & Health*, *24*, 442–451.

Tiffany, S. T., Cox, L. S., & Elash, C. A. (2000). Effects of transdermal nicotine patches on abstinence-induced and cue-elicited craving in cigarette smokers. *Journal of Consulting & Clinical Psychology*, *68*, 233–240.

Tik, M., Sladky, R., Di Bernardi Luft, C., Willinger, D., Hoffmann, A., Banissy, M. J., Bhattacharya, J., & Windischberger, C. (2018). Ultra-high-field fMRI insights on insight: Neural correlates of the Aha!-moment. *Human Brain Mapping, 39,* 3241–3252.

Tinbergen, N. (1951). *The study of instinct.* Oxford University Press.

Ting, F., Buyukozwer Dawkins, M., Stavans, M., & Baillargeon, R. (2020). Principles and concepts in early moral cognition. In J. Decety (Ed.), *The social brain: A developmental perspective.* MIT Press.

Titchener, E. B. (1899). Structural and functional psychology. *Philosophical Review, 8,* 290–299.

Todd, A. R., Galinsky, A. D., & Bodenhausen, G. V. (2012). Perspective taking undermines stereotype maintenance processes: Evidence from social memory, behavior explanation, and information solicitation. *Social Cognition, 30,* 94–108.

Todorov, A., Pakrashi, M., & Oosterhof, N. N. (2009). Evaluating faces on trustworthiness after minimal exposure time. *Social Cognition, 27,* 813–833.

Tolin, D. F. (2014). Beating a dead dodo bird: Looking at signal vs. noise in cognitive-behavioral therapy for anxiety disorders. *Clinical Psychology: Science and Practice, 21,* 351–362.

Tolman, C. W. (1968). The role of the companion in social facilitation of animal behavior. In E. C. Simmel, R. A. Hoppe, & G. A. Milton (Eds.), *Social facilitation and imitative behavior* (pp. 33–54). Allyn & Bacon.

Tomasello, M. (2017). What did we learn from the ape language studies? In B. Hare & S. Yamamoto (Eds.), *Bonobos: Unique in mind, brain, and behavior* (pp. 95–104). Oxford University Press.

Tomkins, S. S. (1962). *Affect, imagery, and consciousness* (Vol. 1). Springer.

Tomlinson-Keasey, C., & Little, T. D. (1990). Predicting educational attainment, occupational achievement, intellectual skill, and personal adjustment among gifted men and women. *Journal of Educational Psychology, 82,* 442–455.

Torrance, E. P. (1981). Empirical validation of criterion-referenced indicators of creative ability through a longitudinal study. *Creative Child and Adult Quarterly, 6,* 136–140.

Towler, G. (1986). From zero to one hundred: Coaction in a natural setting. *Perceptual and Motor Skills, 62,* 377–378.

Trafimow, D., Triandis, H. C., & Goto, S. G. (1991). Some tests of the distinction between the private self and the collective self. *Journal of Personality and Social Psychology, 60,* 649–655.

Trahan, L. H., Stuebing, K. K., Fletcher, J. M., & Hiscock, M. (2014). The Flynn effect: A meta-analysis. *Psychological Bulletin, 140,* 1332–1360.

Travis, F., & Wallace, R. K. (1999). Autonomic and EEG patterns during eyes-closed rest and transcendental meditation (TM) practice: The basis for a neural model of TM practice. *Consciousness and Cognition, 8,* 302–318.

Treiman, R. A., Clifton, C., Meyer, A. S., & Wurm, L. H. (2003). Language comprehension and production. In A. Healy & R. Proctor (Eds.), *Handbook of psychology: Vol. 4 Experimental psychology* (pp. 527–547). Wiley.

Trivers, R. L. (1985). *Social evolution.* Benjamin/Cummings.

Trull, T. J., & McCrae, R. R. (1994). A five-factor perspective on personality disorder research. In P. T. Costa Jr. & T. A. Widiger (Eds.), *Personality disorders and the five-factor model of personality.* American Psychological Association.

Trzesniewski, K. H., & Donnellan, M. B. (2010). Rethinking "Generation Me": A study of cohort effects from 1976–2006. *Perspectives on Psychological Science, 5,* 58–75.

Tuckman, B. W. (1998). Using tests as an incentive to motivate procrastinators to study. *Journal of Experimental Education, 66,* 141–147.

Tulving, E. (1983). *Elements of episodic memory.* Oxford University Press.

Tulving, E. (2002). Episodic memory: From mind to brain. *Annual Review of Psychology, 53,* 1–25.

Tulving, E., & Pearlstone, Z. (1966). Availability versus accessibility of information in memory for words. *Journal of Verbal Learning and Verbal Behavior, 5,* 381–391.

Turati, C. (2004). Why faces are not special to newborns: An alternative account of the face preference. *Current Directions in Psychological Science, 13,* 5–8.

Turiel, E. (2015). Moral development. In R. M. Lerner (Ed.), *Handbook of child psychology and developmental science: Vol. 1. Theory and method* (7th ed., pp. 484–522). Wiley.

Turner, T. J., & Ortony, A. (1992). Basic emotions: Can conflicting criteria converge? *Psychological Review, 99,* 566–571.

Tversky, A., & Kahneman, D. (1973). On the psychology of prediction. *Psychological Review, 80,* 237–251.

Tversky, A., & Kahneman, D. (1974). Decision making under uncertainty: Heuristics and biases. *Science, 185,* 1124–1131.

Tversky, A., & Kahneman, D. (1983). Extensional versus intuitive reasoning: The conjunction fallacy in probability judgment. *Psychological Review, 90,* 293–315.

Twenge, J. M. (2009). Change over time in obedience: The jury's still out, but it might be decreasing. *American Psychologist, 64,* 28–31.

Twenge, J. M. (2014). *Generation me: Why today's young Americans are more confident, assertive, entitled—and more miserable than ever before* (2nd ed.). Atria Books.

Twenge, J. M., Zhang, L., & Im, C. (2004). It's beyond my control: A cross-temporal meta-analysis of increasing externality in locus of control, 1960–2002. *Personality and Social Psychology Review, 8,* 308–319.

Tyrell, F. A., Wheeler, L. A., Gonzales, N. A., Dumka, L., & Millsap, R. (2016). Family influences on Mexican American adolescents' romantic relationships: Moderation by gender and culture. *Journal of Research on Adolescence, 26,* 142–158.

Ulrich, R. E. (1991). Commentary: Animal rights, animal wrongs and the question of balance. *Psychological Science, 2,* 197–201.

Uno, Y., & Coyle, J. T. (2019). Glutamate hypothesis in schizophrenia. *Psychiatry and Clinical Neurosciences, 73,* 204–215.

Unsworth, N. M., Redick, T. S., Heitz, R. P., Broadway, J. M., & Engle, R. W. (2009). Complex working memory span tasks and higher-order cognition: A latent-variable analysis of the relationship between processing and storage. *Memory, 17,* 635–654.

U.S. Census Bureau. (2018). *Current population survey, annual social and economic supplements, 1947 to 2018.* https://www.census.gov/content/dam/Census/library/visualizations/time-series/demo/families-and-households/ms-2.pdf

Vadillo, M. A., Gold, N., & Osman, M. (2016). The bitter truth about sugar and willpower: The limited evidential value of the glucose model of ego depletion. *Psychological Science, 27,* 1207–1214.

Valenzuela, M., & Sachdev, P. (2009). Can cognitive exercise prevent the onset of dementia? Systematic review of randomized clinical trials with longitudinal follow-up. *The American Journal of Geriatric Psychiatry, 17,* 179–187.

Valli, K., & Revonsuo, A. (2009). The threat simulation theory in light of recent empirical evidence: A review. *American Journal of Psychology, 122,* 17–38.

van der Klaauw, A. A., & Farooqi, S. (2015). The hunger genes: Pathways to obesity. *Cell, 161,* 119–132.

van Deurzen, E., & Arnold-Baker, C. (Eds.). (2018). *Existential therapy. Distinctive features.* Routledge.

Van Doornen, L. J., & Van Blokland, R. (1987). Serum-cholesterol: Sex-specific psychological correlates during rest and stress. *Journal of Psychosomatic Research, 31,* 239–249.

Van Houtte, M. (2004). Why boys achieve less at school than girls: The difference between boys' and girls' academic culture. *Educational Studies, 30,* 159–173.

van Veen, V., Krug, M. K., Schooler, J. W., & Carter, C. S. (2009). Neural activity predicts attitude change in cognitive dissonance. *Nature Neuroscience, 12,* 1469–1475.

Vannucci, A., Simpson, E. G., Gagnon, S., & McCauley Ohannessian, C. (2020, February). Social media use and risky behaviors in adolescents: A meta-analysis. *Journal of Adolescence, 79,* 258–274. doi: 10.1016/j.adolescence.2020.01.014

Veenstra, L., Bushman, B. J., & Koole, S. L. (2018). The facts on the furious: A brief review of the psychology of trait anger. *Current Opinion in Psychology, 19,* 98–103.

Vélez-Agosto, N. M., Soto-Crespo, J. G., Vizcarrondo-Oppenheimer, M., Vega-Molina, S., & Coll, C. G. (2017, September). Bronfenbrenner's bioecological theory revision: Moving culture from the macro into the micro. *Perspectives on Psychological Science, 12*(5), 900–910. doi: 10.1177/1745691617704397

Verrusio, W., Ettorrre, E., Vincenzini, E., Cacciafesta, M., & Mercarelli, O. (2015). The Mozart effect: A quantitative EEG study. *Consciousness and Cognition, 35,* 150–155.

Vinson, D. W., Dale, R., & Jones, M. N. (2019). Decision contamination in the wild: Sequential dependencies in online review ratings. *Behavior Research Methods, 51,* 1477–1484.

Visser, B. A., Ashton, M. C., & Vernon, P. A. (2006). Beyond *g:* Putting multiple intelligences theory to the test. *Intelligence, 34,* 487–502.

Volkow, N.D., Wang, G.-J., Newcorn, J. H., Kollins, S. J., Wigal, T. L., Telang, F., Fowler, J. S., Goldstein, R. Z., Klein, N., Logan, J., Wong, C., & Swanson, J. M. (2011). Motivation deficit in ADHD is associated with dysfunction of the dopamine pathway. *Molecular Psychiatry, 16,* 1147–1154.

Vollenweider, F. X., & Kometer, M. (2010). The neurobiology of psychedelic drugs: Implications for the treatment of mood disorders. *Nature Reviews Neuroscience, 11,* 642–651.

Volz, L. J., & Gazzaniga, M. S. (2017). Interaction in isolation: 50 years of insights from split-brain patients. *Brain, 140,* 2051–2060.

von Bartheld, C. S., Bahney, J., & Herculano-Houzel, S. (2016). The search for true numbers of neurons and glial cells in the human brain: A review of 150 years of cell counting. *Journal of Comparative Neurology, 18,* 3865–3895.

von Dawans, B., Spenthof, I., Zimmer, P., & Domes, G.. (2020). Acute psychosocial stress modulates the detection of sensitivity for facial emotions. *Experimental Psychology, 67*(2), 140–149.

von Frisch, K. (1967). *The dance language and orientation of bees.* Belknap Press.

Von Hippel, W., & Trivers, R. (2011). The evolution and psychology of self-deception. *Behavioral and Brain Sciences, 34,* 1–56.

Voss, J. L., Bridge, D. J., Cohen, N. J., & Walker, J. A. (2017). A closer look at the hippocampus and memory. *Trends in Cognitive Sciences, 21,* 577–588.

Vukasovic, T., & Bratko, D. (2015). Heritability of personality. *Psychological Bulletin, 141,* 769–785.

Vygotsky, L. S. (1978). *Mind in society: The development of higher psychological processes.* Harvard University Press.

Wagemans, F. M. A., Brandt, M. J., & Zeelenberg, M. (2018). Disgust sensitivity is primarily associated with purity-based moral judgments. *Emotion, 18*(2), 277–289.

Wagenaar, W. A. (1986). My memory: A study of autobiographical memory over six years. *Cognitive Psychology, 18,* 225–252.

Wagenmakers, E.-J., Beek, T., Dijkhoff, L., Gronau, Q. F., Acosta, A., Adams, R. B., Jr., Albohn, D. N., Allard, E. S., Benning, S. D., Blouin-Hudon, E.-M., Bulnes, L. C., Caldwell, T. L., Calin-Jageman, R. J., Capaldi, C. A., Carfagno, N. S., Chasten, K. T., Cleeremans, A., Connell, L., DeCicco, J. M., . . . Zwaan, R. A. (2016). Registered Replication Report: Strack, Martin, & Stepper (1988). *Perspectives on Psychological Science, 11,* 917–928.

Wagman, J. B., & Blau, J. J. C. (Eds.). (2020).*Perception as information detection: Reflections on Gibson's ecological approach to visual perception.* Routledge.

Wagman, J. B., & Morgan, L. L. (2010). Perceived maximum reaching height reflects anticipated changes in reaching ability. *Psychonomic Bulletin & Review, 17,* 905–909.

Wahba, M. A., & Bridwell, L. G. (1976). Maslow reconsidered: A review of research on the need hierarchy theory. *Organizational Behavior and Human Performance, 15,* 212–240.

Wai, J., & Putallaz, M. (2011). The Flynn effect puzzle: A 30-year examination from the right tail of the ability distribution provides some missing pieces. *Intelligence, 39,* 443–455.

Waldman, I. D., Weinberg, R. A., & Scarr, S. (1994). Racial-group differences in IQ in the Minnesota Transracial Adoption Study: A reply to Levin and Lynn. *Intelligence, 19,* 29–44.

Walen, S. T., DiGuiseppe, R., & Dryden, W. (1992). *A practitioner's guide to rational-emotive therapy.* Oxford University Press.

Walker, E., Kestler, L., Bollini, A., & Hochman, K. M. (2004). Schizophrenia: Etiology and course. *Annual Review of Psychology, 55,* 401–430.

Walker, L. J. (1989). A longitudinal study of moral reasoning. *Child Development, 60,* 157–166.

Walker, M. P., & Stickgold, R. (2006). Sleep, memory, and plasticity. *Annual Review of Psychology, 57,* 139–166.

Wallhagen, M. I., Strawbridge, W., & Shema, S. (1997). *Perceived control: Mental health correlates in a population-based aging cohort* [Paper presentation]. Gerontological Society of America 50th Annual Scientific Meeting.

Walter, H. J., Li, R., Wagman, J.B., & Stoffregen, T. A. (2019). Adaptive perception of changes in affordances for walking on a ship at sea. *Human Movement Science, 64,* 28–37.

Walter, H. J., Wagman, J. B., Stergiou, N., Erkmen, N., & Stoffregen, T. A. (2017). Dynamic perception of dynamic affordances: Walking on a ship at sea. *Experimental Brain Research, 235,* 517–524. doi: 10.1007/s0022-016-4810-6

Walters, J. M., & Gardner, H. (1986). The theory of multiple intelligences: Some issues and answers. In R. J. Sternberg & R. K. Wagner (Eds.), *Practical intelligence: Nature and origins of competence in the everyday world* (pp. 163–182). Cambridge University Press.

Wampold, B. E., Fluckiger, C., Del Re, A. C., Yulish, N. E., Frost, N. D., Pace, B. T., Goldberg, S. B., Miller, S. D., Baardseth, T. P., Laska, K. M., & Hilsenroth, M. J. (2017). In pursuit of truth: A critical examination of meta-analyses of cognitive behavior therapy. *Psychotherapy Research, 27,* 14–32.

Wampold, B. E., Mondin, G. W., Moody, M., Stich, F., Benson, K., & Ahn, H. (1997). A meta-analysis of outcome studies comparing bona fide psychotherapies: Empirically, "all must have prizes." *Psychological Bulletin, 122,* 203–215.

Wandell, B. A., & Winawer, J. (2011). Imaging retinotopic maps in the human brain. *Vision Research, 51,* 718–737.

Wang, X. (2018). Cortical coding of auditory features. *Annual Review of Neuroscience, 41,* 527–552. doi: 10.1146/annurev-neuro-072116-031302

Warne, R. T., Astle, M. C., & Hill, J. C. (2018). What do undergraduates learn about human intelligence? An analysis of introductory psychology textbooks. *Archives of Scientific Psychology, 6,* 32–50.

Washburn, M. F. (1908). *The animal mind.* Macmillan.

Waterhouse, L. (2006). Multiple intelligences, the Mozart effect, and emotional intelligence: A critical review. *Educational Psychologist, 41,* 207–225.

Watson, J. B. (1913). Psychology as a behaviorist views it. *Psychological Review, 20,* 158–177.

Watson, J. B. (1919). *Psychology from the standpoint of a behaviorist.* Lippincott.

Watson, J. B. (1930). *Behaviorism.* Norton.

Watson, J. B., & Rayner, R. (1920). Conditioned emotional reactions. *Journal of Experimental Psychology, 3,* 1–14.

Webb, C. E., Turney, I. C., & Dennis, N. A. (2016). What's the gist? The influence of schemas on the neural correlates underlying true and false memories. *Neuropsychologia, 93,* 61–75.

Webb, E. J., Campbell, D. T., Schwartz, R. D., Sechrist, L., & Grove, J. B. (1981). *Nonreactive research in the social sciences.* Houghton Mifflin.

Webb, W. B. (1981). The return of consciousness. *G. Stanley Hall Lecture Series, 1,* 129–152.

Weber, R., & Crocker, J. (1993). Cognitive processes in the revision of stereotypic beliefs. *Journal of Personality and Social Psychology, 45,* 961–977.

Wegener, D. T., & Carlston, D. E. (2005). Cognitive processes in attitude formation and change. In D. Albarracín, B. Johnson, & M. Zanna (Eds.), *The handbook of attitudes* (pp. 493–542). Erlbaum.

Wegner, D. M. (1994). Ironic processes of mental control. *Psychological Review, 101,* 34–52.

Weiden, P. J. (2007). EPS profiles: The atypical antipsychotics are not all the same. *Journal of Psychiatric Practice, 13,* 13–24.

Weinberg, R. A., Scarr, S., & Waldman, I. D. (1992). The Minnesota Transracial Adoption Study: A follow-up of IQ test performance at adolescence. *Intelligence, 16,* 117–135.

Weingarten, H. P. (1983). Conditioned cues elicit feeding in sated rats: A role for learning in meal initiation. *Science, 220,* 431–433.

Weinstein, E. (2018). The social media see-saw: Positive and negative influences on adolescents' affective well-being. *New Media & Society, 20,* 3597–3623.

Weisberg, D. S., Hopkins, E. J., & Taylor, J. C. V. (2018). People's explanatory preferences for scientific phenomena. *Cognitive Research: Principles and Implications, 3*(44), 1–14.

Weiss, J. M. (1977). Psychosomatic disorders: Psychological and behavioral influences on gastrointestinal lesions in animal models. In J. D. Maser & M. E. P. Seligman (Eds.), *Psychopathology: Experimental models* (pp. 232–269). Freeman.

Weiss, K., Friedman, S. H., & Shand, J. P. (2019). Insanity: A legal and cinematic diagnosis. *The Journal of Nervous and Mental Disease, 207,* 749–754.

Weiten, W. (1995). *Psychology: Themes and variations* (3rd ed.). Brooks/Cole.

Wellman, H. M. (2011). Developing a theory of mind. In U. Goswami (Ed.) *The Wiley-Blackwell handbook of childhood cognitive development* (pp. 258–284). Blackwell.

Wells, A., & Carter, K. (2006). Generalized anxiety disorder. In A. Carr & M. McNulty (Eds.), *The handbook of adult clinical psychology: An evidence-based practice approach.* Routledge/Taylor & Francis Group.

Werker, J. F., & Tees, R. C. (1999). Influences on infant speech processing: Toward a new synthesis. *Annual Review of Psychology, 50,* 509–535.

Wernicke, C. (1874). *Der Aphasische Symptomenkomplex.* Cohn & Weigert.

Westbrook, M., Creswell, J. D., Tabibnia, G., Julson, E., Kober, H., & Tindle, H. A. (2013). Mindful attention reduces neural and self-reported cue-induced craving in smokers. *Social, Cognitive, and Affective Neuroscience, 8,* 73–74.

Wever, E. G. (1949). *Theory of hearing.* Wiley.

Wexler, M., & van Boxtel, J. (2005). Depth perception by the active observer. *Trends in Cognitive Sciences, 9,* 431–438.

Wheeler, L., & Kim, Y. (1997). What is beautiful is culturally good: The physical attractiveness stereotype has different content in collectivistic cultures. *Personality & Social Psychology Bulletin, 23,* 795–800.

Wheeler, M. A., & McMillan, C. T. (2001). Focal retrograde amnesia and the episodic-semantic distinction. *Cognitive, Affective, & Behavioral Neuroscience, 1,* 22–37.

Whitbourne, S. K. (1985). *The aging body.* Springer.

Whitbourne, S. K., Zuschlag, M. K., Elliot, L. B., & Waterman, A. S. (1992). Psychosocial development in adulthood: A 22-year sequential study. *Journal of Personality and Social Psychology, 63*, 260–271.

Whitely, B. E., Jr. (1990). The relationship of heterosexuals' attributions for the causes of homosexuality to attitudes toward lesbians and gay men. *Personality and Social Psychology Bulletin, 16*, 367–377.

Whorf, B. L. (1956). *Language, thought, and reality: Selected writings of Benjamin Lee Whorf*. Wiley.

Widiger, T. A., Crego, C., Rojas, S. L., & Oltmanns, J. R. (2018). Basic personality model. *Current Opinion in Psychology, 21*, 18–22.

Widiger, T. A., & Gore, W. L. (2014). Mental disorders as discrete clinical conditions: Dimensional versus categorical classification. In D. C. Beidel, B. C. Frueh, & M. Hersen (Eds.), *Adult psychopathology and diagnosis* (pp. 3–33). Wiley.

Wiederman, M. W. (2015). Sexual script theory: Past, present, and future. In J. DeLamater & R. F. Plante (Eds.), *Handbook of the sociology of sexualities* (pp. 7–22). Springer.

Wigfield, A. (1994). Expectancy-value theory of achievement motivation: A developmental perspective. *Educational Psychology Review, 6*, 49–78.

Williams, D. A., Overmier, J. B., & LoLordo, V. M. (1992). A reevaluation of Rescorla's early dictums about Pavlovian conditioned inhibition. *Psychological Bulletin, 111*, 275–290.

Williams, K. D. (2009). Ostracism: A temporal need-threat model. In M. Zanna (Ed.), *Advances in experimental social psychology* (pp. 279–314). Academic Press.

Williams, K. D., & Nida, S. A. (2011). Ostracism: Consequences and coping. *Current Directions in Psychological Science, 20*, 71–75.

Williams, L. M. (1992). Adult memories of childhood abuse: Preliminary findings from a longitudinal study. *The Advisor, 5*, 19–20.

Williams, M. J., & Tiedens, L. Z. (2016, February). The subtle suspension of backlash: A meta-analysis of penalties for women's implicit and explicit dominance behavior. *Psychological Bulletin, 142*(2), 165–197. doi: 10.1037/bul0000039

Williams, T., & Williams, K. (2010). Self-efficacy and performance in mathematics: Reciprocal determinism in 33 nations. *Journal of Educational Psychology, 102*, 453–466.

Willoughby, B. J., & Busby, D. M. (2016). In the eye of the beholder: Exploring variations in the perceptions of pornography. *The Journal of Sex Research, 53*, 678–688.

Willoughby, T., Adachi, P. J. C., & Good, M. (2012). A longitudinal study of the association between violent video game play and aggression among adolescents. *Developmental Psychology, 48*, 1044–1057.

Wilson, E. O. (1963, May). Pheromones. *Scientific American, 208*, 100–114.

Winikoff, B. (1983). Nutritional patterns, social choices, and health. In D. Mechanic (Ed.), *Handbook of health, health care, and the health professions* (pp. 81–98). Free Press.

Winkielman, P., & Berridge, K. C. (2004). Unconscious emotion. *Current Directions in Psychological Science, 13*, 120–123.

Wissler, C. (1901). *The correlation of mental and physical tests. Psychological Review, Monograph Supplement 3* (Vol. 6).

Witherington, D. C., Campos, J. J., Anderson, D. I., Lejeune, L., & Seah, E. (2005). Avoidance of heights on the visual cliff in newly walking infants. *Infancy, 7*, 285–298.

Witt, J. K. (2011). Action's effect on perception. *Current Directions in Psychological Science, 20*, 201–206.

Wixted, J. T., & Wells, G. L. (2017). The relationship between eyewitness confidence and identification accuracy: A new synthesis. *Psychological Science in the Public Interest, 18*, 10–65.

Wollberg, Z., & Newman, J. D. (1972). Auditory cortex of squirrel monkey: Response patterns of single cells to species-specific vocalizations. *Science, 175*, 212–214.

Wolpe, J. (1958). *Psychotherapy by reciprocal inhibition*. Stanford University Press.

Wolpe, J. (1975). Foreword. In B. Sloane, F. Staples, A. Cristol, N. Yorkston, & K. Whipple (Eds.), *Psychotherapy versus behavior therapy*. Harvard University Press.

Wolpe, J. (1982). *The practice of behavior therapy*. Pergamon.

Wong, W. I., & Hines, M. (2015). Effects of gender color-coding on toddlers' gender-typical toy play. *Archives of Sexual Behavior, 44*, 1233–1242.

Woodhouse, S., Dykas, M. J., & Cassidy, J. (2012, May). Loneliness and peer relations in adolescence. *Review of Social Development, 21*(2). doi: 10.1111/j.1467-9507.2011.00611.x

Woods, S. C., & D'Alessio, D. A. (2008). Central control of body weight and appetite. *Journal of Clinical Endocrinology & Metabolism, 93*, S37–S50.

Woods, S. C., Schwartz, M. W., Baskin, D. G., & Seeley, R. J. (2000). Food intake and the regulation of body weight. *Annual Review of Psychology, 51*, 255–277.

Woolley, H. T. (1910). Psychological literature: A review of the recent literature on the psychology of sex. *Psychological Bulletin, 7*, 335–342.

Woolley, K., & Fishbach, A. (2018). About time: Earlier rewards increase intrinsic motivation. *Journal of Personality and Social Psychology, 114*, 877–890.

Worringham, C. J., & Messick, D. M. (1983). Social facilitation of running: An unobtrusive study. *Journal of Social Psychology, 121*, 23–29.

Wright, A. G. C., Aslinger, E. N., Bellamy, B., Edershile, E. A., & Woods, W. C. (2020). Daily stress and hassles. In K. L. Harkness & E. P. Hayden (Eds.), *The Oxford handbook of stress and mental health* (pp. 27–44). Oxford University Press.

Wundt, W. (1896). *Outlines of psychology* (Judd, Trans.). Stechart.

Wyatt, T. D. (2015) The search for human pheromones: The lost decades and the necessity of returning to first principles. *Proceedings of the Royal Society, 282*, 2994.

Wyer, N. A. (2007). Motivational influences on compliance with and consequences of instructions to suppress stereotypes. *Journal of Experimental Social Psychology, 43*, 417–424.

Wynne, C. D. L. (2007). What the ape said. *Ethology, 113*, 411–413.

Wyra, M., & Lawson, M. J. (2018). Foreign language vocabulary learning using the keyword method: Strategy and meta-strategy knowledge. *Language Learning Journal, 46*, 1–17.

Xu, F. (2019). Towards a rational constructivist theory of cognitive development. *Psychological Review, 126,* 841–864. 10.1037/rev0000153">doi: 10.1037/rev0000153

Yadollahpour, A., Mirzayan, M., & Rashidi, S. (2017). Quantitative EEG for early and differential diagnosis of bipolar disorders: A comprehensive review of the literature. *International Journal of Mental Health and Addiction, 15,* 387–393.

Yalom, I. D. (2005). *The theory and practice of group psychotherapy* (5th ed.). Basic Books.

Yapko, M. D. (1994). Suggestibility and repressed memories of abuse: A survey of psychotherapists' beliefs. *American Journal of Clinical Hypnosis, 36,* 163–179.

Yates, F. A. (1966). *The art of memory.* University of Chicago Press.

Yoo, G., Leach, A., Woods, R., Holt, T., & Hansen, G. (2020, September 18). Computed tomography practice standards for severe pediatric traumatic brain injury in the emergency department: A national survey. *Journal of Child & Adolescent Trauma.* Advance online publication. https://doi.org/10.1007/s40653-020-00317-x

Young, L., Bechara, A., Tranel, D., Damasio, H., Hauser, M., & Damasio, A. (2010). Damage to ventromedial prefrontal cortex impairs judgment of harmful intent. *Neuron, 65,* 845–851.

Yu, H., McCoach, D. B., Gottfried, A. W., & Gottfried, A. E. (2018). Stability of intelligence from infancy through adolescence: An autoregressive latent variable model. *Intelligence, 69,* 8–15.

Zachar, P., Krueger, R. F., & Kendler, K. S. (2016). Personality disorders in DSM-5: An oral history. *Psychological Medicine, 46,* 1–10.

Zahorik, D. M., Houpt, K. A., & Swartzman-Andert, J. (1990). Taste-aversion learning in three species of ruminants. *Applied Animal Behaviour Science, 26,* 27–39.

Zajonc, R. B. (1968). Attitudinal effects of mere exposure. *Journal of Personality and Social Psychology, 9,* Monograph Supplement (No. 2, part 2).

Zajonc, R. B. (2001). Mere exposure: A gateway to the subliminal. *Current Directions in Psychological Science, 10,* 224–228.

Zajonc, R. B., Heingartner, A., & Herman, E. M. (1969). Social enhancement and impairment of performance in the cockroach. *Journal of Personality and Social Psychology, 13,* 83–92.

Zajonc, R. B., Murphy, S. T. & McIntosh, D. N. (1993). Brain temperature and subjective emotional experience. In M. Lewis & J. M. Haviland (Eds.), *Handbook of emotions* (pp. 209–220). Guilford Press.

Zatorre, R. J. (2005). Finding the missing fundamental. *Nature, 436,* 1093–1094.

Zeidner, M., Roberts, R. D., & Matthews, G. (2008). The science of emotional intelligence: Current consensus and controversies. *European Psychologist, 13,* 64–78.

Zelazo, P. R., Zelazo, N. A., & Kolb, S. (1972). "Walking" in the newborn. *Science, 176,* 314–315.

Zhang, J., Sun-Waterhouse, D., Su, G., & Zhao, M. (2019). New insight into umami receptor, umami/umami-enhancing peptides and their derivatives: A review. *Trends in Food Science & Technology, 88,* 429–438. doi: 10.1016/j.tifs.2019.04.008

Zhu, M., Urhahne, D., & Rubie-Davies, C. M. (2018). The longitudinal effects of teacher judgement and different treatment on students' academic outcomes. *Educational Psychology, 38*(5), 648–668. https://doi.org/10.1080/01443410.2017.1412399

Zilkha, N., Scott, N., & Kimchi, T. (2017). Sexual dimorphism of parental care: From genes to behavior. *Annual Review of Neuroscience, 40,* 273–305.

Zimbardo, P. (2007). *The Lucifer effect: Understanding how good people turn evil.* Random House.

Zuroff, D. C., & Blatt, S. J. (2006). The therapeutic relationship in the brief treatment of depression: Contributions to clinical improvement and enhanced adaptive capacities. *Journal of Consulting and Clinical Psychology, 74,* 130–140.

Zwann, R. A., Pecher, D., Paolacci, G., Bouwmeester, S., Verkoeijen, P., Dijkstra, K., & Zeelenberg, R. (2018). Participant nonnaivete and the reproducibility of cognitive psychology. *Psychonomic Bulletin & Review, 25,* 1968–1972.

Zwir, I., Arnedo, J., Del-Val, C., Pulkki-Råback, L., Konte, B., Yang, S. S., Romero-Zaliz, R., Hintsanen, M., Cloninger, K. M., Garcia, D., Svrakic, D. M., Rozsa, S., Martinez, M., Lyytikäinen, L.-P., Giegling, I., Kähönen, M., Hernandez-Cuervo, H., Seppälä, I., Raitoharju, E., . . . Cloninger, C. R. (2020, October). Uncovering the complex genetics of human character. *Molecular Psychiatry, 25*(10), 2295–2312. doi: https://doi.org/10.1038/s41380-018-0263-6

NAME INDEX

Insight therapies, 4, 16, 546–47, 555, 562, 564, 568, 571, 575–76, 578–79
Instincts, 422–24, 429, 458, 461, 561
Intellectual ability, 351, 366–67, 372–74, 379, 384
Intellectual development, 111, 122–23, 126
Intellectual disabilities, 365–66, 372, 375, 385, 510
Intelligence, 38, 40, 50, 91, 94–95, 349–85, 388–89, 413, 415, 488, 496, 498, 501
  analytic, 359–60
  conceptualize, 351, 358, 360
  measuring, 352, 373, 378
Intelligence quotient. See IQ
Intelligence scores, 94, 375–76, 587
Intelligence tests, 38, 45, 277, 354, 356–57, 363–64, 366–70, 373, 375, 377–78
  standardized, 359, 374, 377
Interactions, peer, 131, 134–35, 591
Interference, 69, 209, 226, 276, 297–98, 300, 303, 306, 482, 488
Internal functions, 64–65, 88, 95, 97, 204, 211
Interneurons, 65–67, 98
Interpersonal attraction, 497–99
Interpretation, stable, 149–50, 168, 183, 188
Intimacy, 135–36, 279, 443, 499–502
Intrinsic motivation, 420, 426–27, 461
IQ (intelligence quotient), 350, 362–69, 372–78, 380–85
IQ scores, 363–67, 373, 375, 377–80, 384
IQ tests, 367, 372–75, 378, 382, 384
Items, 163–64, 271, 276–78, 281–83, 287, 292, 296, 303–5, 341–42, 362, 369

Just noticeable difference, 186–87

Labeling effects, 368, 514
Laboratory studies, 34, 260, 300, 591
Language, 12–13, 65, 78, 80, 82, 148–50, 152, 187, 278, 309–18, 320–22, 345, 350, 416, 448–49
  human, 313, 322, 448
Language abilities, 320–22
Language comprehension, 84, 86, 310–11, 315, 317–18
Language development, 120, 128, 310, 317–18, 320–22, 343, 371
  formal, 317–18
Language processing, 82, 84, 86, 273, 305
Language researchers, 314–15, 317, 343
Learn, 234–37, 241–43, 245, 247–51, 253, 258–62, 265, 267–68, 295–98, 303–4, 311, 327–29, 356, 401, 405–7, 424, 536–37, 563–65, 572–73, 578–79
Learner, 364, 489–90
Learning, 7, 9–10, 20–21, 24, 26, 28, 96, 111, 134, 233–68, 285, 296–98, 537, 564–65, 600
Learning language, 22, 24, 310–11, 317–18, 343, 345
Left hemisphere, 84, 86–87, 155–56, 175, 313
Letters, 161, 164, 204, 273, 275–77, 280, 289, 313, 332–33, 337, 340
Level of arousal, 448–49
Levels, low, 128, 155, 160, 208, 406–7, 430, 460, 595
Life events, 587–90, 602, 612–14
  stressful, 596–97
Lightning, 235, 238, 249
Literal ordering of words, 315, 343, 345
Locus of control, 406–7, 418
Longitudinal studies, 218, 373
Love, 332, 336, 402, 404, 422, 427, 439, 449, 456–57, 494, 499–502, 504, 561–62
LSD, 220–22, 229, 231

Magnetic resonance imaging. See MRI
Major depressive episode, 524, 543
MDMA, 220
Measurement of individual differences, 18, 369, 372
Measurements of intelligence, 353, 373
Measures, 36–40, 42–44, 47, 49, 60, 132–33, 195–96, 264, 273–75, 351–54, 356, 358–63, 366–73, 381–84, 389, 392–94, 539–40, 576, 588
Measures of behavior, 42–43, 45, 58, 60, 410
Measures of central tendency, 39, 58
Measuring individual differences, 350–51, 360, 381, 383
Measuring personality, 388–89, 396, 415–16
Medications, 7, 11, 71, 203, 527, 531, 548–51, 553–54, 567–68, 574, 577, 579
Meditation, 194, 196, 223, 226–29, 231–32, 600, 603
Meeting biological needs, 420–21, 429, 438, 456–57, 459
Memories, 9–10, 16, 18–20, 24, 49, 70–71, 77–78, 80–82, 115, 220–21, 225, 228–32, 269–307, 354–56, 363, 425, 465–67, 522, 553, 555
  false, 78, 292, 295
  recover, 35–36
  repressed, 36, 298, 399, 401
  stored, 270, 287, 305–6
Memory tests, 279, 289, 301, 523
Mental ability, 13, 117, 141, 210, 352–54, 357–58, 375, 381–82
Mental events, 13, 15, 18–19
Mental health professionals, 509, 513, 516, 520–21, 524, 526, 530, 536, 538–39, 546, 551–53, 571, 574–75
Mental processes, 13–14, 16, 20, 71, 73–74, 79, 87, 92, 216, 289–90, 381
Message components, 149–50, 155, 175, 187–88
Messages, 48–49, 65–69, 72–74, 76, 97, 148–51, 160, 175, 177–78, 181–82, 184, 187–90, 196–97, 204, 230, 272, 477–78, 480–81, 503
  environmental, 178, 274–75, 303
  genetic, 92–93, 380
  unattended, 196–98
Method of loci, 284, 287, 306
Midbrain, 79–81, 84, 98
Mind, 2–11, 13–17, 19–23, 25, 27–28, 30–32, 38, 64, 199, 227–28, 294–95, 298, 337–38, 340–42, 346, 396–97, 416–18, 546–48, 555–57, 610–11
  human, 13, 20, 24, 95, 195, 322, 327, 332, 388, 397
Mind and body, 11, 25, 27
Mindfulness, 194, 227–28, 600
Mind wandering, 194–95, 200
Minnesota Multiphasic Personality Inventory (MMPI), 394, 396, 413, 415, 417–18
Mirror neurons, 83, 85, 261
Modern psychology, 2, 5, 10, 13, 15, 19, 22, 24–25, 27–28
Monkeys, 56, 81, 127–28, 156–57, 261, 268, 302, 536, 538
Mood, 219, 447, 454–55, 472–73, 475, 531, 551–52, 574–75, 598–99, 605, 607, 610–11
Mood disorders, 531, 533, 542
Moral development, 123–26, 142, 144
Mother, 90, 92, 101–3, 126–30, 141, 143, 254, 399–401, 509, 537
Motivation, 47, 50, 52, 81, 400–401, 404, 407, 419–22, 424, 426, 446, 456, 458–59, 461, 477–78
Motor development, 105–6, 110, 141
Motor neurons, 65–66, 70–71, 83, 98
MRI (magnetic resonance imaging), 78–79, 97–98
Multiple intelligences, 357–60, 363, 367, 382, 385
Multiple-intelligences approach, 358, 381
Muscles, 66, 70–72, 74, 86, 89, 97, 152, 180, 447–48, 457, 460, 596, 600
Music, classical, 370–71